I WAS BORN A SLAVE

**The Library of
Black America**

I Was Born a Slave

AN ANTHOLOGY OF CLASSIC SLAVE NARRATIVES

VOLUME TWO
1849–1866

EDITED BY
Yuval Taylor

FOREWORD BY
Charles Johnson

First published in Great Britain in 1999 by Payback Press, an imprint of Canongate Books Ltd, 14 High Street, Edinburgh EH1 1TE.

10 9 8 7 6 5 4 3 2 1

British Library Cataloguing-in-Publication Data
A catalogue record for this book is available upon request from the British Library.

ISBN 0 86241 904 2

In thinking of America, I sometimes find myself admiring her bright blue sky—her grand old woods—her fertile fields—her beautiful rivers—her mighty lakes, and star-crowned mountains. But my rapture is soon checked, my joy is soon turned to mourning. When I remember that all is cursed with the infernal spirit of slaveholding, robbery and wrong,—when I remember that with the waters of her noblest rivers, the tears of my brethren are borne to the ocean, disregarded and forgotten, and that her most fertile fields drink daily of the warm blood of my outraged sisters, I am filled with unutterable loathing, and led to reproach myself that any thing could fall from my lips in praise of such a land. America will not allow her children to love her. She seems bent on compelling those who would be her warmest friends, to be her worst enemies. May God give her repentance, before it is too late, is the ardent prayer of my heart. I will continue to pray, labor and wait, believing that she cannot always be insensible to the dictates of justice, or deaf to the voice of humanity.

FREDERICK DOUGLASS, letter to William Lloyd Garrison, January 1, 1846

If it were not for the stripes on my back which were made while I was a slave, I would in my will, leave my skin a legacy to the government, desiring that it might be taken off and made into parchment, and then bind the constitution of glorious happy *and free* America. Let the skin of an American slave, bind the charter of American Liberty.

WILLIAM GRIMES, *Life of William Grimes, the Runaway Slave,* 1824

The author . . . sends out this history—presenting as it were his *own body,* with the marks and scars of the tender mercies of slave drivers upon it . . .

AUSTIN STEWARD, *Twenty-Two Years a Slave, and Forty Years a Freeman,* 1857

Hot weather brings out snakes and slaveholders, and I like one class of the venomous creatures as little as I do the other. What a comfort it is, to be free to *say* so!

HARRIET JACOBS, *Incidents in the Life of a Slave Girl,* 1861

CONTENTS

I s slavery America's original sin?
Despite the end of legal bondage 135 years ago, we are reminded of this national tragedy, and rightly, nearly every day through President Clinton's oft-stated feelings of shame about slavery, or black demands for reparations (or at least an apology), or countless books and magazine and newspaper articles that ground their interpretation of every aspect of contemporary black American life on the complexities of the Peculiar Institution. Adjoa Aiyetoro, director of the National Conference of Black Lawyers, reminds us of its lingering effects in a *Seattle Post-Intelligencer* article (June 29, 1997) when he says, "One of the issues we deal with every day is the vestiges of our enslavement, and our post-enslavement treatment in this country has been such that it has beat us down as a people in so many ways."

Perhaps those "vestiges" might have disappeared if Congress had passed after the Civil War a famous bit of legislation known as Senate Bill No. 60, which not only would have provided emergency relief for black freemen, but also "three million acres of good land" in Florida, Mississippi, and Arkansas for their settlement. In a January 18, 1866, edition of the *Congressional Globe*, senator Lyman Trumball, a Republican from Connecticut, argued that "A homestead is worth more to these people than almost anything else. . . . I think that if it were in our power to secure a homestead to every family that has been made free by the constitutional amendment, we would do more for the colored race than by any other act we could do." This "forty acres and a mule" bill put America's racial future, one might say, squarely at a crossroads. If approved, it might have done much to heal the devastating wounds of slavery and assist an impoverished, landless people in their transition from bondage to a fuller participation in American life, particularly in the area of economic development. But the bill was vetoed by President Andrew Johnson, who argued that "it was never intended that they [ex-slaves] should thenceforth be fed, clothed, educated and sheltered by the United States. The idea on which the slaves were assisted to freedom was that, on becoming free, they would be a self-sustaining population. Any legislation that shall imply that they are not expected to attain a self-sustaining condition must have a tendency injurious alike to their character and their prospects."

With that veto an opportunity was forever lost for both newly freed bondsmen, many of whom would feel slavery was restored after the end of Reconstruction, and for whites, who for the next hundred years were able to sweep under the rug the question of racial justice. Not until the 1960s does the Peculiar Institution become the major premise, the algorithm, the single governing principle for *any* and *all* discussions about white dominance and the condition of blacks in this country. This monistic shift that made slavery the primary causal explanation behind everything black people are and are not, do and don't do, came about because the forgetfulness of whites, we might say, was studied. Since its rediscovery, first by academics in the 1960s, then by popular culture in the 1970s (remember the popularity of Alex Haley's *Roots*), slavery has been—and will continue to be—our obsession, partly because from the period of Reconstruction forward the Plantation School of writers, films like *Gone With the Wind,* and insouciant white Americans in general deliberately denied or downplayed the monstrous practices in the slaughterhouse of slavery. (Blacks often soft-pedaled them too before the 1960s, hoping to put the past behind them and keep moving forward, as when Martin Luther King, Jr., proclaimed, "The Negro understands and forgives and is ready to forget the past.") No event in American history—from the appearance of the first twenty black indentured servants sold off a Dutch ship at Jamestown in 1619 to the present debate on the future of affirmative action—can be properly understood without referencing the agony blacks endured as human chattel.

Everyone is stained, directly or indirectly, by those three hundred years of systematic oppression, including immigrants who arrived from Europe well after Abraham Lincoln's 1863 Emancipation Proclamation. Yet many Americans, blacks among them, sometimes feel weary from being reminded of events that ended so long ago, weary of being accused, weary of being called co-conspirators in crimes that took place before they were born. But they can object to our obsession with American slavery no more than one can object to our equally passionate interest in the hows and whys of the Holocaust. Still, I believe we should clarify a point or two, if only for the sake of fidelity to the enormous complexity of the three-thousand-year-old historical record on human bondage.

First of all, slavery is *humanity's* original sin.

It is safe to say that every country and culture, Eastern and Western, has at some benighted hour in its history enslaved other human beings. This execrable institution was not widely questioned as wrong until the eighteenth century, and then only in a Europe that had experienced the Enlightenment, and by Quaker abolitionists. As Thomas Sowell points out in *Race and Culture,* we owe the word "slave" itself to the *Slavs,* who were forced into bondage in Europe and the Ottoman Empire. Africa has its own long history of black-on-black slavery, one that includes the Ashanti tribe, which prospered by selling Africans to the Europeans. And even today Australia's Anti-Slavery Society suggests that this most evil of human practices is inexpugnable. The Society estimates there are 35,000 religious slaves in West Africa, girls as young as eight years old, who are sexually exploited by so-called holy men. Recently two *Baltimore Sun* reporters went to war-torn Sudan and bought the freedom of two boys, Garang Deng Kuot (age ten) and his brother Akok (twelve), from an Arab trader in Manyiel, a village in the southern province of Bahr el Ghazal; they purchased the brothers for five hundred dollars apiece, the cash equivalent of five cows. Adding to this evidence of slavery's interminable presence among our species, more than three hundred slaves in 1997 were returned to their families in southern Sudan with money raised by a Canadian evangelical television program called "100 Huntley Street" and the Swiss-based Christian Solidarity International. "It was women and children," explained Cal Bombay, vice president of Crossroads

Christian Communications, in an article in *The Seattle Times* (April 2, 1997). "Some of the boys were up to 13 years old, and some of the women had been forcibly circumcised. . . . Some had been mutilated. One girl had her lip cut off."

Although we, as Americans, condemn slavery on our shores as the worst crime against humankind, it remains a firm and healthy institution, as hideous as ever, half a world away. There is little if any Yankee anger, outrage, or activism aimed at ending it. Sadly—and ironically—we seem less concerned about slavery present than we are with slavery past, and I suspect the reason for this can be found in one of the uncomfortable, messy conundrums of human nature, made even more conflicted when we factor in the phenomena of color, white guilt, and black accusation. African societies are *different* from our own. There, we have nonwhites enslaving nonwhites, and many Americans (white and black) shrug helplessly and hypocritically, kvetching, "Who are *we* to condemn the practices of a foreign people?" But in America two centuries ago the barbarism of bondage fused with the profound, primal, emblematic masks of White and Black—a Manichean division between Self and racial Other, thereby casting this social evil in stark, even apocalyptically theatrical figures.

By now we know—or *should* know—that Race is an illusion, a construct of culture. "Race has no basic biological reality," reported Jonathan Marks, a Yale University biologist, in a recent Knight-Ridder newspaper article. "The human species simply doesn't come packaged that way." Other scientists in that same 1996 article agreed with Marks, among them Stanford geneticist Luigi Cavalli-Sforza, who said, "The characteristics that we see with the naked eye that help us distinguish individuals from different continents are, in reality, skin-deep. Whenever we look under the veneer we find that the differences that seem so conspicuous to us are really trivial."

Those differences were not trivial, of course, to white slaveholders who in the early nineteenth century needed "natural" (to their way of thinking) justifications—or biblical ones—for the profitable institution of slavery. We know the history of race theory. We know when this effort to "categorize" human lives began, and how ludicrous its early attempts were. Whites identified a score of "races," even among those now considered white. For example, Italians were not accepted as "white" until the mid-nineteenth century; the Irish were perceived as a separate race until the mid-1800s; and it is not until the end of that century that Jews slowly began to be accepted into the exclusive club of "whiteness" (obviously by the 1930s their inclusion was still not widely accepted in Europe). Many of these racial categories were based on geographic regions, not genetic differences. Even the critical intellect of a W.E.B. Du Bois was taken in by the lie of racial essentialism as late as the twentieth century when, in his essay "The Conservation of Races," he claims that each race has its own unique "message" for civilization. My point, if it isn't clear yet, is that Race is *maya*. Illusion. A chimera constructed for reasons of social, political, and economic domination. Yet it is this illusion that distinguished slavery in the American South from all other histories of bondage and led to its being called "The *Peculiar* Institution."

Peculiar, indeed.

Unlike slavery among the Greeks and Romans, in Africa or the Far East, the existence of this institution in America from 1619 through 1865 is tempered by not only the volatile factor of race but also, in 1776, by the ideals of freedom that fueled the revolt of the colonists against King George. Thomas Jefferson wrote, then struck from an early draft of the Declaration of Independence, a paragraph condemning slavery. The Founders, who were slaveholders, time and again framed their outrage at England by comparing themselves to slaves. In a word, from the beginning of the Republic to the Civil War, the American soul was schizophrenically divided between desiring the profits that came from this ancient social arrangement and its own belief that "We hold these truths to be self-evident, that all men are created equal, that they are endowed by their Creator with certain unalienable Rights, that among these are Life, Liberty and the pursuit of Happiness." Could any slaveholding state be *more* "peculiar" and at odds with itself than this? Historian Gordon Woods observes, "Before the revolution, Americans like every other people took slavery for granted. But slavery came under indictment as a result of the same principles that produced the American founding. In a sense, the prospect of the Civil War is implicitly contained in the Declaration of Independence."

Before that final conflict in the 1860s, America was a crazy quilt of blacks who were free and unfree. Given its principles, the nation's future *hinged* on the status of the Negro, whose presence in this republic, whose slave revolts, slave narratives, and relentless resistance to bondage forced a fledgling nation to confront the implicit universality of its most cherished ideals—indeed, to better understand its own soul. Such a conflict could only produce a maddeningly complex, even Kafkaesque social world. There were Negroes born free in the North, who devoted their lives to agitating for the cause of abolition. There were others who were freed by their masters, only to be kidnapped back into bondage, especially after the passage of the Fugitive Slave Act. There were still others, like Anthony Johnson, a seventeenth-century black Virginia planter, who after his manumission from indentured servitude began accumulating property and owned a black slave, John Casor. And of course there were ex-slaves who escaped from slavery—with and without the help of the Abolitionists—and lived to tell the daring tale of their adventures in thrilling narratives that comprise one of the truly indigenous genres of literature produced in America: a body of works that, like a tree, provides the roots from which spring in the late nineteenth century branches leading to the rich traditions of black autobiography and the black novel.

In this outstanding two-volume collection, *I Was Born a Slave,* editor Yuval Taylor places before us slave narratives that captured the complexities of this very Peculiar Institution and created a powerful literary tradition. These are seminal texts for understanding slavery. And ourselves. As a novelist, teacher, storyteller, and screenwriter, I have worked with many of these classic narratives, particularly for my second novel, *Oxherding Tale* (1982), which used the form common to all these stories as the springboard for a philosophical tale that explored bondage on several levels—physical, political, psychological, metaphysical, and spiritual. Then, as now, I find this literary form—with its structural similarities to the Puritan narrative, which place the slave narrative in a tradition stretching back to St. Augustine's *Confessions*—*more* than fascinating. I revisit them frequently, and I'm happy to admit their crucial influence on PBS dramas I've written, such as "Booker" (Wonderworks, 1985).

No American's education can be called complete if these works are missing from his understanding—specifically the narratives of Olaudah Equiano, whose declaration, "When you make men slaves you compel them to live with you in a state of war," rings as true for our time as it did for his; and that of Frederick Douglass, of whom James Russell Lowell said, "The very *look* of Douglass was an irresistible logic against the oppression of his race" (italics mine); as well as the stirring stories of William Wells Brown, Josiah Henson, Nat Turner, and Charles Ball.

We owe Yuval Taylor our thanks for bringing together so many of these intriguing documents—some long out of print, others appearing here for the first time since their original publication. On these pages you will find firsthand witnesses—many unique voices—to the shame that was slavery. But you will find as well adventure, ingenious escapes, humor (yes, that is here too), and the full, ambiguous range of the human spirit, its darkness and breathtaking triumphs.

You will find, in a word, our collective stories as Americans.

CHARLES JOHNSON
SEATTLE, 1998

NO matter how many years may pass, the stigma of slavery will remain ineradicably imprinted on our country. It was an established fact long before our birth as a nation; it caused our greatest war; it has shadowed every struggle, defeat, and victory of our land. Whites still apologize for it; blacks still resent it; and we are all oppressed by its legacy.

The slaves whose narratives are collected here tried to redeem the burden of that oppression. They transformed themselves from victims into agents of resistance just by telling their stories and protesting the vast injustice that was being done to them. Together, they established a popular literary genre, sold hundreds of thousands of books, and inflamed antislavery sentiment. On the whole, they did not write for posterity—they intended a more immediate impact—yet they produced works of lasting literary and historical value. In doing so, they performed an act of liberation.

I hope this anthology can further this act by making these invaluable documents available once again in a compact, affordable edition. I hope it can liberate these works from their isolation in libraries, used-book stores, and difficult-to-read microfilms. I hope it will prove, once and for all, that the contribution of the slaves to our literature was not only two or three works of uncommon power, but a whole body of inventive, lucid, thoughtful, and passionate works of art.

Between the importation of the first documented shipload of Africans to Virginia in 1619 to the death of the last former slave in the 1970s, some six thousand North American slaves told their own stories in writing or in written interviews.[1] The majority of these accounts are brief (many were included in periodicals, collections, or other books), but approximately 150 of them were separately published as books or pamphlets ranging from eight pages to two volumes.[2]

These separately published narratives fall into three relatively distinct periods. From the 1770s to the 1820s, the narrators for the most part conceived of their lives as adventures or spiritual journeys, rather than as illustrations of a pernicious institution; in the titles of their books they called themselves Africans, not slaves.

But beginning in 1824, with the publication of the *Life of William Grimes, the Runaway Slave,* the reverse became the case. The slave narrative began to show distinct signs of being a cohesive genre that used the autobiographical form to enlighten the world about the facts of slavery. Over the years the narratives also became increasingly novelistic—those published after 1852, the date of Harriet Beecher Stowe's *Uncle Tom's Cabin,* were far more likely to employ fictionalized dialogue.

The abolitionist slave narratives written during the genre's heyday—over eighty were published between 1836 and the end of the Civil War in 1865—exhibit a large number of common elements. The typical narrative includes a preface describing it as a "plain, unvarnished tale";[3] the first sentence begins, "I was born . . . "; the plot includes, among other events, a slave auction, the separation of the narrator from his family, an exceptionally strong and proud slave who refuses to be whipped, and at least two escapes, one of them successful; and the narrative concludes with an appendix of some kind.[4] Yet because the experience and voice of each slave was unique, most of the narratives avoid being formulaic.[5]

After the Civil War, the narratives underwent a fundamental shift in tone. The righteousness and anger of the classic narratives were muted; the plots ended with the narrator adjusting to newfound freedoms, rather than calling for them from exile; and certain aspects of slave life began to seem quaint, in keeping with the imagery of the Sambo tales and minstrel shows then popular. This loss of urgency can be to some degree attributed to a change in the purpose of the narratives: rather than trying to convince their audience of slavery's evils, the writers attempted to present a balanced picture of their lives for the edification of readers. And thematically, the emphasis on *freedom* in the classic narratives was replaced by a corresponding emphasis on *progress*.[6]

Whether before or after emancipation, the slave narrative, with very few exceptions, was written or dictated by a *former* slave. Especially before the end of the Civil War, these narrators by no means represented a cross section of the slave population. In the history of the institution in the United States, probably between 1 and 2 percent of the slave population managed to escape. The narrators thus tended to be unusually brave, physically strong, resourceful, and imaginative individuals. Most of them hailed from near the Mason-Dixon line. They were often literate; a large number had served as "house slaves" and had thus acquired some of their masters' knowledge of the world; most had excellent memories and superb analytic skills. In addition, a disproportionate number of narrators were mulattos, who constituted only between 7 and 12 percent of the slave population—mulattos were not only more likely to be house slaves, but it was easier for them to pass as white when escaping.[7] The narrators varied in age from their early twenties (Moses Roper) to their mid-seventies (James Mars). Between 10 and 12 percent of them were women (however, only one self-penned narrative of a female American slave was published before 1865—Harriet Jacobs's 1861 *Incidents in the Life of a Slave Girl*).

More than half of the separately published slave narratives were penned by the slaves themselves,[8] and many were also self-published. A large number, however, were dictated by the slave to an amanuensis or editor, usually a white man. In many cases, as John W. Blassingame has shown, there is good reason to believe that the amanuensis hewed carefully to the words of the slave.[9] Sometimes editors added passages based on their own research. And occasionally the slave's story was more or less rewritten. For example, the *Narrative of Henry Box Brown* (1849) features the following words on the title page: "Written from a Statement of Facts Made by Himself. With remarks upon the remedy for slavery by Charles Stearns";[10] and the *Narrative of Sojourner Truth* (1850) is a third-person biography written by Olive Gilbert.

"The function of the slave narrative," writes Crispin Sartwell, "is apparently straightforward: resistance to oppression by speaking the truth"[11]—or, to quote a current catchphrase, "speaking truth to power." But this is the *central* goal, not the only one. Considering the great variety of narratives, one might name seven distinct functions: to document the conditions of slavery; to persuade the reader of its evils; to impart religious inspiration; to affirm the narrator's personhood; to redefine what it means to be black; to earn money; and, last but not least, to delight or fascinate the reader.

Although in the first half of this century slave narratives were disparaged as biased or fictionalized, in the 1970s scholars began to recognize that they are the richest firsthand source for information about plantation life.[12] The goal of documentation is evident in the titles of certain narratives, such as *Slavery in the United States* (Charles Ball, 1836), or *Slave Life in Georgia* (John Brown, 1855); in many of the appendices to the narratives, which draw from a wide variety of documentary material; and in sections of the narratives that spell out in detail the daily regimen of the slave, the method of growing crops, what and when the slaves ate, the different kinds of whips, and so on. Later narratives are especially explicit about this purpose: in his introduction, James Mars says his reason for publishing his narrative (1864) is that "many of the people now on the stage of life do not know that slavery ever lived in Connecticut"; in his preface, Louis Hughes (1897) asks, "To what purpose is the story which follows?" and responds, "the narrator presents his story . . . in the hope that it may add something of accurate information regarding the character and influence of an institution which for two hundred years dominated the country."[13]

Many narratives constituted political appeals; publishing a narrative could be as political an act as giving an abolitionist speech. Some—for example, Samuel Ringgold Ward's *Autobiography of a Fugitive Negro* (1855) or the first half of the *Narrative of Henry Box Brown*—are little more than abolitionist rhetoric in a narrative frame. Although many a narrative called itself a "plain, unvarnished tale," few were without some kind of exhortation or apostrophe on the evils of slavery and its conflict with Christian principles or those upon which this country was founded.

While edifying or inspirational matter was at times linked with political persuasion, the narratives were often fundamentally religious in character. For example, in the quasi-mystical *Incidents in the Life of Solomon Bayley* (1820) the narrator, a fugitive slave, is tendered divine protection by a circle of birds in the woods; and the *Life of John Thompson* (1856) concludes with a sermon that allegorizes the narrator's experiences aboard a whaling vessel. Some of the narratives are explicit about their religious or inspirational aims: near the beginning of his narrative, Bayley exclaims, "O! that all people would come to admire him [God] for his goodness and declare his wonders which he doth for the children of men";[14] and in his preface to *The Fugitive Blacksmith* (1849), James W. C. Pennington declares, "Especially have I felt anxious to save professing Christians, and my brethren in the ministry, from falling into a great mistake."

The slave not only identified writing with his newfound freedom, but his book with his newfound selfhood. Austin Steward (1857) goes so far as to say, "The author . . . sends out this history—presenting as it were his *own body,* with the marks and scars of the tender mercies of slave drivers upon it."[15] Slaves were, of course, property, and therefore did not own themselves; they were also forbidden to read and write. Self-expression, then, was one of the greatest boons of freedom—witness the joy of Harriet Jacobs's exclamation, "What a comfort it is, to be free to *say* so!" Even if they did not put it into words, many a fugitive slave may have easily concluded that the mere act of writing was the ultimate act of self-affirmation, the ultimate denial of enslavement. As Annette Niemtzow puts it, "I write, therefore I am, says the slave autobiographer."[16]

The literature of the slavery era is replete with stereotypes of docile, idiotic, or savage Negroes, and one of the functions of slave narratives was to counteract such racist views. The very appearance of a book written by a black man could well confound white readers; as Sartwell notes, "the notion of black authorship, particularly early on, was vexed: it appeared to many people to be *a priori* impossible; it was as if we had discovered a book by a baboon." Beyond that, slaves needed to redefine themselves against the prevailing notion, broadcast by Southern slaveholders and accepted by many in the North, that slaves were "happy darkies gratefully accept[ing] the protection of fatherly masters."[17] The narratives are notable for their complete lack of, as Kenny J. Williams puts it, "lush green fields with singing slaves working hard but happily [near] the big plantation house staffed by authoritarian house slaves and beautiful women in billowing gowns."[18]

Naturally, the act of publication was usually influenced by pecuniary motives. Moses Grandy (1844) is one of several narrators who made this explicit: "Whatever profit may be obtained by the sale of this book . . . will be faithfully employed in redeeming my remaining children and relatives from the dreadful condition of slavery."[19] Another was William Grimes, who said at the end of his narrative, "I hope some will buy my books from charity; but I am no beggar. I am now entirely destitute of property; where and how I shall live I don't know." James Mars concluded the second edition of his narrative with these words: "I am now in my seventy-sixth year of life, and as my joints are stiff with old age and hard labor, finding so ready a sale for my pamphlets, I am induced to take this method to get a living, as I can walk about from house to house." The "Advertisement to the Second Edition" (1838) of Moses Roper's narrative states that its sale will help the author "create a fund which may enable him to qualify himself to instruct the heathen"; six years later Roper wrote, "by the sale of my book . . . [I] have paid for my education and supported myself."[20] As Williams points out, the words "written by himself" on the title pages of so many slave narratives "were used not only to assure the reader of reliability but also make certain that the reader was aware that the author would receive any monetary value from the sale of the book."[21]

The most explicitly denied function, yet the one to which slave narratives most owe their success, was their capacity to delight or fascinate the reader. To "delight and instruct" were the two standard aims of many eighteenth- and nineteenth-century narrative works, whether fiction or factual. Daniel Defoe, for example, writes in his preface to *Moll Flanders* (1722), "There is in this Story abundance of delightful Incidents, and all of them usefully apply'd. There is an agreeable turn Artfully given them in the relating, that naturally Instructs the Reader either one way or other." The slave narratives, however, very rarely make explicit any such aim to delight the reader, or make any claims for their artfulness. For example, Olaudah Equiano, whose masterful narrative (1789) appears to owe a good deal to Defoe,[22] implicitly denies the fact that his narrative "abound[s] in great or striking events." He spells out the goals of his narrative as follows: "If it affords satisfaction to my numerous friends . . . or in the smallest degree promotes the interests of humanity, the ends for which it was undertaken will be fully attained." In his dedication to Great Britain's Parliament, he states that "the chief design" of his narrative "is to excite in your august assemblies a sense of compassion for the miseries which the Slave-Trade has entailed on my unfortunate countrymen." However, large portions of his narrative have no relation whatever to the slave trade. Lastly, he admits,

> I am sensible I ought to entreat your pardon for addressing to you a work so wholly devoid of literary merit; but, as the production of an unlettered African, who is actuated by the hope of becoming an instrument towards the relief of his suffering countrymen, I trust that *such a man,* pleading to *such a cause,* will be acquitted of boldness and presumption.

Of course this kind of statement can be attributed to literary modesty, which is as old as literature itself; it is nevertheless striking how many narratives similarly insist upon their lack of literary merit, and that almost none of them purport to delight as well as instruct.[23] The *Narrative of the Life of J. D. Green* (1864), for example, clearly aims to amuse the reader with the many farcical incidents it describes; but one would never guess that from the prefatory material, which simply invokes the "horrors" of slavery.

The method of storytelling in the narratives—often reminiscent of adventure stories or sentimental novels—implies that delighting the audience was indeed one of their goals. While this goal may constitute a primary claim on readers' attention, however, it may have been seen at the time as detracting from their *central* goal (speaking truth to power). In the eighteenth and nineteenth centuries, when the conventions used to distinguish fiction from nonfiction were not as clear as those of today, it was important that the narratives deny being even remotely fictional—especially since a number of fictional slave narratives were published in the period as well.[24] As William L. Andrews writes:

> As a class, no group of American autobiographers has been received with more skepticism and resistance than the ex-slave. . . . Black autobiographers [were forced] to invent devices and strategies that would endow their stories with the appearance of authenticity. . . . The reception of [the black autobiographer's] narrative as truth depended on the degree to which his artfulness could hide his art.[25]

But their power to fascinate, delight, and thrill is a primary reason the slave narratives were so widely read. It seems that they were popular among both men and women, young and old, black and white, Northerners, Southerners (as evidenced by the scores of proslavery Confederate romances published to rebut slave narratives),[26] British, and, considering the number of translations into a host of languages, practically all literate people. In short, their appeal was universal. An 1855 issue of *Putnam's Monthly* explained:

> Our English literature has recorded many an example of genius struggling against adversity, . . . yet none of these are so impressive as the case of the solitary slave, in a remote district, surrounded by none but enemies, conceiving the project of his escape, teaching himself to read and write to facilitate it, accomplishing it at last, and subsequently raising himself to a leadership in a great movement in behalf of his brethren.[27]

Other readers remarked on the narratives' romantic nature. The transcendentalist minister Theodore Parker, in his oration on "The American Scholar," said, "there is one portion of our permanent literature . . . which is wholly indigenous and original. . . . I mean the Lives of Fugitive Slaves. . . . All the original romance of Americans is in them, not in the white man's novel."[28] Angelina Grimké wrote to Theodore Dwight Weld, "We rejoiced to hear of the fugitives' escape from bondage, tho' some of the pleasure was abridged by the caution to keep these things close. . . . Many and many a tale of romantic horror can the slaves tell."[29] And Senator Charles Sumner called the fugitive slaves "among the heroes of our age. Romance has no storms of more thrilling interest than theirs. Classical antiquity has preserved no examples of adventurous trial more worthy of renown."[30] Part trickster, part pilgrim, the fugitive slave—wandering the wilderness and defying death on a quasi-religious quest for freedom—proved indeed to be the ideal American hero. And his narrative was just what readers were thirsting for.

The first slave narrative, that of James Gronniosaw,[31] went through twelve editions between 1772 and 1800. Olaudah Equiano's went through thirteen editions between 1789 and 1794—including translations into Dutch, German, and Russian—and twenty-two editions by 1837. *The Confessions of Nat Turner* (1831) is said to have sold between forty and fifty thousand copies. Charles Ball's narrative went through at least ten editions in twenty-five years. Moses Roper's went through eleven editions, selling thirty thousand copies between 1837 and 1844. Frederick Douglass's 1845 *Narrative* went through seven U.S. and nine British editions in five years, selling over thirty thousand copies by 1860; his 1855 *My Bondage and My Freedom* sold five thousand copies in two days, and his 1881 *Life and Times* went through another dozen editions. William Wells Brown's went through four American editions between 1847 and 1849, selling ten thousand copies; it sold another eleven thousand in England. The first version of Josiah Henson's narrative (1849) sold six thousand copies in three years, well before his name became associated with that of Stowe's Uncle Tom; publishers estimated that one hundred thousand copies of the various versions of his narrative had been sold by the century's end, and it was translated into Welsh, French, Swedish, Dutch, and German. Solomon Northup's sold twenty-seven thousand copies in 1853 and 1854. And James Mars's 1864 narrative went into a thirteenth edition in 1876.[32] (For purposes of comparison, here are a few other sales figures from the 1850s: the most popular novel of the nineteenth century, *Uncle Tom's Cabin,* sold three hundred thousand copies in its first year; Longfellow's *Hiawatha* sold fifty thousand copies in five months; Hawthorne's *The Scarlet Letter* sold between thirteen and fourteen thousand copies in thirteen years; and *Walden, Moby Dick,* and *Leaves of Grass* sold fewer than two thousand copies each.)

Judging solely from these numbers, these ten slave narrators (all represented in this anthology) were probably the most popular. (If we consider *Up from Slavery* [1901] a slave narrative—although only its first chapter discusses slavery[33]— Booker T. Washington would share that status.) However, the number of editions is a problematic indication of popularity. In the case of James Mars, for example, this number can probably be attributed more to the persistence of the author in hand-selling what were no doubt small print runs than to a truly widespread popularity. At any rate, a score of other narratives went through between three and five editions each—including those of Venture Smith (1798), Thomas Cooper (1832), James Williams (*A Narrative of Events,* 1837), James Williams (*Narrative of James Williams,* 1838),[34] Elleanor Eldridge (1838), Lunsford Lane (1842), Moses Grandy (1843), Lewis and Milton Clarke (1845–46), Henry Bibb (1849), James W. C. Pennington (1849), Thomas H. Jones (1849), Sojourner Truth (1850), John Brown (1855), Peter Randolph (1855), Austin Steward (1856), and Jacob Stroyer (1879).

In the first half of this century slave narratives fell out of print and, because they were products of African American consciousness, were largely ignored by scholars of American history. But black writers have always appreciated them for their striking originality, complexity, and power. Nineteenth-century works influenced by slave narratives include Stowe's *Uncle Tom's Cabin* (1852); William Wells Brown's *Clotel* (1853); Harriet Wilson's *Our Nig* (1859); Martin R. Delaney's *Blake* (1861); and Mark Twain's *The Adventures of Huckleberry Finn* (1884); the number of twentieth-century works is too large to count, but some of the more prominent titles include James Weldon Johnson's *Autobiography of an Ex-Colored Man* (1912); Claude McKay's *Home to Harlem* (1928); Arna Bontemps's *Black Thunder* (1936); Zora Neale Hurston's *Their Eyes Were Watching God* (1937); W. E. B. Du Bois's *Dusk of Dawn* (1940); Richard Wright's *Black Boy* (1945); Ralph Ellison's *Invisible Man* (1952); James Baldwin's *Go Tell It on the Mountain* (1953); *The Autobiography of Malcolm X* (1965); Margaret Walker's *Jubilee* (1966); Maya Angelou's *I Know Why the Caged Bird Sings* (1970); Ernest Gaines's *The Autobiography of Miss Jane Pittman* (1971); Alex Haley's *Roots* (1976); Ishmael Reed's *Flight to Canada* (1976); Charles Johnson's *Oxherding Tale* (1982); Sherley Anne Williams's *Dessa Rose* (1986); Toni Morrison's *Beloved* (1987); and Caryl Philips's *Cambridge* (1991). Indeed, most if not all postbellum African American prose works are descended from the slave narrative, not only because it was the first distinctive African American literary genre, but because of its potent mixture of storytelling, racial awareness, social critique, and self-reflection—elements characteristic of the greatest black literary achievements.

While the narratives describe well the social, economic, legal, and labor conditions of the slaves, they also frequently refer to larger political matters. Their reading can thus be enhanced by a concise look at the major personalities, events, and trends relating to the development of the institution of slavery and the rise of abolitionism in the United States and Great Britain.[35]

If the United States was "conceived in Liberty," as Lincoln's Gettysburg Address would have it, it was no less conceived in *slavery,* which had stained the New World from the moment of its discovery. Christopher Columbus wrote of the Caribbean natives that "there are no better people. . . . They love their neighbors as themselves, and they have the sweetest speech in the world; and are gentle and always laughing";[36] but he did not hesitate to impress them for service on his ships, thus more or less enslaving them. John Smith, the leader of the early British colonists, had been enslaved himself, in Turkey; as if establishing a pattern for the distant future, he killed his master and fled northward. In Jamestown, Virginia, frustrated by the unwillingness of the colonists to endure hard labor, he was dismissed from the governorship; his replacement, Sir Thomas Dale, as Frederick Law Olmsted later wrote, "ordered them all, gentle and simple, to work in gangs under overseers, and threatened to shoot the first man who refused to labor, or was disobedient."[37]

Shortly thereafter Africans were introduced to the British settlements—the first documented shipload arrived in Virginia in 1619, but some may have been landed even earlier.[38] Numerous black slaves were in Spanish Florida by that time, and tens of thousands in the West Indies; but only small numbers of Africans were shipped to the British colonies prior to the 1680s. Not until 1661 were these legally called slaves, and indeed many of them were only indentured servants. At first, mulatto children followed the condition of the father, just as in the French, Dutch, Danish, German, Spanish, and Portuguese colonies; however, in 1662 Virginia enacted a law that the children of slaves should follow the condition of the mother, thus essentially licensing the rape of female slaves by their masters. Soon thereafter, it was lawful in Virginia to do almost anything to one's slaves—even kill them.[39]

It took little time for these and other pernicious effects of the institution to be noticed, especially with the massive importation of Africans between 1680 and 1750. For example, when the colony of Georgia was founded in 1733, slavery was prohibited within its borders. William Byrd II, a prominent Virginia farmer and slaveholder, perceptively predicted the future of Southern slavery in a 1736 letter to John Perceval, Earl of Egmont:

> I am sensible of many bad consequences of multiplying these Ethiopians amongst us. They blow up the pride, & ruin the industry of our white people, who seing a rank of poor creatures below them, detest work for fear it shoud make them look like slaves. . . .
>
> Another unhappy effect of many Negros, is, the necessity of being severe. Numbers make them insolent, & then foul means must do, what fair will not. . . . Yet even this is terrible to a good naturd man, who must submit to be either a fool or a fury. And this will be more our unhappy case, the more Negros are increast amongst us.[40]

But the institution of slavery was not widely questioned until the late eighteenth century. After all, it predates recorded history. Slave labor was used in building the Egyptian pyramids, and the Bible includes laws concerning the treatment—and manumission—of slaves. Modern slavery had its origins in the fifteenth century, when the Portuguese—followed by the British, Dutch, French, and Spanish—began to exploit Africans as slaves. And while it was in the Americas that their use was most widespread, it was in Europe that Enlightenment ideas led to the rise of abolitionism.

It was under the influence of those ideas that Thomas Jefferson, a slaveholder himself, wrote, in a subsequently stricken section of his Declaration of Independence, that King George III had "waged cruel war against human nature itself, violating its most sacred rights of life and liberty in the persons of a distant people who never offended him, captivating and carrying them into slavery in another hemisphere." But despite protestations such as these, and despite the tens of thousands of slaves who ran away during the American Revolution, slaves numbered 20 percent of the U.S. population by 1790, and the next two decades would witness the largest importation of Africans yet.

In 1787 the U.S. constitution declared a slave to count as three-fifths of a person in calculating representation for the states, thus granting a vastly disproportionate share of power to slaveholders. Ninety percent of the slaves lived in the South, where slavery had become an integral part of the plantation system of agriculture; and by 1804, in large part due to the influence of Quakers, all except one of the Northern states (Delaware) had at least begun to abolish slavery. It had become abundantly clear by this time that slavery was the great factor dividing the northern from the southern states. By 1808 the African slave trade had been outlawed by both the British Empire and the United States (though the illegal slave trade flourished for a long time thereafter), and in 1833, slavery itself, which had been abolished in England in 1772, was abolished throughout the British Empire. But in the United States, slavery was not only seemingly irrevocable, but had come to be seen as the overriding political, economic, and social issue of the age.

In the North, the 1830s witnessed the rise of the abolitionist movement, which grew out of the evangelical religious revivals of the 1820s. In 1829 David Walker, a free black man, published his seminal *Appeal,* one of the most vigorous denunciations of slavery ever written. The first issue of William Lloyd Garrison's *The Liberator,* a radical abolitionist journal, followed in 1831. The American Anti-Slavery Society, which grew out of Garrison's New England Anti-Slavery Society, was organized two years later in Philadelphia, primarily by Garrison and Arthur and Lewis Tappan, a few months after the abolition of slavery in the British Empire. Arthur Tappan, who had made a fortune in the dry-goods business, was the first president of the society; but Garrison, who was already famous for his intemperate language, dominated it. He would become president of the society in 1843, and retain that position—while continuing to publish his paper—until the end of the Civil War. The society integrated its black and white members, advocated nonviolence, and included in its goals equal rights for free blacks. In 1835 it launched a massive propaganda campaign, flooding the slave states with abolitionist literature, sending agents throughout the North to organize antislavery societies, and petitioning Congress to abolish slavery in the District of Columbia.

The mood quickly turned violent. Mobs attacked the abolitionists in the North; in the South their pamphlets were suppressed; the House of Representatives enacted a gag rule that prevented the discussion of antislavery proposals; and in 1837 the abolitionist editor Elijah P. Lovejoy was murdered while a mob destroyed his press for the fourth time. Despite these setbacks, by 1838 almost a quarter-million Americans belonged to antislavery societies.

In the South the suppression of freedoms was fed by fear. In 1831 Nat Turner had led the Southampton Insurrection in Virginia, killing between fifty-seven and sixty-five whites in the most deadly slave revolt in U.S. history. This uprising, like earlier ones led by Gabriel Prosser and Denmark Vesey, sparked violent reprisals and the passage of more oppressive laws throughout the South. In Virginia, for example, black ministers were forbidden to preach, education for free blacks was denied, and free blacks who had left the state could not return. Similarly, after the Denmark Vesey insurrection, black sailors landing in South Carolina were locked up in jail until their vessels put out to sea.

The North-South divide was further encouraged by the passage of a series of federal laws supposedly designed to delimit slavery. The Missouri Compromise, passed by Congress in 1820 and 1821, included a provision prohibiting slavery in the remainder of the Louisiana Purchase north of 36° 30' (the southern boundary of Missouri); the Compromise of 1850 included the admission of California as a free state, the prohibition of the slave trade in the District of Columbia, and a more stringent fugitive slave law; and the Kansas-Nebraska Act of 1854, in contravention to the Missouri Compromise, allowed Kansas and Nebraska, both of which were north of the line, to decide themselves the question of slavery in their respective territories. While all of these laws purported to be compromises between Northern and Southern congressmen, they all favored the South, and did little to calm the conflict between the regions, instead entrenching each side more adamantly in its respective position. The key figures in enacting these compromises were Henry Clay, Daniel Webster, John C. Calhoun, and Stephen Douglas.

Henry Clay was at various times Speaker of the Senate, Speaker of the House, and secretary of state; he has been called the Great Pacificator and the Great Compromiser. Although he grew up in Virginia and Kentucky and represented the latter state in Congress, he was no apologist for slavery, denouncing extremists in both North and South. If there was one man most responsible for the Missouri Compromise and the Compromise of 1850, it was Clay.

Daniel Webster represented Massachusetts in Congress, both as representative and senator, through four decades; his speeches in Congress and his eloquent public addresses brought him acclaim as the greatest orator of his time, and he served as secretary of state under William Henry Harrison, John Tyler, and Millard Fillmore. His overriding concern was the preservation of the Union in the face of increasing sectionalism; when he backed the Compromise of 1850, which included the worst of the fugitive slave laws, he was reviled by antislavery groups in the North.

John C. Calhoun was a South Carolina congressman, secretary of war under President Monroe, vice president under John Quincy Adams and Andrew Jackson, and the preeminent spokesman for the South. It was Calhoun who directed the passage of the ordinance of nullification in South Carolina in 1832, declaring that the state had the power to nullify a Federal tariff. He was the most eloquent—and most extreme—defender of the doctrine of states' rights, proclaiming a position of absolute state sovereignty in dramatic debates with Daniel Webster; and he was equally eloquent in defending slavery. His theories later served as the foundation of the Confederate constitution.

Stephen Douglas served fourteen years as Illinois senator and originated the doctrine of popular sovereignty embodied in the Kansas-Nebraska Act, in which each state would decide for itself the question of slavery. Also a great orator, he found himself caught between the demands of his state and those of his party; he won the 1860 Democratic presidential nomination only after Southern delegates withdrew to nominate their own candidate, John C. Breckenridge.

Legislative compromises were not the only ways that Americans tried to resolve the slavery issue. The American Colonization Society was set up to deal with the problem of free blacks, who did not enjoy the same freedoms as whites anywhere in the United States, by resettling them in Africa. The society received support from Henry Clay, and in 1819 Congress appropriated one hundred thousand dollars for returning blacks to Africa. The result was the founding of Liberia in 1821. Abraham Lincoln would later profess to be in favor of colonization. But the movement was savagely attacked by abolitionists, who argued that it strengthened slavery in the South by removing free blacks; and blacks themselves were unenthusiastic about the project, maintaining that they were Americans, not Africans.[41]

In contrast to the compromisers and colonizationists, the abolitionists were largely unconcerned about making peace or preserving the Union. They boasted such national figures as Theodore Dwight Weld, James Birney, John Greenleaf Whittier, Wendell Phillips, Frederick Douglass, Charles Sumner, and William Henry Seward. Weld, who with Garrison was perhaps the most important abolitionist, organized agents for the American Anti-Slavery Society, edited its paper (the *Emancipator*), directed the national campaign to send antislavery petitions to Congress, and wrote the widely popular *American Slavery As It Is* (1839), a seminal influence on *Uncle Tom's Cabin*. Birney, a Kentuckian, freed his slaves in 1834, helped organize the Kentucky Anti-Slavery Society, became executive secretary of the American Anti-Slavery Society, and was nominated for the presidency by the abolitionist Liberty Party in 1840 and 1844. Whittier, a Massachusetts Quaker, was, along with Longfellow, one of the most popular American poets of the nineteenth century; he was also an active abolitionist, running for Congress on the Liberty ticket in 1842, helping to found the Republican Party, and serving as the amanuensis for the 1838 *Narrative of James Williams, An American Slave*. Phillips was a dynamic abolitionist lecturer, advocating not only an end to slavery, but the dissolution of the Union and the granting to blacks of land, education, and full civil rights. Douglass wrote three important slave narratives; edited his own abolitionist newspaper, *The North Star*, for seventeen years; lectured widely; was elected president of the New England Anti-Slavery Society; and organized Massachusetts blacks to fight in the Civil War. Sumner was a U.S. senator from Massachusetts for twenty-three years, during which time he attacked the fugitive slave laws, denounced the Kansas-Nebraska act, delivered notable antislavery speeches, and helped organize the Republican Party. Seward served two terms as governor of New York State, two terms as U.S. senator, and became secretary of state under Abraham Lincoln—during most of which he vociferously opposed slavery.

The 1850s witnessed a huge rise in the popularity of abolitionism. The 1793 fugitive slave law, providing for the return between states of escaped slaves, had been loosely enforced, with some Northern states allowing fugitives trials before their return and others forbidding state officials to capture them. So, as part of the Compromise of 1850, a new fugitive slave law was passed, commanding "all good citizens" to "aid and assist" Federal marshals in recapturing fugitive slaves, and imposing extraordinarily heavy penalties upon anyone who assisted a slave to escape. When captured, any black could be taken before a special commissioner, where he would be denied a jury trial, his testimony would not be admitted, and the affidavit of anyone claiming ownership would be sufficient to establish it in the eyes of the law. Thus all free blacks, whether fugitives or not, were put in danger of being enslaved. The result was an increase in kidnappings, in active resistance to the law, and in antislavery feeling in the North. Abolitionists, who had been widely considered extremists, finally started to gain widespread popularity.

Meanwhile the cotton the slaves produced had become not only the United States' leading export, but exceeded in value all other exports combined. After the slave trade was outlawed in 1807 approximately one million slaves were moved from the states that produced less cotton (Maryland, Virginia, the Carolinas) to those that produced more (Georgia, Alabama, Mississippi, Louisiana, Texas)—a migration almost twice as large as that from Africa to the British colonies and the United States. With the increase in cotton production, the price of slaves went up,[42] to such an extent that by 1860 capital investment in slaves in the South—who now numbered close to four million, or one-third of the population—exceeded the value of all other capital worth, including land.

Due to the increased economic importance of slavery, and in reaction to the North's ever more ardent condemnations of it, between 1830 and 1860 manumission was increasingly prohibited in Southern states, freed blacks were expelled, black churches were eliminated, and penalties for hurting or killing blacks were largely ignored. Proslavery literature was vigorously disseminated, the possession of abolitionist literature was made a serious crime, freedom of speech regarding slavery was effectively curtailed, and prices were even put on the heads of Garrison, Arthur Tappan, and other leading abolitionists. The large majority of slaves were still owned by a small minority of landowners—only one quarter of Southern whites owned slaves, and only 12 percent of those owned more than twenty. But whether slaveholders or not, whites now wielded absolute power over blacks.

In the dozen years before the Civil War, three important factors exacerbated the conflict over slavery and made secession inevitable: the increasing appeal of abolitionism; legal changes; and armed conflict between pro- and antislavery factions.

The rising popularity of slave narratives in the fifteen years before the Civil War is only one example of the power of abolitionist literature. *Uncle Tom's Cabin,* based in part on slave narratives, cannot be underestimated as a factor in turning Northerners against slavery. It sold over three hundred thousand copies in one year and helped bring respect to the antislavery movement worldwide. Its influence was so strong that upon meeting the author Lincoln is said to have commented, "So this is the little lady who made this great war."

The Underground Railroad is another potent instance of the success of abolitionists in altering public perceptions of slavery. As even a cursory reading of the narratives of fugitive slaves will indicate, the major factor in their escapes was their own resourcefulness, although the assistance of free blacks, Quakers, and sympathetic Northern sailors certainly helped. The stories of the Underground Railroad, on the contrary, created the impression that a highly systematic and secret organization, run mostly by white abolitionists, conducted a majority of the fugitive slaves along secret routes from the South to the North. No such nationally coordinated organization existed; and regional Underground Railroads were responsible for a relatively small number of successful escapes. The Underground Railroad was partially a propaganda device to dramatize abolitionist heroism, thereby attracting followers in the North and increasing alarm in the South.

The most important change in the legal status of blacks was the decision by the Supreme Court in the 1857 Dred Scott case that Congress had no power to prohibit slavery in the territories, that the Missouri Compromise was unconstitutional, and that a black "whose ancestors were . . . sold as slaves" was not entitled to the rights of a Federal citizen and therefore had no standing in court. According to Chief Justice Roger B. Taney, who gave the majority decision, blacks had not been citizens at the time of the adoption of the Constitution and had not become citizens of the nation since. By coming down strongly on the side of the South in the question of slavery in the territories, the decision caused a decisive split in the Democratic Party.

The Kansas-Nebraska Act of 1854 had already caused considerable violence in "bleeding Kansas." Both proslavery and antislavery groups pushed settlers into Kansas, hoping to influence elections. Each camp founded its own towns, Lawrence and Topeka being antislavery and Leavenworth and Atchison proslavery. The first elections were won by the proslavery group, but armed Missourians had intimidated voters and stuffed ballot boxes. Then the legislature ousted all free-state members, removed the governor, and adopted proslavery statutes. In retaliation, the abolitionists set up a rival government, and a bloody local war ensued—all despite the fact that slaves in Kansas in 1856 probably numbered only four hundred at most.

One of the most active abolitionists in Kansas was John Brown, who killed five proslavery men in the Pottawatomie massacre in 1856. Three years later, with twenty-one followers, he captured the U.S. arsenal at Harper's Ferry, Virginia (now West Virginia), imprisoned the inhabitants, and took possession of the town, intending to liberate the slaves by setting up an armed stronghold to which they could flee and from which revolts could be initiated. The U.S. Marines assaulted the arsenal, however, killing ten of Brown's men and wounding Brown himself. Brown, who was hanged after a spectacular trial, became a martyr of the abolitionist cause, galvanizing the North with his boldness; his raid so alarmed slaveholders that the whole South began to ready itself for war.

Lincoln's election, the Civil War, and the emancipation of the slaves need not be addressed here, since they are largely immaterial to the narratives included in this anthology, and since the basic facts are widely known. Suffice it to note that slavery in the United States by no means ended at the close of the Civil War in 1865. Although they were not called *slavery,* the post-Reconstruction Southern practices of peonage, forced convict labor, and to a lesser degree sharecropping essentially continued the institution of slavery well into the twentieth century, and were in some ways even worse. (Peonage, for example, was a complex system in which a black man would be arrested for "vagrancy," another word for unemployment, ordered to pay a fine he could not afford, and incarcerated. A plantation owner would pay his fine and "hire" him until he could afford to pay off the fine himself. The peon was then forced to work, locked up at night, and, if he ran away, chased by bloodhounds until recaptured. One important difference between peonage and slavery was that while slaves had considerable monetary value for the plantation owner, peons had almost none, and could therefore be mistreated—and even murdered—without monetary loss.) However, these practices were ignored by post-emancipation slave narratives, which aimed to emphasize the progress blacks had made since emancipation and to minimize their status as victims.

This anthology collects into two volumes the twenty most important and interesting separately published English-language slave narratives. They are unabridged from their first editions and supplemented with introductions and annotations. As a whole, the collection represents the most comprehensive attempt ever undertaken to make this body of literature widely available.

The anthology's title, *I Was Born a Slave,* is taken from the heartbreaking first sentence of Harriet Jacobs's narrative: "I was born a slave; but I never knew it until six years of happy childhood had passed away." *The Experiences of Thomas H. Jones, who was a Slave for Forty-Three Years* also begins, "I was born a slave. My recollections of early life are associated with poverty, suffering and shame."[43] Washington's *Up From Slavery* begins with these five words as well; and, as previously noted, most of the narratives begin with the words "I was born." As James Olney points out, "Escaped slaves . . . in the face of an imposed non-identity and non-existence were impelled to assert over and over, 'I *was* born.'"[44] (It should be noted that three of the narrators included here—Gronniosaw, Equiano, and Northup—were *not* born slaves.)

The selection of the narratives is necessarily a personal one. A number of factors went into it; in order of importance, they are: readability, literary quality, historical importance, authenticity, relevance, uniqueness, length, and scarcity. A few words are in order about each of these criteria.

The first, readability, is no doubt the most subjective. Some of the narratives, I felt, might prove difficult for today's reader to get through. I have excluded the extremely polemic narratives, such as those of Samuel Ringgold Ward and Peter Randolph, for this reason, as well as those by narrators, such as Richard Allen, who put little emphasis on the development of character, setting, or the overall shape of their work.

Literary quality, as a criterion, is closely allied to readability. However, it also takes into account other important questions. Are the meanings of the narrative on or below the surface? Are the characters one-, two-, or three-dimensional? Does the narrative have emotional impact? Is the author's style original or cliché ridden? Is his perspective obvious or thought provoking? Is the narrative monotonous or does it offer variety?

Although there have been a number of books written on slave narratives, few of them subject the individual narratives to the kind of close and rigorous literary analysis that scholars have long performed on the works of other writers of the era.[45] Until the middle of this century, in fact, slave narratives were commonly considered unreliable, tendentious, and subliterate. Most treatments of the last fifty years examine slave narratives either as historical documents— straightforward, uncomplicated texts with little merit as literature—or as a more-or-less homogeneous literary genre rather than one that encompasses a wide range of works. And there have been few claims made for their status as "literature," except, of course, for individual narratives: those of Olaudah Equiano, Frederick Douglass, and Harriet Jacobs have often been acknowledged as masterpieces of their kind. In my opinion, a number of others merit similar approbation. Certainly not all of the narratives collected here are works of genius. But more than a few deserve the same standing in the canon of American literature as certain contemporary narrative works by Cooper, Hawthorne, Melville, Poe, and Stowe.[46]

I determined the historical importance of a work by considering both its popularity at the time of its publication (see p. xx) and how often it has been cited by later historians and scholars of the slave narrative tradition. The ten most cited and discussed narratives appear to be those of Equiano, Douglass, William Wells Brown, Bibb, Henson, Pennington, Northup, William and Ellen Craft, Jacobs, and Washington; all but the last are included herein.

When I set out to compile this volume I had no intention of excluding post–Civil War narratives; and if this collection had been three volumes rather than two, I would have certainly included several.[47] However, in neither quality nor importance did these narratives measure up to the twenty I have decided to include, for they lack the urgency of the narratives written between 1820 and 1861. Frances Smith Foster describes them as "cheerleading exercises to urge continued opportunites for integration of blacks into American society or to depict black contributions to the Horatio Alger tradition. Their descriptions of slavery were mild and offered as 'historical' evidence only."[48] And William Andrews writes, "The postbellum slave narrator treat[s] slavery more as an economic proving ground than an existential battleground. . . . The agenda of the postbellum slave narrative thus emphasizes unabashedly the tangible contribution that blacks made to the South, in and after slavery."[49] The narrative of James Mars, although written before the end of the Civil War, may give the reader a hint of the tone of some of the postbellum narratives—rather than looking forward to a time of freedom, it looks back to a now-vanished past.

A narrative written by the slave himself was more likely to be included in this collection than one dictated to an amanuensis; I excluded narratives whose authenticity is even more problematic, such as the U.S. edition of Henry Box Brown's narrative and The Narrative of Sojourner Truth, for although these books were written with the cooperation of the subject, large portions of them are not autobiographical. (Nat Turner's *Confessions,* which I did include, presents a similar problem, but to a lesser degree.) As a result, thirteen out of these twenty narratives were written by the slaves themselves rather than in collaboration with white editors.

I believe, however, that the question of authorship has little bearing on literary quality. It has long been traditional among literary critics to exclude "as-told-to's" from the canon. Andrews, for example, argues:

> Should an autobiography whose written composition was literally out of the hands of its black narrator be discussed on an equal footing with those autobiographies that were autonomously authored by the black subject himself or herself? Many so-called edited narratives of ex-slaves ought to be treated as ghostwritten accounts insofar as literary analysis is concerned. . . . It was the editor who controlled the manuscript and thus decided how a "statement of facts" became a "fiction of factual representation," a readable, convincing, and moving autobiography. . . . It would be naive to accord dictated oral narratives the same discursive status as autobiographies composed and written by the subjects of the stories themselves. . . . Would not ex-slaves have been inhibited . . . when talking to whites, particularly when the latter's confidence and favor were so necessary to a narrative's publication?[50]

While a collaborative effort, however, might compromise the authenticity or "blackness" of a text, in many cases it can enrich it considerably. After all, every black cultural product in our history has been necessarily mediated to some degree by white culture and its institutions, making claims of authenticity somewhat problematic. Furthermore, why should a jointly authored book be any less subject to literary analysis than one written by a single author? As for "inhibitions," I cannot believe that a slave would be any more inhibited telling his story to a white editor—especially one who had expressed considerable interest in him, his story, and his future—than writing his story for an anonymous white audience; and a comparison between edited and single-authored slave narratives will, I believe, bear this out. Can one characterize Solomon Northup, for example—whose narrative affirms that "the oppressors of my people are a pitiless and unrelenting race"—as inhibited? One need not go as far as Foster to find her comments on this matter worth repeating:

> Why, I wondered, should I refrain from serious consideration of these works until I could verify who wrote what word at what time and under what circumstances? . . . Why the overwhelming need to verify that the author of record did in fact insert each comma and comment? . . . I decided that I did not have to delay a consideration of the text and social context of slave narratives until I had first answered the riddle of who really wrote them. As far as I was concerned, such questions needed to be pursued by those who considered them important. For me, they had the same relevance as trying to establish the exact date of John Keats's death when it was the "Ode to a Grecian Urn" that engaged my imagination and stimulated my curiosity.[51]

Many of the richest and most compelling twentieth-century black autobiographies, from Ethel Waters's *His Eye Is on the Sparrow* to *The Autobiography of Malcolm X,* have been as-told-to's. Without these, and without the narratives of

Gronniosaw, Turner, Ball, the Clarke brothers, Henson, Northup, and John Brown, the world of black literature would be a significantly poorer place.[52]

Also problematic to my selection were those autobiographical works by former slaves that had little relevance to the questions of slavery. For example, although the first chapter of Booker T. Washington's *Up from Slavery,* "A Slave Among Slaves," is an extraordinary piece of writing, the rest of the book says next to nothing about the matter.

Because slave narratives, as a genre, have so many elements in common, I tried to select only narratives that were in some way truly outstanding. I therefore excluded some slightly less interesting narratives, such as Austin Steward's or Isaac Mason's, although they certainly have unique qualities. Length was also a factor—which again mitigated against the inclusion of Austin Steward—as was the amount of prefatory and appended material: the less, the better. I was more inclined to include narratives that are scarce than those that are readily available, such as those of Venture Smith, Sojourner Truth, Elizabeth Keckley, or Booker T. Washington. The anthology includes two narratives—those of J. D. Green and William Parker—that have never been reprinted in full, and close to half of them are currently out of print elsewhere.

I read and reread dozens of narratives before making the final selection, and I regret that for reasons of space I was unable to include the narratives of Venture Smith, Solomon Bayley, Mary Prince, James Williams (1838), Lunsford Lane, Sojourner Truth, Frederick Douglass (*My Bondage and My Freedom,* 1855), Austin Steward, Elizabeth Keckley, and Louis Hughes. All of these are well worth reading, and all are either in print or available on-line; complete citations and short descriptions of each will be found in part I of the bibliography. I also regret that more women are not represented in these pages; the sex of the narrator was not a factor in my selection.

Lastly, I was influenced in my selection by certain ideals shared by many contemporary black thinkers. All too often slaves have been portrayed as victims—by writers stretching from Olmsted, Stowe, and Twain in the nineteenth century[53] to Stanley Elkins and William Styron in our own recent past. Typical of this view is the recent debate about whether the U.S. government should "apologize" for slavery. The narratives in this anthology present the testimony of slaves who saw themselves less as victims than as members of a resistance movement. In my selection, I favored those slaves who actively resisted the fate the white man had decreed for them—rebellious slaves such as Frederick Douglass and Harriet Jacobs, even killers such as Nat Turner and William Parker. (Instead of apologizing, shouldn't the government *honor* slaves such as these?) This is another reason postbellum narratives did not make the cut. Before emancipation, for a slave to tell his own story was an act of resistance, not reflection. And perhaps that explains why these narratives still possess so much power over a century after their initial publication.

In presenting the narratives I have followed some simple rules. First, each narrative is absolutely unabridged. From cover to cover, every word and illustration is presented intact (with two minor exceptions: to save space, I have left out half-title pages and copyright pages, unless they contain material of special interest); only the most obvious typographical errors have been corrected. Second, the text is usually that of the first edition.[54] Later editions almost always contained additional material, much of which seems superfluous, especially considering space constraints. Where material added in later editions might more fully explain some portion of the earlier edition, it is noted in the annotations. Douglass, William Wells Brown, and Henson each published several substantially different narratives; because the first of these is invariably the most succinct and immediate, it is the one included here.

Each narrative is introduced with a few words of biographical detail, publication history, and interpretation. All footnotes in the text appeared in the original edition; all endnotes are mine. In the endnotes, citations are brief; full citations are given in the bibliography at the end of each volume. Sources for the endnotes are cited at the close of each note, unless the source is a general reference work.

I have annotated with dates (where available) and a brief biography all persons mentioned whom contemporaneous readers might have been expected to know, except for the most obvious (Shakespeare, Lincoln, Frederick Douglass, etc.). Also annotated are geographical details and eighteenth- and nineteenth-century words that may have vanished from today's dictionaries. Where the narrator quotes a poem, address, or literary phrase I have done my best to locate and annotate its source, although in some cases I have not succeeded. Where the author misspelled names or made factual errors, I have annotated corrections. Lastly, the annotations often contain historical details about events discussed in the narrative that for one reason or another the author did not fully elucidate.

A reader who attempts to read all twenty of these narratives in a short time may become frustrated by a certain amount of repetition (most pronounced in the first quarter or so of each narrative). In order to help the reader plan which narratives to read in which order, I have given brief descriptions of each below.

- The 1772 autobiography of **James Albert Ukawsaw Gronniosaw** was the first slave narrative, and was both popular and influential. Gronniosaw's experience in slavery was benign, but as a free man he was taken advantage of and ill treated. A profound Calvinist, he imbues with religious significance his adventures in Africa, New York, Amsterdam, England, and with a Caribbean privateer.
- **Olaudah Equiano** published one of the most famous and influential black autobiographies, a conversion/captivity/slave narrative that functions as a travel book, adventure tale, and apologia as well. It includes an extraordinarily wide range of experiences and accomplishments, from his abduction from an idyllic African land to his assimilation into British high society, all unified by his sense of black pride.
- **William Grimes** suffered under ten different owners, was haunted by ghosts and ridden by a witch, went on a hunger strike, tried to break his own leg, and was accused of thievery, pimping, and rape. His may be the most complex and

disconsolate of the narratives, for Grimes did not heroically triumph over adversity, but instead succumbed to it.

- **Nat Turner,** believing himself a divinely guided prophet, led the deadliest slave revolt in U.S. history. His *Confessions* were taken down by a slaveowner who tried to paint Turner as the devil incarnate. Turner's graphic account of his religious visions and the systematic murder of scores of white men, women, and children is disturbing, audacious, and revolutionary in its implications.

- **Charles Ball**'s is the longest and most detailed antebellum slave narrative: no other source more fully describes plantation life from the slave's point of view. But it reads like an exceptionally well written adventure novel. It includes hair-raising escapes, kidnapping attempts, wild animals, military action, an unusual and chilling tale of black-on-white crime and its consequences, and a surprising twist at the end.

- **Moses Roper** was the first fugitive slave to widely publicize his experiences to British audiences. His horrifyingly vivid and popular self-penned narrative is notable for the nightmarish and ingenious tortures practiced upon him by his master Mr. Gooch, whose name soon became a popular symbol for the worst kind of slaveholder.

- **Frederick Douglass**'s *Narrative,* the first of his three autobiographies, is the most widely studied slave narrative. In it, Douglass equates identity, freedom, and literacy; displays unparalleled rhetorical skills; presents a stirring and persuasive abolitionist argument; and transforms himself into the embodiment of the fugitive slave and a potent symbol of liberty.

- **Lewis and Milton Clarke** were two of the most engaging slave storytellers. With their unique blend of biting sarcasm, self-deprecation, a colloquial manner, and an ability to see the comic side of things, their vivid narratives inspire both sympathy and laughter.

- **William Wells Brown,** who later became the first African American novelist and playwright, traveled up and down the Mississippi River as the manservant of a slave trader, witnessing horrific abuses of power and gaining an unparalleled education into the modus operandi of slavery. In his masterfully understated and quietly subversive book he presents himself as a signifying trickster rather than an epic hero.

- Although **Josiah Henson** later became known as "the original Uncle Tom," he was not at all obsequious—he just had a misplaced sense of duty. His narrative is straightforward, well constructed, and consistently surprising; in its various versions, it proved to be the most popular slave narrative of the nineteenth century.

- After **Henry Bibb** escaped from slavery, he kept going back—to try to rescue his wife and child. His affecting memoir, full of trickery, bravery, idealism, and pathos, doubles as a love story and a frontier adventure narrative.

- **James W. C. Pennington** was a well-known abolitionist minister and one of the most educated and literate black men of his time. His narrative, which is concerned primarily with questions of property and ownership, eloquently relates a thrilling and at times droll escape from bondage that shows he was as resourceful and inventive as any trickster-slave.

- **Solomon Northup** was a free black man of New York who was kidnapped, sold, and held as a slave in one of the remotest regions of the South for a period of twelve years. His book combines a mastery of detail with an unusual richness and strength of language; it was one of the fastest-selling and most popular narratives.
- **John Brown**'s is the most brutal of these narratives. Not for the faint of heart, it reads in parts like a litany of horrors—he was even experimented upon by a doctor who wanted to see how deep his black skin went.
- **John Thompson** was one of several slave narrators who professed to have had direct experience of God. His self-published story details a remarkable spiritual adventure, involving violent resistance to slavery, divine visitations, and an unforgettable sea voyage to Africa aboard a whaling vessel.
- **William and Ellen Craft** perpetrated one of the most ingenious and unusual methods of escape in the history of slavery. The pair became heroes, about whom speeches were made and poems written. William Craft proved to be a masterful writer—persuasive, erudite, and witty; his narrative successfully blurs distinctions between white and black, master and slave, man and woman.
- **Harriet Jacobs** was the first female slave to write her own autobiography—perhaps the most intimate and emotionally compelling slave narrative of all. In it she gives the lie to previous depictions of female slaves as sexual victims, redefining traditional roles and using her sexuality to avenge herself upon her lustful master. The result is a slave narrative that reads like a novel, heartbreaking yet inspiring.
- **Jacob D. Green** was the only slave narrator to make full use of the trickster tradition. A Brer Rabbit–like figure, he exposes both blacks and whites to his often cruel and usually hilarious pranks. His narrative is full of reversals, of sudden shifts between humor and horror, laughter and violence.
- **James Mars** was probably the only slave narrator to spend his entire life north of the Mason-Dixon line. Although he recollects his early life with tranquility, it was full of strong action: Mars escaped from one master, defied another, and insisted on his equality with whites. His is a coming-of-age story in which maturity arrives with the act of resistance.
- **William Parker** led an armed group of ex-slaves in battling would-be kidnappers; in 1851 they struck what many then considered the first blow of the Civil War. Among slave narratives, Parker's is perhaps the strongest example of black self-determination and quasi-revolutionary activity. Whether engaging in verbal braggadocio or physical battle, Parker never backed down, and his bravado made him an irresistible force.

For those interested in further reading, I highly recommend the following studies, to which I am greatly indebted: William L. Andrews's *To Tell a Free Story,* by far the best literary analysis of early black autobiography; Charles T. Davis and Henry Louis Gates, Jr.'s *The Slave's Narrative,* a collection of insightful essays; Francis Smith Foster's *Witnessing Slavery,* a consideration of the literary genre of the slave narrative; Marion Wilson Starling's *The Slave Narrative,* the pioneering and invaluable 1946 study that initiated serious attention to the genre; Blyden Jackson's *A History of Afro-American Literature, Volume I*, an elegantly written survey covering 1746–1895; Charles H. Nichols's *Many Thousands Gone*, John W. Blassingame's *The Slave Community*, and Eugene D. Genovese's *Roll, Jordan, Roll*, which all explore what slave narratives tell us about slavery; and *The Oxford Companion to African American Literature*, edited by Andrews, Foster, and Trudier Harris. In addition, three superlative anthologies should be read as companions to this one: John W. Blassingame's *Slave Testimony*, a collection of briefer narratives, letters, interviews, and speeches; Dorothy Porter's *Early Negro Writing, 1760–1837*, which includes almost every important short text of the period; and Vincent Carretta's *Unchained Voices*, which collects the work of black authors of the eighteenth century. The bibliography at the end of this volume gives a complete list of sources.

In closing, I would like to acknowledge and thank: Samuel Baker, who advised me about academic standards, provided me with background information about eighteenth- and nineteenth-century English literature, and went over much of my writing herein; Vincent Carretta, who helped with questions concerning the eighteenth-century narratives; Charles Johnson, who graciously provided both encouragement and a foreword that serves as a post hoc foundation for this book; Curt Matthews, who enabled me to embark on this project and has been tremendously supportive; Linda Matthews, my publisher and copyeditor, who has helped to organize my time and keep me sane when faced with deadlines; Jerry Morreale, who scanned the majority of the narratives; the folks at www.mudcat.org, who helped with questions about slave songs; Joan Sommers, who designed the anthology; my brother, Jonathan Taylor, and Katherine Wolff, who helped me access some of the scarcer narratives; the University of Chicago Library, which has been my primary resource; my wife, Kathryn Anne Duys, whose sustenance, advice, and inspiration have been invaluable; and my daughter, Thalia, whose cheerfulness helped me see that these pages contain not only the woes of oppression but the joys of being alive.

---

1. Starling, in *Slave Narrative*, provides "a bibliographic guide to the location of 6006 narrative records" (xviii, 337–356).

2. William Andrews writes that "approximately sixty-five American slave narratives were published in book or pamphlet form before 1865. Between the Civil War and the onset of the depression, at least fifty more ex-slaves saw their autobiographies in print" (Andrews, "Representation," 78). On the other hand, the reliable scholar John Blassingame writes, "Between 1760 and 1947 more than two hundred book-length autobiographies of southern former slaves were published in the United States and England" (Blassingame, *Slave Testimony*, 681). I find Andrews's estimate of 115 narratives quite low, given the number of pre-1865 slave narratives he lists in the bibliography of *To Tell a Free Story*, and given Blassingame's count of sixty-seven post-1860 narratives (Ibid., xli). Blassingame's figure of two hundred, however, seems quite high, even if one includes "book-length" autobiographies published in periodicals. A truly comprehensive bibliography of all known separately published slave narratives—one that would exclude autobiographies of blacks who were not slaves, fictional narratives, and biographies—has yet to be compiled.

3. This phrase, however often it appears in the narratives, was never written by the slave

himself, but always by a white editor or writer of appended material. It derives from Shakespeare's *Othello.* Olney, "'I Was Born,'" 166.

4. Ibid., 152–154.

5. James Olney, an eminent theorist of autobiography, scholar of slave narratives, and author of *Metaphors of Self* and *Tell Me Africa,* claims otherwise, calling slave narratives invariant and repetitive, and maintaining that "the slave narrative, with very few exceptions, tends to exhibit a highly conventional, rigidly fixed form that bears much the same relationship to autobiography in a full sense as painting by numbers bears to painting as a creative act. . . . The slave narratives do not qualify as either autobiography or literature, . . . and they have no real place in American Literature" (Ibid., 148–150, 168). One of the primary purposes of this anthology is to present evidence that Olney is gravely mistaken.

6. The best discussion of postbellum narratives is probably William Andrews's "The Representation of Slavery and the Rise of Afro-American Literary Realism, 1865–1920."

7. Foster, *Witnessing Slavery,* 128–131.

8. To be more precise, slightly less than half of the antebellum narratives, and almost all of the postbellum narratives, were self-penned.

9. Blassingame, *Slave Testimony,* xviii–xlii.

10. However, Brown also published a substantially different narrative in England in 1851, whose title page features the words, "Written by Himself."

11. Sartwell, *Act Like You Know,* 21.

12. Probably the most important step in this recognition was the publication of John W. Blassingame's *The Slave Community* in 1972, which defended slave narratives in the following words: "If historians seek to provide some understanding of the past experiences of slaves, then the autobiography must be their point of departure" (367).

13. Hughes, *Thirty Years a Slave,* 3.

14. Bayley, *Narrative,* 591.

15. Steward, *Twenty-Two Years,* xii.

16. Niemtzow, "Problematic of Self," 98.

17. Sartwell, *Act Like You Know,* 21, 22.

18. Williams, *They Also Spoke,* 89.

19. Grandy, *Narrative,* 42.

20. Roper, *Narrative* [2d British ed.], iii; Roper, "Anti-Slavery Society," 134.

21. Williams, *They Also Spoke,* 88.

22. Costanzo, *Surprizing Narrative,* 49.

23. The later versions of Josiah Henson's narrative constitute something of an exception to this rule, at least according to one reading of the opening of the 1858 edition (see Doyle, "Rhetorical Art," 89); the fact that Henson's was also the most popular slave narrative of all is probably not entirely coincidental.

24. The most prominent of these are probably *The Slave; or Memoirs of Archy Moore* (Richard Hildreth, 1836) and *Autobiography of a Female Slave* (Mattie Griffith, 1857); there were at least five others. On the other hand, some nonfiction slave narratives, such as those of Charles Ball and Harriet Jacobs, were long suspected of being fiction.

25. Andrews, *Free Story,* 2–3.

26. Davis and Gates, *Slave's Narrative,* xvii.

27. "Life and Bondage," 30–31.

28. Davis and Gates, *Slave's Narrative,* xxi.

29. Cited in Goldsby, "'I Disguised My Hand,'" 30.

30. Davis and Gates, *Slave's Narrative,* xxii.

31. The 1760 *Narrative of the Uncommon Sufferings and Surprizing Deliverance of Briton Hammon, a Negro Man,* a fourteen-page pamphlet, has been frequently cited as the first slave narrative; however, as several scholars have pointed out, Hammon may well have been a free man—he refers to himself as a servant, not a slave. His narrative begins, "On Monday, 25th day of December, 1747, with the leave of my Master, I went from Marshfield, with an Intention to go a Voyage to Sea . . ." This use of the word *master* may have confused historians of the genre—an employer was also usually called *master* in the eighteenth century. Hammon's

supposed status as a slave is difficult to reconcile with his obtaining leave to go to sea, his receipt of wages for his work aboard ship, or his failure to mention his slave status in his narrative. Of course, more research remains to be done. See Carretta, *Unchained Voices*, 20, 24–25; Dziwas, "Hammon, Briton," 1178–1179; Davis, "Hammon, Briton," 281. If Hammon was not a slave, then Gronniosaw's narrative, which has usually been considered the second slave narrative, becomes the first.

32. Many of these figures are cited in Bontemps, *Great Slave Narratives*, xviii; Davis and Gates, *Slave's Narrative*, xvii; Foster, *Witnessing Slavery*, 22; Gates, *Classic Slave Narratives*, xi; and Nichols, *Many Thousand Gone*, xiv–xv. Others are from Andrews, *Free Story*, 97; Carretta, *Unchained Voices*, 54; Jackson, *History*, 117; Low and Clift, *Encyclopedia of Black America*, 793; Potkay and Burr, *Black Atlantic Writers*, 162–163; Starling, *Slave Narrative*, 278; or are based on cards in the National Union Catalog.

33. "Many critics and historians regard [*Up from Slavery*] as the last great slave narrative authored in the United States" (Andrews, "Slave Narrative," 667). Frances Smith Foster, on the other hand, emphatically states, "Washington was encouraging his readers to place his work in the slave narrative tradition. It was not a slave narrative, however. Washington was born about five years before the Emancipation Proclamation and admits little personal knowledge about slavery" (Foster, *Witnessing Slavery*, 151).

34. There were at least four different narratives by slaves named James Williams.

35. Most of the information in the history that follows was gleaned from Chernow and Vallasi, *Columbia Encyclopedia*; Franklin and Moss, *From Slavery to Freedom*; Johnson et al., *Africans in America*; Kolchin, *American Slavery*; Low and Clift, *Encyclopedia of Black America*; and Salzman et al., *Encyclopedia*, unless otherwise noted.

36. *Diario*, Folio 47r, December 25, 1492.

37. Olmsted, *Seaboard Slave States*, I:241–246.

38. Davis, "A Big Business," 50.

39. Olmsted, *Seaboard Slave States*, I:259–261.

40. Byrd, *Correspondence*, 487–488.

41. On this last point, see Quarles, *Black Abolitionists*.

42. This was not a slow and steady increase—just prior to the panic of 1837, the average price of a prime field hand went up to $1,300 in New Orleans; it then fell to $800 in 1843 and gradually escalated again to $1,800 by 1860.

43. Jones, *Experiences*, 5.

44. Olney, "'I Was Born,'" 172.

45. The best treatment of the slave narratives as literature is doubtless William L. Andrews's *To Tell a Free Story: The First Century of Afro-American Autobiography, 1760–1865*.

46. As Kenny J. Williams writes, "The uniqueness of the slave narrative is to be found in its ability to combine various motifs of American literature and American ideology into a new and different form. Much of the prose in the America of the seventeenth and eighteenth centuries as well as that of the early years of the nineteenth century had emphasized not only religious but also political freedom. . . . These concepts were combined with the elements of the sentimental and adventure stories of the early years of the nineteenth century and the melodramatic works of the latter part of the century. Hence the link between the two periods is found not in the work of Emerson, Thoreau, Hawthorne, or Melville but rather in the work of a group of Negro writers . . ." Williams, *They Also Spoke*, 83.

47. William Parker's narrative might be considered postbellum since it was first published in 1866; it is also the only narrative included in this anthology that was published in a journal—*The Atlantic Monthly*—rather than as a book or pamphlet. However, Parker's narrative was clearly written prior to the Civil War, and, considering its length, he may have intended it to be published separately.

48. Foster, *Witnessing Slavery*, 150.

49. Andrews, "Representation," 85.

50. Andrews goes so far as to refrain from analyzing certain coauthored texts: "Lacking a way of distilling an authorial essence from the clouded stream of edited and dictated Afro-American autobiographies, I shall reserve close analytic readings for autonomously authored

black texts." *Free Story*, 19–22. In his bibliography, Andrews even lists the narratives of John Brown, Charles Ball, and Solomon Northup under the names of the amanuenses rather than the narrator (he does not, however, list Gronniosaw's, Turner's, Henson's, or Lewis and Milton Clarke's narratives in this way), despite ample internal evidence that the slaves participated heavily in their creation.

51. Foster, *Witnessing Slavery*, xix.

52. I may be somewhat defensive on this point because, like the nineteenth-century amanuenses, I am a white person responsible for publishing black autobiographies. Sartwell claims that the amanuensis "at once frees the slave to speak for himself and reasserts white power over that expression" (Sartwell, *Act Like You Know*, 23). But because these narratives were all previously published, I empower these black authors *without* a corresponding assertion of "white power" over their expression.

53. For a contrasting nineteenth-century view, see Thomas Wentworth Higginson's *Black Rebellion*. Higginson was practically unique among writers of his time in focussing on rebellious, rather than victimized, slaves.

54. Certain first editions were difficult to locate, and later editions were used instead in the following instances. The edition of Moses Roper's narrative included here is the first *American* edition, although the first *British* edition preceded it; I have not been able to ascertain the extent of the differences between them, but the differences between the first American and *second* British are extensive. Due to limited access to the first editions of Charles Ball's, Henry Bibb's, James W. C. Pennington's, John Brown's, and James Mars's narratives, I have based my text on the second editions, deleting material that was not in the first. The edition of Lewis and Milton Clarke's joint narrative included here is indeed the first, but Lewis Clarke had published an earlier edition on his own.

HENRY BIBB

HENRY BIBB (1815–54) ran away from slavery at least half a dozen times, but every time he gained his freedom, he returned to the South to try to rescue his wife and child. His affecting memoir, full of adventure, idealism, and pathos, is perhaps the only slave narrative which doubles as a kind of love story. As Marion Starling has written, "The story of [Bibb's] struggles to take his family to freedom is one of the outstanding records of human devotion in the literature of the slave."[1]

Bibb's conflicting desires for family and freedom made his condition tragic whether a slave or a free man. Marriage is the central theme of his narrative— as William Andrews points out, while Frederick Douglass and other narrators could leave slavery without looking back and immediately assume a new existence, "when Henry Bibb reached Ohio he could not reject, cast off, and forget the past; he was in fundamental ways 'married' to it and identified with it."[2] Bibb's burden of guilt was enormous: he writes, "If ever there was any one act of my life while a slave, that I have to lament over it is that of being a father and a husband of slaves."

Bibb clearly harbored much less guilt over his use of deceit to escape from slavery, however often he asks the reader to excuse his misbehavior—instead, he took pride in his resourcefulness. A picaresque hero or trickster, he relied on ingenuity, cunning, and a readiness to lie, steal, or disguise himself in order to evade his pursuers. His extensive travels from slavery to freedom through the westernmost states of his day give his autobiography—which features encounters with wolves and Indians, gamblers and professional slave hunters—the flavor of popular frontier adventure stories.

The *Narrative*, which incidentally contains in its prefatory documents perhaps "the most elaborate guarantee of authenticity found in the slave narrative canon,"[3] went through three American editions in 1849 and 1850, achieving its success in part due to excellent reviews:

> Of all the narratives that have been published no one exceeds this in thrilling interest; and of all the subjects of them, no one appears to have seen and suffered so much as Mr. Bibb. It is a book for the rising generation in particular; and we could wish that as many copies of it might be sold during the present year, as there are slaves in the United States (*The Liberator*).

> Did we not know the author, and know from the best of proof that the book is a true narrative, on reading it we should pronounce it a novel. The reader may rely upon its truth, and yet he will find it so full of touching incidents, daring adventures, and hair-breadth escapes, that he will find his attention held spell-bound, from the time he begins until he has finished the little volume (*The True Wesleyan*).

Argument provokes argument, reason is met by sophistry. But narratives of slaves go right to the hearts of men. . . . The book is written with perfect artlessness, and the man who can read it unmoved must be fit for treasons, stratagems and spoils (*The Chronotype*).

It also received encomiums in *The New York Evangelist, The New York Tribune,* and Douglass's *The North Star*.[4]

For the six years prior to its publication, as John Blassingame has written, Bibb had

joined Frederick Douglass and William Wells Brown as one of the most effective antislavery speakers. A master of humor and pathos, Bibb impressed on his audiences all of the contradictions inherent in slavery. In one report of a lecture he gave, a journalist declared that the audience "cheered, clapped, stamped, laughed, and wept, by turns."[5]

And Benjamin Quarles testifies:

Lewis Tappan, who had heard all of the leading orators in the movement, found it impossible to listen to Bibb without feeling his heart swell with the deepest hatred of slavery. . . . A master of pathos, Bibb often sang "The mother's lament," a piece purportedly sung by slaves about to be sold. At the end of a lecture by Bibb at the Baptist Church in Blackiston, Massachusetts, the entire audience stood up, signifying their desire to hear him again.[6]

After the passage of the Fugitive Slave Act of 1850, Bibb and his wife fled to Canada. There, in the space of four years, he founded Canada's first black newspaper, *The Voice of the Fugitive;* became one of the foremost leaders of the Canadian black community; established a school, a Methodist church, and educational and antislavery societies; collaborated with the Underground Railroad in helping escaped slaves find safe haven; purchased, together with Josiah Henson, a two-thousand-acre tract of land near Windsor, Ontario, to become a center for black culture; organized the North American Convention of Colored People in opposition to the colonization movement; published the stories of fugitive slaves and the writings of Martin Delaney, the pioneering black nationalist; and found a Canadian home for his mother and three of his brothers who had successfully escaped from bondage.

NARRATIVE

OF THE

LIFE AND ADVENTURES

OF

HENRY BIBB,

AN AMERICAN SLAVE

WRITTEN BY HIMSELF.

WITH

AN INTRODUCTION

BY LUCIUS C. MATLACK.[7]

———————

NEW YORK:

PUBLISHED BY THE AUTHOR; 5 SPRUCE STREET.

1849.

INTRODUCTION.

FROM the most obnoxious substances we often see spring forth, beautiful and fragrant, flowers of every hue, to regale the eye, and perfume the air. Thus, frequently, are results originated which are wholly unlike the cause that gave them birth. An illustration of this truth is afforded by the history of American Slavery.

Naturally and necessarily, the enemy of literature, it has become the prolific theme of much that is profound in argument, sublime in poetry, and thrilling in narrative. From the soil of slavery itself have sprung forth some of the most brilliant productions, whose logical levers will ultimately upheave and overthrow the system. Gushing fountains of poetic thought, have started from beneath the rod of violence, that will long continue to slake the feverish thirst of humanity outraged, until swelling to a flood it shall rush with wasting violence over the ill-gotten heritage of the oppressor. Startling incidents authenticated, far excelling fiction in their touching pathos, from the pen of self-emancipated slaves, do now exhibit slavery in such revolting aspects, as to secure the execrations of all good men, and become a monument more enduring than marble, in testimony strong as sacred writ against it.

Of the class last named, is the narrative of the life of Henry Bibb, which is equally distinguished as a revolting portrait of the hideous slave system, a thrilling narrative of individual suffering, and a triumphant vindication of the slave's manhood and mental dignity. And all this is associated with unmistakable traces of originality and truthfulness.

To many, the elevated style, purity of diction, and easy flow of language, frequently exhibited, will appear unaccountable and contradictory, in view of his want of early mental culture. But to the thousands who have listened with delight to his speeches on anniversary and other occasions, these same traits will be noted as unequivocal evidence of originality. Very few men present in their written composition, so perfect a transcript of their style as is exhibited by Mr. Bibb.

Moreover, the writer of this introduction is well acquainted with his handwriting and style. The entire manuscript I have examined and prepared for the press. Many of the closing pages of it were written by Mr. Bibb in my office. And the whole is preserved for inspection now. An examination of it will show that no alteration of sentiment, language or style, was necessary to make it what it now is, in the hands of the reader. The work of preparation for the press was that of orthography and punctuation merely, an arrangement of the chapters, and a table of contents—little more than falls to the lot of publishers generally.

The fidelity of the narrative is sustained by the most satisfactory and ample testimony. Time has proved its claims to truth. Thorough investigation has sifted and analysed every essential fact alleged, and demonstrated clearly that this thrilling and eloquent narrative, though stranger than fiction, is undoubtedly true.

It is only necessary to present the following documents to the reader, to sustain this declaration. For convenience of reference, and that they may be more easily understood, the letters will be inserted consecutively, with explanations following the last.

The best preface to these letters, is, the report of a committee appointed to investigate the truth of Mr. Bibb's narrative as he has delivered it in public for years past.

REPORT

Of the undersigned, Committee appointed by the Detroit Liberty Association to investigate the truth of the narrative of Henry Bibb, a fugitive from Slavery, and report thereon:

Mr. Bibb has addressed several assemblies in Michigan, and his narrative is generally known. Some of his hearers, among whom were Liberty men,[8] felt doubt as to the truth of his statements. Respect for their scruples and the obligation of duty to the public induced the formation of the present Committee.

The Committee entered on the duty confided to them, resolved on a searching scrutiny, and an unreserved publication of its result. Mr. Bibb acquiesced in the inquiry with a praiseworthy spirit. He attended before the Committee and gave willing aid to its object. He was subjected to a rigorous examination. Facts—dates—persons—and localities were demanded and cheerfully furnished. Proper inquiry—either by letter, or personally, or through the medium of friends was then made from *every* person, and in *every* quarter likely to elucidate the truth. In fact no test for its ascertainment, known to the sense or experience of the Committee, was omitted. The result was the collection of a large body of testimony from very diversified quarters. Slave owners, slave dealers, fugitives from slavery, political friends and political foes contributed to a mass of testimony, every part of which pointed to a common conclusion—the undoubted truth of Mr. Bibb's statements.

In the Committee's opinion no individual can substantiate the events of his life by testimony more conclusive and harmonious than is now before them in confirmation of Mr. Bibb. The main facts of his narrative, and many of the minor ones are corroborated beyond all question. No inconsistency has been disclosed nor anything revealed to create suspicion. The Committee have no hesitation in declaring their conviction that Mr. Bibb is amply sustained, and is entitled to public confidence and high esteem.

The bulk of testimony precludes its publication, but it is in the Committee's hands for the inspection of any applicant.

> A. L. PORTER,
> C. H. STEWART,
> SILAS M. HOLMES.
> Committee.

Detroit, *April* 22, 1845.

———

From the bulk of testimony obtained, a part only is here introduced. The remainder fully corroborates and strengthens that.

[No. 1. An Extract]   Dawn Mills,[9] Feb. 19th, 1845.

Charles H. Stewart, Esq.
My Dear Brother:
Your kind communication of the 13th came to hand yesterday. I have made inquiries respecting Henry Bibb which may be of service to you. Mr. Wm. Harrison,

to whom you allude in your letter, is here. He is a respectable and worthy man—a man of piety. I have just had an interview with him this evening. He testifies, that he was well acquainted with Henry Bibb in Trimble County, Ky., and that he sent a letter to him by Thomas Henson, and got one in return from him. He says that Bibb came out to Canada some three years ago, and went back to get his wife up, but was betrayed at Cincinnati by a colored man—that he was taken to Louisville but got away—was taken again and lodged in jail, and sold off to New Orleans, or he, (Harrison,) understood that he was taken to New Orleans. He testifies that Bibb is a Methodist man, and says that two persons who came on with him last Summer, knew Bibb. One of these, Simpson Young, is now at Malden. * * *

Very respectfully, thy friend,

HIRAM WILSON.[10]

———

[No. 2.]   BEDFORD, TRIMBLE CO., KENTUCKY.
March 4, 1845.

SIR:—Your letter under date of the 13th ult., is now before me, making some inquiry about a person supposed to be a fugitive from the South, "who is lecturing to your religious community on Slavery and the South."

I am pleased to inform you that I have it in my power to give you the information you desire. The person spoken of by you I have no doubt is Walton, a yellow man, who once belonged to my father, William Gatewood. He was purchased by him from John Sibly, and by John Sibly of his brother Albert G. Sibly, and Albert G. Sibly became possessed of him by his marriage with Judge David White's daughter, he being born Judge White's slave.

The boy Walton at the time he belonged to John Sibly, married a slave of my father's, a mulatto girl, and sometime afterwards solicited him to buy him; the old man after much importuning from Walton, consented to do so, and accordingly paid Sibly eight hundred and fifty dollars. He did not buy him because he needed him, but from the fact that he had a wife there, and Walton on his part promising every thing that my father could desire.

It was not long, however, before Walton became indolent and neglectful of his duty; and in addition to this, he was guilty, as the old man thought, of worse offences. He watched his conduct more strictly, and found he was guilty of disposing of articles from the farm for his own use, and pocketing the money.

He actually caught him one day stealing wheat—he had conveyed one sack full to a neighbor and whilst he was delivering the other my father caught him in the very act.

He confessed his guilt and promised to do better for the future—and on his making promises of this kind my father was disposed to keep him still, not wishing to part him from his wife, for whom he professed to entertain the strongest affection. When the Christmas Holidays came on, the old man, as is usual in this country, gave his negroes a week Holiday. Walton, instead of regaling himself by going about visiting his colored friends, took up his line of march for her Britanic Majesty's dominions.

He was gone about two years I think, when I heard of him in Cincinnati; I repaired thither, with some few friends to aid me, and succeeded in securing him.

He was taken to Louisville, and on the next morning after our arrival there, he escaped, almost from before our face, while we were on the street before the Tavern. He succeeded in eluding our pursuit, and again reached Canada in safety.

Nothing daunted he returned, after a lapse of some twelve or eighteen months, with the intention, as I have since learned, of conducting off his wife and eight or ten more slaves to Canada.

I got news of his whereabouts, and succeeded in recapturing him. I took him to Louisville and together with his wife and child, (she going along with him at her owner's request,) sold him. He was taken from thence to New Orleans—and from hence to Red River, Arkansas—and the next news I had of him he was again wending his way to Canada, and I suppose now is at or near Detroit.

In relation to his character, it was the general opinion here that he was a notorious liar, and a rogue. These things I can procure any number of respectable witnesses to prove.

In proof of it, he says his mother belonged to James Bibb, which is a lie, there not having been such a man about here, much less brother of Secretary Bibb. He says that Bibb's daughter married A. G. Sibly, when the fact is Sibly married Judge David White's daughter, and his mother belonged to White also and is now here, free.

So you will perceive he is guilty of lying for no effect, and what might it not be supposed he would do where he could effect anything by it.

I have been more tedious than I should have been, but being anxious to give you his rascally conduct in full, must be my apology. You are at liberty to publish this letter, or make any use you see proper of it. If you do publish it, let me have a paper containing the publication—at any rate let me hear from you again.

Respectfully yours, &c.,

SILAS GATEWOOD.

To C. H. STEWART, Esq.

————

[No. 3. An Extract.]   CINCINNATI, *March* 10, 1845.

MY DEAR SIR:—Mrs. Path, Nickens and Woodson did not see Bibb on his first visit, in 1837, when he staid with Job Dundy, but were subsequently told of it by Bibb. They first saw him in May, 1838. Mrs. Path remembers this date because it was the month in which she removed from Broadway to Harrison street, and Bibb assisted her to remove. Mrs. Path's garden adjoined Dundy's back yard. While engaged in digging up flowers, she was addressed by Bibb, who was staying with Dundy and who offered to dig them up for her. She hired him to do it. Mrs. Dundy shortly after called over and told Mrs. Path that he was a slave. After that Mrs. Path took him into her house and concealed him. While concealed, he astonished his good protectress by his ingenuity in bottoming chairs with cane. When the furniture was removed, Bibb insisted on helping, and was, after some remonstrances, permitted. At the house on Harrison street, he was employed for several days in digging a cellar, and was so employed when seized on Saturday afternoon by the constables. He held frequent conversations with Mrs. Path and others, in which he gave them the same account which he has given you.

On Saturday afternoon, two noted slave-catching constables, E. V. Brooks and O'Neil, surprised Bibb as he was digging in the cellar. Bibb sprang for the fence and gained the top of it, where he was seized and dragged back. They took him immediately before William Doty, a Justice of infamous notoriety as an accomplice of kidnappers, proved property, paid charges and took him away.

His distressed friends were surprised by his re-appearance in a few days after, the Wednesday following, as they think. He reached the house of Dr. Woods, (a colored man since deceased,) before day-break, and staid until dusk. Mrs. Path, John Woodson and others made up about twelve dollars for him. Woodson accompanied him out of town a mile and bid him "God speed." He has never been here since. Woodson and Clark saw him at Detroit two years ago.

Yours truly,

WILLIAM BIRNEY.

———

[No. 4]   LOUISVILLE, *March* 14, 1845.

MR. STEWART.—Yours of the 1st came to hand on the 13th inst. You wished me to inform you what became of a boy that was in the work-house in the fall of '39. The boy you allude to went by the name of Walton; he had ran away from Kentucky some time before, and returned for his wife —was caught and sold to Garrison; he was taken to Louisiana, I think—he was sold on Red River to a planter. As Garrison is absent in the City of New Orleans at this time, I cannot inform you who he was sold to. Garrison will be in Louisville some time this Spring; if you wish me, I will inquire of Garrison and inform you to whom he was sold, and where his master lives at this time.

Yours,

W. PORTER.

———

[No. 5.]   BEDFORD, TRIMBLE COUNTY, KY
C. H. STEWART, ESQ.,

SIR.—I received your note on the 16th inst., and in accordance with it I write you these lines. You stated that you would wish to know something about Walton H. Bibb, and whether he had a wife and child, and whether they were sold to New Orleans. Sir, before I answer these inquiries, I should like to know who Charles H. Stewart is, and why you should make these inquiries of me, and how you knew who I was, as you are a stranger to me and I must be to you. In your next if you will tell me the intention of your inquiries, I will give you a full history of the whole case.

I have a boy in your county by the name of King, a large man and very black; if you are acquainted with him, give him my compliments, and tell him I am well, and all of his friends. W. H. Bibb is acquainted with him.

I wait your answer.

Your most obedient,

W. H. GATEWOOD

March 17, 1845

———

[No. 6.]   BEDFORD, KENTUCKY, *April* 6th, 1845.
MR. CHARLES H. STEWART.

SIR:—Yours of the 1st March is before me, inquiring if one Walton Bibb, a colored man, escaped from me at Louisville, Ky., in the Spring of 1839. To that inquiry I answer, he did. The particulars are these: He ran off from William Gatewood some time in 1838 I think, and was heard of in Cincinnati. Myself and some others went there and took him, and took him to Louisville for sale, by the directions of his master. While there he made his escape and was gone some time, I think about one year or longer. He came back it was said, to get his wife and child, so report says. He was again taken by his owner; he together with his wife and child was taken to Louisville and sold to a man who traded in negroes, and was taken by him to New Orleans and sold with his wife and child to some man up Red River, so I was informed by the man who sold him. He then ran off and left his wife and child and got back, it seems, to your country. I can say for Gatewood he was a good master, and treated him well. Gatewood bought him from a Mr. Sibly, who was going to send him down the river. Walton, to my knowledge, influenced Gatewood to buy him, and promised if he would, never to disobey him or run off. Who he belongs to now, I do not know. I know Gatewood sold his wife and child at a great sacrifice, to satisfy him. If any other information is necessary I will give it, if required. You will please write me again what he is trying to do in your country, or what he wishes the inquiry from me for.

Yours, truly,

DANIEL S. LANE.

These letters need little comment. Their testimony combined is most harmonious and conclusive. Look at the points established.

1. Hiram Wilson gives the testimony of reputable men now in Canada, who knew Henry Bibb as a slave in Kentucky.

2. Silas Gatewood, with a peculiar relish, fills three pages of foolscap, "being anxious to give his rascally conduct in full," as he says. But he vaults over the saddle and lands on the other side. His testimony is invaluable as an endorsement of Mr. Bibb's truthfulness. He illustrates all the essential facts of this narrative. He also labors to prove him deceitful and a liar.

Deceit in a slave, is only a slight reflex of the stupendous fraud practised by his master. And its indulgence has far more logic in its favor, than the ablest plea ever written for slave holding, under ever such peculiar circumstances. The attempt to prove Mr. Bibb in the lie, is a signal failure, as he never affirmed what Gatewood denies. With this offset, the letter under notice is a triumphant vindication of one, whom he thought there by to injure sadly. As Mr. Bibb has most happily acknowledged the wheat, (see page 194 [page 94 in this edition],) I pass the charge of stealing by referring to the logic there used, which will be deemed convincing.

3. William Birney, Esq., attests the facts of Mr. Bibb's arrest in Cincinnati, and the subsequent escape, as narrated by him, from the declaration of eye witnesses.

4. W. Porter, Jailor, states that Bibb was in the work-house at Louisville, held and sold afterwards to the persons and at the places named in this volume.

6. W. H. Gatewood, with much Southern dignity, will answer no questions, but shows his relation to these matters by naming "King"—saying, "W. H. Bibb is acquainted with him," and promising "a full history of the case."

6. Daniel S. Lane, with remarkable straight-forwardness and stupidity, tells all he knows, and then wants to know what they ask him for. The writer will answer that question. He wanted to prove by two or more witnesses, the truth of his own statements; which has most surely been accomplished.

Having thus presented an array of testimony sustaining the facts alleged in this narrative, the introduction will be concluded by introducing a letter signed by respectable men of Detroit, and endorsed by Judge Wilkins, showing the high esteem in which Mr. Bibb is held by those who know him well where he makes his home. Their testimony expresses their present regard as well as an opinion of his past character. It is introduced here with the greatest satisfaction, as the writer is assured, from an intimate acquaintance with Henry Bibb, that all who know him hereafter will entertain the same sentiments toward him:

DETROIT, *March* 10, 1845.

The undersigned have pleasure in recommending Henry Bibb to the kindness and confidence of Anti-slavery friends in every State. He has resided among us for some years. His deportment, his conduct, and his christian course have won our esteem and affection. The narrative of his sufferings and more early life has been thoroughly investigated by a Committee appointed for the purpose. They sought evidence respecting it in every proper quarter, and their report attested its undoubted truth. In this conclusion we all cordially unite.

H. Bibb has for some years publicly made this narrative to assemblies, whose number cannot be told; it has commanded public attention in this State, and provoked inquiry. Occasionally too we see persons from the South, who knew him in early years, yet not a word or fact worthy of impairing its truth has reached us; but on the contrary, everything tended to its corroboration.

Mr. Bibb's Anti-slavery efforts in this State have produced incalculable benefit. The Lord has blessed him into an instrument of great power. He has labored much, and for very inadequate compensation. Lucrative offers for other quarters did not tempt him to a more profitable field. His sincerity and disinterestedness are therefore beyond suspicion.

We bid him "God-speed," on his route. We bespeak for him every kind consideration. * * * * *

H. HALLOCK,
President of the Detroit Lib. Association.
CULLEN BROWN, *Vice-President.*
S. M. HOLMES, *Secretary.*
J. D. BALDWIN,
CHARLES H. STEWART,
MARTIN WILSON,
WILLIAM BARNUM.

DETROIT, Nov. 11, 1845.

The undersigned, cheerfully concurs with Mr. Hallock and others in their friendly recommendation of Mr. Henry Bibb. The undersigned has known him for many months in the Sabbath School in this City, partly under his charge, and can certify to his correct deportment, and commend him to the sympathies of Christian benevolence.

ROSS WILKINS.[11]

———

The task now performed, in preparing for the press and introducing to the public the narrative of Henry Bibb, has been one of the most pleasant ever required at my hands. And I conclude it with an expression of the hope that it may afford interest to the reader, support to the author in his efforts against slavery, and be instrumental in advancing the great work of emancipation in this country.

LUCIUS C. MATLACK.

NEW YORK CITY, *July* 1st, 1849.

AUTHOR'S PREFACE.

––––––––––––––

THIS work has been written during irregular intervals, while I have been travelling and laboring for the emancipation of my enslaved countrymen. The reader will remember that I make no pretension to literature; for I can truly say, that I have been educated in the school of adversity, whips, and chains. Experience and observation have been my principal teachers, with the exception of three weeks schooling which I have had the good fortune to receive since my escape from the "grave yard of the mind," or the dark prison of human bondage. And nothing but untiring perseverance has enabled me to prepare this volume for the public eye; and I trust by the aid of Divine Providence to be able to make it intelligible and instructive. I thank God for the blessings of Liberty—the contrast is truly great between freedom and slavery. To be changed from a chattel to a human being, is no light matter, though the process with myself practically was very simple. And if I could reach the ears of every slave to-day, throughout the whole continent of America, I would teach the same lesson, I would sound it in the ears of every hereditary bondman, "break your chains and fly for freedom!"

It may be asked why I have written this work, when there has been so much already written and published of the same character from other fugitives? And, why publish it after having told it publicly all through New England and the Western States to multiplied thousands?

My answer is, that in no place have I given orally the detail of my narrative; and some of the most interesting events of my life have never reached the public ear. Moreover, it was at the request of many friends of down-trodden humanity, that I have undertaken to write the following sketch, that light and truth might be spread on the sin and evils of slavery as far as possible. I also wanted to leave my humble testimony on record against this man-destroying system, to be read by succeeding generations when my body shall lie mouldering in the dust.

But I would not attempt by any sophistry to misrepresent slavery in order to prove its dreadful wickedness. For, I presume there are none who may read this narrative through, whether Christians or slaveholders, males or females, but what will admit it to be a system of the most high-handed oppression and tyranny that ever was tolerated by an enlightened nation.

HENRY BIBB.

NARRATIVE

OF THE

LIFE OF HENRY BIBB.

CHAPTER I.

SKETCH OF MY PARENTAGE.—EARLY SEPARATION FROM MY MOTHER.—HARD
FARE.—FIRST EXPERIMENTS AT RUNNING AWAY.—EARNEST LONGING FOR
FREEDOM.—ABHORRENT NATURE OF SLAVERY.

I WAS born May 1815, of a slave mother, in Shelby County, Kentucky,[12] and
was claimed as the property of David White Esq. He came into possession of my
mother long before I was born. I was brought up in the Counties of Shelby,
Henry, Oldham, and Trimble. Or, more correctly speaking, in the above counties, I may safely say, I was *flogged up;* for where I should have received moral,
mental, and religious instruction, I received stripes without number, the object
of which was to degrade and keep me in subordination. I can truly say, that I
drank deeply of the bitter cup of suffering and woe. I have been dragged down
to the lowest depths of human degradation and wretchedness, by Slaveholders.

My mother was known by the name of Milldred Jackson. She is the mother
of seven slaves only, all being sons, of whom I am the eldest. She was also so fortunate or unfortunate, as to have some of what is called the slaveholding blood
flowing in her veins. I know not how much; but not enough to prevent her children though fathered by slaveholders, from being bought and sold in the slave
markets of the South. It is almost impossible for slaves to give a correct account
of their male parentage. All that I know about it is, that my mother informed me
that my fathers name was JAMES BIBB.[13] He was doubtless one of the present
Bibb family of Kentucky; but I have no personal knowledge of him at all, for he
died before my recollection.

The first time I was separated from my mother, I was young and small. I
knew nothing of my condition then as a slave. I was living with Mr. White whose
wife died and left him a widower with one little girl, who was said to be the legitimate owner of my mother, and all her children. This girl was also my playmate when we were children.

I was taken away from my mother, and hired out to labor for various persons, eight or ten years in succession; and all my wages were expended for the

education of Harriet White, my playmate. It was then my sorrows and sufferings commenced. It was then I first commenced seeing and feeling that I was a wretched slave, compelled to work under the lash without wages, and often without clothes enough to hide my nakedness. I have often worked without half enough to eat, both late and early, by day and by night. I have often laid my wearied limbs down at night to rest upon a dirt floor, or a bench, without any covering at all, because I had no where else to rest my wearied body, after having worked hard all the day. I have also been compelled in early life, to go at the bidding of a tyrant, through all kinds of weather, hot or cold, wet or dry, and without shoes frequently, until the month of December, with my bare feet on the cold frosty ground, cracked open and bleeding as I walked. Reader, believe me when I say, that no tongue, nor pen ever has or can express the horrors of American Slavery. Consequently I despair in finding language to express adequately the deep feeling of my soul, as I contemplate the past history of my life. But although I have suffered much from the lash, and for want of food and raiment; I confess that it was no disadvantage to be passed through the hands of so many families, as the only source of information that I had to enlighten my mind, consisted in what I could see and hear from others. Slaves were not allowed books, pen, ink, nor paper, to improve their minds. But it seems to me now, that I was particularly observing, and apt to retain what came under my observation. But more especially, all that I heard about liberty and freedom to the slaves, I never forgot. Among other good trades I learned the art of running away to perfection. I made a regular business of it, and never gave it up, until I had broken the bands of slavery, and landed myself safely in Canada, where I was regarded as a man, and not as a thing.

The first time in my life that I ran away, was for ill treatment, in 1825. I was living with a Mr. Vires, in the village of Newcastle. His wife was a very cross woman. She was every day flogging me, boxing, pulling my ears, and scolding, so that I dreaded to enter the room where she was. This first started me to running away from them. I was often gone several days before I was caught. They would abuse me for going off, but it did no good. The next time they flogged me, I was off again; but after awhile they got sick of their bargain, and returned me back into the hands of my owners. By this time Mr. White had married his second wife. She was what I call a tyrant. I lived with her several months, but she kept me almost half of my time in the woods, running from under the bloody lash. While I was at home she kept me all the time rubbing furniture, washing, scrubbing the floors; and when I was not doing this, she would often seat herself in a large rocking chair, with two pillows about her, and would make me rock her, and keep off the flies. She was too lazy to scratch her own head, and would often make me scratch and comb it for her. She would at other times lie on her bed, in warm weather, and make me fan her while she slept, scratch and rub her feet; but after awhile she got sick of me, and preferred a maiden servant to do such business. I was then hired out again; but by this time I had become much better skilled in running away, and would make calculation to avoid detection, by taking with me a bridle. If any body should see me in the woods, as they have, and asked "what are you doing here sir? you are a runaway?"—I said, "no, sir, I am looking for our old mare;" at other times, "looking for our cows." For such excuses I was let pass. In fact, the only weapon of self defence that I could use successfully, was that of deception. It is use-less for a poor helpless slave, to resist a white man in a slaveholding State. Public opinion and the law is against him; and resistance in many cases is death to the slave, while the law declares, that he shall submit or die.

The circumstances in which I was then placed, gave me a longing desire to be free. It kindled a fire of liberty within my breast which has never yet been quenched. This seemed to be a part of my nature; it was first revealed to me by the inevitable laws of nature's God. I could see that the All-wise Creator, had made man a free, moral, intelligent and accountable being; capable of knowing good and evil. And I believed then, as I believe now, that every man has a right to wages for his labor; a right to his own wife and children; a right to liberty and the pursuit of happiness; and a right to worship God according to the dictates of his own conscience. But here, in the light of these truths, I was a slave, a prisoner for life; I could possess nothing, nor acquire anything but what must belong to my keeper. No one can imagine my feelings in my reflecting moments, but he who has himself been a slave. Oh! I have often wept over my condition, while sauntering through the forest, to escape cruel punishment.

> "No arm to protect me from tyrants aggression;
> No parents to cheer me when laden with grief.
> Man may picture the bounds of the rocks and the rivers,
> The hills and the valleys, the lakes and the ocean,
> But the horrors of slavery, he never can trace."[14]

The term slave to this day sounds with terror to my soul,—a word too ob-noxious to speak—a system too intolerable to be endured. I know this from long and sad experience. I now feel as if I had just been aroused from sleep, and look-ing back with quickened perception at the state of torment from whence I fled. I was there held and claimed as a slave; as such I was subjected to the will and power of my keeper, in all respects whatsoever. That the slave is a human being, no one can deny. It is his lot to be exposed in common with other men, to the calamities of sickness, death, and the misfortunes incident to life. But unlike other men, he is denied the consolation of struggling against external difficulties,

such as destroy the life, liberty, and happiness of himself and family. A slave may be bought and sold in the market like an ox. He is liable to be sold off to a distant land from his family. He is bound in chains hand and foot; and his sufferings are aggravated a hundred fold, by the terrible thought, that he is not allowed to struggle against misfortune, corporeal punishment, insults and outrages committed upon himself and family; and he is not allowed to help himself, to resist or escape the blow, which he sees impending over him.

This idea of utter helplessness, in perpetual bondage, is the more distressing, as there is no period even with the remotest generation when it shall terminate.

CHAPTER II.

A FRUITLESS EFFORT FOR EDUCATION. — THE SABBATH AMONG SLAVES. — DEGRADING
    AMUSEMENTS. — WHY RELIGION IS REJECTED. — CONDITION OF POOR WHITE
    PEOPLE. — SUPERSTITION AMONG SLAVES. — EDUCATION FORBIDDEN.

IN 1833, I had some very serious religious impressions, and there was quite a number of slaves in that neighborhood, who felt very desirous to be taught to read the Bible. There was a Miss Davis, a poor white girl, who offered to teach a Sabbath School for the slaves, notwithstanding public opinion and the law was opposed to it. Books were furnished and she commenced the school; but the news soon got to our owners that she was teaching us to read. This caused quite an excitement in the neighborhood. Patrols* were appointed to go and break it up the next Sabbath. They were determined that we should not have a Sabbath School in operation. For slaves this was called an incendiary movement.

The Sabbath is not regarded by a large number of the slaves as a day of rest. They have no schools to go to; no moral nor religious instruction at all in many localities where there are hundreds of slaves. Hence they resort to some kind of amusement. Those who make no profession of religion, resort to the woods in large numbers on that day to gamble, fight, get drunk, and break the Sabbath. This is often encouraged by slaveholders. When they wish to have a little sport of that kind, they go among the slaves and give them whiskey, to see them dance, "pat juber,"[15] sing and play on the banjo. Then get them to wrestling, fighting, jumping, running foot races, and butting each other like sheep. This is urged on by giving them whiskey; making bets on them; laying chips on one slave's head, and daring another to tip it off with his hand; and if he tipped it off, it would be called an insult, and cause a fight. Before fighting, the parties choose their seconds to stand by them while fighting; a ring or a circle is formed to fight in, and no one is allowed to enter the ring while they are fighting, but their seconds, and the white gentlemen. They are not allowed to fight a duel, nor to use weapons of any kind. The blows are made by kicking, knocking, and butting with their

---

* Police peculiar to the South.

heads; they grab each other by their ears, and jam their heads together like sheep. If they are likely to hurt each other very bad, their masters would rap them with their walking canes, and make them stop. After fighting, they make friends, shake hands, and take a dram together, and there is no more of it.

But this is all principally for want of moral instruction. This is where they have no Sabbath Schools; no one to read the Bible to them; no one to preach the gospel who is competent to expound the Scriptures, except slaveholders. And the slaves, with but few exceptions, have no confidence at all in their preaching, because they preach a pro-slavery doctrine. They say, "Servants be obedient to your masters;—and he that knoweth his masters will and doeth it not, shall be beaten with many stripes;"[16]—means that God will send them to hell, if they disobey their masters. This kind of preaching has driven thousands into infidelity. They view themselves as suffering unjustly under the lash, without friends, without protection of law or gospel, and the green eyed monster tyranny staring them in the face. They know that they are destined to die in that wretched condition, unless they are delivered by the arm of Omnipotence. And they cannot believe or trust in such a religion, as above named.

The poor and loafering class of whites, are about on a par in point of morals with the slaves at the South. They are generally ignorant, intemperate, licentious, and profane. They associate much with the slaves; are often found gambling together on the Sabbath; encouraging slaves to steal from their owners, and sell to them, corn, wheat, sheep, chickens, or any thing of the kind which they can well conceal. For such offences there is no law to reach a slave but lynch law. But if both parties are caught in the act by a white person, the slave is punished with the lash, while the white man is often punished with both lynch and common law. But there is another class of poor white people in the South, who, I

"THE SABBATH AMONG SLAVES."

think would be glad to see slavery abolished in self defence; they despise the institution because it is impoverishing and degrading to them and their children.

The slave holders are generally rich, aristocratic, overbearing; and they look with utter contempt upon a poor laboring man, who earns his bread by the "sweat of his brow," whether he be moral or immoral, honest or dishonest. No matter whether he is white or black; if he performs manual labor for a livelihood, he is looked upon as being inferior to a slaveholder, and but little better off than the slave, who toils without wages under the lash. It is true, that the slaveholder, and non-slaveholder, are living under the same laws in the same State. But the one is rich, the other is poor; one is educated, the other is uneducated; one has houses, land and influence, the other has none. This being the case, that class of the non-slaveholders would be glad to see slavery abolished, but they dare not speak it aloud.

There is much superstition among the slaves. Many of them believe in what they call "conjuration," tricking, and witchcraft; and some of them pretend to understand the art, and say that by it they can prevent their masters from exercising their will over their slaves. Such are often applied to by others, to give them power to prevent their masters from flogging them. The remedy is most generally some kind of bitter root; they are directed to chew it and spit towards their masters when they are angry with their slaves. At other times they prepare certain kinds of powders, to sprinkle about their masters dwellings. This is all done for the purpose of defending themselves in some peaceable manner, although I am satisfied that there is no virtue at all in it. I have tried it to perfection when I was a slave at the South. I was then a young man, full of life and vigor, and was very fond of visiting our neighbors slaves, but had no time to visit only Sundays, when I could get a permit to go, or after night, when I could slip off without being seen. If it was found out, the next morning I was called up to give an account of myself for going off without permission; and would very often get a flogging for it.

I got myself into a scrape at a certain time, by going off in this way, and I expected to be severely punished for it. I had a strong notion of running off, to escape being flogged, but was advised by a friend to go to one of those conjurers, who could prevent me from being flogged. I went and informed him of the difficulty. He said if I would pay him a small sum, he would prevent my being flogged. After I had paid him, he mixed up some alum, salt and other stuff into a powder, and said I must sprinkle it about my master, if he should offer to strike me; this would prevent him. He also gave me some kind of bitter root to chew, and spit towards him, which would certainly prevent my being flogged. According to order I used his remedy, and for some cause I was let pass without being flogged that time.

I had then great faith in conjuration and witchcraft. I was led to believe that I could do almost as I pleased, without being flogged. So on the next Sabbath my conjuration was fully tested by my going off, and staying away until Monday morning, without permission. When I returned home, my master declared that he would punish me for going off; but I did not believe that he could do it while I had this root and dust; and as he approached me, I commenced talking saucy to him. But he soon convinced me that there was no virtue in them. He became so enraged at me for saucing him, that he grasped a handful of switches and punished me severely, in spite of all my roots and powders.

But there was another old slave in that neighborhood, who professed to understand all about conjuration, and I thought I would try his skill. He told me that the first one was only a quack, and if I would only pay him a certain amount in cash, that he would tell me how to prevent any person from striking me. After I had paid him his charge, he told me to go to the cow-pen after night, and get some fresh cow manure, and mix it with red pepper and white people's hair, all to be put into a pot over the fire, and scorched until it could be ground into snuff. I was then to sprinkle it about my master's bedroom, in his hat and boots, and it would prevent him from ever abusing me in any way. After I got it all ready prepared, the smallest pinch of it scattered over a room, was enough to make a horse sneeze from the strength of it; but it did no good. I tried it to my satisfaction. It was my business to make fires in my master's chamber, night and morning. Whenever I could get a chance, I sprinkled a little of this dust about the linen of the bed, where they would breathe it on retiring. This was to act upon them as what is called a kind of love powder, to change their sentiments of anger, to those of love, towards me, but this all proved to be vain imagination. The old man had my money, and I was treated no better for it.

One night when I went in to make a fire, I availed myself of the opportunity of sprinkling a very heavy charge of this powder about my master's bed. Soon after their going to bed, they began to cough and sneeze. Being close around the house, watching and listening, to know what the effect would be, I heard them ask each other what in the world it could be, that made them cough and sneeze so. All the while, I was trembling with fear, expecting every moment I should be called and asked if I knew any thing about it. After this, for fear they might find me out in my dangerous experiments upon them, I had to give them up, for the time being. I was then convinced that running away was the most effectual way by which a slave could escape cruel punishment.

As all the instrumentalities which I as a slave, could bring to bear upon the system, had utterly failed to palliate my sufferings, all hope and consolation fled. I must be a slave for life, and suffer under the lash or die. The influence which this had only tended to make me more unhappy. I resolved that I would be free if running away could make me so. I had heard that Canada was a land of liberty, somewhere in the North; and every wave of trouble that rolled across my breast, caused me to think more and more about Canada, and liberty. But more especially after having been flogged, I have fled to the highest hills of the forest, pressing my way to the North for refuge; but the river Ohio was my limit. To me it was an impassable gulf. I had no rod wherewith to smite the stream, and thereby divide the waters. I had no Moses to go before me and lead the way from bondage to a promised land. Yet I was in a far worse state than Egyptian bondage; for they had houses and land; I had none; they had oxen and sheep; I had none; they had a wise counsel, to tell them what to do, and where to go, and even to go with them; I had none. I was surrounded by opposition on every hand. My friends were few and far between. I have often felt when running away as if I had scarcely a friend on earth.

Sometimes standing on the Ohio River bluff, looking over on a free State, and as far north as my eyes could see, I have eagerly gazed upon the blue sky of the free North, which at times constrained me to cry out from the depths of my soul, Oh! Canada, sweet land of rest—Oh! when shall I get there? Oh, that I had the wings of a dove, that I might soar away to where there is no slavery; no clank-ing of chains, no captives, no lacerating of backs, no parting of husbands and wives; and where man ceases to be the property of his fellow man. These thoughts have revolved in my mind a thousand times. I have stood upon the lofty banks of the river Ohio, gazing upon the splendid steamboats, wafted with all their magnificence up and down the river, and I thought of the fishes of the wa-ter, the fowls of the air, the wild beasts of the forest, all appeared to be free, to go just where they pleased, and I was an unhappy slave!

But my attention was gradually turned in a measure from this subject, by being introduced into the society of young women. This for the time being took my attention from running away, as waiting on the girls appeared to be perfectly congenial to my nature. I wanted to be well thought of by them, and would go to great lengths to gain their affection. I had been taught by the old superstitious slaves, to believe in conjuration, and it was hard for me to give up the notion, for all I had been deceived by them. One of these conjurers, for a small sum agreed to teach me to make any girl love me that I wished. After I had paid him, he told me to get a bull frog, and take a certain bone out of the frog, dry it, and when I got a chance I must step up to any girl whom I wished to make love me, and scratch her somewhere on her naked skin with this bone, and she would be certain to love me, and would follow me in spite of herself; no matter who she might be engaged to, nor who she might be walking with.

So I got me a bone for a certain girl, whom I knew to be under the influence of another young man. I happened to meet her in the company of her lover, one Sunday evening, walking out; so when I act a chance, I fetched her a tremendous rasp across her neck with this bone, which made her jump. But in place of mak-ing her love me, it only made her angry with me. She felt more like running after me to retaliate on me for thus abusing her, than she felt like loving me. After I found there was no virtue in the bone of a frog, I thought I would try some other way to carry out my object. I then sought another counsellor among the old su-perstitious influential slaves; one who professed to be a great friend of mine, told me to get a lock of hair from the head of any girl, and wear it in my shoes: this would cause her to love me above all other persons. As there was another girl whose affections I was anxious to gain, but could not succeed, I thought, without trying the experiment of this hair. I slipped off one night to see the girl, and asked her for a lock of her hair; but she refused to give it. Believing that my success de-pended greatly upon this bunch of hair, I was bent on having a lock before I left that night let it cost what it might. As it was time for me to start home in order to get any sleep that night, I grasped hold of a lock of her hair, which caused her to screech, but I never let go until I had pulled it out. This of course made the girl mad with me, and I accomplished nothing but gained her displeasure.

Such are the superstitious notions of the great masses of southern slaves. It is given to them by tradition, and can never be erased, while the doors of edu-cation are bolted and barred against them. But there is a prohibition by law, of mental and religious instruction. The state of Georgia, by an act of 1770, de-clared "that it shall not be lawful for any number of free negroes, molattoes or mestinos, or even slaves in company with white persons, to meet together for the purpose of mental instruction, either before the rising of the sun or after the going down of the same." 2d Brevard's Digest, 254–5.[17] Similar laws exist in most of the slave States, and patrols are sent out after night and on the Sabbath day to enforce them. They go through their respective towns to prevent slaves from meeting for religious worship or mental instruction.

This is the regulation and law of American Slavery, as sanctioned by the Government of the United States, and without which it could not exist. And almost the whole moral, political, and religious power of the nation are in favor of slavery and aggression, and against liberty and justice. I only judge by their actions, which speak louder than words. Slaveholders are put into the highest offices in the gift of the people in both Church and State, thereby making slave-holding popular and reputable.

CHAPTER III.

MY COURTSHIP AND MARRIAGE. — CHANGE OF OWNER. — MY FIRST BORN. — ITS SUFFERINGS. — MY WIFE ABUSED. — MY OWN ANGUISH.

THE circumstances of my courtship and marriage, I consider to be among the most remarkable events of my life while a slave. To think that after I had determined to carry out the great idea which is so universally and practically acknowledged among all the civilized nations of the earth, that I would be free or die, I suffered myself to be turned aside by the fascinating charms of a female, who gradually won my attention from an object so high as that of liberty; and an object which I held paramount to all others.

But when I had arrived at the age of eighteen, which was in the year of 1833, it was my lot to be introduced to the favor of a mulatto slave girl named Malinda, who lived in Oldham County, Kentucky, about four miles from the residence of my owner. Malinda was a medium sized girl, graceful in her walk, of an extraordinary make, and active in business. Her skin was of a smooth texture, red cheeks, with dark and penetrating eyes. She moved in the highest circle* of slaves, and free people of color. She was also one of the best singers I ever heard, and was much esteemed by all who knew her, for her benevolence, talent and industry. In fact, I considered Malinda to be equalled by few, and surpassed by none, for the above qualities, all things considered.

It is truly marvellous to see how sudden a man's mind can be changed by the charms and influence of a female. The first two or three visits that I paid this dear girl, I had no intention of courting or marrying her, for I was aware that

---

* The distinction among slaves is as marked, as the classes of society are in any aristocratic community. Some refusing to associate with others whom they deem beneath them in point of character, color, condition, or the superior importance of their respective masters.

such a step would greatly obstruct my way to the land of liberty. I only visited Malinda because I liked her company, as a highly interesting girl. But in spite of myself, before I was aware of it, I was deeply in love; and what made this passion so effectual and almost irresistable, I became satisfied that it was reciprocal. There was a union of feeling, and every visit made the impression stronger and stronger. One or two other young men were paying attention to Malinda, at the same time; one of whom her mother was anxious to have her marry. This of course gave me a fair opportunity of testing Malinda's sincerity. I had just about opposition enough to make the subject interesting. That Malinda loved me above all others on earth, no one could deny. I could read it by the warm reception with which the dear girl always met me, and treated me in her mother's house. I could read it by the warm and affectionate shake of the hand, and gentle smile upon her lovely cheek. I could read it by her always giving me the preference of her company; by her pressing invitations to visit even in opposition to her mother's will. I could read it in the language of her bright and sparkling eye, penciled by the unchangable finger of nature, that spake but could not lie. These strong temptations gradually diverted my attention from my actual condition and from liberty, though not entirely.

But oh! that I had only then been enabled to have seen as I do now, or to have read the following slave code, which is but a stereotyped law of American slavery. It would have saved me I think from having to lament that I was a husband and am the father of slaves who are still left to linger out their days in hopeless bondage. The laws of Kentucky, my native State, with Maryland and Virginia, which are said to be the mildest slave States in the Union, noted for their humanity, Christianity and democracy, declare that "Any slave, for rambling in the night, or riding horseback without leave, or running away, may be punished by whipping, cropping and branding in the cheek, or otherwise, not rendering him unfit for labor." "Any slave convicted of petty larceny, murder, or wilfully burning of dwelling houses, may be sentenced to have his right hand cut off; to be hanged in the usual manner, or the head severed from the body, the body divided into four quarters, and head and quarters stuck up in the most public place in the county, where such act was committed."

At the time I joined my wife in holy wedlock, I was ignorant of these ungodly laws; I knew not that I was propogating victims for this kind of torture and cruelty. Malinda's mother was free, and lived in Bedford, about a quarter of a mile from her daughter; and we often met and passed off the time pleasantly. Agreeable to promise, on one Saturday evening, I called to see Malinda, at her mother's residence, with an intention of letting her know my mind upon the subject of marriage. It was a very bright moonlight night; the dear girl was standing in the door, anxiously waiting my arrival. As I approached the door she caught my hand with an affectionate smile, and bid me welcome to her mother's fireside. After having broached the subject of marriage, I informed her of the difficulties which I conceived to be in the way of our marriage; and that I could never engage myself to marry any girl only on certain conditions; near as I can recollect the substance of our conversation upon the subject, it was, that I was religiously inclined; that I intended to try to comply with the requisitions of the gospel, both theoretically and practically through life. Also that I was decided on becoming a free man before I died; and that I expected to get free by running away, and going to Canada, under the British Government. Agreement on those two cardinal questions I made my test for marriage.

I said, "I never will give my heart nor hand to any girl in marriage, until I first know her sentiments upon the all-important subjects of Religion and Liberty. No matter how well I might love her, nor how great the sacrifice in carrying out these God-given principles. And I here pledge myself from this course never to be shaken while a single pulsation of my heart shall continue to throb for Liberty." With this idea Malinda appeared to be well pleased, and with a smile she looked me in the face and said, "I have long entertained the same views, and this has been one of the greatest reasons why I have not felt inclined to enter the married state while a slave; I have always felt a desire to be free; I have long cherished a hope that I should yet be free, either by purchase or running away. In regard to the subject of Religion, I have always felt that it was a good thing, and something that I would seek for at some future period." After I found that Malinda was right upon these all important questions, and that she truly loved me well enough to make me an affectionate wife, I made proposals for marriage. She very modestly declined answering the question then, considering it to be one of a grave character, and upon which our future destiny greatly depended. And notwithstanding she confessed that I had her entire affections, she must have some time to consider the matter. To this I of course consented, and was to meet her on the next Saturday night to decide the question. But for some cause I failed to come, and the next week she sent for me, and on the Sunday evening following I called on her again; she welcomed me with all the kindness of an affectionate lover, and seated me by her side. We soon broached the old subject of marriage, and entered upon a conditional contract of matrimony, viz: that we would marry if our minds should not change within one year; that after marriage we would change our former course and live a pious life; and that we would embrace the earliest opportunity of running away to Canada for our liberty. Clasping each other by the hand, pleding our sacred honor that we would be true, we called on high heaven to witness the rectitude of our purpose. There was nothing that could be more binding upon us as slaves than this; for marriage among American slaves, is disregarded by the laws of this country. It is counted a mere temporary matter; it is a union which may be continued or broken off, with or without the consent of a slaveholder, whether he is a priest or a libertine.

There is no legal marriage among the slaves of the South; I never saw nor heard of such a thing in my life, and I have been through seven of the slave states. A slave marrying according to law, is a thing unknown in the history of American Slavery. And be it known to the disgrace of our country that every slaveholder, who is the keeper of a number of slaves of both sexes, is also the keeper of a house or houses of ill-fame. Licentious white men, can and do, enter at night or day the lodging places of slaves; break up the bonds of affection in families; destroy all their domestic and social union for life; and the laws of the country afford them no protection. Will any man count, if they can be counted, the churches of Maryland, Kentucky, and Virginia, which have slaves connected with them, living in an open state of adultery, never having been married according to the laws of the State, and yet regular members of these various denominations, but more especially the Baptist and Methodist churches? And I hazard nothing in saying, that this state of things exists to a very wide extent in the above states.

I am happy to state that many fugitive slaves, who have been enabled by the aid of an over-ruling providence to escape to the free North with those whom they claim as their wives, notwithstanding all their ignorance and superstition, are not at all disposed to live together like brutes, as they have been compelled to do in slaveholding Churches. But as soon as they get free from slavery they go before some anti-slavery clergyman, and have the solemn ceremony of marriage performed according to the laws of the country. And if they profess religion, and have been baptized by a slaveholding minister, they repudiate it after becoming free, and are rebaptized by a man who is worthy of doing it according to the gospel rule.

The time and place of my marriage, I consider one of the most trying of my life. I was opposed by friends and foes; my mother opposed me because she thought I was too young, and marrying she thought would involve me in trouble and difficulty. My mother-in-law opposed me, because she wanted her daughter to marry a slave who belonged to a very rich man living near by, and who was well known to be the son of his master. She thought no doubt that his master or father might chance to set him free before he died, which would enable him to do a better part by her daughter than I could! And there was no prospect then of my ever being free. But his master has neither died nor yet set his son free, who is now about forty years of age, toiling under the lash, waiting and hoping that his master may die and will him to be free.

The young men were opposed to our marriage for the same reason that Paddy opposed a match when the clergyman was about to pronounce the marriage ceremony of a young couple. He said "if there be any present who have any objections to this couple being joined together in holy wedlock, let them speak now, or hold their peace henceforth." At this time Paddy sprang to his feet and said, "Sir, I object to this." Every eye was fixed upon him. "What is your objection?" said the clergyman. "Faith," replied Paddy, "Sir I want her myself."

The man to whom I belonged was opposed, because he feared my taking off from his farm some of the fruits of my own labor for Malinda to eat, in the shape of pigs, chickens, or turkeys, and would count it not robbery. So we formed a resolution, that if we were prevented from joining in wedlock, that we would run away, and strike for Canada, let the consequences be what they might. But we had one consolation; Malinda's master was very much in favor of the match, but entirely upon selfish principles. When I went to ask his permission to marry Malinda, his answer was in the affirmative with but one condition, which I consider to be too vulgar to be written in this book. Our marriage took place one night during the Christmas holydays; at which time we had quite a festival given us. All appeared to be wide awake, and we had quite a jolly time at my wedding party. And notwithstanding our marriage was without license or sanction of law, we believed it to be honorable before God, and the bed undefiled. Our christmas holydays were spent in matrimonial visiting among our friends, while it should have been spent in running away to Canada, for our liberty. But freedom was little thought of by us, for several months after marriage. I often look back to that period even now as one of the most happy seasons of my life; notwithstanding all the contaminating and heartrending features with which the horrid system of slavery is marked, and must carry with it to its final grave, yet I still look back to that season with sweet remembrance and pleasure, that yet hath power to charm and drive back dull cares which have been accumulated by a thousand painful recollections of slavery. Malinda was to me an affectionate wife. She was with me in the darkest hours of adversity. She was with me in sorrow, and joy, in fasting and feasting, in trial and persecution, in sickness and health, in sunshine and in shade.

Some months after our marriage, the unfeeling master to whom I belonged, sold his farm with the view of moving his slaves to the State of Missouri, regardless of the separation of husbands and wives forever; but for fear of my resuming my old practice of running away, if he should have forced me to leave my wife, by my repeated requests, he was constrained to sell me to his brother, who lived within seven miles of Wm. Gatewood, who then held Malinda as his property. I was permitted to visit her only on Saturday nights, after my work was done, and I had to be at home before sunrise on Monday mornings or take a flogging. He proved to be so oppressive, and so unreasonable in punishing his victims, that I soon found that I should have to run away in self-defence. But he soon began to take the hint, and sold me to Wm. Gatewood the owner of Malinda. With my new residence I confess that I was much dissatisfied. Not that Gatewood was a more cruel master than my former owner—not that I was opposed to living with Malinda, who was then the centre and object of my affections—but to live where I must be eye witness to her insults, scourgings and abuses, such as are common to be inflicted upon slaves, was more than I could bear. If my wife must be exposed to the insults and licentious passions of wicked slavedrivers and overseers; if she must bear the stripes of the lash laid on by an unmerciful tyrant; if this is to be done with impunity, which is frequently done by slaveholders and their abettors, Heaven forbid that I should be compelled to witness the sight.

Not many months after I took up my residence on Wm. Gatewood's plantation, Malinda made me a father. The dear little daughter was called Mary Frances. She was nurtured and caressed by her mother and father, until she was large enough to creep over the floor after her parents, and climb up by a chair before I felt it to be my duty to leave my family and go into a foreign country for a season. Malinda's business was to labor out in the field the greater part of her time, and there was no one to take care of poor little Frances, while her mother was toiling in the field. She was left at the house to creep under the feet of an unmerciful old mistress, whom I have known to slap with her hand the face of little Frances, for crying after her mother, until her little face was left black and blue.

I recollect that Malinda and myself came from the field one summer's day at noon, and poor little Frances came creeping to her mother smiling, but with large tear drops standing in her dear little eyes, sobbing and trying to tell her mother that she had been abused, but was not able to utter a word. Her little face was bruised black with the whole print of Mrs. Gatewood's hand. This print was plainly to be seen for eight days after it was done. But oh! this darling child was a slave; born of a slave mother. Who can imagine what could be the feelings of a father and mother, when looking upon their infant child whipped and tortured with impunity, and they placed in a situation where they could afford it no protection. But we were all claimed and held as property; the father and mother were slaves!

On this same plantation I was compelled to stand and see my wife shamefully scourged and abused by her master; and the manner in which this was done, was so violently and inhumanly committed upon the person of a female, that I despair in finding decent language to describe the bloody act of cruelty. My happiness or pleasure was then all blasted; for it was sometimes a pleasure to be with my little family even in slavery. I loved them as my wife and child. Little Frances was a pretty child; she was quiet, playful, bright, and interesting. She had a keen black eye, and the very image of her mother was stamped upon her cheek; but I could never look upon the dear child without being filled with sorrow and fearful apprehensions, of being separated by slaveholders, because she was a slave, regarded as property. And unfortunately for me, I am the father of a slave, a word too obnoxious to be spoken by a fugitive slave. It calls fresh to my mind the separation of husband and wife; of stripping, tying up and flogging; of tearing children from their parents, and selling them on the auction block. It calls to mind female virtue trampled under foot with impunity. But oh! when I remember that my daughter, my only child, is still there, destined to share the fate of all these calamities, it is too much to bear. If ever there was any one act of my life while a slave, that I have to lament over it is that of being a father and a husband of slaves. I have the satisfaction of knowing that I am only the father of one slave.

CAN A MOTHER FORGET HER SUCKLING CHILD?

THE TENDER MERCIES OF THE WICKED ARE CRUEL

She is bone of my bone, and flesh of my flesh; poor unfortunate child. She was the first and shall be the last slave that ever I will father, for chains and slavery on this earth.

CHAPTER IV.

MY FIRST ADVENTURE FOR LIBERTY.—PARTING SCENE.—JOURNEY UP THE RIVER.— SAFE ARRIVAL IN CINCINNATI.—JOURNEY TO CANADA.—SUFFERING FROM COLD AND HUNGER.—DENIED FOOD AND SHELTER BY SOME.—ONE NOBLE EX- CEPTION.—SUBSEQUENT SUCCESS.—ARRIVAL AT PERRYSBURGH.—I OBTAINED EMPLOYMENT THROUGH THE WINTER.—MY RETURN TO KENTUCKY TO GET MY FAMILY.

IN the fall or winter of 1837 I formed a resolution that I would escape, if possible, to Canada, for my Liberty. I commenced from that hour making preparations for the dangerous experiment of breaking the chains that bound me as a slave. My preparation for this voyage consisted in the accumulation of a little money, perhaps not exceeding two dollars and fifty cents, and a suit which I had never been seen or known to wear before; this last was to avoid detection.

On the twenty-fifth of December, 1837, my long anticipated time had arrived when I was to put into operation my former resolution, which was to bolt for Liberty or consent to die a Slave. I acted upon the former, although I confess it to be one of the most self-denying acts of my whole life, to take leave of an affectionate wife, who stood before me on my departure, with dear little Frances in her arms, and with tears of sorrow in her eyes as she bid me a long farewell. It required all the moral courage that I was master of to suppress my feelings while taking leave of my little family.

Had Malinda known my intention at that time, it would not have been possible for me to have got away, and I might have this day been a slave. Notwithstanding every inducement was held out to me to run away if I would be free, and the voice of liberty was thundering in my very soul, "Be free oh, man! be free," I was struggling against a thousand obstacles which had clustered around my mind to bind my wounded spirit still in the dark prison of mental degradation. My strong attachments to friends and relatives, with all the love of home and birth-place which is so natural among the human family, twined about my heart and were hard to break away from. And withal, the fear of being pursued with guns and blood-hounds, and of being killed, or captured and taken to the extreme South, to linger out my days in hopeless bondage on some cotton or sugar plantation, all combined to deter me. But I had counted the cost, and was fully prepared to make the sacrifice. The time for fulfilling my pledge was then at hand. I must forsake friends and neighbors, wife and child, or consent to live and die a slave.

By the permission of my keeper, I started out to work for myself on Christmas. I went to the Ohio River, which was but a short distance from Bedford. My excuse for wanting to go there was to get work. High wages were offered for hands to work in a slaughter house. But in place of my going to work there, according to promise, when I arrived at the river I managed to find a conveyance to cross over into a free state. I was landed in the village of Madison, Indiana, where steamboats were landing every day and night, passing up and down the river, which afforded me a good opportunity of getting a boat passage to Cincinnati. My anticipation being worked up to the highest pitch, no sooner was the curtain of night dropped over the village, than I secreted myself where no one could see me, and changed my suit ready for the passage. Soon I heard the welcome sound of a Steamboat coming up the river Ohio, which was soon to waft me beyond the limits of the human slave markets of Kentucky. When the boat had landed at Madison, notwithstanding my strong desire to get off, my heart trembled within me in view of the great danger to which I was exposed in taking passage on board of a Southern Steamboat; hence before I took passage, I kneeled down before the Great I Am, and prayed for his aid and protection, which He bountifully bestowed even beyond my expectation; for I felt myself to be unworthy. I then stept boldly on the deck of this splendid swift-running Steamer, bound for the city of Cincinnati. This being the first voyage that I had ever taken on board of a Steamboat, I was filled with fear and excitement, knowing that I was surrounded by the vilest enemies of God and man, liable to be seized and bound hand and foot, by any white man, and taken back into captivity. But I crowded myself back from the light among the deck passengers, where it would be difficult to distinguish me from a white man. Every time during the night that the mate came round with a light after the hands, I was afraid he would see I was a colored man, and take me up; hence I kept from the light as much as possible. Some men love darkness rather than light, because their deeds are evil; but this was not the case with myself; it was to avoid detection in doing right. This was one of the instances of my adventures that my affinity with the Anglo-Saxon race, and even slave-holders, worked well for my escape. But no thanks to them for it. While in their midst they have not only robbed me of my labor and liberty, but they have almost entirely robbed me of my dark complexion. Being so near the color of a slaveholder, they could not, or did not find me out that night among the white passengers. There was one of the deck hands on board called out on his watch, whose hammock was swinging up near by me. I asked him if he would let me lie in it. He said if I would pay him twenty-five cents that I might lie in it until day. I readily paid him the price and got into the hammock. No one could see my face to know whether I was white or colored, while I was in the hammock; but I never closed my eyes for sleep that night. I had often heard of explosions on board of Steamboats; and every time the boat landed, and blowed off steam, I was afraid the boilers had bursted and we should all be killed; but I lived through the night amid the many dangers to which I was exposed. I still maintained my position in the hammock, until the next morning about 8 o'clock, when I heard the passengers saying the boat was near Cincinnati; and by this time I supposed that the attention of the people would be turned to the city, and I might pass off unnoticed. There were no questions asked me while on board the boat. The boat landed about 9 o'clock in the morning in Cincinnati, and I waited until after most of the passengers had gone off of the boat; I then walked as gracefully up street as if I was not running away, until I had got pretty well up Broadway. My object was to go to Canada, but having no knowledge of the road, it was necessary for me to make some inquiry before I left the city. I was afraid to ask a white person, and I could see no colored person to ask. But fortunately for me I found a company of little boys at play in the street, and through these little boys, by asking them indirect questions, I found the residence of a colored man.

"Boys, can you tell me where that old colored man lives who saws wood, and works at jobs around the streets?"

"What is his name?" said one of the boys,

"I forget."

"Is it old Job Dundy?"

"Is Dundy a colored man?"

"Yes, sir."

"That is the very man I am looking for; will you show me where he lives?"

"Yes," said the little boy, and pointed me out the house.

Mr. D. invited me in, and I found him to be a true friend. He asked me if I was a slave from Kentucky, and if I ever intended to go back into slavery? Not knowing yet whether he was truly in favor of slaves running away, I told him that I had just come over to spend my christmas holydays, and that I was going back. His reply was, "my son, I would never go back if I was in your place; you have a right to your liberty." I then asked him how I should get my freedom? He referred me to Canada, over which waved freedom's flag, defended by the British Government, upon whose soil there cannot be the foot print of a slave.

He then commenced telling me of the facilities for my escape to Canada; of the Abolitionists; of the Abolition Societies, and of their fidelity to the cause of suffering humanity. This was the first time in my life that ever I had heard of such people being in existence as the Abolitionists. I supposed that they were a different race of people. He conducted me to the house of one of these warm-hearted friends of God and the slave. I found him willing to aid a poor fugitive on his way to Canada, even to the dividing of the last cent, or morsel of bread if necessary.

These kind friends gave me something to eat, and started me on my way to Canada, with a recommendation to a friend on my way. This was the commencement of what was called the under ground rail road to Canada. I walked with bold courage, trusting in the arm of Omnipotence; guided by the unchangable North Star by night, and inspired by an elevated thought that I was fleeing from a land of slavery and oppression, bidding farewell to handcuffs, whips, thumb-screws and chains.

I travelled on until I had arrived at the place where I was directed to call on an Abolitionist, but I made no stop: so great were my fears of being pursued by the pro-slavery hunting dogs of the South. I prosecuted my journey vigorously for nearly forty-eight hours without food or rest, struggling against external difficulties such as no one can imagine who has never experienced the same: not knowing what moment I might be captured while travelling among strangers, through cold and fear, breasting the north winds, being thinly clad, pelted by the snow storms through the dark hours of the night, and not a house in which I could enter to shelter me from the storm.

The second night from Cincinnati, about midnight, I thought that I should freeze; my shoes were worn through, and my feet were exposed to the bare ground. I approached a house on the road side, knocked at the door, and asked admission to their fire, but was refused. I went to the next house, and was refused the privilege of their fire-side, to prevent my freezing. This I thought was hard treatment among the human family. But—

"Behind a frowning Providence there was a smiling face,"[18]

which soon shed beams of light upon unworthy me.

The next morning I was still found struggling on my way, faint, hungry, lame, and rest-broken. I could see people taking breakfast from the roadside, but I did not dare to enter their houses to get my breakfast, for neither love nor money. In passing a low cottage, I saw the breakfast table spread with all its bounties, and I could see no male person about the house; the temptation for food was greater than I could resist.

I saw a lady about the table, and I thought that if she was ever so much disposed to take me up, that she would have to catch and hold me, and that would have been impossible. I stepped up to the door with my hat off, and asked her if she would be good enough to sell me a sixpence worth of bread and meat. She cut off a piece and brought it to me; I thanked her for it, and handed her the pay, but instead of receiving it, she burst into tears, and said "never mind the money," but gently turned away bidding me go on my journey. This was altogether unexpected to me: I had found a friend in the time of need among strangers, and nothing could be more cheering in the day of trouble than this. When I left that place I started with bolder courage. The next

"NEVER MIND THE MONEY."

night I put up at a tavern, and continued stopping at public houses until my means were about gone. When I got to the Black Swamp in the county of Wood, Ohio, I stopped one night at a hotel, after travelling all day through mud and snow; but I soon found that I should not be able to pay my bill. This was about the time that the "wild-cat banks,"[19] were in a flourishing state, and "shin plasters"* in abundance; they would charge a dollar for one night's lodging.

After I had found out this, I slipped out of the bar room into the kitchen where the landlady was getting supper; as she had quite a number of travellers to cook for that night, I told her if she would accept my services, I would assist her in getting supper; that I was a cook. She very readily accepted the offer, and I went to work.

She was very much pleased with my work, and the next morning I helped her to get breakfast. She then wanted to hire me for all winter, but I refused for fear I might be pursued. My excuse to her was that I had a brother living in Detroit, whom I was going to see on some important business, and after I got that business attended to, I would come back and work for them all winter.

When I started the second morning they paid me fifty cents beside my board, with the understanding that I was to return; but I have not gone back yet.

I arrived the next morning in the village of Perrysburgh, where I found quite a settlement of colored people, many of whom were fugitive slaves. I made

---

* Nickname for temporary paper money.

my case known to them and they sympathized with me. I was a stranger, and they took me in and persuaded me to spend the winter in Perrysburgh, where I could get employment and go to Canada the next spring, in a steamboat which run from Perrysburgh, if I thought it proper so to do.

I got a job of chopping wood during that winter which enabled me to purchase myself a suit, and after paying my board the next spring, I had saved fifteen dollars in cash. My intention was to go back to Kentucky after my wife.

When I got ready to start, which was about the first of May, my friends all persuaded me not to go, but to get some other person to go, for fear I might be caught and sold off from my family into slavery forever. But I could not refrain from going back myself, believing that I could accomplish it better than a stranger.

The money that I had would not pass in the South, and for the purpose of getting it off to a good advantage, I took a steamboat passage to Detroit, Michigan, and there I spent all my money for dry goods, to peddle out on my way back through the State of Ohio. I also purchased myself a pair of false whiskers to put on when I got back to Kentucky, to prevent any one from knowing me after night, should they see me. I then started back after my little family.

CHAPTER V.

My safe arrival at Kentucky.—Surprise and delight to find my family.—
Plan for their escape projected.—Return to Cincinnati.—My be-
trayal by traitors.—Imprisonment in Covington, Kentucky.—Return
to slavery.—Infamous proposal of the slave catchers.—My reply.

I succeeded very well in selling out my goods, and when I arrived in Cincinnati, I called on some of my friends who had aided me on my first escape. They also opposed me in going back only for my own good. But it has ever been characteristic of me to persevere in what I undertake.

I took a Steamboat passage which would bring me to where I should want to land about dark, so as to give me a chance to find my family during the night if possible. The boat landed me at the proper place, and at the proper time accordingly. This landing was about six miles from Bedford, where my mother and wife lived, but with different families. My mother was the cook at a tavern, in Bedford. When I approached the house where mother was living, I remembered where she slept in the kitchen, her bed was near the window.

It was a bright moonlight night, and in looking through the kitchen window, I saw a person lying in bed about where my mother had formerly slept. I rapped on the glass which awakened the person, in whom I recognised my dear mother, but she knew me not, as I was dressed in disguise with my false whiskers on; but she came to the window and asked who I was and what I wanted. But when I took off my false whiskers, and spoke to her, she knew my voice, and quickly sprang to the door, clasping my hand, exclaiming, "Oh! is this my son," drawing me into the room, where I was so fortunate as to find Malinda, and little Frances, my wife and child, whom I had left to find the fair climes of liberty, and whom I was then seeking to rescue from perpetual slavery.

They never expected to see me again in this life. I am entirely unable to describe what my feelings were at that time. It was almost like the return of the prodigal son. There was weeping and rejoicing. They were filled with surprise and fear; with sadness and joy. The sensation of joy at that moment flashed like lightning over my afflicted mind, mingled with a thousand dreadful apprehensions, that none but a heart wounded slave father and husband like myself can possibly imagine. After talking the matter over, we decided it was not best to start with my family that night, as it was very uncertain whether we should get a boat passage immediately. And in case of failure, if Malinda should get back even before daylight the next morning it would have excited suspicion against her, as it was not customary for slaves to leave home at that stage of the week without permission. Hence we thought it would be the most effectual way for her to escape, to start on Saturday night; this being a night on which the slaves of Kentucky are permitted to visit around among their friends, and are often allowed to stay until the afternoon on Sabbath day.

I gave Malinda money to pay her passage on board of a Steamboat to Cincinnati, as it was not safe for me to wait for her until Saturday night; but she was to meet me in Cincinnati, if possible, the next Sunday. Her father was to go with her to the Ohio River on Saturday night, and if a boat passed up during the night she was to get on board at Madison, and come to Cincinnati. If she should fail in getting off that night, she was to try it the next Saturday night. This was the understanding when we separated. This we thought was the best plan for her escape, as there had been so much excitement caused by my running away.

The owners of my wife were very much afraid that she would follow me; and to prevent her they had told her and other slaves that I had been persuaded off by the Abolitionists, who had promised to set me free, but had sold me off to New Orleans. They told the slaves to beware of the abolitionists, that their object was to decoy off slaves and then sell them off in New Orleans. Some of them believed this, and others believed it not; and the owners of my wife were more watchful over her than they had ever been before as she was unbelieving.

This was in the month of June, 1838. I left Malinda on a bright but lonesome Wednesday night. When I arrived at the river Ohio, I found a small craft chained to a tree, in which I ferried myself across the stream.

I succeeded in getting a Steamboat passage back to Cincinnati, where I put up with one of my abolition friends who knew that I had gone after my family, and who appeared to be much surprised to see me again. I was soon visited by several friends who knew of my having gone back after my family. They wished to know why I had not brought my family with me; but after they understood the plan, and that my family was expected to be in Cincinnati within a few days, they thought it the best and safest plan for us to take a stage passage out to Lake Erie. But being short of money, I was not able to pay my passage in the stage, even if it would have prevented me from being caught by the slave hunters of Cincinnati, or save me from being taken back into bondage for life.

These friends proposed helping me by subscription; I accepted their kind offer, but in going among friends to solicit aid for me, they happened to get among traitors, and kidnappers, both white and colored men, who made their living by that kind of business. Several persons called on me and made me small donations, and among them two white men came in professing to be my friends. They told me not to be afraid of them, they were abolitionists. They asked me a great many questions. They wanted to know if I needed any help? and they wanted to know if it could be possible that a man so near white as myself could be a slave? Could it be possible that men would make slaves of their own children? They expressed great sympathy for me, and gave me fifty cents each; by this they gained my confidence. They asked my master's name; where he lived, &c. After which they left the room, bidding me God speed. These traitors, or land pirates, took passage on board of the first Steamboat down the river, in search of my owners. When they found them, they got a reward of three hundred dollars offered for the re-capture of this "stray" which they had so long and faithfully been hunting, by day and by night, by land and by water with dogs and with guns, but all without success. This being the last and only chance for dragging me back into hopeless bondage, time and money was no object when they saw a prospect of my being retaken.

Mr. Gatewood got two of his slaveholding neighbors to go with him to Cincinnati, for the purpose of swearing to anything which might be necessary to change me back into property. They came on to Cincinnati, and with but little effort they soon rallied a mob of ruffians who were willing to become the watch-dogs of slaveholders, for a dram, in connection with a few slavehunting petty constables.

While I was waiting the arrival of my family, I got a job of digging a cellar for the good lady where I was stopping, and while I was digging under the house, all at once I heard a man enter the house; another stept up to the cellar door to where I was at work; he looked in and saw me with my coat off at work. He then rapped over the cellar door on the house side, to notify the one who had entered the house to look for me that I was in the cellar. This strange conduct soon excited suspicion so strong in me, that I could not stay in the cellar and started to come out, but the man who stood by the door, rapped again on the house side, for the other to come to his aid, and told me to stop. I attempted to pass out by him, and he caught hold of me, and drew a pistol, swearing if I did not stop he would shoot me down. By this time I knew that I was betrayed.

I asked him what crime I had committed that I should be murdered.

"I will let you know, very soon," said he.

By this time there were others coming to his aid, and I could see no way by which I could possibly escape the jaws of that hell upon earth.

All my flattering prospects of enjoying my own fire-side, with my little family, were then blasted and gone; and I must bid farewell to friends and freedom forever.

In vain did I look to the infamous laws of the Commonwealth of Ohio, for that protection against violence and outrage, that even the vilest criminal with a white skin might enjoy. But oh! the dreadful thought, that after all my sacrifice and struggling to rescue my family from the hands of the oppressor; that I should be dragged back into cruel bondage to suffer the penalty of a tyrant's law, to endure stripes and imprisonment, and to be shut out from all moral as well as intellectual improvement, and linger out almost a living death.

When I saw a crowd of blood-thirsty, unprincipled slave hunters rushing upon me armed with weapons of death, it was no use for me to undertake to fight my way through against such fearful odds.

But I broke away from the man who stood by with his pistol drawn to shoot me if I should resist, and reached the fence and attempted to jump over it before I was overtaken; but the fence being very high I was caught by my legs before I got over.

I kicked and struggled with all my might to get away, but without success. I kicked a new cloth coat off of his back, while he was holding on to my leg. I kicked another in his eye; but they never let me go until they got more help. By this time, there was a crowd on the out side of the fence with clubs to beat me back. Finally, they succeeded in dragging me from the fence and overpowered me by numbers and choked me almost to death.

These ruffians dragged me through the streets of Cincinnati, to what was called a justice office. But it was more like an office of injustice.

When I entered the room I was introduced to three slaveholders, one of whom was a son of Wm. Gatewood, who claimed me as his property. They pretended to be very glad to see me.

They asked me if I did not want to see my wife and child; but I made no reply to any thing that was said until I was delivered up as a slave. After they were asked a few questions by the court, the old pro-slavery squire very gravely pronounced me to be the property of Mr. Gatewood.

The office being crowded with spectators, many of whom were colored persons, Mr. G. was afraid to keep me in Cincinnati, two or three hours even, until a steamboat got ready to leave for the South. So they took me across the river, and locked me up in Covington jail, for safe keeping. This was the first time in my life that I had been put into a jail. It was truly distressing to my feelings to be locked up in a cold dungeon for no crime. The jailor not being at home, his wife had to act in his place. After my owners had gone back to Cincinnati, the jailor's wife, in company with another female, came into the jail and talked with me very friendly.

I told them all about my situation, and these ladies said they hoped that I might get away again, and went so far as to tell me if I should be kept in the jail that night, there was a hole under the wall of the jail where a prisoner had got out. It was only filled up with loose dirt, they said, and I might scratch it out and clear myself.

This I thought was a kind word from an unexpected friend: I had power to have taken the key from those ladies, in spite of them, and have cleared myself; but knowing that they would have to suffer perhaps for letting me get away, I thought I would wait until after dark, at which time I should try to make my escape, if they should not take me out before that time. But within two or three hours, they came after me, and conducted me on board of a boat, on which we all took passage down to Louisville. I was not confined in any way, but was well

SQUIRE'S OFFICE

guarded by five men, three of whom were slaveholders, and the two young men from Cincinnati, who had betrayed me.

After the boat had got fairly under way, with these vile men standing around me on the upper deck of the boat, and she under full speed carrying me back into a land of torment, I could see no possible way of escape. Yet, while I was permitted to gaze on the beauties of nature, on free soil, as I passed down the river, things looked to me uncommonly pleasant: The green trees and wild flowers of the forest; the ripening harvest fields waving with the gentle breezes of Heaven; and the honest farmers tilling their soil and living by their own toil. These things seem to light upon my vision with a peculiar charm. I was conscious of what must be my fate; a wretched victim for Slavery without limit; to be sold like an ox, into hopeless bondage, and to be worked under the flesh devouring lash during life, without wages.

This was to me an awful thought; every time the boat run near the shore, I was tempted to leap from the deck down into the water, with a hope of making my escape. Such was then my feeling.

But on a moment's reflection, reason with her warning voice overcame this passion by pointing out the dreadful consequences of one's committing suicide. And this I thought would have a very striking resemblance to the act, and I declined putting into practice this dangerous experiment, though the temptation was great.

These kidnapping gentlemen, seeing that I was much dissatisfied, commenced talking to me, by saying that I must not be cast down; they were going to take me back home to live with my family, if I would promise not to run away again.

To this I agreed, and told them that this was all that I could ask, and more than I had expected.

But they were not satisfied with having recaptured me, because they had lost other slaves and supposed that I knew their whereabouts; and truly I did. They wanted me to tell them; but before telling I wanted them to tell who it was that had betrayed me into their hands. They said that I was betrayed by two colored men in Cincinnati, whose names they were backward in telling, because their business in connection with themselves was to betray and catch fugitive slaves for the reward offered. They undertook to justify the act by saying if they had not betrayed me, that somebody else would, and if I would tell them where they could catch a number of other runaway slaves, they would pay for me and set me free, and would then take me in as one of the Club. They said I would soon make money enough to buy my wife and child out of slavery.

But I replied, "No, gentlemen, I cannot commit or do an act of that kind, even if it were in my power so to do. I know that I am now in the power of a master who can sell me from my family for life, or punish me for the crime of running away, just as he pleases: I know that I am a prisoner for life, and have no way of extricating myself; and I also know that I have been deceived and betrayed by men who professed to be my best friends; but can all this justify me in becoming a traitor to others? Can I do that which I complain of others for doing unto me? Never, I trust, while a single pulsation of my heart continues to beat, can I consent to betray a fellow man like myself back into bondage, who has escaped. Dear as I love my wife and little child, and as much as I should like to enjoy freedom and happiness with them, I am unwilling to bring this about by betraying and destroying the liberty and happiness of others who have never offended me!"

I then asked them again if they would do me the kindness to tell me who it was betrayed me into their hands at Cincinnati? They agreed to tell me with the understanding that I was to tell where there was living, a family of slaves at the North, who had run away from Mr. King of Kentucky. I should not have agreed to this, but I knew the slaves were in Canada, where it was not possible for them to be captured. After they had told me the names of the persons who betrayed me, and how it was done, then I told them their slaves were in Canada, doing well. The two white men were Constables, who claimed the right of taking up any strange colored person as a slave; while the two colored kidnappers, under the pretext of being abolitionists, would find out all the fugitives they could, and inform these Constables for which they got a part of the reward, after they had found out where the slaves were from, the name of his master, &c. By the agency of these colored men, they were seized by a band of white ruffians, locked up in jail, and their master sent for. These colored kidnappers, with the Constables, were getting rich by betraying fugitive slaves. This was told to me by one of the Constables, while they were all standing around trying to induce me to engage in the same business for the sake of regaining my own liberty, and that of my wife and child. But my answer even there, under the most trying circumstances, surrounded by the strongest enemies of God and man, was most emphatically in the negative. "Let my punishment be what it may, either with the lash or by selling me away from my friends and home; let my destiny be what you please, I can never engage in this business for the sake of getting free."

They said I should not be sold nor punished with the lash for what I had done, but I should be carried back to Bedford, to live with my wife. Yet when the boat got to where we should have landed, she wafted by without making any stop. I felt awful in view of never seeing my family again; they asked what was the matter? what made me look so cast down? I informed them that I knew I was to be sold in the Louisville slave market, or in New Orleans, and I never expected to see my family again. But they tried to pacify me by promising not to sell me to a slave trader who would take me off to New Orleans; cautioning me at the same time not to let it be known that I had been a runaway. This would very much lessen the value of me in market. They would not punish me by putting irons on my limbs, but would give me a good name, and sell me to some gentleman in Louisville for a house servant. They thought I would soon make money enough to buy myself, and would not part with me if they could get along without. But I had cost them so much in advertising and looking for me, that they were involved by it. In the first place they paid eight hundred and fifty dollars for me; and when I first run away, they paid one hundred for advertising and looking after me; and now they had to pay about forty dollars, expenses travelling to and from Cincinnati, in addition to the three hundred dollars reward; and they were not able to pay the reward without selling me.

I knew then the only alternative left for me to extricate myself was to use deception, which is the most effectual defence a slave can use. I pretended to be satisfied for the purpose of getting an opportunity of giving them the slip.

But oh, the distress of mind, the lamentable thought that I should never again see the face nor hear the gentle voice of my nearest and dearest friends in this life. I could imagine what must be my fate from my peculiar situation. To be sold to the highest bidder, and then wear the chains of slavery down to the grave. The day star of liberty which had once cheered and gladdened my heart in freedom's land, had then hidden itself from my vision, and the dark and dismal frown of slavery had obscured the sunshine of freedom from me, as they supposed for all time to come.

But the understanding between us was, I was not to be tied, chained, nor flogged; for if they should take me into the city handcuffed and guarded by five men the question might be asked what crime I had committed? And if it should be known that I had been a runaway to Canada, it would lessen the value of me at least one hundred dollars.

CHAPTER VI.

ARRIVAL AT LOUISVILLE, KY.—EFFORTS TO SELL ME.—FORTUNATE ESCAPE FROM
THE MAN-STEALERS IN THE PUBLIC STREET.—I RETURN TO BEDFORD, KY.—THE
RESCUE OF MY FAMILY AGAIN ATTEMPTED.—I STARTED ALONE EXPECTING
THEM TO FOLLOW.—AFTER WAITING SOME MONTHS I RESOLVE TO GO BACK
AGAIN TO KENTUCKY.

WHEN the boat arrived at Louisville, the day being too far spent for them to
dispose of me, they had to put up at a Hotel. When we left the boat, they were
afraid of my bolting from them in the street, and to prevent this they took hold
of my arms, one on each side of me, gallanting me up to the hotel with as much
propriety as if I had been a white lady. This was to deceive the people, and prevent my getting away from them.

They called for a bed-room to which I was conducted and locked within.
That night three of them lodged in the same room to guard me. They locked the
door and put the key under the head of their bed. I could see no possible way for
my escape without jumping out of a high three story house window.

It was almost impossible for me to sleep that night in my peculiar situation.
I passed the night in prayer to our Heavenly Father, asking that He would open
to me even the smallest chance for escape.

The next morning after they had taken breakfast, four of them left me in
the care of Dan Lane. He was what might be called one of the watch dogs of Kentucky. There was nothing too mean for him to do. He never blushed to rob a
slave mother of her children, no matter how young or small. He was also cele-

brated for slave selling, kidnapping, and negro hunting. He was well known in that region by the slaves as well as the slaveholders, to have all the qualifications necessary for his business. He was a drunkard, a gambler, a profligate, and a slaveholder.

While the other four were looking around through the city for a purchaser, Dan was guarding me with his bowie knife and pistols. After a while the others came in with two persons to buy me, but on seeing me they remarked that they thought I would run away, and asked me if I had ever run away. Dan sprang to his feet and answered the question for me, by telling one of the most palpable falsehoods that ever came from the lips of a slaveholder. He declared that I had never run away in my life!

Fortunately for me, Dan, while the others were away, became unwell; and from taking salts, or from some other cause, was compelled to leave his room. Off he started to the horse stable which was located on one of the most public streets of Louisville, and of course I had to accompany him. He gallanted me into the stable by the arm, and placed himself back in one of the horses stalls and ordered me to stand by until he was ready to come out.

At this time a thousand thoughts were flashing through my mind with regard to the propriety of trying the springs of my heels, which nature had so well adapted for taking the body out of danger, even in the most extraordinary emergencies. I thought in the attempt to get away by running, if I should not succeed, it could make my condition no worse, for they could but sell me and this they were then trying to do. These thoughts impelled me to keep edging towards the door, though very cautiously. Dan kept looking around after me as if he was not satisfied at my getting so near to the door. But the last I saw of him in the stable was just as he turned his eyes from me; I nerved myself with all the moral courage I could command and bolted for the door, perhaps with the fleetness of a much frightened deer, who never looks behind in time of peril. Dan was left in the stable to make ready for the race, or jump out into the street half dressed, and thereby disgrace himself before the public eye.

It would be impossible for me to set forth the speed with which I run to avoid my adversary; I succeeded in turning a corner before Dan got sight of me, and by fast running, turning corners, and jumping high fences, I was enabled to effect my escape.

In running so swiftly through the public streets, I thought it would be a safer course to leave the public way, and as quick as thought I spied a high board fence by the way and attempted to leap over it. The top board broke and down I came into a hen-coop which stood by the fence. The dogs barked, and the hens flew and cackled so, that I feared it would lead to my detection before I could get out of the yard.

The reader can only imagine how great must have been the excited state of my mind while exposed to such extraordinary peril and danger on every side. In danger of being seized by a savage dog, which sprang at me when I fell into the hen-coop; in danger of being apprehended by the tenants of the lot; in danger of being shot or wounded by any one who might have attempted to stop me, a runaway slave; and in danger on the other hand of being overtaken and getting in conflict with my adversary. With these fearful apprehensions, caution dictated me not to proceed far by day-light in this slaveholding city.

At this moment every nerve and muscle of my whole system was in full stretch; and every facility of the mind brought into action striving to save myself from being re-captured. I dared not go to the forest, knowing that I might be tracked by bloodhounds, and overtaken. I was so fortunate as to find a hiding place in the city which seemed to be pointed out by the finger of Providence. After running across lots, turning corners, and shunning my fellow men, as if they were wild ferocious beasts, I found a hiding place in a pile of boards or scantling, where I kept concealed during that day.

No tongue nor pen can describe the dreadful apprehensions under which I labored for the space of ten or twelve hours. My hiding place happened to be between two workshops, where there were men at work within six or eight feet of me. I could imagine that I heard them talking about me, and at other times thought I heard the footsteps of Daniel Lane in close pursuit. But I retained my position there until 9 or 10 o'clock at night, without being discovered; after which I attempted to find my way out, which was exceedingly difficult. The night being very dark, in a strange city, among slaveholders and slave hunters, to me it was like a person entering a wilderness among wolves and vipers, blindfolded. I was compelled from necessity to enter this place for refuge under the most extraordinary state of excitement, without regard to its geographical position. I found myself surrounded with a large block of buildings, which comprised a whole square, built up mostly on three sides, so that I could see no way to pass out without exposing myself perhaps to the gaze of patrols, or slave catchers.

In wandering around through the dark, I happened to find a calf in a back yard, which was bawling after the cow; the cow was also lowing in another direction, as if they were trying to find each other. A thought struck me that there must be an outlet somewhere about, where the cow and calf were trying to meet. I started in the direction where I heard the lowing of the cow, and I found an arch or tunnel extending between two large brick buildings, where I could see nothing of the cow but her eyes, shining like balls of fire through the dark tunnel, between the walls, through which passed to where she stood. When I entered the streets I found them well lighted up. My heart was gladdened to know there was another chance for my escape. No bird ever let out of a cage felt more like flying, than I felt like running.

Before I left the city, I chanced to find by the way, an old man of color. Supposing him to be a friend, I ventured to make known my situation, and asked him if he would get me a bite to eat. The old man most cheerfully complied with my request. I was then about forty miles from the residence of Wm. Gatewood, where my wife, whom I sought to rescue from slavery, was living. This was also in the direction it was necessary for me to travel in order to get back to the free North. Knowing that the slave catchers would most likely be watching the public highway for me, to avoid them I made my way over the rocky hills, woods and plantations, back to Bedford.

I travelled all that night, guided on my way by the shining stars of heaven alone. The next morning just before the break of day, I came right to a large plantation, about which I secreted myself, until the darkness of the next night began to disappear. The morning larks commenced to chirp and sing merrily—pretty soon I heard the whip crack, and the voice of the ploughman driving in the corn field. About breakfast time, I heard the sound of a horn; saw a number of slaves in the field with a white man, who I supposed to be their overseer. He started to the house before the slaves, which gave me an opportunity to get the attention of one of the slaves, whom I met at the fence, before he started to his breakfast, and made known to him my wants and distresses. I also requested him to bring me a piece of bread if he could when he came back to the field.

The hospitable slave complied with my request. He came back to the field before his fellow laborers, and brought me something to eat, and as an equivolent for his kindness, I instructed him with regard to liberty, Canada, the way of escape, and the facilities by the way. He pledged his word that himself and others would be in Canada, in less than six months from that day. This closed our interview, and we separated. I concealed myself in the forest until about sunset, before I pursued my journey; and the second night from Louisville, I arrived again in the neighborhood of Bedford, where my little family were held in bondage, whom I so earnestly strove to rescue.

I concealed myself by the aid of a friend in that neighborhood, intending again to make my escape with my family. This confidential friend then carried a message to Malinda, requesting her to meet me on one side of the village.

We met under the most fearful apprehensions, for my pursuers had returned from Louisville, with the lamentable story that I was gone, and yet they were compelled to pay three hundred dollars to the Cincinnati slave catchers for re-capturing me there.

Daniel Lane's account of my escape from him, looked so unreasonable to slaveholders, that many of them charged him with selling me and keeping the money; while others believed that I had got away from him, and was then in the neighborhood, trying to take off my wife and child, which was true. Lane declared that in less than five minutes after I run out of the stable in Louisville, he had over twenty men running and looking in every direction after me; but all without success. They could hear nothing of me. They had turned over several tons of hay in a large loft, in search, and I was not to be found there. Dan imputed my escape to my godliness! He said that I must have gone up in a chariot of fire, for I went off by flying; and that he should never again have any thing to do with a praying negro.

Great excitement prevailed in Bedford, and many were out watching for me at the time Malinda was relating to me these facts. The excitement was then so great among the slaveholders—who were anxious to have me re-captured as a means of discouraging other slaves from running away—that time and money were no object while there was the least prospect of their success. I therefore declined making an effort just at that time to escape with my little family. Malinda managed to get me into the house of a friend that night, in the village, where I kept concealed several days seeking an opportunity to escape with Malinda and Frances to Canada.

But for some time Malinda was watched so very closely by white and by colored persons, both day and night, that it was not possible for us to escape together. They well knew that my little family was the only object of attraction that ever had or ever would induce me to come back and risk my liberty over the threshold of slavery—therefore this point was well guarded by the watch dogs of slavery, and I was compelled again to forsake my wife for a season, or surrender, which was suicidal to the cause of freedom, in my judgment.

The next day after my arrival in Bedford, Daniel Lane came to the very house wherein I was concealed and talked in my hearing to the family about my escape from him out of the stable in Louisville. He was near enough for me to have laid my hands on his head while in that house—and the intimidation which this produced on me was more than I could bear. I was also aware of the great temptation of the reward offered to white or colored persons for my apprehension; I was exposed to other calamities which rendered it altogether unsafe for me to stay longer under that roof.

One morning about 2 o'clock, I took leave of my little family and started for Canada. This was almost like tearing off the limbs from my body. When we were about to separate, Malinda clasped my hand exclaiming, "oh my soul! my heart is almost broken at the thought of this dangerous separation. This may be the last time we shall ever see each other's faces in this life, which will destroy all my future prospects of life and happiness forever." At this time the poor unhappy woman burst into tears and wept loudly; and my eyes were not dry. We separated with the understanding that she was to wait until the excitement was all over; after which she was to meet me at a certain place in the State of Ohio; which would not be longer than two months from that time.

"MY HEART IS ALMOST BROKEN."

I succeeded that night in getting a steamboat conveyance back to Cincinnati, or within ten miles of the city. I was apprehensive that there were slave-hunters in Cincinnati, watching the arrival of every boat up the river, expecting to catch me; and the boat landing to take in wood ten miles below the city, I got off and walked into Cincinnati, to avoid detection.

On my arrival at the house of a friend, I heard that the two young men who betrayed me for the three hundred dollars had returned and were watching for me. One of my friends in whom they had great confidence, called on the traitors, after he had talked with me, and asked them what they had done with me. Their reply was that I had given them the slip, and that they were glad of it, because they believed that I was a good man, and if they could see me on my way to Canada, they would give me money to aid me on my escape. My friend assured them that if they would give any thing to aid me on my way, much or little, if they would put the same into his hands, he would give it to me that night, or return it to them the next morning.

They then wanted to know where I was and whether I was in the city; but he would not tell them, but one of them gave him one dollar for me, promising, that if I was in the city, and he would let him know the next morning, he would give me ten dollars.

But I never waited for the ten dollars. I received one dollar of the amount which they got for betraying me, and started that night for the north. Their excuse for betraying me, was, that catching runaways was their business, and if they had not done it somebody else would, but since they had got the reward they were glad that I had made my escape.

Having travelled the road several times from Cincinnati to Lake Erie, I travelled through without much fear or difficulty. My friends in Perrysburgh, who knew that I had gone back into the very jaws of slavery after my family, were much surprised at my return, for they had heard that I was re-captured.

After I had waited three months for the arrival of Malinda, and she came not, it caused me to be one of the most unhappy fugitives that ever left the South. I had waited eight or nine months without hearing from my family. I felt it to be my duty, as a husband and father, to make one more effort. I felt as if I could not give them up to be sacrificed on the "bloody altar of slavery." I felt as if love, duty, humanity and justice, required that I should go back, putting my trust in the God of Liberty for success.

CHAPTER VII.

My safe return to Kentucky. — The perils I encountered there. — Again betrayed, and taken by a mob; ironed and imprisoned. — Narrow escape from death. — Life in a slave prison.

I prepared myself for the journey before named, and started back in the month of July, 1839.

My intention was, to let no person know my business until I returned back to the North. I went to Cincinnati, and got a passage down on board of a boat just as I did the first time, without any misfortune or delay. I called on my mother, and the raising of a dead body from the grave could not have been more surprising to any one than my arrival was to her, on that sad summer's night. She was not able to suppress her feelings. When I entered the room, there was but one other person in the house with my mother, and this was a little slave girl who was asleep when I entered. The impulsive feeling which is ever ready to act itself out at the return of a long absent friend, was more than my bereaved mother could suppress. And unfortunately for me, the loud shouts of joy at that late hour of the night, awakened the little slave girl, who afterwards betrayed me. She kept perfectly still, and never let either of us know that she was awake, in order that she might hear our conversation and report it. Mother informed me where my family was living, and that she would see them the next day, and would make arrangements for us to meet the next night at that house after the people in the village had gone to bed. I then went off and concealed myself during the next day, and according to promise came back the next night about eleven o'clock.

When I got near the house, moving very cautiously, filled with fearful apprehensions, I saw several men walking around the house as if they were looking for some person. I went back and waited about one hour, before I returned, and the number of men had increased. They were still to be seen lurking about this house, with dogs following them. This strange movement frightened me off again, and I never returned until after midnight, at which time I slipped up to the window, and rapped for my mother, who sprang to it and informed me that I was betrayed by the girl who overheard our conversation the night before. She thought that if I could keep out of the way for a few days, the white people would think that this girl was mistaken, or had lied. She had told her old mistress that I was there that night, and had made a plot with my mother to get my wife and child there the next night, and that I was going to take them off to Canada.

I went off to a friend of mine, who rendered me all the aid that one slave could render another, under the circumstances. Thank God he is now free from slavery, and is doing well. He was a messenger for me to my wife and mother, until at the suggestion of my mother, I changed an old friend for a new one, who betrayed me for the sum of five dollars.

We had set the time when we were to start for Canada, which was to be on the next Saturday night. My mother had an old friend whom she thought was true, and she got him to conceal me in a barn, not over two miles from the village. This man brought provisions to me, sent by my mother, and would tell me the news which was in circulation about me, among the citizens. But the poor fellow was not able to withstand the temptation of money.

My owners had about given me up, and thought the report of the slave girl was false; but they had offered a little reward among the slaves for my apprehension. The night before I was betrayed, I met with my mother and wife, and we had set up nearly all night plotting to start on the next Saturday night. I hid myself away in the flax in the barn, and being much rest broken I slept until the next morning about 9 o'clock. Then I was awakened by a mob of blood thirsty slaveholders, who had come armed with all the implements of death, with a determination to reduce me again to a life of slavery, or murder me on the spot.

When I looked up and saw that I was surrounded, they were exclaiming at the top of their voices, "shoot him down! shoot him down!" "If he offers to run, or to resist, kill him!"

I saw it was no use then for me to make any resistance, as I should be murdered. I felt confident that I had been betrayed by a slave, and all my flattering prospects of rescuing my family were gone for ever, and the grim monster slavery with all its horrors was staring me in the face.

I surrendered myself to this hostile mob at once. The first thing done, after they had laid violent hands on me, was to bind my hands behind me with a cord, and rob me of all I possessed.

In searching my pockets, they found my certificate from the Methodist E.[20] Church, which had been given me by my classleader, testifying to my worthiness as a member of that church. And what made the matter look more disgraceful to me, many of this mob were members of the M. E. Church, and they were the persons who took away my church ticket, and then robbed me also of fourteen dollars in cash, a silver watch for which I paid ten dollars, a pocket knife for which I paid seventy-five cents, and a Bible for which I paid sixty-two and one half cents. All this they tyrannically robbed me of, and yet my owner, Wm. Gatewood, was a regular member of the same church to which I belonged.

He then had me taken to a blacksmith's shop, and most wickedly had my limbs bound with heavy irons, and then had my body locked within the cold dungeon walls of the Bedford jail, to be sold to a Southern slave trader.

My heart was filled with grief—my eyes were filled with tears. I could see no way of escape. I could hear no voice of consolation. Slaveholders were coming to the dungeon window in great numbers to ask me questions. Some were rejoicing—some swearing, and others saying that I ought to be hung; while others were in favor of sending both me and my wife to New Orleans. They supposed that I had informed her all about the facilities for slaves to escape to Canada, and that she would tell other slaves after I was gone; hence we must all be sent off to where we could neither escape ourselves nor instruct others the way.

In the afternoon of the same day Malinda was permitted to visit the prison wherein I was locked, but was not permitted to enter the door. When she looked through the dungeon grates and saw my sad situation, which was caused by my repeated adventures to rescue her and my little daughter from the grasp of slavery, it was more than she could bear without bursting in tears. She plead for admission into the cold dungeon where I was confined, but without success. With manacled limbs; with wounded spirit; with sympathising tears and with bleeding heart, I intreated Malinda to weep not for me, for it only added to my grief, which was greater than I could bear.

I have often suffered from the sting of the cruel slave driver's lash on my quivering flesh—I have suffered from corporeal punishment in its various forms—I have mingled my sorrows with those that were bereaved by the ungodly soul drivers—and I also know what it is to shed the sympathetic tear at the grave of a departed friend; but all this is but a mere trifle compared with my sufferings from then to the end of six months subsequent.

The second night while I was in jail, two slaves came to the dungeon grates about the dead hour of night, and called me to the grates to have some conversation about Canada, and the facilities for getting there. They knew that I had travelled over the road, and they were determined to run away and go where they could be free. I of course took great pleasure in giving them directions how and where to go, and they started in less than a week from that time and got clear to Canada. I have seen them both since I came back to the north myself. They were known by the names of King and Jack.

The third day I was brought out of the prison to be carried off with my little family to the Louisville slave market. My hands were fastened together with heavy irons, and two men to guard me with loaded rifles, one of whom led the horse upon which I rode. My wife and child were set upon another nag. After we were all ready to start my old master thought I was not quite safe enough, and ordered one of the boys to bring him a bed cord from the store. He then tied my feet together under the horse, declaring that if I flew off this time, I should fly off with the horse.

Many tears were shed on that occasion by our friends and relatives, who saw us dragged off in irons to be sold in the human flesh market. No tongue could express the deep anguish of my soul when I saw the silent tear drops streaming down the sable cheeks of an aged slave mother, at my departure; and that too, caused by a black hearted traitor who was himself a slave:

> "I love the man with a feeling soul,
> Whose passions are deep and strong;
> Whose cords, when touched with a kindred power,
> Will vibrate loud and long:

> "The man whose word is bond and law—
> Who ne'er for gold or power
> Would kiss the hand that would stab the heart
> In adversity's trying hour."

> "I love the man who delights to help
> The panting, struggling poor:
> The man that will open his heart,
> Nor close against the fugitive at his door.

> "Oh give me a heart that will firmly stand,
> When the storm of affliction shall lower—
> A hand that will never shrink, if grasped,
> In misfortune's darkest hour."

As we approached the city of Louisville, we attracted much attention, my being tied and handcuffed, and a person leading the horse upon which I rode. The horse appeared to be much frightened at the appearance of things in the city, being young and skittish. A carriage passing by jammed against the nag, which caused him to break from the man who was leading him, and in his fright throw me off backwards. My hands being confined with irons, and my feet tied under the horse with a rope, I had no power to help myself. I fell back off of the horse and could not extricate myself from this dreadful condition; the horse kicked with all his might while I was tied so close to his rump that he could only strike me with his legs by kicking.

The breath was kicked out of my body, but my bones were not broken. No one who saw my situation would have given five dollars for me. It was thought by all that I was dead and would never come to life again. When the horse was caught the cords were cut from my limbs, and I was rubbed with whiskey, camphor, &c., which brought me to life again.

Many bystanders expressed sympathy for me in my deplorable condition, and contempt for the tyrant who tied me to the young horse.

I was then driven through the streets of the city with my little family on foot, to jail, wherein I was locked with handcuffs yet on. A physician was then sent for, who doctored me several days before I was well enough to be sold in market.

The jail was one of the most disagreeable places I ever was confined in. It was not only disagreeable on account of the filth and dirt of the most disagreeable kind; but there were bed-bugs, fleas, lice and musquitoes in abundance, to contend with. At night we had to lie down on the floor in this filth. Our food was very scanty, and of the most inferior quality. No gentleman's dog would eat what we were compelled to eat or starve.

I had not been in this prison many days before Madison Garrison, the soul driver, bought me and my family to sell again in the New Orleans slave market. He was buying up slaves to take to New Orleans. So he took me and my little family to the work-house, to be kept under lock and key at work until he had bought up as many as he wished to take off to the South.

The work-house of Louisville was a very large brick building, built on the plan of a jail or State's prison, with many apartments to it, divided off into cells wherein prisoners were locked up after night. The upper apartments were occupied by females, principally. This prison was enclosed by a high stone wall, upon which stood watchmen with loaded guns to guard the prisoners from breaking out, and on either side there were large iron gates.

When Garrison conducted me with my family to the prison in which we were to be confined until he was ready to take us to New Orleans, I was shocked at the horrid sight of the prisoners on entering the yard. When the large iron gate or door was thrown open to receive us, it was astonishing to see so many whites as well as colored men loaded down with irons, at hard labor, under the supervision of overseers.

Some were sawing stone, some cutting stone, and others breaking stone. The first impression which was made on my mind when I entered this place of punishment, made me think of hell, with all its terrors of torment; such as "weeping, wailing, and gnashing of teeth,"[21] which was then the idea that I had of the infernal regions from oral instruction. And I doubt whether there can be a better picture of it drawn, than may be sketched from an American slave prison.

In this prison almost every prisoner had a heavy log chain[22] riveted about his leg. It would indeed be astonishing to a christian man to stand in that prison one half hour and hear and see the contaminating influence of Southern slavery on the body and mind of man—you may there find almost every variety of character to look on. Some singing, some crying, some praying, and others swearing. The people of color who were in there were slaves there without crime, but for safe keeping, while the whites were some of the most abandoned characters living. The keeper took me up to the anvil block and fastened a chain about my leg, which I had to drag after me both day and night during three months. My labor was sawing stone; my food was coarse corn bread and beef shanks and cows heads with pot liquor, and a very scanty allowance of that.

I have often seen the meat spoiled when brought to us, covered with flies and fly blows, and even worms crawling over it, when we were compelled to eat it, or go without any at all. It was all spread out on a long table in separate plates; and at the sound of a bell, every one would take his plate, asking no questions. After hastily eating, we were hurried back to our work, each man dragging a heavy log chain after him to his work.

About a half hour before night they were commanded to stop work, take a bite to eat, and then be locked up in a small cell until the next morning after sunrise. The prisoners were locked in, two together. My bed was a cold stone floor with but little bedding! My visitors were bed-bugs and musquitoes.

CHAPTER VIII.

CHARACTER OF MY PRISON COMPANIONS.—JAIL BREAKING CONTEMPLATED.—DEFEAT OF OUR PLAN.—MY WIFE AND CHILD REMOVED.—DISGRACEFUL PROPOSAL TO HER, AND CRUEL PUNISHMENT.—OUR DEPARTURE IN A COFFLE FOR NEW ORLEANS.—EVENTS OF OUR JOURNEY.

MOST of the inmates of this prison I have described, were white men who had been sentenced there by the law, for depredations committed by them. There was in that prison, gamblers, drunkards, thieves, robbers, adulterers, and even murderers. There were also in the female department, harlots, pickpockets, and adulteresses. In such company, and under such influences, where there was constant swearing, lying, cheating, and stealing, it was almost impossible for a virtuous person to avoid pollution, or to maintain their virtue. No place or places in this country can be better calculated to inculcate vice of every kind than a Southern work house or house of correction.

After a profligate, thief, or a robber, has learned all that they can out of the prison, they might go in one of those prisons and learn something more—they might properly be called robber colleges; and if slaveholders understood this they would never let their slaves enter them. No man would give much for a slave who had been kept long in one of these prisons.

I have often heard them telling each other how they robbed houses, and persons on the high way, by knocking them down, and would rob them, pick their pockets, and leave them half dead. Others would tell of stealing horses, cattle, sheep, and slaves; and when they would be sometimes apprehended, by the aid of their friends, they would break jail. But they could most generally find enough to swear them clear of any kind of villany. They seemed to take great delight in telling of their exploits in robbery. There was a regular combination of them who had determined to resist law, wherever they went, to carry out their purposes.

In conversing with myself, they learned that I was notorious for running away, and professed sympathy for me. They thought that I might yet get to Canada, and be free, and suggested a plan by which I might accomplish it; and one way was, to learn to read and write, so that I might write my self a pass ticket, to go just where I pleased, when I was taken out of the prison; and they taught me secretly all they could while in the prison.

But there was another plan which they suggested to me to get away from slavery; that was to break out of the prison and leave my family. I consented to engage in this plot, but not to leave my family.

By my conduct in the prison, after having been there several weeks, I had gained the confidence of the keeper, and the turnkey. So much so, that when I wanted water or anything of the kind, they would open my door and hand it in to me. One of the turnkeys was an old colored man, who swept and cleaned up the cells, supplied the prisoners with water, &c.

On Sundays in the afternoon, the watchmen of the prison were most generally off, and this old slave, whose name was Stephen, had the prisoners to attend to. The white prisoners formed a plot to break out on Sunday in the afternoon, by making me the agent to get the prison keys from old Stephen.

I was to prepare a stone that would weigh about one pound, tie it up in a rag, and keep it in my pocket to strike poor old Stephen with, when he should open my cell door. But this I would not consent to do, without he should undertake to betray me.

I gave old Stephen one shilling to buy me a water melon, which he was to bring to me in the afternoon. All the prisoners were to be ready to strike, just as soon as I opened their doors. When Stephen opened my door to hand me the melon, I was to grasp him by the collar, raise the stone over his head, and say to him, that if he made any alarm that I should knock him down with the stone. But if he would be quiet he should not be hurt. I was then to take all the keys from him, and lock him up in the cell—take a chisel and cut the chain from my own leg, then unlock all the cells below, and let out the other prisoners, who were all to cut off their chains. We were then to go and let out old Stephen, and make him go off with us. We were to form a line and march to the front gate of the prison with a sledge hammer, and break it open, and if we should be discovered, and there should be any out-cry, we were all to run and raise the alarm of fire, so as to avoid detection. But while we were all listening for Stephen to open the door with the melon, he came and reported that he could not get one, and handed me back the money through the window. All were disappointed, and nothing done. I looked upon it as being a fortunate thing for me, for it was certainly a very dangerous experiment for a slave, and they could never get me to consent to be the leader in that matter again.

A few days after, another plot was concocted to break prison, but it was betrayed by one of the party, which resulted in the most cruel punishment to the prisoners concerned in it; and I felt thankful that my name was not connected with it. They were not only flogged, but they were kept on bread and water alone, for many days. A few days after we were put in this prison, Garrison came and took my wife and child out, I knew not for what purpose, nor to what place, but after the absence of several days I supposed that he had sold them. But one morning, the outside door was thrown open, and Malinda thrust in by the ruthless hand of Garrison, whose voice was pouring forth the most bitter oaths and abusive language that could be dealt out to a female; while her heart-rending shrieks and sobbing, was truly melting to the soul of a father and husband.

The language of Malinda was, "Oh! my dear little child is gone? What shall I do? my child is gone." This most distressing sound struck a sympathetic chord through all the prison among the prisoners. I was not permitted to go to my wife and inquire what had become of little Frances. I never expected to see her again, for I supposed that she was sold.

That night, however, I had a short interview with my much abused wife, who told me the secret. She said that Garrison had taken her to a private house where he kept female slaves for the basest purposes. It was a resort for slave trading profligates and soul drivers, who were interested in the same business.

Soon after she arrived at this place, Garrison gave her to understand what he brought her there for, and made a most disgraceful assault on her virtue, which she promptly repeled; and for which Garrison punished her with the lash, threatening her that if she did not submit that he would sell her child. The next day he made the same attempt, which she resisted, declaring that she would not submit to it; and again he tied her up and flogged her until her garments were stained with blood.

He then sent our child off to another part of the city, and said he meant to sell it, and that she should never see it again. He then drove Malinda before him to the work-house, swearing by his Maker that she should submit to him or die. I have already described her entrance in the prison.

Two days after this he came again and took Malinda out of the prison. It was several weeks before I saw her again, and learned that he had not sold her or the child. At the same time he was buying up other slaves to take to New Orleans. At the expiration of three months he was ready to start with us for the New Orleans slave market, but we never knew when we were to go, until the hour had arrived for our departure.

One Sabbath morning Garrison entered the prison and commanded that our limbs should be made ready for the coffles. They called us up to an anvill block, and the heavy log chains which we had been wearing on our legs during three months, were cut off. I had been in the prison over three months; but he had other slaves who had not been there so long. The hand-cuffs were then put on to our wrists. We were coupled together two and two—the right hand of one to the left hand of another, and a long chain to connect us together.

The other prisoners appeared to be sorry to see us start off in this way. We marched off to the river Ohio, to take passage on board of the steamboat Water

Witch. But this was at a very low time of water, in the fall of 1839. The boat got aground, and did not get off that night; and Garrison had to watch us all night to keep any from getting away. He also had a very large savage dog, which was trained up to catch runaway slaves.

We were more than six weeks getting to the city of New Orleans, in consequence of low water. We were shifted on to several boats before we arrived at the mouth of the river Ohio. But we got but very little rest at night. As all were chained together night and day, it was impossible to sleep, being annoyed by the bustle and crowd of the passengers on board; by the terrible thought that we were destined to be sold in market as sheep or oxen; and annoyed by the galling chains that cramped our wearied limbs, on the tedious voyage. But I had several opportunities to have run away from Garrison before we got to the mouth of the Ohio river. While they were shifting us from one boat to another my hands were some times loosed, until they got us all on board—and I know that I should have broke away had it not been for the sake of my wife and child who was with me. I could see no chance to get them off, and I could not leave them in that condition—and Garrison was not so much afraid of my running away from him while he held on to my family, for he knew from the great sacrifices which I had made to rescue them from slavery, that my attachment was too strong to run off and leave them in his hands, while there was the least hope of ever getting them away with me.

CHAPTER IX.

Our arrival and examination at Vicksburg.—An account of slave sales.—
    Cruel punishment with the paddle.—Attempts to sell myself by Gar-
    rison's direction.—Amusing interview with a slave buyer.—Deacon
    Whitfield's examination.—He purchases the family.—Character of
    the Deacon.

When we arrived at the city of Vicksburg, he intended to sell a portion of his slaves there, and stopped for three weeks trying to sell. But he met with very poor success.

We had there to pass through an examination or inspection by a city officer, whose business it was to inspect slave property that was brought to that market for sale. He examined our backs to see if we had been much scarred by the lash. He examined our limbs, to see whether we were inferior.

As it is hard to tell the ages of slaves, they look in their mouths at their teeth, and prick up the skin on the back of their hands, and if the person is very far advanced in life, when the skin is pricked up, the pucker will stand so many seconds on the back of the hand.

But the most rigorous examinations of slaves by those slave inspectors, is on the mental capacity. If they are found to be very intelligent, this is pronounced the most objectionable of all other qualities connected with the life of a slave. In fact, it undermines the whole fabric of his chattelhood; it prepares for what slaveholders are pleased to pronounce the unpardonable sin when committed by a slave. It lays the foundation for running away, and going to Canada. They also see in it a love for freedom, patriotism, insurrection, bloodshed, and exterminating war against American slavery.

Hence they are very careful to inquire whether a slave who is for sale can read or write. This question has been asked me often by slave traders, and cotton planters, while I was there for market. After conversing with me, they have sworn by their Maker, that they would not have me among their negroes; and that they saw the devil in my eye; I would run away, &c.

I have frequently been asked also, if I had ever run away; but Garrison would generally answer this question for me in the negative. He could have sold my little family without any trouble, for the sum of one thousand dollars. But for fear he might not get me off at so great an advantage, as the people did not like my appearance, he could do better by selling us all together. They all wanted my wife, while but very few wanted me. He asked for me and my family twenty-five hundred dollars, but was not able to get us off at that price.

He tried to speculate on my Christian character. He tried to make it appear that I was so pious and honest that I would not runaway for ill treatment; which was a gross mistake, for I never had religion enough to keep me from running away from slavery in my life.

But we were taken from Vicksburgh, to the city of New Orleans, were we were to be sold at any rate. We were taken to a trader's yard or a slave prison on the corner of St. Joseph street. This was a common resort for slave traders, and planters who wanted to buy slaves; and all classes of slaves were kept there for sale, to be sold in private or public—young or old, males or females, children or parents, husbands or wives.

Every day at 10 o'clock they were exposed for sale. They had to be in trim for showing themselves to the public for sale. Every one's head had to be combed, and their faces washed, and those who were inclined to look dark and rough, were compelled to wash in greasy dish water, in order to make them look slick and lively.

When spectators would come in the yard, the slaves were ordered out to form a line. They were made to stand up straight, and look as sprightly as they could; and when they were asked a question, they had to answer it as promptly as they could, and try to induce the spectators to buy them. If they failed to do this, they were severely paddled after the spectators were gone. The object for using the paddle in the place of a lash was, to conceal the marks which would be made by the flogging. And the object for flogging under such circumstances, is to make the slaves anxious to be sold.

The paddle is made of a piece of hickory timber, about one inch thick, three inches in width, and about eighteen inches in length. The part which is applied to the flesh is bored full of quarter inch auger holes, and every time this is applied to the flesh of the victim, the blood gushes through the holes of the paddle, or a blister makes its appearance. The persons who are thus flogged, are always stripped naked, and their hands tied together. They are then bent over double, their knees are forced between their elbows, and a stick is put through between the elbows and the bend of the legs, in order to hold the victim in that position, while the paddle is applied to those parts of the body which would not be so likely to be seen by those who wanted to buy slaves. (See on page 133 [page 67 in this edition].)

I was kept in this prison for several months, and no one would buy me for fear I would run away. One day while I was in this prison, Garrison got mad with my wife, and took her off in one of the rooms, with his paddle in hand, swearing that he would paddle her; and I could afford her no protection at all, while the strong arm of the law, public opinion and custom, were all against me. I have often heard Garrison say, that he had rather paddle a female, than eat when he was hungry—that it was music for him to hear them scream, and to see their blood run.

After the lapse of several months, he found that he could not dispose of my person to a good advantage, while he kept me in that prison confined among the other slaves. I do not speak with vanity when I say the contrast was so great between myself and ordinary slaves, from the fact that I had enjoyed superior advantages, to which I have already referred. They have their slaves classed off and numbered.

Garrison came to me one day and informed me that I might go out through the city and find myself a master. I was to go to the Hotels, boarding houses, &c.—tell them that my wife was a good cook, wash-woman, &c.,—and that I was a good dining room servant, carriage driver, or porter—and in this way I might find some gentleman who would buy us both; and that this was the only hope of our being sold together.

But before starting me out, he dressed me up in a suit of his old clothes, so as to make me look respectable, and I was so much better dressed than usual that I felt quite gay. He would not allow my wife to go out with me however, for fear we might get away. I was out every day for several weeks, three or four hours in each day, trying to find a new master, but without success.

Many of the old French inhabitants have taken slaves for their wives, in this city, and their own children for their servants. Such commonly are called Creoles. They are better treated than other slaves, and I resembled this class in appearance so much that the French did not want me. Many of them set their mulatto children free, and make slaveholders of them.

At length one day I heard that there was a gentleman in the city from the State of Tennessee, to buy slaves. He had brought down two rafts of lumber for market, and I thought if I could get him to buy me with my family and take us to Tennessee, from there, I would stand a better opportunity to run away again and get to Canada, than I would from the extreme South.

So I brushed up myself and walked down to the river's bank, where the man was pointed out to me standing on board of his raft, I approached him, and after passing the usual compliments I said:

"Sir, I understand that you wish to purchase a lot of servants and I have called to know if it is so."

He smiled and appeared to be much pleased at my visit on such laudable business, supposing me to be a slave trader. He commenced rubbing his hands together, and replied by saying: "Yes sir, I am glad to see you. It is a part of my business here to buy slaves, and if I could get you to take my lumber in part pay I should like to buy four or five of your slaves at any rate. What kind of slaves have you, sir?"

After I found that he took me to be a slave trader I knew that it would be of no use for me to tell him that I was myself a slave looking for a master, for he would have doubtless brought up the same objection that others had brought up,—that I was too white; and that they were afraid that I could read and write; and would never serve as a slave, but run away. My reply to the question respecting the quality of my slaves was, that I did not think his lumber would suit me—that I must have the cash for my negroes, and turned on my heel and left him!

I returned to the prison and informed my wife of the fact that I had been taken to be a slaveholder. She thought that in addition to my light complexion my being dressed up in Garrison's old slave trading clothes might have caused the man to think that I was a slave trader, and she was afraid that we should yet be separated if I should not succeed in finding some body to buy us.

Every day to us was a day of trouble, and every night brought new and fearful apprehensions that the golden link which binds together husband and wife might be broken by the heartless tyrant before the light of another day.

Deep has been the anguish of my soul when looking over my little family during the silent hours of the night, knowing the great danger of our being sold off at auction the next day and parted forever. That this might not come to pass, many have been the tears and prayers which I have offered up to the God of Israel that we might be preserved.

While waiting here to be disposed of, I heard of one Francis Whitfield, a cotton planter, who wanted to buy slaves. He was represented to be a very pious soul, being a deacon of a Baptist church. As the regulations, as well as public opinion generally, were against slaves meeting for religious worship, I thought it would give me a better opportunity to attend to my religious duties should I fall into the hands of this deacon.

So I called on him and tried to show to the best advantage, for the purpose of inducing him to buy me and my family. When I approached him, I felt much pleased at his external appearance—I addressed him in the following words as well as I can remember:

"Sir, I understand you are desirous of purchasing slaves?"

With a very pleasant smile, he replied, "Yes, I do want to buy some, are you for sale?"

"Yes sir, with my wife and one child."

Garrison had given me a note to show wherever I went, that I was for sale, speaking of my wife and child, giving us a very good character of course—and I handed him the note.

After reading it over he remarked, "I have a few questions to ask you, and if you will tell me the truth like a good boy, perhaps I may buy you with your family. In the first place, my boy, you are a little too near white. I want you to tell me now whether you can read or write?"

My reply was in the negative.

"Now I want you to tell me whether you have run away? Don't tell me no stories now, like a good fellow, and perhaps I may buy you."

But as I was not under oath to tell him the whole truth, I only gave him a part of it, by telling him that I had run away once.

He appeared to be pleased at that, but cautioned me to tell him the truth, and asked me how long I stayed away, when I run off?

I told him that I was gone a month.

He assented to this by a bow of his head, and making a long grunt saying, "That's right, tell me the truth like a good boy."

The whole truth was that I had been off in the state of Ohio, and other free states, and even to Canada; besides this I was notorious for running away, from my boyhood.

I never told him that I had been a runaway longer than one month—neither did I tell him that I had not run away more than once in my life; for these questions he never asked me.

I afterwards found him to be one of the basest hypocrites that I ever saw. He looked like a saint—talked like the best of slave holding Christians, and acted at home like the devil.

When he saw my wife and child, he concluded to buy us. He paid for me twelve hundred dollars, and one thousand for my wife and child. He also bought several other slaves at the same time, and took home with him. His residence was in the parish of Claiborn,[23] fifty miles up from the mouth of Red River.

When we arrived there, we found his slaves poor, ragged, stupid, and half-starved. The food he allowed them per week, was one peck of corn for each grown person, one pound of pork, and sometimes a quart of molasses. This was all that they were allowed, and if they got more they stole it.

He had one of the most cruel overseers to be found in that section of country. He weighed and measured out to them, their week's allowance of food every Sabbath morning. The overseer's horn was sounded two hours before daylight for them in the morning, in order that they should be ready for work before daylight. They were worked from daylight until after dark, without stopping but one half hour to eat or rest, which was at noon. And at the busy season of the year, they were compelled to work just as hard on the Sabbath, as on any other day.

CHAPTER X.

Cruel treatment on Whitfield's farm—Exposure of the children—Mode of extorting extra labor—Neglect of the sick—Strange medicine used—Death of our second child.

My first impressions when I arrived on the Deacon's farm, were that he was far more like what the people call the devil, than he was like a deacon. Not many days after my arrival there, I heard the Deacon tell one of the slave girls, that he had bought her for a wife for his boy Stephen, which office he compelled her fully to perform against her will. This he enforced by a threat. At first the poor girl neglected to do this, having no sort of affection for the man—but she was finally forced to it by an application of the driver's lash, as threatened by the Deacon.

The next thing I observed was that he made the slave driver strip his own wife, and flog her for not doing just as her master had ordered. He had a white overseer, and a colored man for a driver, whose business it was to watch and drive the slaves in the field, and do the flogging according to the orders of the overseer.

Next a mulatto girl who waited about the house, on her mistress, displeased her, for which the Deacon stripped and tied her up. He then handed me the lash and ordered me to put it on—but I told him I never had done the like, and hoped he would not compel me to do it. He then informed me that I was to be his overseer, and that he had bought me for that purpose. He was paying a man eight hundred dollars a year to oversee, and he believed I was competent to do the same business, and if I would do it up right he would put nothing harder on me to do; and if I knew not how to flog a slave, he would set me an example by which I might be governed. He then commenced on this poor girl, and gave her two hundred lashes before he had her untied.

After giving her fifty lashes, he stopped and lectured her a while, asking her if she thought that she could obey her mistress, &c. She promised to do all in her power to please him and her mistress, if he would have mercy on her. But this plea was all vain. He commenced on her again; and this flogging was carried on in the most inhuman manner until she had received two hundred stripes on her naked quivering flesh, tied up and exposed to the public gaze of all. And this was the example that I was to copy after.

He then compelled me to wash her back off with strong salt brine, before she was untied, which was so revolting to my feelings, that I could not refrain from shedding tears.

For some cause he never called on me again to flog a slave. I presume he saw that I was not savage enough. The above were about the first items of the Deacon's conduct which struck me with peculiar disgust.

After having enjoyed the blessings of civil and religious liberty for a season, to be dragged into that horrible place with my family, to linger out my existence without the aid of religious societies, or the light of revelation, was more than I could endure. I really felt as if I had got into one of the darkest corners of the earth. I thought I was almost out of humanity's reach, and should never again have the pleasure of hearing the gospel sound, as I could see no way by which I could extricate myself; yet I never omitted to pray for deliverance. I had faith to believe that the Lord could see our wrongs and hear our cries.

I was not used quite as bad as the regular field hands, as the greater part of my time was spent working about the house; and my wife was the cook.

This country was full of pine timber, and every slave had to prepare a light wood torch, over night, made of pine knots, to meet the overseer with, before daylight in the morning. Each person had to have his torch lit, and come with it in his hand to the gin house, before the overseer and driver, so as to be ready to go to the cotton field by the time they could see to pick out cotton. These lights looked beautiful at a distance.

The object of blowing the horn for them two hours before day, was, that they should get their bite to eat, before they went to the field, that they need not stop to eat but once during the day. Another object was, to do up their flogging which had been omitted over night. I have often heard the sound of the slave driver's lash on the backs, of the slaves, and their heart-rending shrieks, which were enough to melt the heart of humanity, even among the most barbarous nations of the earth.

But the Deacon would keep no overseer on his plantation, who neglected to perform this every morning. I have heard him say that he was no better pleased than when he could hear the overseer's loud complaining voice, long before daylight in the morning, and the sound of the driver's lash among the toiling slaves.

This was a very warm climate, abounding with musquitoes, galinippers and other insects which were exceedingly annoying to the poor slaves by night and day, at their quarters and in the field. But more especially to their helpless little children, which they had to carry with them to the cotton fields, where they had to set on the damp ground alone from morning till night, exposed to the scorching rays of the sun, liable to be bitten by poisonous rattle snakes which are plenty in that section of the country, or to be devoured by large alligators, which are often seen creeping through the cotton fields going from swamp to swamp seeking their prey.

The cotton planters generally, never allow a slave mother time to go to the house, or quarter during the day to nurse her child; hence they have to carry them

to the cotton fields and tie them in the shade of a tree, or in clusters of high weeds about in the fields, where they can go to them at noon, when they are allowed to stop work for one half hour. This is the reason why so very few slave children are raised on these cotton plantations, the mothers have no time to take care of them—and they are often found dead in the field and in the quarter for want of the care of their mothers. But I never was eye witness to a case of this kind, but have heard many narrated by my slave brothers and sisters, some of which occurred on the deacon's plantation.

Their plan of getting large quantities of cotton picked is not only to extort it from them by the lash, but hold out an inducement and deceive them by giving small prizes. For example; the overseer will offer something worth one or two dollars to any slave who will pick out the most cotton in one day; dividing the hands off in three classes and offering a prize to the one who will pick out the most cotton in each of the classes. By this means they are all interested in trying to get the prize.

After making them try it over several times and weighing what cotton they pick every night, the overseer can tell just how much every hand can pick. He then gives the present to those that pick the most cotton, and then if they do not pick just as much afterward they are flogged.

I have known the slaves to be so much fatigued from labor that they could scarcely get to their lodging places from the field at night. And then they would have to prepare something to eat before they could lie down to rest. Their corn they had to grind on a hand mill for bread stuff, or pound it in a mortar; and by the time they would get their suppers it would be midnight; then they would herd down all together and take but two or three hours rest, before the overseer's horn called them up again to prepare for the field.

At the time of sickness among slaves they had but very little attention. The master was to be the judge of their sickness, but never had studied the medical profession. He always pronounced a slave who said he was sick, a liar and a hypocrite; said there was nothing the matter, and he only wanted to keep from work.

His remedy was most generally strong red pepper tea, boiled till it was red. He would make them drink a pint cup full of it at one dose. If he should not get better very soon after it, the dose was repeated. If that should not accomplish the object for which it was given, or have the desired effect, a pot or kettle was then put over the fire with a large quantity of chimney soot, which was boiled down until it was as strong as the juice of tobacco, and the poor sick slave was compelled to drink a quart of it.

This would operate on the system like salts, or castor oil. But if the slave should not be very ill, he would rather work as long as he could stand up, than to take this dreadful medicine.

If it should be a very valuable slave, sometimes a physician was sent for and something done to save him. But no special aid is afforded the suffering slave even in the last trying hour, when he is called to grapple with the grim monster death. He has no Bible, no family altar, no minister to address to him the consolations of the gospel, before he launches into the spirit world. As to the burial of slaves, but very little more care is taken of their dead bodies than if they were dumb beasts.

My wife was very sick while we were both living with the Deacon. We expected every day would be her last. While she was sick, we lost our second child, and I was compelled to dig my own child's grave and bury it myself without even a box to put it in.

CHAPTER XI.

I ATTEND A PRAYER MEETING.—PUNISHMENT THEREFOR THREATENED.—I ATTEMPT TO ESCAPE ALONE.—MY RETURN TO TAKE MY FAMILY.—OUR SUFFERINGS.— DREADFUL ATTACK OF WOLVES.—OUR RECAPTURE.

SOME months after Malinda had recovered from her sickness, I got permission from the Deacon, on one Sabbath day, to attend a prayer meeting, on a neighboring plantation, with a few old superanuated slaves, although this was contrary to the custom of the country—for slaves were not allowed to assemble for religious worship. Being more numerous than the whites there was fear of rebellion, and the overpowering of their oppressors in order to obtain freedom.

But this gentleman on whose plantation I attended the meeting was not a Deacon nor a professor of religion. He was not afraid of a few old Christian slaves rising up to kill their master because he allowed them to worship God on the Sabbath day.

We had a very good meeting, although our exercises were not conducted in accordance with an enlightened Christianity; for we had no Bible—no intelligent leader—but a conscience, prompted by our own reason, constrained us to worship God the Creator of all things.

When I returned home from meeting I told the other slaves what a good time we had at our meeting, and requested them to go with me to meeting there on the next Sabbath. As no slave was allowed to go from the plantation on a visit without a written pass from his master, on the next Sabbath several of us went to the Deacon, to get permission to attend that prayer meeting; but he refused to let any go. I thought I would slip off and attend the meeting and get back before he would miss me, and would not know that I had been to the meeting.

When I returned home from the meeting as I approached the house I saw Malinda, standing out at the fence looking in the direction in which I was expected to return. She hailed my approach, not with joy, but with grief. She was weeping under great distress of mind, but it was hard for me to extort from her the reason why she wept. She finally informed me that her master had found out that I had violated his law, and I should suffer the penalty, which was five hundred lashes, on my naked back.

I asked her how he knew that I had gone?

She said I had not long been gone before he called for me and I was not to be found. He then sent the overseer on horseback to the place where we were to meet to see if I was there. But when the overseer got to the place, the meeting was over and I had gone back home, but had gone a nearer route through the woods and the overseer happened not to meet me. He heard that I had been there and hurried back home before me and told the Deacon, who ordered him to take me on the next morning, strip off my clothes, drive down four stakes in the ground and fasten my limbs to them; then strike me five hundred lashes for going to the prayer meeting. This was what distressed my poor companion. She thought it was more than I could bear, and that it would be the death of me. I concluded then to run away—but she thought they would catch me with the blood hounds by their taking my track. But to avoid them I thought I would ride off on one of the Deacon's mules. She thought if I did, they would sell me.

"No matter, I will try it," said I, "let the consequences be what they may. The matter can be no worse than it now is." So I tackled up the Deacon's best mule with his saddle, &c., and started that night and went off eight or ten miles from home. But I found the mule to be rather troublesome, and was like to betray me by braying, especially when he would see cattle, horses, or any thing of the kind in the woods.

The second night from home I camped in a cane break down in the Red river swamp not a great way off from the road, perhaps not twenty rods, exposed to wild ferocious beasts which were numerous in that section of country. On that night about the middle of the night the mule heard the sound of horses feet on the road, and he commenced stamping and trying to break away. As the horses seemed to come nearer, the mule commenced trying to bray, and it was all that I could do to prevent him from making a loud bray there in the woods, which would have betrayed me.

I supposed that it was the overseer out with the dogs looking for me, and I found afterwards that I was not mistaken. As soon as the people had passed by, I mounted the mule and took him home to prevent his betraying me. When I got near by home I stripped off the tackling and turned the mule loose. I then slipt up to the cabin wherein my wife laid and found her awake, much distressed about me. She informed me that they were then out looking for me, and that the Deacon was bent on flogging me nearly to death, and then selling me off from my family. This was truly heart-rending to my poor wife; the thought of our being torn apart in a strange land after having been sold away from all her friends and relations, was more than she could bear.

The Deacon had declared that I should not only suffer for the crime of attending a prayer meeting without his permission, and for running away, but for the awful crime of stealing a jackass, which was death by the law when committed by a negro.

But I well knew that I was regarded as property, and so was the ass; and I thought if one piece of property took off another, there could be no law violated in the act; no more sin committed in this than if one jackass had rode off another.

But after consultation with my wife I concluded to take her and my little daughter with me and they would be guilty of the same crime that I was, so far as running away was concerned; and if the Deacon sold one he might sell us all, and perhaps to the same person.

So we started off with our child that night, and made our way down to the Red river swamps among the buzzing insects and wild beasts of the forest. We wandered about in the wilderness for eight or ten days before we were apprehended, striving to make our way from slavery; but it was all in vain. Our food was parched corn, with wild fruit such as pawpaws, percimmons, grapes, &c. We did at one time chance to find a sweet potato patch where we got a few potatoes; but most of the time, while we were out, we were lost. We wanted to cross the Red river but could find no conveyance to cross in.

I recollect one day of finding a crooked tree which bent over the river or over one fork of the river, where it was divided by an island. I should think that the tree was at least twenty feet from the surface of the water. I picked up my little child, and my wife followed me, saying, "if we perish let us all perish together in the stream." We succeeded in crossing over. I often look back to that dangerous event even now with astonishment, and wonder how I could have run such a risk. What would induce me to run the same risk now? What could induce me now to leave home and friends and go to the wild forest and lay out on the cold ground night after night without covering, and live on parched corn?

What would induce me to take my family and go into the Red river swamps of Louisiana among the snakes and alligators, with all the liabilities of being destroyed by them, hunted down with blood hounds, or lay myself liable to be shot down like the wild beasts of the forest? Nothing I say, nothing but the strongest love of liberty, humanity, and justice to myself and family, would induce me to run such a risk again.

When we crossed over on the tree we supposed that we had crossed over the main body of the river, but we had not proceeded far on our journey before we found that we were on an Island surrounded by water on either side. We made our bed that night in a pile of dry leaves which had fallen from off the trees. We were much rest-broken, wearied from hunger and travelling through briers, swamps and cane-brakes—consequently we soon fell asleep after lying down. About the dead hour of the night I was aroused by the awful howling of a gang of bloodthirsty wolves, which had found us out and surrounded us as their prey, there in the dark wilderness many miles from any house or settlement.

My dear little child was so dreadfully alarmed that she screamed loudly with fear—my wife trembling like a leaf on a tree, at the thought of being devoured there in the wilderness by ferocious wolves.

The wolves kept howling, and were near enough for us to see their glaring eyes, and hear their chattering teeth. I then thought that the hour of death for us was at hand; that we should not live to see the light of another day; for there was no way for our escape. My little family were looking up to me for protection, but I could afford them none. And while I was offering up my prayers to that God who never forsakes those in the hour of danger who trust in him, I thought of Deacon Whitfield; I thought of his profession, and doubted his piety. I thought of his hand-cuffs, of his whips, of his chains, of his stocks, of his thumb-screws, of his slave driver and overseer, and of his religion; I also thought of his opposition to prayer meetings, and of his five hundred lashes promised me for attending a prayer meeting. I thought of God, I thought of the devil, I thought of hell; and I thought of heaven, and wondered whether I should ever see the Deacon there. And I calculated that if heaven was made up of such Deacons, or such persons, it could not be filled with love to all mankind, and with glory and eternal happiness, as we know it is from the truth of the Bible.

The reader may perhaps think me tedious on this topic, but indeed it is one of so much interest to me, that I find myself entirely unable to describe what my own feelings were at that time. I was so much excited by the fierce howling of the savage wolves, and the frightful screams of my little family, that I thought of the future; I thought of the past; I thought the time of my departure had come at last.

My impression is, that all these thoughts and thousands of others, dashed through my mind, while I was surrounded by those wolves. But it seemed to be the will of a merciful providence, that our lives should be spared, and that we should not be destroyed by them.

I had no weapon of defence but a long bowie knife which I had slipped from the Deacon. It was a very splendid blade, about two feet in length, and about two inches in width. This used to be a part of his armor of defence while walking about the plantation among his slaves.

The plan which I took to expel the wolves was a very dangerous one, but it proved effectual. While they were advancing to me, prancing and accumulating in number, apparently of all sizes and grades, who had come to the feast, I thought just at this time, that there was no alternative left but for me to make a charge with my bowie knife. I well knew from the action of the wolves, that if I made no farther resistance, they would soon destroy us, and if I made a break at them, the matter could be no worse. I thought if I must die, I would die striving to protect my little family from destruction, die striving to escape from slavery. My wife took a club in one hand, and her child in the other, while I rushed forth with my bowie knife in hand, to fight off the savage wolves. I made one desperate charge at them, and at the same time making a loud yell at the top of my voice, that caused them to retreat and scatter, which was equivalent to a victory on our part. Our prayers were answered, and our lives spared through the night. We slept no more that night, and the next morning there were no wolves to be seen or heard, and we resolved not to stay on that island another night.

We travelled up and down the river side trying to find a place where we could cross. Finally we found a lot of drift wood clogged together, extending across the stream at a narrow place in the river, upon which we crossed over. But we had not yet surmounted our greatest difficulty. We had to meet one which was far more formidable than the first. Not many days after I had to face the Deacon.

We had been wandering about through the cane brakes, bushes, and briers, for several days, when we heard the yelping of blood hounds, a great way off, but they seemed to come nearer and nearer to us. We thought after awhile that they must be on our track; we listened attentively at the approach. We knew it was no use for us to undertake to escape from them, and as they drew nigh, we heard the voice of a man hissing on the dogs.

After awhile we saw the hounds coming in full speed on our track, and the soul drivers close after them on horse back, yelling like tigers, as they came in sight. The shrill yelling of the savage blood hounds as they drew nigh made the woods echo.

The first impulse was to run to escape the approaching danger of ferocious dogs, and blood thirsty slave hunters, who were so rapidly approaching me with loaded muskets and bowie knives, with a determination to kill or capture me and my family. I started to run with my little daughter in my arms, but stumbled and fell down and scratched the arm of little Frances with a brier, so that it bled very much; but the dear child never cried, for she seemed to know the danger to which we were exposed.

But we soon found that it was no use for us to run. The dogs were soon at our heels, and we were compelled to stop, or be torn to pieces by them. By this time, the soul drivers came charging up on their horses, commanding us to stand still or they would shoot us down.

Of course I surrendered up for the sake of my family. The most abusive

terms to be found in the English language were poured forth on us with bitter oaths. They tied my hands behind me, and drove us home before them, to suffer the penalty of a slaveholder's broken law.

As we drew nigh the plantation my heart grew faint. I was aware that we should have to suffer almost death for running off. I was filled with dreadful apprehensions at the thought of meeting a professed follower of Christ, whom I knew to be a hypocrite! No tongue, no pen can ever describe what my feelings were at that time.

CHAPTER XII.

My sad condition before Whitfeld. — My terrible punishment. — Incidents of a former attempt to escape. — Jack at a farm house. — Six pigs and a turkey. — Our surprise and arrest.

The reader may perhaps imagine what must have been my feelings when I found myself surrounded on the island with my little family, at midnight, by a gang of savage wolves. This was one of those trying emergencies in my life when there was apparently but one step between us and the grave. But I had no cords wrapped about my limbs to prevent my struggling against the impending danger to which I was then exposed. I was not denied the consolation of resisting in self defence, as was now the case. There was no Deacon standing before me, with a loaded rifle, swearing that I should submit to the torturing lash, or be shot down like a dumb beast.

I felt that my chance was by far better among the howling wolves in the

Red river swamp, than before Deacon Whitfield, on the cotton plantation. I was brought before him as a criminal before a bar, without counsel, to be tried and condemned by a tyrant's law. My arms were bound with a cord, my spirit broken, and my little family standing by weeping. I was not allowed to plead my own cause, and there was no one to utter a word in my behalf.

He ordered that the field hands should be called together to witness my punishment, that it might serve as a caution to them never to attend a prayer meeting, or runaway as I had, lest they should receive the same punishment.

At the sound of the overseer's horn, all the slaves came forward and witnessed my punishment. My clothing was stripped off and I was compelled to lie down on the ground with my face to the earth. Four stakes were driven in the ground, to which my hands and feet were tied. Then the overseer stood over me with the lash and laid it on according to the Deacon's order. Fifty lashes were laid on before stopping. I was then lectured with reference to my going to prayer meeting without his orders, and running away to escape flogging.

While I suffered under this dreadful torture, I prayed, and wept, and implored mercy at the hand of slavery, but found none. After I was marked from my neck to my heels, the Deacon took the gory lash, and said he thought there was a spot on my back yet where he could put in a few more. He wanted to give me something to remember him by, he said.

After I was flogged almost to death in this way, a paddle was brought forward and eight or ten blows given me with it, which was by far worse than the lash. My wounds were then washed with salt brine, after which I was let up. A description of such paddles I have already given in another page. I was so badly punished that I was not able to work for several days. After being flogged as described, they took me off several miles to a shop and had a heavy iron collar riveted on my neck with prongs extending above my head, on the end of which there was a small bell. I was not able to reach the bell with my hand. This heavy load of iron I was compelled to wear for six weeks. I never was allowed to lie in the same house with my family again while I was the slave of Whitfield. I either had to sleep with my feet in the stocks, or be chained with a large log chain to a log over night, with no bed or bedding to rest my wearied limbs on, after toiling all day in the cotton field. I suffered almost death while kept in this confinement; and he had ordered the overseer never to let me loose again; saying that I thought of getting free by running off, but no negro should ever get away from him alive.

I have omitted to state that this was the second time I had run away from him; while I was gone the first time, he extorted from my wife the fact that I had been in the habit of running away, before we left Kentucky; that I had been to Canada, and that I was trying to learn the art of reading and writing. All this was against me.

It is true that I was striving to learn myself to write. I was a kind of a house servant and was frequently sent off on errands, but never without a written pass; and on Sundays I have sometimes got permission to visit our neighbor's slaves, and I have often tried to write myself a pass.

Whenever I got hold of an old letter that had been thrown away, or a piece of white paper, I would save it to write on. I have often gone off in the woods and spent the greater part of the day alone, trying to learn to write myself a pass, by writing on the backs of old letters; copying after the pass that had been written by Whitfield; by so doing I got the use of the pen and could form letters as well as I can now, but knew not what they were.

The Deacon had an old slave by the name of Jack whom he bought about the time that he bought me. Jack was born in the State of Virginia. He had some idea of freedom; had often run away, but was very ignorant; knew not where to go for refuge; but understood all about providing something to eat when unjustly deprived of it.

So for ill treatment, we concluded to take a tramp together. I was to be the pilot, while Jack was to carry the baggage and keep us in provisions. Before we started, I managed to get hold of a suit of clothes the Deacon possessed, with his gun, ammunition and bowie knife. We also procured a blanket, a joint of meat, and some bread.

We started in a northern direction, being bound for the city of Little Rock, State of Arkansas. We travelled by night and laid by in the day, being guided by the unchangeable North Star; but at length, our provisions gave out, and it was Jack's place to get more. We came in sight of a large plantation one morning, where we saw people of color, and Jack said he could get something there, among the slaves, that night, for us to eat. So we concealed ourselves, in sight of this plantation until about bed time, when we saw the lights extinguished.

During the day we saw a female slave passing from the dwelling house to the kitchen as if she was the cook; the house being about three rods from the landlord's dwelling. After we supposed the whites were all asleep, Jack slipped up softly to the kitchen to try his luck with the cook, to see if he could get any thing from her to eat.

I would remark that the domestic slaves are often found to be traitors to their own people, for the purpose of gaining favor with their masters; and they are encouraged and trained up by them to report every plot they know of being formed about stealing any thing, or running away, or any thing of the kind; and for which they are paid. This is one of the principal causes of the slaves being divided among themselves, and without which they could not be held in bondage one year, and perhaps not half that time.

I now proceed to describe the unsuccessful attempt of poor Jack to obtain something from the female slave to satisfy hunger. The planter's house was situated on an elevated spot on the side of a hill. The fencing about the house and garden was very crookedly laid up with rails. The night was rather dark and rainy, and Jack left me with the understanding that I was to stay at a certain place until he returned. I cautioned him before he left me to be very careful—and after he started, I left the place where he was to find me when he returned, for fear something might happen which might lead to my detection, should I remain at that spot. So I left it and went off where I could see the house, and that place too.

Jack had not long been gone, before I heard a great noise; a man, crying out with a loud voice, "Catch him! Catch him!" and hissing the dogs on, and they were close after Jack. The next thing I saw, was Jack running for life, and an old white man after him, with a gun, and his dogs. The fence being on sidling ground, and wet with the rain, when Jack run against it he knocked down several pannels of it and fell, tumbling over and over to the foot of the hill; but soon recovered and ran to where he had left me; but I was gone. The dogs were still after him.

There happened to be quite a thicket of small oak shrubs and bushes in the direction he ran. I think he might have been heard running and straddling bushes a quarter of a mile! The poor fellow hurt himself considerably in straddling over bushes in that way, in making his escape.

Finally the dogs relaxed their chase and poor Jack and myself again met in the thick forest. He said when he rapped on the cook-house door, the colored woman came to the door. He asked her if she would let him have a bite of bread if she had it, that he was a poor hungry absconding slave. But she made no reply to what he said but immediately sounded the alarm by calling loudly after her master, saying, "here is a runaway negro!" Jack said that he was going to knock her down but her master was out within one moment, and he had to run for his life.

As soon as we got our eyes fixed on the North Star again, we started on our way. We travelled on a few miles and came to another large plantation, where Jack was determined to get something to eat. He left me at a certain place while he went up to the house to find something if possible.

He was gone some time before he returned, but when I saw him coming, he appeared to be very heavy loaded with a bag of something. We walked off pretty fast until we got some distance in the woods. Jack then stopped and opened his bag in which he had six small pigs. I asked him how he got them without making any noise; and he said that he found a bed of hogs, in which there were the pigs with their mother. While the pigs were sucking he crawled up to them without being discovered by the sow, and took them by their necks one after another, and choked them to death, and slipped them into his bag!

We intended to travel on all that night and lay by the next day in the forest and cook up our pigs. We fell into a large road leading on the direction which we were travelling, and had not proceeded over three miles before I found a white hat lying in the road before me. Jack being a little behind me I stopped until he came up, and showed it to him. He picked it up. We looked a few steps farther and saw a man lying by the way, either asleep or intoxicated, as we supposed.

I told Jack not to take the hat, but he would not obey me. He had only a piece of a hat himself, which he left in exchange for the other. We travelled on about five miles farther, and in passing a house discovered a large turkey sitting on the fence, which temptation was greater than Jack could resist. Notwithstanding he had six very nice fat little pigs on his back, he stepped up and took the turkey off the fence.

By this time it was getting near day-light and we left the road and went off a mile or so among the hills of the forest, where we struck camp for the day. We then picked our turkey, dressed our pigs, and cooked two of them. We got the hair off by singeing them over the fire, and after we had eaten all we wanted, one of us slept while the other watched. We had flint, punk, and powder to strike fire with. A little after dark the next night, we started on our way.

But about ten o'clock that night just as we were passing through a thick skirt of woods, five men sprang out before us with fire-arms, swearing if we moved another step, they would shoot us down; and each man having his gun drawn up for shooting we had no chance to make any defence, and surrendered sooner than run the risk of being killed.

They had been lying in wait for us there, for several hours. They had seen a reward out, for notices were put up in the most public places, that fifty dollars would be paid for me, dead or alive, if I should not return home within so many days. And the reader will remember that neither Jack nor myself was able to read the advertisement. It was of very little consequence with the slave catchers, whether they killed us or took us alive, for the reward was the same to them.

After we were taken and tied, one of the men declared to me that he would have shot me dead just as sure as he lived, if I had moved one step after they com-

manded us to stop. He had his gun level led at my breast, already cocked, and his finger on the trigger. The way they came to find us out was from the circumstance of Jack's taking the man's hat in connection with the advertisement. The man whose hat was taken was drunk; and the next morning when he came to look for his hat it was gone and Jack's old hat lying in the place of it; and in looking round he saw the tracks of two persons in the dust, who had passed during the night, and one of them having but three toes on one foot. He followed these tracks until they came to a large mud pond, in a lane on one side of which a person might pass dry shod; but the man with three toes on one foot had plunged through the mud. This led the man to think there must be runaway slaves, and from out of that neighborhood; for all persons in that settlement knew which side of that mud hole to go. He then got others to go with him, and they followed us until our track left the road. They supposed that we had gone off in the woods to lay by until night, after which we should pursue our course.

After we were captured they took us off several miles to where one of them lived, and kept us over night. One of our pigs was cooked for us to eat that night; and the turkey the next morning. But we were both tied that night with our hands behind us, and our feet were also tied. The doors were locked, and a bedstead was set against the front door, and two men slept in it to prevent our getting out in the night. They said that they knew how to catch runaway negroes, and how to keep them after they were caught.

They remarked that after they found we had stopped to lay by until night, and they saw from our tracks what direction we were travelling, they went about ten miles on that direction, and hid by the road side until we came up that night. That night after all had got fast to sleep, I thought I would try to get out, and I should have succeeded, if I could have moved the bed from the door. I managed to untie myself and crawled under the bed which was placed at the door, and strove to remove it, but in so doing I awakened the men and they got up and confined me again, and watched me until day light, each with a gun in hand.

The next morning they started with us back to Deacon Whitfield's plantation; but when they got within ten miles of where he lived they stopped at a public house to stay over night; and who should we meet there but the Deacon, who was then out looking for me.

The reader may well imagine how I felt to meet him. I had almost as soon come in contact with Satan himself. He had two long poles or sticks of wood brought in to confine us to. I was compelled to lie on my back across one of those sticks with my arms out, and have them lashed fast to the log with a cord. My feet were also tied to the other, and there I had to lie all that night with my back across this stick of wood, and my feet and hands tied. I suffered that night under the most excruciating pain. From the tight binding of the cord the circulation of the blood in my arms and feet was almost entirely stopped. If the night had been much longer I must have died in that confinement.

The next morning we were taken back to the Deacon's farm, and both flogged for going off, and set to work. But there was some allowance made for me on account of my being young. They said that they knew old Jack had persuaded me off, or I never would have gone. And the Deacon's wife begged that

I might be favored some, for that time, as Jack had influenced me, so as to bring up my old habits of running away that I had entirely given up.

CHAPTER XIII.

I am sold to gamblers. — They try to purchase my family. — Our parting scene. — My good usage. — I am sold to an Indian. — His confidence in my integrity manifested.

THE reader will remember that this brings me back to the time the Deacon had ordered me to be kept in confinement until he got a chance to sell me, and that no negro should ever get away from him and live. Some days after this we were all out at the gin house ginning cotton, which was situated on the road side, and there came along a company of men, fifteen or twenty in number, who were Southern sportsmen. Their attention was attracted by the load of iron which was fastened about my neck with a bell attached. They stopped and asked the Deacon what that bell was put on my neck for and he said it was to keep me from running away, &c.

They remarked that I looked as if I might be a smart negro, and asked if he wanted to sell me. The reply was, yes. They then got off their horses and struck a bargain with him for me. They bought me at a reduced price for speculation.

After they had purchased me, I asked the privilege of going to the house to take leave of my family before I left, which was granted by the sportsmen. But the Deacon said I should never again step my foot inside of his yard; and advised the sportsmen not to take the irons from my neck until they had sold me; that if they gave me the least chance I would run away from them, as I did from him. So I was compelled to mount a horse and go off with them as I supposed, never again to meet my family in this life.

We had not proceeded far before they informed me that they had bought me to sell again, and if they kept the irons on me it would be detrimental to the sale, and that they would therefore take off the irons and dress me up like a man, and throw away the old rubbish which I then had on; and they would sell me to some one who would treat me better than Deacon Whitfield. After they had cut off the irons and dressed me up, they crossed over Red River into Texas, where they spent some time horse racing and gambling; and although they were wicked black legs of the basest character, it is but due to them to say, that they used me far better than ever the Deacon did. They gave me plenty to eat and put nothing hard on me to do. They expressed much sympathy for me in my bereavement; and almost every day they gave me money more or less, and by my activity in waiting on them, and upright conduct, I got into the good graces of them all, but they could not get any person to buy me on account of the amount of intelligence which they supposed me to have; for many of them thought that I could read and write. When they left Texas, they intended to go to the Indian Territory west of the Mississippi, to attend a great horse race which was to take place. Not being much out of their way to go past Deacon Whitfield's again, I prevailed on them to call on him for the purpose of trying to purchase my wife and child; and I promised them that if they would buy my wife and child, I would get some person to purchase us from them. So they tried to grant my request by calling on the Deacon, and trying to make the purchase. As we approached the Deacon's plantation, my heart was filled with a thousand painful and fearful apprehensions. I had the fullest confidence in the blacklegs with whom I travelled, believing that they would do according to promise, and go to the fullest extent of their ability to restore peace and consolation to a bereaved family—to re-unite husband and wife, parent and child, who had long been severed by slavery through the agency of Deacon Whitfield. But I knew his determination in relation to myself, and I feared his wicked opposition to a restoration of myself and little family, which he had divided, and soon found that my fears were not without foundation.

When we rode up and walked into his yard, the Deacon came out and spoke to all but myself; and not finding me in tattered rags as a substitute for clothes, nor having an iron collar or bell about my neck, as was the case when he sold me, he appeared to be much displeased.

"What did you bring that negro back here for?" said he.

"We have come to try to buy his wife and child; for we can find no one who is willing to buy him alone; and we will either buy or sell so that the family may be together," said they.

While this conversation was going on, my poor bereaved wife, who never expected to see me again in this life, spied me and came rushing to me through the crowd, throwing her arms about my neck exclaiming in the most sympathetic tones, "Oh! my dear husband! I never expected to see you again!" The poor woman was bathed with tears of sorrow and grief. But no sooner had she reached me, than the Deacon peremptorily commanded her to go to her work. This she did not obey, but prayed that her master would not separate us again, as she was there alone, far from friends and relations whom she should never meet again. And now to take away her husband, her last and only true friend, would be like taking her life!

But such appeals made no impression on the unfeeling Deacon's heart. While he was storming with abusive language, and even using the gory lash with hellish vengeance to separate husband and wife, I could see the sympathetic teardrop, stealing its way down the cheek of the profligate and black-leg, whose object it now was to bind up the broken heart of a wife, and restore to the arms of a bereaved husband, his companion.

They were disgusted at the conduct of Whitfield and cried out shame, even in his presence. They told him that they would give a thousand dollars for my wife and child, or any thing in reason. But no! he would sooner see me to the devil than indulge or gratify me after my having run away from him; and if they did not remove me from his presence very soon, he said he should make them suffer for it.

But all this, and even the gory lash had yet failed to break the grasp of poor Malinda, whose prospect of connubial, social, and future happiness was all at stake. When the dear woman saw there was no help for us, and that we should soon be separated forever, in the name of Deacon Whitfield, and American slavery to meet no more as husband and wife, parent and child—the last and loudest

appeal was made on our knees. We appealed to the God of justice and to the sacred ties of humanity; but this was all in vain. The louder we prayed the harder
he whipped, amid the most heart-rending shrieks from the poor slave mother and
child, as little Frances stood by, sobbing at the abuse inflicted on her mother.

"Oh! how shall I give my husband the parting hand never to meet again?
This will surely break my heart," were her parting words.

I can never describe to the reader the awful reality of that separation—for
it was enough to chill the blood and stir up the deepest feeling of revenge in the
hearts of slaveholding black-legs, who as they stood by, were threatening, some
weeping, some swearing and others declaring vengeance against such treatment
being inflicted on a human being. As we left the plantation, as far as we could
see and hear, the Deacon was still laying on the gory lash, trying to prevent poor
Malinda from weeping over the loss of her departed husband, who was then, by
the hellish laws of slavery, to her, theoretically and practically dead. One of the
black-legs exclaimed that hell was full of just such Deacon's as Whitfield. This
occurred in December, 1840. I have never seen Malinda, since that period. I
never expect to see her again.

"OH! HOW SHALL I GIVE MY HUSBAND THE PARTING HAND NEVER TO MEET AGAIN."

The sportsmen to whom I was sold, showed their sympathy for me not only
by word but by deeds. They said that they had made the most liberal offer to
Whitfield, to buy or sell for the sole purpose of reuniting husband and wife. But
he stood out against it—they felt sorry for me. They said they had bought me to
speculate on, and were not able to lose what they had paid for me. But they
would make a bargain with me, if I was willing, and would lay a plan, by which
I might yet get free. If I would use my influence so as to get some person to buy
me while traveling about with them, they would give me a portion of the money
for which they sold me, and they would also give me directions by which I might
yet run away and go to Canada.

This offer I accepted, and the plot was made. They advised me to act very stupid in language and thought, but in business I must be spry; and that I must persuade men to buy me, and promise them that I would be smart.

We passed through the State of Arkansas and stopped at many places, horse-racing and gambling. My business was to drive a wagon in which they carried their gambling apparatus, clothing, &c. I had also to black boots and attend to horses. We stopped at Fayettville, where they almost lost me, betting on a horse race.

They went from thence to the Indian Territory among the Cherokee Indians, to attend the great races which were to take place there. During the races there was a very wealthy half Indian of that tribe, who became much attached to me, and had some notion of buying me, after hearing that I was for sale, being a slaveholder. The idea struck me rather favorable, for several reasons. First, I thought I should stand a better chance to get away from an Indian than from a white man. Second, he wanted me only for a kind of a body servant to wait on him—and in this case I knew that I should fare better than I should in the field. And my owners also told me that it would be an easy place to get away from. I took their advice for fear I might not get another chance so good as that, and prevailed on the man to buy me. He paid them nine hundred dollars, in gold and silver, for me. I saw the money counted out.

After the purchase was made, the sportsmen got me off to one side, and according to promise they gave me a part of the money, and directions how to get from there to Canada. They also advised me how to act until I got a good chance to run away. I was to embrace the earliest opportunity of getting away, before they should become acquainted with me. I was never to let it be known where I was from, nor where I was born. I was to act quite stupid and ignorant. And when I started I was to go up the boundary line, between the Indian Territory and the States of Arkansas and Missouri, and this would fetch me out on the Missouri river, near Jefferson city, the capital of Missouri. I was to travel at first by night, and to lay by in day light, until I got out of danger.

The same afternoon that the Indian bought me, he started with me to his residence, which was fifty or sixty miles distant. And so great was his confidence in me, that he intrusted me to carry his money. The amount must have been at least five hundred dollars, which was all in gold and silver; and when we stopped over night the money and horses were all left in my charge.

It would have been a very easy matter for me to have taken one of the best horses, with the money, and run off. And the temptation was truly great to a man like myself, who was watching for the earliest opportunity to escape; and I felt confident that I should never have a better opportunity to escape full handed than then.

CHAPTER XIV.

CHARACTER OF MY INDIAN MASTER. — SLAVERY AMONG THE INDIANS LESS CRUEL. — INDIAN CAROUSAL. — ENFEEBLED HEALTH OF MY INDIAN MASTER. — HIS DEATH. —

MY ESCAPE.—ADVENTURE IN A WIGWAM.— SUCCESSFUL PROGRESS TOWARD
LIBERTY.

THE next morning I went home with my new master; and by the way it is only
doing justice to the dead to say, that he was the most reasonable, and humane
slaveholder that I have ever belonged to. He was the last man that pretended to
claim property in my person; and although I have freely given the names and res-
idences of all others who have held me as a slave, for prudential reasons I shall
omit giving the name of this individual.

He was the owner of a large plantation and quite a number of slaves. He
raised corn and wheat for his own consumption only. There was no cotton, tobacco, or anything of the kind produced among them for market. And I found
this difference between negro slavery among the Indians, and the same thing
among the white slaveholders of the South. The Indians allow their slaves enough
to eat and wear. They have no overseers to whip nor drive them. If a slave of-
fends his master, he sometimes, in a heat of passion, undertakes to chastise him;
but it is as often the case as otherwise, that the slave gets the better of the fight,
and even flogs his master;* for which there is no law to punish him; but when
the fight is over that is the last of it. So far as religious instruction is concerned,
they have it on terms of equality, the bond and the free; they have no respect of
persons, they have neither slave laws nor negro pews. Neither do they separate
husbands and wives, nor parents and children. All things considered, if I must be
a slave, I had by far, rather be a slave to an Indian, than to a white man, from
the experience I have had with both.

A majority of the Indians were uneducated, and still followed up their old
heathen traditional notions. They made it a rule to have an Indian dance or frolic,
about once a fortnight; and they would come together far and near to attend these
dances. They would most generally commence about the middle of the afternoon;
and would give notice by the blowing of horns. One would commence blowing
and another would answer, and so it would go all round the neighborhood. When
a number had got together, they would strike a circle about twenty rods in circumference, and kindle up fires about twenty feet apart, all around, in this circle.
In the centre they would have a large fire to dance around, and at each one of the
small fires there would be a squaw to keep up the fire, which looked delightful off
at a distance.

But the most degrading practice of all, was the use of intoxicating drinks,
which were used to a great excess by all that attended these stump dances. At almost all of these fires there was some one with rum to sell. There would be some
dancing, some singing, some gambling, some fighting, and some yelling; and this
was kept up often for two days and nights together.

Their dress for the dance was most generally a great bunch of bird feathers,
coon tails, or something of the kind stuck in their heads, and a great many shells

---

* This singular fact is corroborated in a letter read by the publisher, from an acquaintance while
passing through this country in 1849.

tied about their legs to rattle while dancing. Their manner of dancing is taking hold of each others hands and forming a ring around the large fire in the centre, and go stomping around it until they would get drunk or their heads would get to swimming, and then they would go off and drink, and another set come on. Such were some of the practises indulged in by these Indian slaveholders.

My last owner was in a declining state of health when he bought me; and not long after he bought me he went off forty or fifty miles from home to be doctored by an Indian doctor, accompanied by his wife. I was taken along also to drive the carriage and to wait upon him during his sickness. But he was then so feeble, that his life was of but short duration after the doctor commenced on him.

While he lived, I waited on him according to the best of my ability. I watched over him night and day until he died, and even prepared his body for the tomb, before I left him. He died about midnight and I understood from his friends that he was not to be buried until the second day after his death. I pretended to be taking on at a great rate about his death, but I was more excited about running away, than I was about that, and before daylight the next morning I proved it, for I was on my way to Canada.

I never expected a better opportunity would present itself for my escape. I slipped out of the room as if I had gone off to weep for the deceased, knowing that they would not feel alarmed about me until after my master was buried and they had returned back to his residence. And even then, they would think that I was somewhere on my way home; and it would be at least four or five days before they would make any stir in looking after me. By that time, if I had no bad luck, I should be out of much danger.

After the first day, I laid by in the day and traveled by night for several days and nights, passing in this way through several tribes of Indians. I kept pretty near the boundary line. I recollect getting lost one dark rainy night. Not being able to find the road I came into an Indian settlement at the dead hour of the night. I was wet, wearied, cold and hungry; and yet I felt afraid to enter any of their houses or wigwams, not knowing whether they would be friendly or not. But I knew the Indians were generally drunkards, and that occasionally a drunken white man was found straggling among them, and that such an one would be more likely to find friends from sympathy than an upright man.

So I passed myself off that night as a drunkard among them. I walked up to the door of one of their houses, and fell up against it, making a great noise like a drunken man; but no one came to the door. I opened it and staggered in, falling about, and making a great noise. But finally an old woman got up and gave me a blanket to lie down on.

There was quite a number of them lying about on the dirt floor, but not one could talk or understand a word of the English language. I made signs so as to let them know that I wanted something to eat, but they had nothing, so I had to go without that night. I laid down and pretended to be asleep, but I slept none that night, for I was afraid that they would kill me if I went to sleep. About one hour before day, the next morning, three of the females got up and put into a tin kettle a lot of ashes with water, to boil, and then poured into it about one quart of corn. After letting it stand a few moments, they poured it into a trough, and pounded it into thin hominy. They washed it out, and boiled it down, and called me up to eat my breakfast of it.

After eating, I offered them six cents, but they refused to accept it. I then found my way to the main road, and traveled all that day on my journey, and just at night arrived at a public house kept by an Indian, who also kept a store. I walked in and asked if I could get lodging, which was granted; but I had not been there long before three men came riding up about dusk, or between sunset and dark. They were white men, and I supposed slaveholders. At any rate when they asked if they could have lodging, I trembled for fear they might be in pursuit of me. But the landlord told them that he could not lodge them, but they could get lodging about two miles off, with a white man, and they turned their horses and started.

The landlord asked me where I was traveling to, and where I was from. I told him that I had been out looking at the country; that I had thought of buying land, and that I lived in the State of Ohio, in the village of Perrysburgh. He then said that he had lived there himself, and that he had acted as an interpreter there among the Maumee tribe of Indians for several years. He then asked who I was acquainted with there? I informed him that I knew Judge Hollister, Francis Hollister, J. W. Smith, and others. At this he was so much pleased that he came up and took me by the hand, and received me joyfully, after seeing that I was acquainted with those of his old friends.

I could converse with him understandingly from personal acquaintance, for I had lived there when I first ran away from Kentucky. But I felt it to be my duty to start off the next morning before breakfast, or sunrise. I bought a dozen of eggs, and had them boiled to carry with me to eat on the way. I did not like the looks of those three men, and thought I would get on as fast as possible for fear I might be pursued by them.

I was then about to enter the territory of another slave State, Missouri. I had passed through the fiery ordeal of Sibley, Gatewood, and Garrison, and had even slipped through the fingers of Deacon Whitfield. I had doubtless gone through great peril in crossing the Indian territory, in passing through the various half civilized tribes, who seemed to look upon me with astonishment as I passed along. Their hands were almost invariably filled with bows and arrows, tomahawks, guns, butcher knives, and all the various implements of death which are used by them. And what made them look still more frightful, their faces were often painted red, and their heads muffled with birds feathers, bushes, coons tails and owls heads. But all this I had passed through, and my long enslaved limbs and spirit were then in full stretch for emancipation. I felt as if one more short struggle would set me free.

CHAPTER XV.

Adventure on the Prairie. — I borrow a horse without leave. — Rapid traveling one whole night. — Apology for using other men's horses. — My manner of living on the road.

EARLY in the morning I left the Indian territory as I have already said, for fear I might be pursued by the three white men whom I had seen there over night; but I had not proceeded far before my fears were magnified a hundred fold.

I always dreaded to pass through a prairie, and on coming to one which was about six miles in width, I was careful to look in every direction to see whether there was any person in sight before I entered it; but I could see no one. So I started across with a hope of crossing without coming in contact with any one on the prairie. I walked as fast as I could, but when I got about midway of the prairie, I came to a high spot where the road forked, and three men came up from a low spot as if they had been there concealed. They were all on horse back, and I supposed them to be the same men that had tried to get lodging where I stopped over night. Had this been in timbered land, I might have stood some chance to have dodged them, but there I was, out in the open prairie, where I could see no possible way by which I could escape.

They came along slowly up behind me, and finally passed, and spoke or bowed their heads on passing, but they traveled in a slow walk and kept but a very few steps before me, until we got nearly across the prairie. When we were coming near a plantation a piece off from the road on the skirt of the timbered land, they whipped up their horses and left the road as if they were going across to this plantation. They soon got out of my sight by going down into a valley which lay between us and the plantation. Not seeing them rise the hill to go up to the farm, excited greater suspicion in my mind, so I stepped over on the brow of the hill, where I could see what they were doing, and to my surprise I saw them going right back in the direction they had just came, and they were going very fast. I was then satisfied that they were after me and that they were only going back to get more help to assist them in taking me, for fear that I might kill some of them if they undertook it. The first impression was that I had better leave the road immediately; so I bolted from the road and ran as fast as I could for some distance in the thick forest, and concealed myself for about fifteen or twenty minutes, which were spent in prayer to God for his protecting care and guidance.

My impression was that when they should start in pursuit of me again, they would follow on in the direction which I was going when they left me; and not finding or hearing of me on the road, they would come back and hunt through the woods, and if they could find no track they might go and get dogs to trace me out.

I thought my chance of escape would be better, if I went back to the same side of the road that they first went, for the purpose of deceiving them; as I supposed that they would not suspect my going in the same direction that they went, for the purpose of escaping from them.

So I traveled all that day square off from the road through the wild forest without any knowledge of the country whatever: for I had nothing to travel by but the sun by day, and the moon and stars by night. Just before night I came in sight of a large plantation, where I saw quite a number of horses running at large in a field, and knowing that my success in escaping depended upon my getting out of that settlement within twenty-four hours, to save myself from everlasting slavery, I thought I should be justified in riding one of those horses, that night, if I could catch one. I cut a grape vine with my knife, and made it into a bridle; and shortly after dark I went into the field and tried to catch one of the horses. I got a bunch of dry blades of fodder and walked up softly towards the horses, calling to them "cope," "cope," "cope;" but there was only one out of the number that I was able to get my hand on, and that was an old mare, which I supposed to be the mother of all the rest; and I knew that I could walk faster than she could travel. She had a bell on and was very thin in flesh; she looked gentle and walked on three legs only. The young horses pranced and galloped off. I was not able to get near them, and the old mare being of no use to me, I left them all. After fixing my eyes on the north star I pursued my journey, holding on to my bridle with a hope of finding a horse upon which I might ride that night.

I found a road leading pretty nearly in the direction which I wanted to travel, and I kept it. After traveling several miles I found another large plantation where there was a prospect of finding a horse. I stepped up to the barn-yard, wherein I found several horses. There was a little barn standing with the door open, and I found it quite an easy task to get the horses into the barn, and select out the best looking one of them. I pulled down the fence, led the noble beast out and mounted him, taking a northern direction, being able to find a road which led that way. But I had not gone over three or four miles before I came to a large stream of water which was past fording; yet I could see that it had been forded by the road track, but from high water it was then impassible. As the horse seemed willing to go in I put him through; but before he got in far, he was in water up to his sides and finally the water came over his back and he swam over. I got as wet as could be, but the horse carried me safely across at the proper place. After I got out a mile or so from the river, I came into a large prairie, which I think must have been twenty or thirty miles in width, and the road run across it about in the direction that I wanted to go. I laid whip to the horse, and I think he must have carried me not less than forty miles that night, or before sun rise the next morning. I then stopped him in a spot of high grass in an old field, and took off the bridle. I thanked God, and thanked the horse for what he had done for me, and wished him a safe journey back home.

I know the poor horse must have felt stiff, and tired from his speedy jaunt, and I felt very bad myself, riding at that rate all night without a saddle; but I felt as if I had too much at stake to favor either horse flesh or man flesh. I could indeed afford to crucify my own flesh for the sake of redeeming myself from perpetual slavery.

Some may be disposed to find fault with my taking the horse as I did; but I did nothing more than nine out of ten would do if they were placed in the same circumstances. I had no disposition to steal a horse from any man. But I ask, if a white man had been captured by the Cherokee Indians and carried away from his family for life into slavery, and could see a chance to escape and get back to his family; should the Indians pursue him with a determination to take him back or take his life, would it be a crime for the poor fugitive, whose life, liberty and future happiness were all at stake, to mount any man's horse by the way side, and ride him without asking any questions, to effect his escape? Or who would not do the same thing to rescue a wife, child, father, or mother? Such an act committed by a white man under the same circumstances would not only be pronounced proper, but praiseworthy; and if he neglected to avail himself of such a means of escape he would be pronounced a fool. Therefore from this act I have nothing to regret, for I have done nothing more than any other reasonable person would have done under the same circumstances. But I had good luck from the morning I left the horse until I got back into the State of Ohio. About two miles from where I left the horse, I found a public house on the road, where I stopped and took breakfast. Being asked where I was traveling, I replied that I was going home to Perrysburgh, Ohio, and that I had been out to look at the land in Missouri, with a view of buying. They supposed me to be a native of Ohio, from the fact of my being so well acquainted with its location, its principal cities, inhabitants, &c.

The next night I put up at one of the best hotels in the village where I stopped, and acted with as much independence as if I was worth a million of dollars; talked about buying land, stock and village property, and contrasting it with the same kind of property in the State of Ohio. In this kind of talk they were most generally interested, and I was treated just like other travelers. I made it a point to travel about thirty miles each day on my way to Jefferson city. On several occasions I have asked the landlords where I have stopped over night, if they could tell me who kept the best house where I would stop the next night, which was most generally in a small village. But for fear I might forget, I would get them to give me the name on a piece of paper as a kind of recommend. This would serve as an introduction through which I have always been well received from one landlord to another, and I have always stopped at the best houses, eaten at the first tables, and slept in the best beds. No man ever asked me whether I was bond or free, black or white, rich or poor; but I always presented a bold front and showed the best side out, which was all the pass I had. But when I got within about one hundred miles of Jefferson city, where I expected to take a Steamboat passage to St. Louis, I stopped over night at a hotel, where I met with a young white man who was traveling on to Jefferson City on horse back, and was also leading a horse with a saddle and bridle on.

I asked him if he would let me ride the horse which he was leading, as I was going to the same city? He said that it was a hired horse, that he was paying at the rate of fifty cents per day for it, but if I would pay the same I could ride him. I accepted the offer and we rode together to the city. We were on the road together two or three days, stopped and ate and slept together at the same hotels.

CHAPTER XVI.

Stratagem to get on board the steamer. — My Irish friends. — My success in reaching Cincinnati. — Reflections on again seeing Kentucky. — I get employment in a hotel. — My fright at seeing the gambler who sold me. — I leave Ohio with Mr. Smith. — His letter. — My education.

THE greatest of my adventures came off when I arrived at Jefferson City. There I expected to meet an advertisement for my person; it was there I must cross the river or take a steamboat down; it was there I expected to be interrogated and required to prove whether I was actually a free man or a slave. If I was free, I should have to show my free papers; and if I was a slave I should be required to tell who my master was.

I stopped at a hotel, however, and ascertained that there was a steamboat expected down the river that day for St. Louis. I also found out that there were several passengers at that house who were going down on board of the first boat. I knew that the captain of a steamboat could not take a colored passenger on board of his boat from a slave state without first ascertaining whether such person was bond or free; I knew that this was more than he would dare to do by the laws of the slave states—and now to surmount this difficulty it brought into exercise all the powers of my mind. I would have got myself boxed up as freight, and have been forwarded to St. Louis, but I had no friend that I could trust to do it for me. This plan has since been adopted by some with success. But finally I thought I might possibly pass myself off as a body servant to the passengers going from the hotel down.

So I went to a store and bought myself a large trunk, and took it to the hotel. Soon, a boat came in which was bound to St. Louis, and the passengers started down to get on board. I took up my large trunk, and started along after them as if I was their servant. My heart trembled in view of the dangerous experiment which I was then about to try. It required all the moral courage that I was master of to bear me up in view of my critical condition. The white people that I was following walked on board and I after them. I acted as if the trunk was full of clothes, but I had not a stitch of clothes in it. The passengers went up into the cabin and I followed them with the trunk. I suppose this made the captain think that I was their slave.

I not only took the trunk in the cabin but stood by it until after the boat had started as if it belonged to my owners, and I was taking care of it for them; but as soon as the boat got fairly under way, I knew that some account would have to be given of me, so I then took my trunk down on the deck among the deck passengers to prepare myself to meet the clerk of the boat, when he should come to collect fare from the deck passengers.

Fortunately for me there was quite a number of deck passengers on board, among whom there were many Irish. I insinuated myself among them so as to get into their good graces, believing that if I should get into a difficulty they would stand by me. I saw several of these persons going up to the saloon buying whiskey, and I thought this might be the most effectual way by which I could gain speedily their respect and sympathy. So I participated with them pretty freely for awhile, or at least until after I got my fare settled. I placed myself in a little crowd of them, and invited them all up to the bar with me, stating that it was my treat. This was responded to, and they walked up and drank and I footed the bill. This, of course, brought us into a kind of a union. We sat together and laughed and talked freely. Within ten or fifteen minutes I remarked that I was getting dry again, and invited them up and treated again. By this time I was thought to be one of the most liberal and gentlemanly men on board, by these deck passengers; they were ready to do any thing for me—they got to singing songs, and telling long yarns in which I took quite an active part; but it was all for effect.

By this time the porter came around ringing his bell for all passengers who had not paid their fare, to walk up to the captain's office and settle it. Some of my Irish friends had not yet settled, and I asked one of them if he would be good enough to take my money and get me a ticket when he was getting one for himself, and he quickly replied "yes sir, I will get you a tacket." So he relieved me of my greatest trouble. When they came round to gather the tickets before we got to St. Louis, my ticket was taken with the rest, and no questions were asked me.

The next day the boat arrived at St. Louis; my object was to take passage on board of the first boat which was destined for Cincinnati, Ohio; and as there was a boat going out that day for Pittsburgh, I went on board to make some inquiry about the fare &c., and found the steward to be a colored man with whom I was acquainted. He lived in Cincinnati, and had rendered me some assistance in making my escape to Canada, in the summer of 1838, and he also very kindly aided me then in getting back into a land of freedom. The swift running steamer started that afternoon on her voyage, which soon wafted my body beyond the tyrannical limits of chattel slavery. When the boat struck the mouth of the river Ohio, and I had once more the pleasure of looking on that lovely stream, my heart leaped up for joy at the glorious prospect that I should again be free. Every revolution of the mighty steam-engine seemed to bring me nearer and nearer the "promised land." Only a few days had elapsed, before I was permitted by the smiles of a good providence, once more to gaze on the green hill-tops and valleys of old Kentucky, the State of my nativity. And notwithstanding I was deeply interested while standing on the deck of the steamer looking at the beauties of nature on either side of the river, as she pressed her way up the stream, my very soul was pained to look upon the slaves in the fields of Kentucky, still toiling under their task-masters without pay. It was on this soil I first breathed the free air of Heaven, and felt the bitter pangs of slavery—it was here that I first learned to abhor it. It was here I received the first impulse of human rights—it was here that I first entered my protest against the bloody institution of slavery, by running away from it, and declared that I would no longer work for any man as I had done, without wages.

When the steamboat arrived at Portsmouth, Ohio, I took off my trunk with the intention of going to Canada. But my funds were almost exhausted, so I had to stop and go to work to get money to travel on. I hired myself at the American Hotel to a Mr. McCoy to do the work of a porter, to black boots, &c., for which he was to pay me $12 per month. I soon found the landlord to be bad pay, and not only that, but he would not allow me to charge for blacking boots, although I had to black them after everybody had gone to bed at night, and set them in the barroom, where the gentlemen could come and get them in the morning while I was at other work. I had nothing extra for this, neither would he pay me my regular wages; so I thought this was a little too much like slavery, and devised a plan by which I got some pay for my work.

I made it a point never to blacken all the boots and shoes over night, neither would I put any of them in the bar-room, but lock them up in a room where no one could get them without calling for me. I got a piece of broken vessel, placed it in the room just before the boots, and put into it several pieces of small change, as if it had been given me for boot blacking; and almost every one that came in after their boots, would throw some small trifle into my contribution box, while I was there blacking away. In this way, I made more than my land-lord paid me, and I soon got a good stock of cash again. One morning I blacked a gentleman's boots who came in during the night by a steamboat. After he had put on his boots, I was called into the barroom to button his straps; and while I was performing this service, not thinking to see anybody that knew me, I hap-pened to look up at the man's face and who should it be but one of the very gamblers who had recently sold me. I dropped his foot and bolted from the room as if I had been struck by an electric shock. The man happened not to recognize me, but this strange conduct on my part excited the landlord, who followed me out to see what was the matter. He found me with my hand to my breast, groan-ing at a great rate. He asked me what was the matter; but I was not able to in-form him correctly, but said that I felt very bad indeed. He of course thought I was sick with the colic and ran in the house and got some hot stuff for me, with spice, ginger, &c. But I never got able to go into the bar-room until long after breakfast time, when I knew this man was gone; then I got well.

And yet I have no idea that the man would have hurt a hair of my head; but my first thought was that he was after me. I then made up my mind to leave Portsmouth; its location being right on the border of a slave State.

A short time after this a gentleman put up there over night named Smith, from Perrysburgh, with whom I was acquainted in the North. He was on his way to Kentucky to buy up a drove of fine horses, and he wanted me to go and help him to drive his horses out to Perrysburgh, and said he would pay all my ex-penses if I would go. So I made a contract to go and agreed to meet him the next week, on a set day, in Washington, Ky., to start with his drove to the north. Ac-cordingly at the time I took a steamboat passage down to Maysville, near where I was to meet Mr. Smith with my trunk. When I arrived at Maysville, I found that Washington was still six miles back from the river. I stopped at a hotel and took my breakfast, and who should I see there but a captain of a boat, who saw me but two years previous going down the river Ohio with handcuffs on, in a chain gang; but he happened not to know me. I left my trunk at the hotel and went out to Washington, where I found Mr. Smith, and learned that he was not going to start off with his drove until the next day.

The following letter which was addressed to the committee to investigate the truth of my narrative, will explain this part of it to the reader and corrobo-rate my statements:

MAUMEE CITY, April 5, 1845.

CHAS. H. STEWART, ESQ.

DEAR SIR:—Your favor of 13th February, addressed to me at Perrysburgh, was not received until yesterday; having removed to this place the letter was not forwarded as it should have been. In reply to your inquiry respecting Henry Bibb, I can only say that about the year 1838 I became acquainted with him at Perrysbugh—employed him to do some work by the job which he performed well, and from his apparent honesty and candor, I became much interested in him. About that time he went South for the purpose, as was said, of getting his wife, who was there in slavery. In the spring of 1841, I found him at Portsmouth on the Ohio river, and after much persuasion, employed him to assist my man to drive home some horses and cattle which I was about purchasing near Maysville, Ky. My confidence in him was such that when about half way home I separated the horses from the cattle, and left him with the latter, with money and instructions to hire what help he wanted to get to Perrysburgh. This he accomplished to my entire satisfaction. He worked for me during the summer, and I was unwilling to part with him, but his desire to go to school and mature plans for the liberation of his wife, were so strong that he left for Detroit where he could enjoy the society of his colored brethren. I have heard his story and must say that I have not the least reason to suspect it being otherwise than true, and furthermore, I firmly believe, and have for a long time, that he has the foundation to make himself useful. I shall always afford him all the facilities in my power to assist him, until I hear of something in relation to him to alter my mind.

Yours in the cause of truth,

J. W. SMITH.

When I arrived at Perrysburgh, I went to work for Mr. Smith for several months. This family I found to be one of the most kind-hearted, and unprejudiced that I ever lived with. Mr. and Mrs. Smith lived up to their profession.

I resolved to go to Detroit, that winter, and go to school, in January 1842. But when I arrived at Detroit I soon found that I was not able to give myself a very thorough education. I was among strangers, who were not disposed to show me any great favors. I had every thing to pay for, and clothing to buy, so I graduated within three weeks! And this was all the schooling that I have ever had in my life.

W. C. Monroe was my teacher; to him I went about two weeks only. My occupation varied according to circumstances, as I was not settled in mind about the condition of my bereaved family for several years, and could nor settle myself down at any permanent business. I saw occasionally, fugitives from Kentucky, some of whom I knew, but none of them were my relatives; none could give me the information which I desired most.

CHAPTER XVII.

LETTER FROM W. H. GATEWOOD.—MY REPLY.—MY EFFORTS AS A PUBLIC LECTURER.—SINGULAR INCIDENT IN STEUBENVILLE—MEETING WITH A FRIEND OF WHITFIELD IN MICHIGAN.—OUTRAGE ON A CANAL PACKET.—FRUITLESS EFFORTS TO FIND MY WIFE.

THE first direct information that I received concerning any of my relations, after my last escape from slavery, was communicated in a letter from Wm. H.

Gatewood, my former owner, which I here insert word for word, without any correction:

BEDFORD, TRIMBLE COUNTY, KY.

MR. H. BIBB.

DEAR SIR:—After my respects to you and yours &c., I received a small book which you sent to me that I peroseed and found it was sent by H. Bibb I am a stranger in Detroit and know no man there without it is Walton H. Bibb if this be the man please to write to me and tell me all about that place and the people I will tell you the news here as well as I can your mother is still living here and she is well the people are generally well in this cuntry times are dull and produce low give my compliments to King, Jack, and all my friends in that cuntry I read that book you sent me and think it will do very well—George is sold, I do not know any thing about him I have nothing more at present, but remain yours &c

W. H GATEWOOD.

February 9th, 1844.
P. S. You will please to answer this letter.

Never was I more surprised than at the reception of this letter, it came so unexpected to me. There had just been a State Convention held in Detroit, by the free people of color, the proceedings of which were published in pamphlet form. I forwarded several of them to distinguished slaveholders in Kentucky—one among others was Mr. Gatewood, and gave him to understand who sent it. After showing this letter to several of my anti-slavery friends, and asking their opinions about the propriety of my answering it, I was advised to do it, as Mr. Gatewood had no claim on me as a slave, for he had sold and got the money for me and my family. So I wrote him an answer, as near as I can recollect, in the following language:

"DEAR SIR:—I am happy to inform you that you are not mistaken in the man whom you sold as property, and received pay for as such. But I thank God that I am not property now, but am regarded as a man like yourself, and although I live far north I am enjoying a comfortable living by my own industry. If you should ever chance to be traveling this way, and will call on me, I will use you better than you did me while you held me as a slave. Think not that I have any malice against you, for the cruel treatment which you inflicted on me while I was in your power. As it was the custom of your country, to treat your fellow men as you did me and my little family, I can freely forgive you.

I wish to be remembered in love to my aged mother, and friends; please tell her that if we should never meet again in this life, my prayer shall be to God that we may meet in Heaven, where parting shall be no more.

"You wish to be remembered to King and Jack. I am pleased, sir, to inform you that they are both here, well, and doing well. They are both living in Canada West. They are now the owners of better farms than the men are who once owned them.

You may perhaps think hard of us for running away from slavery, but as to myself, I have but one apology to make for it, which is this: I have only to regret that I did not start at an earlier period. I might have been free long before I was. But you had it in your power to have kept me there much longer than you did. I think it is very probable that I should have been a toiling slave on your plantation to-day, if you had treated me differently.

To be compelled to stand by and see you whip and slash my wife without mercy, when I could afford her no protection, not even by offering myself to suffer the lash in her place, was more than I felt it to be the duty of a slave husband to endure, while the way was open to Canada. My infant child was also frequently flogged by Mrs. Gatewood, for crying, until its skin was bruised literally purple. This kind of treatment was what drove me from home and family, to seek a better home for them. But I am willing to forget the past. I should be pleased to hear from you again, on the reception of this, and should also be very happy to correspond with you often, if it should be agreeable to yourself. I subscribe myself a friend to the oppressed, and Liberty forever.

HENRY BIBB.

WILLIAM GATEWOOD.
Detroit, March 23d, 1844.

The first time that I ever spoke before a public audience, was to give a narration of my own sufferings and adventures, connected with slavery. I commenced in the village of Adrian, State of Michigan, May, 1844. From that up to the present period, the principle part of my time has been faithfully devoted to the cause of freedom—nerved up and encouraged by the sympathy of anti-slavery friends on the one hand, and prompted by a sense of duty to my enslaved countrymen on the other, especially, when I remembered that slavery had robbed me of my freedom—deprived me of education—banished me from my native State, and robbed me of my family.

I went from Michigan to the State of Ohio, where I traveled over some of the Southern counties of that State, in company with Samuel Brooks, and Amos Dresser, lecturing upon the subject of American Slavery. The prejudice of the people at that time was very strong against the abolitionists; so much so that they were frequently mobbed for discussing the subject.

We appointed a series of meetings along on the Ohio River, in sight of the State of Virginia; and in several places we had Virginians over to hear us upon the subject. I recollect our having appointed a meeting in the city of Steubenville, which is situated on the bank of the river Ohio. There was but one known abolitionist living in that city, named George Ore. On the day of our meeting, when we arrived in this splendid city there was not a church, school house, nor hall, that we could get for love or money, to hold our meeting in. Finally, I believe that the whigs consented to let us have the use of their club room, to hold the meeting in; but before the hour had arrived for us to commence, they re-considered the matter, and informed us that we could not have the use of their house for an abolition meeting.

We then got permission to hold forth in the public market house, and even then so great was the hostility of the rabble, that they tried to bluff us off, by threats and epithets. Our meeting was advertised to take place at nine o'clock, A. M. The pro-slavery parties hired a colored man to take a large auction bell, and go all over the city ringing it, and crying, "ho ye! ho ye! Negro auction to take place in the market house, at nine o'clock, by George Ore!" This cry was sounded all over the city, which called out many who would not otherwise have been present. They came to see if it was really the case. The object of the rabble in having the bell rung was, to prevent us from attempting to speak. But at the appointed hour, Bro. Dresser opened the meeting with prayer and Samuel Brooks mounted the block and spoke for fifteen or twenty minutes, after which Mr. Dresser took the block and talked about one hour upon the wickedness of slaveholding. There were not yet many persons present. They were standing off I suppose to see if I was to be offered for sale. Many windows were hoisted and store doors open, and they were looking and listening to what was said. After Mr. Dresser was through, I was called to take the stand. Just at this moment there was no small stir in rushing forward; so much indeed, that I thought they were coming up to mob me. I should think that in less than fifteen minutes there were about one thousand persons standing around, listening. I saw many of them shedding tears while I related the sad story of my wrongs. At twelve o'clock we adjourned the meeting, to meet again at the same place at two P. M. Our afternoon meeting was well attended until nearly sunset, at which time, we saw some signs of a mob and adjourned. The mob followed us that night to the house of Mr. Ore, and they were yelling like tigers, until late that night, around the house, as if they wanted to tear it down.

In the fall of 1844, S. B. Treadwell, of Jackson, and myself, spent two or three months in lecturing through the State of Michigan, upon the abolition of slavery, in a section of country where abolitionists were few and far between. Our meetings were generally appointed in small log cabins, school houses, among the farmers, which were some times crowded full; and where they had no horse teams, it was often the case that there would be four or five ox teams come, loaded down with men, women and children, to attend our meetings.

But the people were generally poor, and in many places not able to give us a decent night's lodging. We most generally carried with us a few pounds of candles to light up the houses wherein we held our meetings after night; for in many places, they had neither candles nor candlesticks. After meeting was out, we have frequently gone from three to eight miles to get lodging, through the dark forest, where there was scarcely any road for a wagon to run on.

I have traveled for miles over swamps, where the roads were covered with logs, without any dirt over them, which has sometimes shook and jostled the wagon to pieces, where we could find no shop or any place to mend it. We would have to tie it up with bark, or take the lines to tie it with, and lead the horse by the bridle. At other times we were in mud up to the hubs of the wheels. I recollect one evening, we lectured in a little village where there happened to be a Southerner present, who was a personal friend of Deacon Whitfield, who became much offended at what I said about his "Bro. Whitfield," and complained about it after the meeting was out.

He told the people not to believe a word that I said, that it was all a humbug. They asked him how he knew? "Ah!" said he, "he has slandered Bro. Whit-field. I am well acquainted with him, we both belonged to one church; and Whit-field is one of the most respectable men in all that region of country." They asked if he (Whitfield) was a slaveholder?

The reply was "yes, but he treated his slaves well."

"Well," said one, "that only proves that he has told us the truth; for all we wish to know, is that there is such a man as Whitfield, as represented by Bibb, and that he is a slave holder."

On the 2d Sept., 1847, I started from Toledo on board the canal packet Erie, for Cincinnati, Ohio. But before going on board, I was waited on by one of the boat's crew, who gave me a card of the boat, upon which was printed, that no pains would be spared to render all passengers comfortable who might favor them with their patronage to Cincinnati. This card I slipped into my pocket, supposing it might be of some use to me. There were several drunken loafers on board go-ing through as passengers, one of whom used the most vulgar language in the cabin, where there were ladies, and even vomited! But he was called a white man, and a southerner, which made it all right. I of course took my place in the cabin with the rest, and there was nothing said against it that night. When the passen-gers went forward to settle their fare I paid as much as any other man, which en-titled me to the same privileges. The next morning at the ringing of the breakfast bell, the proprietor of the packet line, Mr. Samuel Doyle, being on board, invited the passengers to sit up to breakfast. He also invited me personally to sit up to the table. But after we were all seated, and some had began to eat, he came and or-dered me up from the table, and said I must wait until the rest were done.

I left the table without making any reply, and walked out on the deck of the boat. After breakfast the passengers came up, and the cabin boy was sent after me to come to breakfast, but I refused. Shortly after, this man who had ordered me from the table, came up with the ladies. I stepped up and asked him if he was the captain of the boat. His answer was no, that he was one of the proprietors. I then informed him that I was going to leave his boat at the first stopping place, but be-fore leaving I wanted to ask him a few questions: "Have I misbehaved to any one on board of this boat? Have I disobeyed any law of this boat?"

"No," said he.

"Have I not paid you as much as any other passenger through to Cincin-nati?"

"Yes," said he.

"Then I am sure that I have been insulted and imposed upon, on board of this boat, without any just cause whatever."

"No one has misused you, for you ought to have known better than to have come to the table where there were white people."

"Sir, did you not ask me to come to the table?"

"Yes, but I did not know that you was a colored man, when I asked you; and then it was better to insult one man than all the passengers on board of the boat."

"Sir, I do not believe that there is a gentleman or lady on board of this boat who would have considered it an insult for me to have taken my breakfast, and you have imposed upon me by taking my money and promising to use me well, and then to insult me as you have."

"I don't want any of your jaw," said he.

"Sir, with all due respect to your elevated station, you have imposed upon me in a way which is unbecoming a gentleman. I have paid my money, and behaved myself as well as any other man, and I am determined that no man shall impose on me as you have, by deceiving me, without my letting the world know it. I would rather a man should rob me of my money at midnight, than to take it in that way."

I left this boat at the first stopping place, and took the next boat to Cincinnati. On the last boat I had no cause to complain of my treatment. When I arrived at Cincinnati, I published a statement of this affair in the Daily Herald.

The next day Mr. Doyle called on the editor in a great passion.—"Here," said he, "what does this mean."

"What, sir?" said the editor quietly.

"Why, the stuff here, read it and see."

"Read it yourself," answered the editor.

"Well, I want to know if you sympathize with this nigger here."

"Who, Mr. Bibb? Why yes, I think he is a gentleman, and should be used as such."

"Why this is all wrong—all of it."

"Put your finger on the place, and I will right it."

"Well, he says that we took his money, when we paid part back. And if you take his part, why I'll have nothing to do with your paper."

So ended his wrath.

In 1845, the anti-slavery friends of Michigan employed me to take the field as an anti-slavery Lecturer, in that State, during the Spring, Summer, and Fall, pledging themselves to restore to me my wife and child, if they were living, and could be reached by human agency, which may be seen by the following circular from the Signal of Liberty:

TO LIBERTY FRIENDS:—In the Signal of the 28th inst. is a report from the undersigned respecting Henry Bibb. His narrative always excites deep sympathy for himself and favorable bias for the cause, which seeks to abolish the evils he so powerfully portrays. Friends and foes attest his efficiency.

Mr. Bibb has labored much in lecturing, yet has collected but a bare pittance. He has received from Ohio lucrative offers, but we have prevailed on him to remain in this State.

We think that a strong obligation rests on the friends in this State to sustain Mr. Bibb, and restore to him his wife and child. Under the expectation that Michigan will yield to these claims: will support their laborer, and re-unite the long severed ties of husband and wife, parent and child, Mr. Bibb will lecture through the whole State.

Our object is to prepare friends for the visit of Mr. Bibb, and to suggest an effective mode of operations for the whole State.

Let friends in each vicinity appoint a collector—pay to him all contributions for the freedom of Mrs. Bibb and child: then transmit them to us. We will acknowledge them in the Signal, and be responsible for them. We will see that the proper measures for the freedom of Mrs. Bibb and child are taken, and if it be within our means we will accomplish it—nay we will accomplish it, if the objects be living and the friends sustain us. But should we fail, the contributions will be held subject to the order of the donors, less however, by a proportionate deduction of expenses from each.

The hope of this re-union will nerve the heart and body of Mr. Bibb to redoubled effort in a cause otherwise dear to him. And as he will devote his whole time systematically to the anti-slavery cause he must also depend on friends for the means of livelihood. We bespeak for him your hospitality, and such pecuniary contributions as you can afford, trusting that the latter may be sufficient to enable him to keep the field.

A. L. PORTER,
C. H. STEWART,
SILAS M. HOLMES

DETROIT, APRIL 22, 1845.

I have every reason to believe that they acted faithfully in the matter, but without success. They wrote letters in every quarter where they would be likely to gain any information respecting her. There were also two men sent from Michigan in the summer of 1845, down South, to find her if possible, and report—and whether they found out her condition, and refused to report, I am not able to say—but suffice it to say that they never have reported. They were respectable men and true friends of the cause, one of whom was a Methodist minister, and the other a cabinet maker, and both white men.

The small spark of hope which had still lingered about my heart had almost become extinct.

CHAPTER XVIII.

MY LAST EFFORT TO RECOVER MY FAMILY.—SAD TIDINGS OF MY WIFE.—HER DEGRADATION.—I AM COMPELLED TO REGARD OUR RELATION AS DISSOLVED FOREVER.

IN view of the failure to hear any thing of my wife, many of my best friends advised me to get married again, if I could find a suitable person. They regarded my former wife as dead to me, and all had been done that could be.

But I was not yet satisfied myself, to give up. I wanted to know certainly what had become of her. So in the winter of 1845, I resolved to go back to Kentucky, my native State, to see if I could hear anything from my family. And against the advice of all my friends, I went back to Cincinnati, where I took passage on board of a Southern steamboat to Madison, in the State of Indiana, which was only ten miles from where Wm. Gatewood lived, who was my former owner. No sooner had I landed in Madison, than I learned, on inquiry, and from good authority, that my wife was living in a state of adultery with her master, and had been for the last three years. This message she sent back to Kentucky, to her mother and friends. She also spoke of the time and manner of our separation by Deacon Whitfield, my being taken off by the Southern black legs, to where she knew not; and that she had finally given me up. The child she said was still with her. Whitfield had sold her to this man for the above purposes at a high price, and she was better used than ordinary slaves. This was a death blow to all my hopes and pleasant plans. While I was in Madison I hired a white man to go over to Bedford, in Kentucky, where my mother was then living, and bring her over into a free State to see me. I hailed her approach with unspeakable joy. She informed me too, on inquiring whether my family had ever been heard from, that the report which I had just heard in relation to Malinda was substantially true, for it was the same message that she had sent to her mother and friends. And my mother thought it was no use for me to run any more risks, or to grieve myself any more about her.

From that time I gave her up into the hands of an all-wise Providence. As she was then living with another man, I could no longer regard her as my wife. After all the sacrifices, sufferings, and risks which I had run, striving to rescue her from the grasp of slavery; every prospect and hope was cut off. She has ever since been regarded as theoretically and practically dead to me as a wife, for she was living in a state of adultery, according to the law of God and man.

Poor unfortunate woman, I bring no charge of guilt against her, for I know not all the circumstances connected with the case. It is consistent with slavery, however, to suppose that she became reconciled to it, from the fact of her sending word back to her friends and relatives that she was much better treated than she had ever been before, and that she had also given me up. It is also reasonable to suppose that there might have been some kind of attachment formed by living together in this way for years; and it is quite probable that they have other children according to the law of nature, which would have a tendency to unite them stronger together.

In view of all the facts and circumstances connected with this matter, I deem further comments and explanations unnecessary on my part. Finding myself thus isolated in this peculiarly unnatural state, I resolved, in 1846, to spend my days in traveling, to advance the anti-slavery cause. I spent the summer in Michigan, but in the subsequent fall I took a trip to New England, where I spent the winter. And there I found a kind reception wherever I traveled among the friends of freedom.

While traveling about in this way among strangers, I was sometimes sick, with no permanent home, or bosom friend to sympathise or take that care of me which an affectionate wife would. So I conceived the idea that it would be better for me to change my position, provided I should find a suitable person.

In the month of May, 1847, I attended the anti-slavery anniversary in the city of New York, where I had the good fortune to be introduced to the favor of a Miss Mary E. Miles, of Boston; a lady whom I had frequently heard very highly spoken of, for her activity and devotion to the anti-slavery cause, as well as her talents and learning, and benevolence in the cause of reforms, generally. I was very much impressed with the personal appearance of Miss Miles, and was deeply interested in our first interview, because I found that her principles and my own were nearly one and the same. I soon found by a few visits, as well as by letters, that she possessed moral principle, and frankness of disposition, which is often sought for but seldom found. These, in connection with other amiable qualities, soon won my entire confidence and affection. But this secret I kept to myself until I was fully satisfied that this feeling was reciprocal; that there was indeed a congeniality of principles and feeling, which time nor eternity could never change.

When I offered myself for matrimony, we mutually engaged ourselves to each other, to marry in one year, with this condition, viz: that if either party should see any reason to change their mind within that time, the contract should not be considered binding. We kept up a regular correspondence during the time, and in June, 1848, we had the happiness to be joined in holy wedlock. Not in slaveholding style, which is a mere farce, without the sanction of law or gospel; but in accordance with the laws of God and our country. My beloved wife is a bosom friend, a help-meet, a loving companion in all the social, moral, and religious relations of life. She is to me what a poor slave's wife can never be to her husband while in the condition of a slave; for she can not be true to her husband contrary to the will of her master. She can neither be pure nor virtuous, contrary to the will of her master. She dare not refuse to be reduced to a state of adultery at the will of her master; from the fact that the slaveholding law, customs and teachings are all against the poor slaves.

I presume there are no class of people in the United States who so highly appreciate the legality of marriage as those persons who have been held and treated as property. Yes, it is that fugitive who knows from sad experience, what it is to have his wife tyrannically snatched from his bosom by a slaveholding professor of religion, and finally reduced to a state of adultery, that knows how to appreciate the law that repels such high-handed villany. Such as that to which the writer has been exposed. But thanks be to God, I am now free from the hand of the cruel oppressor, no more to be plundered of my dearest rights; the wife of my bosom, and my poor unoffending offspring. Of Malinda I will only add a word in conclusion. The relation once subsisting between us, to which I clung, hoping against hope, for years, after we were torn assunder, not having been sanctioned by any loyal power, cannot be cancelled by a legal process. Voluntarily assumed without law mutually, it was by her relinquished years ago without my knowledge, as before named; during which time I was making every effort to secure her restoration. And it was not until after living alone in the world for more than eight years without a companion known in law or morals, that I changed my condition.

CHAPTER XIX.

COMMENTS ON S. GATEWOOD'S LETTER ABOUT SLAVES STEALING. — THEIR CONDUCT VINDICATED. — COMMENTS ON W. GATEWOOD'S LETTER.

BUT it seems that I am not now beyond the reach of the foul slander of slaveholders. They are not satisfied with selling and banishing me from my native State. As soon as they got news of my being in the free North, exposing their peculiar Institution, a libelous letter was written by Silas Gatewood of Kentucky, a son of one of my former owners, to a Northern Committee, for publication, which he thought would destroy my influence and character. This letter will be found in the introduction.

He has charged me with the awful crime of taking from my keeper and oppressor, some of the fruits of my own labor for the benefit of myself and family.

But while writing this letter he seems to have overlooked the disgraceful fact that he was guilty himself of what would here be regarded highway robbery, in his conduct to me as narrated on page 87 [page 46 in this edition] of this narrative.

A word in reply to Silas Gatewood's letter. I am willing to admit all that is true, but shall deny that which is so basely false. In the first place, he puts words in my mouth that I never used. He says that I represented that "my mother belonged to James Bibb." I deny ever having said so in private or public. He says that I stated that Bibb's daughter married a Sibley. I deny it. He also says that the first time that I left Kentucky for my liberty, I was gone about two years, before I went back to rescue my family. I deny it. I was gone from Dec. 25th, 1837, to May, or June, 1838. He says that I went back the second time for the purpose of taking off my family, and eight or ten more slaves to Canada. This I will not pretend to deny. He says I was guilty of disposing of articles from the farm for my own use, and pocketing the money, and that his father caught me stealing a sack full of wheat. I admit the fact. I acknowledge the wheat.

And who had a better right to eat of the fruits of my own hard earnings than myself? Many a long summer's day have I toiled with my wife and other slaves, cultivating his father's fields, and gathering in his harvest, under the scorching rays of the sun, without half enough to eat, or clothes to wear, and at the same time his meat-house was filled with bacon and bread stuff; his dairy with butter and cheese; his barn with grain, husbanded by the unrequited toil of the slaves. And yet if a slave presumed to take a little from the abundance which he had made by his own sweat and toil, to supply the demands of nature, to quiet the craving appetite which is sometimes almost irresistible, it is called stealing by slaveholders.

But I did not regard it as stealing then, I do not regard it as such now. I hold that a slave has a moral right to eat drink and wear all that he needs, and that it would be a sin on his part to suffer and starve in a country where there is a plenty to eat and wear within his reach. I consider that I had a just right to what I took, because it was the labor of my own hands. Should I take from a neighbor as a freeman, in a free country, I should consider myself guilty of doing wrong before God and man. But was I the slave of Wm. Gatewood to-day, or any other slaveholder, working without wages, and suffering with hunger or for clothing, I should not stop to inquire whether my master would approve of my helping myself to what I needed to eat or wear. For while the slave is regarded as property, how can he steal from his master? It is contrary to the very nature of the relation existing between master and slave, from the fact that there is no law to punish a slave for theft, but lynch law; and the way they avoid that is to hide well. For illustration, a slave from the State of Virginia, for cruel treatment left the State between daylight and dark, being borne off by one of his master's finest horses, and finally landed in Canada, where the British laws recognise no such thing as property in a human being. He was pursued by his owners, who expected to take advantage of the British law by claiming him as a fugitive from justice, and as such he was arrested and brought before the court of Queen's Bench. They swore that he was, at a certain time, the slave of Mr. A., and that he ran away at such a time and stole and brought off a horse. They enquired who the horse belonged to and it was ascertained that the slave and horse both belonged to the same person. The court therefore decided that the horse and the man were both recognised, in the State of Virginia, alike, as articles of property, belonging to the same person—therefore, if there was theft committed on either side, the former must have stolen off the latter—the horse brought away the man, and not the man the horse. So the man was discharged and pronounced free according to the laws of Canada. There are several other letters published in this work upon the same subject, from slaveholders, which it is hardly necessary for me to notice. However, I feel thankful to the writers for the endorsement and confirmation which they have given to my story. No matter what their motives were, they have done me and the anti-slavery cause good service in writing those letters—but more especially the Gatewood's. Silas Gatewood has done more for me than all the rest. He has labored so hard in his long communication in trying to expose me, that he has proved every thing that I could have asked of him; and for which I intend to reward him by forwarding him one of my books, hoping that it may be the means of converting him from a slaveholder to an honest man, and an advocate of liberty for all mankind.

The reader will see in the introduction that Wm. Gatewood writes a more cautious letter upon the subject than his son Silas. "It is not a very easy matter to catch old birds with chaff," and I presume if Silas had the writing of his letter over again, he would not be so free in telling all he knew, and even more, for the sake of making out a strong case. The object of his writing such a letter will doubtless be understood by the reader. It was to destroy public confidence in the victims of slavery, that the system might not be exposed—it was to gag a poor fugitive who had undertaken to plead his own cause and that of his enslaved brethren. It was a feeble attempt to suppress the voice of universal freedom which is now thundering on every gale. But thank God it is too late in the day.

> Go stop the mighty thunder's roar,
> Go hush the ocean's sound,
> Or upward like the eagle soar
> To skies' remotest bound.
>
> And when thou hast the thunder stopped,
> And hushed the ocean's waves,
> Then, freedom's spirit bind in chains,
> And ever hold us slaves.
>
> And when the eagle's boldest feat,
> Thou canst perform with skill,
> Then, think to stop proud freedom's march
> And hold the bondman still.

CHAPTER XX.

Review of my narrative.—Licentiousness a prop of slavery.—A case of mild slavery given.—Its revolting features.—Times of my purchase and sale by professed Christians.—Concluding remarks.

I NOW conclude my narrative, by reviewing briefly what I have written. This little work has been written without any personal aid or a knowledge of the English grammer, which must in part be my apology for many of its imperfections.

I find in several places, where I have spoken out the deep feelings of my soul, in trying to describe the horrid treatment which I have so often received at the hands of slaveholding professors of religion, that I might possibly make a wrong impression on the minds of some northern freemen, who are unacquainted theoretically or practically with the customs and treatment of American slaveholders to their slaves. I hope that it may not be supposed by any, that I have exaggerated in the least, for the purpose of making out the system of slavery worse than it really is, for, to exaggerate upon the cruelties of this system, would be almost impossible; and to write herein the most horrid features of it would not be in good taste for my book.

I have long thought from what has fallen under my own observation while a slave, that the strongest reason why southerners stick with such tenacity to their "peculiar institution," is because licentious white men could not carry out their wicked purposes among the defenceless colored population as they now do, without being exposed and punished by law, if slavery was abolished. Female virtue could not be trampled under foot with impurity, and marriage among the people of color kept in utter obscurity.

On the other hand, lest it should be said by slaveholders and their apologists, that I have not done them the justice to give a sketch of the best side of slavery, if there can be any best side to it, therefore in conclusion, they may have the benefit of the following case, that fell under the observation of the writer. And I challenge America to show a milder state of slavery than this. I once knew a Methodist in the state of Ky., by the name of Young, who was the owner of a large number of slaves, many of whom belonged to the same church with their master. They worshipped together in the same church.

Mr. Young never was known to flog one of his slaves or sell one. He fed and clothed them well, and never over-worked them. He allowed each family a small house to themselves with a little garden spot, whereon to raise their own vegetables; and a part of the day on Saturdays was allowed them to cultivate it.

In process of time he became deeply involved in debt by endorsing notes, and his property was all advertised to be sold by the sheriff at public auction. It consisted in slaves, many of whom were his brothers and sisters in the church.

On the day of sale there were slave traders and speculators on the ground to buy. The slaves were offered on the auction block one after another until they were all sold before their old master's face. The first man offered on the block was an old gray-headed slave by the name of Richard. His wife followed him up to the block, and when they had bid him up to seventy or eighty dollars one of the bidders asked Mr. Young what he could do, as he looked very old and infirm? Mr. Young replied by saying, "he is not able to accomplish much manual labor, from his extreme age and hard labor in early life. Yet I would rather have him than many of those who are young and vigorous; who are able to perform twice as much labor—because I know him to be faithful and trustworthy, a Christian in good standing in my church. I can trust him anywhere with confidence. He has toiled many long years on my plantation and I have always found him faithful.

This giving him a good Christian character caused them to run him up to near two hundred dollars. His poor old companion stood by weeping and pleading that they might not be separated. But the marriage relation was soon dissolved by the sale, and they were separated never to meet again.

Another man was called up whose wife followed him with her infant in her arms, beseeching to be sold with her husband, which proved to be all in vain. After the men were all sold they then sold the women and children. They ordered the first woman to lay down her child and mount the auction block; she refused to give up her little one and clung to it as long as she could, while the cruel lash was applied to her back for disobedience. She pleaded for mercy in the name of God. But the child was torn from the arms of its mother amid the most heart rending shrieks from the mother and child on the one hand, and bitter oaths and cruel lashes from the tyrants on the other. Finally the poor little child was torn from the mother while she was sacrificed to the highest bidder. In this way the sale was carried on from beginning to end.

There was each speculator with his hand-cuffs to bind his victims after the sale; and while they were doing their writings, the Christian portion of the slaves asked permission to kneel in prayer on the ground before they separated, which was granted. And while bathing each other with tears of sorrow on the verge of their final separation, their eloquent appeals in prayer to the Most High seemed to cause an unpleasant sensation upon the ears of their tyrants, who ordered them to rise and make ready their limbs for the coffles. And as they happened not to bound at the first sound, they were soon raised from their knees by the sound of the lash, and the rattle of the chains, in which they were soon taken off by their respective masters,—husbands from wives, and children from parents, never expecting to meet until the judgment of the great day. Then Christ shall say to the slaveholding professors of religion, "Inasmuch as ye did it unto one of the least of these little ones, my brethren, ye did it unto me."[24]

Having thus tried to show the best side of slavery that I can conceive of, the reader can exercise his own judgment in deciding whether a man can be a Bible Christian, and yet hold his Christian brethren as property, so that they may be sold at any time in market, as sheep or oxen, to pay his debts.

During my life in slavery I have been sold by professors of religion several times. In 1836 "Bro." Albert G. Sibley, of Bedford, Kentucky, sold me for $850 to "Bro." John Sibley; and in the same year he sold me to "Bro." Wm. Gatewood of Bedford, for $850. In 1839 "Bro." Gatewood sold me to Madison Garrison, a slave trader, of Louisville, Kentucky, with my wife and child—at a depreciated price because I was a runaway. In the same year he sold me with my family to "Bro." Whitfield, in the city of New Orleans, for $1200. In 1841 "Bro." Whitfield sold me from my family to Thomas Wilson and Co., blacklegs. In the same year they sold me to a "Bro." in the Indian Territory. I think he was a member of the Presbyterian Church. F. E. Whitfield was a deacon in regular standing in the Baptist Church. A. Sibley was a Methodist exhorter of the M. E. Church in good standing. J. Sibley was a class-leader in the same church; and Wm. Gatewood was also an acceptable member of the same church.

Is this Christianity? Is it honest or right? Is it doing as we would be done by? Is it in accordance with the principles of humanity or justice?

I believe slaveholding to be a sin against God and man under all circumstances. I have no sympathy with the person or persons who tolerate and support the system willingly and knowingly, morally, religiously or politically.

Prayerfully and earnestly relying on the power of truth, and the aid of the divine providence, I trust that this little volume will bear some humble part in lighting up the path of freedom and revolutionizing public opinion upon this great subject. And I here pledge myself, God being my helper, ever to contend for the natural equality of the human family, without regard to color, which is but fading *matter*, while *mind* makes the man.

New York City, *May* 1, 1849.

HENRY BIBB.

INDEX.

1. Starling, *Slave Narrative,* 149–150.

2. Andrews, *Free Story,* 158.

3. Stepto, "I Rose and Found," 228.

4. Bibb, *Narrative* (3d ed.), 205–207.

5. Blassingame, "Bibb, Henry Walton," 44.

6. Quarles, *Black Abolitionists,* 61–62.

7. Matlack was a Methodist minister who was deprived of his license to preach for being an ardent abolitionist. He spoke widely on abolitionism, wrote two personal narratives and several histories of Methodism and the antislavery movement, and edited *The Life of Rev. Orange Scott,* who was another abolitionist Methodist minister.

8. Members of the Liberty party (1840–48), an abolitionist political party led by James G. Birney and Gerrit Smith.

9. A black settlement in Canada.

10. One of the trustees of the British American Institute of Science and Industry in Dawn, Canada.

11. Ross Wilkins (1799–1872) was a U.S. district judge in Michigan from 1837 to 1870.

12. In northern Kentucky, just west of Frankfort.

13. James Bibb was a Kentucky state senator.

14. The first and third lines of this poem appear in Abby H. Price's "The Slave-Mother," first published in *The Liberator* in 1843. See Eaklor, *American Antislavery Songs,* 319–320.

15. *Pat juba*—pat rhythms on the knees.

16. See *Colossians* 3:22, *Luke* 12:47.

17. Joseph Brevard (1766–1821), *An Alphabetical Digest of the Public Statute Law of South-Carolina* (1814). An 1800 South Carolina law uses the same wording.

18. William Cowper (1731–1800), "Light Shining Out of Darkness."

19. Between 1840 and 1863 all banking was done by state-chartered institutions; this led to "wildcat" banking in many Western states because of laxity and abuse of state laws. Each bank issued its own currency against little or no security, leading to hyperinflation and over-expanded credit.

20. Episcopal.

21. See *Matthew* 8:12, 13:42, 13:50, 22:13, 24:51, 25:30, and *Luke* 13:28.

22. A chain used for hauling logs.

23. Louisiana; on the Arkansas border.

24. See *Matthew* 25:40.

JAMES W. C. PENNINGTON

JAMES WILLIAM CHARLES PENNINGTON (1807–70) was a well-known abolitionist and minister in the three decades preceding the Civil War, and was one of the most educated and literate black men of his time. Born James Pembroke, he renamed himself Pennington after his escape from slavery in 1828; the name was fitting for a man who had made a steel pen six years earlier, and who would devote many of his best efforts in wielding a pen on behalf of his fellow African Americans.

His 1849 narrative, *The Fugitive Blacksmith,* which eloquently relates a thrilling and at times droll escape from bondage, is concerned primarily with questions of property and ownership. The letter that opens the narrative is devoted to a discussion of the "chattel principle"; Pennington's departure from slavery is precipitated by an incident in which his owner claims to be master of his father's tongue; the book's central event revolves around Pennington's ownership of his history and identity; and the letter that closes the narrative—addressed to his former master—is, as Lucinda MacKethan writes, "spectacularly ironic" in predicting a complete reversal of the master/slave relationship.[1]

Perhaps the most interesting of these is the book's central event, which Pennington highlights by placing it under a subhead reading "GREAT MORAL DILEMMA." In it, he tells a lie as resourceful and inventive as any in the trickster-slave tradition. He then justifies it with a sophisticated argument claiming that the "facts" of his background are his "private property" to do with as he wishes, and, in a radical affirmation of subjectivity, calls his own story "*my* truth." For Pennington as for other slave narrators, such stories were the only things a slave *could* own.[2]

After his escape, Pennington settled in Brooklyn, where he was elected a delegate to the first Negro convention, held in Philadelphia. Educating himself, he became proficient in Latin and Greek, and taught at a school for blacks in Newtown, Long Island. He subsequently tried to enroll at the School of Divinity at Yale University, but was prevented from participating in classes or borrowing books from the library because of his color. He attended lectures nevertheless, and was licensed to preach in 1838.[3]

In 1840 Pennington moved to Hartford, where he was pastor of the Talcott Street Colored Congregational Church, president of the Connecticut State Temperance and Moral Reform Society, and teacher at the North African School. In 1841 he wrote *A Text Book of the Origin and History of the Colored People,* one of the earliest black-authored history books, which was largely devoted to refuting theories of racial inferiority. He continued to be active in the Negro convention meetings, giving speeches and writing articles; and in 1841 he founded and became the first president of the Union Missionary Society (later the American Missionary Association), devoted to bringing the gospel to Africa and other "benighted lands." Named a delegate to both the World Anti Slavery Convention and the first Peace Congress, he traveled to England in 1843, where he made a favorable impression at the convention, met the poet and abolitionist Thomas Campbell as well as many of England's leading divines, and gave lectures across the country.[4]

Meanwhile Pennington had kept the fact that he was a fugitive slave secret from all who knew him, even his own wife, for fear of recapture. In 1844, however, the secret finally leaked out, and he entered into futile negotiations to buy his and his family's freedom. He moved back to New York City in 1848, becoming pastor of the First Colored Presbyterian Church (later called Shiloh). But in 1849, concurrent with a rise in the number of slave catchers in New York, Pennington went to England, hoping to counter the influence there of the American Colonization Society.[5]

In London he published *The Fugitive Blacksmith*, which went through three editions in quick succession between August 1849 and July 1850, selling six thousand copies or more. Reviews were favorable, one condescending reviewer even going so far as to comment, "No man, in the absence of information, could infer that the book before us was the production of a negro. The diction is so pure, the idiom so truly English, the observations generally so just and Christian, occasionally so penetrating and profound, that they could do credit to an Englishman of superior ability and regular education."[6] Pennington's preface to the third edition ingenuously characterized the book as follows:

> My object was to write an unexceptional book of the kind for children in point of matter, and for the masses in point of price. I believe both of these have been gained. I have been gratified also to find that my book has awakened a deep interest in the cause of the *American slave*. Since the second edition was printed, I have been constantly engaged in preaching and lecturing. I have spoken on an average five evenings weekly on slavery, temperance, missions, and Sabbath schools, and preached on an average three times each sabbath. In almost every instance where I have gone into a place, I have found the way prepared by the book. In some cases a single copy had been handed from one to another in the town, and some minister or leading gentleman has been prepared to speak of it at my meeting.[7]

In December 1849 the University of Heidelberg granted Pennington an honorary doctor of divinity degree. His freedom was purchased in May 1850, allowing Pennington to return to the United States. As R. J. M. Blackett writes, he "was now at the zenith of his career, acknowledged as one of the leading black figures in America, a reputation undoubtedly enhanced by his honorary doctorate and his being pastor of the largest black Presbyterian church in the country." He officiated at Frederick Douglass's wedding, played an active role in the Underground Railroad and the New York Vigilance Committee, and raised thousands of dollars for the latter organization.[8]

But his fortunes soon took a turn for the worse. He unsuccessfully brought suit against New York's streetcar companies for their policy of segregation; he was accused of misusing funds he had collected in Britain; and he exposed himself to attack by accepting the post of moderator of the Third Presbytery of New York, a church that had openly endorsed slaveholders' right to membership, and speaking out against non-Christian, or "infidel," abolitionists. Faced with these and other problems, Pennington, who had preached in favor of abstinence from drink, became an alcoholic. He left Shiloh in disgrace in 1856 and returned to his old church in Hartford.[9]

He went to England once again in 1861, where he edited and published the narrative of J. H. Banks, a fugitive Alabama slave. In 1862 he was jailed in Liverpool for a month for the theft of a copy of Pope's translation of the *Odyssey*. Shortly after his return to the United States, he left the Presbyterian church and joined the African Methodist Episcopal church; over the next few years he preached in Natchez, Mississippi; Portland, Maine; and Jacksonville, Florida, where he founded a church and a school. He died in poverty, alone, but still fighting for the betterment of African Americans.[10]

THE

FUGITIVE BLACKSMITH;

OR,

EVENTS IN THE HISTORY

OF

JAMES W. C. PENNINGTON,

PASTOR OF A PRESBYTERIAN CHURCH, NEW YORK,

FORMERLY A SLAVE IN THE STATE OF MARYLAND, UNITED STATES.

———

"Let mine outcasts dwell with thee, Moab; be thou a covert to them from the face of the spoiler.—ISAIAH xvi. 4.

———

LONDON:
CHARLES GILPIN, 5, BISHOPSGATE WITHOUT.

———

1849.

PREFACE.

THE brief narrative I here introduce to the public, consists of outline notes originally thrown together to guide my memory when lecturing on this part of the subject of slavery. This will account for its style, and will also show that the work is not full.

The question may be asked, Why I have published anything so long after my escape from slavery? I answer I have been induced to do so on account of the increasing disposition to overlook the fact, that THE SIN of slavery lies in the chattel principle, or relation. Especially have I felt anxious to save professing Christians, and my brethren in the ministry, from falling into a great mistake. My feelings are always outraged when I hear them speak of "kind masters,"—"Christian masters,"—"the mildest form of slavery,"—"well fed and clothed slaves," as extenuations of slavery; I am satisfied they either mean to pervert the truth, or they do not know what they say. The being of slavery, its soul and body, lives and moves in the chattel principle, the property principle, the bill of sale principle; the cart-whip, starvation, and nakedness, are its inevitable consequences to a greater or less extent, warring with the dispositions of men.

There lies a skein of silk upon a lady's work-table. How smooth and handsome are the threads. But while that lady goes out to make a call, a party of children enter the apartment, and in amusing themselves, tangle the skein of silk, and now who can untangle it? The relation between master and slave is even as delicate as a skein of silk: it is liable to be entangled at any moment.

The mildest form of slavery, if there be such a form, looking at the chattel principle as the definition of slavery, is comparatively the worst form. For it not only keeps the slave in the most unpleasant apprehension, like a prisoner in chains awaiting his trial; but it actually, in a great majority of cases, where kind masters do exist, trains him under the most favourable circumstances the system admits of, and then plunges him into the worst of which it is capable.

It is under the mildest form of slavery, as it exists in Maryland, Virginia, and Kentucky, that the finest specimens of coloured females are reared. There are no mothers who rear, and educate in the natural graces, finer daughters than the Ethiopian women, who have the least chance to give scope to their maternal affections. But what is generally the fate of such female slaves? When they are not raised for the express purpose of supplying the market of a class of economical Louisian and Mississippi gentlemen, who do not wish to incur the expense of rearing legitimate families, they are, nevertheless, on account of their attractions, exposed to the most shameful degradation, by the young masters in the families where it is claimed they are so well off. My master[11] once owned a beautiful girl about twenty-four. She had been raised in a family where her mother was a great favourite. She was her mother's darling child. Her master was a lawyer of eminent abilities and great fame, but owing to habits of intemperance, he failed in business, and my master purchased this girl for a nurse. After he had owned her about a year, one of his sons became attached to her, for no honourable purposes; a fact which was not only well-known among all of the slaves, but which became a source of unhappiness to his mother and sisters.

The result was, that poor Rachel had to be sold to "Georgia." Never shall I forget the heart-rending scene, when one day one of the men was ordered to get "the one-horse cart ready to go into town;" Rachel, with her few articles of clothing, was placed in it, and taken into the very town where her parents lived, and there sold to the traders before their weeping eyes. That same son who had degraded her, and who was the cause of her being sold, acted as salesman, and bill of saleman. While this cruel business was being transacted, my master stood aside, and the girl's father, a pious member and exhorter in the Methodist Church, a venerable grey-headed man, with his hat off, besought that he might be allowed to get some one in the place to purchase his child. But no; my master was invincible. His reply was, "She has offended in my family, and I can only restore confidence by sending her out of hearing." After lying in prison a short time, her new owner took her with others to the far South, where her parents heard no more of her.

Here was a girl born and reared under the mildest form of slavery. Her original master was reputed to be even indulgent. He lived in a town, and was a high bred gentleman, and a lawyer. He had but a few slaves, and had no occasion for an overseer, those negro leeches, to watch and drive them; but when he became embarrassed by his own folly, the chattel principle doomed this girl to be sold at the same sale with his books, house, and horses. With my master she found herself under far more stringent discipline than she had been accustomed to, and finally degraded, and sold where her condition could not be worse, and where she had not the least hope of ever bettering it.

This case presents the legitimate working of the great chattel principle. It is no accidental result—it is the fruit of the tree. You cannot constitute slavery without the chattel principle—and with the chattel principle you cannot save it from these results. Talk not then about kind and christian masters. They are not masters of the system. The system is master of them; and the slaves are their vassals.

These storms rise on the bosom of the calmed waters of the system. You are a slave, a being in whom another owns property. Then you may rise with his pride, but remember the day is at hand when you must also fall with his folly. To-day you may be pampered by his meekness; but to-morrow you will suffer in the storm of his passions.

In the month of September, 1848, there appeared in my study, one morning, in New York City, an aged coloured man of tall and slender form. I saw depicted on his countenance anxiety bordering on despair, still I was confident that he was a man whose mind was accustomed to faith. When I learned that he was a native of my own state, Maryland, having been born in the county of Montgomery, I at once became much interested in him. He had been sent to me by my friend, William Harned, Esq., of the Anti-Slavery Office, 61, John Street. He put into my hand the following bill of distress:—

"Alexander, Virginia, *September 5th,* 1848.

"The bearer, Paul Edmondson, is the father of two girls, Mary Jane and Emily Catherine Edmondson. These girls have been purchased by us, and once sent to the South; and upon the positive assurance that the money for them would be raised if they were brought back, they were returned. Nothing, it appears, has as yet been done in this respect by those who promised, and we are on the very eve of sending them south a second time; and we are candid in saying, that if they go again, we will not regard any promises made in relation to them.

"The father wishes to raise money to pay for them, and intends to appeal to the liberality of the humane and the good to aid him, and has requested us to state in writing *the conditions upon which we will sell his daughters.*

"We expect to start our servants to the South in a few days; if the sum of twelve hundred dollars be raised and paid us in fifteen days, or we be assured of that sum, then we will retain them for twenty-five days more, to give an opportunity for raising the other thousand and fifty dollars, otherwise we shall be compelled to send them along with our other servants.

(Signed)   "BRUIN AND HILL."

The old man also showed me letters from other individuals, and one from the Rev. Matthew A. Turner, pastor of Asbury Chapel, where himself and his daughters were members. He was himself free, but his wife was a slave. Those two daughters were two out of fifteen children he had raised for the owner of his wife. These two girls had been sold, along with four brothers, to the traders, for an attempt to escape to the North, and gain their freedom.

On the next Sabbath evening, I threw the case before my people, and the first fifty dollars of the sum was raised to restore the old man his daughters. Subsequently the case was taken up under the management of a committee of ministers of the Methodist Episcopal Church, consisting of the Rev. G. Peck, D. D., Rev. E. E. Griswold, and Rev. D. Curry, and the entire sum of 2,250 dollars, (£450.) was raised for two girls, fourteen and sixteen years of age!

But why this enormous sum for two mere children? Ah, reader, they were reared under the mildest form of slavery known to the laws of Maryland! The mother is an invalid, and allowed to live with her free husband; but she is a woman of excellent mind, and has bestowed great pains upon her daughters. If you would know, then, why these girls were held at such a price, even to their own father, read the following extract of a letter from one who was actively engaged in behalf of them, and who had several interviews with the traders to induce them to reduce the price, but without success. Writing from Washington, D. C., September 12th, 1848, this gentleman says to William Harned, "The truth is, *and is confessed to be, that their destination is prostitution;* of this you would be satisfied on seeing them: they are of elegant form, and fine faces."

And such, dear reader, is the sad fate of hundreds of my young countrywomen, natives of my native state. Such is the fate of many who are not only reared under the mildest form of slavery, but of those who have been made acquainted with the milder system of the Prince of Peace.

When Christians, and Christian ministers, then, talk about the "mildest form of slavery,"—"Christian masters," &c., I say my feelings are outraged. It is a great mistake to offer these as an extenuation of the system. It is calculated to mislead the public mind. The opinion seems to prevail, that the negro, after having toiled as a slave for centuries to enrich his white brother, to lay the foundation of his proud institutions, after having been sunk as low as slavery can sink him, needs now only a second-rate civilization, a lower standard of civil and religious privileges than the whites claim for themselves.

During the last year or two, we have heard of nothing but revolutions, and the enlargements of the eras of freedom, on both sides of the Atlantic.[12] Our white brethren everywhere are reaching out their hands to grasp more freedom. In the place of absolute monarchies they have limited monarchies, and in the place of limited monarchies they have republics: so tenacious are they of their own liberties.

But when we speak of slavery, and complain of the wrong it is doing us, and ask to have the yoke removed, we are told, "O, you must not be impatient, you must not create undue excitement. You are not so badly off, for many of your masters are kind Christian masters." Yes, sirs, many of our masters are professed Christians; and what advantage is that to us? The grey heads of our fathers are brought down by scores to the grave in sorrow, on account of their young and tender sons, who are sold to the far South, where they have to toil without requite to supply the world's market with *cotton, sugar, rice, tobacco, &c.* Our venerable mothers are borne down with poignant grief at the fate of their children. Our sisters, if not by the law, are by common consent made the prey of vile men, who can bid the highest.

In all the bright achievements we have obtained in the great work of emancipation, if we have not settled the fact that the chattel principle is wrong, and cannot be maintained upon Christian ground, then we have wrought and triumphed to little purpose, and we shall have to do our first work over again.

It is this that has done all the mischief connected with slavery; it is this that threatens still further mischief. Whatever may be the ill or favoured condition of the slave in the matter of mere personal treatment, it is the chattel relation that robs him of his manhood, and transfers his ownership in himself to another. It is this that transfers the proprietorship of his wife and children to another. It is this that throws his family history into utter confusion, and leaves him without a single record to which he may appeal in vindication of his character, or honour. And has a man no sense of honour because he was born a slave? Has he no need of character?

Suppose insult, reproach, or slander, should render it necessary for him to appeal to the history of his family in vindication of his character, where will he find that history? He goes to his native state, to his native county, to his native town; but no where does he find any record of himself *as a man.* On looking at the family record of his old, kind, Christian, master, there he finds his name on a catalogue with the horses, cows, hogs and dogs. However humiliating and degrading it may be to his feelings to find his name written down among the beasts of the field, *that* is just the place, and the *only* place assigned to it by the chattel relation. I beg our Anglo-Saxon brethren to accustom themselves to think that we need something more than mere kindness. We ask for justice, truth and honour as other men do.

My coloured brethren are now widely awake to the degradation which they suffer in having property vested in their persons, and they are also conscious of the deep and corrupting disgrace of having our wives and children owned by other men—men, who have shown to the world that their own virtue is not infallible, and who have given us no flattering encouragement to entrust that of our wives and daughters to them.

I have great pleasure in stating that my dear friend W. W.,[13] spoken of in this narrative, to whom I am so deeply indebted, is still living. I have been twice to see him within four years, and have regular correspondence with him. In one of the last letters I had from him, he authorises me to use his name in connection with this narrative in these words,—"As for using my name, by reference or otherwise, in thy narrative, it is at thy service. I know thee so well James, that I am not afraid of thy making a bad use of it, nor am I afraid or ashamed to have it known that I took thee in and gave thee aid, when I found thee travelling alone and in want.—W. W."

On the second page of the same sheet I have a few lines from his excellent lady, in which she says, "James, I hope thee will not attribute my long silence in writing to indifference. No such feeling can ever exist towards thee in our family. Thy name is mentioned almost every day. Each of the children claims the next letter from thee. It will be for thee to decide which shall have it.—P. W."[14]

In a postscript following this, W. W. says again:—"Understand me, James, that thee is at full liberty to use my name in any way thee wishes in thy narrative. We have a man here from the eastern shore of thy state. He is trying to learn as fast as thee did when here—W. W."

I hope the reader will pardon me for introducing these extracts. My only apology is, the high gratification I feel in knowing that this family has not only been greatly prospered in health and happiness, but that I am upon the most intimate and pleasant terms with all its members, and that they all still feel a deep and cordial interest in my welfare.

There is another distinguished individual whose sympathy has proved very gratifying to me in my situation—I mean that true friend of the negro, *Gerrit Smith, Esq.*[15] I was well acquainted with the family in which Mr. Smith married in Maryland. My attention has been fixed upon him for the last ten years, for I have felt confident that God had set him apart for some great good to the negro. In a letter dated Peterborough, November 7th, 1848, he says:—

"J. W. C. PENNINGTON,

"Slight as is my *personal* acquaintance with you, I nevertheless am well acquainted with you. I am familiar with many passages in your history—all that part of your history extending from the time when, a sturdy blacksmith, you were running away from Maryland oppression, down to the present, when you are the successor of my lamented friend, Theodore S. Wright.[16] Let me add that my acquaintance with you has inspired me with a high regard for your wisdom and integrity."

Give us a few more such men in America, and slavery will soon be numbered among the things that were. A few men who will not only have the moral courage to aim the severing blow at the chattel relation between master and slave, without parley, palliation or compromise; but who have also the christian fidelity to brave public scorn and contumely, to seize a coloured man by the hand, and elevate him to the position from whence the avarice and oppression of the whites have degraded him. These men have the right view of the subject. They see that in every case where the relation between master and slave is broken, slavery is weakened, and that every coloured man elevated, becomes a step in the ladder upon which his whole people are to ascend. They would not have us accept of some modified form of liberty, while the old mischief working chattel relation remains unbroken, untouched and unabrogated.

                                                           J. W. C. PENNINGTON.

13, *Princes Square, London,*
    August 15th, 1849.

CONTENTS.

THE FUGITIVE BLACKSMITH.

CHAPTER I.

MY BIRTH AND PARENTAGE. — THE TREATMENT OF SLAVES GENERALLY IN MARYLAND.

I WAS born in the state of Maryland, which is one of the smallest and most northern of the slave-holding states; the products of this state are wheat, rye, Indian corn, tobacco, with some hemp, flax, &c. By looking at the map, it will be seen that Maryland, like Virginia her neighbour, is divided by the Chesapeake Bay into eastern and western shores. My birthplace was on the eastern shore, where there are seven or eight small counties; the farms are small, and tobacco is mostly raised.[17]

At an early period in the history of Maryland, her lands began to be exhausted by the bad cultivation peculiar to slave states; and hence she soon commenced the business of breeding slaves for the more southern states. This has given an enormity to slavery, in Maryland, differing from that which attaches to the system in Louisiana, and equalled by none of the kind, except Virginia and Kentucky, and not by either of these in extent.

My parents did not both belong to the same owner: my father belonged to a man named ——; my mother belonged to a man named ——.[18] This not only made me a slave, but made me the slave of him to whom my mother belonged; as the primary law of slavery is, that the child shall follow the condition of the mother.

When I was about four years of age, my mother, an older brother and myself, were given to a son of my master, who had studied for the medical profession, but who had now married wealthy, and was about to settle as a wheat planter in Washington County, on the western shore. This began the first of our family troubles that I knew anything about, as it occasioned a separation between my mother and the only two children she then had, and my father, to a distance of about two hundred miles. But this separation did not continue long; my father being a valuable slave, my master was glad to purchase him.

About this time, I began to feel another evil of slavery—I mean the want of parental care and attention. My parents were not able to give any attention to their children during the day. I often suffered much from *hunger* and other similar causes. To estimate the sad state of a slave child, you must look at it as a helpless human being thrown upon the world without the benefit of its natural guardians. It is thrown into the world without a social circle to flee to for hope, shelter, comfort, or instruction. The social circle, with all its heaven-ordained blessings, is of the utmost importance to the *tender child;* but of this, the slave child, however tender and delicate, is robbed.

There is another source of evil to slave children, which I cannot forbear to mention here, as one which early embittered my life,—I mean the tyranny of the master's children. My master had two sons, about the ages and sizes of my older brother and myself. We were not only required to recognise these young sirs as our young masters, but *they* felt themselves to be such; and, in consequence of this feeling, they sought to treat us with the same air of authority that their father did the older slaves.

Another evil of slavery that I felt severely about this time, was the tyranny and abuse of the overseers. These men seem to look with an evil eye upon children. I was once visiting a menagerie, and being struck with the fact, that the lion was comparatively indifferent to every one around his cage, while he eyed with peculiar keenness a little boy I had; the keeper informed me that such was always the case. Such is true of those human beings in the slave states, called overseers. They seem to take pleasure in torturing the children of slaves, long before they are large enough to be put at the hoe, and consequently under the whip.

We had an overseer, named Blackstone; he was an extremely cruel man to the working hands. He always carried a long hickory whip, a kind of pole. He kept three or four of these in order, that he might not at any time be without one.

I once found one of these hickories lying in the yard, and supposing that he had thrown it away, I picked it up, and boy-like, was using it for a horse; he came along from the field, and seeing me with it, fell upon me with the one he then had in his hand, and flogged me most cruelly. From that, I lived in constant dread of that man; and he would show how much he delighted in cruelty by chasing me from my play with threats and imprecations. I have lain for hours in a wood, or behind a fence, to hide from his eye.

At this time my days were extremely dreary. When I was nine years of age, myself and my brother were hired out from home; my brother was placed with a pump-maker, and I was placed with a stonemason. We were both in a town some six miles from home. As the men with whom we lived were not slaveholders, we enjoyed some relief from the peculiar evils of slavery. Each of us lived in a family where there was no other negro.

The slaveholders in that state often hire the children of their slaves out to non-slaveholders, not only because they save themselves the expense of taking care of them, but in this way they get among their slaves useful trades. They put a bright slave-boy with a tradesman, until he gets such a knowledge of the trade as to be able to do his own work, and then he takes him home. I remained with the stonemason until I was eleven years of age: at this time I was taken home. This was another serious period in my childhood; I was separated from my older brother, to whom I was much attached; he continued at his place, and not only learned the trade to great perfection, but finally became the property of the man with whom he lived, so that our separation was permanent, as we never lived nearer after, than six miles. My master owned an excellent blacksmith, who had obtained his trade in the way I have mentioned above. When I returned home at the age of eleven, I was set about assisting to do the mason-work of a new smith's shop. This being done, I was placed at the business, which I soon learned, so as to be called a "first-rate blacksmith." I continued to work at this business for nine years, or until I was twenty-one, with the exception of the last seven months.

In the spring of 1828, my master sold me to a Methodist man, named ———, for the sum of seven hundred dollars. It soon proved that he had not work enough to keep me employed as a smith, and he offered me for sale again. On hearing of this, my old master re-purchased me, and proposed to me to undertake the carpentering business. I had been working at this trade six months with a white workman, who was building a large barn when I left. I will now relate the abuses which occasioned me to fly.

Three or four of our farm hands had their wives and families on other plantations. In such cases, it is the custom in Maryland to allow the men to go on Saturday evening to see their families, stay over the Sabbath, and return on Monday morning, not later than "half-an-hour by sun." To overstay their time is a grave fault, for which, especially at busy seasons, they are punished.

One Monday morning, two of these men had not been so fortunate as to get home at the required time: one of them was an uncle of mine. Besides these, two young men who had no families, and for whom no such provision of time was made, having gone somewhere to spend the Sabbath, were absent. My master was greatly irritated, and had resolved to have, as he said, "a general whipping-match among them."

Preparatory to this, he had a rope in his pocket, and a cowhide in his hand, walking about the premises, and speaking to every one he met in a very insolent manner, and finding fault with some without just cause. My father, among other numerous and responsible duties, discharged that of shepherd to a large and valuable flock of Merino sheep. This morning he was engaged in the tenderest of a shepherd's duties;—a little lamb, not able to go alone, lost its mother; he was feeding it by hand. He had been keeping it in the house for several days. As he stooped over it in the yard, with a vessel of new milk he had obtained, with which to feed it, my master came along, and without the least provocation, began by asking, "Bazil, have you fed the flock?"

"Yes, sir."

"Were you away yesterday?"

"No, sir."

"Do you know why these boys have not got home this morning yet?"

"No, sir, I have not seen any of them since Saturday night."

"By the Eternal, I'll make them know their hour. The fact is, I have too many of you; my people are getting to be the most careless, lazy, and worthless in the country."

"Master," said my father, "I am always at my post; Monday morning never finds me off the plantation."

"Hush, Bazil! I shall have to sell some of you; and then the rest will have enough to do; I have not work enough to keep you all tightly employed; I have too many of you."

All this was said in an angry, threatening, and exceedingly insulting tone. My father was a high spirited man, and feeling deeply the insult, replied to the last expression,—"If I am one too many, sir, give me a chance to get a purchaser, and I am willing to be sold when it may suit you."

"Bazil, I told you to hush!" and suiting the action to the word, he drew forth the "cowhide" from under his arm, fell upon him with most savage cruelty, and inflicted fifteen or twenty severe stripes with all his strength, over his shoulders and the small of his back. As he raised himself upon his toes, and gave the last stripe, he said, "By the * * * I will make you know that I am master of your tongue as well as of your time!"

Being a tradesman, and just at that time getting my breakfast, I was near enough to hear the insolent words that were spoken to my father, and to hear, see, and even count the savage stripes inflicted upon him.

Let me ask any one of Anglo-Saxon blood and spirit, how would you expect a *son* to feel at such a sight?

This act created an open rupture with our family—each member felt the deep insult that had been inflicted upon our head; the spirit of the whole family was roused; we talked of it in our nightly gatherings, and showed it in our daily melancholy aspect. The oppressor saw this, and with the heartlessness that was in perfect keeping with the first insult, commenced a series of tauntings, threatenings, and insinuations, with a view to crush the spirit of the whole family.

Although it was sometime after this event before I took the decisive step, yet in my mind and spirit, I never was a *Slave* after it.

Whenever I thought of the great contrast between my father's employment on that memorable Monday morning, (feeding the little lamb,) and the barbarous conduct of my master, I could not help cordially despising the proud abuser of my sire; and I believe he discovered it, for he seemed to have diligently sought an occasion against me. Many incidents occurred to convince me of this, too tedious to mention; but there is one I will mention, because it will serve to show the state of feeling that existed between us, and how it served to widen the already open breach.

I was one day shoeing a horse in the shop yard. I had been stooping for some time under the weight of the horse, which was large, and was very tired; meanwhile, my master had taken his position on a little hill just in front of me, and stood leaning back on his cane, with his hat drawn over his eyes. I put down the horse's foot, and straightened myself up to rest a moment, and without knowing that he was there, my eye caught his. This threw him into a panic of rage; he would have it that I was watching him. "What are you rolling your white eyes at me for, you lazy rascal?" He came down upon me with his cane, and laid on over my shoulders, arms, and legs, about a dozen severe blows, so that my limbs and flesh were sore for several weeks; and then after several other offensive epithets, left me.

This affair my mother saw from her cottage, which was near; I being one of the oldest sons of my parents, our family was now mortified to the lowest degree. I had always aimed to be trustworthy; and feeling a high degree of mechanical pride, I had aimed to do my work with dispatch and skill, my blacksmith's pride and taste was one thing that had reconciled me so long to remain a slave. I sought to distinguish myself in the finer branches of the business by invention and finish; I frequently tried my hand at making guns and pistols, putting blades in penknives, making fancy hammers, hatchets, swordcanes, &c., &c. Besides I used to assist my father at night in making straw-hats and willow-baskets, by which means we supplied our family with little articles of food, clothing and luxury, which slaves in the mildest form of the system never get from the master; but after this, I found that my mechanic's pleasure and pride were gone. I thought of nothing but the family disgrace under which we were smarting, and how to get out of it.

Perhaps I may as well extend this note a little. The reader will observe that I have not said much about my master's cruel treatment; I have aimed rather to shew the cruelties incident to the system. I have no disposition to attempt to convict him of having been one of the most cruel masters—that would not be true—his prevailing temper was kind, but he was a perpetualist.[19] He was opposed to emancipation; thought free negroes a great nuisance, and was, as respects discipline, a thorough slaveholder. He would not tolerate a look or a word from a slave like insubordination. He would suppress it at once, and at any risk. When he thought it necessary to secure unqualified obedience, he would strike a slave with any weapon, flog him on the bare back, and sell. And this was the kind of discipline he also empowered his overseers and sons to use.

I have seen children go from our plantations to join the chained-gang on its way from Washington to Louisiana; and I have seen men and women flogged—I have seen the overseers strike a man with a hayfork—nay more, men have been maimed by shooting! Some dispute arose one morning between the overseer and one of the farm hands, when the former made at the slave with a hickory club; the slave taking to his heels, started for the woods; as he was crossing the yard, the overseer turned, snatched his gun which was near, and fired at the flying slave, lodging several shots in the calf of one leg. The poor fellow continued his flight, and got into the woods; but he was in so much pain that he was compelled to come out in the evening, and give himself up to his master, thinking he would not allow him to be punished as he had been shot. He was locked up that night; the next morning the overseer was allowed to tie him up and flog him; his master then took his instruments and picked the shot out of his leg, and told him, it served him just right.

My master had a deeply pious and exemplary slave, an elderly man, who one day had a misunderstanding with the overseer, when the latter attempted to flog him. He fled to the woods; it was noon; at evening he came home orderly. The next morning, my master, taking one of his sons with him, a rope and cowhide in his hand, led the poor old man away into the stable; tied him up, and ordered the son to lay on thirty-nine lashes, which he did, making the keen end of the cowhide lap around and strike him in the tenderest part of his side, till the blood sped out, as if a lance had been used.

While my master's son was thus engaged, the sufferer's little daughter, a child six years of age, stood at the door, weeping in agony for the fate of her father. I heard the old man articulating in a low tone of voice; I listened at the intervals between the stripes, and lo! he was praying!

When the last lash was laid on, he was let down; and leaving him to put on his clothes, they passed out of the door, and drove the man's weeping child away! I was mending a hinge to one of the barn doors; I saw and heard what I have stated. Six months after, this same man's eldest daughter, a girl fifteen years old, was sold to slave traders, where he never saw her more.

This poor slave and his wife were both Methodists, so was the wife of the young master who flogged him. My old master was an Episcopalian.

These are only a few of the instances which came under my own notice during my childhood and youth on our plantations; as to those which occurred on other plantations in the neighbourhood, I could state any number.

I have stated that my master was watching the movements of our family very closely. Sometime after the difficulties began, we found that he also had a confidential slave assisting him in the business. This wretched fellow, who was nearly white, and of Irish descent, informed our master of the movements of each member of the family by day and by night, and on Sundays. This stirred the spirit of my mother, who spoke to our fellow-slave, and told him he ought to be ashamed to be engaged in such low business.

Master hearing of this, called my father, mother, and myself before him, and accused us of an attempt to resist and intimidate his "confidential servant." Finding that only my mother had spoken to him, he swore that if she ever spoke another word to him, he would flog her.

I knew my mother's spirit and my master's temper as well. Our social state was now perfectly intolerable. We were on the eve of a general fracas. This last scene occurred on Tuesday; and on Saturday evening following, without counsel or advice from any one, I determined to fly.

CHAPTER II.

THE FLIGHT.

IT was the Sabbath: the holy day which God in his infinite wisdom gave for the rest of both man and beast. In the state of Maryland, the slaves generally have the Sabbath, except in those districts where the evil weed, tobacco, is cultivated; and then, when it is the season for setting the plant, they are liable to be robbed of this only rest.

It was in the month of November, somewhat past the middle of the month. It was a bright day, and all was quiet. Most of the slaves were resting about their quarters; others had leave to visit their friends on other plantations, and were absent. The evening previous I had arranged my little bundle of clothing, and had secreted it at some distance from the house. I had spent most of the forenoon in my workshop, engaged in deep and solemn thought.

It is impossible for me now to recollect all the perplexing thoughts that passed through my mind during that forenoon; it was a day of heartaching to me. But I distinctly remember the two great difficulties that stood in the way of my flight: I had a father and mother whom I dearly loved,—I had also six sisters and four brothers on the plantation. The question was, shall I hide my purpose from them? moreover, how will my flight affect them when I am gone? Will they not be suspected? Will not the whole family be sold off as a disaffected family, as is generally the case when one of its members flies? But a still more trying question was, how can I expect to succeed, I have no knowledge of distance or direction. I know that Pennsylvania is a free state, but I know not where its soil begins, or where that of Maryland ends? Indeed, at this time there was no safety in Pennsylvania, New Jersey, or New York, for a fugitive, except in lurking-places, or under the care of judicious friends, who could be entrusted not only with liberty, but also with life itself.

With such difficulties before my mind, the day had rapidly worn away; and it was just past noon. One of my perplexing questions I had settled—I had re-solved to let no one into my secret; but the other difficulty was now to be met. It was to be met without the least knowledge of its magnitude, except by imagi-nation. Yet of one thing there could be no mistake, that the consequences of a failure would be most serious. Within my recollection no one had attempted to escape from my master; but I had many cases in my mind's eye, of slaves of other planters who had failed, and who had been made examples of the most cruel treatment, by flogging and selling to the far South, where they were never to see their friends more. I was not without serious apprehension that such would be my fate. The bare possibility was impressively solemn; but the hour was now come, and the man must act and be free, or remain a slave for ever. How the im-pression came to be upon my mind I cannot tell; but there was a strange and hor-rifying belief, that if I did not meet the crisis that day, I should be self-doomed—that my ear would be nailed to the door-post for ever. The emotions of that moment I cannot fully depict. Hope, fear, dread, terror, love, sorrow, and deep melancholy were mingled in my mind together; my mental state was one of most painful distraction. When I looked at my numerous family—a beloved father and mother, eleven brothers and sisters, &c.; but when I looked at slavery as such; when I looked at it in its mildest form, with all its annoyances; and above all, when I remembered that one of the chief annoyances of slavery, in the most mild form, is the liability of being at any moment sold into the worst form; it seemed that no consideration, not even that of life itself, could tempt me to give up the thought of flight. And then when I considered the difficulties of the way—the re-ward that would be offered—the human blood-hounds that would be set upon my track—the weariness—the hunger—the gloomy thought, of not only losing all one's friends in one day, but of having to seek and to make new friends in a strange world. But, as I have said, the hour was come, and the man must act, or for ever be a slave.

It was now two o'clock. I stepped into the quarter; there was a strange and melancholy silence mingled with the destitution that was apparent in every part of the house. The only morsel I could see in the shape of food, was a piece of In-dian flour bread,[20] it might be half-a-pound in weight. This I placed in my pocket, and giving a last look at the aspect of the house, and at a few small chil-dren who were playing at the door, I sallied forth thoughtfully and melancholy, and after crossing the barn-yard, a few moments' walk brought me to a small cave, near the mouth of which lay a pile of stones, and into which I had deposited my clothes. From this, my course lay through thick and heavy woods and back lands to ——— town,[21] where my brother lived. This town was six miles dis-tance. It was now near three o'clock, but my object was neither to be seen on the road, or to approach the town by daylight, as I was well-known there, and as any intelligence of my having been seen there would at once put the pursuers on my track. This first six miles of my flight, I not only travelled very slowly, therefore, so as to avoid carrying any daylight to this town; but during this walk another very perplexing question was agitating my mind. Shall I call on my brother as I pass through, and shew him what I am about? My brother was older than I, we were much attached; I had been in the habit of looking to him for counsel.

I entered the town about dark, resolved, all things in view, *not* to shew myself to my brother. Having passed through the town without being recognised, I now found myself under cover of night, a solitary wanderer from home and friends; my only guide was the *north star,* by this I knew my general course northward, but at what point I should strike Penn, or when and where I should find a friend, I knew not. Another feeling now occupied my mind,—I felt like a mariner who has gotten his ship outside of the harbour and has spread his sails to the breeze. The cargo is on board—the ship is cleared—and the voyage I must make; besides, this being my first night, almost every thing will depend upon my clearing the coast before the day dawns. In order to do this my flight must be rapid. I therefore set forth in sorrowful earnest, only now and then I was cheered by the wild hope, that I should somewhere and at sometime be free.

The night was fine for the season, and passed on with little interruption for want of strength, until, about three o'clock in the morning, I began to feel the chilling effects of the dew.

At this moment, gloom and melancholy again spread through my whole soul. The prospect of utter destitution which threatened me was more than I could bear, and my heart began to melt. What substance is there in a piece of dry Indian bread; what nourishment is there in it to warm the nerves of one already chilled to the heart? Will this afford a sufficient sustenance after the toil of the night? But while these thoughts were agitating my mind, the day dawned upon me, in the midst of an open extent of country, where the only shelter I could find, without risking my travel by daylight, was a corn shock, but a few hundred yards from the road, and here I must pass my first day out. The day was an unhappy one; my hiding-place was extremely precarious. I had to sit in a squatting position the whole day, without the least chance to rest. But, besides this, my scanty pittance did not afford me that nourishment which my hard night's travel needed. Night came again to my relief, and I sallied forth to pursue my journey. By this time, not a crumb of my crust remained, and I was hungry and began to feel the desperation of distress.

As I travelled I felt my strength failing and my spirits wavered; my mind was in a deep and melancholy dream. It was cloudy; I could not see my star, and had serious misgivings about my course.

In this way the night passed away, and just at the dawn of day I found a few sour apples, and took my shelter under the arch of a small bridge that crossed the road. Here I passed the second day in ambush.

This day would have been more pleasant than the previous, but the sour apples, and a draught of cold water, had produced anything but a favourable effect; indeed, I suffered most of the day with severe symptoms of cramp. The day passed away again without any further incident, and as I set out at nightfall, I felt quite satisfied that I could not pass another twenty-four hours without nourishment. I made but little progress during the night, and often sat down, and slept frequently fifteen or twenty minutes. At the dawn of the third day I continued my travel. As I had found my way to a public turnpike road during the night, I came very early in the morning to a toll-gate, where the only person I saw, was a lad about twelve years of age. I inquired of him where the road led to. He informed me it led to Baltimore. I asked him the distance, he said it was eighteen miles.

This intelligence was perfectly astounding to me. My master lived eighty miles from Baltimore. I was now sixty-two miles from home. That distance in the right direction, would have placed me several miles across Mason and Dixon's line, but I was evidently yet in the state of Maryland.

I ventured to ask the lad at the gate another question—which is the best way to Philadelphia? Said he, you can take a road which turns off about half-a-mile below this, and goes to Getsburgh, or you can go on to Baltimore and take the packet.

I made no reply, but my thought was, that I was as near Baltimore and Baltimore-packets as would answer my purpose.

In a few moments I came to the road to which the lad had referred, and felt some relief when I had gotten out of that great public highway, "The National Turnpike," which I found it to be.

When I had walked a mile on this road, and when it had now gotten to be about nine o'clock, I met a young man with a load of hay. He drew up his horses, and addressed me in a very kind tone, when the following dialogue took place between us.

"Are you travelling any distance, my friend?"

"I am on my way to Philadelphia."

"Are you free?"

"Yes, sir."

"I suppose, then, you are provided with free papers?"

"No, sir. I have no papers."

"Well, my friend, you should not travel on this road: you will be taken up before you have gone three miles. There are men living on this road who are constantly on the look-out for your people; and it is seldom that one escapes them who attempts to pass by day."

He then very kindly gave me advice where to turn off the road at a certain point, and how to find my way to a certain house, where I would meet with an old gentleman who would further advise me whether I had better remain till night, or go on.

I left this interesting young man; and such was my surprise and chagrin at the thought of having so widely missed my way, and my alarm at being in such a dangerous position, that in ten minutes I had so far forgotten his directions as to deem it unwise to attempt to follow them, lest I should miss my way, and get into evil hands.

I, however, left the road, and went into a small piece of wood, but not finding a sufficient hiding-place, and it being a busy part of the day, when persons were at work about the fields, I thought I should excite less suspicion by keeping in the road, so I returned to the road; but the events of the next few moments proved that I committed a serious mistake.

I went about a mile, making in all two miles from the spot where I met my young friend, and about five miles from the toll-gate to which I have referred, and I found myself at the twenty-four miles' stone from Baltimore. It was now about ten o'clock in the forenoon; my strength was greatly exhausted by reason of the want of suitable food; but the excitement that was then going on in my mind, left me little time to think of my *need* of food. Under ordinary circumstances as a traveller, I should have been glad to see the "Tavern," which was near the mile-stone; but as the case stood with me, I deemed it a dangerous place to pass, much less to stop at. I was therefore passing it as quietly and as rapidly as possible, when from the lot just opposite the house, or sign-post, I heard a coarse stern voice cry, "Halloo!"

I turned my face to the left, the direction from which the voice came, and observed that it proceeded from a man who was digging potatoes. I answered him politely; when the following occurred:—

"Who do *you* belong to?"

"I am free, sir."

"Have you got papers?"

"No, sir."

"Well, you must stop here."

By this time he had got astride the fence, making his way into the road. I said,

"My business is onward, sir, and I do not wish to stop."

"I will see then if you don't stop, you black rascal." He was now in the middle of the road, making after me in a brisk walk.

I saw that a crisis was at hand; I had no weapons of any kind, not even a pocket-knife; but I asked myself, shall I surrender without a struggle. The instinctive answer was "No." What will you do? continue to walk; if he runs after you, run; get him as far from the house as you can, then turn suddenly and smite him on the knee with a stone; that will render him, at least, unable to pursue you.

This was a desperate scheme, but I could think of no other, and my habits as a blacksmith had given my eye and hand such mechanical skill, that I felt quite sure that if I could only get a stone in my hand, and have time to wield it, I should not miss his knee-pan.

He began to breathe short. He was evidently vexed because I did not halt, and I felt more and more provoked at the idea of being thus pursued by a man to whom I had not done the least injury. I had just began to glance my eye about for a stone to grasp, when he made a tiger-like leap at me. This of course brought us to running. At this moment he yelled out "Jake Shouster!" and at the next moment the door of a small house standing to the left was opened, and out jumped a shoemaker girded up in his leather apron, with his knife in hand. He sprang forward and seized me by the collar, while the other seized my arms behind. I was now in the grasp of two men, either of whom were larger bodied than myself, and one of whom was armed with a dangerous weapon.

Standing in the door of the shoemaker's shop, was a third man; and in the potatoe lot I had passed, was still a fourth man. Thus surrounded by superior physical force, the fortune of the day it seemed to me was gone.

My heart melted away, I sunk resistlessly into the hands of my captors, who dragged me immediately into the tavern which was near. I ask my reader to go in with me, and see how the case goes.

GREAT MORAL DILEMMA.

A few moments after I was taken into the bar-room, the news having gone as by electricity, the house and yard were crowded with gossippers, who had left their business to come and see "the runaway nigger." This hastily assembled congregation consisted of men, women, and children, each one had a look to give at, and a word to say about, the "nigger."

But among the whole, there stood one whose name I have never known, but who evidently wore the garb of a man whose profession bound him to speak for the dumb, but he, standing head and shoulders above all that were round about, spoke the first hard sentence against me. Said he, "That fellow is a runaway I know; put him in jail a few days, and you will soon hear where he came from." And then fixing a fiendlike gaze upon me, he continued, "if I lived on this road, *you* fellows would not find such clear running as you do, I'd trap more of you."

But now comes the pinch of the case, the case of conscience to me even at this moment. Emboldened by the cruel speech just recited, my captors enclosed me, and said, "Come now, this matter may easily be settled without you going to jail; who do you belong to, and where did you come from?"

The facts here demanded were in my breast. I knew according to the law of slavery, who I belonged to and where I came from, and I must now do one of three things—I must refuse to speak at all, or I must communicate the fact, or I must tell an untruth. How would an untutored slave, who had never heard of such a writer as Archdeacon Paley,[22] be likely to act in such a dilemma? The first point decided, was, the facts in this case are my private property. These men have no more right to them than a highway robber has to my purse. What will be the consequence if I put them in possession of the facts. In forty-eight hours, I shall have received perhaps one hundred lashes, and be on my way to the Louisiana cotton fields. Of what service will it be to them. They will get a paltry sum of two hundred dollars. Is not my liberty worth more to me than two hundred dollars are to them?

I resolved therefore, to insist that I was free. This not being satisfactory without other evidence, they tied my hands and set out, and went to a magistrate who lived about half a mile distant. It so happened, that when we arrived at his house he was not at home. This was to them a disappointment, but to me it was a relief; but I soon learned by their conversation, that there was still another magistrate in the neighbourhood, and that they would go to him. In about twenty minutes, and after climbing fences and jumping ditches, we, captors and captive, stood before his door, but it was after the same manner as before—he was not at home. By this time the day had worn away to one or two o'clock, and my captors evidently began to feel somewhat impatient of the loss of time. We were about a mile and a quarter from the tavern. As we set out on our return, they began to parley. Finding it was difficult for me to get over fences with my hands tied, they untied me, and said, "Now John," that being the name they had given me, "if you have run away from any one, it would be much better for you to tell us!" but I continued to affirm that I was free. I knew, however, that my situation was very critical, owing to the shortness of the distance I must be from home: my advertisement might overtake me at any moment.

On our way back to the tavern, we passed through a small skirt of wood, where I resolved to make an effort to escape again. One of my captors was walking on either side of me; I made a sudden turn, with my left arm sweeping the legs of one of my captors from under him; I left him nearly standing on his head, and took to my heels. As soon as they could recover they both took after me. We had to mount a fence. This I did most successfully, and making across an open field towards another wood; one of my captors being a long-legged man, was in advance of the other, and consequently nearing me. We had a hill to rise, and during the ascent he gained on me. Once more I thought of self-defence. I am trying to escape peaceably, but this man is determined that I shall not.

My case was now desperate; and I took this desperate thought: "I will run him a little farther from his coadjutor; I will then suddenly catch a stone, and wound him in the breast." This was my fixed purpose, and I had arrived near the point on the top of the hill, where I expected to do the act, when to my surprise and dismay, I saw the other side of the hill was not only all ploughed up, but we came suddenly upon a man ploughing, who as suddenly left his plough and cut off my flight, by seizing me by the collar, when at the same moment my pursuer seized my arms behind. Here I was again in a sad fix. By this time the other pursuer had come up; I was most savagely thrown down on the ploughed ground with my face downward, the ploughman placed his knee upon my shoulders, one of my captors put his upon my legs, while the other tied my arms behind me. I was then dragged up, and marched off with kicks, punches and imprecations.

We got to the tavern at three o'clock. Here they again cooled down, and made an appeal to me to make a disclosure. I saw that my attempt to escape strengthened their belief that I was a fugitive. I said to them, "If you will not put me in jail, I will now tell you where I am from." They promised. "Well," said I, "a few weeks ago, I was sold from the eastern shore to a slave-trader, who had a large gang, and set out for Georgia, but when he got to a town in Virginia, he was taken sick, and died with the small-pox. Several of his gang also died with it, so that the people in the town became alarmed, and did not wish the gang to remain among them. No one claimed us, or wished to have anything to do with us; I left the rest, and thought I would go somewhere and get work."

When I said this, it was evidently believed by those who were present, and notwithstanding the unkind feeling that had existed, there was a murmur of approbation. At the same time I perceived that a panic began to seize some, at the idea that I was one of a small-pox gang. Several who had clustered near me, moved off to a respectful distance. One or two left the bar-room, and murmured, "better let the small-pox nigger go."

I was then asked what was the name of the slave-trader. Without premeditation, I said, "John Henderson."

"John Henderson!" said one of my captors, "I knew him; I took up a yeller boy for him about two years ago, and got fifty dollars. He passed out with a gang about that time, and the boy ran away from him at Frederickstown. What kind of a man was he?"

At a venture, I gave a description of him. "Yes," said he, "that is the man." By this time, all the gossippers had cleared the coast; our friend, "Jake Shouster," had also gone back to his bench to finish his custom work, after having "lost nearly the whole day, trotting about with a nigger tied," as I heard his wife say as she called him home to his dinner. I was now left alone with the man who first called to me in the morning. In a sober manner, he made this proposal to me: "John, I have a brother living in Risterstown, four miles off, who keeps a tavern; I think you had better go and live with him, till we see what will turn up. He wants an ostler." I at once assented to this. "Well," said he, "take something to eat, and I will go with you."

Although I had so completely frustrated their designs for the moment, I knew that it would by no means answer for me to go into that town, where there were prisons, handbills, newspapers, and travellers. My intention was to start with him, but not to enter the town alive.

I sat down to eat; it was Wednesday, four o'clock, and this was the first regular meal I had since Sunday morning. This over, we set out, and to my surprise, he proposed to walk. We had gone about a mile and a-half, and were approaching a wood through which the road passed with a bend. I fixed upon that as the spot where I would either free myself from this man, or die in his arms. I had resolved upon a plan of operation—it was this: to stop short, face about, and commence action; and neither ask or give quarters, until I was free or dead!

We had got within six rods of the spot, when a gentleman turned the corner, meeting us on horseback. He came up, and entered into conversation with my captor, both of them speaking in Dutch, so that I knew not what they said. After a few moments, this gentleman addressed himself to me in English, and I then learned that he was one of the magistrates on whom we had called in the morning; I felt that another crisis was at hand. Using his saddle as his bench, he put on an extremely stern and magisterial-like face, holding up his horse not unlike a field-marshal in the act of reviewing troops, and carried me through a most rigid examination in reference to the statement I had made. I repeated carefully all I had said; at the close, he said, "Well, you had better stay among us a few months, until we see what is to be done with you." It was then agreed that we should go back to the tavern, and there settle upon some further plan. When we arrived at the tavern, the magistrate alighted from his horse, and went into the bar-room. He took another close glance at me, and went over some points of the former examination. He seemed quite satisfied of the correctness of my statement, and made the following proposition: that I should go and live with him for a short time, stating that he had a few acres of corn and potatoes to get in, and that he would give me twenty-five cents per day. I most cheerfully assented to this proposal. It was also agreed that I should remain at the tavern with my captor that night, and that he would accompany me in the morning. This part of the arrangement I did not like, but of course I could not say so. Things being thus arranged, the magistrate mounted his horse, and went on his way home.

It had been cloudy and rainy during the afternoon, but the western sky having partially cleared at this moment, I perceived that it was near the setting of the sun.

My captor had left his hired man most of the day to dig potatoes alone; but the waggon being now loaded, it being time to convey the potatoes into the barn, and the horses being all ready for that purpose, he was obliged to go into the potatoe field and give assistance.

I should say here, that his wife had been driven away by the small-pox panic about three o'clock, and had not yet returned; this left no one in the house, but a boy, about nine years of age.

As he went out, he spoke to the boy in Dutch, which I supposed, from the little fellow's conduct, to be instructions to watch me closely, which he certainly did.

The potatoe lot was across the public road, directly in front of the house; at the back of the house, and about 300 yards distant, there was a thick wood. The circumstances of the case would not allow me to think for one moment of remaining there for the night—the time had come for another effort—but there were two serious difficulties. One was, that I must either deceive or dispatch this boy who is watching me with intense vigilance. I am glad to say, that the latter did not for a moment seriously enter my mind. To deceive him effectually, I left my coat and went to the back door, from which my course would be direct to the wood. When I got to the door, I found that the barn, to which the waggon must soon come, lay just to the right, and over looking the path I must take to the wood. In front of me lay a garden surrounded by a picket fence, to the left of me was a small gate, and that by passing through that gate would throw me into an open field, and give me clear running to the wood; but on looking through the gate, I saw that my captor, being with the team, would see me if I attempted to start before he moved from the position he then occupied. To add to my difficulty the horses had baulked; while waiting for the decisive moment, the boy came to the door and asked me why I did not come in. I told him I felt unwell, and wished him to be so kind as to hand me a glass of water; expecting while he was gone to get it, the team would clear, so that I could start. While he was gone, another attempt was made to start the team but failed; he came with the water and I quickly used it up by gargling my throat and by drinking a part. I asked him to serve me by giving me another glass: he gave me a look of close scrutiny, but went in for the water. I heard him fill the glass, and start to return with it; when the hind end of the waggon cleared the corner of the house, which stood in a range with the fence along which I was to pass in getting to the wood. As I passed out the gate, I "squared my main yard," and laid my course up the line of fence, I cast a last glance over my right shoulder, and saw the boy just perch his head above the garden picket to look after me; I heard at the same time great confusion with the team, the rain having made the ground slippery, and the horses having to cross the road with a slant and rise to get into the barn, it required great effort after they started to prevent their baulking. I felt some assurance that although the boy might give the alarm, my captor could not leave the team until it was in the barn. I heard the horses' feet on the barn-floor, just as I leaped the fence, and darted into the wood.

The sun was now quite down behind the western horizon, and just at this time a heavy dark curtain of clouds was let down, which seemed to usher in haste the night shade. I have never before or since seen anything which seemed to me to compare in sublimity with the spreading of the night shades at the close of that day. My reflections upon the events of that day, and upon the close of it, since I became acquainted with the Bible, have frequently brought to my mind that beautiful passage in the Book of Job, "He holdeth back the face of His throne, and spreadeth a cloud before it."[23]

Before I proceed to the critical events and final deliverance of the next chapter, I cannot forbear to pause a moment here for reflection. The reader may well imagine how the events of the past day affected my mind. You have seen what was done to me; you have heard what was said to me—you have also seen what I have done, and heard what I have said. If you ask me whether I had expected before I left home, to gain my liberty by shedding men's blood, or breaking their limbs? I answer, no! and as evidence of this, I had provided no weapon whatever; not so much as a penknife—it never once entered my mind. I cannot say that I expected to have the ill fortune of meeting with any human being who would attempt to impede my flight.

If you ask me if I expected when I left home to gain my liberty by fabrications and untruths? I answer, no! my parents, slaves as they were, had always taught me, when they could, that "truth may be blamed but cannot be shamed;" so far as their example was concerned, I had no habits of untruth. I was arrested, and the demand made upon me, "Who do you belong to?" knowing the fatal use these men would make of *my* truth, I at once concluded that they had no more right to it than a highwayman has to a traveller's purse.

If you ask me whether I now really believe that I gained my liberty by those lies? I answer, no! I now believe that I should be free, had I told the truth; but, at that moment, I could not see any other way to baffle my enemies, and escape their clutches.

The history of that day has never ceased to inspire me with a deeper hatred of slavery; I never recur to it but with the most intense horror at a system which can put a man not only in peril of liberty, limb, and life itself, but which may even send him in haste to the bar of God with a lie upon his lips.

Whatever my readers may think, therefore, of the history of events of the day, do not admire in it the fabrications; but *see* in it the impediments that often fall into the pathway of the flying bondman. *See* how human bloodhounds gratuitously chase, catch, and tempt him to shed blood and lie; how, when he would do good, evil is thrust upon him.

CHAPTER III.

A DREARY NIGHT IN THE WOODS—CRITICAL SITUATION THE NEXT DAY.

ALMOST immediately on entering the wood, I not only found myself embosomed in the darkness of the night, but I also found myself entangled in a thick forest of undergrowth, which had been quite thoroughly wetted by the afternoon rain.

I penetrated through the wood, thick and thin, and more or less wet, to the distance I should think of three miles. By this time my clothes were all thoroughly soaked through, and I felt once more a gloom and wretchedness; the recollection of which makes me shudder at this distant day. My young friends in this highly favoured Christian country, surrounded with all the comforts of home and parental care, visited by pastors and Sabbath-school teachers, think of the dreary condition of the blacksmith boy in the dark wood that night; and then consider that thousands of his brethren have had to undergo much greater hardships in their flight from slavery.

I was now out of the hands of those who had so cruelly teased me during the day; but a number of fearful thoughts rushed into my mind to alarm me. It was dark and cloudy, so that I could not see the *north star*. How do I know what ravenous beasts are in this wood? How do I know what precipices may be within its bounds? I cannot rest in this wood to-morrow, for it will be searched by those men from whom I have escaped; but how shall I regain the road? How shall I know when I am on the right road again?

These are some of the thoughts that filled my mind with gloom and alarm.

At a venture I struck an angle northward in search of the road. After several hours of zigzag and laborious travel, dragging through briars, thorns and running vines, I emerged from the wood and found myself wading marshy ground and over ditches.

I can form no correct idea of the distance I travelled, but I came to a road, I should think about three o'clock in the morning. It so happened that I came out near where there was as a fork in the road of three prongs.

Now arose a serious query—which is the right prong for me? I was reminded by the circumstance of a superstitious proverb among the slaves, that "the left-hand turning was unlucky," but as I had never been in the habit of placing faith in this or any similar superstition, I am not aware that it had the least weight upon my mind, as I had the same difficulty with reference to the right-hand turning. After a few moments parley with myself, I took the central prong of the road and pushed on with all my speed.

It had not cleared off, but a fresh wind had sprung up; it was chilly and searching. This with my wet clothing made me very uncomfortable; my nerves began to quiver before the searching wind. The barking of mastiffs, the crowing of fowls, and the distant rattling of market waggons, warned me that the day was approaching.

My British reader must remember that in the region where I was, we know nothing of the long hours of twilight you enjoy here. With us the day is measured more by the immediate presence of the sun, and the night by the prevalence of actual darkness.

The day dawned upon me when I was near a small house and barn, situate close to the road side. The barn was too near the road, and too small to afford secure shelter for the day; but as I cast my eye around by the dim light, I could see no wood, and no larger barn. It seemed to be an open country to a wide extent. The sun was travelling so rapidly from his eastern chamber, that ten or fifteen minutes would spread broad daylight over my track. Whether *my* deed was evil, *you* may judge, but I freely confess that I did *then* prefer darkness rather than light; I therefore took to the mow of the little barn at a great risk, as the events of the day will show. It so happened that the barn was filled with corn fodder, newly cured and lately gotten in. You are aware that however quietly one may crawl into such a bed, he is compelled to make much more noise than if it were a feather-bed; and also considerably more than if it were hay or straw. Besides inflicting upon my own excited imagination the belief that I made noise enough to be heard by the inmates of the house who were likely to be rising at the time, I had the misfortune to attract the notice of a little house-dog, such as we call in that part of the world a "fice," on account of its being not only the smallest species of the canine race, but also, because it is the most saucy, noisy, and teasing of all dogs. This little creature commenced a fierce barking. I had at once great fears that the mischievous little thing would betray me; I fully apprehended that as soon as the man of the house arose, he would come and make search in the barn. It now being entirely daylight, it was too late to retreat from this shelter, even if I could have found another; I, therefore, bedded myself down into the fodder as best I could, and entered upon the annoyances of the day, with the frail hope to sustain my mind.

It was Thursday morning; the clouds that had veiled the sky during the latter part of the previous day and the previous night were gone. It was not until about an hour after the sun rose that I heard any out-door movements about the house. As soon as I heard those movements, I was satisfied there was but one man about the house, and that he was preparing to go some distance to work for the day. This was fortunate for me; the busy movements about the yard, and especially the active preparations in the house for breakfast, silenced my unwelcome little annoyer, the fice, until after the man had gone, when he commenced afresh, and continued with occasional intermissions through the day. He made regular sallies from the house to the barn, and after smelling about, would fly back to the house, barking furiously; thus he strove most skilfully throughout the entire day to raise an alarm. There seemed to be no one about the house but one or two small children and the mother, after the man was gone. About ten o'clock my attention was gravely directed to another trial: how I could pass the day without food. The reader will remember it is Thursday, and the only regular meal I have taken since Sunday, was yesterday, in the midst of great agitation, about four o'clock; that since that I have performed my arduous night's travel. At one moment, I had nearly concluded to go and present myself at the door, and ask the woman of the house to have compassion and give me food; but then I feared the consequences might be fatal, and I resolved to suffer the day out. The wind sprang up fresh and cool; the barn being small and the crevices large, my wet clothes were dried by it, and chilled me through and through.

I cannot now, with pen or tongue, give a correct idea of the feeling of wretchedness I experienced; every nerve in my system quivered, so that not a particle of my flesh was at rest. In this way I passed the day till about the middle of the afternoon, when there seemed to be an unusual stir about the public road, which passed close by the barn. Men seemed to be passing in parties on horse-back, and talking anxiously. From a word which I now and then overheard, I had not a shadow of doubt that they were in search of me. One I heard say, "I ought to catch such a fellow, the only liberty he should have for one fortnight, would be ten feet of rope." Another I heard say, "I reckon he is in that wood now." Another said, "Who would have thought that rascal was so 'cute?" All this while the little fice was mingling his voice with those of the horsemen, and the noise of the horses' feet. I listened and trembled.

Just before the setting of the sun, the labouring man of the house returned, and commenced his evening duties about the house and barn; chopping wood, getting up his cow, feeding his pigs, &c., attended by the little brute, who continued barking at short intervals. He came several times into the barn below. While matters were passing thus, I heard the approach of horses again, and as they came up nearer, I was led to believe that all I had heard pass, were returning in one party. They passed the barn and halted at the house, when I recognised the voice of my old captor; addressing the labourer, he asked, "Have you seen a runaway nigger pass here to-day?"

LABOURER.—"No; I have not been at home since early this morning. Where did he come from?"

CAPTOR.—"I caught him down below here yesterday morning. I had him all day, and just at night he fooled me and got away. A party of us have been after him all day; we have been up to the line, but can't hear or see anything of him. I heard this morning where he came from. He is a blacksmith, and a stiff reward is out for him, two hundred dollars."

LAB.—"He is worth looking for."

CAP.—"I reckon so. If I get my clutches on him again, I'll mosey* him down to ——— before I eat or sleep."

Reader, you may if you can, imagine what the state of my mind was at this moment. I shall make no attempt to describe it to you; to my great relief, however, the party rode off, and the labourer after finishing his work went into the house. Hope seemed now to dawn for me once more; darkness was rapidly approaching, but the moments of twilight seemed much longer than they did the evening before. At length the sable covering had spread itself over the earth. About eight o'clock, I ventured to descend from the mow of the barn into the road. The little dog the while began a furious fit of barking, so much so, that I was sure that with what his master had learned about me, he could not fail to believe I was about his premises. I quickly crossed the road, and got into an open field opposite. After stepping lightly about two hundred yards, I halted, and on listening, I heard the door open. Feeling about on the ground, I picked up two stones, and one in each hand I made off as fast as I could, but I heard nothing more that indicated pursuit, and after going some distance I discharged my encumbrance, as from the reduced state of my bodily strength, I could not afford to carry ballast.

---

*An expression which signifies to drive in a hurry.

This incident had the effect to start me under great disadvantage to make a good night's journey, as it threw me at once off the road, and compelled me to encounter at once the tedious and laborious task of beating my way across marshy fields, and to drag through woods and thickets where there were no paths.

After several hours I found my way back to the road, but the hope of making anything like clever speed was out of the question. All I could do was to keep my legs in motion, and this I continued to do with the utmost difficulty. The latter part of the night I suffered extremely from cold. There came a heavy frost; I expected at every moment to fall on the road and perish. I came to a corn-field covered with heavy shocks of Indian corn that had been cut; I went into this and got an ear, and then crept into one of the shocks; eat as much of it as I could, and thought I would rest a little and start again, but weary nature could not sustain the operation of grinding hard corn for its own nourishment, and I sunk to sleep.

When I awoke, the sun was shining around; I started with alarm, but it was too late to think of seeking any other shelter; I therefore nestled myself down, and concealed myself as best I could from the light of day. After recovering a little from my fright, I commenced again eating my whole corn. Grain by grain I worked away at it; when my jaws grew tired, as they often did, I would rest, and then begin afresh. Thus, although I began an early breakfast, I was nearly the whole of the forenoon before I had done.

Nothing of importance occurred during the day, until about the middle of the afternoon, when I was thrown into a panic by the appearance of a party of gunners, who passed near me with their dogs. After shooting one or two birds, however, and passing within a few rods of my frail covering, they went on, and left me once more in hope. Friday night came without any other incident worth naming. As I sallied out, I felt evident benefit from the ear of corn I had nibbled away. My strength was considerably renewed; though I was far from being nourished, I felt that my life was at least safe from death by hunger. Thus encouraged, I set out with better speed than I had made since Sunday and Monday night. I had a presentiment, too, that I must be near free soil. I had not yet the least idea where I should find a home or a friend, still my spirits were so highly elated, that I took the whole of the road to myself; I ran, hopped, skipped, jumped, clapped my hands, and talked to myself. But to the old slaveholder I had left, I said, "Ah! ha! old fellow, I told you I'd fix you."

After an hour or two of such freaks of joy, a gloom would come over me in connexion with these questions, "But where are you going? What are you going to do? What will you do with freedom without father, mother, sisters, and brothers? What will you say when you are asked where you were born? You know nothing of the world; how will you explain the fact of your ignorance?"

These questions made me feel deeply the magnitude of the difficulties yet before me.

Saturday morning dawned upon me; and although my strength seemed yet considerably fresh, I began to feel a hunger somewhat more destructive and pinching, if possible, than I had before. I resolved, at all risk, to continue my travel by day-light, and to ask information of the first person I met.

The events of the next chapter will shew what fortune followed this resolve.

CHAPTER IV.

THE GOOD WOMAN OF THE TOLL-GATE DIRECTS ME TO W. W.—MY RECEPTION BY HIM.

THE resolution of which I informed the reader at the close of the last chapter, being put into practice, I continued my flight on the public road; and a little after the sun rose, I came in sight of a toll-gate again. For a moment all the events which followed my passing a toll-gate on Wednesday morning, came fresh to my recollection, and produced some hesitation; but at all events, said I, I will try again.

On arriving at the gate, I found it attended by an elderly woman, whom I afterwards learned was a widow, and an excellent Christian woman. I asked her if I was in Pennsylvania. On being informed that I was, I asked her if she knew where I could get employ? She said she did not; but advised me to go to W. W., a Quaker, who lived about three miles from her, whom I would find to take an interest in me. She gave me directions which way to take; I thanked her, and bade her good morning, and was very careful to follow her directions.

In about half an hour I stood trembling at the door of W. W. After knocking, the door opened upon a comfortably spread table; the sight of which seemed at once to increase my hunger sevenfold. Not daring to enter, I said I had been sent to him in search of employ. "Well," said he, "Come in and take thy breakfast, and get warm, and we will talk about it; thee must be cold without any coat." "*Come in and take thy breakfast, and get warm!*" These words spoken by a stranger, but with such an air of simple sincerity and fatherly kindness, made an overwhelming impression upon my mind. They made me feel, spite of all my fear and timidity, that I had, in the providence of God, found a friend and a home. He at once gained my confidence; and I felt that I might confide to him a fact which I had, as yet, confided to no one.

From that day to this, whenever I discover the least disposition in my heart to disregard the wretched condition of any poor or distressed persons with whom I meet, I call to mind these words—"*Come in and take thy breakfast, and get warm.*" They invariably remind me of what I was at that time; my condition was as wretched as that of any human being can possibly be, with the exception of the loss of health or reason. I had but four pieces of clothing about my person, having left all the rest in the hands of my captors. I was a starving fugitive, without home or friends—a reward offered for my person in the public papers—pursued by cruel manhunters, and no claim upon him to whose door I went. Had he turned me away, I must have perished. Nay, he took me in, and gave me of his food, and shared with me his own garments. Such treatment I had never before received at the hands of any white man.

A few such men in slaveholding America, have stood, and even now stand, like Abrahams and Lots, to stay its forthcoming and well-earned and just judgment.[24]

The limits of this work compel me to pass over many interesting incidents which occurred during my six months' concealment in that family. I must confine myself only to those which will show the striking providence of God, in directing my steps to the door of W. W., and how great an influence the incidents of that six months has had upon all my subsequent history. My friend kindly gave me employ to saw and split a number of cords of wood, then lying in his yard, for which he agreed with me for liberal pay and board. This inspired me with great encouragement. The idea of beginning to earn something was very pleasant. Next; we confidentially agreed upon the way and means of avoiding surprise, in case any one should come to the house as a spy, or with intention to arrest me. This afforded still further relief, as it convinced me that the whole family would now be on the look out for such persons.

The next theme of conversation was with reference to my education.

"Can thee read or write any, James?" was the question put to me the morning after my arrival, by W. W.

"No, sir, I cannot; my duties as a blacksmith have made me acquainted with the figures on the common mechanics' square. There was a day-book kept in the shop, in which the overseer usually charged the smithwork we did for the neighbours. I have spent entire Sabbaths looking over the pages of that book; knowing the names of persons to whom certain pieces of work were charged, together with their prices, I strove anxiously to learn to write in this way. I got paper, and picked up feathers about the yard, and made ink of ——— berries. My quills being too soft, and my skill in making a pen so poor, that I undertook some years ago to make a steel pen.*[25] In this way I have learnt to make a few of the letters, but I cannot write my own name, nor do I know the letters of the alphabet."

W. W., (*handing a slate and pencil.*)—"Let me see how thee makes letters; try such as thou hast been able to make easily."

A. B. C. L. G.

P. W., (*wife of W. W.*)—"Why, those are better than I can make."

W. W.—"Oh, we can soon get thee in the way, James."

Arithmetic and astronomy became my favourite studies. W. W. was an accomplished scholar; he had been a teacher for some years, and was cultivating a small farm on account of ill-health, which had compelled him to leave teaching. He is one of the most far-sighted and practical men I ever met with. He taught me by familiar conversations, illustrating his themes by diagrams on the slate, so that I caught his ideas with ease and rapidity.

I now began to see, for the first time, the extent of the mischief slavery had done to me. Twenty-one years of my life were gone, never again to return, and I was as profoundly ignorant, comparatively, as a child five years old. This was painful, annoying, and humiliating in the extreme. Up to this time, I recollected to have seen one copy of the New Testament, but the entire Bible I had never seen, and had never heard of the Patriarchs, or of the Lord Jesus Christ. I recollected to have heard two sermons, but had heard no mention in them of Christ, or the way of life by Him. It is quite easy to imagine, then, what was the state of

---

*This attempt was as early as 1822.

my mind, having been reared in total moral midnight; it was a sad picture of mental and spiritual darkness.

As my friend poured light into my mind, I saw the darkness; it amazed and grieved me beyond description. Sometimes I sank down under the load, and became discouraged, and dared not hope that I could ever succeed in acquiring knowledge enough to make me happy, or useful to my fellow-beings.

My dear friend, W. W., however, had a happy tact to inspire me with confidence; and he, perceiving my state of mind, exerted himself, not without success, to encourage me. He cited to me various instances of coloured persons, of whom I had not heard before, and who had distinguished themselves for learning, such as Bannicker, Wheatley, and Francis Williams.[26]

How often have I regretted that the six months I spent in the family of W. W., could not have been six years. The danger of recapture, however, rendered it utterly imprudent that I should remain longer; and early in the month of March, while the ground was covered with the winter's snow, I left the bosom of this excellent family, and went forth once more to try my fortune among strangers.

My dear reader, if I could describe to you the emotions I felt when I left the threshold of W. W.'s door, you could not fail to see how deplorable is the condition of the fugitive slave, often for months and years after he has escaped the immediate grasp of the tyrant. When I left my parents, the trial was great, but I had now to leave a friend who had done more for me than parents could have done as slaves; and hence I felt an endearment to that friend which was heightened by a sense of the important relief he had afforded me in the greatest need, and hours of pleasant and highly profitable intercourse.

About a month previous to leaving the house of W. W., a small circumstance occurred one evening, which I only name to shew the harassing fears and dread in which I lived during most of the time I was there. He had a brother-in-law living some ten miles distant—he was a friend to the slave; he often came unexpectedly and spent a few hours—sometimes a day and a night. I had not, however, ever known him to come at night. One night about nine o'clock, after I had gone to bed, (my lodging being just over the room in which W. W. and his wife were sitting,) I heard the door open and a voice ask, "Where is the boy?" The voice sounded to me like the voice of my master; I was sure it must be his. I sprang and listened for a moment—it seemed to be silent; I heard nothing, and then it seemed to me there was a confusion. There was a window at the head of my bed, which I could reach without getting upon the floor: it was a single sash and opened upon hinges. I quickly opened this window and waited in a perfect tremour of dread for further development. There was a door at the foot of the stairs; as I heard that door open, I sprang for the window, and my head was just out, when the gentle voice of my friend W. W. said, "James?"*
"Here," said I, "—— has come, and he would like to have thee put up his

---

*If W. W. had ascended the stairs without calling, I should certainly have jumped out of the window.

horse." I drew a breath of relief, but my strength and presence of mind did not return for some hours. I slept none that night; for a moment I could doze away, but the voice would sound in my ears, "Where is that boy?" and it would seem to me it must be the tyrant in quest of his weary prey, and would find myself starting again.

From that time the agitation of my mind became so great that I could not feel myself safe. Every day seemed to increase my fear, till I was unfit for work, study or rest. My friend endeavoured, but in vain, to get me to stay a week longer.

The events of the spring proved that I had not left too soon. As soon as the season for travelling fairly opened, active search was made, and my master was seen in a town, twenty miles in advance of where I had spent my six months.

The following curious fact also came out. That same brother-in-law who frightened me, was putting up one evening at a hotel some miles off, and while sitting quietly by himself in one part of the room, he overheard a conversation between a travelling pedler and several gossippers of the neighbourhood, who were lounging away the evening at the hotel.

PEDLER.—"Do you know one W. W. somewhere about here?"

GOSSIPER.—"Yes, he lives ——— miles off."

PED.—"I understand he had a black boy with him last winter, I wonder if he is there yet?"

GOS.—"I don't know, he most always has a runaway nigger with him."

PED.—"I should like to find out whether that fellow is there yet."

BROTHER-IN-LAW. (turning about.)—"What does thee know about that boy?"

PED.—"Well he is a runaway."

BROTHER-IN-LAW.—"Who did he run away from?"

PED.—"From Col ——— in ———."

BROTHER-IN-LAW.—"How did thee find out that fact?"

PED.—"Well, I have been over there peddling."

BROTHER-IN-LAW.—"Where art thou from?"

PED.—"I belong in Conn."

BROTHER-IN-LAW.—"Did thee see the boy's master?"

PED.—"Yes."

BROTHER-IN-LAW.—"What did he offer thee to find the boy?"

PED.—"I agreed to find out where he was, and let him know, and if he got him, I was to receive ———."

BROTHER-IN-LAW.—"How didst thou hear the boy had been with W. W."

PED.—"Oh, he is known to be a notorious rascal for enticing away, and concealing slaves; he'll get himself into trouble yet, the slaveholders are on the look out for him."

BROTHER-IN-LAW.—"W. W. is my brother-in-law; the boy of whom thou speakest is not with him, and to save thee the trouble of abusing him, I can moreover say, he is no rascal."

PED.—"He may not be there now, but it is because he has sent him off. His master heard of him, and from the description, he is sure it must have been his boy. He could tell me pretty nigh where he was; he said he was a fine healthy boy, twenty-one, a first-rate blacksmith; he would not have taken a thousand dollars for him."

Brother-in-law.—"I know not where the boy is, but I have no doubt he is worth more to himself than he ever was to his master, high as he fixes the price on him; and I have no doubt thee will do better to pursue thy peddling honestly, than to neglect it for the sake of serving negro-hunters at a venture."

All this happened within a month or two after I left my friend. One fact which makes this part of the story deeply interesting to my own mind, is, that some years elapsed before it came to my knowledge.

CHAPTER V.

SEVEN MONTHS' RESIDENCE IN THE FAMILY OF J. K. A MEMBER OF THE SOCIETY OF FRIENDS, IN CHESTER COUNTY, PENNSYLVANIA. — REMOVAL TO NEW YORK — BE-COMES A CONVERT TO RELIGION — BECOMES A TEACHER.

On leaving W. W., I wended my way in deep sorrow and melancholy, onward towards Philadelphia, and after travelling two days and a night, I found shelter and employ in the family of J. K., another member of the Society of Friends, a farmer.

The religious atmosphere in this family was excellent. Mrs. K. gave me the first copy of the Holy Scriptures I ever possessed, she also gave me much excellent counsel. She was a preacher in the Society of Friends; this occasioned her with her husband to be much of their time from home. This left the charge of the farm upon me, and besides put it out of their power to render me that aid in my studies which my former friend had. I, however, kept myself closely concealed, by confining myself to the limits of the farm, and using all my leisure time in study. This place was more secluded, and I felt less of dread and fear of discovery than I had before, and although seriously embarrassed for want of an instructor, I realized some pleasure and profit in my studies. I often employed myself in drawing rude maps of the solar system, and diagrams illustrating the theory of solar eclipses. I felt also a fondness for reading the Bible, and committing chapters, and verses of hymns to memory. Often on the Sabbath when alone in the barn, I would break the monotony of the hours by endeavouring to speak, as if I was addressing an audience. My mind was constantly struggling for thoughts, and I was still more grieved and alarmed at its barrenness; I found it gradually freed from the darkness entailed by slavery, but I was deeply and anxiously concerned how I should fill it with useful knowledge. I had a few books, and no tutor.

In this way I spent seven months with J. K., and should have continued longer, agreeably to his urgent solicitation, but I felt that life was fast wearing, and that as I was now free, I must adventure in search of knowledge. On leaving J. K., he kindly gave me the following certificate,—

"East Nautmeal, Chester County, Pennsylvania, *Tenth Month 5th*, 1828.

"I hereby certify, that the bearer, J. W. C. Pennington, has been in my employ seven months, during most of which time I have been from home, leaving my entire business in his trust, and that he has proved a highly trustworthy and industrious young man. He leaves with the sincere regret of myself and family; but as he feels it to be his duty to go where he can obtain education, so as to fit him to be more useful, I cordially commend him to the warm sympathy of the friends of humanity wherever a wise providence may appoint him a home.

    Signed,   "J. K."

Passing through Philadelphia, I went to New York, and in a short time found employ on Long Island, near the city. At this time, the state of things was extremely critical in New York. It was just two years after the general emancipation in that state. In the city it was a daily occurrence for slaveholders from the southern states to catch their slaves, and by certificate from Recorder Riker take them back. I often felt serious apprehensions of danger, and yet I felt also that I must begin the world somewhere.

I was earning respectable wages, and by means of evening schools and private tuition, was making encouraging progress in my studies.

Up to this time, it had never occurred to me that I was a slave in another and a more serious sense. All my serious impressions of mind had been with reference to the slavery from which I had escaped. Slavery had been my theme of thought day and night.

In the spring of 1829, I found my mind unusually perplexed about the state of the slave. I was enjoying rare privileges in attending a Sabbath school; the great value of Christian knowledge began to be impressed upon my mind to an extent I had not been conscious of before. I began to contrast my condition with that of ten brothers and sisters I had left in slavery, and the condition of children I saw sitting around me on the Sabbath, with their pious teachers, with that of 700,000, now 800,440 slave children, who had no means of Christian instruction.

The theme was more powerful than any my mind had ever encountered before. It entered into the deep chambers of my soul, and stirred the most agitating emotions I had ever felt. The question was, what can I do for that vast body of suffering brotherhood I have left behind. To add to the weight and magnitude of the theme, I learnt for the first time, how many slaves there were. The question completely staggered my mind; and finding myself more and more borne down with it, until I was in an agony; I thought I would make it a subject of prayer to God, although prayer had not been my habit, having never attempted it but once.

I not only prayed, but also fasted. It was while engaged thus, that my attention was seriously drawn to the fact that I was a lost sinner, and a slave to Satan; and soon I saw that I must make another escape from another tyrant. I did not by any means forget my fellow-bondmen, of whom I had been sorrowing so deeply, and travailing in spirit so earnestly; but I now saw that while man had been injuring me, I had been offending God; and that unless I ceased to offend him, I could not expect to have his sympathy in my wrongs; and moreover, that I could not be instrumental in eliciting his powerful aid in behalf of those for whom I mourned so deeply.

This may provoke a smile from some who profess to be the friends of the slave, but who have a lower estimate of experimental Christianity than I believe is due to it; but I am not the less confident that sincere prayer to God, proceeding from a few hearts deeply imbued with experimental Christianity about *that time,* has had much to do with subsequent happy results. At that time the 800,000 bondmen in the British Isles had not seen the beginning of the end of their sufferings—at that time, 20,000 who are now free in Canada, were in bonds—at that time, there was no Vigilance Committee to aid the flying slave— at that time, the two powerful Anti-Slavery Societies of America had no being.

I distinctly remember that I felt the need of enlisting the sympathy of God, in behalf of my enslaved brethren; but when I attempted it day after day, and night after night, I was made to feel, that whatever else I might do, I was not qualified to do that, as I was myself alienated from him by wicked works. In short, I felt that I needed the powerful aid of some in my behalf with God, just as much as I did that of my dear friend in Pennsylvania, when flying from man. "If one man sin against another, the judge shall judge him, but if a man sin against God, who shall entreat for him?"

Day after day, for about two weeks, I found myself more deeply convicted of personal guilt before God. My heart, soul and body were in the greatest distress; I thought of neither food, drink or rest, for days and nights together. Burning with a recollection of the wrongs man had done me—mourning for the injuries my brethren were still enduring, and deeply convicted of the guilt of my own sins against God. One evening, in the third week of the struggle, while alone in my chamber, and after solemn reflection for several hours, I concluded that I could never be happy or useful in that state of mind, and resolved that I would try to become reconciled to God. I was then living in the family of an Elder of the Presbyterian Church.[27] I had not made known my feelings to any one, either in the family or out of it; and I did not suppose that any one had discovered my feelings. To my surprise, however, I found that the family had not only been aware of my state for several days, but were deeply anxious on my behalf. The following Sabbath, Dr. Cox[28] was on a visit in Brooklyn to preach, and was a guest in the family; hearing of my case, he expressed a wish to converse with me, and without knowing the plan, I was invited into a room and left alone with him. He entered skilfully and kindly into my feelings, and after considerable conversation he invited me to attend his service that afternoon. I did so, and was deeply interested.

Without detaining the reader with too many particulars, I will only state that I heard the doctor once or twice after this, at his own place of worship in New York City, and had several personal interviews with him, as the result of which, I hope, I was brought to a saving acquaintance with Him, of whom Moses in the Law and the Prophets did write; and soon connected myself with the church under his pastoral care.

I now returned with all my renewed powers to the great theme—slavery. It seemed now as I looked at it, to be more hideous than ever. I saw it now as an evil under the moral government of God—as a sin not only against man, but also against God. The great and engrossing thought with me was, how shall I now employ my time and my talents so as to tell most effectually upon this system of wrong! As I have stated, there was no Anti-Slavery Society then—there was no Vigilance Committee. I had, therefore, to select a course of action, without counsel or advice from any one who professed to sympathize with the slave. Many, many lonely hours of deep meditation have I passed during the years 1828 and 1829, before the great anti-slavery movement. On the questions, What shall I do for the slave? How shall I act so that he will reap the benefit of my time and talents? At one time I had resolved to go to Africa, and to react from there; but without bias or advice from any mortal, I soon gave up that, as looking too much like feeding a hungry man with a long spoon.

At length, finding that the misery, ignorance, and wretchedness of the free coloured people was by the whites tortured into an argument for slavery; finding myself now among the free people of colour in New York, where slavery was so recently abolished; and finding much to do for their elevation, I resolved to give my strength in that direction. And well do I remember the great movement which commenced among us about this time, for the holding of General Conventions,[29] to devise ways and means for their elevation, which continued with happy influence up to 1834, when we gave way to anti-slavery friends, who had then taken up the labouring oar. And well do I remember that the first time I ever saw those tried friends, Garrison, Jocelyn, and Tappan,[30] was in one of those Conventions, where they came to make our acquaintance, and to secure our confidence in some of their preliminary labours.

My particular mode of labour was still a subject of deep reflection; and from time to time I carried it to the Throne of Grace. Eventually my mind fixed upon the ministry as the desire of my whole heart. I had mastered the preliminary branches of English education, and was engaged in studying logic, rhetoric, and the Greek Testament, without a master. While thus struggling in my laudable work, an opening presented itself which was not less surprising than gratifying. Walking on the street one day, I met a friend, who said to me, "I have just had an application to supply a teacher for a school, and I have recommended you." I said, "My dear friend, I am obliged to you for the kindness; but I fear I cannot sustain an examination for that station." "Oh," said he, "try." I said, "I will," and we separated. Two weeks afterwards, I met the trustees of the school, was examined, accepted, and agreed with them for a salary of two hundred dollars per annum; commenced my school, and succeeded. This was five years, three months, and thirteen days after I came from the South.

As the events of my life since that have been of a public professional nature, I will say no more about it. My object in writing this tract is now completed. It has been to shew the reader the hand of God with a slave; and to elicit your sympathy in behalf of the fugitive slave, by shewing some of the untold dangers and hardships through which he has to pass to gain liberty, and how much he needs friends on free soil; and that men who have felt the yoke of slavery, even in its mildest form, cannot be expected to speak of the system otherwise than in terms of the most unqualified condemnation.

There is one sin that slavery committed against me, which I never can forgive. It robbed me of my education; the injury is irreparable; I feel the embarrassment more seriously now than I ever did before. It cost me two years' hard labour, after I fled, to unshackle my mind; it was three years before I had purged my language of slavery's idioms; it was four years before I had thrown off the crouching aspect of slavery; and now the evil that besets me is a great lack of that general information, the foundation of which is most effectually laid in that part of life which I served as a slave. When I consider how much now, more than ever, depends upon sound and thorough education among coloured men, I am grievously overwhelmed with a sense of my deficiency, and more especially as I can never hope now to make it up. If I know my own heart, I have no ambition but to serve the cause of suffering humanity; all that I have desired or sought, has been to make me more efficient for good. So far I have some consciousness that I have done my utmost; and should my future days be few or many, I am reconciled to meet the last account, hoping to be acquitted of any wilful neglect of duty; but I shall have to go to my last account with this charge against the system of slavery, "*Vile monster! thou hast hindered my usefulness, by robbing me of my early education.*"

Oh! what might I have been now, but for this robbery perpetrated upon me as soon as I saw the light. When the monster heard that a man child was born, he laughed, and said, "It is mine." When I was laid in the cradle, he came and looked on my face, and wrote down my name upon his barbarous list of chattels personal, on the same list where he registered his horses, hogs, cows, sheep, and even his *dogs!* Gracious Heaven, is there no repentance for the misguided men who do these things!

The only harm I wish to slaveholders is, that they may be speedily delivered from the guilt of a sin, which, if not repented of, must bring down the judgment of Almighty God upon their devoted heads. The least I desire for the slave is, that he may be speedily released from the pain of drinking a cup whose bitterness I have sufficiently tasted, to know that it is insufferable.

CHAPTER VI.

SOME ACCOUNT OF THE FAMILY I LEFT IN SLAVERY — PROPOSAL TO PURCHASE MYSELF
AND PARENTS — HOW MET BY MY OLD MASTER.

IT is but natural that the reader should wish to hear a word about the family I left behind.

There are frequently large slave families with whom God seems to deal in a remarkable manner. I believe my family is an instance.

I have already stated that when I fled, I left a father, mother, and eleven brothers and sisters. These were all, except my oldest brother, owned by the man from whom I fled. It will be seen at once then how the fear of implicating them embarrassed me in the outset. They suffered nothing, however, but a strong suspicion, until about six months after I had left; when the following circumstance took place:—

When I left my friend W. W. in Pennsylvania to go on north, I ventured to write a letter back to one of my brothers, informing him how I was; and this letter was directed to the care of a white man who was hired on the plantation, who worked in the garden with my father, and who professed a warm friendship to our family; but instead of acting in good faith, he handed the letter to my master. I am sorry that truth compels me to say that that man was an Englishman.

From that day the family were handled most strangely. The history begins thus: they were all sold into Virginia, the adjoining state. This was done lest I should have some plan to get them off; but God so ordered that they fell into kinder hands. After a few years, however, their master became much embarrassed, so that he was obliged to pass them into other hands, at least for a term of years. By this change the family was divided, and my parents, with the greater part of their children, were taken to New Orleans. After remaining there several years at hard labour,—my father being in a situation of considerable trust, they were again taken back to Virginia; and by this means became entitled by the laws of that state to their freedom.[31] Before justice, however, could take its course, their old master in Maryland, as if intent to doom them for ever to bondage, repurchased them; and in order to defeat a similar law in Maryland, by which they would have been entitled to liberty, he obtained from the General Assembly of that state the following special act. This will show not only something of his character as a slaveholder, but also his political influence in the state. It is often urged in the behalf of slaveholders, that the law interposes an obstacle in the way of emancipating their slaves when they wish to do so, but here is an instance which lays open the real philosophy of the whole case. They make the law themselves, and when they find the laws operate more in favour of the slaves than themselves, they can easily evade or change it. Maryland being a slave-exporting state, you will see why they need a law to prohibit the importation of slaves; it is a protection to that sort of trade. This law he wished to evade.

"*An act for the Relief of ——— of ——— County.*
Passed January 17th, 1842.
"Whereas it is represented to this General Assembly that ——— of ——— county, brought into this state from the state of Virginia, sometime in the month of March last, two negro slaves, to wit, ——— and ——— his wife, who are slaves for life, and who were acquired by the said ——— by purchase, and whereas, the said ——— is desirous of retaining said slaves in this state. THEREFORE, BE IT ENACTED, *by the General Assembly* of Maryland, that the said ——— be, and he is hereby authorized to retain said negroes as slaves for life within this state, provided that the said ——— shall within thirty days after the passage of this act, file with the clerk of the ——— county court, a list of said slaves so brought into this state, stating their ages, with an affidavit thereto attached, that the same is a true and faithful list of the slaves so removed, and that they were not brought into this state for the purpose of sale, and that they are slaves for life. And *provided also,* that the sum of fifteen dollars for each slave,

between the ages of twelve and forty-five years, and the sum of five dollars for each slave above the age of forty-five years and under twelve years of age, so brought into this state, shall be paid to the said clerk of ———— county court: to be paid over by him to the treasurer of the western shore, for the use and benefit of the Colonization Society of this state.

State of Connecticut.
Office of Secretary of State.

"I hereby certify, that the foregoing is a true copy of an act passed by the General Assembly of Maryland, January 17th, 1842, as it appears in the printed acts of the said Maryland, in the Library of the state.

In testimony whereof, I have hereunto set my hand and seal of said state, at Hartford, this 17th day of August, 1846.

CHARLES W. BEADLEY,

(SEAL.)   Secretary of State.

Thus, the whole family after being twice fairly entitled to their liberty, even by the laws of two slave states, had the mortification of finding themselves again, not only recorded as slaves for life, but also a premium paid upon them, professedly to aid in establishing others of their fellow-beings in a free republic on the coast of Africa; but the hand of God seems to have been heavy upon the man who could plan such a stratagem to wrong his fellows.

The immense fortune he possessed when I left him, (bating one thousand dollars I brought with me in my own body,) and which he seems to have retained till that time, began to fly, and in a few years he was insolvent, so that he was unable to hold the family, and was compelled to think of selling them again. About this time I heard of their state by an underground railroad passenger, who came from that neighbourhood, and resolved to make an effort to obtain the freedom of my parents, and to relieve myself from liability. For this purpose, after arranging for the means to purchase, I employed counsel to make a definite offer for my parents and myself. To his proposal, the following evasive and offensive answer was returned.

January 12th, 1846.

J. H————, Esq.[32]

"Sir,—Your letter is before me. The ungrateful servant in whose behalf you write, merits no clemency from me. He was guilty of theft when he departed, for which I hope he has made due amends. I have heard he was a respectable man, and calculated to do some good to his fellow-beings. Servants are selling from five hundred and fifty to seven hundred dollars. I will take five hundred and fifty dollars, and liberate him. If my proposition is acceded to, and the money lodged in Baltimore, I will execute the necessary instrument, and deliver it in Baltimore, to be given up on payment being made.

"Yours, &c.,

"————."

"Jim was a first-rate mechanic, (blacksmith) and was worth to me one thousand dollars."

Here he not only refuses to account for my parents, by including them in his return and proposition, but he at the same time attempts to intimidate me by mooting the charge of theft.

I confess I was not only surprised, but mortified, at this result. The hope of being once more united to parents whom I had not seen for sixteen years, and whom I still loved dearly, had so excited my mind, that I disarranged my business relations, disposed of a valuable library of four hundred volumes, and by additional aid obtained among the liberal people of Jamaica, I was prepared to give the extravagant sum of five hundred dollars each for myself, and my father and mother. This I was willing to do, not because I approve of the principle involved as a general rule. But supposing that, as my former master was now an old man not far from his grave, (about which I was not mistaken) and as he knew, by his own shewing, that I was able to do some good, he would be inclined, whatever might have been our former relations and misunderstandings, to meet my reasonable desire to see my parents, and to part this world in reconciliation with each other, as well as with God. I should have rejoiced had his temper permitted him to accede to my offer. But I thought it too bad, a free man of Jesus Christ, living on "free soil," to give a man five hundred dollars for the privilege of being let alone, and to be branded as a thief into the bargain, and that too after I had served him twenty prime years, without the benefit of being taught so much as the alphabet.

I wrote him with my own hand, sometime after this, stating that no proposition would be acceded to by me, which did not include my parents; and likewise fix the sum for myself more reasonable, and also retract the offensive charge; to this he maintained a dignified silence. The means I had acquired by the contributions of kind friends to redeem myself, I laid by, in case the worst should come; and that designed for the purchase of my parents, I used in another kind of operation, as the result of which, my father and two brothers are now in Canada. My mother was sold a second time, south, but she was eventually found. Several of my sisters married free men, who purchased their liberty; and three brothers are owned, by what may be called conscience slaveholders, who hold slaves only for a term of years. My old master has since died; my mother and he are now in the other world together, she is at rest from him. Sometime after his death, I received information from a gentleman, intimate with his heirs, (who are principally females) that the reduced state of the family, afforded not only a good opportunity to obtain a release upon reasonable terms, but also to render the children of my oppressor some pecuniary aid; and much as I had suffered, I must confess this latter was the stronger motive with me, for acceding to their offer made by him.[33]

I have many other deeply interesting particulars touching our family history, but I have detailed as many as prudence will permit, on account of those members who are yet south of Mason and Dixon's line.

I have faith in the hand that has dealt with us so strangely, that all our remaining members will in time be brought together; and then the case may merit a reviewed and enlarged edition of this tract, when other important matter will be inserted.

CHAPTER VII.

THE FEEDING AND CLOTHING OF THE SLAVES IN THE PART OF MARYLAND WHERE I
LIVED, &C.

THE slaves are generally fed upon salt pork, herrings and Indian corn.

The manner of dealing it out to them is as follows: —Each working man, on Monday morning, goes to the cellar of the master where the provisions are kept, and where the overseer takes his stand with some one to assist him, when he, with a pair of steel-yards, weighs out to every man the amount of three-and-a-half pounds, to last him till the ensuing Monday—allowing him just half-a-pound per day. Once in a few weeks there is a change made, by which, instead of the three-and-a-half pounds of pork, each man receives twelve herrings, allowing two a-day. The only bread kind the slaves have is that made of Indian meal. In some of the lower counties, the masters usually give their slaves the corn in the ear; and they have to grind it for themselves by night at hand-mills. But my master had a quantity sent to the grist mill at a time, to be ground into coarse meal, and kept it in a large chest in his cellar, where the woman who cooked for the boys could get it daily. This was baked in large loaves, called "steel poun bread." Sometimes as a change it was made into "Johnny Cake," and then at others into mush.

The slaves had no butter, coffee, tea, or sugar; occasionally they were allowed milk, but not statedly; the only exception to this statement was the "harvest provisions." In harvest, when cutting the grain, which lasted from two to three weeks in the heat of summer, they were allowed some fresh meat, rice, sugar, and coffee; and also their allowance of whiskey.

At the beginning of winter, each slave had one pair of coarse shoes and stockings, one pair of pantaloons, and a jacket.

At the beginning of summer, he had two pair of coarse linen pantaloons and two shirts.

Once in a number of years, each slave, or each man and his wife, had one coarse blanket and enough coarse linen for a "bed-tick." He never had any bedstead or other furniture kind. The men had no hats, waistcoats or handkerchiefs given them, or the women any bonnets. These they had to contrive for themselves. Each labouring man had a small "patch" of ground allowed him; from this he was expected to furnish himself and his boys hats, &c. These patches they had to work by night; from these, also, they had to raise their own provisions, as no potatoes, cabbage, &c., were allowed them from the plantation. Years ago the slaves were in the habit of raising broom-corn, and making brooms to supply the market in the towns; but now of later years great quantities of these and other articles, such as scrubbing-brushes, wooden trays, mats, baskets, and straw hats which the slaves made, are furnished by the shakers and other small manufacturers, from the free states of the north.

Neither my master or any other master, within my acquaintance, made any provisions for the religious instruction of his slaves. They were not worked on the Sabbath. One of the "boys" was required to stay at home and "feed," that is, take care of the stock, every Sabbath; the rest went to see their friends. Those men whose families were on other plantations usually spent the Sabbath with them; some would lie about at home and rest themselves.

When it was pleasant weather my master would ride "into town" to church, but I never knew him to say a word to one of us about going to church, or about our obligations to God, or a future state. But there were a number of pious slaves in our neighbourhood, and several of these my master owned; one of these was an exhorter. He was not connected with a religious body, but used to speak every Sabbath in some part of the neighbourhood. When slaves died, their remains were usually consigned to the grave without any ceremony; but this old gentleman, wherever he heard of a slave having been buried in that way, would send notice from plantation to plantation, calling the slaves together at the grave on the Sabbath, where he'd sing, pray, and exhort. I have known him to go ten or fifteen miles voluntarily to attend these services. He could not read, and I never heard him refer to any Scripture, and state and discourse upon any fundamental doctrine of the gospel; but he knew a number of "spiritual songs by heart," of these he would give two lines at a time very exact, set and lead the tune himself; he would pray with great fervour, and his exhortations were amongst the most impressive I have heard.

The Methodists at one time attempted to evangelize the slaves in our neighbourhood, but the effort was sternly resisted by the masters. They held a Camp Meeting in the neighbourhood, where many of the slaves attended. But one of their preachers for addressing words of comfort to the slaves, was arrested and tried for his life.

My master was very active in this disgraceful affair, but the excellent man, Rev. Mr. G., was acquitted and escaped out of their hands. Still, it was deemed by his brethren to be imprudent for him to preach any more in the place, as some of the more reckless masters swore violence against him. This good man's name is remembered dearly, till this day, by slaves in that county. I met with a fugitive about a year ago, who remembered distinctly the words spoken by Mr. G., and by which his own mind was awakened to a sense of the value of his soul. He said, in the course of his preaching, addressing himself to the slaves, "You have precious immortal souls, that are worth far more to you than your bodies are to your masters;" or words to that effect. But while these words interested many slaves, they also made many masters exceedingly angry, and they tortured his words into an attempt to excite the slaves to rebellion.

Some of my master's slaves who had families, were regularly married, and others were not; the law makes no provision for such marriages, and the only provision made by the master was, that they should obtain his leave. In some cases, after obtaining leave to take his wife, the slave would ask further leave to go to a minister and be married. I never knew trim to deny such a request, and yet, in those cases where the slave did not ask it, he never required him to be married by a minister. Of course, no Bibles, Tracts, or religious books of any kind, were ever given to the slaves; and no ministers or religious instructors were ever known to visit our plantation at any time, either in sickness or in health. When a slave was sick, my master being himself a physician, sometimes attended, and sometimes he called other physicians. Slaves frequently sickened and died, but I never knew any provision made to administer to them the comforts, or to offer to them the hopes of the gospel, or to their friends after their death.

––––––––

There is no one feature of slavery to which the mind recurs with more gloomy impressions, than to its disastrous influence upon the families of the masters, physically, pecuniarily, and mentally.

It seems to destroy families as by a powerful blight, large and opulent slaveholding families, often vanish like a group of shadows at the third or fourth generation. This fact arrested my attention some years before I escaped from slavery, and of course before I had any enlightened views of the moral character of the system. As far back as I can recollect, indeed, it was a remark among slaves, that every generation of slaveholders are more and more inferior. There were several large and powerful families in our county, including that of my master, which affords to my mind a melancholy illustration of this remark. One of the wealthiest slaveholders in the county, was General R., a brother-in-law to my master. This man owned a large and highly valuable tract of land, called R.'s Manor. I do not know how many slaves he owned, but the number was large. He lived in a splendid mansion, and drove his coach and four. He was for some years a member of Congress. He had a numerous family of children.

The family showed no particular signs of decay until he had married a second time, and had considerably increased his number of children. It then became evident that his older children were not educated for active business, and were only destined to be a charge. Of sons, (seven or eight,) not one of them reached the eminence once occupied by the father. The only one that approached to it, was the eldest, who became an officer in the navy, and obtained the doubtful glory of being killed in the Mexican war.

General R. himself ran through his vast estate, died intemperate, and left a widow and large number of daughters, some minors, destitute, and none of his sons fitted for any employment but in the army and navy.

Slaves have a superstitious dread of passing the dilapidated dwelling of a man who has been guilty of great cruelties to his slaves, and who is dead, or moved away. I never felt this dread deeply but once, and that was one Sabbath about sunset, as I crossed the yard of General R.'s residence, which was about two miles from us, after he had been compelled to leave it.

To see the once fine smooth gravel walks, overgrown with grass—the redundances of the shrubbery neglected—the once finely painted pricket fences, rusted and fallen down—a fine garden in splendid ruins—the lofty ceiling of the mansion thickly curtained with cobwebs—the spacious apartments abandoned, while the only music heard within as a substitute for the voices of family glee that once filled it, was the crying cricket and cockroaches! Ignorant slave as I was at that time, I could but pause for a moment, and recur in silent horror to the fact that, a strange reverse of fortune, had lately driven from that proud mansion, a large and once opulent family. What advantage was it now to the members of that family, that the father and head had for near half a century stood high in the counsels of the state, and had the benefit of the unrequited toil of hundreds of his fellowmen, when they were already grappling with the annoyances of that poverty, which he had entailed upon others.

My master's family, in wealth and influence, was not inferior to General R.'s originally. His father was a member of the convention that framed the present constitution of the state; he was, also, for some years chief justice of the state.[34]

My master was never equal to his father, although he stood high at one time. He once lacked but a few votes of being elected Governor of the state: he once sat in the Assembly, and was generally a leading man in his own county. His influence was found to be greatest when exerted in favour of any measure in regard to the control of slaves. He was the first mover in several cruel and rigid municipal regulations in the county, which prohibited slaves from going over a certain number of miles from their master's places on the Sabbath, and from being seen about the town. He once instigated the authorities of the town where he attended service, to break up a Sabbath-school some humane members of the Methodist and Lutheran denominations had set up to teach the free negroes, lest the slaves should get some benefit of it.

But there was a still wider contrast between my master and his own children, eight in number, when I left him. His eldest daughter, the flower of the family, married a miserable and reckless gambler. His eldest son was kind-hearted, and rather a favourite with the slaves on that account; but he had no strength of mind or weight of character. His education was limited, and he had no disposition or tact for business of any kind. He died at thirty-six, intestate; leaving his second wife (a sister to his father's second wife) with several orphan children, a widow with a small estate deeply embarrassed. The second son was once sent to West Point to fit for an officer. After being there a short time, however, he became unsteady, and commenced the study of medicine, but he soon gave that up and preferred to live at home and flog the slaves; and by them was cordially dreaded and disliked, and among themselves he was vulgarly nicknamed on account of his cruel and filthy habits.

These two families will afford a fair illustration of the gloomy history of many others that I could name. This decline of slaveholding families is a subject of observation and daily remark among slaves; they are led to observe every change in the pecuniary, moral, and social state of the families they belong to, from the fact, that as the old master declines, or as his children are married off, they are expecting to fall into their hands, or in case of insolvency on the part of the old master, they expect to be sold; in either case, it involves a change of master—a subject to which they cannot be indifferent. And it is very rarely the case that a slave's condition is benefited by passing from the old master into the hands of one of his children. Owing to the causes I have mentioned, the decline is so rapid and marked, in almost every point of view, that the children of slaveholders are universally inferior to themselves, mentally, morally, physically, as well as pecuniarily, especially so in the latter point of view; and this is a matter of most vital concern to the slaves. The young master not being able to own as many slaves as his father, usually works what he has more severely, and being more liable to embarrassment, the slaves' liability to be sold at an early day is much greater. For the same reason, slaves have a deep interest, generally, in the marriage of a young mistress. Very generally the daughters of slaveholders marry inferior men; men who seek to better their own condition by a wealthy connection. The slaves who pass into the hands of the young master has had some chance to become acquainted with his character, bad as it may be; but the young mistress brings her slaves a new, and sometimes an unknown master. Sometimes these are the sons of already broken down slaveholders. In other cases they are adventurers from the north who remove to the south, and who readily become the most cruel masters.

APPENDIX.

These two letters are simply introduced to show what the state of my feelings was with reference to slavery at the time they were written. I had just heard several facts with regard to my parents, which had awakened my mind to great excitement.

TO MY FATHER, MOTHER, BROTHERS, AND SISTERS.

The following was written in 1844:

DEARLY BELOVED IN BONDS,

About seventeen long years have now rolled away, since in the Providence of Almighty God, I left your embraces, and set out upon a daring adventure in search of freedom. Since that time, I have felt most severely the loss of the sun and moon and eleven stars from my social sky. Many, many a thick cloud of anguish has pressed my brow and sent deep down into my soul the bitter waters of sorrow in consequence. And you have doubtless had your troubles and anxious seasons also about your fugitive star.

I have learned that some of you have been sold, and again taken back by Colonel ———. How many of you are living and together, I cannot tell. My great grief is, lest you should have suffered this or some additional punishment on account of my *Exodus.*

I indulge the hope that it will afford you some consolation to know that your son and brother is yet alive. That God has dealt wonderfully and kindly with me in all my way. He has made me a Christian, and a Christian Minister, and thus I have drawn my support and comfort from that blessed Saviour, who came *to preach good tidings unto the meek, to bind up the broken hearted, to proclaim liberty to the captives, and the opening of the prison to them that are bound. To proclaim the acceptable year of the Lord and the day of vengeance of our God; to comfort all that mourn. To appoint unto them that mourn in Zion, to give unto them beauty for ashes, the oil of joy for mourning, the garment of praise for the spirit of heaviness, that they might be called trees of righteousness, the planting of the Lord that he might be glorified.*[35]

If the course I took in leaving a condition which had become intolerable to me, has been made the occasion of making that condition worse to you in any way, I do most heartily regret such a change for the worse on your part. As I have no means, however, of knowing if such be the fact, so I have no means of making atonement, but by sincere prayer to Almighty God in your behalf, and also by taking this method of offering to you these consolations of the gospel to which I have just referred, and which I have found to be pre-eminently my own stay and support. My dear father and mother; I have very often wished, while administering the Holy Ordinance of Baptism to some scores of children brought forward by doting parents, that I could see you with yours among the number. And you, my brothers and sisters, while teaching hundreds of children and youths in schools over which I have been placed, what unspeakable delight I should have had in having you among the number; you may all judge of my feeling for these past years, when while preaching from Sabbath to Sabbath to congregations, I have not been so fortunate as even to see father, mother, brother, sister, uncle, aunt, nephew, niece, or cousin in my congregations. While visiting the sick, going to the house of mourning, and burying the dead, I have been a constant mourner for you. My sorrow has been that I know you are not in possession of those hallowed means of grace. I am thankful to you for those mild and gentle traits of character which you took such care to enforce upon me in my youthful days. As an evidence that I prize both you and them, I may say that at the age of thirty-seven, I find them as valuable as any lessons I have learned, nor am I ashamed to let it be known to the world, that I am the son of a bond man and a bond woman.

Let me urge upon you the fundamental truths of the Gospel of the Son of God. Let repentance towards God and faith in our Lord Jesus Christ have their perfect work in you, I beseech you. Do not be prejudiced against the gospel because it may be seemingly twisted into a support of slavery. The gospel rightly understood, taught, received, felt and practised, is anti-slavery as it is anti-sin. Just so far and so fast as the true spirit of the gospel obtains in the land, and especially in the lives of the oppressed, will the spirit of slavery sicken and become powerless like the serpent with his head pressed beneath the fresh leaves of the prickly ash of the forest.

There is not a solitary decree of the immaculate God that has been concerned in the ordination of slavery, nor does any possible development of his holy will sanctify it.

He has permitted us to be enslaved according to the invention of wicked men, instigated by the devil, with intention to bring good out of the evil, but He does not, He cannot approve of it. He has no need to approve of it, even on account of the good which He will bring out of it, for He could have brought about that very good in some other way.

God is never straitened; He is never at a loss for means to work. Could He not have made this a great and wealthy nation without making its riches to consist in our blood, bones, and souls? And could He not also have given the gospel to us without making us slaves?

My friends, let us then, in our afflictions, embrace and hold fast the gospel. The gospel is the fulness of God. We have the glorious and total weight of God's moral character in our side of the scale.

The wonderful purple stream which flowed for the healing of the nations, has a branch for us. Nay, is Christ divided? "The grace of God that bringeth salvation hath appeared to (for) all men, teaching us that denying ungodliness and worldly lust, we should live soberly, righteously, and godly in this present world, looking for that blessed hope and glorious appearing of the great God and our Saviour Jesus Christ, who gave himself for us that he might redeem us from all iniquity, and purify unto himself a peculiar people, zealous of good works."—Titus ii. 11–14.

But you say you have not the privilege of hearing of this gospel of which I speak. I know it; and this is my great grief. But you shall have it; I will send it to you by my humble prayer; I can do it; I will beg our heavenly Father, and he will preach this gospel to you in his holy providence.

You, dear father and mother cannot have much longer to live in this troublesome and oppressive world; you cannot bear the yoke much longer. And as you approach another world, how desirable it is that you should have the prospect of a different destiny from what you have been called to endure in this world during a long life.

But it is the gospel that sets before you the hope of such a blessed rest as is spoken of in the word of God, Job iii. 17, 19. "There the wicked cease from troubling, and there the weary be at rest; there the prisoners rest together; they hear not the voice of the oppressors. The small and great are there; and the servant is free from his master."

Father, I know thy eyes are dim with age and weary with weeping, but look, dear father, yet a little while toward that haven. Look unto Jesus, "the author and finisher of thy faith,"[36] for the moment of thy happy deliverance is at hand.

Mother, dear mother, I know, I feel, mother, the pangs of thy bleeding heart, that thou hast endured, during so many years of vexation. Thy agonies are by a genuine son-like sympathy mine; I will, I must, I do share daily in those agonies of thine. But I sincerely hope that with me you bear your agonies to Christ who carries our sorrows.

O come then with me, my beloved family, of weary heart-broken and care-worn ones, to Jesus Christ, "casting all your care upon him, for he careth for you."— 2 Peter v. 7.

With these words of earnest exhortation, joined with fervent prayer to God that He may smooth your rugged way, lighten your burden, and give a happy issue out of all your troubles, I must bid you adieu.

Your son and brother,

JAS. P.

Alias J. W. C. PENNINGTON.

———

To Colonel F—— T——, of H——, Washington County, Md. 1844.

DEAR SIR,

It is now, as you are aware, about seventeen years since I left your house and service, at the age of twenty. Up to that time, I was, according to your rule and claim, your slave. Till the age of seven years, I was, of course, of little or no service to you. At that age, however, you hired me out, and for three years I earned my support; at the age of ten years, you took me to your place again, and in a short time after you put me to work at the blacksmith's trade, at which, together with the carpentering trade, &c., I served you peaceably until the day I left you, with exception of the short time you had sold me to S—— H——, Esq., for seven hundred dollars. It is important for me to say to you, that I have no consciousness of having done you any wrong. I called you master when I was with you from the mere force of circumstances; but I never regarded you as my master. The nature which God gave me did not allow me to believe that you had any more right to me than I had to you, and that was just none at all. And from an early age, I had intentions to free myself from your claim. I never consulted any one about it; I had no advisers or instigators; I kept my own counsel entirely concealed in my own bosom. I never meditated any evil to your person or property, but I regarded you as my oppressor, and I deemed it my duty to get out of your hands by peaceable means.

I was always obedient to your commands. I laboured for you diligently at all times. I acted with fidelity in any matter which you entrusted me. As you sometimes saw fit to entrust me with considerable money, to buy tools or materials, not a cent was ever coveted or kept.

During the time I served you in the capacity of blacksmith, your materials were used economically, your work was done expeditiously, and in the very best style, a style second to no smith in your neighbourhood. In short, sir, you well know that my habits from early life were advantageous to you. Drinking, gambling, fighting, &c., were not my habits. On Sabbaths, holidays, &c., I was frequently at your service, when not even your body-servant was at home.

Times and times again, I have gone on Sunday afternoon to H——, six miles, after your letters and papers, when it was as much my privilege to be "*out of the way*," as it was C——.

But what treatment did you see fit to return me for all this? You, in the most unfeeling manner, abused my father for no cause but speaking a word to you, as a man would speak to his fellow-man, for the sake simply of a better understanding.

You vexed my mother, and because she, as a tender mother would do, showed solicitude for the virtue of her daughters, you threatened her in an insulting brutal manner.

You abused my brother and sister without cause, and in like manner you did to myself; you surmised evil against me. You struck me with your walking-cane, called me insulting names, threatened me, swore at me, and became more and more wrathy in your conduct, and at the time I quitted your place, I had good reason to believe that you were meditating serious evil against me.

Since I have been out of your hands, I have been signally favoured of God, whence I infer that in leaving you, I acted strictly in accordance with his holy will. I have a conscience void of offence towards God and towards all men, yourself not except- cepted. And I verily believe that I have performed a sacred duty to God and myself, and a kindness to you, in taking the blood of my soul peaceably off your soul. And now, dear sir, having spoken somewhat pointedly, I would, to convince you of my perfect good will towards you, in the most kind and respectful terms, remind you of your coming destiny. You are now over seventy years of age, pressing on to eternity with the weight of these seventy years upon you. Is not this enough without the blood of some half-score of souls?

You are aware that your right to property in man is now disputed by the civi- lized world. You are fully aware, also, that the question, whether the Bible sanctions slavery, has distinctly divided this nation in sentiment. On the side of Biblical Anti- slavery, we have many of the most learned, wise and holy men in the land. If the Bible affords no sanction to slavery, (and I claim that it cannot,) then it must be a sin of the deepest dye; and can you, sir, think to go to God in hope with a sin of such mag- nitude upon your soul?

But admitting that the question is yet doubtful, (which I do only for the sake of argument,) still, sir, you will have the critical hazard of this doubt pressing, in no very doubtful way, upon your declining years, as you descend the long and tedious hill of life.

Would it not seem to be exceedingly undesirable to close an eventful probation of seventy or eighty years, and leave your reputation among posterity suspended upon so doubtful an issue? But what, my dear sir, is a reputation among posterity, who are but worms, compared with a destiny in the world of spirits? And it is in light of that destiny that I would now have you look at this subject. You and I, and all that you claim as your slaves, are in a state of probation; our great business is to serve God under His righteous moral government. Master and slave are the subjects of that government, bound by its immutable requirements, and liable to its sanctions in the next world, though enjoying its forbearance in this. You will pardon me then for pressing this point in earnest good faith. You should, at this stage, review your life without political bias, or adherence to long cherished prejudices, and remember that you are soon to meet those whom you have held, and do hold in slavery, at the awful bar of the impartial Judge of all who doeth right. Then what will become of your own doubtful claims? What will be done with those doubts that agitated your mind years ago; will you answer for threatening, swearing, and using the cowhide among your slaves?

What will become of those long groans and unsatisfied complaints of your slaves, for vexing them with insulting words, placing them in the power of dogish and abusive overseers, or under your stripling, misguided, hot-headed son, to drive and whip at pleasure, and for selling parts or whole families to Georgia? They will all meet you at that bar. Uncle James True, Charles Cooper, Aunt Jenny, and the native Africans; Jeremiah, London, and Donmore, have already gone a-head, and only wait your arrival—Sir, I shall meet you there. The account between us for the first twenty years of my life, will have a definite character upon which one or the other will be able to make out a case.

Upon such a review as this, sir, you will, I am quite sure, see the need of seriousness. I assure you that the thought of meeting you in eternity, and before the dread tribunal of God, with a complaint in my mouth against you, is to me of most weighty and solemn character. And you will see that the circumstances from which this thought arises are of equal moment to yourself. Can the pride of leaving your children possessed of long slave states, or the policy of sustaining in the state the institution of slavery, justify you in overlooking a point of moment to your future happiness?

What excuse could you offer at the bar of God, favoured as you have been with the benefits of a refined education, and through a long life with the gospel of love, should you, when arraigned there, find that you have, all your life long, laboured under a great mistake in regard to slavery, and that in this mistake you had died, and only lifted up your eyes in the light of eternity to be corrected, when it was too late to be corrected in any other way.

I could wish to address you (being bred, born, and raised in your family) *as a father in Israel, or as an elder brother in Christ, but I cannot; mockery is a sin.* I can only say then, dear sir, farewell, till I meet you at the bar of God, where Jesus, who died for us, will judge between us. Now his blood can wash out our stain, break down the middle wall of partition, and reconcile us not only to God but to each other, then the word of his mouth, the sentence will set us at one. As for myself, I am quite ready to meet you face to face at the bar of God. I have done you no wrong; I have nothing to fear when we both fall into the hands of the just God.

I beseech you, dear sir, to look well and consider this matter soundly. In yonder world you can have no slaves—you can be no man's master—you can neither sell, buy, or whip, or drive. Are you then, by sustaining the relation of a slaveholder, forming a character to dwell with God in peace?

With kind regards,

I am, sir, yours respectfully,

J. W. C. Pennington.

LIBERTY'S CHAMPION.

BY A FRIEND OF THE AUTHOR'S.

On the wings of the wind he comes, he comes!
   With the rolling billow's speed;
On his breast are the signs of peace and love,
And his soul is nerved with strength from above:
     While his eyes flash fire,
     He burns with desire
   To achieve the noble deed.

To the shores of the free he goes, he goes!
   And smiles as he passes on;
He hears the glad notes of Liberty's song,
And bids the brave sons of freedom be strong.
     While his heart bounds high
     To his crown in the sky,
   He triumphs o'er conquests won.

To the homes of the slave he flies, he flies!
   Where manacled mourners cry;
The bursting groan of the mind's o'erflow,
Transfixed on the dark and speaking brow:
     With a murmuring sound,
     Ascends from the ground,
   To the God that reigns on high.

To his loved Father's throne he hastes, he hastes!
   And pours forth his soul in grief:
Uprising he finds his strength renewed,
And his heart with fervent love is imbued;
     While the heaving sigh,
     And the deep-toned cry,
   Appeal for instant relief.

To the hard oppressor he cries, he cries,
   And points to the bleeding slave;
He tells of the rights of the human soul,
And his eyes with full indignation roll:
     While his heart is moved,
     And the truth is proved,
   He seeks the captive to save.

Again to the foeman he speaks, he speaks,
   But utters his cry in vain;
He breathes no curse, no vengeance seeks,—
For the broken hearts or the anguished shrieks,
     For the mother's pains,
     Or the father's gains,—
   Upon the oppressor's name.

To nations of freemen once more he comes,
    To raise Liberty's banner high;
He tells of the wrongs of the bonded slave.
And cries aloud, 'mid throngs of the brave,
      "O freemen, arise!
      Be faithful and wise,
    And answer the mourner's cry.

In melting strains of love he calls, he calls,
    To the great and good from afar;
Till sympathy wakes to the truthful tale,
And the prayer of the faith, which cannot fail,
      Ascends to heaven,
      And grace is given,
    To nerve for the bloodless war.

The truth with a magic power prevails:
    All hearts are moved to the strife;
In a holy phalanx, and with deathless aim,
They seek a peaceful triumph to gain
      O'er the tyrant's sway,
      In his onward way,
    To raise the fallen to life.

At the mighty voice of the glorious free
    The chain of the oppressor breaks;
The slave from his bondage springs forth to love,
And, standing erect, his eye fixed above,
      He honours his race,
      And in the world's face,
    The language of liberty speaks.

The oppressor no longer owns a right,
    Or property claims in the slave,
    But the world, in the glory of freedom's light,
Beams out from the darkness of wide-spread night;
      Throughout its length,
      In greatness and strength,
    The honour of the free and brave.

———

Printed for CHARLES GILPIN, 5, Bishopgate Street Without.

---

1. See Blackett, *Barriers*, 43; Andrews, *Free Story*, 163–164; MacKethan, "Metaphors of Mastery," 67–68.

2. For a fuller discussion of this portion of Pennington's narrative, see Andrews, *Free Story*, 162–165.

3. Blackett, *Barriers*, 6–11.

4. Ibid., 11–31.

5. Ibid., 31–42.

6. Ibid., 42–45.

7. Bontemps, *Great Slave Narratives,* 204.

8. Blackett, *Barriers,* 46–57.

9. Ibid., 60–73.

10. Ibid., 79–82.

11. Colonel Frisby Tilghman (?–1846) cultivated an estate called Rockland, a 189-acre farm; in 1830, he owned thirty-three slaves. Ibid., 2.

12. Between 1846 and 1849, the United States won Texas, New Mexico, California, Utah, Nevada, and Arizona from Mexico; Liberia was proclaimed an independent republic; King Louis Philippe of France was forced to abdicate, allowing a new republic to be proclaimed; revolutions took place in Vienna, Venice, Berlin, Milan, Parma, Prague, Rome, Dresden, and Baden; the British conquered much of India; and Hungary (unsuccessfully) declared independence from Austria.

13. William Wright, a Quaker of Adams County, Pennsylvania, and leader of the local Underground Railroad. Blackett, *Barriers,* 4.

14. Phoebe Wright. Ibid.

15. Gerrit Smith (1797–1874) was a wealthy philanthropist who built churches, gave generously to schools and colleges, and advocated reforms including sabbath observance, vegetarianism, temperance, women's suffrage, prison reform, and the abolition of slavery. He was friends with William Lloyd Garrison, helped slaves escape to Canada, was nominated for the presidency by the Liberty Pary, and later backed John Brown's raid at Harper's Ferry.

16. Pennington succeeded the Reverend Theodore S. Wright at the pulpit of the First Colored Presbyterian Church in New York City after the latter's death in 1847. Blackett, *Barriers,* 38, 40.

17. Pennington was born in Queen Anne's County. Ibid., 1.

18. Pennington's mother, Nelly, belonged to James Tilghman, Frisby's father; Pennington's father hailed from an adjoining plantation. Ibid.

19. He favored the unlimited perpetuation of black slavery in the United States.

20. Cornmeal bread.

21. Hagerstown.

22. William Paley (1743–1805) was archdeacon of Carlisle and author of *Principles of Moral and Political Philosophy, Horae Paulinae, A View of the Evidences of Christianity,* and *Natural Theology,* among others. He also opposed the slave trade. His commonsense moral textbooks were widely reprinted throughout the first half of the nineteenth century.

23. See *Job* 26:9.

24. Abraham and Lot interceded with God to spare Sodom from destruction. See *Genesis* 18–19.

25. Large-scale production of metal pens did not begin until 1828.

26. Benjamin Banneker (1731–1806) was a black mathematician and scientist who made astronomical calculations and published an annual almanac and a treatise on bees. Phyllis Wheatley (1753–84) was an African-born slave poet and literary prodigy. Francis Williams (c. 1700–?) was the Jamaican-born subject of an experiment by the Duke of Montagu, who sent him to England as a boy to ascertain the intellectual capacities of blacks. He studied classics and, at Cambridge University, mathematics; wrote Latin odes; and ran a school in Jamaica.

27. Pennington was working as a coachman for Adrian Van Sinderen, president of the Brooklyn Colonization Society. Blackett, *Barriers,* 6, 8.

28. Samuel Hanson Cox (1793–1800) was a prominent Presbyterian clergyman and educator who had held passionate antislavery views. At this time he was pastor of the Laight Street Church in New York City. By the date of Pennington's narrative, however, Cox had retracted his antislavery views.

29. In 1831 the first Negro convention was held under the leadership of Richard Allen, bishop of the African Methodist Episcopal Church; Pennington attended, having been elected a delegate by Brooklyn blacks. Blackett, *Barriers,* 7–8.

30. William Lloyd Garrison (1805–79) founded and published *The Liberator* and was president of the American Anti-Slavery Society; he was the most prominent abolitionist leader.

Simeon S. Jocelyn (1794–1879) was an engraver and minister of a black church in New Haven. Arthur Tappan (1786–1865) was a wealthy industrialist and philanthropist who, together with Garrison, founded the American Anti-Slavery Society.

31. A 1778 Virginia law prevented the importation of slaves, providing that any slaves imported were to become free. Hurd, *Law of Freedom,* II:2.

32. John Hooker was a Farmington, Connecticut, lawyer. Blackett, *Barriers,* 31–32.

33. Pennington acceded to an offer from William Clarke, adminstrator of the Tilghman estate, to pay $150 for his freedom; the transaction, however, had not been completed by the time of writing. See Ibid., 51–53, for a discussion of Pennington's efforts to gain his freedom in this manner.

34. James Tilghman (?–1809) also owned seventeen hundred acres of land and sixty slaves. Ibid., 1–2.

35. *Isaiah* 61:1–3.

36. *Hebrews* 12:2.

SOLOMON NORTHUP

SOLOMON NORTHUP (1808–63), as the title page of his narrative indicates, was a free black man of New York who was kidnapped, sold, and held as a slave in one of the most remote regions of the South for a period of twelve years. His book, *Twelve Years a Slave,* is singular in a number of ways: it is perhaps the only slave narrative written from the perspective of a nonslave; it is one of the few to describe the condition of slaves in Louisiana; it combines a mastery of detail with a richness and strength of language rare in the narrative corpus; and it was one of the fastest selling and most popular—the first printing of eight thousand copies was sold within a month of publication, and over thirty thousand copies were sold altogether.[1]

Northup's tale proved unforgettable to his readers. As one of them, Frederick Douglass, said at the time,

> It is a strange history; its truth is stranger than fiction. . . . Think of it: For thirty years a *man,* with all a man's hopes, fears and aspirations—with a wife and children to call him by the endearing names of husband and father—with a home, humble it may be, but still a *home* . . . then for twelve years a *thing,* a chattel personal, classed with mules and horses. . . . Oh! it is horrible. It chills the blood to think that such are.[2]

Another reader, Harriet Beecher Stowe, read about Northup's experiences in a long article published in *The New York Times.* She incorporated Northup's story into *The Key to Uncle Tom's Cabin,* noting, "It is a singular coincidence that this man was carried to a plantation in the Red River country, that same region where the scene of Tom's captivity was laid; and his account of this plantation, his mode of life there, and some incidents which he describes, form a striking parallel to that history."[3] Southerners, too, were impressed by Northup's account— even Edwin Epps, Northup's cruelest master, confessed the narrative's truth to a Union soldier who searched him out during the Civil War.[4]

The narrative was written by David Wilson, a lawyer from the area of Northup's home, Glen Falls, New York. Wilson was a newly elected member of the state legislature, a former superintendent of public schools, and the author of some poetry and local history. The two books he published besides Northup's narrative also concerned local figures with bizarre pasts—one recounted an Indian massacre, the other detailed the life of an insane murderess. Unlike most of the slaves' amanuenses, Wilson was not an active abolitionist; also unlike some others, he composed the book in his own style rather than shaping it according to Northup's dictation, as a comparison of his books has shown.[5] Wilson was faithful, however, to the facts of the story, as well as Northup's sentiments: as Wilson's preface attests, Northup, who was literate, had the opportunity to go over the manuscript carefully and correct anything that seemed inaccurate. At the same time, Wilson's goal seems to have been to outdo the success of *Uncle*

Tom's Cabin, which had been published the year before. This may help explain the presence in *Twelve Years a Slave* of some sentimental and stereotypical passages that seem to come straight out of Stowe.

Northup went on a lecture tour shortly after the book's publication. A typical reaction was published in *The Liberator* in 1855:

> *Twelve Years a Slave* has been widely read in New England, and no narrative of man's experience as a slave . . . is more touching, or better calculated to expose the true character and designs of slaveholders. But it is far more potent to see the man, and hear him, in his clear, manly, straightforward way, speak of slavery as he experienced it, and as he saw it in others. Those who have read his Narrative can scarce fail to desire to see the man . . . and to hear his story from his own lips.[6]

Some time after the narrative was published, a perceptive reader brought to Northup's attention the identity of the two men who kidnapped him and sold him into slavery. Unfortunately, when Northup attempted to prosecute the kidnappers, the trial bogged down in a maze of legal technicalities regarding questions of jurisdiction and the applicability of certain laws to the case. The culprits were never punished. With the three thousand dollars Northup had obtained from the sale of the copyright to his narrative, he purchased some property in Glen Falls and took up his old trade of carpentry.[7]

Solomon Northup

SOLOMON IN HIS PLANTATION SUIT.

TWELVE YEARS A SLAVE.

NARRATIVE

OF

SOLOMON NORTHUP,

A CITIZEN OF NEW-YORK,

KIDNAPPED IN WASHINGTON CITY IN 1841,

AND

RESCUED IN 1853,

FROM A COTTON PLANTATION NEAR THE RED RIVER,
IN LOUISIANA.

AUBURN:
DERBY AND MILLER.
BUFFALO:
DERBY, ORTON AND MULLIGAN.
LONDON:
SAMPSON LOW, SON & COMPANY, 47 LUDGATE HILL.
1853.

TO

HARRIET BEECHER STOWE

WHOSE NAME,

THROUGHOUT THE WORLD, IS IDENTIFIED WITH THE

GREAT REFORM:

THIS NARRATIVE, AFFORDING ANOTHER

𝕶𝖊𝖞 𝖙𝖔 𝖀𝖓𝖈𝖑𝖊 𝕿𝖔𝖒'𝖘 𝕮𝖆𝖇𝖎𝖓,[8]

IS RESPECTFULLY DEDICATED

"Such dupes are men to custom, and so prone
To reverence what is ancient, and can plead
A course of long observance for its use,
That even servitude, the worst of ills,
Because delivered down from sire to son,
Is kept and guarded as a sacred thing.
But is it fit or can it bear the shock
Of rational discussion, that a man
Compounded and made up, like other men,
Of elements tumultuous, in whom lust
And folly in as ample measure meet,
As in the bosom of the slave he rules,
Should be a despot absolute, and boast
Himself the only freeman of his land?"

COWPER.[9]

CONTENTS.

tra" of Dinners—Music and Dancing—Presence of the Mistress—Her Exceeding
Beauty—The Last Slave Dance—William Pierce—Oversleep myself—The Last
Whipping—Despondency—Cold Morning—Epps' Threats—The Passing Car-
riage—Strangers approaching through the Cotton-Field—Last Hour on Bayou

CHAPTER XXI.

The Letter reaches Saratoga—Is forwarded to Anne—Is laid before Henry B.
Northup—The Statute of May 14, 1840—Its Provisions—Anne's Memorial to the
Governor—The affidavits Accompanying it—Senator Soule's Letter—Departure of
the Agent appointed by the Governor—Arrival at Marksville—The Hon. John P.
Waddill—The Conversation on New-York Politics—It suggests a Fortunate Idea—
The Meeting with Bass—The Secret out—Legal Proceedings instituted—Departure
of Northup and the Sheriff from Marksville for Bayou Boeuf—Arrangements on the
Way—Reach Epps' Plantation—Discover his Slaves in the Cotton-Field—The Meet-

CHAPTER XXII.

Arrival in New-Orleans—Glimpse of Freeman—Genois, the Recorder—His Description of Solomon—Reach Charleston Interrupted by Custom House Officers—
Pass through Richmond—Arrival in Washington—Burch Arrested—Shekels and
Thorn—Their Testimony—Burch Acquitted—Arrest of Solomon—Burch withdraws
the Complaint—The Higher Tribunal—Departure from Washington—Arrival at
Sandy Hill—Old Friends and Familiar Scenes—Proceed to Glens Falls—Meeting
with Anne, Margaret, and Elizabeth—Solomon Northup Staunton—Incidents—

LIST OF ILLUSTRATIONS.

EDITOR'S PREFACE.

WHEN the editor commenced the preparation of the following narrative, he did not suppose it would reach the size of this volume. In order, however, to present all the facts which have been communicated to him, it has seemed necessary to extend it to its present length.

Many of the statements contained in the following pages are corroborated by abundant evidence—others rest entirely upon Solomon's assertion. That he has adhered strictly to the truth, the editor, at least, who has had an opportunity of detecting any contradiction or discrepancy in his statements, is well satisfied. He has invariably repeated the same story without deviating in the slightest particular, and has also carefully perused the manuscript, dictating an alteration wherever the most trivial inaccuracy has appeared.

It was Solomon's fortune, during his captivity, to be owned by several masters. The treatment he received while at the "Pine Woods" shows that among slaveholders there are men of humanity as well as of cruelty. Some of them are spoken of with emotions of gratitude—others in a spirit of bitterness. It is believed that the following account of his experience on Bayou Boeuf presents a correct picture of Slavery, in all its lights, and shadows, as it now exists in that locality. Unbiased, as he conceives, by any prepossessions or prejudices, the only object of the editor has been to give a faithful history of Solomon Northup's life, as he received it from his lips.

In the accomplishment of that object, he trusts he has succeeded, notwithstanding the numerous faults of style and of expression it may be found to contain.

DAVID WILSON.

WHITEHALL, N. Y., MAY, 1853.

NARRATIVE OF SOLOMON NORTHUP.

CHAPTER I.

INTRODUCTORY—ANCESTRY—THE NORTHUP FAMILY—BIRTH AND PARENTAGE—
MINTUS NORTHUP—MARRIAGE WITH ANNE HAMPTON—GOOD RESOLUTIONS—
CHAMPLAIN CANAL—RAFTING EXCURSION TO CANADA—FARMING—THE
VIOLIN—COOKING—REMOVAL TO SARATOGA—PARKER AND PERRY—SLAVES AND
SLAVERY—THE CHILDREN—THE BEGINNING OF SORROW.

HAVING been born a freeman, and for more than thirty years enjoyed the blessings of liberty in a free State—and having at the end of that time been kidnapped
and sold into Slavery, where I remained, until happily rescued in the month of
January, 1853, after a bondage of twelve years—it has been suggested that an
account of my life and fortunes would not be uninteresting to the public.

Since my return to liberty, I have not failed to perceive the increasing interest throughout the Northern States, in regard to the subject of Slavery. Works
of fiction, professing to portray its features in their more pleasing as well as more
repugnant aspects, have been circulated to an extent unprecedented, and, as I understand, have created a fruitful topic of comment and discussion.

I can speak of Slavery only so far as it came under my own observation—
only so far as I have known and experienced it in my own person. My object is,
to give a candid and truthful statement of facts: to repeat the story of my life,
without exaggeration, leaving it for others to determine, whether even the pages
of fiction present a picture of more cruel wrong or a severer bondage.

As far back as I have been able to ascertain, my ancestors on the paternal
side were slaves in Rhode Island. They belonged to a family by the name of
Northup, one of whom, removing to the State of New York, settled at Hoosic,
in Rensselaer county. He brought with him Mintus Northup, my father. On the
death of this gentleman, which must have occurred some fifty years ago, my father became free, having been emancipated by a direction in his will.

Henry B. Northup, Esq., of Sandy Hill, a distinguished counselor at law,
and the man to whom, under Providence, I am indebted for my present liberty,
and my return to the society of my wife and children, is a relative of the family
in which my forefathers were thus held to service, and from which they took the
name I bear. To this fact may be attributed the persevering interest he has taken
in my behalf.

Sometime after my father's liberation, he removed to the town of Minerva,
Essex county, N. Y., where I was born, in the month of July, 1808. How long he
remained in the latter place I have not the means of definitely ascertaining. From
thence he removed to Granville, Washington county, near a place known as Sly-
borough, where, for some years, he labored on the farm of Clark Northup, also
a relative of his old master; from thence he removed to the Alden farm, at Moss
Street, a short distance north of the village of Sandy Hill; and from thence to the

farm now owned by Russel Pratt, situated on the road leading from Fort Edward to Argyle, where he continued to reside until his death, which took place on the 22d day of November, 1829. He left a widow and two children—myself, and Joseph, an elder brother. The latter is still living in the county of Oswego, near the city of that name; my mother died during the period of my captivity.

Though born a slave, and laboring under the disadvantages to which my unfortunate race is subjected, my father was a man respected for his industry and integrity, as many now living, who well remember him, are ready to testify. His whole life was passed in the peaceful pursuits of agriculture, never seeking employment in those more menial positions, which seem to be especially allotted to the children of Africa. Besides giving us an education surpassing that ordinarily bestowed upon children in our condition, he acquired, by his diligence and economy, a sufficient property qualification to entitle him to the right of suffrage.[10] He was accustomed to speak to us of his early life; and although at all times cherishing the warmest emotions of kindness, and even of affection towards the family, in whose house he had been a bondsman, he nevertheless comprehended the system of Slavery, and dwelt with sorrow on the degradation of his race. He endeavored to imbue our minds with sentiments of morality, and to teach us to place our trust and confidence in Him who regards the humblest as well as the highest of his creatures. How often since that time has the recollection of his paternal counsels occurred to me, while lying in a slave hut in the distant and sickly regions of Louisiana, smarting with the undeserved wounds which an inhuman master had inflicted, and longing only for the grave which had covered him, to shield me also from the lash of the oppressor. In the church yard at Sandy Hill, an humble stone marks the spot where he reposes, after having worthily performed the duties appertaining to the lowly sphere wherein God had appointed him to walk.

Up to this period I had been principally engaged with my father in the labors of the farm. The leisure hours allowed me were generally either employed over my books, or playing on the violin—an amusement which was the ruling passion of my youth. It has also been the source of consolation since, affording pleasure to the simple beings with whom my lot was cast, and beguiling my own thoughts, for many hours, from the painful contemplation of my fate.

On Christmas day, 1829, I was married to Anne Hampton, a colored girl then living in the vicinity of our residence. The ceremony was performed at Fort Edward, by Timothy Eddy, Esq., a magistrate of that town, and still a prominent citizen of the place. She had resided a long time at Sandy Hill, with Mr. Baird, proprietor of the Eagle Tavern, and also in the family of Rev. Alexander Proudfit, of Salem. This gentleman for many years had presided over the Presbyterian society at the latter place, and was widely distinguished for his learning and piety. Anne still holds in grateful remembrance the exceeding kindness and the excellent counsels of that good man. She is not able to determine the exact line of her descent, but the blood of three races mingles in her veins. It is difficult to tell whether the red, white, or black predominates. The union of them all, however, in her origin, has given her a singular but pleasing expression, such as is rarely to be seen. Though somewhat resembling, yet she cannot properly be styled a quadroon, a class to which, I have omitted to mention, my mother belonged.

I had just now passed the period of my minority, having reached the age of twenty-one years in the month of July previous. Deprived of the advice and assistance of my father, with a wife dependent upon me for support, I resolved to enter upon a life of industry; and notwithstanding the obstacle of color, and the consciousness of my lowly state, indulged in pleasant dreams of a good time coming, when the possession of some humble habitation, with a few surrounding acres, should reward my labors, and bring me the means of happiness and comfort.

From the time of my marriage to this day the love I have borne my wife has been sincere and unabated; and only those who have felt the glowing tenderness a father cherishes for his offspring, can appreciate my affection for the beloved children which have since been born to us. This much I deem appropriate and necessary to say, in order that those who read these pages, may comprehend the poignancy of those sufferings I have been doomed to bear.

Immediately upon our marriage we commenced house-keeping, in the old yellow building then standing at the southern extremity of Fort Edward village, and which has since been transformed into a modern mansion, and lately occupied by Captain Lathrop. It is known as the Fort House. In this building the courts were sometime held after the organization of the county. It was also occupied by Burgoyne in 1777, being situated near the old Fort on the left bank of the Hudson.

During the winter I was employed with others repairing the Champlain Canal, on that section over which William Van Nortwick was superintendent. David McEachron had the immediate charge of the men in whose company I labored. By the time the canal opened in the spring, I was enabled, from the savings of my wages, to purchase a pair of horses, and other things necessarily required in the business of navigation.

Having hired several efficient hands to assist me, I entered into contracts for the transportation of large rafts of timber from Lake Champlain to Troy. Dyer Beckwith and a Mr. Bartemy, of Whitehall, accompanied me on several trips. During the season I became perfectly familiar with the art and mysteries of rafting—a knowledge which afterwards enabled me to render profitable service to a worthy master, and to astonish the simple-witted lumbermen on the banks of the Bayou Boeuf.

In one of my voyages down Lake Champlain, I was induced to make a visit to Canada. Repairing to Montreal, I visited the cathedral and other places of interest in that city, from whence I continued my excursion to Kingston and other towns, obtaining a knowledge of localities, which was also of service to me afterwards, as will appear towards the close of this narrative.

Having completed my contracts on the canal satisfactorily to myself and to my employer, and not wishing to remain idle, now that the navigation of the canal was again suspended, I entered into another contract with Medad Gunn, to cut a large quantity of wood. In this business I was engaged during the winter of 1831–32.

With the return of spring, Anne and myself conceived the project of taking a farm in the neighborhood. I had been accustomed from earliest youth to agricultural labors, and it was an occupation congenial to my tastes. I accordingly entered into arrangements for a part of the old Alden farm, on which my father formerly resided. With one cow, one swine, a yoke of fine oxen I had lately purchased of Lewis Brown, in Hartford, and other personal property and effects, we proceeded to our new home in Kingsbury. That year I planted twenty-five acres of corn, sowed large fields of oats, and commenced farming upon as large a scale as my utmost means would permit. Anne was diligent about the house affairs, while I toiled laboriously in the field.

On this place we continued to reside until 1834. In the winter season I had numerous calls to play on the violin. Wherever the young people assembled to dance, I was almost invariably there. Throughout the surrounding villages my fiddle was notorious. Anne, also, during her long residence at the Eagle Tavern, had become somewhat famous as a cook. During court weeks, and on public occasions, she was employed at high wages in the kitchen at Sherrill's Coffee House.

We always returned home from the performance of these services with money in our pockets; so that, with fiddling, cooking, and farming, we soon found ourselves in the possession of abundance, and, in fact, leading a happy and prosperous life. Well, indeed, would it have been for us had we remained on the farm at Kingsbury; but the time came when the next step was to be taken towards the cruel destiny that awaited me.

In March, 1834, we removed to Saratoga Springs. We occupied a house belonging to Daniel O'Brien, on the north side of Washington street. At that time Isaac Taylor kept a large boarding house, known as Washington Hall, at the north end of Broadway. He employed me to drive a hack, in which capacity I worked for him two years. After this time I was generally employed through the visiting season, as also was Anne, in the United States Hotel, and other public houses of the place. In winter seasons I relied upon my violin, though during the construction of the Troy and Saratoga railroad, I performed many hard days' labor upon it.

I was in the habit, at Saratoga, of purchasing articles necessary for my family at the stores of Mr. Cephas Parker and Mr. William Perry, gentlemen towards whom, for many acts of kindness, I entertained feelings of strong regard. It was for this reason that twelve years afterwards, I caused to be directed to them the letter, which is hereinafter inserted, and which was the means, in the hands of Mr. Northup, of my fortunate deliverance.

While living at the United States Hotel, I frequently met with slaves, who had accompanied their masters from the South. They were always well dressed and well provided for, leading apparently an easy life, with but few of its ordinary troubles to perplex them. Many times they entered into conversation with me on the subject of Slavery. Almost uniformly I found they cherished a secret desire for liberty. Some of them expressed the most ardent anxiety to escape, and consulted me on the best method of effecting it. The fear of punishment, however, which they knew was certain to attend their re-capture and return, in all cases proved sufficient to deter them from the experiment. Having all my life breathed the free air of the North, and conscious that I possessed the same feelings and affections that find a place in the white man's breast; conscious, moreover, of an intelligence equal to that of some men, at least, with a fairer skin. I was too ignorant, perhaps too independent, to conceive how any one could be content to live in the abject condition of a slave. I could not comprehend the justice of that law, or that religion, which upholds or recognizes the principle of Slavery; and never once, I am proud to say, did I fail to counsel any one who came to me, to watch his opportunity, and strike for freedom.

I continued to reside at Saratoga until the spring of 1841. The flattering anticipations which, seven years before, had seduced us from the quiet farm house, on the east side of the Hudson, had not been realized. Though always in comfortable circumstances, we had not prospered. The society and associations at that world-renowned watering place, were not calculated to preserve the simple habits of industry and economy to which I had been accustomed, but, on the contrary, to substitute others in their stead, tending to shiftlessness and extravagance.

At this time we were the parents of three children—Elizabeth, Margaret, and Alonzo. Elizabeth, the eldest, was in her tenth year; Margaret was two years younger, and little Alonzo had just passed his fifth birth-day. They filled our house with gladness. Their young voices were music in our ears. Many an airy castle did their mother and myself build for the little innocents. When not at labor I was always walking with them, clad in their best attire, through the streets and groves of Saratoga. Their presence was my delight; and I clasped them to my bosom with as warm and tender love as if their clouded skins had been as white as snow.

Thus far the history of my life presents nothing whatever unusual—nothing but the common hopes, and loves, and labors of an obscure colored man, making his humble progress in the world. But now I had reached a turning point in my existence—reached the threshold of unutterable wrong, and sorrow, and despair. Now had I approached within the shadow of the cloud, into the thick darkness whereof I was soon to disappear, thenceforward to be hidden from the eyes of all my kindred, and shut out from the sweet light of liberty, for many a weary year.

––––––––––––

CHAPTER II.

THE TWO STRANGERS—THE CIRCUS COMPANY—DEPARTURE FROM SARATOGA—VENTRILOQUISM AND LEGERDEMAIN—JOURNEY TO NEW YORK—FREE PAPERS—BROWN AND HAMILTON—THE HASTE TO REACH THE CIRCUS—ARRIVAL IN WASHINGTON—FUNERAL OF HARRISON—THE SUDDEN SICKNESS—THE TORMENT OF THIRST—THE RECEDING LIGHT—INSENSIBILITY—CHAINS AND DARKNESS.

ONE morning, towards the latter part of the month of March, 1841, having at that time no particular business to engage my attention, I was walking about the village of Saratoga Springs, thinking to myself where I might obtain some present employment, until the busy season should arrive. Anne, as was her usual custom, had gone over to Sandy Hill, a distance of some twenty miles, to take charge of the culinary department at Sherrill's Coffee House, during the session of the court. Elizabeth, I think, had accompanied her. Margaret and Alonzo were with their aunt at Saratoga.

On the corner of Congress street and Broadway, near the tavern, then, and for aught I know to the contrary, still kept by Mr. Moon, I was met by two gentlemen of respectable appearance, both of whom were entirely unknown to me. I have the impression that they were introduced to me by some one of my acquaintances, but who, I have in vain endeavored to recall, with the remark that I was an expert player on the violin.

At any rate, they immediately entered into conversation on that subject, making numerous inquiries touching my proficiency in that respect. My responses being to all appearances satisfactory, they proposed to engage my services for a short period, stating, at the same time, I was just such a person as their business required. Their names, as they afterwards gave them to me, were Merrill Brown and Abram Hamilton, though whether these were their true appellations, I have strong reasons to doubt. The former was a man apparently forty years of age, somewhat short and thick-set, with a countenance indicating shrewdness and intelligence. He wore a black frock coat and black hat, and said he resided either at Rochester or at Syracuse. The latter was a young man of fair complexion and light eyes, and, I should judge, had not passed the age of twenty-five. He was tall and slender, dressed in a snuff-colored coat, with glossy hat, and vest of elegant pattern. His whole apparel was in the extreme of fashion. His appearance was somewhat effeminate, but prepossessing, and there was about him an easy air, that showed he had mingled with the world. They were connected, as they informed me, with a circus company, then in the city of Washington; that they were on their way thither to rejoin it, having left it for a short time to make an excursion northward, for the purpose of seeing the country, and were paying their expenses by an occasional exhibition. They also remarked that they had found much difficulty in procuring music for their entertainments, and that if I would accompany them as far as New-York, they would give me one dollar for each day's services, and three dollars in addition for every night I played at their performances, besides sufficient to pay the expenses of my return from New-York to Saratoga.

I at once accepted the tempting offer, both for the reward it promised, and from a desire to visit the metropolis. They were anxious to leave immediately. Thinking my absence would be brief, I did not deem it necessary to write to Anne whither I had gone; in fact supposing that my return, perhaps, would be as soon as hers. So taking a change of linen and my violin, I was ready to depart. The carriage was brought round—a covered one, drawn by a pair of noble bays, altogether forming an elegant establishment. Their baggage, consisting of three large trunks, was fastened on the rack, and mounting to the driver's seat, while they took their places in the rear, I drove away from Saratoga on the road to Albany, elated with my new position, and happy as I had ever been, on any day in all my life.

We passed through Ballston, and striking the ridge road, as it is called, if my memory correctly serves me, followed it direct to Albany. We reached that city before dark, and stopped at a hotel southward from the Museum. This night I had an opportunity of witnessing one of their performances—the only one, during the whole period I was with them. Hamilton was stationed at the door; I formed the orchestra, while Brown provided the entertainment. It consisted in throwing balls, dancing on the rope, frying pancakes in a hat, causing invisible pigs to squeal, and other like feats of ventriloquism and legerdemain. The audience was extraordinarily sparse, and not of the selectest character at that, and Hamilton's report of the proceeds but a "beggarly account of empty boxes."

Early next morning we renewed our journey. The burden of their conversation now was the expression of an anxiety to reach the circus without delay. They hurried forward, without again stopping to exhibit, and in due course of time, we reached New-York, taking lodgings at a house on the west side of the city, in a street running from Broadway to the river. I supposed my journey was at an end, and expected in a day or two at least, to return to my friends and family at Saratoga. Brown and Hamilton, however, began to importune me to continue with them to Washington. They alleged that immediately on their arrival, now that the summer season was approaching, the circus would set out for the north. They promised me a situation and high wages if I would accompany them. Largely did they expatiate on the advantages that would result to me, and such were the flattering representations they made, that I finally concluded to accept the offer.

The next morning they suggested that, inasmuch as we were about entering a slave State, it would be well, before leaving New-York, to procure free papers. The idea struck me as a prudent one, though I think it would scarcely have occurred to me, had they not proposed it. We proceeded at once to what I understood to be the Custom House. They made oath to certain facts showing I was a free man. A paper was drawn up and handed us, with the direction to take it to the clerk's office. We did so, and the clerk having added something to it, for which he was paid six shillings, we returned again to the Custom House. Some further formalities were gone through with before it was completed, when, paying the officer two dollars, I placed the papers in my pocket, and started with my two friends to our hotel. I thought at the time I must confess, that the papers were scarcely worth the cost of obtaining them—the apprehension of danger to my personal safety never having suggested itself to me in the remotest manner. The clerk, to whom we were directed, I remember, made a memorandum in a large book, which, I presume, is in the office yet. A reference to the entries during the latter part of March, or first of April, 1841, I have no doubt will satisfy the incredulous, at least so far as this particular transaction is concerned.

With the evidence of freedom in my possession, the next day after our arrival in New-York, we crossed the ferry to Jersey City, and took the road to Philadelphia. Here we remained one night, continuing our journey towards Baltimore early in the morning. In due time, we arrived in the latter city, and stopped at a hotel near the railroad depot, either kept by a Mr. Rathbone, or known as the Rathbone House. All the way from New-York, their anxiety to reach the circus seemed to grow more and more intense. We left the carriage at Baltimore, and entering the cars, proceeded to Washington, at which place we arrived just at nightfall, the evening previous to the funeral of General Harrison,[11] and stopped at Gadsby's Hotel, on Pennsylvania Avenue.

After supper they called me to their apartments, and paid me forty-three dollars, a sum greater than my wages amounted to, which act of generosity was in consequence, they said, of their not having exhibited as often as they had given me to anticipate, during our trip from Saratoga. They moreover informed me that it had been the intention of the circus company to leave Washington the next morning, but that on account of the funeral, they had concluded to remain another day. They were then, as they had been from the time of our first meeting, extremely kind. No opportunity was omitted of addressing me in the language of approbation; while, on the other hand, I was certainly much prepossessed in their favor. I gave them my confidence without reserve, and would freely have trusted them to almost any extent. Their constant conversation and manner towards me—their foresight in suggesting the idea of free papers, and a hundred other little acts, unnecessary to be repeated—all indicated that they were friends indeed, sincerely solicitous for my welfare. I know not but they were. I know not but they were innocent of the great wickedness of which I now believe them guilty. Whether they were accessory to my misfortunes—subtle and inhuman monsters in the shape of men—designedly luring me away from home and family, and liberty, for the sake of gold—those who read these pages will have the same means of determining as myself. If they were innocent, my sudden disappearance must have been unaccountable indeed; but revolving in my mind all the attending circumstances, I never yet could indulge, towards them, so charitable a supposition.

After receiving the money from them, of which they appeared to have an abundance, they advised me not to go into the streets that night, inasmuch as I was unacquainted with the customs of the city. Promising to remember their advice, I left them together, and soon after was shown by a colored servant to a sleeping room in the back part of the hotel, on the ground floor. I laid down to rest, thinking of home and wife, and children, and the long distance that stretched between us, until I fell asleep. But no good angel of pity came to my bedside, bidding me to fly—no voice of mercy forewarned me in my dreams of the trials that were just at hand.

The next day there was a great pageant in Washington. The roar of cannon and the tolling of bells filled the air, while many houses were shrouded with crape, and the streets were black with people. As the day advanced, the procession made its appearance, coming slowly through the Avenue, carriage after carriage, in long succession, while thousands upon thousands followed on foot—all moving to the sound of melancholy music. They were bearing the dead body of Harrison to the grave.

From early in the morning, I was constantly in the company of Hamilton and Brown. They were the only persons I knew in Washington. We stood together as the funeral pomp passed by. I remember distinctly how the window glass would break and rattle to the ground, after each report of the cannon they were firing in the burial ground. We went to the Capitol, and walked a long time about the grounds. In the afternoon, they strolled towards the President's House, all the time keeping me near to them, and pointing out various places of interest. As yet, I had seen nothing of the circus. In fact, I had thought of it but little, if at all, amidst the excitement of the day.

My friends, several times during the afternoon, entered drinking saloons, and called for liquor. They were by no means in the habit, however, so far as I knew them, of indulging to excess. On these occasions, after serving themselves, they would pour out a glass and hand it to me. I did not become intoxicated, as may be inferred from what subsequently occurred. Towards evening, and soon after partaking of one of these potations, I began to experience most unpleasant sensations. I felt extremely ill. My head commenced aching—a dull, heavy pain, inexpressibly disagreeable. At the supper table, I was without appetite; the sight and flavor of food was nauseous. About dark the same servant conducted me to the room I had occupied the previous night. Brown and Hamilton advised me to retire, commiserating me kindly, and expressing hopes that I would be better in the morning. Divesting myself of coat and boots merely, I threw myself upon the bed. It was impossible to sleep. The pain in my head continued to increase, until it became almost unbearable. In a short time I became thirsty. My lips were parched. I could think of nothing but water—of lakes and flowing rivers, of brooks where I had stooped to drink, and of the dripping bucket, rising with its cool and overflowing nectar, from the bottom of the well. Towards midnight, as near as I could judge, I arose, unable longer to bear such intensity of thirst. I was a stranger in the house, and knew nothing of its apartments. There was no one up, as I could observe. Groping about at random, I knew not where, I found the way at last to a kitchen in the basement. Two or three colored servants were moving through it, one of whom, a woman, gave me two glasses of water. It afforded momentary relief, but by the time I had reached my room again, the same burning desire of drink, the same tormenting thirst, had again returned. It was even more torturing than before, as was also the wild pain in my head, if such a thing could be. I was in sore distress—in most excruciating agony! I seemed to stand on the brink of madness! The memory of that night of horrible suffering will follow me to the grave.[12]

In the course of an hour or more after my return from the kitchen, I was conscious of some one entering my room. There seemed to be several—a mingling of various voices,—but how many, or who they were, I cannot tell. Whether Brown and Hamilton were among them, is a mere matter of conjecture. I only remember, with any degree of distinctness, that I was told it was necessary to go to a physician and procure medicine, and that pulling on my boots, without coat or hat, I followed them through a long passage-way, or alley, into the open street. It ran out at right angles from Pennsylvania Avenue. On the opposite side there was a light burning in a window. My impression is there were then three persons with me, but it is altogether indefinite and vague, and like the memory of a painful dream. Going towards the light, which I imagined proceeded from a physician's office, and which seemed to recede as I advanced, is the last glimmering recollection I can now recall. From that moment I was insensible. How long I remained in that condition—whether only that night, or many days and nights—I do not know; but when consciousness returned, I found myself alone, in utter darkness, and in chains.

The pain in my head had subsided in a measure, but I was very faint and weak. I was sitting upon a low bench, made of rough boards, and without coat or hat. I was hand-cuffed. Around my ankles also were a pair of heavy fetters. One end of a chain was fastened to a large ring in the floor, the other to the fetters on my ankles. I tried in vain to stand upon my feet. Waking from such a painful trance, it was some time before I could collect my thoughts. Where was I? What was the meaning of these chains? Where were Brown and Hamilton? What had I done to deserve imprisonment in such a dungeon? I could not comprehend. There was a blank of some indefinite period, preceding my awakening in that lonely place, the events of which the utmost stretch of memory was unable to recall. I listened intently for some sign or sound of life, but nothing broke the oppressive silence, save the clinking of my chains, whenever I chanced to move. I spoke aloud, but the sound of my voice startled me. I felt of my pockets, so far as the fetters would allow—far enough, indeed, to ascertain that I had not only been robbed of liberty, but that my money and free papers were also gone! Then did the idea begin to break upon my mind, at first dim and confused, that I had been kidnapped. But that I thought was incredible. There must have been some misapprehension—some unfortunate mistake. It could not be that a free citizen of New-York, who had wronged no man, nor violated any law, should be dealt with thus inhumanly. The more I contemplated my situation, however, the more I became confirmed in my suspicions. It was a desolate thought, indeed. I felt there was no trust or mercy in unfeeling man; and commending myself to the God of the oppressed, bowed my head upon my fettered hands, and wept most bitterly.

CHAPTER III.

PAINFUL MEDITATIONS—JAMES H. BURCH—WILLIAMS' SLAVE PEN IN WASHINGTON—THE LACKEY, RADBURN—ASSERT MY FREEDOM—THE ANGER OF THE TRADER—THE PADDLE AND CAT-O'-NINE-TAILS—THE WHIPPING—NEW ACQUAINTANCES—RAY, WILLIAMS, AND RANDALL—ARRIVAL OF LITTLE EMILY AND HER MOTHER IN THE PEN—MATERNAL SORROWS—THE STORY OF ELIZA.

SOME three hours elapsed, during which time I remained seated on the low bench, absorbed in painful meditations. At length I heard the crowing of a cock, and soon a distant rumbling sound, as of carriages hurrying through the streets, came to my ears, and I knew that it was day. No ray of light, however, penetrated my prison. Finally, I heard footsteps immediately overhead, as of some one walking to and fro. It occurred to me then that I must be in an underground apartment, and the damp, mouldy odors of the place confirmed the supposition. The noise above continued for at least an hour, when, at last, I heard footsteps approaching from without. A key rattled in the lock—a strong door swung back upon its hinges, admitting a flood of light, and two men entered and stood before me. One of them was a large, powerful man, forty years of age, perhaps, with dark, chestnut-colored hair, slightly interspersed with gray. His face was full, his complexion flush, his features grossly coarse, expressive of nothing but cruelty and cunning. He was about five feet ten inches high, of full habit, and, without prejudice, I must be allowed to say, was a man whose whole appearance was sinister and repugnant. His name was James H. Burch,[13] as I learned afterwards—a well-known slave-dealer in Washington; and then, or lately, connected in business, as a partner, with Theophilus Freeman, of New-Orleans. The person who accompanied him was a simple lackey, named Ebenezer Radburn, who acted merely in the capacity of turnkey. Both of these men still live in Washington, or did, at the time of my return through that city from slavery in January last.

The light admitted through the open door enabled me to observe the room in which I was confined. It was about twelve feet square—the walls of solid masonry. The floor was of heavy plank. There was one small window, crossed with great iron bars, with an outside shutter, securely fastened.

An iron-bound door led into an adjoining cell, or vault, wholly destitute of windows, or any means of admitting light. The furniture of the room in which I was, consisted of the wooden bench on which I sat, an old-fashioned, dirty box stove, and besides these, in either cell, there was neither bed, nor blanket, nor any other thing whatever. The door, through which Burch and Radburn entered, led through a small passage, up a flight of steps into a yard, surrounded by a brick wall ten or twelve feet high, immediately in rear of a building of the same width as itself. The yard extended rearward from the house about thirty feet. In one part of the wall there was a strongly ironed door, opening into a narrow, covered passage, leading along one side of the house into the street. The doom of the colored man, upon whom the door leading out of that narrow passage closed, was sealed. The top of the wall supported one end of a roof, which ascended inwards, forming a kind of open shed. Underneath the roof there was a crazy loft all round, where slaves, if so disposed, might sleep at night, or in inclement weather seek shelter from the storm. It was like a farmer's barnyard in most respects, save it was so constructed that the outside world could never see the human cattle that were herded there.

The building to which the yard was attached, was two stories high, fronting on one of the public streets of Washington. Its outside presented only the appearance of a quiet private residence. A stranger looking at it, would never have dreamed of its execrable uses. Strange as it may seem, within plain sight of this same house, looking down from its commanding height upon it, was the Capitol. The voices of patriotic representatives boasting of freedom and equality, and the rattling of the poor slave's chains, almost commingled. A slave pen within the very shadow of the Capitol!

Such is a correct description as it was in 1841, of Williams' slave pen in Washington, in one of the cellars of which I found myself so unaccountably confined.

"Well, my boy, how do you feel now?" said Burch, as he entered through the open door. I replied that I was sick, and inquired the cause of my imprisonment. He answered that I was his slave—that he had bought me, and that he was about to send me to New-Orleans. I asserted, aloud and boldly, that I was a freeman—a resident of Saratoga, where I had a wife and children, who were also free, and that my name was Northup. I complained bitterly of the strange treatment I had received, and threatened, upon my liberation, to have satisfaction for the wrong. He denied that I was free, and with an emphatic oath, declared that I came from Georgia. Again and again I asserted I was no man's slave, and insisted upon his taking off my chains at once. He endeavored to hush me, as if he feared my voice would be overheard. But I would not be silent, and denounced the authors of my imprisonment, whoever they might be, as unmitigated villains. Finding he could not quiet me, he flew into a towering passion. With blasphemous oaths, he called me a black liar, a runaway from Georgia, and every other profane and vulgar epithet that the most indecent fancy could conceive.

During this time Radburn was standing silently by. His business was, to

SCENE IN THE SLAVE PEN AT WASHINGTON.

oversee this human, or rather inhuman stable, receiving slaves, feeding and whipping them, at the rate of two shillings a head per day. Turning to him, Burch ordered the paddle and cat-o'-ninetails to be brought in. He disappeared, and in a few moments returned with these instruments of torture. The paddle, as it is termed in slave-beating parlance, or at least the one with which I first became acquainted, and of which I now speak, was a piece of hard-wood board, eighteen or twenty inches long, moulded to the shape of an old-fashioned pudding stick, or ordinary oar. The flattened portion, which was about the size in circumference of two open hands, was bored with a small auger in numerous places. The cat was a large rope of many strands—the strands unraveled, and a knot tied at the extremity of each.

As soon as these formidable whips appeared, I was seized by both of them, and roughly divested of my clothing. My feet, as has been stated, were fastened to the floor. Drawing me over the bench, face downwards, Radburn placed his heavy foot upon the fetters, between my wrists, holding them painfully to the floor. With the paddle, Burch commenced beating me. Blow after blow was inflicted upon my naked body. When his unrelenting arm grew tired, he stopped and asked if I still insisted I was a free man. I did insist upon it, and then the blows were renewed, faster and more energetically, if possible, than before. When again tired, he would repeat the same question, and receiving the same answer, continue his cruel labor. All this time, the incarnate devil was uttering most fiendish oaths. At length the paddle broke, leaving the useless handle in his hand. Still I would not yield. All his brutal blows could not force from my lips the foul lie that I was a slave. Casting madly on the floor the handle of the broken paddle, he seized the rope. This was far more painful than the other. I struggled with all my power, but it was in vain. I prayed for mercy, but my prayer was only answered with imprecations and with stripes. I thought I must die beneath the lashes of the accursed brute. Even now the flesh crawls upon my bones, as I recall the scene. I was all on fire. My sufferings I can compare to nothing else than the burning agonies of hell!

At last I became silent to his repeated questions. I would make no reply. In fact, I was becoming almost unable to speak. Still he plied the lash without stint upon my poor body, until it seemed that the lacerated flesh was stripped from my bones at every stroke. A man with a particle of mercy in his soul would not have beaten even a dog so cruelly. At length Radburn said that it was useless to whip me any more—that I would be sore enough. Thereupon, Burch desisted, saying, with an admonitory shake of his fist in my face, and hissing the words through his firm-set teeth, that if ever I dared to utter again that I was entitled to my freedom, that I had been kidnapped, or any thing whatever of the kind, the castigation I had just received was nothing in comparison with what would follow. He swore that he would either conquer or kill me. With these consolatory words, the fetters were taken from my wrists, my feet still remaining fastened to the ring; the shutter of the little barred window, which had been opened, was again closed, and going out, locking the great door behind them, I was left in darkness as before.

In an hour, perhaps two, my heart leaped to my throat, as the key rattled in the door again. I, who had been so lonely, and who had longed so ardently to see some one, I cared not who, now shuddered at the thought of man's approach. A human face was fearful to me, especially a white one. Radburn entered, bringing with him, on a tin plate, a piece of shriveled fried pork, a slice of bread and a cup of water. He asked me how I felt, and remarked that I had received a pretty severe flogging. He remonstrated with me against the propriety of asserting my freedom. In rather a patronizing and confidential manner, he gave it to me as his advice, that the less I said on that subject the better it would be for me. The man evidently endeavored to appear kind—whether touched at the sight of my sad condition, or with the view of silencing, on my part, any further expression of my rights, it is not necessary now to conjecture. He unlocked the fetters from my ankles, opened the shutters of the little window, and departed, leaving me again alone.

By this time I had become stiff and sore; my body was covered with blisters, and it was with great pain and difficulty that I could move. From the window I could observe nothing but the roof resting on the adjacent wall. At night I laid down upon the damp, hard floor, without any pillow or covering whatever. Punctually, twice a day, Radburn came in, with his pork, and bread, and water. I had but little appetite, though I was tormented with continual thirst. My wounds would not permit me to remain but a few minutes in any one position; so, sitting, or standing, or moving slowly round, I passed the days and nights. I was heart sick and discouraged. Thoughts of my family, of my wife and children, continually occupied my mind. When sleep overpowered me I dreamed of them—dreamed I was again in Saratoga—that I could see their faces, and hear their voices calling me. Awakening from the pleasant phantasms of sleep to the bitter realities around me, I could but groan and weep. Still my spirit was not broken. I indulged the anticipation of escape, and that speedily. It was impossible, I reasoned, that men could be so unjust as to detain me as a slave, when the truth of my case was known. Burch, ascertaining I was no runaway from Georgia, would certainly let me go. Though suspicions of Brown and Hamilton were not unfrequent, I could not reconcile myself to the idea that they were instrumental to my imprisonment. Surely they would seek me out—they would deliver me from thraldom. Alas! I had not then learned the measure of "man's inhumanity to man," nor to what limitless extent of wickedness he will go for the love of gain.[14]

In the course of several days the outer door was thrown open, allowing me the liberty of the yard. There I found three slaves—one of them a lad of ten years, the others young men of about twenty and twenty-five. I was not long in forming an acquaintance, and learning their names and the particulars of their history.

The eldest was a colored man named Clemens Ray. He had lived in Washington; had driven a hack, and worked in a livery stable there for a long time. He was very intelligent, and fully comprehended his situation. The thought of going south overwhelmed him with grief. Burch had purchased him a few days before, and had placed him there until such time as he was ready to send him to the New-Orleans market. From him I learned for the first time that I was in William's Slave Pen, a place I had never heard of previously. He described to me the uses for which it was designed. I repeated to him the particulars of my unhappy story, but he could only give me the consolation of his sympathy. He also advised me to be silent henceforth on the subject of my freedom, for, knowing the character of Burch, he assured me that it would only be attended with renewed whipping. The next eldest was named John Williams. He was raised in Virginia, not far from Washington. Burch had taken him in payment of a debt, and he constantly entertained the hope that his master would redeem him—a hope that was subsequently realized. The lad was a sprightly child, that answered to the name of Randall. Most of the time he was playing about the yard, but occasionally would cry, calling for his mother, and wondering when she would come. His mother's absence seemed to be the great and only grief in his little heart. He was too young to realize his condition, and when the memory of his mother was not in his mind, he amused us with his pleasant pranks.

At night, Ray, Williams, and the boy, slept in the loft of the shed, while I was locked in the cell. Finally we were each provided with blankets, such as are used upon horses—the only bedding I was allowed to have for twelve years afterwards. Ray and Williams asked me many questions about New-York—how colored people were treated there; how they could have homes and families of their own, with none to disturb and oppress them; and Ray, especially, sighed continually for freedom. Such conversations, however, were not in the hearing of Burch, or the keeper Radburn. Aspirations such as these would have brought down the lash upon our backs.

It is necessary in this narrative, in order to present a full and truthful statement of all the principal events in the history of my life, and to portray the institution of Slavery as I have seen and known it, to speak of well-known places, and of many persons who are yet living. I am, and always was, an entire stranger in Washington and its vicinity—aside from Burch and Radburn, knowing no man there, except as I have heard of them through my enslaved companions. What I am about to say, if false, can be easily contradicted.

I remained in Williams' slave pen about two weeks. The night previous to my departure a woman was brought in, weeping bitterly, and leading by the hand a little child. They were Randall's mother and half-sister. On meeting them he was overjoyed, clinging to her dress, kissing the child, and exhibiting every demonstration of delight. The mother also clasped him in her arms, embraced him tenderly, and gazed at him fondly through her tears, calling him by many an endearing name.

Emily, the child, was seven or eight years old, of light complexion, and with a face of admirable beauty. Her hair fell in curls around her neck, while the style and richness of her dress, and the neatness of her whole appearance indicated she had been brought up in the midst of wealth. She was a sweet child indeed. The woman also was arrayed in silk, with rings upon her fingers, and golden ornaments suspended from her ears. Her air and manners, the correctness and propriety of her language—all showed evidently, that she had sometime stood above the common level of a slave. She seemed to be amazed at finding herself in such a place as that. It was plainly a sudden and unexpected turn of fortune that had brought her there. Filling the air with her complainings, she was hustled, with the children and myself, into the cell. Language can convey but an inadequate impression of the lamentations to which she gave incessant utterance. Throwing herself upon the floor, and encircling the children in her arms, she poured forth such touching words as only maternal love and kindness can suggest. They nestled closely to her, as if *there* only was there any safety or protection. At last they slept, their heads resting upon her lap. While they slumbered, she smoothed the hair back from their little foreheads, and talked to them all night long. She called them her darlings—her sweet babes— poor innocent things, that knew not the misery they were destined to endure. Soon they would have no mother to comfort them—they would be taken from her. What would become of them? Oh! she could not live away from her little Emmy and her dear boy. They had always been good children, and had such loving ways. It would break her heart, God knew, she said, if they were taken from her; and yet she knew they meant to sell them, and, may be, they would be separated, and could never see each other any more. It was enough to melt a heart of stone to listen to the pitiful expressions of that desolate and distracted mother. Her name was Eliza; and this was the story of her life, as she afterwards related it:

She was the slave of Elisha Berry, a rich man, living in the neighborhood of Washington. She was born, I think she said, on his plantation. Years before, he had fallen into dissipated habits, and quarreled with his wife. In fact, soon after the birth of Randall, they separated. Leaving his wife and daughter in the house they had always occupied, he erected a new one nearby, on the estate. Into this house he brought Eliza; and, on condition of her living with him, she and her children were to be emancipated. She resided with him there nine years, with servants to attend upon her, and provided with every comfort and luxury of life. Emily was his child! Finally, her young mistress, who had always remained with her mother at the homestead, married a Mr. Jacob Brooks. At length, for some cause, (as I gathered from her relation,) beyond Berry's control, a division of his property was made. She and her children fell to the share of Mr. Brooks. During the nine years she had lived with Berry, in consequence of the position she was compelled to occupy, she and Emily had become the object of Mrs. Berry and her daughter's hatred and dislike. Berry himself she represented as a man of naturally a kind heart, who always promised her that she should have her freedom, and who, she had no doubt, would grant it to her then, if it were only in his power. As soon as they thus came into the possession and control of the daughter, it became very manifest they would not live long together. The sight of Eliza seemed to be odious to Mrs. Brooks; neither could she bear to look upon the child, half-sister, and beautiful as she was!

The day she was led into the pen, Brooks had brought her from the estate into the city, under pretence that the time had come when her free papers were to be executed, in fulfillment of her master's promise. Elated at the prospect of immediate liberty, she decked herself and little Emmy in their best apparel, and accompanied him with a joyful heart. On their arrival in the city, instead of being baptized into the family of freemen, she was delivered to the trader Burch. The paper that was executed was a bill of sale. The hope of years was blasted in a moment. From the height of most exulting happiness to the utmost depths of wretchedness, she had that day descended. No wonder that she wept, and filled the pen with wailings and expressions of heart-rending woe.

Eliza is now dead. Far up the Red River, where it pours its waters sluggishly through the unhealthy low lands of Louisiana, she rests in the grave at last—the only resting place of the poor slave! How all her fears were realized—how she mourned day and night, and never would be comforted—how, as she predicted, her heart did indeed break, with the burden of maternal sorrow, will be seen as the narrative proceeds.

CHAPTER IV.

ELIZA'S SORROWS—PREPARATION TO EMBARK—DRIVEN THROUGH THE STREETS OF WASHINGTON—HAIL, COLUMBIA—THE TOMB OF WASHINGTON—CLEM RAY— THE BREAKFAST ON THE STEAMER—THE HAPPY BIRDS—AQUIA CREEK—FRED-ERICKSBURGH—ARRIVAL IN RICHMOND—GOODIN AND HIS SLAVE PEN— ROBERT, OF CINCINNATI—DAVID AND HIS WIFE—MARY AND LETHE—CLEM'S RETURN—HIS SUBSEQUENT ESCAPE TO CANADA—THE BRIG ORLEANS—JAMES H. BURCH.

AT intervals during the first night of Eliza's incarceration in the pen, she complained bitterly of Jacob Brooks, her young mistress' husband. She declared that had she been aware of the deception he intended to practice upon her, he never would have brought her there alive. They had chosen the opportunity of getting her away when Master Berry was absent from the plantation. He had always been kind to her. She wished that she could see him; but she knew that even he was unable now to rescue her. Then would she commence weeping again—kissing the sleeping children—talking first to one, then to the other, as they lay in their unconscious slumbers, with their heads upon her lap. So wore the long night away; and when the morning dawned, and night had come again, still she kept mourning on, and would not be consoled.

About midnight following, the cell door opened, and Burch and Radburn entered, with lanterns in their hands. Burch, with an oath, ordered us to roll up our blankets without delay, and get ready to go on board the boat. He swore we would be left unless we hurried fast. He aroused the children from their slumbers with a rough shake, and said they were d—d sleepy, it appeared. Going out into the yard, he called Clem Ray, ordering him to leave the loft and come into the cell, and bring his blanket with him. When Clem appeared, he placed us side by side, and fastened us together with hand-cuffs—my left hand to his right. John Williams had been taken out a day or two before, his master having redeemed him, greatly to his delight. Clem and I were ordered to march, Eliza and the children following. We were conducted into the yard, from thence into the covered passage, and up a flight of steps through a side door into the upper room, where I had heard the walking to and fro. Its furniture was a stove, a few old chairs, and a long table, covered with papers. It was a white-washed room, without any carpet on the floor, and seemed a sort of office. By one of the windows, I remember, hung a rusty sword, which attracted my attention. Burch's trunk was there. In obedience to his orders, I took hold of one of its handles with my unfettered hand, while he taking hold of the other, we proceeded out of the front door into the street in the same order as we had left the cell.

It was a dark night. All was quiet. I could see lights, or the reflection of them, over towards Pennsylvania Avenue, but there was no one, not even a straggler, to be seen. I was almost resolved to attempt to break away. Had I not been hand-cuffed the attempt would certainly have been made, whatever consequence might have followed. Radburn was in the rear, carrying a large stick, and hurrying up the children as fast as the little ones could walk. So we passed, hand-cuffed and in silence, through the streets of Washington—through the Capital of a nation, whose theory of government, we are told, rests on the foundation of man's inalienable right to life, LIBERTY, and the pursuit of happiness! Hail! Columbia, happy land, indeed!

Reaching the steamboat, we were quickly hustled into the hold, among barrels and boxes of freight. A colored servant brought a light, the bell rung, and soon the vessel started down the Potomac, carrying us we knew not where. The bell tolled as we passed the tomb of Washington! Burch, no doubt, with uncovered head, bowed reverently before the sacred ashes of the man who devoted his illustrious life to the liberty of his country.

None of us slept that night but Randall and little Emmy. For the first time Clem Ray was wholly overcome. To him the idea of going south was terrible in the extreme. He was leaving the friends and associations of his youth—everything that was dear and precious to his heart—in all probability never to return. He and Eliza mingled their tears together, bemoaning their cruel fate. For my own part, difficult as it was, I endeavored to keep up my spirits. I resolved in my mind a hundred plans of escape, and fully determined to make the attempt the first desperate chance that offered. I had by this time become satisfied, however, that my true policy was to say nothing further on the subject of my having been born a freeman. It would but expose me to maltreatment, and diminish the chances of liberation.

After sunrise in the morning we were called up on deck to breakfast. Burch took our hand-cuffs off, and we sat down to table. He asked Eliza if she would take a dram. She declined, thanking him politely. During the meal we were all silent—not a word passed between us. A mulatto woman who served at table seemed to take an interest in our behalf—told us to cheer up, and not to be so cast down. Breakfast over, the hand-cuffs were restored, and Burch ordered us out on the stern deck. We sat down together on some boxes, still saying nothing in Burch's presence. Occasionally a passenger would walk out to where we were, look at us for a while, then silently return.

It was a very pleasant morning. The fields along the river were covered with verdure, far in advance of what I had been accustomed to see at that season of the year. The sun shone out warmly; the birds were singing in the trees. The happy birds—I envied them. I wished for wings like them, that I might cleave the air to where my birdlings waited vainly for their father's coming, in the cooler region of the North.

In the forenoon the steamer reached Aquia Creek. There the passengers took stages—Burch and his five slaves occupying one exclusively. He laughed with the children, and at one stopping place went so far as to purchase them a piece of gingerbread. He told me to hold up my head and look smart. That I might, perhaps, get a good master if I behaved myself. I made him no reply. His face was hateful to me, and I could not bear to look upon it. I sat in the corner, cherishing in my heart the hope, not yet extinct, of some day meeting the tyrant on the soil of my native State.

At Fredericksburgh we were transferred from the stage coach to a car, and before dark arrived in Richmond, the chief city of Virginia. At this city we were taken from the cars, and driven through the street to a slave pen, between the railroad depot and the river, kept by a Mr. Goodin. This pen is similar to Williams' in Washington, except it is somewhat larger; and besides, there were two small houses standing at opposite corners within the yard. These houses are usually found within slave yards, being used as rooms for the examination of human chattels by purchasers before concluding a bargain. Unsoundness in a slave, as well as in a horse, detracts materially from his value. If no warranty is given, a close examination is a matter of particular importance to the negro jockey.

We were met at the door of Goodin's yard by that gentleman himself—a short, fat man, with a round, plump face, black hair and whiskers, and a complexion almost as dark as some of his own negroes. He had a hard, stern look, and was perhaps about fifty years of age. Burch and he met with great cordiality. They were evidently old friends. Shaking each other warmly by the hand, Burch remarked he had brought some company, inquired at what time the brig would leave, and was answered that it would probably leave the next day at such an hour. Goodin then turned to me, took hold of my arm, turned me partly round, looked at me sharply with the air of one who considered himself a good judge of property, and as if estimating in his own mind about how much I was worth.

"Well, boy, where did you come from?" Forgetting myself, for a moment, I answered, "From New-York."

"New-York! H—l! what have you been doing up there?" was his astonished interrogatory.

Observing Burch at this moment looking at me with an angry expression that conveyed a meaning it was not difficult to understand, I immediately said, "O, I have only been up that way a piece," in a manner intended to imply that although I might have been as far as New-York, yet I wished it distinctly understood that I did not belong to that free State, nor to any other.

Goodin then turned to Clem, and then to Eliza and the children, examining them severally, and asking various questions. He was pleased with Emily, as was every one who saw the child's sweet countenance. She was not as tidy as when I first beheld her; her hair was now somewhat disheveled; but through its unkempt and soft profusion there still beamed a little face of most surpassing loveliness. "Altogether we were a fair lot—a devilish good lot," he said, enforcing that opinion with more than one emphatic adjective not found in the Christian vocabulary. Thereupon we passed into the yard. Quite a number of slaves, as many as thirty I should say, were moving about, or sitting on benches under the shed. They were all cleanly dressed—the men with hats, the women with handkerchiefs tied about their heads.

Burch and Goodin, after separating from us, walked up the steps at the back part of the main building, and sat down upon the door sill. They entered into conversation, but the subject of it I could not hear. Presently Burch came down into the yard, unfettered me, and led me into one of the small houses.

"You told that man you came from New-York," said he.

I replied, "I told him I had been up as far as New-York, to be sure, but did not tell him I belonged there, nor that I was a freeman. I meant no harm at all, Master Burch. I would not have said it had I thought."

He looked at me a moment as if he was ready to devour me, then turning round went out. In a few minutes he returned. "If ever I hear you say a word about New-York, or about your freedom, I will be the death of you—I will kill you; you may rely on that," he ejaculated fiercely.

I doubt not he understood then better than I did, the danger and the penalty of selling a free man into slavery. He felt the necessity of closing my mouth against the crime he knew he was committing. Of course, my life would not have weighed a feather, in any emergency requiring such a sacrifice. Undoubtedly, he meant precisely what he said.

Under the shed on one side of the yard, there was constructed a rough table, while overhead were sleeping lofts—the same as in the pen at Washington. After partaking at this table of our supper of pork and bread, I was hand-cuffed to a large yellow man, quite stout and fleshy, with a countenance expressive of the utmost melancholy. He was a man of intelligence and information. Chained together, it was not long before we became acquainted with each other's history. His name was Robert. Like myself, he had been born free, and had a wife and two children in Cincinnati. He said he had come south with two men, who had hired him in the city of his residence. Without free papers, he had been seized at Fredericksburgh, placed in confinement, and beaten until he had learned, as I had, the necessity and the policy of silence. He had been in Goodin's pen about three weeks. To this man I became much attached. We could sympathize with, and understand each other. It was with tears and a heavy heart, not many days subsequently, that I saw him die, and looked for the last time upon his lifeless form!

Robert and myself, with Clem, Eliza and her children, slept that night upon our blankets, in one of the small houses in the yard. There were four others, all from the same plantation, who had been sold and were now on their way south, who also occupied it with us. David and his wife, Caroline, both mulattoes, were exceedingly affected. They dreaded the thought of being put into the cane and cotton fields; but their greatest source of anxiety was the apprehension of being separated. Mary, a tall, lithe girl, of a most jetty black, was listless and apparently indifferent. Like many of the class, she scarcely knew there was such a word as freedom. Brought up in the ignorance of a brute, she possessed but little more than a brute's intelligence. She was one of those, and there are very many, who fear nothing but their master's lash, and know no further duty than to obey his voice. The other was Lethe. She was of an entirely different character. She had long, straight hair, and bore more the appearance of an Indian than a negro woman. She had sharp and spiteful eyes, and continually gave utterance to the language of hatred and revenge. Her husband had been sold. She knew not where she was. An exchange of masters, she was sure, could not be for the worse. She cared not whither they might carry her. Pointing to the scars upon her face, the desperate creature wished that she might see the day when she could wipe them off in some man's blood!

While we were thus learning the history of each other's wretchedness, Eliza was seated in a corner by herself, singing hymns and praying for her children. Wearied from the loss of so much sleep, I could no longer bear up against the advances of that "sweet restorer," and laying down by the side of Robert, on the floor, soon forgot my troubles, and slept until the dawn of day.

In the morning, having swept the yard, and washed ourselves, under Goodin's superintendence, we were ordered to roll up our blankets, and make ready for the continuance of our journey. Clem Ray was informed that he would go no further, Burch, for some cause, having concluded to carry him back to Washington. He was much rejoiced. Shaking hands, we parted in the slave pen at Richmond, and I have not seen him since. But, much to my surprise, since my return, I learned that he had escaped from bondage, and on his way to the free soil of Canada, lodged one night at the house of my brother-in-law in Saratoga, informing my family of the place and the condition in which he left me.

In the afternoon we were drawn up, two abreast, Robert and myself in advance, and in this order, driven by Burch and Goodin from the yard, through the streets of Richmond to the brig Orleans. She was a vessel of respectable size, full rigged, and freighted principally with tobacco. We were all on board by five o'clock. Burch brought us each a tin cup and a spoon. There were forty of us in the brig, being all, except Clem, that were in the pen.

With a small pocket knife that had not been taken from me, I began cutting the initials of my name upon the tin cup. The others immediately flocked round me, requesting me to mark theirs in a similar manner. In time, I gratified them all, of which they did not appear to be forgetful.

We were all stowed away in the hold at night, and the hatch barred down. We laid on boxes, or where-ever there was room enough to stretch our blankets on the floor.

Burch accompanied us no farther than Richmond, returning from that point to the capital with Clem. Not until the lapse of almost twelve years, to wit, in January last, in the Washington police office, did I set my eyes upon his face again.

James H. Burch was a slave-trader—buying men, women and children at low prices, and selling them at an advance. He was a speculator in human flesh— a disreputable calling—and so considered at the South. For the present he disappears from the scenes recorded in this narrative, but he will appear again before its close, not in the character of a man-whipping tyrant, but as an arrested, cringing criminal in a court of law, that failed to do him justice.

CHAPTER V.

ARRIVAL AT NORFOLK—FREDERICK AND MARIA—ARTHUR, THE FREEMAN—AP-
POINTED STEWARD—JIM, CUFFEE, AND JENNY—THE STORM—BAHAMA
BANKS—THE CALM—THE CONSPIRACY—THE LONG BOAT—THE SMALL-POX—
DEATH OF ROBERT—MANNING, THE SAILOR—THE MEETING IN THE FORECAS-
TLE—THE LETTER—ARRIVAL AT NEW-ORLEANS—ARTHUR'S RESCUE—
THEOPHILUS FREEMAN, THE CONSIGNEE—PLATT—FIRST NIGHT IN THE
NEW-ORLEANS SLAVE PEN.

AFTER we were all on board, the brig Orleans proceeded down James River. Passing into Chesapeake Bay, we arrived next day opposite the city of Norfolk. While lying at anchor, a lighter approached us from the town, bringing four more slaves. Frederick, a boy of eighteen, had been born a slave, as also had Henry, who was some years older. They had both been house servants in the city. Maria was a rather genteel looking colored girl, with a faultless form, but ignorant and extremely vain. The idea of going to New-Orleans was pleasing to her. She entertained an extravagantly high opinion of her own attractions. Assuming a haughty mien, she declared to her companions, that immediately on our arrival in New-Orleans, she had no doubt, some wealthy single gentleman of good taste would purchase her at once!

But the most prominent of the four, was a man named Arthur. As the lighter approached, he struggled stoutly with his keepers. It was with main force that he was dragged aboard the brig. He protested, in a loud voice, against the treatment he was receiving, and demanded to be released. His face was swollen, and covered with wounds and bruises, and, indeed, one side of it was a complete raw sore. He was forced, with all haste, down the hatchway into the hold. I caught an outline of his story as he was borne struggling along, of which he afterwards gave me a more full relation, and it was as follows: He had long resided in the city of Norfolk, and was a free man. He had a family living there, and was a mason by trade. Having been unusually detained, he was returning late one night to his house in the suburbs of the city, when he was attacked by a gang of persons in an unfrequented street. He fought until his strength failed him. Overpowered at last, he was gagged and bound with ropes, and beaten, until he became insensible. For several days they secreted him in the slave pen at Norfolk— a very common establishment, it appears, in the cities of the South. The night before, he had been taken out and put on board the lighter, which, pushing out from shore, had awaited our arrival. For some time he continued his protestations, and was altogether irreconcilable. At length, however, he became silent. He sank into a gloomy and thoughtful mood, and appeared to be counseling with himself. There was in the man's determined face, something that suggested the thought of desperation.

After leaving Norfolk the hand-cuffs were taken off, and during the day we were allowed to remain on deck. The captain selected Robert as his waiter, and I was appointed to superintend the cooking department, and the distribution of food and water. I had three assistants, Jim, Cuffee and Jenny. Jenny's business was to prepare the coffee, which consisted of corn meal scorched in a kettle, boiled and sweetened with molasses. Jim and Cuffee baked the hoe-cake and boiled the bacon.

Standing by a table, formed of a wide board resting on the heads of the barrels, I cut and handed to each a slice of meat and a "dodger" of the bread, and from Jenny's kettle also dipped out for each a cup of the coffee. The use of plates was dispensed with, and their sable fingers took the place of knives and forks. Jim and Cuffee were very demure and attentive to business, somewhat inflated with their situation as second cooks, and without doubt feeling that there was a great responsibility resting on them. I was called steward—a name given me by the captain.

The slaves were fed twice a day, at ten and five o'clock—always receiving the same kind and quantity of fare, and in the same manner as above described. At night we were driven into the hold, and securely fastened clown.

Scarcely were we out of sight of land before we were overtaken by a violent storm. The brig rolled and plunged until we feared she would go down. Some were sea-sick, others on their knees praying, while some were fast holding to each other, paralyzed with fear. The sea-sickness rendered the place of our confinement loathsome and disgusting. It would have been a happy thing for most of us—it would have saved the agony of many hundred lashes, and miserable deaths at last—had the compassionate sea snatched us that day from the clutches of remorseless men. The thought of Randall and little Emmy sinking down among the monsters of the deep, is a more pleasant contemplation than to think of them as they are now, perhaps, dragging out lives of unrequited toil.

When in sight of the Bahama Banks, at a place called Old Point Compass, or the Hole in the Wall, we were becalmed three days. There was scarcely a breath of air. The waters of the gulf presented a singularly white appearance, like lime water.

In the order of events, I come now to the relation of an occurrence, which I never call to mind but with sensations of regret. I thank God, who has since permitted me to escape from the thralldom of slavery, that through his merciful interposition I was prevented from imbruing my hands in the blood of his creatures. Let not those who have never been placed in like circumstances, judge me harshly. Until they have been chained and beaten—until they find themselves in the situation I was, borne away from home and family towards a land of bondage—let them refrain from saying what they would not do for liberty. How far I should have been justified in the sight of God and man, it is unnecessary now to speculate upon. It is enough to say that I am able to congratulate myself upon the harmless termination of an affair which threatened, for a time, to be attended with serious results.

Towards evening, on the first day of the calm, Arthur and myself were in the bow of the vessel, seated on the windlass. We were conversing together of the probable destiny that awaited us, and mourning together over our misfortunes. Arthur said, and I agreed with him, that death was far less terrible than the living prospect that was before us. For a long time we talked of our children, our past lives, and of the probabilities of escape. Obtaining possession of the brig was suggested by one of us. We discussed the possibility of our being able, in such an event, to make our way to the harbor of New-York. I knew little of the compass; but the idea of risking the experiment was eagerly entertained. The chances, for and against us, in an encounter with the crew, was canvassed. Who could be relied upon, and who could not, the proper time and manner of the attack, were all talked over and over again. From the moment the plot suggested itself I began to hope. I revolved it constantly in my mind. As difficulty after difficulty arose, some ready conceit was at hand, demonstrating how it could be overcome. While others slept, Arthur and I were maturing our plans. At length, with much caution, Robert was gradually made acquainted with our intentions. He approved of them at once, and entered into the conspiracy with a zealous spirit. There was not another slave we dared to trust. Brought up in fear and ignorance as they are, it can scarcely be conceived how servilely they will cringe before a white man's look. It was not safe to deposit so bold a secret with any of them, and finally we three resolved to take upon ourselves alone the fearful responsibility of the attempt.

At night, as has been said, we were driven into the hold, and the hatch barred down. How to reach the deck was the first difficulty that presented itself. On the bow of the brig, however, I had observed the small boat lying bottom upwards. It occurred to me that by secreting ourselves underneath it, we would not be missed from the crowd, as they were hurried down into the hold at night. I was selected to make the experiment, in order to satisfy ourselves of its feasibility. The next evening, accordingly, after supper, watching my opportunity, I hastily concealed myself beneath it. Lying close upon the deck, I could see what was going on around me, while wholly unperceived myself. In the morning, as they came up, I slipped from my hiding place without being observed. The result was entirely satisfactory.

The captain and mate slept in the cabin of the former. From Robert, who had frequent occasion, in his capacity of waiter, to make observations in that quarter, we ascertained the exact position of their respective berths. He further informed us that there were always two pistols and a cutlass lying on the table. The crew's cook slept in the cook galley on deck, a sort of vehicle on wheels, that could be moved about as convenience required, while the sailors, numbering only six, either slept in the forecastle, or in hammocks swung among the rigging.

Finally our arrangements were all completed. Arthur and I were to steal silently to the captain's cabin, seize the pistols and cutlass, and as quickly as possible despatch him and the mate. Robert, with a club, was to stand by the door leading from the deck down into the cabin, and, in case of necessity, beat back the sailors, until we could hurry to his assistance. We were to proceed then as circumstances might require. Should the attack be so sudden and successful as to prevent resistance, the hatch was to remain barred down; otherwise the slaves were to be called up, and in the crowd, and hurry, and confusion of the time, we resolved to regain our liberty or lose our lives. I was then to assume the unaccustomed place of pilot, and, steering northward, we trusted that some lucky wind might bear us to the soil of freedom.

The mate's name was Biddee, the captain's I cannot now recall, though I rarely ever forget a name once heard. The captain was a small, genteel man, erect and prompt, with a proud bearing, and looked the personification of courage. If he is still living, and these pages should chance to meet his eye, he will learn a fact connected with the voyage of the brig, from Richmond to New-Orleans, in 1841, not entered on his log-book.

We were all prepared, and impatiently waiting an opportunity of putting our designs into execution, when they were frustrated[15] by a sad and unforeseen event. Robert was taken ill. It was soon announced that he had the small-pox. He continued to grow worse, and four days previous to our arrival in New-Orleans he died. One of the sailors sewed him in his blanket, with a large stone from the ballast at his feet, and then laying him on a hatchway, and elevating it with tackles above the railing, the inanimate body of poor Robert was consigned to the white waters of the gulf.

We were all panic-stricken by the appearance of the small-pox. The captain ordered lime to be scattered through the hold, and other prudent precautions to be taken. The death of Robert, however, and the presence of the malady, oppressed me sadly, and I gazed out over the great waste of waters with a spirit that was indeed disconsolate.

An evening or two after Robert's burial, I was leaning on the hatchway near the forecastle, full of desponding thoughts, when a sailor in a kind voice asked me why I was so down-hearted. The tone and manner of the man assured me, and I answered, because I was a freeman, and had been kidnapped. He remarked that it was enough to make any one down-hearted, and continued to interrogate me until he learned the particulars of my whole history. He was evidently much interested in my behalf, and, in the blunt speech of a sailor, swore he would aid me all he could, if it "split his timbers." I requested him to furnish me pen, ink and paper, in order that I might write to some of my friends. He promised to obtain them—but how I could use them undiscovered was a difficulty. If I could only get into the forecastle while his watch was off, and the other sailors asleep, the thing could be accomplished. The small boat instantly occurred to me. He thought we were not far from the Balize,[16] at the mouth of the Mississippi, and it was necessary that the letter be written soon, or the opportunity would be lost. Accordingly, by arrangement, I managed the next night to secret myself again under the long-boat. His watch was off at twelve. I saw him pass into the forecastle, and in about an hour followed him. He was nodding over a table, half asleep, on which a sickly light was flickering, and on which also was a pen and sheet of paper. As I entered he aroused, beckoned me to a seat beside him, and pointed to the paper. I directed the letter to Henry B. Northup, of Sandy Hill—stating that I had been kidnapped, was then on board the brig Orleans, bound for New-Orleans; that it was then impossible for me to conjecture my ultimate destination, and requesting he would take measures to rescue me. The letter was sealed and directed, and Manning, having read it, promised to deposit it in the New-Orleans post-office. I hastened back to my place under the long-boat, and in the morning, as the slaves came up and were walking round, crept out unnoticed and mingled with them.

My good friend, whose name was John Manning, was an Englishman by birth, and a noble-hearted, generous sailor as ever walked a deck. He had lived in Boston—was a tall, well-built man, about twenty-four years old, with a face somewhat pock-marked, but full of benevolent expression.

Nothing to vary the monotony of our daily life occurred, until we reached New-Orleans. On coming to the levee, and before the vessel was made fast, I saw Manning leap on shore and hurry away into the city. As he started off he looked back over his shoulder significantly, giving me to understand the object of his errand. Presently he returned, and passing close by me, hunched me with his elbow, with a peculiar wink, as much as to say, "it is all right."

The letter, as I have since learned, reached Sandy Hill. Mr. Northup visited Albany and laid it before Governor Seward, but inasmuch as it gave no definite information as to my probable locality, it was not, at that time, deemed advisable to institute measures for my liberation. It was concluded to delay, trusting that a knowledge of where I was might eventually be obtained.

A happy and touching scene was witnessed immediately upon our reaching the levee. Just as Manning left the brig, on his way to the post-office, two men came up and called aloud for Arthur. The latter, as he recognized them, was almost crazy with delight. He could hardly be restrained from leaping over the brig's side; and when they met soon after, he grasped them by the hand, and clung to them a long, long time. They were men from Norfolk, who had come on to New-Orleans to rescue him. His kidnappers, they informed him, had been arrested, and were then confined in the Norfolk prison. They conversed a few moments with the captain, and then departed with the rejoicing Arthur.

But in all the crowd that thronged the wharf, there was no one who knew or cared for me. Not one. No familiar voice greeted my ears, nor was there a single face that I had ever seen. Soon Arthur would rejoin his family, and have the satisfaction of seeing his wrongs avenged: my family, alas, should I ever see them more? There was a feeling of utter desolation in my heart, filling it with a despairing and regretful sense, that I had not gone down with Robert to the bottom of the sea.

Very soon traders and consignees came on board. One, a tall, thin-faced man, with light complexion and a little bent, made his appearance, with a paper in his hand. Burch's gang, consisting of myself, Eliza and her children, Harry, Lethe, and some others, who had joined us at Richmond, were consigned to him. This gentleman was Mr. Theophilus Freeman. Reading from his paper, he called, "Platt." No one answered. The name was called again and again, but still there was no reply. Then Lethe was called, then Eliza, then Harry, until the list was finished, each one stepping forward as his or her name was called.

"Captain, where's Platt?" demanded Theophilus Freeman.

The captain was unable to inform him, no one being, on board answering to that name.

"Who shipped *that* nigger?" he again inquired of the captain, pointing to me.

"Burch," replied the captain.

"Your name is Platt—you answer my description. Why don't you come forward?" he demanded of me, in an angry tone.

I informed him that was not my name; that I had never been called by it, but that I had no objection to it as I knew of.

"Well, I will learn you your name," said he; "and so you won't forget it either, by ——," he added.

Mr. Theophilus Freeman, by the way, was not a whit behind his partner, Burch, in the matter of blasphemy. On the vessel I had gone by the name of "Steward," and this was the first time I had ever been designated as Platt—the name forwarded by Burch to his consignee. From the vessel I observed the chain-gang at work on the levee. We passed near them as we were driven to Freeman's slave pen. This pen is very similar to Goodin's in Richmond, except the yard was enclosed by plank, standing upright, with ends sharpened, instead of brick walls.

Including us, there were now at least fifty in this pen. Depositing our blankets in one of the small buildings in the yard, and having been called up and fed, we were allowed to saunter about the enclosure until night, when we wrapped our blankets round us and laid down under the shed, or in the loft, or in the open yard, just as each one preferred.

It was but a short time I closed my eyes that night. Thought was busy in my brain. Could it be possible that I was thousands of miles from home—that I had been driven through the streets like a dumb beast—that I had been chained and beaten without mercy—that I was even then herded with a drove of slaves, a slave myself? Were the events of the last few weeks realities indeed?—or was I passing only through the dismal phases of a long, protracted dream? It was no illusion. My cup of sorrow was full to overflowing. Then I lifted up my hands to God, and in the still watches of the night, surrounded by the sleeping forms of my companions, begged for mercy on the poor, forsaken captive. To the Almighty Father of us all—the freeman and the slave—I poured forth the supplications of a broken spirit, imploring strength from on high to bear up against the burden of my troubles, until the morning light aroused the slumberers, ushering in another day of bondage.

CHAPTER VI.

FREEMAN'S INDUSTRY—CLEANLINESS AND CLOTHES—EXERCISING IN THE SHOW ROOM—THE DANCE—BOB, THE FIDDLER—ARRIVAL OF CUSTOMERS—SLAVES EXAMINED—THE OLD GENTLEMAN OF NEW-ORLEANS—SALE OF DAVID, CAROLINE, AND LETHE—PARTING OF RANDALL AND ELIZA—SMALL-POX—THE HOSPITAL—RECOVERY AND RETURN TO FREEMAN'S SLAVE PEN—THE PURCHASER OF ELIZA, HARRY AND PLATT—ELIZA'S AGONY ON PARTING FROM LITTLE EMILY.

THE very amiable, pious-hearted Mr. Theophilus Freeman, partner or consignee of James H. Burch, and keeper of the slave pen in New-Orleans, was out among his animals early in the morning. With an occasional kick of the older men and women, and many a sharp crack of the whip about the ears of the younger slaves, it was not long before they were all astir, and wide awake. Mr. Theophilus Freeman bustled about in a very industrious manner, getting his property ready for the sales-room, intending, no doubt, to do that day a rousing business.

In the first place we were required to wash thoroughly, and those with beards, to shave. We were then furnished with a new suit each, cheap, but clean. The men had hat, coat, shirt, pants and shoes; the women frocks of calico, and handkerchiefs to bind about their heads. We were now conducted into a large room in the front part of the building to which the yard was attached, in order to be properly trained, before the admission of customers. The men were arranged on one side of the room, the women on the other. The tallest was placed at the head of the row, then the next tallest, and so on in the order of their respective heights. Emily was at the foot of the line of women. Freeman charged us to remember our places; exhorted us to appear smart and lively,—sometimes threatening, and again, holding out various inducements. During the day he exercised us in the art of "looking smart," and of moving to our places with exact precision.

After being fed, in the afternoon, we were again paraded and made to dance. Bob, a colored boy, who had some time belonged to Freeman, played on the violin. Standing near him, I made bold to inquire if he could play the "Virginia Reel." He answered he could not, and asked me if I could play. Replying in the affirmative, he handed me the violin. I struck up a tune, and finished it. Freeman ordered me to continue playing, and seemed well pleased, telling Bob that I far excelled him—a remark that seemed to grieve my musical companion very much.

Next day many customers called to examine Freeman's "new lot." The latter gentleman was very loquacious, dwelling at much length upon our several good points and qualities. He would make us hold up our heads, walk briskly back and forth, while customers would feel of our hands and arms and bodies, turn us about, ask us what we could do, make us open our mouths and show our teeth, precisely as a jockey examines a horse which he is about to barter for or purchase. Sometimes a man or woman was taken back to the small house in the yard, stripped, and inspected more minutely. Scars upon a slave's back were considered evidence of a rebellious or unruly spirit, and hurt his sale.

One old gentleman, who said he wanted a coachman, appeared to take a fancy to me. From his conversation with Burch, I learned he was a resident in the city. I very much desired that he would buy me, because I conceived it would not be difficult to make my escape from New-Orleans on some northern vessel. Freeman asked him fifteen hundred dollars for me. The old gentleman insisted it was too much, as times were very hard. Freeman, however, declared that I was sound and healthy, of a good constitution, and intelligent. He made it a point to enlarge upon my musical attainments. The old gentleman argued quite adroitly that there was nothing extraordinary about the nigger, and finally, to my regret, went out, saying he would call again. During the day, however, a number of sales were made. David and Caroline were purchased together by a Natchez planter. They left us, grinning broadly, and in the most happy state of mind, caused by the fact of their not being separated. Lethe was sold to a planter of Baton Rouge, her eyes flashing with anger as she was led away.

The same man also purchased Randall. The little fellow was made to jump, and run across the floor, and perform many other feats, exhibiting his activity and condition. All the time the trade was going on, Eliza was crying aloud, and wringing her hands. She besought the man not to buy him, unless he also bought her self and Emily. She promised, in that case, to be the most faithful slave that ever lived. The man answered that he could not afford it, and then Eliza burst into a paroxysm of grief, weeping plaintively. Freeman turned round to her, savagely, with his whip in his uplifted hand, ordering her to stop her noise, or he would flog her. He would not have such work—such snivelling; and unless she ceased that minute, he would take her to the yard and give her a hundred lashes. Yes, he would take the nonsense out of her pretty quick—if he didn't, might he be d—d. Eliza shrunk before him, and tried to wipe away her tears, but it was all in vain. She wanted to be with her children, she said, the little time she had to live. All the frowns and threats of Freeman, could not wholly silence the afflicted mother. She kept on begging and beseeching them, most piteously, not to separate the three. Over and over again she told them how she loved her boy. A great many times she repeated her former promises—how very faithful and obedient she would be; how hard she would labor day and night, to the last moment of her life, if he would only buy them all together. But it was of no avail; the man could not afford it. The bargain was agreed upon, and Randall must go alone. Then Eliza ran to him; embraced him passionately; kissed him again and again; told him to remember her—all the while her tears falling in the boy's face like rain.

Freeman damned her, calling her a blubbering, bawling wench, and ordered her to go to her place, and behave herself, and be somebody. He swore he wouldn't stand such stuff but a little longer. He would soon give her something to cry about, if she was not mighty careful, and *that* she might depend upon.

The planter from Baton Rouge, with his new purchases, was ready to depart.

"Don't cry, mama. I will be a good boy. Don't cry," said Randall, looking back, as they passed out of the door.

What has become of the lad, God knows. It was a mournful scene indeed. I would have cried myself if I had dared.

That night, nearly all who came in on the brig Orleans, were taken ill. They complained of violent pain in the head and back. Little Emily—a thing unusual with her—cried constantly. In the morning, a physician was called in, but was unable to determine the nature of our complaint. While examining me, and asking questions touching my symptoms, I gave it as my opinion that it was an attack of smallpox—mentioning the fact of Robert's death as the reason of my belief. It might be so indeed, he thought, and he would send for the head physician of the hospital. Shortly, the head physician came—a small, light-haired man, whom they called Dr. Carr. He pronounced it small-pox, whereupon there was much alarm throughout the yard. Soon after Dr. Carr left, Eliza, Emmy, Harry and myself were put into a hack and driven to the hospital—a large white marble building, standing on the outskirts of the city. Harry and I were placed in a room in one of the upper stories. I became very sick. For three days I was entirely blind. While lying in this state one day, Bob came in, saying to Dr. Carr that Freeman had sent him over to inquire how we were getting on. Tell him, said the doctor, that Platt is very bad, but that if he survives until nine o'clock, he may recover.[17]

I expected to die. Though there was little in the prospect before me worth living for, the near approach of death appalled me. I thought I could have been resigned to yield up my life in the bosom of my family, but to expire in the midst of strangers, under such circumstances, was a bitter reflection.

There were a great number in the hospital, of both sexes, and of all ages. In the rear of the building coffins were manufactured. When one died, the bell tolled—a signal to the undertaker to come and bear away the body to the potter's field. Many times, each day and night, the tolling bell sent forth its melancholy voice, announcing another death. But my time had not yet come. The crisis having passed, I began to revive, and at the end of two weeks and two days, returned with Harry to the pen, bearing upon my face the effects of the malady, which to this day continues to disfigure it. Eliza and Emily were also brought back next day in a hack, and again were we paraded in the sales-room, for the inspection and examination of purchasers. I still indulged the hope that the old gentleman in search of a coachman would call again, as he had promised, and purchase me. In that event I felt an abiding confidence that I would soon regain my liberty. Customer after customer entered, but the old gentleman never made his appearance.

At length, one day, while we were in the yard, Freeman came out and ordered us to our places, in the great room. A gentleman was waiting for us as we entered, and inasmuch as he will be often mentioned in the progress of this narrative, a description of his personal appearance, and my estimation of his character, at first sight, may not be out of place.

He was a man above the ordinary height, somewhat bent and stooping forward. He was a good-looking man, and appeared to have reached about the middle age of life. There was nothing repulsive in his presence; but on the other hand, there was something cheerful and attractive in his face, and in his tone of voice. The finer elements were all kindly mingled in his breast, as any one could see. He moved about among us, asking many questions, as to what we could do, and what labor we had been accustomed to; if we thought we would like to live with him, and would be good boys if he would buy us, and other interrogatories of like character.

After some further inspection, and conversation touching prices, he finally offered Freeman one thousand dollars for me, nine hundred for Harry, and seven hundred for Eliza. Whether the small-pox had depreciated our value, or from what cause Freeman had concluded to fall five hundred dollars from the price I was before held at, I cannot say. At any rate, after a little shrewd reflection, he announced his acceptance of the offer.

As soon as Eliza heard it, she was in an agony again. By this time she had become haggard and hollow-eyed with sickness and with sorrow. It would be a relief if I could consistently pass over in silence the scene that now ensued. It recalls memories more mournful and affecting than any language can portray. I have seen mothers kissing for the last time the faces of their dead offspring; I have seen them looking down into the grave, as the earth fell with a dull sound upon their coffins, hiding them from their eyes forever; but never have I seen such an exhibition of intense, unmeasured, and unbounded grief, as when Eliza was parted from her child. She broke from her place in the line of women, and rushing down where Emily was standing, caught her in her arms. The child, sensible of some impending danger, instinctively fastened her hands around her mother's neck, and nestled her little head upon her bosom. Freeman sternly ordered her to be quiet, but she did not heed him. He caught her by the arm and pulled her rudely, but she only clung the closer to the child. Then, with a volley of great oaths, he struck her such a heartless blow, that she staggered backward, and was like to fall. Oh! how piteously then did she beseech and beg and pray that they might not be separated. Why could they not be purchased together? Why not let her have one of her dear children? "Mercy, mercy, master!" she cried, falling on her knees. "Please, master, buy Emily. I can never work any if she is taken from me: I will die."

Freeman interfered again, but, disregarding him, she still plead most earnestly, telling how Randall had been taken from her—how she never him see him again, and now it was too bad—oh, God! it was too bad, too cruel, to take her away from Emily—her pride—her only darling, that could not live, it was so young, without its mother!

Finally, after much more of supplication, the purchaser of Eliza stepped forward, evidently affected, and said to Freeman he would buy Emily, and asked him what her price was.

"What is her *price? Buy* her?" was the responsive interrogatory of Theophilus Freeman. And instantly answering his own inquiry, he added, "I won't sell her. She's not for sale."

The man remarked he was not in need of one so young—that it would be of no profit to him, but since the mother was so fond of her, rather than see them separated, he would pay a reasonable price. But to this humane proposal Freeman was entirely deaf. He would not sell her then on any account whatever. There were heaps and piles of money to be made of her, he said, when she was a few years older. There were men enough in New-Orleans who would give five thousand dollars for such an extra, handsome, fancy piece as Emily would be, rather than not get her. No, no, he would not sell her then. She was a beauty— a picture—a doll—one of the regular bloods—none of your thick-lipped, bullet-headed, cotton-picking niggers—if she was might he be d—d.

When Eliza heard Freeman's determination not to part with Emily, she became absolutely frantic.

"I will *not* go without her. They shall *not* take her from me," she fairly shrieked, her shrieks commingling with the loud and angry voice of Freeman, commanding her to be silent.

Meantime Harry and myself had been to the yard and returned with our blankets, and were at the front door ready to leave. Our purchaser stood near us, gazing at Eliza with an expression indicative of regret at having bought her at the expense of so much sorrow. We waited some time, when, finally, Freeman, out of patience, tore Emily from her mother by main force, the two clinging to each other with all their might.

"Don't leave me, mama—don't leave me," screamed the child, as its mother was pushed harshly forward; "Don't leave me—come back, mama," she still cried, stretching forth her little arms imploringly. But she cried in vain. Out of the door and into the street we were quickly hurried. Still we could hear her calling to her mother, "Come back—don't leave me—come back, mama," until her infant voice grew faint and still more faint, and gradually died away, as distance intervened, and finally was wholly lost.

Eliza never after saw or heard of Emily or Randall. Day nor night, however, were they ever absent from her memory. In the cotton field, in the cabin,

SEPARATION OF ELIZA AND HER LAST CHILD.

always and everywhere, she was talking of them—often *to* them, as if they were actually present. Only when absorbed in that illusion, or asleep, did she ever have a moment's comfort afterwards.

She was no common slave, as has been said. To a large share of natural intelligence which she possessed, was added a general knowledge and information on most subjects. She had enjoyed opportunities such as are afforded to very few of her oppressed class. She had been lifted up into the regions of a higher life. Freedom—freedom for herself and for her offspring, for many years had been her cloud by day, her pillar of fire by night. In her pilgrimage through the wilderness of bondage, with eyes fixed upon that hope-inspiring beacon, she had at length ascended to "the top of Pisgah," and beheld "the land of promise." In an unexpected moment she was utterly overwhelmed with disappointment and despair. The glorious vision of liberty faded from her sight as they led her away into captivity. Now "she weepeth sore in the night, and tears are on her cheeks: all her friends have dealt treacherously with her: they have become her enemies."

CHAPTER VII.

THE STEAMBOAT RODOLPH—DEPARTURE FROM NEW-ORLEANS—WILLIAM FORD—ARRIVAL AT ALEXANDRA, ON RED RIVER—RESOLUTIONS—THE GREAT PINE WOODS—WILD CATTLE—MARTIN'S SUMMER RESIDENCE—THE TEXAS ROAD—ARRIVAL AT MASTER FORD'S—ROSE—MISTRESS FORD—SALLY AND HER CHILDREN—JOHN, THE COOK—WALTER, SAM, AND ANTONY—THE MILLS ON INDIAN CREEK—SABBATH DAYS—SAM'S CONVERSION—THE PROFIT OF KINDNESS—RAFTING—ADAM TAYDEM, THE LITTLE WHITE MAN—CASCALLA AND HIS TRIBE—THE INDIAN BALL—JOHN M. TIBEATS—THE STORM APPROACHING.

ON leaving the New-Orleans slave pen, Harry and I followed our new master through the streets, while Eliza, crying and turning back, was forced along by Freeman and his minions, until we found ourselves on board the steamboat Rodolph, then lying at the levee. In the course of half an hour we were moving briskly up the Mississippi, bound for some point on Red River. There were quite a number of slaves on board beside ourselves, just purchased in the New-Orleans market. I remember a Mr. Kelsow, who was said to be a well known and extensive planter, had in charge a gang of women.

Our master's name was William Ford. He resided then in the "Great Pine Woods," in the parish of Avoyelles, situated on the right bank of Red River, in the heart of Louisiana. He is now a Baptist preacher. Throughout the whole parish of Avoyelles, and especially along both shores of Bayou Boeuf, where he is more intimately known, he is accounted by his fellow-citizens as a worthy minister of God. In many northern minds, perhaps, the idea of a man holding his brother man in servitude, and the traffic in human flesh, may seem altogether incompatible with their conceptions of a moral or religious life. From descriptions of such men as Burch and Freeman, and others hereinafter mentioned, they are led to despise and execrate the whole class of slaveholders, indiscriminately. But I was sometime his slave, and had an opportunity of learning well his character and disposition, and it is but simple justice to him when I say, in my opinion, there never was a more kind, noble, candid, Christian man than William Ford. The influences and associations that had always surrounded him, blinded him to the inherent wrong at the bottom of the system of Slavery. He never doubted the moral right of one man holding another in subjection. Looking through the same medium with his fathers before him, he saw things in the same light. Brought up under other circumstances and other influences, his notions would undoubtedly have been different. Nevertheless, he was a model master, walking uprightly, according to the light of his understanding, and fortunate was the slave who came to his possession. Were all men such as he, Slavery would be deprived of more than half its bitterness.

We were two days and three nights on board the steamboat Rodolph, during which time nothing of particular interest occurred. I was now known as Platt, the name given me by Burch, and by which I was designated through the whole period of my servitude. Eliza was sold by the name of "Dradey." She was so distinguished in the conveyance to Ford, now on record in the recorder's office in New-Orleans.

On our passage I was constantly reflecting on my situation, and consulting with myself on the best course to pursue in order to effect my ultimate escape. Sometimes, not only then, but afterwards, I was almost on the point of disclosing fully to Ford the facts of my history. I am inclined now to the opinion it would have resulted in my benefit. This course was often considered, but through fear of its miscarriage, never put into execution, until eventually my transfer and his pecuniary embarrassments rendered it evidently unsafe. Afterwards, under other masters, unlike William Ford, I knew well enough the slightest knowledge of my real character would consign me at once to the remoter depths of Slavery. I was too costly a chattel to be lost, and was well aware that I would be taken farther on, into some by-place, over the Texan border, perhaps, and sold; that I would be disposed of as the thief disposes of his stolen horse, if my right to freedom was even whispered. So I resolved to lock the secret closely in my heart—never to utter one word or syllable as to who or what I was—trusting in Providence and my own shrewdness for deliverance.

At length we left the steamboat Rodolph at a place called Alexandria, several hundred miles from New-Orleans. It is a small town on the southern shore of Red River. Having remained there over night, we entered the morning train of cars, and were soon at Bayou Lamourie, a still smaller place, distant eighteen miles from Alexandria. At that time it was the termination of the railroad. Ford's plantation was situated on the Texas road, twelve miles from Lamourie, in the Great Pine Woods. This distance, it was announced to us, must be traveled on foot, there being public conveyances no farther. Accordingly we all set out in the company of Ford. It was an excessively hot day. Harry, Eliza, and myself were yet weak, and the bottoms of our feet were very tender from the effects of the small-pox. We proceeded slowly, Ford telling us to take our time and sit down

and rest whenever we desired—a privilege that was taken advantage of quite frequently. After leaving Lamourie and crossing two plantations, one belonging to
Mr. Carnell, the other to a Mr. Flint, we reached the Pine Woods, a wilderness
that stretches to the Sabine River.[18]

The whole country about Red River is low and marshy. The Pine Woods,
as they are called, is comparatively upland, with frequent small intervals, however, running through them. This upland is covered with numerous trees—the
white oak, the chincopin, resembling chestnut, but principally the yellow pine.
They are of great size, running up sixty feet, and perfectly straight. The woods
were full of cattle, very shy and wild, dashing away in herds, with a loud snuff,
at our approach. Some of them were marked or branded, the rest appeared to
be in their wild and untamed state. They are much smaller than northern
breeds, and the peculiarity about them that most attracted my attention was
their horns. They stand out from the sides of the head precisely straight, like
two iron spikes.

At noon we reached a cleared piece of ground containing three or four
acres. Upon it was a small, unpainted, wooden house, a corn crib, or, as we
would say, a barn, and a log kitchen, standing about a rod from the house. It
was the summer residence of Mr. Martin. Rich planters, having large establish-
ments on Bayou Boeuf, are accustomed to spend the warmer season in these
woods. Here they find clear water and delightful shades. In fact, these retreats
are to the planters of that section of the country what Newport and Saratoga are
to the wealthier inhabitants of northern cities.

We were sent around into the kitchen, and supplied with sweet potatoes,
corn-bread, and bacon, while Master Ford dined with Martin in the house. There
were several slaves about the premises. Martin came out and took a look at us,
asking Ford the price of each, if we were green hands, and so forth, and making
inquiries in relation to the slave market generally.

After a long rest we set forth again, following the Texas road, which had
the appearance of being very rarely traveled. For five miles we passed through
continuous woods without observing a single habitation. At length, just as the
sun was sinking in the west, we entered another opening, containing some twelve
or fifteen acres.

In this opening stood a house much larger than Mr. Martin's. It was two
stories high, with a piazza in front. In the rear of it was also a log kitchen, poultry house, corncribs, and several negro cabins. Near the house was a peach orchard, and gardens of orange and pomegranate trees. The space was entirely surrounded by woods, and covered with a carpet of rich, rank verdure. It was a
quiet, lonely, pleasant place—literally a green spot in the wilderness. It was the
residence of my master, William Ford.

As we approached, a yellow girl—her name was Rose—was standing on
the piazza. Going to the door, she called her mistress, who presently came running out to meet her lord. She kissed him, and laughingly demanded if he had
bought "those niggers." Ford said he had, and told us to go round to Sally's cabin
and rest ourselves. Turning the corner of the house, we discovered Sally washing—her two baby children near her, rolling on the grass. They jumped up and

toddled towards us, looked at us a moment like a brace of rabbits, then ran back to their mother as if afraid of us.

Sally conducted us into the cabin, told us to lay down our bundles and be seated, for she was sure that we were tired. Just then John, the cook, a boy some sixteen years of age, and blacker than any crow, came running in, looked steadily in our faces, then turning round, without saying as much as "how d'ye do," ran back to the kitchen, laughing loudly, as if our coming was a great joke indeed.

Much wearied with our walk, as soon as it was dark, Harry and I wrapped our blankets round us, and laid down upon the cabin floor. My thoughts, as usual, wandered back to my wife and children. The consciousness of my real situation; the hopelessness of any effort to escape through the wide forests of Avoyelles, pressed heavily upon me, yet my heart was at home in Saratoga.

I was awakened early in the morning by the voice of Master Ford, calling Rose. She hastened into the house to dress the children, Sally to the field to milk the cows, while John was busy in the kitchen preparing breakfast. In the meantime Harry and I were strolling about the yard, looking at our new quarters. Just after breakfast a colored man, driving three yoke of oxen, attached to a wagon load of lumber, drove into the opening. He was a slave of Ford's, named Walton, the husband of Rose. By the way, Rose was a native of Washington, and had been brought from thence five years before. She had never seen Eliza, but she had heard of Berry, and they knew the same streets, and the same people, either personally, or by reputation. They became fast friends immediately, and talked a great deal together of old times, and of friends they had left behind.

Ford was at that time a wealthy man. Besides his seat in the Pine Woods, he owned a large lumbering establishment on Indian Creek, four miles distant, and also, in his wife's right, an extensive plantation and many slaves on Bayou Boeuf.

Walton had come with his load of lumber from the mills on Indian Creek. Ford directed us to return with him, saying he would follow us as soon as possible. Before leaving, Mistress Ford called me into the storeroom, and handed me, as it is there termed, a tin bucket of molasses for Harry and myself.

Eliza was still ringing her hands and deploring the loss of her children. Ford tried as much as possible to console her—told her she need not work very hard; that she might remain with Rose, and assist the madam in the house affairs.

Riding with Walton in the wagon, Harry and I became quite well acquainted with him long before reaching Indian Creek. He was a "born thrall" of Ford's, and spoke kindly and affectionately of him, as a child would speak of his own father. In answer to his inquiries from whence I came, I told him from Washington. Of that city, he had heard much from his wife, Rose, and all the way plied me with many extravagant and absurd questions.

On reaching the mills at Indian Creek, we found two more of Ford's slaves, Sam and Antony. Sam, also, was a Washingtonian, having been brought out in the same gang with Rose. He had worked on a farm near Georgetown. Antony was a blacksmith, from Kentucky, who had been in his present master's service about ten years. Sam knew Burch, and when informed that he was the trader who had sent me on from Washington, it was remarkable how well we agreed upon the subject of his superlative rascality. He had forwarded Sam, also.

On Ford's arrival at the mill, we were employed in piling lumber, and chopping logs, which occupation we continued during the remainder of the summer.

We usually spent our Sabbaths at the opening, on which days our master would gather all his slaves about him, and read and expound the Scriptures. He sought to inculcate in our minds feelings of kindness towards each other, of dependence upon God—setting forth the rewards promised unto those who lead an upright and prayerful life. Seated in the doorway of his house, surrounded by his man-servants and his maid-servants, who looked earnestly into the good man's face, he spoke of the loving kindness of the Creator, and of the life that is to come. Often did the voice of prayer ascend from his lips to heaven, the only sound that broke the solitude of the place.

In the course of the summer Sam became deeply convicted, his mind dwelling intensely on the subject of religion. His mistress gave him a Bible, which he carried with him to his work. Whatever leisure time was allowed him, he spent in perusing it, though it was only with great difficulty that he could master any part of it. I often read to him, a favor which he well repaid me by many expressions of gratitude. Sam's piety was frequently observed by white men who came to the mill, and the remark it most generally provoked was, that a man like Ford, who allowed his slaves to have Bibles, was "not fit to own a nigger."

He, however, lost nothing by his kindness. It is a fact I have more than once observed, that those who treated their slaves most leniently, were rewarded by the greatest amount of labor. I know it from my own experience. It was a source of pleasure to surprise Master Ford with a greater day's work than was required, while, under subsequent masters, there was no prompter to extra effort but the overseer's lash.

It was the desire of Ford's approving voice that suggested to me an idea that resulted to his profit. The lumber we were manufacturing was contracted to be delivered at Lamourie. It had hitherto been transported by land, and was an important item of expense. Indian Creek, upon which the mills were situated, was a narrow but deep stream emptying into Bayou Boeuf. In some places it was not more than twelve feet wide, and much obstructed with trunks of trees. Bayou Boeuf was connected with Bayou Lamourie. I ascertained the distance from the mills to the point on the latter bayou, where our lumber was to be delivered, was but a few miles less by land than by water. Provided the creek could be made navigable for rafts, it occurred to me that the expense of transportation would be materially diminished.

Adam Taydem, a little white man who had been a soldier in Florida, and had strolled into that distant region, was foreman and superintendent of the mills. He scouted the idea; but Ford, when I laid it before him, received it favorably, and permitted me to try the experiment.

Having removed the obstructions, I made up a narrow raft, consisting of twelve cribs. At this business I think I was quite skillful, not having forgotten my experience years before on the Champlain canal. I labored hard, being extremely anxious to succeed, both from a desire to please my master, and to show Adam Taydem that my scheme was not such a visionary one as he incessantly pronounced it. One hand could manage three cribs. I took charge of the forward three, and commenced poling down the creek. In due time we entered the first bayou, and finally reached our destination in a shorter period of time than I had anticipated.

The arrival of the raft at Lamourie created a sensation, while Mr. Ford loaded me with commendation. On all sides I heard Ford's Platt pronounced the "smartest nigger in the Pine Woods"—in fact I was the Fulton[19] of Indian Creek. I was not insensible to the praise bestowed upon me, and enjoyed, especially, my triumph over Taydem, whose half-malicious ridicule had stung my pride. From this time the entire control of bringing the lumber to Lamourie was placed in my hands until the contract was fulfilled.

Indian Creek, in its whole length, flows through a magnificent forest. There dwells on its shore a tribe of Indians, a remnant of the Chickasaws or Chickopees, if I remember rightly. They live in simple huts, ten or twelve feet square, constructed of pine poles and covered with bark. They subsist principally on the flesh of the deer, the coon, and opossum, all of which are plenty in these woods. Sometimes they exchange venison for a little corn and whisky with the planters on the bayous. Their usual dress is buckskin breeches and calico hunting shirts of fantastic colors, buttoned from belt to chin. They wear brass rings on their wrists, and in their ears and noses. The dress of the squaws is very similar. They are fond of dogs and horses—owning many of the latter, of a small, tough breed—and are skillful riders. Their bridles, girths and saddles were made of raw skins of animals; their stirrups of a certain kind of wood. Mounted astride their ponies, men and women, I have seen them dash out into the woods at the utmost of their speed, following narrow winding paths, and dodging trees, in a manner that eclipsed the most miraculous feats of civilized equestrianism. Circling away in various directions, the forest echoing and re-echoing with their whoops, they would presently return at the same dashing, headlong speed with which they started. Their village was on Indian Creek, known as Indian Castle, but their range extended to the Sabine River. Occasionally a tribe from Texas would come over on a visit, and then there was indeed a carnival in the "Great Pine Woods." Chief of the tribe was Cascalla; second in rank, John Baltese, his son-in-law; with both of whom, as with many others of the tribe, I became acquainted during my frequent voyages down the creek with rafts. Sam and myself would often visit them when the day's task was done. They were obedient to the chief; the word of Cascalla was their law. They were a rude but harmless people, and enjoyed their wild mode of life. They had little fancy for the open country, the cleared lands on the shores of the bayous, but preferred to hide themselves within the shadows of the forest. They worshiped the Great Spirit, loved whisky, and were happy.

On one occasion I was present at a dance, when a roving herd from Texas had encamped in their village. The entire carcass of a deer was roasting before a large fire, which threw its light a long distance among the trees under which they were assembled. When they had formed in a ring, men and squaws alternately, a sort of Indian fiddle set up an indescribable tune. It was a continuous, melancholy kind of wavy sound, with the slightest possible variation. At the first note, if indeed there was more than one note in the whole tune, they circled around, trotting after each other, and giving utterance to a guttural, sing-song noise, equally as nondescript as the music of the fiddle. At the end of the third circuit, they would stop suddenly, whoop as if their lungs would crack, then break from the ring, forming in couples, man and squaw, each jumping backwards as far as possible from the other, then forwards—which graceful feat having been twice or thrice accomplished, they would form in a ring, and go trotting round again. The best dancer appeared to be considered the one who could whoop the loudest, jump the farthest, and utter the most excruciating noise. At intervals, one or more would leave the dancing circle, and going to the fire, cut from the roasting carcass a slice of venison.

In a hole, shaped like a mortar, cut in the trunk of a fallen tree, they pounded corn with a wooden pestle, and of the meal made cake. Alternately they danced and ate. Thus were the visitors from Texas entertained by the dusky sons and daughters of the Chicopees, and such is a description, as I saw it, of an Indian ball in the Pine Woods of Avoyelles.

In the autumn, I left the mills, and was employed at the opening. One day the mistress was urging Ford to procure a loom, in order that Sally might commence weaving cloth for the winter garments of the slaves. He could not imagine where one was to be found, when I suggested that the easiest way to get one would be to make it, informing him at the same time, that I was a sort of "Jack at all trades," and would attempt it, with his permission. It was granted very readily, and I was allowed to go to a neighboring planter's to inspect one before commencing the undertaking. At length it was finished and pronounced by Sally to be perfect. She could easily weave her task of fourteen yards, milk the cows, and have leisure time besides each day. It worked so well, I was continued in the employment of making looms, which were taken down to the plantation on the bayou.

At this time one John M. Tibeats,[20] a carpenter, came to the opening to do some work on master's house. I was directed to quit the looms and assist him. For two weeks I was in his company, planing and matching boards for ceiling, a plastered room being a rare thing in the parish of Avoyelles.

John M. Tibeats was the opposite of Ford in all respects. He was a small, crabbed, quick-tempered, spiteful man. He had no fixed residence that I ever heard of, but passed from one plantation to another, wherever he could find employment. He was without standing in the community, not esteemed by white men, nor even respected by slaves. He was ignorant, withal, and of a revengeful disposition. He left the parish long before I did, and I know not whether he is at present alive or dead. Certain it is, it was a most unlucky day for me that brought us together. During my residence with Master Ford I had seen only the bright side of slavery. His was no heavy hand crushing us to the earth. *He* pointed upwards, and with benign and cheering words addressed us as his fellow-mortals, accountable, like himself, to the Maker of us all. I think of him with affection, and had my family been with me, could have borne his gentle servitude, without murmuring, all my days. But clouds were gathering in the horizon—forerunners of a pitiless storm that was soon to break over me. I was doomed to endure such bitter trials as the poor slave only knows, and to lead no more the comparatively happy life which I had led in the "Great Pine Woods."

CHAPTER VIII.

WILLIAM FORD unfortunately became embarrassed in his pecuniary affairs. A heavy judgement was rendered against him in consequence of his having become security for his brother, Franklin Ford, residing on Red River, above Alexandria, and who had failed to meet his liabilities. He was also indebted to John M. Tibeats to a considerable amount in consideration of his services in building the mills on Indian Creek, and also a weaving-house, corn-mill and other erections on the plantation at Bayou Boeuf, not yet completed. It was therefore necessary, in order to meet these demands, to dispose of eighteen slaves, myself among the number. Seventeen of them, including Sam and Harry, were purchased by Peter Compton, a planter also residing on Red River.

I was sold to Tibeats, in consequence, undoubtedly, of my slight skill as a carpenter. This was in the winter of 1842. The deed of myself from Freeman to Ford, as I ascertained from the public records in New-Orleans on my return, was dated June 23d, 1841. At the time of my sale to Tibeats, the price agreed to be given for me being more than the debt, Ford took a chattel mortgage of four hundred dollars. I am indebted for my life, as will hereafter be seen, to that mortgage.

I bade farewell to my good friends at the opening, and departed with my new master Tibeats. We went down to the plantation on Bayou Boeuf, distant twenty-seven miles from the Pine Woods, to complete the unfinished contract. Bayou Boeuf is a sluggish, winding stream—one of those stagnant bodies of water common in that region, setting back from Red River. It stretches from a point not far from Alexandra, in a south-easterly direction, and following its tortuous course, is more than fifty miles in length. Large cotton and sugar plantations line each shore, extending back to the borders of interminable swamps. It is alive with alligators, rendering it unsafe for swine, or unthinking slave children to stroll along its banks. Upon a bend in this bayou, a short distance from Cheneyville, was situated the plantation of Madam Ford—her brother, Peter Tanner, a great landholder, living on the opposite side.

On my arrival at Bayou Boeuf, I had the pleasure of meeting Eliza, whom I had not seen for several months. She had not pleased Mrs. Ford, being more occupied in brooding over her sorrows than in attending to her business, and had, in consequence, been sent down to work in the fields on the plantation. She had grown feeble and emaciated, and was still mourning for her children. She asked me if I had forgotten them, and a great many times inquired if I still remembered how handsome little Emily was—how much Randall loved her—and wondered if they were living still, and where the darlings could then be. She had sunk beneath the weight of an excessive grief. Her drooping form and hollow cheeks too plainly indicated that she had well nigh reached the end of her weary road.

Ford's overseer on this plantation, and who had the exclusive charge of it, was a Mr. Chapin, a kindly-disposed man, and a native of Pennsylvania. In common with others, he held Tibeats in light estimation, which fact, in connection with the four hundred dollar mortgage, was fortunate for me.

I was now compelled to labor very hard. From earliest dawn until late at night, I was not allowed to be a moment idle. Notwithstanding which, Tibeats was never satisfied. He was continually cursing and complaining. He never spoke to me a kind word. I was his faithful slave, and earned him large wages every day, and yet I went to my cabin nightly, loaded with abuse and stinging epithets.

We had completed the corn mill, the kitchen, and so forth, and were at work upon the weaving-house when I was guilty of an act, in that State punishable with death. It was my first fight with Tibeats. The weaving-house we were erecting stood in the orchard a few rods from the residence of Chapin, or the "great house," as it was called. One night, having worked until it was too dark to see, I was ordered by Tibeats to rise very early in the morning, procure a keg of nails from Chapin, and commence putting on the clapboards. I retired to the cabin extremely tired, and having cooked a supper of bacon and corn cake, and conversed a while with Eliza, who occupied the same cabin, as also did Lawson and his wife Mary, and a slave named Bristol, laid down upon the ground floor, little dreaming of the sufferings that awaited me on the morrow. Before daylight I was on the piazza of the "great house," awaiting the appearance of overseer Chapin. To have aroused him from his slumbers and stated my errand, would have been an unpardonable boldness. At length he came out. Taking off my hat, I informed him Master Tibeats had directed me to call upon him for a keg of nails. Going into the store-room, he rolled it out, at the same time saying, if Tibeats preferred a different size, he would endeavor to furnish them, but that I might use those until further directed. Then mounting his horse, which stood saddled and bridled at the door, he rode away into the field, whither the slaves had preceded him, while I took the keg on my shoulder, and proceeding to the weaving-house, broke in the head, and commenced nailing on the clapboards.

As the day began to open, Tibeats came out of the house to where I was, hard at work. He seemed to be that morning even more morose and disagreeable than usual. He was my master, entitled by law to my flesh and blood, and to exercise over me such tyrannical control as his mean nature prompted; but there was no law that could prevent my looking upon him with intense contempt. I despised both his disposition and his intellect. I had just come round to the keg for a further supply of nails, as he reached the weaving-house.

"I thought I told you to commence putting on weather-boards this morning," he remarked.

"Yes, master, and I am about it," I replied.

"Where?" he demanded.

"On the other side," was my answer.

He walked round to the other side, examined my work for a while, muttering to himself in a fault-finding tone.

"Didn't I tell you last night to get a keg of nails of Chapin?" he broke forth again.

"Yes, master, and so I did; and overseer said he would get another size for you, if you wanted them, when he came back from the field."

Tibeats walked to the keg, looked a moment at the contents, then kicked it violently. Coming towards me in a great passion, he exclaimed,

"G—d d—n you! I thought you *knowed* something."

I made answer: "I tried to do as you told me, master. I didn't mean anything wrong. Overseer said—" But he interrupted me with such a flood of curses that I was unable to finish the sentence. At length he ran towards the house, and going to the piazza, took down one of the overseer's whips. The whip had a short wooden stock, braided over with leather, and was loaded at the butt. The lash was three feet long, or thereabouts, and made of raw-hide strands.

At first I was somewhat frightened, and my impulse was to run. There was no one about except Rachel, the cook, and Chapin's wife, and neither of them were to be seen. The rest were in the field. I knew he intended to whip me, and it was the first time any one had attempted it since my arrival at Avoyelles. I felt, moreover, that I had been faithful—that I was guilty of no wrong whatever, and deserved commendation rather than punishment. My fear changed to anger, and before he reached me I had made up my mind fully not to be whipped, let the result be life or death.

Winding the lash around his hand, and taking hold of the small end of the stock, he walked up to me, and with a malignant look, ordered me to strip.

"Master Tibeats," said I, looking him boldly in the face, "I will *not*." I was about to say something further in justification, but with concentrated vengeance, he sprang upon me, seizing me by the throat with one hand, raising the whip with the other, in the act of striking. Before the blow descended, however, I had caught him by the collar of the coat, and drawn him closely to me. Reaching down, I seized him by the ankle, and pushing him back with the other hand, he fell over on the ground. Putting one arm around his leg, and holding it to my breast, so that his head and shoulders only touched the ground, I placed my foot upon his neck. He was completely in my power. My blood was up. It seemed to course through my veins like fire. In the frenzy of my madness I snatched the whip from his hand. He struggled with all his power; swore that I should not live to see another day; and that he would tear out my heart. But his struggles and his threats were alike in vain. I cannot tell how many times I struck him. Blow after blow fell fast and heavy upon his wriggling form. At length he screamed—cried murder—and at last the blasphemous tyrant called on God for mercy. But he who had never shown mercy did not receive it. The stiff stock of the whip warped round his cringing body until my right arm ached.

Until this time I had been too busy to look about me. Desisting for a moment, I saw Mrs. Chapin looking from the window, and Rachel standing in the kitchen door. Their attitudes expressed the utmost excitement and alarm. His screams had been heard in the field. Chapin was coming as fast as he could ride. I struck him a blow or two more, then pushed him from me with such a well-directed kick that he went rolling over on the ground.

Rising to his feet, and brushing the dirt from his hair, he stood looking at me, pale with rage. We gazed at each other in silence. Not a word was uttered until Chapin galloped up to us.

"What is the matter?" he cried out.

"Master Tibeats wants to whip me for using the nails you gave me," I replied.

"What is the matter with the nails?" he inquired, turning to Tibeats.

Tibeats answered to the effect that they were too large, paying little heed, however, to Chapin's question, but still keeping his snakish eyes fastened maliciously on me.

"I am overseer here", Chapin began. "I told Platt to take them and use them, and if they were not of the proper size I would get others on returning from the field. It is not his fault. Besides, I shall furnish such nails as I please. I hope you will understand *that,* Mr. Tibeats."

Tibeats made no reply, but, grinding his teeth and shaking his fist, swore he would have satisfaction, and that it was not half over yet. Thereupon he walked away, followed by the overseer, and entered the house, the latter talking to him all the while in a suppressed tone, and with earnest gestures.

I remained where I was, doubting whether it was better to fly or abide the result, whatever it might be. Presently Tibeats came out of the house, and, saddling his horse, the only property he possessed besides myself, departed on the road to Cheneyville.

When he was gone, Chapin came out, visibly excited, telling me not to stir, not to attempt to leave the plantation on any account whatever. He then went to the kitchen, and calling Rachel out, conversed with her some time. Coming back, he again charged me with great earnestness not to run, saying my master was a rascal; that he had left on no good errand, and that there might be trouble before night. But at all events, he insisted upon it, I must not stir.

As I stood there, feelings of unutterable agony overwhelmed me. I was conscious that I had subjected myself to unimaginable punishment. The reaction that followed my extreme ebullition of anger produced the most painful sensations of regret. An unfriended, helpless slave—what could I *do,* what could I *say,* to justify, in the remotest manner, the heinous act I had committed, of resenting a *white* man's contumely and abuse. I tried to pray—I tried to beseech my Heavenly Father to sustain me in my sore extremity, but emotion choked my utterance, and I could only bow my head upon my hands and weep. For at least an hour I remained in this situation, finding relief only in tears, when, looking up, I beheld Tibeats, accompanied by two horsemen, coming down the bayou. They rode into the yard, jumped from their horses, and approached me with large whips, one of them also carrying a coil of rope.

"Cross your hands," commanded Tibeats, with the addition of such a shuddering expression of blasphemy as is not decorous to repeat.

"You need not bind me, Master Tibeats, I am ready to go with you anywhere," said I.

One of his companions then stepped forward, swearing if I made the least
resistance he would break my head—he would tear me limb from limb—he
would cut my black throat—and giving wide scope to other similar expressions.
Perceiving any importunity altogether vain, I crossed my hands, submitting
humbly to whatever disposition they might please to make of me. Thereupon
Tibeats tied my wrists, drawing the rope around them with his utmost strength.
Then he bound my ankles in the same manner. In the meantime the other two
had slipped a cord within my elbows, running it across my back, and tying it
firmly. It was utterly impossible to move hand or foot. With a remaining piece
of rope Tibeats made an awkward noose, and placed it about my neck.

"Now, then," inquired one of Tibeats' companions, "where shall we hang
the nigger?"

One proposed such a limb, extending from the body of a peach tree, near

CHAPIN RESCUES SOLOMON FROM HANGING.

the spot where we were standing. His comrade objected to it, alleging it would break, and proposed another. Finally they fixed upon the latter.

During this conversation, and all the time they were binding me, I uttered not a word. Overseer Chapin, during the progress of the scene, was walking hastily back and forth on the piazza. Rachel was crying by the kitchen door, and Mrs. Chapin was still looking from the window. Hope died within my heart. Surely my time had come. I should never behold the light of another day—never behold the faces of my children—the sweet anticipation I had cherished with such fondness. I should that hour struggle through the fearful agonies of death! None would mourn for me—none revenge me. Soon my form would be mouldering in that distant soil, or, perhaps, be cast to the slimy reptiles that filled the stagnant waters of the bayou! Tears flowed down my cheeks, but they only afforded a subject of insulting comment for my executioners.

At length, as they were dragging me towards the tree, Chapin, who had momentarily disappeared from the piazza, came out of the house and walked towards us. He had a pistol in each hand, and as near as I can now recall to mind, spoke in a firm, determined manner, as follows:

"Gentlemen, I have a few words to say. You had better listen to them. Whoever moves that slave another foot from where he stands is a dead man. In the first place, he does not deserve this treatment. It is a shame to murder him in this manner. I never knew a more faithful boy than Platt. You, Tibeats, are in the fault yourself. You are pretty much of a scoundrel, and I know it, and you richly deserve the flogging you have received. In the next place, I have been overseer on this plantation seven years, and, in the absence of William Ford, am master here. My duty is to protect his interests, and that duty I shall perform. You are not responsible—you are a worthless fellow. Ford holds a mortgage on Platt of four hundred dollars. If you hang him he loses his debt. Until that is canceled you have no right to take his life. You have no right to take it any way. There is a law for the slave as well as for the white man. You are no better than a murderer.

"As for you," addressing Cook and Ramsay, a couple of overseers from neighboring plantations, "as for you—begone! If you have any regard for your own safety, I say, begone."

Cook and Ramsay, without a further word, mounted their horses and rode away. Tibeats, in a few minutes, evidently in fear, and overawed by the decided tone of Chapin, sneaked off like a coward, as he was, and mounting his horse, followed his companions.

I remained standing where I was, still bound, with the rope around my neck. As soon as they were gone, Chapin called Rachel, ordering her to run to the field, and tell Lawson to hurry to the house without delay, and bring the brown mule with him, an animal much prized for its unusual fleetness. Presently the boy appeared.

"Lawson," said Chapin, "you must go to the Pine Woods. Tell your master Ford to come here at once—that he must not delay a single moment. Tell him they are trying to murder Platt. Now hurry, boy. Be at the Pine Woods by noon if you kill the mule."

Chapin stepped into the house and wrote a pass. When he returned, Lawson was at the door, mounted on his mule. Receiving the pass, he plied the whip right smartly to the beast, dashed out of the yard, and turning up the bayou on a hard gallop, in less time than it has taken me to describe the scene, was out of sight.

CHAPTER IX.

THE HOT SUN—YET BOUND—THE CORDS SINK INTO MY FLESH—CHAPIN'S UNEASI-
NESS—SPECULATION—RACHEL, AND HER CUP OF WATER—SUFFERING IN-
CREASES—THE HAPPINESS OF SLAVERY—ARRIVAL OF FORD—HE CUTS THE
CORDS WHICH BIND ME, AND TAKES THE ROPE FROM MY NECK—MISERY—THE
GATHERING OF SLAVES IN ELIZA'S CABIN—THEIR KINDNESS—RACHEL REPEATS
THE OCCURRENCES OF THE DAY—LAWSON ENTERTAINS HIS COMPANIONS WITH
AN ACCOUNT OF HIS RIDE—CHAPIN'S APPREHENSIONS OF TIBEATS—HIRED TO
PETER TANNER—PETER EXPOUNDS THE SCRIPTURES—DESCRIPTION OF THE
STOCKS.

As the sun approached the meridian that day it became insufferably warm. Its hot rays scorched the ground. The earth almost blistered the foot that stood upon it. I was without coat or hat, standing bare-headed, exposed to its burning blaze. Great drops of perspiration rolled down my face, drenching the scanty apparel wherewith I was clothed. Over the fence, a very little way off, the peach trees cast their cool, delicious shadows on the grass. I would gladly have given a long year of service to have been enabled to exchange the heated oven, as it were, wherein I stood, for a seat beneath their branches. But I was yet bound, the rope still dangling from my neck, and standing in the same tracks where Tibeats and his comrades left me. I could not move an inch, so firmly had I been bound. To have been enabled to lean against the weaving house would have been a luxury indeed. But it was far beyond my reach, though distant less than twenty feet. I wanted to lie down, but knew I could not rise again. The ground was so parched and boiling hot I was aware it would but add to the discomfort of my situation. If I could have only moved my position, however slightly, it would have been relief unspeakable. But the hot rays of a southern sun, beating all the long summer day on my bare head, produced not half the suffering I experienced from my aching limbs. My wrists and ankles, and the cords of my legs and arms began to swell, burying the rope that bound them into the swollen flesh.

All day Chapin walked back and forth upon the stoop, but not once approached me. He appeared to be in a state of great uneasiness, looking first towards me, and then up the road, as if expecting some arrival every moment. He did not go to the field, as was his custom. It was evident from his manner that he supposed Tibeats would return with more and better armed assistance, perhaps, to renew the quarrel, and it was equally evident he had prepared his mind to defend my life at whatever hazard. Why he did not relieve me—why he suffered me to remain in agony the whole weary day, I never knew. It was not for want of sympathy, I am

certain. Perhaps he wished Ford to see the rope about my neck, and the brutal manner in which I had been bound; perhaps his interference with another's property in
which he had no legal interest might have been a trespass, which would have subjected him to the penalty of the law. Why Tibeats was all day absent was another
mystery I never could divine. He knew well enough that Chapin would not harm
him unless he persisted in his design against me. Lawson told me afterwards, that,
as he passed the plantation of John David Cheney, he saw the three, and that they
turned and looked after him as he flew by. I think his supposition was, that Lawson had been sent out by Overseer Chapin to arouse the neighboring planters, and
to call on them to come to his assistance. He, therefore, undoubtedly, acted on the
principle, that "discretion is the better part of valor," and kept away.

But whatever motive may have governed the cowardly and malignant
tyrant, it is of no importance. There I still stood in the noon-tide sun, groaning
with pain. From long before daylight I had not eaten a morsel. I was growing
faint from pain, and thirst, and hunger. Once only, in the very hottest portion of
the day, Rachel, half fearful she was acting contrary to the overseer's wishes, ventured to me, and held a cup of water to my lips. The humble creature never knew,
nor could she comprehend if she had heard them, the blessings I invoked upon
her, for that balmy draught. She could only say, "Oh, Platt, how I do pity you,"
and then hastened back to her labors in the kitchen.

Never did the sun move so slowly through the heavens—never did it shower
down such fervent and fiery rays, as it did that day. At least, so it appeared to me.
What my meditations were—the innumerable thoughts that thronged through my
distracted brain—I will not attempt to give expression to. Suffice it to say, during
the whole long day I came not to the conclusion, even once, that the southern
slave, fed, clothed, whipped and protected by his master, is happier than the free
colored citizen of the North. To that conclusion I have never since arrived. There
are many, however, even in the Northern States, benevolent and well-disposed
men, who will pronounce my opinion erroneous, and gravely proceed to substantiate the assertion with an argument. Alas! they have never drunk, as I have,
from the bitter cup of slavery. Just at sunset my heart leaped with unbounded joy,
as Ford came riding into the yard, his horse covered with foam. Chapin met him
at the door, and after conversing a short time, he walked directly to me.

"Poor Platt, you are in a bad state," was the only expression that escaped
his lips.

"Thank God!" said I, "thank God, Master Ford, that you have come at last."

Drawing a knife from his pocket, he indignantly cut the cord from my
wrists, arms, and ankles, and slipped the noose from my neck. I attempted to
walk, but staggered like a drunken man, and fell partially to the ground.

Ford returned immediately to the house, leaving me alone again. As he
reached the piazza, Tibeats and his two friends rode up. A long dialogue followed. I could hear the sound of their voices, the mild tones of Ford mingling
with the angry accents of Tibeats, but was unable to distinguish what was said.
Finally the three departed again, apparently not well pleased.

I endeavored to raise the hammer, thinking to show Ford how willing I was
to work, by proceeding with my labors on the weaving house, but it fell from my

nerveless hand. At dark I crawled into the cabin, and laid down. I was in great misery—all sore and swollen—the slightest movement producing excruciating suffering. Soon the hands came in from the field. Rachel, when she went after Lawson, had told them what had happened. Eliza and Mary broiled me a piece of bacon, but my appetite was gone. Then they scorched some corn meal and made coffee. It was all that I could take. Eliza consoled me and was very kind. It was not long before the cabin was full of slaves. They gathered round me, asking many questions about the difficulty with Tibeats in the morning—and the particulars of all the occurrences of the day. Then Rachel came in, and in her simple language, repeated it over again—dwelling emphatically on the kick that sent Tibeats rolling over on the ground—whereupon there was a general titter throughout the crowd. Then she described how Chapin walked out with his pistols and rescued me, and how Master Ford cut the ropes with his knife, just as if he was mad.

By this time Lawson had returned. He had to regale them with an account of his trip to the Pine Woods—how the brown mule bore him faster than a "streak o' lightnin'"—how he astonished everybody as he flew along—how Master Ford started right away—how he said Platt was a good nigger, and they shouldn't kill him, concluding with pretty strong intimations that there was not another human being in the wide world, who could have created such a universal sensation on the road, or performed such a marvelous John Gilpin[21] feat, as he had done that day on the brown mule.

The kind creatures loaded me with the expression of their sympathy—saying Tibeats was a hard, cruel man, and hoping "Massa Ford" would get me back again. In this manner they passed the time, discussing, chatting, talking over and over again the exciting affair, until suddenly Chapin presented himself at the cabin door and called me.

"Platt," said he, "you will sleep on the floor in the great house to-night; bring your blanket with you."

I arose as quickly as I was able, took my blanket in my hand, and followed him. On the way he informed me that he should not wonder if Tibeats was back again before morning—that he intended to kill me—and that he did not mean he should do it without witnesses. Had he stabbed me to the heart in the presence of a hundred slaves, not one of them, by the laws of Louisiana, could have given evidence against him. I laid down on the floor in the "great house"—the first and the last time such a sumptuous resting place was granted me during my twelve years of bondage—and tried to sleep. Near midnight the dog began to bark. Chapin arose, looked from the window, but could discover nothing. At length the dog was quiet. As he returned to his room, he said,

"I believe, Platt, that scoundrel is skulking about the premises somewhere. If the dog barks again, and I am sleeping, wake me."

I promised to do so. After the lapse of an hour or more, the dog re-commenced his clamor, running towards the gate, then back again, all the while barking furiously.

Chapin was out of bed without waiting to be called. On this occasion, he stepped forth upon the piazza, and remained standing there a considerable length of time. Nothing, however, was to be seen, and the dog returned to his kennel.

We were not disturbed again during the night. The excessive pain that I suffered, and the dread of some impending danger, prevented any rest whatever. Whether or not Tibeats did actually return to the plantation that night, seeking an opportunity to wreak his vengeance upon me, is a secret known only to himself, perhaps. I thought then, however, and have the strong impression still, that he was there. At all events, he had the disposition of an assassin—cowering before a brave man's words, but ready to strike his helpless or unsuspecting victim in the back, as I had reason afterwards to know.

At daylight in the morning, I arose, sore and weary, having rested little. Nevertheless, after partaking breakfast, which Mary and Eliza had prepared for me in the cabin, I proceeded to the weaving-house and commenced the labors of another day. It was Chapin's practice, as it is the practice of overseers generally, immediately on arising, to bestride his horse, always saddled and bridled and ready for him—the particular business of some slave—and ride into the field. This morning, on the contrary, he came to the weaving-house, asking if I had seen anything of Tibeats yet. Replying in the negative, he remarked there was something not right about the fellow—there was bad blood in him—that I must keep a sharp watch of him, or he would do me wrong some day when I least expected it.

While he was yet speaking, Tibeats rode in, hitched his horse, and entered the house. I had little fear of him while Ford and Chapin were at hand, but they could not be near me always.

Oh! how heavily the weight of slavery pressed upon me then. I must toil day after day, endure abuse and taunts and scoffs, sleep on the hard ground, live on the coarsest fare, and not only this, but live the slave of a blood-seeking wretch, of whom I must stand henceforth in continued fear and dread. Why had I not died in my young years—before God had given me children to love and live for? What unhappiness and suffering and sorrow it would have prevented. I sighed for liberty; but the bondman's chain was round me, and could not be shaken off. I could only gaze wistfully towards the North, and think of the thousands of miles that stretched between me and the soil of freedom, over which a *black* freeman may not pass.

Tibeats, in the course of half an hour, walked over to the weaving-house, looked at me sharply, then returned without saying anything. Most of the forenoon he sat on the piazza, reading a newspaper and conversing with Ford. After dinner, the latter left for the Pine Woods, and it was indeed with regret that I beheld him depart from the plantation.

Once more during the day Tibeats came to me, gave me some order, and returned.

During the week the weaving-house was completed—Tibeats in the meantime making no allusion whatever to the difficulty—when I was informed he had hired me to Peter Tanner, to work under another carpenter by the name of Myers. This announcement was received with gratification, as any place was desirable that would relieve me of his hateful presence.

Peter Tanner, as the reader has already been informed, lived on the opposite shore, and was the brother of Mistress Ford. He is one of the most extensive planters on Bayou Boeuf, and owns a large number of slaves.

Over I went to Tanner's, joyfully enough. He had heard of my late difficulties—in fact, I ascertained the flogging of Tibeats was soon blazoned far and wide. This affair, together with my rafting experiment, had rendered me somewhat notorious. More than once I heard it said that Platt Ford, now Platt Tibeats—a slave's name changes with his change of master—was "a devil of a nigger." But I was destined to make a still further noise, as will presently be seen, throughout the little world of Bayou Boeuf.

Peter Tanner endeavored to impress upon me the idea that he was quite severe, though I could perceive there was a vein of good humor in the old fellow, after all.

"You're the nigger," he said to me on my arrival—"You're the nigger that flogged your master, eh? You're the nigger that kicks, and holds carpenter Tibeats by the leg, and wallops him, are ye? I'd like to see you hold me by the leg—I should. You're a 'portant character—you're a great nigger—very remarkable nigger, ain't ye? I'd lash you—I'd take the tantrums out of ye. Jest take hold of my leg, if you please. None of your pranks here, my boy, remember *that*. Now go to work, you kickin' rascal," concluded Peter Tanner, unable to suppress a half-comical grin at his own wit and sarcasm.

After listening to this salutation, I was taken charge of by Myers, and labored under his direction for a month, to his and my own satisfaction.

Like William Ford, his brother-in-law, Tanner was in the habit of reading the Bible to his slaves on the Sabbath, but in a somewhat different spirit. He was an impressive commentator on the New Testament. The first Sunday after my coming to the plantation, he called them together, and began to read the twelfth chapter of Luke. When he came to the 47th verse, he looked deliberately around him, and continued—"And that servant which knew his lord's *will*,"—here he paused, looking around more deliberately than before, and again proceeded—"which knew his lord's *will*, and *prepared* not himself"—here was another pause—"*prepared* not himself, neither did *according* to his will, shall be beaten with many *stripes*."

"D'ye hear that?" demanded Peter, emphatically. "*Stripes*," he repeated, slowly and distinctly, taking off his spectacles, preparatory to making a few remarks.

"That nigger that don't take care—that don't obey his lord—that's his master—d'ye see?—that 'ere nigger shall be beaten with many stripes. Now, 'many' signifies a *great* many—forty, a hundred, a hundred and fifty lashes. That's *Scripter!*" and so Peter continued to elucidate the subject for a great length of time, much to the edification of his sable audience.

At the conclusion of the exercises, calling up three of his slaves, Warner, Will and Major, he cried out to me—

"Here, Platt, you held Tibeats by the legs; now I'll see if you can hold these rascals in the same way, till I get back from meetin'."

Thereupon he ordered them to the stocks—a common thing on plantations in the Red River country. The stocks are formed of two planks, the lower one made fast at the ends to two short posts, driven firmly into the ground. At regular distances half circles are cut in the upper edge. The other plank is fastened to one of the posts by a hinge, so that it can be opened or shut down, in the same manner as the blade of a pocket-knife is shut or opened. In the lower edge of the upper plank corresponding half circles are also cut, so that when they close, a row of holes is formed large enough to admit a negro's leg above the ankle, but not large enough to enable him to draw out his foot. The other end of the upper plank, opposite the hinge, is fastened to its post by lock and key. The slave is made to sit upon the ground, when the uppermost prank is elevated, his legs, just above the ankles, placed in the sub-half circles, and shutting it down again, and locking it, he is held secure and fast. Very often the neck instead of the ankle is enclosed. In this manner they are held during the operation of whipping.

Warner, Will and Major, according to Tanner's account of them, were melon-stealing, Sabbath breaking niggers, and not approving of such wickedness, he felt it his duty to put them in the stocks. Handing me the key, himself, Myers, Mistress Tanner and the children entered the carriage and drove away to church at Cheneyville. When they were gone, the boys begged me to let them out. I felt sorry to see them sitting on the hot ground, and remembered my own sufferings in the sun. Upon their promise to return to the stocks at any moment they were required to do so, I consented to release them. Grateful for the lenity shown them, and in order in some measure to repay it, they could do no less, of course, than pilot me to the melon-patch. Shortly before Tanner's return, they were in the stocks again. Finally he drove up, and looking at the boys, said, with a chuckle,—

"Aha! ye havn't been strolling about much to-day, any way. *I'll* teach you what's what. *I'll* tire ye of eating water-melons on the Lord's day, ye Sabbath-breaking niggers."

Peter Tanner prided himself upon his strict religious observances: he was a deacon in the church.

But I have now reached a point in the progress of my narrative, when it becomes necessary to turn away from these light descriptions, to the more grave and weighty matter of the second battle with Master Tibeats, and the flight through the great Pacoudrie Swamp.

CHAPTER X.

RETURN OF TIBEATS—IMPOSSIBILITY OF PLEASING HIM—HE ATTACKS ME WITH A HATCHET—THE STRUGGLE OVER THE BROAD AXE—THE TEMPTATION TO MURDER HIM—ESCAPE ACROSS THE PLANTATION—OBSERVATIONS FROM THE FENCE—TIBEATS APPROACHES, FOLLOWED BY THE HOUNDS—THEY TAKE MY TRACK—THEIR LOUD YELLS—THEY ALMOST OVERTAKE ME—I REACH THE WATER—THE HOUNDS CONFUSED—MOCCASIN SNAKES—ALLIGATORS—NIGHT IN THE "GREAT PACOUDRIE SWAMP"—THE SOUNDS OF LIFE—NORTH-WEST COURSE—EMERGE INTO THE PINE WOODS—SLAVE AND HIS YOUNG MASTER—ARRIVAL AT FORD'S—FOOD AND REST.

AT the end of a month, my services being no longer required at Tanner's I was sent over the bayou again to my master, whom I found engaged in building the cotton press. This was situated at some distance from the great house, in a rather retired place. I commenced working once more in company with Tibeats, being entirely alone with him most part of the time. I remembered the words of Chapin, his precautions, his advice to beware, lest in some unsuspecting moment he might injure me. They were always in my mind, so that I lived in a most uneasy state of apprehension and fear. One eye was on my work, the other on my master. I determined to give him no cause of offence, to work still more diligently, if possible, than I had done, to bear whatever abuse he might heap upon me, save bodily injury, humbly and patiently, hoping thereby to soften in some degree his manner towards me, until the blessed time might come when I should be delivered from his clutches.

The third morning after my return, Chapin left the plantation for Cheneyville, to be absent until night. Tibeats, on that morning, was attacked with one of those periodical fits of spleen and ill-humor to which he was frequently subject, rendering him still more disagreeable and venomous than usual.

It was about nine o'clock in the forenoon, when I was busily employed with the jack-plane on one of the sweeps. Tibeats was standing by the work-bench, fitting a handle into the chisel, with which he had been engaged previously in cutting the thread of the screw.

"You are not planing that down enough," said he.

"It is just even with the line," I replied.

"You're a d—d liar," he exclaimed passionately.

"Oh, well, master," I said, mildly, "I will plane it down more if you say so," at the same time proceeding to do as I supposed he desired. Before one shaving had been removed, however, he cried out, saying I had now planed it too deep—it was too small—I had spoiled the sweep entirely. Then followed curses and imprecations. I had endeavored to do exactly as he directed, but nothing would satisfy the unreasonable man. In silence and in dread I stood by the sweep, holding the jack-plane in my hand, not knowing what to do, and not daring to be idle. His anger grew more and more violent, until, finally, with an oath, such a bitter, frightful oath as only Tibeats could utter, he seized a hatchet from the work-bench and darted towards me, swearing he would cut my head open.

It was a moment of life or death. The sharp, bright blade of the hatchet glittered in the sun. In another instant it would be buried in my brain, and yet in that instant—so quick will a man's thoughts come to him in such a fearful strait—I reasoned with myself. If I stood still, my doom was certain; if I fled, ten chances to one the hatchet, flying from his hand with a too-deadly and unerring aim, would strike me in the back. There was but one course to take. Springing towards him with all my power, and meeting him full half-way, before he could bring down the blow, with one hand I caught his uplifted arm, with the other seized him by the throat. We stood looking each other in the eyes. In his I could see murder. I felt as if I had a serpent by the neck, watching the slightest relaxation of my gripe, to coil itself round my body, crushing and stinging it to death. I thought to scream aloud, trusting that some ear might catch the sound—but Chapin was away; the hands were in the field; there was no living soul in sight or hearing.

The good genius, which thus far through life has saved me from the hands of violence, at that moment suggested a lucky thought. With a vigorous and sudden kick, that brought him on one knee, with a groan, I released my hold upon his throat, snatched the hatchet, and cast it beyond reach.

Frantic with rage, maddened beyond control, he seized a white oak stick, five feet long, perhaps, and as large in circumference as his hand could grasp, which was lying on the ground. Again he rushed towards me, and again I met him, seized him about the waist, and being the stronger of the two, bore him to the earth. While in that position I obtained possession of the stick, and rising, cast it from me, also.

He likewise arose and ran for the broad-axe, on the work-bench. Fortunately, there was a heavy plank lying upon its broad blade, in such a manner that he could not extricate it, before I had sprung upon his back. Pressing him down closely and heavily on the plank, so that the axe was held more firmly to its place, I endeavored, but in vain, to break his grasp upon the handle. In that position we remained some minutes.

There have been hours in my unhappy life, many of them, when the contemplation of death as the end of earthly sorrow—of the grave as a resting place for the tired and worn out body—has been pleasant to dwell upon. But such contemplations vanish in the hour of peril. No man, in his full strength, can stand undismayed, in the presence of the "king of terrors." Life is dear to every living thing; the worm that crawls upon the ground will struggle for it. At that moment it was dear to me, enslaved and treated as I was.

Not able to unloose his hand, once more I seized him by the throat, and this time, with a vice-like gripe that soon relaxed his hold. He became pliant and unstrung. His face, that had been white with passion, was now black from suffocation. Those small serpent eyes that spat such venom, were now full of horror—two great white orbs starting from their sockets!

There was "a lurking devil" in my heart that prompted me to kill the human blood-hound on the spot—to retain the gripe on his accursed throat till the breath of life was gone! I dared not murder him, and I dared not let him live. If I killed him, my life must pay the forfeit—if he lived, my life only would satisfy his vengeance. A voice within whispered me to fly. To be a wanderer among the swamps, a fugitive and a vagabond on the face of the earth, was preferable to the life that I was leading.

My resolution was soon formed, and swinging him from the work-bench to the ground, I leaped a fence near by, and hurried across the plantation, passing the slaves at work in the cotton field. At the end of a quarter of a mile I reached the wood-pasture, and it was a short time indeed that I had been running it. Climbing on to a high fence, I could see the cotton press, the great house, and the space between. It was a conspicuous position, from whence the whole plantation was in view. I saw Tibeats cross the field towards the house, and enter it—then he came out, carrying his saddle, and presently mounted his horse and galloped away.

I was desolate, but thankful. Thankful that my life was spared,—desolate and discouraged with the prospect before me. What would become of me? Who would befriend me? Whither should I fly? Oh, God! Thou who gavest me life, and implanted in my bosom the love of life—who filled it with emotions such as other men, thy creatures, have, do not forsake me. Have pity on the poor slave— let me not perish. If thou dost not protect me, I am lost—lost! Such supplications, silently and unuttered, ascended from my inmost heart to Heaven. But there was no answering voice—no sweet, low tone, coming down from on high, whispering to my soul, "It is I, be not afraid." I was the forsaken of God, it seemed—the despised and hated of men!

In about three-fourths of an hour several of the slaves shouted and made signs for me to run. Presently, looking up the bayou, I saw Tibeats and two others on horse-back, coming at a fast gait, followed by a troop of dogs. There were as many as eight or ten. Distant as I was, I knew them. They belonged on the adjoining plantation. The dogs used on Bayou Boeuf for hunting slaves are a kind of blood-hound, but a far more savage breed than is found in the Northern States. They will attack a negro, at their master's bidding, and cling to him as the common bull-dog will cling to a four footed animal. Frequently their loud bay is heard in the swamps, and then there is speculation as to what point the runaway will be overhauled—the same as a New-York hunter stops to listen to the hounds coursing along the hillsides, and suggests to his companion that the fox will be taken at such a place. I never knew a slave escaping with his life from Bayou Bouef. One reason is, they are not allowed to learn the art of swimming, and are incapable of crossing the most inconsiderable stream. In their flight they can go in no direction but a little way without coming to a bayou, when the inevitable alternative is presented, of being drowned or overtaken by the dogs. In youth I had practised in the clear streams that flow through my native district, until I had become an expert swimmer, and felt at home in the watery element.

I stood upon the fence until the dogs had reached the cotton press. In an instant more, their long, savage yells announced they were on my track. Leaping down from my position, I ran towards the swamp. Fear gave me strength, and I exerted it to the utmost. Every few moments I could hear the yelpings of the dogs. They were gaining upon me. Every howl was nearer and nearer. Each moment I expected they would spring upon my back—expected to feel their long teeth sinking into my flesh. There were so many of them, I knew they would tear me to pieces, that they would worry me, at once, to death. I gasped for breath— gasped forth a half-uttered, choking prayer to the Almighty to save me—to give me strength to reach some wide, deep bayou where I could throw them off the track, or sink into its waters. Presently I reached a thick palmetto bottom. As I fled through them they made a loud rustling noise, not loud enough, however, to drown the voices of the dogs.

Continuing my course due south, as nearly as I can judge, I came at length to water just over shoe. The hounds at that moment could not have been five rods behind me. I could hear them crashing and plunging through the palmettoes, their loud, eager yells making the whole swamp clamorous with the sound. Hope revived a little as I reached the water. If it were only deeper, they might loose the scent, and thus disconcerted, afford me the opportunity of evading them. Luckily, it grew deeper the farther I proceeded—now over my ankles—

now half-way to my knees—now sinking a moment to my waist, and then emerging presently into more shallow places. The dogs had not gained upon me since I struck the water. Evidently they were confused. Now their savage intonations grew more and more distant, assuring me that I was leaving them. Finally I stopped to listen, but the long howl came booming on the air again, telling me I was not yet safe. From bog to bog, where I had stepped, they could still keep upon the track, though impeded by the water. At length, to my great joy, I came to a wide bayou, and plunging in, had soon stemmed its sluggish current to the other side. There, certainly, the dogs would be confounded—the current carrying down the stream all traces of that slight, mysterious scent, which enables the quick-smelling hound to follow in the track of the fugitive.

After crossing this bayou the water became so deep I could not run. I was now in what I afterwards learned was the "Great Pacoudrie Swamp."[22] It was filled with immense trees—the sycamore, the gum, the cotton wood and cypress, and extends, I am informed, to the shore of the Calcasieu river. For thirty or forty miles it is without inhabitants, save wild beasts—the bear, the wild-cat, the tiger, and great slimy reptiles, that are crawling through it everywhere. Long before I reached the bayou, in fact, from the time I struck the water until I emerged from the swamp on my return, these reptiles surrounded me. I saw hundreds of moccasin snakes. Every log and bog—every trunk of a fallen tree, over which I was compelled to step or climb, was alive with them. They crawled away at my approach, but sometimes in my haste, I almost placed my hand or foot upon them. They are poisonous serpents—their bite more fatal than the rattlesnake's. Besides, I had lost one shoe, the sole having come entirely off, leaving the upper only dangling to my ankle.

I saw also many alligators, great and small, lying in the water, or on pieces of floodwood. The noise I made usually startled them, when they moved off and plunged into the deepest places. Sometimes, however, I would come directly upon a monster before observing it. In such cases, I would start back, run a short way round, and in that manner shun them. Straight forward, they will run a short distance rapidly, but do not possess the power of turning. In a crooked race, there is no difficulty in evading them.

About two o'clock in the afternoon, I heard the last of the hounds. Probably they did not cross the bayou. Wet and weary, but relieved from the sense of instant peril, I continued on, more cautious and afraid, however, of the snakes and alligators than I had been in the earlier portion of my flight. Now, before stepping into a muddy pool, I would strike the water with a stick. If the waters moved, I would go around it, if not, would venture through.

At length the sun went down, and gradually night's trailing mantle shrouded the great swamp in darkness. Still I staggered on, fearing every instant I should feel the dreadful sting of the moccasin, or be crushed within the jaws of some disturbed alligator. The dread of them now almost equaled the fear of the pursuing hounds. The moon arose after a time, its mild light creeping through the overspreading branches, loaded with long, pendent moss. I kept traveling forwards until after midnight, hoping all the while that I would soon emerge into some less desolate and dangerous region. But the water grew deeper and the walking more difficult than ever. I perceived it would be impossible to proceed much farther, and knew not, moreover, what hands I might fall into, should I succeed in reaching a human habitation. Not provided with a pass, any white man would be at liberty to arrest me, and place me in prison until such time as my master should "prove property, pay charges, and take me away." I was an estray, and if so unfortunate as to meet a law-abiding citizen of Louisiana, he would deem it his duty to his neighbor, perhaps, to put me forthwith in the pound. Really, it was difficult to determine which I had most reason to fear—dogs, alligators or men!

After midnight, however, I came to a halt. Imagination cannot picture the dreariness of the scene. The swamp was resonant with the quacking of innumerable ducks! Since the foundation of the earth, in all probability, a human footstep had never before so far penetrated the recesses of the swamp. It was not silent now—silent to a degree that rendered it oppressive,—as it was when the sun was shining in the heavens. My midnight intrusion had awakened the feathered tribes, which seemed to throng the morass in hundreds of thousands, and their garrulous throats poured forth such multitudinous sounds—there was such a fluttering of wings—such sullen plunges in the water all around me—that I was affrighted and appalled. All the fowls of the air, and all the creeping things of the earth appeared to have assembled together in that particular place, for the purpose of filling it with clamor and confusion. Not by human dwellings—not in crowded cities alone, are the sights and sounds of life. The wildest places of the earth are full of them. Even in the heart of that dismal swamp, God had provided a refuge and a dwelling place for millions of living things.

The moon had now risen above the trees, when I resolved upon a new project. Thus far I had endeavored to travel as nearly south as possible. Turning about I proceeded in a north-west direction, my object being to strike the Pine Woods in the vicinity of Master Ford's. Once within the shadow of his protection, I felt I would be comparatively safe.

My clothes were in tatters, my hands, face, and body covered with scratches, received from the sharp knots of fallen trees, and in climbing over piles of brush and floodwood. My bare foot was full of thorns. I was besmeared with muck and mud, and the green slime that had collected on the surface of the dead water, in which I had been immersed to the neck many times during the day and night. Hour after hour, and tiresome indeed had they become, I continued to plod along on my north-west course. The water began to grow less deep, and the ground more firm under my feet. At last I reached the Pacoudrie, the same wide bayou I had swam while "outward bound." I swam it again, and shortly after thought I heard a cock crow, but the sound was faint, and it might have been a mockery of the ear. The water receded from my advancing footsteps—now I had left the bogs behind me—now I was on dry land that gradually ascended to the plain, and I knew I was somewhere in the "Great Pine Woods."

Just at day-break I came to an opening—a sort of small plantation—but one I had never seen before. In the edge of the woods I came upon two men, a slave and his young master, engaged in catching wild hogs. The white man I knew would demand my pass, and not able to give him one, would take me into possession. I was too wearied to run again, and too desperate to be taken, and therefore adopted a ruse that proved entirely successful. Assuming a fierce expression, I walked directly towards him, looking him steadily in the face. As I approached, he moved backwards with an air of alarm. It was plain he was much affrighted—that he looked upon me as some infernal goblin, just arisen from the bowels of the swamp!

"Where does William Ford live?" I demanded, in no gentle tone.

"He lives seven miles from here," was the reply.

"Which is the way to his place?" I again demanded, trying to look more fiercely than ever.

"Do you see those pine trees yonder?" he asked, pointing to two, a mile distant, that rose far above their fellows, like a couple of tall sentinels, overlooking the broad expanse of forest.

"I see them," was the answer.

"At the feet of those pine trees," he continued, "runs the Texas road. Turn to the left, and it will lead you to William Ford's."

Without further parley, I hastened forward, happy as he was, no doubt, to place the widest possible distance between us. Striking the Texas road, I turned to the left hand, as directed, and soon passed a great fire, where a pile of logs were burning. I went to it, thinking I would dry my clothes; but the gray light of the morning was fast breaking away,—some passing white man might observe me; besides, the heat overpowered me with the desire of sleep: so, lingering no longer, I continued my travels, and finally, about eight o'clock, reached the house of Master Ford.

The slaves were all absent from the quarters, at their work. Stepping on to the piazza, I knocked at the door, which was soon opened by Mistress Ford. My appearance was so changed—I was in such a wobegone and forlorn condition, she did not know me. Inquiring if Master Ford was at home, that good man made his appearance, before the question could be answered. I told him of my flight, and all the particulars connected with it. He listened attentively, and when I had concluded, spoke to me kindly and sympathetically, and taking me to the kitchen, called John, and ordered him to prepare me food. I had tasted nothing since daylight the previous morning.

When John had set the meal before me, the madam came out with a bowl of milk, and many little delicious dainties, such as rarely please the palate of a slave. I was hungry, and I was weary, but neither food nor rest afforded half the pleasure as did the blessed voices speaking kindness and consolation. It was the oil and the wine which the Good Samaritan in the "Great Pine Woods" was ready to pour into the wounded spirit of the slave, who came to him, stripped of his raiment and half-dead.

They left me in the cabin, that I might rest. Blessed be sleep! It visiteth all alike, descending as the dews of heaven on the bond and free. Soon it nestled to my bosom, driving away the troubles that oppressed it, and bearing me to that shadowy region, where I saw again the faces, and listened to the voices of my children, who, alas, for aught I knew in my waking hours, had fallen into the arms of that *other* sleep, from which they *never* would arouse.

CHAPTER XI.

AFTER a long sleep, sometime in the afternoon I awoke, refreshed, but very sore
and stiff. Sally came in and talked with me, while John cooked me some dinner.
Sally was in great trouble, as well as myself, one of her children being ill, and she
feared it could not survive. Dinner over, after walking about the quarters for a
while, visiting Sally's cabin and looking at the sick child, I strolled into the
madam's garden. Though it was a season of the year when the voices of the birds
are silent, and the trees are stripped of their summer glories in more frigid climes,
yet the whole variety of roses were then blooming there, and the long, luxuriant
vines creeping over the frames. The crimson and golden fruit hung half hidden
amidst the younger and older blossoms of the peach, the orange, the plum, and
the pomegranate; for, in that region of almost perpetual warmth, the leaves are
falling and the buds bursting into bloom the whole year long.

I indulged the most grateful feelings towards Master and Mistress Ford,
and wishing in some manner to repay their kindness, commenced trimming the
vines, and afterwards weeding out the grass from among the orange and pomegranate trees. The latter grows eight or ten feet high, and its fruit, though larger,
is similar in appearance to the jelly-flower. It has the luscious flavor of the straw-
berry. Oranges, peaches, plums, and most other fruits are indigenous to the rich,
warm soil of Avoyelles; but the apple, the most common of them all in colder
latitudes, is rarely to be seen.

Mistress Ford came out presently, saying it was praise-worthy in me, but I
was not in a condition to labor, and might rest myself at the quarters until master should go down to Bayou Boeuf, which would not be that day, and it might
not be the next. I said to her—to be sure, I felt bad, and was stiff, and that my
foot pained me, the stubs and thorns having so torn it, but thought such exercise
would not hurt me, and that it was a great pleasure to work for so good a mistress. Thereupon she returned to the great house, and for three days I was diligent in the garden, cleaning the walks, weeding the flower beds, and pulling up
the rank grass beneath the jessamine vines, which the gentle and generous hand
of my protectress had taught to clamber along the walls.

The fourth morning, having become recruited and refreshed, Master Ford ordered me to make ready to accompany him to the bayou. There was but one saddle horse at the opening, all the others with the mules having been sent down to the plantation. I said I could walk, and bidding Sally and John good-bye, left the opening, trotting along by the horse's side.

That little paradise in the Great Pine Woods was the oasis in the desert, towards which my heart turned lovingly, during many years of bondage. I went forth from it now with regret and sorrow, not so overwhelming, however, as if it had then been given me to know that I should never return to it again.

Master Ford urged me to take his place occasionally on the horse, to rest me; but I said no, I was not tired, and it was better for me to walk than him. He said many kind and cheering things to me on the way, riding slowly, in order that I might keep pace with him. The goodness of God was manifest, he declared, in my miraculous escape from the swamp. As Daniel came forth unharmed from the den of lions, and as Jonah had been preserved in the whale's belly, even so had I been delivered from evil by the Almighty. He interrogated me in regard to the various fears and emotions I had experienced during the day and night, and if I had felt, at any time, a desire to pray. I felt forsaken of the whole world, I answered him, and was praying mentally all the while. At such times, said he, the heart of man turns instinctively towards his Maker. In prosperity, and when there is nothing to injure or make him afraid, he remembers Him not, and is ready to defy Him; but place him in the midst of dangers, cut him off from human aid, let the grave open before him—then it is, in the time of his tribulation, that the scoffer and unbelieving man turns to God for help, feeling there is no other hope, or refuge, or safety, save in his protecting arm.

So did that benignant man speak to me of this life and of the life hereafter; of the goodness and power of God, and of the vanity of earthly things, as we journeyed along the solitary road towards Bayou Boeuf.

When within some five miles of the plantation, we discovered a horseman at a distance, galloping towards us. As he came near I saw that it was Tibeats! He looked at me a moment, but did not address me, and turning about, rode along side by side with Ford. I trotted silently at their horses' heels, listing to their conversation. Ford informed him of my arrival in the Pine Woods three days before, of the sad plight I was in, and of the difficulties and dangers I had encountered.

"Well," exclaimed Tibeats, omitting his usual oaths in the presence of Ford, "I never saw such running before. I'll bet him against a hundred dollars, he'll beat any nigger in Louisiana. I offered John David Cheney twenty-five dollars to catch him, dead or alive, but he outran his dogs in a fair race. Them Cheney dogs ain't much, after all. Dunwoodie's hounds would have had him down before he touched the palmettoes. Somehow the dogs got off the track, and we had to give up the hunt. We rode the horses as far as we could, and then kept on foot till the water was three feet deep. The boys said he was drowned, sure. I allow I wanted a shot at him mightily. Ever since, I have been riding up and down the bayou, but had'nt much hope of catching him—thought he was dead, *sartin*. Oh, he's a cuss to run—that nigger is!"

In this way Tibeats ran on, describing his search in the swamp, the wonderful speed with which I had fled before the hounds, and when he had finished, Master Ford responded by saying, I had always been a willing and faithful boy with him; that he was sorry we had such trouble; that, according to Platt's story, he had been inhumanly treated, and that he, Tibeats, was himself in fault. Using hatchets and broad-axes upon slaves was shameful, and should not be allowed, he remarked. "This is no way of dealing with them, when first brought into the country. It will have a pernicious influence, and set them all running away. The swamps will be full of them. A little kindness would be far more effectual in restraining them, and rendering them obedient, than the use of such deadly weapons. Every planter on the bayou should frown upon such inhumanity. It is for the interest of all to do so. It is evident enough, Mr. Tibeats, that you and Platt cannot live together. You dislike him, and would not hesitate to kill him, and knowing it, he will run from you again through fear of his life. Now, Tibeats, you must sell him, or hire him out, at least. Unless you do so, I shall take measures to get him out of your possession."

In this spirit Ford addressed him the remainder of the distance. I opened not my mouth. On reaching the plantation they entered the great house, while I repaired to Eliza's cabin. The slaves were astonished to find me there, on returning from the field, supposing I was drowned. That night, again, they gathered about the cabin to listen to the story of my adventure. They took it for granted I would be whipped, and that it would be severe, the well-known penalty of running away being five hundred lashes.

"Poor fellow," said Eliza, taking me by the hand, "it would have been better for you if you had drowned. You have a cruel master, and he will kill you yet, I am afraid."

Lawson suggested that it might be, overseer Chapin would be appointed to inflict the punishment, in which case it would not be severe, whereupon Mary, Rachel, Bristol, and others hoped it would be Master Ford, and then it would be no whipping at all. They all pitied me and tried to console me, and were sad in view of the castigation that awaited me, except Kentucky John. There were no bounds to his laughter; he filled the cabin with cachinnations, holding his sides to prevent an explosion, and the cause of his noisy mirth was the idea of my outstripping the hounds. Somehow, he looked at the subject in a comical light. "I *know'd* dey would'nt cotch him, when he run cross de plantation. O, de lor', did'nt Platt pick his feet right up, tho', hey? When dem dogs got whar he was, he was'nt *dar*—haw, haw, haw! O, de lor' a' mity!"—and then Kentucky John relapsed into another of his boisterous fits.

Early the next morning, Tibeats left the plantation. In the course of the forenoon, while sauntering about the gin-house, a tall, good-looking man came to me, and inquired if I was Tibeats' boy, that youthful appellation being applied indiscriminately to slaves even though they may have passed the number of three score years and ten. I took off my hat, and answered that I was.

"How would you like to work for me?" he inquired.

"Oh, I would like to, very much," said I, inspired with a sudden hope of getting away from Tibeats.

"You worked under Myers at Peter Tanner's, didn't you?"

I replied I had, adding some complimentary remarks that Myers had made concerning me.

"Well, boy," said he, "I have hired you of your master to work for me in the 'Big Cane Brake,' thirty-eight miles from here, down on Red River."

This man was Mr. Eldret, who lived below Ford's, on the same side of the bayou. I accompanied him to his plantation, and in the morning started with his slave Sam, and a wagon-load of provisions, drawn by four mules, for the Big Cane, Eldret and Myers having preceded us on horseback. This Sam was a native of Charleston, where he had a mother, brother and sisters. He "allowed"—a common word among both black and white—that Tibeats was a mean man, and hoped, as I most earnestly did also, that his master would buy me.

We proceeded down the south shore of the bayou, crossing it at Carey's plantation; from thence to Huff Power, passing which, we came upon the Bayou Rouge road, which runs towards Red River. After passing through Bayou Rouge Swamp, and just at sunset, turning from the highway, we struck off into the "Big Cane Brake." We followed an unbeaten track, scarcely wide enough to admit the wagon. The cane, such as are used for fishing-rods, were as thick as they could stand. A person could not be seen through them the distance of a rod. The paths of wild beasts run through them in various directions—the bear and the American tiger abounding in these brakes, and wherever there is a basin of stagnant water, it is full of alligators.

We kept on our lonely course through the "Big Cane" several miles, when we entered a clearing, known as "Sutton's Field." Many years before, a man by the name of Sutton had penetrated the wilderness of cane to this solitary place. Tradition has it, that he fled thither, a fugitive, not from service, but from justice. Here he lived alone—recluse and hermit of the swamp—with his own hands planting the seed and gathering in the harvest. One day a band of Indians stole upon his solitude, and after a bloody battle, overpowered and massacred him. For miles the country round, in the slaves' quarters, and on the piazzas of "great houses," where white children listen to superstitious tales, the story goes, that that spot, in the heart of the "Big Cane," is a haunted place. For more than a quarter of a century, human voices had rarely, if ever, disturbed the silence of the clearing. Rank and noxious weeds had overspread the once cultivated field—serpents sunned themselves on the doorway of the crumbling cabin. It was indeed a dreary picture of desolation.

Passing "Sutton's Field," we followed a new-cut road two miles farther, which brought us to its termination. We had now reached the wild lands of Mr. Eldret, where he contemplated clearing up an extensive plantation. We went to work next morning with our cane-knives, and cleared a sufficient space to allow the erection of two cabins—one for Myers and Eldret, the other for Sam, myself, and the slaves that were to join us. We were now in the midst of trees of enormous growth, whose wide-spreading branches almost shut out the light of the sun, while the space between the trunks was an impervious mass of cane, with here and there an occasional palmetto.

The bay and the sycamore, the oak and the cypress, reach a growth unparalleled, in those fertile lowlands bordering the Red River. From every tree, moreover, hang long, large masses of moss, presenting to the eye unaccustomed to them, a striking and singular appearance. This moss, in large quantities, is sent north, and there used for manufacturing purposes.

We cut down oaks, split them into rails, and with these erected temporary cabins. We covered the roofs with the broad palmetto leaf, an excellent substitute for shingles, as long as they last.

The greatest annoyance I met with here were small flies, gnats and mosquitoes. They swarmed the air. They penetrated the porches of the ear, the nose, the eyes, the mouth. They sucked themselves beneath the skin. It was impossible to brush or beat them off. It seemed, indeed, as if they would devour us—carry us away piecemeal, in their small tormenting mouths.

A lonelier spot, or one more disagreeable, than the centre of the "Big Cane Brake," it would be difficult to conceive; yet to me it was a paradise, in comparison with any other place in the company of Master Tibeats. I labored hard, and oft-times was weary and fatigued, yet I could lie down at night in peace, and arise in the morning without fear.

In the course of a fortnight, four black girls came down from Eldret's plantation—Charlotte, Fanny, Cresia and Nelly. They were all large and stout. Axes were put into their hands, and they were sent out with Sam and myself to cut trees. They were excellent choppers, the largest oak or sycamore standing but a brief season before their heavy and well-directed blows. At piling logs, they were equal to any man. There are lumberwomen as well as lumbermen in the forests of the South. In fact, in the region of the Bayou Boeuf they perform their share of all the labor required on the plantation. They plough, drag, drive team, clear wild lands, work on the highway, and so forth. Some planters, owning large cotton and sugar plantations, have none other than the labor of slave women. Such an one is Jim Burns, who lives on the north shore of the bayou, opposite the plantation of John Fogaman.

On our arrival in the brake, Eldret promised me, if I worked well, I might go up to visit my friends at Ford's in four weeks. On Saturday night of the fifth week, I reminded him of his promise, when he told me I had done so well, that I might go. I had set my heart upon it, and Eldret's announcement thrilled me with pleasure. I was to return in time to commence the labors of the day on Tuesday morning.

While indulging the pleasant anticipation of so soon meeting my old friends again, suddenly the hateful form of Tibeats appeared among us. He inquired how Myers and Platt got along together, and was told, very well, and that Platt was going up to Ford's plantation in the morning on a visit.

"Poh, poh!" sneered Tibeats; "it isn't worth while—the nigger will get unsteady. He can't go."

But Eldret insisted I had worked faithfully—that he had given me his promise, and that, under the circumstances, I ought not to be disappointed. They then, it being about dark, entered one cabin and I the other. I could not give up the idea of going; it was a sore disappointment. Before morning I resolved, if Eldret made no objection, to leave at all hazards. At daylight I was at his door, with my blanket rolled up into a bundle, and hanging on a stick over my shoulder, waiting for a pass. Tibeats came out presently in one of his disagreeable moods, washed his face, and going to a stump near by, sat down upon it, apparently busily thinking with himself. After standing there a long time, impelled by a sudden impulse of impatience, I started off.

"Are you going without a pass?" he cried out to me.

"Yes, master, I thought I would," I answered.

"How do you think you'll get there?" demanded he.

"Don't know," was all the reply I made him.

"You'd be taken and sent to jail, where you ought to be, before you got half-way there," he added, passing into the cabin as he said it. He came out soon with the pass in his hand, and calling me a "d—d nigger that deserved a hundred lashes," threw it on the ground. I picked it up, and hurried away right speedily.

A slave caught off his master's plantation without a pass, may be seized and whipped by any white man whom he meets. The one I now received was dated, and read as follows:

"Platt has permission to go to Ford's plantation, on Bayou Boeuf, and return by Tuesday morning.

JOHN M. TIBEATS."

This is the usual form. On the way, a great many demanded it, read it, and passed on. Those having the air and appearance of gentlemen, whose dress indicated the possession of wealth, frequently took no notice of me whatever; but a shabby fellow, an unmistakable loafer, never failed to hail me, and to scrutinize and examine me in the most thorough manner. Catching runaways is sometimes a money-making business. If, after advertising, no owner appears, they may be sold to the highest bidder; and certain fees are allowed the finder for his services, at all events, even if reclaimed. "A mean white," therefore,—a name applied to the species loafer—considers it a god-send to meet an unknown negro without a pass.

There are no inns along the highways in that portion of the State where I sojourned. I was wholly destitute of money, neither did I carry any provisions, on my journey from the Big Cane to Bayou Boeuf; nevertheless, with his pass in his hand, a slave need never suffer from hunger or from thirst. It is only necessary to present it to the master or overseer of a plantation, and state his wants, when he will be sent round to the kitchen and provided with food or shelter, as the case may require. The traveler stops at any house and calls for a meal with as much freedom as if it was a public tavern. It is the general custom of the country. Whatever their faults may be, it is certain the inhabitants along Red River, and around the bayous in the interior of Louisiana are not wanting in hospitality.

I arrived at Ford's plantation towards the close of the afternoon, passing the evening in Eliza's cabin, with Lawson, Rachel, and others of my acquaintance. When we left Washington Eliza's form was round and plump. She stood erect, and in her silks and jewels, presented a picture of graceful strength and elegance. Now she was but a thin shadow of her former self. Her face had become ghastly haggard, and the once straight and active form was bowed down, as if bearing the weight of a hundred years. Crouching on her cabin floor, and clad in the coarse garments of a slave, old Elisha Berry would not have recognized the mother of his child. I never saw her afterwards. Having become useless in the cotton-field, she was bartered for a trifle, to some man residing in the vicinity of Peter Compton's. Grief had gnawed remorselessly at her heart, until her strength was gone; and for that, her last master, it is said, lashed and abused her most unmercifully. But he could not whip back the departed vigor of her youth, nor straighten up that bended body to its full height, such as it was when her children were around her, and the light of freedom was shining on her path.

I learned the particulars relative to her departure from this world, from some of Compton's slaves, who had come over Red River to the bayou, to assist young Madam Tanner during the "busy season." She became at length, they said, utterly helpless, for several weeks lying on the ground floor in a dilapidated cabin, dependent upon the mercy of her fellow thralls for an occasional drop of water, and a morsel of food. Her master did not "knock her on the head," as is sometimes done to put a suffering animal out of misery, but left her unprovided for, and unprotected, to linger through a life of pain and wretchedness to its natural close. When the hands returned from the field one night they found her dead! During the day, the Angel of the Lord, who moveth invisibly over all the earth, gathering in his harvest of departing souls, had silently entered the cabin of the dying woman, and taken her from thence. She was *free* at last!

Next day, rolling up my blanket, I started on my return to the Big Cane. After traveling five miles, at a place called Huff Power, the ever-present Tibeats met me in the road. He inquired why I was going back so soon, and when informed I was anxious to return by the time I was directed, he said I need go no farther than the next plantation, as he had that day sold me to Edwin Epps.[23] We walked down into the yard, where we met the latter gentleman, who examined me, and asked me the usual questions propounded by purchasers. Having been duly delivered over, I was ordered to the quarters, and at the same time directed to make a hoe and axe handle for myself.

I was now no longer the property of Tibeats—his dog, his brute, dreading his wrath and cruelty day and night; and whoever or whatever my new master might prove to be, I could not, certainly, regret the change. So it was good news when the sale was announced, and with a sigh of relief I sat down for the first time in my new abode.

Tibeats soon after disappeared from that section of the country. Once afterwards, and only once, I caught a glimpse of him. It was many miles from Bayou Boeuf. He was seated in the doorway of a low groggery. I was passing, in a drove of slaves, through St. Mary's parish.

CHAPTER XII.

PERSONAL APPEARANCE OF EPPS—EPPS, DRUNK AND SOBER—A GLIMPSE OF HIS HISTORY—COTTON GROWING—THE MODE OF PLOUGHING AND PREPARING GROUND—OF PLANTING, OF HOEING, OF PICKING, OF TREATING RAW HANDS—THE DIFFERENCE IN COTTON PICKERS—PATSEY A REMARKABLE ONE—TASKED ACCORDING TO ABILITY—BEAUTY OF A COTTON FIELD—THE

SLAVE'S LABORS—FEAR OF APPROACHING THE GIN-HOUSE—WEIGHING—
"CHORES"—CABIN LIFE—THE CORN MILL—THE USES OF THE GOURD—FEAR
OF OVERSLEEPING—FEAR CONTINUALLY—MODE OF CULTIVATING CORN—
SWEET POTATOES—FERTILITY OF THE SOIL—FATTENING HOGS—PRESERVING
BACON—RAISING   CATTLE—SHOOTING-MATCHES—GARDEN   PRODUCTS—
FLOWERS AND VERDURE.

EDWIN EPPS, of whom much will be said during the remainder of this history, is a large, portly, heavy-bodied man with light hair, high cheek bones, and a Roman nose of extraordinary dimensions. He has blue eyes, a fair complexion, and is, as I should say, full six feet high. He has the sharp, inquisitive expression of a jockey. His manners are repulsive and coarse, and his language gives speedy and unequivocal evidence that he has never enjoyed the advantages of an education. He has the faculty of saying most provoking things, in that respect even excelling old Peter Tanner. At the time I came into his possession, Edwin Epps was fond of the bottle, his "sprees" sometimes extending over the space of two whole weeks. Latterly, however, he had reformed his habits, and when I left him, was as strict a specimen of temperance as could be found on Bayou Boeuf. When "in his cups," Master Epps was a roystering, blustering, noisy fellow, whose chief delight was in dancing with his "niggers," or lashing them about the yard with his long whip, just for the pleasure of hearing them screech and scream, as the great welts were planted on their backs. When sober, he was silent, reserved and cunning, not beating us indiscriminately, as in his drunken moments, but sending the end of his rawhide to some tender spot of a lagging slave, with a sly dexterity peculiar to himself.

He had been a driver and overseer in his younger years, but at this time was in possession of a plantation on Bayou Huff Power, two and a half miles from Holmesville, eighteen from Marksville, and twelve from Cheneyville. It belonged to Joseph B. Roberts, his wife's uncle, and was leased by Epps. His principal business was raising cotton, and inasmuch as some may read this book who have never seen a cotton field, a description of the manner of its culture may not be out of place.

The ground is prepared by throwing up beds or ridges, with the plough— back-furrowing, it is called. Oxen and mules, the latter almost exclusively, are used in ploughing. The women as frequently as the men perform this labor, feeding, currying, and taking care of their teams, and in all respects doing the field and stable work, precisely as do the ploughboys of the North.

The beds, or ridges, are six feet wide, that is, from water furrow to water furrow. A plough drawn by one mule is then run along the top of the ridge or center of the bed, making the drill, into which a girl usually drops the seed, which she carries in a bag hung round her neck. Behind her comes a mule and harrow, covering up the seed, so that two mules, three slaves, a plough and harrow, are employed in planting a row of cotton. This is done in the months of March and April. Corn is planted in February. When there are no cold rains, the cotton usually makes its appearance in a week. In the course of eight or ten days afterwards the first hoeing is commenced. This is performed in part, also, by the aid of the plough and mule. The plough passes as near as possible to the cotton on both sides, throwing the furrow from it. Slaves follow with their hoes, cutting up the grass and cotton, leaving hills two feet and a half apart. This is called scraping cotton. In two weeks more commences the second hoeing. This time the furrow is thrown towards the cotton. Only one stalk, the largest, is now left standing in each hill. In another fortnight it is hoed the third time, throwing the furrow towards the cotton in the same manner as before, and killing all the grass between the rows. About the first of July, when it is a foot high or thereabouts, it is hoed the fourth and last time. Now the whole space between the rows is ploughed, leaving a deep water furrow in the center. During all these hoeings the overseer or driver follows the slaves on horseback with a whip, such as has been described. The fastest hoer takes the lead row. He is usually about a rod in advance of his companions. If one of them passes him, he is whipped. If one falls behind or is a moment idle, he is whipped. In fact, the lash is flying from morning until night, the whole day long. The hoeing season thus continues from April until July, a field having no sooner been finished once, than it is commenced again.

In the latter part of August begins the cotton picking season. At this time each slave is presented with a sack. A strap is fastened to it, which goes over the neck, holding the mouth of the sack breast high, while the bottom reaches nearly to the ground. Each one is also presented with a large basket that will hold about two barrels. This is to put the cotton in when the sack is filled. The baskets are carried to the field and placed at the beginning of the rows.

When a new hand, one unaccustomed to the business, is sent for the first time into the field, he is whipped up smartly, and made for that day to pick as fast as he can possibly. At night it is weighed, so that his capability in cotton picking is known. He must bring in the same weight each night following. If it falls short, it is considered evidence that he has been laggard, and a greater or less number of lashes is the penalty.

An ordinary day's work is two hundred pounds. A slave who is accustomed to picking, is punished, if he or she brings in a less quantity than that. There is a great difference among them as regards this kind of labor. Some of them seem to have a natural knack, or quickness, which enables them to pick with great celerity, and with both hands, while others, with whatever practice or industry, are utterly unable to come up to the ordinary standard. Such hands are taken from the cotton field and employed in other business. Patsey, of whom I shall have more to say, was known as the most remarkable cotton picker on Bayou Boeuf. She picked with both hands and with such surprising rapidity, that five hundred pounds a day was not unusual for her.

Each one is tasked, therefore, according to his picking abilities, none, however, to come short of two hundred weight. I, being unskillful always in that business, would have satisfied my master by bringing in the latter quantity, while on the other hand, Patsey would surely have been beaten if she failed to produce twice as much.

The cotton grows from five to seven feet high, each stalk having a great many branches, shooting out in all directions, and lapping each other above the water furrow.

There are few sights more pleasant to the eye, than a wide cotton field when it is in the bloom. It presents an appearance of purity, like an immaculate expanse of light, new-fallen snow.

Sometimes the slave picks down one side of a row, and back upon the other, but more usually, there is one on either side, gathering all that has blossomed, leaving the unopened boils for a succeeding picking. When the sack is filled, it is emptied into the basket and trodden down. It is necessary to be extremely careful the first time going through the field, in order not to break the branches off the stalks. The cotton will not bloom upon a broken branch. Epps never failed to inflict the severest chastisement on the unlucky servant who, either carelessly or unavoidably, was guilty in the least degree in this respect.

The hands are required to be in the cotton field as soon as it is light in the morning, and, with the exception of ten or fifteen minutes, which is given them at noon to swallow their allowance of cold bacon, they are not permitted to be a moment idle until it is too dark to see, and when the moon is full, they often times labor till the middle of the night. They do not dare to stop even at dinner time, nor return to the quarters, however late it be, until the order to halt is given by the driver.

The day's work over in the field, the baskets are "toted," or in other words, carried to the gin-house, where the cotton is weighed. No matter how fatigued and weary he may be—no matter how much he longs for sleep and rest—a slave never approaches the gin-house with his basket of cotton but with fear. If it falls short in weight—if he has not performed the full task appointed him, he knows that he must suffer. And if he has exceeded it by ten or twenty pounds, in all probability his master will measure the next day's task accordingly. So, whether he has too little or too much, his approach to the gin-house is always with fear and trembling. Most frequently they have too little, and therefore it is they are not anxious to leave the field. After weighing, follow the whippings; and then the baskets are carried to the cotton house, and their contents stored away like hay, all hands being sent in to tramp it down. If the cotton is not dry, instead of taking it to the gin-house at once, it is laid upon platforms, two feet high, and some three times as wide, covered with boards or plank, with narrow walks running between them.

This done, the labor of the day is not yet ended, by any means. Each one must then attend to his respective chores. One feeds the mules, another the swine—another cuts the wood, and so forth; besides, the packing is all done by candle light. Finally, at a late hour, they reach the quarters, sleepy and overcome with the long day's toil. Then a fire must be kindled in the cabin, the corn ground in the small hand-mill, and supper, and dinner for the next day in the field, prepared. All that is allowed them is corn and bacon, which is given out at the corn-crib and smoke-house every Sunday morning. Each one receives, as his weekly allowance, three and a half pounds of bacon, and corn enough to make a peck of meal. That is all—no tea, coffee, sugar, and with the exception of a very scanty sprinkling now and then, no salt. I can say, from a ten years' residence with Master Epps, that no slave of his is ever likely to suffer from the gout, superinduced by excessive high living. Master Epps' hogs were fed on *shelled* corn—it was thrown out to his "niggers" in the ear. The former, he thought, would fatten faster by shelling, and soaking it in the water—the latter, perhaps, if treated in the same manner, might grow too fat to labor. Master Epps was a shrewd calculator, and knew how to manage his own animals, drunk or sober.

The corn mill stands in the yard beneath a shelter. It is like a common coffee mill, the hopper holding about six quarts. There was one privilege which Master Epps granted freely to every slave he had. They might grind their corn nightly, in such small quantities as their daily wants required, or they might grind the whole week's allowance at one time, on Sundays, just as they preferred. A very generous man was Master Epps!

I kept my corn in a small wooden box, the meal in a gourd; and, by the way, the gourd is one of the most convenient and necessary utensils on a plantation. Besides supplying the place of all kinds of crockery in a slave cabin, it is used for carrying water to the fields. Another, also, contains the dinner. It dispenses with the necessity of pails, dippers, basins, and such tin and wooden superfluities altogether.

When the corn is ground, and fire is made, the bacon is taken down from the nail on which it hangs, a slice cut off and thrown upon the coals to broil. The majority of slaves have no knife, much less a fork. They cut their bacon with the axe at the woodpile. The corn meal is mixed with a little water, placed in the fire, and baked. When it is "done brown," the ashes are scraped off, and being placed upon a chip, which answers for a table, the tenant of the slave hut is ready to sit down upon the ground to supper. By this time it is usually midnight. The same fear of punishment with which they approach the gin-house, possesses them again on lying down to get a snatch of rest. It is the fear of oversleeping in the morning. Such an offence would certainly be attended with not less than twenty lashes. With a prayer that he may be on his feet and wide awake at the first sound of the horn, he sinks to his slumbers nightly.

The softest couches in the world are not to be found in the log mansion of the slave. The one whereon I reclined year after year, was a plank twelve inches wide and ten feet long. My pillow was a stick of wood. The bedding was a coarse blanket, and not a rag or shred beside. Moss might be used, were it not that it directly breeds a swarm of fleas.

The cabin is constructed of logs, without floor or window. The latter is altogether unnecessary, the crevices between the logs admitting sufficient light. In stormy weather the rain drives through them, rendering it comfortless and extremely disagreeable. The rude door hangs on great wooden hinges. In one end is constructed an awkward fire-place.

An hour before day light the horn is blown. Then the slaves arouse, prepare their breakfast, fill a gourd with water, in another deposit their dinner of cold bacon and corn cake, and hurry to the field again. It is an offence invariably followed by a flogging, to be found at the quarters after daybreak. Then the fears and labors of another day begin; and until its close there is no such thing as rest. He fears he will be caught lagging through the day; he fears to approach the gin-house with his basket-load of cotton at night; he fears, when he lies down, that he will oversleep himself in the morning. Such is a true, faithful, unexaggerated

picture and description of the slave's daily life, during the time of cotton-picking, on the shores of Bayou Boeuf.

In the month of January, generally, the fourth and last picking is completed. Then commences the harvesting of corn. This is considered a secondary
crop, and receives far less attention than the cotton. It is planted, as already mentioned, in February. Corn is grown in that region for the purpose of fattening
hogs and feeding slaves; very little, if any, being sent to market. It is the white
variety, the ear of great size, and the stalk growing to the height of eight, and often times ten feet. In August the leaves are stripped off, dried in the sun, bound
in small bundles, and stored away as provender for the mules and oxen. After
this the slaves go through the field, turning down the ear, for the purpose of keeping the rains from penetrating to the grain. It is left in this condition until after
cotton-picking is over, whether earlier or later. Then the ears are separated from
the stalks, and deposited in the corncrib with the husks on; otherwise, stripped
of the husks, the weevil would destroy it. The stalks are left standing in the field.

The Carolina, or sweet potato, is also grown in that region to some extent.
They are not fed, however, to hogs or cattle, and are considered but of small importance. They are preserved by placing them upon the surface of the ground,
with a slight covering of earth or cornstalks. There is not a cellar on Bayou Boeuf.
The ground is so low it would fill with water. Potatoes are worth from two to
three "bits," or shillings a barrel; corn, except when there is an unusual scarcity,
can be purchased at the same rate.

As soon as the cotton and corn crops are secured, the stalks are pulled up,
thrown into piles and burned. The ploughs are started at the same time, throwing up the beds again, preparatory to another planting. The soil, in the parishes
of Rapides and Avoyelles, and throughout the whole country, so far as my observation extended, is of exceeding richness and fertility. It is a kind of marl, of
a brown or reddish color. It does not require those invigorating composts necessary to more barren lands, and on the same field the same crop is grown for
many successive years.

Ploughing, planting, picking cotton, gathering the corn, and pulling and
burning stalks, occupies the whole of the four seasons of the year. Drawing and
cutting wood, pressing cotton, fattening and killing hogs, are but incidental labors.

In the month of September or October, the hogs are run out of the swamps
by dogs, and confined in pens. On a cold morning, generally about New Year's
day, they are slaughtered. Each carcass is cut into six parts, and piled one above
the other in salt, upon large tables in the smoke-house. In this condition it remains a fortnight, when it is hung up, and a fire built, and continued more than
half the time during the remainder of the year. This thorough smoking is necessary to prevent the bacon from becoming infested with worms. In so warm a climate it is difficult to preserve it, and very many times myself and my companions have received our weekly allowance of three pounds and a half, when it was
full of these disgusting vermin.

Although the swamps are overrun with cattle, they are never made the
source of profit, to any considerable extent. The planter cuts his mark upon the
ear, or brands his initials upon the side, and turns them into the swamps, to roam

unrestricted within their almost limitless confines. They are the Spanish breed, small and spike-horned. I have known of droves being taken from Bayou Boeuf, but it is of very rare occurrence. The value of the best cows is about five dollars each. Two quarts at one milking, would be considered an unusual large quantity. They furnish little tallow, and that of a soft, inferior quality. Notwithstanding the great number of cows that throng the swamps, the planters are indebted to the North for their cheese and butter, which is purchased in the New-Orleans market. Salted beef is not an article of food either in the great house, or in the cabin.

Master Epps was accustomed to attend shooting matches for the purpose of obtaining what fresh beef he required. These sports occurred weekly at the neighboring village of Holmesville. Fat beeves are driven thither and shot at, a stipulated price being demanded for the privilege. The lucky marksman divides the flesh among his fellows, and in this manner the attending planters are supplied.

The great number of tame and untamed cattle which swarm the woods and swamps of Bayou Boeuf, most probably suggested that appellation to the French, inasmuch as the term, translated, signifies the creek or river of the wild ox.

Garden products, such as cabbages, turnips and the like, are cultivated for the use of the master and his family. They have greens and vegetables at all times and seasons of the year. "The grass withereth and the flower fadeth"[24] before the desolating winds of autumn in the chill northern latitudes, but perpetual verdure overspreads the hot lowlands, and flowers bloom in the heart of winter, in the region of Bayou Boeuf.

There are no meadows appropriated to the cultivation of the grasses. The leaves of the corn supply a sufficiency of food for the laboring cattle, while the rest provide for themselves all the year in the evergrowing pasture.

There are many other peculiarities of climate, habit, custom, and of the manner of living and laboring at the South, but the foregoing, it is supposed, will give the reader an insight and general idea of life on a cotton plantation in Louisiana. The mode of cultivating cane, and the process of sugar manufacturing, will be mentioned in another place.

CHAPTER XIII.

THE CURIOUS AXE-HELVE—SYMPTOMS OF APPROACHING ILLNESS—CONTINUE TO DECLINE—THE WHIP INEFFECTUAL—CONFINED TO THE CABIN—VISIT BY DR. WINES—ART—PARTIAL RECOVERY—FAILURE AT COTTON PICKING—WHAT MAY BE HEARD ON EPPS' PLANTATION—LASHES GRADUATED—EPPS IN A WHIPPING MOOD—EPPS IN A DANCING MOOD—DESCRIPTION OF THE DANCE—LOSS OF REST NO EXCUSE—EPPS' CHARACTERISTICS—JIM BURNS—REMOVAL FROM HUFF POWER TO BAYOU BOEUF—DESCRIPTION OF UNCLE ABRAM; OF WILEY; OF AUNT PHEBE; OF BOB, HENRY, AND EDWARD; OF PATSEY; WITH A GENEALOGICAL ACCOUNT OF EACH—SOMETHING OF THEIR PAST HISTORY, AND PECULIAR CHARACTERISTICS—JEALOUSY AND LUST—PATSEY, THE VICTIM.

ON my arrival at Master Epps', in obedience to his order, the first business upon which I entered was the making of an axe-helve. The handles in use there are simply a round, straight stick. I made a crooked one, shaped like those to which I had been accustomed at the North. When finished, and presented to Epps, he looked at it with astonishment, unable to determine exactly what it was. He had never before seen such a handle, and when I explained its conveniences, he was forcibly struck with the novelty of the idea. He kept it in the house a long time, and when his friends called, was wont to exhibit it as a curiosity.

It was now the season of hoeing. I was first sent into the corn-field, and afterwards set to scraping cotton. In this employment I remained until hoeing time was nearly passed, when I began to experience the symptoms of approaching illness. I was attacked with chills, which were succeeded by a burning fever. I became weak and emaciated, and frequently so dizzy that it caused me to reel and stagger like a drunken man. Nevertheless, I was compelled to keep up my row. When in health I found little difficulty in keeping pace with my fellow-laborers, but now it seemed to be an utter impossibility. Often I fell behind, when the driver's lash was sure to greet my back, infusing into my sick and drooping body a little temporary energy. I continued to decline until at length the whip became entirely ineffectual. The sharpest sting of the rawhide could not arouse me. Finally, in September, when the busy season of cotton picking was at hand, I was unable to leave my cabin. Up to this time I had received no medicine, nor any attention from my master or mistress. The old cook visited me occasionally, preparing me corn-coffee, and sometimes boiling a bit of bacon, when I had grown too feeble to accomplish it myself.

When it was said that I would die, Master Epps, unwilling to bear the loss, which the death of an animal worth a thousand dollars would bring upon him, concluded to incur the expense of sending to Holmesville for Dr. Wines. He announced to Epps that it was the effect of the climate, and there was a probability of his losing me. He directed me to eat no meat, and to partake of no more food than was absolutely necessary to sustain life. Several weeks elapsed, during which time, under the scanty diet to which I was subjected, I had partially recovered. One morning, long before I was in a proper condition to labor, Epps appeared at the cabin door, and, presenting me a sack, ordered me to the cotton field. At this time I had had no experience whatever in cotton picking. It was an awkward business indeed. While others used both hands, snatching the cotton and depositing it in the mouth of the sack, with a precision and dexterity that was incomprehensible to me, I had to seize the boll with one hand, and deliberately draw out the white, gushing blossom with the other.

Depositing the cotton in the sack, moreover, was a difficulty that demanded the exercise of both hands and eyes. I was compelled to pick it from the ground where it would fall, nearly as often as from the stalk where it had grown. I made havoc also with the branches, loaded with the yet unbroken bolls, the long, cumbersome sack swinging from side to side in a manner not allowable in the cotton field. After a most laborious day I arrived at the gin-house with my load. When the scale determined its weight to be only ninety-five pounds, not half the quantity required of the poorest picker, Epps threatened the severest flogging, but in consideration of my being a "raw hand," concluded to pardon me on that occasion. The following day, and many days succeeding, I returned at night with no better success—I was evidently not designed for that kind of labor. I had not the gift—the dexterous fingers and quick motion of Patsey, who could fly along one side of a row of cotton, stripping it of its undefiled and fleecy whiteness miraculously fast. Practice and whipping were alike unavailing, and Epps, satisfied of it at last, swore I was a disgrace—that I was not fit to associate with a cotton-picking "nigger"—that I could not pick enough in a day to pay the trouble of weighing it, and that I should go into the cotton field no more. I was now employed in cutting and hauling wood, drawing cotton from the field to the gin-house, and performed whatever other service was required. Suffice to say, I was never permitted to be idle.

It was rarely that a day passed by without one or more whippings. This occurred at the time the cotton was weighed. The delinquent, whose weight had fallen short, was taken out, stripped, made to lie upon the ground, face downwards, when he received a punishment proportioned to his offence. It is the literal, unvarnished truth, that the crack of the lash, and the shrieking of the slaves, can be heard from dark till bed time, on Epps' plantation, any day almost during the entire period of the cotton-picking season.

The number of lashes is graduated according to the nature of the case. Twenty-five are deemed a mere brush, inflicted, for instance, when a dry leaf or piece of boll is found in the cotton, or when a branch is broken in the field; fifty is the ordinary penalty following all delinquencies of the next higher grade; one hundred is called severe: it is the punishment inflicted for the serious offence of standing idle in the field; from one hundred and fifty to two hundred is bestowed upon him who quarrels with his cabin-mates, and five hundred, well laid on, besides the mangling of the dogs, perhaps, is certain to consign the poor, unpitied runaway to weeks of pain and agony.

During the two years Epps remained on the plantation at Bayou Huff Power, he was in the habit, as often as once in a fortnight at least, of coming home intoxicated from Holmesville. The shooting-matches almost invariably concluded with a debauch. At such times he was boisterous and half-crazy. Often he would break the dishes, chairs, and whatever furniture he could lay his hands on. When satisfied with his amusement in the house, he would seize the whip and walk forth into the yard. Then it behooved the slaves to be watchful and exceeding wary. The first one who came within reach felt the smart of his lash. Sometimes for hours he would keep them running in all directions, dodging around the corners of the cabins. Occasionally he would come upon one unawares, and if he succeeded in inflicting a fair, round blow, it was a feat that much delighted him. The younger children, and the aged, who had become inactive, suffered then. In the midst of the confusion he would slily take his stand behind a cabin, waiting with raised whip, to dash it into the first black face that peeped cautiously around the corner.

At other times he would come home in a less brutal humor. Then there must be a merry-making. Then all must move to the measure of a tune. Then Master Epps must needs regale his melodious ears with the music of a fiddle.

Then did he become buoyant, elastic, gaily "tripping the light fantastic toe" around the piazza and all through the house.

Tibeats, at the time of my sale, had informed him I could play on the violin. He had received his information from Ford. Through the importunities of Mistress Epps, her husband had been induced to purchase me one during a visit to New-Orleans. Frequently I was called into the house to play before the family, mistress being passionately fond of music.

All of us would be assembled in the large room of the great house, whenever Epps came home in one of his dancing moods. No matter how worn out and tired we were, there must be a general dance. When properly stationed on the floor, I would strike up a tune.

"Dance, you d—d niggers, dance," Epps would shout.

Then there must be no halting or delay, no slow or languid movements; all must be brisk, and lively, and alert. "Up and down, heel and toe, and away we go," was the order of the hour. Epps' portly form mingled with those of his dusky slaves, moving rapidly through all the mazes of the dance.

Usually his whip was in his hand, ready to fall about the ears of the presumptuous thrall, who dared to rest a moment, or even stop to catch his breath. When he was himself exhausted, there would be a brief cessation, but it would be very brief. With a slash, and crack, and flourish of the whip, he would shout again, "Dance, niggers, dance," and away they would go once more, pell-mell, while I, spurred by an occasional sharp touch of the lash, sat in a corner, extracting from my violin a marvelous quick-stepping tune. The mistress often upbraided him, declaring she would return to her father's house at Cheneyville; nevertheless, there were times she could not restrain a burst of laughter, on witnessing his uproarious pranks. Frequently, we were thus detained until almost morning. Bent with excessive toil—actually suffering for a little refreshing rest, and feeling rather as if we could cast ourselves upon the earth and weep, many a night in the house of Edwin Epps have his unhappy slaves been made to dance and laugh.

Notwithstanding these deprivations in order to gratify the whim of an unreasonable master, we had to be in the field as soon as it was light, and during the day perform the ordinary and accustomed task. Such deprivations could not be urged at the scales in extenuation of any lack of weight, or in the cornfield for not hoeing with the usual rapidity. The whippings were just as severe as if we had gone forth in the morning, strengthened and invigorated by a night's repose. Indeed, after such frantic revels, he was always more sour and savage than before, punishing for slighter causes, and using the whip with increased and more vindictive energy.

Ten years I toiled for that man without reward. Ten years of my incessant labor has contributed to increase the bulk of his possessions. Ten years I was compelled to address him with down-cast eyes and uncovered head—in the attitude and language of a slave. I am indebted to him for nothing, save undeserved abuse and stripes.

Beyond the reach of his inhuman thong, and standing on the soil of the free State where I was born, thanks be to Heaven, I can raise my head once more among men. I can speak of the wrongs I have suffered, and of those who inflicted them, with upraised eyes. But I have no desire to speak of him or any other one otherwise than truthfully. Yet to speak truthfully of Edwin Epps would be to say—he is a man in whose heart the quality of kindness or of justice is not found. A rough, rude energy, united with an uncultivated mind and an avaricious spirit, are his prominent characteristics. He is known as a "nigger breaker," distinguished for his faculty of subduing the spirit of the slave, and priding himself upon his reputation in this respect, as a jockey boasts of his skill in managing a refractory horse. He looked upon a colored man, not as a human being, responsible to his Creator for the small talent entrusted to him, but as a "chattel personal," as mere live property, no better, except in value, than his mule or dog. When the evidence, clear and indisputable, was laid before him that I was a free man, and as much entitled to my liberty as he—when, on the day I left, he was informed that I had a wife and children, as dear to me as his own babes to him, he only raved and swore, denouncing the law that tore me from him, and declaring he would find out the man who had forwarded the letter that disclosed the place of my captivity, if there was any virtue or power in money, and would take his life. He thought of nothing but his loss, and cursed me for having been born free. He could have stood unmoved and seen the tongues of his poor slaves torn out by the roots—he could have seen them burned to ashes over a slow fire, or gnawed to death by dogs, if it only brought him profit. Such a hard, cruel, unjust man is Edwin Epps.

There was but one greater savage on Bayou Boeuf than he. Jim Burns' plantation was cultivated, as already mentioned, exclusively by women. That barbarian kept their backs so sore and raw, that they could not perform the customary labor demanded daily of the slave. He boasted of his cruelty, and through all the country round was accounted a more thorough-going, energetic man than even Epps. A brute himself, Jim Burns had not a particle of mercy for his subject brutes, and like a fool, whipped and scourged away the very strength upon which depended his amount of gain.

Epps remained on Huff Power two years, when, having accumulated a considerable sum of money, he expended it in the purchase of the plantation on the east bank of Bayou Boeuf, where he still continues to reside. He took possession of it in 1845, after the holidays were passed. He carried thither with him nine slaves, all of whom, except myself, and Susan, who has since died, remain there yet. He made no addition to this force, and for eight years the following were my companions in his quarters, viz: Abram, Wiley, Phebe, Bob, Henry, Edward, and Patsey. All these, except Edward, born since, were purchased out of a drove by Epps during the time he was overseer for Archy B. Williams, whose plantation is situated on the shore of Red River, not far from Alexandria.

Abram was tall, standing a full head above any common man. He is sixty years of age, and was born in Tennessee. Twenty years ago, he was purchased by a trader, carried into South Carolina, and sold to James Buford, of Williamsburgh county, in that State. In his youth he was renowned for his great strength, but age and unremitting toil have somewhat shattered his powerful frame and enfeebled his mental faculties.

Wiley is forty-eight. He was born on the estate of William Tassle, and for many years took charge of that gentleman's ferry over the Big Black River, in South Carolina.

Phebe was a slave of Buford, Tassle's neighbor, and having married Wiley, he bought the latter, at her instigation. Buford was a kind master, sheriff of the county, and in those days a man of wealth.

Bob and Henry are Phebe's children, by a former husband, their father having been abandoned to give place to Wiley. That seductive youth had insinuated himself into Phebe's affections, and therefore the faithless spouse had gently kicked her first husband out of her cabin door. Edward had been born to them on Bayou Huff Power.

Patsey is twenty-three—also from Buford's plantation. She is in no wise connected with the others, but glories in the fact that she is the offspring of a "Guinea nigger," brought over to Cuba in a slave ship, and in the course of trade transferred to Buford, who was her mother's owner.

This, as I learned from them, is a genealogical account of my master's shaves. For years they had been together. Often they recalled the memories of other days, and sighed to retrace their steps to the old home in Carolina. Troubles came upon their master Buford, which brought far greater troubles upon them. He became involved in debt, and unable to bear up against his failing fortunes, was compelled to sell these, and others of his slaves. In a chain gang they had been driven from beyond the Mississippi to the plantation of Archy B. Williams. Edwin Epps, who, for a long while had been his driver and overseer, was about establishing himself in business on his own account, at the time of their arrival, and accepted them in payment of his wages.

Old Abram was a kind-hearted being—a sort of patriarch among us, fond of entertaining his younger brethren with grave and serious discourse. He was deeply versed in such philosophy as is taught in the cabin of the slave; but the great absorbing hobby of Uncle Abram was General Jackson,[25] whom his young master in Tennessee had followed to the wars. He loved to wander back, in imagination, to the place where he was born, and to recount the scenes of his youth during those stirring times when the nation was in arms. He had been athletic, and more keen and powerful than the generality of his race, but now his eye had become dim, and his natural force abated. Very often, indeed, while discussing the best method of baking the hoe-cake, or expatiating at large upon the glory of Jackson, he would forget where he left his hat, or his hoe, or his basket; and then would the old man be laughed at, if Epps was absent, and whipped if he was present. So was he perplexed continually, and sighed to think that he was growing aged and going to decay. Philosophy and Jackson and forgetfulness had played the mischief with him, and it was evident that all of them combined were fast bringing down the gray hairs of Uncle Abram to the grave.

Aunt Phebe had been an excellent field hand, but latterly was put into the kitchen, where she remained, except occasionally, in a time of uncommon hurry. She was a sly old creature, and when not in the presence of her mistress or her master, was garrulous in the extreme.

Wiley, on the contrary, was silent. He performed his task without murmur or complaint, seldom indulging in the luxury of speech, except to utter a wish that he was away from Epps, and back once more in South Carolina.

Bob and Henry had reached the ages of twenty and twenty-three, and were distinguished for nothing extraordinary or unusual, while Edward, a lad of thirteen, not yet able to maintain his row in the corn or the cotton field, was kept in the great house, to wait on the little Eppses.

Patsey was slim and straight. She stood erect as the human form is capable of standing. There was an air of loftiness in her movement, that neither labor, nor weariness, nor punishment could destroy. Truly, Patsey was a splendid animal, and were it not that bondage had enshrouded her intellect in utter and everlasting darkness, would have been chief among ten thousand of her people. She could leap the highest fences, and a fleet hound it was indeed, that could outstrip her in a race. No horse could fling her from his back. She was a skillful teamster. She turned as true a furrow as the best, and at splitting rails there were none who could excel her. When the order to halt was heard at night, she would have her mules at the crib, unharnessed, fed and curried, before uncle Abram had found his hat. Not, however, for all or any of these, was she chiefly famous. Such lightning-like motion was in her fingers as no other fingers ever possessed, and therefore it was, that in cotton picking time, Patsey was queen of the field.

She had a genial and pleasant temper, and was faithful and obedient. Naturally, she was a joyous creature, a laughing, light-hearted girl, rejoicing in the mere sense of existence. Yet Patsey wept oftener, and suffered more, than any of her companions. She had been literally excoriated. Her back bore the scars of a thousand stripes; not because she was backward in her work, nor because she was of an unmindful and rebellious spirit, but because it had fallen to her lot to be the slave of a licentious master and a jealous mistress. She shrank before the lustful eye of the one, and was in danger even of her life at the hands of the other, and between the two, she was indeed accursed. In the great house, for days together, there were high and angry words, poutings and estrangement, whereof she was the innocent cause. Nothing delighted the mistress so much as to see her suffer, and more than once, when Epps had refused to sell her, has she tempted me with bribes to put her secretly to death, and bury her body in some lonely place in the margin of the swamp. Gladly would Patsey have appeased this unforgiving spirit, if it had been in her power, but not like Joseph, dared she escape from Master Epps, leaving her garment in his hand. Patsey walked under a cloud. If she uttered a word in opposition to her master's will, the lash was resorted to at once, to bring her to subjection; if she was not watchful when about her cabin, or when walking in the yard, a billet of wood, or a broken bottle perhaps, hurled from her mistress' hand, would smite her unexpectedly in the face. The enslaved victim of lust and hate, Patsey had no comfort of her life.

These were my companions and fellow-slaves, with whom I was accustomed to be driven to the field, and with whom it has been my lot to dwell for ten years in the log cabins of Edwin Epps. They, if living, are yet toiling on the banks of Bayou Boeuf, never destined to breathe, as I now do, the blessed air of liberty, nor to shake off the heavy shackles that enthrall them, until they shall lie down forever in the dust.

CHAPTER XIV.

DESTRUCTION OF THE COTTON CROP IN 1845—DEMAND FOR LABORERS IN ST. MARY'S
PARISH—SENT THITHER IN A DROVE—THE ORDER OF THE MARCH—THE GRAND
COTEAU—HIRED TO JUDGE TURNER ON BAYOU SALLE—APPOINTED DRIVER IN
HIS SUGAR HOUSE—SUNDAY SERVICES—SLAVE FURNITURE; HOW OBTAINED—
THE PARTY AT YARNEY'S, IN CENTREVILLE—GOOD FORTUNE—THE CAPTAIN OF
THE STEAMER—HIS REFUSAL TO SECRETE ME—RETURN TO BAYOU BOEUF—
SIGHT OF TIBEATS—PATSEY'S SORROWS—TUMULT AND CONTENTION—HUNT-
ING THE COON AND OPOSSUM—THE CUNNING OF THE LATTER—THE LEAN CON-
DITION OF THE SLAVE—DESCRIPTION OF THE FISH TRAP—THE MURDER OF THE
MAN FROM NATCHEZ—EPPS CHALLENGED BY MARSHALL—THE INFLUENCE OF
SLAVERY—THE LOVE OF FREEDOM.

THE first year of Epps' residence on the bayou, 1845, the caterpillars almost totally destroyed the cotton crop throughout that region. There was little to be
done, so that the slaves were necessarily idle half the time. However, there came
a rumor to Bayou Boeuf that wages were high, and laborers in great demand on
the sugar plantations in St. Mary's parish. This parish is situated on the coast of
the Gulf of Mexico, about one hundred and forty miles from Avoyelles. The Rio
Teche, a considerable stream, flows through St. Mary's to the gulf.

It was determined by the planters, on the receipt of this intelligence, to
make up a drove of slaves to be sent down to Tuckapaw in St. Mary's, for the
purpose of hiring them out in the cane fields. Accordingly, in the month of September, there were one hundred and forty-seven collected at Holmesville,
Abram, Bob and myself among the number. Of these about one-half were
women. Epps, Alonson Pierce, Henry Toler, and Addison Roberts, were the
white men, selected to accompany, and take charge of the drove. They had a two-
horse carriage and two saddle horses for their use. A large wagon, drawn by four
horses, and driven by John, a boy belonging to Mr. Roberts, carried the blankets
and provisions.

About 2 o'clock in the afternoon, having been fed, preparations were made
to depart. The duty assigned me was, to take charge of the blankets and provisions, and see that none were lost by the way. The carriage proceeded in advance,
the wagon following; behind this the slaves were arranged, while the two horsemen brought up the rear, and in this order the procession moved out of
Holmesville.

That night we reached a Mr. McCrow's plantation, a distance of ten or fifteen miles, when we were ordered to halt. Large fires were built, and each one
spreading his blanket on the ground, laid down upon it. The white men lodged
in the great house. An hour before day we were aroused by the drivers coming
among us, cracking their whips and ordering us to arise. Then the blankets were
rolled up, and being severally delivered to me and deposited in the wagon, the
procession set forth again.

The following night it rained violently. We were all drenched, our clothes saturated with mud and water. Reaching an open shed, formerly a gin-house, we found beneath it such shelter as it afforded. There was not room for all of us to lay down. There we remained, huddled together, through the night, continuing our march, as usual, in the morning. During the journey we were fed twice a day, boiling our bacon and baking our corn-cake at the fires in the same manner as in our huts. We passed through Lafayetteville, Mountsville, New-Town, to Centreville, where Bob and Uncle Abram were hired. Our number decreased as we advanced—nearly every sugar plantation requiring the services of one or more.

On our route we passed the Grand Coteau or prairie, a vast space of level, monotonous country, without a tree, except an occasional one which had been transplanted near some dilapidated dwelling. It was once thickly populated, and under cultivation, but for some cause had been abandoned. The business of the scattered inhabitants that now dwell upon it is principally raising cattle. Immense herds were feeding upon it as we passed. In the centre of the Grand Coteau one feels as if he were on the ocean, out of sight of land. As far as the eye can see, in all directions, it is but a ruined and deserted waste.

I was hired to Judge Turner, a distinguished man and extensive planter, whose large estate is situated on Bayou Salle, within a few miles of the gulf. Bayou Salle is a small stream flowing into the bay of Atchafalaya. For some days I was employed at Turner's in repairing his sugar house, when a cane knife was put into my hand, and with thirty or forty others, I was sent into the field. I found no such difficulty in learning the art of cutting cane that I had in picking cotton. It came to me naturally and intuitively, and in a short time I was able to keep up with the fastest knife. Before the cutting was over, however, Judge Tanner transferred me from the field to the sugar house, to act there in the capacity of driver. From the time of the commencement of sugar making to the close, the grinding and boiling does not cease day or night. The whip was given me with directions to use it upon any one who was caught standing idle. If I failed to obey them to the letter, there was another one for my own back. In addition to this my duty was to call on and off the different gangs at the proper time. I had no regular periods of rest, and could never snatch but a few moments of sleep at a time.

It is the custom in Louisiana, as I presume it is in other slave States, to allow the slave to retain whatever compensation he may obtain for services performed on Sundays. In this way, only, are they able to provide themselves with any luxury or convenience whatever. When a slave, purchased, or kidnapped in the North, is transported to a cabin on Bayou Boeuf he is furnished with neither knife, nor fork, nor dish, nor kettle, nor any other thing in the shape of crockery, or furniture of any nature or description. He is furnished with a blanket before he reaches there, and wrapping that around him, he can either stand up, or lie down upon the ground, or on a board, if his master has no use for it. He is at liberty to find a gourd in which to keep his meal, or he can eat his corn from the cob, just as he pleases. To ask the master for a knife, or skillet, or any small convenience of the kind, would be answered with a kick, or laughed at as a joke. Whatever necessary article of this nature is found in a cabin has been purchased with Sunday money. However injurious to the morals, it is certainly a blessing to the physical condition of the slave, to be permitted to break the Sabbath. Otherwise there would be no way to provide himself with any utensils, which seem to be indispensable to him who is compelled to be his own cook.

On cane plantations in sugar time, there is no distinction as to the days of the week. It is well understood that all hands must labor on the Sabbath, and it is equally well understood that those especially who are hired, as I was to Judge Turner, and others in succeeding years, shall receive remuneration for it. It is usual, also, in the most hurrying time of cotton-picking, to require the same extra service. From this source, slaves generally are afforded an opportunity of earning sufficient to purchase a knife, a kettle, tobacco and so forth. The females, discarding the latter luxury, are apt to expend their little revenue in the purchase of gaudy ribbons, wherewithal to deck their hair in the merry season of the holidays.

I remained in St. Mary's until the first of January, during which time my Sunday money amounted to ten dollars. I met with other good fortune, for which I was indebted to my violin, my constant companion, the source of profit, and soother of my sorrows during years of servitude. There was a grand party of whites assembled at Mr. Yarney's, in Centreville, a hamlet in the vicinity of Turner's plantation. I was employed to play for them, and so well pleased were the merry-makers with my performance, that a contribution was taken for my benefit, which amounted to seventeen dollars.

With this sum in possession, I was looked upon by my fellows as a millionaire. It afforded me great pleasure to look at it—to count it over and over again, day after day. Visions of cabin furniture, of water pails, of pocket knives, new shoes and coats and hats, floated through my fancy, and up through all rose the triumphant contemplation, that I was the wealthiest "nigger" on Bayou Boeuf.

Vessels run up the Rio Teche to Centreville. While there, I was bold enough one day to present myself before the captain of a steamer, and beg permission to hide myself among the freight. I was emboldened to risk the hazard of such a step, from overhearing a conversation, in the course of which I ascertained he was a native of the North. I did not relate to him the particulars of my history, but only expressed an ardent desire to escape from slavery to a free State. He pitied me, but said it would be impossible to avoid the vigilant custom house officers in New-Orleans, and that detection would subject him to punishment, and his vessel to confiscation. My earnest entreaties evidently excited his sympathies, and doubtless he would have yielded to them, could he have done so with any kind of safety. I was compelled to smother the sudden flame that lighted up my bosom with sweet hopes of liberation, and turn my steps once more towards the increasing darkness of despair.

Immediately after this event the drove assembled at Centreville, and several of the owners having arrived and collected the monies due for our services, we were driven back to Bayou Boeuf. It was on our return, while passing through a small village, that I caught sight of Tibeats, seated in the door of a dirty grocery, looking somewhat seedy and out of repair. Passion and poor whisky, I doubt not, have ere this laid him on the shelf.

During our absence, I learned from Aunt Phebe and Patsey, that the latter had been getting deeper and deeper into trouble. The poor girl was truly an object of pity. "Old Hogjaw," the name by which Epps was called, when the slaves were by themselves, had beaten her more severely and frequently than ever. As surely as he came from Holmesville, elated with liquor—and it was often in those days—he would whip her, merely to gratify the mistress; would punish her to an extent almost beyond endurance, for an offence of which he himself was the sole and irresistible cause. In his sober moments he could not always be prevailed upon to indulge his wife's insatiable thirst for vengeance.

To be rid of Patsey—to place her beyond sight or reach, by sale, or death, or in any other manner, of late years, seemed to be the ruling thought and passion of my mistress. Patsey had been a favorite when a child, even in the great house. She had been petted and admired for her uncommon sprightliness and pleasant disposition. She had been fed many a time, so Uncle Abram said, even on biscuit and milk, when the madam, in her younger days, was wont to call her to the piazza, and fondle her as she would a playful kitten. But a sad change had come over the spirit of the woman. Now, only black and angry fiends ministered in the temple of her heart, until she could look on Patsey but with concentrated venom.

Mistress Epps was not naturally such an evil woman, after all. She was possessed of the devil, jealousy, it is true, but aside from that, there was much in her character to admire. Her father, Mr. Roberts, resided in Cheneyville, an influential and honorable man, and as much respected throughout the parish as any other citizen. She had been well educated at some institution this side the Mississippi; was beautiful, accomplished, and usually good-humored. She was kind to all of us but Patsey—frequently, in the absence of her husband, sending out to us some little dainty from her own table. In other situations—in a different society from that which exists on the shores of Bayou Boeuf, she would have been pronounced an elegant and fascinating woman. An ill wind it was that blew her into the arms of Epps.

He respected and loved his wife as much as a coarse nature like his is capable of loving, but supreme selfishness always overmastered conjugal affection.

> "He loved as well as baser natures can,
> But a mean heart and soul were in that man."[26]

He was ready to gratify any whim—to grant any request she made, provided it did not cost too much. Patsey was equal to any two of his slaves in the cotton field. He could not replace her with the same money she would bring. The idea of disposing of her, therefore, could not be entertained. The mistress did not regard her at all in that light. The pride of the haughty woman was aroused; the blood of the fiery southern boiled at the sight of Patsey, and nothing less than trampling out the life of the helpless bondwoman would satisfy her.

Sometimes the current of her wrath turned upon him whom she had just cause to hate. But the storm of angry words would pass over at length, and there would be a season of calm again. At such times Patsey trembled with fear, and cried as if her heart would break, for she knew from painful experience, that if mistress should work herself to the red-hot pitch of rage, Epps would quiet her at last with a promise that Patsey should be flogged—a promise he was sure to keep. Thus did pride, and jealousy, and vengeance war with avarice and brute-passion in the mansion of my master, filling it with daily tumult and contention. Thus, upon the head of Patsey—the simpleminded slave, in whose heart God had implanted the seeds of virtue—the force of all these domestic tempests spent itself at last.

During the summer succeeding my return from St. Mary's parish, I conceived a plan of providing myself with food, which, though simple, succeeded beyond expectation. It has been followed by many others in my condition, up and down the bayou, and of such benefit has it become that I am almost persuaded to look upon myself as a benefactor. That summer the worms got into the bacon. Nothing but ravenous hunger could induce us to swallow it. The weekly allowance of meal scarcely sufficed to satisfy us. It was customary with us, as it is with all in that region, where the allowance is exhausted before Saturday night, or is in such a state as to render it nauseous and disgusting, to hunt in the swamps for coon and opossum. This, however, must be done at night, after the day's work is accomplished. There are planters whose slaves, for months at a time, have no other meat than such as is obtained in this manner. No objections are made to hunting, inasmuch as it dispenses with drafts upon the smoke-house, and because every marauding coon that is killed is so much saved from the standing corn. They are hunted with dogs and clubs, slaves not being allowed the use of fire-arms.

The flesh of the coon is palatable, but verily there is nothing in all butcherdom so delicious as a roasted 'possum. They are a round, rather long-bodied, little animal, of a whitish color, with nose like a pig, and caudal extremity like a rat. They burrow among the roots and in the hollows of the gum tree, and are clumsy and slow of motion. They are deceitful and cunning creatures. On receiving the slightest tap of a stick, they will roll over on the ground and feign death. If the hunter leaves him, in pursuit of another, without first taking particular pains to break his neck, the chances are, on his return, he is not to be found. The little animal has outwitted the enemy—has "played 'possum"—and is off. But after a long and hard day's work, the weary slave feels little like going to the swamp for his supper, and half the time prefers throwing himself on the cabin floor without it. It is for the interest of the master that the servant should not suffer in health from starvation, and it is also for his interest that he should not become gross from over-feeding. In the estimation of the owner, a slave is the most serviceable when in rather a lean and lank condition, such a condition as the race-horse is in, when fitted for the course, and in that condition they are generally to be found on the sugar and cotton plantations along Red River.

My cabin was within a few rods of the bayou bank, and necessity being indeed the mother of invention, I resolved upon a mode of obtaining the requisite amount of food, without the trouble of resorting nightly to the woods. This was to construct a fish trap. Having, in my mind, conceived the manner in which it could be done, the next Sunday I set about putting it into practical execution. It may be impossible for me to convey to the reader a full and correct idea of its construction, but the following will serve as a general description:

A frame between two and three feet square is made, and of a greater or less height, according to the depth of water. Boards or slats are nailed on three sides of this frame, not so closely, however, as to prevent the water circulating freely through it. A door is fitted into the fourth side, in such manner that it will slide easily up and down in the grooves cut in the two posts. A movable bottom is then so fitted that it can be raised to the top of the frame without difficulty. In the centre of the movable bottom an auger hole is bored, and into this one end of a handle or round stick is fastened on the under side so loosely that it will turn. The handle ascends from the centre of the movable bottom to the top of the frame, or as much higher as is desirable. Up and down this handle, in a great many places, are gimlet holes, through which small sticks are inserted, extending to opposite sides of the frame. So many of these small sticks are running out from the handle in all directions, that a fish of any considerable dimensions cannot pass through without hitting one of them. The frame is then placed in the water and made stationary.

The trap is "set" by sliding or drawing up the door, and kept in that position by another stick, one end of which rests in a notch on the inner side, the other end in a notch made in the handle, running up from the centre of the movable bottom. The trap is baited by rolling a handful of wet meal and cotton together until it becomes hard, and depositing it in the back part of the frame. A fish swimming through the upraised door towards the bait, necessarily strikes one of the small sticks turning the handle, which displacing the stick supporting the door, the latter falls, securing the fish within the frame. Taking hold of the top of the handle, the movable bottom is then drawn up to the surface of the water, and the fish taken out. There may have been other such traps in use before mine was constructed, but if there were I had never happened to see one. Bayou Boeuf abounds in fish of large size and excellent quality, and after this time I was very rarely in want of one for myself, or for my comrades. Thus a mine was opened—a new resource was developed, hitherto unthought of by the enslaved children of Africa, who toil and hunger along the shores of that sluggish, but prolific stream.

About the time of which I am now writing, an event occurred in our immediate neighborhood, which made a deep impression upon me, and which shows the state of society existing there, and the manner in which affronts are oftentimes avenged. Directly opposite our quarters, on the other side of the bayou, was situated the plantation of Mr. Marshall. He belonged to a family among the most wealthy and aristocratic in the country. A gentleman from the vicinity of Natchez had been negotiating with him for the purchase of the estate. One day a messenger came in great haste to our plantation, saying that a bloody and fearful battle was going on at Marshall's—that blood had been spilled—and unless the combatants were forthwith separated, the result would be disastrous.

On repairing to Marshall's house, a scene presented itself that beggars description. On the floor of one of the rooms lay the ghastly corpse of the man from Natchez, while Marshall, enraged and covered with wounds and blood, was stalking back and forth, "breathing out threatenings and slaughter." A difficulty had arisen in the course of their negotiation, high words ensued, when drawing their weapons, the deadly strife began that ended so unfortunately. Marshall was never placed in confinement. A sort of trial or investigation was had at Marksville, when he was acquitted, and returned to his plantation, rather more respected, as I thought, than ever, from the fact that the blood of a fellow being was on his soul.

Epps interested himself in his behalf, accompanying him to Marksville, and on all occasions loudly justifying him, but his services in this respect did not afterwards deter a kinsman of this same Marshall from seeking his life also. A brawl occurred between them over a gambling-table, which terminated in a deadly feud. Riding up on horseback in front of the house one day, armed with pistols and bowie knife, Marshall challenged him to come forth and make a final settlement of the quarrel, or he would brand him as a coward, and shoot him like a dog the first opportunity. Not through cowardice, nor from any conscientious scruples, in my opinion, but through the influence of his wife, he was restrained from accepting the challenge of his enemy. A reconciliation, however, was effected afterward, since which time they have been on terms of the closest intimacy.

Such occurrences, which would bring upon the parties concerned in them merited and condign punishment in the Northern States, are frequent on the bayou, and pass without notice, and almost without comment. Every man carries his bowie knife, and when two fall out, they set to work hacking and thrusting at each other, more like savages than civilized and enlightened beings.

The existence of Slavery in its most cruel form among them, has a tendency to brutalize the humane and finer feelings of their nature. Daily witnesses of human suffering—listening to the agonizing screeches of the slave—beholding him writhing beneath the merciless lash—bitten and torn by dogs—dying without attention, and buried without shroud or coffin—it cannot otherwise be expected, than that they should become brutified and reckless of human life. It is true there are many kind-hearted and good men in the parish of Avoyelles—such men as William Ford—who can look with pity upon the sufferings of a slave, just as there are, over all the world, sensitive and sympathetic spirits, who cannot look with indifference upon the sufferings of any creature which the Almighty has endowed with life. It is not the fault of the slaveholder that he is cruel, so much as it is the fault of the system under which he lives. He cannot withstand the influence of habit and associations that surround him. Taught from earliest childhood, by all that he sees and hears, that the rod is for the slave's back, he will not be apt to change his opinions in maturer years.

There may be humane masters, as there certainly are inhuman ones—there may be slaves well-clothed, well-fed, and happy, as there surely are those half-clad, half-starved and miserable; nevertheless, the institution that tolerates such wrong and inhumanity as I have witnessed, is a cruel, unjust, and barbarous one. Men may write fictions portraying lowly life as it is, or as it is not—may expatiate with owlish gravity upon the bliss of ignorance—discourse flippantly from arm chairs of the pleasures of slave life; but let them toil with him in the field—sleep with him in the cabin—feed with him on husks; let them behold him scourged, hunted, trampled on, and they will come back with another story in their mouths. Let them know the *heart* of the poor slave—learn his secret thoughts—thoughts he dare not utter in the hearing of the white man; let them sit by him in the silent watches of the night—converse with him in trustful confidence, of "life, liberty, and the pursuit of happiness," and they will find that ninety-nine out of every hundred are intelligent enough to understand their situation, and to cherish in their bosoms the love of freedom, as passionately as themselves.

CHAPTER XV.

LABORS ON SUGAR PLANTATIONS—THE MODE OF PLANTING CANE—OF HOEING CANE—CANE RICKS—CUTTING CANE—DESCRIPTION OF THE CANE KNIFE—WINROWING—PREPARING FOR SUCCEEDING CROPS—DESCRIPTION OF HAWKINS' SUGAR MILL ON BAYOU BOEUF—THE CHRISTMAS HOLIDAYS—THE CARNIVAL SEASON OF THE CHILDREN OF BONDAGE—THE CHRISTMAS SUPPER—RED, THE FAVORITE COLOR—THE VIOLIN, AND THE CONSOLATION IT AFFORDED—THE CHRISTMAS DANCE—LIVELY, THE COQUETTE—SAM ROBERTS, AND HIS RIVALS—SLAVE SONGS—SOUTHERN LIFE AS IT IS—THREE DAYS IN THE YEAR—THE SYSTEM OF MARRIAGE—UNCLE ABRAM'S CONTEMPT OF MATRIMONY.

IN consequence of my inability in cotton-picking, Epps was in the habit of hiring me out on sugar plantations during the season of cane-cutting and sugar-making. He received for my services a dollar a day, with the money supplying my place on his cotton plantation. Cutting cane was an employment that suited me, and for three successive years I held the lead row at Hawkins', leading a gang of from fifty to an hundred hands.

In a previous chapter the mode of cultivating cotton is described. This may be the proper place to speak of the manner of cultivating cane.

The ground is prepared in beds, the same as it is prepared for the reception of the cotton seed, except it is ploughed deeper. Drills are made in the same manner. Planting commences in January, and continues until April. It is necessary to plant a sugar field only once in three years. Three crops are taken before the seed or plant is exhausted.

Three gangs are employed in the operation. One draws the cane from the rick, or stack, cutting the top and flags from the stalk, leaving only that part which is sound and healthy. Each joint of the cane has an eye, like the eye of a potato, which sends forth a sprout when buried in the soil. Another gang lays the cane in the drill, placing two stalks side by side in such manner that joints will occur once in four or six inches. The third gang follows with hoes, drawing earth upon the stalks, and covering them to the depth of three inches.

In four weeks, at the farthest, the sprouts appear above the ground, and from this time forward grow with great rapidity. A sugar field is hoed three times, the same as cotton, save that a greater quantity of earth is drawn to the roots. By the first of August hoeing is usually over. About the middle of September, whatever is required for seed is cut and stacked in ricks, as they are termed. In October it is ready for the mill or sugar-house, and then the general cutting begins. The blade of a cane-knife is fifteen inches long, three inches wide in the middle, and tapering towards the point and handle. The blade is thin, and in order to be at all serviceable must be kept very sharp. Every third hand takes the lead of two others, one of whom is on each side of him. The lead hand, in the first place, with a blow of his knife shears the flags from the stalk. He next cuts off the top down as far as it is green. He must be careful to sever all the green from the ripe part, inasmuch as the juice of the former sours the molasses, and renders it unsalable. Then he severs the stalk at the root, and lays it directly behind him. His right and left hand companions lay their stalks, when cut in the same manner, upon his. To every three hands there is a cart, which follows, and the stalks are thrown into it by the younger slaves, when it is drawn to the sugar-house and ground.

If the planter apprehends a frost, the cane is winrowed. Winrowing is the cutting the stalks at an early period and throwing them lengthwise in the water furrow in such a manner that the tops will cover the butts of the stalks. They will remain in this condition three weeks or a month without souring, and secure from frost. When the proper time arrives, they are taken up, trimmed and carted to the sugarhouse.

In the month of January the slaves enter the field again to prepare for another crop. The ground is now strewn with the tops, and flags cut from the past year's cane. On a dry day fire is set to this combustible refuse, which sweeps over the field, leaving it bare and clean, and ready for the hoes. The earth is loosened about the roots of the old stubble, and in process of time another crop springs up from the last year's seed. It is the same the year following; but the third year the seed has exhausted its strength, and the field must be ploughed and planted again. The second year the cane is sweeter and yields more than the first, and the third year more than the second.

During the three seasons I labored on Hawkins' plantation, I was employed a considerable portion of the time in the sugar-house. He is celebrated as the producer of the finest variety of white sugar. The following is a general description of his sugar-house and the process of manufacture:

The mill is an immense brick building, standing on the shore of the bayou. Running out from the building is an open shed, at least an hundred feet in length and forty or fifty feet in width. The boiler in which the steam is generated is situated outside the main building; the machinery and engine rest on a brick pier, fifteen feet above the floor, within the body of the building. The machinery turns two great iron rollers, between two and three feet in diameter and six or eight feet in length. They are elevated above the brick pier, and roll in towards each other. An endless carrier, made of chain and wood, like leathern belts used in small mills, extends from the iron rollers out of the main building and through the entire length of the open shed. The carts in which the cane is brought from the field as fast as it is cut, are unloaded at the sides of the shed. All along the endless carrier are ranged slave children, whose business it is to place the cane upon it, when it is conveyed through the shed into the main building, where it falls between the rollers, is crushed, and drops upon another carrier that conveys it out of the main building in an opposite direction, depositing it in the top of a chimney upon a fire beneath, which consumes it. It is necessary to burn it in this manner, because otherwise it would soon fill the building, and more especially because it would soon sour and engender disease. The juice of the cane falls into a conductor underneath the iron rollers, and is carried into a reservoir. Pipes convey it from thence into five filterers, holding several hogsheads each. These filterers are filled with bone-black, a substance resembling pulverized charcoal. It is made of bones calcinated in close vessels, and is used for the purpose of decolorizing, by filtration, the cane juice before boiling. Through these five filterers it passes in succession, and then runs into a large reservoir underneath the ground floor, from whence it is carried up, by means of a steam pump, into a clarifier made of sheet iron, where it is heated by steam until it boils. From the first clarifier it is carried in pipes to a second and a third, and thence into close iron pans, through which tubes pass, filled with steam. While in a boiling state it flows through three pans in succession, and is then carried in other pipes down to the coolers on the ground floor. Coolers are wooden boxes with sieve bottoms made of the finest wire. As soon as the syrup passes into the coolers, and is met by the air, it grains, and the molasses at once escapes through the sieves into a cistern below. It is then white or loaf sugar of the finest kind—clear, clean, and as white as snow. When cool, it is taken out, packed in hogsheads, and is ready for market. The molasses is then carried from the cistern into the upper story again, and by another process converted into brown sugar.

There are larger mills, and those constructed differently from the one thus imperfectly described, but none, perhaps, more celebrated than this anywhere on Bayou Boeuf. Lambert, of New-Orleans, is a partner of Hawkins. He is a man of vast wealth, holding, as I have been told, an interest in over forty different sugar plantations in Louisiana.

———————

The only respite from constant labor the slave has through the whole year, is during the Christmas holidays. Epps allowed us three—others allow four, five and six days, according to the measure of their generosity. It is the only time to which they look forward with any interest or pleasure. They are glad when night comes, not only because it brings them a few hours repose, but because it brings them one day nearer Christmas. It is hailed with equal delight by the old and the young; even Uncle Abram ceases to glorify Andrew Jackson, and Patsey forgets her many sorrows, amid the general hilarity of the holidays. It is the time of feasting, and frolicking, and fiddling—the carnival season with the children of bondage. They are the only days when they are allowed a little restricted liberty, and heartily indeed do they enjoy it.

It is the custom for one planter to give a "Christmas supper," inviting the shaves from neighboring plantations to join his own on the occasion; for instance, one year it is given by Epps, the next by Marshall, the next by Hawkins, and so on. Usually from three to five hundred are assembled, coming together on foot, in carts, on horseback, on mules, riding double and triple, sometimes a boy and girl, at others a girl and two boys, and at others again a boy, a girl and an old woman. Uncle Abram astride a mule, with Aunt Phebe and Patsey behind him, trotting towards a Christmas supper, would be no uncommon sight on Bayou Boeuf.

Then, too, "of all days i' the year," they array themselves in their best attire. The cotton coat has been washed clean, the stump of a tallow candle has been applied to the shoes, and if so fortunate as to possess a rimless or a crownless hat, it is placed jauntily on the head. They are welcomed with equal cordiality, however, if they come bare-headed and bare-footed to the feast. As a general thing, the women wear handkerchiefs tied about their heads, but if chance has thrown in their way a fiery red ribbon, or a cast-off bonnet of their mistress' grandmother, it is sure to be worn on such occasions. Red—the deep blood red—is decidedly the favorite color among the enslaved damsels of my acquaintance. If a red ribbon does not encircle the neck, you will be certain to find all the hair of their woolly heads tied up with red strings of one sort or another.

The table is spread in the open air, and loaded with varieties of meat and piles of vegetables. Bacon and corn meal at such times are dispensed with. Sometimes the cooking is performed in the kitchen on the plantation, at others in the shade of wide branching trees. In the latter case, a ditch is dug in the ground, and wood laid in and burned until it is filled with glowing coals, over which chickens, ducks, turkeys, pigs, and not unfrequently the entire body of a wild ox, are roasted. They are furnished also with flour, of which biscuits are made, and often with peach and other preserves, with tarts, and every manner and description of pies, except the mince, that being an article of pastry as yet unknown among them. Only the slave who has lived all the years on his scanty allowance of meal and bacon, can appreciate such suppers. White people in great numbers assemble to witness the gastronomical enjoyments.

They seat themselves at the rustic table—the males on one side, the females on the other. The two between whom there may have been an exchange of tenderness, invariably manage to sit opposite; for the omnipresent Cupid disdains not to hurl his arrows into the simple hearts of slaves. Unalloyed and exulting happiness lights up the dark faces of them all. The ivory teeth, contrasting with their black complexions, exhibit two long, white streaks the whole extent of the table. All round the bountiful board a multitude of eyes roll in ecstacy. Giggling and laughter and the clattering of cutlery and crockery succeed. Cuffee's elbow hunches his neighbor's side, impelled by an involuntary impulse of delight; Nelly shakes her finger at Sambo and laughs, she knows not why, and so the fun and merriment flows on.[27]

When the viands have disappeared, and the hungry maws of the children of toil are satisfied, then, next in the order of amusement, is the Christmas dance. My business on these gala days always was to play on the violin. The African race is a music-loving one, proverbially; and many there were among my fellow-bondsmen whose organs of tune were strikingly developed, and who could thumb the banjo with dexterity; but at the expense of appearing egotistical, I must, nevertheless, declare, that I was considered the Ole Bull of Bayou Boeuf. My master often received letters, sometimes from a distance of ten miles, requesting him to send me to play at a ball or festival of the whites. He received his compensation, and usually I also returned with many picayunes[28] jingling in my pockets—the extra contributions of those to whose delight I had administered. In this manner I became more acquainted than I otherwise would, up and down the bayou. The young men and maidens of Holmesville always knew there was to be a jollification somewhere, whenever Platt Epps was seen passing through the town with his fiddle in his hand. "Where are you going now, Platt?" and "What is coming off tonight, Platt?" would be interrogatories issuing from every door and window, and many a time when there was no special hurry, yielding to pressing importunities, Platt would draw his bow, and sitting astride his mule, perhaps, discourse musically to a crowd of delighted children, gathered around him in the street.

Alas! had it not been for my beloved violin, I scarcely can conceive how I could have endured the long years of bondage. It introduced me to great houses—relieved me of many days' labor in the field—supplied me with conveniences for my cabin—with pipes and tobacco, and extra pairs of shoes, and oftentimes led me away from the presence of a hard master, to witness scenes of jollity and mirth. It was my companion—the friend of my bosom—triumphing loudly when I was joyful, and uttering its soft, melodious consolations when I was sad. Often, at midnight, when sleep had fled affrighted from the cabin, and my soul was disturbed and troubled with the contemplation of my fate, it would sing me a song of peace. On holy Sabbath days, when an hour or two of leisure was allowed, it would accompany me to some quiet place on the bayou bank, and, lifting up its voice, discourse kindly and pleasantly indeed. It heralded my name round the country—made me friends, who, otherwise would not have noticed me—gave me an honored seat at the yearly feasts, and secured the loudest and heartiest welcome of them all at the Christmas dance. The Christmas dance! Oh, ye pleasure-seeking sons and daughters of idleness, who move with measured step, listless and snail-like, through the slow-winding cotillon, if ye wish to look upon the celerity, if not the "poetry of motion"—upon genuine happiness, rampant and unrestrained—go down to Louisiana, and see the slaves dancing in the starlight of a Christmas night.

On that particular Christmas I have now in my mind, a description whereof will serve as a description of the day generally, Miss Lively and Mr. Sam, the first belonging to Stewart, the latter to Roberts, started the ball. It was well known that Sam cherished an ardent passion for Lively, as also did one of Marshall's and another of Carey's boys; for Lively was *lively* indeed, and a heart-breaking coquette withal. It was a victory for Sam Roberts, when, rising from the repast, she gave him her hand for the first "figure" in preference to either of his rivals. They were somewhat crest-fallen, and, shaking their heads angrily, rather intimated they would like to pitch into Mr. Sam and hurt him badly. But not an emotion of wrath ruffled the placid bosom of Samuel as his legs flew like drum-sticks down the outside and up the middle, by the side of his bewitching partner. The whole company cheered them vociferously, and, excited with the applause, they continued "tearing down" after all the others had become exhausted and halted a moment to recover breath. But Sam's superhuman exertions overcame him finally, leaving Lively alone, yet whirling like a top. Thereupon one of Sam's rivals, Pete Marshall, dashed in, and, with might and main, leaped and shuffled and threw himself into every conceivable shape, as if determined to show Miss Lively and all the world that Sam Roberts was of no account.

Pete's affection, however, was greater than his discretion. Such violent exercise took the breath out of him directly, and he dropped like an empty bag. Then was the time for Harry Carey to try his hand; but Lively also soon outwinded him, amidst hurrahs and shouts, fully sustaining her well-earned reputation of being the "fastest gal" on the bayou.

One "set" off, another takes its place, he or she remaining longest on the floor receiving the most uproarious commendation, and so the dancing continues until broad daylight. It does not cease with the sound of the fiddle, but in that case they set up a music peculiar to themselves. This is called "patting," accompanied with one of those unmeaning songs, composed rather for its adaptation to a certain tune or measure, than for the purpose of expressing any distinct idea. The patting is performed by striking the hands on the knees, then striking the hands together, then striking the right shoulder with one hand, the left with the other—all the while keeping time with the feet, and singing, perhaps, this song:

> "Harper's creek and roarin' ribber,
> Thar, my dear, we'll live forebber;
> Den we'll go to de Ingin nation,
> All I want in dis creation,
> Is pretty little wife and big plantation.
> *Chorus.* Up dat oak and down dat ribber,
>   Two overseers and one little nigger"

Or, if these words are not adapted to the tune called for, it may be that "Old Hog Eye" *is*—a rather solemn and startling specimen of versification, not, however, to be appreciated unless heard at the South. It runneth as follows:

> "Who's been here since I've been gone?
> Pretty little gal wid a josey[29] on.
>   Hog Eye!
>   Old Hog Eye,
>   And Hosey too!
>
> Never see de like since I was born,
> Here come a little gal wid a josey on.
>   Hog Eye!
>   Old Hog Eye!
>   And Hosey too!"

Or, may be the following, perhaps, equally nonsensical, but full of melody, nevertheless, as it flows from the negro's mouth:

> "Ebo Dick and Jurdan's Jo,
> Them two niggers stole my yo'.[30]

Chorus. Hop Jim along,
 Walk Jim along,
 Talk Jim along," &c.

Old black Dan, as black as tar,
He dam glad he was not dar.
 Hop Jim along," &c.

During the remaining holidays succeeding Christmas, they are provided with passes, and permitted to go where they please within a limited distance, or they may remain and labor on the plantation, in which case they are paid for it. It is very rarely, however, that the latter alternative is accepted. They may be seen at these times hurrying in all directions, as happy looking mortals as can be found on the face of the earth. They are different beings from what they are in the field; the temporary relaxation, the brief deliverance from fear, and from the lash, producing an entire metamorphosis in their appearance and demeanor. In visiting, riding, renewing old friendships, or, perchance, reviving some old attachment, or pursuing whatever pleasure may suggest itself; the time is occupied. Such is "southern life as it is," *three days in the year,* as I found it—the other three hundred and sixty-two being days of weariness, and fear, and suffering, and unremitting labor.

Marriage is frequently contracted during the holidays, if such an institution may be said to exist among them. The only ceremony required before entering into that "holy estate," is to obtain the consent of the respective owners. It is usually encouraged by the masters of female slaves. Either party can have as many husbands or wives as the owner will permit, and either is at liberty to discard the other at pleasure. The law in relation to divorce, or to bigamy, and so forth, is not applicable to property, of course. If the wife does not belong on the same plantation with the husband, the latter is permitted to visit her on Saturday nights, if the distance is not too far. Uncle Abram's wife lived seven miles from Epps', on Bayou Huff Power. He had permission to visit her once a fortnight, but he was growing old, as has been said, and truth to say, had latterly well nigh forgotten her. Uncle Abram had no time to spare from his meditations on General Jackson—connubial dalliance being well enough for the young and thoughtless, but unbecoming a grave and solemn philosopher like himself.

CHAPTER XVI.

OVERSEERS—HOW THEY ARE ARMED AND ACCOMPANIED—THE HOMICIDE—HIS EXECUTION AT MARKSVILLE—SLAVE DRIVERS—APPOINTED DRIVER ON REMOVING TO BAYOU BOEUF—PRACTICE MAKES PERFECT—EPPS'S ATTEMPT TO CUT PLATT'S THROAT—THE ESCAPE FROM HIM—PROTECTED BY THE MISTRESS—FORBIDS READING AND WRITING—OBTAIN A SHEET OF PAPER AFTER NINE YEARS' EFFORT—THE LETTER—ARMSBY, THE MEAN WHITE—PARTIALLY CONFIDE IN HIM—HIS TREACHERY—EPPS' SUSPICIONS—HOW THEY WERE QUIETED—BURNING THE LETTER—ARMSBY LEAVES THE BAYOU—DISAPPOINTMENT AND DESPAIR.

WITH the exception of my trip to St. Mary's parish, and my absence during the cane-cutting seasons, I was constantly employed on the plantation of Master Epps. He was considered but a small planter, not having a sufficient number of hands to require the services of an overseer, acting in the latter capacity himself. Not able to increase his force, it was his custom to hire during the hurry of cotton-picking.

On larger estates, employing fifty or a hundred, or perhaps two hundred hands, an overseer is deemed indispensable. These gentlemen ride into the field on horseback, without an exception, to my knowledge, armed with pistols, bowie knife, whip, and accompanied by several dogs. They follow, equipped in this fashion, in rear of the slaves, keeping a sharp lookout upon them all. The requisite qualifications in an overseer are utter heartlessness, brutality and cruelty. It is his business to produce large crops, and if that is accomplished, no matter what amount of suffering it may have cost. The presence of the dogs are necessary to overhaul a fugitive who may take to his heels, as is sometimes the case, when faint or sick, he is unable to maintain his row, and unable, also, to endure the whip. The pistols are reserved for any dangerous emergency, there having been instances when such weapons were necessary. Goaded into uncontrollable madness, even the slave will sometimes turn upon his oppressor. The gallows were standing at Marksville last January, upon which one was executed a year ago for killing his overseer. It occurred not many miles from Epps' plantation on Red River. The slave was given his task at splitting rails. In the course of the day the overseer sent him on an errand, which occupied so much time that it was not possible for him to perform the task. The next day he was called to an account, but the loss of time occasioned by the errand was no excuse, and he was ordered to kneel and bare his back for the reception of the lash. They were in the woods alone—beyond the reach of sight or hearing. The boy submitted until maddened at such injustice, and insane with pain, he sprang to his feet, and seizing an axe, literally chopped the overseer in pieces. He made no attempt whatever at concealment, but hastening to his master, related the whole affair, and declared himself ready to expiate the wrong by the sacrifice of his life. He was led to the scaffold, and while the rope was around his neck, maintained an undismayed and fearless bearing, and with his last words justified the act.

Besides the overseer, there are drivers under him, the number being in proportion to the number of hands in the field. The drivers are black, who, in addition to the performance of their equal share of work, are compelled to do the whipping of their several gangs. Whips hang around their necks, and if they fail to use them thoroughly, are whipped themselves. They have a few privileges, however; for example, in cane-cutting the hands are not allowed to sit down long enough to eat their dinners. Carts filled with corn cake, cooked at the kitchen, are driven into the field at noon. The cake is distributed by the drivers, and must be eaten with the least possible delay.

When the slave ceases to perspire, as he often does when taxed beyond his strength, he falls to the ground and becomes entirely helpless. It is then the duty of the driver to drag him into the shade of the standing cotton or cane, or of a neighboring tree, where he dashes buckets of water upon him, and uses other means of bringing out perspiration again, when he is ordered to his place, and compelled to continue his labor.

At Huff Power, when I first came to Epps', Tom, one of Roberts' negroes, was driver. He was a burly fellow, and severe in the extreme. After Epps' removal to Bayou Boeuf, that distinguished honor was conferred upon myself. Up to the time of my departure I had to wear a whip about my neck in the field. If Epps was present, I dared not show any lenity, not having the Christian fortitude of a certain well-known Uncle Tom sufficiently to brave his wrath, by refusing to perform the office. In that way, only, I escaped the immediate martyrdom he suffered, and, withal, saved my companions much suffering, as it proved in the end. Epps, I soon found, whether actually in the field or not, had his eyes pretty generally upon us. From the piazza, from behind some adjacent tree, or other concealed point of observation, he was perpetually on the watch. If one of us had been backward or idle through the day, we were apt to be told all about it on returning to the quarters, and as it was a matter of principle with him to reprove every offence of that kind that came within his knowledge, the offender not only was certain of receiving a castigation for his tardiness, but I likewise was punished for permitting it.

If, on the other hand, he had seen me use the lash freely, the man was satisfied. "Practice makes perfect," truly; and during my eight years' experience as a driver, I learned to handle the whip with marvelous dexterity and precision, throwing the lash within a hair's breadth of the back, the ear, the nose, without, however, touching either of them. If Epps was observed at a distance, or we had reason to apprehend he was as sneaking somewhere in the vicinity, I would commence plying the lash vigorously, when, according to arrangement, they would squirm and screech as if in agony, although not one of them had in fact been even grazed. Patsey would take occasion, if he made his appearance presently, to mumble in his hearing some complaints that Platt was lashing them the whole time, and Uncle Abram, with an appearance of honesty peculiar to himself, would declare roundly I had just whipped them worse than General Jackson whipped the enemy at New-Orleans. If Epps was not drunk, and in one of his beastly humors, this was, in general, satisfactory. If he was, some one or more of us must suffer, as a matter of course. Sometimes his violence assumed a dangerous form, placing the lives of his human stock in jeopardy. On one occasion the drunken madman thought to amuse himself by cutting my throat.

He had been absent at Holmesville, in attendance at a shooting-match, and none of us were aware of his return. While hoeing by the side of Patsey, she exclaimed in a low voice, suddenly, "Platt, d'ye see old Hog-Jaw beckoning me to come to him?"

Glancing sideways, I discovered him in the edge of the field, motioning and grimacing, as was his habit when half-intoxicated. Aware of his lewd intentions, Patsey began to cry. I whispered her not to look up, and to continue at her work, as if she had not observed him. Suspecting the truth of the matter, however, he soon staggered up to me in a great rage.

"What did you say to Pats?" he demanded, with an oath. I made him some evasive answer, which only had the effect of increasing his violence.

"How long have you owned this plantation, *say,* you d—d nigger?" he inquired, with a malicious sneer, at the same time taking hold of my shirt collar with one hand, and thrusting the other into his pocket. "Now I'll cut your black throat; that's what I'll do," drawing his knife from his pocket as he said it. But with one hand he was unable to open it, until finally seizing the blade in his teeth, I saw he was about to succeed, and felt the necessity of escaping from him, for in his present reckless state, it was evident he was not joking, by any means. My shirt was open in front, and as I turned round quickly and sprang from him, while he still retained his gripe, it was stripped entirely from my back. There was no difficulty now in eluding him. He would chase me until out of breath, then stop until it was recovered, swear, and renew the chase again. Now he would command me to come to him, now endeavor to coax me, but I was careful to keep at a respectful distance. In this manner we made the circuit of the field several times, he making desperate plunges, and I always dodging them, more amused than frightened, well knowing that when his sober senses returned, he would laugh at his own drunken folly. At length I observed the mistress standing by the yard fence, watching our half-serious, half-comical manœuvres. Shooting past him, I ran directly to her. Epps, on discovering her, did not follow. He remained about the field an hour or more, during which time I stood by the mistress, having related the particulars of what had taken place. Now, *she* was aroused again, denouncing her husband and Patsey about equally. Finally, Epps came towards the house, by this time nearly sober, walking demurely, with his hands behind his back, and attempting to look as innocent as a child.

As he approached, nevertheless, Mistress Epps began to berate him roundly, heaping upon him many rather disrespectful epithets, and demanding for what reason he had attempted to cut my throat. Epps made wondrous strange of it all, and to my surprise, swore by all the saints in the calendar he had not spoken to me that day.

"Platt, you lying nigger, *have* I?" was his brazen appeal to me.

It is not safe to contradict a master, even by the assertion of a truth. So I was silent, and when he entered the house I returned to the field, and the affair was never after alluded to.

Shortly after this time a circumstance occurred that came nigh divulging the secret of my real name and history, which I had so long and carefully concealed, and upon which I was convinced depended my final escape. Soon after he purchased me, Epps asked me if I could write and read, and on being informed that I had received some instruction in those branches of education, he assured me, with emphasis, if he ever caught me with a book, or with pen and ink, he would give me a hundred lashes. He said he wanted me to understand that he bought "niggers" to work and not to educate. He never inquired a word of my past life, or from whence I came. The mistress, however, cross-examined me frequently about Washington, which she supposed was my native city, and more than once remarked that I did not talk nor act like the other "niggers," and she was sure I had seen more of the world than I admitted.

My great object always was to invent means of getting a letter secretly into the post-office, directed to some of my friends or family at the North. The difficulty of such an achievement cannot be comprehended by one unacquainted with the severe restrictions imposed upon me. In the first place, I was deprived of pen, ink, and paper. In the second place, a slave cannot leave his plantation without a pass, nor will a post-master mail a letter for one without written instructions from his owner. I was in slavery nine years, and always watchful and on the alert, before I met with the good fortune of obtaining a sheet of paper. While Epps was in New-Orleans, one winter, disposing of his cotton, the mistress sent me to Holmesville, with an order for several articles, and among the rest a quantity of foolscap. I appropriated a sheet, concealing it in the cabin, under the board on which I slept.

After various experiments I succeeded in making ink, by boiling white maple bark, and with a feather plucked from the wing of a duck, manufactured a pen. When all were asleep in the cabin, by the light of the coals, lying upon my plank couch, I managed to complete a somewhat lengthy epistle. It was directed to an old acquaintance at Sandy Hill, stating my condition, and urging him to take measures to restore me to liberty. This letter I kept a long time, contriving measures by which it could be safely deposited in the post-office. At length, a low fellow, by the name of Armsby, hitherto a stranger, came into the neighborhood, seeking a situation as overseer. He applied to Epps, and was about the planta-tion for several days. He next went over to Shaw's, near by, and remained with him several weeks. Shaw was generally surrounded by such worthless characters, being himself noted as a gambler and unprincipled man. He had made a wife of his slave Charlotte, and a brood of young mulattoes were growing up in his house. Armsby became so much reduced at last, that he was compelled to labor with the slaves. A white man working in the field is a rare and unusual spectacle on Bayou Boeuf. I improved every opportunity of cultivating his acquaintance privately, desiring to obtain his confidence so far as to be willing to intrust the letter to his keeping. He visited Marksville repeatedly, he informed me, a town some twenty miles distant, and there, I proposed to myself, the letter should be mailed.

Carefully deliberating on the most proper manner of approaching him on the subject, I concluded finally to ask him simply if he would deposit a letter for me in the Marksville post-office the next time he visited that place, without dis-closing to him that the letter was written, or any of the particulars it contained; for I had fears that he might betray me, and knew that some inducement must be held out to him of a pecuniary nature, before it would be safe to confide in him. As late as one o'clock one night I stole noiselessly from my cabin, and, cross-ing the field to Shaw's, found him sleeping on the piazza. I had but a few picayunes—the proceeds of my fiddling performances, but all I had in the world I promised him if he would do me the favor required. I begged him not to expose me if he could not grant the request. He assured me, upon his honor, he would deposit it in the Marksville post-office, and that he would keep it an inviolable secret forever. Though the letter was in my pocket at the time, I dared not then deliver it to him, but stating I would have it written in a day or two, bade him good night, and returned to my cabin. It was impossible for me to expel the sus-picions I entertained, and all night I lay awake, revolving in my mind the safest course to pursue. I was willing to risk a great deal to accomplish my purpose, but should the letter by any means fall into the hands of Epps, it would be a death-blow to my aspirations. I was "perplexed in the extreme."

My suspicions were well-founded, as the sequel demonstrated. The next day but one, while scraping cotton in the field, Epps seated himself on the line fence between Shaw's plantation and his own, in such a position as to overlook the scene of our labors. Presently Armsby made his appearance, and, mounting the fence, took a seat beside him. They remained two or three hours, all of which time I was in an agony of apprehension.

That night, while broiling my bacon, Epps entered the cabin with his rawhide in his hand.

"Well, boy," said he, "I understand I've got a larned nigger, that writes letters, and tries to get white fellows to mail 'em. Wonder if you know who he is?"

My worst fears were realized, and although it may not be considered entirely creditable, even under the circumstances, yet a resort to duplicity and downright falsehood was the only refuge that presented itself.

"Don't know nothing about it, Master Epps," I answered him, assuming an air of ignorance and surprise; "Don't know nothing at all about it, sir."

"Wan't you over to Shaw's night before last?" he inquired.

"No, master," was the reply.

"Hav'nt you asked that fellow, Armsby, to mail a letter for you at Marksville?"

"Why, Lord, master, I never spoke three words to him in all my life. I don't know what you mean."

"Well," he continued, "Armsby told me to-day the devil was among my niggers; that I had one that needed close watching or he would run away; and when I axed him why, he said you come over to Shaw's, and waked him up in the night, and wanted him to carry a letter to Marksville. What have you got to say to that, ha?"

"All I've got to say, master," I replied, "is, there is no truth in it. How could I write a letter without any ink or paper? There is nobody I want to write to, 'cause I haint got no friends living as I know of. That Armsby is a lying, drunken fellow, they say, and nobody believes him anyway. You know I always tell the truth, and that I never go off the plantation without a pass. Now, master, I can see what that Armsby is after, plain enough. Didn't he want you to hire him for an overseer?"

"Yes, he wanted me to hire him," answered Epps.

"That's it," said I, "he wants to make you believe we're all going to run away, and then he thinks you'll hire an overseer to watch us. He just made that story out of whole cloth, 'cause he wants to get a situation. It's all a lie, master, you may depend on't."

Epps mused awhile, evidently impressed with the plausibility of my theory, and exclaimed,

"I'm d—d, Platt, if I don't believe you tell the truth. He must take me for a soft, to think he can come it over me with them kind of yarns, mustn't he? Maybe he thinks he can fool me; maybe he thinks I don't know nothing—can't take care of my own niggers, eh! Soft soap old Epps, eh! Ha, ha, ha! D—n Armsby! Set the dogs on him, Platt," and with many other comments descriptive of Armsby's general character, and his capability of taking care of his own business, and attending to his own "niggers," Master Epps left the cabin. As soon as he was gone I threw the letter in the fire, and, with a desponding and despairing heart, beheld the epistle which had cost me so much anxiety and thought, and which I fondly hoped would have been my forerunner to the land of freedom, writhe and shrivel on its bed of coals, and dissolve into smoke and ashes. Armsby, the treacherous wretch, was driven from Shaw's plantation not long subsequently, much to my relief, for I feared he might renew his conversation, and perhaps induce Epps to credit him.

I knew not now whither to look for deliverance. Hopes sprang up in my heart only to be crushed and blighted. The summer of my life was passing away; I felt I was growing prematurely old; that a few years more, and toil, and grief, and the poisonous miasma of the swamps would accomplish their work on me—would consign me to the grave's embrace, to moulder and be forgotten. Repelled, betrayed, cut off from the hope of succor, I could only prostrate myself upon the earth and groan in unutterable anguish. The hope of rescue was the only light that cast a ray of comfort on my heart. That was now flickering, faint and low; another breath of disappointment would extinguish it altogether, leaving me to grope in midnight darkness to the end of life.

CHAPTER XVII.

WILEY DISREGARDS THE COUNSELS OF AUNT PHEBE AND UNCLE ABRAM, AND IS CAUGHT BY THE PATROLLERS—THE ORGANIZATION AND DUTIES OF THE LATTER—WILEY RUNS AWAY—SPECULATIONS IN REGARD TO HIM—HIS UNEXPECTED RETURN—HIS CAPTURE ON THE RED RIVER, AND CONFINEMENT IN ALEXANDRIA JAIL—DISCOVERED BY JOSEPH B. ROBERTS—SUBDUING DOGS IN ANTICIPATION OF ESCAPE—THE FUGITIVES IN THE GREAT PINE WOODS—CAPTURED BY ADAM TAYDEM AND THE INDIANS—AUGUSTUS KILLED BY DOGS—NELLY, ELDRET'S SLAVE WOMAN—THE STORY OF CELESTE—THE CONCERTED MOVEMENT—LEW CHENEY, THE TRAITOR—THE IDEA OF INSURRECTION.

THE year 1850, down to which time I have now arrived, omitting many occurrences uninteresting to the reader, was an unlucky year for my companion Wiley, the husband of Phebe, whose taciturn and retiring nature has thus far kept him in the background. Notwithstanding Wiley seldom opened his mouth, and revolved in his obscure and unpretending orbit without a grumble, nevertheless the warm elements of sociality were strong in the bosom of that silent "nigger." In the exuberance of his self-reliance, disregarding the philosophy of Uncle Abram, and setting the counsels of Aunt Phebe utterly at naught, he had the foolhardiness to essay a nocturnal visit to a neighboring cabin without a pass.

So attractive was the society in which he found himself, that Wiley took lit-

tle note of the passing hours, and the light began to break in the east before he
was aware. Speeding homeward as fast as he could run, he hoped to reach the
quarters before the horn would sound; but, unhappily, he was spied on the way
by a company of patrollers.

How it is in other dark places of slavery, I do not know, but on Bayou
Boeuf there is an organization of patrollers, as they are styled, whose business it
is to seize and whip any slave they may find wandering from the plantation. They
ride on horseback, headed by a captain, armed, and accompanied by dogs. They
have the right, either by law, or by general consent, to inflict discretionary chastisement upon a black man caught beyond the boundaries of his master's estate
without a pass, and even to shoot him, if he attempts to escape. Each company
has a certain distance to ride up and down the bayou. They are compensated by
the planters, who contribute in proportion to the number of slaves they own. The
clatter of their horses' hoofs dashing by can be heard at all hours of the light, and
frequently they may be seen driving a slave before them, or leading him by a rope
fastened around his neck, to his owner's plantation.

Wiley fled before one of these companies, thinking he could reach his cabin
before they could overtake him; but one of their dogs, a great ravenous hound,
gripped him by the leg, and held him fast. The patrollers whipped him severely,
and brought him, a prisoner, to Epps. From him he received another flagellation
still more severe, so that the cuts of the lash and the bites of the dog rendered
him sore, stiff, and miserable, insomuch he was scarcely able to move. It was impossible in such a state to keep up his row, and consequently there was not an
hour in the day but Wiley felt the sting of his master's rawhide on his raw and
bleeding back. His sufferings became intolerable, and finally he resolved to run
away. Without disclosing his intentions to run away even to his wife Phebe, he
proceeded to make arrangements for carrying his plan into execution. Having
cooked his whole week's allowance, he cautiously left the cabin on a Sunday
night, after the inmates of the quarters were asleep. When the horn sounded in
the morning, Wiley did not make his appearance. Search was made for him in
the cabins, in the corn-crib, in the cotton-house, and in every nook and corner
of the premises. Each of us was examined, touching any knowledge we might
have that could throw light upon his sudden disappearance or present whereabouts. Epps raved and stormed, and mounting his horse, galloped to neighboring plantations, making inquiries in all directions. The search was fruitless.
Nothing whatever was elicited, going to show what had become of the missing
man. The dogs were led to the swamp, but were unable to strike his trail. They
would circle away through the forest, their noses to the ground, but invariably
returned in a short time to the spot from whence they started.

Wiley had escaped, and so secretly and cautiously as to elude and baffle all
pursuit. Days and even weeks passed away, and nothing could be heard of him.
Epps did nothing but curse and swear. It was the only topic of conversation
among us when alone. We indulged in a great deal of speculation in regard to
him, one suggesting he might have been drowned in some bayou, inasmuch as
he was a poor swimmer; another, that perhaps he might have been devoured by
alligators, or stung by the venomous moccasin, whose bite is certain and sudden

death. The warm and hearty sympathies of us all, however, were with poor Wiley, wherever he might be. Many an earnest prayer ascended from the lips of Uncle Abram, beseeching safety for the wanderer.

In about three weeks, when all hope of ever seeing him again was dismissed, to our surprise, he one day appeared among us. On leaving the plantation, he informed us, it was his intention to make his way back to South Carolina—to the old quarters of Master Buford. During the day he remained secreted, sometimes in the branches of a tree, and at night pressed forward through the swamps. Finally, one morning, just at dawn, he reached the shore of Red River. While standing on the bank, considering how he could cross it, a white man accosted him, and demanded a pass. Without one, and evidently a runaway, he was taken to Alexandria, the shire town of the parish of Rapides, and confined in prison. It happened several days after that Joseph B. Roberts, uncle of Mistress Epps, was in Alexandria, and going into the jail, recognized him. Wiley had worked on his plantation, when Epps resided at Huff Power. Paying the jail fee, and writing him a pass, underneath which was a note to Epps, requesting him not to whip him on his return, Wiley was sent back to Bayou Boeuf. It was the hope that hung upon this request, and which Roberts assured him would be respected by his master, that sustained him as he approached the house. The request, however, as may be readily supposed, was entirely disregarded. After being kept in suspense three days, Wiley was stripped, and compelled to endure one of those inhuman floggings to which the poor slave is so often subjected. It was the first and last attempt of Wiley to run away. The long scars upon his back, which he will carry with him to the grave, perpetually remind him of the dangers of such a step.

There was not a day throughout the ten years I belonged to Epps that I did not consult with myself upon the prospect of escape. I laid many plans, which at the time I considered excellent ones, but one after the other they were all abandoned. No man who has never been placed in such a situation, can comprehend the thousand obstacles thrown in the way of the flying slave. Every white man's hand is raised against him—the patrollers are watching for him—the hounds are ready to follow on his track, and the nature of the country is such as renders it impossible to pass through it with any safety. I thought, however, that the time might come, perhaps, when I should be running through the swamps again. I concluded, in that case, to be prepared for Epps' dogs, should they pursue me. He possessed several, one of which was a notorious slave-hunter, and the most fierce and savage of his breed. While out hunting the coon or the opossum, I never allowed an opportunity to escape, when alone, of whipping them severely. In this manner I succeeded at length in subduing them completely. They feared me, obeying my voice at once when others had no control over them whatever. Had they followed and overtaken me, I doubt not they would have shrank from attacking me.

Notwithstanding the certainty of being captured, the woods and swamps are, nevertheless, continually filled with runaways. Many of them, when sick, or so worn out as to be unable to perform their tasks, escape into the swamps, willing to suffer the punishment inflicted for such offences, in order to obtain a day or two of rest.

While I belonged to Ford, I was unwittingly the means of disclosing the hiding-place of six or eight, who had taken up their residence in the "Great Pine Woods." Adam Taydem frequently sent me from the mills over to the opening after provisions. The whole distance was then a thick pine forest. About ten o'clock of a beautiful moonlight night, while walking along the Texas road, returning to the mills, carrying a dressed pig in a bag swung over my shoulder, I heard footsteps behind me, and turning round, beheld two black men in the dress of slaves approaching at a rapid pace. When within a short distance, one of them raised a club, as if intending to strike me; the other snatched at the bag. I managed to dodge them both, and seizing a pine knot, hurled it with such force against the head of one of them that he was prostrated apparently senseless to the ground. Just then two more made their appearance from one side of the road. Before they could grapple me, however, I succeeded in passing them, and taking to my heels, fled, much affrighted, towards the mills. When Adam was informed of the adventure, he hastened straightway to the Indian village, and arousing Cascalla and several of his tribe, started in pursuit of the highwaymen. I accompanied them to the scene of attack, when we discovered a puddle of blood in the road, where the man whom I had smitten with the pine knot had fallen. After searching carefully through the woods a long time, one of Cascalla's men discovered a smoke curling up through the branches of several prostrate pines, whose tops had fallen together. The rendezvous was cautiously surrounded, and all of them taken prisoners. They had escaped from a plantation in the vicinity of Lamourie, and had been secreted there three weeks. They had no evil design upon me, except to frighten me out of my pig. Having observed me passing towards Ford's just at night-fall, and suspecting the nature of my errand, they had followed me, seen me butcher and dress the porker, and start on my return. They had been pinched for food, and were driven to this extremity by necessity. Adam conveyed them to the parish jail, and was liberally rewarded.

Not unfrequently the runaway loses his life in the attempt to escape. Epps' premises were bounded on one side by Carey's, a very extensive sugar plantation. He cultivates annually at least fifteen hundred acres of cane, manufacturing twenty-two or twenty-three hundred hogsheads of sugar; an hogshead and a half being the usual yield of an acre. Besides this he also cultivates five or six hundred acres of corn and cotton. He owned last year one hundred and fifty three field hands, besides nearly as many children, and yearly hires a drove during the busy season from this side the Mississippi.

One of his negro drivers, a pleasant, intelligent boy, was named Augustus. During the holidays, and occasionally while at work in adjoining fields, I had an opportunity of making his acquaintance, which eventually ripened into a warm and mutual attachment. Summer before last he was so unfortunate as to incur the displeasure of the overseer, a coarse, heartless brute, who whipped him most cruelly. Augustus ran away. Reaching a cane rick on Hawkins' plantation, he secreted himself in the top of it. All Carey's dogs were put upon his track—some fifteen of them—and soon scented his footsteps to the hiding place. They surrounded the rick, baying and scratching, but could not reach him. Presently, guided by the clamor of the hounds, the pursuers rode up, when the overseer, mounting on to the rick, drew him forth. As he rolled down to the ground the whole pack plunged upon him, and before they could be beaten off, had gnawed and mutilated his body in the most shocking manner, their teeth having penetrated to the bone in an hundred places. He was taken up, tied upon a mule, and carried home. But this was Augustus' last trouble. He lingered until the next day, when death sought the unhappy boy, and kindly relieved him from his agony.

It was not unusual for slave women as well as slave men to endeavor to escape. Nelly, Eldret's girl, with whom I lumbered for a time in the "Big Cane Brake," lay concealed in Epps' corn crib three days. At night, when his family were asleep, she would steal into the quarters for food, and return to the crib again. We concluded it would no longer be safe for us to allow her to remain, and accordingly she retraced her steps to her own cabin.

But the most remarkable instance of a successful evasion of dogs and hunters was the following: Among Carey's girls was one by the name of Celeste. She was nineteen or twenty, and far whiter than her owner, or any of his offspring. It required a close inspection to distinguish in her features the slightest trace of African blood. A stranger would never have dreamed that she was the descendant of slaves. I was sitting in my cabin late at night, playing a low air on my violin, when the door opened carefully, and Celeste stood before me. She was pale and haggard. Had an apparition arisen from the earth, I could not have been more startled.

"Who are you?" I demanded, after gazing at her a moment.

"I'm hungry; give me some bacon," was her reply.

My first impression was that she was some deranged young mistress, who, escaping from home, was wandering, she knew not whither, and had been attracted to my cabin by the sound of the violin. The coarse cotton slave dress she wore, however, soon dispelled such a supposition.

"What is your name?" I again interrogated.

"My name is Celeste," she answered. "I belong to Carey, and have been two days among the palmettoes. I am sick and can't work, and would rather die in the swamp than be whipped to death by the overseer. Carey's dogs won't follow me. They have tried to set them on. There's a secret between them and Celeste, and they wont mind the devilish orders of the overseer. Give me some meat—I'm starving."

I divided my scanty allowance with her, and while partaking of it, she related how she had managed to escape, and described the place of her concealment. In the edge of the swamp, not half a mile from Epps' house, was as a large space, thousands of acres in extent, thickly covered with palmetto. Tall trees, whose long arms interlocked each other, formed a canopy above them, so dense as to exclude the beams of the sun. It was like twilight always, even in the middle of the brightest day. In the centre of this great space, which nothing but serpents very often explore—a sombre and solitary spot—Celeste had erected a rude hut of dead branches that had fallen to the ground, and covered it with the leaves of the palmetto. This was the abode she had selected. She had no fear of Carey's dogs, any more than I had of Epps'. It is a fact, which I have never been able to explain, that there are those whose tracks the hounds will absolutely refuse to follow. Celeste was one of them.

For several nights she came to my cabin for food. On one occasion our dogs barked as she approached, which aroused Epps, and induced him to reconnoitre the premises. He did not discover her, but after that it was not deemed prudent for her to come to the yard. When all was silent I carried provisions to a certain spot agreed upon, where she would find them.

In this manner Celeste passed the greater part of the summer. She regained her health, and became strong and hearty. At all seasons of the year the howlings of wild animals can be heard at night along the borders of the swamps. Several times they had made her a midnight call, awakening her from slumbers with a growl. Terrified by such unpleasant salutations, she finally concluded to abandon her lonely dwelling; and, accordingly, returning to her master, was scourged, her neck meanwhile being fastened in the stocks, and sent into the field again.

The year before my arrival in the country there was a concerted movement among a number of slaves on Bayou Boeuf, that terminated tragically indeed. It was, I presume, a matter of newspaper notoriety at the time, but all the knowledge I have of it, has been derived from the relation of those living at that period in the immediate vicinity of the excitement. It has become a subject of general and unfailing interest in every slave-hut on the bayou, and will doubtless go down to succeeding generations as their chief tradition. Lew Cheney, with whom I became acquainted—a shrewd, cunning negro, more intelligent than the generality of his race, but unscrupulous and full of treachery—conceived the project of organizing a company sufficiently strong to fight their way against all opposition, to the neighboring territory of Mexico.

A remote spot, far within the depths of the swamp back of Hawkins' plantation, was selected as the rallying point. Lew flitted from one plantation to another, in the dead of night, preaching a crusade to Mexico, and, like Peter the Hermit, creating a furor of excitement wherever he appeared. At length a large number of runaways were assembled; stolen mules, and corn gathered from the fields, and bacon filched from smoke-houses, had been conveyed into the woods. The expedition was about ready to proceed when their hiding place was discovered. Lew Cheney, becoming convinced of the ultimate failure of his project, in order to curry favor with his master, and avoid the consequences which he foresaw would follow, deliberately determined to sacrifice all his companions. Departing secretly from the encampment, he proclaimed among the planters the number collected in the swamp, and, instead of stating truly the object they had in view, asserted their intention was to emerge from their seclusion the first favorable opportunity, and murder every white person along the bayou.

Such an announcement, exaggerated as it passed from mouth to mouth, filled the whole country with terror. The fugitives were surrounded and taken prisoners, carried in chains to Alexandria, and hung by the populace. Not only those, but many who were suspected, though entirely innocent, were taken from the field and from the cabin, and without the shadow of process or form of trial, hurried to the scaffold. The planters on Bayou Boeuf finally rebelled against such reckless destruction of property, but it was not until a regiment of soldiers had arrived from some fort on the Texan frontier, demolished the gallows, and opened the doors of the Alexandria prison, that the indiscriminate slaughter was stayed. Lew Cheney escaped, and was even rewarded for his treachery. He is still living, but his name is despised and execrated by all his race throughout the parishes of Rapides and Avoyelles.

Such an idea as insurrection, however, is not new among the enslaved population of Bayou Boeuf. More than once I have joined in serious consultation, when the subject has been discussed, and there have been times when a word from me would have placed hundreds of my fellow-bondsmen in an attitude of defiance Without arms or ammunition, or even with them, I saw such a step would result in certain defeat, disaster and death, and always raised my voice against it.

During the Mexican war I well remember the extravagant hopes that were excited. The news of victory filled the great house with rejoicing, but produced only sorrow and disappointment in the cabin. In my opinion—and I have had opportunity to know something of the feeling of which I speak—there are not fifty slaves on the shores of Bayou Boeuf, but would hail with unmeasured delight the approach of an invading army.

They are deceived who flatter themselves that the ignorant and debased slave has no conception of the magnitude of his wrongs. They are deceived who imagine that he arises from his knees, with back lacerated and bleeding, cherishing only a spirit of meekness and forgiveness. A day may come—it *will* come, if his prayer is heard—a terrible day of vengeance when the master in his turn will cry in vain for mercy.

CHAPTER XVIII.

O'NIEL, THE TANNER—CONVERSATION WITH AUNT PHEBE OVERHEARD—EPPS IN THE TANNING BUSINESS—STABBING OF UNCLE ABRAM—THE UGLY WOUND—EPPS IS JEALOUS—PATSEY IS MISSING—HER RETURN FROM SHAW'S—HARRIET, SHAW'S BLACK WIFE—EPPS ENRAGED—PATSEY DENIES HIS CHARGES—SHE IS TIED DOWN NAKED TO FOUR STAKES—THE INHUMAN FLOGGING—FLAYING OF PATSEY—THE BEAUTY OF THE DAY—THE BUCKET OF SALT WATER—THE DRESS STIFF WITH BLOOD—PATSEY GROWS MELANCHOLY—HER IDEA OF GOD AND ETERNITY—OF HEAVEN AND FREEDOM—THE EFFECT OF SLAVE-WHIPPING—EPPS' OLDEST SON—"THE CHILD IS FATHER TO THE MAN."

WILEY suffered severely at the hands of Master Epps, as has been related in the preceding chapter, but in this respect he fared no worse than his unfortunate companions. "Spare the rod," was an idea scouted by our master. He was constitutionally subject to periods of ill-humor, and at such times, however little provocation there might be, a certain amount of punishment was inflicted. The circumstances attending the last flogging but one that I received, will show how trivial a cause was sufficient with him for resorting to the whip.

A Mr. O'Niel, residing in the vicinity of the Big Pine Woods, called upon

Epps for the purpose of purchasing me. He was a tanner and currier by occupation, transacting an extensive business, and intended to place me at service in some department of his establishment, provided he bought me. Aunt Phebe, while preparing the dinner-table in the great house, overheard their conversation. On returning to the yard at night, the old woman ran to meet me, designing, of course, to overwhelm me with the news. She entered into a minute repetition of all she had heard, and Aunt Phebe was one whose ears never failed to drink in every word of conversation uttered in her hearing. She enlarged upon the fact that "Massa Epps was g'wine to sell me to a tanner ober in de Pine Woods," so long and loudly as to attract the attention of the mistress, who, standing unobserved on the piazza at the time, was listening to our conversation.

"Well, Aunt Phebe," said I, "I'm glad of it. I'm tired of scraping cotton, and would rather be a tanner. I hope he'll buy me."

O'Niel did not effect a purchase, however, the parties differing as to price, and the morning following his arrival, departed homewards. He had been gone but a short time me, when Epps made his appearance in the field. Now nothing will more violently enrage a master, especially Epps, than the intimation of one of his servants that he would like to leave him. Mistress Epps had repeated to him my expressions to Aunt Phebe the evening previous, as I learned from the latter afterwards, the mistress having mentioned to her that she had overheard us. On entering the field, Epps walked directly to me.

"So, Platt, you're tired of scraping cotton, are you? You would like to change your master, eh? You're fond of moving round—traveler—ain't ye? Ah, yes—like to travel for your health, may be? Feel above cotton-scraping, I 'spose. So you're going into the tanning business? Good business—devilish fine business. Enterprising nigger! B'lieve I'll go into that business myself. Down on your knees, and strip that rag off your back! I'll try my hand at tanning."

I begged earnestly, and endeavored to soften him with excuses, but in vain. There was no other alternative; so kneeling down, I presented my bare back for the application of the lash.

"How do you like *tanning?*" he exclaimed, as the rawhide descended upon my flesh. "How do you like *tanning?*" he repeated at every blow. In this manner he gave me twenty or thirty lashes, incessantly giving utterance to the word "tanning," in one form of expression or another. When sufficiently "tanned," he allowed me to arise, and with a half-malicious laugh assured me, if I still fancied the business, he would give me further instruction in it whenever I desired. This time, he remarked, he had only given me a short lesson in "*tanning*"—the next time he would "curry me down."[31]

Uncle Abram, also, was frequently treated with great brutality, although he was one of the kindest and most faithful creatures in the world. He was my cabin-mate for years. There was a benevolent expression in the old man's face, pleasant to behold. He regarded us with a kind of parental feeling, always counseling us with remarkable gravity and deliberation.

Returning from Marshall's plantation one afternoon, whither I had been sent on some errand of the mistress, I found him lying on the cabin floor, his clothes saturated with blood. He informed me that he had been stabbed! While spreading cotton on the scaffold, Epps came home intoxicated from Holmesville. He found fault with every thing, giving many orders so directly contrary that it was impossible to execute any of them. Uncle Abram, whose faculties were growing dull, became confused, and committed some blunder of no particular consequence. Epps was so enraged thereat, that, with drunken recklessness, he flew upon the old man, and stabbed him in the back. It was a long, ugly wound, but did not happen to penetrate far enough to result fatally. It was sewed up by the mistress, who censured her husband with extreme severity, not only denouncing his inhumanity, but declaring that she expected nothing else than that he would bring the family to poverty—that he would kill all the slaves on the plantation in some of his drunken fits.

It was no uncommon thing with him to prostrate Aunt Phebe with a chair or stick of wood; but the most cruel whipping that ever I was doomed to witness—one I can never recall with any other emotion than that of horror—was inflicted on the unfortunate Patsey.

It has been seen that the jealousy and hatred of Mistress Epps made the daily life of her young and agile slave completely miserable. I am happy in the belief that on numerous occasions I was the means of averting punishment from the inoffensive girl. In Epps' absence the mistress often ordered me to whip her without the remotest provocation. I would refuse, saying that I feared my master's displeasure, and several times ventured to remonstrate with her against the treatment Patsey received. I endeavored to impress her with the truth that the latter was not responsible for the acts of which she complained, but that she being a slave, and subject entirely to her master's will, he alone was answerable.

At length "the green-eyed monster" crept into the soul of Epps also, and then it was that he joined with his wrathful wife in an infernal jubilee over the girl's miseries.

On a Sabbath day in hoeing time, not long ago, we were on the bayou bank, washing our clothes, as was our usual custom. Presently Patsey was missing. Epps called aloud, but there was no answer. No one had observed her leaving the yard, and it was a wonder with us whither she had gone. In the course of a couple of hours she was seen approaching from the direction of Shaw's. This man, as has been intimated, was a notorious profligate, and withal not on the most friendly terms with Epps. Harriet, his black wife, knowing Patsey's troubles, was kind to her, in consequence of which the latter was in the habit of going over to see her every opportunity. Her visits were prompted by friendship merely, but the suspicion gradually entered the brain of Epps, that another and a baser passion led her thither—that it was not Harriet she desired to meet, but rather the unblushing libertine, his neighbor. Patsey found her master in a fearful rage on her return. His violence so alarmed her that at first she attempted to evade direct answers to his questions, which only served to increase his suspicions. She finally, however, drew herself up proudly, and in a spirit of indignation boldly denied his charges.

"Missus don't give me soap to wash with, as she does the rest," said Patsey, "and you know why. I went over to Harriet's to get a piece," and saying this, she drew it forth from a pocket in her dress and exhibited it to him. "That's what I went to Shaw's for, Massa Epps," continued she; "the Lord knows that was all."

"You lie, you black wench!" shouted Epps.

"I *don't* lie, massa. If you kill me, I'll stick to that."

"Oh! I'll fetch you down. I'll learn you to go to Shaw's. I'll take the starch out of ye," he muttered fiercely through his shut teeth.

Then turning to me, he ordered four stakes to be driven into the ground, pointing with the toe of his boot to the places where he wanted them. When the stakes were driven down, he ordered her to be stripped of every article of dress. Ropes were then brought, and the naked girl was laid upon her face, her wrists and feet each tied firmly to a stake. Stepping to the piazza, he took down a heavy whip, and placing it in my hands, commanded me to lash her. Unpleasant as it was, I was compelled to obey him. Nowhere that day, on the face of the whole earth, I venture to say, was there such a demoniac exhibition witnessed as then ensued.

THE STAKING OUT AND FLOGGING OF THE GIRL PATSEY.

Mistress Epps stood on the piazza among her children, gazing on the scene with an air of heartless satisfaction. The slaves were huddled together at a little distance, their countenances indicating the sorrow of their hearts. Poor Patsey prayed piteously for mercy, but her prayers were vain. Epps ground his teeth, and stamped upon the ground, screaming at me, like a mad fiend, to strike *harder*.

"Strike harder, or *your* turn will come next, you scoundrel," he yelled.

"Oh, mercy, massa!—oh! have mercy, *do*. Oh, God! pity me," Patsey exclaimed continually, struggling fruitlessly, and the flesh quivering at every stroke.

When I had struck her as many as thirty times, I stopped, and turned round toward Epps, hoping he was satisfied; but with bitter oaths and threats, he ordered me to continue. I inflicted ten or fifteen blows more. By this time her back was covered with long welts, intersecting each other like net work. Epps was yet furious and savage as ever, demanding if she would like to go to Shaw's again, and swearing he would flog her until she wished she was in h—l. Throwing down the whip, I declared I could punish her no more. He ordered me to go on, threatening me with a severer flogging than she had received, in case of refusal. My heart revolted at the inhuman scene, and risking the consequences, I absolutely refused to raise the whip. He then seized it himself, and applied it with ten-fold greater force than I had. The painful cries and shrieks of the tortured Patsey, mingling with the loud and angry curses of Epps, loaded the air. She was terribly lacerated—I may say, without exaggeration, literally flayed. The lash was wet with blood, which flowed down her sides and dropped upon the ground. At length she ceased struggling. Her head sank listlessly on the ground. Her screams and supplications gradually decreased and died away into a low moan. She no longer writhed and shrank beneath the lash when it bit out small pieces of her flesh. I thought that she was dying!

It was the Sabbath of the Lord. The fields smiled in the warm sunlight—the birds chirped merrily amidst the foliage of the trees—peace and happiness seemed to reign everywhere, save in the bosoms of Epps and his panting victim and the silent witnesses around him. The tempestuous emotions that were raging there were little in harmony with the calm and quiet beauty of the day. I could look on Epps only with unutterable loathing and abhorrence, and thought within myself—"Thou devil, sooner or later, somewhere in the course of eternal justice, thou shalt answer for this sin!"

Finally, he ceased whipping from mere exhaustion, and ordered Phebe to bring a bucket of salt and water. After washing her thoroughly with this, I was told to take her to her cabin. Untying the ropes, I raised her in my arms. She was unable to stand, and as her head rested on my shoulder, she repeated many times, in a faint voice scarcely perceptible, "Oh, Platt—oh, Platt!" but nothing further. Her dress was replaced, but it clung to her back, and was soon stiff with blood. We laid her on some boards in the hut, where she remained a long time, with eyes closed and groaning in agony. At night Phebe applied melted tallow to her wounds, and so far as we were able, all endeavored to assist and console her. Day after day she lay in her cabin upon her face, the sores preventing her resting in any other position.

A blessed thing it would have been for her—days and weeks and months of misery it would have saved her—had she never lifted up her head in life again. Indeed, from that time forward she was not what she had been. The burden of a deep melancholy weighed heavily on her spirits. She no longer moved with that buoyant and elastic step—there was not that mirthful sparkle in her eyes that formerly distinguished her. The bounding vigor—the sprightly, laughter-loving spirit of her youth, were gone. She fell into a mournful and desponding mood, and oftentimes would start up in her sleep, and with raised hands, plead for mercy. She became more silent than she was, toiling all day in our midst, not uttering a word. A care-worn, pitiful expression settled on her face, and it was her humor now to weep, rather than rejoice. If ever there was a broken heart—one crushed and blighted by the rude grasp of suffering misfortune—it was Patsey's.

She had been reared no better than her master's beast—looked upon merely as a valuable and handsome animal—and consequently possessed but a limited amount of knowledge. And yet a faint light cast its rays over her intellect, so that it was not wholly dark. She had a dim perception of God and of eternity, and a still more dim perception of a Saviour who had died even for such as her. She entertained but confused notions of a future life—not comprehending the distinction between the corporeal and spiritual existence. Happiness, in her mind, was exemption from stripes—from labor—from the cruelty of masters and overseers. Her idea of the joy of heaven was simply *rest*, and is fully expressed in these of a melancholy bard:

> "I ask no paradise on high,
>   With cares on earth oppressed,
> The only heaven for which I sigh,
>   Is rest, eternal rest."

It is a mistaken opinion that prevails in some quarters that the slave does not understand the term—does not comprehend the idea of freedom. Even on Bayou Boeuf, where I conceive slavery exists in its most abject and cruel form—where it exhibits features altogether unknown in more northern States—the most ignorant of them generally know full well its meaning. They understand the privileges and exemptions that belong to it—that it would bestow upon them the fruits of their own labors, and that it would secure to them the enjoyment of domestic happiness. They do not fail to observe the difference between their own condition and the meanest white man's, and to realize the injustice of the laws which place it in his power not only to appropriate the profits of their industry, but to subject them to unmerited and unprovoked punishment, without remedy, or the right to resist, or to remonstrate.

Patsey's life, especially after her whipping, was one long dream of liberty. Far away, to her fancy an immeasurable distance, she knew there was a land of freedom. A thousand times she had heard that somewhere in the distant North there were no slaves—no masters. In her imagination it was an enchanted region, the Paradise of the earth. To dwell where the black man may work for himself—live in his own cabin—till his own soil, was a blissful dream of Patsey's—a dream, alas! the fulfillment of which she can never realize.

The effect of these exhibitions of brutality on the household of the slave-holder, is apparent. Epps' oldest son is an intelligent lad of ten or twelve years of age. It is pitiable, sometimes, to see him chastising, for instance, the venerable Uncle Abram. He will call the old man to account, and if in his childish judge-ment it is necessary, sentence him to a certain number of lashes, which he pro-ceeds to inflict with much gravity and deliberation. Mounted on his pony, he of-ten rides into the field with his whip, playing the overseer, greatly to his father's delight. Without discrimination, at such times, he applies the rawhide, urging the slaves forward with shouts, and occasional expressions of profanity, while the old man laughs, and commends him as a thorough-going boy.

"The child is father to the man," and with such training, whatever may be his natural disposition, it cannot well be otherwise than that, on arriving at ma-turity, the sufferings and miseries of the slave will be looked upon with entire in-difference. The influence of the iniquitous system necessarily fosters an unfeeling and cruel spirit, even in the bosoms of those who, among their equals, are re-garded as humane and generous.

Young Master Epps possessed some noble qualities, yet no process of rea-soning could lead him to comprehend, that in the eye of the Almighty there is no distinction of color. He looked upon the black man simply as an animal, differ-ing in no respect from any other animal, save in the gift of speech and the pos-session of somewhat higher instincts, and, therefore, the more valuable. To work like his father's mules—to be whipped and kicked and scourged through life—to address the white man with hat in hand, and eyes bent servilely on the earth, in his mind, was the natural and proper destiny of the slave. Brought up with such ideas—in the notion that we stand without the pale of humanity—no won-der the oppressors of my people are a pitiless and unrelenting race.

CHAPTER XIX.

AVERY, ON BAYOU ROUGE—PECULIARITY OF DWELLINGS—EPPS BUILDS A NEW HOUSE—BASS, THE CARPENTER—HIS NOBLE QUALITIES—HIS PERSONAL AP-PEARANCE AND ECCENTRICITIES—BASS AND EPPS DISCUSS THE QUESTION OF SLAVERY—EPPS' OPINION OF BASS—I MAKE MYSELF KNOWN TO HIM—OUR CON-VERSATION—HIS SURPRISE—THE MIDNIGHT MEETING ON THE BAYOU BANK—BASS' ASSURANCES—DECLARES WAR AGAINST SLAVERY—WHY I DID NOT DIS-CLOSE MY HISTORY—BASS WRITES LETTERS—COPY OF HIS LETTER TO MESSRS. PARKER AND PERRY—THE FEVER OF SUSPENSE—DISAPPOINTMENTS—BASS EN-DEAVORS TO CHEER ME—MY FAITH IN HIM.

IN the month of June, 1852, in pursuance of a previous contract, Mr. Avery, a carpenter of Bayou Rouge, commenced the erection of a house for Master Epps. It has previously been stated that there are no cellars on Bayou Boeuf; on the other hand, such is the low and swampy nature of the ground, the great houses are usually built upon spiles. Another peculiarity is, the rooms are not plastered, but the ceiling and sides are covered with matched cypress boards, painted such color as most pleases the owner's taste. Generally the plank and boards are sawed by slaves with whip-saws, there being no waterpower upon which mills might be built within many miles. When the planter erects for himself a dwelling, therefore, there is plenty of extra work for his slaves. Having had some experience under Tibeats as a carpenter, I was taken from the field altogether, on the arrival of Avery and his hands.

Among them was one to whom I owe an immeasurable debt of gratitude. Only for him, in all probability, I should have ended my days in slavery. He was my deliverer—a man whose true heart overflowed with noble and generous emotions. To the last moment of my existence I shall remember him with feelings of thankfulness. His name was Bass, and at that time he resided in Marksville. It will be difficult to convey a correct impression of his appearance or character. He was a large man, between forty and fifty years old, of light complexion and light hair. He was very cool and self-possessed, fond of argument, but always speaking with extreme deliberation. He was that kind of person whose peculiarity of manner was such that nothing he uttered ever gave offence. What would be intolerable, coming from the lips of another, could be said by him with impunity. There was not a man on Red River, perhaps, that agreed with him on the subject of politics or religion, and not a man, I venture to say, who discussed either of those subjects half as much. It seemed to be taken for granted that he would espouse the unpopular side of every local question, and it always created amusement rather than displeasure among his auditors, to listen to the ingenious and original manner in which he maintained the controversy. He was a bachelor—an "old bachelor," according to the true acceptation of the term—having no kindred living, as he knew of, in the world. Neither had he any permanent abiding place—wandering from one State to another, as his fancy dictated. He had lived in Marksville three or four years, and in the prosecution of his business as a carpenter; and in consequence, likewise, of his peculiarities, was quite extensively known throughout the parish of Avoyelles. He was liberal to a fault; and his many acts of kindness and transparent goodness of heart rendered him popular in the community, the sentiment of which he unceasingly combated.

He was a native of Canada, from whence he had wandered in early life, and after visiting all the principal localities in the northern and western States, in the course of his peregrinations, arrived in the unhealthy region of the Red River. His last removal was from Illinois. Whither he has now gone, I regret to be obliged to say, is unknown to me. He gathered up his effects and departed quietly from Marksville the day before I did, the suspicions of his instrumentality in procuring my liberation rendering such a step necessary. For the commission of a just and righteous act he would undoubtedly have suffered death, had he remained within reach of the slave-whipping tribe on Bayou Boeuf.

One day, while working on the new house, Bass and Epps became engaged in a controversy, to which, as will be readily supposed, I listened with absorbing interest. They were discussing the subject of Slavery.

"I tell you what it is Epps," said Bass, "it's all wrong—all wrong, sir—there's no justice nor righteousness in it. I wouldn't own a slave if I was rich as

Croesus, which I am not, as is perfectly well understood, more particularly among my creditors. *There's* another humbug—the credit system—humbug, sir; no credit—no debt. Credit leads a man into temptation. Cash down is the only thing that will deliver him from evil. But this question of *Slavery;* what *right* have you to your niggers when you come down to the point?"

"What right!" said Epps, laughing; "why, I bought 'em, and paid for 'em."

"Of *course* you did; the law says you have the right to hold a nigger, but begging the law's pardon, it *lies.* Yes, Epps, when the law says that it's a *liar,* and the truth is not in it. Is every thing right because the law allows it? Suppose they'd pass a law taking away your liberty and making you a slave?"

"Oh, that ain't a supposable case," said Epps, still laughing; "hope you don't compare me to a nigger, Bass."

"Well," Bass answered gravely, "no, not exactly. But I have seen niggers before now as good as I am, and I have no acquaintance with any white man in these parts that I consider a whit better than myself. Now, in the sight of God, what is the difference, Epps, between a white man and a black one?"

"All the difference in the world," replied Epps. "You might as well ask what the difference is between a white man and a baboon. Now, I've seen one of them critters in Orleans that knowed just as much as any nigger I've got. You'd call them feller citizens, I s'pose?"—and Epps indulged in a loud laugh at his own wit.

"Look here, Epps," continued his companion; "you can't laugh me down in that way. Some men are witty, and some ain't so witty as they think they are. Now let me ask you a question. Are all men created free and equal as the Declaration of Independence holds they are?"

"Yes," responded Epps, "but all men, niggers, and monkeys *ain't;*" and hereupon he broke forth into a more boisterous laugh than before.

"There are monkeys among white people as well as black, when you come to that," coolly remarked Bass. "I know some white men that use arguments no sensible monkey would. But let that pass. These niggers are human beings. If they don't know as much as their masters, whose fault is it? They are not *allowed* to know anything. You have books and papers, and can go where you please, and gather intelligence in a thousand ways. But your slaves have no privileges. You'd whip one of them if caught reading a book. They are held in bondage, generation after generation, deprived of mental improvement, and who can expect them to possess much knowledge? If they are not brought down to a level with the brute creation, you slaveholders will never be blamed for it. If they are baboons, or stand no higher in the scale of intelligence than such animals, you and men like you will have to answer for it. There's a sin, a fearful sin, resting on this nation, that will not go unpunished forever. There will be a reckoning yet—yes, Epps, there's a day coming that will burn as an oven. It may be sooner or it may be later, but it's a coming as sure as the Lord is just."

"If you lived up among the Yankees in New-England," said Epps, "I expect you'd be one of them cursed fanatics that know more than the constitution, and go about peddling clocks and coaxing niggers to run away."

"If I was in New-England," returned Bass, "I would be just what I am here.

I would say that Slavery was an iniquity, and ought to be abolished. I would say there was no reason nor justice in the law, or the constitution that allows one man to hold another man in bondage. It would be hard for you to lose your property, to be sure, but it wouldn't be half as hard as it would be to lose your liberty. You have no more right to your freedom, in exact justice, than Uncle Abram yonder. Talk about black skin, and black blood; why, how many slaves are there on this bayou as white as either of us? And what difference is there in the color of the soul? Pshaw! the whole system is as absurd as it is cruel. You may own niggers and be hanged, but I wouldn't own one for the best plantation in Louisiana."

"You like to hear yourself talk, Bass, better than any man I know of. You would argue that black was white, or white black, if any body would contradict you. Nothing suits you in this world, and I don't believe you will be satisfied with the next, if you should have your choice in them."

Conversations substantially like the foregoing were not unusual between the two after this; Epps drawing him out more for the purpose of creating a laugh at his expense, than with a view of fairly discussing the merits of the question. He looked upon Bass, as a man ready to say anything merely for the pleasure of hearing his own voice; as somewhat self-conceited, perhaps, contending against his faith and judgment, in order, simply, to exhibit his dexterity in argumentation.

He remained at Epps', through the summer, visiting Marksville generally once a fortnight. The more I saw of him, the more I became convinced he was a man in whom I could confide. Nevertheless, my previous ill-fortune had taught me to be extremely cautious. It was not my place to speak to a white man except when spoken to, but I omitted no opportunity of throwing myself in his way, and endeavored constantly in every possible manner to attract his attention. In the early part of August he and myself were at work alone in the house, the other carpenters having left, and Epps being absent in the field. Now was the time, if ever, to broach the subject, and I resolved to do it, and submit to whatever consequences might ensue. We were busily at work in the afternoon, when I stopped suddenly and said—

"Master Bass, I want to ask you what part of the country you came from?"

"Why, Platt, what put that into your head?" he answered. "You wouldn't know if I should tell you." After a moment or two he added—"I was born in Canada; now guess where that is."

"Oh, I know where Canada is," said I, "I have been there myself."

"Yes, I expect you are well acquainted all through that country", he remarked, laughing incredulously.

"As sure as I live, Master Bass," I replied, "I have been there. I have been in Montreal and Kingston, and Queenston, and a great many places in Canada, and I have been in York State, too—in Buffalo, and Rochester, and Albany, and can tell you the names of the villages on the Erie canal and the Champlain canal."

Bass turned round and gazed at me a long time without uttering a syllable.

"How came you here?" he inquired, at length,

"Master Bass," I answered, "if justice had been done, I never would have been here."

"Well, how's this?" said he. "Who are you? You have been in Canada sure enough; I know all the places you mention. How did you happen to get here? Come, tell me all about it."

"I have no friends here," was my reply, "that I can put confidence in. I am afraid to tell you, though I don't believe you would tell Master Epps if I should."

He assured me earnestly he would keep every word I might speak to him a profound secret, and his curiosity was evidently strongly excited. It was a long story, I informed him, and would take some time to relate it. Master Epps would be back soon, but if he would see me that night after all were asleep, I would repeat it to him. He consented readily to the arrangement, and directed me to come into the building where we were then at work, and I would find him there. About midnight, when all was still and quiet, I crept cautiously from my cabin, and silently entering the unfinished building, found him awaiting me.

After further assurances on his part that I should not be betrayed, I began a relation of the history of my life and misfortunes. He was deeply interested, asking numerous questions in reference to localities and events. Having ended my story I besought him to write to some of my friends at the North, acquainting them with my situation, and begging them to forward free papers, or take such steps as they might consider proper to secure my release. He promised to do so, but dwelt upon the danger of such an act in case of detection, and now impressed upon me the great necessity of strict silence and secrecy. Before we parted our plan of operation was arranged.

We agreed to meet the next night at a specified place among the high weeds on the bank of the bayou, some distance from master's dwelling. There he was write down on paper the names and address of several persons, old friends in the North, to whom he would direct letters during his next visit to Marksville. It was not deemed prudent to meet in the new house, inasmuch as the light it would be necessary to use might possibly be discovered. In the course of the day I managed to obtain a few matches and a piece of candle, unperceived, from the kitchen, during a temporary absence of Aunt Phebe. Bass had pencil and paper in his tool chest.

At the appointed hour we met on the bayou bank, and creeping among the high weeds, I lighted the candle, while he drew forth pencil and paper and prepared for business. I gave him the names of William Perry, Cephas Parker and Judge Marvin, all of Saratoga Springs, Saratoga county, New-York. I had been employed by the latter in the United States Hotel, and had transacted business with the former to a considerable extent, and trusted that at least one of them would be still living at that place. He carefully wrote the names, and then remarked, thoughtfully—

"It is so many years since you left Saratoga, all these men may be dead, or may have removed. You say you obtained papers at the custom house in New-York. Probably there is a record of them there, and I think it would be well to write and ascertain."

I agreed with him, and again repeated the circumstances related heretofore, connected with my visit to the custom house with Brown and Hamilton. We lingered on the bank of the bayou an hour or more, conversing upon the subject which now engrossed our thoughts. I could no longer doubt his fidelity, and freely spoke to him of the many sorrows I had borne in silence, and so long. I spoke of my wife and children, mentioning their names and ages, and dwelling upon the unspeakable happiness it would be to clasp them to my heart once more before I died. I caught him by the hand, and with tears and passionate entreaties implored him to befriend me—to restore me to my kindred and to liberty—promising I would weary Heaven the remainder of my life with prayers that it would bless and prosper him. In the enjoyment of freedom—surrounded by the associations of youth, and restored to the bosom of my family—that promise is not yet forgotten, nor shall it ever be so long as I have strength to raise my imploring eyes on high.

> "Oh, blessings on his kindly voice and on his silver hair,
> And blessings on his whole life long, until he meet me there."[32]

He overwhelmed me with assurances of friendship and faithfulness, saying he had never before taken so deep an interest in the fate of any one. He spoke of himself in a somewhat mournful tone, as a lonely man, a wanderer about the world—that he was growing old, and must soon reach the end of his earthly journey, and lie down to his final rest without kith or kin to mourn for him, or to remember him—that his life was of little value to himself, and henceforth should be devoted to the accomplishment of my liberty, and to an unceasing warfare against the accursed shame of Slavery.

After this time we seldom spoke to, or recognized each other. He was, moreover, less free in his conversation with Epps on the subject of Slavery. The remotest suspicion that there was any unusual intimacy—any secret understanding between us—never once entered the mind of Epps, or any other person, white or black, on the plantation.

I am often asked, with an air of incredulity, how I succeeded so many years in keeping from my daily and constant companions the knowledge of my true name and history. The terrible lesson Burch taught me, impressed indelibly upon my mind the danger and uselessness of asserting I was a freeman. There was no possibility of any slave being able to assist me, while, on the other hand, there *was* a possibility of his exposing me. When it is recollected the whole current of my thoughts, for twelve years, turned to the contemplation of escape, it will not be wondered at, that I was always cautious and on my guard. It would have been an act of folly to have proclaimed my *right* to freedom; it would only have subjected me to severer scrutiny—probably have consigned me to some more distant and inaccessible region than even Bayou Boeuf. Edwin Epps was a person utterly regardless of a black man's rights or wrongs—utterly destitute of any natural sense of justice, as I well knew. It was important, therefore, not only as regarded my hope of deliverance, but also as regarded the few personal priviliges I was as permitted to enjoy, to keep from him the history of my life.

The Saturday night subsequent to our interview at the water's edge, Bass went home to Marksville. The next day, being Sunday, he employed himself in his own room writing letters. One he directed to the Collector of Customs at

New-York, another to Judge Marvin, and another to Messrs. Parker and Perry jointly. The latter was the one which led to my recovery. He subscribed my true name, but in the postscript intimated I was not the writer. The letter itself shows that he considered himself engaged in a dangerous undertaking—no less than running "the risk of his life, if detected." I did not see the letter before it was mailed, but have since obtained a copy, which is here inserted:

"Bayou Boeuf, August 15, 1852.
"Mr. WILLIAM PERRY or MR. CEPHAS PARKER:
"Gentlemen—It having been a long time since I have seen or heard from you, and not knowing that you are living, it is with uncertainty that I write to you, but the necessity of the case must be my excuse.
"Having been born free, just across the river from you, I am certain you must know me, and I am here now a slave. I wish you to obtain free papers for me, and forward them to me at Marksville, Louisiana, Parish of Avoyelles, and oblige
"Yours,   SOLOMON NORTHUP.

"The way I came to be a slave, I was taken sick in Washington City, and was insensible for some time. When I recovered my reason, I was robbed of my free-papers, and in irons on my way to this State, and have never been able to get any one to write for me until now; and he that is writing for me runs the risk of his life if detected."

The allusion to myself in the work recently issued, entitled "A Key to Uncle Tom's Cabin," contains the first part of this letter, omitting the postscript. Neither are the full names of the gentlemen to whom it is directed correctly stated, there being a slight discrepancy, probably a typographical error. To the postscript more than to the body of the communication am I indebted for my liberation, as will presently be seen.

When Bass returned from Marksville he informed me of what he had done. We continued our midnight consultations, never speaking to each other through the day, excepting as it was necessary about the work. As nearly as he was able to ascertain, it would require two weeks for the letter to reach Saratoga in due course of mail, and the same length of time for an answer to return. Within six weeks, at the farthest, we concluded, an answer would arrive, if it arrived at all. A great many suggestions were now made, and a great deal of conversation took place between us, as to the most safe and proper course to pursue on receipt of the free papers. They would stand between him and harm, in case we were overtaken and arrested leaving the country altogether. It would be no infringement of law, however much it might provoke individual hostility, to assist a freeman to regain his freedom.

At the end of four weeks he was again at Marksville, but no answer had arrived. I was sorely disappointed, but still reconciled myself with the reflection that sufficient length of time had not yet elapsed—that there might have been delays—and that I could not reasonably expect one so soon. Six, seven, eight, and ten weeks passed by, however, and nothing came. I was in a fever of suspense whenever Bass visited Marksville, and could scarcely close my eyes until his return. Finally my master's house was finished, and the time came when Bass must leave me. The night before his departure I was wholly given up to despair. I had clung to him as a drowning man clings to the floating spar, knowing if it ships from his grasp he must forever sink beneath the waves. The all-glorious hope, upon which I had laid such eager hold, was crumbling to ashes in my hands. I felt as if sinking down, down, amidst the bitter waters of Slavery, from the unfathomable depths of which I should never rise again.

The generous heart of my friend and benefactor was touched with pity at the sight of my distress. He endeavored to cheer me up, promising to return the day before Christmas, and if no intelligence was received in the meantime, some further step would be undertaken to effect our design. He exhorted me to keep up my spirits—to rely upon his continued efforts in my behalf, assuring me, in most earnest and impressive language, that my liberation should, from thenceforth, be the chief object of his thoughts.

In his absence the time passed slowly indeed. I looked forward to Christmas with intense anxiety and impatience. I had about given up the expectation of receiving any answer to the letters. They might have miscarried, or might have been misdirected. Perhaps those at Saratoga, to whom they had been addressed, were all dead; perhaps, engaged in their pursuits, they did not consider the fate of an obscure, unhappy black man of sufficient importance to be noticed. My whole reliance was in Bass. The faith I had in him was continually re-assuring me, and enabled me to stand up against the tide of disappointment that had overwhelmed me.

So wholly was I absorbed in reflecting upon my situation and prospects, that the hands with whom I labored in the field often observed it. Patsey would ask me if I was sick, and Uncle Abram, and Bob, and Wiley frequently expressed a curiosity to know what I could be thinking about so steadily. But I evaded their inquiries with some light remark, and kept my thoughts locked closely in my breast.

CHAPTER XX.

BASS FAITHFUL TO HIS WORD—HIS ARRIVAL ON CHRISTMAS EVE—THE DIFFICULTY OF OBTAINING AN INTERVIEW—THE MEETING IN THE CABIN—NON-ARRIVAL OF THE LETTER—BASS ANNOUNCES HIS INTENTION TO PROCEED NORTH—CHRISTMAS—CONVERSATION BETWEEN EPPS AND BASS—YOUNG MISTRESS MCCOY, THE BEAUTY OF BAYOU BOEUF—THE "NE PLUS ULTRA" OF DINNERS—MUSIC AND DANCING—PRESENCE OF THE MISTRESS—HER EXCEEDING BEAUTY—THE LAST SLAVE DANCE—WILLIAM PIERCE—OVERSLEEP MYSELF—THE LAST WHIPPING—DESPONDENCY—COLD MORNING—EPPS' THREATS—THE PASSING CARRIAGE—STRANGERS APPROACHING THROUGH THE COTTON-FIELD—LAST HOUR ON BAYOU BOEUF.

FAITHFUL to his word, the day before Christmas, just at night-fall, Bass came riding into the yard.

"How are you," said Epps, shaking him by the hand, "glad to see you."

He would not have been *very* glad had he known the object of his errand.

"Quite well, quite well," answered Bass. "Had some business out on the bayou, and concluded to call and see you, and stay over night."

Epps ordered one of the slaves to take charge of his horse, and with much talk and laughter they passed into the house together; not, however, until Bass had looked at me significantly, as much as to say, "Keep dark, we understand each other." It was ten o'clock at night before the labors of the day were performed, when I entered the cabin. At that time Uncle Abram and Bob occupied it with me. I laid down upon my board and feigned I was asleep. When my companions had fallen into a profound slumber, I moved stealthily out of the door, and watched, and listened attentively for some sign or sound from Bass. There I stood until long after midnight, but nothing could be seen or heard. As I suspected, he dared not leave the house, through fear of exciting the suspicion of some of the family. I judged, correctly, he would rise earlier than was his custom, and take the opportunity of seeing me before Epps was up. Accordingly I aroused Uncle Abram an hour sooner than usual, and sent him into the house to build a fire, which, at that season of the year, is a part of Uncle Abram's duties.

I also gave Bob a violent shake, and asked him if he intended to sleep till noon, saying master would be up before the mules were fed. He knew right well the consequence that would follow such an event, and, jumping to his feet, was at the horse-pasture in a twinkling.

Presently, when both were gone, Bass slipped into the cabin.

"No letter yet, Platt," said he. The announcement fell upon my heart like lead.

"Oh, *do* write again, Master Bass," I cried; "I will give you the names of a great many I know. Surely they are not all dead. Surely some one will pity me."

"No use," Bass replied, "no use. I have made up my mind to that. I fear the Marksville post-master will mistrust something, I have inquired so often at his office. Too uncertain—too dangerous."

"Then it is all over," I exclaimed. "Oh, my God, how can I end my days here!"

"You're not going to end them here," he said, "unless you die very soon. I've thought this matter all over, and have come to a determination. There are more ways than one to manage this business, and a better and surer way than writing letters. I have a job or two on hand which can be completed by March or April. By that time I shall have a considerable sum of money, and then, Platt, I am going to Saratoga myself."

I could scarcely credit my own senses as the words fell from his lips. But he assured me, in a manner that left no doubt of the sincerity of his intention, that if his life was spared until spring, he should certainly undertake the journey.

"I have lived in this region long enough," he continued; "I may as well be in one place as another. For a long time I have been thinking of going back once more to the place where I was born. I'm tired of Slavery as well as you. If I can succeed in getting you away from here, it will be a good act that I shall like to think of all my life. And I *shall* succeed, Platt; I'm *bound* to do it. Now let me tell you what I want. Epps will be up soon, and it won't do to be caught here. Think of a great many men at Saratoga and Sandy Hill, and in that neighborhood, who once knew you. I shall make excuse to come here again in the course of the winter, when I will write down their names. I will then know who to call on when I go north. Think of all you can. Cheer up! Don't be discouraged. I'm with you, life or death. Good-bye. God bless you," and saying this he left the cabin quickly, and entered the great house.

It was Christmas morning—the happiest day in the whole year for the slave. That morning he need not hurry to the field, with his gourd and cotton-bag. Happiness sparkled in the eyes and overspread the countenances of all. The time of feasting and dancing had come. The cane and cotton fields were deserted. That day the clean dress was to be donned—the red ribbon displayed; there were to be re-unions, and joy and laughter, and hurrying to and fro. It was to be a day of *liberty* among the children of Slavery. Wherefore they were happy, and rejoiced.

After breakfast Epps and Bass sauntered about the yard, conversing upon the price of cotton, and various other topics.

"Where do your niggers hold Christmas?" Bass inquired.

"Platt is going to Tanners to-day. His fiddle is in great demand. They want him at Marshall's Monday, and Miss Mary McCoy, on the old Norwood plantation, writes me a note that she wants him to play for her niggers Tuesday."

"He is rather a smart boy, ain't he?" said Bass. "Come here, Platt," he added, looking at me as I walked up to them, as if he had never thought before to take any special notice of me.

"Yes," replied Epps, taking hold of my arm and feeling it, "there isn't a bad joint in him. There ain't a boy on the bayou worth more than he is—perfectly sound, and no bad tricks. D—n him, he isn't like other niggers; doesn't look like 'em—don't act like 'em. I was offered seventeen hundred dollars for him last week."

"And didn't take it?" Bass inquired, with an air of surprise.

"Take it—no; devilish clear of it. Why, he's a reg'lar genius; can make a plough beam, wagon tongue—anything, as well as you can. Marshall wanted to put up one of his niggers agin him and raffle for them, but I told him I would see the devil have him first."

"I don't see anything remarkable about him," Bass observed.

"Why, just feel of him, now," Epps rejoined. "You don't see a boy very often put together any closer than he is. He's a thin-skin'd cuss, and won't bear as much whipping as some; but he's got the muscle in him, and no mistake."

Bass felt of me, turned me round, and made a thorough examination, Epps all the while dwelling on my good points. But his visitor seemed to take but little interest finally in the subject, and consequently it was dropped. Bass soon departed, giving me another sly look of recognition and significance, as he trotted out of the yard.

When he was gone I obtained a pass, and started for Tanner's—not Peter Tanner's, of whom mention has previously been made, but a relative of his. I played during the day and most of the night, spending the next day, Sunday, in my cabin. Monday I crossed the bayou to Douglas Marshall's, all Epps' slaves accompanying me, and on Tuesday went to the old Norwood place, which is the third plantation above Marshall's, on the same side of the water.

This estate is now owned by Miss Mary McCoy, a lovely girl, some twenty years of age. She is the beauty and the glory of Bayou Bouef. She owns about a hundred working hands, besides a great many house servants, yard boys, and young children. Her brother-in-law, who resides on the adjoining estate, is her general agent. She is beloved by all her slaves, and good reason indeed have they to be thankful that they have fallen into such gentle hands. Nowhere on the bayou are there such feasts, such merrymaking, as at young Madam McCoy's. Thither, more than to any other place, do the old and the young for miles around love to repair in the time of the Christmas holidays; for nowhere else can they find such delicious repasts; nowhere else can they hear a voice speaking to them so pleasantly. No one is so well beloved—no one fills so large a space in the hearts of a thousand slaves, as young Madam McCoy, the orphan mistress of the old Norwood estate.

On my arrival at her place, I found two or three hundred had assembled. The table was prepared in a long building, which she had erected expressly for her slaves to dance in. It was covered with every variety of food the country afforded, and was pronounced by general acclamation to be the rarest of dinners. Roast turkey, pig, chicken, duck, and all kinds of meat, baked, boiled, and broiled, formed a line the whole length of the extended table, while the vacant spaces were filled with tarts, jellies, and frosted cake, and pastry of many kinds. The young mistress walked around the table, smiling and saying a kind word to each one, and seemed to enjoy the scene exceedingly.

When the dinner was over the tables were removed to make room for the dancers. I tuned my violin and struck up a lively air; while some joined in a nimble reel, others patted and sang their simple but melodious songs, filling the great room with music mingled with the sound of human voices and the clatter of many feet.

In the evening the mistress returned, and stood in the door a long time, looking at us. She was magnificently arrayed. Her dark hair and eyes contrasted strongly with her clear and delicate complexion. Her form was slender but commanding, and her movement was a combination of unaffected dignity and grace. As she stood there, clad in her rich apparel, her face animated with pleasure, I thought I had never looked upon a human being half so beautiful. I dwell with delight upon the description of this fair and gentle lady, not only because she inspired me with emotions of gratitude and admiration, but because I would have the reader understand that all slave-owners on Bayou Boeuf are not like Epps, or Tibeats, or Jim Burns. Occasionally can be found, rarely it may be, indeed, a good man like William Ford, or an angel of kindness like young Mistress McCoy.

Tuesday concluded the three holidays Epps yearly allowed us. On my way home, Wednesday morning, while passing the plantation of William Pierce, that gentleman hailed me, saying he had received a line from Epps, brought down by William Varnell, permitting him to detain me for the purpose of playing for his slaves that night. It was the last time I was destined to witness a slave dance on the shores of Bayou Boeuf. The party at Pierce's continued their jollification until broad daylight, when I returned to my master's house, somewhat wearied with the loss of rest, but rejoicing in the possession of numerous bits and picayunes,[33] which the whites, who were pleased with my musical performances, had contributed.

On Saturday morning, for the first time in years, I overslept myself. I was frightened on coming out of the cabin to find the slaves were already in the field. They had preceded me some fifteen minutes. Leaving my dinner and water-gourd, I hurried after them as fast as I could move. It was not yet sunrise, but Epps was on the piazza as I left the hut, and cried out to me that it was a pretty time of day to be getting up. By extra exertion my row was up when he came out after breakfast. This, however, was no excuse for the offence of oversleeping. Bidding me strip and lie down, he gave me ten or fifteen lashes, at the conclusion of which he inquired if I thought, after that, I could get up sometime in the *morning*. I expressed myself quite positively that I *could*, and, with back stinging with pain, went about my work.

The following day, Sunday, my thoughts were upon Bass, and the probabilities and hopes which hung upon his action and determination. I considered the uncertainty of life; that if it should be the will of God that he should die, my prospect of deliverance, and all expectation of happiness in this world, would be wholly ended and destroyed. My sore back, perhaps, did not have a tendency to render me unusually cheerful. I felt down-hearted and unhappy all day long, and when I laid down upon the hard board at night, my heart was oppressed with such a load of grief, it seemed that it must break.

Monday morning, the third of January, 1853, we were in the field betimes. It was a raw, cold morning, such as is unusual in that region. I was in advance, Uncle Abram next to me, behind him Bob, Patsey and Wiley, with our cotton-bags about our necks. Epps happened (a rare thing, indeed,) to come out that morning without his whip. He swore, in a manner that would shame a pirate, that we were doing nothing. Bob ventured to say that his fingers were so numb with cold he couldn't pick fast. Epps cursed himself for not having brought his rawhide, and declared that when he came out again he would warm us well; yes, he would make us all hotter than that fiery realm in which I am sometimes compelled to believe he will himself eventually reside.

With these fervent expressions, he left us. When out of hearing, we commenced talking to each other, saying how hard it was to be compelled to keep up our tasks with numb fingers; how unreasonable master was, and speaking of him generally in no flattering terms. Our conversation was interrupted by a carriage passing rapidly towards the house. Looking up, we saw two men approaching us through the cotton-field.

Having now brought down this narrative to the last hour I was to spend on Bayou Boeuf—having gotten through my last cotton picking, and about to bid Master Epps farewell—I must beg the reader to go back with me to the month of August; to follow Bass' letter on its long journey to Saratoga; to learn the effect it produced—and that, while I was repining and despairing in the slave hut of Edwin Epps, through the friendship of Bass and the goodness of Providence, all things were working together for my deliverance.

CHAPTER XXI.

THE LETTER REACHES SARATOGA—IS FORWARDED TO ANNE—IS LAID BEFORE HENRY B. NORTHUP—THE STATUTE OF MAY 14, 1840—ITS PROVISIONS— ANNE'S MEMORIAL TO THE GOVERNOR—THE AFFIDAVITS ACCOMPANYING IT—SENATOR SOULE'S LETTER—DEPARTURE OF THE AGENT APPOINTED BY THE GOVERNOR—ARRIVAL AT MARKSVILLE—THE HON. JOHN P. WADDILL— THE CONVERSATION ON NEW-YORK POLITICS—IT SUGGESTS A FORTUNATE IDEA—THE MEETING WITH BASS—THE SECRET OUT—LEGAL PROCEEDINGS IN- STITUTED—DEPARTURE OF NORTHUP AND THE SHERIFF FROM MARKSVILLE FOR BAYOU BOEUF—ARRANGEMENTS ON THE WAY—REACH EPPS' PLANTA- TION—DISCOVER HIS SLAVES IN THE COTTON-FIELD—THE MEETING—THE FAREWELL.

I AM indebted to Mr. Henry B. Northup and others for many of the particulars contained in this chapter.

The letter written by Bass, directed to Parker and Perry, and which was de- posited in the post-office in Marksville on the 15th day of August, 1852, arrived at Saratoga in the early part of September. Some time previous to this, Anne had removed to Glens Falls, Warren county, where she had charge of the kitchen in Carpenter's Hotel. She kept house, however, lodging with our children, and was only absent from them during such time as the discharge of her duties in the ho- tel required.

Messrs. Parker and Perry, on receipt of the letter, forwarded it immediately to Anne. On reading it the children were all excitement, and without delay has- tened to the neighboring village of Sandy Hill, to consult Henry B. Northup, and obtain his advice and assistance in the matter.

Upon examination, that gentleman found among the statutes of the State an act providing for the recovery of free citizens from slavery. It was passed May 14, 1840, and is entitled "An act more effectually to protect the free citizens of this State from being kidnapped or reduced to slavery." It provides that it shall be the duty of the Governor, upon the receipt of satisfactory information that any free citizen or inhabitant of this State, is wrongfully held in another State or Territory of the United States, upon the allegation or pretence that such person is a slave, or by color of any usage or rule of law is deemed or taken to be a slave, to take such measures to procure the restoration of such person to liberty, as he shall deem necessary. And to that end, he is authorized to appoint and employ an agent, and directed to furnish him with such credentials and instructions as will be likely to accomplish the object of his appointment. It requires the agent so appointed to proceed to collect the proper proof to establish the right of such person to his freedom; to perform such journeys, take such measures, institute such legal proceedings, &c., as may be necessary to return such person to this State, and charges all expenses incurred in carrying the act into effect, upon moneys not otherwise appropriated in the treasury.*

It was necessary to establish two facts to the satisfaction of the Governor: First, that I was a free citizen of New-York; and secondly, that I was wrongfully held in bondage. As to the first point, there was no difficulty, all the older inhabitants in the vicinity being ready to testify to it. The second point rested entirely upon the letter to Parker and Perry, written in an unknown hand, and upon the letter penned on board the brig Orleans, which, unfortunately, had been mislaid or lost.

A memorial was prepared, directed to his excellency, Governor Hunt, setting forth her marriage, my departure to Washington city; the receipt of the letters; that I was a free citizen, and such other facts as were deemed important, and was signed and verified by Anne. Accompanying this memorial were several affidavits of prominent citizens of Sandy Hill and Fort Edward, corroborating fully the statements it contained, and also a request of several well known gentlemen to the Governor, that Henry B. Northup be appointed agent under the legislative act.

On reading the memorial and affidavits, his excellency took a lively interest in the matter, and on the 23d day of November, 1852, under the seal of the State, "constituted, appointed and employed Henry B. Northup, Esq., an agent, with full power to effect" my restoration, and to take such measures as would be most likely to accomplish it, and instructing him to proceed to Louisiana with all convenient dispatch.†

The pressing nature of Mr. Northup's professional and political engagements delayed his departure until December. On the fourteenth day of that month he left Sandy Hill, and proceeded to Washington. The Hon. Pierre Soule, Senator in Congress from Louisiana, Hon. Mr. Conrad, Secretary of War, and Judge Nelson, of the Supreme Court of the United States, upon hearing a statement of the facts, and examining his commission, and certified copies of the memorial and affidavits, furnished him with open letters to gentlemen in Louisiana, strongly urging their assistance in accomplishing the object of his appointment.

Senator Soule especially interested himself in the matter, insisting, in forcible language, that it was the duty and interest of every planter in his State to aid in restoring me to freedom, and trusted the sentiments of honor and justice in the bosom of every citizen of the commonwealth would enlist him at once in my behalf. Having obtained these valuable letters, Mr. Northup returned to Baltimore, and proceeded from thence to Pittsburgh. It was his original intention, under advice of friends at Washington, to go directly to New Orleans, and consult the authorities of that city. Providentially, however, on arriving at the mouth of Red River, he changed his mind. Had he continued on, he would not

---

*See Appendix A.
†See Appendix B.

have met with Bass, in which case the search for me would probably have been fruitless.

Taking passage on the first steamer that arrived, he pursued his journey up Red River, a sluggish, winding stream, flowing through a vast region of primitive forests and impenetrable swamps, almost wholly destitute of inhabitants. About nine o'clock in the forenoon, January 1st, 1853, he left the steamboat at Marksville, and proceeded directly to Marksville Court House, a small village four miles in the interior.

From the fact that the letter to Messrs. Parker and Perry was post-marked at Marksville, it was supposed by him that I was in that place or its immediate vicinity. On reaching this town, he at once laid his business before the Hon. John P. Waddill, a legal gentleman of distinction, and a man of fine genius and most noble impulses. After reading the letters and documents presented him, and listening to a representation of the circumstances under which I had been carried away into captivity, Mr. Waddill at once proffered his services, and entered into the affair with great zeal and earnestness. He, in common with others of like elevated character, looked upon the kidnapper with abhorrence. The title of his fellow parishioners and clients to the property which constituted the larger proportion of their wealth, not only depended upon the good faith in which slave sales were transacted, but he was a man in whose honorable heart emotions of indignation were aroused by such an instance of injustice.

Marksville, although occupying a prominent position, and standing out in impressive italics on the map of Louisiana, is, in fact, but a small and insignificant hamlet. Aside from the tavern, kept by a jolly and generous boniface, the court house, inhabited by lawless cows and swine in the seasons of vacation, and a high gallows, with its dissevered rope dangling in the air, there is little to attract the attention of the stranger.

Solomon Northup was a name Mr. Waddill had never heard, but he was confident that if there was a slave bearing that appellation in Marksville or vicinity, his black boy Tom would know him. Tom was accordingly called, but in all his extensive circle of acquaintances there was no such personage.

The letter to Parker and Perry was dated at Bayou Boeuf. At this place, therefore, the conclusion was, I must be sought. But here a difficulty suggested itself, of a very grave character indeed. Bayou Boeuf, at its nearest point, was twenty-three miles distant, and was the name applied to the section of country extending between fifty and a hundred miles, on both sides of that stream. Thousands and thousands of slaves resided upon its shores, the remarkable richness and fertility of the soil having attracted thither a great number of planters. The information in the letter was so vague and indefinite as to render it difficult to conclude upon any specific course of proceeding. It was finally determined, however, as the only plan that presented any prospect of success, that Northup and the brother of Waddill, a student in the office of the latter, should repair to the Bayou, and traveling up one side and down the other its whole length, inquire at each plantation for me. Mr. Waddill tendered the use of his carriage, and it was definitely arranged that they should start upon the excursion early Monday morning.

It will be seen at once that this course, in all probability, would have resulted unsuccessfully. It would have been impossible for them to have gone into the fields and examine all the gangs at work. They were not aware that I was known only as Platt; and had they inquired of Epps himself, he would have stated truly that he knew nothing of Solomon Northup.

The arrangement being adopted however, there was nothing further to be done until Sunday had elapsed. The conversation between Messrs. Northup and Waddill, in the course of the afternoon, turned upon New-York politics.

"I can scarcely comprehend the nice distinctions and shades of political parties in your State," observed Mr. Waddill. "I read of soft-shells and hard-shells, hunkers and barnburners, woolly-heads and silver-grays, and am unable to understand the precise difference between them. Pray, what is it?"

Mr. Northup, re-filling his pipe, entered into quite an elaborate narrative of the origin of the various sections of parties, and concluded by saying there was another party in New-York, known as free-soilers or abolitionists. "You have seen none of those in this part of the country, I presume?" Mr. Northup remarked.

"Never, but one," answered Waddill, laughingly. "We have one here in Marksville, an eccentric creature, who preaches abolitionism as vehemently as any fanatic at the North. He is a generous, inoffensive man, but always maintaining the wrong side of an argument. It affords us a deal of amusement. He is an excellent mechanic, and almost indispensable in this community. He is a carpenter. His name is Bass."

Some further good-natured conversation was had at the expense of Bass' peculiarities, when Waddill all at once fell into a reflective mood, and asked for the mysterious letter again.

"Let me see—l-e-t m-e s-e-e!" he repeated, thoughtfully to himself, running his eyes over the letter once more. " 'Bayou Boeuf, August 15.' August 15—post-marked here. 'He that is writing for me—' Where did Bass work last summer?" he inquired, turning suddenly to his brother. His brother was unable to inform him, but rising, left the office, and soon returned with the intelligence that "Bass worked last summer somewhere on Bayou Boeuf."

"He is the man," bringing down his hand emphatically on the table, "who can tell us all about Solomon Northup," exclaimed Waddill.

Bass was immediately searched for, but could not be found. After some inquiry, it was ascertained he was at the landing on Red River. Procuring a conveyance, young Waddill and Northup were not long in traversing the few miles to the latter place. On their arrival, Bass was found, just on the point of leaving, to be absent a fortnight or more. After an introduction, Northup begged the privilege of speaking to him privately a moment. They walked together towards the river, when the following conversation ensued:

"Mr. Bass," said Northup, "allow me to ask you if you were on Bayou Boeuf last August?"

"Yes, sir, I was there in August," was the reply.

"Did you write a letter for a colored man as that place to some gentleman in Saratoga Springs?"

"Excuse me, sir, if I say that is none of your business," answered Bass, stopping and looking his interrogator searchingly in the face.

"Perhaps I am rather hasty, Mr. Bass; I beg your pardon; but I have come from the State of New-York to accomplish the purpose the writer of a letter dated the 15th of August, post-marked at Marksville, had in view. Circumstances have led me to think that you are perhaps the man who wrote it. I am in search of Solomon Northup. If you know him, I beg you to inform me frankly where he is, and I assure you the source of any information you may give me shall not be divulged, if you desire it not to be."

A long time Bass looked his new acquaintance steadily in the eyes, without opening his lips. He seemed to be doubting in his own mind if there was not an attempt to practice some deception upon him. Finally he said, deliberately—

"I have done nothing to be ashamed of. I am the man who wrote the letter. If you have come to rescue Solomon Northup, I am glad to see you."

"When did you last see him, and where is he?" Northup inquired.

"I last saw him Christmas, a week ago to-day. He is the slave of Edwin Epps, a planter on Bayou Boeuf, near Holmesville. He is not known as Solomon Northup; he is called Platt."

The secret was out—the mystery was unraveled. Through the thick, black cloud, amid whose dark and dismal shadows I had walked twelve years, broke the star that was to light me back to liberty. All mistrust and hesitation were soon thrown aside, and the two men conversed long and freely upon the subject uppermost in their thoughts. Bass expressed the interest he had taken in my behalf—his intention of going north in the Spring, and declaring that he had resolved to accomplish my emancipation, if it were in his power. He described the commencement and progress of his acquaintance with me, and listened with eager curiosity to the account given him of my family, and the history of my early life. Before separating, he drew a map of the bayou on a strip of paper with a piece of red chalk, showing the locality of Epps' plantation, and the road leading most directly to it.

Northup and his young companion returned to Marksville, where it was determined to commence legal proceedings to test the question of my right to freedom. I was made plaintiff, Mr. Northup acting as my guardian, and Edwin Epps defendant. The process to be issued was in the nature of replevin, directed to the sheriff of the parish, commanding him to take me into custody, and detain me until the decision of the court. By the time the papers were duly drawn up, it was twelve o'clock at night—too late to obtain the necessary signature of the Judge, who resided some distance out of town. Further business was therefore suspended until Monday morning.

Everything, apparently, was moving along swimmingly, until Sunday afternoon, when Waddill called at Northup's room to express his apprehension of difficulties they had not expected to encounter. Bass had become alarmed, and had placed his affairs in the hands of a person at the landing, communicating to him his intention of leaving the State.[34] This person had betrayed the confidence reposed in him to a certain extent, and a rumor began to float about the town, that the stranger at the hotel, who had been observed in the company of lawyer

Waddill, was after one of old Epps' slaves, over on the bayou. Epps was known at Marksville, having frequent occasion to visit that place during the session of the courts, and the fear entertained by Mr. Northup's adviser was, that intelligence would be conveyed to him in the night, giving him an opportunity of secreting me before the arrival of the sheriff.

This apprehension had the effect of expediting matters considerably. The sheriff, who lived in one direction from the village, was requested to hold himself in readiness immediately after midnight, while the Judge was informed he would be called upon at the same time. It is but justice to say, that the authorities at Marksville cheerfully rendered all the assistance in their power.

As soon after midnight as bail could be perfected, and the Judge's signature obtained, a carriage, containing Mr. Northup and the sheriff, driven by the landlord's son, rolled rapidly out of the village of Marksville, on the road towards Bayou Boeuf.

It was supposed that Epps would contest the issue involving my right to liberty, and it therefore suggested itself to Mr. Northup, that the testimony of the sheriff, describing my first meeting with the former, might perhaps become material on the trial. It was accordingly arranged during the ride, that, before I had an opportunity of speaking to Mr. Northup, the sheriff should propound to me certain questions agreed upon, such as the number and names of my children, the name of my wife before marriage, of places I knew at the North, and so forth. If my answers corresponded with the statements given him, the evidence must necessarily be considered conclusive.

At length, shortly after Epps had left the field, with the consoling assurance that he would soon return and *warm* us, as was stated in the conclusion of the preceding chapter, they came in sight of the plantation, and discovered us at work. Alighting from the carriage, and directing the driver to proceed to the great house, with instructions not to mention to any one the object of their errand until they met again, Northup and the sheriff turned from the highway, and came towards us across the cotton field. We observed them, on looking up at the carriage—one several rods in advance of the other. It was a singular and unusual thing to see white men approaching us in that manner, and especially at that early hour in the morning, and Uncle Abram and Patsey made some remarks, expressive of their astonishment. Walking up to Bob, the sheriff inquired:

"Where's the boy they call Platt?"

"Thar he is, massa," answered Bob, pointing to me, and twitching off his hat.

I wondered to myself what business he could possibly have with me, and turning round, gazed at him until he had approached within a step. During my long residence on the bayou, I had become familiar with the face of every planter within many miles; but this man was an utter stranger—certainly I had never seen him before.

"Your name is Platt, is it?" he asked.

"Yes, master," I responded.

Pointing towards Northup, standing a few rods distant, he demanded— "Do you know that man?"

I looked in the direction indicated, and as my eyes rested on his countenance, a world of images thronged my brain; a multitude of well-known faces—Anne's, and the dear children's, and my old dead father's; all the scenes and associations of childhood and youth; all the friends of other and happier days, appeared and disappeared, flitting and floating like dissolving shadows before the vision of my imagination, until at last the perfect memory of the man recurred to me, and throwing up my hands towards Heaven, I exclaimed, in a voice louder than I could utter in a less exciting moment—

"*Henry B. Northup!* Thank God—thank God!"

In an instant I comprehended the nature of his business, and felt that the hour of my deliverance was at hand. I started towards him, but the sheriff stepped before me.

"Stop a moment," said he; "have you any other name than Platt?"

"Solomon Northup is my name, master," I replied.

"Have you a family?" he inquired.

"I *had* a wife and three children."

"What were your children's names?"

"Elizabeth, Margaret and Alonzo."

"And your wife's name before her marriage?"

"Anne Hampton."

"Who married you?"

"Timothy Eddy, of Fort Edward."

"Where does that gentleman live?" again pointing to Northup, who remained standing in the same place where I had first recognized him.

"He lives in Sandy Hill, Washington county, New York," was the reply.

He was proceeding to ask further questions, but I pushed past him, unable longer to restrain myself. I seized my old acquaintance by both hands. I could not speak. I could not refrain from tears.

"Sol," he said at length, "I'm glad to see you."

I essayed to make some answer, but emotion choked all utterance, and I was silent. The slaves, utterly confounded, stood gazing upon the scene, their open mouths and rolling eyes indicating the utmost wonder and astonishment. For ten years I had dwelt among them, in the field and in the cabin, borne the same hardships, partaken the same fare, mingled my griefs with theirs, participated in the same scanty joys; nevertheless, not until this hour, the last I was to remain among them, had the remotest suspicion of my true name, or the slightest knowledge of my real history been entertained by any one of them.

Not a word was spoken for several minutes, during which time I clung fast to Northup, looking up into his face, fearful I should awake and find it all a dream.

"Throw down that sack," Northup added, finally, "your cotton-picking days are over. Come with us to the man you live with."

I obeyed him, and walking between him and the sheriff, we moved towards the great house. It was not until we had proceeded some distance that I had recovered my voice sufficiently to ask if my family were all living. He informed me he had seen Anne, Margaret and Elizabeth but a short time previously; that

Alonzo was also living, and all were well. My mother, however, I could never see again. As I began to recover in some measure from the sudden and great excitement which so overwhelmed me, I grew faint and weak, insomuch it was with difficulty I could walk. The sheriff took hold of my arm and assisted me, or I think I should have fallen. As we entered the yard, Epps stood by the gate, conversing with the driver. That young man, faithful to his instructions, was entirely unable to give him the least information in answer to his repeated inquiries of what was going on. By the time we reached him he was almost as much amazed and puzzled as Bob or Uncle Abram.

Shaking hands with the sheriff, and receiving an introduction to Mr. Northup, he invited them into house, ordering me, at the same time, to bring in some wood. It was some time before I succeeded in cutting an armful, having, somehow, unaccountably lost the power of wielding the axe with any manner of precision. When I entered with it at last, the table was strewn with papers, from one of which Northup was reading. I was probably longer than necessity required, in placing the sticks upon the fire, being particular as to the exact

SCENE IN THE COTTON FIELD—SOLOMON DELIVERED UP.

position of each individual one of them. I heard the words, "the said Solomon Northup," and "the deponent further says," and "free citizen of New-York," repeated frequently, and from these expressions understood that the secret I had so long retained from Master and Mistress Epps, was finally developing. I lingered as long as prudence permitted, and was about leaving the room, when Epps inquired,

"Platt, do you know this gentleman?"

"Yes, master," I replied, "I have known him as long as I can remember."

"Where does he live?"

"He lives in New-York."

"Did you ever live there?"

"Yes, master—born and bred there."

"You was free, then. Now you d—d nigger," he exclaimed, "why did you not tell me that when I bought you?"

"Master Epps," I answered, in a somewhat different tone than the one in which I had been accustomed to address him—"Master Epps, you did not take the trouble to ask me; besides, I told one of my owners—the man that kidnapped me—that I was free, and was whipped almost to death for it."

"It seems there has been a letter written for you by somebody. Now, who is it?" he demanded, authoritatively. I made no reply.

"I say, who wrote that letter?" he demanded again.

"Perhaps I wrote it myself", I said.

"You haven't been to Marksville post-office and back before light, I know."

He insisted upon my informing him, and I insisted I would not. He made many vehement threats against the man, whoever he might be, and intimated the bloody and savage vengeance he would wreak upon him, when he found him out. His whole manner and language exhibited a feeling of anger towards the unknown person who had written for me, and of fretfulness at the idea of losing so much property. Addressing Mr. Northup, he swore if he had only had an hour's notice of his coming, he would have saved him the trouble of taking me back to New-York; that he would have run me into the swamp, or some other place out of the way, where all the sheriffs on earth couldn't have found me.

I walked out into the yard, and was entering the kitchen door, when something struck me in the back. Aunt Phebe, emerging from the back door of the great house with a pan of potatoes, had thrown one of them with unnecessary violence, thereby giving me to understand that she wished to speak to me a moment confidentially. Running up to me, she whispered in my ear with great earnestness,

"Lor a'mity, Platt! what d'ye think? Dem two men come after ye. Heard'em tell massa you free—got wife and tree children back thar whar you come from. Goin' wid 'em? Fool if ye don't—wish I could go," and Aunt Phebe ran on in this manner at a rapid rate.

Presently Mistress Epps made her appearance in the kitchen. She said many things to me, and wondered why I had not told her who I was. She expressed her regret, complimenting me by saying she had rather lose any other servant on the plantation. Had Patsey that day stood in my place, the measure of my mistress' joy would have overflowed. Now there was no one left who could mend a chair or a piece of furniture—no one who was of any use about the house—no one who could play for her on the violin—and Mistress Epps was actually affected to tears.

Epps had called to Bob to bring up his saddle horse. The other slaves, also, overcoming their fear of the penalty, had left their work and come to the yard. They were standing behind the cabins, out of sight of Epps. They beckoned me to come to them, and with all the eagerness of curiosity, excited to the highest pitch, conversed with and questioned me. If I could repeat the exact words they uttered, with the same emphasis—if I could paint their several attitudes, and the expression of their countenances—it would be indeed an interesting picture. In their estimation, I had suddenly arisen to an immeasurable height—had become a being of immense importance.

The legal papers having been served, and arrangements made with Epps to meet them the next day at Marksville, Northup and the sheriff entered the carriage to return to the latter place. As I was about mounting to the driver's seat, the sheriff said I ought to bid Mr. and Mrs. Epps good-bye. I ran back to the piazza where they were standing, and taking off my hat, said,

"Good-bye, missis."

"Good-bye, Platt," said Mrs. Epps, kindly.

"Good-bye, master."

"Ah! you d—d nigger," muttered Epps, in a surly, malicious tone of voice, "you needn't feel so cussed tickled—you ain't gone yet—I'll see about this business at Marksville to-morrow."

I was only a "*nigger*" and knew my place, but felt as strongly as if I had been a white man, that it would have been an inward comfort, had I dared to have given him a parting kick. On my way back toward the carriage, Patsey ran from behind a cabin and threw her arms about my neck.

"Oh! Platt," she cried, tears streaming down her face, "you're goin' to be free—you're goin' way off yonder where we'll neber see ye any more. You've saved me a good many whippins, Platt; I'm glad you're goin' to be free—but oh! de Lord, de Lord! what'll become of me?"

I disengaged myself from her, and entered the carriage. The driver cracked his whip and away we rolled. I looked back and saw Patsey, with drooping head, half reclining on the ground; Mrs. Epps was on the piazza; Uncle Abram, and Bob, and Wiley, and Aunt Phebe stood by the gate, gazing after me. I waved my hand, but the carriage turned a bend of the bayou, hiding them from my eyes forever.

We stopped a moment at Carey's sugar house, where a great number of slaves were at work, such an establishment being a curiosity to a Northern man. Epps dashed by us on horseback at full speed—on the way, as we learned next day, to the "Pine Woods," to see William Ford, who had brought me into the country.

Tuesday, the fourth of January, Epps and his counsel, the Hon. H. Taylor,

Northup, Waddill, the Judge and sheriff of Avoyelles, and myself, met in a room in the village of Marksville. Mr. Northup stated the facts in regard to me, and presented his commission, and the affidavits accompanying it. The sheriff described the scene in the cotton field. I was also interrogated at great length. Finally, Mr. Taylor assured his client that he was satisfied, and that litigation would not only be expensive, but utterly useless. In accordance with his advice, a paper was drawn up and signed by the proper parties, wherein Epps acknowledged he was satisfied of my right to freedom, and formally surrendered me to the authorities of New-York. It was also stipulated that it be entered of record in the recorder's office of Avoyelles.*

Mr. Northup and myself immediately hastened to the landing, and taking passage on the first steamer that arrived, were soon floating down Red River, up which, with such desponding thoughts, I had been borne twelve years before.

CHAPTER XXII.

ARRIVAL IN NEW-ORLEANS—GLIMPSE OF FREEMAN—GENOIS, THE RECORDER—HIS DESCRIPTION OF SOLOMON—REACH CHARLESTON INTERRUPTED BY CUSTOM HOUSE OFFICERS—PASS THROUGH RICHMOND—ARRIVAL IN WASHINGTON—BURCH ARRESTED—SHEKELS AND THORN—THEIR TESTIMONY—BURCH ACQUITTED—ARREST OF SOLOMON—BURCH WITHDRAWS THE COMPLAINT—THE HIGHER TRIBUNAL—DEPARTURE FROM WASHINGTON—ARRIVAL AT SANDY HILL—OLD FRIENDS AND FAMILIAR SCENES—PROCEED TO GLENS FALLS—MEETING WITH ANNE, MARGARET, AND ELIZABETH—SOLOMON NORTHUP STAUNTON—INCIDENTS—CONCLUSION.

As the steamer glided on its way towards New-Orleans, *perhaps* I was not happy—*perhaps* there was no difficulty in restraining myself from dancing round the deck—perhaps I did not feel grateful to the man who had come so many hundred miles for me—perhaps I did not light his pipe, and wait and watch his word, and run at his slightest bidding. If I didn't—well, no matter.

We tarried at New-Orleans two days. During that time I pointed out the locality of Freeman's slave pen, and the room in which Ford purchased me. We happened to meet Theophilus in the street, but I did not think it worth while to renew acquaintance with him. From respectable citizens we ascertained he had become a low, miserable rowdy—a broken-down, disreputable man.

We also visited the recorder, Mr. Genois, to whom Senator Soule's letter was directed, and found him a man well deserving the wide and honorable reputation that he bears. He very generously furnished us with a sort of legal pass, over his signature and seal of office, and as it contains the recorder's description of my personal appearance, it may not be amiss to insert it here. The following is a copy:

---

*See Appendix C.

"State of Louisiana—City of New-Orleans:
Recorder's Office, Second District.

"To all to whom these presents shall come:—

"This is to certify that Henry B. Northup, Esquire, of the county of Washington, New-York, has produced before me due evidence of the freedom of Solomon, a mulatto man, aged about forty-two years, five feet, seven inches and six lines, woolly hair, and chestnut eyes, who is a native born of the State of New-York. That the said Northup, being about bringing the said Solomon to his native place, through the southern routes, the civil authorities are requested to let the aforesaid colored man Solomon pass unmolested, he demeaning well and properly.

"Given under my hand and the seal of the city of New-Orleans this 7th January, 1853.

[L. S.]   "TH. GENOIS, Recorder."

On the 8th we came to Lake Pontchartrain, by railroad, and, in due time, following the usual route, reached Charleston. After going on board the steamboat, and paying our passage at this city, Mr. Northup was called upon by a custom-house officer to explain why he had not registered his servant. He replied that he had no servant—that, as the agent of New-York, he was accompanying a free citizen of that State from slavery to freedom, and did not desire nor intend to make any registry whatever. I conceived from his conversation and manner, though I may perhaps be entirely mistaken, that no great pains would be taken to avoid whatever difficulty the Charleston officials might deem proper to create. At length, however, we were permitted to proceed, and, passing through Richmond, where I caught a glimpse of Goodin's pen, arrived in Washington January 17th, 1853.

We ascertained that both Burch and Radburn were still residing in that city. Immediately a complaint was entered with a police magistrate of Washington, against James H. Burch, for kidnapping and selling me into slavery. He was arrested upon a warrant issued by Justice Goddard, and returned before Justice Mansel, and held to bail in the sum of three thousand dollars. When first arrested, Burch was much excited, exhibiting the utmost fear and alarm, and before reaching the justice's office on Louisiana Avenue, and before knowing the precise nature of the complaint, begged the police to permit him to consult Benjamin O. Shekels, a slave trader of seventeen years' standing, and his former partner. The latter became his bail.

At ten o'clock, the 18th of January, both parties appeared before the magistrate. Senator Chase, of Ohio,[35] Hon. Orville Clark, of Sandy Hill, and Mr. Northup acted as counsel for the prosecution, and Joseph H. Bradley for the defence.

Gen. Orville Clark was called and sworn as a witness, and testified that he had known me from childhood, and that I was a free man, as was my father before me. Mr. Northup then testified to the same, and proved the facts connected with his mission to Avoyelles.

Ebenezer Radburn was then sworn for the prosecution, and testified he was forty-eight years old; that he was a resident of Washington, and had known Burch fourteen years; that in 1841 he was keeper of Williams' slave pen; that he remembered the fact of my confinement in the pen that year. At this point it was admitted by the defendant's counsel, that I had been placed in the pen by Burch in the spring of 1841, and hereupon the prosecution rested.

Benjamin O. Shekels was then offered as a witness by the prisoner. Benjamin is a large, coarse-featured man, and the reader may perhaps get a somewhat correct conception of him by reading the exact language he used in answer to the first question of defendant's lawyer. He was asked the place of his nativity, and his reply, uttered in a sort of rowdyish way, was in these very words—

"I was born in Ontario county, New-York, and *weighed fourteen pounds!*"

Benjamin was a prodigious baby! He further testified that he kept the Steamboat Hotel in Washington in 1841, and saw me there in the spring of that year. He was proceeding to state what he had heard two men say, when Senator Chase raised a legal objection, to wit, that the sayings of third persons, being hearsay, was improper evidence. The objection was overruled by the Justice, and Shekels continued, stating that two men came to his hotel and represented they had a colored man for sale; that they had an interview with Burch; that they stated they came from Georgia, but he did not remember the county; that they gave a full history of the boy, saying he was a bricklayer, and played on the violin; that Burch remarked he would purchase if they could agree; that they went out and brought the boy in, and that I was the same person. He further testified, with as much unconcern as if it was the truth, that I represented I was born and bred in Georgia; that one of the young men with me was my master; that I exhibited a great deal of regret at parting with him, and he believed "got into tears!"—nevertheless, that I insisted my master had a right to sell me; that he *ought* to sell me; and the remarkable reason I gave was, according to Shekels, because he, my master, "had been gambling and on a spree!"

He continued, in these words, copied from the minutes taken on the examination: "Burch interrogated the boy in the usual manner, told him if he purchased him he should send him south. The boy said he had no objection, that in fact he would like to go south. Burch paid $650 for him, to my knowledge. I don't know what name was given him, but think it was not Solomon. Did not know the name of either of the two men. They were in my tavern two or three hours, during which time the boy played on the violin. The bill of sale was signed in my bar-room. It was a *printed blank, filled up by Burch.* Before 1838 Burch was my partner. Our business was buying and selling slaves. After that time he was a partner of Theophilus Freeman, of New-Orleans. Burch bought here—Freeman sold there!"

Shekels, before testifying, had heard my relation of the circumstances connected with the visit to Washington with Brown and Hamilton, and therefore, it was, undoubtedly, he spoke of "two men," and of my playing on the violin. Such was his fabrication, utterly untrue, and yet there was found in Washington a man who endeavored to corroborate him.

Benjamin A. Thorn testified he was at Shekels' in 1841, and saw a colored boy playing on a fiddle. "Shekels said he was for sale. Heard his master tell him he should sell him. The boy acknowledged to me he was a slave. I was not present when the money was paid. Will not swear positively this is the boy. The master *came near shedding tears: I think the boy did!* I have been engaged in the business of taking slaves south, off and on, for twenty years. When I can't do that I do something else."

I was then offered as a witness, but, objection being made, the court decided my evidence inadmissible. It was rejected solely on the ground that I was a colored man—the fact of my being a free citizen of New-York not being disputed.

Shekels having testified there was a bill of sale executed, Burch was called upon by the prosecution to produce it, inasmuch as such a paper would corroborate the testimony of Thorn and Shekels. The prisoner's counsel saw the necessity of exhibiting it, or giving some reasonable explanation for its non-production. To effect the latter, Burch himself was offered as a witness in his own behalf. It was contended by counsel for the people, that such testimony should not be allowed—that it was in contravention of every rule of evidence, and if permitted would defeat the ends of justice. His testimony, however, was received by the court! He made oath that such a bill of sale had been drawn up and signed, *but he had lost it, and did not know what had become of it!* Thereupon the magistrate was requested to dispatch a police officer to Burch's residence, with directions to bring his books, containing his bills of sales for the year 1841. The request was granted, and before any measure could be taken to prevent it, the officer had obtained possession of the books, and brought them into court. The sales for the year 1841 were found, and carefully examined, but no sale of myself, by any name, was discovered!

Upon this testimony the court held the fact to be established, that Burch came innocently and honestly by me, and accordingly he was discharged.

An attempt was then made by Burch and his satellites, to fasten upon me the charge that I had conspired with the two white men to defraud him—with what success, appears in an extract taken from an article in the New-York Times, published a day or two subsequent to the trial: "The counsel for the defendant had drawn up, before the defendant was discharged, an affidavit, signed by Burch, and had a warrant out against the colored man for a conspiracy with the two white men before referred to, to defraud Burch out of six hundred and twenty-five dollars. The warrant was served, and the colored man arrested and brought before officer Goddard. Burch and his witnesses appeared in court, and H. B. Northup appeared as counsel for the colored man, stating he was ready to proceed as counsel on the part of the defendant, and asking no delay whatever. Burch, after consulting privately a short time with Shekels, stated to the magistrate that he wished him to dismiss the complaint, as he would not proceed farther with it. Defendant's counsel stated to the magistrate that if the complaint was withdrawn, it must be without the request or consent of the defendant. Burch then asked the magistrate to let him have the complaint and the warrant, and he took them. The counsel for the defendant objected to his receiving them, and insisted they should remain as part of the records of the court, and that the court should endorse the proceedings which had been had under the process. Burch delivered them up, and the court rendered a judgment of discontinuance by the request of the prosecutor, and filed it in his office."

There may be those who will affect to believe the statement of the slave-trader—those, in whose minds his allegations will weigh heavier than mine. I am a poor colored man—one of a down-trodden and degraded race, whose humble voice may not be heeded by the oppressor—but *knowing* the truth, and with a full sense of my accountability, I do solemnly declare before men, and before God, that any charge or assertion, that I conspired directly or indirectly with any person or persons to sell myself; that any other account of my visit to Washington, my capture and imprisonment in Williams' slave pen, than is contained in these pages, is utterly and absolutely false. I never played on the violin in Washington. I never was in the Steamboat Hotel, and never saw Thorn or Shekels, to my knowledge, in my life, until last January. The story of the trio of slave-traders is a fabrication as absurd as it is base and unfounded. Were it true, I should not have turned aside on my way back to liberty for the purpose of prosecuting Burch. I should have *avoided* rather than sought him. I should have known that such a step would have resulted in rendering me infamous. Under the circumstances—longing as I did to behold my family, and elated with the prospect of returning home—it is an outrage upon probability to suppose I would have run the hazard, not only of exposure, but of a criminal prosecution and conviction, by voluntarily placing myself in the position I did, if the statements of Burch and his confederates contain a particle of truth. I took pains to seek him out, to confront him in a court of law, charging him with the crime of kidnapping; and the only motive that impelled me to this step, was a burning sense of the wrong he had inflicted upon me, and a desire to bring him to justice. He was acquitted, in the manner, and by such means as have been described. A human tribunal has permitted him to escape; but there is another and a higher tribunal, where false testimony will not prevail, and where I am willing, so far at least as these statements are concerned, to be judged at last.

We left Washington on the 20th of January, and proceeding by the way of Philadelphia, New-York, and Albany, reached Sandy Hill in the night of the 21st. My heart overflowed with happiness as I looked around upon old familiar scenes, and found myself in the midst of friends of other days. The following morning I started, in company with several acquaintances, for Glens Falls, the residence of Anne and our children.

As I entered their comfortable cottage, Margaret was the first that met me. She did not recognize me. When I left her, she was but seven years old, a little prattling girl, playing with her toys. Now she was grown to womanhood—was married, with a bright-eyed boy standing by her side. Not forgetful of his enslaved, unfortunate grand-father, she had named the child Solomon Northup Staunton. When told who I was, she was overcome with emotion, and unable to speak. Presently Elizabeth entered the room, and Anne came running from the hotel, having been informed of my arrival. They embraced me, and with tears flowing down their cheeks, hung upon my neck. But I draw a veil over a scene which can better be imagined than described.

When the violence of our emotions had subsided to a sacred joy—when the household gathered round the fire, that sent out its warm and crackling comfort through the room, we conversed of the thousand events that had occurred—the hopes and fears, the joys and sorrows, the trials and troubles we had each experienced during the long separation. Alonzo was absent in the western part of the State. The boy had written to his mother a short time previous, of the prospect of his obtaining sufficient money to purchase my freedom. From his earliest years, that had been the chief object of his thoughts and his ambition. They knew I was in bondage. The letter written on board the brig, and Clem Ray himself, had given them that information. But where I was, until the arrival of Bass' letter, was a matter of conjecture. Elizabeth and Margaret once returned from school—so Anne informed me—weeping bitterly. On inquiring the cause of the children's sorrow, it was found that, while studying geography, their attention had been attracted to the picture of slaves working in the cotton-field, and an overseer following them with his whip. It reminded them of the sufferings father might be, and, as it happened, actually *was,* enduring in the South. Numerous

ARRIVAL HOME, AND FIRST MEETING WITH HIS WIFE AND CHILDREN.

incidents, such as these, were related—incidents showing they still held me in constant remembrance, but not, perhaps, of sufficient interest to the reader, to be recounted.

My narrative is at an end. I have no comments to make upon the subject of Slavery. Those who read this book may form their own opinions of the "peculiar institution." What it may be in other States, I do not profess to know; what it is in the region of Red River, is truly and faithfully delineated in these pages. This is no fiction, no exaggeration. If I have failed in anything, it has been in presenting to the reader too prominently the bright side of the picture. I doubt not hundreds have been as unfortunate as myself; that hundreds of free citizens have been kidnapped and sold into slavery, and are at this moment wearing out their lives on plantations in Texas and Louisiana. But I forbear. Chastened and subdued in spirit by the sufferings I have borne, and thankful to that good Being through whose mercy I have been restored to happiness and liberty, I hope henceforward to lead an upright though lowly life, and rest at last in the church yard where my father sleeps.[36]

ROARING RIVER.

A REFRAIN OF THE RED RIVER PLANTATION.

"Harper's creek and roarin' ribber,
Thar, my dear, we'll live forebber;
Den we'll go to de Ingin nation,
All I want in dis creation,
Is pretty little wife and big plantation.

CHORUS.
Up dat oak and down dat ribber,
Two overseers and one little nigger."

APPENDIX.

A.—Page 292.

CHAP. 375.

An act more effectually to protect the free citizens of this State from being kidnapped, or reduced to Slavery.

[Passed May 14, 1840]

The People of the State of New-York, represented in Senate and Assembly, do enact as follows:

§1. Whenever the Governor of this State shall receive information satisfactory to him that any free citizen or any inhabitant of this State has been kidnapped or transported away out of this State, into any other State or Territory of the United States, for the purpose of being there held in slavery; or that such free citizen or inhabitant is wrongfully seized, imprisoned or held in slavery in any of the States or Territories of the United States, on the allegation or pretence that such a person is a slave, or by color of any usage or rule of law prevailing in such State or Territory, is deemed or taken to be a slave, or not entitled of right to the personal liberty belonging to a citizen; it shall be the duty of the said Governor to take such measures as he shall deem necessary to procure such person to be restored to his liberty and returned to this State. The Governor is hereby authorized to appoint and employ such agent or agents as he shall deem necessary to effect the restoration and return of such person; and shall furnish the said agent with such credentials and instructions as will be likely to accomplish the object of his appointment. The Governor may determine the compensation to be allowed to such agent for his services besides his necessary expenses.

§2. Such agent shall proceed to collect the proper proof to establish the right of such person to his freedom, and shall perform such journeys, take such measures, institute and procure to be prosecuted such legal proceedings, under the direction of the Governor, as shall be necessary to procure such person to be restored to his liberty and returned to this State.

§3. The accounts for all services and expenses incurred in carrying this act into effect shall be audited by the Comptroller, and paid by the Treasurer on his warrant, out of any moneys in the treasury of this State not otherwise appropriated. The Treasurer may advance, on the warrant of the Comptroller, to such agent, such sum or sums as the Governor shall certify to be reasonable advances to enable him to accomplish the purposes of his appointment, for which advance such agent shall account, on the final audit of his warrant.

§4. This act shall take effect immediately.

B.—Page 292.

MEMORIAL OF ANNE.

To His Excellency, the Governor of the State of New-York:

The memorial of Anne Northup, of the village of Glens Falls, in the county of Warren, State aforesaid, respectfully sets forth—

That your memorialist, whose maiden name was Anne Hampton, was forty-four years old on the 14th day of March last, and was married to Solomon Northup, then of Fort Edward, in the county of Washington and State aforesaid, on the 25th day of December, A. D. 1828, by Timothy Eddy, then a Justice of the Peace. That the said Solomon, after such marriage, lived and kept house with your memorialist in said town until 1830, when he removed with his said family to the town of Kingsbury in said county, and remained there about three years, and then removed to Saratoga Springs in the State aforesaid, and continued to reside in said Saratoga Springs and the adjoining town until about the year 1841, as near as the time can be recollected, when the said Solomon started to go to the city of Washington, in the District of Columbia, since which time your memorialist has never seen her said husband.

And your memorialist further states, that in the year 1841 she received information by a letter directed to Henry B. Northup, Esq., of Sandy Hill, Washington county, New-York, and post-marked at New-Orleans, that said Solomon had been kidnapped in Washington, put on board of a vessel, and was then in such vessel in New-Orleans, but could not tell how he came in that situation, nor what his destination was.

That your memorialist ever since the last mentioned period has been wholly unable to obtain any information of where the said Solomon was, until the month of September last, when another letter was received from the said Solomon, post-marked at Marksville, in the parish of Avoyelles, in the State of Louisiana, stating that he was held there as a slave, which statement your memorialist believes to be true.

That the said Solomon is about forty-five years of age, and never resided out of the State of New-York, in which State he was born, until the time he went to Washington city, as before stated. That the said Solomon Northup is a free citizen of the State of New-York, and is now wrongfully held in slavery, in or near Marksville, in the parish of Avoyelles, in the State of Louisiana, one of the United States of America, on the allegation or pretence that the said Solomon is a slave.

And your memorialist further states that Mintus Northup was the reputed father of said Solomon, and was a negro, and died at Fort Edward, on the 22d day of November, 1829; that the mother of said Solomon was a mulatto, or three quarters white, and died in the county of Oswego, New-York, some five or six years ago, as your memorialist was informed and believes, and never was a slave.

That your memorialist and her family are poor and wholly unable to pay or sustain any portion of the expenses of restoring the said Solomon to his freedom.

Your excellency is entreated to employ such agent or agents as shall be deemed necessary to effect the restoration and return of said Solomon Northup, in pursuance of an act of the Legislature of the State of New-York, passed May 14th, 1840, entitled "An act more effectually to protect the free citizens of this State from being kidnappd or reduced to slavery." And your memorialist will ever pray.

    (Signed,)   ANNE NORTHUP.
Dated November 19, 1852.

STATE OF NEW-YORK:
> Washington county, ss.

Anne Northup, of the village of Glens Falls, in the county of Warren, in said State, being duly sworn, doth depose and say that she signed the above memorial, and that the statements therein contained are true.

(Signed,)   ANNE NORTHUP.

Subscribed and sworn before me this
> 19th November, 1852.
> CHARLES HUGHES, Justice Peace.

We recommend that the Governor appoint Henry B. Northup, of the village of Sandy Hill, Washington county, New-York, as one of the agents to procure the restoration and return of Solomon Northup, named in the foregoing memorial of Anne Northup.

Dated at Sandy Hill, Washington Co., N. Y.,
> November 20, 1852.   (Signed,)

PETER HOLBROOK,	DANIEL SWEET,
B. F. HOAG,	ALMON CLARK,
CHARLES HUGHES,	BENJAMIN FERRIS,
E. D. BAKER,	JOSIAH H. BROWN
ORVILLE CLARK.	

STATE OF NEW-YORK:
> Washington County, ss:

Josiah Hand, of the village of Sandy Hill, in said county, being duly sworn, says, he is fifty-seven years old, and was born in said village, and has always resided there; that he has known Mintus Northup and his son Solomon, named in the annexed memorial of Anne Northup, since previous to the year 1816; that Mintus Northup then, and until the time of his death, cultivated a farm in the towns of Kingsbury and Fort Edward, from the time deponent first knew him until he died; that said Mintus and his wife, the mother of said Solomon Northup, were reported to be free citizens of New-York, and deponent believes they were so free; that said Solomon Northup was born in said county of Washington, as deponent believes, and was married Dec. 25th, 1828, in Fort Edward aforesaid, and his said wife and three children—two daughters and one son—are now living in Glens Falls, Warren county, New-York, and that the said Solomon Northup always resided in said county of Washington, and its immediate vicinity, until about 1841, since which time deponent has not seen him, but deponent has been credibly informed, and as he verily believes truly, the said Solomon is now wrongfully held as a slave in the State of Louisiana. And deponent further says that Anne Northup, named in the said memorial, is entitled to credit, and deponent believes the statements contained in her said memorial are true.

(Signed,)   JOSIAH HAND.

Subscribed and sworn before me this
19th day of November, 1852,   CHARLES HUGHES, Justice Peace.

STATE OF NEW-YORK:
> Washington county, ss:

Timothy Eddy, of Fort Edward, in said county, being duly sworn, says he is now over — years old, and has been a resident of said town more than — years last past, and that he was well acquainted with Solomon Northup, named in the annexed memorial of Anne Northup, and with his father, Mintus Northup, who was a negro,—the wife of said Mintus was a mulatto woman; that said Mintus Northup and his said wife and family, two sons, Joseph and Solomon, resided in said town of Fort Edward for several years before the year 1828, and said Mintus died in said town A.D. 1829, as deponent believes. And deponent further says that he was a Justice of the Peace in said town in the year 1828, and as such Justice of the Peace, he, on the 25th day of Dec'r, 1828, joined the said Solomon Northup in marriage with Anne Hampton, who is the same person who has subscribed the annexed memorial. And deponent expressly says, that said Solomon was a free citizen of the State of New-York, and always lived in said State, until about the year A.D. 1840, since which time deponent has not seen him, but has recently been informed, and as deponent believes truly, that said Solomon Northup is wrongfully held in slavery in or near Marksville, in the parish of Avoyelles, in the State of Louisiana. And deponent further says, that said Mintus Northup was nearly sixty years old at the time of his death, and was, for more than thirty years next prior to his death, a free citizen of the State of New-York.

And this deponent further says, that Anne Northup, the wife of said Solomon Northup, is of good character and reputation, and her statements, as contained in the memorial hereto annexed, are entitled to full credit.

(Signed,)   TIMOTHY EDDY.

Subscribed and sworn before me this
19th day of November, 1852,   TIM'Y STOUGHTON, Justice

STATE OF NEW-YORK:
        Washington County, ss:
        Henry B. Northup, of the village of Sandy Hill, in said county, being duly sworn, says, that he is forty-seven years old, and has always lived in said county; that he knew Mintus Northup, named in the annexed memorial, from deponent's earliest recollection until the time of his death, which occurred at Fort Edward, in said county, in 1829; that deponent knew the children of said Mintus, viz, Solomon and Joseph; that they were both born in the county of Washington aforesaid, as deponent believes; that deponent was well acquainted with said Solomon, who is the same person named in the annexed memorial of Anne Northup, from his childhood; and that said Solomon always resided in said county of Washington and the adjoining counties until about the year 1841; that said Solomon could read and write; that said Solomon and his mother and father were free citizens of the State of New-York; that sometime about the year 1841 this deponent received a letter from said Solomon, post-marked New-Orleans, stating that while on business at Washington city, he had been kidnapped, and his free papers taken from him, and he was then on board a vessel, in irons, and was claimed as a slave, and that he did not know his destination, which the deponent believes to be true, and he urged this deponent to assist in procuring his restoration to freedom; that deponent has lost or mislaid said letter, and cannot find it; that deponent has since endeavored to find where said Solomon was, but could get no farther trace of him until Sept. last, when this deponent ascertained by a letter purporting to have been written by the direction of said Solomon, that said Solomon was held and claimed as a slave in or near Marksville, in the parish of Avoyelles, Louisiana, and

that this deponent verily believes that such information is true, and that said Solomon is now wrongfully held in slavery at Marksville aforesaid.

(Signed,)   HENRY B. NORTHUP.

Subscribed and sworn to before me
this 20th day of November, 1852, CHARLES HUGHES, J. P.

STATE OF NEW-YORK:
           Washington County, ss

Nicholas C. Northup, of the village of Sandy Hill, in said county, being duly sworn, doth depose and say, that he is now fifty-eight years of age, and has known Solomon Northup, mentioned in the annexed memorial of Ann Northup, ever since he was born. And this deponent saith that said Solomon is now about forty-five years old, and was born in the county of Washington aforesaid, or in the county of Essex, in said State, and always resided in the State of New-York until about the year 1841, since which time deponent has not seen him or known where he was, until a few weeks since, deponent was informed, and believes truly, that said Solomon was held in slavery in the State of Louisiana. Deponent further says, that said Solomon was married in the town of Fort Edward, in said county, about twenty-four years ago, and that his wife and two daughters and one son now reside in the village of Glens Falls, county of Warren, in said State of New-York. And this deponent swears positively that said Solomon Northup is a citizen of said State of New-York, and was born free, and from his earliest infancy lived and resided in the counties of Washington, Essex, Warren and Saratoga, in the State of New-York, and that his said wife and children have never resided out of said counties since the time said Solomon was married; that deponent knew the father of said Solomon Northup; that said father was a negro, named Mintus Northup, and died in the town of Fort Edward, in the county of Washington, State of New-York, on the 22d day of November, A.D. 1829, and was buried in the grave-yard in Sandy Hill aforesaid; that for more than thirty years before his death he lived in the counties of Essex, Washington and Rensselaer and State of New-York, and left a wife and two sons, Joseph and the said Solomon, him surviving; that the mother of said Solomon was a mulatto woman, and is now dead, and died, as deponent believes, in Oswego county, New-York, within five or six years past. And this deponent further states, that the mother of the said Solomon Northup was not a slave at the time of the birth of said Solomon Northup, and has not been a slave at any time within the last fifty years.

(Signed,)   N. C. NORTHUP.

Subscribed and sworn before me this 19th day
of November, 1852.   CHARLES HUGHES, Justice Peace.

STATE OF NEW-YORK:
           Washington County, ss.

Orville Clark, of the village of Sandy Hill, in the county of Washington, State of New-York, being duly sworn, doth depose and say—that he, this deponent, is over fifty years of age; that in the years 1810 and 1811, or most of the time of those years, this deponent resided at Sandy Hill, aforesaid, and at Glens Falls; that this deponent then knew Mintus Northup, a black or colored man; he was then a free man, as this deponent believes and always understood; that the wife of said Mintus Northup, and mother of Solomon, was a free woman; that from the year 1818 until the time of the death of said Mintus Northup, about the year 1829, this deponent was very well acquainted with the said Mintus Northup; that he was a respectable man in the community in which he resided, and was a free man, so taken and esteemed by all his acquaintances; that this deponent has also been and was acquainted with his son Solomon Northup, from the said year 1818 until he left this part of the country, about the year 1840 or 1841; that he married Anne Hampton, daughter of William Hampton, a near neighbor of this deponent; that the said Anne, wife of said Solomon, is now living and resides in this vicinity; that the said Mintus Northup and William Hampton were both reputed and esteemed in this community as respectable men. And this deponent saith that the said Mintus Northup and his family, and the said William Hampton and his family, from the earliest recollection and acquaintance of this deponent with him (as far back as 1810,) were always reputed, esteemed, and taken to be, and this deponent believes, truly so, free citizens of the State of New-York. This deponent knows the said William Hampton, under the laws of this State, was entitled to vote at our elections, and he believes the said Mintus Northup also was entitled as a free citizen with the property qualification. And this deponent further saith, that the said Solomon Northup, son of said Mintus, and husband of said Anne Hampton, when he left this State, was at the time thereof a free citizen of the State of New-York. And this deponent further saith, that said Anne Hampton, wife of Solomon Northup, is a respectable woman, of good character, and I would believe her statements, and do believe the facts set forth in her memorial to his excellency, the Governor, in relation to her said husband, are true.

    (Signed,)   ORVILLE CLARK.
Sworn before me, November
19th, 1852.

        U. G. Paris, Justice of the Peace.

State of New-York:
       Washington County, ss.

    Benjamin Ferris, of the village of Sandy Hill, in said county, being duly sworn, doth depose and say—that he is now fifty-seven years old, and has resided in said village forty-five years; that he was as well acquainted with Mintus Northup, named in the annexed memorial of Anne Northup, from the year 1816 to the time of his death, which occurred at Fort Edward, in the fall of 1829; that he knew the children of the said Mintus, namely, Joseph Northup and Solomon Northup, and that the said Solomon is the same person named in said memorial; that said Mintus resided in the said county of Washington to the time of his death, and was, during all that time, a free citizen of the said State of New-York, as deponent verily believes; that said memorialist, Anne Northup, is a woman of good character, and the statement contained in her memorial is entitled to credit.

    (Signed)   BENJAMIN FERRIS.
Sworn before me, November
19th, 1852.

        U. G. Paris, Justice of the Peace.

State of New-York:
       Executive Chamber, Albany, Nov. 30, 1852.

    I hereby certify that the foregoing is a correct copy of certain proofs filed in the Executive Department, upon which I have appointed Henry B. Northup an Agent of this State, to take proper proceedings in behalf of Solomon Northup therein mentioned.

    (Signed,)   WASHINGTON HUNT.

By the Governor.
    J. F. R., Private Secretary.

STATE OF NEW-YORK:
        Executive Department.
WASHINGTON HUNT, *Governor of the State of New-York, to whom it may concern, greeting:*
    Whereas, I have received information on oath, which is satisfactory to me, that Solomon Northup, who is a free citizen of this State, is wrongfully held in slavery, in the State of Louisiana:
    And whereas, it is made my duty, by the laws of this State, to take such measures as I shall deem necessary to procure any citizen so wrongfully held in slavery, to be restored to his liberty and returned to this State:
    Be it known, that in pursuance of chapter 375 of the laws of this State, passed in 1840, I have constituted, appointed and employed Henry B. Northup, Esquire, of the county of Washington, in this State, an Agent, with full power to effect the restoration of said Solomon Northup, and the said Agent is hereby authorized and empowered to institute such proper and legal proceedings, to procure such evidence, retain such counsel, and finally to take such measures as will be most likely to accomplish the object of his said appointment.
    He is also instructed to proceed to the State of Louisiana with all convenient dispatch, to execute the agency hereby created.
    In witness whereof, I have hereunto subscribed my name, and affixed the privy seal of the State, at Albany, this 23d day of November, in the year of our Lord 1852.
    (Signed,)   WASHINGTON HUNT.
JAMES F. RUGGLES, Private Secretary.

————

C.—Page 301.

STATE OF LOUISIANA:
        Parish of Avoyelles.
    Before me, Aristide Barbin, Recorder of the parish of Avoyelles, personally came and appeared Henry B. Northup, of the county of Washington, State of New-York, who hath declared that by virtue of a commission to him as agent of the State of New-York, given and granted by his excellency, Washington Hunt, Governor of the said State of New-York, bearing date the 23d day of November, 1852, authorizing and empowering him, the said Northup, to pursue and recover from slavery a free man of color, called Solomon Northup, who is a free citizen of the State of New-York, and who was kidnapped and sold into slavery, in the State of Louisiana, and now in the possession of Edwin Epps, of the State of Louisiana, of the Parish of Avoyelles; he, the said agent, hereto signing, acknowledges that the said Edwin has this day given and surrendered to him as such agent, the said Solomon Northup, free man of color, as aforesaid, in order that he be restored to his freedom, and carried back to the said State of New-York, pursuant to said commission, the said Edwin Epps being satisfied from the proofs produced by said agent, that the said Solomon Northup is entitled to his freedom. The parties consenting that a certified copy of said power of attorney be annexed to this act.
    Done and signed at Marksville, parish of Avoyelles, this fourth day of January,

one thousand eight hundred and fifty-three, in the presence of the undersigned, legal and competent witnesses, who have also hereto signed.

      (Signed,)   HENRY B. NORTHUP.

                                                        EDWIN EPPS.

                                              ADE. BARBIN, Recorder.

Witnesses:

      H. TAYLOR,

      JOHN P. WADDILL.

STATE OF LOUISIANA:

      Parish of Avoyelles.

      I do hereby certify the foregoing to be a true and correct copy of the original on file and of record in my office.

[L. S.]   (Given under my hand and seal of office as Recorder in and for the parish of Avoyelles, this 4th day of January, A.D. 1853.

      (Signed,)   ADE. BARBIN, Recorder.

THE END

1. Eakin and Logsdon, *Twelve Years,* xiv; Born, "Solomon Northup," 540.

2. Cited in Eakin and Logsdon, *Twelve Years,* ix.

3. Stowe, *Key,* 174.

4. Logsdon, "Northup, Solomon," 474.

5. Eakin and Logsdon, *Twelve Years,* xiii–xiv.

6. Cited in Starling, *Slave Narrative,* 174.

7. Eakin and Logsdon, *Twelve Years,* xvii–xxiii; Logsdon, "Northup, Solomon," 474.

8. Harriet Beecher Stowe's 1853 *A Key to Uncle Tom's Cabin* is a large compendium of documentary material in support of the incidents and settings of her novel *Uncle Tom's Cabin.*

9. William Cowper (1731–1800), *The Task.* Cowper was a forerunner of the British romantic poets, and wrote a number of antislavery verses. *The Task* (1785) was probably his most famous poem.

10. Until 1821, New Yorkers had to own property valued at one hundred dollars or more in order to vote; afterward, however, the qualification rose to $250 for blacks and was dropped altogether for whites. Eakin and Logsdon, *Twelve Years,* 5.

11. William Henry Harrison (1773–1844), then U.S. president.

12. These symptoms were most likely caused by a dose of belladonna, laudanum, or a combination of the two. Eakin and Logsdon, *Twelve Years,* 18.

13. Actually James H. Birch. Ibid., 21.

14. As Northup would learn well after his return to freedom, "Brown and Hamilton" were indeed responsible for Northup's kidnapping. They were positively identified as Alexander Merrill and Joseph Russell in 1854. Shortly after Northup's disappearance, they had been seen in Baltimore by an old acquaintance, Thaddeus St. John, who had previously noticed their Negro friend. Now the pair sported recent haircuts, clean-shaven faces, new clothes, ivory canes, and gold watches. When St. John jokingly suggested that they must have sold their former companion for $500, Merrill told him to raise the price by $150. Ibid., xvii–xviii.

15. Although Northup was frustrated in his designs to seize the brig *Orleans,* its sister ship, the *Creole,* was seized by its slave passengers in October 1841, several months after Northup's departure from the same port. Logsdon, "Northup, Solomon," 473.

16. A village for ship pilots.

17. The initial symptoms of smallpox include fever, aching, and prostration. An eruption then occurs, which spreads over the entire body; within a week, the lesions become blisterlike and pustular.

18. The Sabine marks the Texas-Louisiana border.

19. Robert Fulton (1765–1815) built the first commercially successful steamboat, and was popularly considered its inventor.

20. Actually John M. Tibaut. Eakin and Logsdon, *Twelve Years,* 73.

21. A character from William Cowper's comic poem, "The Diverting History of John Gilpin," who was seated on a capricious and very speedy runaway horse.

22. Actually the Cocodrie (crocodile) Swamp. Eakin and Logsdon, *Twelve Years,* 103.

23. For fifteen hundred dollars. Ibid., 120.

24. *Isaiah* 40:7.

25. General (and later President) Andrew Jackson (1767–1845) was the greatest American military hero of the War of 1812.

26. Caroline Elizabeth Sarah Norton (1808–77), "A Destiny."

27. The character of Sambo, a widespread stereotype of plantation blacks throughout nineteenth- and early twentieth-century culture, included imagery much like that found here. As John W. Blassingame puts it, "Indolent, faithful, humorous, loyal, dishonest, superstitious, improvident, and musical, Sambo was inevitably a clown and congenitally docile." *Slave Community,* 225.

28. See note 33, below.

29. Jersey.

30. Probably *ewe,* which is still pronounced *yo* in many parts of the South.

31. To curry is to prepare tanned hides for use by coloring them.

32. Alfred, Lord Tennyson (1809–92), "Conclusion."

33. The bit was a Spanish *real,* equivalent to one-eighth of a dollar; the picayune was a Spanish half-*real,* one-sixteenth of a dollar.

34. Samuel Bass actually remained in hiding in Marksville in the home of a free black woman until his death of natural causes eight months later. Eakin and Logsdon, *Twelve Years,* 233; Logsdon, "Northup, Solomon," 474.

35. Salmon Portland Chase (1808–73) defended fugitives so often he became known as "attorney general for runaway slaves." He was later elected governor of Ohio, served as Lincoln's secretary of the treasury, and became chief justice in 1864.

36. This wish was sadly disregarded, and Northup was not buried next to his father. Eakin and Logsdon, *Twelve Years,* xxiii.

JOHN BROWN

FROM A COLODION BY J. DUDMAN.

JOHN BROWN (1818– ?; not to be confused with the abolitionist John Brown, of Harper's Ferry fame) underwent—and witnessed—the most brutal treatment described in any slave narrative. Not for the faint of heart, his *Slave Life in Georgia* is in part a litany of horrors. As William Andrews points out, the narrative

> achieves the unpleasant distinction of unveiling the most appalling atrocities yet seen in Afro-American autobiography. . . . The prose of *Slave Life in Georgia* renders the unspeakable almost commonplace. In addition to the many floggings, paddlings, brandings, and burnings recounted in his story, Brown exposed in clinical detail a manifestation of 19th-century racism that is particularly chilling to the consciousness of post-Holocaust readers: sickening "experiments" done on Brown himself by a renowned Georgia doctor intent on ascertaining "how deep my black skin went."[1]

Brown's treatment of these horrors in his narrative is admirably matter-of-fact, even at times understated. His cool, unemotional demeanor, much like that of Moses Roper, renders his account more believable—and more chilling. The narrative, however, is not unrelentingly bleak: it is enriched by Brown's almost comic geographical ignorance and his unforgettable description of his first meal with the Quakers.

John Brown was illiterate; his narrative was written by Louis A. Chamerovzow, a British abolitionist editor. It went through two identical editions in 1855, both British, and was translated into Dutch and German, but was not published in the United States until this century.

SLAVE LIFE IN GEORGIA:

A NARRATIVE

OF THE

LIFE, SUFFERINGS, AND ESCAPE

OF

JOHN BROWN,

𝔄 𝔉𝔲𝔤𝔦𝔱𝔦𝔳𝔢 𝔖𝔩𝔞𝔳𝔢,

NOW IN ENGLAND.

EDITED BY

L. A. CHAMEROVZOW,[2]

SECRETARY OF THE BRITISH AND FOREIGN ANTI-SLAVERY SOCIETY.

LONDON:
MAY BE HAD ON APPLICATION TO THE EDITOR,
AT No. 27, NEW BROAD STREET,
AND OF ALL BOOKSELLERS.

1855.

PREFACE.

THE Editor is conscious that the following Narrative has only its truthfulness to recommend it to favourable consideration. It is nothing more than it purports to be, namely; a plain, unvarnished tale of real Slave-life, conveyed as nearly as possible in the language of the subject of it, and written under his dictation. It would have been easy to fill up the outline of the picture here and there, with dark shadows, and to impart a heightened dramatic colouring to some of the incidents; but he preferred allowing the narrator to speak for himself, and the various events recorded to tell their own tale. He believes few persons will peruse it unmoved; or arise from a perusal of it without feeling an increased abborrence of the inhuman system under which, at this hour, in the United States of America alone, three millions and a half of men, women, and children, are held as "chattels personal," by thirty-seven thousand and fifty-five individuals, many of them professing Ministers of the Gospel, and defenders of "the peculiar institution."

In undertaking to prepare this volume for the press, the Editor's object was two-fold, namely; to advance the anti-slavery cause by the diffusion of information; and to promote the success of the project John Brown has formed, to advance himself by his own exertions, and to set an example to others of his "race." If by the little the Editor has done to render the volume interesting, he should secure for it a fair meed of popular favour, these two objects will be certainly accomplished, and his labour will not have been expended in vain.

27, *New Broad Street,*
  London, January, 1855.

CHAPTER I.

MY CHILDHOOD AND FIRST TROUBLES.

MY name is John Brown. How I came to take it, I will explain in due time. When in Slavery, I was called Fed. Why I was so named, I cannot tell. I never knew myself by any other name, nor always by that; for it is common for slaves to answer to any name, as it may suit the humour of the master. I do not know how old I am, but think I may be any age between thirty-five and forty. I fancy I must be about thirty-seven or eight; as nearly as I can guess. I was raised on Betty Moore's estate, in Southampton County, Virginia,[3] about three miles from Jerusalem Court house and the little Nottoway river. My mother belonged to Betty Moore. Her name was Nancy; but she was called Nanny. My father's name was Joe. He was owned by a planter named Benford, who lived at Northampton, in the same State. I believe my father and his family were bred on Benford's plantation. His father had been stolen from Africa. He was of the Eboe tribe.[4] I remember seeing him once, when he came to visit my mother. He was very black. I never saw him but that one time, and though I was quite small, I have a distinct recollection of him. He and my mother were separated, in consequence of his master's going further off, and then my mother was forced to take another husband. She had three children by my father; myself, and a brother and sister, twins. My brother's name was Silas, and my sister's Lucy. My mother's second husband's name was Lamb. He was the property of a neighbouring planter and miller named Collier. By him she had three children; two boys, Curtis and Cain, and a girl between them called Iraene. We all lived together with our mother, in a log cabin, containing two rooms, one of which we occupied; the other being inhabited by my mother's niece, Annikie, and her children. It had a mud floor; the sides were of wattle and daub, and the roof was thatched over. Our sleeping place was made by driving a forked stake into the floor, which served to support a cross piece of wood, one end of it resting in the crotch, the other against the shingle that formed the wall. A plank or two across, over the top, completed the bed-room arrangements, with the exception of another plank on which we laid straw or cotton-pickings, and over that a blanket.

Our mistress Betty Moore was an old, big woman, about seventy, who wore spectacles and took snuff. I remember her very well, for she used to call us children up to the big house every morning, and give us a dose of garlic and rue to keep us "wholesome," as she said, and make us "grow likely for market." After swallowing our dose, she would make us run round a great sycamore tree in the yard, and if we did not run fast enough to please her, she used to make us nimbler by laying about us with a cow-hide. She always carried this instrument dangling at her side, like ladies in this country wear their scissors. It was painted blue, and we used to call it the "blue lizard." She used to like to see her people constantly employed, and would make us all set to work at night, after our day's labour was over, picking the seed out of cotton. We had a hard time of it with the old lady.

At this period, my principal occupation was to nurse my little brother whilst my mother worked in the field. Almost all slave children have to do the nursing; the big taking care of the small, who often come poorly off in consequence. I know this was my little brother's case. I used to lay him in the shade, under a tree, sometimes, and go to play, or curl myself up under a hedge, and take a sleep. He would wake me by his screaming, when I would find him covered with ants, or musquitos, or blistered from the heat of the sun, which having moved round whilst I was asleep, would throw the shadow of the branches in another direction, leaving the poor child quite exposed.

The children of both sexes usually run about quite naked, until they are from ten to twelve years of age. I have seen them as old as twelve, going about in this state, or with only an old shirt, which they would put on when they had to go anywhere very particular for their mistress, or up to the great house.

The clothing of the men consists of a pair of thin cotton pantaloons, and a shirt of the same material, two of each being allowed them every year. The women wear a shirt similar to the men's, and a cotton petticoat, which is kept on by means of braces passing over their shoulders. But when they are in the field, the shirt is thrown aside. They also have two suits allowed them every year. These, however, are not enough. They are made of the lowest quality of material, and get torn in the bush, so that the garments soon become useless, even for purposes of the barest decency. We slaves feel that this is not right, and we grow up with very little sense of shame; but immorality amongst ourselves is not common, for all that.

Betty Moore had three daughters. The eldest was married to one Burrell Williams, who acted as Betty's overseer. The second was the wife of one James Davis; and the third was unmarried, when I first began to notice the persons about us. At last the third got married to one Billy Bell, and then I experienced my first serious tribulation.

According to the will left by old Moore, the slave-property was to be equally divided amongst the mother and the three daughters, when the youngest married. About a month after this event, it began to be talked about that the distribution was soon going to take place. I remember well the grief this caused us to feel, and how the women and the men used to whisper to one another when they thought nobody was by, and meet at night, or get together in the field when they had an opportunity, to talk about what was coming. They would speculate, too, on the prospects they had of being separated; to whose lot they and their children were likely to fall, and whether the husbands would go with their wives. The women who had young children cried very much. My mother did, and took to kissing us a good deal oftener. This uneasiness increased as the time wore on, for though we did not know when the great trouble would fall upon us, we all knew it would come, and were looking forward to it with very sorrowful hearts. At last, one afternoon, James Davis, the husband of Betty's second daughter, rode into the yard. This man had a dreadful name for cruelty. He was the terror of his own negroes, as well as of his neighbour's. When we young ones saw him, we ran away and hid ourselves. In the evening orders came to the negroes, at their quarters, to be up at the big house by nine the next morning. Then we knew our great trouble was come.

It was a bright, sun-shiny morning, in the autumn season, at about the commencement of tobacco-cutting time. At the appointed hour, nearly the whole of us had congregated in the great yard, under the big sycamore tree. A fourth part of the negroes on the estate, had been kept back by Betty Moore, as her share, her husband's will giving her the right of making a selection. Besides these, she had taken my brother Silas and my sister Lucy, whom she reserved on behalf of her eldest daughter, the wife of Burrell Williams. They were fine, strong children, and it was arranged they should remain with Betty till she died, and then revert to Burrell Williams. All who were there stood together, facing the Executors, or Committee as they were called, who sat on chairs under the same sycamore tree I have spoken of. Burrell Williams, James Davis, and Billy Bell, held themselves aloof, and did not in any manner interfere with the proceedings of the Committee, who told us off into three lots, each lot consisting of about twenty-five or thirty, as near as I can recollect. As there was a good deal of difference in the value of the slaves, individually, some being stronger than others, or more likely, the allotments were regulated so as to equalize the value of each division. For instance, my brother Silas and my sister Lucy, who belonged rightly to the gang of which I and my mother and other members of the family formed a part, were replaced by two of my cousin Annikie's children, a boy and a girl; the first called Henry, the other Mason, who were weak and sickly. When the lots had been told off, the names of the men, women, and children composing them were written on three slips of paper, and these were put into a hat. Burrell Williams then came forward and drew. James Davis followed, and Billy Bell came last. The lot in which I and my mother were, was drawn by James Davis. Each slip was then signed by the Committee, and the lot turned over to the new owner.

By about two o'clock, the business was concluded, and we were permitted to have the rest of the day to ourselves. It was a heart-rending scene when we all got together again, there was so much crying and wailing. I really thought my mother would have died of grief at being obliged to leave her two children, her mother, and her relations behind. But it was of no use lamenting, and as we were to start early next morning, the few things we had were put together that night, and we completed our preparations for parting for life by kissing one another over and over again, and saying good bye till some of us little ones fell asleep.

CHAPTER II.

MY NEW MASTER: AND HOW HE CAME TO SELL ME.

WE were aroused by times in the morning, and were soon ready to set off on our journey. Our destination was Northampton, about forty-five miles from our old home. We expected to be two days on the road, and as there were a good many little children, who could not walk so far, the smallest of these were put into a waggon, which our new master, James Davis, helped to drive. He rode by it on horseback, his wife keeping along with the older coloured people, in her carriage. The weather was very fine, and we went slowly on, many of us looking back sadly at the place we were leaving, and with which we were so familiar. At noon we drew up by the roadside to breakfast off hoe-cake[5] and water, after which we started again, and walked on until dark. We camped out in the wood by the highway that night, James Davis and his wife putting up at a planter's in the neighbourhood, who sent relay parties to watch us. We collected a lot of dried sticks, and made a fire, in which the women baked some Johnny-cake which they made from our allowance of corn. When we had supped, we raked together the leaves into heaps, under the trees, and laid down upon them, covering ourselves with whatever blanketing we could muster. The children slept in the waggon.

At day-break we started afresh, and continued our journey until noon, when we stopped to eat. We had baked sufficient Johnny-cake over night, for the mid-day meal next day, so we were not long refreshing. To encourage us to make good speed, we were promised a feast of boiled black-eyed peas and bacon-rinds as soon as we got to Northampton, and some of us got a cut with the whip. Any how, we reached James Davis' that afternoon, at about four o'clock. We had our peas and bacon-rinds, and some hard cider was served out to us into the bargain. I remember it very well, for it gave me a very violent cholic. After supper we were driven to our quarters.

And here I may as well tell what kind of man our new master was. He was of small stature, and thin, but very strong. He had sandy hair, fierce gray eyes, a very red face, and chewed tobacco. His countenance had a very cruel expression, and his disposition was a match for it. He was, indeed, a very bad man, and used to flog us dreadfully. He would make his slaves work on one meal a day, until quite night, and after supper, set them to burn brush or to spin cotton. We worked from four in the morning till twelve before we broke our fast, and from that time to eleven or twelve at night. I should say that on the average, and taking all the year round, we labored eighteen hours a day well told. He was a captain of the patrol, which went out every Wednesday and Saturday night, hunting "stray niggers," and to see that none of the neighbours' people were from quarters.

Our allowance of food was one peck of corn a week to each full-grown slave. We never had meat of any kind, and our usual drink was water. Sometimes, however, we got a drink of sour milk or a little hard cider. We used to make our corn into homminy, hoe and Johnny-cake, and sometimes parch it, and eat it without any other preparation. The corn was always of inferior quality, and weevil-eaten, so that though we got a peck, it did not yield in meal what it would have done had it been sound. Its outside value might have been about three-pence English money.

The morning after our arrival, my mother was set to plough, and I was put to grub and hoe. She also had other very hard work to do, such as making fences, grubbing bushes, fetching and burning brush, and such like. I had the same kind of work to do, though being small, I could only help my mother a very little, except in the tobacco-fields, where I was of most use, picking off tobacco-worms from the leaves. This was, also, the principal occupation of the children, from the time they could get about to do any thing at all, until they grew old and strong enough to go to harder work.

I said our master was very cruel. I will give one instance of the fact. I and my little brother Curtis were sent up one day to the house. Passing through the grounds, where there was a large number of water-melons, they tempted us, we being very thirsty. So we took one and ate it. The value of it was not half a far-thing. We did not know we were seen. James Davis, however, was not far from us, and soon overtook us. He swore at us for thieving his property, and as I was the biggest, and had taken the fruit, he at once set to flogging me with the cow-hide, and continued doing so until he was tired out, and I could scarcely move. I did not get over that beating for a very long while.

I remained at James Davis's for nearly eighteen months. Once during that period, I remember he took me into the town to a tavern kept by one Captain Jemmy Duprey. There was a negro speculator there, on the look-out for bar-gains, but he would not have me. I did not know where I was going, when my master took me with him, but when I got back I told my mother, who cried over me, and said she was very glad I had not been sold away from her.

But the time arrived when we were to be finally separated. Owing to a con-siderable rise in the price of cotton, there came a great demand for slaves in Geor-gia. One day a negro speculator named Starling Finney arrived at James Davis's place. He left his drove on the highway, in charge of one of his companions, and made his way up to our plantation, prospecting for negroes. It happened that James Davis had none that suited Finney, but being in want of money, as he was building a new house, and Finney being anxious for a deal, my master called me up and offered to sell me. I was then about or nearly ten years of age, and after some chaffering about terms, Finney agreed to purchase me by the pound.

How I watched them whilst they were driving this bargain! and how I spec-ulated upon the kind of man he was who sought to buy me! His venomous coun-tenance inspired me with mortal terror, and I almost felt the heavy thong of the great riding-whip he held in his hand, twisting round my shoulders. He was a large, tall fellow, and might have killed me easily with one blow from his huge fist. He had left his horse at the gate, and when the bargain for me was struck, he went out and led him to the door, where he took the saddle off. I wondered what this was for, though suspicious that it had something to do with me; nor had I long to wait before I knew. A ladder was set upright against the end of the building, outside, to one rong of which they made a stilyard[6] fast. The first thing Finney did was to weigh his saddle, the weight of which he knew, to see whether the stilyard was accurately adjusted. Having satisfied himself of this, a rope was brought, both ends of which were tied together, so that it formed a large noose or loop. This was hitched over the hook of the stilyard, and I was seated in the loop. After I had been weighed, there was a deduction made for the rope. I do not recollect what I weighed, but the price I was sold for amounted to three hun-dred and ten dollars. Within five minutes after, Finney paid the money, and I was marched off. I looked round and saw my poor mother stretching out her hands after me. She ran up, and overtook us, but Finney, who was behind me, and be-tween me and my mother, would not let her approach, though she begged and prayed to be allowed to kiss me for the last time, and bid me good bye. I was so stupified with grief and fright, that I could not shed a tear, though my heart was bursting. At last we got to the gate, and I turned round to see whether I could not get a chance of kissing my mother. She saw me, and made a dart forward to meet me, but Finney gave me a hard push, which sent me spinning through the gate. He then slammed it to and shut it in my mother's face. That was the last time I ever saw her, nor do I know whether she is alive or dead at this hour.

We were in a lane now, about a hundred and fifty yards in length, and which led from the gate to the highway. I walked on before Finney, utterly unconscious of any thing. I seemed to have become quite bewildered. I was aroused from this state of stupor by seeing that we had reached the main road, and had come up with a gang of negroes, some of whom were hand-cuffed two and two, and fastened to a long chain running between the two ranks. There were also a good many women and children, but none of these were chained. The children seemed to be all above ten years of age, and I soon learnt that they had been purchased in different places, and were for the most part strangers to one another and to the negroes in the coffle.[7] They were waiting for Finney to come up. I fell into the rank, and we set off on our journey to Georgia.

CHAPTER III.

I AM SOLD AGAIN. HOW I FARED.

OUR journey lasted six weeks, as we made a good many stoppages by the way, to enable the speculator, Finney, to buy up, and change away, and dispose of his slaves. I do not recollect the names of all the places we passed through. We crossed the Roanoke river by ferry, and went on to Halifax, and from there to Raleigh in North Carolina. Several incidents occurred on the road, of which I will relate only two.

When I joined the coffle, there was in it a negro woman named Critty, who had belonged to one Hugh Benford. She was married, in the way that slaves are, but as she had no children, she was compelled to take a second husband. Still she did not have any offspring. This displeased her master, who sold her to Finney. Her anguish was intense, and within about four days from the time I saw her first, she died of grief. It happened in the night, whilst we were encamped in the woods. We set off in the morning, leaving her body there. We noticed, however, that two of Finney's associates remained behind, as we conjectured to dispose of the corpse. They fetched up with us again about two hours after.

The other incident was the stealing of a young negro girl. An old lady whose name I do not remember, and who was going into Georgia, travelled with the drove for the sake of society. She was accompanied by her waiting-maid, a young woman about twenty years of age, and of smart appearance. When we stopped at night, the old lady would be driven to some planter's house to lodge, and her horses be sent back to feed with ours. The girl remained with us. This was cheaper for the old lady than having to pay for the keep of her horses and her maid. In the morning her horses would be sent to the place where she had lodged, and she would drive on until she overtook us on the road, and then take up her maid. Finney determined to steal this girl. One morning, we being then on our way through South Carolina, the old lady's horses were sent as usual, to the house where she had staid the night, and we went on. Instead, however, of keeping the direct road, Finney turned off and went through the woods, so that we gave the poor girl's mistress the slip. She was then forced to get up in the waggon with Finney, who brutally ill-used her, and permitted his companions to treat her in the same manner. This continued for several days, until we got to Augusta, in the state of Georgia, where Finney sold her. Our women talked about this very much, and many of them cried, and said it was a great shame.

At last we stopped at one Ben Tarver's place in Jones' County, Georgia. This man was a Methodist Minister, and had a cotton plantation, and a good many slaves. He had a great name for possessing the fastest cotton-picking negroes in the whole county, and they were frequently set to work with others against time for wagers. He had an overseer who did the best part of his flogging, but he used the cow-hide himself occasionally, and they said he hit worse than the overseer; but I cannot say if it was so, as he never flogged me. I know he did not give his slaves any thing to eat till noon-day, and then no more again until nine at night. They got corn, which they made into cake, but I never knew them to have any meat, and as far as I was able to learn, I do not think any was given to them. He was reputed to be a very bad master, but a very good preacher.

During the time I staid there, which was two weeks, Finney used to take out his slaves every day, to try and sell them, bringing those back whom he failed to dispose of. Those who did not go out with Finney, for the market, were made to work in Tarver's cotton-fields, but they did not get any thing extra to eat, though he profited by their labour. In these two weeks Finney disposed of a good many of his drove, and he became anxious to sell the rest, for he wanted to take another journey into Virginia, on a fresh speculation. One day I was dressed in a new pair of pantaloons and a new shirt, made from part of the tilt[8] of a waggon in which we children sometimes slept. I soon found out why I was made so smart, for I was taken to Millidgeville, with some other lads, and there put up at auction.

This happened to me some time in the month of March. The sale took place in a kind of shed. The auctioneer did not like my appearance. He told Finney in private, who was holding me by the hand, that I was old and hard-looking, and not well grown, and that I should not fetch a price. In truth I was not much to look at. I was worn down by fatigue and poor living till my bones stuck up almost through my skin, and my hair was burnt to a brown red from exposure to the sun. I was not, however, very well pleased to hear myself run down. I remember Finney answered the auctioneer that I should be sure to grow a big-made man, and bade him, if he doubted his judgment, examine my feet, which were large, and proved that I would be strong and stout some day. My looks and my condition, nevertheless, did not recommend me, and I was knocked down to a man named Thomas Stevens, for three hundred and fifty dollars: so Finney made forty dollars by me. Thomas Stevens could not pay cash for me, so I went back to Ben Tarver's that night, but next morning Finney and one of his associates, Hartwell Tarver, Ben's brother, took me round to Stevens' place, and the money having been paid, I was again handed over to a new master.

Thomas Stevens' plantation was on the Clinton road, in Baldwin County, and about eight miles from Millidgeville. He was a man of middle height, with a fair skin, but had black hair. He was of Welsh origin. His countenance always wore a laughing expression, but this did not indicate his disposition, which was dreadfully savage. Still, he always laughed, even when in a passion. In fact, at such times, and they were very frequent, he laughed more than at any other. Originally he had been a poor jobbing carpenter. He then set up a still, and made some money by distilling whiskey. He next purchased a plantation and stocked it with negroes, continuing his trade as a maltster of Indian corn, and a distiller. He was a very bad and a dishonest man, and used to force his negroes to go out at night and steal corn from his neighbours. His plan was to gain their negroes over by a present of whiskey. They would then agree to have a quantity of corn ready at a specified place and by a certain hour, which he would then send his own people to fetch away. He always took good care, however, to keep out of the way himself when the stealing was going on, so that if any of his slaves should be caught, he might take sides against them, and his own dishonesty not be suspected. The stolen corn used to be carried to his mill, which was about half a mile from his still-house, where it was taken in by an old negro named Uncle Billy, who had to account for all that was brought. Stevens contrived to keep a pretty correct account himself, for as he was a great rogue, he had no confidence in anybody, and was always trying to prevent himself from being cheated.

I was sent to the still-house, and placed under Uncle Billy. I had to carry whiskey from the still-house to the store, and meal from the mill-house to the still. I also had to carry his breakfast to a slave of the name of John Glasgow, who was at that time employed up in the woods chopping billets[9] for the still. This lasted the whole winter, during which season only, the still was worked. It could not be done in the summer, because the heat turned the malted meal sour and rendered it useless for making whiskey. When the time came for "pitching the crop," that is, for putting in seeds, I was set to labour in the fields along with the rest, clearing the ground, cutting down corn-stalks and burning them, and such like. I was not used to this heavy work; besides which my heart was heavy thinking of my mother and my relations, and I got down-hearted and discouraged, which made me forget my duties, and do what I was set about very indifferently. Then my master would flog me severely, and swear at me the most abominable oaths. I used to feel very bad, and wish to die, and only for John Glasgow I think it must have come to that soon.

I was one of the gang that worked with John Glasgow, who used to tell me not to cry after my father and mother, and relatives, for I should never see them any more. He encouraged me to try and forget them, for my own sake, and to do what I was bidden. He said I must try, too, to be honest and upright, and if I ever could get to England, where he came from, and conducted myself properly, folks would respect me as much as they did a white man. These kind words from

John Glasgow, gave me better heart, and inspired me with a longing to get to England, which I made up my mind I would try and do some day. I got along a little better after a while, but for all that my master would flog me for the least thing.

One day, and not long after I had been there, a sudden heavy fresh[10] in the river caused the mill-dam to overflow, and the mill-door being locked, nobody could get in to raise the flood-gate. I was sent to the house to fetch the key. The house was about a mile off, and I ran every step of the way there. Indeed, I ran so fast, that I lost an old hat I used to wear, for I would not stay to pick it up. My mistress made me take a horse out of the stable to get back quicker, so I was not gone very long in all. After the flood-gates were opened, Stevens came to me, and called me to him from the spring-head where I was, cleaning out the leaves from the water-troughs. This spring-head was up the side of a hill, and troughs were laid down from it to the still-house, on tall stakes, so as to throw the water up to the top of the still-house. Stevens was standing at the bottom of the hill and I went down to him. He began swearing at me directly, and asked me why I did not run when he sent me to fetch the key.

"I did run, Sir," I said.

"You ran, did you, Sir?" said he again, with another oath.

"Yes, Sir," I answered.

"Oh, you ran, did you?" And as he said this he took out his knife and cut a hickory rod from the hedge, with which he beat me until it was destroyed.

"Now, Sir, you tell me you ran, eh?" he asked.

"Yes, Sir," I answered; for I would not tell him to the contrary, though the blood was trickling down my back.

"Oh, you ran, did you?" he said again, and cut another rod, with which he beat me as before.

I do not know how it was that the pain did not make me cry. It did not, however, but seemed to harden me; or perhaps my feelings were benumbed, for you may be whipped sometimes till sensation is almost gone. When he saw I did not cry, he swore at me louder, and said,

"Why don't you cry, Sir, why don't you cry?"

It was of no use his asking me, for I could not cry, and would not answer.

He cut a third rod, and repeating the same questions, "why I didn't run," when I was sent after the key, and "why I didn't cry," beat me with it till that was worn out.

In this way he cut five rods, all of which he used upon my poor back in the same way. Uncle Billy was in the still-house, whilst Stevens was punishing me in this manner, and came running up.

"Oh, Massa," he said, "don't kill the poor boy. Perhaps he hasn't got sense to cry. Don't, please, Massa; please don't kill him."

Uncle Billy usually had some influence with Stevens, because he received the stolen corn up at the meal-house, and knew a great deal about Stevens' business. But on this occasion his entreaties were all thrown away, for my master only swore the louder and hit me the harder. Uncle Billy wrung his hands and went down on his knees to him, still it was not of any use. I think he would have killed me, had not Hartwell Tarver just then rode up to tell him that Starling Finney had arrived from Virginia with a new drove of negroes, and was waiting at Ben Tarver's, to give him (Stevens) the pick of them. He was cutting another hickory rod when Hartwell Tarver came up, and took off his attention from me. I verily believe I owe my life to that accident. I was very bad after this heavy flogging, but I got over it after a while.

Another time Stevens went to see a man hanged at Millidgeville, and his wife set me to cut broomcorn[11] during his absence. I accidentally broke the knife, in two places, in an attempt I made to cut more stalks in a handful, and so get through more work. I took the knife up to his wife, but when her husband came back she told him I had done it for devilment, that I might not have to do any more work. So he called me up and asked me about it. I told him the truth, and showed him how the accident happened. It was easy to see I was telling the truth, but he called me many horrible names, swore I was lying, and flogged me for an hour with the cow-hide.

Stevens seemed to have a spite against me, especially after a particular time, when a mare in the team I used to drive died. She got overheated in the field, and would not eat her corn when I put her up at noon. I noticed it when I took her out again, in about an hour after, not knowing she was not fit to work. She dropped down and died in the plough. I was sent to tell my master to come and see the mare, and on my way, stopped in the stable, and shifted the uneaten corn out of the mare's bin into another, substituting the cobs that the other horse had left. I did this lest Stevens should go into the stable and see that the mare had not eaten her corn, and he should flog me for taking her out under those circumstances. The artifice succeeded so far, that he attributed the mare's death to her being overheated in the sun; but this did not save me from a very severe flogging.

From this time he led me a dreadful life, and became so savage to me, I used to dread to see him coming. I had only too good reason for my fears.

I was ploughing one day, some long time after the mare died, with what we call a buzzard plough. It is made so as to cut under the roots of the grass and weeds that choke the cotton, and must be used carefully, or it will go too deep, and leave the roots of the cotton-plant exposed to the sun, when the plant will wither and die. The share was loose on the helve, and would not run true, so I could not do my work quickly or well, as I had to keep stooping down to set the share true. Stevens saw me, came up, and asked me why I did not plough better. I explained to him why, and shewed him that the plough ran foul. I stooped for this purpose, and was cleaning the dirt off from the share with my hands, when he viciously raised his foot, which was heavily shod, and unexpectedly dealt me a kick with all his might. The blow struck me right between the eyes, breaking the bone of my nose, and cutting the leaders[12] of the right eye, so that it turned quite round in its socket. I was stunned for the moment, and fell, my mouth filling with blood, which also poured from my nose and eyes. In spite of the pain, and though I could scarcely see, I got up and resumed my work, continuing it until the evening. John Glasgow then doctored my eye. He washed the blood from my face, and got a ball of tallow, and an old handkerchief from Aunt Sally, the cook up at the house. He gently pressed the ball of tallow, made warm, against the displaced eye, until he forced it back into its proper position, when he put some cotton over it, and bound it up with the handkerchief. In about a fortnight I was able to have the bandage removed, but my eye remained very bad, and it was more than two months before I could use it at all. The other eye was also seriously affected, the inflammation having extended to it. I have never been able to see so well since, and cannot now look long at print without suffering much pain. The letters seem cloudy. To this day my right eye has remained out of its proper place.

CHAPTER IV.

THE STORY OF JOHN GLASGOW.

I MUST interrupt my own narrative here, to relate the story of John Glasgow. I had it from his own lips; and acting on the advice of the Secretary of the *British and Foreign Anti-Slavery Society,* I have made a declaration in his presence, before a notary public, to the effect that, as given below, the narrative is substantially correct. I stated the facts to the Secretary of the Society, some time ago, and he introduced them in the *Anti-Slavery Reporter* for July 1853.

John Glasgow was a native of Demerara,[13] born of free negro parents, whose free condition he inherited as well as their complexion. When quite small he took to the sea, first as a cabin-boy; working his way up until he stood A.B.S.[14] on the ship's register. His first voyages were made on board the small coasters that trade between the West-India Islands, but he abandoned the coasting-trade after a few years, and went to and fro to England, improving his opportunities so much, that he saved money, and was regarded as a prosperous man. He then sought a wife. In the immediate neighbourhood of Liverpool—the port he had most frequented—there resided a small farmer who had a daughter. She is said not to have belied the adage which is so complimentary to Lancashire, in respect of its maidens. On the other hand, John Glasgow was a fine fellow, tall of stature and powerful in frame, having a brave look and a noble carriage. He was, moreover, upright in conduct, and of thrifty habits. In fact, save in one particular, he was altogether such a youth as would be most likely to find favour in the eyes of the "Lancashire witches." But, alas, John was as black as a coal, and though many admired, none of the Liverpool lasses would "have him for a husband at any price:" at least so the report went out, when it became bruited that he was going to marry the farmer's daughter. For his part, John said, when he heard it, "that he had never asked them to have him." He felt, in fact, quite happy in the affection of the girl he had chosen, and who had consented to take him for a partner, in spite of his complexion and very woolly hair. So they were married, the young woman's relatives taking her view of matters, and coinciding in the opinion that it was wise in her to marry the man she loved, whose sterling qualities she had learned to appreciate.

Being married, however, was not all. John had saved money, it is true, but not sufficient to support a wife in idleness. On the other hand, his spouse's relatives were not in a position to assist them much. They were in a small way; and though the farmer worked hard a-field, and his dame tended the dairy and sold eggs and butter at market, their united labours, aided by the good wife's economy, proved barely adequate to meet the expenses of a large family, or left but the smallest surplus sometimes to put by against the contingency of failing crops. Thus the young couple saw that they must depend upon their own exertions, and they set to work accordingly. Through the father's interest, they got into a small farm in the neighbourhood, and John Glasgow invested his savings in the purchase of three horses, a plough, and a cart. As his wife had been accustomed to farming operations, she agreed to attend to the concerns of the farm; whilst John—who, though well acquainted with the economy of a vessel, from her kelson[15] to her signal halyards, knew nothing at all about farming—determined to continue his calling, and therefore engaged himself as an able-bodied seaman, on board one of the many vessels trading between Liverpool and the West Indies. At the end of his second voyage he found himself the father of a fine brown baby, over which he shed many tears when the time came for him to leave port again. But John and his wife prospered, he in his vocation, she at her farm; and as he had managed to add trade to navigation, there seemed to be a prospect of his amassing wealth in the course of a few years. Indeed, had he only known how to read and write, he might have been mate long ago.

In the year 1830, John Glasgow, being then about twenty-five years of age, engaged to go out to Savannah, in Georgia, in an English vessel, and under an English captain, for a cargo of rice. He was now the father of two children, and his heart yearned more strongly towards them and his wife than it had ever done before. He seemed to be impressed with a foreboding of evil, and half repented having put his mark to the ship's articles. But his wife encouraged him, reminding him of his promise to her that this should be his last voyage to so distant a country, and that on his return he was to confine his trips to the English coast, and never go far from home again. So John kissed his wife and children, and the vessel left the Mersey with a favourable breeze, bearing him away with a sadder heart than he had ever had under similar circumstances. The voyage was prosperous, and the passage a rapid one: too much so for John Glasgow's happiness, as it turned out.

The black law of Georgia, like that of South Carolina, is no respecter of freedom, if it present itself with a coloured skin; and poor John, a freeman born, a British subject, and unoffending, was seized, handcuffed like a common felon, conveyed to gaol, and incarcerated until the vessel that brought him to the port should discharge her cargo, be re-laden, and on the point of sailing away again. What his feelings under such a trial were, may be left to the reader to imagine. He had learnt, only too late, that his fate was in the hands of the captain: though, as he had faithfully served him, he doubted not but he would pay the gaol fees and save him from slavery. Unhappily the ship was detained considerably beyond the time the captain had reckoned upon, owing to delays in the procuring of the cargo. Slave-labour was dear, and the captain had to pay high wages to the slave who had been hired to him to do John Glasgow's work, while John lay pining in gaol, desiring nothing so much as that he might be doing it himself. The captain was displeased at being thus imposed upon, especially when he thought of the wages he would have to pay to John Glasgow; and matters in his mind were not improved when, the time having come for the ship to sail, he found that the gaol-fees for John's release had run up enormously high, and with what he had already paid and would have to pay, made so considerable a sum, that, looking at the whole matter commercially, to hand over so much money was wholly out of the question: and considering it humanely, was out of the question too. Besides he was "only a nigger after all;" so the captain refused to pay the gaol-fees: he set sail without John, leaving him, as yet, in ignorance of his dreadful fate.

Poor John's wife and children! They were already expecting him home, on the day he was taken out of the gaol and sold on the auction-block for three hundred and fifty dollars, to Thomas Stevens, of Baldwin County, Georgia. He would have fetched more than three times as much, but being "a green hand," he was not worth it. Well, he was marched off to the plantation, and set to work. Here he soon realized the extent of his misfortune. His "brave look," when spoken to, offended his master, who swore he "would flog his nigger pride out of him;" and poor John had to suffer for having the look and carriage of a free man. When he had been some three or four years on the plantation, his master bade him take a wife. John told him he had one in England, and two dear children. Then his master flogged him for saying so, and for insisting upon it that he was free and a British subject. At last, to save his poor body from the torture of the cow-hide and the paddle, he promised his master never to say as much again, and to look out for a wife. In Jones County, and about five miles from Stevens' plantation, there lived another planter named John Ward. John Glasgow, having to go backwards and forwards on errands, saw and at length selected a young, bright, coloured girl named Nancy, and they were married, in the way that slaves are; that is, nominally. This did not please Stevens, because Nancy being Ward's property, her children would be Ward's also: so John was flogged for marrying Nancy, instead of one of Stevens' "likely gals," and was forbidden to visit her. Still he contrived to do so without his master's discovering it. The young woman was of a very sweet disposition, it seems, and knew all about John's misfortunes, and his having a wife and children in England. She was very kind to him, and would weep over him, as she dressed his sore and bleeding back when he crept to her log cabin at dead of night; so it was no wonder he came to love her and the three children she bore him, whilst all the time talking of his English wife and children, whom he should never see more: never, never.

One Christmas-day—a holiday for all—he thought he would slip away from the other slaves who were having a feast before Stevens' house, and go see Nancy. Accordingly, watching his opportunity, he soon succeeded in getting away, unobserved as he fancied. Not so, however. His master saw him, but instead of calling him back, maliciously allowed him to get a good distance off, when beckoning to him three other slaves, myself, March, and Jack, (of whom I shall say more presently,) they started in pursuit, and soon came up with the object of their search. John Glasgow struggled ineffectually to release himself from the grasp of his comrades, though he knew full well they were only obeying their tyrant master. He was secured and brought back to quarters, and the other slaves were called together to witness the infliction upon him of a punishment called *bucking*. The poor fellow having been stripped stark naked, his hands were fast tied and brought down over his knees, he being compelled, for this purpose, to assume a sitting posture, with his knees doubled up under his chin. A stout stake was then thrust under his hams, so that he was rendered completely powerless. In this position he was turned first on one side then on the other, and flogged with willow switches and the cow-hide, until the blood ran down in streams and settled under him in puddles. For three mortal hours he endured this inhuman punishment, groaning piteously all the time, whilst his master looked on and chuckled. At last he was taken out of the buck, and his lacerated body washed down with salt, red pepper, and water. It was two weeks before he went to work again.

Severe as this torture was, it did not smother John Glasgow's affection for the poor mulatto girl who shared his sorrows, and who was, perhaps, the only human being to whom he durst unburden his whole soul. As soon as he felt able to go so far, that is, in about three months, he made another attempt to see her, was missed, pursued and caught. Then Thomas Stevens swore a fearful oath that he would cure him of "wife-hunting. If he must have a wife, there was a plenty of likely yellow gals on the plantation for such as he to choose from. He might have the pick of 'em. But he (Stevens) wasn't going to let his niggers breed for another man's benefit, not he: so if John couldn't get a wife off the plantation he shouldn't have one at all. But he'd cure him of Nancy any how."

The unfortunate fellow was taken to the whipping-post, which on Stevens' estate consisted of two solid uprights, some ten feet high, with a cross-beam at the top, forming a kind of gallows. Along the cross-beam were three or four massive iron cleets, to which pulleys were fixed, having a fine but closely-twisted cord passing over them. John Glasgow having been stripped, as on the previous occasion, the end of one of these cords was tightly fastened round his wrists. His left foot was then drawn up and tied, toes downwards, to his right knee, so that his left knee formed an angle by means of which, when swung up, his body could conveniently be turned. An oaken stake, about two feet long, was now driven into the ground beneath the cross-beam of the whipping-post, and made sharp at the top with a draw-knife. He was then hoisted up by his hands, by means of the pulley and rope, in such wise that his body swung by its own weight, his hands being high over his head and his right foot level with the pointed end of the oaken "stob" or stake.

I may here state that this punishment is called the picket, and by being swung in this manner, the skin of the victim's back is stretched till it shines, and cuts more readily under the lash: on the other hand, if the unhappy sufferer, swinging "between heaven and earth" as it is called, desires to rest, he can do so only by placing the foot that is at liberty on the sharp end of the stake. The excessive pain caused by being flogged while suspended, and the nausea excited by twirling round, causes the victim of the "picket" to seek temporary relief by staying himself on the "stob." On his doing so, for ever so brief a space, one of the bystanders taking hold of the bent knee, and using it as a handle, gives the unfortunate a twirl, and sends him spinning round on the hard point of the stake, which perforates the heel or the sole of the foot, as the case may be, quite to the bone.

John Glasgow thus suspended was flogged and twisted for an hour, receiving "five licks" or strokes of the raw cow-hide at a time, with an interval of two or three minutes between, to allow him "to come to, and to fetch his breath." His shrieks and groans were most agonizing, and could be heard, at first, a mile and a quarter off, but as the punishment proceeded, they subsided into moans scarcely audible at the distance of fifty paces. All Stevens' slaves were made to stand by during the infliction of the torture, and some of them took turns at the whipping, according to the instructions of their master, who swore he would serve them the same if they refused, or ever disobeyed him as "that cussed nigger there had done." At the end of an hour he was "dropped from the gallows," his back being fearfully lacerated, his wrists deeply cut with the cord, and his foot pierced through in three places. Beneath the beam there was a pool of coagulated blood, whilst the oaken stake was dyed red with that which had streamed from his foot. He could not stand, much less walk, so they carried him to his quarters, where the usual application of salt and water, and red pepper, was made to his wounds, and he was left to die or to recover, as might be. It was a month before he stirred from his plank, five months more elapsed ere he could walk. Ever after he had a limp in his gait.

I made my escape from Thomas Stevens', about two years after this horrible punishment had been inflicted on John Glasgow. I do not know whether the husband and the wife ever met again. The last I know of John's history is, that in 1840, or thereabouts, the poor fellow was felling a white oak in the woods, which in falling struck him on his right thigh, just above the knee, and broke it in two. As he was thus rendered comparatively useless for field-work, Thomas Stevens gave him to his son John, who kept him to shell corn off the cob.

Should this narrative by chance meet the eye of any person to whom John Glasgow's name or the circumstances of his disappearance are familiar, and lead to a discovery of the whereabouts of the poor fellow's English wife and children, let such a one write forthwith, to the Secretary of the *British and Foreign Anti-Slavery Society,* who will place the parties in communication with such friends as may be anxious to take steps in this distressing case. One of my chief regrets is that I cannot remember the name of the place where John's wife lived. To John I owe a debt of gratitude, for he it was who taught me to love and to seek liberty.*

---

*This narrative has been slightly altered. As it originally appeared in the *Anti-Slavery Reporter,* the Editor spoke. In the present instance it is John Brown. (ED.)

CHAPTER V.

DR. HAMILTON'S EXPERIMENTS UPON ME. MY MASTER DIES,
AND I AGAIN CHANGE HANDS.

I HAD been fourteen years with Stevens, suffering all the time very much from his ill-treatment of me, when he fell ill. I do not know what his malady was. It must have been serious, for they called in to treat him one Doctor Hamilton, who lived in Jones County, and who had a great name. He cured Stevens, who was so pleased, that he told the Doctor to ask him any favour, and it should be granted. Now it so happened that this Doctor Hamilton had been trying a great number of experiments, for the purpose of finding out the best remedies for sun-stroke. I was, it seems, a strong and likely subject to be experimented upon, and the Doctor having fixed the thing in his mind, asked Stevens to lend me to him. This he did at once, never caring to inquire what was going to be done with me. I myself did not know. Even if I had been made aware of the nature of the trials I was about to undergo, I could not have helped myself. There was nothing for it but passive resignation, and I gave myself up in ignorance and in much fear.

Yet, it was not without curiosity I watched the progress of the preparations the Doctor caused to be made. He ordered a hole to be dug in the ground, three feet and a half deep by three feet long, and two feet and a half wide. Into this pit a quantity of dried red oak bark was cast, and fire set to it. It was allowed to burn until the pit became heated like an oven, when the embers were taken out. A plank was then put across the bottom of the pit, and on that a stool. Having tested, with a thermometer, the degree to which the pit was heated, the Doctor bade me strip, and get in; which I did, only my head being above the ground. He then gave me some medicine which he had prepared, and as soon as I was on the stool, a number of wet blankets were fastened over the hole, and scantlings laid across them. This was to keep in the heat. It soon began to tell upon me; but though I tried hard to keep up against its effects, in about half an hour I fainted. I was then lifted out and revived, the Doctor taking a note of the degree of heat when I left the pit. I used to be put in between daylight and dark, after I had done my day's work; for Stevens was not a man to lose more of the labour of his slaves than he could help. Three or four days afterwards, the experiment was repeated, and so on for five or six times, the Doctor allowing me a few days' rest between each trial. His object was to ascertain which of the medicines he administered to me on these occasions, enabled me to withstand the greatest degree of heat. He found that cayenne-pepper tea accomplished this object; and a very nice thing he made of it. As soon as he got back home, he advertised that he had discovered a remedy for sun-stroke. It consisted of pills, which were to be dissolved in a dose of cayenne-pepper tea, without which, he said, the pills would not produce any effect. Nor do I see how they should have done so, for they were only made of common flour. However, he succeeded in getting them into general use, and as he asked a good price, he soon realized a large fortune.

Having completed his series of experiments upon me, in the heated pit, and allowed me some days' rest, I was put on a diet, and then, during a period of about three weeks, he bled me every other day. At the end of that time he found I was failing, so he left off, and I got a month's rest, to regain a little strength. At the expiration of that time, he set to work to ascertain how deep my black skin went. This he did by applying blisters to my hands, legs and feet, which bear the scars to this day. He continued until he drew up the dark skin from between the upper and the under one. He used to blister me at intervals of about two weeks. He also tried other experiments upon me, which I cannot dwell upon.

Altogether, and from first to last, I was in his hands, under treatment, for about nine months, at the end of which period I had become so weak, that I was no longer able to work in the fields. I had never been allowed to knock off, I ought to say, during the whole of this time, though my bodily strength failed daily. Stevens always kept me employed: at hard work as long as I could do it, and at lighter labour, as my strength went away. At last, finding that the Doctor's experiments had so reduced me that I was useless in the field, he put me to his old trade of carpentering and joinery, which I took to very readily, and soon got a liking for.

I do not know what made Stevens so cruel-hearted to us poor slaves. We all led a dreadful life; I did, I know; and this made me more and more anxious to get away. In this I was encouraged by one Buck Hurd, who was what is called a nigger-stealer. He belonged to a club, the head of which was a man of the name of Murrell, in Tennessee. This club was a company of "nigger and pony-stealers," and was composed of a great many persons. They had stations in various parts of the country, at convenient distances, and when a member of the club succeeded in stealing away a negro or a pony, he would pass him on as quickly as he could to the nearest stations, from which point he would be forwarded to another, and so on, till the negro or the horse was quite safely disposed of. By this system of stations they would run off a "nigger or a pony," three hundred miles sometimes, without stopping. The partners, or agents, belonging to this club, were always on the lookout for negroes and horses, and Buck Hurd used frequently to come round to our quarters of a night, and try to entice some of us away. I heard him say, more than once, that Murrell had got slaves to run from one master, and after selling them to another, would induce them to run from him, and then sell them to a third; and that he had been known to sell the same "nigger" three or four times over. One of them, whom he had so sold, he was like to get into trouble about. The masters heard about it, and Murrell became alarmed. He did not know what to do with the stolen man—though he kept him closely concealed—fearing that the various masters should claim their property, and the facts come out. So he got the poor fellow to go down to the spring, in the woods, after some water, and there shot him.

But although I heard all these things, I was so hard used, that I gave in, and consented to run off with Buck. We started one night, walking on as fast as we could, until daylight, when we took to the woods and lay down to rest. I cannot say how far we went, for I was ignorant of that part of the country. I know it was a long way, for we were out some days, walking at night, and hiding in the woods and swamps by day. At last, however, we reached the station Buck Hurd had been making for, and there we heard that Murrell had been found out and was then in the States' prison. This frightened Buck, who said I must go back. I agreed to do so if he would get my master to promise not to flog me. To this he consented, and we made our way for home. On the road, however, Buck called at his own house, and took a gun and a dog, to make it appear as though he had been out nigger hunting and caught me. At any rate he told Stevens so when we got to the house, and Stevens believed him and paid him thirty dollars for catching and bringing me home. Before he gave me up, he made me promise I would not run away any more. This I did, telling a downright lie, for I meant running off if ever I got the chance. However, I did not get flogged that time, and thought I had been very lucky.

I may here state that negro stealing is quite a trade in the States, and that it is carried on to a great extent.

Not very long after this, Stevens was struck with paralysis. He lost the use of one side, and of his speech. I was called in to watch and tend him, but I did not think it my duty to understand all he tried to say. This made him very savage. He would sometimes get my hand between his foot and the bed, and try to grind the bones. When the "people" learnt he was not likely to recover, they were much pleased, and used to be very merry at quarters, for they knew they could not have a worse master. At last he died, and very glad we all were. I know I was; and even now, at this distance of time, when my troubles are all over, I cannot help feeling that the world was well rid of him. I only hope he did not go where there is any chance of my meeting with him again. He was buried, any how, nobody regretting him; not even his old dog, who wagged his tail when the coffin went by his kennel.

He left his property to his son Decatur Stevens.

CHAPTER VI.

JOHN MORGAN.

BEFORE I narrate what befel me next, I may perhaps as well mention a few facts which will serve to shew the workings of the system of Slavery.

I do not think people know what Slavery means. It is not possible they should be able to understand how wicked a thing it is, and how it affects the free, as well as the bond. Now, the poor whites are worse off in the Slave States than they ever can be in the Free States, because in the Slave States labour is made shameful, and a man does not like to go to work in his own fields for fear folks should look down upon him. So it happens that when these poor whites cannot obtain a living honestly, which they very seldom do, they get the slaves in their neighbourhood to steal corn, poultry, and such like, from their masters, and bring these things to them: corn especially. The slaves steal, because they are so poorly fed. They know very well that they cannot get the corn they steal ground, without a danger of their being found out, so they are very glad to bargain to receive back in meal, half or less of what they pilfer in the husk. This system is carried on to a very great extent; and as the parties to it are interested in keeping the secret, it is not often the masters find out how much they are robbed. I never considered it wicked to steal, because I looked upon what I took as part of what was due to me for my labour. But whenever I was trusted with my master's property, money, or cattle, or any thing of this sort, I always had a kind of pride to keep a good account of what was given me to take care of.

Another result of Slavery is, that it makes the slaveholders jealous of every man who works with free labour. If such a man comes amongst them, they are sure to try to get rid of him, and they mostly succeed, some how or other. I will illustrate this by a case that came under my own knowledge.

John Morgan was a large, robust man from Scotland, who came to settle in Baldwin County, on an estate adjoining Stevens' plantation. I had been with Stevens about ten years when Morgan came into our neighbourhood. He did not like Slavery, though he was not what people called an Abolitionist. He came quite resolved to employ only free-labour, and he hired free men, both coloured and white, to whom he paid regular wages, as agreed upon between them. He did much better than the planters his neighbours. His cotton was much better, and fetched a higher price in the market. The reason was that his men were not forced to pick the cotton in the wet, so the fibre came out cleaner. He made a good deal of money, and it was known to all the people about, that he said free-labour was better and more profitable than slave-labour. He was a good man, too, of a kind, Christian disposition, and always spoke gently to the black folks as well as to the white. The planters got jealous of him, because he always had the best of the market, and they began to frown upon him. They said he would spoil all their niggers, injure the settlement, and damage the system of Slavery, so he must be got rid of. They used to get together and talk the matter over, and they met in this way a good many times. We slaves knew something was going on, but we durst not say a word. At last Stevens was spoken to. They asked him to try and "get shut" of Morgan. Stevens said he would consider how it was to be done. Some days after, he told them he had hit upon a plan. It was to buy his land. It seems the plan met their views, for they got very merry over it, and went away laughing and joking. But Morgan did not all at once fall into the trap. He declined parting with his land, because it was bringing him in a good living. Stevens, however, offered him a double price. The bait took, and he was paid in promissory notes. Soon after the purchase was completed, he left his own farm-house, on the estate, and went to live in a smaller dwelling on the top of an adjoining hill, quite away from any other inhabited house, though still in the neighbourhood of the plantations. He soon found out that he had been tricked, for when the bills he held fell due, the parties who had signed them did not meet the demand, and Morgan could not get his money. On his applying to them, and complaining of the hardship of his case, they laughed at him; and when he threatened he would take the law of them, they defied him. And well they might, as they knew they could secure the lawyers on their side.

Well, John Morgan went to law, bringing suits against the parties who owed him the money. On their side, they bribed the lawyers, besides setting them against Morgan by saying that he was a friend of the niggers; so he could not get his case fairly heard. In this way they kept the suits going on, until Morgan's means were exhausted, and he was thrown out of court, being unable to go on any further. So he was completely ruined.

He now had nothing to live upon, and at last was compelled to do as the other poor whites did; that is, to depend chiefly upon the coloured people. One day he came round to the back of our farm, where we were ploughing. A man named Jack, one of our fellow-slaves, was driving the team, and as he turned the horses' heads, Morgan tapped the fence with a stick, to attract his notice. Jack stopped, and Morgan then asked him whether he could not get him a little corn. Jack said "Yes," and they agreed that he should bring it round in a sack on a certain night, to a place they named. Morgan then went away. Jack, however, wanted somebody to help him, so he asked another man of the name of March, whether he would lend a hand, and he should have a share. March promised, but instead of doing it, he told Stevens, in order that he might make a friend of him and not get flogged so often. Stevens laid his plans accordingly.

About three days after, Stevens called me to him. It was in the evening, and quite dark: that is, there was no moon, but the stars were shining brightly. He had his gun in his hand, and he bade me take a stout hickory club, and follow him. We went on till we came to a certain place on the highway, where we got into the bushes and hid ourselves. We had lain there about half an hour when we heard footsteps. I knew they were Jack's, and could tell he carried a load. Jack stopped near where we were, and we saw he had a sack of corn. He set down the sack, but we did not take any heed of him. Presently we heard somebody else coming. I felt very bad then, for I knew it was Morgan, and that there would be a scuffle. As soon as he and Jack met, my master poked me with the muzzle of his gun, and whispered me to leap out of the bushes into the road and lay hold of Morgan. I was obliged to do his bidding, knowing he had his gun, and fearing he would shoot me if I did not obey him. As soon as Jack heard a noise in the bushes, he ran off, and the next moment I had seized fast hold of Morgan. The poor fellow struggled very hard to get away, but Stevens was by my side, shouting to me to hold on, and dodging round me and Morgan as we fought, and wrestled. I do not know whether he thought Morgan would get away, but all at once, and whilst we were still tusseling, he lowered his gun, and discharged it. I thought I was shot, the fire and smoke were so close to me, but at the same moment Morgan gave a leap right out of my arms, and fell with a loud cry flat upon his face in the road. He had received the whole contents of the piece in his right side. Hardly knowing what I was doing, I took to my heels, and never stopped till I got safe to quarters, where I remained for about an hour and a half. I was very much terrified at what had taken place, and feared lest Stevens should accuse me of having killed Morgan, so I thought I would run round and tell his wife all about it, and she would then be able to clear me. I listened whether I could hear any one about, and as all seemed quiet, I slipped out, and made my way to her house, as fast as I could. It was between eleven and twelve when I knocked at the door. She was up, and dressed, and seemed to be expecting her husband. I told her my master had shot a man that evening, and that I was sure it was her husband. She could not speak, but burst out crying. I told her where he was lying, and then ran back to my quarters.

It seems she was afraid to go out that night; but quite early in the morning she went down to the place, with three poor white men named Elias Cammel, James Cammel, and Bill Cannon. They found the poor fellow quite stiff dead, about a hundred and fifty yards from the spot where he had fallen. He had struggled hard, and they had traced him by his blood to the hedge where he had at last dropped down for good. The men who came were his friends, and they buried him in Cannon's wood, just across a little creek. They all persuaded Morgan's widow to take the case in hand, and lay an information against Stevens, so she went to a magistrate to get a warrant. But the magistrate asked her on whose evidence the warrant was to be granted. She told him that it was on that of Stevens' man, Fed; meaning me. He refused then to give her a warrant, because, as I was a slave, my evidence would not be received in the Courts. She said it was very hard, for she knew I had told the truth; but he still refused, and sent her away, saying that "if she brought five hundred nigger witnesses, he would not give her a warrant." The poor woman was obliged to go then, and at last she got so frightened, lest Stevens should kill her too, that she quitted her house, and left that neighbourhood, quite ruined, a widow, and with two young children.

When I last heard of her, she was going about, up and down the country with them, begging.

CHAPTER VII.

SOMETHING ABOUT SOME OF MY FELLOW-SLAVES.

I SPOKE of Jack in the last chapter. I have something to tell about him and others, my companions in Slavery.

Stevens had bought Jack of a man named Jem Mallet, who lived about two miles from my master's. Of course he was obliged to leave his wife behind, and Stevens forbade his going to see her. However, Jack used to manage to creep out of a night and visit her, always taking care to be back betimes. Stevens at last got a suspicion of the truth, from seeing Jack's track across the field, and soon found him out. Next day he got all the people together, and had Jack stripped and tied up to a rough red oak tree, his hands being made fast round the tree, so that he embraced it. Stevens then took a branding-iron, marked T. S., which he heated red hot at the kitchen fire, and applied to the fleshy part of Jack's loins. The poor fellow screamed awfully, and began to move round the tree. Stevens was afraid this would cause him to make what is called a miss-letter, so he followed Jack round the tree till the iron was quite buried in the flesh. Jack tore round the rough tree, the smoke from his burning flesh rising high and white above the top; he all the time screaming, and master swearing. At last the branding was done, and Jack was loosed, when we saw that in going round the tree, he had torn all the flesh from his chest, which was bleeding dreadfully. But he was obliged to go to his work directly, for all that, and I remember he anointed with soap the wound the brand had made. He was afterwards compelled to take a young woman named Hannah, as a wife, and to abandon his former one. By Hannah he had a good many children, but after he had been with her about eight years, he was sold away from her and their children, to one Robert Ware, of Decatur Town, in De Kalb County, Georgia, about ten miles from Stevens' place.

It is all very well for Mrs. Tyler to say that families are not often separated. I know better than that, and so does she.[16]

On one occasion, Jack's wife (Hannah) could not get her task of spinning cotton done. Stevens called her up, and after swearing at and abusing her, made her strip stark naked, and then forced her to hug the shed post; that is, to clasp it round. He then made her husband go round and hold her hands, whilst he flogged her with the cow-hide some seventy or eighty lashes, after which he turned her loose. She was about twenty-five years old.

On another occasion he cruelly flogged her and another slave woman named Mimey. It was one Sunday morning, and they were down at the spring washing their clothes. They quarrelled, and master hearing their noise came running down. He made them strip off all their garments, and sent me for the cow-hide, with which he beat them till he could not wag his arm any longer, they crying out all the time.

Amongst us we had a negro named Primus. His father and mother had been stolen right from Africa. They both belonged to a Methodist minister, the Reverend Mr. Woods, who lived on Fishing-Creek, about three miles from Stevens'. He had bought them off a slave-ship, directly they were landed. The vessel had come into the port of Savannah. The father was from Golah.[17] The woman came from the Coast of Guinea. Woods owned a great many negroes. He was a cotton planter as well as a preacher, but folks used to say his cotton was worth more than his sermons. When Primus was about twenty-four, he was sold to Stevens for six hundred dollars. Stevens bought him of Woods, about two years after he had purchased me. Doctor Woods was a tall, pleasant looking man, and was said to treat his slaves kindly. Primus had never known what cruel usage was, and did not shew fear of a white man, as the other negroes did. Stevens therefore made up his mind to tame him down, and used him all the more cruelly. Now this Doctor Woods had a son named Elisha, who owned a negro girl of the name of Annikie. He sold this girl to Stevens. Primus had married Annikie, and was very fond of her. It used to cut him to the heart to see her flogged, which Stevens often used to do. He treated them both so cruelly, indeed, that at last Primus made up his mind to have done with it. One day he tied a brace round his arm, and cut a vein, then ran home to kill Annikie, hoping they might both die together. But he bled too much, and Uncle Billy having seen him, loosed the cord, and saved his life. He hallooed after Primus as he was running home, and he was caught, and taken to the home-house. Weak as he was from loss of blood, he was picketed, and turned loose.

It seems that Primus took a dislike to Uncle Billy from that time, because Billy had told upon him. He threatened to be revenged some day, and soon after Stevens heard of it. He got Tom and Elijah Wilson, neighbouring planters, to come in and help punish him; so they came one day and laid hold of him, Stevens assisting them. They stretched him, face downwards, on a carpenter's bench, his hands being tied underneath, as tightly as the cords could be drawn. They then cut his clothes off his back, and Stevens took a cobbing paddle and laid on to him as long as he could stand. This paddle is a piece of wood from eighteen inches to two feet long, having a handle about eight inches in length. It is made of oak, one end being broad and flat, and between five and six inches in width, with eight holes drilled through it. Before being used, it is wetted and rubbed in sand. When Stevens got tired, he handed the instrument over to John Wilson. During the infliction of this punishment, all of us slaves were made to stand by. Every blow they struck raised eight blisters, the blood starting underneath them, quite black. They paddled him in this way, five minutes at a time, each of them, for about an hour; long before which, Primus was befooled. Then Stevens took a raw cow-hide and flogged him across the blisters till they burst, the blood flying out all over him, and round about the bench on to the ground. When he had flogged him till the poor fellow's back and loins were like a jelly, they rubbed the parts with red pepper and salt and water, and sent him to quarters. It was a horrible scene; the man screaming till he could not scream any longer. The punishment was awful, and it otherwise dreadfully injured him. However, after a long time, he got over it.

Another day he was sent for something to the still-house. Stevens was there and spoke to him, but Primus did not hear him. Stevens snatched up a barrel-stave, and immediately dealt him such a blow, that he fell like an ox. He laid there senseless for full two hours. Stevens got alarmed, and taking out his knife, cut him across the arm, to make him bleed. Billy threw whiskey in his face, and at last he came to, but he did not recover himself for several days. He always was subject to fits after that, and used to go about as though he was half foolish. I am sure I wonder now he was not quite a lunatic with such horrible treatment. Two years after, he was quite "a done up nigger;" and Stevens finding him useless, gave him to his son-in-law, Billy Gay. He died three years after, in a fit.

I might add many other instances of cruel usage of slaves, but I have perhaps stated enough for the present. It may be thought that the female slaves are perhaps, as a rule, less badly treated. This is not the case. Men and women, boys and girls, receive the same kind of punishments, or I would say rather, that the same kind of tortures are inflicted upon them. I know full well that women in a state of pregnancy are not spared from the infliction of the most dreadful scourgings, with the cow-hide, the bull-whip, and the cobbing-paddle. Thousands of them never bring their burden into the world, and numbers of negro infants are overlaid and smothered by their mothers at night, in consequence of their having been overworked in the day.

Mrs. Stowe has told something about Slavery. I think she must know a great deal more than she has told. I know more than I dare to tell.

CHAPTER VIII.

I MAKE AN ATTEMPT TO ESCAPE. HOW IT ENDED.

DECATUR STEVENS, my new master, to whom I had been willed, turned out to be a good deal worse than his father. He was naturally a stupid man, and had received no education to brighten him up. Under him we all led a terrible life. My mind had long been made up to run away. I was constantly dwelling on what John Glasgow had told me about freedom, and England, and becoming a man. During my old master's lifetime, I had frequently hidden away in the woods and swamps; sometimes for a few days only; at others for a fortnight at a stretch; and once for a whole month. I used to sneak out at night from my hiding-place and steal corn, fruit, and such like. As long as it lasted, the release from the severe labour put upon me was quite grateful; and though I always got cruelly flogged on my return, the temptation to get a rest this way was too great to be resisted. It may be asked why I did not go right off when once I had made a start. I may as well tell the truth. I was frightened to take a long journey. I did not know the country, but I did know that if my master caught me and brought me back, I should get perhaps paddled or scourged nearly to death. I was, nevertheless, always on the look-out for a fair chance of escaping, and treasured up in my memory such scraps of information as I could draw out of the people that came to the plantation; especially the new hands. Decatur Stevens did not like to sell me, because I was too valuable to him. He used to say of me, that nothing came amiss to me; and in this, for once, he told the truth; for I may say, without unduly boasting, that at farming, at carpentering, and at any and all kinds of labour, I was a match for any two hands he could bring against me. In fact, I could and used to do two men's work, when I returned from my lying-out. At such times I could only compare myself to a man gone lunatic. Knowing Stevens would not sell me, and having made up my mind to suffer any amount of flogging, I grew defiant of my master, but I determined I would be killed in defending myself if he should use me too hard. I also took to studying his countenance, until I became so accustomed to its expression and to his ways, that I could always tell whether he intended mischief. At such times I would get out of the way. The older I grew, and the stronger, the less fearful I became; and then I noticed that my master got frightened of me, lest I should run away. All this, however, did not save my poor back; but whenever Stevens wanted to spite me, he would not ask the men to hold me, for fear I should kill them, but used to creep up very slily, and hit me unawares, or throw sticks, chunks, and big stones at me, which sometimes hit and hurt me, and sometimes missed me and injured another. All this I bore. I wanted to get a clear start, for my mind was bent upon making tracks for England, which I fancied was not very far away. So I put up with the floggings and the ill-usage, and bided my time.

I remember once he wanted to punish me for a spite he had. He and I had been watching each other a good many days, and I had contrived to dodge him out of his revenge.

At length he invited one Jessie Cleveland, who lived in De Kalb county, and five or six more of his companions, to go a fishing with him. He took me and the other negroes to draw the seine through the river. We were to fish at night, so we lighted a great fire on the bank, and whilst they sat down by it, drinking, and smoking, and feasting, we went on fishing by torch-light. We remained at it the whole night, and Stevens kept on forcing us to drink rum until we were all drunk, like himself and his companions. At eight o'clock in the morning we left off, and then, seeing I could not help myself by running away, he set to and flogged me with a hickory rod: and how he did beat me that morning—oh dear!

At length I determined to be off. John Glasgow had been given away about two years before, to Stevens' son John. When he went I lost my only friend. But all he had told me rested on my mind. My whole thoughts dwelt upon England, and as things seemed to be getting worse with me, I considered the time was come for me to make a bold start for liberty.

Accordingly I laid in, by degrees, a stock of corn-bread, and having obtained a forged pass from a poor white man, for which I gave him an old hen, I stole off one night, about two months after I had procured the pass, and made for the high road, which I thought would lead me straight to England. I walked on all night, and when morning came hid myself in the wood, starting again when it began to get dusk. I went on this way a great many nights, keeping to the main road, and concealing myself by day in the woods or swamps. My only direction was to take the biggest road. One night I came to one, which, after I had followed it for some time—still under the impression that it would take me to England—brought me to a dead stop, at a stone quarry, at the foot of the Blue Ridge of mountains. I staid here all night, walking about to keep clear of the wild cats, panthers, and cat-a-mounts which I could hear prowling about, and whose growling alarmed me very much. When morning broke I began to consider what I should do. I knew that I ought to go northwards, but having nothing to guide me, I began to look about for signs. I soon noticed that on one side of the trees the moss was drier and shorter than it was on the other, and I concluded it was the sun which had burnt it up, and checked its growth, and that the dry moss must therefore be on the south side. I examined a good many trees, and finding these signs on most of them, I set off in the direction towards which the long, green moss pointed, and went on, until late in the day, without any thing happening to me, when all of a sudden I heard a man chopping wood. I soon came up to him. He was a white man, and he asked me where I was going.

"Into Ohio," said I.

"Are you free?" he asked.

"Yes, Sir," I answered.

"Where's your pass, Sir?" he said.

I took out the pass I had spoken of, and handed it to him. He saw at once that it was forged, and told me so. I drew out of him that a genuine pass was always signed by a great many individuals, and countersigned by the clerk of the district court, besides bearing the seal. He added, in answer to questions from me, that I was in Tennessee, and that no pass signed by one person would be of any use to enable me to go out of one State into another. I felt that I was caught, and hardly knew what to do. The man spoke very loud and strong at first, but I suppose there was something in my manner that made him feel timid, for he presently began to talk more softly, trying to calm me down. At last he said, if I would go home with him, he would see no harm came to me, and he would provide me with proper passes to take me through Tennessee, Kentucky, and Ohio. He said he would number each, so that I might not mistake one for the other, and he advised me to throw them away, one by one, after they had served my turn. At length I agreed to go home with him. I remained there until night. His name was Posey, I afterwards learned. He went away in the early part of the evening to fetch the passes, as he said; but as the time wore on without his making his appearance, I began to get uncomfortable. I was pondering what I should do, when he suddenly came in, with five other men having guns. Then I knew I had been betrayed, and must give up.

The first thing Posey did was to bid me cross my hands before me. I did so. He then took a log chain and fastened it round my leg. When he had me fast, he began to question me in his old rough way.

"Who do you belong to, Sir?" he said.

I told him that Decatur Stevens was my master.

"Where does he live?" he asked then.

"In Georgia, Sir," I answered.

"Then what are you doing here?" was his next question.

"I got lost, Sir," I replied.

"Oh! You got lost, did you?" he said. "And pray, Sir, did you come here on purpose to get lost?"

"No, Sir," I answered. "I got lost before I got here. I got lost before I saw you."

They consulted together a few minutes, and then one of them said they would put me in a safe place where I should not "get lost very soon," and where the dogs could not catch me. We all set out together then, and I soon found I was going to be taken to the jail. I now began to consider whether I might not get out of their hands if I tried, for my mind was quite made up not to give up the hope of effecting my escape, so long as I saw there remained ever so slight a chance in my favour. I therefore began to talk with my captors, one of whom was named Wiggins, and another Arres. I told them I thought they were going to do a very foolish thing in taking me to jail. If they put me there, and sent for my master, he would pay them for catching me, but he would have to give the jailer his fees; but if they kept me safe somewhere, and sent for Stevens to fetch me away, they might get more out of him, on account of the trouble that would be saved him getting me out of jail again. This idea seemed to find favour with them, and at last they agreed that I should be conveyed to Wiggins' house, and that Arres should go to Stevens and tell him about me. Having made up their mind to this, Arres took my bundle of clothes to his place, and set off, we turning into a road that led to Wiggins' house.

I remained nearly a week at Wiggins'. Every night he used to chain me to the post of the bed on which he slept, fastening me to the wall in the day-time, by means of a staple driven through it. I always remained here until after suppertime, with a little girl who was set to watch me. At the end of two or three days we became quite great friends, and I made up my mind to try and befool her, and get away if I could. One evening I pretended to be sulky, and would not answer her when she spoke to me. At last I stared at her very hard, till I noticed she seemed to get a little alarmed, when I told her that she must not talk to me, or look at me, for if any body did so, when I felt as I did then, I should be sure to go mad. I saw she became more alarmed than before, and presently she moved away, and sat down with her back towards me. Still she would peep round over her shoulder, every now and then, when I would shake my head, and glare at her, and rattle my chain, till she turned her head again.

I ought to state that all this was part of a plan I had made up in my mind. In order to fasten me up, some workmen had been employed to cut a hole in the wall, to fix the staple and secure my chain. They had left a chisel on the ground, which I had seen, and when I was taken away, the first night, to be fastened to Wiggins' bed-post, I threw my old blanket over the chisel to prevent any body else from spying it out. Next morning I drew it and my blanket to me, and laid upon them, and when night came, left it, as before, concealed by the blanket. In the course of the week, and from the moment I concluded to try again for liberty, I had constantly sent the little girl I have mentioned backwards and forwards to her father, telling him I wanted him to lead me out. In a few days he got tired of coming so often, and at length did not pay any heed to my messages. I had calculated upon this circumstance, which I felt might serve me, when the time came to take advantage of it.

On the evening in question, having quite succeeded in turning away my little jailer's attention from me, I thought the time was come for making another attempt to escape. I had heard that Arres was looked for every day, and, of course, my master with him. Wiggins was in the kitchen, which was thirty yards away from the dwelling-house, and I knew it would take but a very little while for the child to run there and back: but on the use I could make of those few minutes I felt all my present hopes of getting away depended. Watching my opportunity, I took the chisel and the whaffle-irons which the cook had left standing in the chimney-corner, and with the two tried to break a link of my chain. The whaffle-irons failed, so I put them down, and reached over to get an old pan-handle that did service as a poker. With it I succeeded in breaking the chain. I waited a few moments to fetch breath, for my heart beat so, at the thought that I was so far free, that I could scarcely sit still. Presently I told the child to go and tell her father I wanted him. She gave me one look and started off. No sooner was she gone than I made off too, only in another direction, bounding like a hare over every thing that came in my way.

After running a good distance, I stopped to listen for sounds, and to breathe, for I was quite blown. I could hear nothing, and concluded I was safe for the present. It was now past ten, and as I had no money nor clothes, nor any thing to eat, I thought I would go round to Posey's, and try and get my bundle. I found my way there, for I knew the direction of the house, and that it was not more than a mile from Wiggins', with no house or dwelling between them. When I got up to it I listened at the windows, and soon discovered that Posey was at home, so that any chance of getting my bundle was gone. What to do I did not know. To pursue my own inclination, and try to complete my escape, I felt would be exposing myself to certain re-capture, and most severe punishment; for I knew I could not remain long in the neighbourhood, and that it would be raised in search of me as soon as morning broke. On the other hand, I concluded that if I were to go back to my master I might get a flogging, but that another more favourable chance of escaping might offer, and my going back of my own accord, as I had done before, would perhaps be in my favour. After weighing the chances over in my mind, I determined to return into Georgia and give myself up, trying to harden myself to meet the consequences.

So I set off back, and after a journey of several days, travelling by night to avoid being caught, and resting by day, I got to the plantation and delivered myself into the hands of my master, telling him he was to do with me what he pleased.

It pleased him to tie me up and give me a dreadful flogging; and so ended my second determined attempt to escape from slavery.

CHAPTER IX.

MORE TRIBULATION.

HAVING got over this trouble, I began to ponder on what means I should employ to ensure the success of my next attempt to escape; for I was still bent upon accomplishing my object. I determined to do all that I could to delude my master into the belief that I was cured of running off, and by appearing very humble and submissive, first gain his confidence. I dare say the good people who read this confession will think I was very wicked, and I do not mean to say it is not wrong to deceive; but I do not think any one should judge me too harshly for following the example that was set by everybody around me. My master was always deceiving us slaves. If he promised us any thing we never got it, except it happened to be a flogging; and I must say he always kept his word in that. We used to know we were cheated, when having done our best, he swore we had skulked, and cowhided us for it. His dealings with everybody were all on the same principle of trying to over-reach them. Then we could not help seeing many things we knew to be wrong, and which we could have set right if our evidence had been taken; but whenever it suited our master's purpose to require us to lie, we were obliged to do as he wished, or take the consequences. In fact, we felt we were living under a system of cheating, and lying, and deceit; and being taught no better, we grew up in it, and did not see the wrong of it, so long as we were not acting against one another. I am sure that, as a rule, any one of us who would have thought nothing of stealing a hog, or a sack of corn, from our master, would have allowed himself to be cut to pieces rather than betray the confidence of his fellow-slave; and, perhaps, my mentioning this fact may be taken as a set-off against the systematic deception we practised, in self-defence, on our master.

Having made up my mind now to cheat Stevens into a good opinion of me, I took to answering him very humbly, and pretended to be frightened of him. Every thing he bade me do, I did, until at length he got to think the last flogging he had given me, had done me good, and made me submissive. Then he would chuckle and crow over me, thinking it a great victory to have succeeded, as he thought, in breaking down my spirit. Indeed, the experiment in my case seemed so satisfactory, that he thought he would try it on two rather unruly "boys" named Alfred and Harry. One day he sent them to catch four mules which were loose in the stable. This was only a pretext, for he beckoned me to him, and we followed them in. When we were in, he set his back against the door, and, drawing a bit of cord from under his coat, told me to catch the "boys," as he intended to flog them. As soon as they saw what he was after, they began dodging round and under the mules, I trying my hardest to lay hold of them. The mules, in running, rubbed against Decatur, and pushed him away from the door, which was no sooner open, than boys and mules bolted, master swearing at me for letting them get away, and declaring that I had done so for the purpose. I told him I had done just the contrary; but in spite of all I could say, he got into a towering rage, and as I was going out at the door, leaped on my back, holding me fast round the neck, and calling out to Aunt Sally—one of the old negro women—to bring him down his gun. Aunt Sally ran into the house, and presently I saw her come out of it, holding up the gun that my master's father had shot poor Morgan with. I do not know whether Decatur intended to shoot me, but I know I became dreadfully alarmed, and without being scarcely aware of what I did, I tipped him down off my shoulders, and he fell to the ground, severely hurting his neck. I immediately took to my heels and escaped into the wood near the plantation. I staid here all day, in fear and trembling, thinking of the law which punishes, with the loss of his right arm, any slave who shall inflict injury on or raise his arm against his master.[18] By the time night had fallen I became so miserable, that I resolved to drown myself, and proceeded to the river for that purpose. When I got there, however, and saw the water looked so cold and so deep, my resolution was shaken. I candidly confess I did not like the prospect, even though death seemed preferable to the life I was leading, with its hourly miseries, and almost daily punishments. But I reflected that so long as I had life, there was hope; so I turned my back upon the river, and made my way to our old apple-orchard, where I laid down, and dozed till morning.

I wandered about here three days, eating berries—for there was no fruit—until, at the end of that time, I was well nigh famished. I then concluded to return to my master, and to meet the consequences of his displeasure. I went round to where the coloured people were at work, who advised me to make for the house by the way of the spring, and I should see what was going on, and what was in store for me. Accordingly I bent my steps in that direction, until I came to a little knoll or rising ground, from which I could overlook the plantation and buildings. I saw two posts set upright in the ground, and a cross-beam reaching from one to the other, to which a block and a rope were attached. I concluded Stevens was going to hang me, so I set off running. I had, however, been perceived, and I soon found that I was being hunted down with dogs. I looked behind, and saw my master and a good many strange people, some on horses and some on foot, who were exciting the hounds to follow me. These were gaining fast upon me, but I observed that they minded the strange people, or any one who urged them on, so I determined I would give them the slip if I could. As they came up, I began to halloo and shout to them as lustily as any body, all the while running as fast as I could.

"Catch him, fellow," said I, urging the dogs on; "catch him; hey, fellow, hey, fellow; catch him."

The poor animals wagged their tails, and, excited by me, ran right ahead, quite fooled, and jumping and looking about, as though they sought to find out what we were all after. But at this moment, Billy Curtis, a planter, who was one of the party, and who was well mounted, rode up and struck me on the head with a dogwood club. The blow felled me, as though I had been shot, completely stunning me. When I recovered, I found myself stretched on the ground, my head bleeding fearfully, and my master standing over me, with his foot on my forehead. The scar that blow made, I retain to this day.

I was now forced to get up, when they drove me to where I had seen the posts. Here they tied my hands and feet together, and passing the rope through the block and pulleys, hoisted me up and began to swing me backwards and forwards. Billy Curtis stood on one side, with a bull-whip in his hand, and David Barrett on the other, with a cow-hide. My master stood a little further off, laughing, and as Curtis and Barrett could not whip and swing me too, a negro was set to keep me going. As I swung past them, these men hit me each a lick with their whips, and they continued doing so until I fainted, when I was taken down.

But I was not done with yet.

Many people say that half of what Mrs. Stowe and others have written about the punishments inflicted on slaves is untrue. I wish, for the sake of those who are now in bonds, that it were so. Unfortunately it is too true; and I believe half of what is done to them never comes to light. This is what happened to me next.

To prevent my running away any more, Stevens fixed bells and horns on my head. This is not by any means an uncommon punishment. I have seen many slaves wearing them. A circle of iron, having a hinge behind, with a staple and padlock before, which hang under the chin, is fastened round the neck. Another circle of iron fits quite close round the crown of the head. The two are held together in this position by three rods of iron, which are fixed in each circle. These rods, or horns, stick out three feet above the head, and have a bell attached to each. The bells and horns do not weigh less than from twelve to fourteen pounds. When Stevens had fixed this ornament on my head, he turned me loose, and told me I might run off now if I liked.

I wore the bells and horns, day and night, for three months, and I do not think any description I could give of my sufferings during this time would convey any thing approaching to a faint idea of them. Let alone that their weight made my head and neck ache dreadfully, especially when I stooped to my work, at night I could not lie down to rest, because the horns prevented my stretching myself, or even curling myself up; so I was obliged to sleep crouching. Of course it was impossible for me to attempt to remove them, or to get away, though I still held to my resolution to make another venture as soon as I could see my way of doing it. Indeed, during those three long months, I thought more of John Glasgow, and getting off to England, than I had ever done all the time before, with such a firm purpose. I collected and arranged in my mind all the scraps of information I had been able to procure from others, or that I had acquired myself; and concealed, in the trunk of an old tree, a bundle of clothes and a flint and steel and tinder-horn: for though my case seemed desperate, I clung to hope, with a tenacity which now surprises me. It was a blessed consolation, and only for it I must have died.

CHAPTER X.

I MAKE ANOTHER ATTEMPT TO ESCAPE.

I OWE it to an accidental circumstance that I got rid, at last, of my uncomfortable head-dress.

After wearing it for about three months, I was set to pack corn into a crib. The bells and horns, however, prevented me from getting into the crib, so Decatur took them off, and set them down by the side of the corn-crib, ready for me to have them on again. It was one Saturday evening, and I had heard there was going to be a camp-meeting a little way off. To this I determined to go. I had frequently heard of these meetings, and often longed to attend one of them, but had never yet done so. Instead of packing the corn, as I was bidden, I took the opportunity—being now released from my bells and horns—to go to the camp-meeting, where I remained all night. Whilst there I turned over in my mind the chances I had of escaping, and concluded the favourable time had come for me to renew my attempt. In order to throw Stevens off his guard, I thought I would go back next morning, as if he saw me, after lying out all night, he would believe I did not intend running off, as I had not taken advantage of that opportunity. It was a part of my calculation to run away under circumstances which should leave my master under the impression of my having gone off in a fright. Had I disappeared without any apparently sufficient cause, a hue and cry would have been raised after me directly. So I returned home early on Sunday morning.

When Decatur came round, a little later in the forenoon, and saw that I had not done my task, he began to swear at me dreadfully, and to threaten me. But I was a much stronger man than he, and if I looked as wicked as I felt, whilst he was abusing me so, I think it must have been from fear he did not put his threats into execution. I was a match for two such men as he, any day, and he knew it. He looked at me and at the bells and horns, which remained standing by the corn-crib, but I suppose he felt it was of no use for him to try to put them on again without help. I quite believe he intended to do so, in his sly way, by bringing two or three of the hands in suddenly to seize and hold me whilst he put them on. Any how, he made no attempt now, but kept on swearing at and calling me dreadful names. He presently shouted to Minney, an old negro woman, and the mother of thirteen children, to come and do my work. The poor old creature began to run towards him, but she did not run fast enough to please him, so, stooping down, he picked up a huge white flint stone, and hove it at her. It struck her on the arm, and broke it just above the wrist. She shrieked out with the pain, but that only made our savage master laugh. I would gladly have saved the old woman that blow, had it been in my power, for I felt that Decatur had vented upon her the spite he had against me. I was, however, in danger myself, and seeing the other women come round the poor creature, I ran away and hid myself in the wood.

I lay concealed here until dark, pondering in my mind which way I should go. I at length resolved to take a road westward. I had come to know the road from Stevens' to Cass-ville, because we slaves used to have to take bacon to the Altoonah gold mines to sell to the miners. Cass-ville must be quite two hundred miles from Millidgeville, and I knew every step of the road. We also used to go to New Echota, in the Cherokee purchase, on the Ooestennala river. A very large body of Indians, gathered from this territory, had been located there sometime between 1836 and 1838, where they remained six months, under guard, being on their way to their new location in Arkansas. There were some thousands in all, under the chiefs John Ross and John Ridge. Stevens used to send us to these people to sell them provisions, generally causing his son-in-law, Joe Stokes, to accompany us. So it was I came to know there was a good road open for me thus far.

As soon as it was dark enough to make it safe, I set out once more on my travels, with a full determination either to gain my freedom, or to die in the attempt.

The incidents of my journey, during the first eight or ten days, were not of sufficient note to need my dwelling particularly upon them. My plan was to walk all night, and to hide myself in the day. I used to listen with painful attention for the sounds of footsteps, and when I heard, or fancied I heard a noise, I would conceal myself behind a log, or in a tree, or anywhere else, until the party had gone by, or my fears were allayed. I kept myself from starving by grubbing up sweet potatoes out of the fields by the way-side, which I cooked in a fire I made with dry sticks. When I came to such a field, I would get as many potatoes as I could conveniently carry for store; but as they were heavy and cumbersome, it may be supposed the stock I obtained on such occasions was not very large. In this way I travelled on out of Georgia into Alabama, until I reached a place, which I afterwards learned is called Tuscumbia, on the Tennessee river. I remember this place very well, for close to Tuscumbia there is a bubbling spring, and the landing-place is about two miles lower down.

When I got here, I became afraid to continue travelling by land. I considered what I should do; and concluding at last that the river must run into the sea, and that if I once got to the seaside, I should be sure to find some Englishmen there who would tell me the way to England, I determined to construct a raft, and float myself down upon it.

The reader will bear in mind that at this time I did not know where England was, but, foolishly enough, believed it was not very far off. Had I known where the Tennessee river would have floated me to, I should probably have turned off in some other direction. But I now look upon my ignorance of the fact, at that time, as a happy circumstance, to which I am, in all probability, indebted for my liberty.

I now sought out a place of concealment, which I soon discovered, in the wood, not far from the landing-place, and here I watched for float-wood as it came down the river. I procured three sticks of this timber, each being about fifteen feet long, and perhaps a foot and a half in diameter. These I dragged into shallow water, and bound firmly together with the blue grapevine, which grew in abundance in the wood; and having completed the raft, which was about five feet wide, I made it fast under the bushes that grew quite close down to the riverside, hanging quite over the water.

Prowling about at night, I had paid a visit to an old warehouse or shed that had been abandoned at the landing-place, it being now the fall-season, and the water in the river low. Here I found an old wedge-axe, and a piece of sheet-iron, that I afterwards conjectured had been part of the funnel of a steam-vessel; for, I need scarcely observe, I had not, at this time, ever seen a steamer. The iron was a good find for me, for I at once perceived that it would serve me to kindle a fire upon; so I took it into the wood, and hammered it out flat on a log; and very useful I found it. I afterwards rummaged up a board, which I fashioned into a paddle with my jack-knife, and having picked out a pole of timber, to help me further in navigating my raft, my preparations for starting were complete.

I pushed off that evening, as soon as it became dark enough to allow of my doing so safely. I had put some sand on the iron plate, and made preparations to kindle a fire on it, so that any one by chance noticing me going down the river, might take me for a fisherman. The next morning I beached my raft at a convenient spot, and having jumped ashore, pulled it up under the bushes and brush, so as effectually to conceal it. I then laid down and slept, and after I had rested, sauntered about until nightfall, when I put off again.

I was about nine days going down the river in this manner. During that time I saw several people, but do not think they caught sight of me, because I was so very cautious not to shew myself. I travelled always by night, concealing myself by day. I usually selected a place to land, in the neighbourhood of dwellings, as I was almost certain to find potatoe-fields near them. To these I paid as frequent visits as I could, prudently, bringing away with me as many potatoes as would last me for a couple or three days, and which I stored away on my raft. These, roasted, were my only food during the nine days, with one exception. One night my raft ran foul of a line stretched across the water. I traced it with my paddle and pole, and found it had a good many other smaller lines attached to it, each having a hook at the end. On one of them was a cat-fish, which I appropriated, and off which I made a famous feast.

At the end of about nine days I found the water becoming too deep for my pole, and the river widening considerably. Still I contrived to keep on, by using my paddle industriously, and not going far from the banks, until one evening, and whilst I was wondering where the great water, opening beyond, would take me to, I heard all of a sudden a great roaring and splashing. Almost directly after I saw two big, red eyes coming down full upon me, raised, as it appeared, only just above the level of the water. I also saw showers of sparks shooting up in the air, mingling with red fiery smoke—all, as I thought, being belched up by this strange monster, as he came along, hissing and heaving, and splashing up the water. I fell into a horrible fear, for I verily believed it to be Old Sam,* and that he had waylaid and was going to catch me. With all the trouble in the world I reached the bank, and leaped ashore, and abandoning my raft, took to my heels, and ran on towards some lights I had noticed; which I afterwards found were those of a town called Paducah,[19] about a mile from where I had landed, in my terror.

I had reached the Ohio river.

I need not inform my readers that the monster I took to be the devil was only a steam-boat. It seems to me now very foolish that I should have been so frightened; but if they had been placed in the same circumstances, and been as ignorant as I was, they would have felt quite as much alarmed, I am sure.

CHAPTER XI.

FORTUNE AND MISFORTUNE.

WHEN I look back upon the events of my life, I fancy I can perceive the directing hand of Providence in all that befel me at this particular time. My very ignorance may have proved one means of my safety, for if I had not been terrified into abandoning my raft, I do not see how I could have escaped again speedily falling into the hands of my enemies. The circumstances of my escape show me now, that every thing worked together for my ultimate good, though I did not, at the time, think so, nor easily reconcile myself to the various misfortunes which befel me, and delayed my obtaining my freedom.

Had it been broad day instead of quite dark, when I left my raft to be carried away by the current, my appearance in Paducah would certainly had led to my re-capture. I was dirty and miserable-looking from fatigue, travelling, and want of sufficient food, and my clothes were all worn and ragged. I got into the town, however, at an hour when few people were about, and it was easier for me to avoid them. After resting to take breath, I determined to look out for a barber's shop. In the United States, the barbers are generally coloured men, and I concluded I should be in safer hands with one of my own race. So I strolled about, up and down the streets, peeping in at doors and windows, until at length I found what I was seeking. After a moment's hesitation I knocked gently at the door. It was presently opened by a black man, who no sooner saw me, than he understood by my looks that I wanted assistance. He at once invited me in, and immediately closed and fastened the door.

Having made me take a seat he asked me which way I was going.

---

*The negroes so call the devil.—ED.

"My master's gone down to New Orleans," I said, "and I want to join him again."

I knew he did not believe me, and that he saw I was telling him a lie; but I felt afraid to tell him the truth right out.

"You're a runaway," he answered, almost directly. "Where have you come from?"

I did not hesitate now to confess the fact; and as I thought he looked friendly, I told him my story from beginning to end, in as few words as I could, he listening attentively all the while. When I had finished, he said:

"You mustn't stop here: it would be dangerous for both of us. You can sleep here to-night, however, and I will try to get you away in the morning. But if you were seen, and it were found out I was helping you off, it would break me up."

Concluding I was hungry, he gave me some fried fish and some hoe-cake for supper. I need not say I ate heartily. We chatted for an hour or so, and I learnt his name, and that he was a free man from Illinois. I must not repeat his name, but if ever this book reaches him, he will remember me, and I wish him to know that I have always thought of him with gratitude for his kindness to me that night, and for his fidelity to me in my sore trouble.

He put me to sleep on his sofa, but I could not close my eyes for fear, as well as for a kind of shivering, brought on by my long exposure to cold and wet. If I slept at all, it was only by snatches, so that I felt quite relieved when morning came. My benefactor then informed me he had been making inquiries, and there was a steamer ready to start for New Orleans, on board of which I must go. She was called the *Neptune*. I did not desire any thing better than to be off, fancying still that if I got safely to New Orleans I should find no difficulty in reaching England. Accordingly I jumped up, and after a hurried breakfast, made the best of my way to the quay, where I soon saw the steamer.

I went straight on board, and saw the Captain, to whom I repeated the story of my master's having gone on to New Orleans; that I had missed him, and wanted to join him as soon as possible. He did not say much then, being very busy, and I went and stood aside, trying to avoid notice. After we started, he began walking about, contriving to draw near to me every now and then, when he would fix his eyes on me in a very doubting way. At length we got to the fork of the Mississippi, below Paducah and Cairo, where the Ohio joins it. Here there is, in the last-named river, a flat shallow, and here the steamer took ground, knocking off her two iron-chimneys, and receiving other damage. The confusion and bustle caused by this accident diverted the Captain's attention from me, for a time, and were quite a relief to me from his constant watching. After a while we got free again, and he recommenced walking the deck, as before. He also began to put questions to me now and then; asking about my master; wanting to know his name; where he lived; the names of his neighbours, and such like, all of which questions I strove to answer as unconcernedly and as satisfactorily as I could. I noticed him, however, to shake his head as he turned away, and I concluded he doubted my story, and that having his suspicions of my being a runaway, he would sell me as soon as we reached our destination. So I made up my mind to the worst, resolving, notwithstanding, to give him the slip, if I could.

I have said I thought England was near New Orleans, for I had always heard it spoken of as being "only just across the water." Whilst on board, I endeavoured to ascertain how far it was from New Orleans, and whether there would be any difficulty in my getting from there to England. I felt much relieved when the men told me I had only to "step across" from New Orleans to England, and quite hugged myself in the anticipation of so soon being beyond the reach of the slave-holders. But it was not long before I discovered that, taking advantage of my ignorance and simplicity, they had poked fun at me, and altogether misled me.

In about four or five days, and at about nine in the morning, we reached New Orleans. Oh, how my poor heart did beat, as the steamer drew near to the wharf side, and I saw the negroes at work. I then began to suspect all was not right, and my fears of the Captain increased every minute. There was great confusion on deck, as soon as the steamer was made fast, so many people coming on board, and so much running backwards and forwards. Watching for an opportunity when the Captain's back was turned, and his attention engaged by parties conversing with him, I slunk to the gangway, and walked off in the crowd, increasing my pace as I got further from the quay. I made for a place where I saw a number of cotton-waggons, tended by the drivers, who were all, or nearly all, of my own colour. They were carting cotton from the dock to the presses, and seemed very busy. I went up to them, and after asking a few questions, learnt that I was in the very heart of slavery, and further off from England than when I was in Georgia. They were not long in discovering me to be a runaway, and told me I should be certain to be taken up before night, and put into the calaboose or prison; and that I should be flogged every morning until I told the name of my master. Under these circumstances I did not know what to do, but having asked them a few questions about the city, I set off again, thinking, as I went along, what I should do for the best.

I had ascertained, of the men I have alluded to, that Murrell and Buck Hurd were well known in New Orleans, and I now thought that if I could meet with either of them, I might perhaps get them to sell me, and to say nothing about it, as they would pocket a good sum by the sale, and I might get a good master. It makes me smile, now, to think of the slender hope there was of my running up against either of these men; though at the time I felt quite sanguine that they must be there, and that every thing would fall out as I wished. But it did not, quite.

After wandering about for some time, without meeting the parties I was seeking, it occurred to me to look out for some one like them; or for a party who might be likely to fall in with the plan I had imagined for getting myself sold, in order to save my back, and preserve any chances of escape a change of masters might bring me. I had nothing to guide me in this apparently mad search, but an instinctive knowledge of character which I had acquired from a long habit of studying the expression of the countenance. Nor will this surprise my readers when they bear in mind how closely I had been forced to watch the changes of my master's physiognomy, as well as those of the parties he associated with, so as to frame my conduct in accordance with what I had reason to believe was their prevailing mood at any given time. Anyhow, I may say, without boasting, that a

man's countenance is my guide to his disposition, and I have found my judgment
in this respect so unfailing, that I would never act contrary to it. With this idea
in my mind then, and looking at the folks I met, I walked on, until I came to a
large street, and almost ran up against the man whom I felt I wanted most at that
moment. He was young, and indifferently well dressed, his clothes looking dusty
and tumbled. He had a gold-headed cane in his hand, and walked lazily, with
rather an irregular step. I observed that he looked sleepy, and that his eyes were
blood-shotten and puffy, as though he had been up all night. I set him down in
my mind for a gambler and a drunkard, of whom I had seen many such at
Stevens', and I concluded he might want money: so I stopped him.

"Master," said I, speaking low, "I've run away, Sir."

He stopped short and looked at me a moment very hard.

"Run away?" he exclaimed.

"Yes, Sir," I answered.

"Where from, Sir?" he asked, speaking roughly.

"From the State of Georgia, Sir," I replied.

"Well, Sir," said he then, "what's that to me?"

"Sir," I made reply, "I thought may be you would take me and sell me, and
put the money in your pocket, so that my old master may never get me any
more."

"Hum!" he said. "What part of Georgia have you come from?"

I told him I used to live in Baldwin County, and that my name was Benford; and he then asked me a great many questions, mentioning the names of
people I knew, and amongst others that of Dr. Hamilton. He seemed satisfied I
told him the truth, and bade me remain where I was for five minutes, and he
would go and see what he could do.

This occurred not far from the St. Charles' Hôtel, opposite to which there
was—as I subsequently found out—an auction-room for the sale of negroes. He
went in, and presently came out with another man, whom I afterwards learnt
was Theophilus Freeman the negro-trader. It was a crafty thing the stranger did,
to bring Freeman out to me. By so doing he avoided observation, and gave the
trader an opportunity of striking a bargain without being over-heard by any
other dealer. Freeman looked at me a minute, and then examined me, but did
not at first seem disposed to purchase me. He found fault with my age and my
appearance, and said I should not go off well, as I was not smart-looking enough.
The young man then informed him I was a carpenter, and I added that I was a
good workman, and worth any man's money. Freeman upon this asked what the
young man, my supposed master, wanted for me, and was told eight hundred
dollars, and that I was quite a bargain at that price. The trader did not make any
remark about the sum, but asked to see the bill of sale relating to me. The young
man answered that he had no bill of sale of me; his father had given me to him,
so there had been no need of one. He added that really he did not want to part
with me, for I was a "thorough good boy;" but he had been gambling; had lost
a large sum, and was quite hard up for cash, so he had no other alternative but
to raise money by disposing of me. Freeman replied that he was very sorry for
him, but without a bill of sale he would not give more than four hundred dollars

for me. This made the young man very angry, and he swore at Freeman, and cursed him for being so hard; but after more chaffering, seeing that Freeman was firm, he consented to take the sum offered: so the bargain was struck upon the spot, and they both conducted me to the negro-pen, where I was shut up with other slaves, after being treated to a meal of cold bacon and cabbage.

CHAPTER XII.

THE SLAVE-PEN IN NEW ORLEANS.

I HAVE stated that the slave-pen to which I was taken, stood facing the St. Charles' Hôtel. It had formerly been an old Bank. It consisted of a block of houses forming a square, and covering perhaps an acre of ground. The centre of this square had been filled quite up with rubbish and stones, as high as the back of the first floor of the houses, so as to form a solid foundation for the yard of the pen, which, it will be understood, was level with the first floor, and nicely gravelled for the slaves to take exercise in. The houses themselves were built upon brick pillars or piers, the spaces between which had been converted into stores. Of these there were a great number, one of them being used as the negro auction-room.

The accommodation for the negroes consisted of three tiers of rooms, one above the other, the yard I have spoken of being common to all. There were two entrances to the pen, one for the "niggers," the other for visiters and buyers. The windows in front, which overlooked the street, were heavily barred, as were those which overlooked the yard. It was an awfully gloomy place, notwithstanding the bustle that was always going on in it.

I may as well describe here the order of the daily proceedings, as during the whole time I remained in the pen, they were, one day with the other, pretty much the same.

A mulatto named Bob Freeman, and who was called the Steward, had charge of the arrangements that concerned the slaves. He had a great deal of power of a particular kind, and did very nearly what he liked in the way of making them comfortable or otherwise; shutting them up if he disliked them, or they displeased him: according as they were favourites with him or not. The pen would contain about five hundred, and was usually full. The men were separated from the women, and the children from both; but the youngest and handsomest females were set apart as the concubines of the masters, who generally changed mistresses every week.

I could relate, in connection with this part of my subject, some terrible things I know of, that happened, and lay bare some most frightful scenes of immorality and vice which I witnessed; but I abstain, for reasons which my readers will, I hope, appreciate. I think it only right, however, to mention the above fact, that people may get a glimpse of the dreadful fate which awaits the young slave women who are sold away South, where the slave-pen is only another name for a brothel.

As may be imagined, the slaves are brought from all parts; are of all sorts, sizes, and ages, and arrive in various states of fatigue and condition; but they soon improve in their looks, as they are regularly fed, and have plenty to eat. As soon as we were roused in the morning, there was a general washing, and combing, and shaving, pulling out of grey hairs, and dyeing the hair of those who were too grey to be plucked without making them bald. When this was over—and it was no light business—we used to breakfast, getting bread, and bacon, and coffee, of which a sufficiency was given to us, that we might plump up and become sleek. Bob would then proceed to instruct us how to show ourselves off, and afterwards form us into companies, according to our size; those who were nearly of the same height and make being put into separate lots; the men, the women, and the children of both sexes, being divided off all alike. In consequence of this arrangement, the various members of a family were of necessity separated, and would often see the last of one another in that dreadful show-room. The buying commenced at about ten in the morning, and lasted till one, during which time we were obliged to be sitting about in our respective companies, ready for inspection. At one we used to go to dinner, our usual food being a repetition of the morning meal, varied with vegetables, and a little fruit sometimes. After dinner we were compelled to walk, and dance, and kick about in the yard for exercise; and Bob, who had a fiddle, used to play up jigs for us to dance to. If we did not dance to his fiddle, we used to have to do so to his whip, so no wonder we used our legs handsomely, though the music was none of the best. When our exercises were over, we used to be "sized out" again, ready for the afternoon sale, which commenced at three, and ended at six. This over, we had tea, and were then free to do what we liked in the pen, until Bob rang us off to bed at ten.

Of course our ranks were constantly thinned by sales, and as constantly recruited by fresh arrivals. Amongst other "nigger speculators" whom I remember bringing in their coffles, were Williams from Washington, and Redford and Kelly from Kentucky, and M'Cargo from Richmond, in Virginia, who was Freeman's partner. It was surprising what large gangs they brought in, frequently filling the pen.

At the top of the building there was an attic called the "flogging-room." It was quite empty. Screwed into the floor were several rows of wooden cleets, for the purpose of reaving[20] cords through. The name of the room tells what used to be done here. Every day there was flogging going on. It is a rule amongst "nigger dealers," not to flog with any instrument that will cut the skin, because this would depreciate the value of the "property;" therefore the punishment is inflicted with what is called a "flopping paddle." The "flop" is of leather, about a foot-and-a-half long, and as broad as the palm of the hand; perhaps a little broader: the handle is of wood, and about two feet long. Men, women, and girls are all punished alike. They are brought in and stripped stark naked, and laid flat on the floor, with their face downwards, their hands being made fast to the cleets by means of the cords. Sometimes their feet are bound in the same manner, but usually a negro, who is called in for the purpose, holds the victim's feet down by main force, whilst the whipper lays on, "flop, flop, flop," for half an hour, which is the usual time the flogging lasts. The punishment is dreadfully severe, for all no blood is drawn. I have frequently been forced to come in and hold the feet of women and girls, and sometimes to "flop" them, as well as men; but I was never myself punished in this manner. "Flopping" was inflicted for various offences, especially the unpardonable one of "not speaking up and looking bright and smart" when the buyers were choosing.

As the importance of "looking bright" under such circumstances may not be readily understood by the ordinary run of readers, I may as well explain that the price a slave fetches depends, in a great measure, upon the general appearance he or she presents to the intending buyer. A man or a woman may be well made, and physically faultless in every respect, yet their value be impaired by a sour look, or a dull, vacant stare, or a general dulness of demeanour. For this reason the poor wretches who are about to be sold, are instructed to look "spry and smart:" to hold themselves well up, and put on a smiling, cheerful countenance. They are also told to speak up for, and recommend themselves; to conceal any defects they may have, and especially not to tell their age when they are getting past the active period of life. It is quite a truism that "a nigger never knows when he was born," for though he may be quite certain of the year, and might swear to it blindfold, he must say he is just as old as his master chooses to bid him do, or he will have to take the consequences. It may be conceived that "nigger trading" is as much a calling as any other, and that there is an enormous amount of cheating and roguery in it. There are "nigger jockeys" as well as horse jockeys, and as many tricks are played off to sell a bad or an unsound "nigger," as there are to palm off a diseased horse; and the man who succeeds in "shoving off a used up nigger," as one sound in wind and limb, takes as much pride in boasting of it, as the horse dealer does who has taken in a green-horn with a wall-eyed pony. Of course these "tricks of the trade" are known, and every means are employed to defeat attempts at dishonest sales. I dare not—for decency's sake—detail the various expedients that are resorted to by dealers to test the soundness of a male or a female slave. When I say that they are handled in the grossest manner, and inspected with the most elaborate and disgusting minuteness, I have said enough for the most obtuse understanding to fill up the outline of the horrible picture. What passes behind the screen in the auction-room, or in the room where the dealer is left alone with the "chattels" offered to him to buy, only those who have gone through the ordeal can tell. But God has recorded the wickedness that is done there, and punishment will assuredly fall upon the guilty.

I do not think any pen could describe the scene that takes place at a negro auction. The companies, regularly "sized out," are forced to stand up, as the buyers come up to them, and to straighten themselves as stiffly as they can. When spoken to, they must reply quickly, with a smile on their lips, though agony is in their heart, and the tear trembling in their eye. They must answer every question, and do as they are bid, to show themselves off; dance, jump, walk, leap, squat, tumble, and twist about, that the buyer may see they have no stiff joints, or other physical defect. Here may be seen husbands separated from their wives, only by the width of the room, and children from their parents, one or both, witnessing the driving of the bargain that is to tear them asunder for ever, yet not a word of lamentation or anguish must escape from them; nor when the deed is consummated, dare they bid one another good-bye, or take one last embrace. Even the poor, dear, little children, who are crying and wringing their hands after "daddy and mammy," are not allowed to exchange with them a parting caress. Nature, however, will not be thus controlled, and in spite of the terrors of the paddle and the cow-hide, the most fearful scenes of anguish and confusion too often take place, converting the auction-room into a perfect Bedlam of despair. I cannot think of it without a cold shiver. I often dream of it, and as often dwell upon it in the day-time.

Oh, that the fine ladies of England could see with my eyes!

CHAPTER XIII.

I AM ONCE MORE SOLD.

I HAD been sold to Freeman under the name of Benford, by which name I was known during the time I remained in the pen, and here, therefore, I lost that of Fed. The very same evening of the day on which I became Freeman's property, the young man who had sold me to him, came to the pen, on a pretence of business. He soon found me out, and asked me to run off with him to Mobile. I refused to do so. I felt afraid, and did not want to incur the risk of encountering fresh difficulties, let alone that I had my own plan of escape to carry out. I noticed that he was better dressed than when I met him in the morning, so I concluded he had rigged himself out afresh with some of the money he had received for me. He saw I was determined not to fall in with his proposal, so he did not press it. He kept on talking to me, however, about indifferent matters, I wondering what he wanted, when I observed that his attention seemed directed to Freeman and Mac Cargo, (whom I have already mentioned,) and who were playing cards in the gambling saloon. Every now and then, Mac Cargo, who lost, would run across into his own room, and take a handful of gold out of his trunk, with which he would return, to stake and play again. We could see all this very plainly, as the rooms were on the same landing. The young man then set me to watch, giving me instructions to cough if any body stirred, and I saw him go into Mac Cargo's chamber, straight to the trunk, the lid of which he lifted just high enough to allow his hand to go in. He presently returned with a great handful of the gold pieces six of which he gave to me, and then went away into the gambling and drinking room.

I took the money and concealed it. I did not see there was any wrong in it. I said to myself it had been got by selling "niggers," and I had as much right to it as anybody. I am free to confess now that the morality of my argument was none of the highest, but I judged according to the notions I had at that time. I do not know what became of the young man, as I was removed next day; nor did I ever learn his name.

The gold proved very serviceable. Being in want of tobacco, I asked the mulatto steward, Bob Freeman, to buy me some, and gave him one of the gold pieces for that purpose. He did so, and brought me the change honestly. Finding I had money, he selected me to accompany him out to purchase provisions, and the friendship and liking he showed for me ultimately induced his masters, Freeman and Mac Cargo, to place confidence in me too. I used to go everywhere with Bob, especially when he had to take negroes down to the smith's, to have their irons taken off or new ones put on. By taking advantage of the opportunities thus afforded me, I contrived to get a good deal of information, which I treasured up for use at a future time; for I still cherished my project of escape.

I remember one day a coloured man named George being brought in, heavily ironed. As usual, Bob and I went with him to the smith's, to have the irons removed, and on the way I asked him why he had been so heavily ironed. He said it was for running away. I questioned him then more closely, and learnt he had come down the Mississippi. He informed me of the route he had taken, and in answer to further questions, told me that I might always know the Mississippi river, because its waters are muddy, and that if I kept to the muddy water, going up the stream, it would take me into Missouri. This was, in my circumstances, a most useful practical hint. I did not neglect profiting by it when the time came.

In like manner I picked up, from others, a good stock of valuable knowledge, and began to have a more definite idea of what was before me. I saw that my success would depend as much upon my prudence as upon my resolution, and as I now knew that my best chance would be to make for the north, I directed my attention to the best means of getting there.

I could very considerably extend the dimensions of this narrative, were I to relate all the incidents that occurred to me during the three months I remained in the slave-pen at New Orleans. At some future time, I may add to what this book contains. For the present, I wish to confine myself, as much as possible, to the narration of those things which more immediately relate to myself. One particular circumstance, however, occurred there, which I will just mention, as illustrating the working of the system under which I was.

It is a regulation established in New Orleans by the local authorities, to imprison strange negroes or coloured people who come into the city, should they be unable or unwilling to give such an account of themselves as shall be satisfactory to the police. Of course slaves do not often come without their masters, so that the regulation is especially oppressive to the free coloured people who may be compelled, in pursuit of their lawful calling, to visit the city. One day Freeman met a young woman, whom he knew. She was a beautiful mulatto; a perfect lady, and the *wife* and slave of a gentleman in Natchez, from which place she had come. Freeman probably threatened her, for he knew that by taking advantage of his knowledge of her, the law gave him a power over her; so to escape the ignominy of working in the public streets, in what is called "the chain-gang," she was compelled to have her trunks conveyed to his place, to let it be supposed she belonged to him, and to stay with him till his Natchez drove came in; which was nearly a fortnight.

From what I have related of the pen, it will be seen that when once a man is in it, there is little hope of his effecting his escape. Still, a few do so, notwithstanding the sharp look-out that is kept after them. I remember one slipping through our fingers. He had been sold as a "guaranteed nigger;" that is, warranted not to run away. In such cases, should the man "bolt," the seller is obliged to refund the sum he received for him. Bob and I had to conduct this man down to the ship, as he was going to a cotton farm. We took him, and saw him quite safely on board, but half-an-hour after, his new master came to look for him. Bob and I were sent to help in the search, but we never found him; so Freeman was obliged to "cash up" for him. I remember feeling envious of that "boy."

Although I had been in the pen now so long, and been put up to sale a good many times, I had not yet found a purchaser. One reason of this was that Mac Cargo and Freeman demanded a heavy price for me, but also in some measure because I did not care to speak up for myself, so that my looks did not recommend me to buyers. Freeman knew I should fetch a price when the spring-crops came on, as I was a good carpenter, so he was in no hurry at first. But as the time wore on, and he found I did not go off, he began to suspect the truth, and he and Mac Cargo got angry, and in my hearing said I did not care to try and sell myself, but that if I did not do so soon, they must make me. I knew very well what that threat meant. I had used the flopping-paddle too often not to understand; so I thought I ought to make up my mind now to save my back, by endeavouring to find a master.

Accordingly I began to draw Bob, and having learnt from him that there would be buyers from up the Mississippi, in a few days, I determined to pick one out, if I got the chance. I wanted to go in that direction, for reasons which should be plain to my readers; and when at last Bob told me the buyers were come, I felt quite excited with hope, and eager to meet them.

So I was put up again in the auction-room, and I took good care to look my brightest and answer my smartest. Such a character I gave myself, never a "nigger" had before. I was careful, however, to draw out the buyers, in order to learn what they wanted me for; which I judged of by the questions they put to me. One day a man came in, and I was called out and made to stand in the middle of the floor. His name was Jepsey James. He was a great, big robust man, with dark features, and wore a long, shabby blanket coat. His countenance was very sour-looking, and I did not at all like the looks of him. It seems, however, that mine pleased him, so he had me out, and felt my limbs, and squinted at me till my eyes ached staring back at him, and asked me all sorts of questions, which I answered quite smartly. At last he struck a bargain for me, and I was sold to him for twelve hundred dollars.

My new master bought a good many others, besides myself, who were at once chained and handcuffed. Freeman guaranteed me, so I was not served so; and when I learnt that he and my new master placed confidence in me, I made it a point of honour not to try and get away, so long as we were in the city, though had I been so minded, there was no lack of opportunities. Bob and I were charged with the conducting of the drove to the quay. We shipped on board the steamer *Oceola,* when Bob and I parted company. We were soon off, and at about four in the afternoon of the second day, we reached a landing, within a stone's throw of Jepsey James' house, just below the *Shirt-tail* bend in the Mississippi.

CHAPTER XIV.

HOW I GOT AWAY FROM JEPSEY JAMES'.

MY new master's place was distant about a hundred and fifty yards from the landing. He and his family dwelt in a dirty log hut, which formed the principal building in a group of about thirty negro picket cabins, the whole enclosed within a large "yard," about four acres in extent. These cabins were made of four crotches set upright in the ground, with cypress slabs across. The floor was of plank laid on the bare earth. It was an uncomfortable, prison-looking sort of a place, and the sight of it did not cheer me much. His wife was a small, fiery woman, and as good a "man of business" as himself. They were both rich, and had about a hundred and fifty slaves. The farm was a cotton farm. James grew nothing else.

After we reached our quarters, we got supper and turned in to rest. At four next morning we were roused up by the "nigger bell." It hung upon a post in the yard, twenty feet high, and was rung by a rope. It was, I think, the month of February, for it was towards the close of cotton-picking time, and we all went out into the field to pick cotton from the bole, the children from ten years of age going out with us. We picked until twelve o'clock, when the cotton was weighed by a negro driver named Jeff, and we got our first meal, consisting of potatoe soup, made of Indian corn meal and potatoes, boiled up. It is called "lob-lolly," or "mush," or "stirt-about." A pint was served out to each hand. It was brought into the field in wooden pails, and each slave being provided with a tin pannikin[21] buckled round his waist, the distribution and disposal of the mess did not take long. After the meal, we set to again until night-fall, when our baskets were weighed a second time, and each hand's picking for the day told up. I had out-picked all the new hands. The rule is a hundred pounds for each hand. The first day I picked five pounds over this quantity; much to my sorrow as I found, in the long run, for as I picked so well at first, more was exacted of me, and if I flagged a minute, the whip was liberally applied to keep me up to the mark. By being driven in this way, I at last got to pick a hundred and sixty pounds a day. My good picking, however, made it worse for me, for, being an old picker, I did well at first; but the others, being new at the work, were flogged till they fetched up with me; by which time I had done my best, and then got flogged for not doing better.

I may here observe that the women pick much faster than the men, their fingers being naturally more nimble; but as their baskets get filled, they become heavier to lift, and they lose time in removing them from place to place, so that by the time evening comes the men have fetched up with or out-picked them. The baskets are hamper-shaped, and contain from eighty-five to a hundred and twenty-five pounds. For every pound that is found short of the task, the punishment is one stroke of the bull-whip. I never got flogged for short weight, but many of the others did, poor things; and dreadful was the punishment they received, for the bull-whip is a dreadful instrument of torture, which I may as well describe in this place.

First a stock is chosen of a convenient length, the butt of which is loaded with lead, to give the whip force. The stock is then cleverly split to within a foot or so of the butt, into twelve strips. A piece of tanned leather, divided into eight strips, is then drawn on the stock, so that the split lengths of the wooden stock and the strips of leather can be plaited together. This is done very regularly, until the leather tapers down to quite a fine point, the whip being altogether about six feet long, and as limber and lithsome as a snake. The thong does not bruise, but cuts; and those who are expert in the use of it, can do so with such dexterity, as to only just raise the skin and draw blood, or cut clean through to the bone. I have seen a board, a quarter of an inch thick, cut through with it, at one blow. I have also seen a man fasten a bullet to the end of the thong, and after giving the whip a whirl round his head, send the thong whizzing forward, and drive the bullet into a door. This fearful instrument is called a "bull-whip," because it is the master of all whips. It is also employed to "whip down" savage bulls, or unruly cattle. I have seen many a horse cut with it right through the hollow of the flank, and the animal brought quivering to the ground. The way of using it is to whirl it round the head until the thong acquires a certain forward power, and then to let the end of the thong fall across the back, or on the part intended to be cut, the arm being drawn back with a kind of sweep. But although it is so formidable an instrument, it is seldom employed on slaves in such a manner as to disable them, for the "licks" are always regulated to an extreme nicety, so as only to cut the flesh and draw blood. But this is quite bad enough, and my readers will readily comprehend that with the fear of this punishment ever before us at Jepsey James', it was no wonder we did our utmost to make up our daily weight of cotton in the hamper.

After our day's picking was done, we got for supper the same quantity of "mush" as we had for breakfast in the morning, and this was the only kind of food we had during the whole time I was with Jepsey James, except what we could steal.

We went on picking cotton for two weeks, by the end of which time the season was at an end. We then were set to packing, and I was put in the jin-house.

I suppose I had the misfortune to get a run of bad masters. Jepsey was as bad as any of my former ones, and things were done at his place which makes my blood curdle to speak of. For instance, he would flog women when they were in a certain delicate condition, previously causing a hole to be dug in the ground for them to lie in more conveniently, so as not to injure the burden they were carrying. I have myself witnessed this, and even been forced to hold them down. The poor women were dreadfully hard worked. I have known them to be taken in travail when in the field, and immediately after their trouble was over, compelled to return to work. One of these women I well remember. She was as white as Ellen Craft:[22] that is, she might have passed for a white person without much fear of detection. There were, however, it seems, but very few births on Jepsey James' plantation, the female slaves being over-driven and over-worked.

Several instances of cruelty occurred whilst I was there, of which I will relate one or two.

Thomas James, Jep's second son, had cast his eyes on a handsome young negro girl, to whom he made dishonest overtures. She would not submit to him, and finding he could not overcome her, he swore he would be revenged. One night he called her out of the jin-house, and then bade me and two or three more, strip her naked; which we did. He then made us throw her down on her face, in front of the door, and hold her whilst he flogged her—the brute—with the bull-whip, cutting great gashes of flesh out of her person, at every blow, from five to six inches long. The poor unfortunate girl screamed most awfully all the time, and writhed under our strong arms, rendering it necessary for us to use our united strength to hold her down. He flogged her for half an hour, until he nearly killed her, and then left her, to crawl away to her cabin.

Poor girl! How my heart bled for her!

Another time John James, another of Jep's sons, and a married man, sought the wife of a slave named Abram. In order to gain access more easily to the man's cabin, he set a tree on fire, and then sent Abram to watch the fence, lest it should catch and burn down. Abram suspected John James' design upon his wife, and that this was a mere pretext to get rid of him for a while. His cabin was a full mile from the spot he had to watch, but he felt so uneasy about home, that instead of stopping at the fire, he ran to and from the fence to his hut. The consequence was that the fence—which was of solid wood—took fire, and burnt for the distance of three quarters of a mile. I mention this circumstance, because it happened on a certain Saturday night, when I had made preparations to run off on the Sunday, and I was compelled instead, to set to splitting timber to make the fence good. By "preparations," I mean that I had been looking out for chances, and made up a plan in my mind for taking a fresh start.

Jepsey James had all along inspired me with dread, and my old determination to get away from slavery had been quickened by sundry conversations I overheard on several occasions, all having reference to me.

One day master came in with a "nigger hunter" and his six dogs. He wished to frighten me: at least I concluded so. I had been sullen for some days, and he had observed it. On this occasion, he addressed one of the hands named Amos:

"Amos," he said, "when are any of you niggers going to run off again?"

"We does n't want to run away, Sir," Amos answered.

"Oh yes you do," said master. "You'd better run off, some of you. We've got some of the right kind of dogs now to fetch you back, quicker a heap than you can run a-head. You'd better start, some of you. In less than two days we'll bring you back."

He looked at me very hard and suspiciously whilst he spoke: so, said I to myself:

"Old fellow, you're speaking at me, I know. But I'll give you and your dogs a chance to track me yet, any how."

On another occasion I overheard him speaking to his son John, with whom, by the way, I was a bit of a favourite. He said I looked hard, as though I should give him some trouble to break me in. He added that I must be flogged, to see how I should stand it, and that it would have to be done before the summer came on, or the bushes sprouted into leaf, as, if I were flogged then, and should run off, it would be more difficult to find me out.

These conversations did not hold out a very encouraging prospect for me, and I therefore determined to be off as soon as I could. I arranged my plan in my head, which was to keep up the Mississippi, and make for the North as rapidly as possible. I only now waited for the favourable moment to start.

I have stated what circumstance prevented me from setting off on the day I had fixed upon for making the attempt. On the Monday night, however, having now been at Jepsey James' three months, I started on my travels once more. I watched until the negro quarters had been inspected, then skulked out into the yard, where I had observed a small skiff. I dragged it down to the water, and crossed over to the Arkansas side, the river here being about a mile in width. Having reached the bank, I turned the skiff adrift. I had chosen this mode of making my escape, because I knew the skiff would be missed, and that James would naturally conclude I had gone towards New Orleans, and would hunt for me in that direction, never suspecting I should go up stream. I think I was right in this conjecture. Any how, here I was safe for the present, and I at once set off walking as hard as I could put foot to the ground.

CHAPTER XV.

HOW I CAME TO BE JOHN BROWN.

DURING my journey I observed the plan I had followed on former occasions; namely, walking by night, and lying by for rest and concealment in the day, sleeping behind logs, like a wild man. I guided my course by following the muddy waters of the Mississippi, but I was frequently baulked by coming to inlets or *bayous*. These are considerably lower than the bed of the river, and are full of alligators. I used to hear these creatures at night, snorting and plashing about in the water—to my mortal terror—for I did not know but that I might, at any moment, unexpectedly fall into their hungry jaws. When I came to one of these *bayous* I would follow the bank until I came to a ferry. Here I would stop, and watching an opportunity, draw the staple that kept the boat fastened, and cross over in the boat to the opposite side, where I would leave it. I would then go down that bank until I reached the Mississippi again. I lived, or rather sustained life, by eating raw corn, potatoes, pine roots, and sassafras buds. The country I passed through appeared to be quite thinly inhabited; there was, however, plenty of wood and reed cane, so that I found no sort of difficulty in hiding myself, even quite close down to the water's edge. From these places of concealment I used to watch the steamers going up and down the river; and these served to guide me in my course, for I knew they must start from somewhere, and I hoped that I might find friends there, and rest for a time.

At last I reached a great town where the steamers were in large numbers. I cannot say, with any accuracy, how long I was getting to it; many weary days and nights I know. I judge it must have taken me at least three months. Being at a loss what to do, or where to go, without information, I took courage, and went on board one of the steamers. It was early in the morning, and there were not very many people about, on deck; but my appearance excited the suspicion of the captain, who pointed me out to the mate, and said I looked like a runaway. I observed them closely without appearing to do so, and went to the cook, who was a coloured man, to beg something to eat. He gave me some bread and beef. I also learnt that the name of the steamer was the *Ellen Kirkman,* and that the great town was St. Louis, in Missouri. The cook asked me a great many questions, but I did not like to answer him too freely; especially as I was watched by the captain and the mate, who had now both placed themselves at the bow of the boat, evidently with the intention of capturing me, as they concluded I must pass them to get ashore. The *Ellen Kirkman* was one of the outside vessels. I had made my way to her, because I thought there would be less chance of my being noticed by the along shore people. Seeing how closely I was watched, and feeling quite satisfied that the captain and the mate intended me a mischief, I made up my mind how to circumvent them; and watching a favourable moment, suddenly slipped off on the opposite side of the vessel, at the stern, and crossed the other steamers till I reached the shore. As soon as I felt land again, I walked off at a tolerably rapid pace down the quay, and turned sharp round into the first street.

It was Sunday morning, and the people were going to meeting. I noticed a number of coloured people walking all in one direction, towards a chapel, where some more were going in: for the State I was now in, bordering on a Free State, they were permitted the right—denied to them in other Slave States—to worship God like other folks. To avoid suspicion, I went in too and sat down, and waited till the meeting was over, and all the congregation gone, with the exception of the deacons and other principal men belonging to it. I followed them out, and after we had gone on a little way they closed up and began talking to me. They soon discovered me to be a stranger, and one of them then invited me to go home with him. I gladly accepted his offer, and he fed me, and gave me a hat and a clean shirt. I told him I was suspected of being a runaway, but was not. I did not like to tell him the truth, being afraid of getting him into trouble. In the afternoon I went to meeting again, staying till it broke up. I had learnt, of the friend who received me in the morning, the name of the minister of the chapel. It was Cole, and I did think of going to him, but gave up the idea, lest I might expose him to danger for helping me. All this I thought of whilst in chapel, and at last made up my mind to leave the town as soon as it got dark. When I set off, however, I found the watch about, and became alarmed, as I knew they would capture me without ceremony. I therefore slunk back to the house of the man I have referred to, and, quite unknown to him, concealed myself all night in the outhouse. Here I put on the clean shirt. I had a bundle with me, containing an old waistcoat, an old Kentucky coat, which I had procured at New Orleans, an old pair of trowsers, and an old shirt. I dressed myself in these things and put up my old ones in the bundle, intending to throw them away.

In the morning I went down to the water-side, and, on my way, disposed of my bundle on the top of a pile of steam-boat shafts and boilers. When I got to the quay I asked for work, saying I was a carpenter. I might have hired myself over and over again, but I really did not want to do so. I only wanted to avoid suspicion, and get safe into the woods again, so I asked such a high price for my labour that nobody would hire me. I soon found, however, that my conduct in this respect excited suspicion, therefore I at last accepted of a job, undertaking to come the next morning and bring my weekly pass; for I had, in reply to the questions put to me, given out that I was not free, but was allowed by my master to hire myself out: a thing that is often done. In this way I avoided many embarrassing questions, and got the opportunity of acquiring some very useful scraps of information; to do which, indeed, was one of my principal objects in coming down to the quay.

After striking my bargain, and sauntering about awhile, I started off till I came to the woods, a mile and a half from the town, where I remained the rest of the day. As soon as it got dark, I took the same road back, intending to return into the town; but I became alarmed, and coming to a steam-mill between two ferries, I crept along on my hands and knees to a place where I had noticed, in the morning, a little boat fastened to a tree, and which it was now my object to get. It lay between the two ferries, and nearly opposite to the upper point of an island that lies between St. Louis and the Illinois bank. I reached the boat, jumped into it, snapped the chain by a rude jerk, and put off. The current was rapid and very strong, and the river of considerable width, and full of snags. My object was to make the upper point of the island, for if I failed, and struck it at any other part, I knew that the current would draw me down to the steam-boat wharf again, where I should be discovered by the watch. It was with the utmost difficulty I avoided the snags, but at length I touched the island, at the spot I have mentioned. On reaching the bank I encountered another difficulty. The current had undermined the turf, and made it so rotten, that I could not land, not being able to make the boat fast. I was so exhausted, too, by the efforts I had made to reach the Illinois side, that before I recovered myself, I drifted quite three quarters of a mile down, to a place where the stump of a tree stuck up, at the water's edge. Here I succeeded in securing the boat, and when the current brought her gunwale on, close enough to the bank, I leaped ashore.

By this time it was daylight, and therefore dangerous for me to be seen; but I had no alternative save to walk on till I should reach a convenient place of concealment. I had not proceeded very far, before I saw a white man, to whom I made up.

"If you please, Sir," said I, "do you know of a coloured man living away about here?"

"What name?" asked he.

"Well, Sir," I answered, "I can't remember his name. I've forgotten it. But I was told he used to live about here."

"Name Caesar?" asked the stranger.

"That's it, I think," said I.

"Well, yes, there's a coloured man of that name does live on this side. He's down away yonder, a good bit, cutting walnut cord-wood. If you go on, you're sure to meet with him."

With my heart leaping almost into my throat, I thanked the man, and went on, and some time after came to the place where Caesar was very busy plying his axe. We were not long in coming to an understanding. I told him my story; he gave me shelter in his shanty, shared his food with me, and I sat with him till dark. I learnt from him that he was the only coloured man who lived on that side, close to the river, for there was no business doing there; so although the question I had put to the white man was quite a natural one, under the circumstances in which I was placed, I had every reason to congratulate myself on having been so fortunate as to fall in with Caesar at this particular time.

This good fellow gave me the most precise information about the country, advising me what roads to take, and what towns to avoid. He advised me not to make for Chicago; to avoid Springfield, and to go to Indianapolis by way of Vandalia.[23] He also directed me to call at a place, the name of which, I think, is Rockville, where I should find a coloured man, a friend of his, from North Carolina, on whose aid I might rely. Accordingly I set off again at night, walking until day-break, through a small prairie, extending between the Mississippi and the forks of the Springfield and Vandalia roads. By the time it was light, however, I had not got further than about seven miles from the river, the road through the prairie being cut up into deep ruts by waggons and carts, and all filled with mud and water. As it was not safe for me to continue my journey, I looked about for a place of concealment, and soon found one, in the lock of a high wooden fence, the end of which went down to the water's edge. Here I intended staying till night. I made my walking-stick serve as a seat, by fixing it across the timbers of the fence, and then crouched down, so as to avoid being seen as much as possible; but, overcome by fatigue, I fell asleep.

I was awakened by a voice, crying out—

"Hallo, old fellow! Are you asleep?"

I looked up, and remembering the advice I had received from Caesar, never to look frightened if I should be surprised by any one, I answered, without getting up:

"No, I'm not asleep! I was asleep till you waked me, though."

The party who spoke to me was a common-sized man, who had perched himself up on the top of the fence, which was from seven to eight feet high, and made of split timbers, ten feet and a half long. He held a fowling-piece across his lap, and had I started off, could easily have shot me, for I must have run before him, the fence preventing my getting away in one direction, the water in the other, and the prairie in a third.

"Which way are you going?" he asked.

"I'm not going anywhere," I replied. "I'm sitting down."

Bethinking myself that I ought to show a reason for being asleep so early in the morning, I scrambled up, and pretended to be drunk, staggering, and reeling, and looking foolishly at him.

"Hie, old fellow!" he said, then; "you've been drinking, I reckon."

"Yes, Sir, been drinking a little," I answered.

"Do you live in this part of the country?" he inquired.

"Oh no! My home is in Buffalo," I made answer; for Caesar had told me to say so, if any one asked me such a question. "I've been following the water, and I got away round to New Orleans, and from there to St. Louis. Now I'm going on through the country, on by Vandalia, to see my cousin."

"Well, old fellow," the man said; "you had better hire yourself out to me. Don't you want to cut some cord wood?"

"What sort of pay will you give me?" said I.

"Half a dollar a-day," he answered.

"What will you pay me in?" I asked.

"Well, would n't you like to have a gun?"

"What sort of a gun?"

"This one," he said, patting the one he held.

"That gun's of no account," I said; and here I staggered again.

"It's very good to shoot ducks with," he made answer.

"Oh," I said; "the land's so wet that you can't travel by it, let alone going into the water after ducks. But I think I'll take your offer, for the weather is so bad, I don't suppose I shall be able to get along very well."

"Well," he answered, "you go up to the house yonder, and I'll go to Vandalia road to get some eggs."

So saying, he jumped down from the fence and went on.

The house was half a mile from this place. I made straight for it, but the mistress of the house, who was in the horse-yard, would not let me in when I knocked at the door. I suppose she was afraid, for I know she saw me as I was going by. I turned from the door, and observing that the men in the field had stopped their horses, and were leaning against the handles of their ploughs, watching me, I thought it best to go up boldly to them, so as to avert suspicion. I pretended to want work, and in answer to their questions, told them I was a carpenter and joiner. They said they did not want any mechanical workman, but that if I went on the Springfield road, down under the Bluff, there was a man there would employ me. As I saw woods in the direction they pointed out, their advice suited me very well; so I went on till I got into the woods on the Springfield road. Here I found a chunk of a blown-down tree. I got behind it, and as it was crooked, I could, by lying down, very conveniently peep out from under the crook. I watched to see whether any persons were following me, or dogging my steps, but saw no one; so I remained till dark, when I set off again.

I had been wringing wet now for forty-eight hours, and when I got up, was all of a shiver; but I went on, notwithstanding, till morning came, by which time I was in the high road to Vandalia, having crossed the woods in the night. At last I reached the place to which Caesar had directed me. Here I soon made out the man I wanted. I got a rest at his dwelling, and induced him to get me a free pass, for which I made him take an old watch. With that pass I assumed the name of John Brown, which I have retained ever since.

CHAPTER XVI.

I AM ADVERTISED AS A RUN-AWAY.

HAVING now assumed such a name as I could safely travel by, I set off for Vandalia, which took me a week to reach, walking by night, and lying by in concealment in the day, to recruit myself by such sleep and rest as I could snatch. I ran very short of food the whole time, and experienced many serious difficulties from my ignorance of the roads, and my fears of being captured. I found the rivers a serious obstacle, too, for I did not always light upon canoes, ferries, or the proper fording-places. I incurred great risk besides, in seeking information respecting the best roads to distant places. My plan, however, was to lurk about in the neighbourhood of some isolated dwelling, until it was quite late in the night, and people were fast asleep. I would then knock them up out of their beds, when they would hasten to the window, and look out, half awake, to see what was the matter. I would then put the questions I wanted answered, and as they could not see my colour in the dark, I never found them backward in replying, as they seemed always in too great a hurry to get back to bed. In this manner, and though I was in constant fear, I contrived to steer pretty clear of danger, keeping by the high-road from Vandalia, until I reached Terrehaute, on the Wabash river.

I crossed this river in a canoe which I found moored to the bank. It was in the night, and I had to walk about until morning, keeping a sharp look-out all round. I watched until I saw a coloured man, whom I addressed, and to whom I told my story. In the course of conversation we found out that the preacher at St. Louis was his brother. He was quite glad to hear of him through me, and took me home, where he gave me some refreshment. But I could not remain with him, he said, as it would expose him to danger, so he directed me to a settlement of coloured people, situated at about three miles from his place, where he intimated I could remain a while in safety. I reached it without difficulty, and passing my-self off as a free man, staid in the place for two weeks, doing jobs of carpentering, at the end of which time I found it desirable to start off again on my travels, in consequence of the people's suspicions becoming excited by my answers to their questions. So I set off for Indianapolis, the road to which I had ascertained.

Here I got a great fright. I chanced to fall in with a coloured man who was out white-washing. On my accosting him he looked at me very hard, and presently informed me I was in great and immediate danger, for that there were advertisements out, giving an accurate description of my person, and offering a very large sum for my apprehension. This was, indeed, sad news for me, though I might have expected it. Jepsey James had issued the notices, and sent them flying all through the country by means of the steamers and other modes of transmitting information. My friend—and a true friend he proved to me; may God bless him!—told me it would be more than his life was worth if we were seen together; but for all that, he took me to his house, and concealed me till night. On our way he pointed out the placards on the walls, and read what they said; and sure enough my master had drawn my picture so well, that nobody could have mistaken me, unless he had been blind. When we reached his house, he gave me plenty to eat—not before I wanted it—and what I required then still more, good advice, of which he was not sparing. He told me that so many slaves were escaping from slavery, that the slave-holders were all roused, and determined to deal a terrible revenge on the first one they caught running off. Those in the more Southern states had sent forward to their friends north, who were all on the look-out to help them in defence of their common interests. A great many runaways had been traced to that neighbourhood, which was all in a commotion in consequence. He added that the Quakers were known to have helped off the runaways, by the Underground Railroad, and that they had been brought into great trouble through it, and through having otherwise protected the coloured people. Numbers of them, he said, had been ruined by law-suits, which the slave-holders had brought against them; others had had their farm-houses burnt down, their woods and plantations set on fire, their crops destroyed, their stock driven off; and many of them had been themselves seriously injured by the violence of mobs. Still, they kept on helping off as many slaves as ever, because they felt it to be their duty to do so, and nothing would turn them from it.

I felt very much distressed to hear of these things; and though I had never seen any of the people he spoke about, my gratitude to them was unbounded, for I felt that if I could once get into their hands, I should be safe. I have since learnt to love them, for what they did for me then, and for what they have done for me since. The memory of their kind deeds will ever live in my heart while it beats.

My friend gave me a full account of the Underground Railroad, for as I did not understand any thing about it, I asked him a good many questions. I have been permitted to add, in another chapter, a brief history of it, penned by the Editor of my Narrative. I have met with, I may say, many hundreds of persons in England, who do not know more about the Underground Railroad than I did once; and to those who are in similar ignorance, that chapter will be as interesting as any that relates to myself.

My good friend also informed me in what direction I should go that night, in order to reach a certain town on Blue River, within, say a hundred miles of Carthage,[24] and where one of the managers of the line resided. He gave me his name, and precise instructions to find out his residence; but, for obvious reasons, I do not think it prudent to mention his name, or that of the town in which he lived; nay, perhaps lives now. His was the first station of the Underground line, in that part of the country, and it was absolutely necessary for me to reach it that night. It was thirty miles from my friend's house, and he impressed upon me the necessity of making up my mind to accomplish the distance before day-break, or I should certainly be lost; that is, captured. Of course, with such a prospect before me, I had every inducement to task my remaining strength to the utmost, in order to cover the ground within the time, though, it being now the month of August, the space between night-fall and day-break was not any too long for me to do what was before me. As soon, however, as it set in quite dusk to make it safe for me to go, I took leave of my benefactor, and set out with a stout heart.

What I endured of anxiety that night will never be effaced from my memory. I had received general instructions for my guidance on the road, and been told what villages I should have to go through. But in order to avoid incurring unnecessary risk, when I reached a village, instead of passing through it, I would make a turn and go round it, endeavouring to strike the road a little beyond. This did not always succeed. More than once, after going right round one side of a village, and coming to a road, my heart misgave me, and in obedience to a secret presentiment that all was not right, and which I found it impossible to resist, I turned back, and beat about until I struck another road, even retracing my steps, more than once, until I came to the road that left no misgiving on my mind, when I would go on again as brave as a lion.

Many people will say I was superstitious. And so I was. But the feeling was a kind of instinct, whose cautions, even at the present day, I cannot help minding.

In this way I walked and ran the whole night, but as day broke I had the satisfaction of seeing afar off, the town I was making for, and very soon after, I enjoyed the still greater pleasure of finding myself in a place of safety.

CHAPTER XVII.

I AM BOOKED TO CANADA, EXPRESS, BY THE UNDERGROUND RAILROAD.

I HAD been instructed by my friend to seek out a certain coloured man, on my arrival at the town in which I now was, and where there was a considerable settlement of Quakers. He had given me a very precise description of the spot where his house stood, and by what signs I should know it. Accordingly I lost no time in seeking it, and soon found it out. My new friend was at home, and on my making myself known to him, which I did by mentioning the name of our mutual acquaintance, he knew what I wanted. He then gave me directions to go to a certain house, which he pointed out to me, where I should be in safety. He could not accompany me, as that would have been imprudent, and have exposed him to danger. I made straight for the place, and, on being seen, was instantly taken in.

Between nine and ten months had now elapsed since I left Decatur Stevens', the whole of which time had been one of sore trial to me. Having, however, brought my readers with me to a place of rest, I wish to dwell a little on this part of my history, for what happened to me here, forms an era in my life.

I was introduced by two sturdy young men to their father, as "another of the travellers bound to the North Star." The old man laid a hand upon my shoulder, and taking my other hand in his, gave me a welcome, and then conducting me into the parlour, introduced me to his wife. It was now past sun-rise, and they were about going to breakfast. I was, however, taken to an upper room, where I had a good wash, in a white basin, and where clean linen and a complete suit of clothes were brought to me. After refreshing myself by this wholesome change, I was re-conducted to the parlour, and seated at the table.

It was the first time in my life I had found myself in such grand company. I was so completely abashed, and felt so out of my element, that I had no eyes, no ears, no understanding. I was quite bewildered. As to eating, it was out of the question.

"Come, friend John Brown, thee must eat," said the kind old lady, heaping my plate up with fried ham and eggs. "Thee need'nt be afraid of eating."

"I'm sure thee must be hungry'" added the old gentleman, handing me a great chunk of bread. "Eat away, and don't thee be afraid. We have plenty more in the house."

But it was all of no use, and though an hour or even half an hour before, I had felt that I could devour any thing, the smoking coffee, ham, eggs, and sausages, and the nice white bread could not tempt me. For a good half hour this continued: they pressing me to eat, and I quite unable to do so. At last I began, and picked a bit now and then, receiving encouragement as my courage seemed to increase. My appetite came with my courage, and then—oh! how I did eat!

I fear my readers may think I exaggerate when I tell them that "I ate straight on for an entire hour, quite steady." I demolished all the ham and eggs and sausages they placed before me, with their due accompaniment of bread, and then a round of cold salt beef was brought up, from which I was helped abundantly. I could not but notice the looks of my new friends. The old gentleman would cough and wipe his eyes now and then, and the younger folks keep exchanging glances with one another. The old lady, fearing I should do myself an injury, made several ineffectual attempts to draw my attention off.

"Friend John Brown, we wish to talk with thee, as soon as thou can," she said; "we want to hear all about thee."

"Yes, ma'am," I answered, without leaving off: "you can go on, ma'am; I can talk and eat too."

I dare not say how long I might have gone on. I had not eaten a meal for so long, that now it seemed as though I never could satisfy my craving. At last the old lady said, decidedly:

"Friend, John Brown, thee must n't take it unkindly, but thee must n't eat any more now. Thou can'st have some more in the day-time if thou like; but thou wilt make thyself ill, if thou take more now."

And so I was obliged to give in.

A chapter from the Scriptures was read after breakfast, which, including my "spell" at the table, had lasted two hours from the time we sat down.

I was then conducted into a safe retreat, where there was a comfortable bed provided for me, into which I got, and soon fell asleep. I slept until I was awakened at three in the afternoon, when I was taken down to dinner. After that we sat and chatted until supper-time, and then I went to bed again. In the middle of the night I awoke, and finding myself in a strange place, became alarmed. It was a clear, starlight night, and I could see the walls of my room, and the curtains all of a dazzling whiteness around me. I felt so singularly happy, however, notwithstanding the fear I was in, at not being able to make out where I was, that I could only conclude I was in a dream, or a vision, and for some minutes I could not rid my mind of this idea. At last I became alive to the truth; that I was in a friend's house, and that I really was free and safe.

I had never learnt to pray; but if what passed in my heart that night was not prayer, I am sure I shall never pray as long as I live.

I cannot describe the blessed happiness I enjoyed in my benefactor's family, during the time I remained there, which was from the Friday morning to the Saturday night week. So happy I never can be again, because I do not think the circumstances in which I may be placed, will ever be of a nature to excite similar feelings in my breast.

At length the time came for me to go, though I was not previously told it was necessary for my own safety that I should quit my benefactors. On the Saturday afternoon week, there had been some talk of the camp of the coloured people, near, where they met for worship, and I was asked, quite cursorily, whether I would like to go and see it. I answered in the affirmative. When it was quite dark—perhaps it might be eight o'clock—I was called out to the door, as if to go and see the camp. There I saw three saddle-horses, on one of which one of the old gentleman's sons was mounted, holding the second horse by the bridle. The other son held the third horse, and was dismounted.

"Friend John," he said, "it is not safe for thee to stay any longer; nor for us to keep thee. Come, jump up."

There was no alternative but for me to get across the beast that had been provided for me. I did so, not without suspicion that I was going to be taken back into slavery. I hope I may be forgiven for entertaining such a thought; but after all I had passed through, I was not ready to place implicit confidence even in those who treated me as a friend. I am sure I am now very sorry for ever having suspected my noble saviours.

They placed me between them, and off we set as hard as our animals could go. We frightened a lot of coloured people in a village we passed through, who were coming from their Saturday night's meeting; and not a few persons opened their doors to come and stare at us, we made such a clatter. At about twelve we reached our destination; the first station of the Underground line from headquarters.

I remember very well the odd reception we met with, at the hands of the bluff old Quaker who received us:

"What! Only one, and coming at this time of night. Why I've room and food ready for a dozen. But come in, come in and rest."

My conductors remained talking till half-past one, when they took leave of us. After they were gone, I sat up till three, telling the family of my escape and adventures, and then I retired to bed. The next day, being Sunday, the family went to Meeting. They brought in to dinner a middle-aged, strong-built Friend, who talked with me a good deal. At about three in the afternoon, I was told that horses were ready, and that I must start with this gentleman, as we had a good way to go. It came very suddenly upon me, to leave so soon, but I complied, of course, and we set off.

All that afternoon, the whole night, and the whole of the next day, we travelled, only stopping at times to let our beasts graze. I suppose we went a hundred miles, crossing the Wabash again, and going through the Indian reserve on our way. At last, at about three on the Monday afternoon, we reached the station; and glad enough I was.

My Quaker friend of the pleasant countenance and sturdy frame, remained till next afternoon, when he started back. Finding I was safe, for the present, I thought I would stay here awhile. Accordingly I set to splitting rails, with my host's son, and shooting squirrels. But the suspicion of the folks around became excited, so that after I had been here a fortnight, I found it safer to start again. I was encouraged to do so by my host; and having been provided with an ample supply of corn-bread, and meat, I set off to another place, which my friends indicated, about a hundred miles off. I was three or four days getting to it, but was received kindly; and here I should have remained awhile, but was informed it would be unsafe; so after resting four days, during which time I worked splitting rails, I set off one morning for Marshall, in Michigan.

It would not interest my readers much to follow me on my journey, for nothing of any consequence occurred to me. I travelled chiefly by night, that being the safest time. Indeed, I made very light of any real privations I now experienced. The sense of present security, and the certainty of freedom awaiting me, more than compensated me for temporary inconveniences. I felt quite happy, knowing I should meet with none but friends on my road to Canada. My way seemed perfectly clear, and the only description I can give of my sensations, is, that I felt like a new man.

I arrived in Marshall one morning, and was in search of a certain Friend, when I was hailed, as I was going down the street, by a number of coloured people who were building a chapel, and who had been hired to do the work by a Mr. Fitch. They asked me various questions, and I soon discovered that, like myself, they were fugitives from slavery. Their names were Samuel Patterson, Noel Johnson, Thomas Smith, a man named Samuel, Elias Earle, and Thomas Christopher. They told me I need not fear any thing, as I was now quite out of danger, and asked me whether I would join them, and work for my living. I readily consented, and accordingly I was set to carry bricks and mortar. On the third day I felt unaccountably dull, and something told me not to go to my work, so, instead, I went into the woods to cut timber for the same building, which occupation suited me better, I being a carpenter. I had been there about half the day, when some one came and told me that the props of the chapel had given way, and that the men had only escaped by a sort of miracle.

Another curious circumstance also happened whilst I was employed here. Two of my mates, Noel Johnson and Thomas Smith, had belonged to one John Shelby, of Lexington, in Kentucky. They had been willed to his son-in-law, one West, and he had removed them into Missouri, whence they had run off. West traced them to Marshall (where I fell in with them,) after they had been there quite two years, and one day made his appearance for the purpose of claiming and taking them back into slavery. When we heard of it, we determined to stand by them; and all rose, as one man, to defend them, and prevent them from being carried off. Finding us so resolute, West became very much alarmed, and actually appealed to his former slave, Johnson, for protection. Johnson at once extended it to him; took him home and gave him some dinner, and afterwards got him safely away.

But to return to myself. I remained in Marshall until the chapel was completed—that is, for about a twelvemonth—and then made straight for Detroit. Here I fell in with one Mr. Joseph Teague, captain of a party of Cornish miners, who were fitting out to explore the copper region on Lake Superior. I engaged myself to Captain Teague, believing that I should be safer with Englishmen in the mines than anywhere else. He was a native of Redruth, in Cornwall, where he resided when at home. He had come over under contract, to test the copper-mines belonging to Jones & Co., of Boston. We went from Detroit to

Copper Harbour, by Mackinaw and Sault St. Mary, and thence to the mouth of the Ontonagon River, Michigan. From this place we went to Cyrus Mindenhall's location, and afterwards to the Porcupine Mountains.[25] I remained working in the mines, as a miner's carpenter, for eighteen months, when Captain Teague started to return to England. I engaged to follow him almost immediately, and to join him in Redruth; but having heard a great deal, since I had been in this part of the country, of the Dawn Institute, at Dawn, Canada West,[26] I wished first to see something of it. Accordingly I made my way to it, and remained five or six months, working at the saw-mill. I helped to saw the walnut timber which was sent to the Great Exhibition in Hyde Park, in 1851, and exhibited in the Canadian department, where I afterwards saw it again; and I also constructed a floating self-acting car-way, designed to draw timber from the water to the saw, which answered very well, and for which I was praised.

I had not reason to be pleased with the manner in which the affairs of the Dawn Institute were managed. I will not mention names, because I do not want to speak disparagingly of any body. But, in consequence, I left Dawn, sooner than I intended, and having a little money to receive for work that I had done, I secured a berth on board the *Parliament,* Captain Brown, bound from Boston to Liverpool. We left the former port the last week in July 1850, and reached Liverpool on the 10th of August, after a surprising run of fifteen days.

Thus, after all my trials and sufferings, I found myself at last safely landed in the town where poor John Glasgow left his wife and children so many years before.

I lost no time in making my way to Redruth, as I was anxious to begin work under my old captain and friend, Joe Teague. To my great grief, when I reached the town, I learned that he had never returned to England, but had died in Boston. I saw his son William, however, and a friend of the captain's, one Mr. Richardson, and also the clergyman of the parish, from all of whom I obtained testimonials. There are now miners working in the mines there, with whom I worked in those of Lake Superior. Their names are Thomas Champion, Thomas Williams, James Vivian, Richard George, William George, Thomas Polkinghorn, and Richard Pascoe, who, with Captain Teague and his son Joseph, were in my mine, and worked by my side.

I staid two months at Redruth, earning enough to maintain me by reciting my adventures in meetings got up for me by my Cornish friends. I then went to Bristol, where I procured employment at a carpenter's shop. I remained here four weeks, but though I worked hard, I did not see my way to rising, as a man, so I went to Heywood, in Lancashire, and engaged myself to Mr. John Mills, a builder. I worked here until I found that there is prejudice against colour in England, in some classes, as well as more generally in America; and as I had an object to accomplish—of which I shall speak presently—I thought I had better make my way to London, and set about seeking the means of carrying that object out. With this view I quitted my employment, after a proper understanding with Mr. Mills, with whom I was on the best of terms, and reached the metropolis, one Wednesday evening, some time in April 1851.

CHAPTER XVIII.

THE CULTIVATION OF COTTON, TOBACCO, AND RICE.

BEFORE I address myself to set forth what is now the grand object of my life; the object to which I wish to devote the rest of my days, and the best of my energies; and before I venture to present my own reflections on Slavery, and my views as to what should be done to put it down, it may be useful that I should present my readers with a brief account of the mode of cultivating Cotton, and Tobacco, and Rice, as practised in the plantations on which I have myself worked, or have had opportunities of visiting.

COTTON being the staple production of the Southern States, much attention is paid to its cultivation. When the price rises in the English market, even but half a farthing a pound, the poor slaves immediately feel the effects, for they are harder driven, and the whip is kept more constantly going. I often think that if the ladies in this country could see the slave women, and girls, and even little children, picking the cotton in the fields, till the blood runs from the tips of their fingers, where they have been pricked by the hard pod; or if they could see them dragging their baskets, all trembling, to the scale, for fear their weight should be short, and they should get the flogging which in such a case they know they must expect; or if they could see them, as I often have, bent double with constant stooping, and scourged on their bare back when they attempted to rise to straighten themselves for a moment: I say, if the ladies of this country could see this, or witness the infliction of what are called slight punishments on these unfortunate creatures, they would, I am sure, never in their lives wear another article made of slave-grown cotton.

But I am, perhaps, wandering a little from the subject immediately before me.

In the fall-season the ground is pulverized with the plough, with a view to cut up and destroy the worms and other insects which usually infest the cotton-fields, and which would, unless killed, commit great havoc in the growing season. These worms are large, thick creatures, that burrow in the ground till spring-time, when they come out and nip off the young plants quite close. When we see them we tear them in two.

In March, the ground, having lain fallow during the winter, is ridged by throwing three furrows into one ridge, in which state it is left until April, when the ridge is split by a small plough, and the cotton seed sown by hand in the drill. The ridges are four feet apart, and a man used to sowing, can cast the seed to a distance of from five to eight feet straight before him. He is followed by a harrowing party, the harrow having two teeth. These rake the earth over the seed in the drill, whilst the hinder part of the harrow smoothes it over. In five or six days, in open weather, the seed generally shews itself, and when it has come up a little strong, it is chopped out with the hoe, in spaces from ten to twelve inches apart; ten or a dozen stalks being left in each bunch. A small plough, called the bull-tongued plough, is then run along up one side of the drills and down the other, so as to fill up the hoe-holes, and cover the crab-grass. The latter soon springs again, and is very troublesome to keep under. When it shews, the people go round with heavy hoes to scrape it down, and trim off the young grass. It is then ploughed again with the bull-tongued plough, to break what are called the "baulks," or hard ground, between the drills, as the ground must be kept open to admit moisture and air, without which the young plants would shrivel up and die.

The cotton plant does not begin to grow very fast until the roots strike the sub-soil, which they do in about three weeks or a month. Meanwhile, all hands—men, women, and children—have to thin out the plants by hand-picking, a most painful process, because of the constant stooping. They are compelled to go across a thirty, forty, or fifty acre field without straightening themselves one minute, and with the burning sun striking their head and back, and the heat reflected upwards from the soil into their faces. It will take a good hand, from an hour to an hour and a half, to hand-pick such a row. The next thing done is to hoe up the ground close to the roots, and hoe out the grass and weeds. The overseer, or "nigger-driver," or the master himself sometimes, goes round to see that this is properly done; and for every sprig of grass or stray weed that has been left in the row which has been thus "dressed," the slave who has left it gets a flogging more or less severe. The hands usually go into the field at five in the morning, and work till twelve, when they get breakfast, for which an hour is allowed. At one they return to the fields, and work till it becomes too dark to distinguish any thing.

When the plant is about six weeks old it begins to branch out; but it requires no other tending or dressing than I have described, until the bole or blossom begins to open, which is about the end of July. It ripens very quickly, and keeps on blossoming and ripening till the frost comes in and stops the blooming. It is extremely sensitive to cold, and should be picked as much as possible when there is no wet upon it, either dew or rain. No wonder, then, that this is a busy time in the fields, and that every hand picks his fastest. Every thing depends upon the care with which it is picked, and the season in which it is done. Dew or wet makes the cotton yellow and streaky, and when gathered in this state it must be dried in the sun. The frost, on the other hand, checks the growth, and makes the fibre short and dark. If it is left too long in the bole, the cup opens and throws out the cotton, which then looks like so much snow falling in a stream from each over-ripe blossom, and the heat, and wind, and dust damage it, each in its way; besides which, the bole being very brittle, breaks up into little pieces as soon as it is touched, filling the fibre with woody particles. For these reasons, when the plant is just ripening, all hands are set to pick it, as this is the most favourable time. The women pick cleaner and better than the men generally, because their fingers are more delicate and taper, and they can more easily lay hold of the cotton as it lies snug in the pod. Many people may think it is a very light, pleasant occupation, but it is not; for let alone the large quantity that each slave must pick every day, the bole of the plant when split by ripeness, pricks the fingers, even when you are very careful, and lacerates the flesh round the nails so as to cause a great soreness: besides which, the constant stooping is terribly irksome and painful, even to the strongest-backed man.

On rainy days the people do not pick at all, but are sent into the jin-house to jin and pack. The jinning is for the purpose of separating the seed, which lies closely embedded in the wool, and is not easy to get out. The jins I have seen employed are the roller and saw-jins. Sometimes, however, the seed is extracted by hand-picking. This is usually done at night, more to keep the slaves employed than because it is the most expeditious mode of performing this operation; though, for saving the fibre, nothing can come up to it.

The seed is used to make oil from, and also oil-cake, on which sheep and horned cattle will do very well; but it is ruination to hogs. Sometimes, too, the seed is crushed and mixed up in the "mush" that is given to the negroes; but it is unwholesome, and soon brings them out in sores. I have been made to eat it, thus mixed, in my food, until I broke out in great ulcers, from my ankle-bone upwards. Experiments have been tried to ascertain what quantity a "nigger" could bear to swallow in this manner. It was found that a very little soon sent him a long way out of the reach of his master for ever; so, unless a man wants to kill his "niggers," or make them unfit for work, or to spite them, I do not think he would try the thing on any very large scale.

The cotton being jinned, is now ready for packing. There are two ways of doing this; box-packing and bag-packing. The former mode is done in this wise. A box of convenient dimensions is prepared, say about five feet by three; in a word, of the same size as the bales which any one may see lying on the wharves in Liverpool. This box is open at top and bottom, and a packing-cloth, made of what is called "gunny,"[27] is placed inside, having cords which pass underneath, and hang over the sides of the box. The latter is placed beneath a screw-press, or one weighted by hydraulic pressure, and the cotton is thrown into the box, as regularly and evenly as possible, and pressed down quite hard, so that its bulk is reduced to the narrowest compass. The cords are then brought round and fastened, and the bale is ready for shipment. Each bale may weigh, on an average, about four hundred pounds.

Bag-packing is a different operation. It takes five yards of "gunny" to make a bag. In the mouth of the bag a hoop is sewn. There is a hole in the floor, through which the bag is dropped, so that it hangs by the hoop. The cotton is now packed into it by hand, as fast as it comes from the jin, and rammed down with a packing-iron. This implement is a bar of iron from four feet and a half to five feet long, and about an inch and a half thick, of an eight-sided shape all the way down to the bottom, where it is flattened out at the end into the form of a wedge, till it is only about a quarter of an inch thick. This must be constantly used, or the cotton, which is naturally elastic, will "swell back," and the bag will not weigh the right weight, namely, from three hundred and fifty pounds, or over. The packer has no guide but the hardness of the cotton to go by; so that it is pretty much guess-work with him. If his bag should be short in weight, or he does not keep up with the jin, he gets a flogging. The average day's packing is two bags for each man. Packing is very hard, oppressive work. The dust and fibres fly about in thick clouds, and get into the chest, checking respiration, and injuring the lungs very seriously. It is a common thing for the slaves to sicken off with chest diseases, acquired in the packing-room or jin-house, and to hear them wheezing and coughing like broken-winded horses, as they crawl about to the work that is killing them.

As a closing remark on the subject of cotton-growing, I may say that cotton-lands work out in two years, when they require rest. Corn is sown on them for a rotation, one year, which is often ploughed in green. The fourth year the land is quite fit for another sowing of cotton. The average produce per acre varies more than any thing else that is grown.

I will now give an account of the cultivation of TOBACCO.

In the month of February they begin what is called "burning the beds," that is, the dry brush is burnt off from the beds intended to be sown and planted. The ground is then broken up with the grubbing-hoe, an implement something like a pick-axe, only that it is four inches wide, and heavy. The ground must be well manured before it is broken up, because the tobacco-plant is greedy of food, and likes good living. Indeed, without it, it would soon pine, and grow up a starveling. The usual manure is that from the stable or the cattle-pen. It is better to break up the ground with the grubbing-hoe, because it pulverizes the soil more effectually; but it is sometimes done with the plough. When the seed-beds have been properly broken up, they are raked level, and the tobacco-seed, having been previously mixed with weak wood-ashes, is sown broad-cast over them. The first rain that comes, settles the seed into the ground, and if the weather is warm, it springs up in about five days. During this interval, the ground is being still further prepared to receive the young plants, which have to be transplanted. Mounds are raised, called tobacco-hills, about three or four inches above the level of the soil, and about four feet in area. This is to permit the water to flow off from the plants, otherwise they would be drowned. A very little water will do this, so great care is necessary. In about a fortnight or three weeks the plant is fit to remove from the bed into the field, and when the favourable moment arrives, all the hands, men, women, and children, are forced to set to, transplanting as hard as they can, working early and late, Sundays as well as week-days; for when young the seedling is very delicate, and unless it is transplanted just at the proper time, it dies. The transplanting time lasts from the middle of April through May. Two seedlings are generally planted in each hill, and when they have struck, that is, rooted, the weakest is pulled up. As soon as it begins to grow, the ground has to be kept constantly stirred around the roots, or it would clod; and it must also be kept free from weeds. It is a terrible hard time for the slaves, young and old, but especially for the small children, who are better able to creep amongst the plants and pick out the weeds with their little fingers, than grown-up men and women are; and they are also, for the same reason, more suitable to do the transplanting. It comes very hard at times, too, to the old slaves, some of whom I have seen, who, from constant stooping, could not stand straight up to save their lives. The driver is very sharp and active during this season; and if he sees a hand "straighten" from his work, that is, stand up a minute to rest his back, down comes the bull-whip, across the shoulders of the unfortunate man or woman, with a loud crack like a pistol-shot.

The next process is called "priming," that is, pulling off the lower, scorched and withered leaves, which are left on the ground. We have also to look for a worm called the "bud-worm," a grub that nips off the sprouting plant and conceals itself in the ground, and which as much damages the plant in its present state, as the one I have previously mentioned does in its earlier stage of growth. We also now flat-weed the hills, that is, hoe up the grass that grows about the plants, with a flat hoe, after which the ground is well ploughed between the hills, in order to enable the fibres of the roots to spread kindly.

By this time, the plant is getting strong; but now it is requisite to be more vigilant than ever, for the tobacco-fly is looking out for a place to lay her eggs. She comes out of an evening, and lays one on each leaf. If the egg is not picked off, it is hatched by the next night, and in two days there is a caterpillar, or grub, as big as a man's little finger. Early every morning gangs are sent round, children and all, to hunt for the eggs and grubs, and pick them off, as also for any worms that may be about.

Disgusting as it may seem, the slaves have to pull these grubs in two. They are tough and "blobby," and are very filthy things to handle. I have, however, known my old master, James Davis, go round, and if, after the plants had been picked, he found a grub left, he would call to the slave in whose row he had found it, and forcing his mouth open, rub the vermin against his teeth, to teach him to have sharper eyes in future.

Another good hoeing is now also given to the plants, and if any of them are high enough to "top," the bud is nipped off. This "topping," however, is systematically done, as the plant shoots. It has the effect of strengthening it, and causing buds to spring out at the sides, which are all nipped, in order to prevent blossoming, and to cause the leaves to grow luxuriantly. When the plant is getting ripe, the leaves become "snarly," like a bull's face. They are tried every morning, by doubling them up between the finger and the thumb. If the leaf breaks, it is ripe, and then comes gathering time.

The plant is now slit down the stalk, close to the ground, with a long knife, fashioned like a chase-knife, and then cut off. It is then set butt upwards, and left to wither, when it is picked up, thrown across the arm, carried to a pile, and laid flat. Here it remains until it has heated. It is next shaken and hung on a tobacco-scaffold. This is formed of sticks about eight feet long, driven into the ground. The upper end of them is crotched, or forked, and smaller sticks are laid in them. Across these the tobacco is hung, the cleft in the plant keeping it fast, and the leaves hanging downwards, the tips of them being about five feet from the ground. When the plant is first gathered it is as green as a cabbage, and has to be left on the scaffold until it turns brown. Should it "cure green," a fire is made underneath the scaffold, which is kept burning until the leaves dry, and are ready to crumble to pieces when touched. As soon as any signs of damp appear in the atmosphere, the tobacco is gathered and put into barns. Here all the slaves set to—children and all—pulling the leaves off the stalks, and tying them up into bundles, called "hands," the stalks being thrown aside for manure. Some "knowing ones," called "sorters," are selected to pick out the different qualities: that which is known by the name of "bird's-eye," is merely the ordinary leaf cut up, stem and all, the stem constituting the "eye:" the sort called "Cavendish" is the same ordinary leaf, only stripped from the stem, then rolled up and pressed under a screw-press.

The best tobacco is grown in Virginia, and the land on which it is grown requires rest every other year.

I will now say a little about the growth of RICE, which is perhaps the most unhealthy occupation in which a slave can be engaged.

It is usually grown on low lands, which are useless for any other purpose, and which are easy to flood, either naturally or by sluices constructed for that purpose. In the spring the slaves take hoes, about ten to twelve inches wide in the blade, and draw, in the mud, trenches of the same width, and about an inch deep, with the corner of the hoe. These trenches are very regular, and in them the rice is sown in the month of March. The seed is covered in lightly by drawing the back of the hoe over the ground, and in about a week the plant peeps up. There is a kind of grass, called bull-grass, which is very troublesome in rice-fields, as it springs up amongst the rice, and between the rows or "in-steps," and being of singularly rapid growth, would soon choke the rice. This grass has to be hoed out of the insteps, and pulled up as it springs amongst the rice. Should any be left, the slaves are most severely flogged. When the plant is about half leg high, the land is flooded to the depth of from six to eight inches. The growing crop remains under water three or four days, during which time the slaves are obliged to go into these swamps, grubbing up the grass between the rows. It is awful work. Men, women, and children are all employed incessantly, for it is a busy time. They work naked, or nearly so, and contract all sorts of maladies. There is the muddy soil into which you sink knee-deep, and which sends up the foulest smell and vapour, causing fever and sickness. The heat, too, from the sun overhead, reflected back into your face from the water, is intolerably painful, frequently bringing on giddiness and sun-stroke. Then the feet get water-poisoned, or you take the toe or ground-itch, when the flesh cracks and cankers. You also catch the "chiggers," a small insect that punctures the skin under the toe, where it deposits an egg. This soon turns into a live, but very minute, maggot, which breeds in the flesh very fast, causing a great lump to swell up, and an unendurable irritation. You have also to run the risk of getting bitten by all kinds of water-reptiles, and are sure to have some sickness or other. Fevers, agues, rheumatism, pleurisies, asthmas, and consumptions, are amongst the maladies the slaves contract in the rice-swamps, and numerous deaths result. It is very much more trying than either cotton or tobacco cultivation.

But bad as the work is whilst the water lies on the land, it is as nothing compared with what it becomes after the water is drawn off, when the slaves have to go in and weed with their fingers. The stench is much worse, and the labour heavier, because the feet stick in the miry ground, and it is difficult to drag them out. During the growth of the rice the land is flooded three times. The hands are regularly tasked—every man, woman, and child having their allotted portion of ground marked, or, as it is called, "staked" out, and that portion he or she must do. The usual task is one acre for a man, three-quarters of an acre for the women, and proportionately less for the children; or a certain number of them are told off to one man's or one woman's task, as the case may be. It must not be supposed, however, that the masters are very particular about keeping to any average. It is not an uncommon thing, by any means, for the task to be doubled, for it is always "staving times" with them; they are always in a hurry to get the crops in, and always in a hurry to get them out.

The overseer or "nigger driver" is also ever near by, with his long shot-gun to bring down a run-away, and with his bunch of "chinkey-pen"[28] switches. These are roasted to make them tough, and are from four to six feet long. They "lick" the body very badly, scratching and tearing the skin as they are drawn across it. More flogging, perhaps, takes place in a rice-field than in any other, on account of the hands leaving grass in the "in-steps," the whole of which it is impossible to root up.

The plant ripens its seed towards the latter part of August, and through September. It is then cut, and left to dry or "cure," and when dried, it is stacked away in long ricks. During winter the rice is thrashed out, then gathered up, and put into large mortars, to be beaten. Each mortar will contain about a bushel. It is pounded to loosen the husk, which is very hard to get off. Sometimes it is passed through a mill. After this it is sieved, riddled, and fanned; the broken, that is useless for sale, is given to the negroes, and the rest is put up into barrels, ready for sending to market.

CHAPTER XIX.

A FEW WORDS ON THE TREATMENT OF SLAVES.

IT will be expected of me that I should say something concerning the general treatment of slaves, as far as my own experience goes. I have had a little, and consider myself qualified to speak. I have been a slave nearly all my life, and seen as much of the system as any body. I have not narrated half of what I know, for there are some things I could not speak of in a public way. The little I have told may afford an insight into the system of Slavery, but it is only a "small peep." I have suffered enough myself, but others have endured and are daily enduring, perhaps, much more. When will it end?

It is not true—so far as my experience goes—to say that the masters treat their slaves well, because it is their interest to do so. The cattle are better treated than we are. They have warm stables to lie down in; they are tended and regularly fed, and get plenty to eat; and their owners know that if they over-work them they will knock up and die. But they never seem to know when we are over-worked, or to care about it when they do know. If we fall off our work, they call us idle, and whip us up to their mark. They look upon us only as working cattle, but seem to act on the principle that there are no bounds to human endurance. Half the floggings I have had at any one time would have killed the strongest horse. Our huts, or what are called the "nigger quarters," are only of logs, with a flooring of mud, like I have described in the opening chapter of this narrative. The wind and the rain will come in, and the smoke will not go out. We are indifferently clad, being nearly naked half our time; and our doctor, when we are sick, is generally some old "Aunt" or "Uncle" who has "caught" a little experience from others; and that not of the best. Our food is insufficient, and of bad quality. We never get but two meals a day: breakfast at twelve, and supper when our work is done. The general allowance is a peck of Indian corn a week, which may cost at the rate of about a shilling a bushel. It ought to be good, sound corn; but, more frequently than not, it is shrivelled up, and does not give any thing like what it ought in meal. Once a fortnight, or perhaps once a week, we get about two ounces to a quarter of a pound of old bacon, which is generally alive with "skippers,"[29] or honey-combed by them. If we did not steal, we could scarcely live. I believe every master is plundered of corn, hogs, chickens, turkeys, and such like, to a very large extent, by his slaves. They are forced to do it. Hunger drives them to it, though they know they will be flogged if they are found out. But the fear of punishment, instead of deterring them from committing thefts, only makes them more cunning in trying not to be found out.

I could say a good deal, too, about the laws, but I should have to write a large book if I did. One thing I know, and that includes all. The laws are made for the master, not for the slave. How should it be otherwise, when, in the eye of the law, the slave is only a "chattel?" It is all nonsense to say that the law protects the slave. It does no such thing for the slave; indeed, even a coloured free man cannot give evidence against a white man, so that even murder on the person of a slave cannot be brought home to the man who commits it. The law says you may give a slave thirty-nine lashes if he is found roaming about without a pass. I warrant that ten with the bull-whip, properly laid on, will cut any man's life out; and this is twenty-nine "licks" within the law. Flogging niggers has got to be a science almost. But niggers are not all alike. Some will stand harder than others; and if those that are weak should die under a licking that another has had and got over, where is the law that can touch the master? There is no cruelty under the sun that hard-hearted men can devise, that has not been employed to bring "niggers" into subjection. The masters call the slave a "chattel," but they know and feel he is a man, and they try all they can to tame him, and break down his spirit, and the law supports him in it.

Then the work. The time a slave works depends upon his master. I do not think we get, as a general rule, more than five hours' rest; if that can be called rest which is nothing but a broken doze. All the time we are at work, we work in right down earnest. No matter whether it is by the day, under the overseer's eye and whip, or by the piece; for slaves are often set to labour by the task, both in the cotton and the rice-fields. This is a great deal harder than working in the ordinary way, because the amount of labour required to be done, is usually fully equal to what an able-bodied slave, male or female, can accomplish, work as hard as they may. Some work harder than others. This makes it worse for the rest, as what these do is adopted as a guide or standard for the others, who are strained to the utmost to keep pace with the nimbler hands. My old master, Stevens, had a way of his own to get the most out of his folks, at task-work. He would pick out two or more of the strongest and sturdiest, and excite them to race at hoeing or picking, for an old hat, or something of the sort. He would stand with his watch in his hand, observing their movements, whilst they hoed or picked across a certain space he had marked out. The man who won the prize set the standard for the rest. Whatever he did, within a given time, would be multiplied by a certain rule, for the day's work, and every man's task would be staked out accordingly.

I have heard it said by some people who want to make out that this system of task-work is the best for the slave, that when his task is done he has the rest of the day to himself. And so he has; but then he never gets done till night-fall, and often cannot finish his task at all, and is then so fatigued he can scarcely crawl to his wretched cabin. He is very glad, when he gets there, to throw himself down and sleep. Many and many a time I have gone to sleep without my supper, quite dead beat with fatigue: and I am a strong man. Then, again, you are never sure but the overseer or the master will find fault with your work, and make you go over it again to mend it, besides giving you a flogging for your negligence. There is often too good reason for fault-finding; and no wonder. The task is usually so heavy, that in the hurry to get through the day's work, the ground will not be clean hoed, or the plants will be broken: faults which never escape severe punishment. But the system of task-work is not, I think, usual, except on the smaller plantations, where the master does his own overseeing and flogs his own "niggers;" which some of them like to do. There is an economy in this system, because it enables the master to do without an overseer. After he has ascertained the speed of his "niggers" in hoeing, picking cotton, or such like, he tasks and leaves them. He has then only to go over their work, and can at once detect if any of the hands have fallen off; and as each had his task, he is in no difficulty to find out the delinquent. The ordinary day's labour in hoeing, at task-work, is about from eight to ten rows across a fifteen acre field, the rows being about four feet apart, when the cotton is growing. If it is a ten acre field, there are more rows; if a twenty acre field, fewer. I set, what, from hard experience, I know to be the average. The task for women is from seven to eight rows of fifteen acres across, or in the same proportion as the men. It is very laborious work. It breaks the back, as the body is constantly bent, and the arms are continually going; the perspiration, meanwhile, streams from every pore of the body till the whole of it, head, hair, and all, are covered with a crust of mud. When the cotton is older in growth, the day's labour is increased one-third, or thereabouts, as by this time the weeds and grass are pretty well under. In North Carolina and in Virginia, the tasking system is not so bad as in Georgia and in South Carolina. Where there is overseeing, the negroes are driven as hard as possible, but the work is done less regularly, and by fits and starts. The negroes will flag and rest if they can get the chance. Whilst they do so, one of the number is usually set to watch the overseer, and when he sees them coming, they have a signal, and all hands fall to again as fast as they can. Some days he is not in a flogging humour, and then he will ease off the hands a little. On others it is just the reverse. Then, again, there is all the difference in the work. Some fields are easy; some hard; some have more grass; others more roots; and it very often happens that the hands are hardest pressed where the land is most difficult to clean, and that they are eased off when the work is comparatively light. In picking cotton, an ordinary fair day's pick is a hundred pounds. In Georgia, a day's task picking is a hundred and fifty pounds: in Mississippi about two hundred. In hoeing corn, thirty-five rows of ten acres across is a task. The hoers are generally led by the fastest hand, and the rest are compelled to strain their utmost to keep up with him. I have no hesitation in saying that the task system is very bad indeed for the negroes; and any one who considers the facts I have given, must, I think, come to the same conclusion.

Having alluded to the food and lodging of slaves, I may, perhaps, put in a word here about their raiment. We get two suits a year, consisting of a cotton shirt of coarse cloth, and pantaloons of the same; the whole cost of which does not exceed half a crown. We get a blanket once a year, and sometimes only once in two years; value not more than from one shilling and six-pence to two shillings. I should say that the cost of a negro's clothing does not exceed eight shillings a year, and that his rations do not cost more than a shilling a week; so that Three Pounds sterling will cover his keep and clothing. There is then his first cost to be considered. But the calculation of the master is, that in two years one slave earns enough to buy another; that is, that he pays for himself, and henceforward all he earns, over and above the expense of keeping him, is clear profit.

Before I close this chapter, I wish to add a remark or two about the slave-trade. It is supposed that there are no slaves imported into the South from Africa. I am quite sure that the reverse is the case. There was a planter lived on an estate adjoining my old master, Stevens. His name was Zachariah Le Mar, and he was called Squire. That man had, to my knowledge, five hundred of them, all fresh from Africa, and I know that new ones were constantly brought in. We call them "Salt-backs." I remember, too, that one day, being still at Stevens', I was down in our apple-orchard shooting red-headed wood-peckers with a bow and arrow. John Glasgow was with me, and there came across to see him, one Tony Wilson, a negro belonging to John Wilson, whose farm adjoined our's; and one Boatswain Smith, another negro, who belonged to a Doctor Smith, living three miles from us. They were native Africans, and could speak English only very imperfectly. They met in the orchard, and had not long been in conversation, before Tony Wilson discovered that Boatswain Smith was the very man who had sold him from his country, within the last two years. He got into a great rage, and fell upon Smith directly, and they both began to fight, butting at one another furiously. We had a great deal of trouble to part them, but we succeeded at last, and learnt that they had both been brought direct to Savannah in Georgia, with a great many more. Boatswain Smith had been kidnapped not very long after he had been the means of sending his countryman into Slavery. This little incident may serve as a proof of the fact I am quite sure would be borne out by close inquiry, that the slave-trade is still carried on between the Coast of Africa and the Slave States of the American Union.

CHAPTER XX.

MY REFLECTIONS.

WHEN I think of all I have gone through, and of the millions of men, women, and children I have left behind me in slavery, every one of whom may be undergoing similar or even greater sufferings, I ask myself when this is all to end? and how it is to be ended? I look upon it that slavery is kept up entirely by those who make it profitable as a system of labour. Bad as slaveholders are, if they did not find their account in working slaves, they would soon leave off doing it. Their badness arises out of the system. They must get work out of their "niggers" any how, or else they will not get profit. To make them work they must have complete control over them, and the laws are framed with an eye to this object. Now, "niggers" will work well enough for themselves, but they do not care to work for the benefit of another, unless they are forced to do it. And who can blame them? In order to compel them to labour for the sole advantage of another, the whip and all sorts of coercive means are employed, and this is how the cruelty begins. A man soon gets hardened into it, and then he can go any lengths. Cruelty is inseparable from slavery, as a system of forced labour; for it is only by it, or through fear of it, that enough work is got out of slaves to make it profitable to keep them. Every slave works against his heart, because he knows he is labouring for the benefit of another man. But my firm belief is, that, if they were set free to-morrow, the most part of them would work for the planters ten times better for fair wages than they do for cow-hidings, and that the masters would find themselves much better off. It is all very well to talk about kind masters. I do not say there are none. On the contrary, I believe there are a few, though I never had the experience of them. But if there are any, they are good in spite of the laws, which would make the best master bad, because they give him such an almighty power over his slaves, he cannot help abusing it. If he does not do so himself, those about him do; and that brings it to the same thing, as far as we are concerned. It is not of any use to talk to the slaveholder about the wrongfulness of holding slaves. The chinking of the dollars in his pocket makes such a noise that he cannot hear you; and so long as his pocket is full you may talk, but he only keeps on never minding you. Now, if you could prevent his getting the dollars, he would begin to think there must be something very wrong in slave-holding; and as the dollars slipped away, his notion of the system's being wrong would grow bigger and bigger, till he would be so full of it he could not but abandon it. And this is what I should like folks—especially the anti-slavery folks—to understand better than it seems to me they do.

I have often been asked how we slaves, being so ignorant, come to know that holding a human creature as a slave is wrong and wicked. I say that, putting the cruelties of the system out of the question, we cannot be made to understand how any man can hold another man as a slave, and do right. A slave is not a human being in the eye of the law, and the slaveholder looks upon him just as what the law makes him; nothing more, and perhaps even something less. But God made every man to stand upright before him, and if the slave law throws that man down; tramples upon him; robs him of his right, as a man, to the use of his own limbs, of his own faculties, of his own thoughts; shuts him out of the world up in a world of his own, where all is darkness, and cruelty, and degradation, and where there is no hope to cheer him on; reducing him, as the law says, to a "chattel," then the law unmakes God's work; the slaveholder lends himself to it, and not all the reasonings or arguments that can be strung together, on a text or on none, can make the thing right. I have heard long preachments from ministers of the Gospel to try and shew that slavery is not a wrong system; but some-how they could not fix it right to my mind, and they always seemed to me to have a hard matter to bring it square to their own. When I have been asked the question, I have had in my mind the death-bed scenes I have witnessed of slaveholders, who all their lives had rioted in cruelty to their slaves, but who, when the dark hour came, could not leave the world without asking pardon of those they had ill-used.

There was my old master Thomas Stevens. Ever so many times before he really did die, he thought his time was come. But though he made a mistake on all these occasions, and recovered from his illnesses, in his frights he sent for us all and asked us to forgive him. Many a time he would exclaim, that he wished "he'd never seen a nigger." I remember his calling old Aunt Sally to him, and begging and praying of her to get the devil away from behind the door, and such like. It is a common belief amongst us that all the masters die in an awful fright, for it is usual for the slaves to be called up on such occasions to say they forgive them for what they have done. So we come to think their minds must be dreadfully uneasy about holding slaves, and therefore there cannot be any good in it. All this may seem to be trifling, but it is the truth. In our ignorance, we have no light but what comes to us through these little chinks, and I only give what I have myself experienced.

Then, again, when the masters die, we cannot but feel that somebody is stronger than they are. The masters always try to make us believe that they are superior to us in every thing, and a different order of beings, almost next to God himself. They do this to make us fear them. I will just relate an anecdote that may illustrate this point.

My old master Stevens once missed a hen, and wanted to find out who had stolen it. We were all called up and asked about it, but nobody knew any thing of it. He said that it was of no use trying to deceive him, for he should be sure to find out the thief. He got a lot of slips of paper, all of the same length, and made us each take one, telling us that the paper would grow in the hands of him who had stolen the hen. Next day we were all called up again to give him our slip of paper, and he at once picked out the thief, who, it seems, being afraid his should grow, tore off a bit of his slip, and so convicted himself. We found this out afterwards, of course; but at the time, we thought he must be a wizard at the very least, and we dreaded him all the more.

To such tricks as these the masters stoop, in order to acquire an influence over their slaves. But when we see them sick, and hear them cry out with pain and fear on their death-bed, just like we do when we are being flogged, we understand that there is some one superior to them, who can make them feel pain and torment too; so, after all, we come at last to learn that they are only poor human creatures like ourselves.

So this is the way we get to learn that there is something wrong in slaveholding. When a man cannot die happy, it is a sure sign his mind is heavy about something, and our masters do not leave us in doubt what it is.

But, as I have already said, slaveholders are not sensible to moral arguments, because they believe their interests are bound up in maintaining the system of slavery. I would not advise the anti-slavery party to leave off arguing out the question on moral grounds; but I would urge them to pay a little more attention to the commercial part of the subject. I do not hesitate to say, that so long as anti-slavery people, or those who profess anti-slavery sentiments, continue to use up slave-grown articles, the slaveholders will keep on, thinking their professions are hollow. I do not see how the system is to be put down except by undermining it. I mean by underselling it in the markets of the world. I believe there is very little or no difficulty in getting free-labour Sugar and Rice. The chief difficulty is in procuring a sufficient supply of free-labour Cotton. Yet there is no doubt, that if proper encouragement were given, a very large quantity could be soon procured from Africa, where it grows wild, and might be very cheaply cultivated; or from the West Indies; or from India; or from Australia. I have been spoken to by many gentlemen who are interested in this subject; but they complain of the indifference of the anti-slavery public, who will not pay a small advance on the price of an article made of free-labour cotton; nor encourage enterprises set on foot to increase the supplies of the raw staple. But they will cry over the sufferings of the poor slave, who labours under the lash, from morning till night, in the cotton, rice, or sugar-cane fields, and who, when these commodities rise ever so little in price, soon has the figure scored into his flesh, and so finds out the markets have improved. I am quite convinced that if slavery is to be put down, one of the most certain means—if it is not, indeed, the only one—is to reduce the value of its products in the markets, by bringing into them as much cotton, sugar, rice, &c.—but especially cotton—as can be raised by free-labour. This cannot be done all at once; but it can be done. To do it well, it must be set about in right down earnest, and systematically; and I intend to devote the rest of my days to doing my part.

I do not want charity help. Thank God, I am a strong man yet, in spite of the privations, hardships, and sufferings I have undergone. I have no education, and until I can settle down I am not likely to pick much up. But I have just that sort of experience which I believe I could turn to account were the field open. I am what is called a "handy fellow." I am a good carpenter, and can make just what machinery I want, give me only tools. I understand all about the growth of cotton, from the time of preparing the land to receive the seed, till the wool is jinned and packed. I am a good judge of its quality, too, and know what is the best kind of jin for the various sorts. I do not say this for the sake of boasting. My knowledge has not come naturally to me. I have acquired it in a very hard school, and I want to turn it to account.

And why do I say I do not ask for charity-help? Because I feel that with a fair field I can earn my own living. I want to do it. I want to rise. I do not want to stay in this country any longer than is necessary for me to get enough money to purchase me some tools, and to set me going in the world. I hope to realize sufficient for this by the sale of my Narrative, and intend to place myself under the guidance of the good friends I have found, and who have promised to use their influence and interest in my behalf, to secure me a fair chance. I want to show the world that a "nigger" has quite as much will, and energy, and purpose in him, as any white man, if you only give him fair play. I also want to show my

coloured brethren who are in Canada, that they might do something great for
our people in the South, by turning their attention to growing cotton in the West
Indies or in Africa. By so doing, they would strike slavery a hard blow, just where
it is most likely to feel it. I have been to Canada, and though the coloured people there may, some of them, be doing tolerably well, snow does not agree with
their complexion. They ought to look into the future. They ought to consider
those they have left behind them, and how they can help them. My opinion is,
they could do so better in the West Indies or in Africa, than in Canada. Cotton
is the King of Slavery. So long as there is a good market for slave-grown cotton,
so long will it pay slave-holders to produce it. The coloured people must do their
own work. If they stand by till other folks do it for them, slavery may take a long
lease yet. But only let them once come to this conclusion, that they have a work
to do, and set about it in earnest, and Slavery may call in all the doctors the South
can muster—including old Sam himself—but it must die, in spite of every thing
they can do to keep it alive.

CHAPTER XXI.

THE UNDERGROUND RAILROAD.

(From the *Anti-Slavery Reporter,* April 1853.)

NO railroad in the world deserves greater encouragement than the one which bears
this name, at once so peculiar and so expressive. It was originally projected to connect the Southern States of the American Union with the Northern: Slavery with
Freedom. It may be said properly to commence at what is technically known as Mason and Dixon's line; that is at the junction of the Slave States with the Free States:
and to terminate at the southern frontier of Canada. Its course is by no means regular, for it has to encounter the Alleghany range of mountains and several considerable rivers, including the Ohio. Lake Erie too lies in its track, nor is it altogether independent of forests. In spite, however, of all these, and numerous minor obstacles,
the line has been constructed with admirable skill, as they can testify whose circumstances have compelled them to avail themselves of this mode of transit. Travelling
by it cannot strictly be said to be either pleasant or altogether safe; yet the traffic is
greatly on the increase. It is exclusively a passenger traffic; the trains are all express,
and strange to add, run all one way, namely, from South towards the North: there
are no *return tickets*. The stations are numerous, but by no means conspicuous. The
principal aim of the projectors having been to get the line itself into good working
condition, the stations were selected for convenience more than for show. They lie
from ten to fifteen miles apart, having nothing in their external appearance to distinguish them particularly, though they are never, or very rarely missed. Once the
passenger is fairly on the line, he seldom fails reaching his ultimate destination. Owing to the great danger and the numerous difficulties that attend the running of a
train, extreme caution is requisite in regulating the hour of its departure, and no small
amount of ingenuity and dexterity is brought into play to secure the safety of the passengers. The character of the train varies according to circumstances and the

exigencies of the case; but in this respect, comfort is disregarded as a matter of tri-fling importance, in comparison with the principal object, which is individual secu-rity. The Underground Railroad being for the exclusive use of slaves, who are run-ning for freedom, its managers are not known, in a general way. It is rather a point with them to evade popularity, for detection would bring with it no end of fines and imprisonment. Yet they derive no pecuniary advantage from what is called "the for-warding business." They work, like noble heroes as they are, for suffering and op-pressed humanity, and for no other reward than the satisfaction of their conscience. The station-masters belong to almost every class of society, and are dispersed all over the regions through which the underground line passes: for its branches are very nu-merous, and require extensive and constant supervision, not only to prevent acci-dents, (that is, seizures,) but also to gather information. It frequently happens that a train is kept waiting several days, sometimes two or three weeks, when the "danger" signal has been made, which usually means "look out for slave-hunters." Then it is that the self-possession, the courage, and the resources of the particular station-master who has the convoy under his care, are largely drawn upon. His situation at these times is most critical, for though the cunning and daring of the reckless and ex-perienced slave-hunter may be baffled, it is a far more difficult feat to delude the sagacity of the four-footed colleagues that frequently accompany him, and who can "snuff a nigger an eternal distance off, and nose him out anywhere," so admirably are they trained to their cruel work. It may be observed, by way of parenthesis, that the above quotation is a genuine recommendation of "some prime dogs," that were advertised for sale a short time since in the New Orleans Picayune. It illustrates at once the nature of the advertiser's trade, and the peculiar qualities of his blood-hounds. But the runaways and their friends possess a secret which enables them to deceive even the keen scent of these fierce animals, and it is at no time more service-able than when the hunters are nearest to their prey. Instances have been known of fugitives being tracked to the very thresh-hold of their lurking-place, yet lying close in safety, until the dogs, utterly baffled, have cast off again with a wild howl of dis-appointment. Such, however, have been trying times for all parties. As may be imag-ined, the travellers by this line have frequent recourse to disguises; and exciting in-deed are the narrations of hair-breadth escapes, under similar circumstances, and admirable the acts of heroism to which they have led. Perhaps no fact is more wor-thy of being dwelt upon in this place than the fidelity of the station-masters to their trust. No pecuniary consideration has hitherto induced them to violate a secret in-volving the fate of so many thousands of their fellow-creatures, and it is not reckon-ing too much upon their future fidelity, to say that they never will; though the pass-ing of the Fugitive-slave Law has increased the risks of their undertaking, and raised the price of blood. The slave-owners would doubtless pay a heavy sum to the man who would point out to them exactly where the underground line commences, and thus enable them to complete its survey for their own purposes. But Abolition knows its duty better. When Emancipation has taken place, the Managers of the Under-ground Line will make them a present of the secret.

A word now on the origin of the "underground railroad to Freedom," the pro-jector of which, like many more benefactors of the human species, fell a victim to his philanthropy. His name—and long will it and his memory live, in the hearts of the friends of humanity—was Charles Turner Torrey. He was born in Scituate, Massa-chusetts, November the 1st, 1813. At the tender age of four, he became an orphan, but was received by his maternal grand-parents, and subsequently educated at Exeter Academy, Yale College, and Andover Seminary. He finally settled in the ministry at Providence, Rhode Island, but did not long remain there. He continued his labours in various places, until in 1842 we find him in the prison of Annapolis, Maryland. The Reverend Mr. Torrey's uncompromising views as an Abolitionist were well known. He had urged them with all the energy of his strong mind and earnest convictions. With his fine talents, improved by learning and observation; his clear and intensely active intellect; and a heart full of sympathy and genial humanity, he could not but be an energetic and zealous advocate of any cause; and devoting himself, as he did, to that of Abolition, no wonder its friends held him in more than ordinary esteem, or that the pro-slavery party marked him as a man to be feared and to be punished if the opportunity presented itself; as indeed it soon did. In 1842, the slaveholders of Maryland convened a meeting at Annapolis, for the purpose of making what further aggressions they could devise, upon the rights of the free-coloured people of this State. (A similar meeting has recently been held in Virginia, Carolina Co. for a similar purpose, which has resulted in the passing of resolutions, that, if carried out, will reduce this class of its citizens to slavery.) Mr. Torrey, ever active, repaired to the place of assembly at Annapolis, and took his seat in the gallery, where he was soon observed, taking notes of the proceedings; his intention being to publish a report of them in an anti-slavery paper. For this offence, in a free country with a free press, he was incarcerated for a week. During his imprisonment, his busy thoughts were directed to devising some plan by which slaves might be assisted in effecting their escape. The idea all at once occurred to him, that if a number of persons resident in the Free States, and located at convenient distances from one another, could be induced to pledge themselves to help forward fugitive slaves to Canada, it would be the means of preventing numerous run-aways from being recaptured and carried back into Slavery. Having determined upon the general outline of the plan, he was no sooner released than he commenced operations for carrying it out in all its details. In this he was so successful, that before many weeks the underground line was completed from Mason and Dixon's boundary to Canada, a distance varying from two hundred to above five hundred miles, with all its complicated machinery of vigilance committees, spies, pilots, conveyances, and signals. It had not yet received a name, but the number of slaves who effected their escape increased so enormously, in consequence of the facilities "the line" afforded them, that the slave-holders took the alarm. In vain, however, they redoubled their vigilance, and multiplied their precautions and their measures. Though they even succeeded in tracking the fugitives to the Ohio, all traces of them disappeared there. They were all amazement; and at length, as a solution of the mystery that attended the disappearance of their property at this point, they jumped to the conclusion that the Abolitionists had prepared a subterranean railroad, by means of which they ran off fugitive slaves. The term was a happy one, and "the Underground Railroad to Freedom" was at once adopted by the Abolitionists as the most appropriate name for so extraordinary an enterprise. From first to last, that is, in about two years, Mr. Torrey was individually instrumental in running off nearly four hundred slaves, the greater part of whom would probably, "but for his exertions," he writes, "have died in slavery."

On the 25th of June, 1844, Mr. Torrey was arrested at Baltimore, (Maryland,) at the instance of one Bushrod Taylor, of Winchester, (Virginia,) who swore that Mr. Torrey had helped sundry slaves of his (the complainant's) to escape. Governor

M'Donnell, without further inquiry, at once issued an order for Torrey's arrest and incarceration. Immediately upon this, a second complaint was lodged against him by a man of most infamous character, named Heckrotte, for having aided two of his victims to escape. The chief evidence to sustain the second charge was that of two *professional slave-catchers,* men of notoriously bad repute, and whose entire testimony, in so far as it implicated Mr. Torrey, was a tissue of falsehoods concocted for the occasion. Had he succeeded in disappointing the malignity of the parties who, it is strongly suspected, set on Taylor and Heckrotte, by proving the perjury of themselves and their witnesses, a requisition from the State of Virginia itself impended over him, ready to be enforced as soon as he was released from jail. This measure, however, became unnecessary, for poor Torrey died. During his incarceration, and rather with a view to terminate the severe privations he was designedly subjected to, than to evade a trial, he sought to escape, but his attempt was frustrated, the plan having been betrayed by a fellow prisoner of the name of Doyle, a notorious negro-trader. At length he was brought up. The proceedings lasted three days; November 29th and the two succeeding days. He was found guilty on the perjured testimony of the witnesses suborned to establish the charge, and sentenced to six years' imprisonment in the Penitentiary. In the autumn of 1845 his health began to fail, and on the 9th May, 1846, he died, at the early age of thirty-three, a victim to the intense malignity of the slave-power.

From the published reports of the proceedings, it would appear that every effort was made to procure a conviction. In the case of Taylor, who had sworn to the identity of Torrey, it subsequently came out that he had never set eyes on him until *after* his arrest. In that of Heckrotte, whose accomplices swore that Torrey had actually himself enticed the slaves away, it was satisfactorily established that he had never seen them until they were thirty miles beyond Baltimore; and he might at any time have cleared himself from this second charge, by giving up the name of the party (a lady) who planned their escape; but this he refused to do. As, however, it was elicited that Torrey had really aided slaves in running off, the establishment of the general fact was considered sufficient to fix him with the guilt of the particular offences for which he was tried; hence his condemnation. The whole affair created intense excitement; the sentence was regarded as vindictive, and when Torrey died, the event shed a general gloom over the circles that were familiar with him and his efforts in the anti-slavery cause. A public ceremonial graced the passage of his remains to their last resting-place at Mount Auburn, Boston, where a monument has since been erected to his memory. The Committee of the British and Foreign Anti-Slavery Society also marked their high respect for him, and their deep sympathy with his mourning friends, in a series of resolutions embodying these sentiments, and recording their protest against the vile and unholy system to the malignity of which he fell a sacrifice.

Torrey's death did not, however, in the least degree affect the success of the "underground railroad." From the period of its establishment to that of the passing of the Fugitive Slave-law, the average number of passengers by it exceeded a thousand a year. But since 1850, the number has greatly increased, not only owing to the fact becoming known to the slave-community through various channels, that if a fugitive only strike a certain track, he will find friends to help him on to Canada, but also because that atrocious enactment has roused a spirit of opposition to the power which carried it through the Senate, and which has by its means attempted to convert the Free States into man-traps, and free citizens into man-stealers and kidnappers for the South. The escapes are at present so much on the increase, that the slave-owners are adopting the most active measures to check the traffic by the underground line.

It may be readily conceived that to accomplish the safe transit of a convoy, much precaution and forethought are indispensable. Usually, means are taken to signal, from one station to another, the arrival and the departure of each train of passengers; (for as such we will consider the runaways:) so that the lookers-out at the station a-head may be on the watch. The main difficulty is to convey the travellers across the rivers. The ordinary ferry-boats would not, for obvious reasons, be the most eligible water-conveyance. Against this contingency due provision is made, and "pilots" are appointed for this special service, whose duty it is to lie in wait at or near the place which has been signalled as the point for which the convoy will make. This service involves much anxious and patient watching, as the safety of the fugitives wholly depends upon their meeting with the expected "pilot" at the specified crossing-place. We will illustrate, by two anecdotes, the danger and accidents incidental to a trip by the underground line, and the consequences of slips by the way.

At a certain village on the Ohio river, not a hundred miles from Cincinnati, and in Ohio State, there came one evening in the spring of 1851, to the house of an Abolitionist—one of the managers of the underground line—a fugitive-slave seeking shelter. He was soon at home, and informed our friend that himself and nineteen others had just escaped out of Kentucky. At a particular place they were to have fallen in with a "pilot." They had reached it but found no pilot there. Not knowing what to do, and dreading discovery, he had broken away from his companions, and wandered on in the dark in search of a secure hiding-place. It is needless to add, that he found one with our friend the Abolitionist, who forthwith despatched him to Canada. The next day the village was in an uproar. The Kentuckians, the masters of the run-aways, accompanied by their friends, invaded the place in search of their lost property. They had tracked them to the village, and now threatened vengeance against the coloured people and the known Abolitionists for enticing away their slaves. Being armed to the teeth, with bowie-knives, revolvers, and rifles, their presence and threatening manner caused great excitement and alarm, for they effected a forcible entry into the premises of every suspected person. It was fortunate for our friend the Abolitionist that he had already dismissed his *protégé* on the road to freedom. Meanwhile, the Abolitionists were not idle, but sent out scouts in various directions, in order to ascertain what had become of the missing nineteen. Their efforts, however, proved unsuccessful. They only ascertained that the pilot, who had come from another town, had repaired to the appointed place, expecting the fugitives there at a particular time. After waiting considerably beyond the hour specified, and finding they did not arrive, he concluded they would not come that night, and returned home. It was supposed, that finding they had missed their expected guide, the slaves had taken to the woods, where they would disperse and lie concealed, and hopes were entertained that they might still elude the vigilance of their pursuers. It ultimately turned out that this was not the fact. On their arrival near the appointed place, they had sent one of their number on to look for the pilot. Finding him not there, they strayed about in the dark until dawn, when they took refuge in a sugar-house owned by a Methodist. The sequel is soon told. This man finding them there, and tempted by the large reward which was offered for their recovery, quietly assembled a few of his neighbours, and captured the whole gang. They were all surrendered into the hands of their owners, and again consigned to slavery and to the horrible punishments inflicted on recaptured runaways. Amongst them was a mother and her seven children.

The second adventure had a more cheerful termination.

Some three or four years since a party of fugitives had reached Oberlin, Ohio, a few miles south of Lake Erie. They were congratulating themselves on their security, seeing they were so near to Canada, when, to their utter dismay, intelligence came that the slave-hunters were on their track, and already near the building where they had found a temporary resting-place. No time was to be lost if they were to be saved. The managers of this branch of the underground line—chiefly students belonging to the Oberlin Institute—immediately devised a plan for rescuing the fugitives, which they as speedily put into execution. A carriage was procured into which the slave-hunters, who were now near enough to perceive what was passing, saw the party enter of which they were in search. They counted their number, and took note of their sex. The carriage drove rapidly off, the slave-hunters following in hot pursuit. The pace was terrific; but the latter gained on their prey, and succeeded in overtaking the whole party as they got into the next town. They were taken, carriage and all, to the court-house, when they were thrust into a room, to await the arrival of the magistrate. Here they were accommodated, as a special favour, with a little water. In due time, the magistrate having inspected his law-books for the purpose of ascertaining how the statutes had provided for such a case, the delinquents were summoned before him; when lo! the whole party presented themselves with perfectly white, and it must be added, indecorously grinning faces. The slave-hunters at once perceived the *ruse* which had been practised upon them. In their eagerness they had only noticed the colour, the garb, the number, and the apparent sex of the parties who had rushed with such precipitancy into the carriage. As these tallied with the description of the fugitives, they thought of nothing but of their recapture. It need scarcely be explained, that the lads were indebted for their sable hue, to a convenient chimney, and to the slaves themselves for their disguise. The magistrate, however, who was not at all in the secret, looked gravely at the young men, and then at the slave-hunters, asking whether they claimed these white people as their slaves. Now although a coloured man may be arrested, carried before a judge, and claimed as a slave, with perfect impunity, (his discharge of course depending upon his disproving the fact of his being the claimant's property,) it is an extremely grave offence so to treat a white. Probably if the slave-hunters who had been thus tricked, could have safely revenged themselves upon the young men, by subjecting them to even a temporary imprisonment, until they had procured the requisite proof of their own identity, they would not have scrupled to assert a claim to them. But this would have been too serious an affair. They had, therefore, no other alternative but to reply that they had been duped, and that the young men were free. This they accordingly did, and hastily withdrew, amidst the derisive shouts of the assembled crowd.

Meanwhile the party of real fugitives were sent on to Canada by the Underground Railroad.

May it prosper until emancipation leaves it no more work to do, or until it has run off every slave now in bondage.

DECLARATION.

[The following Declaration of John Brown, made before a Notary Public of the City of London, and setting forth the facts relating to the seizure, enslavement, and torturing of John Glasgow, a free-born British subject, is inserted here, in order that any person disposed, to make inquiries respecting John Glasgow's English wife and family, may have legal evidence on which to proceed.]

To all to whom these Presents shall come. I, ALEXANDER RIDGWAY, of London, Notary Public by Royal Authority duly admitted and sworn (and by the Statute 5th and 6th William the 4th, chapter 62, especially empowered in this behalf), do hereby certify that on the day of the date hereof before me at my Office, No. 28, Royal Exchange, in the City of London personally came and appeared Mr. John Brown of No. 26, Stonecutter Street Farringdon Street in the County of Middlesex Carpenter and Joiner named and described in the Declaration hereunto annexed vouched for to me by Louis Alexis Chamerovzow Esq. as being a person well-known and worthy of full credit and by solemn declaration which the said John Brown then made before me he did solemnly and sincerely declare to be true the several matters and things mentioned and contained in the said annexed Declaration.

(Seal)

In Testimony whereof I have set unto my hand and Notarial Seal and have caused mentioned and referred to in and by the said Declaration to be hereunto also annexed. Dated in London the Twenty-ninth day of May One thousand eight hundred and fifty-four.
ALEXANDER RIDGWAY,
Notary Public.

I, JOHN BROWN, of No. 26 Stonecutter Street, Farringdon Street, in the City of London, Carpenter and Joiner, formerly known by the single name of Fed, do solemnly and sincerely declare as follows: I was born, as I believe, about the year One thousand eight hundred and eighteen, in a state of slavery, upon an estate called "Betty Moore's plantation," in Southampton County in the state of Virginia, about three miles from Jerusalem Court House in the said county. I was sold when ten years of age or thereabouts to one Starling Finnie, a negro speculator, and by him re-sold a few weeks after to Thomas Stevens, of Baldwyn County, in the State of Georgia, whose plantation was situated within eight miles of Millageville, in the said county. I well remember that on my arrival in this plantation I found a slave named John Glasgow, who was then a new hand, having been recently purchased at a slave auction at Savannah. It was reported and believed amongst the slaves on the plantation that this John Glasgow had been a free British subject, and this circumstance, which caused some to chuckle and others to sympathize, has tended to fix the following facts strongly in my recollection. He also felt for me in my grief at parting from my former relations, and endeavouring to console me as best he could, frequently spoke to me of his own previous history, particularly of his residence and relatives in England. These are the facts

I thus learnt and believe. John Glasgow was a native of Demerara, born of free negro-parents: when quite small he took to the sea, first as cabin boy, working his way up till he became an able-bodied seaman, and was so rated on the ships' books. His first voyages were made on board the small coasters that trade between the West-India Islands; but he abandoned the coasting trade after a few years, and went to and fro to England, improving his opportunities so much that he saved money and was regarded as a prosperous man. He then sought a wife. In the immediate neighbourhood of Liverpool, the port he had most frequented, there resided a small farmer who had a daughter. John Glasgow was a fine fellow, tall of stature and powerful in frame, having a brave look and a noble carriage. The farmer's daughter married him with the approbation of her relatives. Having saved money, John Glasgow, through the father's interest, got into a small farm in the neighbourhood, and purchased (as he was fond of repeating to the slaves) three horses, a plough and a cart. As his wife had been accustomed to farming operations she agreed to attend to the concerns of the farm, whilst he, finding that he knew nothing at all about farming, determined to continue his calling, and engaged himself as an able-bodied seaman on board one of the many vessels trading between Liverpool and the West Indies. At the end of his second voyage he found himself a father, and from this time he and his wife continued to prosper, he in his vocation, she at her farm. About the year One thousand eight hundred and twenty-nine, being then about twenty-five years of age, he engaged to go out to Savannah, in Georgia, in an English vessel, and under an English captain, for a cargo of rice: he was now the father of two children. He sailed, and in due course arrived with his vessel at Savannah. By virtue of certain provisions of the Black Law of Georgia, like that of South Carolina, John Glasgow, though a free-born British subject, was conveyed to gaol, and incarcerated until the vessel that brought him to the port should discharge her cargo, be re-laden, and on the point of sailing away again. By the same provisions he would then have been released on payment of the gaol fees by the captain. The ship was detained considerably beyond the time the captain had reckoned upon, owing to delays in procuring the cargo. Slave labour was dear, and the captain had to pay high wages to the slave who had been hired to him to do John Glasgow's work. When, therefore, the time came for the ship to set sail, he found that the gaol fees for John's release had run up enormously high, so the captain refused to pay them, and set sail without him. John Glasgow was then taken out of the gaol and sold on the auction block for three hundred and fifty dollars to Thomas Stevens, on whose plantation I found him as above described. From this point I can declare to the facts stated as within my personal knowledge. I remember his naturally brave look: this offended his master, who swore he "would flog his nigger pride out of him." When he had been some three or four years on the plantation his master bade him take a wife. John told him he had one in England, and two children. Then his master flogged him for saying so and for insisting upon it he was free, and a British subject. At last, to save his body from the cow-hide and the paddle, he promised his master never to say as much again, and to look out for a wife. In Jones County, and about five miles from Stevens' plantation, there lived another planter named John Ward. John Glasgow having to go backwards and forwards on errands, saw and at length selected a young coloured girl named Nancy, and they were married in the way that slaves are, that is, nominally. This did not please Stevens, because Nancy, be-

ing Ward's property, her children would be Ward's also; so John was flogged for
marrying Nancy instead of one of Stevens' "likely gals," and was forbidden to visit
her: still he contrived to do so without his master's discovering it. The young
woman was of a very sweet disposition, and knew all about John's misfortunes
and his having a wife and children in England: she was very kind to him. On
Christmas Day, a holiday for all, he thought he would slip away from the other
slaves who were having a feast before Stevens' house, and go see Nancy. Accordingly, watching his opportunity, he soon succeeded in getting away. His master
saw him, but instead of calling him back, allowed him to get a good distance off,
when, beckoning to him three other slaves, of whom I, declarant, was one, they
started in pursuit, and soon came up with the object of their search. John Glasgow struggled ineffectually to release himself. He was secured and brought back
to quarters, and the other slaves were called together to witness the infliction upon
him of a punishment called bucking. Having been stripped stark naked, his hands
were fast tied and brought down over his knees, he being compelled for this purpose to assume a sitting posture with his knees doubled up under his chin. A stout
stake was then thrust under his hams, so that he was rendered completely powerless. In this position he was turned first on one side then on the other, and flogged
with willow switches by me, the declarant, and with the cow-hide by his master
until the blood ran down in streams and settled under him in puddles. For three
hours he endured this punishment, groaning piteously all the time, whilst his master looked on and chuckled. At last he was taken out of the buck, and his lacerated body washed down with salt, red pepper, and water. It was two weeks before he went to work again.

Severe as this torture was, it did not smother John Glasgow's affection for the
poor mulatto girl who shared his sorrows. As soon as he felt able to go so far, that
is in about three months, he made another attempt to see her, was missed, pursued,
and caught. Then Thomas Stevens swore an oath that he would cure him of "wife-
hunting. If he must have a wife, there was a plenty of likely yellow gals on the plantation for such as he to choose from. He might have the pick of 'em. But he (Stevens)
wasn't going to let his niggers breed for another man's benefit, not he: so if he (John)
couldn't get a wife off the plantation, he should't have one at all; but he'd cure him
of Nancy any how."

John Glasgow was taken to the whipping post, which, on Stevens' estate, consisted of two solid uprights, some ten feet high, with a cross-beam at the top, forming a kind of gallows. Along the cross-beam were three or four massive iron cleets,
to which pulleys were fixed, having a fine but closely twisted cord passing over them.
John Glasgow, having been stripped as on the previous occasion, the end of one of
these cords was tightly fastened round his wrists. His left foot was then drawn up
and tied, toes downwards, to his right knee, so that his left knee formed an angle by
means of which, when swung up, his body could conveniently be turned. An oaken
stake about two feet long was now driven into the ground beneath the cross beam of
the whipping post, and made sharp at the top with a draw-knife. He was then hoisted
up by his hands by means of the pulley and rope in such wise that his body swung
by its own weight, his hands being high over his head and his right foot level with
the pointed end of the oaken "stob," or stake.

This punishment is called "the Picket," and by the body being swung in this
manner the skin of the back is stretched till it shines and cuts more readily under

the lash: on the other hand, if the negro, swinging "between heaven and earth," as it is called, desires to rest, he can do so only by placing the foot that is at liberty on the sharp end of the stake. The excessive pain caused by being flogged while suspended, and the nausea excited by twirling round, causes the person undergoing "the picket" to seek temporary relief by staying himself on the "stob." On his doing so for ever so brief a space, one of the bystanders, taking hold of the bent knee and using it as a handle, gives him a twirl and sends him spinning round on the hard point of the stake, which perforates the heel or sole of the foot, as the case may be, quite to the bone.

John Glasgow, thus suspended, was flogged and twisted for an hour, receiving "five licks," or strokes of the raw cow-hide at a time, with an interval of two or three minutes between, to allow him "to come to and to fetch his breath." His shrieks and groans were most agonizing, and could be heard at first a mile and a quarter off, but as the punishment proceeded they subsided into moans scarcely audible at the distance of fifty paces. All Stevens' slaves were made to stand by during the infliction of the torture, and some of them took turns at the whipping, according to the instructions of their master, who swore he would serve them the same if they refused, or ever disobeyed him as "that cussed nigger there had done." At the end of an hour he was "dropped from the beam," his back being fearfully lacerated, his wrists deeply cut with the cord, and his foot pierced through in three places. Beneath the beam there was a pool of coagulated blood, whilst the oaken stake was dyed red with that which had streamed from his foot. He could not stand, much less walk, so they carried him to his quarters, where the usual application of salt and water and red pepper was made to his wounds. It was a month before he stirred from his plank, and five months elapsed ere he could walk. Ever after he had a limp in his gait. I made my escape from Thomas Stevens' plantation some time after this punishment had been inflicted on John Glasgow, and the last I know of his history is, that in One thousand eight hundred and forty, or thereabouts, the poor fellow was felling a white oak in the woods, which in falling struck him on his right thigh, just above the knee, and broke it in two. As he was thus rendered comparatively useless for field work, Thomas Stevens gave him to his son John, who kept him to shell corn off the cob. Lastly, I declare, in respect to myself personally, that upon my escape from Mr. Stevens' plantation I passed into the free state of Michigan, and there remained for about three years with a company of Cornish miners. Thence I went to Canada, and after remaining in the Dawn Institution for some months, came to England, led by the descriptions of John Glasgow and the suggestions of Captain Joe Teague, Captain of the mine in Michigan, a native of Redruth in Cornwall.

And I make this solemn declaration, conscientiously believing the same to be true, and by virtue of the provisions of an Act made and passed in the Sixth year of the reign of His Majesty King William the Fourth, intituled, "An Act to repeal an Act of the present Session of Parliament, intituled 'An Act for the more effectual abolition of Oaths and Affirmations taken and made in various departments of the State, and to substitute declarations in lieu thereof, and for the more entire suppression of voluntary and extra-judicial Oaths and Affidavits, and to make other provisions for the abolition of unnecessary Oaths.'"

Declared at my Office, No. 28 North side of the Royal Exchange, in the City of London, this twenty-ninth day of May, One thousand eight hundred and fifty-four.

JOHN BROWN.

Before me,
ALEXANDER RIDGWAY,
Notary Public.

JOHN BROWN'S TESTIMONIALS.

WE the undersigned do certify our knowledge of John Brown, who was a Slave in America, in the state of Georgia, and was four times sold. He came to Lake Superior, for refuge, in 1847, and was employed by our Company. He was employed by our Company for one year and a half; during that time we found him quiet, honest, and industrious. His object in coming to England was to see Captain Joseph Teague, by whom he was promised support. Unfortunately the Captain died in America, and J. Brown not knowing of his death till he came to Redruth, Cornwall, by that means he is thrown out in a strange country for a little support. We have helped him all that lay in our power, and would heartily do more for him if we could. We have heard him several times lecture on Slavery and also on Teetotalism. We hope the object he seeks will induce the sympathy of English Christians.

Dated, Redruth,
February 26th, 1851.

JAMES VIVIAN, Redruth.
RICHARD PASCOE, Redruth.
THOMAS WILLIAMS, Redruth.
THOMAS CHAMPION, Redruth.

――――

St. Austell, March 20th, 1851.

I beg to testify to my firm conviction of the forestated case of John Brown. When he called on me in the first instance, there happened to be a relative of the said Captain Teague present, who, after very considerable conversation, expressed his full conviction of his, J. B. having been engaged under his relative, Captain Teague. I believe John Brown is entitled to sympathy and assistance from common humanity, especially from Christians.

SAMUEL BARLOW.

――――

Bodmin, March 25th, 1851.

The bearer, John Brown, has been in this town a few days, and lectured in the Union Hall to a large assemblage of persons, to whom he delivered a narrative of his life during the time that he was a slave in the State of Georgia.

I privately questioned him previous to this, as to the treatment received by slaves from their masters, the route he pursued at the time of his escape, &c.; and having resided in those parts for several years, I have a firm conviction in my own mind as to the truth of his statements and the sincerity of his objects.

CHARLES PEARSE,
House Surveyor.

———

Liskeard, 3d Month, 31st, 1851.

Having conversed with John Brown, a coloured man, now here, but who was formerly a slave in the United States, I have reason to be satisfied, from the accounts which he gives of persons and places that are known to me in that country, that he is not an impostor; and judging from his conduct while here, I am disposed to encourage him to spread the knowledge of the cruelties of Slavery, and recommend him to the kind notice of the public, trusting that he will continue to conduct himself well.

JOHN ALLEN.

———

Plymouth, April 12th, 1851.

The undersigned are desirous of recommending John Brown to the notice of philanthropists in other parts of England which he may visit.

From an examination of his testimonials, as well as from their own observation, they are fully satisfied of his veracity, and consider the object he has in view worthy of the support and encouragement of all friends of the Negro race.

J. B. has addressed a crowded meeting at the Guildhall, and his simple narrative of his sufferings in his escape from Slavery was listened to with great interest and attention.

E. JONES, *Independent Minister.*
RICHARD BISHOP, *Draper.*
WILLIAM SMITH.
CHARLES FOX HINTON, *Chemist.*
HENRY HEYDON, *Printer and Stationer.*

———

John Brown, a fugitive slave, has been giving an interesting account at public meetings in Exeter of his sufferings in Slavery, and escape therefrom. We believe him to be a person fully deserving of credit.

R. WERE FOX.
JOHN DYMOND.
THOMAS HINCKS.
SAMUEL DAVIS.

Exeter. { There is no date to this testimonial, but it will easily be seen that it closely follows the above.—ED.

———

27, *New Broad Street, London,*
20th June, 1851.

The bearer of this, John Brown, has been recommended to me as an honest and industrious man. The information I have received privately about him is quite satisfactory.

JOHN SCOBLE,
Secretary of the Anti-Slavery Society.

3, *Winchester Buildings, June 23d, 1851.*

John Brown has brought very satisfactory testimonials to me, and from what I have seen of him, he appears to be a steady and deserving character.

EDMUND FRY.
ELIHU BURRITT.

———

Wrexham, May 5th, 1852.

Although I was entirely unacquainted with the bearer, John Brown, until his arrival in Wrexham, I am so satisfied with the high testimonials he brings with him, that I have no hesitation of aiding my name to those by which he is already recommended to the public.

JOSEPH CLARE.

———

27, *New Broad Street, 18th May, 1853.*

I am desirous of adding my testimony to those which John Brown, the bearer, already has in his possession. I have had many opportunities, as extraordinary as they were unexpected, of testing the accuracy of his narrative of his life and sufferings, and am quite satisfied that he is altogether trustworthy in this respect.

I also believe him to be a man of upright views and sound principles, and who is most anxious to do something for his race, in calling attention to the capabilities of the free negroes of Canada to grow cotton in Africa and in Australia. He is directing their energies in the right way, and is also advancing the Anti-Slavery cause; for in proportion as free labour can be made to compete with slave labour, especially in the article of cotton, will Slavery be undermined.

I hope he will meet with consideration from all the friends of the slave.

L. A. CHAMEROVZOW,
Secretary of the British and Foreign Anti-Slavery Society.

The bearer, John Brown, is a total abstainer.

———

Reading, 11 mo., 24, 1851.

W. WESTMACOTT,
Goddard's Arms Hotel,
Swindon.

John Brown spent about a week here, during which time I saw some little of him, and he took a meal or two at my house. I looked over his testimonials, and know several of the parties whose names are attached to them, and fully satisfied myself that he was worthy of the attention of the friends of the poor slave. I presided at a meeting here, which was satisfactory. I understand that he is now wishing to excite a sympathy for the slaves of America, and raise a little fund for himself that will enable him to get to Canada; and I hope the people of Swindon will do their little to provide him the means for this purpose.

I am, respectfully,

GEORGE PALMER.

———

February 19th, 1852.

I have examined Mr. John Brown's testimonials, and, as far as I can judge, they appear to me to be correct, and that he is a deserving person.

Wm. Ker.

The Parsonage,
Tipton.

———

February 21st, 1852.

My dear Sir,

The bearer of this note, Mr. John Brown, has presented me with testimonials in his favour; among these is a note from yourself, stating that you have examined him, and think him a deserving person. If you think any thing can be done for him or his cause—which, from extraneous appearance, is certainly a good one—I shall be happy to give the use of my room for the purpose of a lecture, &c.

I am, dear Sir,
Yours very respectfully,
Richard Warmington.

The Rev. W. Ker, M.A.

———

Bridgewater, March 31st, 1853.

Dear Sir,

The bearer, Mr. John Brown, an escaped slave, is desirous of visiting Manchester, in order to advance what appears to me a very practical plan for the amelioration of the condition of the coloured population of America. His testimonials, which I have examined, seem to me to recommend him strongly, and his plan shows him to be a man of strong mind.

I am sure you will exert your influence on his behalf, and if you can procure him a favourable opportunity of advocating his views in Manchester you will oblige.

Yours most sincerely,
S. Alfred Steinthal.

Rev. J. R. Beard, D.D.

———

The testimonials which John Brown has produced satisfy us that his narrative is a truthful one, and as such, its being related must give a very affecting picture of American slavery, and tend to increase the feeling of abhorrence of that system of iniquity.

E. Wigham,
Secretary to the Edinburgh Ladies'
Emancipation Society.

10th mo., 1853.

———

John Brown, a fugitive Slave, happily escaped from that hell of sin and misery, "a Slave State," waited on me some weeks ago. His testimonials—some from persons known to me in this country and in America—established his truthfulness to my conviction. I presided at a meeting which he addressed with interesting power, especially considering his being shut out from the mental training enjoyed by the "Free." He gave a simple, graphic narrative of his escape, &c. The audience was gratified. I introduced him to my friend, the Rev. William Parlane, of Tranent. John addressed a meeting in Tranent with approval, and also at Prestonpans. I gave him a testimonial, and I thus repeat it for the following reason.

Mr. Smith, one of the Magistrates of Glasgow, wrote me that John had been shewing his testimonials, had, after a few minutes' interval, returned to the shop, saying some one had rudely jostled him on the street, and, on searching, he found that his pocket-book, containing all his testimonials, had been abstracted. The Messrs. Smith, knowing that John could not have been in improper company, that his tale was true, took means, by advertisement, &c., for the recovery of John's testimonials. Finding all efforts vain, they kindly applied to me and others for duplicates; hence this minuteness on my part—the more, that I have since conversed with Mr. Smith at large on poor John's misfortune.

John professes to be practically acquainted with the rearing of cotton from the seed to the bale, and I should think him, from his constitutional strength and energy, well fitted to superintend the operative department, in the valuable scheme of raising Free Labour Cotton, say in Natal, or Australia, or India.

JOHN RITCHIE.

19, Salisbury Road, Edinburgh,
17th Nov. 1853.

_____

173, Irongate, Glasgow,
November 18, 1853.

The bearer, John Brown, a self-emancipated negro, called upon me on Saturday last, 12th inst., and shewed me several testimonials of a highly satisfactory character. He had not left my place of business above fifteen minutes, when he returned, saying he had been jostled by a man in Argyle Street, and he immediately discovered the loss of his pocket-book and all his certificates: fortunately no money was stolen, however. We immediately gave notice to the police, and got bills printed and posted, but no appearance of the missing book and contents has yet been discovered. In these circumstances I have procured for him one or two duplicates of his testimonials from his friends in Edinburgh, and have much pleasure in giving my own. John Brown seems a most worthy, honest man, and I hope he may be successful in obtaining the support requisite to reach Natal, or some other of our colonies, where his knowledge of cotton growing and packing may be turned to good account.

I should have stated that the time at which J. B. called on me was early in the afternoon, I think between two and three o'clock.

JOHN SMITH,
Secretary, Glasgow New Association
for the Abolition of Slavery.

_____

Glasgow, 18th Nov. 1853.

The bearer, John Brown, having been robbed of his pocket-book on the public streets of this city, and during daylight, has thereby been deprived of all his testimonials to character, and other papers, but, happily for him, the pocket-book contained no money; and we, the Subscribers, having seen the said testimonials, hereby certify that they were of the most satisfactory description, and cannot but express our regret that he should have been thus deprived of them, inasmuch as the want of these documents must obviously be to him a most serious deprivation. In these circumstances, we shall be glad if this certificate may be of any service to him.

(Signed)   WM. SMEAL,

Sec. and Treas. to the Glasgow Emancipation Soc.

ANDREW PATON.

JOHN KNOX.

————

John Brown states that he escaped from slavery in the year 1847, was employed in a copper mine in Michigan, United States, for eighteen months, in Canada, as a carpenter, eight months. He has also gained his bread in the same line of business in this country, but latterly he has been giving lectures, detailing the slave system, and giving a history of his life. In these departments he has given proof of industry, and a determination to gain his bread by his own efforts, and not to be burthensome to any one. John Brown is desirous of being sent out to the west coast of Africa, where he could teach the farmers and labourers to grow cotton, as he professes *thoroughly* to understand this process in *all* its parts, and can even make the machinery used in dressing cotton. I much wish to see John Brown placed in this situation, where, in the course of time, the Slave Trade may be stopped by employing the natives in their own country as free labourers. In Africa wages are so low as to afford grounds to expect that cotton-growers would be able to rival those in the United States, and thus to compel them to abandon slavery.

I know that the Secretary of the Anti-Slavery Society in London has a good opinion of J. B., and intends to promote his views; and all that I hear and see induces me to believe that he is an industrious, honest man, who is desirous to do well.

JOHN WIGHAM, JUN.

10, *Salisbury Road, Edinburgh.*

26th day of Eleventh Month, 1853.

————

John Brown, the bearer of this, gives a most interesting narrative of his sufferings while in a state of slavery, and his escape to Canada, after many fruitless attempts, which brought on him severe punishment. My full persuasion is that he is an honest man, and that his statements may be relied on. In his projected attempts to raise Free-Labour Cotton on the coast of Africa, though I am not competent to decide on the merits of the plan, I sincerely wish him success.

J. Brown delivered a lecture at the Mechanics' Institute in this town, on Monday evening last, on which occasion I took the chair. The attendance was good; and the simplicity and shrewd common sense with which he delivered his statements and made his remarks, very strongly interested the audience.

B. GODWIN, D.D.

Bradford, Yorkshire,
March 10, 1854.

————

Concurring in the views expressed by Dr. Godwin, on the other side, respecting John Brown, I think that he claims the kind and judicious notice of those who may have it in their power to aid him in his object.

BENJ. SEEBOHM.

Bradford, 3 *mo.* 11, 1854.

1. Andrews, *Free Story,* 183.

2. Louis Alexis Chamerovzow (?–c. 1876) was secretary of the British and Foreign Anti-Slavery Society from 1852 through 1869. He presided over the antislavery lecture certification system, encouraged blacks to tour England, and fought a variety of legislative and diplomatic battles. Ripley, *Black Abolitionist Papers,* I:384; Merrill & Ruchamer, *Letters of Garrison,* IV:310.

3. In southeast Virginia, on the North Carolina border.

4. From Benin.

5. A thin bread made of cornmeal, water, and salt, originally baked on a hoe.

6. A stillion: a stand for a cask.

7. A gang of slaves chained together.

8. Canvas cover.

9. Sticks of firewood.

10. Freshet.

11. A canelike grass.

12. Tendons or sinews.

13. In British Guiana.

14. Able-bodied seaman.

15. A beam running lengthwise above a ship's keel.

16. Julia Gardiner Tyler, wife of ex-President John Tyler, wrote a letter defending slavery that appeared in the February 1853 *Southern Literary Messenger,* in which she stated that the separation of slave families was "of rare occurrence and then attended by peculiar circumstances." As a result of her letter, for a brief moment Tyler became a national figure and a Southern heroine, with over fifty newspapers, North and South, printing favorable notices of the article. Seager, *and Tyler too,* 402–405.

17. Probably Angola.

18. This is a myth. Dismemberment was actually a very unusual legal punishment, and was limited to the state of Missouri. The slave code of Georgia in fact stated, "If any slave shall *presume* to strike *any white* person, such slave . . . shall for the *first* offence suffer such punishment as the said justice or justices shall in his or their discretion think fit, not extending to life or limb; and for the *second* offence suffer DEATH." Stroud, *Laws,* 68, 88.

19. Kentucky.

20. To reeve is to pass a rope through a hole.

21. A small saucepan.

22. Ellen Craft (1826–91) was a light-skinned mulatto famous for having disguised herself as a white slaveowner in order to escape from slavery. See her narrative, pp. II:481–531.

23. In south-central Illinois.

24. In east-central Indiana.

25. In Michigan's Upper Peninsula.

26. Canada West later became the province of Ontario. Dawn was founded in 1842 as an all-black colony; Josiah Henson (see pp. I:719–756) was the man most responsible for its initial success. Its main attraction was the British-American Institute, which occupied three hundred acres; another fifteen hundred were owned by black settlers, who came to number five hundred or more. The sawmill Brown refers to was one of Henson's own projects, and was mismanaged in his absence.

27. A coarse fabric, such as burlap.

28. Chinquapin.

29. Maggots.

JOHN THOMPSON

JOHN THOMPSON (1812–?), in his preface, explains that he read other slave narratives before writing his own, and he clearly modeled his first few chapters upon them. However, he was one of the small but significant number of slaves who professed to have had direct experience of God, and that experience evidently reshaped his narrative following its conventional opening. His story—which he wrote and printed himself without the benefit of any editor or advisor[1]—became a remarkable spiritual adventure, involving violent resistance to slavery, divine visitations, and an unforgettable sea voyage. In order to escape fugitive slave hunters, Thompson boarded a whaling vessel in New Bedford and sailed to Africa. His experiences form a curious parallel to those of Melville, who also boarded a New Bedford whaler at about the same time; interestingly, both writers imbued their travel accounts with allegorical significance. Abandoning the rhetoric of abolitionism, Thompson concludes with a sermon comparing the soul's progress with that of a ship; and only at the very end does he ingeniously work in references to slavery and freedom. His narrative eschews consistency, instead transforming itself as it moves, in a pilgrim's progress, from the worldly to the divine.

The narrative was well received when published—a review in *The Liberator* commented, "The unusual opportunities which John Thompson enjoyed of acquiring an education by stealth have enabled him to tell his story in a clear, connected, and interesting manner."[2] But it only went through one edition and was not reprinted for over a century.

THE

LIFE OF JOHN THOMPSON,

A FUGITIVE SLAVE;

CONTAINING HIS HISTORY OF 25 YEARS IN BONDAGE, AND
HIS PROVIDENTIAL ESCAPE.

WRITTEN BY HIMSELF.

WORCESTER:
PUBLISHED BY JOHN THOMPSON.
MDCCCLVI.

PREFACE.

_____

IT would be an unprecedented act to send into the world a work of the magnitude of this volume, without a preface; and I am glad to avail myself of the opportunity, which custom not only allows but prescribes, to say something of the work before you. Its history is as follows: It was suggested to me about two years since, after relating to many the main facts relative to my bondage and escape to the land of freedom, that it would be a desirable thing to put these facts into permanent form. I first sought to discover what had been said by other partners in bondage once, but in freedom now, and from what States they came. I found many of my brethren from other and remote States, had written on the subject, but scarcely any from Maryland. I am aware that now, when public opinion makes it no martyrdom to denounce slavery, there are multitudes of men that grow bold, and wield a powerful weapon against this great evil; and even school boys daringly denounce a system, the enormity of which they cannot appreciate, surely I thought it may be permitted to one who has worn the galling yoke of bondage, to say something of its pains, and something of that freedom which, if he should not succeed in accurately defining, he can truly say he will ever admire and love.

JOHN THOMPSON.

WORCESTER, MASS., MAY, 1856.

Life of John Thompson, a Fugitive Slave.

CHAP. I.

I WAS born in Maryland, in 1812, and was slave to a Mrs. Wagar. She had four sons and two daughters. The sons were all farmers, owning large tracts of land; which were well stocked with slaves, and other animal property!

When her youngest son, James H., was about forty or forty-five years of age, he owned the plantation upon which he and his mother lived, and on which I was born. On this plantation were about two hundred slaves, young and old; of which fifty belonged to him, and the remainder to his mother; but all were in his charge.

Mr. J. H. W. had two children, John and Elizabeth. His wife died before I could remember, leaving the children under the supervision of the Grandmother. Elizabeth was about thirteen, and John ten years of age.

My parents had seven children, five sons and two daughters. My father and mother were field hands. My younger sister was house girl and ladies' maid, while the elder was given to one of the sons. The rest of us were too small to work, the eldest being only eleven years old.

The first act of slavery which I recorded in my memory, was the sale of my elder sister, who belonged to Henry Wagar, brother to J. H., and who lived three miles from our plantation. My mother heard of the sale, which was on Saturday, and on Sunday took us with her to see our beloved sister, who was then in the yard with the trader's drove, preparatory to being removed far south, on the Monday following. After travelling six miles, we arrived at our place of destination. Mother, approaching the door of the trader's house, fell upon her knees, in tears begging to be permitted to see her imprisoned daughter, who was soon to be dragged away from her embrace, probably to be seen no more in the flesh. It was not his custom to admit slaves into his yard to see their friends; but at this time, his heart seemed to be moved with compassion, for he opened the door, telling us to go in, which we did.

Here, the first thing that saluted my ears, was the rattling of the chains upon the limbs of the poor victims. It seemed to me to be a hell upon earth, emblematical of that dreadful dungeon where the wicked are kept, until the day of God's retribution, and where their torment ascends up forever and ever.

As soon as my sister saw our mother, she ran to her and fell upon her neck, but was unable to speak a word. There was a scene which angels witnessed; there were tears which, I believe, were bottled and placed in God's depository, there to be reserved until the day when He shall pour His wrath upon this guilty nation.

The trader, becoming uneasy at this exciting scene, and fearing the rest of the drove would become dissatisfied with their situations, permitted sister to leave the yard for a few moments, to keep mother's company. He did not watch her, as I thought he would have done, but permitted her to go about with mother, and even to accompany us part of our way towards home. He ordered dinner for us, but not one of us could eat one mouthful. I thought my heart would break, as the time drew near for our departure. I dreaded the time when I should bid farewell to my beloved sister, never more to see her face, never more to meet her in the paternal circle, never more to hear her fervent prayer to the throne of God.

I watched the sun, as it seemed to descend behind the western hills; but this did not stop its progress. The time soon arrived when we must go. When mother was about to bid farewell to my sister, and reached out her hand to grasp hers, she burst into a flood of tears, exclaiming aloud. "Lord, have mercy upon me!"

The trader, seeing such parental affection, as he stood by, hung down his head and wiped the tears from his eyes; and to relieve himself from a scene so affecting, he said, "Mary, you can go some way with your mother, and return soon."

Turning to mother, he said, "old woman, I will do the best I can for your daughter; I will sell her to a good master."

We then left the house. After going with us two miles, sister Mary, in obedience to orders and her promise, could go no farther, and she said, "Mother, I suppose I must go back."

Here another heart-rending scene took place. I well remember her parting words, "Mother," she said, "don't grieve, for though we are separated in body, our separation is only for a season, and if we are faithful we shall meet again where partings are no more. Mother, will you try to meet me?"

We all promised to do so. We then parted, and have never heard directly from her since. She was, as we afterwards understood, taken to Alabama, and sold at public auction. But, if I am faithful, I shall see her again.

> Hark and hear the captive pleading,
>   Listen to her plaintive cry,
> While in floods her tears are falling;
>   Must I, in my bondage die?
> When I dwelt in my own country,
>   With my children by my side,
> Cruel white men coming on me,
>   Dragg'd me o'er the deep so wide.
> Oft I think of my sweet children,
>   And my dear companion too;
> If on earth I no more see them,
>   And have bid a last adieu,
> I must try to live so faithful
>   To that God who rules above,
> That I may obtain His favor,
>   And may dwell with Him in love.
> I must wait until that moment,
>   When the trump of God shall sound;

Calling nations all together,
    Then to hear their final doom!
There I'll see my dear companion,
    Whom long since I bade adieu;
There I'll see my smiling children,
    And my blessed Jesus, too!
Then let cares, like a wild deluge,
    Roll across this mortal frame;
Death will soon burst off my fetters,
    Soon 'twill break the tyrant's chain;
Then I'll pass from grace to glory,
    Then I'll sing my suffering o'er;
For then grief, and pain, and sorrow,
    Shall be felt and known no more.

CHAP. II.

ALL the slaves, both men and women, except those about the house, were forced to work in the field. We raised corn, wheat and tobacco.

The provision for each slave, per week, was a peck of corn, two dozens of herrings, and about four pounds of meat. The children, under eight years of age, were not allowed anything. The women were allowed four weeks of leisure at child birth; after which, they were compelled to leave their infants to provide for themselves, and to the mercy of Providence, while they were again forced to labor in the field, sometimes a mile from the house.

Often the older children had to take care of the younger. Sometimes the mother, until her babe was about three or four months old, if she had a kind and humane overseer, could come to the house once between meals, and nurse her child; but such favors were but seldom granted. More frequently the mother must take her child with her to the field, place it at the side where she could see it as she came to the end of the row; moving it along as she moved from row to row.

The slaves were called out from their quarters at daylight. The breakfast must be prepared and eaten before going to work, and if not done before the overseer called them to the field, they must go without it; and often the children, being asleep at this time, were of course obliged to go without their breakfast.

The slaves' clothing was, in winter, one shirt, pants and jacket, without lining, shoes and stockings. In summer, one shirt and one pair of pants of coarse linen.

When the tobacco is ripe, or nearly so, there are frequently worms in it, about two inches long, and as large as one's thumb. They have horns, and are called tobacco worms. They are very destructive to the tobacco crops, and must be carefully picked off by the hands, so as not to break the leaves, which are very easily broken. But careful as the slaves may be, they cannot well avoid leaving some of these worms on the plants. It was a custom of Mr. Wagar to follow after the slaves, to see if he could find any left, and if so, to compel the person in whose row they were found, to eat them. This was done to render them more careful. It may seem incredible to my readers, but it is a fact.

My mistress and her family were all Episcopalians. The nearest church was five miles from our plantation, and there was no Methodist church nearer than ten miles. So we went to the Episcopal church, but always came home as we went, for the preaching was above our comprehension, so that we could understand but little that was said. But soon the Methodist religion was brought among us, and preached in a manner so plain that the way-faring man, though a fool, could not err therein.

This new doctrine produced great consternation among the slaveholders. It was something which they could not understand. It brought glad tidings to the poor bondman; it bound up the broken-hearted; it opened the prison doors to them that were bound, and let the captive go free.

As soon as it got among the slaves, it spread from plantation to plantation, until it reached ours, where there were but few who did not experience religion. The slaveholders, becoming much alarmed at this strange phenomenon, called a meeting, at which they appointed men to patrol the country, and break up these religious assemblies. This was done, and many a poor victim had his back severely cut, for simply going to a prayer meeting.

At length, Mr. Wagar bought at auction a man named Martin, who was a fiddler. As slaves are very fond of dancing, our master thought that fiddling would bring them back to their former ignorant condition, and bought this man for that purpose. It had the desired effect upon most of them, and what the whip failed to accomplish, the fiddle completed, for it is no easy matter to drive a soul from God by cruelty, when it may easily be drawn away by worldly pleasures; and fiddling I think is better appropriated to this purpose, than anything else I could mention.

CHAP. III.

MR. W. was a very cruel slave driver. He would whip unreasonably and without cause. He was often from home, and not unfrequently three or four weeks at a time, leaving the plantation, at such times, in care of the overseer. When he returned, he sometimes ordered all the slaves to assemble at the house, when he would whip them all round; a little whipping being, as he thought, necessary, in order to secure the humble submission of the slaves.

Sometimes he forced one slave to flog another, the husband his wife; the mother her daughter; or the father his son. This practice seemed very amusing to himself and his children, especially to his son, John, who failed not to walk in his father's footsteps, by carrying into effect the same principle, until he became characteristically a tyrant.

When at home from school, he would frequently request his grandmother's permission, to call all the black children from their quarters to the house, to sweep and clear the yard from weeds, &c., in order that he might oversee them.

Then, whip in hand, he walked about among them, and sometimes lashed the poor little creatures, who had on nothing but a shirt, and often nothing at all, until the blood streamed down their backs and limbs, apparently for no reason whatever, except to gratify his own cruel fancy.

This was pleasing to his father and grandmother, who, accordingly, considered him a very smart boy indeed! Often, my mother, after being in the field all day, upon returning at night, would find her little children's backs mangled by the lash of John Wagar, or his grandmother; for if any child dared to resist the boy, she would order the cook to lash it with a cowhide, kept for that purpose.

I well remember the tears of my poor mother, as they fell upon my back, while she was bathing and dressing my wounds. But there was no redress for her grievance, she had no appeal for justice, save to high heaven; for if she complained, her own back would be cut in a similar manner.

Sometimes she wept and sobbed all night, but her tears must be dried and her sobs hushed, ere the overseer's horn sounded, which it did at early dawn, lest they should betray her. And she, unrefreshed, must shake off her dull slumbers, and repair, at break of day, to the field, leaving her little ones to a similar, or perhaps, worse fate on the coming day, and dreading a renewal of her own sorrows the coming evening. Great God, what a succession of crimes! Is there no balm in Gilead; is there no physician there, that thy people can be healed?[3]

Martin, the fiddler, was bought for a term of ten years, after which he was to be freed. He was a good hand, was called a faithful, humble servant, and was much liked by all who knew him. His term was now expired, according to the bill of sale. Of this he was fully sensible, but his administrator being at the distance of seventy-five miles from him, Martin had no means of seeing him, nor of informing him that he was still held in bondage, beyond the time of contract.

Therefore, feeling himself at liberty, he consequently began to manifest some signs of his freedom; for, when the overseer would drive him as usual, he wanted him to understand that what he now did was optional with himself, since he was now a free man, and had been such for eighteen months.

The overseer took this as an insult, but would not correct him himself, for he feared the action of Martin's administrator. Accordingly he complained to Mr. W., upon his return from a journey, upon which he had been absent. Martin was immediately called up, together with all the slaves, that they might witness the punishment to which he was subjected, in order that it might prove a warning to any one who might fancy himself free.

None knew at the time why they were called; they only knew that some one, and perhaps all, were to be whipped. And immediately each one began to inquire within himself, is it I? They began to consider if they had done anything worthy of punishment. Their doubts and fears were, however, soon ended by the lot falling on Martin, who was ordered to cross his hands. This was in the barn yard. He, having had his coarse shirt removed, and his pants fastened about his hips, was swung up to a beam by his hands, in the open shed, when the overseer was ordered to lash him with a cowhide. Every stroke laid open the flesh upon his back, and caused the blood to flow. His shrieks and piteous cries of "Lord, have mercy on me!" were heard at distant plantations. But they were of no avail;

there was no mercy in the iron heart of his tormentor. It seemed as if death alone could terminate his sufferings. But at length God heard his cry, and sent deliverance. By a weak and unexpected means, He confounded the mighty.

John, who at this time was about fifteen years of age, was out gunning, at a distance from the house. He heard the piercing shrieks of the victim, and hastened to the spot, where the frightful scene was being enacted.

"What is the overseer whipping Martin for," he inquired of his father.

His father answered the question only by bidding him go to the house. Instead of obeying, John cocked his gun, exclaiming "by God, I'll kill that overseer!" at the same time pointing the weapon at the overseer, and bidding his father to stand out of his way.

The overseer, becoming frightened, ran to Mr. Wagar for safety, well knowing that John would execute his threat, and that separated from Mr. W. there was no safety for him.

"Put up that gun, John," said his father.

"No I won't," replied John, "stand away, stand away, I'll kill that d——d overseer!"

The father was afraid to go towards his own son, lest in the frenzy of exasperation, he should murder him. So the overseer, conducted by Mr. W., for safety, left the farm for two days, until John's anger was appeased. Martin was then cut down by John, but was not able to work for several days.

About four or five months after this occurrence, his administrator arrived at the plantation. He seemed much surprised that Martin had been held so long over his time, and said that Mr. W. should pay him for it. He said nothing of the unjust punishment Martin had received, and whether there was ever any redress for it, I never knew. Martin left this plantation for a better one.

This was the only good act of John Wagar, of which I ever knew. Ever afterwards he was fully equal to his father in cruelty. Not many years afterwards, he whipped a slave woman to death, for taking a glass of rum out of his jug, which he thought he had lost.

This woman's husband generally kept liquor in his house, where some was found, when search was made in the slave's quarters for the lost rum. She said that her husband had bought it, but her assertion was not credited. Her husband belonged to a Mr. Morton, about five miles distant, and came on Saturdays to see his wife. The woman's name was Minta; she was the mother of six children. She was whipped to make her confess she was guilty, when she was not; and she finally confessed. He whipped her one half hour, to force a confession; after which he whipped another half hour for a crime which she never committed. This caused her death, which occurred three days after.

This was about the commencement of John's administration, for after he had finished his education and returned home, his father gave up the management of the plantation to him.

While young and attending school, his uncle gave him a beautiful little pony, saddle and bridle. Then this young gentleman must have a private body servant for himself, and he claimed the honor of making choice of one for himself, from among the slave children. Accordingly he made choice of myself.

Then my business was to wait upon him, attend to his horse, and go with him to and from school; for neglect of which, as he fancied, I often got severe floggings from him. Still, I did not wish my situation changed, for I considered my station a very high one; preferring an occasional licking, to being thrown out of office.

Being a gentleman's body servant, I had nothing more to do with plantation affairs, and, consequently, thought myself much superior to those children who had to sweep the yard. I was about twelve years old when given to John Wagar.

CHAP. IV.

FIDDLING and dancing being done away with among the slaves, by the disappearance of Martin's fiddle, Christianity seemed to gain ground, and a glorious revival of religion sprang up, which required another legal provision to suppress. This was the new provision: that the patrolers should search the slave quarters, on every plantation, from whence, if they found any slaves absent after night fall, they should receive, when found, thirty-nine lashes upon the naked back. When the slaves were caught, if a constable were present, he could administer the punishment immediately. If no constable were present, then the truant slave must be taken before a justice of the peace, where he must receive not less than five, nor more than thirty-nine lashes, unless he could show a pass, either from his master or his overseer. Many were thus whipped, both going to and returning from night meetings; or, worse still, often taken from their knees while at prayer, and cruelly whipped.

But this did not stop the progress of God's mighty work, for he had laid the foundation for the building, and his workmen determined to carry on the work until the capstone was laid.

Many slaves were sold farther south, for going to meetings. They would sometimes travel four or five miles, attend meeting and return in time for the overseer's horn.

Mr. Wagar had a valuable slave named Aaron, a carpenter by trade, and an excellent workman; a man of true piety and great physical strength. He never submitted to be flogged, unless compelled by superior force; and although he was often whipped, still it did not conquer his will, nor lessen his bravery; so that, whenever his master attempted to whip him, it was never without the assistance of, at least, five or six men. Such men there were who were always ready to lend their aid in such emergencies. Aaron was too valuable to shoot, and his master did not wish to sell him; but at last, growing tired of calling on help to whip a slave, and knowing that neglecting to do this would appear like a submission to the negro, which in time might prove dangerous, since other slaves, becoming unruly, might resist him, until he could not flog any of them without help. He finally concluded to sell Aaron, much as he disliked it.

The slave was at work at the time, sawing heavy timber, to build a barn. The manner of sawing such timber, at the South, is by what they call a whip saw.

A scaffold, about ten feet high, being erected, the logs to be sawed are placed thereon, when one man is placed above, and another below, who alternately pull and push the saw, thus forcing it through the logs.

Aaron was busy at this kind of work, when he observed several strange visitors approaching him, whose business he did not at first suspect. He was requested to come down from the scaffold, as one of the gentlemen wished to talk with him about building a barn. He at once refused to comply with the request, for having seen the same trader before, he soon surmised his business, and supposed that he, himself, was sold.

At this refusal, they commenced pelting him with stones, chips, or whatever else they could find to throw at him, until they finally forced him down. He sprang from the scaffold, axe in hand, and commenced trying to cut his way through them; but, being defeated, he was knocked down, put in irons, taken to the drove yard, and beaten severely, but not until he had badly wounded two of his captors.

His wife, being at the house spinning wool, did not hear of this until night. In the anguish of her heart, she ran, weeping bitterly, from one plantation to another, in search of some kind slaveholder who would buy her husband. But, alas, she could find none.

Aaron was kept confined in the jail yard two weeks, during every day of which he was whipped. Finally he broke jail and made his escape. The trader came early next morning to his jail, but Aaron was not there. At that time the slaves knew little of the friendly guidance of the north star, and therefore lingered about in swamps and among bushes, where they were fed by their fellow servants during the night, instead of fleeing to the north.

In this way Aaron remained concealed nearly one year, after which his wife got a man to purchase him, a running. Then Uncle Aaron came home to his new master, where he was when I left the South.

Matters continued in about the same course until the year 1822, when a change took place on our plantation, caused by the death of old Mistress, which event happened in October of that year. Now her slaves must be divided among her children and grand children. Now we must pass into other hands, some for better, some for worse.

The estate was divided the same month in which old Mistress died. The slaves were also divided, and each one was to go to his new home on the first of January, 1823. My father's family fell to Mr. George Thomas, who was a cruel man, and all the slaves feared much that they should fall to him. He was a very bad man. He fed his slaves well, but drove and whipped them most unmercifully, and not unfrequently selling them.

The time drew near for our departure, and sorrowful it was. Every heart was sad; every countenance downcast. Parents looking upon their darling children would say, "is it possible that I must soon bid them adieu, possibly forever!" Some rejoiced in hope of a better situation, while others mourned, fearing a worse one. Christmas came, but without bringing the usual gladness and joy. We met together in prayer meeting, and petitioned for heavenly strength to sustain our feeble frames. These were continued during holiday week, from Christmas to New Year's day, when slaves are not to be molested; consequently, no patrolers annoyed us.

New Year's, that sorrowful day for us, at length arrived. Each one weeping while they went round, taking leave of parents or children, for some children and parents were separated, as were also husbands and wives. Our meetings were now broken up, and our separation accomplished.

CHAP. V.

I WAS about fourteen years of age when the change mentioned in the last chapter, occurred. John Wagar claimed me by promise, as he said my grandmother gave me to him; and, consequently, bade me keep out of sight, when they came for my father's family. This I did by hiding myself until the rest were all gone. I did this willingly, as I did not want to go to Mr. Thomas. Indeed, I had rather forego the pleasure of being with my parents than live with him. So I remained behind.

I had lived securely upon the old plantation about three months, when one day I was sent on an errand, two or three miles from home. There I met Mr. Thomas, who said to me, "where are you going?" I answered his question, when he said, "You belong to me; come, go home with me." I told him I wished to return with my errand, but he said "No; go right home to my house, where your father and mother are. Don't you want to see your mother?" I replied that I did, for I was afraid to answer any other way.

This Mr. George Thomas had married my old Mistress's daughter, and we fell to him in right of his wife. I went home with him with a heavy heart.

When John Wagar heard of this event, he said I belonged to him and should come back; but he could not accomplish his purpose in this, for being left to Mrs. Thomas, he could not hold me. He then tried to buy me, but my new master would not sell me, to him.

Soon after my arrival in the family, Mr. Thomas let me to one of his sons, named Henry, who was a doctor, to attend his horse. This son was unmarried, lived a bachelor, and kept a cook and waiter. The cook belonged neither to him nor his father, but was hired. She was a good looking mulatto, and was married to a right smart, intelligent man, who belonged to the doctor's uncle. One night, coming home in haste, and wishing to see his wife, he sent me up stairs to request her to come down. Upon going up, I found she was in a room with the doctor, the door of which was fast. This I thoughtlessly told her husband, who, upon her coming down a moment after, upbraided her for it. She denied it, and afterwards told the doctor, but not till I had gone to my mother, sick, up to the old man's plantation.

The doctor was a very intemperate man. As soon as his cook told him her story, he came to his father with the complaint, that I had left him without his consent; upon which his father told him to flog me. He ordered me out to the barn, when I was scarcely able to hold up my head, and had to be led by my brother.

Without saying what he wanted of me, he stripped off my clothes and then whipped me, beating me over the head until I became senseless, and life was nearly extinct. I was carried to my mother's quarters, where I lay five weeks, unable to move without assistance. When I finally recovered, I did not return to him, as he did not wish it, but remained with my mother four years.

My father was a very pious man, never complaining, but bearing every thing patiently, and praying for grace and fortitude to help him to overcome his trials, which he believed would one day be ended. He was a good servant and an affectionate parent. But new trials and sorrows soon broke upon this quiet family.

My sister, whose name I must not mention, as she is now in the North, and like myself, not out of danger, was old Mistress's house maid. She possessed both grace and beauty, and to-day, thank God, is a living monument in his temple. She was given to Mrs. Thomas as her maid, and was much prized, because a gift from her mother; but especially because she knew her to be a virtuous girl.

She had found it impossible to long keep a maid of this stamp, for none could escape the licentious passions of her husband, who was the father of about one-fourth of the slaves on his plantation, by his slave women. Mrs. Thomas strove every way to shield my sister from this monster, but he was determined to accomplish his brutal designs.

One day during his wife's absence on a visit to her friends, being, as he thought, a good opportunity, he tried to force my sister to submit to his wishes. This she defeated by a resistance so obstinate, that he, becoming enraged, ordered two of his men to take her to the barn, where he generally whipped his slaves; there to strip off her clothes and whip her, which was done, until the blood stood in puddles under her feet.

Upon his wife's return, Mr. Thomas told her that my sister had been whipped for neglect of duty. Of this Mrs. Thomas did not complain, as she had no objection to necessary floggings. But similar scenes occuring quite often, our Mistress began to suspect that sister was not in fault, especially as in her presence she never neglected her business, and these complaints only came during her absence. Besides, she knew well her husband's former practices, and at last began to suspect that these and my sister's pretended faults, were in some way connected. Accordingly, she began to question her maid concerning her offences, who, fearing to tell her plainly, knowing it would be certain death to her, answered in low and trembling terms, "I must not tell you, but you may know what it is all for. If I have done anything Madam, contrary to your wishes, and do not suit you please sell me, but do not kill me without cause. Old Mistress, your mother, who is dead, and I trust in heaven, took great pains to bring me up a virtuous girl, and I will die before I will depart from her dying counsel given, as you well know, while we were standing by her dying bed."

These words so affected Mrs. Thomas, that she fainted and was carried to her bed, to which she was confined by sickness five or six weeks. Her husband's conduct still persisted in, finally caused her death, which occurred four years after.

Mistress told sister that she had best get married, and that if she would, she would give her a wedding. Soon after, a very respectable young man, belonging to Mr. Bowman, a wealthy planter, and reputed to be a good master, began to court my sister. This very much pleased Mistress, who wished to hasten the marriage. She determined that her maid should be married, not as slaves usually are, but that with the usual matrimonial ceremonies should be tied the knot to be broken only by death.

The Sabbath was appointed for the marriage, which was to take place at the Episcopal Church. I must here state that no slave can be married lawfully, without a line from his or her owner. Mistress and all the family, except the old man, went to church to witness the marriage ceremony, which was to be performed by their minister, parson Reynolds. The master of Josiah, my sister's destined husband, was also at the wedding, for he thought a great deal of his man.

Mistress returned delighted from the wedding, for she thought she had accomplished a great piece of work. But the whole affair only enraged her unfeeling husband, who, to be revenged upon the maid, proposed to sell her. To this his wife refused consent. Although Mrs. T. had never told him her suspicions, or what my sister had said, yet he suspected the truth, and determined to be revenged. Accordingly, during another absence of Mistress, he again cruelly whipped my sister. A continued repetition of these things finally killed our Mistress, who the doctor said, died of a broken heart.

After the death of this friend, sister ran away, leaving behind her husband and one child, and finally found her way to the North. None of our family ever heard from her afterwards, until I accidentally met her in the streets in Philadelphia. My readers can imagine what a meeting ours must have been. She is again married and in prosperity.

CHAP. VI.

MY master, George Thomas, was a man of wealth, his farm consisting of about one thousand acres of land, well stocked with slaves. He was as inhuman as he was rich, and would whip when no particle of fault existed on the part of the slave. He would not employ an overseer who did not practice whipping one or more slaves at least once a day; if not a man, then some weak or gray-headed woman. Any overseer who would not agree to these terms, could find no employment on Mr. Thomas's farm.

The third year after our arrival upon his plantation, he hired an overseer from Virginia, who was a man after his own heart, and who commenced the work of bloodshed soon after his arrival. He, however, soon met with his match.

On the plantation was a slave named Ben, who was highly prized by Mr. T., being, as he thought, the best and most faithful servant on the farm. Ben was a resolute and brave man, and did not fear death. Such courage did not suit the overseer, who wanted each slave to tremble with fear when he addressed him. Ben was too high-minded for such humiliation before any insignificant overseer. He had philosophically concluded that death, is but death any way, and that one might as well die by hanging as whipping; so he resolved not to submit to be whipped by the overseer.

One day in the month of November, when the slaves were in the field gathering corn, which Ben was carting to the barn, the overseer thought he did not drive his oxen fast enough. As soon then as Ben came within hearing of his voice, while returning from the barn, where he had just discharged his load, to the field, the overseer bellowed to him to drive faster. With this order Ben attempted to comply, by urging his beasts to their utmost speed. But all was of no avail. As soon as they met, the overseer struck Ben upon the head with the butt of his whip, felling him to the ground. But before he could repeat the blow, Ben sprang from the ground, seized his antagonist by the throat with one hand, while he felled him to the ground with the other; then jumping upon his breast, he commenced choking and beating him at the same time, until he had nearly killed him. In fact he probably would have killed his enemy, had not two of the slaves hastened to his rescue, which they with difficulty accomplished, so firm and determined was Ben's hold of him. For a while the discomfited man was senseless, his face became of the blackness of his hat, while the blood streamed down his face.

When he had recovered his senses, and was able to walk, he started for the house, to relate this sad circumstance to Mr. Thomas. Ben loaded his cart and followed after. No sooner had he entered the barn, than his master sprang forward to seize him; but Ben eluded his grasp and fled to the woods, where he remained about three weeks, when he returned to his work.

No allusion was made to the circumstance for about five weeks, and Ben supposed all was past and forgotten. At length a rainy time came on, during which the hands could neither labor in the field nor elsewhere out of doors, but were forced to work in the corn-house, shelling the corn. While all were thus busily employed, the doors closed, there entered five strong white men, besides our master, armed with pistols, swords, and clubs. What a shocking sight! thus to take one poor unarmed negro, these men must be employed, and the county aroused to action.

Ben was soon bound in hemp enough, comparatively speaking, to rig a small vessel. Thus bound, he was led to the place of torture, where he was whipped until his entrails could be seen moving within his body. Poor Ben! his crime, according to the laws of Maryland, was punishable with death; a penalty far more merciful than the one he received.

The manner of whipping on Mr. Thomas's plantation, was to bind the victim fast, hands, body and feet, around a hogshead or cask, so that he was unable to move. After Ben was thus flogged, he said, "I wish I had killed the overseer, then I should have been hung, and an end put to my pain. If I have to do the like again, I will kill him and be hung at once!"

Ben was, for five weeks, unable to walk, or sit, or lie down. He could only rest upon his knees and elbows, and his wounds became so offensive, that no person could long remain in his presence. He crawled about upon his hands and knees, gritting his teeth with pain and vengeance, and often exclaiming, "How I wish I had taken his life!"

After this, Mr. Thomas forbade his overseers meddling with Ben, telling them that he would kill them if they did; also, that he was a good hand, and needed no driving. When Ben got well, Mr. Thomas knowing his disposition, was afraid to go near or speak to him; consequently, he was sent to a distant part of the farm to work by himself, nor was he ever again struck by master or overseer.

Ben was a brave fellow, nor did this flogging lessen his bravery in the least. Nor is Ben the only brave slave at the South; there are many there who would rather be shot than whipped by any man.

After I had learned to read, I was very fond of reading newspapers, when I could get them. One day in the year 1830, I picked up a piece of old newspaper containing the speech of J. Q. Adams, in the U.S. Senate, upon a petition of the ladies of Massachusetts, praying for the abolition of slavery in the District of Columbia.[4] This I kept hid away for some months, and read it until it was so worn that I could scarce make out the letters.

While reading this speech, my heart leaped with joy. I spent many Sabbaths alone in the woods, meditating upon it. I then found out that there was a place where the negro was regarded as a man, and not as a brute; where he might enjoy the "inalienable right of life, liberty, and the pursuit of happiness"; and where he could walk unfettered throughout the length and breadth of the land.

These thoughts were constantly revolving in my mind, and I determined to see, ere long, the land from whence echoed that noble voice; where man acknowledged a difference between his brother man and a beast; and where I could "worship God under my own vine and fig tree, with none to molest or make afraid."[5]

Little did Mr. Adams know, when he was uttering that speech, that he was "opening the eyes of the blind"; that he was breaking the iron bands from the limbs of one poor slave, and setting the captive free. But bread cast upon the waters, will be found and gathered after many days.

But Mr. Adams has gone from hope to reward, and while his mortal body is laying in the dust of the earth, awaiting the summons for the re-union of soul and body, his spirit is with God in his kingdom above.

CHAP. VII.

NEAR our plantation lived as cruel a planter as ever God suffered to live, named doctor Jackson; who was the owner of a large farm, with several slaves. He was destitute of heart, soul, and conscience; while his wife was of the same character. She often induced him to ill-treat the slaves, especially those about the house; she being as ready to complain of them, as he was to punish them.

One day, she became displeased with Sarah, her cook, and wanted her husband to whip her. She said to Sarah, "I swear I will make your master whip you, as soon as he comes to the house"; to which Sarah replied, "Those who will swear, will lie!" This reply she reported to the doctor upon his return; upon which he tied Sarah up and whipped her, until the flesh so cleaved from the bone, that it might easily have been scraped off with the hand; while the blood stood in puddles under her feet.

After taking her down, he anointed her lacerated back with a mixture of grease and tar, which was a new application; the usual one being strong brine.

For a long time after this, the poor creature could neither walk nor stand, and it was dreadful to see her crawling about in such painful agony. To Mrs. Jackson, however, it was a delightful sight, for she seemed to gloat over the sight of such bloody, mangled victims. Her cook had often before been flogged, but never so much to her satisfaction.

I was one day sent upon an errand to the doctor's house, and being acquainted, I did not ask permission to enter, but went in unannounced at the dining-room door. There I saw a little slave girl, about eight years of age, running about the room; while Mrs. Jackson was following and lashing her, and the blood running upon the floor! The child's offense was breaking a dish!!

On another side of our plantation lived another tyrant, by name Clinton Hanley; who also had a large farm well stocked with slaves. In his cruelty, this man had invented a somewhat different way of punishing his slaves, from that practised by most masters. He whipped severely, drove hard, and fed poorly. In cold weather he sent his slaves, both men and women, through the snow, without shoes, to cut wood.

He had one slave, named Mary, who was thus sent out to cut wood, until her feet were so frozen and cracked, that she could be tracked by her blood. To punish her, he one day ordered two men to lift up the fence and put her head under, while he sat upon it to increase the weight. While thus occupied, he was suddenly seized with a violent pain at his heart, of which he died within three days.

I was hired out one year to a Mr. Compton, who was a kind master; feeding and clothing well, and seldom beating his slaves, of which he owned about one hundred able bodied and intelligent men and women. His wife was equally as kind as a Mistress.

Mr. Compton was a sportsman, and very fond of gaming, horse racing and drinking. His slaves were all religious, and much attached to their master and mistress. They were allowed to hold their prayer meetings unmolested, in their own quarters, and I felt thankful that I had once more got among Christians.

Mr. Compton finally got so in debt, by his extravagance, that he was obliged to sell his slaves to pay his creditors. The slaves, little suspecting for what purpose, were sent down to town to pack tobacco. While busily engaged at this work, the warehouse door was suddenly closed, to prevent their escaping; when about sixty of them were fettered and put on board a schooner, then lying at anchor in the river, for the express purpose of conveying them far to the South. Only three were fortunate enough to make their escape. The women and children were brought down from the farm in wagons, and put on board the vessel.

But O! reader, could you have seen those men, loaded down with irons, as they passed weeping from the warehouse, you must have exclaimed, "Great God, how long wilt thou suffer this sin to remain upon the earth?"

The three men who made their escape, were sold to new masters.

Mrs. Compton, being from home at the time, knew nothing of this transaction until her return. When she first heard of it, she fainted; but upon recovering exclaimed, in the anguish of her heart, "O, my people; husband, my heart will break!"

But her tears were of no avail; it was too late; the vessel, freighted with its human cargo, had already weighed anchor, and was under sail. Wafted by the northern breeze she gallantly sailed down the stream at the rate of nine knots per hour; while the multitude stood upon the banks and watched her disappearance, tears of pity flowing down their cheeks.

She soon vanished from their sight. But God, who has his ways in the wind, and manages the sea, had his purpose fixed; so thought one of the slaves, who, in his faith, raised his cry of petition to the living God; so while some were dancing to please the captain and crew, others were crying.

The vessel ran well for about four days, when suddenly the sky became overcast with dense black clouds, from whence flashed the forked lightnings, and pealed the fearful thunders. The raging billows lashed into fury, rolled mountain high, until there seemed no possible escape from the frowns of a sin-avenging God. The captain summoned all hands on board, and the vessel was finally driven upon a sand beach, near one of the West India Islands, where all on board, except one of the sailors, was saved. And thus did these slaves obtain their freedom. The trader himself was not on board, having gone by land, to the place where he expected to meet the slaves, after giving them in charge to another person.

From this time to the day of her death, Mrs. Compton always wore the marks of a sorrowful woman, while her husband became a miserable wretch. In consequence of his inability to pay my year's wages, I only remained with him until Christmas; after which I was hired out to Richard Thomas, my mistress's brother; who was the most humane of the family, and who, notwithstanding he liked to whip them himself, did not choose that any one else should chastise his slaves. I lived with him two years.

He had a hired plantation about thirty-five miles from his father's, where were my father, mother and five brothers; all having been hired out to him. Here I had an opportunity of improving in my education, for many of the planters in this region were not only rich, but humane, and many of their slaves could read and write. Miserable loafing white people were scarce in that vicinity, their services not being needed. Neither was slave hunting much practised, therefore there was no patroling, and the land being less cursed by cruelty, was rich and fertile; producing in abundance corn, wheat, and tobacco, together with cotton enough for home consumption.

Religion also flourished in that region, where there were no Catholic churches, but only Methodists and Episcopalians. Finally the masters concluded to build a church for their slaves. So they united in the work and soon had a large church, under the superintendance of a white preacher; although a colored man could preach in it, if qualified and licensed by the whites. The congregation was large. Many white people went there to hear the colored ones sing and praise God, and were often much affected by their simple but earnest devotion.

Mr. Thomas, being a lawyer of great reputation and extensive practise, was necessarily often called from home on business, disconnected with his farm; consequently he employed an overseer to attend to this and the slaves. This overseer was a very proud and haughty fellow, made so by this sudden promotion; he never before having held such an office, which made him fancy himself, if not a god, at least an emperor!

Our living, which before had been decent, he soon entirely changed; frequently allowing us but one meal of victuals a day, consisting of corn bread, sometimes baked in the ashes, with two salted herring. This was to be eaten before going to the field in the morning, and we were called at break of day, after which we had no more until our return at night. Now you must know, reader, that chopping wood all day, upon an empty stomach, is not what it is cracked up to be!

One cold winter's day in February he sent us to the woods to chop. I worked until I became so hungry and faint, that I thought I could stand it no longer, when I resolved to go to the house for something to eat; or failing, to die in the attempt. Some of the hands promising to follow me, I started, supposing them close at hand; but I soon found myself alone, they having backed out, their courage failing. They thought, as I had troubled the waters, I might drink them alone; but they declined to partake of such bitter streams.

Before I reached the house, the overseer saw me and inquired where I was bound, to which I replied, "to the house, for something to eat." He ordered me back, but I, being homeward bound, and under full sail, thought best not to 'bout ship, so he ran after me, caught me by the back of the neck, struck me with the butt end of the whip upon my head, but did not fell me to the ground. I seized hold of the whip, wrung it from his hand, threw him upon the ground, clenched him somewhere about the throat, and for a few moments stopped his mortal respiration.

When I released him, he lost no time in running for the house, to tell his story to master Richard; after which he hastened back to the woods. I went to our quarters, ate my corn cake and herrings, and returned to the chopping. Nothing was said; the silence of the grave seemed to reign around, broken only by the sound of the axes. The men seemed to cut more wood that afternoon, than at other times they had for a whole day.

Next morning upon going, as usual, to the stable to attend to the horses, the overseer followed me, entered the stable and shut the door. He took from his pocket a rope, and ordered me to cross my hands, which I refused to do; upon which he seized a tobacco stick about four feet long and two inches thick, with which he struck and brought me to the ground. He then sprang upon me, for the purpose of tying my hands, but did not succeed, for I rose to my feet with him upon my back, shook off my uncomfortable load, and in turn mounted his back, wrung the stick from his hand, and with it commenced beating him.

As soon as he could escape from my hands, he opened the stable door and ran for the house; from whence I soon saw him returning in great haste, accompanied by master Richard; who, coming up to me, bade me surrender. I did so, and he tied my hands across each other, then tied me to one of the beams in the barn, and told the overseer to whip me. Accordingly he divested himself of his coat, rolled up his sleeves, and commenced flogging with all his might. But after giving me about ten cuts, to his extreme disappointment, he was told to desist, as that was sufficient.

I thought much of being thus punished for nothing, and resolved that, should the overseer again attempt to whip me, I would kill him and abide the consequences. I therefore told master Richard, that I had rather die than again be whipped; that the punishment of death was not so dreadful, and I should know next time what to do. "What will you do, sir?" said he. I replied, "You alone have the right to correct me, sir. Had you been made acquainted with all the facts in the case, you would not have had me whipped so; and if the overseer strikes me again, I will kill him and be hung at once, that there may be an end of me." He bade me hold my tongue, and go to work; after which, turning to the overseer, he said, "Whenever that fellow disobeys, I wish you to inform me, that I may learn what is the fault; I do not wish you to flog him; I know he is a good hand, and needs no flogging to make him work."

After this, we had three meals a day, larger in proportion, and everything went on well, until the following July, when a difficulty arose between master and overseer.

CHAP. VIII.

My young master, being very fond of work himself, did not like to see lazy men around him. Whenever he came to the field, he always busied himself about something, while the overseer stood with his whip under his arm, and his hands in his pockets, or sat under a shady tree and read the newspapers. I well knew this would not last very long, and had the overseer known his employer as well as I did, he would not thus have hazarded his best interest by an indulgence in such laziness, as finally dethroned him.

Master Richard, coming into the field one day, found the overseer, as usual, sitting at his ease under a pleasant tree, which at once irritated him. Addressing the overseer, as he was thus enjoying his comfort, he asked, "Why have not the ploughs been used in this field, where they are so much needed, instead of yonder, where they are less needed?"

The overseer made some paltry reply, not so well suited to master's dignity, as to the purpose which he had in contemplation, which was to discharge him immediately; a thing which, according to contract, he could not do. Directly, upon hearing the answer, he seized a stick which lay near, and with it aimed a violent blow at the overseer's head, which, however, he fortunately dodged, when he ran from the field, left the plantation, and was seen there no more.

My father was then put overseer, an office which he did not long fill, as in October following he sickened and died. His death was much lamented by all his fellow slaves, as well as by his master, Richard, who gave him every possible attention during his sickness, employing the best physicians to attend upon him. He called to see him three or four times each day, and sometimes sat by his bedside hours at a time, apparently striving to prevent the extinction of the vital spark; but all to no purpose, for the great Master had called for him, and he must obey the summons.

My father lived an exemplary life, and died a triumphant death, leaving to posterity a bright evidence of his acceptance with God. And, thank heaven, his prayers over me, a careless, hardened sinner, were not as seed sown upon a rock, but as bread cast upon the waters, to be seen and gathered after many days.

Immediately after the decease of this faithful slave, master Richard directed my brother to take his horse and go up to old master's plantation, and inform his sister Elizabeth, our mistress, that his father, John, her slave, was dead. As soon as she received the tidings, she came in her carriage to her brother's, but only to look on the lifeless clay of my father. "Oh!" she exclaimed, as she gazed upon the lifeless form, "I had rather lose all my other slaves, than to lose John."

My brother was now put overseer, and made an excellent one. The crops, in their abundance, were gathered and safely secured.

We now removed about forty miles to another plantation, in Prince George county, a neighborhood as different from that we had just left, as Alabama is from Kentucky. Here our master married a Miss Barber, very rich and equally cruel. I think she was about as bad a woman as ever lived. She soon spoiled her husband's disposition, inducing in him the practice of the surrounding planters, to whip occasionally, whether there was a cause or not. They considered whipping as essential to the good of the soul as the body; and therefore sometimes indispensably necessary.

My old grey-headed mother, now cook, was the first victim to the uncontrollable, hellish passions of her new mistress. My mother had always borne the reputation, in old mistress's time, of a very good cook; but she could not suit this tyrannical mistress, do the best she could. Indeed, nothing was so pleasant to her as the smell of negro blood! Entering the kitchen, she would beat my mother with shovel, tongs, or whatever other weapon lay within her reach, until exhausted herself; then, upon her husband's return, she would complain to him, and cause him to strip and whip the victim until she was unable longer to stand. My feelings, upon hearing her shrieks and pleadings, may better be imagined than described. Sometimes she would, in this way, have all her servants whipped.

While upon the other plantation, I spared no exertions to learn to read and write, both of which I could now do tolerably well; and although I spent all my Sundays in study, still, master did not know that I could do either. One day he sent me with a note to a gentleman, requiring an answer by the bearer. The answer I put into my pocket with some writing of my own, one of which was the copy of a pass I had received from my master long before, to go to visit a friend. This copy I accidentally handed him, instead of the answering note, not perceiving my mistake until he exclaimed, "What is this?" Immediately I discovered my mistake, and handed him the right paper. He kept both. At the time he said no more to me, but soon communicated the fact to his sister, pressing her to sell me, which she at length consented to do, empowering him to transact the business in reference to the sale. The next morning, while I was preparing feed for the horses in the stables, he, with four other white men, armed with bludgeons and pistols, came upon me. I looked about me for some means of resistance, but seeing none, concluded there was no way for me but to surrender.

My hands were at once tied, after which I was taken to another part of the barn, where they commenced whipping me; but the switches proving brittle, two of them were broken at once. This so enraged my master that he cursed the switches, and swore he had something that would not break. This was a cowhide, which he went and brought from the house, I, meanwhile, hanging suspended between the heavens and the earth, for no crime save what he himself was guilty of, namely, education. He finally concluded, however, not to whip me, lest it might injure my sale, and therefore ordered one of the other slaves to take me down, and prepare me to go to Alexandria.

All being ready, he called for me to be brought out. As I passed the house door in crossing the yard, bound in chains, his wife came out and ordered me to stop a moment, while she delivered to me her farewell message.

"Well, John," she began, "you are going to be sold!" "Yes, madam, I suppose so," was my reply.

"I am sorry," she continued, "that you are so disobedient to your master Richard, and if you will promise me to do better, I will plead with him not to sell you."

I answered, "Madam, I have done the best I am able for him, and cannot, to save my life, do better; willingly would I do so, if I could. I do not know why he wishes to sell me."

While I was speaking, he came out, being ready to start for the slave market. He said to his wife, "I don't wish you to speak to him, for I am going to sell him; sister Elizabeth gave me leave to do so, and I shall do it." "He has promised me to do better, and I do not wish him sold," said his wife.

"I don't want to hear any of his promises, he has made them before," was his reply.

While this conversation was going on, a coachman from the lower plantation rode up, and handed master Richard a note, saying that Miss Elizabeth had changed her mind, and did not wish me sold, and that if he did not want me any longer, to send me home to her. Thus was the affair knocked into a cocked hat.[6]

He took the rope from my hands, and bade me go to work, a command which I joyfully obeyed; but feeling no gratitude to him, since, had it been in his power, he would have sold me. I finished my year with him, after which, on Christmas, I returned to my mistress.

CHAP. IX.

THE following year, I was hired to Mr. Wm. Barber, a Catholic himself, as were also his slaves, all except myself. He adhered strictly to his religious profession, praying three or four times each day, and every Sunday morning calling up his slaves to attend prayer, to which call I refused to respond. This refusal in me, caused in him a strong dislike to me, insomuch that he seemed to dislike me, and hate to see me worse than the devil, against whom he prayed so devoutly.

I was very fond of singing Methodist hymns while at work, especially if I was alone, the sound of which threw him into spasms of anger. He accordingly treated me worse than any other slave upon the plantation, all of whom were treated bad enough. Our allowance was a quart of meal and two herrings per day. Our dinner was sent to us in the fields, both in hot and cold weather. None of our friends were ever permitted to come to the farm to see us.

On Easter, it being holiday among the slaves, a negro belonging to Mr. Charles Gardner, not knowing our master's rules, called to see his mother and sister, whom Mr. Barber had hired, and whom he had not seen for a long time. Our master happening to get a glimpse of this negro, pitched upon him and endeavored to collar him. The black, being a strong active fellow, and understanding what we call the "Virginia hoist," seized and threw his assailant over his head to the distance of five feet, where he struck the ground so that his nose ploughed the earth some distance! Before the discomfited master could rise from the ground, the slave had effected his escape.

But poor David's back must smart for his dexterity. Master imagined that I invited David to our plantation for the purpose of retaliating some of my grievances, so I must share his fate. A difficulty now arose, for as master professed to be a Christian, he could not consistently whip without a cause, which he could not readily find, since he could not prove that I was in any way implicated in David's crime.

Still, he could not rest satisfied until I was flogged, and therefore tried every way to find fault with me, which I knowing, did my best to prevent. But all effort to please, on my part, was useless. He sent me, one very cold day, a mile from the house to cut rails. The snow was about six inches deep. I had shoes and stockings, but still, as I had no chance to warm my feet from break of day until night, my dinner being sent me, which I was obliged to eat frozen, my feet were nearly frozen, and I was completely chilled. Mr. Barber watched me the whole day, except while away at dinner, which he hastened through as fast as possible, that he might not long lose sight of me.

When it grew dark he started for the house, bidding me follow, as it was time to feed the cattle. As I was so cold, I thought I would kindle a fire and warm me before going. I did so, and then started for the house. When passing through the yard, on my way to the cowpen, I met Mr. B. returning, he having been there waiting for me. He, being a holy man! did not swear directly, but said, "Confound you, where have you been?" accompanying the question by a blow from a four foot stick across my head.

I tried to explain the reason of my delay, but he would not listen, and continued beating me. At last I caught hold of the stick, wrenched it from his hands, struck him over the head, and knocked him down, after which I choked him until he was as black as I am. When I let him up, he ran for his gun; but when he returned I had fled to parts unknown to him. I kept away about two weeks, staying in the woods during the day, and coming to the quarters at night for something to eat.

Mr. Barber, however, needing my services, as it was a very busy time, told the slaves, if they saw me, to tell me to come home, and that he would not whip me. This was to me a very welcome message, for I was tired of my life in the woods, and I immediately returned home. I went to work, as usual, thinking all was right; but soon found myself very much mistaken.

I worked about three weeks, during which I accomplished six weeks labor. One day, while busily engaged, hoeing up new ground, I saw two men coming towards me, whom I soon recognized as constables, both of whom I well knew. Upon approaching near me, the constable for our district said, "John, you must come with me."

I dropped my hoe and followed him. When I reached the house, I found poor David standing bound like a sheep dumb before its shearers. We were put up stairs to await Mr. B.'s orders, who was not then ready. The rope was tied so tight around David's wrists as to stop the circulation of the blood, and give him excruciating pain. He begged to have the rope loosened, but the officer having him in charge, would not gratify him. The other constable, however, soon come and relieved him.

Mr. Barber being ready, we set off for the magistrate's office, which was about three miles from our house. David and I were tied together, his left being tied to my right hand. On the way the constable said to me, "John, I always thought you was a good negro; what have you been doing? You ought to behave so well as not to need whipping."

I replied, "I have done nothing wrong, and if I am whipped, it shall be the last time on that farm?"

"What will you do?" asked Mr. Barber. "Run away," I answered. "When we are done with you, you will not be able to run far," said he. "Well sir, if you whip me so that I am unable to walk, I can do you no good; but if I can walk, I will take the balance of the year to myself, and go home to my mistress, at Christmas."

He did not relish this kind of talk, for he did not wish to pay my wages and not have my service, so he told me to shut my head or he would break it. Of course I said no more.

We soon arrived at the dreaded place, and were left seated in the piazza awaiting our trial, a constable being present to watch us. I asked him for a drink of water, when he said, "Would you not like a glass of brandy?" a drink very acceptable on such occasions. I replied in the affirmative, when he brought out a half-pint tumbler nearly full, of which I drank the whole. This roused my courage, and I felt brave. My expected punishment was not half as much dreaded as before.

The court being ready, we were brought before his honor, Justice Barber, uncle to my master. David was first tried, declared guilty, and sentenced to have 39 lashes well laid upon his bare back.

My case was next in order, but Mr. Barber, instead of preferring any charge against me, told the Judge he would forgive me this time, as he thought I would do better in future. Upon this the old man, raising his spectacles and looking at me, said, "Do you think you can behave, so as not to have to be brought before me again?" "Yes sir," I answered quickly. "Well sir," he said, "go home to your work, and if you are brought before me again, I will order the skin all taken from your back!"

The rope was taken off my hands, and I was told to go in peace and sin no more. I waited to see the fate of poor David. He was taken to the whipping post, strung up until his toes scarce touched the ground, his back stripped and whipped until the blood flowed in streams to the ground. When he was taken down he staggered like a drunken man. We returned together, talking over the matter on the way. He said, "O, I wish I could die! I am whipped for no fault of my own. I wish I had killed him, and been hung at once; I should have been better off." I felt sorry for him.

I determined then, if he struck me again, I would kill him. I expected another attack, and accordingly planned where I would conceal his body, where it would not readily be found, in case no one saw me perform the act. But God overruled. He had his destiny fixed, and no mortal could resist it,—no mortal arm could stay his mighty purpose. But I must hasten to the close of the year.

Mr. Barber had a most luxuriant crop of tobacco nearly ripe and ready for the harvest. Tobacco is so delicate a plant, that it will not stand the frost, and if exposed to it is thereby rendered nearly useless. Our crops had all been gathered except two fields, when by a sudden change in the wind to the north, it became so cold as to threaten a frost, which would probably destroy the tobacco remaining in the field. Mr. Barber feared this, and notwithstanding it was the Sabbath, ordered his slaves to go and secure the remainder of the crop.

Soon all hands were in the field at work. No other farmer in the neighborhood went out, all, excepting Mr. B. being willing to trust their crops to Him who had given them; although many had larger quantities exposed. Being angry with the great Omnipotent for this threatening arrangement of his providence, Mr. Barber fell to beating his slaves on the Lord's day. But his suspected enemy did not come; his fears were groundless. The night cleared off warm, and no frost came.

> "God moves in a mysterious way,
> "His wonders to perform;
> "He plants his footsteps in the sea,
> "And rides upon the storm.
> "Deep and unfathomable mine
> "Of never failing skill;
> "He treasures up his bright design,
> "And works his sovereign will.
> "Ye fearful saints, fresh courage take;
> "The clouds ye so much dread
> "Are big with mercy, and shall break
> "With blessings on your head.
>
> "Judge not the Lord with feeble sense,
> "But trust him for his grace;
> "Behind a frowning providence
> "He hides a smiling face.
> "His purposes will ripen fast,
> "Unfolding every hour;
> "The bud may have a bitter taste,
> "But sweet will be the flower.
> "Blind unbelief is sure to err,
> "And scan his works in vain;
> "God is his own interpreter,
> "And he will make it plain."[7]

We worked until midnight on Sunday, and secured all the crops, as Mr. B. thought.

The manner of curing tobacco is, to hang it up in the barn, and put a hot fire under it, so as to cure it gradually. But the heat must be in proportion to the dampness of the tobacco.

All things being regulated, Mr. B. began to boast of the security of his great crops. The following Saturday, at three o'clock, P. M., he told his slaves that they might have the remainder of that day to compensate for the previous Sabbath, when they had worked.

The same day, while preparing to go to confession, as usual, one of the slaves ran in and told him that the barn was on fire! I looked from the kitchen door, saw the smoke bursting from the roof, and ran to the spot. Master got there before me, and within three minutes all the slaves were upon the spot; but seeing it would be of no avail, they did not attempt to enter the barn.

Mr. Barber, moved by his usual ambition, rushed in, notwithstanding the slaves tried to persuade him of the danger, and plead with him to desist; but, blinded by the god of this world, he would not listen to their entreaties, and rushed in just as the roof was ready to fall! When they beheld the awful sight, the wails of the slaves might have been heard fully two miles.

He was caught by the end of the roof only, as it fell, from which, in a minute or two, he made his escape, his clothes all on fire. He was taken to the house, but died the next Sunday week. Before he died, however, like Nebuchadnezzar of old, he acknowledged that God reigns among the kingdoms of men.[8]

This sad event transpired in the month of October, after which nothing more worthy of note occurred while I remained in the family, which was until Christmas. After this I returned to my mistress, who gave me a note permitting me to get myself another home.

CHAP. X.

I NOW called to see a Mr. James Burkit, who had formerly been very rich, but who, by dissipation, had spent all his property, and become quite poor. He was willing to hire me, and sent word to my mistress to that effect. I commenced work there on the first day of January.

There were but few slaves upon this plantation, upon which every thing seemed in an unprosperous condition; fences broken down and fields overrun with weeds. I went to work, and soon had things in better order, which so much pleased my employer, that he made me foreman on the plantation.

The father of Mr. Burkit, who died when James was very young, was a very rich man, and had the reputation among the slaves, of having been a very good master, and of having freed a portion of his slaves at his decease, one family of whom I knew. The balance of his slaves was divided among his heirs.

One of these freed slaves, by name George Nichols, was a very delicate young man, unfit for field labor, and therefore brought up waiter in the old man's family. George being an expert hand at his business, was hired out to a man in Washington city, where he was when his old old master died, and where he had been for several years previous.

As soon as the father died, his heirs tried to break the will, and thus again enslave those who had thereby been set free. Mr. Burkit was especially recommended to sell George immediately, as he had been so long out of the state, that, according to the laws of Maryland, he was free already, independent of the will. To accomplish this, Mr. Burkit hastened directly to Washington, and went to a hotel kept by Mr. Brown, where George lived, whom he desired to see. George was at work in a distant part of the house, but upon receiving the message that some one wished to see him, he hastened to the bar-room, where he was both surprised and pleased to see his master James. "How *do* you do, Master James?" he inquired, smilingly, and reached out his hand to grasp that of his young master.

"I am well, how do you do, George?" was the reply.

"Very well, I thank you, sir," said poor George, and began to inquire for his parents, whom he had not seen for several years. They were very well, Mr. B. said, and then added, "George, I am about to be married, and have come for you to go to Halifax to serve as waiter at my wedding."

At this George was much pleased, thinking it highly complimentary that his young master had come so far for him, to serve at the wedding.

When Mr. Burkit made known to Mr. Brown, the hotel keeper, that he intended to sell George far south, that gentleman was much surprised, and said, "Why, Mr Burkit, you don't mean to take George from me at this time; you will ruin me. Congress is in session, my house is full of boarders, and he is my best waiter; I cannot well get along without him. If you wish to sell him, I will buy, and give you as much for him as you can get elsewhere."

But Mr. Burkit would not sell him to Mr. Brown. George heard and knew nothing of this conversation. When he was ready, he came to the bar-room with his small bundle of clothes under his arm, and soon started off with his master James. Mr. Brown called the latter back and said, "Mr. Burkit, I will give you one hundred dollars more than any other man for George; or I will give you eight hundred now. No other man will give as much, for one unacquainted with him would not give over six hundred. To look at him, he appears like a very delicate boy, and indeed, he is fit only for a waiter; consequently worth more to a person in my business, than to a planter. As I know what he can do, I will give more than a stranger would." To all these offers Mr. Burkit turned a deaf ear, and again started off.

On account of his tender feet, George had to wear soft slippers, suitable only to be worn within doors. On the way to the vessel, which was waiting to receive them, George said, "Master James, will you please to get me another pair of slippers? These I have on will be unfit to wear at your wedding." "O yes, George, you shall have a pair," was the reply.

After they got on board the vessel, George said, "master James, you have forgotten my slippers." "G—d d—n you, if you ask for slippers, I will break your d—n head!" was his only answer. Then George knew, for the first time, that he was to be sold. His master continued, "you have been a gentleman in Washington long enough, now if you ask me for anything, I will beat out your d—d brains with a handspike!" George now felt that his case was hopeless.

The vessel soon arrived in port, when George was put in irons, and confined in a slave pen among a drove of slaves, in New Market. This dreadful news was soon sent to his mother, who lived at a considerable distance, but who hastened at once to see and bathe in tears her child.

When she reached the pen, she was conducted up stairs to a room, in the middle of which was a long staple driven into the floor, with a large ring attached to it, having four long chains fastened to that. To these were attached shorter chains, to which the slaves were made fast by rings around their ankles. Men, women and children were huddled in this room together, awaiting the arrival of more victims, as the drove was not full.

In this miserable condition did Mrs. Nichols, who had served out her time, find her son; who was as much entitled to his freedom as she was to hers. And in this condition she left him forever! Would that the Rev. Dr. Adams[9] and others, who paint slavery in such glowingly beautiful colors, could have seen this, and have heard the agonizing cries of that mother and child, at parting! Think of these things, ye men of God!

The trader told the poor mother, that if she could find any one to buy her son, he would sell him for just what he gave, five hundred dollars, as he was not what he wanted, and he only bought him to gratify Mr. Burkit. He continued, "I want only strong able-bodied slaves, as the best can only live five or six years at longest, and your son, being so delicate, I shall get little for him."

George then said, "Mother, don't grieve for me, it is for no crime that I have done; it is only because I was to be free. But if you will please send to Washington, as soon as possible, and ask Mr. Brown, the gentleman that I lived with, to buy me, I know he will gladly do so. Tell him I have one hundred and fifty dollars in my trunk, in my room at the hotel, which he can use towards paying for me."

The old woman hastened from New Market, which lies on the eastern shore of Maryland, between Cambridge and Vienna, to her own home, a distance of fifteen miles. Upon reaching home, she hastened to a friend, as she thought, (though he wore a friendly face, and possessed an enemy's heart,) to whom she related her sad story, requesting him to write for her to Mr. Brown at Washington, which he promised to do. She supposed he had done so, and waited anxiously for an answer; but none ever came, and the poor young man was carried away, where he has never since been seen or heard from by his heart-broken mother. The name of this supposed friend was Annalds. He was an old man, and a member of the Methodist church. Of course the colored people had great confidence in him, on account of his supposed piety, as he made loud professions, and talked high of heaven. But it was all hypocrisy, God in the face, and the devil in the heart; for he cheated the poor free blacks out of their rightful wages whenever he got a chance.

The plantation adjoining Mr. Burkit's was owned by a very rich planter, Robert Dennis, Esq. He was a very kind master, always treated his slaves well, would neither whip them himself, nor suffer another person to do so, and would not sell them. Consequently, he was much beloved by his slaves, who regarded him as a father.

He had a great number of well looking slaves, men, women and children, over whom he would have no overseer, but trusted all to them in cultivating his large tracts of land; nor did they ever betray his trust or give him any trouble. But at length happened a sad event to these slaves, at the death of their much beloved master. Sorrow now filled their hearts, and spread a gloom over the whole plantation; for now, like other slaves, they must be separated and sold from their friends and families, some, perhaps, to cruel masters. They knew the estate was somewhat in debt, and expected to have to be sold to cancel it, at least part of them.

This would have been done but for Miss Betsey, who could not endure the idea of seeing her grandfather's devoted slaves sold to pay debts which they had no hand in contracting. She watched for an opportunity, when, unseen by the white people, she could go to the slaves' quarters; and having found one, she immediately hastened there, and told them that she had some bad news for them, but dared not communicate it until they pledged themselves not to betray her, which they readily did, as they did not wish to bring harm upon her, which they knew they should do by telling of her.

She then told them that there was some dispute about the settlement of the estate, which, it was thought, could not be settled without selling them all; which, she said, she could not bear to see done.

They all exclaimed at once, "What shall we do?" She answered frankly, "You had better make your escape." They said they knew not where to go, nor how to do. She told them that their Christmas holidays were near at hand, when they would have permission to go to visit their friends and relatives. She recommended them then to obtain of their master John, passes for this purpose, each of which was to be for a different direction from the others. Then leave for the free States.

Most of them did as she directed, obtained their passes, left for the free States, and have not since been seen at their old home.

Miss Betsey in this performed a good deed, yet she was soon after betrayed, and that, too, by a slave. An old woman, whose sons escaped with the rest, made a terrible fuss, crying and lamenting to a great rate, and saying that Miss Betsey had sent all her children off to the "Jarsers"; (meaning New Jersey, which was the only free State of which she seemed to have any idea,) and she should never see them again. She continued in this way until it came to the ears of the white people, who inquired of Miss Betsey about it. She denied all knowledge of the matter, and said, "Cousin John, do you think I would advise the slaves to run away? I have said nothing to them about being sold. Old Priss, you know, is always drunk, and knows not what she says."

This partially quieted the heirs, but did not remove all suspicion, and they still thought that Miss Betsey was in some way concerned in the affair. So when the estate was divided, they did not give her as much as would wrap around her finger, and she lived a poor girl for several years.

Subsequently she removed to Baltimore, where she married a poor man.

But God remembered her. Each of the blacks whom she helped to escape from bondage, upon hearing of her poverty, and her place of residence, sent her fifty dollars, eight hundred dollars in all, as a token of their thankfulness and gratitude.

Those who did not leave, according to her direction, were all sold.

CHAP. XI.

I WAS next hired out to Mr. Hughes, who was, comparatively, a poor man, having but one working slave of his own; the rest on his farm being all hired. His accommodations for his workmen were good; we all ate at the kitchen table.

I had not been long at this place, before it became known that I could read and write, upon which I was forbidden to visit the slaves on any of the neighboring plantations. One man, who had several pretty girls upon his farm, that I was fond of visiting, as soon as he learned that I was sometimes there, tried to catch me to whip me. But I always managed to elude him, and yet to have him know that I had been there, after I had gone away.

This provoked him most desperately, and determined him to catch me at any rate. So he employed the patrolers to watch for me, catch me if possible, and by all means bring me to him before flogging me, that he might enjoy the pleasure by sharing in it. For a long time their efforts proved unavailing. I was often in his house, in the room adjoining that in which he then was, and while the patrolers were searching the quarters.

At last, however, fortune seemed to favor him. One night, at an unusually early hour for the patrolers to be abroad, I was at one of his slave quarters, while the patrolers were at the other. One of the girls ran and told me of this, and said farther, that they would be down there soon. This, you may well guess, was no very pleasant news to me, especially as I was at the time cozily seated beside a pretty young lady. And as ladies you know, love bravery, so I did not like to hasten my usual steps, lest it should appear like cowardice; still, I knew delays were dangerous.

I considered a moment, and finally started, thinking it my safest course; but I had not proceeded more than five feet from the door, before the enemy were upon me. There was another colored man in the quarter at the same time, who, if caught, was as liable to be whipped as myself; still, I was their special object of pursuit, as Mr. Bowlding had promised them twenty-five dollars, if they caught me on his place.

When we saw the patrollers, we both started at full speed, Ben, the other colored man, being about fifty yards ahead, and they after us. They continued the chase about a quarter of a mile, after which they returned; but, still thinking them at my heels, I continued my flight a mile, Ben still in advance. As soon as I discovered that we were alone, I called to Ben to stop; but he, thinking it was the voice of one of his pursuers, only put on more steam, until, finally, he ran against a rail fence, (the night being very dark,) knocked down two lengths of it, and fell upon it himself, which stopped his career until I came up, explained all, and banished his fears.

We stopped awhile to rest ourselves, and consult upon our farther course. I concluded best for me to go home, but he decided upon returning to the quarters, thinking the patrollers would now be gone, and he did not like to forego a pleasant chat with the ladies, especially as he had come so far for that express purpose. He thought this step would efface from the ladies' minds this appearance of his cowardice, and restore his reputation for heroism, because no person is allowed to possess gentlemanly bravery and valor at the South, who will run from the face of any man, or will not even courageously look death in the face, with all its terrors. I did not for a moment doubt that the company of ladies was pleasant, and that a display of heroism was a pretty sure pathway to their favor; still, I thought the preservation of a sound back, was not a thing to be overlooked, or treated lightly, so I determined to proceed homeward, which determination, as the sequel will show, proved a wise one. Ben returned to the quarters, and while standing in the yard, rehearsing the particulars of his flight, the patrollers suddenly came upon him, and seized him behind by the collar of his jacket. This garment being loose, he threw his arms back and ran out of it. And now followed another chase, in which, as before, Ben was victorious, and reached home in safety.

The affair passed off, and I supposed was ended, until about two weeks afterwards, when one day, being at work near the house, I saw two horsemen ride up to the stile, dismount and enter the house. Very soon Mr. Hughes came to the door, and requested me to come to the house. I did so, when, to my surprise, I found the horsemen were constables.

Mr. Hughes, turning to me, said, "John, these gentlemen have come to take you before a magistrate, to testify to what you know concerning the wheat that was found at Mr. Bowlding's, on the night that you ran from there." I replied, "I know nothing of the wheat, as I saw and heard of none." "Well," he said, "you will only be required to tell of what you know. Do you know the consequence of taking a false oath?"

"Yes, sir," I replied. "Well, what is it?" he asked. "I shall go to hell," I answered. "Yes, and that is not all," he said, "you will also have your ears cropped."

Turning to the constable, he said, "Mr. Waters, please send him home as soon as you are through with him, for I am very busy and need him." He added, to me, "hurry home as soon as they get done with you; do you hear?" "Yes sir," I answered. Upon this we started.

We had to go about a mile, mostly through the woods, and they, fearing I would seize this opportunity, so good a one, to try to escape, began to cut jokes to amuse me. But I had no idea of trying to escape, as I did not expect a whipping, knowing that, although a constable may seize and flog a slave, if caught from home after nightfall without a pass; still, according to law, they have no right to take him before a justice and whip him for being from home at any time, that being exclusively the master's or overseer's privilege. So I went on cheerfully.

When I reached the place of trial, I saw a large collection of people, it be-

ing the day for magistrates' meetings, and among the rest, the girl I was courting, brought there for the purpose of humbling my pride, and mortifying me. For
you must think, reader, that it would be rather mortifying to be stripped and
flogged in the presence of a girl, especially, after cutting such a swell as I had.
Many of the crowd came expressly to see me whipped, for they thought I assumed too much of the gentleman.

Ben's case came on first, but neither of us were allowed to be present, but
were kept in the yard during the trial and giving the sentence. Although, in the
North it is customary to have a defendant present, to hear his case stated, yet,
we were denied this, and were only informed of our sentence, after it had been
passed.

Ben's sentence was to receive ten stripes, five for his first, and as many for
his second offence. While being whipped, he dropped his handkerchief, which
the constable picked up and handed to him, upon which he exclaimed, "D—n
the handkerchief." This being reported to the justice, five stripes more were
added to his first sentence, thus, making fifteen in all.

I was next brought forward, to receive five stripes, when I saw several
smile, and heard them say to the constable, "Put it on well!" I was stretched up
and fastened to the limb of a tree, just so that my toes could touch the ground.
Every stroke buried the lash in my flesh.

When I was released, instead of returning to Mr. Hughes', I went to see
my mistress, she being then at her brother Richard's. I arrived there about eight
o'clock in the evening, went into the kitchen, and told the servant that I wanted
to see mistress; who, upon hearing of it, came directly out, and expressed much
joy at seeing me, saying: "How do you do, John?" I told her that I was almost
dead. "What is the matter?" she inquired. I answered, "I am whipped almost to
death." "By whom?" she asked. "By the constable, before the magistrate." "For
what?" said she. I then related to her the whole story.

She rushed into the house, and told her brother of the affair, who sent for
me to come in and repeat the story again to him. I did so, and also pulled off my
jacket, and showed them my shirt, wet with blood. This so affected my mistress,
that she commenced walking the floor, and weeping, saying meanwhile, that she
was imposed upon, because she was a lone girl, and had no one to take an interest in her affairs; that if her father was alive, they would sooner thrust their
heads into the fire, than treat her so. She did not believe this was for any fault of
mine, but simply because they grudged her her property.

This roused master Richard at once, for when she spoke of her father, and
her lonely condition, it touched him in a tender point. Now it will be recollected,
that this man was a lawyer, and he was feared rather than respected by most who
knew him. He bade me go home, but told me not to go to work until he came. I
went home and to bed, pretending to be very sick, so that when Mr. Hughes
called next morning for me to go to work, I was unable to get up. About 10
o'clock master Richard, mounted upon a fine horse, rode up, and asked to see
Mr. Hughes. This gentleman immediately came out, and invited him to alight
and enter the house, which invitation was declined, as, he said, all his business
could be transacted there.

He inquired if Mr. Hughes knew how cruelly I had been beaten, and received for answer that he did not. That he only knew that two constables came there, bringing a warrant to take me before a magistrate, in relation to some wheat that had been found at Mr. Thomas Bowlding's.

Master Richard inquired the names of the constables and magistrates, and whatever else Mr. Hughes knew concerning the matter; after which he asked for me. Upon being called, I went out, when master Richard told me to go over to the magistrate's, which I did, reaching there before he did.

When he entered the office, he asked to see the justice's docket or books, which were shown him; but the magistrate seeing me, suspected something wrong, and commenced explaining before being asked. Master Richard said nothing, until he had finished examining the documents, where, failing to find any charge, he inquired what was the complaint alleged against me.

Oh! he said, there was no regular complaint; but Mr. Hughes said I would not work and attend to my duty at home, and Mr. Bowlding complained that I went to his plantation and kept the girls up all night, so that they were unfit for service next day; so he thought he would order me a few stripes, just to frighten and keep me in order.

"That, then, is all, sir?" inquired master Richard, contemptuously. He then bade me take off my shirt, and exhibit my bruised back, after which he added to the justice, "Now, sir, please look at his back! is that merely to frighten him? You had no right to do this, and I will make it cost you more than he is worth!"

In the meantime, the constable came up, upon seeing whom, master Richard went towards him, asking, "Why did you whip my sister's negro in such a manner?" "Because it was my duty," was the answer. "Then, sir, it is my duty to give you just such an one," said master Richard, at the same time drawing his pistol, cocking and presenting it to the affrighted constable. "And," he continued, "I will blow out your brains, if you move!" He then, with his horsewhip, lashed the constable as much as he thought he needed, the fellow making not the least resistance.

I went home to Mr. Hughes' as well as ever, nor was I again troubled by patrollers, while I remained in his employ. He one day said to me, "John, now I hope you will stay at home. You have caused more disturbance in the neighborhood, than any one before; have caused Mr. Simpson to be turned out of office, and to be obliged to pay more than you are worth. I would not have you another year as a gift, and shall be glad when your time is up." So at Christmas, I left Mr. Hughes, and went to a new place.

CHAP. XII.

My new master's name was Mr. Horken. He was a tolerably good man, so far as whipping was concerned; but fed his slaves most miserably, giving them meat only once each month.

At the plantation where I lived two years previously, I became acquainted with three slaves, who had now determined to make an effort to gain their freedom, by starting for the free States. They came down to see me, and try to induce me to go with them, they intending to start in about three weeks; but they exacted from me a promise of secrecy in regard to the whole matter. I had not as yet fully made up my mind to make an attempt for my freedom, therefore did not give a positive promise to accompany them. I had known several, who, having made the attempt, had failed, been brought back, whipped, and then sold far to the South. Such considerations somewhat discouraged me from making the attempt.

As the time drew near for them to start, they came again to know my decision. I told them that I had consulted my mother, whose fears for my success were so great, that she had persuaded me not to go. These three friends were very religious persons, one of them being a Methodist preacher. He, in particular, urged me very strongly to accompany them, saying that he had full confidence in the surety of the promises of God, who had said that heaven and earth should pass away, before one jot of his word should fail; that he had often tried God, and never knew him to fail; consequently he believed he was able to carry him safely to the land of freedom, and accordingly he was determined to go. Still I was afraid to risk myself on such uncertain promises; I dared not trust an unseen God.

This visit to me was on Sunday, and they had planned to start the Saturday night following, and travel the next Sunday and Monday. It was not uncommon for slaves to go away on Saturday and not return until the following Tuesday, feigning sickness as an excuse, though this pretence not unfrequently subjected them to a flogging. So that very little alarm was felt for a slave's absence until Wednesday, unless his previous conduct had excited suspicion.

On the night on which they intended to start, accompanied by several of their fellow slaves, they repaired to an open lot of ground. Others, prompted by curiosity, followed, until quite a large concourse was assembled. Here they knelt in prayer to the great God of Heaven and Earth, invoking Him to guard them through every troublesome scene of this life, and go with them to their journey's end. Afterwards they sang a parting hymn, bidding their companions no other farewell, the hymn being exactly appropriate to the occasion. It was one of the old camp-meeting songs:—

> "Farewell my dear brethren, I bid you farewell!
> I am going to travel the way to excel;
> I am going to travel the wilderness through,
> Therefore, my dear brethren, I bid you adieu!
>
> The thought of our parting doth cause me to grieve,
> So well do I love you; still you I must leave;
> Though we live at a distance, and you I no more see,
> On the banks of old Canaan united we will be."

I well remember the evening of their departure. It was a beautiful night, the moon poured a flood of silver light, and the stars shone brilliantly upon their pathway, seeming like witness of God's presence, and an encouragement that he would guide them to their journey's end.

After they had gone, I began to regret that I had so much distrusted God, and had not accompanied them, and these regrets weighed so heavily upon my mind, that I could not rest day or night.

Wednesday came, and with it uproar and confusion, for three slaves were missing, of whom no one could give any account. Search was instantly made, which was, of course, unavailing, since they were already safe in some free State. Who would have thought that those contented negroes would have left their masters, preferring freedom to slavery? But they are in Canada.

Some time after this, master Richard concluded to sell his plantation, and with his slaves remove to Mississippi, my mistress consenting that he might take hers also. So he, one day, told me that I could have my choice, go with him or be sold. I told him I would not leave him to go to any one else in the known world. He then said that he would hire me out the next year, upon conditions that my employer should release me to him whenever he called for me. So when my year with Mr. Horken was up, I was hired to Dr. Johns upon the above conditions.

It was rumored about that I had given the three escaped slaves passes, it being known that I could write a tolerable hand. But master Richard looked into the affair, and finding no evidence against me, the subject was dismissed.

I lived with Dr. Johns from the commencement of the year, until the middle of June. About this time two more slaves attempted to escape, but were overtaken, caught, and brought back. It was said they had passes, but of the truth of this I am not sure, as the slaveholders reported many stories to implicate me in guilt. But God fought my battle.

To make matters appear still more in my disfavor, one slave, whom I never knew, told his master that I was going to run away, and had been trying to persuade him to go; that my master was going to remove me South, but that I intended to leave for the free States.

These were facts; but how this slave came by them I never knew, as I had only confided them to one man, and he came off with me. I left home on Saturday night, and on Sunday several slaves were arrested and put in irons, suspected of intentions of trying to escape with me. I was about three miles from home, and knew nothing of all this, though they were hunting for me.

I felt very melancholy all day Sunday, yet knew not the cause. Early Monday morning, the constables were at Dr. Johns', waiting my arrival, to take me; but I did not go home that morning, nor have I ever since been there. Still, it was my intention to have gone, but God overruled that intention by a better.

I started early on Monday to return to the doctor's, and got within a mile of that place, to a fork of the roads, when suddenly my steps were arrested, and a voice seemed to say, don't go any farther in that direction. I stopped, considered a moment, and concluded that it was mere fancy or conceit. So I started on again; but the same feelings returned with redoubled force.

What can all this mean? I queried within myself; these sensations so strange and unusual; yet so strong and irresistable? It was God, warning me to avoid danger by not going home. So I turned upon my footsteps, and immediately these feelings left me. I sat down by the side of the road to reason upon the matter, when, for the first time, I felt an entire confidence in God, and prayed in faith.

I now made a third attempt to go home. But upon reaching the same spot, I was more uncontrollably effected than before. I became nearly blind, my head swam, and I could scarcely stand. I now felt satisfied that it was the working of an unseen God, and really think that had I still persisted in my attempts to go forward in that direction, I should have fallen as one dead, in the road.

I therefore went into the woods and stayed until night, when I went to a neighboring slave's quarters, where I got something to eat. After this, I started for Mr. Morton's plantation, where Uncle Harry's wife lived, and which was near Dr. Johns'. Harry was a carpenter, and was at work for the doctor, therefore I knew that I could learn through him the whole state of affairs there, as he came home to stay nights.

As soon as I entered the house, Uncle Harry exclaimed, "John, what have you been doing?" "Nothing," I answered. He then said, "the whole plantation, at the doctor's, is in an uproar about you, as they say you have been giving passes to slaves, to help them run away, which you also intend to do yourself; and, accordingly, the constables have been on the watch for you these two days. I saw your old mother to-day, who was running from one road to the other, to meet you, to prevent your coming home, lest they should catch you. Now I don't know what you will do, as they have advertised you, offering three hundred dollars for your arrest; so the patrollers will be looking for you; consequently you had better not stop here long. I promised your mother to try and see you to-night."

He told his wife to give me something to eat, but told me it would not be safe for me to stay there to eat it. I moved slowly away, but he hastened my footsteps, as did the angel those of good old Lot,[10] for surely danger was at my heels.

Now my morning's feelings were fully explained. I knew it was the hand of God, working in my behalf; it was his voice warning me to escape from the danger towards which I was hastening. Who would not praise such a God? Great is the Lord, and greatly to be praised.

I felt renewed confidence and faith, for I believed that God was in my favor, and now was the time to test the matter. About two rods from Uncle Harry's house I fell upon my knees, and with hands uplifted to high heaven, related all the late circumstances to the Great King, saying that the whole world was against me without a cause, besought his protection, and solemnly promised to serve him all the days of my life. I received a spiritual answer of approval; a voice like thunder seeming to enter my soul, saying, I am your God and am with you; though the whole world be against you, I am more than the world; though wicked men hunt you, trust in me, for I am the Rock of your Defence.

Had my pursuers then been near, they must have heard me, for I praised God at the top of my voice. I was determined to take him at his word, and risk the consequences.

I retired to my hiding place in the woods until the next night, when I returned to Uncle Harry's, that I might see or hear from my mother. I found her there waiting for me. She had brought food in her pocket for me.

I inquired if the patrollers had been there in search of me, and was told that they had not as yet, but would, doubtless, be there that night.

My mother appeared almost heart-broken. She did not wish me to go away, and had been to master Richard about me, who had promised to inquire into the accusations against me, and if there was not sufficient proof to substantiate them, they could not injure me. But he recommended that I should keep out of sight for the present, and if he could do nothing else in my favor, he would so manage, that when he was ready to go South, I could be got off with him. I thought this a very wise plan too, in case I desired to go South; but I had fully resolved to go North.

I did not, however, communicate this resolution to mother, as I saw she was not in a proper condition to receive it. She promised to go again to master Richard, and come and let me know the result of her visit. But I knew I should never again see her, and that I was then probably taking my last look of her—this side the grave.

Upon leaving me, she took my hand, and in a voice choked by sobs, gave me her parting blessing. My heart was so full that I could scarcely endure this, and but for the support of God, I must have fainted. I now returned to my hiding place, leaving word with Uncle Harry, where the friend who had promised to come away with me, might find me.

As soon as he heard he came directly to see me, for he had been anxious lest I should go off without him.

CHAP. XIII.

THIS friend lived about eight miles from my hiding place, to which he walked after his day's work was ended. He wished me to go home and stay with him until he was ready to leave. I was very glad to do this, as he had a secure place, where they would least expect to find me. We had appointed two different times before this to start, and had been disappointed; still, his determination was firm to go.

I left my old hiding place, where I had spent one comfortable week, in solemn meditation and sweet communion with God, and went home with my friend.

He was coachman to his master, and had a room above the kitchen, which no one entered but himself, and where he concealed me. His master drove, whipped, and clothed his slaves most unmercifully, but fed them uncommonly well; consequently, my friend was able to feed me well, while I was his guest, he often coming to his room unseen, to see if I needed any thing.

He went one night to the neighborhood where I had lived, but returned with very discouraging news. Three hundred dollars had been offered for me, and I had been advertised in all the papers; therefore, he thought my way so much hedged in, that my escape was impossible, and finally concluded not to try himself. I did not care so much for the advertisement, as for this determination of his, which rather discouraged me, for I knew he was a shrewd man, also, that his business had often taken him from home in different directions; therefore, I thought he would know more of the way than myself, and I had accordingly, waited long for, and relied much upon, him. But my trust in Him who will not forsake in time of need, was greater; so I resolved to try the road alone and abide the consequences.

I passed most of my time in supplication to my Great Conductor, until the next Friday, the time appointed for my departure. The most discouraging thing seemed my ignorance of the direction I ought to pursue. I knew well that dangers thickly beset the pathway, and that should I miss my way, it would be almost certain failure to inquire it of a white man; also, that I must starve rather than ask one for food.

Various were the suggestions which the enemy of souls continually presented to my mind, to weaken my trust in God; but, like Abraham of old, I drove them away, still held my confidence, and prayed incessantly. The all-important Friday now came, and I thought it necessary to make one more trial, a third covenant with God, since it is said a threefold cord is not easily broken. So I again inquired of Him relative to this undertaking, and was soon spiritually convinced that He was still with me, and would so continue to the end of my journey; so I fully and finally committed myself to his charge, and determined to start that night.

About three o'clock in the afternoon my friend came in with the good tidings that he had changed his mind, and concluded to accompany me, which quite encouraged me, though it did not change my trust from divine to human aid. The evening came, and with it my friend, true to his promise. He said, "Come, let us be going; I believe God's promise is sufficient, and I will try Him, and see what He will do for me. Let us trust everything to him and serve him better. If we are taken, he has power to provide a way for our escape."

We started about 8 o'clock in the evening. After travelling about three miles, we saw many horses feeding near the road, and concluding that four legs were better adapted to speed than two, we took one apiece. We went to a barn and took two blankets, but while hunting for bridles, were routed and chased some distance by the faithful watch dogs of the farm. Then we concluded to go to nature's manufactory; so we cut grape vines, made for ourselves bridles, mounted our horses, and rode at full speed until day-break, after which we turned them loose, leaving them to shift for themselves, and thanking them for their aid to us. I think we must have travelled at least forty miles that night; yet, strange to say, did not meet a single person.

The following day we travelled rapidly, and, about four o'clock, P. M., reached Washington city. I went to a store and bought a pair of shoes, and on the way met a colored man with whom I was acquainted, we having been raised on the same farm. He inquired what wind blew me there at that time of year, it not being holiday time. I knew this man was a Christian, and therefore that it was safe to trust him, which is not true of all, since there are as many treacherous colored, as white men. I told him I had started for the free States, and thought to go to Baltimore by steamboat; but he said that would be impossible.

I asked what I should do; to which he replied that *he* could not tell, but pointing to a house near by, said, "There lives Mrs. R., a free woman, and one of God's true children, who has travelled there many times, and can direct you. You may depend upon what she tells you."

I went as directed, and inquired for Mrs. R. She invited me to enter, and asked where I was from; upon which I related my whole history, during the recital of which tears ran down her cheeks. When I ended, she said, "let us pray." We knelt before God, when such a prayer as I never heard from mortal lips, fell from hers. I felt God's presence sensibly.

After the prayer was concluded, she gave us a very good dinner. I asked for pen and ink, and prepared to write a pass, upon which she said, "Lay aside those earthly, selfish dependencies; God cannot work when you depend partly on self; you must put your trust entirely in Him, believing him to be all-sufficient. If you will do this," she added, with raised hands, "I will give my head for a chopping block, if he does not carry you safely through, for I never knew him to fail."

She then gave us directions for our journey, naming the dangerous places which we were to avoid; after which we started with renewed courage. After travelling about two miles we came to a bridge, upon which were many hands at work, under the supervision of a "boss." They did not address us, although they looked steadily at us, as if they wished to do so.

This was a toll bridge, at which footmen paid two cents, but when we crossed, the toll man was in so high dispute with a teamster, who had just crossed, that he did not notice us. Thus God paid our toll.

About a mile beyond this, we came to a place where were several Irishmen quarrying stone. They stopped work as we approached, looked hard at us, and I heard them say, "Here come two negroes who look like runaways; we can make a penny apiece off them, let's take them up." This was a trying time, and exercised all the faith of which we were possessed. But faith is the substance of things hoped for, and the evidence of things not seen; by it the elders obtained a good report.[11]

But notwithstanding the suggestions of these men and our passing near them, still they did not molest us, although they followed us with their eyes, as far as they could see us. This was another Ebenezer for us to raise, in token of God's deliverance;[12] so when we were out of their sight, we knelt and offered up our thanksgiving to God for this great salvation.

Three miles farther on we passed a village tavern, at the door of which stood a stage coach loaded with passengers, of the driver of which we inquired the way to a certain town. We had travelled about a mile in the direction he designated, when we saw two horsemen following us, in great haste. We suspected they were in pursuit of us, but as there were no woods near, saw no means of escape.

As they came up they said, "Boys, where are you going?" We named the town which was about three miles distant. "You will not get there to-night," said one. "No, sir, we don't expect it," I answered.

They kept along with us for about a mile. I soon suspected their object was to arrest us, that they dared not attempt it alone, but that they hoped to meet some one who would assist them. One of them entered a tavern, which we passed, but finding no help there, came out and continued on with us.

After awhile one of them rode on ahead of us, when the other tried to check him by saying, "We must not go so fast, they will take another road." This verified our suspicions that they were after us.

My companion began to complain that it was now a gone case with us, and said he wished he had not come. I reproved him for this faithlessness; told him if this was his course of procedure, that we should soon be taken up, and reminded him of his promise to trust in God, let danger assume whatever shape it might. I told him my confidence remained unshaken, that I had no reason at all to doubt. Upon this he braved up, and went on cheerfully.

When we approached the town of Rockville, our undesirable companions rode off at full speed, thinking, doubtless, that we should be foolish enough to follow. We thought it wisest, however, as soon as they were out of sight, to take the woods until night. But whilst resting under the bushes, we observed two boys approaching, one black the other white. The latter exclaimed at once, "There are two runaways, I will go and tell my father."

The boys went directly to a man who was near by ploughing, and informed against us. We saw that to remain there would be unsafe, so we resumed our journey. As we stood on a hill near Rockville, we could look down into the village, where we saw many people, apparently awaiting our arrival; therefore we presumed the two horsemen had only gone ahead to prepare for our reception.

We saw a colored man near by, of whom we inquired what course we could take to go around the village; but he would give us no information whatever. So we decided that our best way was to venture directly through the town, and had started to do so, when a colored man, who was driving a wood team, seeing that we were strangers, and guessing we were runaways, came near and said to us, "I see you are strangers, and I hope you will excuse my boldness in addressing you. I wish to say, that you had best not go through the village, unless you have the necessary papers. Whether you have such documents you best know. No colored man can pass here, without being subjected to a close examination."

We thanked him, and gave him to understand that we felt our cases to be nearly desperate, and wished him to tell us the best way to go around the town. He kindly told us, and we started to follow his directions, which were to go through the woods and enter the main road again, on the other side of the town.

But we had proceeded but a little way into the wood, when, to our surprise, we saw coming towards us, down the road, a great number of men, some on foot, others on horses, who had probably seen us as we left the road for the wood. We fell back farther into the woods, but it being large timber, with few bushes, we had little chance of concealment, and were truly in a bad fix.

We at last found an old tree, which had fallen so that the trunk was supported by the limbs about two feet from the ground. Under this we crawled and lay flat upon our faces, as being the safest place we could find, and little safety there seemed to me in this, for I thought a man a hundred yards off might have seen us, with half an eye.

We saw the huntsmen and their dogs within ten yards of us, and even heard them say, "They must be near this place!" We lay still, and held God to his promise, though when danger came so near, our hopes began to vanish, and like Israel we began to mourn. But stand still and see the salvation of God, which he will show thee to-day.[13]

Presently one man said, "I think they have gone farther into the woods. There is no place of concealment here, and besides the dogs would find them." Oh, foolish man! God bestowed their senses and he can take them away. He can touch one nerve of the brain, and directly their understanding is lost.

They finally went farther into the woods, listening to their dogs, who seemed as anxious as their masters, to find us; but they could not hit upon the right trail We remained under the friendly tree from five in the afternoon until ten in the evening; when, thinking all was safe, after returning God our thanks, we left our hiding place, and pursued our journey, determining to travel here-after no more by day.

CHAP. XIV.

ABOUT three miles farther on we discovered two horses saddled, standing tied in the wood near the road, which, we soon discovered, were the same upon which the men rode who had overtaken us before we reached Rockville. We knew them by the pieces of buffalo skin on their saddles. Their riders had evidently left them and concealed themselves near by, to watch the road, thinking we should leave our hiding places after dark, and resume our journey.

Upon making this discovery we entered a rye field, through which we passed, still keeping the road in sight. Thus we went on for two or three hours, through fields, bushes and swamps, until worn out with fatigue and hunger, we were forced to lie down to rest. Here we soon fell asleep, and did not awake until day-light. It was now Sunday. After praying we resumed our journey, taking the road.

Uncertain ourselves whether we were in the right or wrong way, we could only trust to the guidance of the Great Pilot as we travelled onward, and when we were hungry we prayed for spiritual food, which seemed to strengthen and fill us.

We now saw a colored man sitting upon the fence, about a mile from us, whom we approached, when he immediately accosted us in these words: "Good morning, my friends, I have been sitting here for about an hour, unable to move with all the effort I could make, when I ought to have been at home, (as I am a coachman,) preparing my horses and carriage to take the people to church. I now feel why I have been thus forced against my will to remain here; it is that I may help you. And now tell me what I can do for you, for as God liveth I will do it if possible."

We told him that we had been travelling since Friday, without any food, and were now nearly famishing. Pointing to a farmer's house, he said, "Go there and inquire for my wife; tell her I sent you that she might give you something to eat. She is the cook for the farm."

We thanked him, and started to follow his directions. Upon reaching the house, we saw the overseer standing in the yard, who scrutinized us very closely and suspiciously. Nevertheless we inquired for the cook, who soon made her appearance, when we did our errand; and although she quickly answered, "I don't see why he should send you here, for I have nothing for you to eat, and he knows it;" still, we could see that we had awakened her sympathy, and that she only answered thus indifferently because of the overseer.

He, however, told her to give us some breakfast; upon which she took us into the kitchen, while he started instantly to get help to take us. The cook suspected as much, and told us so, and the slaves immediately concealed us very carefully. Soon the overseer returned with his help, and inquired for us, when the slaves told him that we went away soon after he did. He inquired in what direction, and when they had told him, he started off in hot haste in pursuit.

The slaves expressed great astonishment that we had come so far without getting taken up, but told us to keep still, and they would take care of us. At night a free colored man took us through unfrequented paths, to escape the vigilance of the overseer, until we reached Fredericktown, when he said he could go no further, as, if we were taken and he found in our company, it would ruin him. Moreover, he was fearful we could not get through the town, as no colored man was allowed to pass through after nightfall. Therefore, to avoid creating suspicion and being arrested, we decided to part company for the present, I to go through the town on one side, and my companion on the other.

Before parting from our kind conductor, we knelt down and besought God to conduct us on our way, and shield us from all harm; and again we made a mutual promise, to place all our trust in divine strength. We saw many people as we passed through the town, none of whom noticed us, until we were about to leave it, when we perceived a large and noisy crowd, apparently intoxicated, coming towards us.

We left the road until they had passed, when we again resumed our journey together. We soon came to a fork in the roads, when, not knowing which to take, we pulled down a guideboard and ascertained; after which we went on until daybreak, when we took shelter in the woods during the day on Monday.

The following night we travelled without interruption, and on Tuesday lay all day concealed in a rye field. We travelled Tuesday night until within five miles of Baltimore, when we missed our way. Here again we had an instance of God's care for us, for had the night been one hour longer, we should probably have reached Baltimore, and been taken.

But, early in the morning we met a colored man, who, as we hesitated to answer him when he asked where we were going, said we need not fear him, as he was friendly, and would not hurt a hair of our heads. Thus assured we revealed to him our secret, when he exclaimed, "My friends, you are running directly to destruction! That is the road to Baltimore, which is but five miles distant, where you will certainly fall into the hands of your enemies, who are on the sharp lookout for all such chances, therefore you had best take a different route."

We were truly alarmed, for day now broke suddenly and unexpectedly upon us, from a hitherto dark and cloudy sky. We knew not what to do, as there was no forest large enough in sight, in which to conceal ourselves, so we besought our new friend to direct us, which he did by pointing out to us a poor, dismal looking old frame in a small wood, occupied by a free colored man.

Thither we went, and were kindly received by the man's family, who gave us food, of which we were in great need. My feet and ankles were so much swollen, that we found it necessary to remain here two days, about which we felt many misgivings since the man was often intoxicated, when he was very communicative, and I feared he might unintentionally, if in no other way, betray us, for I knew no dependence could be placed on a drunken man.

Friday night we started again, the man having told us what route to take; and that when we reached the Susquehanna, we should have no other means of crossing but to steal a boat for that purpose. The next day as we lay concealed near the road, under the bushes, we could hear the people converse as they passed.

We finally concluded not to go on this way any farther, as the chance of stealing a boat was a very hazardous one, but to return to the place from whence we last started, and see if we could not obtain some better instructions. On our way back, we passed a house from which a man hailed us with, "Hallo, boys, where are you going? stop awhile." I said we were going home, and had no time to stop. This was about midnight.

As we heard him call his dogs, we left the road and went through the wheat fields to the woods, where we soon heard him pass at full speed, with his dogs. We hastened to our friend's house, but he advised us not to lose a moment in making our way off, as they would most likely come to search his house, knowing him to be a free man. He directed us by another route, which was a very dangerous one, being watched constantly to the borders of Pennsylvania; but told us to go to another free colored man, six miles distant, who could perhaps direct us better.

He cautioned us about passing a house, which he carefully described to us, in which lived a negro buyer, who watched to catch runaways. But, notwithstanding his caution, we unluckily found ourselves almost at the door of his house, before we were aware of it. We however passed it unperceived.

Early next morning we arrived at the house to which we had been directed, and called up the owner. As soon as I heard him speak, I knew him to be a man of God, for his words betrayed him. He called his wife to come quickly and prepare food, for two wayworn and hungry travellers, which she hastened to do. Now, who told this man of our necessities? for we had not. But never refuse to entertain strangers, for some have thus entertained angels unawares.

When the table was spread ready for breakfast, the old man approaching the throne of grace, with eyes uplifted towards heaven, repeated the following hymn, which the whole family joined in singing:—

> "And are we yet alive?
> See we each other's face?
> Glory and praise to Jesus give,
> For his redeeming grace.

> Preserved by power divine,
> To full salvation here;
> Again in Jesus' praise we join,
> And in his sight appear.
> What troubles have we seen,
> What conflicts have we passed?
> Dangers without and fears within?
> Since we assembled last.
> But out of all the Lord
> Hath brought us by his love;
> And still he doth his help afford,
> And hides our lives above."[14]

While they were singing, the mighty power of God filled my frame like electricity, so that whereas I had before been hungry and weak, I now felt the strength of a giant; I could no longer restrain my feelings.

This was Sunday morning, and the family started soon after breakfast for the Methodist church, which was three miles distant, taking my friend and leaving me locked up in the house, for my limbs were so swollen that it was deemed advisable that I should rest during the day. Four others accompanied them on their return, towards one of whom my heart leaped for joy as soon as I saw him, for I felt that he was a servant of the Most High. He instantly grasped my hand, saying, "Have you faith in the Lord Jesus Christ?" I answered in the affirmative, when he continued, "Well, God has brought you thus far, and he will conduct you safely to the land of freedom."

After dinner and a round of prayers, we started on our way, these friends accompanying us. We were supposed to be some of their neighbors, whom, having been with them to church, they were accompanying homeward. They continued with us until dark, taking us through fields and by-paths. When they left us, they said we were within two nights' travel of the Pennsylvania line, but cautioned us against one dangerous place, which having passed, we should probably have little more to fear.

This was a large two storied white house standing near the road, about two rods from which stood a barn thatched with rye straw. The owner's business was to catch slaves, for which purpose he kept well trained dogs, who having once got on our track, would follow for miles, and the master would shoot us if we did not surrender, therefore we should be careful to avoid this place, in particular.

Our friends left us, and we went on, but before we knew it we had passed the barn, and were near the house. As soon as we perceived our mistake, we took to the fields. Everything was still about the house, until I, in attempting to get over a fence, broke down, when I made so much noise as to rouse the dogs, which presently began to bark. This brought out the master, who tried to urge them on, but, strange to say, though they ran to and fro, they could not strike our trail.

We did not venture into the public road again that night. The next day we lay by, and at eight o'clock in the evening again started, hoping to reach port before morning.

Our friends had told us, that when we reached the Baltimore turnpike, leading into Pennsylvania, that we were then over the line. About three o'clock in the morning we came to a shanty, on the edge of a wood, so small and mean that I thought no person inhabiting it would have the courage to attempt our arrest. My friend objected to going to the house, but I wanted to inquire the way, having got somewhat bewildered. So I went and knocked at the door, until a surly voice called out, "Who's there?" "A friend," I answered. "What does the friend want?" he inquired. "To know if he is on the direct road to the Baltimore turnpike, and how far it is there," I said. "Yes, go on, it is about half a mile," he said, in a voice which plainly denoted that he did not wish to be disturbed by night rovers, though a price of three hundred dollars was on the head of the one then at his door.

We pursued our course, and shortly came to the much desired turnpike, when we clasped glad hands, and went on the next mile or two, rejoicing and praising God for this deliverance. We now imagined ourselves out of danger, but were mistaken, for after passing York we came to a village called Berlin, where we were attacked by a Dutchman, who came running out of a carpenter's shop and grasped me by the shoulder, at the same time muttering over some lingo, wholly incomprehensible to me.

But I looked at him so furiously, at the same time thrusting my hand into my pocket, as if after some weapon of defence, that he became so frightened as to loose his grasp, and run backwards as if his life was in danger. I followed him to the great amusement of the by-standers, who were looking on to see him take me.

I supposed my companion was close by, but when I turned round I saw him about six rods distant, walking off at a rapid speed, and leaving me to do the best I could alone. This cowardice somewhat enraged me, but when I overtook him he so excused himself that I forgave him, knowing that his spirit was willing, but his flesh was weak.

CHAP. XV.

WE at last reached Columbia, Pennsylvania, where we intended to stop and hire out to work. But the people advised us to go on farther, as already there were two slave hunters in the place in pursuit of two fugitives, whom they had traced to that place. Accordingly we started again the following night, and after travelling about ten miles, reached the house of an elderly quaker, who offered us a home with him until he could get places for us. These he soon procured, and we went to work; and oh, how sweet the reflection that I was working for myself. We remained here about six months, when we were again routed by the arrival of slave hunters, who had already taken two women and some children, and were in pursuit of other fugitives. In consequence of this, many of the colored people were leaving this for safer parts of the country; so we concluded to go to Philadelphia.

I went first, and my friend soon followed. We had not been there many days, before he was met and recognized by a lady, in Chestnut Street; but he feigned ignorance of her, and did not answer when she addressed him. He came directly and told me of the affair, which at first gave me great alarm, but as we heard nothing more from her, our fears gradually subsided.

My friend soon married, and not long after moved to Massachusetts, whither he was driven by one day seeing his old master in one of the streets of Philadelphia, peering into the face of every colored man who happened to pass.

I soon got into bad company, and forgot the goodness of that Being who had shown me so much kindness, who had stuck by me closer than a brother, through all my wanderings, and who had finally brought me from bondage to a land of freedom. I often now reflect upon my ungratefulness towards him.

One night, while returning from my day's labor, I fell into meditation upon the past blessings of God to me. When I reached home I looked in the Bible to find something applicable to my case, when I, almost immediately, opened at Luke's Gospel, 15th chapter and 18th verse, "I will arise and go to my father."

I felt a heavy load resting upon my heart; I felt as if I had neglected the Saviour, and God had forever withdrawn his spirit from me. I knelt in prayer, and like Jacob, wrestled manfully. I continued in this state six weeks, until the meeting of the Methodist Conference, which took place in the Bethel Church, in Philadelphia. When it commenced I was sick, and had been confined to my bed two weeks. I heard people talk of the great revival, and of the excellent preaching they were having, and though I was then confined to my bed by sickness, and the rain was falling fast, still I was resolved to go to church, for I felt that my soul was at stake, and I did go, notwithstanding friends tried to prevail on me to remain at home.

I took my seat in a dark corner of the church, while the congregation were singing for their own amusement. Presently a tall man entered, went into the pulpit, and read the following hymn:

> "Hark, my soul! it is the Lord;
> It is the Saviour, hear his word;
> Jesus speaks, he speaks to thee,
> He says, poor sinner, love thou me.
>
> I delivered thee when bound,
> And when wounded healed thy wound;
> Sought thee wandering, set thee right,
> Turned thy darkness into light.
>
> Can a woman's tender care
> Cease towards the child she bare?
> Yes, she may forgetful be,
> But I will remember thee."[15]

He lined the hymn so that all could sing, during which he often called the attention of the congregation to the sentiment, to all which I paid great attention, for my mind was forcibly carried back to the state of bondage from which I had just escaped, and the many manifestations of God's mercies to me throughout the journey. The hymn was not sung by wood or brass, but by mortal tongues, which were more charming in their harmony than ten thousand stringed instruments. This hymn was so precisely suited to my case that I began to feel much better.

The preacher, Rev. Josiah Gilbert, of Baltimore, then arose, taking for his text, "O, praise the Lord, for He is good, and His mercies endure forever." Never before nor since have I heard such a sermon. The load was removed from my heart, and I found myself standing up in the church, praising God, for it seemed to me a heaven upon earth to my soul.

I felt nothing more of my sickness, and next day went to my work, tending for brick-layers. The following night, at the meeting the question was put if any person wished to join the church. No person went about among the crowd to drag others to the altar, or to force them to say they had religion, when they had none; yet one hundred and twenty, like noble volunteers, forced their way to the altar, and gave in their names, shouting the praises of Immanuel's God,[16] while the preacher was recording them.

I joined the church that same night. O, memorable night! Would that I could bring thee back, that I might live thee over again! But thou art gone, and I can only live over thy blessings in memory. But they will not so flee.

I married the same year, and for a time everything seemed to go on well. God gave me a companion who loved Him, and we soon had a family altar in our lowly habitation. Sickness and sorrow however came. Several slaves near by were arrested and taken to the South, so I finally concluded best for me to go to sea, and accordingly removed to New York city for that purpose.

MANY of my friends have expressed a curiosity to learn how I, being a slave, obtained an education; to gratify which I will now relate some incidents in my past life, which I have not done in the foregoing pages.

When about eight years of age, I was sent to the school house with the white children, to carry their dinners, it being a distance of two miles, and therefore too far for them to go home for them. There were two of these children relatives of my master, whose father had once been rich, but who, through misfortune, left his children almost penniless at his decease.

Little Henry, one of the children, was one morning, while walking leisurely to school, repeating over his lesson, when I said to him, "How I would like to read like you." "Would you?" said he, "Then I will learn you." I told him, if his Uncle knew it, he would forbid it.

"I know it," he answered, "But I will not tell him; for he would then stop you from going with me, and I would have to carry my own dinners!" Thereupon we made a mutual promise to reveal our secret to no person.

Henry was about my own age, being the elder of the two children; his sister, Jane, being about five years old. He commenced teaching me from his book my letters. We sometimes started an hour or two before school time, that we might have more leisure for our undertaking. We had a piece of woods to pass on our way, which also facilitated the practical operation of our plans, as we could, by going into them, escape the observation of the other school children, or of passers by in the road. We even sometimes took Jane to the school house, leaving her to play with the other children, while we returned to our school in the woods, until the school bell rang.

I made such rapid progress that Henry was encouraged and delighted. When my father knew of the matter, he gave Henry some money with which to purchase me a book, which he did of one of the scholars, who, being advanced into a higher lesson, had no longer use for this book.

I now lost no time, but studied my lessons every leisure moment, at all convenient times. I went thus with the children to school about three years, when I became the body servant of John Wagar, and had to give my attention to him and his horse.

John being six miles from home, at a boarding school, was only at home from Saturdays until Mondays. During his absence I had to attend to his pony, and do small jobs about the house, which did not prevent my continuing my studies, although my opportunities to do so were not now as good as formerly; still, my little teacher improved every chance that offered of giving his instructions.

I soon got through my first book, Webster's Spelling Book,[17] after which Henry bought me the Introduction to the English Reader.[18] He also commenced setting me copies, as he thought it time I was commencing to write, though he still kept me at reading until I had nearly completed my second book, when our school was broken up by the return of John Wagar from the boarding school, he having completed his education.

John, whose father was very rich, hardly treated Henry, a poor orphan boy, with common courtesy or decency, and was unwilling even to sit and eat with him at table. Mrs. Ashton, Henry's mother, noticed this conduct of John's, and also that his father sided with him in all his complaints against Henry, and knowing the cause she did not wish longer to remain where she was; so she, with the children, removed to Alexandria, where Henry is now doing a large dry goods business, in which, by honesty and skill, he has accumulated considerable wealth.

When Henry was about to leave the plantation, he said to me, "I am sorry, John, that I cannot teach you longer, as I had intended to learn you through the English Reader, and also to write a good hand. But you must not forget what you have learned, and try to improve what you can by yourself."

This parting filled my heart with sorrow, for I loved Henry Ashton like a brother. I followed him with my eyes until distance closed the view; and my affectionate prayers and good wishes always have, and always will, follow him, for to him I owe the rudiments of one of my greatest blessings, my education. Through this I have been enabled to read the Word of God, and thereby learn the way of salvation; and though I could never repay these services, yet God has doubly paid him, for before I left Maryland his name ranked among the most respectable and wealthy of country merchants.

After this I continued to read and write at every opportunity, often carrying my book in my hat, that I might lose no chance of using it. When I was with Richard Thomas, in the south part of the State, I became acquainted with a poor Englishman, who lived near the plantation. He, seeing my strong desire to learn, proposed to instruct me, after exacting from me a promise of secrecy in the matter. He continued to teach me from the first of March until the October following, when he and his daughter, (his whole family,) died.

After that I had no teacher until I went to Philadelphia, where I attended evening schools during the winters of my stay in that city.

CHAP. XVI.

VOYAGE TO THE INDIAN OCEAN.

WHEN I reached New York, in consequence of my inexperience I could get no berth on shipboard, as they only wanted to employ able seamen, so I was advised to go to New Bedford, where green hands were more wanted, and where, I was told, I could go free of expense.

Accordingly, next morning, in care of an agent, I started on board a vessel bound for that port. When I arrived there, I was told I could only go before the mast as a raw hand, as a great responsibility rested upon the cook, or steward, of a whaling vessel, bound upon a long voyage, one of which places I preferred and solicited.

I soon saw there was no chance for me with that master, so I went to the office of Mr. Gideon Allen, who was fitting out a ship for sea, and wanted both cook and steward. I approached him with much boldness, and asked if he would like to employ a good steward, to which he replied in the affirmative, asking me at the same time if I was one.

I told him I thought I was. So, without much parleying we agreed upon the price, when he took me down to the vessel, gave to my charge the keys of the cabin, and I went to work as well as I knew how.

The following day the Captain, Mr. Aaron C. Luce, come on board with Mr. Allen, who introduced me to him as the captain of the ship, with whom I was going to sea. The captain looked at me very suspiciously, as much as to say, you know nothing of the duties of the office you now fill.

At the house where I boarded was a cook, who, in consequence of deformed feet, could not obtain a berth, as the captains and ship owners thought he would thereby be disenabled for going aloft when necessity required it. This man told me that if I would get him a place as cook, he could and would give me all needful instruction in reference to my office.

I was pleased with an offer which promised so well for me, and accordingly recommended him to Mr. Allen for cook, who, supposing I knew the man, and that all was right, hired him.

The Milwood, on which we were to sail, was a splendid vessel, called a three boat ship. She was arranged to carry 3500 bbls.[19] of oil, with a crew numbering twenty-five hands, with four principal officers, captain and three mates, and three boatswains, who are termed subordinate officers. All things being in readiness, the hands were summoned on board, when, at the pilot's command, she was loosed from her moorings at the dock, floated out of the harbor, and with well filled sails, stood out to sea.

The thoughts of the voyage and of the responsibilities which I had taken upon myself, were anything but pleasant. I knew that I was wholly ignorant of a steward's duties, and consequently expected to incur the captain's just displeasure for my assurance and imposition, since at sea every man is expected to know his own duty, and fill his own station, without begging aid from others. But again I reflected that God was all sufficient, at sea as well as upon the land, so I put my trust in him, fully confident that he would bring me out more than victorious.

As I bid my family farewell, and left the American shore, I thought over the following lines:

> Jesus, at thy command,
>   I launch into the deep;
> And leave my native land,
>   Where sin lulls all to sleep.
> For thee I would this world resign,
> And sail to Heaven with thee and thine.
>
> Thou art my pilot, wise;
>   My compass is thy word;
> My soul each storm defies,
>   Whilst I have such a Lord.
> I trust his faithfulness and power,
> To save me in a trying hour.
>
> Though rocks and quicksands deep,
>   Through all my passage lie;
> Yet Christ will safely keep,
>   And guide me with his eye.
> My anchor, hope, shall firm abide,
> And everlasting storms outride.[20]

Soon after the pilot left us I became very sea sick, and unable to attend to my duties, which, consequently, all devolved upon the cook, he having promised to assist me. But of this he soon grew tired, and complained to the captain, hoping to get my place; so he told him I was a greenhorn, had never been to sea before, and knew nothing of a steward's office.

The captain, who had been deceived by my sickness, now came into the cabin very angry, and said to me, "What is the matter with you?" I told him I was sick.

"Have you ever been at sea before?" he asked. I told him I never had, upon which he asked how I came to ship as steward? I answered, "I am a fugitive slave from Maryland, and have a family in Philadelphia; but fearing to remain there any longer, I thought I would go a whaling voyage, as being the place where I stood least chance of being arrested by slave hunters. I had become somewhat experienced in cooking by working in hotels, inasmuch that I thought I could fill the place of steward."

This narrative seemed to touch his heart, for his countenance at once assumed a pleasing expression. Thus God stood between me and him, and worked in my defence.

He told me that had circumstances been different, he should have flogged me for my imposition; but now bade me go on deck, where I could inhale the fresh air, and I should soon be well. I did so and soon recovered.

The captain became as kind as a father to me, often going with me to the cabin, and when no one was present, teaching me to make pastries and sea messes. He had a cook book, from which I gained much valuable information.

I was soon able to fulfill my duty to the gratification and satisfaction of the captain, though much to the surprise of the whole crew, who, knowing I was a raw hand, wondered how I had so soon learned my business. But I could never suit the mate, do the best I could, for he wanted me put before the mast, and for more than four months kept a grudge against me. The cook also, disappointed in not getting my place, often complained of me to my enemy, the mate. And not satisfied with this, he had the baseness to forbid my going to the galley to look after my cooking, and it was often spoiled. But I bore all with patience, as I knew that I had two good friends, in the captain and God. This trouble was, however, soon removed, for the cook was taken sick before we reached Fayal,[21] where he was left in charge of the American Consul, to be sent home.

When we had been about three weeks out, we captured a sperm whale, which furnished eighty-five bbls. of oil, which we sent home from Fayal, where we remained just long enough to discharge the oil, and take on board a fresh supply of water and vegetables, which required about three days.

Shortly after leaving this place, while the captain was aloft one day, the mate became so much exasperated with me as to beat me. He took hold of me, whereupon I threw him down, but did not strike him. Upon entering the cabin, the captain found me in tears, and inquired the cause. I told him that, do the best I could, I was unable to please the mate, who had been beating me now, for no cause of which I was conscious. He told me to do my duty to the best of my ability, and he would take care of the rest.

He then went upon deck, and inquired of the mate of what I was guilty deserving a flogging; who replied that I was unfit to be in the cabin, and ought to be before the mast; that I was too much of a gentleman to be at sea. Whereupon the captain told him not to lay a finger upon me again, for I was his steward, and the mate had no control over me, which he wished him, the mate, to plainly understand. The captain allowed I was green enough, but said that I was willing to do the best I knew; that when the mate first went to sea, he was as green as I was, and that every man must have a chance to learn before he could do his duty.

The mate accused the captain of partiality to me, upon which the captain gave him to understand that he was master of the vessel, and should treat each man as he deserved, from the mate to the cook. After this I soon fell in favor with the mate and all the crew. The mate was a resolute man, and a good whaleman. Being steward I was not obliged to go in the boats for whales unless I chose, or unless some one of the hands was unable to go, whose place I was to fill, of necessity.

The manner of arranging the boats in a ship of this character, is as follows: Three boats, ready fitted, are kept swinging in the cranes alongside the ship; these are called the starboard, larboard and waist boats. Each is manned by six men, including the officer, and each has its regular crew. The captain commands the starboard, the first mate the larboard, and the second mate the waist boat. The third mate commands the captain's boat, when the latter does not go.

Each boat carries five oars, the officer steering, while the harpooner, who is termed the boatswain, rows the bow oar, until the whale is fastened with the harpoon, which operation is performed by this person. This being done, the boat-steerer goes aft and takes the officer's place, while that person goes forward to kill the whale; which is done with a sharp spear, about six feet long, called a lance.

The harpoon is sharp, and barbed at one end, so that when it has once entered the animal, it is difficult to draw it out again, and has attached to its other end a pole, two inches thick and five feet long. Attached to this is a line 75 or 100 fathoms in length, which is coiled into the bow of the boat. Sometimes these lines have two harpoons attached, so that if one misses the whale, another can be ready to take effect, before the creature is beyond their reach. The lance is fixed to a line in a similar manner, by which it may be drawn out of the animal, as it is repeatedly thrust into him, until he is killed by bleeding to death; a process sometimes requiring two or three hours for its completion.

The boats remain beside the dead animal until the ships come to them, for they are generally unable to tow him to the ship, in consequence of his great weight. When brought alongside the vessel, a chain, called the fluke chain, is fastened around his tail, which is towards the bow of the vessel, by which means he is made secure to it. From his carcass are then cut large junks[22] of oily substance, called blubber, which is from twelve to eighteen inches in thickness, and is the only fleshy part of any value. These junks are hoisted upon deck, and placed in cauldron kettles, that the oil may be tried and pressed from them; after which, the refuse is thrown upon the fire and used for fuel.

There are five different kinds of whale: the sperm, the right, the humpback, the finback, and the sulphur bottom, of which but three are much caught, the sperm, the right and the humpback. The first is found in warm climates, the last in temperate, but the right in cold. Two men are generally placed aloft as "look-outs," while the ship is cruising for whales, which may often be seen at a distance of two miles, usually by their spouting, which is sometimes repeated as often as every half minute. The whale can neither stay long above nor below the water, without changing.

When the whale is discovered, the signal is given to the captain, or the officer upon the deck watch, in the following manner: The man aloft says, "There she blows." The officer inquires "Where away?" "Two points of the weather beam, sir," is the reply, or whatever direction the animal may be. This signal is repeated every time the whale spouts, until the officer goes aloft, to determine of what kind the animal is.

Part of the crew are always on the watch, while the others are asleep below. Orders are now given to call all hands on deck, which being done, each boat's crew stations itself by its boat, until orders are given for lowering them away. When within reach of the whale, the officer in command gives orders for the harpooner to throw his instrument, which he does until the animal is fastened. The whale can only be killed by lancing him under the fin, which is the work of much skill and practice.

The whale is a monster, terrible in his fury, but harmless when left alone; able to shiver the boat in atoms by one stroke of his tail, and when in agony roaring like a lion in the forest. Hence the officer in the boat should have as much skill in the art of whaling, as a military commander in the art of warfare, since the safety of the crew rests with him.

CHAP. XVII.

AFTER leaving Fayal, we sailed for St. Paul's Island,[23] stopping a short time at the Cape de Verdes, where right whales were said to be numerous. We had pleasant weather for about three weeks.

One day, while standing upon the deck, looking upon the broad expanse of waters spread out around me, and meditating upon the works of the Omnipotent and Omniscient Deity, my soul was suddenly so filled with the Holy Ghost, that I exclaimed aloud, "Glory to God and the Lamb forever!" I continued in this strain until captain Luce, coming unexpectedly behind me, asked what was the matter with me? I told him my soul had caught new fire from the burning altar of God, until I felt happy, soul and body.

Directly he commenced cracking jokes at me, but I soon left his presence and returned to the cabin, where I could be, for a while, alone, and where I could obtain spiritual strength to enable me to stand before wicked men. There is no better time to pray, than when God is ready to answer; when he stands knocking at the door of our hearts, pleading for entrance. He works upon our right hand and our left, and we perceive him not.

The captain, being in a very pleasant mood, one day, came into the cabin, and asked me if I ever prayed for him? to which I replied I did. "Do you think that your prayer is answered?" he asked, "for I don't. I don't think they ascend higher than the foreyard." I told him that bread cast upon the waters, was sometimes found and gathered after many days. He laughingly asked me if I prayed that the ship might get a load of oil? I told him I always prayed for the blessing of God on the ship in general. He said if he had to go home without a load of oil, which he expected to do, that he should call me a hypocrite.

While he was talking, the man on the lookout cried out, "There she blows," upon which he ran upon deck, and found there were four whales in sight, not more than three-fourths of a mile distant. The mate, who was below, springing from his bed, said, "Steward, will you go in my boat?" I replied I would. "Then," said he, "Stand by the boat."

The boats being lowered, we started for the whales. The mate rushed among them, and fastened one; the captain soon followed, and fastened another; and at last, the second mate to another! They all furnished 239 bbls. of oil. This was a day of rejoicing for all hands, as we had not seen a whale before for more than five weeks. The mate, who had before been my enemy, now became my friend, and during the remainder of the voyage treated me like a man.

On our way to the Dutch Banks, whither the captain concluded to go, because of the abundance of whales there, we caught two, and fastened upon a third, which, however, got loose. When we arrived at the Banks, we found plenty of whales, and many vessels there for the purpose of taking them; but which, in consequence of stormy weather, had hitherto been unsuccessful, and for the same reason we only took three.

For about three weeks the storm raged most furiously, the wind became a hurricane, the waves rolled and dashed mountain high, sweeping our boats from their hangings, and dashing them in pieces; while the sun was hid by dark and portentuous clouds.

All hands looked upon the captain as their deliverer, while he stood looking at the clouds, seemingly with deprecating vengeance. But it was the work of our God, whom the winds obey, and to whom the sea does homage. Well might the Scripture say, "He has his ways in the whirlwinds, and his paths are known to the mighty deep."[24] He looks, and the fearfully threatening clouds hide their deformed faces; He speaks, and the winds are hushed in profound silence; He commands, and the lofty billows lowly bow their heads.

The storm being over, we sailed for St. Pauls, where we took several whales; but had two of our boats stove to pieces, in encounters with them. The Captain and first mate's boats were frequently injured in this way; but the second mate generally kept in the background until the danger and bustle were passed. Here I again had time to reflect upon past blessings; while calmness prevails, the mariner should prepare for a storm; for the storm, which gathers slowly, accumulates more fury than a sudden, transient blast.

> "Whene'er becalmed I lie,
>   And storms forbear to toss;
>   Be thou, dear Lord, still nigh,
>   Lest I should suffer loss:
> For more the treacherous calm I dread,
> Than tempest, bursting overhead."

Captain Luce was a good seaman and captain, and a man of reliable judgment. He would allow no swearing on board his vessel; he looked upon the sailors as his children, and they in turn regarded him with affectionate esteem. The mate was a man of quick passions, easily excited, but as easily calmed.

He one night entered the cabin, where I was, while I was singing one of the songs of Zion, and being in a melancholy mood, he asked me to sing for him; with which request I gladly complied, by commencing a new song, which I had recently learned in Philadelphia. He instantly stopped me, saying he did not wish to hear any new hymn, but some old and substantial one; upon which I sang the following:

"Before Jehovah's awful throne,
　Ye nations bow with sacred awe;
Know that the Lord is God alone:
　He can create and he destroy.

His sovereign power, without our aid,
　Made us of clay, and formed us men;
And when, like wandering sheep, we strayed,
　He brought us to his fold again.

Wide as the world is his command,
　Vast as eternity his love;
Firm as a rock his truth shall stand,
　When rolling years shall cease to move."[25]

While I was singing, tears came into his eyes, and when I ceased, he exclaimed, "Oh! steward, had I the religion which I think you have, I would not part with it for all the world!" This was a very unexpected compliment to me, from a man in so high a station, and encouraged me to pray on and hope continually.

After the whaling season at St. Pauls was ended, we went to the Crowsett Island,[26] where it was very cold, and where the fogs continued a long time, without intermission. We had good success in whaling there, but the weather was so unfavorable, that the hands soon became disabled by scurvey, to that degree that we were obliged to put into port sooner than the captain had intended. So we sailed towards Madagascar, where one remarkable circumstance occurred.

We had a sailor on board named Smith, who told me the reason for his coming on this voyage, was, that being in company with some firemen, in Brooklyn, who had committed a crime in which he was implicated, he had adopted this as the best means of eluding the vigilance of the officers, who were in pursuit of him, and who had taken some of the company.

I told him that he could not so easily escape from God, that the remembrance of his crime would still pursue him, and that unless he repented, he must expect severe punishment, both here and hereafter: to all which he only replied by laughing in my face.

Soon after this conversation a whale was seen, and Smith belonged to one of the boats sent in pursuit. The animal was harpooned, but stove the boat, and broke loose. In the encounter, Smith came near losing his life. When they returned, I thought it a good time to again refresh his memory, in reference to his crime. While the fright lasted, he seemed somewhat penitent, but the feeling soon passed away, like the fleeting time.

Not long after, a similar circumstance happened to him, which was as soon forgotten. But a repetition of them, made him afraid to go in the boat, so he excused himself to the captain, upon the plea that he had cut his finger and could not row; whereupon the mate, to whose boat he belonged, gladly took me in his place; when we, in a short time, captured four whales, with no accident.

Just before we left this Island, another whale was seen, when the captain ordered Smith to go in his usual place, notwithstanding he attempted, as usual, to excuse himself, upon the ground of his inability to row: to all which the captain turned a deaf ear. They soon came up with the whale and harpooned him, when he stove the boat all in pieces, throwing the crew all into the sea, where they were struggling for their lives, by clinging to pieces of wreck or whatever else they could reach. The other boats at the time, were at a great distance from this scene, one of them being already fastened to another whale.

Smith strove manfully to keep himself above water, until finding his strength failing, he made for a piece of the wreck, on which were already three persons, but which could not sustain a fourth; so those first in possession of the frail support, thinking three lives of more consequence than one, as the only means of self-preservation, pushed Smith off into the deep, and would not permit him to grasp their piece of wreck.

The poor fellow was for a time quite at a loss what course to pursue, but time pressed, his strength was fast failing, and he must make some effort, even though he perish in the attempt, it could be no worse, since he must surely perish if he remained where he was. The whale was then lying quietly upon the water, near by. Quick as thought Smith conceived the hazardous plan of saving himself, by clinging to that enemy, which he had just been using all his power and skill to destroy, and as quickly grasped the line attached to the harpoon, which was still sticking in the whale, and by its help climbed upon his back, where, holding by the handle of the harpoon, he rested securely until a boat came and took him off! Then was the moment when Smith, in the agony, and from the depths of his heart, cried, "Lord save, or I perish!" and Heaven heard the rebel's prayer, and held that mighty leviathan, and made him the means of his persecutor's preservation! For as soon as Smith was taken off his back, he went down and came up again a half mile distant.

This terrible fright lasted Smith nearly two weeks, during which I again reminded him of his crime, and of his wanderings from the path of rectitude. I strove to make him realize how wonderfully the Lord had preserved his life, and how mercifully He had dealt with him; to all which Smith replied, by promising that henceforth he would serve the Lord better.

We reached Madagascar, which is an African island, and of immense dimensions I am told, about the first of May; but I cannot give my readers a geographical description of it, as I only went about five miles inland; nor need I, for it might weary their patience, while to speak of some of the manners and customs of the inhabitants, might mantle with blushes the cheek of morality. The soil is rich, producing in abundance rice, cotton, corn, sugar cane, &c.

The natives are black, with long straight hair, slender forms, and remarkable for their longevity. They are cunning and much disposed to plunder. Their religion is Mahomedan, though they practice many Jewish rites, such as sacrifice and burnt offerings, for which purpose they raise many cattle. They consider the white man a superhuman being, who can hold converse with the Almighty, who will speak to him as He will not to them. One day they stood looking with amazement at the mate, as he was taking the sun's altitude with a quadrant. When he had finished his observations, he offered the instrument to several of them, all of whom refused it, saying, God would not talk to them as he did to white men!

I was much gratified, upon conversing with them, to learn that they had some faint knowledge of the true and living God, and believed Mahomet was only a mediator between God and man. A woman, who I least expected would possess any such knowledge, gave me to understand that she believed God dwelt above in the heavens, and that at some future time he would come to judge the world.

Wednesday was my day to go on shore, and Thursday the cook's day. But being one day on shore, I learned that the following day was one devoted by the natives to sacrificial offerings, which I would not tell the cook, lest curiosity should prompt him to go to see them, and thus deprive me of a chance. So I paid him to stay and do my cabin work, and let me go on shore again that day.

This offering was to secure the blessing of their Hokerbarro, or God, on the king and his family. The sacrifice was performed in this manner: three poles, 15 or 20 feet in length, with shorter ones lying across them, were placed three feet above the ground. When this was done, the sacrificial bullock was brought to look upon it, after which he was killed, his blood caught in a calabash, or gourd, for a separate offering, and his flesh cut in pieces and laid upon the poles, under which a fire was kindled, around which the natives danced, clapping their hands while it was burning, the whole performance being accompanied by numerous ceremonies. The sacrifice ends with the sunset, but as my duty required my attendance on shipboard before that time, I did not witness its conclusion.

We remained in Madagascar three weeks to repair the ship, which was damaged at sea. While lying in port four of the crew escaped, and were concealed on shore by the natives; who afterwards came and betrayed them to the captain for a price. The mate, with a boat's crew of Portuguese, was sent for them, with whom they not only refused to return, but severely cut and bruised them. Afterwards the captain, with the captains of five other vessels, then lying in port, went for them, conducted by the natives, who knew their place of concealment, in a native hut.

When he discovered them, the captain calmly told them he wished them to return with him to their duty on board the vessel, to which they readily gave their assent, saying they would have gone before had he sent Americans for them, but that they would not willingly submit to be fettered by Portuguese.

When they reached the ship, they were placed in irons, and put upon criminal's allowance until the next morning, when it was expected they would receive their deserved punishment. Our captain did not wish to flog them, as he thought he could inflict some other punishment which would prove more salutary and efficacious; but, being pressingly urged by captain Burton, of the ship Sally Ann, and others, to do so, he finally flogged three of them, among whom was Smith; while one, who was not concerned in resisting the Portuguese, was suffered to go without his flogging. But before we were ready to leave Madagascar, this very man again escaped from the vessel, by lying upon a plank and paddling himself along with his hands, he having previously arranged with the crew of the ship to which he was going, to receive him on board and conceal him, which they did, until she was ready to sail for New London, whither she was bound, loaded with oil.

CHAP. XVIII.

WE cruised around the coast of Africa for whales, but finding none, put into the port of Johanna,[27] where we again met the ship Sally Ann, captain Burton, who had the reputation of being a very cruel man.

While lying in port, six or seven of his men, taking with them provisions, a compass, quadrant, chart, nautical almanac, spy glass, and other useful implements of navigation, one morning before daylight, took a boat and made off, intending to go to Mohilla, one of the Comoro Islands, about ten miles from Johanna. But before they were out of sight, they were discovered from the ship.

Now, there is a reef of rocks running about one and a half miles out to sea, from the port of Johanna, which are, at all times, very dangerous, in consequence of the heavy seas which are constantly breaking over them. When captain Burton discovered and gave chase to his deserting crew, they ran at once among these reefs, and thus escaped, he not daring to follow them, but returning to his ship much fatigued and exasperated.

It seemed that the Johannicans and Mohillans had been at war with each other, and consequently no intercourse was permitted between the islands. Captain Burton offered the Johanna king a large reward, if he would catch his runaways, and deliver them up to him when he returned from a short cruise, which he was now obliged to make, and from which he should return in about three weeks. But the king, fearing to approach the shores of his enemy's island, only cruised about his own, and of course with no success; so he finally gave up the search, and the ship was obliged to put out to sea without them, though the captain swore he would have them, if they went to hell!

Five days afterwards they discovered a sperm whale, after which they immediately gave chase. He went down and finally came up very near the captain's boat, when he gave orders to harpoon him, which the boatsteerer immediately did, and fastened him. The captain then went forward to lance him, when the whale struck him so violent a blow with his tail, as to break both his legs, without injuring another person. He was taken directly to Johanna, but there being no surgeon there, he was obliged to remain in this painful situation, until an English vessel, having one on board, came into port. But by this time his limbs were so badly swollen, that one of them could not be properly set, so he was taken to Cape Town, from whence he was sent to America. Three of his runaway crew were taken on board a French vessel, nearly in a state of starvation, while the rest actually perished.

We lay in this port about a week. It is a very ancient town, the houses of one story, mostly built of stone, and seldom having any windows. The inhabitants are Arabs, Malays and Africans. They are of a light brown complexion, and have regular features. Their religion is Mahomedan, the rites of which they scrupulously observe. They are exceedingly jealous of their females, insomuch that they will not permit them to speak to any man, out of their own family circle. They wear sad countenances, but are very hospitable. They have large and splendidly decorated temples, the floors of which are covered with striped matting, of their own manufacture.

One of the natives, who seemed a man of some influence and high moral standing, one day invited me to visit, with him, one of these temples; which invitation I gladly accepted. When we reached the door, my conductor stopped to speak to a person who I supposed was a priest, as he sat by a table on which lay a book and many papers, from which he was reading in a tuneful voice. A stone trough was standing beside the church.

I bolted at once into the temple, without hesitation, but was as soon brought back and told that I had defiled it, in consequence of not purifying myself before entering. The priest seemed very much offended, but led me to the trough, in which was a constantly changing supply of clean, fresh water, and bade me wash my hands and feet before entering.

I was told that my sacrilegious entrance, unpurified, would oblige them to perform an extra sacrifice, by way of atonement. I regretted much that I had unwittingly been the cause of so much trouble, and thought an acknowledgment a sufficient sacrifice, but I was mistaken.

After being properly prepared, I was allowed to enter and remain during their service. I was astonished at the reverence and humility with which they approached the throne of grace, for they fell flat upon their faces.

Many things might be said concerning the manners and customs prevalent on this Island, as also concerning its towns; but my business is to describe my voyage to the Indian Ocean, to which I will now return.

We left this Island, and sailed in the direction of New Zealand, near which we cruised five weeks, taking several whales in the time. Four other vessels were in company with us here, each of which went in for himself, taking whales.

During one of our whaling adventures, I unwillingly consented to accompany the mate, at his request. I attributed most of the accidents to his carelessness; notwithstanding, he was called a skillful whaleman, therefore I did not like to go with him. He would rush to attack a whale, like a restless horse to battle, harpooning him without any regard to order or formality, lest some other boat should secure him first. We here took three whales in one week.

We one day fell in with a ship from Sag Harbor, having on board the dead bodies of two men, the captain of which came on board the Milwood, one beautiful Sabbath morning, when the sea was as smooth as glass, to ask our captain and such of the crew as chose to accompany him, to go on board his ship and attend their funeral.

I went and witnessed what is, probably, one of the most solemn and affecting of scenes,—a burial at sea. All who witnessed it were affected with sadness. When all was ready for the final ceremony, the bodies were taken to the waist gangway, where they were lashed upon boards, lying upon their backs, with heavy bags of sand attached to their feet, after which they were committed to the waves, and instantly sank into the vast deep. Captain Luce performed the religious services with great solemnity.

After cruising in these seas about two months, we put into a harbor on New Zealand, where we stayed one week, and then went to New Holland[28] for the cure of the scurvy, with which the sailors were badly afflicted, in consequence of having been so long exposed to an atmosphere loaded with saline vapors, and of being so long fed upon salted food. Eating raw potatoes is considered by some an excellent remedy for this disease, which commences with an irruption of the skin, and ends in putrefaction, if not arrested in season to prevent.

Another remedy, and one to which our sailors were subjected, is reckoned very good, namely: to bury the patient in the ground, all but his head, for a while. After the diseased ones had thus been cured, we cruised for a long time with no success, and finally returned to the Crowsett Islands; but even here were unsuccessful.

We had now been at sea over two years, and had completed our cargo, all save 50 bbls., when our captain decided to cruise towards home, keeping up a sharp lookout, until we were beyond the whaling ground. This decision filled me with joy, for I yearned to see my long unseen family.

The captain said to me one day, when we had been sometime homeward bound, "Steward, I thought you promised us a full cargo to return with, which you see we have not got; so I must think you a hypocrite!" I told him I still believed my prayers would be answered, and that we should yet have a full cargo.

About two weeks after this, while the ship, with all her canvas spread, and with a fair wind, was running after the rate of nine knots an hour, the man aloft saw two whales in the distance. The captain had offered ten dollars for a whale that would furnish 50 bbls. of oil, and each man was desirous of winning the prize. Preparations were soon made to give chase to the whales, who were still at a considerable distance from the ship.

The mate's boat soon fastened one whale, but while the captain was striving to fasten the other, he stove the boat and tumbled the crew into the water. The mate's crew, however, after killing their whale, took after this, and finally secured him, while the second mate's boat picked up the almost despairing crew. The two whales filled 150 bbls. with oil, so that there was not place in the ship to stow it, without throwing over some of the provisions to make room. We then went into Soldonna[29] for refreshment, and while there lost four of our crew by desertion.

We next stopped at St. Helena,[30] which renowned place I was very glad to see, and took occasion to visit the residence and tomb of the Emperor Napoleon. But I discovered nothing very remarkable at either place, therefore will not weary my readers with unimportant description. After one week's stay we left St. Helena for the American coast.

About three days out from this island, we spoke a ship, recently from home, by which the captain learned that since he left home his wife had given birth to a son. This filled him with joy, and made him so anxious to reach home, that he ordered the mate to put the ship under all the sail which she would bear.

The wind blew so furiously that it sometimes seemed as if the sails must all be carried away; but like a gallant bark, the ship safely outrode the whole, and arrived at New Bedford. No pilot being in sight, we had to fire twenty rounds from the cannon as a signal, before we could raise one. At last, however, to our great joy, a pilot boat hove in sight, dancing over the waves, when shouts were heard, "O, sir, we shall soon get into harbor!" Then the joyful hymn was sung:—

"By faith I see the land,
    The port of endless rest;
My soul, each sail expand,
    And fly to Jesus' breast,
Oh! may I gain that heavenly shore,
Where winds and waves disturb no more."

But our singing was soon turned into sighing, our joy into sadness, for our pilot, being unacquainted with the New Bedford channel, could only take us in sight of the city, where we were left nearly two days to brood over our bitter disappointment.

How often do professed ministers of the Christian Church pretend to lead the anxious soul to the haven of eternal rest, when they are themselves ignorant of the way, and of course leave him in the gulf of despair to mourn his sad disappointment. But the right pilot came at last and took us into New Bedford, and Oh, what joy filled my soul, when I was once more permitted to enter the congregation of the righteous, and to hear the sound of the Gospel Trumpet.

But my bliss was not complete, for I had a family in Philadelphia, whom I must hasten to see, that they might participate in my joy, and unite with me in praises to God for my safe preservation through so long a voyage; so, as soon as I received my wages, I left New Bedford. Before I left, the captain and mate both called to see me, the former giving me ten, and the latter five dollars, telling me to live faithful until death, and asking me to pray for them, which I promised to do, then bade them farewell, and left for Philadelphia.

CHAP. XIX.

WHILE at sea and learning the uses of the various nautical instruments, I also studied their spiritual application, for nothing else so much resembles the passage of a Christian from earth to glory, as a gallant ship under full sail for some distant port. The parallel between ships and souls, of course does not extend to their original structure or nature, since one is mere inert matter, fashioned by human skill, visible and perishable; while the other is immortal, invisible, and the direct handiwork of God.

Simplicity of nature must ever insure immortality under a government where the annihilation of created beings is impossible. Yet numerous are the circumstances in which the parallel will hold, and where the propriety of the metaphor is apparent. Let us contemplate some few of these for a moment, for time would fail us to review the curious machine in all its parts, and speak of its accommodating and beautiful comparison with the faculties of a rational soul; or to the grace of one regenerated and sanctified by the spirit of God.

Pleasant and entertaining as it might be, to consider how this metaphorical ship uses conscience for its helm, the understanding for its rudder, judgment and reason for its masts, its affections for sails; how education stands in the place of carving and gilding; how the passions represent too full sails, thus producing danger from foundering; how pride represents the too taut rigging; how assumed professions represent deceptive and ruinous false colors; yet, we must necessarily waive all such considerations.

Still, we must pause to admire the excellence of the model of this work of God, as much the highest of all this lower creation, as a ship is superior to every other work of human art. Nor can any words sufficiently deplore that misfortune by which, on its first being launched upon the ocean of life, this noble vessel was dashed on the rocks of presumption, and thus, in an unlucky moment, condemned and cast away utterly unfit for service.

How poor a pilot is man, even with his highest knowledge and ability, and how unfit to take his soul into his own keeping. And how magnanimous the grace of the generous Owner, who, instead of destroying that insignificant wreck, as might have been expected, was pleased to repair the ruins; notwithstanding he was well aware it would be a work of more difficulty and labor, than to construct an entirely new one, which could have been done by a word; while to restore the old wreck, would cost the greatest treasure in heaven, the life of the great owner and builder's only begotten and well beloved son! Oh, amazing love! that could so highly value things so worthless; things only fitted to be cast into the den of wild and furious beasts, or the dreary abode of unclean birds!

From the Omnipotent Power and Infinite Skill of the divine undertaker of the work, as well as the invaluable price given to defray the expenses, reason would immediately conclude, that in rebuilding this moral and spiritual structure, which was shipwrecked in Adam, but redeemed in Christ, no pains would be spared, nor anything omitted, which would be necessary to complete the work on which Jehovah's heart was set, and to make the second structure more glorious than the first.

Nor was the conclusion unfounded, for every material was purchased by the blood of the Son of God, and laid in bountifully by the gracious owner. Every piece is hewn by the law in the work of conviction; every faculty purged from sin and guilt by the great atonement, received by faith in Christ Jesus; every plank bent by the fire of divine love, all fitted to their places by the invincible energy of sovereign grace, and the structure is completed according to the model prepared in the council of peace, and published in the gospel, which divine illumination is made visible to the mental eye, through which it is received into the heart, and leaves its impress there. Destined for a voyage of vast importance, in seas beset with dangers and perils, this new vessel will find nothing more needful than a strong and sound bottom.

If faith is not genuine and enduring; if those principles typified by the planks and timbers of a ship, be rotten or unsound at heart, not consistent with each other, and not shaped so as to lie compactly; or if each is not well secured by bolts of the endurable metal of eternal truth from the mine of divine revelation; if all is not carefully caulked with the powerful cement of unfailing love and redeeming blood; in a word, if Christ is not the sole foundation, and his righteousness the grand security, then on the slightest trial, the seams open, the vessel bilges, and every soul on board is lost.

From the hour of active conversion, the redeemed soul is launched upon the deep, and moves in a new element. As she proceeds onward, and greater depths surround her, the amazing wonders of divine counsel appear more manifest, which had hitherto been unknown and unfathomed by any human line; the latent corruptions within its own recesses appear more terrible as farther explored, and every new glimpse still more affrights and humbles; while the mysterious and inexplicable depths of divine Providence, with its mercies, judgments, and deliverances also rise to view.

She floats on an ocean of trouble, where temptations inflame the appetite, and weaken good resolutions, as worms pierce through and destroy the bottom of a vessel. Trials follow each other, as wave succeeds wave; nor should we feel ourselves alone, nor more sorely tempted than others, in this, since it is the experience of every one who floats upon life's ocean billows. When our sorrows are mitigated, our thankfulness should increase; and when the clouds of grief become thicker and darker, it should wean us more effectually from earthly things, and kindle within us a more ardent desire for heavenly things.

Nor should the Christian repine at his afflictions, for he could not well do without them, since no means is more effectual to weaken the force of inate sin, or to wean him from his earthly idols, even as the heat of a furnace keeps the seething metal in commotion, while it separates and drives off the dross; or the unceasing rolling of the restless ocean, which, I am told serves to keep its waters pure. In contemplating the fickleness of this uncertain world, let us not fail to draw instruction therefrom.

Bound, as she is, to take a voyage on this restless, troubled ocean, the spiritual ship must not only be furnished with rigging suited to such a bottom as I have described, but she must also be provided with all necessary nautical instruments before she can safely put to sea; and oh, how carefully has her gracious owner been, that all her wants should be supplied.

An invariable and unfailing compass is furnished by the Sacred Scriptures, whose direction may be safely followed in the darkest night. The divine illumination will serve as a quadrant by which the Christian may discover his own latitude, and his position in regard to the path of rectitude and duty; but in vain will the most experienced seaman attempt to do this, unless his sun shines, and his horizon is clear.

How often, by persuading men to neglect the use of this quadrant, and thereby lose their true situation, has satan decoyed men to accept his pilotage, and trust to his skill, until he had led them clear out of the right course, to the very mouth of the gulf of despondency, among rocks and quicksands on all sides.

Through the spy glass of faith, the Christian may discover his faithful starry guides, although the heavens be shrouded in clouds; or may descry the approaching enemy, and avoid him; or may discover the far off haven of security. In the same manner self-examination may supply to the believing soul a line and lead, whereby to sound the waters, discover the way, and learn his distance, both from the port of departure and that to which he is bound.

A longing to arrive at a blessed end of the voyage, serves as an hour glass, by which he may mark the swiftly passing hours, and so reckon his time, that he may be able to give a correct account of it to the great ship owner; especially as he is sensible that not one hour can pass unremarked. This glass also admonishes him to set the watch at the exact minute, lest the steersman sleep at his helm, the hands slacken their diligence in duty, the vessel lose its way, or storms or enemies come unawares and find it unprepared. Precious moments, how swiftly they fly, every wave of the wing hastening us onward to eternity. Oh, that Christians would more carefully note their falling sands, and renew their watch more frequently. Failing to do this, caused David's penitential agony, and Peter's bitter tears of anguish.

To often try the pump is no less necessary than to change the watch, for which purpose is given sincere repentance, such as sinks to the bottom of the heart, searches out every lust and evil desire, brings it to the surface, and casts it out, as does the pump-rod the stagnant bilge-water, which, if allowed to remain, would finally sink the vessel.

On the ocean of life, where we are constantly meeting vessels, steering in every possible direction, would that Christians would show the same courtesy and kindness to each other, that seamen of every nation and under all colors, do. Then, with what true interest would they hail each other, with what courtesy answer when asked where they were bound, and with what good wishes send them on their way to their place of destination. With what truthfulness would they give an account of their voyage, of their adventures, of their cargo, and also of their reasons for the hope that is within them, with fear and meekness; so that believers might in this way become comforters, helpers, and directors to each other.

And that they might be thoroughly furnished for so good a work, their gracious owner has put on board a silver trumpet, whose sound is never false nor unreliable. I mean the Gospel, which brings glad tidings to all within sound of its voice, and speaks in a language which people of all nations can understand. In this language all may converse together, however much they may differ in other things; and all imbued with its spirit will gladly bear each other company, and hold communion together, in so far as time and circumstances will allow.

Defensive arms, also, are necessary for the safety of the voyage, and accordingly, see how completely the thoughtful owner has equipped the ship at his own expense. A full inventory of the armory may be found recorded in Ephesians, 6: 14–18.[31]

But all else would fail were a cable and anchor wanting, both which are supplied, the one by hope, the other by faith. Thus completed and supplied with every necessary, the good ship takes in her lading. The various gifts and graces of the Holy Ghost, together with the hopes and comforts arising from their exercise; the bracelets, the signets, and stuffs, the evidences and manifestations of the divine favor; goodly pearls selected from the treasury of unsearchable riches in Christ Jesus, all the special furniture, privileges, enjoyments, and experiences of the true believer, purchased for him by the blood of his dying Redeemer, are now put on board by orders of the Spirit of Sanctification: while, at the same time, every needful store is furnished by the precious promises and glorious truths of the gospel, of which a spirit of faith and prayer keeps the key, from whence the believer may daily draw and drink of the waters of Life; and upon which he may fare sumptuously every day.

Bound for the port of endless rest, the soul thus equipped receives sailing orders from the inspired oracles, which, at the same time, commands her to forsake all, to deny herself, to take up the cross, and to follow the Lamb whithersoever he goeth. If sincerely desirous to proceed, she will be very careful to have all things in readiness, and all hands in waiting for a favorable wind, without which the truest helm or the ablest steersman will be of no avail. Oh, Christian friends, were we but as earnest for the port of glory, as the mariner is for some earthly port, we should not often be found loitering or off our duty. Our prayers would ascend with every breath, that the heavenly gale would spring up, and awake the church from her lethargic slumbers.

How carefully then should we accompany our prayers with watching, heedfully marking every changeful appearance of the sky. How eagerly should we seize the first favorable moment, when the long wished for opportunity of sailing was in our power. Eager for departure, we would not willingly lose one fair breeze, knowing that without this all previous preparations were fruitless. Nor must the fairest gale entice us to sea without the heavenly pilot; for without thee, blessed Jesus, we can do nothing; to thee we must turn in every difficulty, and upon thee call in every time of danger. We dare trust no other at the helm, because no other can safely steer us past the rocks and quicksands. How kind thy promise, to be with us when passing through deep and dangerous waters. How gracious thy word which engages never to leave nor forsake us. We will confidently leave our feeble vessel entirely to thy guiding care, to shape its course and direct its way; nor will we dread the greatest danger, with thy hand upon the helm, believing no hidden rock can escape thy penetrating eye, nor any storm or danger surpass thy skill, or counteract thy unbounded power.

The hour arrives, all is in readiness, the pilot gives the signal, the anchor is weighed, and with all sails set, our bark proceeds to sea. What more majestic sight than a gallant ship, under full sail, wafted by a fair gale, proudly cutting her way through the vast deep? And so of the Holy Ghost, spreading every sail, that the kindly gales of the spirit of all grace, may waft it safe to the heavenly port, while the beams of the sun of Righteousness gild and brighten the scene.

Such halcyon days are sometimes vouchsafed to the young convert, just starting on life's new voyage. Oh, how should he improve them while within his reach, by preparing for the coming change! But alas! the treachery of the heart sometimes perverts such favors into occasions of spiritual pride. Then may be seen displayed the colors of mere profession; the streamers of confidence flying; the top gallant sails of self-conceit hoisted; the haughty royals set, and the vessel of self-righteousness mounted loftily on the waves.

Alas! how many have been thus wrecked in a vainglorious moment; and life has paid the forfeit of such insolence of heart, disdaining to proportion the sail to the ballast. Such an abuse of mercy could not escape the all-penetrating eye. The golden season suddenly expires, and is succeeded by a dead calm. The poor self-admirer lays his head in the lap of some bewitching Delilah, who lulls him to sleep with her siren songs.

Now all the Christian graces lie dormant; all precepts, ordinances and means are lost on a person so fascinated; while the rolling billows serve only to rock him into a deeper sleep. With no guide at the helm, such a ship gains nothing in her course. Could conscience only gain a hearing, all hands would quickly be roused to prepare for the coming storm; the leisure of the threatening calm would not be consumed in slothfulness.

Instead of inactivity and delay, when dangers threaten, the real, active believer is on the alert. While becalmed, he is examining his stores and cargo, patching his sails, and splicing his rigging. Spy glass in hand, he is searching for a clear coast. His journal is revised and his reckoning adjusted, his quadrant applied and his observations compared. Did we but judiciously employ the hour of tranquility, we should have little to fear from tempests.

But while all hands are negligently folded in security, and thoughtlessness fills the dreams of all, the change comes, contrary winds arise, obstacles spring up, difficulties beset the way, and all where least expected. Now we are forced by adversity to lower those sails, which, in the season of sunshine we hoisted, just to gain applause. Like Babylon, which, in its pride, vainly exalted itself, and was finally humbled. Dan. 5: 20. Ob. 1: 3.[32]

But notwithstanding adverse winds may blow, the faithful mariner will not haul in all sail, and lash the helm, thus leaving his vessel to the sport of fate. On the contrary, he will lose no chance of taking advantage of every fair breeze, to do which he will trim his sails to the wind, laying his course as near as possible, even though he cannot lay it direct. With the Bible in his hand for his compass, he steers his way, going not to the conclaves of councils, nor to the decrees of earthly potentates for his creed or the rule of his duty.

Disdaining to be the slave of popularity, he will neither embrace opinions because of their fashionableness, nor trim his principles to suit the times, nor yet follow the multitude to do evil. By experience he is taught to trust no mere professions, but like the panting slave fleeing from the bondman's chains and dungeon, he is suspicious of even a brother fugitive, who says he is travelling the same road, lest he should be betrayed. For freedom, like eternal life, is precious, and a true man will risk every power of body or mind to escape the snares of satan, and secure an everlasting rest at the right hand of God.

THE END.

1. Starling, *Slave Narrative*, 180.
2. *The Liberator* 26 (August 22, 1956):138; cited in Ibid.
3. See *Jeremiah* 8:22.
4. John Quincy Adams (1767–1848), U.S. president (1825–29), was a courageous opponent of slavery from 1835 until his death. There are a number of inaccuracies in Thompson's recollection. Adams's first act as a congressman, on December 12, 1831 (not 1830), was to present petitions from ladies of Pennsylvania (not Massachusetts) to the House of Representatives (not the Senate) to abolish slavery and the slave trade in the District of Columbia; he then stated his opposition to those parts of the petitions that supported abolishing slavery in the District altogether.

5. *Micah* 4:4.

6. Ruined, spoiled.

7. William Cowper (1731–1800), "God Moves in a Mysterious Way."

8. See *Daniel* 4:34.

9. Rev. Nehemiah Adams (1806–78), author of *A South-Side View of Slavery; or, Three Months at the South, in 1854*.

10. See *Genesis* 19:15.

11. See *Hebrews* 11:1.

12. When the Israelites defeated the Philistines near Mizpah, the prophet Samuel set up a stone there, and called it Eben-ezer, saying, "Hitherto hath the Lord helped us." See *1 Samuel* 7:12.

13. *Exodus* 14:13.

14. A Methodist hymn by Charles Wesley (1707–88).

15. Adapted from Cowper, "Lovest Thou Me?"

16. *Isaiah* 7:14: "Behold, a virgin shall conceive, and bear a son, and shall call his name Immanuel." Also see *Matthew* 1:23.

17. Noah Webster (1758–1843) wrote *The American Spelling Book; Containing, the Rudiments of the English Language, for the Use of Schools in the United States* (one of several alternate titles), first published in 1783 and reissued in numerous editions throughout the late eighteenth and nineteenth centuries.

18. Lindley Murray (1745–1826) wrote the *Introduction to the English Reader: or, A Selection of Pieces, in Prose and Poetry; Calculated to Improve the Younger Classes of Learners in Reading; and to Imbue Their Minds with Love of Virtue. To Which Are Added, Rules and Observations for Assisting Children to Read with Propriety*. It was first published in 1801, and went through numerous editions throughout the first half of the nineteenth century.

19. Barrels.

20. Anonymous Methodist hymn, first published in 1774 in Lady Huntingdon's *Collection of Hymns*.

21. Fayal Island is the westernmost of the central Azores.

22. Lumps, chunks.

23. An outlying dependency of Madagascar, in the southern Indian Ocean, about 2,800 miles from the southeast African coast.

24. Not a precise quote, but a conflation of *Nahum* 1:3 and *Psalms* 77:19.

25. Isaac Watts (1674–1748), "Before Jehovah's Awful Throne."

26. The Crozet Islands form an archipelago in the subantarctic zone of the south Indian Ocean, about 1,500 miles off the southeast coast of Africa.

27. One of the Comoro Islands in the Indian Ocean, off northwest Madagascar; also called Anjouan Island.

28. An earlier name for Australia.

29. Saldanha Bay, on the Atlantic coast of South Africa.

30. A British island in the south Atlantic Ocean, 1,695 miles northwest of Cape Town.

31. This list includes such items as "the breastplate of righteousness," "the shield of faith," "the helmet of slavation," and "the sword of the Spirit."

32. *Daniel* 5:20: "But when his heart was lifted up, and his mind hardened in pride, he was deposed from his kingly throne, and they took his glory from him." *Obadiah* 1:3: "The pride of thine heart hath deceived thee, thou that dwellest in the clefts of the rock, whose habitation is high; that saith in his heart, Who shall bring me down to the ground?"

WILLIAM AND ELLEN CRAFT

WILLIAM AND ELLEN CRAFT (c. 1826–1900; 1826–91) adopted one of the most ingenious and unusual methods of escape in history of American slavery: Ellen disguised herself as a white male slaveowner while William pretended to be her slave as they rode the public rails north to Philadelphia. With the support of black abolitionist and ex-slave William Wells Brown, the pair became immensely popular as lecturers both in the United States and England because of interest in their spectacular story. The abolitionist statesman Wendell Phillips was among several who spoke on their behalf: "We would look in vain through the most trying times of our Revolutionary history for an incident of courage and noble daring to equal that of the escape of William and Ellen Craft; and future historians and poets would tell this story as one of the most thrilling in the nation's annals."[1]

The Liberator's account of a February 1849 lecture in New Bedford emphasized the romantic nature of their appeal:

> An expression of astonishment arose from the audience, as Ellen and her husband stood before them. Could it be possible that she was held as a slave? There she was, in the language of the slaveholder's advertisement, "with regular features, straight hair, and so light as not to be distinguished from a white woman."
>
> A lady in the audience wanted to know if they called her a "nigger" at the South. "Oh, yes," said she, "they didn't call me anything else; they said it would make me proud.". . .
>
> William, the husband, is a noble specimen of a man; he is said to resemble Cinques, the Amistad hero; he certainly does in his love of liberty; you may see it in his eyes.[2]

The publicity given their story caused so much concern among Southerners that for years young masters traveling north accompanied by a single slave were regarded with suspicion.[3] As Arna Bontemps has written, "Apparently no two slaves in their flight for freedom ever thrilled the world so much as did this handsome young couple. . . . They became heroes, about whom speeches were made and poems written."[4]

It wasn't until twelve years after their escape that they published their narrative. In that time, they made speaking tours in England with their friend William Wells Brown, and staged a mock slave auction at the Crystal Palace Exhibition of 1851. Because of her almost white skin, Ellen became a living symbol of the barbarity of slavery, and sketches depicting her disguised as a man were circulated widely. In a letter published in the Boston Liberator, Ellen tried to dispel rumors started by southerners that she had left her husband and longed to return to slavery, stating plainly that she would rather starve in England "a free-woman, than be a slave for the best man that ever breathed upon the American Continent." In addition to lecturing, the Crafts opened an import-export business in fancy goods in west London.[5]

Meanwhile William, at one time a complete illiterate, had become an accomplished writer, persuasive, erudite, and witty, a master at depicting memorable characters and scenes. He was indeed the sole author of his narrative, as Marion Wilson Starling and John W. Blassingame have shown by comparing it to the letters he wrote prior to the Civil War.[6] While his frequent quotations from poetry and allusions to British authors may seem to stem from a desire to impress the reader, citation on this order was common in nineteenth-century British works. A contemporary analogy might be the writer who frequently quotes from popular songs.

In his narrative, Craft is intent on blurring distinctions between white and black, master and slave, man and woman.[7] He does so by not simply recounting his and his wife's escape, but by using the words *master* and *he* to describe his wife, and by the selection of the stories he tells to fill out his narrative. The result was one of the first black-authored books to center on the phenomenon of passing for white, thus helping to engender a tradition that includes such works as James Weldon Johnson's *The Autobiography of an Ex-Colored Man,* Walter White's *Flight,* and Charles Johnson's *Oxherding Tale.*

In 1863, William Craft traveled twice to Dahomey in West Africa and met with the King in order to try to persuade him to outlaw slavery and human sacrifice. His second visit lasted three-and-a-half years, during which time he opened a school.[8] He returned to England in 1867, having lost all his money in the African enterprise, and moved to Boston in 1869 with Ellen and three of their children. They then returned to Georgia with their five children the following year to set up a Southern Industrial School and Labor Enterprise, financed by abolitionists. When this was burned down by the Ku Klux Klan, the Crafts bravely bought an eighteen-hundred-acre plantation in Bryan County, Georgia, financing it with loans and the proceeds from William's continued lectures in the North. On the plantation they founded the Woodville Co-Operative Farm School; sixteen families lived there, growing rice, corn, and cotton. But the Crafts were nothing like the plantation owners who had once been their masters. Their school was founded to help poor blacks who had no notion of how to raise crops, and in order to run it, they went deeply into debt.[9] As William Craft wrote in 1875:

> Altogether the school is highly appreciated by the colored people. There are seventy-five boys and girls on our books, most of whom attend regularly. Thirty pupils reside here. The others come from the neighborhood free. . . . The school is poorly off for furniture, having nothing but a pine table and coarse forms. Nearly without compensation, my wife and sons have worked very hard to get the children on.[10]

But their efforts were doomed to failure. White neighbors coordinated a powerful campaign against the Crafts, who lost a rigged libel suit. Unable to raise further funds for their school, they were forced to close it in 1878. They remained on the plantation, getting deeper and deeper into debt, until their deaths.[11]

RUNNING A THOUSAND MILES FOR FREEDOM

OR, THE ESCAPE

OF

WILLIAM AND ELLEN CRAFT

FROM SLAVERY.

"Slaves cannot breathe in England: if their lungs
Receive our air, that moment they are free;
They touch our country, and their shackles fall."

COWPER.[12]

LONDON:
WILLIAM TWEEDIE, 337, STRAND.
———
1860.

ELLEN CRAFT, THE FUGITIVE SLAVE.

PREFACE.

HAVING heard while in Slavery that "God made of one blood all nations of men,"[13] and also that the American Declaration of Independence says, that "We hold these truths to be self-evident, that all men are created equal; that they are endowed by their Creator with certain inalienable rights; that among these, are life, liberty, and the pursuit of happiness;" we could not understand by what right we were held as "chattels." Therefore, we felt perfectly justified in undertaking the dangerous and exciting task of "running a thousand miles" in order to obtain those rights which are so vividly set forth in the Declaration.

I beg those who would know the particulars of our journey, to peruse these pages.

This book is not intended as a full history of the life of my wife, nor of myself; but merely as an account of our escape; together with other matter which I hope may be the means of creating in some minds a deeper abhorrence of the sinful and abominable practice of enslaving and brutifying our fellow-creatures.

Without stopping to write a long apology for offering this little volume to the public, I shall commence at once to pursue my simple story.

W. CRAFT.

12, CAMBRIDGE ROAD,
  HAMMERSMITH,
    LONDON.

RUNNING A THOUSAND MILES FOR FREEDOM.

PART I.

"God gave us only over beast, fish, fowl,
Dominion absolute; that right we hold
By his donation. But man over man
He made not lord; such title to himself
Reserving, human left from human free."

MILTON.[14]

MY wife and myself were born in different towns in the State of Georgia, which is one of the principal slave States. It is true, our condition as slaves was not by any means the worst; but the mere idea that we were held as chattels, and deprived of all legal rights—the thought that we had to give up our hard earnings to a tyrant, to enable him to live in idleness and luxury—the thought that we could not call the bones and sinews that God gave us our own: but above all, the fact that another man had the power to tear from our cradle the new-born babe and sell it in the shambles like a brute, and then scourge us if we dared to lift a finger to save it from such a fate, haunted us for years.

But in December, 1848, a plan suggested itself that proved quite successful, and in eight days after it was first thought of we were free from the horrible trammels of slavery, rejoicing and praising God in the glorious sunshine of liberty.

My wife's first master was her father, and her mother his slave, and the latter is still the slave of his widow.

Notwithstanding my wife being of African extraction on her mother's side, she is almost white—in fact, she is so nearly so that the tyrannical old lady to whom she first belonged became so annoyed, at finding her frequently mistaken for a child of the family, that she gave her when eleven years of age to a daughter, as a wedding present.[15] This separated my wife from her mother, and also from several other dear friends. But the incessant cruelty of her old mistress made the change of owners or treatment so desirable, that she did not grumble much at this cruel separation.

It may be remembered that slavery in America is not at all confined to persons of any particular complexion; there are a very large number of slaves as white as any one; but as the evidence of a slave is not admitted in court against a free white person, it is almost impossible for a white child, after having been kidnapped and sold into or reduced to slavery, in a part of the country where it is not known (as often is the case), ever to recover its freedom.

I have myself conversed with several slaves who told me that their parents were white and free; but that they were stolen away from them and sold when quite young. As they could not tell their address, and also as the parents did not know what had become of their lost and dear little ones, of course all traces of each other were gone.

The following facts are sufficient to prove, that he who has the power, and is inhuman enough to trample upon the sacred rights of the weak, cares nothing for race or colour:—

In March, 1818, three ships arrived at New Orleans, bringing several hundred German emigrants from the province of Alsace, on the lower Rhine. Among them were Daniel Muller and his two daughters, Dorothea and Salomé, whose mother had died on the passage. Soon after his arrival, Muller, taking with him his two daughters, both young children, went up the river to Attakapas parish, to work on the plantation of John F. Miller. A few weeks later, his relatives, who had remained at New Orleans, learned that he had died of the fever of the country. They immediately sent for the two girls; but they had disappeared, and the relatives, notwithstanding repeated and persevering inquiries and researches, could find no traces of them. They were at length given up for dead. Dorothea was never again heard of; nor was any thing known of Salomé from 1818 till 1843.

In the summer of that year, Madame Karl, a German woman who had come over in the same ship with the Mullers, was passing through a street in New Orleans, and accidentally saw Salomé in a wine-shop, belonging to Louis Belmonte, by whom she was held as a slave. Madame Karl recognised her at once, and carried her to the house of another German woman, Mrs. Schubert, who was Salomé's cousin and godmother, and who no sooner set eyes on her than, without having any intimation that the discovery had been previously made, she unhesitatingly exclaimed, "My God! here is the long-lost Salomé Muller."

The *Law Reporter,* in its account of this case, says:—

"As many of the German emigrants of 1818 as could be gathered together were brought to the house of Mrs. Schubert, and every one of the number who had any recollection of the little girl upon the passage, or any acquaintance with her father and mother, immediately identified the woman before them as the long-lost Salomé Muller. By all these witnesses, who appeared at the trial, the identity was fully established. The family resemblance in every feature was declared to be so remarkable, that some of the witnesses did not hesitate to say that they should know her among ten thousand; that they were as certain the plaintiff was Salomé Muller, the daughter of Daniel and Dorothea Muller, as of their own existence."

Among the witnesses who appeared in Court was the midwife who had assisted at the birth of Salomé. She testified to the existence of certain peculiar marks upon the body of the child, which were found, exactly as described, by the surgeons who were appointed by the Court to make an examination for the purpose.

There was no trace of African descent in any feature of Salomé Muller. She had long, straight, black hair, hazel eyes, thin lips, and a Roman nose. The complexion of her face and neck was as dark as that of the darkest brunette. It appears, however, that, during the twenty-five years of her servitude, she had been exposed to the sun's rays in the hot climate of Louisiana, with head and neck unsheltered, as is customary with the female slaves, while labouring in the cotton or the sugar field. Those parts of her person which had been shielded from the sun were comparatively white.

Belmonte, the pretended owner of the girl, had obtained possession of her by an act of sale from John F. Miller, the planter in whose service Salomé's father died. This Miller was a man of consideration and substance, owning large sugar estates, and bearing a high reputation for honour and honesty, and for indulgent treatment of his slaves. It was testified on the trial that he had said to Belmonte, a few weeks after the sale of Salomé, "that she was white, and had as much right to her freedom as any one, and was only to be retained in slavery by care and kind treatment." The broker who negotiated the sale from Miller to Belmonte, in 1838, testified in Court that he then thought, and still thought, that the girl was white!

The case was elaborately argued on both sides, but was at length decided in favour of the girl, by the Supreme Court declaring that "she was free and white, and therefore unlawfully held in bondage."

The Rev. George Bourne, of Virginia, in his *Picture of Slavery,* published in 1834, relates the case of a white boy who, at the age of seven, was stolen from his home in Ohio, tanned and stained in such a way that he could not be distinguished from a person of colour, and then sold as a slave in Virginia. At the age of twenty, he made his escape, by running away, and happily succeeded in rejoining his parents.

I have known worthless white people to sell their own free children into slavery; and, as there are good-for-nothing white as well as coloured persons everywhere, no one, perhaps, will wonder at such inhuman transactions: particularly in the Southern States of America, where I believe there is a greater want of humanity and high principle amongst the whites, than among any other civilized people in the world.

I know that those who are not familiar with the working of "the peculiar institution," can scarcely imagine any one so totally devoid of all natural affection as to sell his own offspring into returnless bondage. But Shakspeare, that great observer of human nature, says:—

> "With caution judge of probabilities.
> Things deemed unlikely, e'en impossible,
> Experience often shows us to be true."

My wife's new mistress was decidedly more humane than the majority of her class. My wife has always given her credit for not exposing her to many of the worst features of slavery. For instance, it is a common practice in the slave States for ladies, when angry with their maids, to send them to the calybuce[16] sugar-house, or to some other place established for the purpose of punishing slaves, and have them severely flogged; and I am sorry it is a fact, that the villains to whom those defenceless creatures are sent, not only flog them as they are ordered, but frequently compel them to submit to the greatest indignity. Oh! if there is any one thing under the wide canopy of heaven, horrible enough to stir a man's soul, and to make his very blood boil, it is the thought of his dear wife, his unprotected sister, or his young and virtuous daughters, struggling to save themselves from falling a prey to such demons!

It always appears strange to me that any one who was not born a slave-holder, and steeped to the very core in the demoralizing atmosphere of the South-ern States, can in any way palliate slavery. It is still more surprising to see virtu-ous ladies looking with patience upon, and remaining indifferent to, the existence of a system that exposes nearly two millions of their own sex in the manner I have mentioned, and that too in a professedly free and Christian country. There is, however, great consolation in knowing that God is just, and will not let the oppressor of the weak, and the spoiler of the virtuous, escape unpunished here and hereafter.

I believe a similar retribution to that which destroyed Sodom is hanging over the slaveholders. My sincere prayer is that they may not provoke God, by persisting in a reckless course of wickedness, to pour out his consuming wrath upon them.

I must now return to our history.

My old master had the reputation of being a very humane and Christian man, but he thought nothing of selling my poor old father, and dear aged mother, at separate times, to different persons, to be dragged off never to behold each other again, till summoned to appear before the great tribunal of heaven. But, oh! what a happy meeting it will be on that day for those faithful souls. I say a happy meeting, because I never saw persons more devoted to the service of God than they. But how will the case stand with those reckless traffickers in human flesh and blood, who plunged the poisonous dagger of separation into those lov-ing hearts which God had for so many years closely joined together—nay, sealed as it were with his own hands for the eternal courts of heaven? It is not for me to say what will become of those heartless tyrants. I must leave them in the hands of an all-wise and just God, who will, in his own good time, and in his own way, avenge the wrongs of his oppressed people.

My old master also sold a dear brother and a sister, in the same manner as he did my father and mother. The reason he assigned for disposing of my par-ents, as well as of several other aged slaves, was, that "they were getting old, and would soon become valueless in the market, and therefore he intended to sell off all the old stock, and buy in a young lot." A most disgraceful conclusion for a man to come to, who made such great professions of religion!

This shameful conduct gave me a thorough hatred, not for true Christian-ity, but for slaveholding piety.

My old master, then, wishing to make the most of the rest of his slaves, ap-prenticed a brother and myself out to learn trades: he to a blacksmith, and my-self to a cabinet-maker. If a slave has a good trade, he will let or sell for more than a person without one, and many slaveholders have their slaves taught trades on this account. But before our time expired, my old master wanted money; so he sold my brother, and then mortgaged my sister, a dear girl about fourteen years of age, and myself, then about sixteen, to one of the banks, to get money to speculate in cotton. This we knew nothing of at the moment; but time rolled on, the money became due, my master was unable to meet his payments; so the bank had us placed upon the auction stand and sold to the highest bidder.

My poor sister was sold first: she was knocked down to a planter who resided at some distance in the country. Then I was called upon the stand. While the auctioneer was crying the bids, I saw the man that had purchased my sister getting her into a cart, to take her to his home. I at once asked a slave friend who was standing near the platform, to run and ask the gentleman if he would please to wait till I was sold, in order that I might have an opportunity of bidding her good-bye. He sent me word back that he had some distance to go, and could not wait.

I then turned to the auctioneer, fell upon my knees, and humbly prayed him to let me just step down and bid my last sister farewell. But, instead of granting me this request, he grasped me by the neck, and in a commanding tone of voice, and with a violent oath, exclaimed, "Get up! You can do the wench no good; therefore there is no use in your seeing her."

On rising, I saw the cart in which she sat moving slowly off; and, as she clasped her hands with a grasp that indicated despair, and looked pitifully round towards me, I also saw the large silent tears trickling down her cheeks. She made a farewell bow, and buried her face in her lap. This seemed more than I could bear. It appeared to swell my aching heart to its utmost. But before I could fairly recover, the poor girl was gone;—gone, and I have never had the good fortune to see her from that day to this! Perhaps I should have never heard of her again, had it not been for the untiring efforts of my good old mother, who became free a few years ago by purchase, and, after a great deal of difficulty, found my sister residing with a family in Mississippi. My mother at once wrote to me, informing me of the fact, and requesting me to do something to get her free; and I am happy to say that, partly by lecturing occasionally, and through the sale of an engraving of my wife in the disguise in which she escaped, together with the extreme kindness and generosity of Miss Burdett Coutts, Mr. George Richardson of Plymouth, and a few other friends, I have nearly accomplished this. It would be to me a great and ever-glorious achievement to restore my sister to our dear mother, from whom she was forcibly driven in early life.

I was knocked down to the cashier of the bank to which we were mortgaged,[17] and ordered to return to the cabinet shop where I previously worked.

But the thought of the harsh auctioneer not allowing me to bid my dear sister farewell, sent red-hot indignation darting like lightning through every vein. It quenched my tears, and appeared to set my brain on fire, and made me crave for power to avenge our wrongs! But alas! we were only slaves, and had no legal rights; consequently we were compelled to smother our wounded feelings, and crouch beneath the iron heel of despotism.

I must now give the account of our escape; but, before doing so, it may be well to quote a few passages from the fundamental laws of slavery; in order to give some idea of the legal as well as the social tyranny from which we fled.

According to the law of Louisiana, "A slave is one who is in the power of a master to whom he belongs. The master may sell him, dispose of his person, his industry, and his labour; he can do nothing, possess nothing, nor acquire anything but what must belong to his master."—*Civil Code*, art. 35.

In South Carolina it is expressed in the following language:—"Slaves shall be deemed, sold, taken, reputed and judged in law to be *chattels personal* in the hands of their owners and possessors, and their executors, administrators, and assigns, *to all intents, constructions, and purposes whatsoever.*"—2 *Brevard's Digest,* 229.

The Constitution of Georgia has the following (Art. 4, sec. 12):—"Any person who shall maliciously dismember or deprive a slave of life, shall suffer such punishment as would be inflicted in case the like offence had been committed on a free white person, and on the like proof, except in case of insurrection of such slave, and unless SUCH DEATH SHOULD HAPPEN BY ACCIDENT IN GIVING SUCH SLAVE MODERATE CORRECTION."—*Prince's Digest,* 559.

I have known slaves to be beaten to death, but as they died under "moderate correction," it was quite lawful; and of course the murderers were not interfered with.

"If any slave, who shall be out of the house or plantation where such slave shall live, or shall be usually employed, or without some white person in company with such slave, shall *refuse to submit* to undergo the examination of *any white* person, (let him be ever so drunk or crazy), it shall be lawful for such white person to pursue, apprehend, and moderately correct such slave; and if such slave shall assault and strike such white person, such slave may be *lawfully killed.*"— 2 *Brevard's Digest,* 231.

"Provided always," says the law, "that such striking be not done by the command and in the defence of the person or property of the owner, or other person having the government of such slave; in which case the slave shall be wholly excused."

According to this law, if a slave, by the direction of his overseer, strike a white person who is beating said overseer's pig, "the slave shall be wholly excused." But, should the bondman, of his own accord, fight to defend his wife, or should his terrified daughter instinctively raise her hand and strike the wretch who attempts to violate her chastity, he or she shall, saith the model republican law, suffer death.

From having been myself a slave for nearly twenty-three years, I am quite prepared to say, that the practical working of slavery is worse than the odious laws by which it is governed.

At an early age we were taken by the persons who held us as property to Maçon, the largest town in the interior of the State of Georgia, at which place we became acquainted with each other for several years before our marriage; in fact, our marriage was postponed for some time simply because one of the unjust and worse than Pagan laws under which we lived compelled all children of slave mothers to follow their condition. That is to say, the father of the slave may be the President of the Republic; but if the mother should be a slave at the infant's birth, the poor child is ever legally doomed to the same cruel fate.

It is a common practice for gentlemen (if I may call them such), moving in the highest circles of society, to be the fathers of children by their slaves, whom they can and do sell with the greatest impunity; and the more pious, beautiful, and virtuous the girls are, the greater the price they bring, and that too for the most infamous purposes.

Any man with money (let him be ever such a rough brute), can buy a beautiful and virtuous girl, and force her to live with him in a criminal connexion; and as the law says a slave shall have no higher appeal than the mere will of the master, she cannot escape, unless it be by flight or death.

In endeavouring to reconcile a girl to her fate, the master sometimes says that he would marry her if it was not unlawful.* However, he will always consider her to be his wife, and will treat her as such; and she, on the other hand, may regard him as her lawful husband; and if they have any children, they will be free and well educated.

I am in duty bound to add, that while a great majority of such men care nothing for the happiness of the women with whom they live, nor for the children of whom they are the fathers, there are those to be found, even in that heterogeneous mass of licentious monsters, who are true to their pledges. But as the woman and her children are legally the property of the man, who stands in the anomalous relation to them of husband and father, as well as master, they are liable to be seized and sold for his debts, should he become involved.

There are several cases on record where such persons have been sold and separated for life. I know of some myself, but I have only space to glance at one.

I knew a very humane and wealthy gentleman, that bought a woman, with whom he lived as his wife. They brought up a family of children, among whom were three nearly white, well educated, and beautiful girls.

On the father being suddenly killed it was found that he had not left a will; but, as the family had always heard him say that he had no surviving relatives, they felt that their liberty and property were quite secured to them, and, knowing the insults to which they were exposed, now their protector was no more, they were making preparations to leave for a free State.

But, poor creatures, they were soon sadly undeceived. A villain residing at a distance, hearing of the circumstance, came forward and swore that he was a relative of the deceased; and as this man bore, or assumed, Mr. Slator's name, the case was brought before one of those horrible tribunals, presided over by a second Judge Jeffreys, and calling itself a court of justice, but before whom no coloured person, nor an abolitionist, was ever known to get his full rights.

A verdict was given in favour of the plaintiff, whom the better portion of the community thought had wilfully conspired to cheat the family.

The heartless wretch not only took the ordinary property, but actually had the aged and friendless widow, and all her fatherless children, except Frank, a fine young man about twenty-two years of age, and Mary, a very nice girl, a little younger than her brother, brought to the auction stand and sold to the highest bidder. Mrs. Slator had cash enough, that her husband and master left, to purchase the liberty of herself and children; but on her attempting to do so, the pusillanimous scoundrel, who had robbed them of their freedom, claimed the money as his property; and, poor creature, she had to give it up. According to

---

*It is unlawful in the slave States for any one of purely European descent to intermarry with a person of African extraction; though a white man may live with as many coloured women as he pleases without materially damaging his reputation in Southern society.

law, as will be seen hereafter, a slave cannot own anything. The old lady never recovered from her sad affliction.

At the sale she was brought up first, and after being vulgarly criticised, in the presence of all her distressed family, was sold to a cotton planter, who said he wanted the "proud old critter to go to his plantation, to look after the little woolly heads, while their mammies were working in the field."

When the sale was over, then came the separation, and

"O, deep was the anguish of that slave mother's heart,
When called from her darlings for ever to part;
The poor mourning mother of reason bereft,
Soon ended her sorrows, and sank cold in death."[18]

Antoinette, the flower of the family, a girl who was much beloved by all who knew her, for her Christ-like piety, dignity of manner, as well as her great talents and extreme beauty, was bought by an uneducated and drunken slave-dealer.

I cannot give a more correct description of the scene, when she was called from her brother to the stand, than will be found in the following lines—

"Why stands she near the auction stand?
    That girl so young and fair;
What brings her to this dismal place?
    Why stands she weeping there?

Why does she raise that bitter cry?
    Why hangs her head with shame,
As now the auctioneer's rough voice
    So rudely calls her name!

But see! she grasps a manly hand,
    And in a voice so low,
As scarcely to be heard, she says,
    "My brother, must I go?"

A moment's pause: then, midst a wail
    Of agonizing woe,
His answer falls upon the ear,—
    "Yes, sister, you must go!

No longer can my arm defend,
    No longer can I save
My sister from the horrid fate
    That waits her as a SLAVE!"

Blush, Christian, blush! for e'en the dark
    Untutored heathen see
Thy inconsistency, and lo!
    They scorn thy God, and thee![19]

The low trader said to a kind lady who wished to purchase Antoinette out of his hands, "I reckon I'll not sell the smart critter for ten thousand dollars; I always wanted her for my own use." The lady, wishing to remonstrate with him, commenced by saying, "You should remember, Sir, that there is a just God." Hoskens not understanding Mrs. Huston, interrupted her by saying, "I does, and guess its monstrous kind an' him to send such likely niggers for our convenience." Mrs. Huston finding that a long course of reckless wickedness, drunkenness, and vice, had destroyed in Hoskens every noble impulse, left him.

Antoinette, poor girl, also seeing that there was no help for her, became frantic. I can never forget her cries of despair, when Hoskens gave the order for her to be taken to his house, and locked in an upper room. On Hoskens entering the apartment, in a state of intoxication, a fearful struggle ensued. The brave Antoinette broke loose from him, pitched herself head foremost through the window, and fell upon the pavement below.

Her bruised but unpolluted body was soon picked up—restoratives brought—doctor called in; but, alas! it was too late: her pure and noble spirit had fled away to be at rest in those realms of endless bliss, "where the wicked cease from troubling, and the weary are at rest."[20]

Antoinette like many other noble women who are deprived of liberty, still

> "Holds something sacred, something undefiled;
> Some pledge and keepsake of their higher nature.
> And, like the diamond in the dark, retains
> Some quenchless gleam of the celestial light."[21]

On Hoskens fully realizing the fact that his victim was no more, he exclaimed "By thunder I am a used-up man!" The sudden disappointment, and the loss of two thousand dollars, was more than he could endure: so he drank more than ever, and in a short time died, raving mad with *delirium tremens.*

The villain Slator said to Mrs. Huston, the kind lady who endeavoured to purchase Antoinette from Hoskens, "Nobody needn't talk to me 'bout buying them ar likely niggers, for I'm not going to sell em." "But Mary is rather delicate," said Mrs. Huston, "and, being unaccustomed to hard work, cannot do you much service on a plantation." "I don't want her for the field," replied Slator, "but for another purpose." Mrs. Huston understood what this meant, and instantly exclaimed, "Oh, but she is your cousin!" "The devil she is!" said Slator; and added, "Do you mean to insult me Madam, by saying that I am related to niggers?" "No," replied Mrs. Huston, "I do not wish to offend you, Sir. But wasn't Mr. Slator, Mary's father, your uncle?" "Yes, I calculate he was," said Slator; "but I want you and everybody to understand that I'm no kin to his niggers." "Oh, very well," said Mrs. Huston; adding, "Now what will you take for the poor girl?" "Nothin'," he replied; "for, as I said before, I'm not goin' to sell, so you needn't trouble yourself no more. If the critter behaves herself, I'll do as well by her as any man."

Slator spoke up boldly, but his manner and sheepish look clearly indicated that

> "His heart within him was at strife
>   With such accursed gains;
> For he knew whose passions gave her life,
>   Whose blood ran in her veins."

> "The monster led her from the door,
>   He led her by the hand,
> To be his slave and paramour
>   In a strange and distant land!"[22]

Poor Frank and his sister were handcuffed together, and confined in prison. Their dear little twin brother and sister were sold, and taken where they knew not. But it often happens that misfortune causes those whom we counted dearest to shrink away; while it makes friends of those whom we least expected to take any interest in our affairs. Among the latter class Frank found two comparatively new but faithful friends to watch the gloomy paths of the unhappy little twins.

In a day or two after the sale, Slator had two fast horses put to a large light van, and placed in it a good many small but valuable things belonging to the distressed family. He also took with him Frank and Mary, as well as all the money for the spoil; and after treating all his low friends and bystanders, and drinking deeply himself, he started in high glee for his home in South Carolina. But they had not proceeded many miles, before Frank and his sister discovered that Slator was too drunk to drive. But he, like most tipsy men, thought he was all right; and as he had with him some of the ruined family's best brandy and wine, such as he had not been accustomed to, and being a thirsty soul, he drank till the reins fell from his fingers, and in attempting to catch them he tumbled out of the vehicle, and was unable to get up. Frank and Mary there and then contrived a plan by which to escape. As they were still handcuffed by one wrist each, they alighted, took from the drunken assassin's pocket the key, undid the iron bracelets, and placed them upon Slator, who was better fitted to wear such ornaments. As the demon lay unconscious of what was taking place, Frank and Mary took from him the large sum of money that was realized at the sale, as well as that which Slator had so very meanly obtained from their poor mother. They then dragged him into the woods, tied him to a tree, and left the inebriated robber to shift for himself, while they made good their escape to Savannah. The fugitives being white, of course no one suspected that they were slaves.

Slator was not able to call any one to his rescue till late the next day; and as there were no railroads in that part of the country at that time, it was not until late the following day that Slator was able to get a party to join him for the chase. A person informed Slator that he had met a man and woman, in a trap, answering to the description of those whom he had lost, driving furiously towards Savannah. So Slator and several slavehunters on horseback started off in full tilt, with their bloodhounds, in pursuit of Frank and Mary.

On arriving at Savannah, the hunters found that the fugitives had sold the horses and trap, and embarked as free white persons, for New York. Slator's disappointment and rascality so preyed upon his base mind, that he, like Judas, went and hanged himself.

As soon as Frank and Mary were safe, they endeavoured to redeem their good mother. But, alas! she was gone; she had passed on to the realm of spirit life.

In due time Frank learned from his friends in Georgia where his little brother and sister dwelt. So he wrote at once to purchase them, but the persons with whom they lived would not sell them. After failing in several attempts to buy them, Frank cultivated large whiskers and moustachios, cut off his hair, put on a wig and glasses, and went down as a white man, and stopped in the neighbourhood where his sister was; and after seeing her and also his little brother, arrangements were made for them to meet at a particular place on a Sunday, which they did, and got safely off.

I saw Frank myself, when he came for the little twins. Though I was then quite a lad, I well remember being highly delighted by hearing him tell how nicely he and Mary had served Slator.

Frank had so completely disguised or changed his appearance that his little sister did not know him, and would not speak till he showed their mother's likeness; the sight of which melted her to tears,—for she knew the face. Frank might have said to her

> "'O, Emma! O, my sister, speak to me!
> Dost thou not know me, that I am thy brother?
> Come to me, little Emma, thou shalt dwell
> With me henceforth, and know no care or want.'
> Emma was silent for a space, as if
> 'Twere hard to summon up a human voice."

Frank and Mary's mother was my wife's own dear aunt.

After this great diversion from our narrative, which I hope dear reader, you will excuse, I shall return at once to it.

My wife was torn from her mother's embrace in childhood, and taken to a distant part of the country. She had seen so many other children separated from their parents in this cruel manner, that the mere thought of her ever becoming the mother of a child, to linger out a miserable existence under the wretched system of American slavery, appeared to fill her very soul with horror; and as she had taken what I felt to be an important view of her condition, I did not, at first, press the marriage, but agreed to assist her in trying to devise some plan by which we might escape from our unhappy condition, and then be married.

We thought of plan after plan, but they all seemed crowded with insurmountable difficulties. We knew it was unlawful for any public conveyance to take us as passengers, without our master's consent. We were also perfectly aware of the startling fact, that had we left without this consent the professional slave-hunters would have soon had their ferocious bloodhounds baying on our track, and in a short time we should have been dragged back to slavery, not to fill the more favourable situations which we had just left, but to be separated for life, and put to the very meanest and most laborious drudgery; or else have been tortured to death as examples, in order to strike terror into the hearts of others, and thereby prevent them from even attempting to escape from their cruel taskmasters. It is a fact worthy of remark, that nothing seems to give the slave-holders so much pleasure as the catching and torturing of fugitives. They had much rather take the keen and poisonous lash, and with it cut their poor trembling victims to atoms, than allow one of them to escape to a free country, and expose the infamous system from which he fled.

The greatest excitement prevails at a slave-hunt. The slaveholders and their hired ruffians appear to take more pleasure in this inhuman pursuit than English sportsmen do in chasing a fox or a stag. Therefore, knowing what we should have been compelled to suffer, if caught and taken back, we were more than anxious to hit upon a plan that would lead us safely to a land of liberty.

But, after puzzling our brains for years, we were reluctantly driven to the sad conclusion, that it was almost impossible to escape from slavery in Georgia, and travel 1,000 miles across the slave States. We therefore resolved to get the consent of our owners, be married, settle down in slavery, and endeavour to make ourselves as comfortable as possible under that system; but at the same time ever to keep our dim eyes steadily fixed upon the glimmering hope of liberty, and earnestly pray God mercifully to assist us to escape from our unjust thraldom.

We were married, and prayed and toiled on till December, 1848, at which time (as I have stated) a plan suggested itself that proved quite successful, and in eight days after it was first thought of we were free from the horrible trammels of slavery, and glorifying God who had brought us safely out of a land of bondage.

Knowing that slaveholders have the privilege of taking their slaves to any part of the country they think proper, it occurred to me that, as my wife was nearly white, I might get her to disguise herself as an invalid gentleman, and assume to be my master, while I could attend as his slave, and that in this manner we might effect our escape.[23] After I thought of the plan, I suggested it to my wife, but at first she shrank from the idea. She thought it was almost impossible for her to assume that disguise, and travel a distance of 1,000 miles across the slave States. However, on the other hand, she also thought of her condition. She saw that the laws under which we lived did not recognize her to be a woman, but a mere chattel, to be bought and sold, or otherwise dealt with as her owner might see fit. Therefore the more she contemplated her helpless condition, the more anxious she was to escape from it. So she said, "I think it is almost too much for us to undertake; however, I feel that God is on our side, and with his assistance, notwithstanding all the difficulties, we shall be able to succeed. Therefore, if you will purchase the disguise, I will try to carry out the plan."

But after I concluded to purchase the disguise, I was afraid to go to any one to ask him to sell me the articles. It is unlawful in Georgia for a white man to trade with slaves without the master's consent. But, notwithstanding this, many persons will sell a slave any article that he can get the money to buy. Not that they sympathize with the slave, but merely because his testimony is not admitted in court against a free white person.

Therefore, with little difficulty I went to different parts of the town, at odd times, and purchased things piece by piece, (except the trowsers which she found necessary to make,) and took them home to the house where my wife resided. She being a ladies' maid, and a favourite slave in the family, was allowed a little room to herself; and amongst other pieces of furniture which I had made in my overtime, was a chest of drawers; so when I took the articles home, she locked them up carefully in these drawers. No one about the premises knew that she had anything of the kind. So when we fancied we had everything ready the time was fixed for the flight. But we knew it would not do to start off without first getting our master's consent to be away for a few days. Had we left without this, they would soon have had us back into slavery, and probably we should never have got another fair opportunity of even attempting to escape.

Some of the best slaveholders will sometimes give their favourite slaves a few days' holiday at Christmas time; so, after no little amount of perseverance on my wife's part, she obtained a pass from her mistress, allowing her to be away for a few days. The cabinet-maker with whom I worked gave me a similar paper, but said that he needed my services very much, and wished me to return as soon as the time granted was up. I thanked him kindly; but somehow I have not been able to make it convenient to return yet; and, as the free air of good old England agrees so well with my wife and our dear little ones, as well as with myself, it is not at all likely we shall return at present to the "peculiar institution" of chains and stripes.

On reaching my wife's cottage she handed me her pass, and I showed mine, but at that time neither of us were able to read them. It is not only unlawful for slaves to be taught to read, but in some of the States there are heavy penalties attached, such as fines and imprisonment, which will be vigorously enforced upon any one who is humane enough to violate the so-called law.

The following case will serve to show how persons are treated in the most enlightened slaveholding community.

"INDICTMENT.

COMMONWEALTH OF VIRGINIA, NORFOLK COUNTY, *ss.* } *In the Circuit Court.* The Grand Jurors empannelled and sworn to inquire of offences committed in the body of the said County on their oath present, that Margaret Douglass, being an evil disposed person, not having the fear of God before her eyes, but moved and instigated by the devil, wickedly, maliciously, and feloniously, on the fourth day of July, in the year of our Lord one thousand eight hundred and fifty-four, at Norfolk, in said County, did teach a certain black girl named Kate to read in the Bible, to the great displeasure of Almighty God, to the pernicious example of others in like case offending, contrary to the form of the statute in such case made and provided, and against the peace and dignity of the Commonwealth of Virginia. "VICTOR VAGABOND, *Prosecuting Attorney.*"

"On this indictment Mrs. Douglass was arraigned as a necessary matter of form, tried, found guilty of course; and Judge Scalawag, before whom she was tried, having consulted with Dr. Adams, ordered the sheriff to place Mrs. Douglass in the prisoner's box, when he addressed her as follows: 'Margaret Douglass, stand up. You are guilty of one of the vilest crimes that ever disgraced society; and the jury have found you so. You have taught a slave girl to read in the Bible. No enlightened society can exist where such offences go unpunished. The Court, in your case, do not feel for you one solitary ray of sympathy, and they will inflict on you the utmost penalty of the law. In any other civilized country you would have paid the forfeit of your crime with your life, and the Court have only to regret that such is not the law in this country. The sentence for your offence is, that you be imprisoned one month in the county jail, and that you pay the costs of this prosecution. Sheriff, remove the prisoner to jail.' On the publication of these proceedings, the Doctors of Divinity preached each a sermon on the necessity of obeying the laws; the *New York Observer* noticed with much pious gladness a revival of religion on Dr. Smith's plantation in Georgia, among his slaves; while the *Journal of Commerce* commended this political preaching of the Doctors of Divinity because it favoured slavery. Let us do nothing to offend our Southern brethren."

However, at first, we were highly delighted at the idea of having gained permission to be absent for a few days; but when the thought flashed across my wife's mind, that it was customary for travellers to register their names in the visitors' book at hotels, as well as in the clearance or Custom-house book at Charleston, South Carolina—it made our spirits droop within us.

So, while sitting in our little room upon the verge of despair, all at once my wife raised her head, and with a smile upon her face, which was a moment before bathed in tears, said, "I think I have it!" I asked what it was. She said, "I think I can make a poultice and bind up my right hand in a sling, and with propriety ask the officers to register my name for me." I thought that would do.

It then occurred to her that the smoothness of her face might betray her; so she decided to make another poultice, and put it in a white handkerchief to be worn under the chin, up the cheeks, and to tie over the head. This nearly hid the expression of the countenance, as well as the beardless chin.

The poultice is left off in the engraving, because the likeness could not have been taken well with it on.

My wife, knowing that she would be thrown a good deal into the company of gentlemen, fancied that she could get on better if she had something to go over the eyes; so I went to a shop and bought a pair of green spectacles. This was in the evening.

We sat up all night discussing the plan, and making preparations. Just before the time arrived, in the morning, for us to leave, I cut off my wife's hair square at the back of the head, and got her to dress in the disguise and stand out on the floor. I found that she made a most respectable looking gentleman.

My wife had no ambition whatever to assume this disguise, and would not have done so had it been possible to have obtained our liberty by more simple means; but we knew it was not customary in the South for ladies to travel with male servants; and therefore, notwithstanding my wife's fair complexion, it would have been a very difficult task for her to have come off as a free white lady, with me as her slave; in fact, her not being able to write would have made this quite impossible. We knew that no public conveyance would take us, or any other slave, as a passenger, without our master's consent. This consent could never be obtained to pass into a free State. My wife's being muffled in the poultices, &c., furnished a plausible excuse for avoiding general conversation, of which most Yankee travellers are passionately fond.

There are a large number of free negroes residing in the southern States; but in Georgia (and I believe in all the slave States,) every coloured person's complexion is *primâ facie* evidence of his being a slave; and the lowest villain in the country, should he be a white man, has the legal power to arrest, and question, in the most inquisitorial and insulting manner, any coloured person, male or female, that he may find at large, particularly at night and on Sundays, without a written pass, signed by the master or some one in authority; or stamped free papers, certifying that the person is the rightful owner of himself.

If the coloured person refuses to answer questions put to him, he may be beaten, and his defending himself against this attack makes him an outlaw, and if he be killed on the spot, the murderer will be exempted from all blame; but after the coloured person has answered the questions put to him, in a most humble and pointed manner, he may then be taken to prison; and should it turn out, after further examination, that he was caught where he had no permission or legal right to be, and that he has not given what they term a satisfactory account of himself, the master will have to pay a fine. On his refusing to do this, the poor slave may be legally and severely flogged by public officers. Should the prisoner prove to be a free man, he is most likely to be both whipped and fined.

The great majority of slaveholders hate this class of persons with a hatred that can only be equalled by the condemned spirits of the infernal regions. They have no mercy upon, nor sympathy for, any negro whom they cannot enslave. They say that God made the black man to be a slave for the white, and act as though they really believed that all free persons of colour are in open rebellion to a direct command from heaven, and that they (the whites) are God's chosen agents to pour out upon them unlimited vengeance. For instance, a Bill has been introduced in the Tennessee Legislature to prevent free negroes from travelling on the railroads in that State. It has passed the first reading. The bill provides that the President who shall permit a free negro to travel on any road within the jurisdiction of the State under his supervision shall pay a fine of 500 dollars; any conductor permitting a violation of the Act shall pay 250 dollars; provided such free negro is not under the control of a free white citizen of Tennessee, who will vouch for the character of said free negro in a penal bond of one thousand dollars. The State of Arkansas has passed a law to banish all free negroes from its bounds, and it came into effect on the 1st day of January, 1860. Every free negro found there after that date will be liable to be sold into slavery, the crime of freedom being unpardonable. The Missouri Senate has before it a bill providing that all free negroes above the age of eighteen years who shall be found in the State after September, 1860, shall be sold into slavery; and that all such negroes as shall enter the State after September, 1861, and remain there twenty-four hours, shall also be sold into slavery for ever. Mississippi, Kentucky, and Georgia, and in fact, I believe, all the slave States, are legislating in the same manner. Thus the slaveholders make it almost impossible for free persons of colour to get out of the slave States, in order that they may sell them into slavery if they don't go. If no white persons travelled upon railroads except those who could get some one to vouch for their character in a penal bond of one thousand dollars, the railroad companies would soon go to the "wall." Such mean legislation is too low for comment; therefore I leave the villainous acts to speak for themselves.

But the Dred Scott decision is the crowning act of infamous Yankee legislation. The Supreme Court, the highest tribunal of the Republic, composed of nine Judge Jeffries's, chosen both from the free and slave States, has decided that no coloured person, or persons of African extraction, can ever become a citizen of the United States, or have any rights which white men are bound to respect. That is to say, in the opinion of this Court, robbery, rape, and murder are not crimes when committed by a white upon a coloured person.[24]

Judges who will sneak from their high and honourable position down into the lowest depths of human depravity, and scrape up a decision like this, are wholly unworthy the confidence of any people. I believe such men would, if they had the power, and were it to their temporal interest, sell their country's independence, and barter away every man's birthright for a mess of pottage. Well may Thomas Campbell say—

> United States, your banner wears,
>   Two emblems,—one of fame,
> Alas, the other that it bears
>   Reminds us of your shame!
> The white man's liberty in types
>   Stands blazoned by your stars;
> But what's the meaning of your stripes?
>   They mean your Negro-scars.[25]

When the time had arrived for us to start, we blew out the lights, knelt down, and prayed to our Heavenly Father mercifully to assist us, as he did his people of old, to escape from cruel bondage; and we shall ever feel that God heard and answered our prayer. Had we not been sustained by a kind, and I sometimes think special, providence, we could never have overcome the mountainous difficulties which I am now about to describe.

After this we rose and stood for a few moments in breathless silence,—we were afraid that some one might have been about the cottage listening and watching our movements. So I took my wife by the hand, stepped softly to the door, raised the latch, drew it open, and peeped out. Though there were trees all around the house, yet the foliage scarcely moved; in fact, everything appeared to be as still as death. I then whispered to my wife, "Come my dear, let us make a desperate leap for liberty!" But poor thing, she shrank back, in a state of trepidation. I turned and asked what was the matter; she made no reply, but burst into violent sobs, and threw her head upon my breast. This appeared to touch my very heart, it caused me to enter into her feelings more fully than ever. We both saw the many mountainous difficulties that rose one after the other before our view, and knew far too well what our sad fate would have been, were we caught and forced back into our slavish den. Therefore on my wife's fully realizing the solemn fact that we had to take our lives, as it were, in our hands, and contest every inch of the thousand miles of slave territory over which we had to pass, it made her heart almost sink within her, and, had I known them at that time, I would have repeated the following encouraging lines, which may not be out of place here—

"The hill, though high, I covet to ascend,
The *difficulty will not me offend;*
For I perceive the way to life lies here:
Come, pluck up heart, let's neither faint nor fear;
Better, though difficult, the right way to go,—
Than wrong, though easy, where the end is woe."[26]

However, the sobbing was soon over, and after a few moments of silent prayer she recovered her self-possession, and said, "Come, William, it is getting late, so now let us venture upon our perilous journey."

We then opened the door, and stepped as softly out as "moonlight upon the water." I locked the door with my own key, which I now have before me, and tiptoed across the yard into the street. I say tiptoed, because we were like persons near a tottering avalanche, afraid to move, or even breathe freely, for fear the sleeping tyrants should be aroused, and come down upon us with double vengeance, for daring to attempt to escape in the manner which we contemplated.

We shook hands, said farewell, and started in different directions for the railway station. I took the nearest possible way to the train, for fear I should be recognized by some one, and got into the negro car in which I knew I should have to ride; but my *master* (as I will now call my wife) took a longer way round, and only arrived there with the bulk of the passengers. He obtained a ticket for himself and one for his slave to Savannah, the first port, which was about two hundred miles off. My master then had the luggage stowed away, and stepped into one of the best carriages.

But just before the train moved off I peeped through the window, and, to my great astonishment, I saw the cabinet-maker with whom I had worked so long, on the platform. He stepped up to the ticket-seller, and asked some question, and then commenced looking rapidly through the passengers, and into the carriages. Fully believing that we were caught, I shrank into a corner, turned my face from the door, and expected in a moment to be dragged out. The cabinet-maker looked into my master's carriage, but did not know him in his new attire, and, as God would have it, before he reached mine the bell rang, and the train moved off.

I have heard since that the cabinet-maker had a presentiment that we were about to "make tracks for parts unknown;" but, not seeing me, his suspicions vanished, until he received the startling intelligence that we had arrived safely in a free State.

As soon as the train had left the platform, my master looked round in the carriage, and was terror-stricken to find a Mr. Cray—an old friend of my wife's master, who dined with the family the day before, and knew my wife from childhood—sitting on the same seat.

The doors of the American railway carriages are at the ends. The passengers walk up the aisle, and take seats on either side; and as my master was engaged in looking out of the window, he did not see who came in.

My master's first impression, after seeing Mr. Cray, was, that he was there for the purpose of securing him. However, my master thought it was not wise to give any information respecting himself, and for fear that Mr. Cray might draw him into conversation and recognise his voice, my master resolved to feign deafness as the only means of self-defence.

After a little while, Mr. Cray said to my master, "It is a very fine morning, sir." The latter took no notice, but kept looking out of the window. Mr. Cray soon repeated this remark, in a little louder tone, but my master remained as before. This indifference attracted the attention of the passengers near, one of whom laughed out. This, I suppose, annoyed the old gentleman; so he said, "I will make him hear;" and in a loud tone of voice repeated, "It is a very fine morning, sir."

My master turned his head, and with a polite bow said, "Yes," and commenced looking out of the window again.

One of the gentlemen remarked that it was a very great deprivation to be deaf. "Yes," replied Mr. Cray, "and I shall not trouble that fellow any more." This enabled my master to breathe a little easier, and to feel that Mr. Cray was not his pursuer after all.

The gentlemen then turned the conversation upon the three great topics of discussion in first-class circles in Georgia, namely, Niggers, Cotton, and the Abolitionists.

My master had often heard of abolitionists, but in such a connection as to cause him to think that they were a fearful kind of wild animal. But he was highly delighted to learn, from the gentlemen's conversation, that the abolitionists were persons who were opposed to oppression; and therefore, in his opinion, not the lowest, but the very highest, of God's creatures.

Without the slightest objection on my master's part, the gentlemen left the carriage at Gordon, for Milledgeville (the capital of the State).

We arrived at Savannah early in the evening, and got into an omnibus, which stopped at the hotel for the passengers to take tea. I stepped into the house and brought my master something on a tray to the omnibus, which took us in due time to the steamer, which was bound for Charleston, South Carolina.

Soon after going on board, my master turned in; and as the captain and some of the passengers seemed to think this strange, and also questioned me respecting him, my master thought I had better get out the flannels and opodeldoc[27] which we had prepared for the rheumatism, warm them quickly by the stove in the gentleman's saloon, and bring them to his berth. We did this as an excuse for my master's retiring to bed so early.

While at the stove one of the passengers said to me, "Buck, what have you got there?" "Opodeldoc, sir," I replied. "I should think it's opo*devil*," said a lanky swell, who was leaning back in a chair with his heels upon the back of another, and chewing tobacco as if for a wager; "it stinks enough to kill or cure twenty men. Away with it, or I reckon I will throw it overboard!"

It was by this time warm enough, so I took it to my master's berth, remained there a little while, and then went on deck and asked the steward where

I was to sleep. He said there was no place provided for coloured passengers, whether slave or free. So I paced the deck till a late hour, then mounted some cotton bags, in a warm place near the funnel, sat there till morning, and then went and assisted my master to get ready for breakfast.

He was seated at the right hand of the captain, who, together with all the passengers, inquired very kindly after his health. As my master had one hand in a sling, it was my duty to carve his food. But when I went out the captain said, "You have a very attentive boy, sir; but you had better watch him like a hawk when you get on to the North. He seems all very well here, but he may act quite differently there. I know several gentlemen who have lost their valuable niggers among them d—d cut-throat abolitionists."

Before my master could speak, a rough slavedealer, who was sitting opposite, with both elbows on the table, and with a large piece of broiled fowl in his fingers, shook his head with emphasis, and in a deep Yankee tone, forced through his crowded mouth the words, "Sound doctrine, captain, very sound." He then dropped the chicken into the plate, leant back, placed his thumbs in the armholes of his fancy waistcoat, and continued, "I would not take a nigger to the North under no consideration. I have had a deal to do with niggers in my time, but I never saw one who ever had his heel upon free soil that was worth a d—n." "Now stranger," addressing my master, "if you have made up your mind to sell that ere nigger, I am your man; just mention your price, and if it isn't out of the way, I will pay for him on this board with hard silver dollars." This hard-featured, bristly-bearded, wire-headed, red-eyed monster, staring at my master as the serpent did at Eve, said, "What do you say, stranger?" He replied, "I don't wish to sell, sir; I cannot get on well without him."

"You will have to get on without him if you take him to the North," continued this man; "for I can tell ye, stranger, as a friend, I am an older cove[28] than you, I have seen lots of this ere world, and I reckon I have had more dealings with niggers than any man living or dead. I was once employed by General Wade Hampton,[29] for ten years, in doing nothing but breaking 'em in; and everybody knows that the General would not have a man that didn't understand his business. So I tell ye, stranger, again, you had better sell, and let me take him down to Orleans. He will do you no good if you take him across Mason's and Dixon's line; he is a keen nigger, and I can see from the cut of his eye that he is certain to run away." My master said, "I think not, sir; I have great confidence in his fidelity." "Fidevil," indignantly said the dealer, as his fist came down upon the edge of the saucer and upset a cup of hot coffee in a gentleman's lap. (As the scalded man jumped up the trader quietly said, "Don't disturb yourself, neighbour; accidents will happen in the best of families.") "It always makes me mad to hear a man talking about fidelity in niggers. There isn't a d—d one on 'em who wouldn't cut sticks,[30] if he had half a chance."

By this time we were near Charleston; my master thanked the captain for his advice, and they all withdrew and went on deck, where the trader fancied he became quite eloquent. He drew a crowd around him, and with emphasis said, "Cap'en, if I was the President of this mighty United States of America, the greatest and freest country under the whole univarse, I would never let no man, I don't care who he is, take a nigger into the North and bring him back here, filled to the brim, as he is sure to be, with d—d abolition vices, to taint all quiet niggers with the hellish spirit of running away. These air, cap'en, my flat-footed, every day, right up and down sentiments, and as this is a free country, cap'en, I don't care who hears 'em; for I am a Southern man, every inch on me to the backbone." "Good!" said an insignificant-looking individual of the slave-dealer stamp. "Three cheers for John C. Calhoun and the whole fair sunny South!" added the trader. So off went their hats, and out burst a terrific roar of irregular but continued cheering. My master took no more notice of the dealer. He merely said to the captain that the air on deck was too keen for him, and he would therefore return to the cabin.

While the trader was in the zenith of his eloquence, he might as well have said, as one of his kith did, at a great Filibustering[31] meeting, that "When the great American Eagle gets one of his mighty claws upon Canada and the other into South America, and his glorious and starry wings of liberty extending from the Atlantic to the Pacific, oh! then, where will England be, ye gentlemen? I tell ye, she will only serve as a pocket-handkerchief for Jonathan[32] to wipe his nose with."

On my master entering the cabin he found at the breakfast-table a young southern military officer, with whom he had travelled some distance the previous day.

After passing the usual compliments the conversation turned upon the old subject,—niggers.

The officer, who was also travelling with a manservant, said to my master, "You will excuse me, Sir, for saying I think you are very likely to spoil your boy by saying 'thank you' to him. I assure you, sir, nothing spoils a slave so soon as saying, 'thank you' and 'if you please' to him. The only way to make a nigger toe the mark, and to keep him in his place, is to storm at him like thunder, and keep him trembling like a leaf. Don't you see, when I speak to my Ned, he darts like lightning; and if he didn't I'd skin him."

Just then the poor dejected slave came in, and the officer swore at him fearfully, merely to teach my master what he called the proper way to treat me.

After he had gone out to get his master's luggage ready, the officer said, "That is the way to speak to them. If every nigger was drilled in this manner, they would be as humble as dogs, and never dare to run away."

The gentleman urged my master not to go to the North for the restoration of his health, but to visit the Warm Springs in Arkansas.

My master said, he thought the air of Philadelphia would suit his complaint best; and, not only so, he thought he could get better advice there.

The boat had now reached the wharf. The officer wished my master a safe and pleasant journey, and left the saloon.

There were a large number of persons on the quay waiting the arrival of the steamer: but we were afraid to venture out for fear that some one might recognize me; or that they had heard that we were gone, and had telegraphed to have us stopped. However, after remaining in the cabin till all the other passengers were gone, we had our luggage placed on a fly, and I took my master by the arm, and with a little difficulty he hobbled on shore, got in and drove off to the best hotel, which John C. Calhoun,[33] and all the other great southern fire-eating statesmen, made their head-quarters while in Charleston.

On arriving at the house the landlord ran out and opened the door: but judging, from the poultices and green glasses, that my master was an invalid, he took him very tenderly by one arm and ordered his man to take the other.

My master then eased himself out, and with their assistance found no trouble in getting up the steps into the hotel. The proprietor made me stand on one side, while he paid my master the attention and homage he thought a gentleman of his high position merited.

My master asked for a bed-room. The servant was ordered to show a good one, into which we helped him. The servant returned. My master then handed me the bandages, I took them downstairs in great haste, and told the landlord my master wanted two hot poultices as quickly as possible. He rang the bell, the servant came in, to whom he said, "Run to the kitchen and tell the cook to make two hot poultices right off, for there is a gentleman upstairs very badly off indeed!"

In a few minutes the smoking poultices were brought in. I placed them in white handkerchiefs, and hurried upstairs, went into my master's apartment, shut the door, and laid them on the mantel-piece. As he was alone for a little while, he thought he could rest a great deal better with the poultices off. However, it was necessary to have them to complete the remainder of the journey. I then ordered dinner, and took my master's boots out to polish them. While doing so I entered into conversation with one of the slaves. I may state here, that on the sea-coast of South Carolina and Georgia the slaves speak worse English than in any other part of the country. This is owing to the frequent importation, or smuggling in, of Africans, who mingle with the natives. Consequently the language cannot properly be called English or African, but a corruption of the two.

The shrewd son of African parents to whom I referred said to me, "Say, brudder, way you come from, and which side you goin day wid dat ar little don up buckra" (white man)?

I replied, "To Philadelphia."

"What!" he exclaimed, with astonishment, "to Philumadelphy?"

"Yes," I said.

"By squash! I wish I was going wid you! I hears um say dat dare's no slaves way over in dem parts; is um so?"

I quietly said, "I have heard the same thing."

"Well," continued he, as he threw down the boot and brush, and, placing his hands in his pockets, strutted across the floor with an air of independence— "Gorra Mighty, dem is de parts for Pompey; and I hope when you get dare you will stay, and nebber follow dat buckra back to dis hot quarter no more, let him be eber so good."

I thanked him; and just as I took the boots up and started off, he caught my hand between his two, and gave it a hearty shake, and, with tears streaming down his cheeks, said:—

"God bless you, broder, and may de Lord be wid you. When you gets de freedom, and sitin under your own wine and fig-tree, don't forget to pray for poor Pompey."

I was afraid to say much to him, but I shall never forget his earnest request, nor fail to do what little I can to release the millions of unhappy bondmen, of whom he was one.

At the proper time my master had the poultices placed on, came down, and seated himself at a table in a very brilliant dining-room, to have his dinner. I had to have something at the same time, in order to be ready for the boat; so they gave me my dinner in an old broken plate, with a rusty knife and fork, and said, "Here, boy, you go in the kitchen." I took it and went out, but did not stay more than a few minutes, because I was in a great hurry to get back to see how the invalid was getting on. On arriving I found two or three servants waiting on him; but as he did not feel able to make a very hearty dinner, he soon finished, paid the bill, and gave the servants each a trifle, which caused one of them to say to me, "Your massa is a big bug"—meaning a gentleman of distinction—"he is the greatest gentleman dat has been dis way for dis six months." I said, "Yes, he is some pumpkins," meaning the same as "big bug."

When we left Maçon, it was our intention to take a steamer at Charleston through to Philadelphia; but on arriving there we found that the vessels did not run during the winter, and I have no doubt it was well for us they did not; for on the very last voyage the steamer made that we intended to go by, a fugitive was discovered secreted on board, and sent back to slavery. However, as we had also heard of the Overland Mail Route, we were all right. So I ordered a fly to the door, had the luggage placed on; we got in, and drove down to the Custom-house Office, which was near the wharf where we had to obtain tickets, to take a steamer for Wilmington, North Carolina. When we reached the building, I helped my master into the office, which was crowded with passengers. He asked for a ticket for himself and one for his slave to Philadelphia. This caused the principal officer—a very mean-looking, cheese-coloured fellow, who was sitting there—to look up at us very suspiciously, and in a fierce tone of voice he said to me, "Boy, do you belong to that gentleman?" I quickly replied, "Yes, sir" (which was quite correct). The tickets were handed out, and as my master was paying for them the chief man said to him, "I wish you to register your name here, sir, and also the name of your nigger, and pay a dollar duty on him."

My master paid the dollar, and pointing to the hand that was in the poultice, requested the officer to register his name for him. This seemed to offend the "high-bred" South Carolinian. He jumped up, shaking his head; and, cramming his hands almost through the bottom of his trousers pockets, with a slave-bullying air, said, "I shan't do it."

This attracted the attention of all the passengers. Just then the young military officer with whom my master travelled and conversed on the steamer from Savannah stepped in, somewhat the worse for brandy; he shook hands with my master, and pretended to know all about him. He said, "I know his kin (friends) like a book;" and as the officer was known in Charleston, and was going to stop there with friends, the recognition was very much in my master's favour.

The captain of the steamer, a good-looking jovial fellow, seeing that the gentleman appeared to know my master, and perhaps not wishing to lose us as passengers, said in an off-hand sailor-like manner, "I will register the gentleman's name, and take the responsibility upon myself." He asked my master's name. He said, "William Johnson." The names were put down, I think, "Mr. Johnson and slave." The captain said, "It's all right now, Mr. Johnson." He thanked him kindly, and the young officer begged my master to go with him, and have something to drink and a cigar; but as he had not acquired these accomplishments, he excused himself, and we went on board and came off to Wilmington, North Carolina. When the gentleman finds out his mistake, he will, I have no doubt, be careful in future not to pretend to have an intimate acquaintance with an entire stranger. During the voyage the captain said, "It was rather sharp shooting this morning, Mr. Johnson. It was not out of any disrespect to you, sir; but they make it a rule to be very strict at Charleston. I have known families to be detained there with their slaves till reliable information could be received respecting them. If they were not very careful, any d—d abolitionist might take off a lot of valuable niggers."

My master said, "I suppose so," and thanked him again for helping him over the difficulty.

We reached Wilmington the next morning, and took the train for Richmond, Virginia. I have stated that the American railway carriages (or cars, as they are called), are constructed differently to those in England. At one end of some of them, in the South, there is a little apartment with a couch on both sides for the convenience of families and invalids; and as they thought my master was very poorly, he was allowed to enter one of these apartments at Petersburg, Virginia, where an old gentleman and two handsome young ladies, his daughters, also got in, and took seats in the same carriage. But before the train started, the gentleman stepped into my car, and questioned me respecting my master. He wished to know what was the matter with him, where he was from, and where he was going. I told him where he came from, and said that he was suffering from a complication of complaints, and was going to Philadelphia, where he thought he could get more suitable advice than in Georgia.

The gentleman said my master could obtain the very best advice in Philadelphia. Which turned out to be quite correct, though he did not receive it from physicians, but from kind abolitionists who understood his case much better. The gentleman also said, "I reckon your master's father hasn't any more such faithful and smart boys as you." "O, yes, sir, he has," I replied, "lots on 'em." Which was literally true. This seemed all he wished to know. He thanked me, gave me a ten-cent piece, and requested me to be attentive to my good master. I promised that I would do so, and have ever since endeavoured to keep my pledge. During the gentleman's absence, the ladies and my master had a little cosy chat. But on his return, he said, "You seem to be very much afflicted, sir." "Yes, sir," replied the gentleman in the poultices. "What seems to be the matter with you, sir; may I be allowed to ask?" "Inflammatory rheumatism, sir." "Oh! that is very bad, sir," said the kind gentleman: "I can sympathise with you; for I know from bitter experience what the rheumatism is." If he did, he knew a good deal more than Mr. Johnson.

The gentleman thought my master would feel better if he would lie down and rest himself; and as he was anxious to avoid conversation, he at once acted upon this suggestion. The ladies politely rose, took their extra shawls, and made a nice pillow for the invalid's head. My master wore a fashionable cloth cloak, which they took and covered him comfortably on the couch. After he had been lying a little while the ladies, I suppose, thought he was asleep; so one of them gave a long sigh, and said, in a quiet fascinating tone, "Papa, he seems to be a very nice young gentleman." But before papa could speak, the other lady quickly said, "Oh! dear me, I never felt so much for a gentleman in my life!" To use an American expression, "they fell in love with the wrong chap."

After my master had been lying a little while he got up, the gentleman assisted him in getting on his cloak, the ladies took their shawls, and soon they were all seated. They then insisted upon Mr. Johnson taking some of their refreshments, which of course he did, out of courtesy to the ladies. All went on enjoying themselves until they reached Richmond, where the ladies and their father left the train. But, before doing so, the good old Virginian gentleman, who appeared to be much pleased with my master, presented him with a recipe, which he said was a perfect cure for the inflammatory rheumatism. But the invalid not being able to read it, and fearing he should hold it upside down in pretending to do so, thanked the donor kindly, and placed it in his waistcoat pocket. My master's new friend also gave him his card, and requested him the next time he travelled that way to do him the kindness to call; adding, "I shall be pleased to see you, and so will my daughters." Mr. Johnson expressed his gratitude for the proffered hospitality, and said he should feel glad to call on his return. I have not the slightest doubt that he will fulfil the promise whenever that return takes place. After changing trains we went on a little beyond Fredericksburg, and took a steamer to Washington.

At Richmond, a stout elderly lady, whose whole demeanour indicated that she belonged (as Mrs. Stowe's Aunt Chloe expresses it) to one of the "firstest families," stepped into the carriage, and took a seat near my master. Seeing me passing quickly along the platform, she sprang up as if taken by a fit, and exclaimed, "Bless my soul! there goes my nigger, Ned!"

My master said, "No; that is my boy."

The lady paid no attention to this; she poked her head out of the window, and bawled to me, "You Ned, come to me, sir, you runaway rascal!"

On my looking round she drew her head in, and said to my master, "I beg your pardon, sir, I was sure it was my nigger; I never in my life saw two black pigs more alike than your boy and my Ned."

After the disappointed lady had resumed her seat, and the train had moved off, she closed her eyes, slightly raising her hands, and in a sanctified tone said to my master, "Oh! I hope, sir, your boy will not turn out to be so worthless as my Ned has. Oh! I was as kind to him as if he had been my own son. Oh! sir, it grieves me very much to think that after all I did for him he should go off without having any cause whatever."

"When did he leave you?" asked Mr. Johnson.

"About eighteen months ago, and I have never seen hair or hide of him since."

"Did he have a wife?" enquired a very respectable-looking young gentleman, who was sitting near my master and opposite to the lady.

"No, sir; not when he left, though he did have one a little before that. She was very unlike him; she was as good and as faithful a nigger as any one need wish to have. But, poor thing! she became so ill, that she was unable to do much work; so I thought it would be best to sell her, to go to New Orleans, where the climate is nice and warm."

"I suppose she was very glad to go South for the restoration of her health?" said the gentleman.

"No; she was not," replied the lady, "for niggers never know what is best for them. She took on a great deal about leaving Ned and the little nigger; but, as she was so weakly, I let her go."

"Was she good-looking?" asked the young passenger, who was evidently not of the same opinion as the talkative lady, and therefore wished her to tell all she knew.

"Yes; she was very handsome, and much whiter than I am; and therefore will have no trouble in getting another husband. I am sure I wish her well. I asked the speculator who bought her to sell her to a good master. Poor thing! she has my prayers, and I know she prays for me. She was a good Christian, and always used to pray for my soul. It was through her earliest prayers," continued the lady, "that I was first led to seek forgiveness of my sins, before I was converted at the great camp-meeting."

This caused the lady to snuffle and to draw from her pocket a richly embroidered handkerchief, and apply it to the corner of her eyes. But my master could not see that it was at all soiled.

The silence which prevailed for a few moments was broken by the gentleman's saying, "As your 'July' was such a very good girl, and had served you so faithfully before she lost her health, don't you think it would have been better to have emancipated her?"

"No, indeed I do not!" scornfully exclaimed the lady, as she impatiently crammed the fine handkerchief into a little work-bag. "I have no patience with people who set niggers at liberty. It is the very worst thing you can do for them. My dear husband just before he died willed all his niggers free. But I and all our friends knew very well that he was too good a man to have ever thought of doing such an unkind and foolish thing, had he been in his right mind, and, therefore we had the will altered as it should have been in the first place."

"Did you mean, madam," asked my master, "that willing the slaves free was unjust to yourself, or unkind to them?"

"I mean that it was decidedly unkind to the servants themselves. It always seems to me such a cruel thing to turn niggers loose to shift for themselves, when there are so many good masters to take care of them. As for myself," continued the considerate lady, "I thank the Lord my dear husband left me and my son well provided for. Therefore I care nothing for the niggers, on my own account, for they are a great deal more trouble than they are worth, I sometimes wish that there was not one of them in the world; for the ungrateful wretches are always running away. I have lost no less than ten since my poor husband died. It's ruinous, sir!"

"But as you are well provided for, I suppose you do not feel the loss very much," said the passenger.

"I don't feel it at all," haughtily continued the good soul; "but that is no reason why property should be squandered. If my son and myself had the money for those valuable niggers, just see what a great deal of good we could do for the poor, and in sending missionaries abroad to the poor heathen, who have never heard the name of our blessed Redeemer. My dear son who is a good Christian minister has advised me not to worry and send my soul to hell for the sake of niggers; but to sell every blessed one of them for what they will fetch, and go and live in peace with him in New York. This I have concluded to do. I have just been to Richmond and made arrangements with my agent to make clean work of the forty that are left."

"Your son being a good Christian minister," said the gentleman, "It's strange he did not advise you to let the poor negroes have their liberty and go North."

"It's not at all strange, sir; it's not at all strange. My son knows what's best for the niggers; he has always told me that they were much better off than the free niggers in the North. In fact, I don't believe there are any white labouring people in the world who are as well off as the slaves."

"You are quite mistaken, madam," said the young man. "For instance, my own widowed mother, before she died, emancipated all her slaves, and sent them to Ohio, where they are getting along well. I saw several of them last summer myself."

"Well," replied the lady, "freedom may do for your ma's niggers, but it will never do for mine; and, plague them, they shall never have it; that is the word, with the bark on it."

"If freedom will not do for your slaves," replied the passenger, "I have no doubt your Ned and the other nine negroes will find out their mistake, and return to their old home.

"Blast them!" exclaimed the old lady, with great emphasis, "if I ever get them, I will cook their infernal hash, and tan their accursed black hides well for them! God forgive me," added the old soul, "the niggers will make me lose all my religion!"

By this time the lady had reached her destination. The gentleman got out at the next station beyond. As soon as she was gone, the young Southerner said to my master, "What a d—d shame it is for that old whining hypocritical humbug to cheat the poor negroes out of their liberty! If she has religion, may the devil prevent me from ever being converted!"

For the purpose of somewhat disguising myself, I bought and wore a very good second-hand white beaver,[34] an article which I had never indulged in before. So just before we arrived at Washington, an uncouth planter, who had been watching me very closely, said to my master, "I reckon, stranger, you are 'spiling' that ere nigger of yourn, by letting him wear such a devilish fine hat. Just look at the quality on it; the President couldn't wear a better. I should just like to go and kick it overboard." His friend touched him, and said, "Don't speak so to a gentleman." "Why not?" exclaimed the fellow. He grated his short teeth, which appeared to be nearly worn away by the incessant chewing of tobacco, and said, "It always makes me itch all over, from head to toe, to get hold of every d—d nigger I see dressed like a white man. Washington is run away with *spiled* and free niggers. If I had my way I would sell every d—d rascal of 'em way down South, where the devil would be whipped out on 'em."

This man's fierce manner made my master feel rather nervous, and therefore he thought the less he said the better; so he walked off without making any reply. In a few minutes we were landed at Washington, where we took a conveyance and hurried off to the train for Baltimore.

We left our cottage on Wednesday morning, the 21st of December, 1848, and arrived at Baltimore, Saturday evening, the 24th (Christmas Eve). Baltimore was the last slave port of any note at which we stopped.

On arriving there we felt more anxious than ever, because we knew not what that last dark night would bring forth. It is true we were near the goal, but our poor hearts were still as if tossed at sea; and, as there was another great and dangerous bar to pass, we were afraid our liberties would be wrecked, and, like the ill-fated *Royal Charter,* go down for ever just off the place we longed to reach.

They are particularly watchful at Baltimore to prevent slaves from escaping into Pennsylvania, which is a free State. After I had seen my master into one of the best carriages, and was just about to step into mine, an officer, a full-blooded Yankee of the lower order, saw me. He came quickly up, and, tapping me on the shoulder, said in his unmistakable native twang, together with no little display of his authority, "Where are you going, boy?" "To Philadelphia, sir," I humbly replied. "Well, what are you going there for?" "I am travelling with my master, who is in the next carriage, sir." "Well, I calculate you had better get him out; and be mighty quick about it, because the train will soon be starting. It is against my rules to let any man take a slave past here, unless he can satisfy them in the office that he has a right to take him along."

The officer then passed on and left me standing upon the platform, with my anxious heart apparently palpitating in the throat. At first I scarcely knew which way to turn. But it soon occurred to me that the good God, who had been with us thus far, would not forsake us at the eleventh hour. So with renewed hope I stepped into my master's carriage, to inform him of the difficulty. I found him sitting at the farther end, quite alone. As soon as he looked up and saw me, he smiled. I also tried to wear a cheerful countenance, in order to break the shock of the sad news. I knew what made him smile. He was aware that if we were fortunate we should reach our destination at five o'clock the next morning, and this made it the more painful to communicate what the officer had said; but, as there was no time to lose, I went up to him and asked him how he felt. He said "Much better," and that he thanked God we were getting on so nicely. I then said we were not getting on quite so well as we had anticipated. He anxiously and quickly asked what was the matter. I told him. He started as if struck by lightning, and exclaimed, "Good Heavens! William, is it possible that we are, after all, doomed to hopeless bondage?" I could say nothing, my heart was too full to speak, for at first I did not know what to do. However we knew it would never do to turn back to the "City of Destruction," like Bunyan's *Mistrust* and *Timorous,* because they saw lions in the narrow way after ascending the hill Difficulty; but press on, like noble *Christian* and *Hopeful,* to the great city in which dwelt a few "shining ones."[35] So, after a few moments, I did all I could to encourage my companion, and we stepped out and made for the office: but how or where my master obtained sufficient courage to face the tyrants who had power to blast all we held dear, heaven only knows! Queen Elizabeth could not have been more terror-stricken, on being forced to land at the traitors' gate leading to the Tower,[36] than we were on entering that office. We felt that our very existence was at stake, and that we must either sink or swim. But, as God was our present and mighty helper in this as well as in all former trials, we were able to keep our heads up and press forwards.

On entering the room we found the principal man, to whom my master said, "Do you wish to see me, sir?" "Yes," said this eagle-eyed officer; and he added, "It is against our rules, sir, to allow any person to take a slave out of Baltimore into Philadelphia, unless he can satisfy us that he has a right to take him along." "Why is that?" asked my master, with more firmness than could be expected. "Because, sir," continued he, in a voice and manner that almost chilled our blood, "if we should suffer any gentleman to take a slave past here into Philadelphia; and should the gentleman with whom the slave might be travelling turn out not to be his rightful owner; and should the proper master come and prove that his slave escaped on our road, we shall have him to pay for; and, therefore, we cannot let any slave pass here without receiving security to show, and to satisfy us, that it is all right."

This conversation attracted the attention of the large number of bustling passengers. After the officer had finished, a few of them said, "Chit, chit, chit;" not because they thought we were slaves endeavouring to escape, but merely because they thought my master was a slaveholder and invalid gentleman, and therefore it was wrong to detain him. The officer, observing that the passengers sympathised with my master, asked him if he was not acquainted with some gentleman in Baltimore that he could get to endorse for him, to show that I was his property, and that he had a right to take me off. He said, "No;" and added, "I bought tickets in Charleston to pass us through to Philadelphia, and therefore you have no right to detain us here." "Well, sir," said the man, indignantly, "right or no right, we shan't let you go." These sharp words fell upon our anxious hearts like the crack of doom, and made us feel that hope only smiles to deceive.

For a few moments perfect silence prevailed. My master looked at me, and I at him, but neither of us dared to speak a word, for fear of making some blunder that would tend to our detection. We knew that the officers had power to throw us into prison, and if they had done so we must have been detected and driven back, like the vilest felons, to a life of slavery, which we dreaded far more than sudden death.

We felt as though we had come into deep waters and were about being overwhelmed, and that the slightest mistake would clip asunder the last brittle thread of hope by which we were suspended, and let us down for ever into the dark and horrible pit of misery and degradation from which we were straining every nerve to escape. While our hearts were crying lustily unto Him who is ever ready and able to save, the conductor of the train that we had just left stepped in. The officer asked if we came by the train with him from Washington; he said we did, and left the room. Just then the bell rang for the train to leave; and had it been the sudden shock of an earthquake it could not have given us a greater thrill. The sound of the bell caused every eye to flash with apparent interest, and to be more steadily fixed upon us than before. But, as God would have it, the officer all at once thrust his fingers through his hair, and in a state of great agitation said, "I really don't know what to do; I calculate it is all right." He then told the clerk to run and tell the conductor to "let this gentleman and slave pass;" adding, "As he is not well, it is a pity to stop him here. We will let him go." My master thanked him, and stepped out and hobbled across the platform as quickly as possible. I tumbled him unceremoniously into one of the best carriages, and leaped into mine just as the train was gliding off towards our happy destination.

We thought of this plan about four days before we left Maçon; and as we had our daily employment to attend to, we only saw each other at night. So we sat up the four long nights talking over the plan and making preparations.

We had also been four days on the journey; and as we travelled night and day, we got but very limited opportunities for sleeping. I believe nothing in the world could have kept us awake so long but the intense excitement, produced by the fear of being retaken on the one hand, and the bright anticipation of liberty on the other.

We left Baltimore about eight o'clock in the evening; and not being aware of a stopping-place of any consequence between there and Philadelphia, and also knowing that if we were fortunate we should be in the latter place early the next morning, I thought I might indulge in a few minutes' sleep in the car; but I, like Bunyan's Christian in the arbour, went to sleep at the wrong time, and took too long a nap. So, when the train reached Havre de Grace, all the first-class passengers had to get out of the carriages and into a ferry-boat, to be ferried across the Susquehanna river, and take the train on the opposite side.

The road was constructed so as to be raised or lowered to suit the tide. So they rolled the luggage-vans on to the boat, and off on the other side; and as I was in one of the apartments adjoining a baggage-car, they considered it unnecessary to awaken me, and tumbled me over with the luggage. But when my master was asked to leave his seat, he found it very dark, and cold, and raining. He missed me for the first time on the journey. On all previous occasions, as soon as the train stopped, I was at hand to assist him. This caused many slaveholders to praise me very much: they said they had never before seen a slave so attentive to his master: and therefore my absence filled him with terror and confusion; the children of Israel could not have felt more troubled on arriving at the Red Sea. So he asked the conductor if he had seen anything of his slave. The man being somewhat of an abolitionist, and believing that my master was really a slaveholder, thought he would tease him a little respecting me. So he said, "No, sir; I haven't seen anything of him for some time: I have no doubt he has run away, and is in Philadelphia, free, long before now." My master knew that there was nothing in this; so he asked the conductor if he would please to see if he could find me. The man indignantly replied, "I am no slave-hunter; and as far as I am concerned everybody must look after their own niggers." He went off and left the confused invalid to fancy whatever he felt inclined. My master at first thought I must have been kidnapped into slavery by some one, or left, or perhaps killed on the train. He also thought of stopping to see if he could hear anything of me, but he soon remembered that he had no money. That night all the money we had was consigned to my own pocket, because we thought, in case there were any pickpockets about, a slave's pocket would be the last one they would look for. However, hoping to meet me some day in a land of liberty, and as he had the tickets, he thought it best upon the whole to enter the boat and come off to Philadelphia, and endeavour to make his way alone in this cold and hollow world as best he could. The time was now up, so he went on board and came across with feelings that can be better imagined than described.

After the train had got fairly on the way to Philadelphia, the guard came into my car and gave me a violent shake, and bawled out at the same time, "Boy, wake up!" I started, almost frightened out of my wits. He said, "Your master is scared half to death about you." That frightened me still more—I thought they had found him out; so I anxiously inquired what was the matter. The guard said, "He thinks you have run away from him." This made me feel quite at ease. I said, "No, sir; I am satisfied my good master doesn't think that." So off I started to see him. He had been fearfully nervous, but on seeing me he at once felt much better. He merely wished to know what had become of me.

On returning to my seat, I found the conductor and two or three other persons amusing themselves very much respecting my running away. So the guard said, "Boy, what did your master want?"* I replied, "He merely wished to know what had become of me." "No," said the man, "that was not it; he thought you had taken French leave, for parts unknown. I never saw a fellow so badly scared about losing his slave in my life. Now," continued the guard, "let me give you a little friendly advice. When you get to Philadelphia, run away and leave that cripple, and have your liberty." "No, sir," I indifferently replied, "I can't promise to do that." "Why not?" said the conductor, evidently much surprised; "don't you want your liberty?" "Yes, sir," I replied; "but I shall never run away from such a good master as I have at present."

One of the men said to the guard, "Let him alone; I guess he will open his eyes when he gets to Philadelphia, and see things in another light." After giving me a good deal of information, which I afterwards found to be very useful, they left me alone.

I also met with a coloured gentleman on this train, who recommended me to a boarding-house that was kept by an abolitionist, where he thought I would be quite safe, if I wished to run away from my master. I thanked him kindly, but of course did not let him know who we were. Late at night, or rather early in the morning, I heard a fearful whistling of the steam-engine; so I opened the window and looked out, and saw a large number of flickering lights in the distance, and

---

*I may state here that every man slave is called boy till he is very old, then the more respectable slaveholders call him uncle. The women are all girls till they are aged, then they are called aunts. This is the reason why Mrs. Stowe calls her characters Uncle Tom, Aunt Chloe, Uncle Tiff, &c.

heard a passenger in the next carriage—who also had his head out of the window—say to his companion, "Wake up, old horse, we are at Philadelphia!"

The sight of those lights and that announcement made me feel almost as happy as Bunyan's Christian must have felt when he first caught sight of the cross. I, like him, felt that the straps that bound the heavy burden to my back began to pop, and the load to roll off. I also looked, and looked again, for it appeared very wonderful to me how the mere sight of our first city of refuge should have all at once made my hitherto sad and heavy heart become so light and happy. As the train speeded on, I rejoiced and thanked God with all my heart and soul for his great kindness and tender mercy, in watching over us, and bringing us safely through.

As soon as the train had reached the platform, before it had fairly stopped, I hurried out of my carriage to my master, whom I got at once into a cab, placed the luggage on, jumped in myself, and we drove off to the boarding-house which was so kindly recommended to me. On leaving the station, my master—or rather my wife, as I may now say—who had from the commencement of the journey borne up in a manner that much surprised us both, grasped me by the hand, and said, "Thank God, William, we are safe!" and then burst into tears, leant upon me, and wept like a child. The reaction was fearful. So when we reached the house, she was in reality so weak and faint that she could scarcely stand alone. However, I got her into the apartments that were pointed out, and there we knelt down, on this Sabbath, and Christmas-day,—a day that will ever be memorable to us,—and poured out our heartfelt gratitude to God, for his goodness in enabling us to overcome so many perilous difficulties, in escaping out of the jaws of the wicked.

PART II.

AFTER my wife had a little recovered herself, she threw off the disguise and assumed her own apparel. We then stepped into the sitting-room, and asked to see the landlord. The man came in, but he seemed thunderstruck on finding a fugitive slave and his wife, instead of a "young cotton planter and his nigger." As his eyes travelled round the room, he said to me, "Where is your master?" I pointed him out. The man gravely replied, "I am not joking, I really wish to see your master." I pointed him out again, but at first he could not believe his eyes; he said "he knew that was not the gentleman that came with me."

But, after some conversation, we satisfied him that we were fugitive slaves, and had just escaped in the manner I have described. We asked him if he thought it would be safe for us to stop in Philadelphia. He said he thought not, but he would call in some persons who knew more about the laws than himself. He then went out, and kindly brought in several of the leading abolitionists of the city, who gave us a most hearty and friendly welcome amongst them. As it was in December, and also as we had just left a very warm climate,[37] they advised us not to go to Canada as we had intended, but to settle at Boston in the United States. It is true that the constitution of the Republic has always guaranteed the slaveholders the right to come into any of the so-called free States, and take their fugitives back to southern Egypt. But through the untiring, uncompromising, and manly efforts of Mr. Garrison, Wendell Phillips, Theodore Parker, and a host of other noble abolitionists of Boston and the neighbourhood, public opinion in Massachusetts had become so much opposed to slavery and to kidnapping, that it was almost impossible for any one to take a fugitive slave out of that State.

So we took the advice of our good Philadelphia friends, and settled at Boston. I shall have something to say about our sojourn there presently.

Among other friends we met with at Philadelphia, was Robert Purves, Esq., a well educated and wealthy coloured gentleman, who introduced us to Mr. Barkley Ivens, a member of the Society of Friends, and a noble and generous-hearted farmer, who lived at some distance in the country.

This good Samaritan at once invited us to go and stop quietly with his family, till my wife could somewhat recover from the fearful reaction of the past journey. We most gratefully accepted the invitation, and at the time appointed we took a steamer to a place up the Delaware river, where our new and dear friend met us with his snug little cart, and took us to his happy home. This was the first act of great and disinterested kindness we had ever received from a white person.

The gentleman was not of the fairest complexion, and therefore, as my wife was not in the room when I received the information respecting him and his anti-slavery character, she thought of course he was a quadroon like herself. But on arriving at the house, and finding out her mistake, she became more nervous and timid than ever.

As the cart came into the yard, the dear good old lady, and her three charming and affectionate daughters, all came to the door to meet us. We got out, and the gentleman said, "Go in, and make yourselves at home; I will see after the baggage." But my wife was afraid to approach them. She stopped in the yard, and said to me, "William, I thought we were coming among coloured people?" I replied, "It is all right; these are the same." "No," she said, "it is not all right, and I am not going to stop here; I have no confidence whatever in white people, they are only trying to get us back to slavery." She turned round and said, "I am going right off." The old lady then came out, with her sweet, soft, and winning smile, shook her heartily by the hand, and kindly said, "How art thou, my dear? We are all very glad to see thee and thy husband. Come in, to the fire; I dare say thou art cold and hungry after thy journey."

We went in, and the young ladies asked if she would like to go upstairs and "fix" herself before tea. My wife said, "No, I thank you; I shall only stop a little while." "But where art thou going this cold night?" said Mr. Ivens, who had just stepped in. "I don't know," was the reply. "Well, then," he continued, "I think thou hadst better take off thy things and sit near the fire; tea will soon be ready." "Yes, come Ellen," said Mrs. Ivens, "let me assist thee;" (as she commenced undoing my wife's bonnet-strings;) "don't be frightened, Ellen, I shall not hurt a single hair of thy head. We have heard with much pleasure of the marvellous escape of thee and thy husband, and deeply sympathise with thee in all that thou hast undergone. I don't wonder at thee, poor thing, being timid; but thou needs not fear us; we would as soon send one of our own daughters into slavery as thee; so thou mayest make thyself quite at ease!" These soft and soothing words fell like balm upon my wife's unstrung nerves, and melted her to tears; her fears and prejudices vanished, and from that day she has firmly believed that there are good and bad persons of every shade of complexion.

After seeing Sally Ann and Jacob, two coloured domestics, my wife felt quite at home. After partaking of what Mrs. Stowe's Mose and Pete called a "busting supper," the ladies wished to know whether we could read. On learning we could not, they said if we liked they would teach us. To this kind offer, of course, there was no objection. But we looked rather knowingly at each other, as much as to say that they would have rather a hard task to cram anything into our thick and matured sculls.

However, all hands set to and quickly cleared away the tea-things, and the ladies and their good brother brought out the spelling and copy books and slates, &c., and commenced with their new and green pupils. We had, by stratagem, learned the alphabet while in slavery, but not the writing characters; and, as we had been such a time learning so little, we at first felt that it was a waste of time for any one at our ages to undertake to learn to read and write. But, as the ladies were so anxious that we should learn, and so willing to teach us, we concluded to give our whole minds to the work, and see what could be done. By so doing, at the end of the three weeks we remained with the good family we could spell and write our names quite legibly. They all begged us to stop longer; but, as we were not safe in the State of Pennsylvania, and also as we wished to commence doing something for a livelihood, we did not remain.

When the time arrived for us to leave for Boston, it was like parting with our relatives. We have since met with many very kind and hospitable friends, both in America and England; but we have never been under a roof where we were made to feel more at home, or where the inmates took a deeper interest in our well-being, than Mr. Barkley Ivens and his dear family. May God ever bless them, and preserve each one from every reverse of fortune!

We finally, as I have stated, settled at Boston, where we remained nearly two years, I employed as cabinet-maker and furniture broker, and my wife at her needle; and, as our little earnings in slavery were not all spent on the journey, we were getting on very well, and would have made money, if we had not been compelled by the General Government, at the bidding of the slaveholders, to break up business, and fly from under the Stars and Stripes to save our liberties and our lives.

In 1850, Congress passed the Fugitive Slave Bill, an enactment too infamous to have been thought of or tolerated by any people in the world, except the unprincipled and tyrannical Yankees. The following are a few of the leading features of the above law; which requires, under heavy penalties, that the inhabitants of the *free* States should not only refuse food and shelter to a starving, hunted human being, but also should assist, if called upon by the authorities, to seize the unhappy fugitive and send him back to slavery.

In no case is a person's evidence admitted in Court, in defence of his liberty, when arrested under this law.

If the judge decides that the prisoner is a slave, he gets ten dollars; but if he sets him at liberty, he only receives five.

After the prisoner has been sentenced to slavery, he is handed over to the United States Marshal, who has the power, at the expense of the General Government, to summon a sufficient force to take the poor creature back to slavery, and to the lash, from which he fled.

Our old masters sent agents to Boston after us. They took out warrants, and placed them in the hands of the United States Marshal to execute. But the following letter from our highly esteemed and faithful friend, the Rev. Samuel May, of Boston, to our equally dear and much lamented friend, Dr. Estlin of Bristol, will show why we were not taken into custody.

> "21, *Cornhill, Boston,*
> "*November 6th,* 1850.

"My dear Mr Estlin,

"I trust that in God's good providence this letter will be handed to you in safety by our good friends, William and Ellen Craft. They have lived amongst us about two years, and have proved themselves worthy, in all respects, of our confidence and regard. The laws of this republican and Christian land (tell it not in Moscow, nor in Constantinople) regard them only as slaves—chattels—personal property. But they nobly vindicated their title and right to freedom, two years since, by winning their way to it; at least, so they thought. But now, the slave power, with the aid of Daniel Webster[38] and a band of lesser traitors, has enacted a law, which puts their dearly-bought liberties in the most imminent peril; holds out a strong temptation to every mercenary and unprincipled ruffian to become their kidnapper; and has stimulated the slaveholders generally to such desperate acts for the recovery of their fugitive property, as have never before been enacted in the history of this government.

"Within a fortnight, two fellows from Maçon, Georgia, have been in Boston for the purpose of arresting our friends William and Ellen.[39] A writ was served against them from the United States District Court;[40] but it was not served by the United States Marshal; why not, is not certainly known: perhaps through fear, for a general feeling of indignation, and a cool determination not to allow this young couple to be taken from Boston into slavery, was aroused, and pervaded the city.[41] It is understood that one of the judges told the Marshal that he would not be authorised in breaking the door of Craft's house. Craft kept himself close within the house, armed himself, and awaited with remarkable composure the event.[42] Ellen, in the meantime, had been taken to a retired place out of the city.[43] The Vigilance Committee (appointed at a late meeting in Fanueil Hall) enlarged their numbers, held an almost permanent session, and appointed various subcommittees to act in different ways. One of these committees called repeatedly on Messrs. Hughes and Knight, the slave-catchers, and requested and advised them to leave the city. At first they peremptorily refused to do so, ''till they got hold of the niggers.' On complaint of different persons, these two fellows were several times arrested, carried before one of our county courts, and held to bail on charges of 'conspiracy to kidnap,' and of 'defamation,' in calling William and Ellen '*slaves*.'[44] At length, they became so alarmed, that they left the city by an indirect route, evading the vigilance of many persons who were on the look-out for them. Hughes, at one time, was near losing his life at the hands of an infuriated coloured man.[45] While these men remained in the city, a prominent whig gentleman sent word to William Craft, that if he would submit peaceably to an arrest, he and his wife should be bought from their owners, cost what it might. Craft replied, in effect, that he was in a measure the representative of all the other fugitives in Boston, some 200 or 300 in number; that, if he gave up, they would all be at the mercy of the slave-catchers, and must fly from the city at any sacrifice; and that, if his freedom could be bought for two cents, he would not consent to compromise the matter in such a way. This event has stirred up the slave spirit of the country, south and north; the United States government is determined to try its hand in enforcing the Fugitive Slave law; and William and Ellen Craft would be prominent objects of the slaveholders' vengeance. Under these circumstances, it is the almost unanimous opinion of their best friends, that they should quit America as speedily as possible, and seek an asylum in England! Oh! shame, shame upon us, that Americans, whose fathers fought against Great Britain, in order to be FREE, should have to acknowledge this disgraceful fact! God gave us a fair and goodly heritage in this land, but man has cursed it with his devices and crimes against human souls and human rights. Is America the 'land of the free, and the home of the brave?' God knows it is not; and we know it too. A brave young man and a virtuous young woman must fly the American shores, and seek, under the shadow of the British throne, the enjoyment of 'life, liberty, and the pursuit of happiness.'

"But I must pursue my plain, sad story. All day long, I have been busy planning a safe way for William and Ellen to leave Boston. We dare not allow them to go on board a vessel, even in the port of Boston; for the writ is yet in the Marshal's hands, and he *may* be waiting an opportunity to serve it; so I am expecting to accompany them to-morrow to Portland, Maine, which is beyond the reach of the Marshal's authority; and there I hope to see them on board a British steamer.

"This letter is written to introduce them to you. I know your infirm health; but I am sure, if you were stretched on your bed in your last illness, and could lift your hand at all, you would extend it to welcome these poor hunted fellow-creatures. Henceforth, England is their nation and their home. It is with real regret for our personal loss in their departure, as well as burning shame for the land that is not worthy of them, that we send them away, or rather allow them to go. But, with all the resolute courage they have shown in a most trying hour, they themselves see it is the part of a foolhardy rashness to attempt to stay here longer.

"I must close; and with many renewed thanks for all your kind words and deeds towards us,

"I am, very respectfully yours,
"SAMUEL MAY, JUN."

Our old masters, having heard how their agents were treated at Boston, wrote to Mr. Filmore, who was then President of the States, to know what he could do to have us sent back to slavery. Mr. Filmore said that we should be returned. He gave instructions for military force to be sent to Boston to assist the officers in making the arrest.[46] Therefore we, as well as our friends (among whom was George Thompson, Esq., late M.P. for the Tower Hamlets—the slave's long-tried, self-sacrificing friend, and eloquent advocate) thought it best, at any sacrifice, to leave the mock-free Republic, and come to a country where we and our dear little ones can be truly free.—"No one daring to molest or make us afraid."[47] But, as the officers were watching every vessel that left the port to prevent us from escaping, we had to take the expensive and tedious overland route to Halifax.

We shall always cherish the deepest feelings of gratitude to the Vigilance Committee of Boston (upon which were many of the leading abolitionists), and also to our numerous friends, for the very kind and noble manner in which they assisted us to preserve our liberties and to escape from Boston, as it were like Lot from Sodom, to a place of refuge, and finally to this truly free and glorious country; where no tyrant, let his power be ever so absolute over his poor trembling victims at home, dare come and lay violent hands upon us or upon our dear little boys (who had the good fortune to be born upon British soil), and reduce us to the legal level of the beast that perisheth. Oh! may God bless the thousands of unflinching, disinterested abolitionists of America, who are labouring through evil as well as through good report, to cleanse their country's escutcheon from the foul and destructive blot of slavery, and to restore to every bondman his God-given rights; and may God ever smile upon England and upon England's good, much-beloved, and deservedly-honoured Queen, for the generous protection that is given to unfortunate refugees of every rank, and of every colour and clime.

On the passing of the Fugitive Slave Bill, the following learned doctors, as well as a host of lesser traitors, came out strongly in its defence.

The Rev. Dr. Gardiner Spring, an eminent Presbyterian Clergyman of New York, well known in this country by his religious publications, declared from the pulpit that, "if by one prayer he could liberate every slave in the world he would not dare to offer it."

The Rev. Dr. Joel Parker, of Philadelphia, in the course of a discussion on the nature of Slavery, says, "What, then, are the evils inseparable from slavery? There is not one that is not equally inseparable from depraved human nature in other lawful relations."

The Rev. Moses Stuart, D.D., (late Professor in the Theological College of Andover), in his vindication of this Bill, reminds his readers that "many Southern slaveholders are true *Christians*." That "sending back a fugitive to them is not like restoring one to an idolatrous people." That "though we may *pity* the fugitive, yet the Mosaic Law does not authorize the rejection of the claims of the slaveholders to their stolen or strayed *property*."

The Rev. Dr. Spencer, of Brooklyn, New York, has come forward in support of the "Fugitive Slave Bill," by publishing a sermon entitled the "Religious Duty of Obedience to the Laws," which has elicited the highest encomiums from Dr. Samuel H. Cox, the Presbyterian minister of Brooklyn (notorious both in this country and America for his sympathy with the slaveholder).

The Rev. W. M. Rogers, an orthodox minister of Boston, delivered a sermon in which he says, "When the slave asks me to stand between him and his master, what does he ask? He asks me to murder a nation's life; and I will not do it, because I have a conscience,—because there is a God." He proceeds to affirm that if resistance to the carrying out of the "Fugitive Slave Law" should lead the magistracy to call the citizens to arms, their duty was to obey and "if ordered to take human life, in the name of God to take it;" and he concludes by admonishing the fugitives to "hearken to the Word of God, and to count their own masters worthy of all honour."

The Rev. William Crowell, of Waterfield, State of Maine, printed a Thanksgiving Sermon of the same kind, in which he calls upon his hearers not to allow "excessive sympathies for a few hundred fugitives to blind them so that they may risk increased suffering to the millions already in chains."

The Rev. Dr. Taylor, an Episcopal Clergyman of New Haven, Connecticut, made a speech at a Union Meeting, in which he deprecates the agitation on the law, and urges obedience to it; asking,—"Is that article in the Constitution contrary to the law of Nature, of nations, or to the will of God? Is it so? Is there a shadow of reason for saying it? I have not been able to discover it. Have I not shown you it is lawful to deliver up, in compliance with the laws, fugitive slaves, for the high, the great, the momentous interests of those [Southern] States?"

The Right Rev. Bishop Hopkins, of Vermont, in a Lecture at Lockport, says, "It was warranted by the Old Testament;" and inquires, "What effect had the Gospel in doing away with slavery? None whatever." Therefore he argues, as it is expressly permitted by the Bible, it does not in itself involve any sin; but that every Christian is authorised by the Divine Law to own slaves, provided they were not treated with unnecessary cruelty.

The Rev. Orville Dewey, D.D., of the Unitarian connexion, maintained in his lectures that the safety of the Union is not to be hazarded for the sake of the African race. He declares that, for his part, he would send his own brother or child into slavery, if needed to preserve the Union between the free and the slave-holding States; and, counselling the slave to similar magnanimity, thus exhorts him:—"*Your right to be free is not absolute, unqualified, irrespective of all consequences. If my espousal of your claim is likely to involve your race and mine together in disasters infinitely greater than your personal servitude, then you ought not to be free. In such a case personal rights ought to be sacrificed to the general good. You yourself ought to see this, and be willing to suffer for a while—one for many.*"

If the Doctor is prepared, he is quite at liberty to sacrifice his "personal rights to the general good." But, as I have suffered a long time in slavery, it is hardly fair for the Doctor to advise me to go back. According to his showing, he ought rather to take my place. That would be practically carrying out his logic, as respects "suffering awhile—one for many."

In fact, so eager were they to prostrate themselves before the great idol of slavery, and, like Baalam, to curse instead of blessing the people whom God had brought out of bondage, that they in bringing up obsolete passages from the Old Testament to justify their downward course, overlooked, or would not see, the following verses, which show very clearly, according to the Doctor's own textbook, that the slaves have a right to run away, and that it is unscriptural for any one to send them back.

In the 23rd chapter of Deuteronomy, 15th and 16th verses, it is thus written:—"Thou shalt not deliver unto his master the servant which is escaped from his master unto thee. He shall dwell with thee, even among you, in that place which he shall choose in one of thy gates, where it liketh him best: thou shalt not oppress him."

"Hide the outcast. Bewray not him that wandereth. Let mine outcasts dwell with thee. Be thou a covert to them from the face of the spoiler."—(Isa. xvi. 3, 4.)

The great majority of the American ministers are not content with uttering sentences similar to the above, or remaining wholly indifferent to the cries of the poor bondman; but they do all they can to blast the reputation, and to muzzle the mouths, of the few good men who dare to beseech the God of mercy "to loose the bonds of wickedness, to undo the heavy burdens, and let the oppressed go free." These reverend gentlemen pour a terrible cannonade upon "Jonah," for refusing to carry God's message against Nineveh, and tell us about the whale in which he was entombed; while they utterly overlook the existence of the whales which trouble their republican waters, and know not that they themselves are the "Jonahs" who threaten to sink their ship of state, by steering in an unrighteous direction. We are told that the whale vomited up the runaway prophet. This would not have seemed so strange, had it been one of the above lukewarm Doctors of Divinity whom he had swallowed; for even a whale might find such a morsel difficult of digestion.

> "I venerate the man whose heart is warm,
> Whose hands are pure; whose doctrines and whose life
> Coincident, exhibit lucid proof
> That he is honest in the sacred cause."
>
> "But grace abused brings forth the foulest deeds,
> As richest soil the most luxuriant weeds."[48]

I must now leave the reverend gentlemen in the hands of Him who knows best how to deal with a recreant ministry.

I do not wish it to be understood that all the ministers of the States are of the Baalam stamp. There are those who are as uncompromising with slaveholders as Moses was with Pharaoh, and, like Daniel, will never bow down before the great false God that has been set up.

On arriving at Portland, we found that the steamer we intended to take had run into a schooner the previous night, and was lying up for repairs; so we had to wait there, in fearful suspense, for two or three days. During this time, we had the honour of being the guest of the late and much lamented Daniel Oliver, Esq., one of the best and most hospitable men in the State. By simply fulfilling the Scripture injunction, to take in the stranger, &c., he ran the risk of incurring a penalty of 2,000 dollars, and twelve months' imprisonment.

But neither the Fugitive Slave Law, nor any other Satanic enactment, can ever drive the spirit of liberty and humanity out of such noble and generous-hearted men.

May God ever bless his dear widow, and eventually unite them in His courts above!

We finally got off to St. John's, New Brunswick, where we had to wait two days for the steamer that conveyed us to Windsor, Nova Scotia.

On going into a hotel at St. John's, we met the butler in the hall, to whom I said, "We wish to stop here to-night." He turned round, scratching his head, evidently much put about. But thinking that my wife was white, he replied, "We have plenty of room for the lady, but I don't know about yourself; we never take in coloured folks." "Oh, don't trouble about me," I said; "if you have room for the lady, that will do; so please have the luggage taken to a bed-room." Which was immediately done, and my wife went upstairs into the apartment.

After taking a little walk in the town, I returned, and asked to see the "lady." On being conducted to the little sitting-room, where she then was, I entered without knocking, much to the surprise of the whole house. The "lady" then rang the bell, and ordered dinner for two. "Dinner for two, mum!" exclaimed the waiter, as he backed out of the door. "Yes, for two," said my wife. In a little while the stout, red-nosed butler, whom we first met, knocked at the door. I called out, "Come in." On entering, he rolled his whisky eyes at me, and then at my wife, and said, in a very solemn tone, "Did you order dinner for two, mum?" "Yes, for two," my wife again replied. This confused the chubby butler more than ever; and, as the landlord was not in the house, he seemed at a loss what to do.

When dinner was ready, the maid came in and said, "Please mum, the Missis wishes to know whether you will have dinner up now, or wait till your friend arrives?" "I will have it up at once, if you please." "Thank you, mum," continued the maid, and out she glided.

After a good deal of giggling in the passage, some one said, "You are in for it, butler, after all; so you had better make the best of a bad job." But before dinner was sent up, the landlord returned, and having heard from the steward of the steamer by which we came that we were bound for England, the proprietor's native country, he treated us in the most respectful manner.

At the above house, the boots[49] (whose name I forget) was a fugitive slave, a very intelligent and active man, about forty-five years of age. Soon after his marriage, while in slavery, his bride was sold away from him, and he could never learn where the poor creature dwelt. So after remaining single for many years, both before and after his escape, and never expecting to see again, nor even to hear from, his long-lost partner, he finally married a woman at St. John's. But, poor fellow, as he was passing down the street one day, he met a woman; at the first glance they nearly recognized each other; they both turned round and stared, and unconsciously advanced, till she screamed and flew into his arms. Her first words were, "Dear, are you married?" On his answering in the affirmative, she shrank from his embrace, hung her head, and wept. A person who witnessed this meeting told me it was most affecting.

This couple knew nothing of each other's escape or whereabouts. The woman had escaped a few years before to the free States, by secreting herself in the hold of a vessel; but as they tried to get her back to bondage, she fled to New Brunswick for that protection which her native country was too mean to afford.

The man at once took his old wife to see his new one, who was also a fugitive slave, and as they all knew the workings of the infamous system of slavery, they could (as no one else can,) sympathise with each other's misfortune.

According to the rules of slavery, the man and his first wife were already divorced, but not morally; and therefore it was arranged between the three that he should live only with the lastly married wife, and allow the other one so much a week, as long she requested his assistance.

After staying at St. John's two days, the steamer arrived, which took us to Windsor, where we found a coach bound for Halifax. Prejudice against colour forced me on the top in the rain. On arriving within about seven miles of the town, the coach broke down and was upset. I fell upon the big crotchety driver, whose head stuck in the mud; and as he "always objected to niggers riding inside with white folks," I was not particularly sorry to see him deeper in the mire than myself. All of us were scratched and bruised more or less. After the passengers had crawled out as best they could, we all set off, and paddled through the deep mud and cold and rain, to Halifax.

On leaving Boston, it was our intention to reach Halifax at least two or three days before the steamer from Boston touched there, *en route* for Liverpool; but, having been detained so long at Portland and St. John's, we had the misfortune to arrive at Halifax at dark, just two hours after the steamer had gone; consequently we had to wait there a fortnight, for the *Cambria*.

The coach was patched up, and reached Halifax with the luggage, soon after the passengers arrived. The only respectable hotel that was then in the town had suspended business, and was closed; so we went to the inn, opposite the market, where the coach stopped: a most miserable, dirty hole it was.

Knowing that we were still under the influence of the low Yankee prejudice, I sent my wife in with the other passengers, to engage a bed for herself and husband. I stopped outside in the rain till the coach came up. If I had gone in and asked for a bed they would have been quite full. But as they thought my wife was white, she had no difficulty in securing apartments, into which the luggage was afterwards carried. The landlady, observing that I took an interest in the baggage, became somewhat uneasy, and went into my wife's room, and said to her, "Do you know the dark man downstairs?" "Yes, he is my husband." "Oh! I mean the black man—the *nigger?*" "I quite understand you; he is my husband." "My God!" exclaimed the woman as she flounced out and banged to the door. On going upstairs, I heard what had taken place: but, as we were there, and did not mean to leave that night, we did not disturb ourselves. On our ordering tea, the landlady sent word back to say that we must take it in the kitchen, or in our bed-room, as she had no other room for "niggers." We replied that we were not particular, and that they could sent it up to our room,—which they did.

After the pro-slavery persons who were staying there heard that we were in, the whole house became agitated, and all sorts of oaths and fearful threats were heaped upon the "d—d niggers, for coming among white folks." Some of them said they would not stop there a minute if there was another house to go to.

The mistress came up the next morning to know how long we wished to stop. We said a fortnight. "Oh! dear me, it is impossible for us to accommodate you, and I think you had better go: you must understand, I have no prejudice myself; I think a good deal of the coloured people, and have always been their friend; but if you stop here we shall lose all our customers, which we can't do nohow." We said we were glad to hear that she had "no prejudice," and was such a staunch friend to the coloured people. We also informed her that we would be sorry for her "customers" to leave on our account; and as it was not our intention to interfere with anyone, it was foolish for them to be frightened away. However, if she would get us a comfortable place, we would be glad to leave. The landlady said she would go out and try. After spending the whole morning in canvassing the town, she came to our room and said, "I have been from one end of the place to the other, but everybody is full." Having a little fore-taste of the vulgar prejudice of the town, we did not wonder at this result. How-ever, the landlady gave me the address of some respectable coloured families, whom she thought, "under the circumstances," might be induced to take us. And, as we were not at all comfortable—being compelled to sit, eat and sleep, in the same small room—we were quite willing to change our quarters.

I called upon the Rev. Mr. Cannady, a truly good-hearted Christian man, who received us at a word; and both he and his kind lady treated us handsomely, and for a nominal charge.

My wife and myself were both unwell when we left Boston, and, having taken fresh cold on the journey to Halifax, we were laid up there under the doc-tor's care, nearly the whole fortnight. I had much worry about getting tickets, for they baffled us shamefully at the Cunard office. They at first said that they did not book till the steamer came; which was not the fact. When I called again, they said they knew the steamer would come full from Boston, and therefore we had "bet-ter try to get to Liverpool by other means." Other mean Yankee excuses were made; and it was not till an influential gentleman, to whom Mr. Francis Jackson, of Boston, kindly gave us a letter, went and rebuked them, that we were able to secure our tickets. So when we went on board my wife was very poorly, and was also so ill on the voyage that I did not believe she could live to see Liverpool.

However, I am thankful to say she arrived; and, after laying up at Liver-pool very ill for two or three weeks, gradually recovered.

It was not until we stepped upon the shore at Liverpool that we were free from every slavish fear.

We raised our thankful hearts to Heaven, and could have knelt down, like the Neapolitan exiles, and kissed the soil; for we felt that from slavery

> "Heaven sure had kept this spot of earth uncurs'd,
> To show how all things were created first."

In a few days after we landed, the Rev. Francis Bishop and his lady came and invited us to be their guests; to whose unlimited kindness and watchful care my wife owes, in a great degree, her restoration to health.

We enclosed our letter from the Rev. Mr. May to Mr. Estlin, who at once wrote to invite us to his house at Bristol. On arriving there, both Mr. and Miss Estlin received us as cordially as did our first good Quaker friends in Pennsylva-nia. It grieves me much to have to mention that he is no more. Everyone who knew him can truthfully say—

> "Peace to the memory of a man of worth,
> A man of letters, and of manners too!
> Of manners sweet as Virtue always wears
> When gay Good-nature dresses her in smiles."[50]

It was principally through the extreme kindness of Mr. Estlin, the Right Hon. Lady Noel Byron, Miss Harriet Martineau, Mrs. Reid, Miss Sturch, and a few other good friends, that my wife and myself were able to spend a short time at a school in this country, to acquire a little of that education which we were so shamefully deprived of while in the house of bondage. The school is under the supervision of the Misses Lushington, daughters of the Right Hon. Stephen Lushington, D.C.L. During our stay at the school we received the greatest attention from every one; and I am particularly indebted to Thomas Wilson, Esq., of Bradmore House, Chiswick, (who was then the master,) for the deep interest he took in trying to get me on in my studies. We shall ever fondly and gratefully cherish the memory of our endeared and departed friend, Mr. Estlin. We, as well as the Anti-Slavery cause, lost a good friend in him. However, if departed spirits in Heaven are conscious of the wickedness of this world, and are allowed to speak, he will never fail to plead in the presence of the angelic host, and before the great and just Judge, for downtrodden and outraged humanity.

> "Therefore I cannot think thee wholly gone;
>   The better part of thee is with us still;
> Thy soul its hampering clay aside hath thrown,
>   And only freer wrestles with the ill.
>
> "Thou livest in the life of all good things;
>   What words thou spak'st for Freedom shall not die;
> Thou sleepest not, for now thy Love hath wings
>   To soar where hence thy hope could hardly fly.
>
> "And often, from that other world, on this
>   Some gleams from great souls gone before may shine,
> To shed on struggling hearts a clearer bliss,
>   And clothe the Right with lustre more divine.
>
> "Farewell! good man, good angel now! this hand
>   Soon, like thine own, shall lose its cunning, too;
> Soon shall this soul, like thine, bewildered stand,
>   Then leap to thread the free unfathomed blue."
>
> —James Russell Lowell.[51]

In the preceding pages I have not dwelt upon the great barbarities which are practised upon the slaves; because I wish to present the system in its mildest form, and to show that the "tender mercies of the wicked are cruel." But I do now, however, most solemnly declare, that a very large majority of the American slaves are over-worked, under-fed, and frequently unmercifully flogged.

I have often seen slaves tortured in every conceivable manner. I have seen them hunted down and torn by bloodhounds. I have seen them shamefully beaten, and branded with hot irons. I have seen them hunted, and even burned alive at the stake, frequently for offences that would be applauded if committed by white persons for similar purposes.

In short, it is well known in England, if not all over the world, that the Americans, as a people, are notoriously mean and cruel towards all coloured persons, whether they are bond or free.

> "Oh, tyrant, thou who sleepest
> On a volcano, from whose pent-up wrath,
> Already some red flashes bursting up,
> Beware!"

1. *The Liberator* 19 (2 February 1849). Cited in Blackett, *Barriers,* 90.

2. *The Liberator* 19 (16 February 1849): 27. Cited in Starling, *Slave Narrative,* 235–236.

3. Starling, *Slave Narrative,* 238.

4. Bontemps, *Great Slave Narratives,* 269.

5. Blackett, *Barriers,* 98, 101–103; Gara, "Craft, Ellen," 140.

6. Starling, *Slave Narrative,* 237; Blassingame, *Slave Testimony,* xxxix.

7. Andrews, *Free Story,* 213.

8. For a fascinating discussion of Craft's involvement with Africa, see Blackett, *Barriers,* 108–121.

9. Gara, "Craft, Ellen," 140; Freedman, *Running,* xv–xvii; Blackett, *Barriers,* 122–130.

10. Boston *Daily Advertiser,* July 30, 1875. Cited in Freedman, *Running,* xvii–xviii.

11. Blackett, *Barriers,* 130–136.

12. William Cowper (1731–1800), *The Task.* Cowper was a forerunner of the British romantic poets, and wrote a number of antislavery verses. *The Task* (1785) was probably his most famous poem.

13. *Acts* 17:26.

14. John Milton (1608–74), *Paradise Lost.*

15. Ellen Craft's father was also her master, Major James C. Smith of Macon, one of the incorporators of that city in 1823. The daughter referred to was Eliza C. Smith; in 1837 she married Dr. Robert Collins, and Ellen was given to the pair as a wedding present. A prominent citizen of Macon, Collins owned the Monroe & Bibb Banking Company (where William's master worked), more than ten thousand acres of farmland, and, by the time of his death in 1861, 102 slaves. Freedman, *Running,* iii–iv; Blackett, *Barriers,* 88.

16. Calaboose, or prison-house.

17. Ira H. Taylor. Freedman, *Running,* iv.

18. Jesse Hutchinson, "The Bereaved Mother" (1844).

19. Anonymous, "The Slave-Auction—A Fact." In *Garland of Freedom,* III:54–55; Brown, *Anti-Slavery Harp,* 24.

20. *Job* 3:17.

21. Henry Wadsworth Longfellow (1807–82), "The Spanish Student."

22. Longfellow, "The Quadroon Girl."

23. As Blyden Jackson points out, it would have been impractical for Ellen Craft to pose as a white woman rather than a man: "Young white women in the antebellum South, as in America of all generations, were not in the habit of traipsing around the countryside, whatever their condition, accompanied only by equally young male blacks, free or slave." Jackson, *History,* 149.

24. *Scott v. Sandford,* 1857. While the decision did indeed rob blacks of citizenship, thereby preventing them from bringing suit in federal court, it did not legalize crimes against blacks.

25. "Epigram to the United States of North America." Campbell (1777–1844) was an important Scottish poet.

26. Bunyan, *The Pilgrim's Progress.* See note 35, below.

27. A liniment composed usually of alcohol, soap, camphor, and rosemary.

28. Fellow.

29. Hampton (c. 1752–1835) was a soldier in the American Revolution and War of 1812 who also served as a U.S. congressman. The wealthiest planter of his day, he developed large cotton plantations in South Carolina and sugar plantations in Mississippi.

30. Run away.

31. A filibuster was an American adventurer who led armed expeditions, without governmental consent, into countries with whom America was at peace. There were a series of such filibustering expeditions into Cuba, Mexico, and Central and South America in the years before the Civil War.

32. A personification of America.

33. Calhoun (1782–1850) was congressman, secretary of war, vice president, and leader of the proslavery faction in Congress.

34. A silk hat.

35. John Bunyan (1628–88) was a British author best known for his masterpiece *The Pilgrim's Progress from This World to That Which Is to Come* (1678–84), of which this is a plot summary.

36. On March 18, 1553, Elizabeth, not yet queen, was arrested on suspicion of conspiring with Sir Thomas Wyatt to overthrow Queen Mary's regime. She was imprisoned in the Tower of London for several months.

37. William Still, the black chairman of the Acting Vigilant Committee of the Philadelphia branch of the Underground Railway, wrote in his book *The Underground Rail Road* (1872) that the "constant strain and pressure on Ellen's nerves" had caused her to be "physically very much prostrated" (370). Freedman, *Running*, 5.

38. Daniel Webster (1782–1852), congressman, secretary of state, and one of America's greatest orators, backed the Compromise of 1850 out of concern for the preservation of the Union; because the Compromise included the worst of the fugitive slave laws, he was reviled as a traitor by abolitionists.

39. These were Willis Hughes, a slave-hunter and jailer, and John Knight, who had worked with William Craft in a cabinet shop in Macon and had come to identify him. Acording to Rev. Theodore Parker, who was the Crafts' Boston minister, Knight tried to trap William by going to the cabinet shop where he worked, pretending to be his friend; he suggested that William give him a tour of Boston, then tried to lure him to his hotel, pretending to have news of Ellen's mother. William, however, was properly suspicious of Knight and refused to accompany him. Freedman, *Running*, vi; Blackett, *Barriers*, 93.

40. The writ of arrest charged William Craft as a thief, having stolen himself and the clothes he wore. Freedman, *Running*, vii.

41. In fact, large meetings were held, where blacks pledged to protect the Crafts and appealed to the legislature to arrest Hughes and Knight. According to one observer, the black inhabitants of homes on Belknap and Cambridge streets were armed with guns, swords, and knives. Blackett, *Barriers*, 92–93.

42. Friends also stood watch. One reporter observed that "no man could approach within 100 years of Craft's shop without being seen by a hundred eyes, and a signal would call a powerful body at a moment's warning." William Craft was later taken to a friend's, where kegs of gunpowder were put in the basement in case of an attack. Ibid., 92.

43. Specifically to Brookline, Massachusetts. Ibid.

44. Hughes's bail for each of these three "crimes" (one slander and two kidnapping attempts) was set at ten thousand dollars, but was paid by a sympathetic Bostonian. Freedman, *Running*, vii; Blackett, *Barriers*, 93.

45. When Hughes was released from jail, a black man broke the glass of his carriage and was about to shoot him when one of the Vigilance Committee pulled him away, seeking to avoid violence. Nonetheless, militants chased the carriage for a long distance. The Vigilance Committee proceeded to issue posters graphically describing Hughes and Knight in an attempt to harass them enough to force them to leave Boston. Finally, after being watched constantly, shouted at, and warned by Rev. Parker of further violence, they left for New York. Freedman, *Running*, vii–viii.

46. From Rev. Parker's journal: "Talk in the newspapers about the President sending on 600 or 700 soldiers to dragoon us into keeping the Fugitive Slave Law! The Bostonians remember how that business of quartering soldiers on us in time of peace worked in the last century! It is worthwhile to read Hutchinson and Adams." (This "talk" was just that, and the president carried out no such intention.) Before the Crafts departed Boston, the Reverend performed a somewhat radical abolitionist marriage ceremony because, as he wrote, "their marriage lacks the solemnity of law." In it, he put a Bible into William's left hand, and a sword (actually a "California knife") into his right, telling him "if the worst came to the worst to use that to save his wife's liberty, or her life, if he could effect it in no other way." Ibid., ix–xi.

47. *Micah* 4:4.

48. Cowper, "Expostulation."

49. A servant who shines shoes.

50. Cowper, *The Task.*

51. "Elegy on the Death of Dr. Channing." Lowell (1819–91) was an important American poet and a friend of the abolitionist cause.

HARRIET JACOBS (LINDA BRENT)

HARRIET JACOBS (c. 1813–97) was the first female slave to write her own autobiography, for previous narratives of female slaves had been penned by others.[1] Published at the tail end of the antebellum era, her *Incidents in the Life of a Slave Girl* is perhaps the most intimate and emotionally compelling slave narrative of all.

The idea for it may have been suggested to her when she was working in the antislavery reading room, office, and bookstore she and her brother had established above the Rochester offices of Frederick Douglass's newspaper *The North Star*. The Quaker reformer Amy Post, with whom Jacobs lived for nine months, was her confidante, and urged her to publish her history to boost abolitionist sentiment. Although Jacobs had probably read many slave narratives while working in the reading room, she felt hesitant about writing her own.[2]

After leaving Rochester, she was employed to take care of the children of a prominent New York writer, Nathaniel Parker Willis, and it was in his home that she began to compose her memoirs. But because Willis was proslavery, Jacobs kept her writing secret, working only at night and refusing to discuss her book with her employers. At first she had planned to dictate her narrative to Harriet Beecher Stowe, but Stowe's careless response led Jacobs to feel that Stowe "had betrayed her as a woman, denigrated her as a mother, and threatened her as a writer," as her biographer Jean Fagan Yellin puts it.[3] In 1854, Jacobs wrote to Post:

> as yet I have not written a single page by daylight[.] Mrs W[illis] dont know from my lips that I am writing for a Book and has never seen a line of what I have written . . . with the care of the little baby the big Babies and at the household calls I have but a little time to think or write but I have tried in my poor way to do my best and that is not much . . . just now the poor Book is in its Chrysalis state and though I can never make it a butterfly I am satisfied to have it creep meekly among some of the humbler bugs . . .[4]

Jacobs also began writing short pieces on the sexual abuse of slave women, some of which appeared anonymously in Horace Greeley's New York *Tribune*.[5] By 1857, the manuscript was substantially completed. She wrote Post:

> I have My dear friend—Striven faithfully to give a true and just account of my own life in Slavery—God knows I have tried to do it in a Christian spirit—there are some things that I might have made plainer I know—Woman can whisper—her cool wrongs into the ear of a very dear friend—much easier than she can record them for the world to read—I have left nothing out but what I thought—the world might believe that a Slave Woman was too willing to pour out—that she might gain their sympathies[.] I ask nothing—I have placed myself before you to be judged as a woman whether I deserve your pity or contempt—I have another object in view—it is to come

to you just as I am a poor Slave Mother—not to tell you what I have heard but what I have seen—and what I have suffered—and if their [sic] is any sympathy to give— let it be given to the thousands—of of [sic] Slave Mothers that are still in bondage— suffering far more than I have— . . .[6]

For several years she tried to get her book into print, but publishers were reluctant to take it without an endorsement from a prominent writer. So she sent the book to Lydia Maria Child, one of the most famous female writers in the country and a prominent abolitionist, who arranged for the book's publication by a Boston publisher, and worked on the manuscript herself. Child wrote to Jacobs in 1860:

> I have very little occasion to alter the language, which is wonderfully good, for one whose opportunities for education have been so limited. . . . But I am copying a great deal of it, for the purpose of transposing sentences and pages, so as to bring the story into continuous *order,* and the remarks into *appropriate* places. I think you will see that this renders the story much more clear and entertaining.

She explained to another friend, "I abridged, and struck out superfluous words sometimes; but I don't think I altered fifty words in the whole volume. . . . I put the savage cruelties into one chapter, entitled 'neighboring planters,' in order that those who shrink from 'supping upon horrors' might omit them, without interrupting the thread of the story."

Unfortunately the publisher went bankrupt; so Jacobs bought the plates and published the book herself. It appeared in early February 1861, only two months before the outbreak of the war to end slavery.[7]

For Jacobs, however, slavery was less a political fact than a physical condition. The abolitionists, as Mary Titus points out, described "slavery as a poison or disease that affects both the body and politic of the nation and the body natural of each citizen." Jacobs's master had been a doctor whose "treatment" worsened her condition to an unbearable degree. From her point of view, all of society under slavery was sick; and in her book she "painfully questions whether health—personal or national—can ever be regained after the long illness of slavery."[8]

In the face of this poisonous atmosphere, Jacobs refused to give in to slavery's dictates, and maintained complete control over her body, even at the sacrifice of her virtue. Time and again she deliberately diverged from the conduct that was considered proper for a woman in her position. As a result her book is, as Hazel Carby has written, "the most sophisticated, sustained narrative dissection of the conventions of true womanhood by a black author before emancipation."[9]

In her struggles for freedom, Jacobs frequently received support from her family, from the black community, and from a number of women, both black and white. Unlike many male slave narrators, who represented themselves as solitary figures in a wilderness, Jacobs acted in concert with her family and friends, forming, by the end of her tale, a kind of "American sisterhood."[10] But this companionship coexisted with an ever present and often overpowering sense of loneliness, secrecy, and deprivation. Not even the Gothic novels of the time described more stifling and oppressive conditions than those that Jacobs suffered during the years prior to her departure from the South. Characteristically, in this period Jacobs began to write, imagining herself a free woman in the North while simultaneously enacting a trickster's revenge upon her master. As William Andrews puts it, "In her garret, where she reads and sews, she wields a literary needle that injects her master's mind (instead of her own) with poisonous 'delusions.'"[11] In this act, as in many others, Jacobs gave the lie to previous depictions of slave women, who were usually portrayed as helpless sexual victims. Instead, Jacobs continually reversed the words and roles expected of her.

The unconventionality of her narrative begins with her title. The substitution of *Incidents* for *Narrative* highlights her intention to tell an *incomplete* narrative—*necessarily* incomplete since the limits imposed by the conventions of the era prevented her from fully revealing her sexual history. The title page, with the name of its author conspicuously absent, also signifies Jacobs's conscious decision to depart from the documentary conventions of the slave narrative. Except in the cases of well-known figures such as Amy and Isaac Post (and in one other case—that of the treacherous slave girl Jenny[12]), Jacobs uses pseudonyms in place of characters' real names, naming herself Linda Brent and her master Dr. Flint. In the documentary slave narrative, even the most gruesome, excruciating details are usually spelled out in full; but Jacobs takes an almost Jamesian approach by concentrating on the psychological rather than the physical effects of her sexual oppression. These departures from tradition—as well as many others—show Jacobs shaping her narrative to resemble a novel.

Unlike most narratives but like most novels, Jacobs's book is full of dialogue—in fact Andrews claims that "there is more dialogue in *Incidents* than in any other black autobiography of the antebellum era." This dialogue gives Jacobs an opportunity to describe verbal sparring matches between herself and her master, in which she asserts the right to speak certain words forbidden to her, to "define herself through language," and to redefine her master's words—particularly the word *love*—in her favor.[13] But what is uttered in *Incidents* may be less important than what is not uttered. Jacobs's world is one of secrets—secrets kept not only from her foes, but from the most cherished members of her family. They circumscribe her existence and pervade her narrative, with its pseudonyms, elisions, deceptions, and subterfuges. These methods, not the straightforward path, lead to insight, freedom, and actualization for Jacobs. As Jacqueline Goldsby points out, in this context, "the true nature of slavery can be revealed only through disguise and masquerade."[14]

No matter how much her narrative resembles a novel, however, through her protagonist's actions Jacobs also defies the conventions of the mid-nineteenth-century women's novel. And these conventions were well defined. In the novel of seduction, the heroine, a genteel young lady, is virtuous, but helpless; she falls prey to an unscrupulous man; she yields herself to him; and she dies.[15] Jacobs, by contrast, subverts the sexual roles she has been given, politicizes her sexuality, and uses it as a weapon.[16] It is small wonder that Jacobs only found a large readership over one hundred years after her book's publication.

During that century, *Incidents* was in turn neglected and suspected of being fictional; its authorship was also called into question. It probably influenced Frances Ellen Watkins Harper's pioneering novel *Iola Leroy; Or, Shadows Up-*

lifted (1892), which in turn influenced Zora Neal Hurston and other black women writers.[17] But it was not reprinted until 1973; and it was not until 1981 that it was finally authenticated by Jean Yellin, who dug up a treasure trove of information about Jacobs and the characters and events of her narrative. In the critical edition that Yellin published in 1987, she also included a sophisticated literary analysis of the book. She concluded:

> *Incidents,* like the great American romances, transforms the conventions of literature. In Jacobs's hand, the passive female of the captivity narratives acts to save herself; in her hand, the slave narrative is changed from the story of a hero who single-handedly seeks freedom and literacy to the story of a hero tightly bound to family and community who seeks freedom and a home for her children. In her hand, the pathetic seduced "tragic mulatto" of white fiction is metamorphosed from a victim of white male deception and fickleness into an inexperienced girl making desperate choices in her struggle for autonomy; the "mammy" of white fiction becomes not the white babies' nurse but the nurturer and liberator of her own children. In her hand, the madwoman in the attic sanely plots for her freedom; instead of studying self-control within the domestic setting, the young woman learns to engage in political action. Harriet Jacobs tells a story new in black literature, in women's writings, and in American letters: a woman's "true and just account of my own life in slavery."[18]

But by the end of her narrative, Jacobs had not yet reached her goal. She was free from the laws of slavery, but economic and social chains still bound her. The heroic quest for home—a place of freedom, privacy, and family—that had dominated her tale was left unfulfilled.[19]

A year after its publication in the United States, *Incidents* was published in England under the title *The Deeper Wrong*. Reviews were encouraging: the *Weekly Anglo-African* wrote, "It is the 'oft told tale' of American slavery, in another and more revolting phase than that which is generally seen: More revolting because it is of the spirit and not the flesh."[20] Describing Jacobs's visit to London in 1858, the *Anti-Slavery Advocate* wrote:

> Between two and three years ago, a coloured woman, about as dark as a southern Spaniard or Portuguese, aged about five-and-forty, and with a kind and pleasing expression of countenance, called on us. . . . We had an excellent opportunity of becoming acquainted with one of the truest heroines we have ever met with. Her manners were marked by refinement and sensibility, and by an utter absence of pretence or affectation; and we were deeply touched by the circumstances of her early life which she then communicated, and which exactly coincide with those of the volume now before us.[21]

Although her narrative only went through one printing, Jacobs apparently became well known among abolitionists. Beginning in 1862, she, along with other black women of note, worked to aid the "contraband," the black refugees following the Union Army through the South. Over the 1860s, she and her daughter worked in Washington, Alexandria, and Savannah, distributing clothing and supplies; organizing schools, nursing homes, and orphanages; and reporting on their own work in the northern press. Harriet Jacobs was named to the executive committee of the feminist Women's Loyal National League, and her daughter Louisa lectured for the radical American Equal Rights Association.

Confronted with antiblack violence in the South, they moved to Cambridge, Massachusetts, where they ran a boardinghouse; but in the mid-1870s they moved back down to Washington, where Jacobs died on March 7, 1897. She is buried in Mount Auburn Cemetery, Cambridge.[22]

INCIDENTS

IN THE

LIFE OF A SLAVE GIRL.

WRITTEN BY HERSELF.

"Northerners know nothing at all about Slavery. They think it is perpetual bondage only. They have no conception of the depth of *degradation* involved in that word, Slavery; if they had, they would never cease their efforts until so horrible a system was overthrown."

A WOMAN OF NORTH CAROLINA.[23]

"Rise up, ye women that are at ease! Hear my voice, ye careless daughters! Give ear unto my speech."

ISAIAH xxxii. 9.

EDITED BY L. MARIA CHILD.[24]

BOSTON:
PUBLISHED FOR THE AUTHOR.
1861.

PREFACE BY THE AUTHOR.

READER, be assured this narrative is no fiction. I am aware that some of my adventures may seem incredible; but they are, nevertheless, strictly true. I have not exaggerated the wrongs inflicted by Slavery; on the contrary, my descriptions fall far short of the facts. I have concealed the names of places, and given persons fictitious names. I had no motive for secrecy on my own account, but I deemed it kind and considerate towards others to pursue this course.

I wish I were more competent to the task I have undertaken. But I trust my readers will excuse deficiencies in consideration of circumstances. I was born and reared in Slavery; and I remained in a Slave State twenty-seven years. Since I have been at the North, it has been necessary for me to work diligently for my own support, and the education of my children. This has not left me much leisure to make up for the loss of early opportunities to improve myself; and it has compelled me to write these pages at irregular intervals, whenever I could snatch an hour from household duties.

When I first arrived in Philadelphia, Bishop Paine[25] advised me to publish a sketch of my life, but I told him I was altogether incompetent to such an undertaking. Though I have improved my mind somewhat since that time, I still remain of the same opinion; but I trust my motives will excuse what might otherwise seem presumptuous. I have not written my experiences in order to attract attention to myself; on the contrary, it would have been more pleasant to me to have been silent about my own history. Neither do I care to excite sympathy for my own sufferings. But I do earnestly desire to arouse the women of the North to a realizing sense of the condition of two millions of women at the South, still in bondage, suffering what I suffered, and most of them far worse. I want to add my testimony to that of abler pens to convince the people of the Free States what Slavery really is. Only by experience can any one realize how deep, and dark, and foul is that pit of abominations. May the blessing of God rest on this imperfect effort in behalf of my persecuted people!

LINDA BRENT.

INTRODUCTION BY THE EDITOR.

———————

THE author of the following autobiography is personally known to me, and her conversation and manners inspire me with confidence. During the last seventeen years, she has lived the greater part of the time with a distinguished family in New York, and has so deported herself as to be highly esteemed by them. This fact is sufficient, without further credentials of her character. I believe those who know her will not be disposed to doubt her veracity, though some incidents in her story are more romantic than fiction.

At her request, I have revised her manuscript; but such changes as I have made have been mainly for purposes of condensation and orderly arrangement. I have not added any thing to the incidents, or changed the import of her very pertinent remarks. With trifling exceptions, both the ideas and the language are her own. I pruned excrescences a little, but otherwise I had no reason for changing her lively and dramatic way of telling her own story. The names of both persons and places are known to me; but for good reasons I suppress them.

It will naturally excite surprise that a woman reared in Slavery should be able to write so well. But circumstances will explain this. In the first place, nature endowed her with quick perceptions. Secondly, the mistress, with whom she lived till she was twelve years old, was a kind, considerate friend, who taught her to read and spell. Thirdly, she was placed in favorable circumstances after she came to the North; having frequent intercourse with intelligent persons, who felt a friendly interest in her welfare, and were disposed to give her opportunities for self-improvement.

I am well aware that many will accuse me of indecorum for presenting these pages to the public; for the experiences of this intelligent and much-injured woman belong to a class which some call delicate subjects, and others indelicate. This peculiar phase of Slavery has generally been kept veiled; but the public ought to be made acquainted with its monstrous features, and I willingly take the responsibility of presenting them with the veil withdrawn. I do this for the sake of my sisters in bondage, who are suffering wrongs so foul, that our ears are too delicate to listen to them. I do it with the hope of arousing conscientious and reflecting women at the North to a sense of their duty in the exertion of moral influence on the question of Slavery, on all possible occasions. I do it with the hope that every man who reads this narrative will swear solemnly before God that, so far as he has power to prevent it, no fugitive from Slavery shall ever be sent back to suffer in that loathsome den of corruption and cruelty.

L. MARIA CHILD.

CONTENTS.

INCIDENTS

IN THE

LIFE OF A SLAVE GIRL,

SEVEN YEARS CONCEALED.

I.

CHILDHOOD.

I WAS born a slave; but I never knew it till six years of happy childhood had passed away. My father[26] was a carpenter, and considered so intelligent and skilful in his trade, that, when buildings out of the common line were to be erected, he was sent for from long distances, to be head workman. On condition of paying his mistress two hundred dollars a year, and supporting himself, he was allowed to work at his trade, and manage his own affairs. His strongest wish was to purchase his children; but, though he several times offered his hard earnings for that purpose, he never succeeded. In complexion my parents were a light shade of brownish yellow, and were termed mulattoes. They lived together in a comfortable home; and, though we were all slaves, I was so fondly shielded that I never dreamed I was a piece of merchandise, trusted to them for safe keeping, and liable to be demanded of them at any moment. I had one brother, William,[27] who was two years younger than myself—a bright, affectionate child. I had also a great treasure in my maternal grandmother,[28] who was a remarkable woman in many respects. She was the daughter of a planter in South Carolina, who, at his death, left her mother and his three children free, with money to go to St. Augustine, where they had relatives. It was during the Revolutionary War; and they were captured on their passage, carried back, and sold to different purchasers. Such was the story my grandmother used to tell me; but I do not remember all the particulars. She was a little girl when she was captured and sold to the keeper of a large hotel.[29] I have often heard her tell how hard she fared during childhood. But as she grew older she evinced so much intelligence, and was so faithful, that her master and mistress could not help seeing it was for their interest to take care of such a valuable piece of property. She became an indispensable personage in the household, officiating in all capacities, from cook and wet nurse to seamstress. She was much praised for her cooking; and her nice crackers became so famous in the neighborhood that many people were desirous of obtaining them. In consequence of numerous requests of this kind, she asked permission of

544

her mistress to bake crackers at night, after all the household work was done; and she obtained leave to do it, provided she would clothe herself and her children from the profits. Upon these terms, after working hard all day for her mistress, she began her midnight bakings, assisted by her two oldest children. The business proved profitable; and each year she laid by a little, which was saved for a fund to purchase her children. Her master died, and the property was divided among his heirs. The widow had her dower in the hotel, which she continued to keep open. My grandmother remained in her service as a slave; but her children were divided among her master's children. As she had five, Benjamin,[30] the youngest one, was sold, in order that each heir might have an equal portion of dollars and cents. There was so little difference in our ages that he seemed more like my brother than my uncle. He was a bright, handsome lad, nearly white; for he inherited the complexion my grandmother had derived from Anglo-Saxon ancestors. Though only ten years old, seven hundred and twenty dollars were paid for him. His sale was a terrible blow to my grandmother; but she was naturally hopeful, and she went to work with renewed energy, trusting in time to be able to purchase some of her children. She had laid up three hundred dollars, which her mistress one day begged as a loan, promising to pay her soon. The reader probably knows that no promise or writing given to a slave is legally binding; for, according to Southern laws, a slave, *being* property, can *hold* no property. When my grandmother lent her hard earnings to her mistress, she trusted solely to her honor. The honor of a slaveholder to a slave!

To this good grandmother I was indebted for many comforts. My brother Willie and I often received portions of the crackers, cakes, and preserves, she made to sell; and after we ceased to be children we were indebted to her for many more important services.

Such were the unusually fortunate circumstances of my early childhood. When I was six years old, my mother[31] died; and then, for the first time, I learned, by the talk around me, that I was a slave. My mother's mistress[32] was the daughter of my grandmother's mistress. She was the foster sister of my mother; they were both nourished at my grandmother's breast. In fact, my mother had been weaned at three months old, that the babe of the mistress might obtain sufficient food. They played together as children; and, when they became women, my mother was a most faithful servant to her whiter foster sister. On her death-bed her mistress promised that her children should never suffer for any thing; and during her lifetime she kept her word. They all spoke kindly of my dead mother, who had been a slave merely in name, but in nature was noble and womanly. I grieved for her, and my young mind was troubled with the thought who would now take care of me and my little brother. I was told that my home was now to be with her mistress; and I found it a happy one. No toilsome or disagreeable duties were imposed upon me. My mistress was so kind to me that I was always glad to do her bidding, and proud to labor for her as much as my young years would permit. I would sit by her side for hours, sewing diligently, with a heart as free from care as that of any free-born white child. When she thought I was tired, she would send me out to run and jump; and away I bounded, to gather berries or flowers to decorate her room. Those were happy days—too happy to last. The slave child had no thought for the morrow; but there came that blight, which too surely waits on every human being born to be a chattel.

When I was nearly twelve years old, my kind mistress sickened and died. As I saw the cheek grow paler, and the eye more glassy, how earnestly I prayed in my heart that she might live! I loved her; for she had been almost like a mother to me. My prayers were not answered. She died, and they buried her in the little churchyard, where, day after day, my tears fell upon her grave.

I was sent to spend a week with my grandmother. I was now old enough to begin to think of the future; and again and again I asked myself what they would do with me. I felt sure I should never find another mistress so kind as the one who was gone. She had promised my dying mother that her children should never suffer for any thing; and when I remembered that, and recalled her many proofs of attachment to me, I could not help having some hopes that she had left me free. My friends were almost certain it would be so. They thought she would be sure to do it, on account of my mother's love and faithful service. But, alas! we all know that the memory of a faithful slave does not avail much to save her children from the auction block.

After a brief period of suspense, the will of my mistress was read, and we learned that she had bequeathed me to her sister's daughter, a child of five years old.[33] So vanished our hopes. My mistress had taught me the precepts of God's Word: "Thou shalt love thy neighbor as thyself."[34] "Whatsoever ye would that men should do unto you, do ye even so unto them."[35] But I was her slave, and I suppose she did not recognize me as her neighbor. I would give much to blot out from my memory that one great wrong. As a child, I loved my mistress; and, looking back on the happy days I spent with her, I try to think with less bitterness of this act of injustice. While I was with her, she taught me to read and spell; and for this privilege, which so rarely falls to the lot of a slave, I bless her memory.

She possessed but few slaves; and at her death those were all distributed among her relatives. Five of them were my grandmother's children, and had shared the same milk that nourished her mother's children. Notwithstanding my grandmother's long and faithful service to her owners, not one of her children escaped the auction block. These God-breathing machines are no more, in the sight of their masters, than the cotton they plant, or the horses they tend.

II.

THE NEW MASTER AND MISTRESS.

DR. FLINT,[36] a physician in the neighborhood, had married the sister of my mistress, and I was now the property of their little daughter. It was not without murmuring that I prepared for my new home; and what added to my unhappiness, was the fact that my brother William was purchased by the same family. My father, by his nature, as well as by the habit of transacting business as a skilful mechanic, had more of the feelings of a freeman than is common among slaves. My brother was a spirited boy; and being brought up under such influences, he early detested the name of master and mistress. One day, when his father and his mistress both happened to call him at the same time, he hesitated between the two; being perplexed to know which had the strongest claim upon his obedience. He finally concluded to go to his mistress. When my father reproved him for it, he said, "You both called me, and I didn't know which I ought to go to first."

"You are *my* child," replied our father, "and when I call you, you should come immediately, if you have to pass through fire and water."

Poor Willie! He was now to learn his first lesson of obedience to a master. Grandmother tried to cheer us with hopeful words, and they found an echo in the credulous hearts of youth.

When we entered our new home we encountered cold looks, cold words, and cold treatment. We were glad when the night came. On my narrow bed I moaned and wept, I felt so desolate and alone.

I had been there nearly a year, when a dear little friend of mine was buried. I heard her mother sob, as the clods fell on the coffin of her only child, and I turned away from the grave, feeling thankful that I still had something left to love. I met my grandmother, who said, "Come with me, Linda;" and from her tone I knew that something sad had happened. She led me apart from the people, and then said, "My child, your father is dead." Dead! How could I believe it? He had died so suddenly I had not even heard that he was sick.[37] I went home with my grandmother. My heart rebelled against God, who had taken from me mother, father, mistress, and friend. The good grandmother tried to comfort me. "Who knows the ways of God?" said she. "Perhaps they have been kindly taken from the evil days to come." Years afterwards I often thought of this. She promised to be a mother to her grandchildren, so far as she might be permitted to do so; and strengthened by her love, I returned to my master's. I thought I should be allowed to go to my father's house the next morning; but I was ordered to go for flowers, that my mistress's house might be decorated for an evening party. I spent the day gathering flowers and weaving them into festoons, while the dead body of my father was lying within a mile of me. What cared my owners for that? he was merely a piece of property. Moreover, they thought he had spoiled his children, by teaching them to feel that they were human beings. This was blasphemous doctrine for a slave to teach; presumptuous in him, and dangerous to the masters.

The next day I followed his remains to a humble grave beside that of my dear mother. There were those who knew my father's worth, and respected his memory.

My home now seemed more dreary than ever. The laugh of the little slave-children sounded harsh and cruel. It was selfish to feel so about the joy of others. My brother moved about with a very grave face. I tried to comfort him, by saying, "Take courage, Willie; brighter days will come by and by."

"You don't know any thing about it, Linda," he replied. "We shall have to stay here all our days; we shall never be free."

I argued that we were growing older and stronger, and that perhaps we might, before long, be allowed to hire our own time, and then we could earn money to buy our freedom. William declared this was much easier to say than to do; moreover, he did not intend to *buy* his freedom. We held daily controversies upon this subject.

Little attention was paid to the slaves' meals in Dr. Flint's house. If they could catch a bit of food while it was going, well and good. I gave myself no trouble on that score, for on my various errands I passed my grandmother's house, where there was always something to spare for me. I was frequently threatened with punishment if I stopped there; and my grandmother, to avoid detaining me, often stood at the gate with something for my breakfast or dinner. I was indebted to *her* for all my comforts, spiritual or temporal. It was *her* labor that supplied my scanty wardrobe. I have a vivid recollection of the linsey-woolsey dress given me every winter by Mrs. Flint. How I hated it! It was one of the badges of slavery.

While my grandmother was thus helping to support me from her hard earnings, the three hundred dollars she had lent her mistress were never repaid. When her mistress died, her son-in-law, Dr. Flint, was appointed executor. When grandmother applied to him for payment, he said the estate was insolvent, and the law prohibited payment. It did not, however, prohibit him from retaining the silver candelabra, which had been purchased with that money. I presume they will be handed down in the family, from generation to generation.

My grandmother's mistress had always promised her that, at her death, she should be free; and it was said that in her will she made good the promise. But when the estate was settled, Dr. Flint told the faithful old servant that, under existing circumstances, it was necessary she should be sold.

On the appointed day,[38] the customary advertisement was posted up, proclaiming that there would be a "public sale of negroes, horses, &c." Dr. Flint called to tell my grandmother that he was unwilling to wound her feelings by putting her up at auction, and that he would prefer to dispose of her at private sale. My grandmother saw through his hypocrisy; she understood very well that he was ashamed of the job. She was a very spirited woman, and if he was base enough to sell her, when her mistress intended she should be free, she was determined the public should know it. She had for a long time supplied many families with crackers and preserves; consequently, "Aunt Marthy," as she was called, was generally known, and every body who knew her respected her intelligence and good character. Her long and faithful service in the family was also well known, and the intention of her mistress to leave her free. When the day of sale came, she took her place among the chattels, and at the first call she sprang upon the auction-block. Many voices called out, "Shame! Shame! Who is going to sell *you*, aunt Marthy? Don't stand there! That is no place for *you*." Without saying a word, she quietly awaited her fate. No one bid for her. At last, a feeble voice said, "Fifty dollars." It came from a maiden lady,[39] seventy years old, the sister of my grandmother's deceased mistress. She had lived forty years under the same roof with my grandmother; she knew how faithfully she had served her owners, and how cruelly she had been defrauded of her rights; and she resolved to protect her. The auctioneer waited for a higher bid; but her wishes were respected; no one bid above her. She could neither read nor write; and when the bill of sale was made out, she signed it with a cross. But what consequence was that, when she had a big heart overflowing with human kindness? She gave the old servant her freedom.

At that time, my grandmother was just fifty years old. Laborious years had passed since then; and now my brother and I were slaves to the man who had defrauded her of her money, and tried to defraud her of her freedom. One of my mother's sisters, called Aunt Nancy,[40] was also a slave in his family. She was a kind, good aunt to me; and supplied the place of both housekeeper and waiting maid to her mistress. She was, in fact, at the beginning and end of every thing.

Mrs. Flint,[41] like many southern women, was totally deficient in energy. She had not strength to superintend her household affairs; but her nerves were so strong, that she could sit in her easy chair and see a woman whipped, till the blood trickled from every stroke of the lash. She was a member of the church; but partaking of the Lord's supper did not seem to put her in a Christian frame of mind. If dinner was not served at the exact time on that particular Sunday, she would station herself in the kitchen, and wait till it was dished, and then spit in all the kettles and pans that had been used for cooking. She did this to prevent the cook and her children from eking out their meagre fare with the remains of the gravy and other scrapings. The slaves could get nothing to eat except what she chose to give them. Provisions were weighed out by the pound and ounce, three times a day. I can assure you she gave them no chance to eat wheat bread from her flour barrel. She knew how many biscuits a quart of flour would make, and exactly what size they ought to be.

Dr. Flint was an epicure. The cook never sent a dinner to his table without fear and trembling; for if there happened to be a dish not to his liking, he would either order her to be whipped, or compel her to eat every mouthful of it in his presence. The poor, hungry creature might not have objected to eating it; but she did object to having her master cram it down her throat till she choked.

They had a pet dog, that was a nuisance in the house. The cook was ordered to make some Indian mush for him. He refused to eat, and when his head was held over it, the froth flowed from his mouth into the basin. He died a few minutes after. When Dr. Flint came in, he said the mush had not been well cooked, and that was the reason the animal would not eat it. He sent for the cook, and compelled her to eat it. He thought that the woman's stomach was stronger than the dog's; but her sufferings afterwards proved that he was mistaken. This poor woman endured many cruelties from her master and mistress; sometimes she was locked up, away from her nursing baby, for a whole day and night.

When I had been in the family a few weeks, one of the plantation slaves was brought to town, by order of his master. It was near night when he arrived, and Dr. Flint ordered him to be taken to the work house, and tied up to the joist, so that his feet would just escape the ground. In that situation he was to wait till the doctor had taken his tea. I shall never forget that night. Never before, in my life, had I heard hundreds of blows fall, in succession, on a human being. His piteous groans, and his "O, pray don't, massa," rang in my ear for months afterwards. There were many conjectures as to the cause of this terrible punishment. Some said master accused him of stealing corn; others said the slave had quarrelled with his wife, in presence of the overseer, and had accused his master of being the father of her child. They were both black, and the child was very fair.

I went into the work house next morning, and saw the cowhide still wet with blood, and the boards all covered with gore. The poor man lived, and continued to quarrel with his wife. A few months afterwards Dr. Flint handed them both over to a slave-trader. The guilty man put their value into his pocket, and had the satisfaction of knowing that they were out of sight and hearing. When the mother was delivered into the trader's hands, she said, "You *promised* to treat me well." To which he replied, "You have let your tongue run too far; damn you!" She had forgotten that it was a crime for a slave to tell who was the father of her child.

From others than the master persecution also comes in such cases. I once saw a young slave girl dying soon after the birth of a child nearly white. In her agony she cried out, "O Lord, come and take me!" Her mistress stood by, and mocked at her like an incarnate fiend. "You suffer, do you?" she exclaimed. "I am glad of it. You deserve it all, and more too."

The girl's mother said, "The baby is dead, thank God; and I hope my poor child will soon be in heaven, too."

"Heaven!" retorted the mistress. "There is no such place for the like of her and her bastard."

The poor mother turned away, sobbing. Her dying daughter called her, feebly, and as she bent over her, I heard her say, "Don't grieve so, mother; God knows all about it; and HE will have mercy upon me."

Her sufferings, afterwards, became so intense, that her mistress felt unable to stay; but when she left the room, the scornful smile was still on her lips. Seven children called her mother. The poor black woman had but the one child, whose eyes she saw closing in death, while she thanked God for taking her away from the greater bitterness of life.

III.

THE SLAVES' NEW YEAR'S DAY.

DR. FLINT owned a fine residence in town, several farms, and about fifty slaves,[42] besides hiring a number by the year.

Hiring-day at the south takes place on the 1st of January. On the 2d, the slaves are expected to go to their new masters. On a farm, they work until the corn and cotton are laid. They then have two holidays. Some masters give them a good dinner under the trees. This over, they work until Christmas eve. If no heavy charges are meantime brought against them, they are given four or five holidays, whichever the master or overseer may think proper. Then comes New

Year's eve; and they gather together their little alls, or more properly speaking, their little nothings, and wait anxiously for the dawning of day. At the appointed hour the grounds are thronged with men, women, and children, waiting, like criminals, to hear their doom pronounced. The slave is sure to know who is the most humane, or cruel master, within forty miles of him.

It is easy to find out, on that day, who clothes and feeds his slaves well; for he is surrounded by a crowd, begging, "Please, massa, hire me this year. I will work *very* hard, massa."

If a slave is unwilling to go with his new master, he is whipped, or locked up in jail, until he consents to go, and promises not to run away during the year. Should he chance to change his mind, thinking it justifiable to violate an extorted promise, woe unto him if he is caught! The whip is used till the blood flows at his feet; and his stiffened limbs are put in chains, to be dragged in the field for days and days!

If he lives until the next year, perhaps the same man will hire him again, without even giving him an opportunity of going to the hiring-ground. After those for hire are disposed of, those for sale are called up.

O, you happy free women, contrast *your* New Year's day with that of the poor bond-woman! With you it is a pleasant season, and the light of the day is blessed. Friendly wishes meet you every where, and gifts are showered upon you. Even hearts that have been estranged from you soften at this season, and lips that have been silent echo back, "I wish you a happy New Year." Children bring their little offerings, and raise their rosy lips for a caress. They are your own, and no hand but that of death can take them from you.

But to the slave mother New Year's day comes laden with peculiar sorrows. She sits on her cold cabin door, watching the children who may all be torn from her the next morning; and often does she wish that she and they might die before the day dawns. She may be an ignorant creature, degraded by the system that has brutalized her from childhood; but she has a mother's instincts, and is capable of feeling a mother's agonies.

On one of these sale days, I saw a mother lead seven children to the auction-block. She knew that *some* of them would be taken from her; but they took *all.* The children were sold to a slave-trader, and their mother was bought by a man in her own town. Before night her children were all far away. She begged the trader to tell her where he intended to take them; this he refused to do. How *could* he, when he knew he would sell them, one by one, wherever he could command the highest price? I met that mother in the street, and her wild, haggard face lives to-day in my mind. She wrung her hands in anguish, and exclaimed, "Gone! All gone! Why *don't* God kill me?" I had no words wherewith to comfort her. Instances of this kind are of daily, yea, of hourly occurrence.

Slaveholders have a method, peculiar to their institution, of getting rid of *old* slaves, whose lives have been worn out in their service. I knew an old woman, who for seventy years faithfully served her master. She had become almost helpless, from hard labor and disease. Her owners moved to Alabama, and the old black woman was left to be sold to any body who would give twenty dollars for her.

IV.

THE SLAVE WHO DARED TO FEEL LIKE A MAN.

Two years had passed since I entered Dr. Flint's family, and those years had brought much of the knowledge that comes from experience, though they had afforded little opportunity for any other kinds of knowledge.

My grandmother had, as much as possible, been a mother to her orphan grandchildren. By perseverance and unwearied industry, she was now mistress of a snug little home, surrounded with the necessaries of life. She would have been happy could her children have shared them with her. There remained but three children and two grandchildren, all slaves. Most earnestly did she strive to make us feel that it was the will of God: that He had seen fit to place us under such circumstances; and though it seemed hard, we ought to pray for contentment.

It was a beautiful faith, coming from a mother who could not call her children her own. But I, and Benjamin, her youngest boy, condemned it. We reasoned that it was much more the will of God that we should be situated as she was. We longed for a home like hers. There we always found sweet balsam for our troubles. She was so loving, so sympathizing! She always met us with a smile, and listened with patience to all our sorrows. She spoke so hopefully, that unconsciously the clouds gave place to sunshine. There was a grand big oven there, too, that baked bread and nice things for the town, and we knew there was always a choice bit in store for us.

But, alas! even the charms of the old oven failed to reconcile us to our hard lot. Benjamin was now a tall, handsome lad, strongly and gracefully made, and with a spirit too bold and daring for a slave. My brother William, now twelve years old, had the same aversion to the word master that he had when he was an urchin of seven years. I was his confidant. He came to me with all his troubles. I remember one instance in particular. It was on a lovely spring morning, and when I marked the sunlight dancing here and there, its beauty seemed to mock my sadness. For my master, whose restless, craving, vicious nature roved about day and night, seeking whom to devour, had just left me, with stinging, scorching words; words that scathed ear and brain like fire. O, how I despised him! I thought how glad I should be, if some day when he walked the earth, it would open and swallow him up, and disencumber the world of a plague.

When he told me that I was made for his use, made to obey his command in *every* thing; that I was nothing but a slave, whose will must and should surrender to his, never before had my puny arm felt half so strong.

So deeply was I absorbed in painful reflections afterwards, that I neither saw nor heard the entrance of any one, till the voice of William sounded close beside me. "Linda," said he, "what makes you look so sad? I love you. O, Linda, isn't this a bad world? Every body seems so cross and unhappy. I wish I had died when poor father did."

I told him that every body was *not* cross, or unhappy; that those who had pleasant homes, and kind friends, and who were not afraid to love them, were happy. But we, who were slave-children, without father or mother, could not expect to be happy. We must be good, perhaps that would bring us contentment.

"Yes," he said, "I try to be good; but what's the use? They are all the time troubling me." Then he proceeded to relate his afternoon's difficulty with young master Nicholas.[43] It seemed that the brother of master Nicholas had pleased himself with making up stories about William. Master Nicholas said he should be flogged, and he would do it. Whereupon he went to work; but William fought bravely, and the young master, finding he was getting the better of him, undertook to tie his hands behind him. He failed in that likewise. By dint of kicking and fisting, William came out of the skirmish none the worse for a few scratches.

He continued to discourse on his young master's *meanness;* how he whipped the *little* boys, but was a perfect coward when a tussle ensued between him and white boys of his own size. On such occasions he always took to his legs. William had other charges to make against him. One was his rubbing up pennies with quicksilver, and passing them off for quarters of a dollar on an old man who kept a fruit stall. William was often sent to buy fruit, and he earnestly inquired of me what he ought to do under such circumstances. I told him it was certainly wrong to deceive the old man, and that it was his duty to tell him of the impositions practised by his young master. I assured him the old man would not be slow to comprehend the whole, and there the matter would end. William thought it might with the old man, but not with *him.* He said he did not mind the smart of the whip, but he did not like the *idea* of being whipped.

While I advised him to be good and forgiving I was not unconscious of the beam in my own eye. It was the very knowledge of my own shortcomings that urged me to retain, if possible, some sparks of my brother's God-given nature. I had not lived fourteen years in slavery for nothing. I had felt, seen, and heard enough, to read the characters, and question the motives, of those around me. The war of my life had begun; and though one of God's most powerless creatures, I resolved never to be conquered. Alas, for me!

If there was one pure, sunny spot for me, I believed it to be in Benjamin's heart, and in another's, whom I loved with all the ardor of a girl's first love. My owner knew of it, and sought in every way to render me miserable. He did not resort to corporal punishment, but to all the petty, tyrannical ways that human ingenuity could devise.

I remember the first time I was punished. It was in the month of February. My grandmother had taken my old shoes, and replaced them with a new pair. I needed them; for several inches of snow had fallen, and it still continued to fall. When I walked through Mrs. Flint's room, their creaking grated harshly on her refined nerves. She called me to her, and asked what I had about me that made such a horrid noise. I told her it was my new shoes. "Take them off," said she; "and if you put them on again, I'll throw them into the fire."

I took them off, and my stockings also. She then sent me a long distance, on an errand. As I went through the snow, my bare feet tingled. That night I was very hoarse; and I went to bed thinking the next day would find me sick, perhaps dead. What was my grief on waking to find myself quite well!

I had imagined if I died, or was laid up for some time, that my mistress would feel a twinge of remorse that she had so hated "the little imp," as she styled me. It was my ignorance of that mistress that gave rise to such extravagant imaginings.

Dr. Flint occasionally had high prices offered for me; but he always said, "She don't belong to me. She is my daughter's property, and I have no right to sell her." Good, honest man! My young mistress was still a child, and I could look for no protection from her. I loved her, and she returned my affection. I once heard her father allude to her attachment to me; and his wife promptly replied that it proceeded from fear. This put unpleasant doubts into my mind. Did the child feign what she did not feel? or was her mother jealous of the mite of love she bestowed on me? I concluded it must be the latter. I said to myself, "Surely, little children are true."

One afternoon I sat at my sewing, feeling unusual depression of spirits. My mistress had been accusing me of an offence, of which I assured her I was perfectly innocent; but I saw, by the contemptuous curl of her lip, that she believed I was telling a lie.

I wondered for what wise purpose God was leading me through such thorny paths, and whether still darker days were in store for me. As I sat musing thus, the door opened softly, and William came in. "Well, brother," said I, "what is the matter this time?"

"O Linda, Ben and his master have had a dreadful time!" said he.

My first thought was that Benjamin was killed. "Don't be frightened, Linda," said William; "I will tell you all about it."

It appeared that Benjamin's master had sent for him, and he did not immediately obey the summons. When he did, his master was angry, and began to whip him. He resisted. Master and slave fought, and finally the master was thrown. Benjamin had cause to tremble; for he had thrown to the ground his master—one of the richest men in town. I anxiously awaited the result.

That night I stole to my grandmother's house, and Benjamin also stole thither from his master's. My grandmother had gone to spend a day or two with an old friend living in the country.

"I have come," said Benjamin, "to tell you good by. I am going away."

I inquired where.

"To the north," he replied.

I looked at him to see whether he was in earnest. I saw it all in his firm, set mouth. I implored him not to go, but he paid no heed to my words. He said he was no longer a boy, and every day made his yoke more galling. He had raised his hand against his master, and was to be publicly whipped for the offence. I reminded him of the poverty and hardships he must encounter among strangers. I told him he might be caught and brought back; and that was terrible to think of.

He grew vexed, and asked if poverty and hardships with freedom, were not preferable to our treatment in slavery. "Linda," he continued, "we are dogs here;

foot-balls, cattle, every thing that's mean. No, I will not stay. Let them bring me back. We don't die but once."

He was right; but it was hard to give him up. "Go," said I, "and break your mother's heart."

I repented of my words ere they were out.

"Linda," said he, speaking as I had not heard him speak that evening, "how *could* you say that? Poor mother! be kind to her, Linda; and you, too, cousin Fanny."

Cousin Fanny was a friend who had lived some years with us.

Farewells were exchanged, and the bright, kind boy, endeared to us by so many acts of love, vanished from our sight.

It is not necessary to state how he made his escape. Suffice it to say, he was on his way to New York when a violent storm overtook the vessel. The captain said he must put into the nearest port. This alarmed Benjamin, who was aware that he would be advertised in every port near his own town. His embarrassment was noticed by the captain. To port they went. There the advertisement met the captain's eye. Benjamin so exactly answered its description, that the captain laid hold on him, and bound him in chains. The storm passed, and they proceeded to New York. Before reaching that port Benjamin managed to get off his chains and throw them overboard. He escaped from the vessel, but was pursued, captured, and carried back to his master.

When my grandmother returned home and found her youngest child had fled, great was her sorrow; but, with characteristic piety, she said, "God's will be done." Each morning, she inquired if any news had been heard from her boy. Yes, news *was* heard. The master was rejoicing over a letter, announcing the capture of his human chattel.

That day seems but as yesterday, so well do I remember it. I saw him led through the streets in chains, to jail. His face was ghastly pale, yet full of determination. He had begged one of the sailors to go to his mother's house and ask her not to meet him. He said the sight of her distress would take from him all self-control. She yearned to see him, and she went; but she screened herself in the crowd, that it might be as her child had said.

We were not allowed to visit him; but we had known the jailer for years, and he was a kind-hearted man. At midnight he opened the jail door for my grandmother and myself to enter, in disguise. When we entered the cell not a sound broke the stillness. "Benjamin, Benjamin!" whispered my grandmother. No answer. "Benjamin!" she again faltered. There was a jingle of chains. The moon had just risen, and cast an uncertain light through the bars of the window. We knelt down and took Benjamin's cold hands in ours. We did not speak. Sobs were heard, and Benjamin's lips were unsealed; for his mother was weeping on his neck. How vividly does memory bring back that sad night! Mother and son talked together. He asked her pardon for the suffering he had caused her. She said she had nothing to forgive; she could not blame his desire for freedom. He told her that when he was captured, he broke away, and was about casting himself into the river, when thoughts of *her* came over him, and he desisted. She asked if he did not also think of God. I fancied I saw his face grow fierce in the moonlight. He answered, "No, I did not think of him. When a man is hunted like a wild beast he forgets there is a God, a heaven. He forgets every thing in his struggle to get beyond the reach of the bloodhounds."

"Don't talk so, Benjamin," said she. "Put your trust in God. Be humble, my child, and your master will forgive you."

"Forgive me for *what*, mother? For not letting him treat me like a dog? No! I will never humble myself to him. I have worked for him for nothing all my life, and I am repaid with stripes and imprisonment. Here I will stay till I die, or till he sells me."

The poor mother shuddered at his words. I think he felt it; for when he next spoke, his voice was calmer. "Don't fret about me, mother. I ain't worth it," said he. "I wish I had some of your goodness. You bear every thing patiently, just as though you thought it was all right. I wish I could."

She told him she had not always been so; once, she was like him; but when sore troubles came upon her, and she had no arm to lean upon, she learned to call on God, and he lightened her burdens. She besought him to do likewise.

We overstaid our time, and were obliged to hurry from the jail.

Benjamin had been imprisoned three weeks, when my grandmother went to intercede for him with his master. He was immovable. He said Benjamin should serve as an example to the rest of his slaves; he should be kept in jail till he was subdued, or be sold if he got but one dollar for him. However, he afterwards relented in some degree. The chains were taken off, and we were allowed to visit him.

As his food was of the coarsest kind, we carried him as often as possible a warm supper, accompanied with some little luxury for the jailer.

Three months elapsed, and there was no prospect of release or of a purchaser. One day he was heard to sing and laugh. This piece of indecorum was told to his master, and the overseer was ordered to re-chain him. He was now confined in an apartment with other prisoners, who were covered with filthy rags. Benjamin was chained near them, and was soon covered with vermin. He worked at his chains till he succeeded in getting out of them. He passed them through the bars of the window, with a request that they should be taken to his master, and he should be informed that he was covered with vermin.

This audacity was punished with heavier chains, and prohibition of our visits.

My grandmother continued to send him fresh changes of clothes. The old ones were burned up. The last night we saw him in jail his mother still begged him to send for his master, and beg his pardon. Neither persuasion nor argument could turn him from his purpose. He calmly answered, "I am waiting his time."

Those chains were mournful to hear.

Another three months passed, and Benjamin left his prison walls. We that loved him waited to bid him a long and last farewell. A slave trader had bought him. You remember, I told you what price he brought when ten years of age. Now he was more than twenty years old, and sold for three hundred dollars. The master had been blind to his own interest. Long confinement had made his face too pale, his form too thin; moreover, the trader had heard something of his character, and it did not strike him as suitable for a slave. He said he would give any price if the handsome lad was a girl. We thanked God that he was not.

Could you have seen that mother clinging to her child, when they fastened the irons upon his wrists; could you have heard her heart-rending groans, and seen her bloodshot eyes wander wildly from face to face, vainly pleading for mercy; could you have witnessed that scene as I saw it, you would exclaim, *Slavery is damnable!*

Benjamin, her youngest, her pet, was forever gone! She could not realize it. She had had an interview with the trader for the purpose of ascertaining if Benjamin could be purchased. She was told it was impossible, as he had given bonds not to sell him till he was out of the state. He promised that he would not sell him till he reached New Orleans.

With a strong arm and unvaried trust, my grandmother began her work of love. Benjamin must be free. If she succeeded, she knew they would still be separated; but the sacrifice was not too great. Day and night she labored. The trader's price would treble that he gave; but she was not discouraged.

She employed a lawyer to write to a gentleman, whom she knew, in New Orleans. She begged him to interest himself for Benjamin, and he willingly favored her request. When he saw Benjamin, and stated his business, he thanked him; but said he preferred to wait a while before making the trader an offer. He knew he had tried to obtain a high price for him, and had invariably failed. This encouraged him to make another effort for freedom. So one morning, long before day, Benjamin was missing. He was riding over the blue billows, bound for Baltimore.

For once his white face did him a kindly service. They had no suspicion that it belonged to a slave; otherwise, the law would have been followed out to the letter, and the *thing* rendered back to slavery. The brightest skies are often overshadowed by the darkest clouds. Benjamin was taken sick, and compelled to remain in Baltimore three weeks. His strength was slow in returning; and his desire to continue his journey seemed to retard his recovery. How could he get strength without air and exercise? He resolved to venture on a short walk. A by-street was selected, where he thought himself secure of not being met by any one that knew him; but a voice called out, "Halloo, Ben, my boy! what are you doing *here?*"

His first impulse was to run; but his legs trembled so that he could not stir. He turned to confront his antagonist, and behold, there stood his old master's next door neighbor! He thought it was all over with him now; but it proved otherwise. That man was a miracle. He possessed a goodly number of slaves, and yet was not quite deaf to that mystic clock, whose ticking is rarely heard in the slaveholder's breast.

"Ben, you are sick," said he. "Why, you look like a ghost. I guess I gave you something of a start. Never mind, Ben, I am not going to touch you. You had a pretty tough time of it, and you may go on your way rejoicing for all me. But I would advise you to get out of this place plaguy quick, for there are several gentlemen here from our town." He described the nearest and safest route to New York, and added, "I shall be glad to tell your mother I have seen you. Good by, Ben."

Benjamin turned away, filled with gratitude, and surprised that the town he hated contained such a gem—a gem worthy of a purer setting.

This gentleman was a Northerner by birth, and had married a southern lady. On his return, he told my grandmother that he had seen her son, and of the service he had rendered him.

Benjamin reached New York safely, and concluded to stop there until he had gained strength enough to proceed further. It happened that my grandmother's only remaining son had sailed for the same city on business for his mistress. Through God's providence, the brothers met. You may be sure it was a happy meeting. "O Phil,"[44] exclaimed Benjamin, "I am here at last." Then he told him how near he came to dying, almost in sight of free land, and how he prayed that he might live to get one breath of free air. He said life was worth something now, and it would be hard to die. In the old jail he had not valued it; once, he was tempted to destroy it; but something, he did not know what, had prevented him; perhaps it was fear. He had heard those who profess to be religious declare there was no heaven for self-murderers; and as his life had been pretty hot here, he did not desire a continuation of the same in another world. "If I die now," he exclaimed, "thank God, I shall die a freeman!"

He begged my uncle Phillip not to return south; but stay and work with him, till they earned enough to buy those at home. His brother told him it would kill their mother if he deserted her in her trouble. She had pledged her house, and with difficulty had raised money to buy him. Would he be bought?

"No, never!" he replied. "Do you suppose, Phil, when I have got so far out of their clutches, I will give them one red cent? No! And do you suppose I would turn mother out of her home in her old age? That I would let her pay all those hard-earned dollars for me, and never to see me? For you know she will stay south as long as her other children are slaves. What a good mother! Tell her to buy *you*, Phil. You have been a comfort to her, and I have been a trouble. And Linda, poor Linda; what'll become of her? Phil, you don't know what a life they lead her. She has told me something about it, and I wish old Flint was dead, or a better man. When I was in jail, he asked her if she didn't want *him* to ask my master to forgive me, and take me home again. She told him, No; that I didn't want to go back. He got mad, and said we were all alike. I never despised my own master half as much as I do that man. There is many a worse slaveholder than my master; but for all that I would not be his slave."

While Benjamin was sick, he had parted with nearly all his clothes to pay necessary expenses. But he did not part with a little pin I fastened in his bosom when we parted. It was the most valuable thing I owned, and I thought none more worthy to wear it. He had it still.

His brother furnished him with clothes, and gave him what money he had.

They parted with moistened eyes; and as Benjamin turned away, he said, "Phil, I part with all my kindred." And so it proved. We never heard from him again.

Uncle Phillip came home; and the first words he uttered when he entered the house were, "Mother, Ben is free! I have seen him in New York." She stood looking at him with a bewildered air. "Mother, don't you believe it?" he said, laying his hand softly upon her shoulder. She raised her hands, and exclaimed, "God be praised! Let us thank him." She dropped on her knees, and poured forth her heart in prayer. Then Phillip must sit down and repeat to her every word Benjamin had said. He told her all; only he forbore to mention how sick and pale her darling looked. Why should he distress her when she could do him no good?

The brave old woman still toiled on, hoping to rescue some of her other children. After a while she succeeded in buying Phillip. She paid eight hundred dollars, and came home with the precious document that secured his freedom. The happy mother and son sat together by the old hearthstone that night, telling how proud they were of each other, and how they would prove to the world that they could take care of themselves, as they had long taken care of others. We all concluded by saying, "He that is *willing* to be a slave, let him be a slave."

————————

V.

THE TRIALS OF GIRLHOOD.

DURING the first years of my service in Dr. Flint's family, I was accustomed to share some indulgences with the children of my mistress. Though this seemed to me no more than right, I was grateful for it, and tried to merit the kindness by the faithful discharge of my duties. But I now entered on my fifteenth year—a sad epoch in the life of a slave girl. My master began to whisper foul words in my ear. Young as I was, I could not remain ignorant of their import. I tried to treat them with indifference or contempt. The master's age, my extreme youth, and the fear that his conduct would be reported to my grandmother, made him bear this treatment for many months. He was a crafty man, and resorted to many means to accomplish his purposes. Sometimes he had stormy, terrific ways, that made his victims tremble; sometimes he assumed a gentleness that he thought must surely subdue. Of the two, I preferred his stormy moods, although they left me trembling. He tried his utmost to corrupt the pure principles my grandmother had instilled. He peopled my young mind with unclean images, such as only a vile monster could think of. I turned from him with disgust and hatred. But he was my master. I was compelled to live under the same roof with him—where I saw a man forty years my senior daily violating the most sacred commandments of nature. He told me I was his property; that I must be subject to his will in all things. My soul revolted against the mean tyranny. But where could I turn for protection? No matter whether the slave girl be as black as ebony or as fair as her mistress. In either case, there is no shadow of law to protect her from insult, from violence, or even from death; all these are inflicted by fiends who bear the shape of men. The mistress, who ought to protect the helpless victim, has no other feelings towards her but those of jealousy and rage. The degradation, the wrongs, the vices, that grow out of slavery, are more than I can describe. They are greater than you would willingly believe. Surely, if you credited one half the truths that are told you concerning the helpless millions suffering in this cruel bondage, you at the north would not help to tighten the yoke. You surely would refuse to do for the master, on your own soil, the mean and cruel work which trained bloodhounds and the lowest class of whites do for him at the south.

Every where the years bring to all enough of sin and sorrow; but in slavery the very dawn of life is darkened by these shadows. Even the little child, who is accustomed to wait on her mistress and her children, will learn, before she is twelve years old, why it is that her mistress hates such and such a one among the slaves. Perhaps the child's own mother is among those hated ones. She listens to violent outbreaks of jealous passion, and cannot help understanding what is the cause. She will become prematurely knowing in evil things. Soon she will learn to tremble when she hears her master's footfall. She will be compelled to realize that she is no longer a child. If God has bestowed beauty upon her, it will prove her greatest curse. That which commands admiration in the white woman only hastens the degradation of the female slave. I know that some are too much brutalized by slavery to feel the humiliation of their position; but many slaves feel it most acutely, and shrink from the memory of it. I cannot tell how much I suffered in the presence of these wrongs, nor how I am still pained by the retrospect. My master met me at every turn, reminding me that I belonged to him, and swearing by heaven and earth that he would compel me to submit to him. If I went out for a breath of fresh air, after a day of unwearied toil, his footsteps dogged me. If I knelt by my mother's grave, his dark shadow fell on me even there. The light heart which nature had given me became heavy with sad forebodings. The other slaves in my master's house noticed the change. Many of them pitied me; but none dared to ask the cause. They had no need to inquire. They knew too well the guilty practices under that roof; and they were aware that to speak of them was an offence that never went unpunished.

I longed for some one to confide in. I would have given the world to have laid my head on my grandmother's faithful bosom, and told her all my troubles. But Dr. Flint swore he would kill me, if I was not as silent as the grave. Then, although my grandmother was all in all to me, I feared her as well as loved her. I had been accustomed to look up to her with a respect bordering upon awe. I was very young, and felt shamefaced about telling her such impure things, especially as I knew her to be very strict on such subjects. Moreover, she was a woman of a high spirit. She was usually very quiet in her demeanor; but if her indignation was once roused, it was not very easily quelled. I had been told that she once chased a white gentleman with a loaded pistol, because he insulted one of her daughters. I dreaded the consequences of a violent outbreak; and both pride and fear kept me silent. But though I did not confide in my grandmother, and even evaded her vigilant watchfulness and inquiry, her presence in the neighborhood was some protection to me. Though she had been a slave, Dr. Flint was afraid of her. He dreaded her scorching rebukes. Moreover, she was known and patronized by many people; and he did not wish to have his villany made public. It was lucky for me that I did not live on a distant plantation, but in a town not so large that the inhabitants were ignorant of each other's affairs. Bad as are the laws and customs in a slaveholding community, the doctor, as a professional man, deemed it prudent to keep up some outward show of decency.

O, what days and nights of fear and sorrow that man caused me! Reader, it is not to awaken sympathy for myself that I am telling you truthfully what I suffered in slavery. I do it to kindle a flame of compassion in your hearts for my sisters who are still in bondage, suffering as I once suffered.

I once saw two beautiful children playing together. One was a fair white child; the other was her slave, and also her sister. When I saw them embracing each other, and heard their joyous laughter, I turned sadly away from the lovely sight. I foresaw the inevitable blight that would fall on the little slave's heart. I knew how soon her laughter would be changed to sighs. The fair child grew up to be a still fairer woman. From childhood to womanhood her pathway was blooming with flowers, and overarched by a sunny sky. Scarcely one day of her life had been clouded when the sun rose on her happy bridal morning.

How had those years dealt with her slave sister, the little playmate of her childhood? She, also, was very beautiful; but the flowers and sunshine of love were not for her. She drank the cup of sin, and shame, and misery, whereof her persecuted race are compelled to drink.

In view of these things, why are ye silent, ye free men and women of the north? Why do your tongues falter in maintenance of the right? Would that I had more ability! But my heart is so full, and my pen is so weak! There are noble men and women who plead for us, striving to help those who cannot help themselves. God bless them! God give them strength and courage to go on! God bless those, every where, who are laboring to advance the cause of humanity!

VI.

THE JEALOUS MISTRESS.

I WOULD ten thousand times rather that my children should be the half-starved paupers of Ireland than to be the most pampered among the slaves of America. I would rather drudge out my life on a cotton plantation, till the grave opened to give me rest, than to live with an unprincipled master and a jealous mistress. The felon's home in a penitentiary is preferable. He may repent, and turn from the error of his ways, and so find peace; but it is not so with a favorite slave. She is not allowed to have any pride of character. It is deemed a crime in her to wish to be virtuous.

Mrs. Flint possessed the key to her husband's character before I was born. She might have used this knowledge to counsel and to screen the young and the innocent among her slaves; but for them she had no sympathy. They were the objects of her constant suspicion and malevolence. She watched her husband with unceasing vigilance; but he was well practised in means to evade it. What he could not find opportunity to say in words he manifested in signs. He invented more than were ever thought of in a deaf and dumb asylum. I let them pass, as if I did not understand what he meant; and many were the curses and threats bestowed on me for my stupidity. One day he caught me teaching myself to write.

He frowned, as if he was not well pleased; but I suppose he came to the conclusion that such an accomplishment might help to advance his favorite scheme. Before long, notes were often slipped into my hand. I would return them, saying, "I can't read them, sir." "Can't you?" he replied; "then I must read them to you." He always finished the reading by asking, "Do you understand?" Sometimes he would complain of the heat of the tea room, and order his supper to be placed on a small table in the piazza. He would seat himself there with a well-satisfied smile, and tell me to stand by and brush away the flies. He would eat very slowly, pausing between the mouthfuls. These intervals were employed in describing the happiness I was so foolishly throwing away, and in threatening me with the penalty that finally awaited my stubborn disobedience. He boasted much of the forbearance he had exercised towards me, and reminded me that there was a limit to his patience. When I succeeded in avoiding opportunities for him to talk to me at home, I was ordered to come to his office, to do some errand. When there, I was obliged to stand and listen to such language as he saw fit to address to me. Sometimes I so openly expressed my contempt for him that he would become violently enraged, and I wondered why he did not strike me. Circumstanced as he was, he probably thought it was better policy to be forbearing. But the state of things grew worse and worse daily. In desperation I told him that I must and would apply to my grandmother for protection. He threatened me with death, and worse than death, if I made any complaint to her. Strange to say, I did not despair. I was naturally of a buoyant disposition, and always I had a hope of somehow getting out of his clutches. Like many a poor, simple slave before me, I trusted that some threads of joy would yet be woven into my dark destiny.

I had entered my sixteenth year, and every day it became more apparent that my presence was intolerable to Mrs. Flint. Angry words frequently passed between her and her husband. He had never punished me himself, and he would not allow any body else to punish me. In that respect, she was never satisfied; but, in her angry moods, no terms were too vile for her to bestow upon me. Yet I, whom she detested so bitterly, had far more pity for her than he had, whose duty it was to make her life happy. I never wronged her, or wished to wrong her; and one word of kindness from her would have brought me to her feet.

After repeated quarrels between the doctor and his wife, he announced his intention to take his youngest daughter, then four years old, to sleep in his apartment. It was necessary that a servant should sleep in the same room, to be on hand if the child stirred. I was selected for that office, and informed for what purpose that arrangement had been made. By managing to keep within sight of people, as much as possible, during the day time, I had hitherto succeeded in eluding my master, though a razor was often held to my throat to force me to change this line of policy. At night I slept by the side of my great aunt, where I felt safe. He was too prudent to come into her room. She was an old woman, and had been in the family many years. Moreover, as a married man, and a professional man, he deemed it necessary to save appearances in some degree. But he resolved to remove the obstacle in the way of his scheme; and he thought he had planned it so that he should evade suspicion. He was well aware how much I prized my refuge by the side of my old aunt, and he determined to dispossess me of it. The first night the doctor had the little child in his room alone. The next morning, I was ordered to take my station as nurse the following night. A kind Providence interposed in my favor. During the day Mrs. Flint heard of this new arrangement, and a storm followed. I rejoiced to hear it rage.

After a while my mistress sent for me to come to her room. Her first question was, "Did you know you were to sleep in the doctor's room?"

"Yes, ma'am."

"Who told you?"

"My master."

"Will you answer truly all the questions I ask?"

"Yes, ma'am."

"Tell me, then, as you hope to be forgiven, are you innocent of what I have accused you?"

"I am."

She handed me a Bible, and said, "Lay your hand on your heart, kiss this holy book, and swear before God that you tell me the truth."

I took the oath she required, and I did it with a clear conscience.

"You have taken God's holy word to testify your innocence," said she. "If you have deceived me, beware! Now take this stool, sit down, look me directly in the face, and tell me all that has passed between your master and you."

I did as she ordered. As I went on with my account her color changed frequently, she wept, and sometimes groaned. She spoke in tones so sad, that I was touched by her grief. The tears came to my eyes; but I was soon convinced that her emotions arose from anger and wounded pride. She felt that her marriage vows were desecrated, her dignity insulted; but she had no compassion for the poor victim of her husband's perfidy. She pitied herself as a martyr; but she was incapable of feeling for the condition of shame and misery in which her unfortunate, helpless slave was placed.

Yet perhaps she had some touch of feeling for me; for when the conference was ended, she spoke kindly, and promised to protect me. I should have been much comforted by this assurance if I could have had confidence in it; but my experiences in slavery had filled me with distrust. She was not a very refined woman, and had not much control over her passions. I was an object of her jealousy, and, consequently, of her hatred; and I knew I could not expect kindness or confidence from her under the circumstances in which I was placed. I could not blame her. Slaveholders' wives feel as other women would under similar circumstances. The fire of her temper kindled from small sparks, and now the flame became so intense that the doctor was obliged to give up his intended arrangement.

I knew I had ignited the torch, and I expected to suffer for it afterwards; but I felt too thankful to my mistress for the timely aid she rendered me to care much about that. She now took me to sleep in a room adjoining her own. There I was an object of her especial care, though not of her especial comfort, for she spent many a sleepless night to watch over me. Sometimes I woke up, and found her bending over me. At other times she whispered in my ear, as though it was her husband who was speaking to me, and listened to hear what I would answer. If she startled me, on such occasions, she would glide stealthily away; and the next morning she would tell me I had been talking in my sleep, and ask who I was talking to. At last, I began to be fearful for my life. It had been often threatened; and you can imagine, better than I can describe, what an unpleasant sensation it must produce to wake up in the dead of night and find a jealous woman bending over you. Terrible as this experience was, I had fears that it would give place to one more terrible.

My mistress grew weary of her vigils; they did not prove satisfactory. She changed her tactics. She now tried the trick of accusing my master of crime, in my presence, and gave my name as the author of the accusation. To my utter astonishment, he replied, "I don't believe it; but if she did acknowledge it, you tortured her into exposing me." Tortured into exposing him! Truly, Satan had no difficulty in distinguishing the color of his soul! I understood his object in making this false representation. It was to show me that I gained nothing by seeking the protection of my mistress; that the power was still all in his own hands. I pitied Mrs. Flint. She was a second wife, many years the junior of her husband; and the hoary-headed miscreant was enough to try the patience of a wiser and better woman. She was completely foiled, and knew not how to proceed. She would gladly have had me flogged for my supposed false oath; but, as I have already stated, the doctor never allowed any one to whip me. The old sinner was politic. The application of the lash might have led to remarks that would have exposed him in the eyes of his children and grandchildren. How often did I rejoice that I lived in a town where all the inhabitants knew each other! If I had been on a remote plantation, or lost among the multitude of a crowded city, I should not be a living woman at this day.

The secrets of slavery are concealed like those of the Inquisition. My master was, to my knowledge, the father of eleven slaves. But did the mothers dare to tell who was the father of their children? Did the other slaves dare to allude to it, except in whispers among themselves? No, indeed! They knew too well the terrible consequences.

My grandmother could not avoid seeing things which excited her suspicions. She was uneasy about me, and tried various ways to buy me; but the never-changing answer was always repeated: "Linda does not belong to *me*. She is my daughter's property, and I have no legal right to sell her." The conscientious man! He was too scrupulous to *sell* me; but he had no scruples whatever about committing a much greater wrong against the helpless young girl placed under his guardianship, as his daughter's property. Sometimes my persecutor would ask me whether I would like to be sold. I told him I would rather be sold to any body than to lead such a life as I did. On such occasions he would assume the air of a very injured individual, and reproach me for my ingratitude. "Did I not take you into the house, and make you the companion of my own children?" he would say. "Have I ever treated you like a negro? I have never allowed you to be punished, not even to please your mistress. And this is the recompense I get, you ungrateful girl!" I answered that he had reasons of his own for screening me from punishment, and that the course he pursued made my mistress hate me and persecute me. If I wept, he would say, "Poor child! Don't cry! don't cry! I will make peace for you with your mistress. Only let me arrange matters in my own way. Poor, foolish girl! you don't know what is for your own good. I would cherish you. I would make a lady of you. Now go, and think of all I have promised you."

I did think of it.

Reader, I draw no imaginary pictures of southern homes. I am telling you the plain truth. Yet when victims make their escape from this wild beast of Slavery, northerners consent to act the part of bloodhounds, and hunt the poor fugitive back into his den, "full of dead men's bones, and all uncleanness."[45] Nay, more, they are not only willing, but proud, to give their daughters in marriage to slaveholders. The poor girls have romantic notions of a sunny clime, and of the flowering vines that all the year round shade a happy home. To what disappointments are they destined! The young wife soon learns that the husband in whose hands she has placed her happiness pays no regard to his marriage vows. Children of every shade of complexion play with her own fair babies, and too well she knows that they are born unto him of his own household. Jealousy and hatred enter the flowery home, and it is ravaged of its loveliness.

Southern women often marry a man knowing that he is the father of many little slaves. They do not trouble themselves about it. They regard such children as property, as marketable as the pigs on the plantation; and it is seldom that they do not make them aware of this by passing them into the slavetrader's hands as soon as possible, and thus getting them out of their sight. I am glad to say there are some honorable exceptions.

I have myself known two southern wives who exhorted their husbands to free those slaves towards whom they stood in a "parental relation;" and their request was granted. These husbands blushed before the superior nobleness of their wives' natures. Though they had only counselled them to do that which it was their duty to do, it commanded their respect, and rendered their conduct more exemplary. Concealment was at an end, and confidence took the place of distrust.

Though this bad institution deadens the moral sense, even in white women, to a fearful extent, it is not altogether extinct. I have heard southern ladies say of Mr. Such a one, "He not only thinks it no disgrace to be the father of those little niggers, but he is not ashamed to call himself their master. I declare, such things ought not to be tolerated in any decent society!"

VII.

THE LOVER.

WHY does the slave ever love? Why allow the tendrils of the heart to twine around objects which may at any moment be wrenched away by the hand of violence? When separations come by the hand of death, the pious soul can bow in resignation, and say, "Not my will, but thine be done, O Lord!" But when the ruthless hand of man strikes the blow, regardless of the misery he causes, it is hard to be submissive. I did not reason thus when I was a young girl. Youth will be youth. I loved, and I indulged the hope that the dark clouds around me would turn out a bright lining. I forgot that in the land of my birth the shadows are too dense for light to penetrate. A land

> "Where laughter is not mirth; nor thought the mind;
> Nor words a language; nor e'en men mankind.
> Where cries reply to curses, shrieks to blows,
> And each is tortured in his separate hell."[46]

There was in the neighborhood a young colored carpenter; a free born man. We had been well acquainted in childhood, and frequently met together afterwards. We became mutually attached, and he proposed to marry me. I loved him with all the ardor of a young girl's first love. But when I reflected that I was a slave, and that the laws gave no sanction to the marriage of such, my heart sank within me. My lover wanted to buy me; but I knew that Dr. Flint was too wilful and arbitrary a man to consent to that arrangement. From him, I was sure of experiencing all sorts of opposition, and I had nothing to hope from my mistress. She would have been delighted to have got rid of me, but not in that way. It would have relieved her mind of a burden if she could have seen me sold to some distant state, but if I was married near home I should be just as much in her husband's power as I had previously been,—for the husband of a slave has no power to protect her. Moreover, my mistress, like many others, seemed to think that slaves had no right to any family ties of their own; that they were created merely to wait upon the family of the mistress. I once heard her abuse a young slave girl, who told her that a colored man wanted to make her his wife. "I will have you peeled and pickled,[47] my lady," said she, "if I ever hear you mention that subject again. Do you suppose that I will have you tending *my* children with the children of that nigger?" The girl to whom she said this had a mulatto child, of course not acknowledged by its father. The poor black man who loved her would have been proud to acknowledge his helpless offspring.

Many and anxious were the thoughts I revolved in my mind. I was at a loss what to do. Above all things, I was desirous to spare my lover the insults that had cut so deeply into my own soul. I talked with my grandmother about it, and partly told her my fears. I did not dare to tell her the worst. She had long suspected all was not right, and if I confirmed her suspicions I knew a storm would rise that would prove the overthrow of all my hopes.

This love-dream had been my support through many trials; and I could not bear to run the risk of having it suddenly dissipated. There was a lady in the neighborhood, a particular friend of Dr. Flint's, who often visited the house. I had a great respect for her, and she had always manifested a friendly interest in me. Grandmother thought she would have great influence with the doctor. I went to this lady, and told her my story. I told her I was aware that my lover's being a free-born man would prove a great objection; but he wanted to buy me; and if Dr. Flint would consent to that arrangement, I felt sure he would be willing to pay any reasonable price. She knew that Mrs. Flint disliked me; therefore, I ventured to suggest that perhaps my mistress would approve of my being sold, as that would rid her of me. The lady listened with kindly sympathy, and promised to do her utmost to promote my wishes. She had an interview with the doctor, and I believe she pleaded my cause earnestly; but it was all to no purpose.

How I dreaded my master now! Every minute I expected to be summoned to his presence; but the day passed, and I heard nothing from him. The next morning, a message was brought to me: "Master wants you in his study." I found the door ajar, and I stood a moment gazing at the hateful man who claimed a right to rule me, body and soul. I entered, and tried to appear calm. I did not want him to know how my heart was bleeding. He looked fixedly at me, with an expression which seemed to say, "I have half a mind to kill you on the spot." At last he broke the silence, and that was a relief to both of us.

"So you want to be married, do you?" said he, "and to a free nigger."

"Yes, sir."

"Well, I'll soon convince you whether I am your master, or the nigger fellow you honor so highly. If you must have a husband, you may take up with one of my slaves."

What a situation I should be in, as the wife of one of *his* slaves, even if my heart had been interested!

I replied, "Don't you suppose, sir, that a slave can have some preference about marrying? Do you suppose that all men are alike to her?"

"Do you love this nigger?" said he, abruptly.

"Yes, sir."

"How dare you tell me so!" he exclaimed, in great wrath. After a slight pause, he added, "I supposed you thought more of yourself; that you felt above the insults of such puppies."

I replied, "If he is a puppy I am a puppy, for we are both of the negro race. It is right and honorable for us to love each other. The man you call a puppy never insulted me, sir; and he would not love me if he did not believe me to be a virtuous woman."

He sprang upon me like a tiger, and gave me a stunning blow. It was the first time he had ever struck me; and fear did not enable me to control my anger. When I had recovered a little from the effects, I exclaimed, "You have struck me for answering you honestly. How I despise you!"

There was silence for some minutes. Perhaps he was deciding what should be my punishment; or, perhaps, he wanted to give me time to reflect on what I had said, and to whom I had said it. Finally, he asked, "Do you know what you have said?"

"Yes, sir; but your treatment drove me to it."

"Do you know that I have a right to do as I like with you,—that I can kill you, if I please?"

"You have tried to kill me, and I wish you had; but you have no right to do as you like with me."

"Silence!" he exclaimed, in a thundering voice. "By heavens, girl, you forget yourself too far! Are you mad? If you are, I will soon bring you to your senses. Do you think any other master would bear what I have borne from you this morning? Many masters would have killed you on the spot. How would you like to be sent to jail for your insolence?"

"I know I have been disrespectful, sir," I replied; "but you drove me to it; I couldn't help it. As for the jail, there would be more peace for me there than there is here."

"You deserve to go there," said he, "and to be under such treatment, that you would forget the meaning of the word *peace*. It would do you good. It would take some of your high notions out of you. But I am not ready to send you there yet, notwithstanding your ingratitude for all my kindness and forbearance. You have been the plague of my life. I have wanted to make you happy, and I have been repaid with the basest ingratitude; but though you have proved yourself incapable of appreciating my kindness, I will be lenient towards you, Linda. I will give you one more chance to redeem your character. If you behave yourself and do as I require, I will forgive you and treat you as I always have done; but if you disobey me, I will punish you as I would the meanest slave on my plantation. Never let me hear that fellow's name mentioned again. If I ever know of your speaking to him, I will cowhide you both; and if I catch him lurking about my premises, I will shoot him as soon as I would a dog. Do you hear what I say? I'll teach you a lesson about marriage and free niggers! Now go, and let this be the last time I have occasion to speak to you on this subject."

Reader, did you ever hate? I hope not. I never did but once; and I trust I never shall again. Somebody has called it "the atmosphere of hell;" and I believe it is so.

For a fortnight the doctor did not speak to me. He thought to mortify me; to make me feel that I had disgraced myself by receiving the honorable addresses of a respectable colored man, in preference to the base proposals of a white man. But though his lips disdained to address me, his eyes were very loquacious. No animal ever watched its prey more narrowly than he watched me. He knew that I could write, though he had failed to make me read his letters; and he was now troubled lest I should exchange letters with another man. After a while he became weary of silence; and I was sorry for it. One morning, as he passed through the hall, to leave the house, he contrived to thrust a note into my hand. I thought I had better read it, and spare myself the vexation of having him read it to me. It expressed regret for the blow he had given me, and reminded me that I myself was wholly to blame for it. He hoped I had become convinced of the injury I was doing myself by incurring his displeasure. He wrote that he had made up his mind to go to Louisiana; that he should take several slaves with him, and intended I should be one of the number. My mistress would remain where she was; therefore I should have nothing to fear from that quarter. If I merited kindness from him, he assured me that it would be lavishly bestowed. He begged me to think over the matter, and answer the following day.

The next morning I was called to carry a pair of scissors to his room. I laid them on the table, with the letter beside them. He thought it was my answer, and did not call me back. I went as usual to attend my young mistress to and from school. He met me in the street, and ordered me to stop at his office on my way back. When I entered, he showed me his letter, and asked me why I had not answered it. I replied, "I am your daughter's property, and it is in your power to send me, or take me, wherever you please." He said he was very glad to find me so willing to go, and that we should start early in the autumn. He had a large practice in the town, and I rather thought he had made up the story merely to frighten me. However that might be, I was determined that I would never go to Louisiana with him.

Summer passed away, and early in the autumn Dr. Flint's eldest son was sent to Louisiana to examine the country, with a view to emigrating. That news did not disturb me. I knew very well that I should not be sent with *him*. That I had not been taken to the plantation before this time, was owing to the fact that his son was there. He was jealous of his son; and jealousy of the overseer had kept him from punishing me by sending me into the fields to work. Is it strange that I was not proud of these protectors? As for the overseer, he was a man for whom I had less respect than I had for a bloodhound.

Young Mr. Flint did not bring back a favorable report of Louisiana, and I heard no more of that scheme. Soon after this, my lover met me at the corner of the street, and I stopped to speak to him. Looking up, I saw my master watching us from his window. I hurried home, trembling with fear. I was sent for, immediately, to go to his room. He met me with a blow. "When is mistress to be married?" said he, in a sneering tone. A shower of oaths and imprecations followed. How thankful I was that my lover was a free man! that my tyrant had no power to flog him for speaking to me in the street!

Again and again I revolved in my mind how all this would end. There was no hope that the doctor would consent to sell me on any terms. He had an iron will, and was determined to keep me, and to conquer me. My lover was an intelligent and religious man. Even if he could have obtained permission to marry me while I was a slave, the marriage would give him no power to protect me from my master. It would have made him miserable to witness the insults I should have been subjected to. And then, if we had children, I knew they must "follow the condition of the mother." What a terrible blight that would be on the heart of a free, intelligent father! For *his* sake, I felt that I ought not to link his fate with my own unhappy destiny. He was going to Savannah to see about a little property left him by an uncle; and hard as it was to bring my feelings to it, I earnestly entreated him not to come back. I advised him to go to the Free States, where his tongue would not be tied, and where his intelligence would be of more avail to him. He left me, still hoping the day would come when I could be bought. With me the lamp of hope had gone out. The dream of my girlhood was over. I felt lonely and desolate.

Still I was not stripped of all. I still had my good grandmother, and my affectionate brother. When he put his arms round my neck, and looked into my eyes, as if to read there the troubles I dared not tell, I felt that I still had something to love. But even that pleasant emotion was chilled by the reflection that he might be torn from me at any moment, by some sudden freak of my master. If he had known how we loved each other, I think he would have exulted in separating us. We often planned together how we could get to the north. But, as William remarked, such things are easier said than done. My movements were very closely watched, and we had no means of getting any money to defray our expenses. As for grandmother, she was strongly opposed to her children's undertaking any such project. She had not forgotten poor Benjamin's sufferings, and she was afraid that if another child tried to escape, he would have a similar or a worse fate. To me, nothing seemed more dreadful than my present life. I said to myself, "William *must* be free. He shall go to the north, and I will follow him." Many a slave sister has formed the same plans.

VIII.

WHAT SLAVES ARE TAUGHT TO THINK OF THE NORTH.

SLAVEHOLDERS pride themselves upon being honorable men; but if you were to hear the enormous lies they tell their slaves, you would have small respect for their veracity. I have spoken plain English. Pardon me. I cannot use a milder term. When they visit the north, and return home, they tell their slaves of the runaways they have seen, and describe them to be in the most deplorable condition. A slaveholder once told me that he had seen a runaway friend of mine in New York, and that she besought him to take her back to her master, for she was literally dying of starvation; that many days she had only one cold potato to eat, and at other times could get nothing at all. He said he refused to take her, because he knew her master would not thank him for bringing such a miserable wretch to his house. He ended by saying to me, "This is the punishment she brought on herself for running away from a kind master."

This whole story was false. I afterwards staid with that friend in New York, and found her in comfortable circumstances. She had never thought of such a thing as wishing to go back to slavery. Many of the slaves believe such stories, and think it is not worth while to exchange slavery for such a hard kind of freedom. It is difficult to persuade such that freedom could make them useful men, and enable them to protect their wives and children. If those heathen in our Christian land had as much teaching as some Hindoos, they would think otherwise. They would know that liberty is more valuable than life. They would begin to understand their own capabilities, and exert themselves to become men and women.

But while the Free States sustain a law which hurls fugitives back into slavery, how can the slaves resolve to become men? There are some who strive to protect wives and daughters from the insults of their masters; but those who have such sentiments have had advantages above the general mass of slaves. They have been partially civilized and Christianized by favorable circumstances. Some are bold enough to *utter* such sentiments to their masters. O, that there were more of them!

Some poor creatures have been so brutalized by the lash that they will sneak out of the way to give their masters free access to their wives and daughters. Do you think this proves the black man to belong to an inferior order of beings? What would *you* be, if you had been born and brought up a slave, with generations of slaves for ancestors? I admit that the black man *is* inferior. But what is it that makes him so? It is the ignorance in which white men compel him to live; it is the torturing whip that lashes manhood out of him; it is the fierce bloodhounds of the South, and the scarcely less cruel human bloodhounds of the north, who enforce the Fugitive Slave Law. *They* do the work.

Southern gentlemen indulge in the most contemptuous expressions about the Yankees, while they, on their part, consent to do the vilest work for them, such as the ferocious bloodhounds and the despised negro-hunters are employed to do at home. When southerners go to the north, they are proud to do them honor; but the northern man is not welcome south of Mason and Dixon's line, unless he suppresses every thought and feeling at variance with their "peculiar institution." Nor is it enough to be silent. The masters are not pleased, unless they obtain a greater degree of subservience than that; and they are generally accommodated. Do they respect the northerner for this? I trow not. Even the slaves despise "a northern man with southern principles;" and that is the class they generally see. When northerners go to the south to reside, they prove very apt scholars. They soon imbibe the sentiments and disposition of their neighbors, and generally go beyond their teachers. Of the two, they are proverbially the hardest masters.

They seem to satisfy their consciences with the doctrine that God created the Africans to be slaves. What a libel upon the heavenly Father, who "made of one blood all nations of men!"[48] And then who *are* Africans? Who can measure the amount of Anglo-Saxon blood coursing in the veins of American slaves?

I have spoken of the pains slaveholders take to give their slaves a bad opinion of the north; but, notwithstanding this, intelligent slaves are aware that they have many friends in the Free States. Even the most ignorant have some confused notions about it. They knew that I could read; and I was often asked if I had seen any thing in the newspapers about white folks over in the big north, who were trying to get their freedom for them. Some believe that the abolitionists have already made them free, and that it is established by law, but that their masters prevent the law from going into effect. One woman begged me to get a newspaper and read it over. She said her husband told her that the black people had sent word to the queen of 'Merica that they were all slaves; that she didn't believe it, and went to Washington city to see the president about it. They quarrelled; she drew her sword upon him, and swore that he should help her to make them all free.

That poor, ignorant woman thought that America was governed by a Queen, to whom the President was subordinate. I wish the President was subordinate to Queen Justice.

IX.

SKETCHES OF NEIGHBORING SLAVEHOLDERS.[49]

THERE was a planter in the country, not far from us, whom I will call Mr. Litch.[50] He was an ill-bred, uneducated man, but very wealthy. He had six hundred slaves, many of whom he did not know by sight. His extensive plantation was managed by well-paid overseers. There was a jail and a whipping post on his grounds; and whatever cruelties were perpetrated there, they passed without comment. He was so effectually screened by his great wealth that he was called to no account for his crimes, not even for murder.

Various were the punishments resorted to. A favorite one was to tie a rope round a man's body, and suspend him from the ground. A fire was kindled over him, from which was suspended a piece of fat pork. As this cooked, the scalding drops of fat continually fell on the bare flesh. On his own plantation, he required very strict obedience to the eighth commandment.[51] But depredations on the neighbors were allowable, provided the culprit managed to evade detection or suspicion. If a neighbor brought a charge of theft against any of his slaves, he was browbeaten by the master, who assured him that his slaves had enough of every thing at home, and had no inducement to steal. No sooner was the neighbor's back turned, than the accused was sought out, and whipped for his lack of discretion. If a slave stole from him even a pound of meat or a peck of corn, if detection followed, he was put in chains and imprisoned, and so kept till his form was attenuated by hunger and suffering.

A freshet once bore his wine cellar and meat house miles away from the plantation. Some slaves followed, and secured bits of meat and bottles of wine. Two were detected; a ham and some liquor being found in their huts. They were summoned by their master. No words were used, but a club felled them to the ground. A rough box was their coffin, and their interment was a dog's burial. Nothing was said.

Murder was so common on his plantation that he feared to be alone after nightfall. He might have believed in ghosts.

His brother, if not equal in wealth, was at least equal in cruelty. His bloodhounds were well trained. Their pen was spacious, and a terror to the slaves. They were let loose on a runaway, and, if they tracked him, they literally tore the flesh from his bones. When this slaveholder died, his shrieks and groans were so frightful that they appalled his own friends. His last words were, "I am going to hell; bury my money with me."

After death his eyes remained open. To press the lids down, silver dollars were laid on them. These were buried with him. From this circumstance, a rumor went abroad that his coffin was filled with money. Three times his grave was opened, and his coffin taken out. The last time, his body was found on the ground, and a flock of buzzards were pecking at it. He was again interred, and a sentinel set over his grave. The perpetrators were never discovered.

Cruelty is contagious in uncivilized communities. Mr. Conant, a neighbor of Mr. Litch, returned from town one evening in a partial state of intoxication. His body servant gave him some offence. He was divested of his clothes, except his shirt, whipped, and tied to a large tree in front of the house. It was a stormy night in winter. The wind blew bitterly cold, and the boughs of the old tree crackled under falling sleet. A member of the family, fearing he would freeze to death, begged that he might be taken down; but the master would not relent. He remained there three hours; and, when he was cut down, he was more dead than alive. Another slave, who stole a pig from this master, to appease his hunger, was terribly flogged. In desperation, he tried to run away. But at the end of two miles, he was so faint with loss of blood, he thought he was dying. He had a wife, and he longed to see her once more. Too sick to walk, he crept back that long distance on his hands and knees. When he reached his master's, it was night. He had not strength to rise and open the gate. He moaned, and tried to call for help. I had a friend living in the same family. At last his cry reached her. She went out and found the prostrate man at the gate. She ran back to the house for assistance, and two men returned with her. They carried him in, and laid him on the floor. The back of his shirt was one clot of blood. By means of lard, my friend loosen it from the raw flesh. She bandaged him, gave him cool drink, and left him to rest. The master said he deserved a hundred more lashes. When his own labor was stolen from him, he had stolen food to appease his hunger. This was his crime.

Another neighbor was a Mrs. Wade. At no hour of the day was there cessation of the lash on her premises. Her labors began with the dawn, and did not cease till long after nightfall. The barn was her particular place of torture. There she lashed the slaves with the might of a man. An old slave of hers once said to me, "It is hell in missis's house. 'Pears I can never get out. Day and night I prays to die."

The mistress died before the old woman, and, when dying, entreated her husband not to permit any one of her slaves to look on her after death. A slave who had nursed her children, and had still a child in her care, watched her chance, and stole with it in her arms to the room where lay her dead mistress. She gazed a while on her, then raised her hand and dealt two blows on her face, saying, as she did so, "The devil is got you *now*!" She forgot that the child was looking on. She had just begun to talk; and she said to her father, "I did see ma, and mammy did strike ma, so," striking her own face with her little hand. The master was startled. He could not imagine how the nurse could obtain access to the room where the corpse lay; for he kept the door locked. He questioned her. She confessed that what the child had said was true, and told how she had procured the key. She was sold to Georgia.

In my childhood I knew a valuable slave, named Charity, and loved her, as all children did. Her young mistress married, and took her to Louisiana. Her little boy, James, was sold to a good sort of master. He became involved in debt, and James was sold again to a wealthy slaveholder, noted for his cruelty. With this man he grew up to manhood, receiving the treatment of a dog. After a severe whipping, to save himself from further infliction of the lash, with which he was threatened, he took to the woods. He was in a most miserable condition— cut by the cowskin, half naked, half starved, and without the means of procuring a crust of bread.

Some weeks after his escape, he was captured, tied, and carried back to his master's plantation. This man considered punishment in his jail, on bread and water, after receiving hundreds of lashes, too mild for the poor slave's offence. Therefore he decided, after the overseer should have whipped him to his satisfaction, to have him placed between the screws of the cotton gin, to stay as long as he had been in the woods. This wretched creature was cut with the whip from his head to his feet, then washed with strong brine, to prevent the flesh from mortifying, and make it heal sooner than it otherwise would. He was then put into the cotton gin, which was screwed down, only allowing him room to turn on his side when he could not lie on his back. Every morning a slave was sent with a piece of bread and bowl of water, which were placed within reach of the poor fellow. The slave was charged, under penalty of severe punishment, not to speak to him.

Four days passed, and the slave continued to carry the bread and water. On the second morning, he found the bread gone, but the water untouched. When he had been in the press four days and five nights, the slave informed his master that the water had not been used for four mornings, and that a horrible stench came from the gin house. The overseer was sent to examine into it. When the press was unscrewed, the dead body was found partly eaten by rats and vermin. Perhaps the rats that devoured his bread had gnawed him before life was extinct. Poor Charity! Grandmother and I often asked each other how her affectionate heart would bear the news, if she should ever hear of the murder of her son. We had known her husband, and knew that James was like him in manliness and intelligence. These were the qualities that made it so hard for him to be a plantation slave. They put him into a rough box, and buried him with less feeling than would have been manifested for an old house dog. Nobody asked any questions. He was a slave; and the feeling was that the master had a right to do what he pleased with his own property. And what did *he* care for the value of a slave? He had hundreds of them. When they had finished their daily toil, they must hurry to eat their little morsels, and be ready to extinguish their pine knots before nine o'clock, when the overseer went his patrol rounds. He entered every cabin, to see that men and their wives had gone to bed together, lest the men, from over-fatigue, should fall asleep in the chimney corner, and remain there till the morning horn called them to their daily task. Women are considered of no value, unless they continually increase their owner's stock. They are put on a par with animals. This same master shot a woman through the head, who had run away and been brought back to him. No one called him to account for it. If a slave resisted being whipped, the bloodhounds were unpacked, and set upon him, to tear his flesh from his bones. The master who did these things was highly educated, and styled a perfect gentleman. He also boasted the name and standing of a Christian, though Satan never had a truer follower.

I could tell of more slaveholders as cruel as those I have described. They are not exceptions to the general rule. I do not say there are no humane slaveholders. Such characters do exist, notwithstanding the hardening influences around them. But they are "like angels' visits—few and far between."[52]

I knew a young lady who was one of these rare specimens. She was an orphan, and inherited as slaves a woman and her six children. Their father was a free man. They had a comfortable home of their own, parents and children living together. The mother and eldest daughter served their mistress during the day, and at night returned to their dwelling, which was on the premises. The young lady was very pious, and there was some reality in her religion. She taught her slaves to lead pure lives, and wished them to enjoy the fruit of their own industry. *Her* religion was not a garb put on for Sunday, and laid aside till Sunday returned again. The eldest daughter of the slave mother was promised in marriage to a free man; and the day before the wedding this good mistress emancipated her, in order that her marriage might have the sanction of *law*.

Report said that this young lady cherished an unrequited affection for a man who had resolved to marry for wealth. In the course of time a rich uncle of hers died. He left six thousand dollars to his two sons by a colored woman, and the remainder of his property to this orphan niece. The metal soon attracted the magnet. The lady and her weighty purse became his. She offered to manumit her slaves—telling them that her marriage might make unexpected changes in their destiny, and she wished to insure their happiness. They refused to take their freedom, saying that she had always been their best friend, and they could not be so happy any where as with her. I was not surprised. I had often seen them in their comfortable home, and thought that the whole town did not contain a happier family. They had never felt slavery; and, when it was too late, they were convinced of its reality.

When the new master claimed this family as his property, the father became furious, and went to his mistress for protection. "I can do nothing for you now, Harry," said she. "I no longer have the power I had a week ago. I have succeeded in obtaining the freedom of your wife; but I cannot obtain it for your children." The unhappy father swore that nobody should take his children from him. He concealed them in the woods for some days; but they were discovered and taken. The father was put in jail, and the two oldest boys sold to Georgia. One little girl, too young to be of service to her master, was left with the wretched mother. The other three were carried to their master's plantation. The eldest soon became a mother; and, when the slaveholder's wife looked at the babe, she wept bitterly. She knew that her own husband had violated the purity she had so carefully inculcated. She had a second child by her master, and then he sold her and his offspring to his brother. She bore two children to the brother, and was sold again. The next sister went crazy. The life she was compelled to lead drove her mad. The third one became the mother of five daughters. Before the birth of the fourth the pious mistress died. To the last, she rendered every kindness to the slaves that her unfortunate circumstances permitted. She passed away peacefully, glad to close her eyes on a life which had been made so wretched by the man she loved.

This man squandered the fortune he had received, and sought to retrieve his affairs by a second marriage; but, having retired after a night of drunken debauch, he was found dead in the morning. He was called a good master; for he fed and clothed his slaves better than most masters, and the lash was not heard on his plantation so frequently as on many others. Had it not been for slavery, he would have been a better man, and his wife a happier woman.

No pen can give an adequate description of the all-pervading corruption produced by slavery. The slave girl is reared in an atmosphere of licentiousness and fear. The lash and the foul talk of her master and his sons are her teachers. When she is fourteen or fifteen, her owner, or his sons, or the overseer, or perhaps all of them, begin to bribe her with presents. If these fail to accomplish their

purpose, she is whipped or starved into submission to their will. She may have
had religious principles inculcated by some pious mother or grandmother, or
some good mistress; she may have a lover, whose good opinion and peace of
mind are dear to her heart; or the profligate men who have power over her may
be exceedingly odious to her. But resistance is hopeless.

> "The poor worm
> Shall prove her contest vain. Life's little day
> Shall pass, and she is gone!"[53]

The slaveholder's sons are, of course, vitiated, even while boys, by the unclean influences every where around them. Nor do the master's daughters always
escape. Severe retributions sometimes come upon him for the wrongs he does to
the daughters of the slaves. The white daughters early hear their parents quarrelling about some female slave. Their curiosity is excited, and they soon learn
the cause. They are attended by the young slave girls whom their father has cor-
rupted; and they hear such talk as should never meet youthful ears, or any other
ears. They know that the women slaves are subject to their father's authority in
all things; and in some cases they exercise the same authority over the men slaves.
I have myself seen the master of such a household whose head was bowed down
in shame; for it was known in the neighborhood that his daughter had selected
one of the meanest slaves on his plantation to be the father of his first grandchild.
She did not make her advances to her equals, nor even to her father's more intelligent servants. She selected the most brutalized, over whom her authority
could be exercised with less fear of exposure. Her father, half frantic with rage,
sought to revenge himself on the offending black man; but his daughter, fore-
seeing the storm that would arise, had given him free papers, and sent him out
of the state.

In such cases the infant is smothered, or sent where it is never seen by any
who know its history. But if the white parent is the *father*, instead of the mother,
the offspring are unblushingly reared for the market. If they are girls, I have indicated plainly enough what will be their inevitable destiny.

You may believe what I say; for I write only that whereof I know. I was
twenty-one years in that cage of obscene birds. I can testify, from my own experience and observation, that slavery is a curse to the whites as well as to the
blacks. It makes the white fathers cruel and sensual; the sons violent and licentious; it contaminates the daughters, and makes the wives wretched. And as for
the colored race, it needs an abler pen than mine to describe the extremity of their
sufferings, the depth of their degradation.

Yet few slaveholders seem to be aware of the widespread moral ruin occasioned by this wicked system. Their talk is of blighted cotton crops—not of the
blight on their children's souls.

If you want to be fully convinced of the abominations of slavery, go on a
southern plantation, and call yourself a negro trader. Then there will be no concealment; and you will see and hear things that will seem to you impossible
among human beings with immortal souls.

X.

A PERILOUS PASSAGE IN THE SLAVE GIRL'S LIFE.

AFTER my lover went away, Dr. Flint contrived a new plan. He seemed to have an idea that my fear of my mistress was his greatest obstacle. In the blandest tones, he told me that he was going to build a small house for me, in a secluded place, four miles away from the town. I shuddered; but I was constrained to listen, while he talked of his intention to give me a home of my own, and to make a lady of me. Hitherto, I had escaped my dreaded fate, by being in the midst of people. My grandmother had already had high words with my master about me. She had told him pretty plainly what she thought of his character, and there was considerable gossip in the neighborhood about our affairs, to which the open-mouthed jealousy of Mrs. Flint contributed not a little. When my master said he was going to build a house for me, and that he could do it with little trouble and expense, I was in hopes something would happen to frustrate his scheme; but I soon heard that the house was actually begun. I vowed before my Maker that I would never enter it. I had rather toil on the plantation from dawn till dark; I had rather live and die in jail, than drag on, from day to day, through such a living death. I was determined that the master, whom I so hated and loathed, who had blighted the prospects of my youth, and made my life a desert, should not, after my long struggle with him, succeed at last in trampling his victim under his feet. I would do any thing, every thing, for the sake of defeating him. What *could* I do? I thought and thought, till I became desperate, and made a plunge into the abyss.

And now, reader, I come to a period in my unhappy life, which I would gladly forget if I could. The remembrance fills me with sorrow and shame. It pains me to tell you of it; but I have promised to tell you the truth, and I will do it honestly, let it cost me what it may. I will not try to screen myself behind the plea of compulsion from a master; for it was not so. Neither can I plead ignorance or thoughtlessness. For years, my master had done his utmost to pollute my mind with foul images, and to destroy the pure principles inculcated by my grandmother, and the good mistress of my childhood. The influences of slavery had had the same effect on me that they had on other young girls; they had made me prematurely knowing, concerning the evil ways of the world. I knew what I did, and I did it with deliberate calculation.

But, O, ye happy women, whose purity has been sheltered from childhood, who have been free to choose the objects of your affection, whose homes are protected by law, do not judge the poor desolate slave girl too severely! If slavery had been abolished, I, also, could have married the man of my choice; I could have had a home shielded by the laws; and I should have been spared the painful task of confessing what I am now about to relate; but all my prospects had been blighted by slavery. I wanted to keep myself pure; and, under the most adverse circumstances, I tried hard to preserve my self-respect; but I was struggling alone in the powerful grasp of the demon Slavery; and the monster proved too strong for me. I felt as if I was forsaken by God and man; as if all my efforts must be frustrated; and I became reckless in my despair.

I have told you that Dr. Flint's persecutions and his wife's jealousy had given rise to some gossip in the neighborhood. Among others, it chanced that a white unmarried gentleman had obtained some knowledge of the circumstances in which I was placed. He knew my grandmother, and often spoke to me in the street. He became interested for me, and asked questions about my master, which I answered in part. He expressed a great deal of sympathy, and a wish to aid me. He constantly sought opportunities to see me, and wrote to me frequently. I was a poor slave girl, only fifteen years old.

So much attention from a superior person was, of course, flattering; for human nature is the same in all. I also felt grateful for his sympathy, and encouraged by his kind words. It seemed to me a great thing to have such a friend. By degrees, a more tender feeling crept into my heart. He was an educated and eloquent gentleman; too eloquent, alas, for the poor slave girl who trusted in him. Of course I saw whither all this was tending. I knew the impassable gulf between us; but to be an object of interest to a man who is not married, and who is not her master, is agreeable to the pride and feelings of a slave, if her miserable situation has left her any pride or sentiment. It seems less degrading to give one's self, than to submit to compulsion. There is something akin to freedom in having a lover who has no control over you, except that which he gains by kindness and attachment. A master may treat you as rudely as he pleases, and you dare not speak; moreover, the wrong does not seem so great with an unmarried man, as with one who has a wife to be made unhappy. There may be sophistry in all this; but the condition of a slave confuses all principles of morality, and, in fact, renders the practice of them impossible.

When I found that my master had actually begun to build the lonely cottage, other feelings mixed with those I have described. Revenge, and calculations of interest, were added to flattered vanity and sincere gratitude for kindness. I knew nothing would enrage Dr. Flint so much as to know that I favored another; and it was something to triumph over my tyrant even in that small way. I thought he would revenge himself by selling me, and I was sure my friend, Mr. Sands,[54] would buy me. He was a man of more generosity and feeling than my master, and I thought my freedom could be easily obtained from him. The crisis of my fate now came so near that I was desperate. I shuddered to think of being the mother of children that should be owned by my old tyrant. I knew that as soon as a new fancy took him, his victims were sold far off to get rid of them; especially if they had children. I had seen several women sold, with his babies at the breast. He never allowed his offspring by slaves to remain long in sight of himself and his wife. Of a man who was not my master I could ask to have my children well supported; and in this case, I felt confident I should obtain the boon. I also felt quite sure that they would be made free. With all these thoughts revolving in my mind, and seeing no other way of escaping the doom I so much dreaded, I made a headlong plunge. Pity me, and pardon me, O virtuous reader! You never knew what it is to be a slave; to be entirely unprotected by law or custom; to have the laws reduce you to the condition of a chattel, entirely subject to the will of another. You never exhausted your ingenuity in avoiding the snares, and eluding the power of a hated tyrant; you never shuddered at the sound of his footsteps, and trembled within hearing of his voice. I know I did wrong. No one can feel it more sensibly than I do. The painful and humiliating memory will haunt me to my dying day. Still, in looking back, calmly, on the events of my life, I feel that the slave woman ought not to be judged by the same standard as others.

The months passed on. I had many unhappy hours. I secretly mourned over the sorrow I was bringing on my grandmother, who had so tried to shield me from harm. I knew that I was the greatest comfort of her old age, and that it was a source of pride to her that I had not degraded myself, like most of the slaves. I wanted to confess to her that I was no longer worthy of her love; but I could not utter the dreaded words.

As for Dr. Flint, I had a feeling of satisfaction and triumph in the thought of telling *him*. From time to time he told me of his intended arrangements, and I was silent. At last, he came and told me the cottage was completed, and ordered me to go to it. I told him I would never enter it. He said, "I have heard enough of such talk as that. You shall go, if you are carried by force; and you shall remain there."

I replied, "I will never go there. In a few months I shall be a mother."

He stood and looked at me in dumb amazement, and left the house without a word. I thought I should be happy in my triumph over him. But now that the truth was out, and my relatives would hear of it, I felt wretched. Humble as were their circumstances, they had pride in my good character. Now, how could I look them in the face? My self-respect was gone! I had resolved that I would be virtuous, though I was a slave. I had said, "Let the storm beat! I will brave it till I die." And now, how humiliated I felt!

I went to my grandmother. My lips moved to make confession, but the words stuck in my throat. I sat down in the shade of a tree at her door and began to sew. I think she saw something unusual was the matter with me. The mother of slaves is very watchful. She knows there is no security for her children. After they have entered their teens she lives in daily expectation of trouble. This leads to many questions. If the girl is of a sensitive nature, timidity keeps her from answering truthfully, and this well-meant course has a tendency to drive her from maternal counsels. Presently, in came my mistress, like a mad woman, and accused me concerning her husband. My grandmother, whose suspicions had been previously awakened, believed what she said. She exclaimed, "O Linda! has it come to this? I had rather see you dead than to see you as you now are. You are a disgrace to your dead mother." She tore from my fingers my mother's wedding ring and her silver thimble. "Go away!" she exclaimed, "and never come to my house, again." Her reproaches fell so hot and heavy, that they left me no chance to answer. Bitter tears, such as the eyes never shed but once, were my only answer. I rose from my seat, but fell back again, sobbing. She did not speak to me; but the tears were running down her furrowed cheeks, and they scorched me like fire. She had always been so kind to me! *So* kind! How I longed to throw myself at her feet, and tell her all the truth! But she had ordered me to go, and never to come there again. After a few minutes, I mustered strength, and started to obey her. With what feelings did I now close that little gate, which I used to open with such an eager hand in my childhood! It closed upon me with a sound I never heard before.

Where could I go? I was afraid to return to my master's. I walked on recklessly, not caring where I went, or what would become of me. When I had gone four or five miles, fatigue compelled me to stop. I sat down on the stump of an old tree. The stars were shining through the boughs above me. How they mocked me, with their bright, calm light! The hours passed by, and as I sat there alone a chilliness and deadly sickness came over me. I sank on the ground. My mind was full of horrid thoughts. I prayed to die; but the prayer was not answered. At last, with great effort I roused myself, and walked some distance further, to the house of a woman who had been a friend of my mother. When I told her why I was there, she spoke soothingly to me; but I could not be comforted. I thought I could bear my shame if I could only be reconciled to my grandmother. I longed to open my heart to her. I thought if she could know the real state of the case, and all I had been bearing for years, she would perhaps judge me less harshly. My friend advised me to send for her. I did so; but days of agonizing suspense passed before she came. Had she utterly forsaken me? No. She came at last. I knelt before her, and told her the things that had poisoned my life; how long I had been persecuted; that I saw no way of escape; and in an hour of extremity I had become desperate. She listened in silence. I told her I would bear any thing and do any thing, if in time I had hopes of obtaining her forgiveness. I begged of her to pity me, for my dead mother's sake. And she did pity me. She did not say, "I forgive you;" but she looked at me lovingly, with her eyes full of tears. She laid her old hand gently on my head, and murmured, "Poor child! Poor child!"

XI.

THE NEW TIE TO LIFE.

I RETURNED to my good grandmother's house. She had an interview with Mr. Sands. When she asked him why he could not have left her one ewe lamb,— whether there were not plenty of slaves who did not care about character,—he made no answer; but he spoke kind and encouraging words. He promised to care for my child, and to buy me, be the conditions what they might.

I had not seen Dr. Flint for five days. I had never seen him since I made the avowal to him. He talked of the disgrace I had brought on myself; how I had sinned against my master, and mortified my old grandmother. He intimated that if I had accepted his proposals, he, as a physician, could have saved me from exposure. He even condescended to pity me. Could he have offered wormwood more bitter? He, whose persecutions had been the cause of my sin!

"Linda," said he, "though you have been criminal towards me, I feel for you, and I can pardon you if you obey my wishes. Tell me whether the fellow you wanted to marry is the father of your child. If you deceive me, you shall feel the fires of hell."

I did not feel as proud as I had done. My strongest weapon with him was gone. I was lowered in my own estimation, and had resolved to bear his abuse in silence. But when he spoke contemptuously of the lover who had always treated me honorably; when I remembered that but for *him* I might have been a virtuous, free, and happy wife, I lost my patience. "I have sinned against God and myself," I replied; "but not against you."

He clinched his teeth, and muttered, "Curse you!" He came towards me, with ill-suppressed rage, and exclaimed, "You obstinate girl! I could grind your bones to powder! You have thrown yourself away on some worthless rascal. You are weak-minded, and have been easily persuaded by those who don't care a straw for you. The future will settle accounts between us. You are blinded now; but hereafter you will be convinced that your master was your best friend. My lenity towards you is a proof of it. I might have punished you in many ways. I might have had you whipped till you fell dead under the lash. But I wanted you to live; I would have bettered your condition. Others cannot do it. You are my slave. Your mistress, disgusted by your conduct, forbids you to return to the house; therefore I leave you here for the present; but I shall see you often. I will call tomorrow."

He came with frowning brows, that showed a dissatisfied state of mind. After asking about my health, he inquired whether my board was paid, and who visited me. He then went on to say that he had neglected his duty; that as a physician there were certain things that he ought to have explained to me. Then followed talk such as would have made the most shameless blush. He ordered me to stand up before him. I obeyed. "I command you," said he, "to tell me whether the father of your child is white or black." I hesitated. "Answer me this instant!" he exclaimed. I did answer. He sprang upon me like a wolf, and grabbed my arm as if he would have broken it. "Do you love him?" said he, in a hissing tone.

"I am thankful that I do not despise him," I replied.

He raised his hand to strike me; but it fell again. I don't know what arrested the blow. He sat down, with lips tightly compressed. At last he spoke. "I came here," said he, "to make you a friendly proposition; but your ingratitude chafes me beyond endurance. You turn aside all my good intentions towards you. I don't know what it is that keeps me from killing you." Again he rose, as if he had a mind to strike me.

But he resumed. "On one condition I will forgive your insolence and crime. You must henceforth have no communication of any kind with the father of your child. You must not ask any thing from him, or receive any thing from him. I will take care of you and your child. You had better promise this at once, and not wait till you are deserted by him. This is the last act of mercy I shall show towards you."

I said something about being unwilling to have my child supported by a man who had cursed it and me also. He rejoined, that a woman who had sunk to my level had no right to expect any thing else. He asked, for the last time, would I accept his kindness? I answered that I would not.

"Very well," said he; "then take the consequences of your wayward course. Never look to me for help. You are my slave, and shall always be my slave. I will never sell you, that you may depend upon."

Hope died away in my heart as he closed the door after him. I had calculated that in his rage he would sell me to a slave-trader; and I knew the father of my child was on the watch to buy me.

About this time my uncle Phillip was expected to return from a voyage. The day before his departure I had officiated as bridesmaid to a young friend. My heart was then ill at ease, but my smiling countenance did not betray it. Only a year had passed; but what fearful changes it had wrought! My heart had grown gray in misery. Lives that flash in sunshine, and lives that are born in tears, receive their hue from circumstances. None of us know what a year may bring forth.

I felt no joy when they told me my uncle had come. He wanted to see me, though he knew what had happened. I shrank from him at first; but at last consented that he should come to my room. He received me as he always had done. O, how my heart smote me when I felt his tears on my burning cheeks! The words of my grandmother came to my mind,—"Perhaps your mother and father are taken from the evil days to come." My disappointed heart could now praise God that it was so. But why, thought I, did my relatives ever cherish hopes for me? What was there to save me from the usual fate of slave girls? Many more beautiful and more intelligent than I had experienced a similar fate, or a far worse one. How could they hope that I should escape?

My uncle's stay was short, and I was not sorry for it. I was too ill in mind and body to enjoy my friends as I had done. For some weeks I was unable to leave my bed. I could not have any doctor but my master, and I would not have him sent for. At last, alarmed by my increasing illness, they sent for him. I was very weak and nervous; and as soon as he entered the room, I began to scream. They told him my state was very critical. He had no wish to hasten me out of the world, and he withdrew.

When my babe[55] was born, they said it was premature. It weighed only four pounds; but God let it live. I heard the doctor say I could not survive till morning. I had often prayed for death; but now I did not want to die, unless my child could die too. Many weeks passed before I was able to leave my bed. I was a mere wreck of my former self. For a year there was scarcely a day when I was free from chills and fever. My babe also was sickly. His little limbs were often racked with pain. Dr. Flint continued his visits, to look after my health; and he did not fail to remind me that my child was an addition to his stock of slaves.

I felt too feeble to dispute with him, and listened to his remarks in silence. His visits were less frequent; but his busy spirit could not remain quiet. He employed my brother in his office, and he was made the medium of frequent notes and messages to me. William was a bright lad, and of much use to the doctor. He had learned to put up medicines, to leech, cup, and bleed. He had taught himself to read and spell. I was proud of my brother; and the old doctor suspected as much. One day, when I had not seen him for several weeks, I heard his steps approaching the door. I dreaded the encounter, and hid myself. He inquired for me, of course; but I was nowhere to be found. He went to his office, and despatched William with a note. The color mounted to my brother's face when he gave it to me; and he said, "Don't you hate me, Linda, for bringing you these things?" I told him I could not blame him; he was a slave, and obliged to obey his master's will. The note ordered me to come to his office. I went. He demanded to know where I was when he called. I told him I was at home. He flew into a passion, and said he knew better. Then he launched out upon his usual themes,— my crimes against him, and my ingratitude for his forbearance. The laws were laid down to me anew, and I was dismissed. I felt humiliated that my brother should stand by, and listen to such language as would be addressed only to a slave. Poor boy! He was powerless to defend me; but I saw the tears, which he vainly strove to keep back. This manifestation of feeling irritated the doctor. William could do nothing to please him. One morning he did not arrive at the office so early as usual; and that circumstance afforded his master an opportunity to vent his spleen. He was put in jail. The next day my brother sent a trader to the doctor, with a request to be sold. His master was greatly incensed at what he called his insolence. He said he had put him there to reflect upon his bad conduct, and he certainly was not giving any evidence of repentance. For two days he harassed himself to find somebody to do his office work; but every thing went wrong without William. He was released, and ordered to take his old stand, with many threats, if he was not careful about his future behavior.

As the months passed on, my boy improved in health. When he was a year old, they called him beautiful. The little vine was taking deep root in my existence, though its clinging fondness excited a mixture of love and pain. When I was most sorely oppressed I found a solace in his smiles. I loved to watch his infant slumbers; but always there was a dark cloud over my enjoyment. I could never forget that he was a slave. Sometimes I wished that he might die in infancy. God tried me. My darling became very ill. The bright eyes grew dull, and the little feet and hands were so icy cold that I thought death had already touched them. I had prayed for his death, but never so earnestly as I now prayed for his life; and my prayer was heard. Alas, what mockery it is for a slave mother to try to pray back her dying child to life! Death is better than slavery. It was a sad thought that I had no name to give my child. His father caressed him and treated him kindly, whenever he had a chance to see him. He was not unwilling that he should bear his name; but he had no legal claim to it; and if I had bestowed it upon him, my master would have regarded it as a new crime, a new piece of insolence, and would, perhaps, revenge it on the boy. O, the serpent of Slavery has many and poisonous fangs!

XII.

FEAR OF INSURRECTION.[56]

NOT far from this time Nat Turner's insurrection broke out;[57] and the news threw our town into great commotion. Strange that they should be alarmed, when their slaves were so "contented and happy"! But so it was.

It was always the custom to have a muster every year. On that occasion every white man shouldered his musket. The citizens and the so-called country gentlemen wore military uniforms. The poor whites took their places in the ranks in every-day dress, some without shoes, some without hats. This grand occasion had already passed; and when the slaves were told there was to be another muster, they were surprised and rejoiced. Poor creatures! They thought it was going to be a holiday. I was informed of the true state of affairs, and imparted it to the few I could trust. Most gladly would I have proclaimed it to every slave; but I dared not. All could not be relied on. Mighty is the power of the torturing lash.

By sunrise, people were pouring in from every quarter within twenty miles of the town. I knew the houses were to be searched; and I expected it would be done by country bullies and the poor whites. I knew nothing annoyed them so much as to see colored people living in comfort and respectability; so I made arrangements for them with especial care. I arranged every thing in my grandmother's house as neatly as possible. I put white quilts on the beds, and decorated some of the rooms with flowers. When all was arranged, I sat down at the window to watch. Far as my eye could reach, it rested on a motley crowd of soldiers. Drums and fifes were discoursing martial music. The men were divided into companies of sixteen, each headed by a captain. Orders were given, and the wild scouts rushed in every direction, wherever a colored face was to be found.

It was a grand opportunity for the low whites, who had no negroes of their own to scourge. They exulted in such a chance to exercise a little brief authority, and show their subserviency to the slaveholders; not reflecting that the power which trampled on the colored people also kept themselves in poverty, ignorance, and moral degradation. Those who never witnessed such scenes can hardly believe what I know was inflicted at this time on innocent men, women, and children, against whom there was not the slightest ground for suspicion. Colored people and slaves who lived in remote parts of the town suffered in an especial manner. In some cases the searchers scattered powder and shot among their clothes, and then sent other parties to find them, and bring them forward as proof that they were plotting insurrection. Every where men, women, and children were whipped till the blood stood in puddles at their feet. Some received five hundred lashes; others were tied hands and feet, and tortured with a bucking paddle,[58] which blisters the skin terribly. The dwellings of the colored people, unless they happened to be protected by some influential white person, who was nigh at hand, were robbed of clothing and every thing else the marauders thought worth carrying away. All day long these unfeeling wretches went round, like a troop of demons, terrifying and tormenting the helpless. At night, they formed themselves into patrol bands, and went wherever they chose among the colored people, acting out their brutal will. Many women hid themselves in woods and swamps, to keep out of their way. If any of the husbands or fathers told of these outrages, they were tied up to the public whipping post, and cruelly scourged for telling lies about white men. The consternation was universal. No two people that had the slightest tinge of color in their faces dared to be seen talking together.

I entertained no positive fears about our household, because we were in the midst of white families who would protect us. We were ready to receive the soldiers whenever they came. It was not long before we heard the tramp of feet and the sound of voices. The door was rudely pushed open; and in they tumbled, like a pack of hungry wolves. They snatched at every thing within their reach. Every box, trunk, closet, and corner underwent a thorough examination. A box in one of the drawers containing some silver change was eagerly pounced upon. When I stepped forward to take it from them, one of the soldiers turned and said angrily, "What d'ye foller us fur? D'ye s'pose white folks is come to steal?"

I replied, "You have come to search; but you have searched that box, and I will take it, if you please."

At that moment I saw a white gentleman who was friendly to us; and I called to him, and asked him to have the goodness to come in and stay till the search was over. He readily complied. His entrance into the house brought in the captain of the company, whose business it was to guard the outside of the house, and see that none of the inmates left it. This officer was Mr. Litch, the wealthy slaveholder whom I mentioned, in the account of neighboring planters, as being notorious for his cruelty. He felt above soiling his hands with the search. He merely gave orders; and, if a bit of writing was discovered, it was carried to him by his ignorant followers, who were unable to read.

My grandmother had a large trunk of bedding and table cloths. When that was opened, there was a great shout of surprise; and one exclaimed, "Where'd the damned niggers git all dis sheet an' table clarf?"

My grandmother, emboldened by the presence of our white protector, said, "You may be sure we didn't pilfer 'em from *your* houses."

"Look here, mammy," said a grim-looking fellow without any coat, "you seem to feel mighty gran' 'cause you got all them 'ere fixens. White folks oughter have 'em all."

His remarks were interrupted by a chorus of voices shouting, "We's got 'em! We's got 'em! Dis 'ere yeller gal's got letters!"

There was a general rush for the supposed letter, which, upon examination, proved to be some verses written to me by a friend. In packing away my things, I had overlooked them. When their captain informed them of their contents, they seemed much disappointed. He inquired of me who wrote them.

I told him it was one of my friends. "Can you read them?" he asked. When I told him I could, he swore, and raved, and tore the paper into bits. "Bring me all your letters!" said he, in a commanding tone. I told him I had none. "Don't be afraid," he continued, in an insinuating way. "Bring them all to me. Nobody shall do you any harm." Seeing I did not move to obey him, his pleasant tone changed to oaths and threats. "Who writes to you? half free niggers?" inquired he. I replied, "O, no; most of my letters are from white people. Some request me to burn them after they are read, and some I destroy without reading."

An exclamation of surprise from some of the company put a stop to our conversation. Some silver spoons which ornamented an old-fashioned buffet had just been discovered. My grandmother was in the habit of preserving fruit for many ladies in the town, and of preparing suppers for parties; consequently she had many jars of preserves. The closet that contained these was next invaded, and the contents tasted. One of them, who was helping himself freely, tapped his neighbor on the shoulder, and said, "Wal done! Don't wonder de niggers want to kill all de white folks, when dey live on 'sarves" [meaning preserves]. I stretched out my hand to take the jar, saying, "You were not sent here to search for sweetmeats."

"And what *were* we sent for?" said the captain, bristling up to me. I evaded the question.

The search of the house was completed, and nothing found to condemn us. They next proceeded to the garden, and knocked about every bush and vine, with no better success. The captain called his men together, and, after a short consultation, the order to march was given. As they passed out of the gate, the captain turned back, and pronounced a malediction on the house. He said it ought to be burned to the ground, and each of its inmates receive thirty-nine lashes. We came out of this affair very fortunately; not losing any thing except some wearing apparel.

Towards evening the turbulence increased. The soldiers, stimulated by drink, committed still greater cruelties. Shrieks and shouts continually rent the air. Not daring to go to the door, I peeped under the window curtain. I saw a mob dragging along a number of colored people, each white man, with his musket upraised, threatening instant death if they did not stop their shrieks. Among the prisoners was a respectable old colored minister. They had found a few parcels of shot in his house, which his wife had for years used to balance her scales. For this they were going to shoot him on Court House Green. What a spectacle was that for a civilized country! A rabble, staggering under intoxication, assuming to be the administrators of justice!

The better class of the community exerted their influence to save the innocent, persecuted people; and in several instances they succeeded, by keeping them shut up in jail till the excitement abated. At last the white citizens found that their own property was not safe from the lawless rabble they had summoned to protect them. They rallied the drunken swarm, drove them back into the country, and set a guard over the town.

The next day, the town patrols were commissioned to search colored people that lived out of the city; and the most shocking outrages were committed with perfect impunity. Every day for a fortnight, if I looked out, I saw horsemen with some poor panting negro tied to their saddles, and compelled by the lash to keep up with their speed, till they arrived at the jail yard. Those who had been whipped too unmercifully to walk were washed with brine, tossed into a cart, and carried to jail. One black man, who had not fortitude to endure scourging, promised to give information about the conspiracy. But it turned out that he knew nothing at all. He had not even heard the name of Nat Turner. The poor fellow had, however, made up a story, which augmented his own sufferings and those of the colored people.[59]

The day patrol continued for some weeks, and at sundown a night guard was substituted. Nothing at all was proved against the colored people, bond or free. The wrath of the slaveholders was somewhat appeased by the capture of

Nat Turner.[60] The imprisoned were released. The slaves were sent to their masters, and the free were permitted to return to their ravaged homes. Visiting was strictly forbidden on the plantations. The slaves begged the privilege of again meeting at their little church in the woods, with their burying ground around it. It was built by the colored people, and they had no higher happiness than to meet there and sing hymns together, and pour out their hearts in spontaneous prayer. Their request was denied, and the church was demolished. They were permitted to attend the white churches, a certain portion of the galleries being appropriated to their use. There, when every body else had partaken of the communion, and the benediction had been pronounced, the minister said, "Come down, now, my colored friends." They obeyed the summons, and partook of the bread and wine, in commemoration of the meek and lowly Jesus, who said, "God is your Father, and all ye are brethren."[61]

XIII.

THE CHURCH AND SLAVERY.

AFTER the alarm caused by Nat Turner's insurrection had subsided, the slaveholders came to the conclusion that it would be well to give the slaves enough of religious instruction to keep them from murdering their masters. The Episcopal clergyman[62] offered to hold a separate service on Sundays for their benefit. His colored members were very few, and also very respectable—a fact which I presume had some weight with him. The difficulty was to decide on a suitable place for them to worship. The Methodist and Baptist churches admitted them in the afternoon; but their carpets and cushions were not so costly as those at the Episcopal church. It was at last decided that they should meet at the house of a free colored man, who was a member.

I was invited to attend, because I could read. Sunday evening came, and, trusting to the cover of night, I ventured out. I rarely ventured out by daylight, for I always went with fear, expecting at every turn to encounter Dr. Flint, who was sure to turn me back, or order me to his office to inquire where I got my bonnet, or some other article of dress. When the Rev. Mr. Pike came, there were some twenty persons present. The reverend gentleman knelt in prayer, then seated himself, and requested all present, who could read, to open their books, while he gave out the portions he wished them to repeat or respond to.

His text was, "Servants, be obedient to them that are your masters according to the flesh, with fear and trembling, in singleness of your heart, as unto Christ."[63]

Pious Mr. Pike brushed up his hair till it stood upright, and, in deep, solemn tones, began: "Hearken, ye servants! Give strict heed unto my words. You are rebellious sinners. Your hearts are filled with all maimer of evil. 'Tis the devil who tempts you. God is angry with you, and will surely punish you, if you don't forsake your wicked ways. You that live in town are eye-servants behind your master's back. Instead of serving your masters faithfully, which is pleasing in the sight of your heavenly Master, you are idle, and shirk your work. God sees you. You tell lies. God hears you. Instead of being engaged in worshipping him, you are hidden away somewhere, feasting on your master's substance; tossing coffee-grounds with some wicked fortuneteller, or cutting cards with another old hag. Your masters may not find you out, but God sees you, and will punish you. O, the depravity of your hearts! When your master's work is done, are you quietly together, thinking of the goodness of God to such sinful creatures? No; you are quarrelling, and tying up little bags of roots to bury under the door-steps to poison each other with. God sees you. You men steal away to every grog shop to sell your master's corn, that you may buy rum to drink. God sees you. You sneak into the back streets, or among the bushes, to pitch coppers. Although your masters may not find you out, God sees you; and he will punish you. You must forsake your sinful ways, and be faithful servants. Obey your old master and your young master—your old mistress and your young mistress. If you disobey your earthly master, you offend your heavenly Master. You must obey God's commandments. When you go from here, don't stop at the corners of the streets to talk, but go directly home, and let your master and mistress see that you have come."

The benediction was pronounced. We went home, highly amused at brother Pike's gospel teaching, and we determined to hear him again. I went the next Sabbath evening, and heard pretty much a repetition of the last discourse. At the close of the meeting, Mr. Pike informed us that he found it very inconvenient to meet at the friend's house, and he should be glad to see us, every Sunday evening, at his own kitchen.

I went home with the feeling that I had heard the Reverend Mr. Pike for the last time. Some of his members repaired to his house, and found that the kitchen sported two tallow candles; the first time, I am sure, since its present occupant owned it, for the servants never had any thing but pine knots. It was so long before the reverend gentleman descended from his comfortable parlor that the slaves left, and went to enjoy a Methodist shout. They never seem so happy as when shouting and singing at religious meetings. Many of them are sincere, and nearer to the gate of heaven than sanctimonious Mr. Pike, and other long-faced Christians, who see wounded Samaritans, and pass by on the other side.

The slaves generally compose their own songs and hymns; and they do not trouble their heads much about the measure. They often sing the following verses:

> "Old Satan is one busy ole man;
>   He rolls dem blocks all in my way;
> But Jesus is my bosom friend;
>   He rolls dem blocks away.

> "If I had died when I was young,
>   Den how my stam'ring tongue would have sung;
> But I am ole, and now I stand
>   A narrow chance for to tread dat heavenly land."

I well remember one occasion when I attended a Methodist class meeting. I went with a burdened spirit, and happened to sit next a poor, bereaved mother, whose heart was still heavier than mine. The class leader was the town constable—a man who bought and sold slaves, who whipped his brethren and sisters of the church at the public whipping post, in jail or out of jail. He was ready to perform that Christian office any where for fifty cents. This white-faced, black-hearted brother came near us, and said to the stricken woman, "Sister, can't you tell us how the Lord deals with your soul? Do you love him as you did formerly?"

She rose to her feet, and said, in piteous tones, "My Lord and Master, help me! My load is more than I can bear. God has hid himself from me, and I am left in darkness and misery." Then, striking her breast, she continued, "I can't tell you what is in here! They've got all my children. Last week they took the last one. God only knows where they've sold her. They let me have her sixteen years, and then——O! O! Pray for her brothers and sisters! I've got nothing to live for now. God make my time short!"

She sat down, quivering in every limb. I saw that constable class leader become crimson in the face with suppressed laughter, while he held up his handkerchief, that those who were weeping for the poor woman's calamity might not see his merriment. Then, with assumed gravity, he said to the bereaved mother, "Sister, pray to the Lord that every dispensation of his divine will may be sanctified to the good of your poor needy soul!"

The congregation struck up a hymn, and sung as though they were as free as the birds that warbled round us,—

> "Ole Satan thought he had a mighty aim;
> He missed my soul, and caught my sins.
> Cry Amen, cry Amen, cry Amen to God!
>
> "He took my sins upon his back;
> Went muttering and grumbling down to hell.
> Cry Amen, cry Amen, cry Amen to God!
>
> "Ole Satan's church is here below.
> Up to God's free church I hope to go.
> Cry Amen, cry Amen, cry Amen to God!"

Precious are such moments to the poor slaves. If you were to hear them at such times, you might think they were happy. But can that hour of singing and shouting sustain them through the dreary week, toiling without wages, under constant dread of the lash?

The Episcopal clergyman, who, ever since my earliest recollection, had been a sort of god among the slaveholders, concluded, as his family was large, that he must go where money was more abundant. A very different clergyman[64] took his place. The change was very agreeable to the colored people, who said, "God has sent us a good man this time." They loved him, and their children followed him, for a smile or a kind word. Even the slaveholders felt his influence. He brought to the rectory five slaves. His wife taught them to read and write, and to be useful to her and themselves. As soon as he was settled, he turned his attention to the needy slaves around him. He urged upon his parishioners the duty of having a meeting expressly for them every Sunday, with a sermon adapted to their comprehension. After much argument and importunity, it was finally agreed that they might occupy the gallery of the church on Sunday evenings. Many colored people, hitherto unaccustomed to attend church, now gladly went to hear the gospel preached. The sermons were simple, and they understood them. Moreover, it was the first time they had ever been addressed as human beings. It was not long before his white parishioners began to be dissatisfied. He was accused of preaching better sermons to the negroes than he did to them. He honestly confessed that he bestowed more pains upon those sermons than upon any others; for the slaves were reared in such ignorance that it was a difficult task to adapt himself to their comprehension. Dissensions arose in the parish. Some wanted he should preach to them in the evening, and to the slaves in the afternoon. In the midst of these disputings his wife died, after a very short illness. Her slaves gathered round her dying bed in great sorrow. She said, "I have tried to do you good and promote your happiness; and if I have failed, it has not been for want of interest in your welfare. Do not weep for me; but prepare for the new duties that lie before you. I leave you all free. May we meet in a better world." Her liberated slaves were sent away, with funds to establish them comfortably.[65] The colored people will long bless the memory of that truly Christian woman. Soon after her death her husband preached his farewell sermon, and many tears were shed at his departure.

Several years after, he passed through our town and preached to his former congregation. In his afternoon sermon he addressed the colored people. "My friends," said he, "it affords me great happiness to have an opportunity of speaking to you again. For two years I have been striving to do something for the colored people of my own parish; but nothing is yet accomplished. I have not even preached a sermon to them. Try to live according to the word of God, my friends. Your skin is darker than mine; but God judges men by their hearts, not by the color of their skins." This was strange doctrine from a southern pulpit. It was very offensive to slaveholders. They said he and his wife had made fools of their slaves, and that he preached like a fool to the negroes.

I knew an old black man, whose piety and childlike trust in God were beautiful to witness. At fifty-three years old he joined the Baptist church. He had a most earnest desire to learn to read. He thought he should know how to serve God better if he could only read the Bible. He came to me, and begged me to teach him. He said he could not pay me, for he had no money; but he would bring me nice fruit when the season for it came. I asked him if he didn't know it was contrary to law; and that slaves were whipped and imprisoned for teaching each other to read. This brought the tears into his eyes. "Don't be troubled, uncle Fred," said I. "I have no thoughts of refusing to teach you. I only told you of the law, that you might know the danger, and be on your guard." He thought he could plan to come three times a week without its being suspected. I selected a quiet nook, where no intruder was likely to penetrate, and there I taught him his A, B, C. Considering his age, his progress was astonishing. As soon as he could spell in two syllables he wanted to spell out words in the Bible. The happy smile that illuminated his face put joy into my heart. After spelling out a few words, he paused, and said, "Honey, it 'pears when I can read dis good book I shall be nearer to God. White man is got all de sense. He can larn easy. It ain't easy for ole black man like me. I only wants to read dis book, dat I may know how to live; den I hab no fear 'bout dying."

I tried to encourage him by speaking of the rapid progress he had made. "Hab patience, child," he replied. "I larns slow."

I had no need of patience. His gratitude, and the happiness I imparted, were more than a recompense for all my trouble.

At the end of six months he had read through the New Testament, and could find any text in it. One day, when he had recited unusually well, I said, "Uncle Fred, how do you manage to get your lessons so well?"

"Lord bress you, chile," he replied. "You nebber gibs me a lesson dat I don't pray to God to help me to understan' what I spells and what I reads. And he *does* help me, chile. Bress his holy name!"

There are thousands, who, like good uncle Fred, are thirsting for the water of life; but the law forbids it, and the churches withhold it. They send the Bible to heathen abroad, and neglect the heathen at home. I am glad that missionaries go out to the dark corners of the earth; but I ask them not to overlook the dark corners at home. Talk to American slaveholders as you talk to savages in Africa. Tell *them* it is wrong to traffic in men. Tell them it is sinful to sell their own children, and atrocious to violate their own daughters. Tell them that all men are brethren, and that man has no right to shut out the light of knowledge from his brother. Tell them they are answerable to God for sealing up the Fountain of Life from souls that are thirsting for it.

There are men who would gladly undertake such missionary work as this; but, alas! their number is small. They are hated by the south, and would be driven from its soil, or dragged to prison to die, as others have been before them. The field is ripe for the harvest, and awaits the reapers. Perhaps the great grandchildren of uncle Fred may have freely imparted to them the divine treasures, which he sought by stealth, at the risk of the prison and the scourge.

Are doctors of divinity blind, or are they hypocrites? I suppose some are the one, and some the other; but I think if they felt the interest in the poor and the lowly, that they ought to feel, they would not be so *easily* blinded. A clergyman who goes to the south, for the first time, has usually some feeling, however vague, that slavery is wrong. The slaveholder suspects this, and plays his game accordingly. He makes himself as agreeable as possible; talks on theology, and other kindred topics. The reverend gentleman is asked to invoke a blessing on a table loaded with luxuries. After dinner he walks round the premises, and sees the beautiful groves and flowering vines, and the comfortable huts of favored household slaves. The southerner invites him to talk with these slaves. He asks them if they want to be free, and they say, "O, no, massa." This is sufficient to satisfy him. He comes home to publish a "South-Side View of Slavery,"[66] and to complain of the exaggerations of abolitionists. He assures people that he has been to the south, and seen slavery for himself; that it is a beautiful "patriarchal institution;" that the slaves don't want their freedom; that they have hallelujah meetings, and other religious privileges.

What does *he* know of the half-starved wretches toiling from dawn till dark on the plantations? of mothers shrieking for their children, torn from their arms by slave traders? of young girls dragged down into moral filth? of pools of blood around the whipping post? of hounds trained to tear human flesh? of men screwed into cotton gins to die? The slaveholder showed him none of these things, and the slaves dared not tell of them if he had asked them.

There is a great difference between Christianity and religion at the south. If a man goes to the communion table, and pays money into the treasury of the church, no matter if it be the price of blood, he is called religious. If a pastor has offspring by a woman not his wife, the church dismiss him, if she is a white woman; but if she is colored, it does not hinder his continuing to be their good shepherd.

When I was told that Dr. Flint had joined the Episcopal church, I was much surprised. I supposed that religion had a purifying effect on the character of men; but the worst persecutions I endured from him were after he was a communicant. The conversation of the doctor, the day after he had been confirmed, certainly gave *me* no indication that he had "renounced the devil and all his works." In answer to some of his usual talk, I reminded him that he had just joined the church. "Yes, Linda," said he. "It was proper for me to do so. I am getting in years, and my position in society requires it, and it puts an end to all the damned slang. You would do well to join the church, too, Linda."

"There are sinners enough in it already," rejoined I. "If I could be allowed to live like a Christian, I should be glad."

"You can do what I require; and if you are faithful to me, you will be as virtuous as my wife," he replied.

I answered that the Bible didn't say so.

His voice became hoarse with rage. "How dare you preach to me about your infernal Bible!" he exclaimed. "What right have you, who are my negro, to talk to me about what you would like, and what you wouldn't like? I am your master, and you shall obey me."

No wonder the slaves sing,—

"Ole Satan's church is here below;
Up to God's free church I hope to go."

XIV.

ANOTHER LINK TO LIFE.

I HAD not returned to my master's house since the birth of my child. The old man raved to have me thus removed from his immediate power; but his wife vowed, by all that was good and great, she would kill me if I came back; and he did not doubt her word. Sometimes he would stay away for a season. Then he would come and renew the old threadbare discourse about his forbearance and my ingratitude. He labored, most unnecessarily, to convince me that I had lowered myself. The venomous old reprobate had no need of descanting on that theme. I felt humiliated enough. My unconscious babe was the ever-present witness of my shame. I listened with silent contempt when he talked about my having forfeited *his* good opinion; but I shed bitter tears that I was no longer worthy of being respected by the good and pure. Alas! slavery still held me in its poisonous grasp. There was no chance for me to be respectable. There was no prospect of being able to lead a better life.

Sometimes, when my master found that I still refused to accept what he called his kind offers, he would threaten to sell my child. "Perhaps that will humble you," said he.

Humble *me!* Was I not already in the dust? But his threat lacerated my heart. I knew the law gave him power to fulfil it; for slaveholders have been cunning enough to enact that "the child shall follow the condition of the *mother*," not of the *father;* thus taking care that licentiousness shall not interfere with avarice. This reflection made me clasp my innocent babe all the more firmly to my heart. Horrid visions passed through my mind when I thought of his liability to fall into the slave trader's hands. I wept over him, and said, "O my child! perhaps they will leave you in some cold cabin to die, and then throw you into a hole, as if you were a dog."

When Dr. Flint learned that I was again to be a mother, he was exasperated beyond measure. He rushed from the house, and returned with a pair of shears. I had a fine head of hair; and he often railed about my pride of arranging it nicely. He cut every hair close to my head, storming and swearing all the time. I replied to some of his abuse, and he struck me. Some months before, he had pitched me down stairs in a fit of passion; and the injury I received was so serious that I was unable to turn myself in bed for many days. He then said, "Linda, I swear by God I will never raise my hand against you again;" but I knew that he would forget his promise.

After he discovered my situation, he was like a restless spirit from the pit. He came every day; and I was subjected to such insults as no pen can describe. I would not describe them if I could; they were too low, too revolting. I tried to keep them from my grandmother's knowledge as much as I could. I knew she had enough to sadden her life, without having my troubles to bear. When she saw the doctor treat me with violence, and heard him utter oaths terrible enough to palsy a man's tongue, she could not always hold her peace. It was natural and motherlike that she should try to defend me; but it only made matters worse.

When they told me my new-born babe was a girl,[67] my heart was heavier than it had ever been before. Slavery is terrible for men; but it is far more terrible for women. Superadded to the burden common to all, *they* have wrongs, and sufferings, and mortifications peculiarly their own.

Dr. Flint had sworn that he would make me suffer, to my last day, for this new crime against *him*, as he called it; and as long as he had me in his power he kept his word. On the fourth day after the birth of my babe, he entered my room suddenly, and commanded me to rise and bring my baby to him. The nurse who took care of me had gone out of the room to prepare some nourishment, and I was alone. There was no alternative. I rose, took up my babe, and crossed the room to where he sat. "Now stand there," said he, "till I tell you to go back!" My child bore a strong resemblance to her father, and to the deceased Mrs. Sands, her grandmother. He noticed this; and while I stood before him, trembling with weakness, he heaped upon me and my little one every vile epithet he could think of. Even the grandmother in her grave did not escape his curses. In the midst of his vituperations I fainted at his feet. This recalled him to his senses. He took the baby from my arms, laid it on the bed, dashed cold water in my face, took me up, and shook me violently, to restore my consciousness before any one entered the room. Just then my grandmother came in, and he hurried out of the house. I suffered in consequence of this treatment; but I begged my friends to let me die, rather than send for the doctor. There was nothing I dreaded so much as his presence. My life was spared; and I was glad for the sake of my little ones. Had it not been for these ties to life, I should have been glad to be released by death, though I had lived only nineteen years.

Always it gave me a pang that my children had no lawful claim to a name. Their father offered his; but, if I had wished to accept the offer, I dared not while my master lived. Moreover, I knew it would not be accepted at their baptism. A Christian name they were at least entitled to; and we resolved to call my boy for our dear good Benjamin, who had gone far away from us.

My grandmother belonged to the church; and she was very desirous of having the children christened. I knew Dr. Flint would forbid it, and I did not venture to attempt it. But chance favored me. He was called to visit a patient out of town, and was obliged to be absent during Sunday. "Now is the time," said my grandmother; "we will take the children to church, and have them christened."

When I entered the church, recollections of my mother came over me, and I felt subdued in spirit. There she had presented me for baptism, without any reason to feel ashamed. She had been married, and had such legal rights as slavery allows to a slave. The vows had at least been sacred to *her,* and she had never violated them. I was glad she was not alive, to know under what different circumstances her grandchildren were presented for baptism. Why had my lot been so different from my mother's? *Her* master had died when she was a child; and she remained with her mistress till she married. She was never in the power of any master; and thus she escaped one class of the evils that generally fall upon slaves.

When my baby was about to be christened, the former mistress of my father stepped up to me, and proposed to give it her Christian name. To this I added the surname of my father, who had himself no legal right to it; for my grandfather on the paternal side was a white gentleman. What tangled skeins are the genealogies of slavery! I loved my father; but it mortified me to be obliged to bestow his name on my children.

When we left the church, my father's old mistress invited me to go home with her. She clasped a gold chain round my baby's neck. I thanked her for this kindness; but I did not like the emblem. I wanted no chain to be fastened on my daughter, not even if its links were of gold. How earnestly I prayed that she might never feel the weight of slavery's chain, whose iron entereth into the soul!

XV.

CONTINUED PERSECUTIONS.

MY children grew finely; and Dr. Flint would often say to me, with an exulting smile, "These brats will bring me a handsome sum of money one of these days."

I thought to myself that, God being my helper, they should never pass into his hands. It seemed to me I would rather see them killed than have them given up to his power. The money for the freedom of myself and my children could be obtained; but I derived no advantage from that circumstance. Dr. Flint loved money, but he loved power more. After much discussion, my friends resolved on making another trial. There was a slaveholder about to leave for Texas, and he was commissioned to buy me. He was to begin with nine hundred dollars, and go up to twelve. My master refused his offers. "Sir," said he, "she don't belong to me. She is my daughter's property, and I have no right to sell her. I mistrust that you come from her paramour. If so, you may tell him that he cannot buy her for any money; neither can he buy her children."

The doctor came to see me the next day, and my heats beat quicker as he entered. I never had seen the old man tread with so majestic a step. He seated himself and looked at me with withering scorn. My children had learned to be afraid of him. The little one would shut her eyes and hide her face on my shoulder whenever she saw him; and Benny, who was now nearly five years old, often inquired, "What makes that bad man come here so many times? Does he want to hurt us?" I would clasp the dear boy in my arms, trusting that he would be free before he was old enough to solve the problem. And now, as the doctor sat there so grim and silent, the child left his play and came and nestled up by me. At last my tormentor spoke. "So you are left in disgust, are you?" said he. "It is no more than I expected. You remember I told you years ago that you would be treated so. So he is tired of you? Ha! ha! ha! The virtuous madam don't like to hear about it, does she? Ha! ha! ha!" There was a sting in his calling me virtuous madam. I no longer had the power of answering him as I had formerly done. He continued: "So it seems you are trying to get up another intrigue. Your new paramour came to me, and offered to buy you; but you may be assured you will not succeed. You are mine; and you shall be mine for life. There lives no human being that can take you out of slavery. I would have done it; but you rejected my kind offer."

I told him I did not wish to get up any intrigue; that I had never seen the man who offered to buy me.

"Do you tell me I lie?" exclaimed he, dragging me from my chair. "Will you say again that you never saw that man?"

I answered, "I do say so."

He clinched my arm with a volley of oaths. Ben began to scream, and I told him to go to his grandmother.

"Don't you stir a step, you little wretch!" said he. The child drew nearer to me, and put his arms round me, as if he wanted to protect me. This was too much for my enraged master. He caught him up and hurled him across the room. I thought he was dead, and rushed towards him to take him up.

"Not yet!" exclaimed the doctor. "Let him lie there till he comes to."

"Let me go! Let me go!" I screamed, "or I will raise the whole house." I struggled and got away; but he clinched me again. Somebody opened the door, and he released me. I picked up my insensible child, and when I turned my tormentor was gone. Anxiously I bent over the little form, so pale and still; and when the brown eyes at last opened, I don't know whether I was very happy.

All the doctor's former persecutions were renewed. He came morning, noon, and night. No jealous lover ever watched a rival more closely than he watched me and the unknown slaveholder, with whom he accused me of wishing to get up an intrigue. When my grandmother was out of the way he searched every room to find him.

In one of his visits, he happened to find a young girl, whom he had sold to a trader a few days previous. His statement was, that he sold her because she had been too familiar with the overseer. She had had a bitter life with him, and was glad to be sold. She had no mother, and no near ties. She had been torn from all her family years before. A few friends had entered into bonds for her safety, if the trader would allow her to spend with them the time that intervened between her sale and the gathering up of his human stock. Such a favor was rarely granted. It saved the trader the expense of board and jail fees, and though the amount was small, it was a weighty consideration in a slave-trader's mind.

Dr. Flint always had an aversion to meeting slaves after he had sold them. He ordered Rose out of the house; but he was no longer her master, and she took no notice of him. For once the crushed Rose was the conqueror. His gray eyes flashed angrily upon her; but that was the extent of his power. "How came this girl here?" he exclaimed. "What right had you to allow it, when you knew I had sold her?"

I answered "This is my grandmother's house, and Rose came to see her. I have no right to turn any body out of doors, that comes here for honest purposes."

He gave me the blow that would have fallen upon Rose if she had still been his slave. My grandmother's attention had been attracted by loud voices, and she entered in time to see a second blow dealt. She was not a woman to let such an outrage, in her own house, go unrebuked. The doctor undertook to explain that I had been insolent. Her indignant feelings rose higher and higher, and finally boiled over in words. "Get out of my house!" she exclaimed. "Go home, and take care of your wife and children, and you will have enough to do, without watching my family."

He threw the birth of my children in her face, and accused her of sanctioning the life I was leading. She told him I was living with her by compulsion of his wife; that he needn't accuse her, for he was the one to blame; he was the one who had caused all the trouble. She grew more and more excited as she went on. "I tell you what, Dr. Flint," said she, "you ain't got many more years to live, and you'd better be saying your prayers. It will take 'em all, and more too, to wash the dirt off your soul."

"Do you know whom you are talking to?" he exclaimed.

She replied, "Yes, I know very well who I am talking to."

He left the house in a great rage. I looked at my grandmother. Our eyes met. Their angry expression had passed away, but she looked sorrowful and weary—weary of incessant strife. I wondered that it did not lessen her love for me; but if it did she never showed it. She was always kind, always ready to sympathize with my troubles. There might have been peace and contentment in that humble home if it had not been for the demon Slavery.

The winter passed undisturbed by the doctor. The beautiful spring came; and when Nature resumes her loveliness, the human soul is apt to revive also. My drooping hopes came to life again with the flowers. I was dreaming of freedom again; more for my children's sake than my own. I planned and I planned. Obstacles hit against plans. There seemed no way of overcoming them; and yet I hoped.

Back came the wily doctor. I was not at home when he called. A friend had invited me to a small party, and to gratify her I went. To my great consternation, a messenger came in haste to say that Dr. Flint was at my grandmother's, and insisted on seeing me. They did not tell him where I was, or he would have come and raised a disturbance in my friend's house. They sent me a dark wrapper; I threw it on and hurried home. My speed did not save me; the doctor had gone away in anger. I dreaded the morning, but I could not delay it; it came, warm and bright. At an early hour the doctor came and asked me where I had been last night. I told him. He did not believe me, and sent to my friend's house to ascertain the facts. He came in the afternoon to assure me he was satisfied that I had spoken the truth. He seemed to be in a facetious mood, and I expected some jeers were coming. "I suppose you need some recreation," said he, "but I am surprised at your being there, among those negroes. It was not the place for *you*. Are you *allowed* to visit such people?"

I understood this covert fling at the white gentleman who was my friend; but I merely replied, "I went to visit my friends, and any company they keep is good enough for me."

He went on to say, "I have seen very little of you of late, but my interest in you is unchanged. When I said I would have no more mercy on you I was rash. I recall my words. Linda, you desire freedom for yourself and your children, and you can obtain it only through me. If you agree to what I am about to propose, you and they shall be free. There must be no communication of any kind between you and their father. I will procure a cottage, where you and the children can live together. Your labor shall be light, such as sewing for my family. Think what is offered you, Linda—a home and freedom! Let the past be forgotten. If I have been harsh with you at times, your wilfulness drove me to it. You know I exact obedience from my own children, and I consider you as yet a child."

He paused for an answer, but I remained silent.

"Why don't you speak?" said he. "What more do you wait for?"

"Nothing, sir."

"Then you accept my offer?"

"No, sir."

His anger was ready to break loose; but he succeeded in curbing it, and replied, "You have answered without thought. But I must let you know there are two sides to my proposition; if you reject the bright side, you will be obliged to take the dark one. You must either accept my offer, or you and your children shall be sent to your young master's plantation, there to remain till your young mistress is married; and your children shall fare like the rest of the negro children. I give you a week to consider of it."

He was shrewd; but I knew he was not to be trusted. I told him I was ready to give my answer now.

"I will not receive it now," he replied. "You act too much from impulse. Remember that you and your children can be free a week from to-day if you choose."

On what a monstrous chance hung the destiny of my children! I knew that my master's offer was a snare, and that if I entered it escape would be impossible. As for his promise, I knew him so well that I was sure if he gave me free papers, they would be so managed as to have no legal value. The alternative was inevitable. I resolved to go to the plantation. But then I thought how completely I should be in his power, and the prospect was apalling. Even if I should kneel before him, and implore him to spare me, for the sake of my children, I knew he would spurn me with his foot, and my weakness would be his triumph.

Before the week expired, I heard that young Mr. Flint was about to be married to a lady of his own stamp. I foresaw the position I should occupy in his establishment. I had once been sent to the plantation for punishment, and fear of the son had induced the father to recall me very soon. My mind was made up; I was resolved that I would foil my master and save my children, or I would perish in the attempt. I kept my plans to myself; I knew that friends would try to dissuade me from them, and I would not wound their feelings by rejecting their advice.

On the decisive day the doctor came, and said he hoped I had made a wise choice.

"I am ready to go to the plantation, sir," I replied.

"Have you thought how important your decision is to your children?" said he.

I told him I had.

"Very well. Go to the plantation, and my curse go with you," he replied. "Your boy shall be put to work, and he shall soon be sold; and your girl shall be raised for the purpose of selling well. Go your own ways!" He left the room with curses, not to be repeated.

As I stood rooted to the spot, my grandmother came and said, "Linda, child, what did you tell him?"

I answered that I was going to the plantation.

"*Must* you go?" said she. "Can't something be done to stop it?"

I told her it was useless to try; but she begged me not to give up. She said she would go to the doctor, and remind him how long and how faithfully she had served in the family, and how she had taken her own baby from her breast to nourish his wife. She would tell him I had been out of the family so long they would not miss me; that she would pay them for my time, and the money would procure a woman who had more strength for the situation than I had. I begged her not to go; but she persisted in saying, "He will listen to *me,* Linda." She went, and was treated as I expected. He coolly listened to what she said, but denied her request. He told her that what he did was for my good, that my feelings were entirely above my situation, and that on the plantation I would receive treatment that was suitable to my behavior.

My grandmother was much cast down. I had my secret hopes; but I must fight my battle alone. I had a woman's pride, and a mother's love for my children; and I resolved that out of the darkness of this hour a brighter dawn should rise for them. My master had power and law on his side; I had a determined will. There is might in each.

XVI.

SCENES AT THE PLANTATION.

EARLY the next morning I left my grandmother's with my youngest child. My boy was ill, and I left him behind. I had many sad thoughts as the old wagon jolted on. Hitherto, I had suffered alone; now, my little one was to be treated as a slave. As we drew near the great house, I thought of the time when I was formerly sent there out of revenge. I wondered for what purpose I was now sent. I could not tell. I resolved to obey orders so far as duty required; but within myself, I determined to make my stay as short as possible. Mr. Flint was waiting to receive us, and told me to follow him up stairs to receive orders for the day. My little Ellen was left below in the kitchen. It was a change for her, who had always been so carefully tended. My young master said she might amuse herself in the yard. This was kind of him, since the child was hateful to his sight. My task was to fit up the house for the reception of the bride. In the midst of sheets, tablecloths, towels, drapery, and carpeting, my head was as busy planning, as were my fingers with the needle. At noon I was allowed to go to Ellen. She had sobbed herself to sleep. I heard Mr. Flint say to a neighbor, "I've got her down here, and I'll soon take the town notions out of her head. My father is partly to blame for her nonsense. He ought to have broke her in long ago." The remark was made within my hearing, and it would have been quite as manly to have made it to my face. He *had* said things to my face which might, or might not, have surprised his neighbor if he had known of them. He was "a chip of the old block."

I resolved to give him no cause to accuse me of being too much of a lady, so far as work was concerned. I worked day and night, with wretchedness before me. When I lay down beside my child, I felt how much easier it would be to see her die than to see her master beat her about, as I daily saw him beat other little ones. The spirit of the mothers was so crushed by the lash, that they stood by, without courage to remonstrate. How much more must I suffer, before I should be "broke in" to that degree?

I wished to appear as contented as possible. Sometimes I had an opportunity to send a few lines home; and this brought up recollections that made it difficult, for a time, to seem calm and indifferent to my lot. Notwithstanding my efforts, I saw that Mr. Flint regarded me with a suspicious eye. Ellen broke down under the trials of her new life. Separated from me, with no one to look after her, she wandered about, and in a few days cried herself sick. One day, she sat under the window where I was at work, crying that weary cry which makes a mother's heart bleed. I was obliged to steel myself to bear it. After a while it ceased. I looked out, and she was gone. As it was near noon, I ventured to go down in search of her. The great house was raised two feet above the ground. I looked under it, and saw her about midway, fast asleep. I crept under and drew her out. As I held her in my arms, I thought how well it would be for her if she never waked up; and I uttered my thought aloud. I was startled to hear some one say, "Did you speak to me?" I looked up, and saw Mr. Flint standing beside me. He said nothing further, but turned, frowning, away. That night he sent Ellen a biscuit and a cup of sweetened milk. This generosity surprised me. I learned afterwards, that in the afternoon he had killed a large snake, which crept from under the house; and I supposed that incident had prompted his unusual kindness.

The next morning the old cart was loaded with shingles for town. I put Ellen into it, and sent her to her grandmother. Mr. Flint said I ought to have asked his permission. I told him the child was sick, and required attention which I had no time to give. He let it pass; for he was aware that I had accomplished much work in a little time.

I had been three weeks on the plantation, when I planned a visit home. It must be at night, after every body was in bed. I was six miles from town, and the road was very dreary. I was to go with a young man, who, I knew, often stole to town to see his mother. One night, when all was quiet, we started. Fear gave speed to our steps, and we were not long in performing the journey. I arrived at my grandmother's. Her bed room was on the first floor, and the window was open, the weather being warm. I spoke to her and she awoke. She let me in and closed the window, lest some late passer-by should see me. A light was brought, and the whole household gathered round me, some smiling and some crying. I went to look at my children, and thanked God for their happy sleep. The tears fell as I leaned over them. As I moved to leave, Benny stirred. I turned back, and whispered, "Mother is here." After digging at his eyes with his little fist, they opened, and he sat up in bed, looking at me curiously. Having satisfied himself that it was I, he exclaimed, "O mother! you ain't dead, are you? They didn't cut off your head at the plantation, did they?"

My time was up too soon, and my guide was waiting for me. I laid Benny back in his bed, and dried his tears by a promise to come again soon. Rapidly we retraced our steps back to the plantation. About half way we were met by a company of four patrols. Luckily we heard their horse's hoofs before they came in sight, and we had time to hide behind a large tree. They passed, hallooing and shouting in a manner that indicated a recent carousal. How thankful we were that they had not their dogs with them! We hastened our footsteps, and when we arrived on the plantation we heard the sound of the hand-mill. The slaves were grinding their corn. We were safely in the house before the horn summoned them to their labor. I divided my little parcel of food with my guide, knowing that he had lost the chance of grinding his corn, and must toil all day in the field.

Mr. Flint often took an inspection of the house, to see that no one was idle. The entire management of the work was trusted to me, because he knew nothing about it; and rather than hire a superintendent he contented himself with my arrangements. He had often urged upon his father the necessity of having me at the plantation to take charge of his affairs, and make clothes for the slaves; but the old man knew him too well to consent to that arrangement.

When I had been working a month at the plantation, the great aunt of Mr. Flint came to make him a visit. This was the good old lady who paid fifty dollars for my grandmother, for the purpose of making her free, when she stood on the auction block. My grandmother loved this old lady, whom we all called Miss Fanny. She often came to take tea with us. On such occasions the table was spread with a snow-white cloth, and the china cups and silver spoons were taken from the old-fashioned buffet. There were hot muffins, tea rusks, and delicious sweetmeats. My grandmother kept two cows, and the fresh cream was Miss Fanny's delight. She invariably declared that it was the best in town. The old ladies had cosey times together. They would work and chat, and sometimes, while talking over old times, their spectacles would get dim with tears, and would have to be taken off and wiped. When Miss Fanny bade us good by, her bag was filled with grandmother's best cakes, and she was urged to come again soon.

There had been a time when Dr. Flint's wife came to take tea with us, and when her children were also sent to have a feast of "Aunt Marthy's" nice cooking. But after I became an object of her jealousy and spite, she was angry with grandmother for giving a shelter to me and my children. She would not even speak to her in the street. This wounded my grandmother's feelings, for she could not retain ill will against the woman whom she had nourished with her milk when a babe. The doctor's wife would gladly have prevented our intercourse with Miss Fanny if she could have done it, but fortunately she was not dependent on the bounty of the Flints. She had enough to be independent; and that is more than can ever be gained from charity, however lavish it may be.

Miss Fanny was endeared to me by many recollections, and I was rejoiced to see her at the plantation. The warmth of her large, loyal heart made the house seem pleasanter while she was in it. She staid a week, and I had many talks with her. She said her principal object in coming was to see how I was treated, and whether any thing could be done for me. She inquired whether she could help me in any way. I told her I believed not. She condoled with me in her own peculiar way; saying she wished that I and all my grandmother's family were at rest in our graves, for not until then should she feel any peace about us. The good old soul did not dream that I was planning to bestow peace upon her, with regard to myself and my children; not by death, but by securing our freedom.

Again and again I had traversed those dreary twelve miles, to and from the town; and all the way, I was meditating upon some means of escape for myself and my children. My friends had made every effort that ingenuity could devise to effect our purchase, but all their plans had proved abortive. Dr. Flint was suspicious, and determined not to loosen his grasp upon us. I could have made my escape alone; but it was more for my helpless children than for myself that I longed for freedom. Though the boon would have been precious to me, above all price, I would not have taken it at the expense of leaving them in slavery. Every trial I endured, every sacrifice I made for their sakes, drew them closer to my heart, and gave me fresh courage to beat back the dark waves that rolled and rolled over me in a seemingly endless night of storms.

The six weeks were nearly completed, when Mr. Flint's bride was expected to take possession of her new home. The arrangements were all completed, and Mr. Flint said I had done well. He expected to leave home on Saturday, and return with his bride the following Wednesday. After receiving various orders from him, I ventured to ask permission to spend Sunday in town. It was granted; for which favor I was thankful. It was the first I had ever asked of him, and I intended it should be the last. It needed more than one night to accomplish the project I had in view; but the whole of Sunday would give me an opportunity. I spent the Sabbath with my grandmother. A calmer, more beautiful day never came down out of heaven. To me it was a day of conflicting emotions. Perhaps it was the last day I should ever spend under that dear, old sheltering roof! Perhaps these were the last talks I should ever have with the faithful old friend of my whole life! Perhaps it was the last time I and my children should be together! Well, better so, I thought, than that they should be slaves. I knew the doom that awaited my fair baby in slavery, and I determined to save her from it, or perish in the attempt. I went to make this vow at the graves of my poor parents, in the burying-ground of the slaves. "There the wicked cease from troubling, and there the weary be at rest. There the prisoners rest together; they hear not the voice of the oppressor; the servant is free from his master."[68] I knelt by the graves of my parents, and thanked God, as I had often done before, that they had not lived to witness my trials, or to mourn over my sins. I had received my mother's blessing when she died; and in many an hour of tribulation I had seemed to hear her voice, sometimes chiding me, sometimes whispering loving words into my wounded heart. I have shed many and bitter tears, to think that when I am gone from my children they cannot remember me with such entire satisfaction as I remembered my mother.

The graveyard was in the woods, and twilight was coming on. Nothing broke the death-like stillness except the occasional twitter of a bird. My spirit was overawed by the solemnity of the scene. For more than ten years I had frequented this spot, but never had it seemed to me so sacred as now. A black stump, at the head of my mother's grave, was all that remained of a tree my father had planted. His grave was marked by a small wooden board, bearing his name, the letters of which were nearly obliterated. I knelt down and kissed them, and poured forth a prayer to God for guidance and support in the perilous step I was about to take. As I passed the wreck of the old meeting house, where, before Nat Turner's time, the slaves had been allowed to meet for worship, I seemed to hear my father's voice come from it, bidding me not to tarry till I reached freedom or the grave. I rushed on with renovated hopes. My trust in God had been strengthened by that prayer among the graves.

My plan was to conceal myself at the house of a friend, and remain there a few weeks till the search was over. My hope was that the doctor would get discouraged, and, for fear of losing my value, and also of subsequently finding my children among the missing, he would consent to sell us; and I knew somebody would buy us. I had done all in my power to make my children comfortable during the time I expected to be separated from them. I was packing my things, when grandmother came into the room, and asked what I was doing. "I am putting my things in order," I replied. I tried to look and speak cheerfully; but her watchful eye detected something beneath the surface. She drew me towards her, and asked me to sit down. She looked earnestly at me, and said, "Linda, do you want to kill your old grandmother? Do you mean to leave your little, helpless children? I am old now, and cannot do for your babies as I once did for you."

I replied, that if I went away, perhaps their father would be able to secure their freedom.

"Ah, my child," said she, "don't trust too much to him. Stand by your own children, and suffer with them till death. Nobody respects a mother who forsakes her children; and if you leave them, you will never have a happy moment. If you go, you will make me miserable the short time I have to live. You would be taken and brought back, and your sufferings would be dreadful. Remember poor Benjamin. Do give it up, Linda. Try to bear a little longer. Things may turn out better than we expect."

My courage failed me, in view of the sorrow I should bring on that faithful, loving old heart. I promised that I would try longer, and that I would take nothing out of her house without her knowledge.

Whenever the children climbed on my knee, or laid their heads on my lap, she would say, "Poor little souls! what would you do without a mother? She don't love you as I do." And she would hug them to her own bosom, as if to reproach me for my want of affection; but she knew all the while that I loved them better than my life. I slept with her that night, and it was the last time. The memory of it haunted me for many a year.

On Monday I returned to the plantation, and busied myself with preparations for the important day. Wednesday[69] came. It was a beautiful day, and the faces of the slaves were as bright as the sunshine. The poor creatures were merry. They were expecting little presents from the bride, and hoping for better times under her administration. I had no such hopes for them. I knew that the young wives of slaveholders often thought their authority and importance would be best established and maintained by cruelty; and what I had heard of young Mrs. Flint gave me no reason to expect that her rule over them would be less severe than that of the master and overseer. Truly, the colored race are the most cheerful and forgiving people on the face of the earth. That their masters sleep in safety is owing to their superabundance of heart; and yet they look upon their sufferings with less pity than they would bestow on those of a horse or a dog.

I stood at the door with others to receive the bridegroom and bride. She was a handsome, delicate-looking girl, and her face flushed with emotion at sight of her new home. I thought it likely that visions of a happy future were rising before her. It made me sad; for I knew how soon clouds would come over her sunshine. She examined every part of the house, and told me she was delighted with the arrangements I had made. I was afraid old Mrs. Flint had tried to prejudice her against me, and I did my best to please her.

All passed off smoothly for me until dinner time arrived. I did not mind the embarrassment of waiting on a dinner party, for the first time in my life, half so much as I did the meeting with Dr. Flint and his wife, who would be among the guests. It was a mystery to me why Mrs. Flint had not made her appearance at the plantation during all the time I was putting the house in order. I had not met her, face to face, for five years, and I had no wish to see her now. She was a praying woman, and, doubtless, considered my present position a special answer to her prayers. Nothing could please her better than to see me humbled and trampled upon. I was just where she would have me—in the power of a hard, unprincipled master. She did not speak to me when she took her seat at table; but her satisfied, triumphant smile, when I handed her plate, was more eloquent than words. The old doctor was not so quiet in his demonstrations. He ordered me here and there, and spoke with peculiar emphasis when he said "your *mistress*." I was drilled like a disgraced soldier. When all was over, and the last key turned, I sought my pillow, thankful that God had appointed a season of rest for the weary.

The next day my new mistress began her housekeeping. I was not exactly appointed maid of all work; but I was to do whatever I was told. Monday evening came. It was always a busy time. On that night the slaves received their weekly allowance of food. Three pounds of meat, a peck of corn, and perhaps a dozen herring were allowed to each man. Women received a pound and a half of meat, a peck of corn, and the same number of herring. Children over twelve years old had half the allowance of the women. The meat was cut and weighed by the foreman of the field hands, and piled on planks before the meat house. Then the second foreman went behind the building, and when the first foreman called out, "Who takes this piece of meat?" he answered by calling somebody's name. This method was resorted to as a means of preventing partiality in distributing the meat. The young mistress came out to see how things were done on her plantation, and she soon gave a specimen of her character. Among those in waiting for their allowance was a very old slave, who had faithfully served the Flint family through three generations. When he hobbled up to get his bit of meat, the mistress said he was too old to have any allowance; that when niggers were too old to work, they ought to be fed on grass. Poor old man! He suffered much before he found rest in the grave.

My mistress and I got along very well together. At the end of a week, old Mrs. Flint made us another visit, and was closeted a long time with her daughter-in-law. I had my suspicions what was the subject of the conference. The old doctor's wife had been informed that I could leave the plantation on one condition, and she was very desirous to keep me there. If she had trusted me, as I deserved to be trusted by her, she would have had no fears of my accepting that condition. When she entered her carriage to return home, she said to young Mrs. Flint, "Don't neglect to send for them as quick as possible." My heart was on the watch all the time, and I at once concluded that she spoke of my children. The doctor came the next day, and as I entered the room to spread the tea table,

I heard him say, "Don't wait any longer. Send for them to-morrow." I saw through the plan. They thought my children's being there would fetter me to the spot, and that it was a good place to break us all in to abject submission to our lot as slaves. After the doctor left, a gentleman called, who had always manifested friendly feelings towards my grandmother and her family. Mr. Flint carried him over the plantation to show him the results of labor performed by men and women who were unpaid, miserably clothed, and half famished. The cotton crop was all they thought of. It was duly admired, and the gentleman returned with specimens to show his friends. I was ordered to carry water to wash his hands. As I did so, he said, "Linda, how do you like your new home?" I told him I liked it as well as I expected. He replied, "They don't think you are contented, and to-morrow they are going to bring your children to be with you. I am sorry for you, Linda. I hope they will treat you kindly." I hurried from the room, unable to thank him. My suspicions were correct. My children were to be brought to the plantation to be "broke in."

To this day I feel grateful to the gentleman who gave me this timely information. It nerved me to immediate action.

XVII.

THE FLIGHT.

MR. FLINT was hard pushed for house servants, and rather than lose me he had restrained his malice. I did my work faithfully, though not, of course, with a willing mind. They were evidently afraid I should leave them. Mr. Flint wished that I should sleep in the great house instead of the servants' quarters. His wife agreed to the proposition, but said I mustn't bring my bed into the house, because it would scatter feathers on her carpet. I knew when I went there that they would never think of such a thing as furnishing a bed of any kind for me and my little one. I therefore carried my own bed, and now I was forbidden to use it. I did as I was ordered. But now that I was certain my children were to be put in their power, in order to give them a stronger hold on me, I resolved to leave them that night. I remembered the grief this step would bring upon my dear old grandmother; and nothing less than the freedom of my children would have induced me to disregard her advice. I went about my evening work with trembling steps. Mr. Flint twice called from his chamber door to inquire why the house was not locked up. I replied that I had not done my work. "You have had time enough to do it," said he. "Take care how you answer me!"

I shut all the windows, locked all the doors, and went up to the third story, to wait till midnight. How long those hours seemed, and how fervently I prayed that God would not forsake me in this hour of utmost need! I was about to risk every thing on the throw of a die; and if I failed, O what would become of me and my poor children? They would be made to suffer for my fault.

At half past twelve I stole softly down stairs. I stopped on the second floor, thinking I heard a noise. I felt my way down into the parlor, and looked out of the window. The night was so intensely dark that I could see nothing. I raised the window very softly and jumped out. Large drops of rain were falling, and the darkness bewildered me. I dropped on my knees, and breathed a short prayer to God for guidance and protection. I groped my way to the road, and rushed towards the town with almost lightning speed. I arrived at my grandmother's house, but dared not see her. She would say, "Linda, you are killing me;" and I knew that would unnerve me. I tapped softly at the window of a room, occupied by a woman, who had lived in the house several years. I knew she was a faithful friend, and could be trusted with my secret. I tapped several times before she heard me. At last she raised the window, and I whispered, "Sally, I have run away. Let me in, quick." She opened the door softly, and said in low tones, "For God's sake, don't. Your grandmother is trying to buy you and de chillern. Mr. Sands was here last week. He tole her he was going away on business, but he wanted her to go ahead about buying you and de chillern, and he would help her all he could. Don't run away, Linda. Your grandmother is all bowed down wid trouble now."

I replied, "Sally, they are going to carry my children to the plantation to-morrow; and they will never sell them to any body so long as they have me in their power. Now, would you advise me to go back?"

"No, chile, no," answered she. "When dey finds you is gone, dey won't want de plague ob de chillern; but where is you going to hide? Dey knows ebery inch ob dis house."

I told her I had a hiding-place, and that was all it was best for her to know. I asked her to go into my room as soon as it was light, and take all my clothes out of my trunk, and pack them in hers; for I knew Mr. Flint and the constable would be there early to search my room. I feared the sight of my children would be too much for my full heart; but I could not go out into the uncertain future without one last look. I bent over the bed where lay my little Benny and baby Ellen. Poor little ones! fatherless and motherless! Memories of their father came over me. He wanted to be kind to them; but they were not all to him, as they were to my womanly heart. I knelt and prayed for the innocent little sleepers. I kissed them lightly, and turned away.

As I was about to open the street door, Sally laid her hand on my shoulder, and said, "Linda, is you gwine all alone? Let me call your uncle."

"No, Sally," I replied, "I want no one to be brought into trouble on my account."

I went forth into the darkness and rain. I ran on till I came to the house of the friend who was to conceal me.

Early the next morning Mr. Flint was at my grandmother's inquiring for me. She told him she had not seen me, and supposed I was at the plantation. He watched her face narrowly, and said, "Don't you know any thing about her running off?" She assured him that she did not. He went on to say, "Last night she ran off without the least provocation. We had treated her very kindly. My wife liked her. She will soon be found and brought back. Are her children with you?" When told that they were, he said, "I am very glad to hear that. If they are here, she cannot be far off. If I find out that any of my niggers have had any thing to do with this damned business, I'll give 'em five hundred lashes." As he started to go to his father's, he turned round and added, persuasively, "Let her be brought back, and she shall have her children to live with her."

The tidings made the old doctor rave and storm at a furious rate. It was a busy day for them. My grandmother's house was searched from top to bottom. As my trunk was empty, they concluded I had taken my clothes with me. Before ten o'clock every vessel northward bound was thoroughly examined, and the law against harboring fugitives was read to all on board. At night a watch was set over the town. Knowing how distressed my grandmother would be, I wanted to send her a message; but it could not be done. Every one who went in or out of her house was closely watched. The doctor said he would take my children, unless she became responsible for them; which of course she willingly did. The next day was spent in searching. Before night, the following advertisement was posted at every corner, and in every public place for miles round:—

"$300 REWARD! Ran away from the subscriber, an intelligent, bright, mulatto girl, named Linda, 21 years of age. Five feet four inches high. Dark eyes, and black hair inclined to curl; but it can be made straight. Has a decayed spot on a front tooth. She can read and write, and in all probability will try to get to the Free States. All persons are forbidden, under penalty of the law, to harbor or employ said slave. $150 will be given to whoever takes her in the state, and $300 if taken out of the state and delivered to me, or lodged in jail.

DR. FLINT."[70]

XVIII.

MONTHS OF PERIL.

THE search for me was kept up with more perseverence than I had anticipated. I began to think that escape was impossible. I was in great anxiety lest I should implicate the friend who harbored me. I knew the consequences would be frightful; and much as I dreaded being caught, even that seemed better than causing an innocent person to suffer for kindness to me. A week had passed in terrible suspense, when my pursuers came into such close vicinity that I concluded they had tracked me to my hiding-place. I flew out of the house, and concealed myself in a thicket of bushes. There I remained in an agony of fear for two hours. Suddenly, a reptile of some kind seized my leg. In my fright, I struck a blow which loosened its hold, but I could not tell whether I had killed it; it was so dark, I could not see what it was; I only knew it was something cold and slimy. The pain I felt soon indicated that the bite was poisonous. I was compelled to leave my place of concealment, and I groped my way back into the house. The pain had become intense, and my friend was startled by my look of anguish. I asked her to prepare a poultice of warm ashes and vinegar, and I applied it to my leg, which was already much swollen. The application gave me some relief, but the swelling did not abate. The dread of being disabled was greater than the physical pain I endured. My friend asked an old woman, who doctored among the slaves, what was good for the bite of a snake or a lizard. She told her to steep a dozen coppers in vinegar, over night, and apply the cankered vinegar to the inflamed part.*

I had succeeded in cautiously conveying some messages to my relatives. They were harshly threatened, and despairing of my having a chance to escape, they advised me to return to my master, ask his forgiveness, and let him make an example of me. But such counsel had no influence with me. When I started upon this hazardous undertaking, I had resolved that, come what would, there should be no turning back. "Give me liberty, or give me death,"[71] was my motto. When my friend contrived to make known to my relatives the painful situation I had been in for twenty-four hours, they said no more about my going back to my master. Something must be done, and that speedily; but where to turn for help, they knew not. God in his mercy raised up "a friend in need."

Among the ladies who were acquainted with my grandmother, was one who had known her from childhood, and always been very friendly to her. She had also known my mother and her children, and felt interested for them. At this crisis of affairs she called to see my grandmother, as she not unfrequently did. She observed the sad and troubled expression of her face, and asked if she knew where Linda was, and whether she was safe. My grandmother shook her head, without answering. "Come, Aunt Martha," said the kind lady, "tell me all about it. Perhaps I can do something to help you." The husband of this lady held many slaves, and bought and sold slaves. She also held a number in her own name; but she treated them kindly, and would never allow any of them to be sold. She was unlike the majority of slaveholders' wives. My grandmother looked earnestly at her. Something in the expression of her face said "Trust me!" and she did trust her. She listened attentively to the details of my story, and sat thinking for a while. At last she said, "Aunt Martha, I pity you both. If you think there is any chance of Linda's getting to the Free States, I will conceal her for a time. But first you must solemnly promise that my name shall never be mentioned. If such a thing should become known, it would ruin me and my family. No one in my house must know of it, except the cook. She is so faithful that I would trust my own life with her; and I know she likes Linda. It is a great risk; but I trust no harm will come of it. Get word to Linda to be ready as soon as it is dark, before the patrols are out. I will send the housemaids on errands, and Betty shall go to meet Linda." The place where we were to meet was designated and agreed upon. My grandmother was unable to thank the lady for this noble deed; overcome by her emotions, she sank on her knees and sobbed like a child.

I received a message to leave my friend's house at such an hour, and go to a certain place where a friend would be waiting for me. As a matter of prudence no names were mentioned. I had no means of conjecturing who I was to meet,

---

*The poison of a snake is a powerful acid, and is counteracted by powerful alkalies, such as potash, ammonia, &c. The Indians are accustomed to apply wet ashes, or plunge the limb into strong lie. White men, employed to lay out railroads in snaky places, often carry ammonia with them as an antidote.—EDITOR.

or where I was going. I did not like to move thus blindfolded, but I had no choice. It would not do for me to remain where I was. I disguised myself, summoned up courage to meet the worst, and went to the appointed place. My friend Betty was there; she was the last person I expected to see. We hurried along in silence. The pain in my leg was so intense that it seemed as if I should drop; but fear gave me strength. We reached the house and entered unobserved. Her first words were: "Honey, now you is safe. Dem devils ain't coming to search *dis* house. When I get you into missis' safe place, I will bring some nice hot supper. I specs you need it after all dis skeering." Betty's vocation led her to think eating the most important thing in life. She did not realize that my heart was too full for me to care much about supper.

The mistress came to meet us, and led me up stairs to a small room over her own sleeping apartment. "You will be safe here, Linda," said she; "I keep this room to store away things that are out of use. The girls are not accustomed to be sent to it, and they will not suspect any thing unless they hear some noise. I always keep it locked, and Betty shall take care of the key. But you must be very careful, for my sake as well as your own; and you must never tell my secret; for it would ruin me and my family. I will keep the girls busy in the morning, that Betty may have a chance to bring your breakfast; but it will not do for her to come to you again till night. I will come to see you sometimes. Keep up your courage. I hope this state of things will not last long." Betty came with the "nice hot supper," and the mistress hastened down stairs to keep things straight till she returned. How my heart overflowed with gratitude! Words choked in my throat; but I could have kissed the feet of my benefactress. For that deed of Christian womanhood, may God forever bless her!

I went to sleep that night with the feeling that I was for the present the most fortunate slave in town. Morning came and filled my little cell with light. I thanked the heavenly Father for this safe retreat. Opposite my window was a pile of feather beds. On the top of these I could lie perfectly concealed, and command a view of the street through which Dr. Flint passed to his office. Anxious as I was, I felt a gleam of satisfaction when I saw him. Thus far I had outwitted him, and I triumphed over it. Who can blame slaves for being cunning? They are constantly compelled to resort to it. It is the only weapon of the weak and oppressed against the strength of their tyrants.

I was daily hoping to hear that my master had sold my children; for I knew who was on the watch to buy them. But Dr. Flint cared even more for revenge than he did for money. My brother William, and the good aunt who had served in his family twenty years, and my little Benny, and Ellen, who was a little over two years old, were thrust into jail, as a means of compelling my relatives to give some information about me. He swore my grandmother should never see one of them again till I was brought back. They kept these facts from me for several days. When I heard that my little ones were in a loathsome jail, my first impulse was to go to them. I was encountering dangers for the sake of freeing them, and must I be the cause of their death? The thought was agonizing. My benefactress tried to soothe me by telling me that my aunt would take good care of the children while they remained in jail. But it added to my pain to think that the good old aunt, who had always been so kind to her sister's orphan children, should be shut up in prison for no other crime than loving them. I suppose my friends feared a reckless movement on my part, knowing, as they did, that my life was bound up in my children. I received a note from my brother William. It was scarcely legible, and ran thus: "Wherever you are, dear sister, I beg of you not to come here. We are all much better off than you are. If you come, you will ruin us all. They would force you to tell where you had been, or they would kill you. Take the advice of your friends; if not for the sake of me and your children, at least for the sake of those you would ruin."

Poor William! He also must suffer for being my brother. I took his advice and kept quiet. My aunt was taken out of jail at the end of a month, because Mrs. Flint could not spare her any longer. She was tired of being her own house-keeper. It was quite too fatiguing to order her dinner and eat it too. My children remained in jail, where brother William did all he could for their comfort. Betty went to see them sometimes, and brought me tidings. She was not permitted to enter the jail; but William would hold them up to the grated window while she chatted with them. When she repeated their prattle, and told me how they wanted to see their ma, my tears would flow. Old Betty would exclaim, "Lors, chile! what's you crying 'bout? Dem young uns vil kill you dead. Don't be so chick'n hearted! If you does, you vil nebber git thro' dis world."

Good old soul! She had gone through the world childless. She had never had little ones to clasp their arms round her neck; she had never seen their soft eyes looking into hers; no sweet little voices had called her mother; she had never pressed her own infants to her heart, with the feeling that even in fetters there was something to live for. How could she realize my feelings? Betty's husband loved children dearly, and wondered why God had denied them to him. He ex-pressed great sorrow when he came to Betty with the tidings that Ellen had been taken out of jail and carried to Dr. Flint's. She had the measles a short time be-fore they carried her to jail, and the disease had left her eyes affected. The doc-tor had taken her home to attend to them. My children had always been afraid of the doctor and his wife. They had never been inside of their house. Poor little Ellen cried all day to be carried back to prison. The instincts of childhood are true. She knew she was loved in the jail. Her screams and sobs annoyed Mrs. Flint. Before night she called one of the slaves, and said, "Here, Bill, carry this brat back to the jail. I can't stand her noise. If she would be quiet I should like to keep the little minx. She would make a handy waiting-maid for my daughter by and by. But if she staid here, with her white face, I suppose I should either kill her or spoil her. I hope the doctor will sell them as far as wind and water can carry them. As for their mother, her ladyship will find out yet what she gets by running away. She hasn't so much feeling for her children as a cow has for its calf. If she had, she would have come back long ago, to get them out of jail, and save all this expense and trouble. The good-for-nothing hussy! When she is caught, she shall stay in jail, in irons, for one six months, and then be sold to a sugar plantation. I shall see her broke in yet. What do you stand there for, Bill? Why don't you go off with the brat? Mind, now, that you don't let any of the niggers speak to her in the street!"

When these remarks were reported to me, I smiled at Mrs. Flint's saying that she should either kill my child or spoil her. I thought to myself there was very little danger of the latter. I have always considered it as one of God's special providences that Ellen screamed till she was carried back to jail.

That same night Dr. Flint was called to a patient, and did not return till near morning. Passing my grandmother's, he saw a light in the house, and thought to himself, "Perhaps this has something to do with Linda." He knocked, and the door was opened. "What calls you up so early?" said he. "I saw your light, and I thought I would just stop and tell you that I have found out where Linda is. I know where to put my hands on her, and I shall have her before twelve o'clock." When he had turned away, my grandmother and my uncle looked anxiously at each other. They did not know whether or not it was merely one of the doctor's tricks to frighten them. In their uncertainty, they thought it was best to have a message conveyed to my friend Betty. Unwilling to alarm her mistress, Betty resolved to dispose of me herself. She came to me, and told me to rise and dress quickly. We hurried down stairs, and across the yard, into the kitchen. She locked the door, and lifted up a plank in the floor. A buffalo skin and a bit of carpet were spread for me to lie on, and a quilt thrown over me. "Stay dar," said she, "till I sees if dey know 'bout you. Dey say dey vil put thar hans on you afore twelve o'clock. If dey *did* know whar you are, dey won't know *now*. Dey'll be disapinted dis time. Dat's all I got to say. If dey comes rummagin 'mong *my* tings, dey'll get one bressed sarssin from dis 'ere nigger." In my shallow bed I had but just room enough to bring my hands to my face to keep the dust out of my eyes; for Betty walked over me twenty times in an hour, passing from the dresser to the fireplace. When she was alone, I could hear her pronouncing anathemas over Dr. Flint and all his tribe, every now and then saying, with a chuckling laugh, "Dis nigger's too cute for 'em dis time." When the housemaids were about, she had sly ways of drawing them out, that I might hear what they would say. She would repeat stories she had heard about my being in this, or that, or the other place. To which they would answer, that I was not fool enough to be staying round there; that I was in Philadelphia or New York before this time. When all were abed and asleep, Betty raised the plank, and said, "Come out, chile; come out. Dey don't know nottin 'bout you. 'Twas only white folks' lies, to skeer de niggers."

Some days after this adventure I had a much worse fright. As I sat very still in my retreat above stairs, cheerful visions floated through my mind. I thought Dr. Flint would soon get discouraged, and would be willing to sell my children, when he lost all hopes of making them the means of my discovery. I knew who was ready to buy them. Suddenly I heard a voice that chilled my blood. The sound was too familiar to me, it had been too dreadful, for me not to recognize at once my old master. He was in the house, and I at once concluded he had come to seize me. I looked round in terror. There was no way of escape. The voice receded. I supposed the constable was with him, and they were searching the house. In my alarm I did not forget the trouble I was bringing on my generous benefactress. It seemed as if I were born to bring sorrow on all who befriended me, and that was the bitterest drop in the bitter cup of my life. After a while I heard approaching footsteps; the key was turned in my door. I braced myself against the wall to keep from falling. I ventured to look up, and there stood my kind benefactress alone. I was too much overcome to speak, and sunk down upon the floor.

"I thought you would hear your master's voice," she said; "and knowing you would be terrified, I came to tell you there is nothing to fear. You may even indulge in a laugh at the old gentleman's expense. He is so sure you are in New York, that he came to borrow five hundred dollars to go in pursuit of you. My sister had some money to loan on interest. He has obtained it, and proposes to start for New York to-night. So, for the present, you see you are safe. The doctor will merely lighten his pocket hunting after the bird he has left behind."

XIX.

THE CHILDREN SOLD.

THE doctor came back from New York, of course without accomplishing his purpose. He had expended considerable money, and was rather disheartened. My brother and the children had now been in jail two months, and that also was some expense. My friends thought it was a favorable time to work on his discouraged feelings. Mr. Sands sent a speculator to offer him nine hundred dollars for my brother William, and eight hundred for the two children. These were high prices, as slaves were then selling; but the offer was rejected. If it had been merely a question of money, the doctor would have sold any boy of Benny's age for two hundred dollars; but he could not bear to give up the power of revenge. But he was hard pressed for money, and he revolved the matter in his mind. He knew that if he could keep Ellen till she was fifteen, he could sell her for a high price; but I presume he reflected that she might die, or might be stolen away. At all events, he came to the conclusion that he had better accept the slave-trader's offer. Meeting him in the street, he inquired when he would leave town. "To-day, at ten o'clock," he replied. "Ah, do you go so soon?" said the doctor; "I have been reflecting upon your proposition, and I have concluded to let you have the three negroes if you will say nineteen hundred dollars." After some parley, the trader agreed to his terms. He wanted the bill of sale drawn up and signed immediately, as he had a great deal to attend to during the short time he remained in town. The doctor went to the jail and told William he would take him back into his service if he would promise to behave himself; but he replied that he would rather be sold. "And you *shall* be sold, you ungrateful rascal!" exclaimed the doctor. In less than an hour the money was paid, the papers were signed, sealed, and delivered, and my brother and children were in the hands of the trader.

It was a hurried transaction; and after it was over, the doctor's characteristic caution returned. He went back to the speculator, and said, "Sir, I have come to lay you under obligations of a thousand dollars not to sell any of those negroes in this state." "You come too late," replied the trader; "our bargain is closed." He had, in fact, already sold them to Mr. Sands, but he did not mention it. The doctor required him to put irons on "that rascal, Bill," and to pass through the back streets when he took his gang out of town. The trader was privately instructed to concede to his wishes. My good old aunt went to the jail to bid the children good by, supposing them to be the speculator's property, and that she should never see them again. As she held Benny in her lap, he said, "Aunt Nancy, I want to show you something." He led her to the door and showed her a long row of marks, saying, "Uncle Will taught me to count. I have made a mark for every day I have been here, and it is sixty days. It is a long time; and the speculator is going to take me and Ellen away. He's a bad man. It's wrong for him to take grandmother's children. I want to go to my mother."

My grandmother was told that the children would be restored to her, but she was requested to act as if they were really to be sent away. Accordingly, she made up a bundle of clothes and went to the jail. When she arrived, she found William handcuffed among the gang, and the children in the trader's cart. The scene seemed too much like reality. She was afraid there might have been some deception or mistake. She fainted, and was carried home.

When the wagon stopped at the hotel, several gentlemen came out and proposed to purchase William, but the trader refused their offers, without stating that he was already sold. And now came the trying hour for that drove of human beings, driven away like cattle, to be sold they knew not where. Husbands were torn from wives, parents from children, never to look upon each other again this side the grave. There was wringing of hands and cries of despair.

Dr. Flint had the supreme satisfaction of seeing the wagon leave town, and Mrs. Flint had the gratification of supposing that my children were going "as far as wind and water would carry them." According to agreement, my uncle followed the wagon some miles, until they came to an old farm house. There the trader took the irons from William, and as he did so, he said, "You are a damned clever fellow. I should like to own you myself. Them gentlemen that wanted to buy you said you was a bright, honest chap, and I must git you a good home. I guess your old master will swear to-morrow, and call himself an old fool for selling the children. I reckon he'll never git their mammy back agin. I expect she's made tracks for the north. Good by, old boy. Remember, I have done you a good turn. You must thank me by coaxing all the pretty gals to go with me next fall. That's going to be my last trip. This trading in niggers is a bad business for a fellow that's got any heart. Move on, you fellows!" And the gang went on, God alone knows where.

Much as I despise and detest the class of slave-traders, whom I regard as the vilest wretches on earth, I must do this man the justice to say that he seemed to have some feeling. He took a fancy to William in the jail, and wanted to buy him. When he heard the story of my children, he was willing to aid them in getting out of Dr. Flint's power, even without charging the customary fee.

My uncle procured a wagon and carried William and the children back to town. Great was the joy in my grandmother's house! The curtains were closed, and the candles lighted. The happy grandmother cuddled the little ones to her bosom. They hugged her, and kissed her, and clapped their hands, and shouted. She knelt down and poured forth one of her heartfelt prayers of thanksgiving to

God. The father was present for a while, and though such a "parental relation" as existed between him and my children takes slight hold of the hearts or consciences of slaveholders, it must be that he experienced some moments of pure joy in witnessing the happiness he had imparted.

I had no share in the rejoicings of that evening. The events of the day had not come to my knowledge. And now I will tell you something that happened to me; though you will, perhaps, think it illustrates the superstition of slaves. I sat in my usual place on the floor near the window, where I could hear much that was said in the street without being seen. The family had retired for the night, and all was still. I sat there thinking of my children, when I heard a low strain of music. A band of serenaders were under the window, playing "Home, sweet home."[72] I listened till the sounds did not seem like music, but like the moaning of children. It seemed as if my heart would burst. I rose from my sitting posture, and knelt. A streak of moonlight was on the floor before me, and in the midst of it appeared the forms of my two children. They vanished; but I had seen them distinctly. Some will call it a dream, others a vision. I know not how to account for it, but it made a strong impression on my mind, and I felt certain something had happened to my little ones.

I had not seen Betty since morning. Now I heard her softly turning the key. As soon as she entered, I clung to her, and begged her to let me know whether my children were dead, or whether they were sold; for I had seen their spirits in my room, and I was sure something had happened to them. "Lor, chile," said she, putting her arms round me; "you's got de high-sterics. I'll sleep wid you tonight, 'cause you'll make a noise, and ruin missis. Something has stirred you up mightily. When you is done cryin, I'll talk wid you. De chillern is well, and mighty happy. I seed 'em myself. Does dat satisfy you? Dar, chile, be still! Somebody vill hear you." I tried to obey her. She lay down, and was soon sound asleep; but no sleep would come to my eyelids.

At dawn, Betty was up and off to the kitchen. The hours passed on, and the vision of the night kept constantly recurring to my thoughts. After a while I heard the voices of two women in the entry. In one of them I recognized the housemaid. The other said to her, "Did you know Linda Brent's children was sold to the speculator yesterday. They say ole massa Flint was mighty glad to see 'em drove out of town; but they say they've come back agin. I 'specs it's all their daddy's doings. They say he's bought William too. Lor! how it will take hold of ole massa Flint! I'm going roun' to aunt Marthy's to see 'bout it."

I bit my lips till the blood came to keep from crying out. Were my children with their grandmother, or had the speculator carried them off? The suspense was dreadful. Would Betty *never* come, and tell me the truth about it? At last she came, and I eagerly repeated what I had overheard. Her face was one broad, bright smile. "Lor, you foolish ting!" said she. "I'se gwine to tell you all 'bout it. De gals is eating thar breakfast, and missus tole me to let her tell you; but, poor creeter! t'aint right to keep you waitin', and I'se gwine to tell you. Brudder, chillern, all is bought by de daddy! I'se laugh more dan nuff, tinking 'bout ole massa Flint. Lor, how he *vill* swar! He's got ketched dis time, any how; but I must be getting out o' dis, or dem gals vill come and ketch *me*."

Betty went off laughing; and I said to myself, "Can it be true that my children are free? I have not suffered for them in vain. Thank God!"

Great surprise was expressed when it was known that my children had returned to their grandmother's. The news spread through the town, and many a kind word was bestowed on the little ones.

Dr. Flint went to my grandmother's to ascertain who was the owner of my children, and she informed him. "I expected as much," said he. "I am glad to hear it. I have had news from Linda lately, and I shall soon have her. You need never expect to see *her* free. She shall be my slave as long as I live, and when I am dead she shall be the slave of my children. If I ever find out that you or Phillip had any thing to do with her running off I'll kill him. And if I meet William in the street, and he presumes to look at me, I'll flog him within an inch of his life. Keep those brats out of my sight!"

As he turned to leave, my grandmother said something to remind him of his own doings. He looked back upon her, as if he would have been glad to strike her to the ground.

I had my season of joy and thanksgiving. It was the first time since my childhood that I had experienced any real happiness. I heard of the old doctor's threats, but they no longer had the same power to trouble me. The darkest cloud that hung over my life had rolled away. Whatever slavery might do to me, it could not shackle my children. If I fell a sacrifice, my little ones were saved. It was well for me that my simple heart believed all that had been promised for their welfare. It is always better to trust than to doubt.

XX.

NEW PERILS.

THE doctor, more exasperated than ever, again tried to revenge himself on my relatives. He arrested uncle Phillip on the charge of having aided my flight. He was carried before a court, and swore truly that he knew nothing of my intention to escape, and that he had not seen me since I left my master's plantation. The doctor then demanded that he should give bail for five hundred dollars that he would have nothing to do with me. Several gentlemen offered to be security for him; but Mr. Sands told him he had better go back to jail, and he would see that he came out without giving bail.

The news of his arrest was carried to my grandmother, who conveyed it to Betty. In the kindness of her heart, she again stowed me away under the floor; and as she walked back and forth, in the performance of her culinary duties, she talked apparently to herself, but with the intention that I should hear what was going on. I hoped that my uncle's imprisonment would last but few days; still I was anxious. I thought it likely Dr. Flint would do his utmost to taunt and insult him, and I was afraid my uncle might lose control of himself, and retort in some way that would be construed into a punishable offence; and I was well aware that in court his word would not be taken against any white man's. The search for me was renewed. Something had excited suspicions that I was in the vicinity. They searched the house I was in. I heard their steps and their voices. At night, when all were asleep, Betty came to release me from my place of confinement. The fright I had undergone, the constrained posture, and the dampness of the ground, made me ill for several days. My uncle was soon after taken out of prison; but the movements of all my relatives, and of all our friends, were very closely watched.

We all saw that I could not remain where I was much longer. I had already staid longer than was intended, and I knew my presence must be a source of perpetual anxiety to my kind benefactress. During this time, my friends had laid many plans for my escape, but the extreme vigilance of my persecutors made it impossible to carry them into effect.

One morning I was much startled by hearing somebody trying to get into my room. Several keys were tried, but none fitted. I instantly conjectured it was one of the housemaids; and I concluded she must either have heard some noise in the room, or have noticed the entrance of Betty. When my friend came, at her usual time, I told her what had happened. "I knows who it was," said she. "'Pend upon it, 'twas dat Jenny. Dat nigger allers got de debble in her." I suggested that she might have seen or heard something that excited her curiosity.

"Tut! tut! chile!" exclaimed Betty, "she ain't seen notin', nor hearn notin'. She only 'spects someting. Dat's all. She wants to fine out who hab cut and make my gownd. But she won't nebber know. Dat's sartin. I'll git missis to fix her."

I reflected a moment, and said, "Betty, I must leave here to-night."

"Do as you tink best, poor chile," she replied. "I'se mighty 'fraid dat 'ere nigger vill pop on you some time."

She reported the incident to her mistress, and received orders to keep Jenny busy in the kitchen till she could see my uncle Phillip. He told her he would send a friend for me that very evening. She told him she hoped I was going to the north, for it was very dangerous for me to remain any where in the vicinity. Alas, it was not an easy thing, for one in my situation, to go to the north. In order to leave the coast quite clear for me, she went into the country to spend the day with her brother, and took Jenny with her. She was afraid to come and bid me good by, but she left a kind message with Betty. I heard her carriage roll from the door, and I never again saw her who had so generously befriended the poor, trembling fugitive! Though she was a slaveholder, to this day my heart blesses her!

I had not the slightest idea where I was going. Betty brought me a suit of sailor's clothes,—jacket, trowsers, and tarpaulin hat. She gave me a small bundle, saying I might need it where I was going. In cheery tones, she exclaimed, "I'se so glad you is gwine to free parts! Don't forget ole Betty. P'raps I'll come 'long by and by."

I tried to tell her how grateful I felt for all her kindness, but she interrupted me. "I don't want no tanks, honey. I'se glad I could help you, and I hope de good Lord vill open de path for you. I'se gwine wid you to de lower gate. Put your hands in your pockets, and walk ricketty, like de sailors."

I performed to her satisfaction. At the gate I found Peter, a young colored man, waiting for me. I had known him for years. He had been an apprentice to my father, and had always borne a good character. I was not afraid to trust to him. Betty bade me a hurried good by, and we walked off. "Take courage, Linda," said my friend Peter. "I've got a dagger, and no man shall take you from me, unless he passes over my dead body."

It was a long time since I had taken a walk out of doors, and the fresh air revived me. It was also pleasant to hear a human voice speaking to me above a whisper. I passed several people whom I knew, but they did not recognize me in my disguise. I prayed internally that, for Peter's sake, as well as my own, nothing might occur to bring out his dagger. We walked on till we came to the wharf. My aunt Nancy's husband was a seafaring man, and it had been deemed necessary to let him into our secret. He took me into his boat, rowed out to a vessel not far distant, and hoisted me on board. We three were the only occupants of the vessel. I now ventured to ask what they proposed to do with me. They said I was to remain on board till near dawn, and then they would hide me in Snaky Swamp, till my uncle Phillip had prepared a place of concealment for me. If the vessel had been bound north, it would have been of no avail to me, for it would certainly have been searched. About four o'clock, we were again seated in the boat, and rowed three miles to the swamp. My fear of snakes had been increased by the venomous bite I had received, and I dreaded to enter this hiding-place. But I was in no situation to choose, and I gratefully accepted the best that my poor, persecuted friends could do for me.

Peter landed first, and with a large knife cut a path through bamboos and briers of all descriptions. He came back, took me in his arms, and carried me to a seat made among the bamboos. Before we reached it, we were covered with hundreds of mosquitos. In an hour's time they had so poisoned my flesh that I was a pitiful sight to behold. As the light increased, I saw snake after snake crawling round us. I had been accustomed to the sight of snakes all my life, but these were larger than any I had ever seen. To this day I shudder when I remember that morning. As evening approached, the number of snakes increased so much that we were continually obliged to thrash them with sticks to keep them from crawling over us. The bamboos were so high and so thick that it was impossible to see beyond a very short distance. Just before it became dark we procured a seat nearer to the entrance of the swamp, being fearful of losing our way back to the boat. It was not long before we heard the paddle of oars, and the low whistle, which had been agreed upon as a signal. We made haste to enter the boat, and were rowed back to the vessel. I passed a wretched night; for the heat of the swamp, the mosquitos, and the constant terror of snakes, had brought on a burning fever. I had just dropped asleep, when they came and told me it was time to go back to that horrid swamp. I could scarcely summon courage to rise. But even those large, venomous snakes were less dreadful to my imagination than the white men in that community called civilized. This time Peter took a quantity of tobacco to burn, to keep off the mosquitos. It produced the desired effect on them, but gave me nausea and severe headache. At dark we returned to the vessel. I had been so sick during the day, that Peter declared I should go home that night, if the devil himself was on patrol. They told me a place of concealment had been provided for me at my grandmother's. I could not imagine how it was possible to hide me in her house, every nook and corner of which was known to the Flint family. They told me to wait and see. We were rowed ashore, and went boldly through the streets, to my grandmother's. I wore my sailor's clothes, and had blackened my face with charcoal. I passed several people whom I knew. The father of my children came so near that I brushed against his arm; but he had no idea who it was.

"You must make the most of this walk," said my friend Peter, "for you may not have another very soon."

I thought his voice sounded sad. It was kind of him to conceal from me what a dismal hole was to be my home for a long, long time.

XXI.

THE LOOPHOLE OF RETREAT.[73]

A SMALL shed had been added to my grandmother's house years ago. Some boards were laid across the joists at the top, and between these boards and the roof was a very small garret, never occupied by any thing but rats and mice. It was a pent roof, covered with nothing but shingles, according to the southern custom for such buildings. The garret was only nine feet long and seven wide. The highest part was three feet high, and sloped down abruptly to the loose board floor. There was no admission for either light or air. My uncle Philip, who was a carpenter, had very skilfully made a concealed trap-door, which communicated with the storeroom. He had been doing this while I was waiting in the swamp. The storeroom opened upon a piazza. To this hole I was conveyed as soon as I entered the house. The air was stifling; the darkness total. A bed had been spread on the floor. I could sleep quite comfortably on one side; but the slope was so sudden that I could not turn on the other without hitting the roof. The rats and mice ran over my bed; but I was weary, and I slept such sleep as the wretched may, when a tempest has passed over them. Morning came. I knew it only by the noises I heard; for in my small den day and night were all the same. I suffered for air even more than for light. But I was not comfortless. I heard the voices of my children. There was joy and there was sadness in the sound. It made my tears flow. How I longed to speak to them! I was eager to look on their faces; but there was no hole, no crack, through which I could peep. This continued darkness was oppressive. It seemed horrible to sit or lie in a cramped position day after day, without one gleam of light. Yet I would have chosen this, rather than my lot as a slave, though white people considered it an easy one; and it was so compared with the fate of others. I was never cruelly over-worked; I was never lacerated with the whip from head to foot; I was never so beaten and bruised that I could not turn from one side to the other; I never had my heel-strings cut to prevent my running away; I was never chained to a log and forced to drag it about, while I toiled in the fields from morning till night; I was never branded with hot iron, or torn by bloodhounds. On the contrary, I had always been kindly treated, and tenderly cared for, until I came into the hands of Dr. Flint. I had never wished for freedom till then. But though my life in slavery was comparatively devoid of hardships, God pity the woman who is compelled to lead such a life!

My food was passed up to me through the trap-door my uncle had contrived; and my grandmother, my uncle Phillip, and aunt Nancy would seize such opportunities as they could, to mount up there and chat with me at the opening. But of course this was not safe in the daytime. It must all be done in darkness. It was impossible for me to move in an erect position, but I crawled about my den for exercise. One day I hit my head against something, and found it was a gimlet. My uncle had left it sticking there when he made the trap-door. I was as rejoiced as Robinson Crusoe could have been at finding such a treasure. It put a lucky thought into my head. I said to myself, "Now I will have some light. Now I will see my children." I did not dare to begin my work during the daytime, for feat of attracting attention. But I groped round; and having found the side next the street, where I could frequently see my children, I stuck the gimlet in and waited for evening. I bored three rows of holes, one above another; then I bored out the interstices between. I thus succeeded in making one hole about an inch long and an inch broad. I sat by it till late into the night, to enjoy the little whiff of air that floated in. In the morning I watched for my children. The first person I saw in the street was Dr. Flint. I had a shuddering, superstitious feeling that it was a bad omen. Several familiar faces passed by. At last I heard the merry laugh of children, and presently two sweet little faces were looking up at me, as though they knew I was there, and were conscious of the joy they imparted. How I longed to *tell* them I was there!

My condition was now a little improved. But for weeks I was tormented by hundreds of little red insects, fine as a needle's point, that pierced through my skin, and produced an intolerable burning. The good grandmother gave me herb teas and cooling medicines, and finally I got rid of them. The heat of my den was intense, for nothing but thin shingles protected me from the scorching summer's sun. But I had my consolations. Through my peeping-hole I could watch the children, and when they were near enough, I could hear their talk.

Aunt Nancy brought me all the news she could hear at Dr. Flint's. From her I learned that the doctor had written to New York to a colored woman, who had been born and raised in our neighborhood, and had breathed his contaminating atmosphere. He offered her a reward if she could find out any thing about me. I know not what was the nature of her reply; but he soon after started for New York in haste, saying to his family that he had business of importance to transact. I peeped at him as he passed on his way to the steamboat. It was a satisfaction to have miles of land and water between us, even for a little while; and it was a still greater satisfaction to know that he believed me to be in the Free States. My little den seemed less dreary than it had done. He returned, as he did from his former journey to New York, without obtaining any satisfactory information. When he passed our house next morning, Benny was standing at the gate. He had heard them say that he had gone to find me, and he called out, "Dr. Flint, did you bring my mother home? I want to see her." The doctor stamped his foot at him in a rage, and exclaimed, "Get out of the way, you little damned rascal! If you don't, I'll cut off your head."

Benny ran terrified into the house, saying, "You can't put me in jail again. I don't belong to you now." It was well that the wind carried the words away from the doctor's ear. I told my grandmother of it, when we had our next conference at the trap-door; and begged of her not to allow the children to be impertinent to the irascible old man.

Autumn came, with a pleasant abatement of heat. My eyes had become accustomed to the dim light, and by holding my book or work in a certain position near the aperture I contrived to read and sew. That was a great relief to the tedious monotony of my life. But when winter came, the cold penetrated through the thin shingle roof, and I was dreadfully chilled. The winters there are not so long, or so severe, as in northern latitudes; but the houses are not built to shelter from cold, and my little den was peculiarly comfortless. The kind grandmother brought me bed-clothes and warm drinks. Often I was obliged to lie in bed all day to keep comfortable; but with all my precautions, my shoulders and feet were frostbitten. O, those long, gloomy days, with no object for my eye to rest upon, and no thoughts to occupy my mind, except the dreary past and the uncertain future! I was thankful when there came a day sufficiently mild for me to wrap myself up and sit at the loophole to watch the passers by. Southerners have the habit of stopping and talking in the streets, and I heard many conversations not intended to meet my ears. I heard slave-hunters planning how to catch some poor fugitive. Several times I heard allusions to Dr. Flint, myself, and the history of my children, who, perhaps, were playing near the gate. One would say, "I wouldn't move my little finger to catch her, as old Flint's property." Another would say, "I'll catch *any* nigger for the reward. A man ought to have what belongs to him, if he *is* a damned brute." The opinion was often expressed that I was in the Free States. Very rarely did any one suggest that I might be in the vicinity. Had the least suspicion rested on my grandmother's house, it would have been burned to the ground. But it was the last place they thought of. Yet there was no place, where slavery existed, that could have afforded me so good a place of concealment.

Dr. Flint and his family repeatedly tried to coax and bribe my children to tell something they had heard said about me. One day the doctor took them into a shop, and offered them some bright little silver pieces and gay handkerchiefs if they would tell where their mother was. Ellen shrank away from him, and would not speak; but Benny spoke up, and said, "Dr. Flint, I don't know where my mother is. I guess she's in New York; and when you go there again, I wish you'd ask her to come home, for I want to see her; but if you put her in jail, or tell her you'll cut her head off, I'll tell her to go right back."

XXII.

CHRISTMAS FESTIVITIES.

CHRISTMAS was approaching. Grandmother brought me materials, and I busied myself making some new garments and little playthings for my children. Were it not that hiring day is near at hand, and many families are fearfully looking forward to the probability of separation in a few days, Christmas might be a happy season for the poor slaves. Even slave mothers try to gladden the hearts of their little ones on that occasion. Benny and Ellen had their Christmas stockings filled. Their imprisoned mother could not have the privilege of witnessing their surprise and joy. But I had the pleasure of peeping at them as they went into the street with their new suits on. I heard Benny ask a little playmate whether Santa Claus brought him any thing. "Yes," replied the boy; "but Santa Claus ain't a real man. It's the children's mothers that put things into the stockings." "No, that can't be," replied Benny, "for Santa Claus brought Ellen and me these new clothes, and my mother has been gone this long time."

How I longed to tell him that his mother made those garments, and that many a tear fell on them while she worked!

Every child rises early on Christmas morning to see the Johnkannaus.[74] Without them, Christmas would be shorn of its greatest attraction. They consist of companies of slaves from the plantations, generally of the lower class. Two athletic men, in calico wrappers, have a net thrown over them, covered with all manner of bright-colored stripes. Cows' tails are fastened to their backs, and their heads are decorated with horns. A box, covered with sheepskin, is called the gumbo box. A dozen beat on this, while others strike triangles and jawbones, to which bands of dancers keep time. For a month previous they are composing songs, which are sung on this occasion. These companies, of a hundred each, turn out early in the morning, and are allowed to go round till twelve o'clock, begging for contributions. Not a door is left unvisited where there is the least chance of obtaining a penny or a glass of rum. They do not drink while they are out, but carry the rum home in jugs, to have a carousal. These Christmas donations frequently amount to twenty or thirty dollars. It is seldom that any white man or child refuses to give them a trifle. If he does, they regale his ears with the following song:—

> "Poor massa, so dey say;
> Down in de heel, so dey say;
> Got no money, so dey say;
> Not one shillin, so dey say;
> God A'mighty bress you, so dey say."

Christmas is a day of feasting, both with white and colored people. Slaves, who are lucky enough to have a few shillings, are sure to spend them for good eating; and many a turkey and pig is captured, without saying, "By your leave, sir." Those who cannot obtain these, cook a 'possum, or a raccoon, from which savory dishes can be made. My grandmother raised poultry and pigs for sale; and it was her established custom to have both a turkey and a pig roasted for Christmas dinner.

On this occasion, I was warned to keep extremely quiet, because two guests had been invited. One was the town constable, and the other was a free colored man, who tried to pass himself off for white, and who was always ready to do any mean work for the sake of currying favor with white people. My grandmother had a motive for inviting them. She managed to take them all over the house. All the rooms on the lower floor were thrown open for them to pass in and out; and after dinner, they were invited up stairs to look at a fine mocking bird my uncle had just brought home. There, too, the rooms were all thrown open, that they might look in. When I heard them talking on the piazza, my heart almost stood still. I knew this colored man had spent many nights hunting for me. Every body knew he had the blood of a slave father in his veins; but for the sake of passing himself off for white, he was ready to kiss the slaveholders' feet. How I despised him! As for the constable, he wore no false colors. The duties of his office were despicable, but he was superior to his companion, inasmuch as he did not pretend to be what he was not. Any white man, who could raise money enough to buy a slave, would have considered himself degraded by being a constable; but the office enabled its possessor to exercise authority. If he found any slave out after nine o'clock, he could whip him as much as he liked; and that was a privilege to be coveted. When the guests were ready to depart, my grandmother gave each of them some of her nice pudding, as a present for their wives. Through my peep-hole I saw them go out of the gate, and I was glad when it closed after them. So passed the first Christmas in my den.

XXIII.

STILL IN PRISON.

WHEN spring returned, and I took in the little patch of green the aperture commanded, I asked myself how many more summers and winters I must be condemned to spend thus. I longed to draw in a plentiful draught of fresh air, to stretch my cramped limbs, to have room to stand erect, to feel the earth under my feet again. My relatives were constantly on the lookout for a chance of escape; but none offered that seemed practicable, and even tolerably safe. The hot summer came again, and made the turpentine drop from the thin roof over my head.

During the long nights I was restless for want of air, and I had no room to toss and turn. There was but one compensation; the atmosphere was so stifled that even mosquitos would not condescend to buzz in it. With all my detestation of Dr. Flint, I could hardly wish him a worse punishment, either in this world or that which is to come, than to suffer what I suffered in one single summer. Yet the laws allowed *him* to be out in the free air, while I, guiltless of crime, was pent up here, as the only means of avoiding the cruelties the laws allowed him to inflict upon me! I don't know what kept life within me. Again and again, I thought I should die before long; but I saw the leaves of another autumn whirl through the air, and felt the touch of another winter. In summer the most terrible thunder storms were acceptable, for the rain came through the roof, and I rolled up my bed that it might cool the hot boards under it. Later in the season, storms sometimes wet my clothes through and through, and that was not comfortable when the air grew chilly. Moderate storms I could keep out by filling the chinks with oakum.

But uncomfortable as my situation was, I had glimpses of things out of doors, which made me thankful for my wretched hiding-place. One day I saw a slave pass our gate, muttering, "It's his own, and he can kill it if he will." My grandmother told me that woman's history. Her mistress had that day seen her baby for the first time, and in the lineaments of its fair face she saw a likeness to her husband. She turned the bondwoman and her child out of doors, and forbade her ever to return. The slave went to her master, and told him what had happened. He promised to talk with her mistress, and make it all right. The next day she and her baby were sold to a Georgia trader.

Another time I saw a woman rush wildly by, pursued by two men. She was a slave, the wet nurse of her mistress's children. For some trifling offence her mistress ordered her to be stripped and whipped. To escape the degradation and the torture, she rushed to the river, jumped in, and ended her wrongs in death.

Senator Brown, of Mississippi, could not be ignorant of many such facts as these, for they are of frequent occurrence in every Southern State. Yet he stood up in the Congress of the United States, and declared that slavery was "a great moral, social, and political blessing; a blessing to the master, and a blessing to the slave!"[75]

I suffered much more during the second winter than I did during the first. My limbs were benumbed by inaction, and the cold filled them with cramp. I had a very painful sensation of coldness in my head; even my face and tongue stiffened, and I lost the power of speech. Of course it was impossible, under the circumstances, to summon any physician. My brother William came and did all he could for me. Uncle Phillip also watched tenderly over me; and poor grandmother crept up and down to inquire whether there were any signs of returning life. I was restored to consciousness by the dashing of cold water in my face, and found myself leaning against my brother's arm, while he bent over me with streaming eyes. He afterwards told me he thought I was dying, for I had been in an unconscious state sixteen hours. I next became delirious, and was in great danger of betraying myself and my friends. To prevent this, they stupefied me with drugs. I remained in bed six weeks, weary in body and sick at heart. How to get medical advice was the question. William finally went to a Thompsonian doctor,[76] and described himself as having all my pains and aches. He returned with herbs, roots, and ointment. He was especially charged to rub on the ointment by a fire; but how could a fire be made in my little den? Charcoal in a furnace was tried, but there was no outlet for the gas, and it nearly cost me my life. Afterwards coals, already kindled, were brought up in an iron pan, and placed on bricks. I was so weak, and it was so long since I had enjoyed the warmth of a fire, that those few coals actually made me weep. I think the medicines did me some good; but my recovery was very slow. Dark thoughts passed through my mind as I lay there day after day. I tried to be thankful for my little cell, dismal as it was, and even to love it, as part of the price I had paid for the redemption of my children. Sometimes I thought God was a compassionate Father, who would forgive my sins for the sake of my sufferings. At other times, it seemed to me there was no justice or mercy in the divine government. I asked why the curse of slavery was permitted to exist, and why I had been so persecuted and wronged from youth upward. These things took the shape of mystery, which is to this day not so clear to my soul as I trust it will be hereafter.

In the midst of my illness, grandmother broke down under the weight of anxiety and toil. The idea of losing her, who had always been my best friend and a mother to my children, was the sorest trial I had yet had. O, how earnestly I prayed that she might recover! How hard it seemed, that I could not tend upon her, who had so long and so tenderly watched over me!

One day the screams of a child nerved me with strength to crawl to my peeping-hole, and I saw my son covered with blood. A fierce dog, usually kept chained, had seized and bitten him. A doctor was sent for, and I heard the groans and screams of my child while the wounds were being sewed up. O, what torture to a mother's heart, to listen to this and be unable to go to him!

But childhood is like a day in spring, alternately shower and sunshine. Before night Benny was bright and lively, threatening the destruction of the dog; and great was his delight when the doctor told him the next day that the dog had bitten another boy and been shot. Benny recovered from his wounds; but it was long before he could walk.

When my grandmother's illness became known, many ladies, who were her customers, called to bring her some little comforts, and to inquire whether she had every thing she wanted. Aunt Nancy one night asked permission to watch with her sick mother, and Mrs. Flint replied, "I don't see any need of your going. I can't spare you." But when she found other ladies in the neighborhood were so attentive, not wishing to be outdone in Christian charity, she also sallied forth, in magnificent condescension, and stood by the bedside of her who had loved her in her infancy, and who had been repaid by such grievous wrongs. She seemed surprised to find her so ill, and scolded uncle Phillip for not sending for Dr. Flint. She herself sent for him immediately, and he came. Secure as I was in my retreat, I should have been terrified if I had known he was so near me. He pronounced my grandmother in a very critical situation, and said if her attending physician wished it, he would visit her. Nobody wished to have him coming to the house at all hours, and we were not disposed to give him a chance to make out a long bill.

As Mrs. Flint went out, Sally told her the reason Benny was lame was, that a dog had bitten him. "I'm glad of it," replied she. "I wish he had killed him. It would be good news to send to his mother. *Her* day will come. The dogs will grab *her* yet." With these Christian words she and her husband departed, and, to my great satisfaction, returned no more.

I heard from uncle Phillip, with feelings of unspeakable joy and gratitude, that the crisis was passed and grandmother would live. I could now say from my heart, "God is merciful. He has spared me the anguish of feeling that I caused her death."

XXIV.

THE CANDIDATE FOR CONGRESS.

THE summer had nearly ended, when Dr. Flint made a third visit to New York, in search of me. Two candidates were running for Congress, and he returned in season to vote. The father of my children was the Whig candidate. The doctor had hitherto been a stanch Whig; but now he exerted all his energies for the defeat of Mr. Sands. He invited large parties of men to dine in the shade of his trees, and supplied them with plenty of rum and brandy. If any poor fellow drowned his wits in the bowl, and, in the openness of his convivial heart, proclaimed that he did not mean to vote the Democratic ticket, he was shoved into the street without ceremony.

The doctor expended his liquor in vain. Mr. Sands was elected; an event which occasioned me some anxious thoughts. He had not emancipated my children, and if he should die they would be at the mercy of his heirs. Two little voices, that frequently met my ear, seemed to plead with me not to let their father depart without striving to make their freedom secure. Years had passed since I had spoken to him. I had not even seen him since the night I passed him, unrecognized, in my disguise of a sailor. I supposed he would call before he left, to say something to my grandmother concerning the children, and I resolved what course to take.

The day before his departure for Washington I made arrangements, towards evening, to get from my hiding-place into the storeroom below. I found myself so stiff and clumsy that it was with great difficulty I could hitch from one resting place to another. When I reached the storeroom my ankles gave way under me, and I sank exhausted on the floor. It seemed as if I could never use my limbs again. But the purpose I had in view roused all the strength I had. I crawled on my hands and knees to the window, and, screened behind a barrel, I waited for his coming. The clock struck nine, and I knew the steamboat would leave between ten and eleven. My hopes were failing. But presently I heard his voice, saying to some one, "Wait for me a moment. I wish to see aunt Martha." When he came out, as he passed the window, I said, "Stop one moment, and let me speak for my children." He started, hesitated, and then passed on, and went out of the gate. I closed the shutter I had partially opened, and sank down behind the barrel. I had suffered much; but seldom had I experienced a keener pang than I then felt. Had my children, then, become of so little consequence to him? And had he so little feeling for their wretched mother that he would not listen a moment while she pleaded for them? Painful memories were so busy within me, that I forgot I had not hooked the shutter, till I heard some one opening it. I looked up. He had come back. "Who called me?" said he, in a low tone. "I did," I replied. "Oh, Linda," said he, "I knew your voice; but I was afraid to answer, lest my friend should hear me. Why do you come here? Is it possible you risk yourself in this house? They are mad to allow it. I shall expect to hear that you are all ruined." I did not wish to implicate him, by letting him know my place of concealment; so I merely said, "I thought you would come to bid grandmother good by, and so I came here to speak a few words to you about emancipating my children. Many changes may take place during the six months you are gone to Washington, and it does not seem right for you to expose them to the risk of such changes. I want nothing for myself; all I ask is, that you will free my children, or authorize some friend to do it, before you go."

He promised he would do it, and also expressed a readiness to make any arrangements whereby I could be purchased.

I heard footsteps approaching, and closed the shutter hastily. I wanted to crawl back to my den, without letting the family know what I had done; for I knew they would deem it very imprudent. But he stepped back into the house, to tell my grandmother that he had spoken with me at the storeroom window, and to beg of her not to allow me to remain in the house over night. He said it was the height of madness for me to be there; that we should certainly all be ruined. Luckily, he was in too much of a hurry to wait for a reply, or the dear old woman would surely have told him all.

I tried to go back to my den, but found it more difficult to go up than I had to come down. Now that my mission was fulfilled, the little strength that had supported me through it was gone, and I sank helpless on the floor. My grandmother, alarmed at the risk I had run, came into the storeroom in the dark, and locked the door behind her. "Linda," she whispered, "where are you?"

"I am here by the window," I replied. "I *couldn't* have him go away without emancipating the children. Who knows what may happen?"

"Come come, child," said she, "it won't do for you to stay here another minute. You've done wrong; but I can't blame you, poor thing!"

I told her I could not return without assistance, and she must call my uncle. Uncle Phillip came, and pity prevented him from scolding me. He carried me back to my dungeon, laid me tenderly on the bed, gave me some medicine, and asked me if there was any thing more he could do. Then he went away, and I was left with my own thoughts—starless as the midnight darkness around me.

My friends feared I should become a cripple for life; and I was so weary of my long imprisonment that, had it not been for the hope of serving my children, I should have been thankful to die; but, for their sakes, I was willing to bear on.

XXV.

COMPETITION IN CUNNING.

Dr. Flint had not given me up. Every now and then he would say to my grandmother that I would yet come back, and voluntarily surrender myself; and that when I did, I could be purchased by my relatives, or any one who wished to buy me. I knew his cunning nature too well not to percieve that this was a trap laid for me; and so all my friends understood it. I resolved to match my cunning against his cunning. In order to make him believe that I was in New York, I resolved to write him a letter dated from that place. I sent for my friend Peter, and asked him if he knew any trustworthy seafaring person, who would carry such a letter to New York, and put it in the post office there. He said he knew one that he would trust with his own life to the ends of the world. I reminded him that it was a hazardous thing for him to undertake. He said he knew it, but he was willing to do any thing to help me. I expressed a wish for a New York paper, to ascertain the names of some of the streets. He run his hand into his pocket, and said, "Here is half a one, that was round a cap I bought of a pedler yesterday." I told him the letter would be ready the next evening. He bade me good by, adding, "Keep up your spirits, Linda; brighter days will come by and by."

My uncle Phillip kept watch over the gate until our brief interview was over. Early the next morning, I seated myself near the little aperture to examine the newspaper. It was a piece of the New York Herald; and, for once, the paper that systematically abuses the colored people, was made to render them a service. Having obtained what information I wanted concerning streets and numbers, I wrote two letters, one to my grandmother, the other to Dr. Flint. I reminded him how he, a gray-headed man, had treated a helpless child, who had been placed in his power, and what years of misery he had brought upon her. To my grandmother, I expressed a wish to have my children sent to me at the north, where I could teach them to respect themselves, and set them a virtuous example; which a slave mother was not allowed to do at the south. I asked her to direct her answer to a certain street in Boston, as I did not live in New York, though I went there sometimes. I dated these letters ahead, to allow for the time it would take to carry them, and sent a memorandum of the date to the messenger. When my friend came for the letters, I said, "God bless and reward you, Peter, for this disinterested kindness. Pray be careful. If you are detected, both you and I will have to suffer dreadfully. I have not a relative who would dare to do it for me." He replied, "You may trust to me, Linda. I don't forget that your father was my best friend, and I will be a friend to his children so long as God lets me live."

It was necessary to tell my grandmother what I had done, in order that she might be ready for the letter, and prepared to hear what Dr. Flint might say about my being at the north. She was sadly troubled. She felt sure mischief would come of it. I also told my plan to aunt Nancy, in order that she might report to us what was said at Dr. Flint's house. I whispered it to her through a crack, and she whispered back, "I hope it will succeed. I shan't mind being a slave all *my* life, if I can only see you and the children free."

I had directed that my letters should be put into the New York post office on the 20th of the month. On the evening of the 24th my aunt came to say that Dr. Flint and his wife had been talking in a low voice about a letter he had received, and that when he went to his office he promised to bring it when he came to tea. So I concluded I should hear my letter read the next morning. I told my grandmother Dr. Flint would be sure to come, and asked her to have him sit near a certain door, and leave it open, that I might hear what he said. The next morning I took my station within sound of that door, and remained motionless as a statue. It was not long before I heard the gate slam, and the well-known footsteps enter the house. He seated himself in the chair that was placed for him, and said, "Well, Martha, I've brought you a letter from Linda. She has sent me a letter, also. I know exactly where to find her; but I don't choose to go to Boston for her. I had rather she would come back of her own accord, in a respectable manner. Her uncle Phillip is the best person to go for her. With *him,* she would feel perfectly free to act. I am willing to pay his expenses going and returning. She shall be sold to her friends. Her children are free; at least I suppose they are; and when you obtain her freedom, you'll make a happy family. I suppose, Martha, you have no objection to my reading to you the letter Linda has written to you."

He broke the seal, and I heard him read it. The old villain! He had suppressed the letter I wrote to grandmother, and prepared a substitute of his own, the purport of which was as follows:—

"Dear Grandmother: I have long wanted to write to you; but the disgraceful manner in which I left you and my children made me ashamed to do it. If you knew how much I have suffered since I ran away, you would pity and forgive me. I have purchased freedom at a dear rate. If any arrangement could be made for me to return to the south without being a slave, I would gladly come. If not, I beg of you to send my children to the north. I cannot live any longer without them. Let me know in time, and I will meet them in New York or Philadelphia, whichever place best suits my uncle's convenience. Write as soon as possible to your unhappy daughter,

LINDA."

"It is very much as I expected it would be," said the old hypocrite, rising to go. "You see the foolish girl has repented of her rashness, and wants to return. We must help her to do it, Martha. Talk with Phillip about it. If he will go for her, she will trust to him, and come back. I should like an answer tomorrow. Good morning, Martha."

As he stepped out on the piazza, he stumbled over my little girl. "Ah, Ellen, is that you?" he said, in his most gracious manner. "I didn't see you. How do you do?"

"Pretty well, sir," she replied. "I heard you tell grandmother that my mother is coming home. I want to see her."

"Yes, Ellen, I am going to bring her home very soon," rejoined he; "and you shall see her as much as you like, you little curly-headed nigger."

This was as good as a comedy to me, who had heard it all; but grandmother was frightened and distressed, because the doctor wanted my uncle to go for me.

The next evening Dr. Flint called to talk the matter over. My uncle told him that from what he had heard of Massachusetts, he judged he should be mobbed if he went there after a runaway slave. "All stuff and nonsense, Phillip!" replied the doctor. "Do you suppose I want you to kick up a row in Boston? The business can all be done quietly. Linda writes that she wants to come back. You are her relative, and she would trust *you*. The case would be different if I went. She might object to coming with *me*; and the damned abolitionists, if they knew I was her master, would not believe me, if I told them she had begged to go back. They would get up a row; and I should not like to see Linda dragged through the streets like a common negro. She has been very ungrateful to me for all my kindness; but I forgive her, and want to act the part of a friend towards her. I have no wish to hold her as my slave. Her friends can buy her as soon as she arrives here."

Finding that his arguments failed to convince my uncle, the doctor "let the cat out of the bag," by saying that he had written to the mayor of Boston, to ascertain whether there was a person of my description at the street and number from which my letter was dated. He had omitted this date in the letter he had made up to read to my grandmother. If I had dated from New York, the old man would probably have made another journey to that city. But even in that dark region, where knowledge is so carefully excluded from the slave, I had heard enough about Massachusetts to come to the conclusion that slaveholders did not consider it a comfortable place to go to in search of a runaway. That was before the Fugitive Slave Law[77] was passed; before Massachusetts had consented to become a "nigger hunter" for the south.

My grandmother, who had become skittish by seeing her family always in danger, came to me with a very distressed countenance, and said, "What will you do if the mayor of Boston sends him word that you haven't been there? Then he will suspect the letter was a trick; and maybe he'll find out something about it, and we shall all get into trouble. O Linda, I wish you had never sent the letters."

"Don't worry yourself, grandmother," said I. "The mayor of Boston won't trouble himself to hunt niggers for Dr. Flint. The letters will do good in the end. I shall get out of this dark hole some time or other."

"I hope you will, child," replied the good, patient old friend. "You have been here a long time; almost five years; but whenever you do go, it will break your old grandmother's heart. I should be expecting every day to hear that you were brought back in irons and put in jail. God help you, poor child! Let us be thankful that some time or other we shall go "where the wicked cease from troubling, and the weary are at rest."[78] My heart responded, Amen.

The fact that Dr. Flint had written to the mayor of Boston convinced me that he believed my letter to be genuine, and of course that he had no suspicion of my being any where in the vicinity. It was a great object to keep up this delusion, for it made me and my friends feel less anxious, and it would be very convenient whenever there was a chance to escape. I resolved, therefore, to continue to write letters from the north from time to time.

Two or three weeks passed, and as no news came from the mayor of Boston, grandmother began to listen to my entreaty to be allowed to leave my cell, sometimes, and exercise my limbs to prevent my becoming a cripple. I was allowed to slip down into the small storeroom, early in the morning, and remain there a little while. The room was all filled up with barrels, except a small open space under my trap-door. This faced the door, the upper part of which was of glass, and purposely left uncurtained, that the curious might look in. The air of this place was close; but it was so much better than the atmosphere of my cell, that I dreaded to return. I came down as soon as it was light, and remained till eight o'clock, when people began to be about, and there was danger that some one might come on the piazza. I had tried various applications to bring warmth and feeling into my limbs, but without avail. They were so numb and stiff that it was a painful effort to move; and had my enemies come upon me during the first mornings I tried to exercise them a little in the small unoccupied space of the storeroom, it would have been impossible for me to have escaped.

XXVI.

IMPORTANT ERA IN MY BROTHER'S LIFE.

I MISSED the company and kind attentions of my brother William, who had gone to Washington with his master, Mr. Sands. We received several letters from him, written without any allusion to me, but expressed in such a manner that I knew he did not forget me. I disguised my hand, and wrote to him in the same manner. It was a long session; and when it closed, William wrote to inform us that Mr. Sands was going to the north, to be gone some time, and that he was to accompany him. I knew that his master had promised to give him his freedom, but no time had been specified. Would William trust to a slave's chances? I remembered how we used to talk together, in our young days, about obtaining our freedom, and I thought it very doubtful whether he would come back to us.

Grandmother received a letter from Mr. Sands, saying that William had proved a most faithful servant, and he would also say a valued friend; that no mother had ever trained a better boy. He said he had travelled through the Northern States and Canada; and though the abolitionists had tried to decoy him away, they had never succeeded. He ended by saying they should be at home shortly.

We expected letters from William, describing the novelties of his journey, but none came. In time, it was reported that Mr. Sands would return late in the autumn, accompanied by a bride. Still no letters from William. I felt almost sure I should never see him again on southern soil; but had he no word of comfort to send to his friends at home? to the poor captive in her dungeon? My thoughts wandered through the dark past, and over the uncertain future. Alone in my cell, where no eye but God's could see me, I wept bitter tears. How earnestly I prayed to him to restore me to my children, and enable me to be a useful woman and a good mother!

At last the day arrived for the return of the travellers. Grandmother had made loving preparations to welcome her absent boy back to the old hearthstone. When the dinner table was laid, William's plate occupied its old place. The stage coach went by empty. My grandmother waited dinner. She thought perhaps he was necessarily detained by his master. In my prison I listened anxiously, expecting every moment to hear my dear brother's voice and step. In the course of the afternoon a lad was sent by Mr. Sands to tell grandmother that William did not return with him; that the abolitionists had decoyed him away. But he begged her not to feel troubled about it, for he felt confident she would see William in a few days. As soon as he had time to reflect he would come back, for he could never expect to be so well off at the north as he had been with him.

If you had seen the tears, and heard the sobs, you would have thought the messenger had brought tidings of death instead of freedom. Poor old grandmother felt that she should never see her darling boy again. And I was selfish. I thought more of what I had lost, than of what my brother had gained. A new anxiety began to trouble me. Mr. Sands had expended a good deal of money, and would naturally feel irritated by the loss he had incurred. I greatly feared this might injure the prospects of my children, who were now becoming valuable property. I longed to have their emancipation made certain. The more so, because their master and father was now married. I was too familiar with slavery not to know that promises made to slaves, though with kind intentions, and sincere at the time, depend upon many contingencies for their fulfilment.

Much as I wished William to be free, the step he had taken made me sad and anxious. The following Sabbath was calm and clear; so beautiful that it seemed like a Sabbath in the eternal world. My grandmother brought the children out on the piazza, that I might hear their voices. She thought it would comfort me in my despondency; and it did. They chatted merrily, as only children can. Benny said, "Grandmother, do you think uncle Will has gone for good? Won't he ever come back again? May be he'll find mother. If he does, *won't* she be glad to see him! Why don't you and uncle Phillip, and all of us, go and live where mother is? I should like it; wouldn't you, Ellen?"

"Yes, I should like it," replied Ellen; "but how could we find her? Do you know the place, grandmother? I don't remember how mother looked—do you, Benny?"

Benny was just beginning to describe me when they were interrupted by an old slave woman, a near neighbor, named Aggie. This poor creature had witnessed the sale of her children, and seen them carried off to parts unknown, without any hopes of ever hearing from them again. She saw that my grandmother had been weeping, and she said, in a sympathizing tone, "What's the matter, aunt Marthy?"

"O Aggie," sue replied, "it seems as if I shouldn't have any of my children or grandchildren left to hand me a drink when I'm dying, and lay my old body in the ground. My boy didn't come back with Mr. Sands. He staid at the north."

Poor old Aggie clapped her hands for joy. "Is *dat* what you's crying fur?" she exclaimed. "Git down on your knees and bress de Lord! I don't know whar my poor chillern is, and I nebber 'spect to know. You don't know whar poor Linda's gone to; but you *do* know whar her brudder is. He's in free parts; and dat's de right place. Don't murmur at de Lord's doings, but git down on your knees and tank him for his goodness."

My selfishness was rebuked by what poor Aggie said. She rejoiced over the escape of one who was merely her fellow-bondman, while his own sister was only thinking what his good fortune might cost her children. I knelt and prayed God to forgive me; and I thanked him from my heart, that one of my family was saved from the grasp of slavery.

It was not long before we received a letter from William. He wrote that Mr. Sands had always treated him kindly, and that he had tried to do his duty to him faithfully. But ever since he was a boy, he had longed to be free; and he had already gone through enough to convince him he had better not lose the chance that offered. He concluded by saying, "Don't worry about me, dear grandmother. I shall think of you always; and it will spur me on to work hard and try to do right. When I have earned money enough to give you a home, perhaps you will come to the north, and we can all live happy together."

Mr. Sands told my uncle Phillip the particulars about William's leaving him. He said, "I trusted him as if he were my own brother, and treated him as kindly. The abolitionists talked to him in several places; but I had no idea they could tempt him. However, I don't blame William. He's young and inconsiderate, and those Northern rascals decoyed him. I must confess the scamp was very bold about it. I met him coming down the steps of the Astor House with his trunk on his shoulder, and I asked him where he was going. He said he was going to change his old trunk. I told him it was rather shabby, and asked if he didn't need some money. He said, No, thanked me, and went off. He did not return so soon as I expected; but I waited patiently. At last I went to see if our trunks were packed, ready for our journey. I found them locked, and a sealed note on the table informed me where I could find the keys. The fellow even tried to be religious. He wrote that he hoped God would always bless me, and reward me for my kindness; that he was not unwilling to serve me; but he wanted to be a free man; and that if I thought he did wrong, he hoped I would forgive him. I intended to give him his freedom in five years. He might have trusted me. He has shown himself ungrateful; but I shall not go for him, or send for him. I feel confident that he will soon return to me."

I afterwards heard an account of the affair from William himself. He had not been urged away by abolitionists. He needed no information they could give him about slavery to stimulate his desire for freedom. He looked at his hands, and remembered that they were once in irons. What security had he that they would not be so again? Mr. Sands was kind to him; but he might indefinitely postpone the promise he had made to give him his freedom. He might come under pecuniary embarrassments, and his property be seized by creditors; or he might die, without making any arrangements in his favor. He had too often known such accidents to happen to slaves who had kind masters, and he wisely resolved to make sure of the present opportunity to own himself. He was scrupulous about taking any money from his master on false presences; so he sold his best clothes to pay for his passage to Boston. The slaveholders pronounced him a base, ungrateful wretch, for thus requiting his master's indulgence. What would *they* have done under similar circumstances?

When Dr. Flint's family heard that William had deserted Mr. Sands, they chuckled greatly over the news. Mrs. Flint made her usual manifestations of Christian feeling, by saying, "I'm glad of it. I hope he'll never get him again. I like to see people paid back in their own coin. I reckon Linda's children will have to pay for it. I should be glad to see them in the speculator's hands again, for I'm tired of seeing those little niggers march about the streets."

XXVII.

NEW DESTINATION FOR THE CHILDREN.

MRS. FLINT proclaimed her intention of informing Mrs. Sands who was the father of my children. She likewise proposed to tell her what an artful devil I was;

that I had made a great deal of trouble in her family; that when Mr. Sands was at the north, she didn't doubt I had followed him in disguise, and persuaded William to run away. She had some reason to entertain such an idea; for I had written from the north, from time to time, and I dated my letters from various places. Many of them fell into Dr. Flint's hands, as I expected they would; and he must have come to the conclusion that I travelled about a good deal. He kept a close watch over my children, thinking they would eventually lead to my detection.

A new and unexpected trial was in store for me. One day, when Mr. Sands and his wife were walking in the street, they met Benny. The lady took a fancy to him, and exclaimed, "What a pretty little negro! Whom does he belong to?"

Benny did not hear the answer; but he came home very indignant with the stranger lady, because she had called him a negro. A few days afterwards, Mr. Sands called on my grandmother, and told her he wanted her to take the children to his house. He said he had informed his wife of his relation to them, and told her they were motherless; and she wanted to see them.

When he had gone, my grandmother came and asked what I would do. The question seemed a mockery. What *could* I do? They were Mr. Sands's slaves, and their mother was a slave, whom he had represented to be dead. Perhaps he thought I was. I was too much pained and puzzled to come to any decision; and the children were carried without my knowledge.

Mrs. Sands had a sister from Illinois staying with her. This lady, who had no children of her own, was so much pleased with Ellen, that she offered to adopt her, and bring her up as she would a daughter. Mrs. Sands wanted to take Benjamin. When grandmother reported this to me, I was tried almost beyond endurance. Was this all I was to gain by what I had suffered for the sake of having my children free? True, the prospect *seemed* fair; but I knew too well how lightly slaveholders held such "parental relations." If pecuniary troubles should come, or if the new wife required more money than could conveniently be spared, my children might be thought of as a convenient means of raising funds. I had no trust in thee, O Slavery! Never should I know peace till my children were emancipated with all due formalities of law.

I was too proud to ask Mr. Sands to do any thing for my own benefit; but I could bring myself to become a supplicant for my children. I resolved to remind him of the promise he had made me, and to throw myself upon his honor for the performance of it. I persuaded my grandmother to go to him, and tell him I was not dead, and that I earnestly entreated him to keep the promise he had made me; that I had heard of the recent proposals concerning my children, and did not feel easy to accept them; that he had promised to emancipate them, and it was time for him to redeem his pledge. I knew there was some risk in thus betraying that I was in the vicinity; but what will not a mother do for her children? He received the message with surprise, and said, "The children are free. I have never intended to claim them as slaves. Linda may decide their fate. In my opinion, they had better be sent to the north. I don't think they are quite safe here. Dr. Flint boasts that they are still in his power. He says they were his daughter's property, and as she was not of age when they were sold, the contract is not legally binding."

So, then, after all I had endured for their sakes, my poor children were between two fires; between my old master and their new master! And I was powerless. There was no protecting arm of the law for me to invoke. Mr. Sands proposed that Ellen should go, for the present, to some of his relatives,[79] who had removed to Brooklyn, Long Island. It was promised that she should be well taken care of, and sent to school. I consented to it, as the best arrangement I could make for her. My grandmother, of course, negotiated it all; and Mrs. Sands knew of no other person in the transaction. She proposed that they should take Ellen with them to Washington, and keep her till they had a good chance of sending her, with friends, to Brooklyn. She had an infant daughter. I had had a glimpse of it, as the nurse passed with it in her arms. It was not a pleasant thought to me, that the bondwoman's child should tend her free-born sister; but there was no alternative. Ellen was made ready for the journey. O, how it tried my heart to send her away, so young, alone, among strangers! Without a mother's love to shelter her from the storms of life; almost without memory of a mother! I doubted whether she and Benny would have for me the natural affection that children feel for a parent. I thought to myself that I might perhaps never see my daughter again, and I had a great desire that she should look upon me, before she went, that she might take my image with her in her memory. It seemed to me cruel to have her brought to my dungeon. It was sorrow enough for her young heart to know that her mother was a victim of slavery, without seeing the wretched hiding-place to which it had driven her. I begged permission to pass the last night in one of the open chambers, with my little girl. They thought I was crazy to think of trusting such a young child with my perilous secret. I told them I had watched her character, and I felt sure she would not betray me; that I was determined to have an interview, and if they would not facilitate it, I would take my own way to obtain it. They remonstrated against the rashness of such a proceeding; but finding they could not change my purpose, they yielded. I slipped through the trap-door into the storeroom, and my uncle kept watch at the gate, while I passed into the piazza and went up stairs, to the room I used to occupy. It was more than five years since I had seen it; and how the memories crowded on me! There I had taken shelter when my mistress drove me from her house; there came my old tyrant, to mock, insult, and curse me; there my children were first laid in my arms; there I had watched over them, each day with a deeper and sadder love; there I had knelt to God, in anguish of heart, to forgive the wrong I had done. How vividly it all came back! And after this long, gloomy interval, I stood there such a wreck!

In the midst of these meditations, I heard footsteps on the stairs. The door opened, and my uncle Phillip came in, leading Ellen by the hand. I put my arms round her, and said, "Ellen, my dear child, I am your mother." She drew back a little, and looked at me; then, with sweet confidence, she laid her cheek against mine, and I folded her to the heart that had been so long desolated. She was the first to speak. Raising her head, she said, inquiringly, "You really *are* my mother?" I told her I really was; that during all the long time she had not seen me, I had loved her most tenderly; and that now she was going away, I wanted to see her and talk with her, that she might remember me. With a sob in her voice, she said, "I'm glad you've come to see me; but why didn't you ever come before? Benny and I have wanted so much to see you! He remembers you, and sometimes he tells me about you. Why didn't you come home when Dr. Flint went to bring you?"

I answered, "I couldn't come before, dear. But now that I am with you, tell me whether you like to go away." "I don't know," said she, crying. "Grandmother says I ought not to cry; that I am going to a good place, where I can learn to read and write, and that by and by I can write her a letter. But I shan't have Benny, or grandmother, or uncle Phillip, or any body to love me. Can't you go with me? O, *do* go, dear mother!"

I told her I couldn't go now; but sometime I would come to her, and then she and Benny and I would live together, and have happy times. She wanted to run and bring Benny to see me now. I told her he was going to the north, before long, with uncle Phillip, and then I would come to see him before he went away. I asked if she would like to have me stay all night and sleep with her. "O, yes," she replied. Then, turning to her uncle, she said, pleadingly, "*May* I stay? Please, uncle! She is my own mother." He laid his hand on her head, and said, solemnly, "Ellen, this is the secret you have promised grandmother never to tell. If you ever speak of it to any body, they will never let you see your grandmother again, and your mother can never come to Brooklyn." "Uncle," she replied, "I will never tell." He told her she might stay with me; and when he had gone, I took her in my arms and told her I was a slave, and that was the reason she must never say she had seen me. I exhorted her to be a good child, to try to please the people where she was going, and that God would raise her up friends. I told her to say her prayers, and remember always to pray for her poor mother, and that God would permit us to meet again. She wept, and I did not check her tears. Perhaps she would never again have a chance to pour her tears into a mother's bosom. All night she nestled in my arms, and I had no inclination to slumber. The moments were too precious to lose any of them. Once, when I thought she was asleep, I kissed her forehead softly, and she said, "I am not asleep, dear mother."

Before dawn they came to take me back to my den. I drew aside the window curtain, to take a last look of my child. The moonlight shone on her face, and I bent over her, as I had done years before, that wretched night when I ran away. I hugged her close to my throbbing heart; and tears, too sad for such young eyes to shed, flowed down her cheeks, as she gave her last kiss, and whispered in my ear, "Mother, I will never tell." And she never did.

When I got back to my den, I threw myself on the bed and wept there alone in the darkness. It seemed as if my heart would burst. When the time for Ellen's departure drew nigh, I could hear neighbors and friends saying to her, "Good by, Ellen. I hope your poor mother will find you out. *Won't* you be glad to see her!" She replied, "Yes, ma'am;" and they little dreamed of the weighty secret that weighed down her young heart. She was an affectionate child, but naturally very reserved, except with those she loved, and I felt secure that my secret would be safe with her. I heard the gate close after her, with such feelings as only a slave mother can experience. During the day my meditations were very sad. Sometimes I feared I had been very selfish not to give up all claim to her, and let her go to

Illinois, to be adopted by Mrs. Sands's sister. It was my experience of slavery that decided me against it. I feared that circumstances might arise that would cause her to be sent back. I felt confident that I should go to New York myself; and then I should be able to watch over her, and in some degree protect her.

Dr. Flint's family knew nothing of the proposed arrangement till after Ellen was gone, and the news displeased them greatly. Mrs. Flint called on Mrs. Sands's sister to inquire into the matter. She expressed her opinion very freely as to the respect Mr. Sands showed for his wife, and for his own character, in acknowledging those "young niggers." And as for sending Ellen away, she pronounced it to be just as much stealing as it would be for him to come and take a piece of furniture out of her parlor. She said her daughter was not of age to sign the bill of sale, and the children were her property; and when she became of age, or was married, she could take them, wherever she could lay hands on them.

Miss Emily Flint, the little girl to whom I had been bequeathed, was now in her sixteenth year. Her mother considered it all right and honorable for her, or her future husband, to steal my children; but she did not understand how any body could hold up their heads in respectable society, after they had purchased their own children, as Mr. Sands had done. Dr. Flint said very little. Perhaps he thought that Benny would be less likely to be sent away if he kept quiet. One of my letters, that fell into his hands, was dated from Canada; and he seldom spoke of me now. This state of things enabled me to slip down into the storeroom more frequently, where I could stand upright, and move my limbs more freely.

Days, weeks, and months passed, and there came no news of Ellen. I sent a letter to Brooklyn, written in my grandmother's name, to inquire whether she had arrived there. Answer was returned that she had not. I wrote to her in Washington; but no notice was taken of it. There was one person there, who ought to have had some sympathy with the anxiety of the child's friends at home; but the links of such relations as he had formed with me, are easily broken and cast away as rubbish. Yet how protectingly and persuasively he once talked to the poor, helpless slave girl! And how entirely I trusted him! But now suspicions darkened my mind. Was my child dead, or had they deceived me, and sold her?

If the secret memoirs of many members of Congress should be published, curious details would be unfolded. I once saw a letter from a member of Congress to a slave, who was the mother of six of his children. He wrote to request that she would send her children away from the great house before his return, as he expected to be accompanied by friends. The woman could not read, and was obliged to employ another to read the letter. The existence of the colored children did not trouble this gentleman, it was only the fear that friends might recognize in their features a resemblance to him.

At the end of six months, a letter came to my grandmother, from Brooklyn. It was written by a young lady in the family, and announced that Ellen had just arrived. It contained the following message from her: "I do try to do just as you told me to, and I pray for you every night and morning." I understood that these words were meant for me; and they were a balsam to my heart. The writer closed her letter by saying, "Ellen is a nice little girl, and we shall like to have her with us. My cousin, Mr. Sands, has given her to me, to be my little waiting maid.

I shall send her to school, and I hope some day she will write to you herself." This letter perplexed and troubled me. Had my child's father merely placed her there till she was old enough to support herself? Or had he given her to his cousin, as a piece of property? If the last idea was correct, his cousin might return to the south at any time, and hold Ellen as a slave. I tried to put away from me the painful thought that such a foul wrong could have been done to us. I said to myself, "Surely there must be *some* justice in man;" then I remembered, with a sigh, how slavery perverted all the natural feelings of the human heart. It gave me a pang to look on my light-hearted boy. He believed himself free; and to have him brought under the yoke of slavery, would be more than I could bear. How I longed to have him safely out of the reach of its power!

XXVIII.

AUNT NANCY.

I HAVE mentioned my great-aunt, who was a slave in Dr. Flint's family, and who had been my refuge during the shameful persecutions I suffered from him. This aunt had been married at twenty years of age; that is, as far as slaves *can* marry. She had the consent of her master and mistress, and a clergyman performed the ceremony. But it was a mere form, without any legal value. Her master or mistress could annul it any day they pleased. She had always slept on the floor in the entry, near Mrs. Flint's chamber door, that she might be within call. When she was married, she was told she might have the use of a small room in an outhouse. Her mother and her husband furnished it. He was a seafaring man, and was allowed to sleep there when he was at home. But on the wedding evening, the bride was ordered to her old post on the entry floor.

Mrs. Flint, at that time, had no children; but she was expecting to be a mother, and if she should want a drink of water in the night, what could she do without her slave to bring it? So my aunt was compelled to lie at her door, until one midnight she was forced to leave, to give premature birth to a child. In a fortnight she was required to resume her place on the entry door, because Mrs. Flint's babe needed her attentions. She kept her station there through summer and winter, until she had given premature birth to six children; and all the while she was employed as night-nurse to Mrs. Flint's children. Finally, toiling all day, and being deprived of rest at night, completely broke down her constitution, and Dr. Flint declared it was impossible she could ever become the mother of a living child. The fear of losing so valuable a servant by death, now induced them to allow her to sleep in her little room in the out-house, except when there was sickness in the family. She afterwards had two feeble babes, one of whom died in a few days, and the other in four weeks. I well remember her patient sorrow as she held the last dead baby in her arms. "I wish it could have lived," she said; "it is not the will of God that any of my children should live. But I will try to be fit to meet their little spirits in heaven."

Aunt Nancy was housekeeper and waiting-maid in Dr. Flint's family. Indeed, she was the *factotum* of the household. Nothing went on well without her. She was my mother's twin sister, and, as far as was in her power, she supplied a mother's place to us orphans. I slept with her all the time I lived in my old master's house, and the bond between us was very strong. When my friends tried to discourage me from running away, she always encouraged me. When they thought I had better return and ask my master's pardon, because there was no possibility of escape, she sent me word never to yield. She said if I persevered I might, perhaps, gain the freedom of my children; and even if I perished in doing it, that was better than to leave them to groan under the same persecutions that had blighted my own life. After I was shut up in my dark cell, she stole away, whenever she could, to bring me the news and say something cheering. How often did I kneel down to listen to her words of consolation, whispered through a crack! "I am old, and have not long to live," she used to say; "and I could die happy if I could only see you and the children free. You must pray to God, Linda, as I do for you, that he will lead you out of this darkness." I would beg her not to worry herself on my account; that there was an end of all suffering sooner or later, and that whether I lived in chains or in freedom, I should always remember her as the good friend who had been the comfort of my life. A word from her always strengthened me; and not me only. The whole family relied upon her judgment, and were guided by her advice.

I had been in my cell six years when my grandmother was summoned to the bedside of this, her last remaining daughter. She was very ill, and they said she would die. Grandmother had not entered Dr. Flint's house for several years. They had treated her cruelly, but she thought nothing of that now. She was grateful for permission to watch by the death-bed of her child. They had always been devoted to each other; and now they sat looking into each other's eyes, longing to speak of the secret that had weighed so much on the hearts of both. My aunt had been stricken with paralysis. She lived but two days, and the last day she was speechless. Before she lost the power of utterance, she told her mother not to grieve if she could not speak to her; that she would try to hold up her hand, to let her know that all was well with her. Even the hard-hearted doctor was a little softened when he saw the dying woman try to smile on the aged mother, who was kneeling by her side. His eyes moistened for a moment, as he said she had always been a faithful servant, and they should never be able to supply her place. Mrs. Flint took to her bed, quite overcome by the shock. While my grandmother sat alone with the dead, the doctor came in, leading his youngest son, who had always been a great pet with aunt Nancy, and was much attached to her. "Martha," said he, "aunt Nancy loved this child, and when he comes where you are, I hope you will be kind to him, for her sake." She replied, "Your wife was my foster-child, Dr. Flint, the foster-sister of my poor Nancy, and you little know me if you think I can feel any thing but good will for her children."

"I wish the past could be forgotten, and that we might never think of it," said he; "and that Linda would come to supply her aunt's place. She would be worth more to us than all the money that could be paid for her. I wish it for your sake also, Martha. Now that Nancy is taken away from you, she would be a great comfort to your old age."

He knew he was touching a tender chord. Almost choking with grief, my grandmother replied, "It was not I that drove Linda away. My grandchildren are gone; and of my nine children only one is left. God help me!"

To me, the death of this kind relative was an inexpressible sorrow. I knew that she had been slowly murdered; and I felt that my troubles had helped to finish the work. After I heard of her illness, I listened constantly to hear what news was brought from the great house; and the thought that I could not go to her made me utterly miserable. At last, as uncle Phillip came into the house, I heard some one inquire, "How is she?" and he answered, "She is dead." My little cell seemed whirling round, and I knew nothing more till I opened my eyes and found uncle Phillip bending over me. I had no need to ask any questions. He whispered, "Linda, she died happy." I could not weep. My fixed gaze troubled him. "Don't look *so,*" he said. "Don't add to my poor mother's trouble. Remember how much she has to bear, and that we ought to do all we can to comfort her." Ah, yes, that blessed old grandmother, who for seventy-three years had borne the pelting storms of a slave-mother's life. She did indeed need consolation!

Mrs. Flint had rendered her poor foster-sister childless, apparently without any compunction; and with cruel selfishness had ruined her health by years of incessant, unrequited toil, and broken rest. But now she became very sentimental. I suppose she thought it would be a beautiful illustration of the attachment existing between slaveholder and slave, if the body of her old worn-out servant was buried at her feet. She sent for the clergyman and asked if he had any objection to burying aunt Nancy in the doctor's family burial-place. No colored person had ever been allowed interment in the white people's burying-ground, and the minister knew that all the deceased of our family reposed together in the old graveyard of the slaves. He therefore replied, "I have no objection to complying with your wish; but perhaps aunt Nancy's *mother* may have some choice as to where her remains shall be deposited."

It had never occurred to Mrs. Flint that slaves could have any feelings. When my grandmother was consulted, she at once said she wanted Nancy to lie with all the rest of her family, and where her own old body would be buried. Mrs. Flint graciously complied with her wish, though she said it was painful to her to have Nancy buried away from *her.* She might have added with touching pathos, "I was so long *used* to sleep with her lying near me, on the entry floor."

My uncle Phillip asked permission to bury his sister at his own expense; and slaveholders are always ready to grant *such* favors to slaves and their relatives. The arrangements were very plain, but perfectly respectable. She was buried on the Sabbath, and Mrs. Flint's minister read the funeral service. There was a large concourse of colored people, bond and free, and a few white persons who had always been friendly to our family. Dr. Flint's carriage was in the procession; and when the body was deposited in its humble resting place, the mistress dropped a tear, and returned to her carriage, probably thinking she had performed her duty nobly.

It was talked of by the slaves as a mighty grand funeral. Northern travellers, passing through the place, might have described this tribute of respect to the humble dead as a beautiful feature in the "patriarchal institution;" a touching proof of the attachment between slaveholders and their servants; and tender-hearted Mrs. Flint would have confirmed this impression, with handkerchief at her eyes. *We* could have told them a different story. We could have given them a chapter of wrongs and sufferings, that would have touched their hearts, if they *had* any hearts to feel for the colored people. We could have told them how the poor old slave-mother had toiled, year after year, to earn eight hundred dollars to buy her son Phillip's right to his own earnings; and how that same Phillip paid the expenses of the funeral, which they regarded as doing so much credit to the master. We could also have told them of a poor, blighted young creature, shut up in a living grave for years, to avoid the tortures that would be inflicted on her, if she ventured to come out and look on the face of her departed friend.

All this, and much more, I thought of, as I sat at my loophole, waiting for the family to return from the grave; sometimes weeping, sometimes falling asleep, dreaming strange dreams of the dead and the living.

It was sad to witness the grief of my bereaved grandmother. She had always been strong to bear, and now, as ever, religious faith supported her. But her dark life had become still darker, and age and trouble were leaving deep traces on her withered face. She had four places to knock for me to come to the trap-door, and each place had a different meaning. She now came oftener than she had done, and talked to me of her dead daughter, while tears trickled slowly down her furrowed cheeks. I said all I could to comfort her; but it was a sad reflection, that instead of being able to help her, I was a constant source of anxiety and trouble. The poor old back was fitted to its burden. It bent under it, but did not break.

XXIX.

PREPARATIONS FOR ESCAPE.

I HARDLY expect that the reader will credit me, when I affirm that I lived in that little dismal hole, almost deprived of light and air, and with no space to move my limbs, for nearly seven years. But it is a fact; and to me a sad one, even now; for my body still suffers from the effects of that long imprisonment, to say nothing of my soul. Members of my family, now living in New York and Boston, can testify to the truth of what I say.

Countless were the nights that I sat late at the little loophole scarcely large enough to give me a glimpse of one twinkling star. There, I heard the patrols and slave-hunters conferring together about the capture of runaways, well knowing how rejoiced they would be to catch me.

Season after season, year after year, I peeped at my children's faces, and heard their sweet voices, with a heart yearning all the while to say, "Your mother is here." Sometimes it appeared to me as if ages had rolled away since I entered upon that gloomy, monotonous existence. At times, I was stupefied and listless; at other times I became very impatient to know when these dark years would end, and I should again be allowed to feel the sunshine, and breathe the pure air.

After Ellen left us, this feeling increased. Mr. Sands had agreed that Benny might go to the north whenever his uncle Phillip could go with him; and I was anxious to be there also, to watch over my children, and protect them so far as I was able. Moreover, I was likely to be drowned out of my den, if I remained much longer; for the slight roof was getting badly out of repair, and uncle Phillip was afraid to remove the shingles, lest some one should get a glimpse of me. When storms occurred in the night, they spread mats and bits of carpet, which in the morning appeared to have been laid out to dry; but to cover the roof in the daytime might have attracted attention. Consequently, my clothes and bedding were often drenched; a process by which the pains and aches in my cramped and stiffened limbs were greatly increased. I revolved various plans of escape in my mind, which I sometimes imparted to my grandmother, when she came to whisper with me at the trap-door. The kind-hearted old woman had an intense sympathy for runaways. She had known too much of the cruelties inflicted on those who were captured. Her memory always flew back at once to the sufferings of her bright and handsome son, Benjamin, the youngest and dearest of her flock. So, whenever I alluded to the subject, she would groan out, "O, don't think of it, child. You'll break my heart." I had no good old aunt Nancy now to encourage me; but my brother William and my children were continually beckoning me to the north.

And now I must go back a few months in my story. I have stated that the first of January was the time for selling slaves, or leasing them out to new masters. If time were counted by heart-throbs, the poor slaves might reckon years of suffering during that festival so joyous to the free. On the New Year's day preceding my aunt's death, one of my friends, named Fanny, was to be sold at auction, to pay her master's debts. My thoughts were with her during all the day, and at night I anxiously inquired what had been her fate. I was told that she had been sold to one master, and her four little girls to another master, far distant; that she had escaped from her purchaser, and was not to be found. Her mother was the old Aggie I have spoken of. She lived in a small tenement belonging to my grandmother, and built on the same lot with her own house. Her dwelling was searched and watched, and that brought the patrols so near me that I was obliged to keep very close in my den. The hunters were somehow eluded; and not long afterwards Benny accidentally caught sight of Fanny in her mother's hut. He told his grandmother, who charged him never to speak of it, explaining to him the frightful consequences; and he never betrayed the trust. Aggie little dreamed that my grandmother knew where her daughter was concealed, and that the stooping form of her old neighbor was bending under a similar burden of anxiety and fear; but these dangerous secrets deepened the sympathy between the two old persecuted mothers.

My friend Fanny and I remained many weeks hidden within call of each other; but she was unconscious of the fact. I longed to have her share my den, which seemed a more secure retreat than her own; but I had brought so much trouble on my grandmother, that it seemed wrong to ask her to incur greater risks. My restlessness increased. I had lived too long in bodily pain and anguish of spirit. Always I was in dread that by some accident, or some contrivance, slavery would succeed in snatching my children from me. This thought drove me nearly frantic, and I determined to steer for the North Star at all hazards. At this crisis, Providence opened an unexpected way for me to escape. My friend Peter came one evening, and asked to speak with me. "Your day has come, Linda," said he. "I have found a chance for you to go to the Free States. You have a fortnight to decide." The news seemed too good to be true; but Peter explained his arrangements, and told me all that was necessary was for me to say I would go. I was going to answer him with a joyful yes, when the thought of Benny came to my mind. I told him the temptation was exceedingly strong, but I was terribly afraid of Dr. Flint's alleged power over my child, and that I could not go and leave him behind. Peter remonstrated earnestly. He said such a good chance might never occur again; that Benny was free, and could be sent to me; and that for the sake of my children's welfare I ought not to hesitate a moment. I told him I would consult with uncle Phillip. My uncle rejoiced in the plan, and bade me go by all means. He promised, if his life was spared, that he would either bring or send my son to me as soon as I reached a place of safety. I resolved to go, but thought nothing had better be said to my grandmother till very near the time of departure. But my uncle thought she would feel it more keenly if I left her so suddenly. "I will reason with her," said he, "and convince her how necessary it is, not only for your sake, but for hers also. You cannot be blind to the fact that she is sinking under her burdens." I was not blind to it. I knew that my concealment was an ever-present source of anxiety, and that the older she grew the more nervously fearful she was of discovery. My uncle talked with her, and finally succeeded in persuading her that it was absolutely necessary for me to seize the chance so unexpectedly offered.

The anticipation of being a free woman proved almost too much for my weak frame. The excitement stimulated me, and at the same time bewildered me. I made busy preparations for my journey, and for my son to follow me. I resolved to have an interview with him before I went, that I might give him cautions and advice, and tell him how anxiously I should be waiting for him at the north. Grandmother stole up to me as often as possible to whisper words of counsel. She insisted upon my writing to Dr. Flint, as soon as I arrived in the Free States, and asking him to sell me to her. She said she would sacrifice her house, and all she had in the world, for the sake of having me safe with my children in any part of the world. If she could only live to know *that* she could die in peace. I promised the dear old faithful friend that I would write to her as soon as I arrived, and put the letter in a safe way to reach her; but in my own mind I resolved that not another cent of her hard earnings should be spent to pay rapacious slaveholders for what they called their property. And even if I had not been unwilling to buy what I had already a right to possess, common humanity would have prevented me from accepting the generous offer, at the expense of turning my aged relative out of house and home, when she was trembling on the brink of the grave.

I was to escape in a vessel; but I forbear to mention any further paticulars. I was in readiness, but the vessel was unexpectedly detained several days. Meantime, news came to town of a most horrible murder committed on a fugitive slave, named James. Charity, the mother of this unfortunate young man, had been an old acquaintance of ours. I have told the shocking particulars of his death, in my description of some of the neighboring slaveholders. My grandmother, always nervously sensitive about runaways, was terribly frightened. She felt sure that a similar fate awaited me, if I did not desist from my enterprise. She sobbed, and groaned, and entreated me not to go. Her excessive fear was somewhat contagious, and my heart was not proof against her extreme agony. I was grievously disappointed, but I promised to relinquish my project.

When my friend Peter was apprised of this, he was both disappointed and vexed. He said, that judging from our past experience, it would be a long time before I had such another chance to throw away. I told him it need not be thrown away; that I had a friend concealed near by, who would be glad enough to take the place that had been provided for me. I told him about poor Fanny, and the kind-hearted, noble fellow, who never turned his back upon any body in distress, white or black, expressed his readiness to help her. Aggie was much surprised when she found that we knew her secret. She was rejoiced to hear of such a chance for Fanny, and arrangements were made for her to go on board the vessel the next night. They both supposed that I had long been at the north, therefore my name was not mentioned in the transaction. Fanny was carried on board at the appointed time, and stowed away in a very small cabin. This accommodation had been purchased at a price that would pay for a voyage to England. But when one proposes to go to fine old England, they stop to calculate whether they can afford the cost of the pleasure; while in making a bargain to escape from slavery, the trembling victim is ready to say, "Take all I have, only don't betray me!"

The next morning I peeped through my loophole, and saw that it was dark and cloudy. At night I received news that the wind was ahead, and the vessel had not sailed. I was exceedingly anxious about Fanny, and Peter too, who was running a tremendous risk at my instigation. Next day the wind and weather remained the same. Poor Fanny had been half dead with fright when they carried her on board, and I could readily imagine how she must be suffering now. Grandmother came often to my den, to say how thankful she was I did not go. On the third morning she rapped for me to come down to the storeroom. The poor old sufferer was breaking down under her weight of trouble. She was easily flurried now. I found her in a nervous, excited state, but I was not aware that she had forgotten to lock the door behind her, as usual. She was exceedingly worried about the detention of the vessel. She was afraid all would be discovered, and then Fanny, and Peter, and I, would all be tortured to death, and Phillip would be utterly ruined, and her house would be torn down. Poor Peter! If he should die such a horrible death as the poor slave James had lately done, and all for his kindness in trying to help me, how dreadful it would be for us all! Alas, the thought was familiar to me, and had sent many a sharp pang through my heart. I tried to suppress my own anxiety, and speak soothingly to her. She brought in some allusion to aunt Nancy, the dear daughter she had recently buried, and then she lost all control of herself. As she stood there, trembling and sobbing, a voice from the piazza called out, "Whar is you, aunt Marthy?" Grandmother was startled, and in her agitation opened the door, without thinking of me. In stepped Jenny, the mischievous housemaid, who had tried to enter my room, when I was concealed in the house of my white benefactress. "I's bin huntin ebery whar for you, aunt Marthy," said she. "My missis wants you to send her some crackers." I had slunk down behind a barrel, which entirely screened me, but I imagined that Jenny was looking directly at the spot, and my heart beat violently. My grand mother immediately thought what she had done, and went out quickly with Jenny to count the crackers, locking the door after her. She returned to me, in a few minutes, the perfect picture of despair. "Poor child!" she exclaimed, "my carelessness has ruined you. The boat ain't gone yet. Get ready immediately, and go with Fanny. I ain't got another word to say against it now; for there's no telling what may happen this day."

Uncle Phillip was sent for, and he agreed with his mother in thinking that Jenny would inform Dr. Flint in less than twenty-four hours. He advised getting me on board the boat, if possible; if not, I had better keep very still in my den, where they could not find me without tearing the house down. He said it would not do for him to move in the matter, because suspicion would be immediately excited; but he promised to communicate with Peter. I felt reluctant to apply to him again, having implicated him too much already; but there seemed to be no alternative. Vexed as Peter had been by my indecision, he was true to his generous nature, and said at once that he would do his best to help me, trusting I should show myself a stronger woman this time.

He immediately proceeded to the wharf, and found that the wind had shifted, and the vessel was slowly beating down stream. On some pretext of urgent necessity, he offered two boatmen a dollar apiece to catch up with her. He was of lighter complexion than the boatmen he hired, and when the captain saw them coming so rapidly, he thought officers were pursuing his vessel in search of the runaway slave he had on board. They hoisted sails, but the boat gained upon them, and the indefatigable Peter sprang on board.

The captain at once recognized him. Peter asked him to go below, to speak about a bad bill he had given him. When he told his errand, the captain replied, "Why, the woman's here already; and I've put her where you or the devil would have a tough job to find her."

"But it is another woman I want to bring," said Peter. "*She* is in great distress, too, and you shall be paid any thing within reason, if you'll stop and take her."

"What's her name?" inquired the captain.

"Linda," he replied.

"That's the name of the woman already here," rejoined the captain. "By George! I believe you mean to betray me."

"O!" exclaimed Peter, "God knows I wouldn't harm a hair of your head. I am too grateful to you. But there really *is* another woman in great danger. Do have the humanity to stop and take her!"

After a while they came to an understanding. Fanny, not dreaming I was any where about in that region, had assumed my name, though she called herself Johnson. "Linda is a common name," said Peter, "and the woman I want to bring is Linda Brent."

The captain agreed to wait at a certain place till evening, being handsomely paid for his detention.

Of course, the day was an anxious one for us all. But we concluded that if Jenny had seen me, she would be too wise to let her mistress know of it; and that she probably would not get a chance to see Dr. Flint's family till evening, for I knew very well what were the rules in that household. I afterwards believed that she did not see me; for nothing ever came of it, and she was one of those base characters that would have jumped to betray a suffering fellow being for the sake of thirty pieces of silver.[80]

I made all my arrangements to go on board as soon as it was dusk. The intervening time I resolved to spend with my son. I had not spoken to him for seven years, though I had been under the same roof, and seen him every day, when I was well enough to sit at the loophole. I did not dare to venture beyond the storeroom; so they brought him there, and locked us up together, in a place concealed from the piazza door. It was an agitating interview for both of us. After we had talked and wept together for a little while, he said, "Mother, I'm glad you're going away. I wish I could go with you. I knew you was here; and I have been *so* afraid they would come and catch you!"

I was greatly surprised, and asked him how he had found it out.

He replied, "I was standing under the eaves, one day, before Ellen went away, and I heard somebody cough up over the wood shed. I don't know what made me think it was you, but I did think so. I missed Ellen, the night before she went away; and grandmother brought her back into the room in the night; and I thought maybe she'd been to see *you,* before she went, for I heard grandmother whisper to her, 'Now go to sleep; and remember never to tell.' "

I asked him if he ever mentioned his suspicions to his sister. He said he never did; but after he heard the cough, if he saw her playing with other children on that side of the house, he always tried to coax her round to the other side, for fear they would hear me cough, too. He said he had kept a close lookout for Dr. Flint, and if he saw him speak to a constable, or a patrol, he always told grandmother. I now recollected that I had seen him manifest uneasiness, when people were on that side of the house, and I had at the time been puzzled to conjecture a motive for his actions. Such prudence may seem extraordinary in a boy of twelve years, but slaves, being surrounded by mysteries, deceptions, and dangers, early learn to be suspicious and watchful, and prematurely cautious and cunning. He had never asked a question of grandmother, or uncle Phillip, and I had often heard him chime in with other children, when they spoke of my being at the north.

I told him I was now really going to the Free States, and if he was a good, honest boy, and a loving child to his dear old grandmother, the Lord would bless him, and bring him to me, and we and Ellen would live together. He began to tell me that grandmother had not eaten any thing all day. While he was speaking, the door was unlocked, and she came in with a small bag of money, which she wanted me to take. I begged her to keep a part of it, at least, to pay for Benny's being sent to the north; but she insisted, while her tears were falling fast, that I should take the whole. "You may be sick among strangers," she said, "and they would send you to the poorhouse to die." Ah, that good grandmother!

For the last time I went up to my nook. Its desolate appearance no longer chilled me, for the light of hope had risen in my soul. Yet, even with the blessed prospect of freedom before me, I felt very sad at leaving forever that old homestead, where I had been sheltered so long by the dear old grandmother; where I had dreamed my first young dream of love; and where, after that had faded away, my children came to twine themselves so closely round my desolate heart. As the hour approached for me to leave, I again descended to the storeroom. My grandmother and Benny were there. She took me by the hand, and said, "Linda, let us pray." We knelt down together, with my child pressed to my heart, and my other arm round the faithful, loving old friend I was about to leave forever. On no other occasion has it ever been my lot to listen to so fervent a supplication for mercy and protection. It thrilled through my heart, and inspired me with trust in God.

Peter was waiting for me in the street. I was soon by his side, faint in body, but strong of purpose. I did not look back upon the old place, though I felt that I should never see it again.

XXX.

NORTHWARD BOUND.

I NEVER could tell how we reached the wharf. My brain was all of a whirl, and my limbs tottered under me. At an appointed place we met my uncle Phillip, who had started before us on a different route, that he might reach the wharf first, and give us timely warning if there was any danger. A row-boat was in readiness. As I was about to step in, I felt something pull me gently, and turning round I saw Benny, looking pale and anxious. He whispered in my ear, "I've been peeping into the doctor's window, and he's at home. Good by, mother. Don't cry; I'll come." He hastened away. I clasped the hand of my good uncle, to whom I owed so much, and of Peter, the brave, generous friend who had volunteered to run such terrible risks to secure my safety. To this day I remember how his bright face beamed with joy, when he told me he had discovered a safe method for me to escape. Yet that intelligent, enterprising, noble-hearted man was a chattel! liable, by the laws of a country that calls itself civilized, to be sold with horses and pigs! We parted in silence. Our hearts were all too full for words!

Swiftly the boat glided over the water. After a while, one of the sailors said, "Don't be down-hearted, madam. We will take you safely to your husband, in ———." At first I could not imagine what he meant; but I had presence of mind to think that it probably referred to something the captain had told him; so I thanked him, and said I hoped we should have pleasant weather.

When I entered the vessel the captain came forward to meet me. He was an elderly man, with a pleasant countenance. He showed me to a little box of a cabin, where sat my friend Fanny. She started as if she had seen a spectre. She gazed on me in utter astonishment, and exclaimed, "Linda, can this be *you?* or is it your ghost?" When we were locked in each other's arms, my overwrought feelings could no longer be restrained. My sobs reached the ears of the captain, who came and very kindly reminded us, that for his safety, as well as our own, it would be prudent for us not to attract any attention. He said that when there was a sail in sight he wished us to keep below; but at other times, he had no objection to our being on deck. He assured us that he would keep a good lookout, and if we acted prudently, he thought we should be in no danger. He had represented us as women going to meet our husbands in ———. We thanked him, and promised to observe carefully all the directions he gave us.

Fanny and I now talked by ourselves, low and quietly, in our little cabin. She told me of the sufferings she had gone through in making her escape, and of her terrors while she was concealed in her mother's house. Above all, she dwelt on the agony of separation from all her children on that dreadful auction day. She could scarcely credit me, when I told her of the place where I had passed nearly seven years. "We have the same sorrows," said I. "No," replied she, "you are going to see your children soon, and there is no hope that I shall ever even hear from mine."

The vessel was soon under way, but we made slow progress. The wind was against us. I should not have cared for this, if we had been out of sight of the town; but until there were miles of water between us and our enemies, we were filled with constant apprehensions that the constables would come on board. Neither could I feel quite at ease with the captain and his men. I was an entire stranger to that class of people, and I had heard that sailors were rough, and sometimes cruel. We were so completely in their power, that if they were bad men, our situation would be dreadful. Now that the captain was paid for our passage, might he not be tempted to make more money by giving us up to those who claimed us as property? I was naturally of a confiding disposition, but slavery had made me suspicious of every body. Fanny did not share my distrust of the captain or his men. She said she was afraid at first, but she had been on board three days while the vessel lay in the dock, and nobody had betrayed her, or treated her otherwise than kindly.

The captain soon came to advise us to go on deck for fresh air. His friendly and respectful manner, combined with Fanny's testimony, reassured me, and we went with him. He placed us in a comfortable seat, and occasionally entered into conversation. He told us he was a Southerner by birth, and had spent the greater part of his life in the Slave States, and that he had recently lost a brother who traded in slaves. "But," said he, "it is a pitiable and degrading business, and I always felt ashamed to acknowledge my brother in connection with it." As we passed Snaky Swamp, he pointed to it, and said, "There is a slave territory that defies all the laws." I thought of the terrible days I had spent there, and though it was not called Dismal Swamp, it made me feel very dismal as I looked at it.

I shall never forget that night. The balmy air of spring was so refreshing! And how shall I describe my sensations when we were fairly sailing on Chesapeake Bay? O, the beautiful sunshine! the exhilarating breeze! and I could enjoy them without fear or restraint. I had never realized what grand things air and sunlight are till I had been deprived of them.

Ten days after we left land we were approaching Philadelphia. The captain said we should arrive there in the night, but he thought we had better wait till morning, and go on shore in broad daylight, as the best way to avoid suspicion.

I replied, "You know best. But will you stay on board and protect us?"

He saw that I was suspicious, and he said he was sorry, now that he had brought us to the end of our voyage, to find I had so little confidence in him. Ah, if he had ever been a slave he would have known how difficult it was to trust a white man. He assured us that we might sleep through the night without fear; that he would take care we were not left unprotected. Be it said to the honor of this captain, Southerner as he was, that if Fanny and I had been white ladies, and our passage lawfully engaged, he could not have treated us more respectfully. My intelligent friend, Peter, had rightly estimated the character of the man to whose honor he had intrusted us.

The next morning I was on deck as soon as the day dawned. I called Fanny to see the sun rise, for the first time in our lives, on free soil; for such I *then* believed it to be. We watched the reddening sky, and saw the great orb come up slowly out of the water, as it seemed. Soon the waves began to sparkle, and every thing caught the beautiful glow. Before us lay the city of strangers. We looked at each other, and the eyes of both were moistened with tears. We had escaped from slavery, and we supposed ourselves to be safe from the hunters. But we were alone in the world, and we had left dear ties behind us; ties cruelly sundered by the demon Slavery.

XXXI.

INCIDENTS IN PHILADELPHIA.

I HAD heard that the poor slave had many friends at the north. I trusted we should find some of them. Meantime, we would take it for granted that all were friends, till they proved to the contrary. I sought out the kind captain, thanked him for his attentions, and told him I should never cease to be grateful for the service he had rendered us. I gave him a message to the friends I had left at home, and he promised to deliver it. We were placed in a row-boat, and in about fifteen minutes were landed on a wood wharf in Philadelphia. As I stood looking round, the friendly captain touched me on the shoulder, and said, "There is a respectable-looking colored man behind you. I will speak to him about the New York trains, and tell him you wish to go directly on." I thanked him, and asked him to direct me to some shops where I could buy gloves and veils. He did so, and said he would talk with the colored man till I returned. I made what haste I could. Constant exercise on board the vessel, and frequent rubbing with salt water, had nearly restored the use of my limbs. The noise of the great city confused me, but I found the shops, and bought some double veils and gloves for Fanny and myself. The shopman told me they were so many levies. I had never heard the word before, but I did not tell him so. I thought if he knew I was a stranger he might ask me where I came from. I gave him a gold piece, and when he returned the change, I counted it, and found out how much a levy was.[81] I made my way back to the wharf, where the captain introduced me to the colored man, as the Rev. Jeremiah Durham, minister of Bethel church. He took me by the hand, as if I had been an old friend. He told us we were too late for the morning cars to New York, and must wait until the evening, or the next morning. He invited me to go home with him, assuring me that his wife would give me a cordial welcome; and for my friend he would provide a home with one of his neighbors. I thanked him for so much kindness to strangers, and told him if I must be detained, I should like to hunt up some people who formerly went from our part of the country. Mr. Durham insisted that I should dine with him, and then he would assist me in finding my friends. The sailors came to bid us good by. I shook their hardy hands, with tears in my eyes. They had all been kind to us, and they had rendered us a greater service than they could possibly conceive of.

I had never seen so large a city, or been in contact with so many people in the streets. It seemed as if those who passed looked at us with an expression of curiosity. My face was so blistered and peeled, by sitting on deck, in wind and sunshine, that I thought they could not easily decide to what nation I belonged.

Mrs. Durham met me with a kindly welcome, without asking any questions. I was tired, and her friendly manner was a sweet refreshment. God bless her! I was sure that she had comforted other weary hearts, before I received her sympathy. She was surrounded by her husband and children, in a home made sacred by protecting laws. I thought of my own children, and sighed.

After dinner Mr. Durham went with me in quest of the friends I had spoken of. They went from my native town, and I anticipated much pleasure in looking on familiar faces. They were not at home, and we retraced our steps through streets delightfully clean. On the way, Mr. Durham observed that I had spoken to him of a daughter I expected to meet; that he was surprised, for I looked so young he had taken me for a single woman. He was approaching a subject on which I was extremely sensitive. He would ask about my husband next, I thought, and if I answered him truly, what would he think of me? I told him I had two children, one in New York the other at the south. He asked some further questions, and I frankly told him some of the most important events of my life. It was painful for me to do it; but I would not deceive him. If he was desirous of being my friend, I thought he ought to know how far I was worthy of it. "Excuse me, if I have tried your feelings," said he. "I did not question you from idle curiosity. I wanted to understand your situation, in order to know whether I could be of any service to you, or your little girl. Your straight-forward answers do you credit; but don't answer every body so openly. It might give some heartless people a pretext for treating you with contempt."

That word *contempt* burned me like coals of fire. I replied, "God alone knows how I have suffered; and He, I trust, will forgive me. If I am permitted to have my children, I intend to be a good mother, and to live in such a manner that people cannot treat me with contempt."

"I respect your sentiments," said he. "Place your trust in God, and be governed by good principles, and you will not fail to find friends."

When we reached home, I went to my room, glad to shut out the world for a while. The words he had spoken made an indelible impression upon me. They brought up great shadows from the mournful past. In the midst of my meditations I was startled by a knock at the door. Mrs. Durham entered, her face all beaming with kindness, to say that there was an anti-slavery friend down stairs, who would like to see me. I overcame my dread of encountering strangers, and went with her. Many questions were asked concerning my experiences, and my escape from slavery; but I observed how careful they all were not to say any thing that might wound my feelings. How gratifying this was, can be fully understood only by those who have been accustomed to be treated as if they were not included within the pale of human beings. The anti-slavery friend had come to inquire into my plans, and to offer assistance, if needed. Fanny was comfortably established, for the present, with a friend of Mr. Durham. The Anti-Slavery Society agreed to pay her expenses to New York. The same was offered to me, but I declined to accept it; telling them that my grandmother had given me sufficient to pay my expenses to the end of my journey. We were urged to remain in Philadelphia a few days, until some suitable escort could be found for us. I gladly accepted the proposition, for I had a dread of meeting slaveholders, and some dread also of railroads. I had never entered a railroad car in my life, and it seemed to me quite an important event.

That night I sought my pillow with feelings I had never carried to it before. I verily believed myself to be a free woman. I was wakeful for a long time, and I had no sooner fallen asleep, than I was roused by fire-bells. I jumped up, and hurried on my clothes. Where I came from, every body hastened to dress themselves on such occasions. The white people thought a great fire might be used as a good opportunity for insurrection, and that it was best to be in readiness; and the colored people were ordered out to labor in extinguishing the flames. There was but one engine in our town, and colored women and children were often required to drag it to the river's edge and fill it. Mrs. Durham's daughter slept in the same room with me, and seeing that she slept through all the din, I thought it was my duty to wake her. "What's the matter?" said she, rubbing her eyes.

"They're screaming fire in the streets, and the bells are ringing," I replied.

"What of that?" said she, drowsily. "We are used to it. We never get up, without the fire is very near. What good would it do?"

I was quite surprised that it was not necessary for us to go and help fill the engine. I was an ignorant child, just beginning to learn how things went on in great cities.

At daylight, I heard women crying fresh fish, berries, radishes, and various other things. All this was new to me. I dressed myself at an early hour, and sat at the window to watch that unknown tide of life. Philadelphia seemed to me a wonderfully great place. At the breakfast table, my idea of going out to drag the engine was laughed over, and I joined in the mirth.

I went to see Fanny, and found her so well contented among her new friends that she was in no haste to leave. I was also very happy with my kind hostess. She had had advantages for education, and was vastly my superior. Every day, almost every hour, I was adding to my little stock of knowledge. She took me out to see the city as much as she deemed prudent. One day she took me to an artist's room, and showed me the portraits of some of her children. I had never seen any paintings of colored people before, and they seemed to me beautiful.

At the end of five days, one of Mrs. Durham's friends offered to accompany us to New York the following morning. As I held the hand of my good hostess in a parting clasp, I longed to know whether her husband had repeated to her what I had told him. I supposed he had, but she never made any allusion to it. I presume it was the delicate silence of womanly sympathy.

When Mr. Durham handed us our tickets, he said, "I am afraid you will have a disagreeable ride; but I could not procure tickets for the first class cars."

Supposing I had not given him money enough, I offered more. "O, no," said he, "they could not be had for any money. They don't allow colored people to go in the first-class cars."

This was the first chill to my enthusiasm about the Free States. Colored people wore allowed to ride in a filthy box, behind white people, at the south, but there they were not required to pay for the privilege. It made me sad to find how the north aped the customs of slavery.

We were stowed away in a large, rough car, with windows on each side, too high for us to look out without standing up. It was crowded with people, apparently of all nations. There were plenty of beds and cradles, containing screaming and kicking babies. Every other man had a cigar or pipe in his mouth, and jugs of whiskey were handed round freely. The fumes of the whiskey and the dense tobacco smoke were sickening to my senses, and my mind was equally nauseated by the coarse jokes and ribald songs around me. It was a very disagreeable ride. Since that time there has been some improvement in these matters.

XXXII.

THE MEETING OF MOTHER AND DAUGHTER.

WHEN we arrived in New York, I was half crazed by the crowd of coachmen calling out, "Carriage, ma'am?" We bargained with one to take us to Sullivan Street for twelve shillings. A burly Irishman stepped up and said, "I'll tak' ye for sax shillings." The reduction of half the price was an object to us, and we asked if he could take us right away. "Troth an I will, ladies," he replied. I noticed that the hackmen smiled at each other, and I inquired whether his conveyance was decent. "Yes, it's dacent it is, marm. Devil a bit would I be after takin' ladies in a cab that was not dacent." We gave him our checks. He went for the baggage, and soon reappeared, saying, "This way, if you plase, ladies." We followed, and found our trunks on a truck, and we were invited to take our seats on them. We told him that was not what we bargained for, and he must take the trunks off. He swore they should not be touched till we had paid him six shillings. In our situation it was not prudent to attract attention, and I was about to pay him what he required, when a man near by shook his head for me not to do it. After a great ado we got rid of the Irishman, and had our trunks fastened on a hack. We had been recommended to a boarding-house in Sullivan Street, and thither we drove. There Fanny and I separated. The Anti-Slavery Society provided a home for her, and I afterwards heard of her in prosperous circumstances. I sent for an old friend from my part of the country, who had for some time been doing business in New York. He came immediately. I told him I wanted to go to my daughter, and asked him to aid me in procuring an interview.

I cautioned him not to let it be known to the family that I had just arrived from the south, because they supposed I had been at the north seven years. He told me there was a colored woman in Brooklyn who came from the same town I did, and I had better go to her house, and have my daughter meet me there. I accepted the proposition thankfully, and he agreed to escort me to Brooklyn. We crossed Fulton ferry, went up Myrtle Avenue, and stopped at the house he designated. I was just about to enter, when two girls passed. My friend called my attention to them. I turned, and recognized in the eldest, Sarah, the daughter of a woman who used to live with my grandmother, but who had left the south years ago. Surprised and rejoiced at this unexpected meeting, I threw my arms round her, and inquired concerning her mother.

"You take no notice of the other girl," said my friend. I turned, and there stood my Ellen! I pressed her to my heart, then held her away from me to take a look at her. She had changed a good deal in the two years since I parted from her. Signs of neglect could be discerned by eyes less observing than a mother's. My friend invited us all to go into the house; but Ellen said she had been sent of an errand, which she would do as quickly as possible, and go home and ask Mrs. Hobbs to let her come and see me. It was agreed that I should send for her the next day. Her companion, Sarah, hastened to tell her mother of my arrival. When I entered the house, I found the mistress of it absent, and I waited for her return. Before I saw her, I heard her saying, "Where is Linda Brent? I used to know her father and mother." Soon Sarah came with her mother. So there was quite a company of us, all from my grandmother's neighborhood. These friends gathered round me and questioned me eagerly. They laughed, they cried, and they shouted. They thanked God that I had got away from my persecutors and was safe on Long Island. It was a day of great excitement. How different from the silent days I had passed in my dreary den!

The next morning was Sunday. My first waking thoughts were occupied with the note I was to send to Mrs. Hobbs, the lady with whom Ellen lived. That I had recently come into that vicinity was evident; otherwise I should have sooner inquired for my daughter. It would not do to let them know I had just arrived from the south, for that would involve the suspicion of my having been harbored there, and might bring trouble, if not ruin, on several people.

I like a straightforward course, and am always reluctant to resort to subterfuges. So far as my ways have been crooked, I charge them all upon slavery. It was that system of violence and wrong which now left me no alternative but to enact a falsehood. I began my note by stating that I had recently arrived from Canada, and was very desirous to have my daughter come to see me. She came and brought a message from Mrs. Hobbs, inviting me to her house, and assuring me that I need not have any fears. The conversation I had with my child did not leave my mind at ease. When I asked if she was well treated, she answered yes; but there was no heartiness in the tone, and it seemed to me that she said it from an unwillingness to have me troubled on her account. Before she left me, she asked very earnestly, "Mother, when will you take me to live with you?" It made me sad to think that I could not give her a home till I went to work and earned the means; and that might take me a long time. When she was placed with Mrs. Hobbs, the agreement was that she should be sent to school. She had been there two years, and was now nine years old, and she scarcely knew her letters. There was no excuse for this, for there were good public schools in Brooklyn, to which she could have been sent without expense.

She staid with me till dark, and I went home with her. I was received in a friendly manner by the family, and all agreed in saying that Ellen was a useful, good girl. Mrs. Hobbs looked me coolly in the face, and said, "I suppose you know that my cousin, Mr. Sands, has *given* her to my eldest daughter. She will make a nice waiting-maid for her when she grows up." I did not answer a word. How *could* she, who knew by experience the strength of a mother's love, and who was perfectly aware of the relation Mr. Sands bore to my children,—how *could* she look me in the face, while she thrust such a dagger into my heart?

I was no longer surprised that they had kept her in such a state of ignorance. Mr. Hobbs had formerly been wealthy, but he had failed, and afterwards obtained a subordinate situation in the Custom House. Perhaps they expected to return to the south some day; and Ellen's knowledge was quite sufficient for a slave's condition. I was impatient to go to work and earn money, that I might change the uncertain position of my children. Mr. Sands had not kept his promise to emancipate them. I had also been deceived about Ellen. What security had I with regard to Benjamin? I felt that I had none.

I returned to my friend's house in an uneasy state of mind. In order to protect my children, it was necessary that I should own myself. I called myself free, and sometimes felt so; but I knew I was insecure. I sat down that night and wrote a civil letter to Dr. Flint, asking him to state the lowest terms on which he would sell me; and as I belonged by law to his daughter, I wrote to her also, making a similar request.

Since my arrival at the north I had not been unmindful of my dear brother William. I had made diligent inquiries for him, and having heard of him in Boston, I went thither. When I arrived there, I found he had gone to New Bedford. I wrote to that place, and was informed he had gone on a whaling voyage, and would not return for some months. I went back to New York to get employment near Ellen. I received an answer from Dr. Flint, which gave me no encouragement. He advised me to return and submit myself to my rightful owners, and then any request I might make would be granted. I lent this letter to a friend, who lost it; otherwise I would present a copy to my readers.

XXXIII.

A HOME FOUND.

My greatest anxiety now was to obtain employment. My health was greatly improved, though my limbs continued to trouble me with swelling whenever I walked much. The greatest difficulty in my way was, that those who employed strangers required a recommendation; and in my peculiar position, I could, of course, obtain no certificates from the families I had so faithfully served.

One day an acquaintance told me of a lady[82] who wanted a nurse for her babe, and I immediately applied for the situation. The lady told me she preferred to have one who had been a mother, and accustomed to the care of infants. I told her I had nursed two babes of my own. She asked me many questions, but, to my great relief, did not require a recommendation from my former employers. She told me she was an English woman, and that was a pleasant circumstance to me, because I had heard they had less prejudice against color than Americans entertained. It was agreed that we should try each other for a week. The trial proved satisfactory to both parties, and I was engaged for a month.

The heavenly Father had been most merciful to me in leading me to this place. Mrs. Bruce was a kind and gentle lady, and proved a true and sympathizing friend. Before the stipulated month expired, the necessity of passing up and down stairs frequently, caused my limbs to swell so painfully, that I became unable to perform my duties. Many ladies would have thoughtlessly discharged me; but Mrs. Bruce made arrangements to save me steps, and employed a physician to attend upon me. I had not yet told her that I was a fugitive slave. She noticed that I was often sad, and kindly inquired the cause. I spoke of being separated from my children, and from relatives who were dear to me; but I did not mention the constant feeling of insecurity which oppressed my spirits. I longed for some one to confide in; but I had been so deceived by white people, that I had lost all confidence in them. If they spoke kind words to me, I thought it was for some selfish purpose. I had entered this family with the distrustful feelings I had brought with me out of slavery; but ere six months had passed, I found that the gentle deportment of Mrs. Bruce and the smiles of her lovely babe were thawing my chilled heart. My narrow mind also began to expand under the influences of her intelligent conversation, and the opportunities for reading, which were gladly allowed me whenever I had leisure from my duties. I gradually became more energetic and more cheerful.

The old feeling of insecurity, especially with regard to my children, often threw its dark shadow across my sunshine. Mrs. Bruce offered me a home for Ellen; but pleasant as it would have been, I did not dare to accept it, for fear of offending the Hobbs family. Their knowledge of my precarious situation placed me in their power; and I felt that it was important for me to keep on the right side of them, till, by dint of labor and economy, I could make a home for my children. I was far from feeling satisfied with Ellen's situation. She was not well cared for. She sometimes came to New York to visit me; but she generally brought a request from Mrs. Hobbs that I would buy her a pair of shoes, or some article of clothing. This was accompanied by a promise of payment when Mr. Hobbs's salary at the Custom House became due; but some how or other the pay-day never came. Thus many dollars of my earnings were expended to keep my child comfortably clothed. That, however, was a slight trouble, compared with the fear that their pecuniary embarrassments might induce them to sell my precious young daughter. I knew they were in constant communication with

Southerners, and had frequent opportunities to do it. I have stated that when Dr. Flint put Ellen in jail, at two years old, she had an inflammation of the eyes, occasioned by measles. This disease still troubled her; and kind Mrs. Bruce proposed that she should come to New York for a while, to be under the care of Dr. Elliott, a well known oculist. It did not occur to me that there was any thing improper in a mother's making such a request; but Mrs. Hobbs was very angry, and refused to let her go. Situated as I was, it was not politic to insist upon it. I made no complaint, but I longed to be entirely free to act a mother's part towards my children. The next time I went over to Brooklyn, Mrs. Hobbs, as if to apologize for her anger, told me she had employed her own physician to attend to Ellen's eyes, and that she had refused my request because she did not consider it safe to trust her in New York. I accepted the explanation in silence; but she had told me that my child *belonged* to her daughter, and I suspected that her real motive was a fear of my conveying her property away from her. Perhaps I did her injustice; but my knowledge of Southerners made it difficult for me to feel otherwise.

Sweet and bitter were mixed in the cup of my life, and I was thankful that it had ceased to be entirely bitter. I loved Mrs. Bruce's babe. When it laughed and crowed in my face, and twined its little tender arms confidingly about my neck, it made me think of the time when Benny and Ellen were babies, and my wounded heart was soothed. One bright morning, as I stood at the window, tossing baby in my arms, my attention was attracted by a young man in sailor's dress, who was closely observing every house as he passed. I looked at him earnestly. Could it be my brother William? It *must* be he—and yet, how changed![83] I placed the baby safely, flew down stairs, opened the front door, beckoned to the sailor, and in less than a minute I was clasped in my brother's arms. How much we had to tell each other ! How we laughed, and how we cried, over each other's adventures! I took him to Brooklyn, and again saw him with Ellen, the dear child whom he had loved and tended so carefully, while I was shut up in my miserable den. He staid in New York a week. His old feelings of affection for me and Ellen were as lively as ever. There are no bonds so strong as those which are formed by suffering together.

XXXIV.

THE OLD ENEMY AGAIN.

MY young mistress, Miss Emily Flint, did not return any answer to my letter requesting her to consent to my being sold. But after a while, I received a reply, which purported to be written by her younger brother. In order rightly to enjoy the contents of this letter, the reader must bear in mind that the Flint family supposed I had been at the north many years. They had no idea that I knew of the doctor's three excursions to New York in search of me; that I had heard his voice, when he came to borrow five hundred dollars for that purpose; and that I had seen him pass on his way to the steamboat. Neither were they aware that all the particulars of aunt Nancy's death and burial were conveyed to me at the time they occurred. I have kept the letter, of which I herewith subjoin a copy:—

"Your letter to sister was received a few days ago. I gather from it that you are desirous of returning to your native place, among your friends and relatives. We were all gratified with the contents of your letter; and let me assure you that if any members of the family have had any feeling of resentment towards you, they feel it no longer. We all sympathize with you in your unfortunate condition, and are ready to do all in our power to make you contented and happy. It is difficult for you to return home as a free person. If you were purchased by your grandmother, it is doubtful whether you would be permitted to remain, although it would be lawful for you to do so. If a servant should be allowed to purchase herself, after absenting herself so long from her owners, and return free, it would have an injurious effect. From your letter, I think your situation must be hard and uncomfortable. Come home. You have it in your power to be reinstated in our affections. We would receive you with open arms and tears of joy. You need not apprehend any unkind treatment, as we have not put ourselves to any trouble or expense to get you. Had we done so, perhaps we should feel otherwise. You know my sister was always attached to you, and that you were never treated as a slave. You were never put to hard work, nor exposed to field labor. On the contrary, you were taken into the house, and treated as one of us, and almost as free; and we, at least, felt that you were above disgracing yourself by running away. Believing you may be induced to come home voluntarily has induced me to write for my sister. The family will be rejoiced to see you; and your poor old grandmother expressed a great desire to have you come, when she heard your letter read. In her old age she needs the consolation of having her children round her. Doubtless you have heard of the death of your aunt. She was a faithful servant, and a faithful member of the Episcopal church. In her Christian life she taught us how to live—and, O, too high the price of knowledge, she taught us how to die! Could you have seen us round her death bed, with her mother, all mingling our tears in one common stream, you would have thought the same heartfelt tie existed between a master and his servant, as between a mother and her child. But this subject is too painful to dwell upon. I must bring my letter to a close. If you are contented to stay away from your old grandmother, your child, and the friends who love you, stay where you are. We shall never trouble ourselves to apprehend you. But should you prefer to come home, we will do all that we can to make you happy. If you do not wish to remain in the family, I know that father, by our persuasion, will be induced to let you be purchased by any person you may choose in our community. You will please answer this as soon as possible, and let us know your decision. Sister sends much love to you. In the mean time believe me your sincere friend and well wisher."

This letter was signed by Emily's brother, who was as yet a mere lad. I knew, by the style, that it was not written by a person of his age, and though the writing was disguised, I had been made too unhappy by it, in former years, not to recognize at once the hand of Dr. Flint. O, the hypocrisy of slaveholders! Did the old fox suppose I was goose enough to go into such a trap? Verily, he relied too much on "the stupidity of the African race." I did not return the family of

Flints any thanks for their cordial invitation—a remissness for which I was, no doubt, charged with base ingratitude.

Not long afterwards I received a letter from one of my friends at the south, informing me that Dr. Flint was about to visit the north. The letter had been delayed, and I supposed he might be already on the way. Mrs. Bruce did not know I was a fugitive. I told her that important business called me to Boston, where my brother then was, and asked permission to bring a friend to supply my place as nurse, for a fortnight. I started on my journey immediately; and as soon as I arrived, I wrote to my grandmother that if Benny came, he must be sent to Boston. I knew she was only waiting for a good chance to send him north, and, fortunately, she had the legal power to do so, without asking leave of any body. She was a free woman; and when my children were purchased, Mr. Sands preferred to have the bill of sale drawn up in her name. It was conjectured that he advanced the money, but it was not known. At the south, a gentleman may have a shoal of colored children without any disgrace; but if he is known to purchase them, with the view of setting them free, the example is thought to be dangerous to their "peculiar institution," and he becomes unpopular.

There was a good opportunity to send Benny in a vessel coming directly to New York. He was put on board with a letter to a friend, who was requested to see him off to Boston. Early one morning, there was a loud rap at my door, and in rushed Benjamin, all out of breath. "O mother!" he exclaimed, "here I am! I run all the way; and I come all alone. How d'you do?"

O reader, can you imagine my joy? No, you cannot, unless you have been a slave mother. Benjamin rattled away as fast as his tongue could go. "Mother, why don't you bring Ellen here? I went over to Brooklyn to see her, and she felt very bad when I bid her good by. She said, 'O Ben, I wish I was going too.' I thought she'd know ever so much; but she don't know so much as I do; for I can read, and she can't. And, mother, I lost all my clothes coming. What can I do to get some more? I 'spose free boys can get along here at the north as well as white boys."

I did not like to tell the sanguine, happy little fellow how much he was mistaken. I took him to a tailor, and procured a change of clothes. The rest of the day was spent in mutual asking and answering of questions, with the wish constantly repeated that the good old grandmother was with us, and frequent injunctions from Benny to write to her immediately, and be sure to tell her every thing about his voyage, and his journey to Boston.

Dr. Flint made his visit to New York, and made every exertion to call upon me, and invite me to return with him; but not being able to ascertain where I was, his hospitable intentions were frustrated, and the affectionate family, who were waiting for me with "open arms," were doomed to disappointment.

As soon as I knew he was safely at home, I placed Benjamin in the care of my brother William, and returned to Mrs. Bruce. There I remained through the winter and spring, endeavoring to perform my duties faithfully, and finding a good degree of happiness in the attractions of baby Mary, the considerate kindness of her excellent mother, and occasional interviews with my darling daughter.

But when summer came, the old feeling of insecurity haunted me. It was necessary for me to take little Mary out daily, for exercise and fresh air, and the city was swarming with Southerners, some of whom might recognize me. Hot weather brings out snakes and slaveholders, and I like one class of the venomous creatures as little as I do the other. What a comfort it is, to be free to *say* so!

XXXV.

PREJUDICE AGAINST COLOR.

It was a relief to my mind to see preparations for leaving the city. We went to Albany in the steamboat Knickerbocker. When the gong sounded for tea, Mrs. Bruce said, "Linda, it is late, and you and baby had better come to the table with me." I replied, "I know it is time baby had her supper, but I had rather not go with you, if you please. I am afraid of being insulted." "O no, not if you are with *me*," she said. I saw several white nurses go with their ladies, and I ventured to do the same. We were at the extreme end of the table. I was no sooner seated, than a gruff voice said, "Get up! You know you are not allowed to sit here." I looked up, and, to my astonishment and indignation, saw that the speaker was a colored man. If his office required him to enforce the by-laws of the boat, he might, at least, have done it politely. I replied, "I shall not get up, unless the captain comes and takes me up." No cup of tea was offered me, but Mrs. Bruce handed me hers and called for another. I looked to see whether the other nurses were treated in a similar manner. They were all properly waited on.

Next morning, when we stopped at Troy for breakfast, every body was making a rush for the table. Mrs. Bruce said, "Take my arm, Linda, and we'll go in together." The landlord heard her, and said, "Madam, will you allow your nurse and baby to take breakfast with my family?" I knew this was to be attributed to my complexion; but he spoke courteously, and therefore I did not mind it.

At Saratoga we found the United States Hotel crowded, and Mr. Bruce took one of the cottages belonging to the hotel. I had thought, with gladness, of going to the quiet of the country, where I should meet few people, but here I found myself in the midst of a swarm of Southerners. I looked round me with fear and trembling, dreading to see some one who would recognize me. I was rejoiced to find that we were to stay but a short time.

We soon returned to New York, to make arrangements for spending the remainder of the summer at Rockaway. While the laundress was putting the clothes in order, I took an opportunity to go over to Brooklyn to see Ellen. I met her going to a grocery store, and the first words she said, were, "O, mother, don't go to Mrs. Hobbs's. Her brother, Mr. Thorne,[84] has come from the south, and may be he'll tell where you are." I accepted the warning. I told her I was going away with Mrs. Bruce the next day, and would try to see her when I came back.

Being in servitude to the Anglo-Saxon race, I was not put into a "Jim Crow car," on our way to Rockaway, neither was I invited to ride through the streets on the top of trunks in a truck; but every where I found the same manifestations of that cruel prejudice, which so discourages the feelings, and represses the energies of the colored people. We reached Rockaway before dark, and put up at the Pavilion—a large hotel, beautifully situated by the sea-side—a great resort of the fashionable world. Thirty or forty nurses were there, of a great variety of nations. Some of the ladies had colored waiting-maids and coachmen, but I was the only nurse tinged with the blood of Africa. When the tea bell rang, I took little Mary and followed the other nurses. Supper was served in a long hall. A young man, who had the ordering of things, took the circuit of the table two or three times, and finally pointed me to a seat at the lower end of it. As there was but one chair, I sat down and took the child in my lap. Whereupon the young man came to me and said, in the blandest manner possible, "Will you please to seat the little girl in the chair, and stand behind it and feed her? After they have done, you will be shown to the kitchen, where you will have a good supper."

This was the climax! I found it hard to preserve my self-control, when I looked round, and saw women who were nurses, as I was, and only one shade lighter in complexion, eyeing me with a defiant look, as if my presence were a contamination. However, I said nothing. I quietly took the child in my arms, went to our room, and refused to go to the table again. Mr. Bruce ordered meals to be sent to the room for little Mary and I. This answered for a few days; but the waiters of the establishment were white, and they soon began to complain, saying they were not hired to wait on negroes. The landlord requested Mr. Bruce to send me down to my meals, because his servants rebelled against bringing them up, and the colored servants of other boarders were dissatisfied because all were not treated alike.

My answer was that the colored servants ought to be dissatisfied with *themselves,* for not having too much self-respect to submit to such treatment; that there was no difference in the price of board for colored and white servants, and there was no justification for difference of treatment. I staid a month after this, and finding I was resolved to stand up for my rights, they concluded to treat me well. Let every colored man and woman do this, and eventually we shall cease to be trampled under foot by our oppressors.

XXXVI.

THE HAIRBREADTH ESCAPE.

AFTER we returned to New York, I took the earliest opportunity to go and see Ellen. I asked to have her called down stairs; for I supposed Mrs. Hobbs's southern brother might still be there, and I was desirous to avoid seeing him, if possible. But Mrs. Hobbs came to the kitchen, and insisted on my going up stairs. "My brother wants to see you," said she, "and he is sorry you seem to shun him. He knows you are living in New York. He told me to say to you that he owes thanks to good old aunt Martha for too many little acts of kindness for him to be base enough to betray her grandchild."

This Mr. Thorne had become poor and reckless long before he left the south, and such persons had much rather go to one of the faithful old slaves to borrow a dollar, or get a good dinner, than to go to one whom they consider an equal. It was such acts of kindness as these for which he professed to feel grateful to my grandmother. I wished he had kept at a distance, but as he was here, and knew where I was, I concluded there was nothing to be gained by trying to avoid him; on the contrary, it might be the means of exciting his ill will. I followed his sister up stairs. He met me in a very friendly manner, congratulated me on my escape from slavery, and hoped I had a good place, where I felt happy.

I continued to visit Ellen as often as I could. She, good thoughtful child, never forgot my hazardous situation, but always kept a vigilant lookout for my safety. She never made any complaint about her own inconveniences and troubles; but a mother's observing eye easily perceived that she was not happy. On the occasion of one of my visits I found her unusually serious. When I asked her what was the matter, she said nothing was the matter. But I insisted upon knowing what made her look so very grave. Finally, I ascertained that she felt troubled about the dissipation that was continually going on in the house. She was sent to the store very often for rum and brandy, and she felt ashamed to ask for it so often; and Mr. Hobbs and Mr. Thorne drank a great deal, and their hands trembled so that they had to call her to pour out the liquor for them. "But for all that," said she, "Mr. Hobbs is good to me, and I can't help liking him. I feel sorry for him." I tried to comfort her, by telling her that I had laid up a hundred dollars, and that before long I hoped to be able to give her and Benjamin a home, and send them to school. She was always desirous not to add to my troubles more than she could help, and I did not discover till years afterwards that Mr. Thorne's intemperance was not the only annoyance she suffered from him. Though he professed too much gratitude to my grandmother to injure any of her descendants, he had poured vile language into the ears of her innocent great-grandchild.

I usually went to Brooklyn to spend Sunday afternoon. One Sunday, I found Ellen anxiously waiting for me near the house. "O, mother," said she, "I've been waiting for you this long time. I'm afraid Mr. Thorne has written to tell Dr. Flint where you are. Make haste and come in. Mrs. Hobbs will tell you all about it!"

The story was soon told. While the children were playing in the grape-vine arbor, the day before, Mr. Thorne came out with a letter in his hand, which he tore up and scattered about. Ellen was sweeping the yard at the time, and having her mind full of suspicions of him, she picked up the pieces and carried them to the children, saying, "I wonder who Mr. Thorne has been writing to."

"I'm sure I don't know, and don't care," replied the oldest of the children; "and I don't see how it concerns you."

"But it does concern me," replied Ellen; "for I'm afraid he's been writing to the south about my mother."

They laughed at her, and called her a silly thing, but good-naturedly put the fragments of writing together, in order to read them to her. They were no sooner arranged, than the little girl exclaimed, "I declare, Ellen, I believe you are right."

The contents of Mr. Thorne's letter, as nearly as I can remember, were as follows: "I have seen your slave, Linda, and conversed with her. She can be taken very easily, if you manage prudently. There are enough of us here to swear to her identity as your property. I am a patriot, a lover of my country, and I do this as an act of justice to the laws." He concluded by informing the doctor of the street and number where I lived. The children carried the pieces to Mrs. Hobbs, who immediately went to her brother's room for an explanation. He was not to be found. The servants said they saw him go out with a letter in his hand, and they supposed he had gone to the post office. The natural inference was, that he had sent to Dr. Flint a copy of those fragments. When he returned, his sister accused him of it, and he did not deny the charge. He went immediately to his room, and the next morning he was missing. He had gone over to New York, before any of the family were astir.

It was evident that I had no time to lose; and I hastened back to the city with a heavy heart. Again I was to be torn from a comfortable home, and all my plans for the welfare of my children were to be frustrated by that demon Slavery! I now regretted that I never told Mrs. Bruce my story. I had not concealed it merely on account of being a fugitive; that would have made her anxious, but it would have excited sympathy in her kind heart. I valued her good opinion, and I was afraid of losing it, if I told her all the particulars of my sad story. But now I felt that it was necessary for her to know how I was situated. I had once left her abruptly, without explaining the reason, and it would not be proper to do it again. I went home resolved to tell her in the morning. But the sadness of my face attracted her attention, and, in answer to her kind inquiries, I poured out my full heart to her, before bed time. She listened with true womanly sympathy, and told me she would do all she could to protect me. How my heart blessed her!

Early the next morning, Judge Vanderpool and Lawyer Hopper[85] were consulted. They said I had better leave the city at once, as the risk would be great if the case came to trial. Mrs. Bruce took me in a carriage to the house of one of her friends, where she assured me I should be safe until my brother could arrive, which would be in a few days. In the interval my thoughts were much occupied with Ellen. She was mine by birth, and she was also mine by Southern law, since my grandmother held the bill of sale that made her so. I did not feel that she was safe unless I had her with me. Mrs. Hobbs, who felt badly about her brother's treachery, yielded to my entreaties, on condition that she should return in ten days. I avoided making any promise. She came to me clad in very thin garments, all outgrown, and with a school satchel on her arm, containing a few articles. It was late in October, and I knew the child must suffer; and not daring to go out in the streets to purchase any thing, I took off my own flannel skirt and converted it into one for her. Kind Mrs. Bruce came to bid me good by, and when she saw that I had taken off my clothing for my child, the tears came to her eyes. She said, "Wait for me, Linda," and went out. She soon returned with a nice warm shawl and hood for Ellen. Truly, of such souls as hers are the kingdom of heaven.

My brother reached New York on Wednesday. Lawyer Hopper advised us to go to Boston by the Stonington route, as there was less Southern travel in that direction. Mrs. Bruce directed her servants to tell all inquirers that I formerly lived there, but had gone from the city.

We reached the steamboat Rhode Island in safety. That boat employed colored hands, but I knew that colored passengers were not admitted to the cabin. I was very desirous for the seclusion of the cabin, not only on account of exposure to the night air, but also to avoid observation. Lawyer Hopper was waiting on board for us. He spoke to the stewardess, and asked, as a particular favor, that she would treat us well. He said to me, "Go and speak to the captain yourself by and by. Take your little girl with you, and I am sure that he will not let her sleep on deck." With these kind words and a shake of the hand he departed.

The boat was soon on her way, bearing me rapidly from the friendly home where I had hoped to find security and rest. My brother had left me to purchase the tickets, thinking that I might have better success than he would. When the stewardess came to me, I paid what she asked, and she gave me three tickets with clipped corners. In the most unsophisticated manner I said, "You have made a mistake; I asked you for cabin tickets. I cannot possibly consent to sleep on deck with my little daughter." She assured me there was no mistake. She said on some of the routes colored people were allowed to sleep in the cabin, but not on this route, which was much travelled by the wealthy. I asked her to show me to the captain's office, and she said she would after tea. When the time came, I took Ellen by the hand and went to the captain, politely requesting him to change our tickets, as we should be very uncomfortable on deck. He said it was contrary to their custom, but he would see that we had berths below; he would also try to obtain comfortable seats for us in the cars; of that he was not certain, but he would speak to the conductor about it, when the boat arrived. I thanked him, and returned to the ladies' cabin. He came afterwards and told me that the conductor of the cars was on board, that he had spoken to him, and he had promised to take care of us. I was very much surprised at receiving so much kindness. I don't know whether the pleasing face of my little girl had won his heart, or whether the stewardess inferred from Lawyer Hopper's manner that I was a fugitive, and had pleaded with him in my behalf.

When the boat arrived at Stonington, the conductor kept his promise, and showed us to seats in the first car, nearest the engine. He asked us to take seats next the door, but as he passed through, we ventured to move on toward the other end of the car. No incivility was offered us, and we reached Boston in safety.

The day after my arrival was one of the happiest of my life. I felt as if I was beyond the reach of the bloodhounds; and, for the first time during many years, I had both my children together with me. They greatly enjoyed their reunion, and laughed and chatted merrily. I watched them with a swelling heart. Their every motion delighted me.

I could not feel safe in New York, and I accepted the offer of a friend, that we should share expenses and keep house together. I represented to Mrs. Hobbs that Ellen must have some schooling, and must remain with me for that purpose. She felt ashamed of being unable to read or spell at her age, so instead of sending her to school with Benny, I instructed her myself till she was fitted to enter an intermediate school. The winter passed pleasantly, while I was busy with my needle, and my children with their books.

XXXVII.

A VISIT TO ENGLAND.

IN the spring, sad news came to me. Mrs. Bruce was dead. Never again, in this world, should I see her gentle face, or hear her sympathizing voice. I had lost an excellent friend, and little Mary had lost a tender mother. Mr. Bruce wished the child to visit some of her mother's relatives in England, and he was desirous that I should take charge of her. The little motherless one was accustomed to me, and attached to me, and I thought she would be happier in my care than in that of a stranger. I could also earn more in this way than I could by my needle. So I put Benny to a trade, and left Ellen to remain in the house with my friend and go to school.

We sailed from New York, and arrived in Liverpool after a pleasant voyage of twelve days. We proceeded directly to London, and took lodgings at the Adelaide Hotel. The supper seemed to me less luxurious than those I had seen in American hotels; but my situation was indescribably more pleasant. For the first time in my life I was in a place where I was treated according to my deportment, without reference to my complexion. I felt as if a great millstone had been lifted from my breast. Ensconced in a pleasant room, with my dear little charge, I laid my head on my pillow, for the first time, with the delightful consciousness of pure, unadulterated freedom.

As I had constant care of the child, I had little opportunity to see the wonders of that great city; but I watched the tide of life that flowed through the streets, and found it a strange contrast to the stagnation in our Southern towns. Mr. Bruce took his little daughter to spend some days with friends in Oxford Crescent, and of course it was necessary for me to accompany her. I had heard much of the systematic method of English education, and I was very desirous that my dear Mary should steer straight in the midst of so much propriety. I closely observed her little playmates and their nurses, being ready to take any lessons in the science of good management. The children were more rosy than American children, but I did not see that they differed materially in other respects. They were like all children—sometimes docile and sometimes wayward.

We next went to Steventon, in Berkshire. It was a small town, said to be the poorest in the county. I saw men working in the fields for six shillings, and seven shillings, a week, and women for sixpence, and seven-pence, a day, out of which they boarded themselves. Of course they lived in the most primitive manner; it could not be otherwise, where a woman's wages for an entire day were not sufficient to buy a pound of meat. They paid very low rents, and their clothes were made of the cheapest fabrics, though much better than could have been procured in the United States for the same money. I had heard much about the oppression of the poor in Europe. The people I saw around me were, many of them, among the poorest poor. But when I visited them in their little thatched cottages, I felt that the condition of even the meanest and most ignorant among them was vastly superior to the condition of the most favored slaves in America. They labored hard; but they were not ordered out to toil while the stars were in the sky, and driven and slashed by an overseer, through heat and cold, till the stars shone out again. Their homes were very humble; but they were protected by law. No insolent patrols could come, in the dead of night, and flog them at their pleasure. The father, when he closed his cottage door, felt safe with his family around him. No master or overseer could come and take from him his wife, or his daughter. They must separate to earn their living; but the parents knew where their children were going, and could communicate with them by letters. The relations of husband and wife, parent and child, were too sacred for the richest noble in the land to violate with impunity. Much was being done to enlighten these poor people. Schools were established among them, and benevolent societies were active in efforts to ameliorate their condition. There was no law forbidding them to learn to read and write; and if they helped each other in spelling out the Bible, they were in no danger of thirty-nine lashes, as was the case with myself and poor, pious, old uncle Fred. I repeat that the most ignorant and the most destitute of these peasants was a thousand fold better off than the most pampered American slave.

I do not deny that the poor are oppressed in Europe. I am not disposed to paint their condition so rose-colored as the Hon. Miss Murray paints the condition of the slaves in the United States.[86] A small portion of *my* experience would enable her to read her own pages with anointed eyes. If she were to lay aside her title, and, instead of visiting among the fashionable, become domesticated, as a poor governess, on some plantation in Louisiana or Alabama, she would see and hear things that would make her tell quite a different story.

My visit to England is a memorable event in my life, from the fact of my having there received strong religious impressions. The contemptuous manner in which the communion had been administered to colored people, in my native place; the church membership of Dr. Flint, and others like him; and the buying and selling of slaves, by professed ministers of the gospel, had given me a prejudice against the Episcopal church. The whole service seemed to me a mockery and a sham. But my home in Steventon was in the family of a clergyman, who was a true disciple of Jesus. The beauty of his daily life inspired me with faith in the genuineness of Christian professions. Grace entered my heart, and I knelt at the communion table, I trust, in true humility of soul.

I remained abroad ten months, which was much longer than I had anticipated. During all that time, I never saw the slightest symptom of prejudice against color. Indeed, I entirely forgot it, till the time came for us to return to America.

XXXVIII.

RENEWED INVITATIONS TO GO SOUTH.

WE had a tedious winter passage, and from the distance spectres seemed to rise up on the shores of the United States. It is a sad feeling to be afraid of one's native country. We arrived in New York safely, and I hastened to Boston to look after my children. I found Ellen well, and improving at her school; but Benny was not there to welcome me. He had been left at a good place to learn a trade, and for several months every thing worked well. He was liked by the master, and was a favorite with his fellow-apprentices; but one day they accidentally discovered a fact they had never before suspected—that he was colored! This at once transformed him into a different being. Some of the apprentices were Americans, others American-born Irish; and it was offensive to their dignity to have a "nigger" among them, after they had been told that he *was* a "nigger." They began by treating him with silent scorn, and finding that he returned the same, they resorted to insults and abuse. He was too spirited a boy to stand that, and he went off. Being desirous to do something to support himself, and having no one to advise him, he shipped for a whaling voyage. When I received these tidings I shed many tears, and bitterly reproached myself for having left him so long. But I had done it for the best, and now all I could do was to pray to the heavenly Father to guide and protect him.

Not long after my return, I received the following letter from Miss Emily Flint, now Mrs. Dodge:[87]—

"In this you will recognize the hand of your friend and mistress. Having heard that you had gone with a family to Europe, I have waited to hear of your return to write to you. I should have answered the letter you wrote to me long since, but as I could not then act independently of my father, I knew there could be nothing done satisfactory to you. There were persons here who were willing to buy you and run the risk of getting you. To this I would not consent. I have always been attached to you, and would not like to see you the slave of another, or have unkind treatment. I am married now, and can protect you. My husband expects to move to Virginia this spring, where we think of settling. I am very anxious that you should come and live with me. If you are not willing to come, you may purchase yourself; but I should prefer having you live with me. If you come, you may, if you like, spend a month with your grandmother and friends, then come to me in Norfolk, Virginia. Think this over, and write as soon as possible, and let me know the conclusion. Hoping that your children are well, I remain you friend and mistress."

Of course I did not write to return thanks for this cordial invitation. I felt insulted to be thought stupid enough to be caught by such professions.

> " 'Come up into my parlor,' said the spider to the fly;
> ''Tis the prettiest little parlor that ever you did spy.' "[88]

It was plain that Dr. Flint's family were apprised of my movements, since they knew of my voyage to Europe. I expected to have further trouble from them; but having eluded them thus far, I hoped to be as successful in future. The money I had earned, I was desirous to devote to the education of my children, and to secure a home for them. It seemed not only hard, but unjust, to pay for myself. I could not possibly regard myself as a piece of property. Moreover, I had worked many years without wages, and during that time had been obliged to depend on my grandmother for many comforts in food and clothing. My children certainly belonged to me; but though Dr. Flint had incurred no expense for their support, he had received a large sum of money for them. I knew the law would decide that

I was his property, and would probably still give his daughter a claim to my children; but I regarded such laws as the regulations of robbers, who had no rights that I was bound to respect.

The Fugitive Slave Law had not then passed. The judges of Massachusetts had not then stooped under chains to enter her courts of justice, so called. I knew my old master was rather skittish of Massachusetts. I relied on her love of freedom, and felt safe on her soil. I am now aware that I honored the old Commonwealth beyond her deserts.

XXXIX.

THE CONFESSION.

FOR two years my daughter and I supported ourselves comfortably in Boston. At the end of that time, my brother William offered to send Ellen to a boarding school. It required a great effort for me to consent to part with her, for I had few near ties, and it was her presence that made my two little rooms seem home-like. But my judgment prevailed over my selfish feelings. I made preparations for her departure. During the two years we had lived together I had often resolved to tell her something about her father; but I had never been able to muster sufficient courage. I had a shrinking dread of diminishing my child's love. I knew she must have curiosity on the subject, but she had never asked a question. She was always very careful not to say any thing to remind me of my troubles. Now that she was going from me, I thought if I should die before she returned, she might hear my story from some one who did not understand the palliating circumstances; and that if she were entirely ignorant on the subject, her sensitive nature might receive a rude shock.

When we retired for the night, she said, "Mother, it is very hard to leave you alone. I am almost sorry I am going, though I do want to improve myself. But you will write to me often; won't you, mother?"

I did not throw my arms round her. I did not answer her. But in a calm, solemn way, for it cost me great effort, I said, "Listen to me, Ellen; I have something to tell you!" I recounted my early sufferings in slavery, and told her how nearly they had crushed me. I began to tell her how they had driven me into a great sin, when she clasped me in her arms, and exclaimed, "O, don't, mother! Please don't tell me any more."

I said, "But, my child, I want you to know about your father."

"I know all about it, mother," she replied; "I am nothing to my father, and he is nothing to me. All my love is for you. I was with him five months in Washington, and he never cared for me. He never spoke to me as he did to his little Fanny. I knew all the time he was my father, for Fanny's nurse told me so; but she said I must never tell any body, and I never did. I used to wish he would take me in his arms and kiss me, as he did Fanny; or that he would sometimes smile at me, as he did at her. I thought if he was my own father, he ought to love me.

I was a little girl then, and didn't know any better. But now I never think any thing about my father. All my love is for you." She hugged me closer as she spoke, and I thanked God that the knowledge I had so much dreaded to impart had not diminished the affection of my child. I had not the slightest idea she knew that portion of my history. If I had, I should have spoken to her long before; for my pent-up feelings had often longed to pour themselves out to some one I could trust. But I loved the dear girl better for the delicacy she had manifested towards her unfortunate mother.

The next morning, she and her uncle started on their journey to the village in New York, where she was to be placed at school.[89] It seemed as if all the sunshine had gone away. My little room was dreadfully lonely. I was thankful when a message came from a lady, accustomed to employ me, requesting me to come and sew in her family for several weeks. On my return, I found a letter from brother William. He thought of opening an anti-slavery reading room in Rochester, and combining with it the sale of some books and stationery; and he wanted me to unite with him. We tried it, but it was not successful. We found warm anti-slavery friends there, but the feeling was not general enough to support such an establishment.[90] I passed nearly a year in the family of Isaac and Amy Post,[91] practical believers in the Christian doctrine of human brotherhood. They measured a man's worth by his character, not by his complexion. The memory of those beloved and honored friends will remain with me to my latest hour.

XL.

THE FUGITIVE SLAVE LAW.

MY brother, being disappointed in his project, concluded to go to California; and it was agreed that Benjamin should go with him. Ellen liked her school, and was a great favorite there. They did not know her history, and she did not tell it, because she had no desire to make capital out of their sympathy. But when it was accidently discovered that her mother was a fugitive slave, every method was used to increase her advantages and diminish her expenses.

I was alone again. It was necessary for me to be earning money, and I preferred that it should be among those who knew me. On my return from Rochester, I called at the house of Mr. Bruce, to see Mary, the darling little babe that had thawed my heart, when it was freezing into a cheerless distrust of all my fellow-beings. She was growing a tall girl now, but I loved her always. Mr. Bruce had married again, and it was proposed that I should become nurse to a new infant.[92] I had but one hesitation, and that was my feeling of insecurity in New York, now greatly increased by the passage of the Fugitive Slave Law. However, I resolved to try the experiment. I was again fortunate in my employer. The new Mrs. Bruce was an American, brought up under aristocratic influences, and still living in the midst of them; but if she had any prejudice against color, I was never made aware of it; and as for the system of slavery, she had a most hearty dislike of it. No sophistry of Southerners could blind her to its enormity. She was a person of excellent principles and a noble heart. To me, from that hour to the present, she has been a true and sympathizing friend. Blessings be with her and hers!

About the time that I reëntered the Bruce family, an event occurred of disastrous import to the colored people. The slave Hamlin, the first fugitive that came under the new law, was given up by the bloodhounds of the north to the bloodhounds of the south.[93] It was the beginning of a reign of terror to the colored population. The great city rushed on in its whirl of excitement, taking no note of the "short and simple annals of the poor." But while fashionables were listening to the thrilling voice of Jenny Lind[94] in Metropolitan Hall, the thrilling voices of poor hunted colored people went up, in an agony of supplication, to the Lord, from Zion's church.[95] Many families, who had lived in the city for twenty years, fled from it now. Many a poor washerwoman, who, by hard labor, had made herself a comfortable home, was obliged to sacrifice her furniture, bid a hurried farewell to friends, and seek her fortune among strangers in Canada. Many a wife discovered a secret she had never known before—that her husband was a fugitive, and must leave her to insure his own safety. Worse still, many a husband discovered that his wife had fled from slavery years ago, and as "the child follows the condition of its mother," the children of his love were liable to be seized and carried into slavery. Every where, in those humble homes, there was consternation and anguish. But what cared the legislators of the "dominant race" for the blood they were crushing out of trampled hearts?

When my brother William spent his last evening with me, before he went to California, we talked nearly all the time of the distress brought on our oppressed people by the passage of this iniquitous law; and never had I seen him manifest such bitterness of spirit, such stern hostility to our oppressors. He was himself free from the operation of the law; for he did not run from any Slaveholding State, being brought into the Free States by his master. But I was subject to it; and so were hundreds of intelligent and industrious people all around us. I seldom ventured into the streets; and when it was necessary to do an errand for Mrs. Bruce, or any of the family, I went as much as possible through back streets and by-ways. What a disgrace to a city calling itself free, that inhabitants, guiltless of offence, and seeking to perform their duties conscientiously, should be condemned to live in such incessant fear, and have nowhere to turn for protection! This state of things, of course, gave rise to many impromptu vigilance committees. Every colored person, and every friend of their persecuted race, kept their eyes wide open. Every evening I examined the newspapers carefully, to see what Southerners had put up at the hotels. I did this for my own sake, thinking my young mistress and her husband might be among the list; I wished also to give information to others, if necessary; for if many were "running to and fro," I resolved that "knowledge should be increased."[96]

This brings up one of my Southern reminiscences, which I will here briefly relate. I was somewhat acquainted with a slave named Luke, who belonged to a wealthy man in our vicinity. His master died, leaving a son and daughter heirs to his large fortune. In the division of the slaves, Luke was included in the son's portion. This young man became a prey to the vices growing out of the "patriarchal institution," and when he went to the north, to complete his education, he carried his vices with him. He was brought home, deprived of the use of his limbs, by excessive dissipation. Luke was appointed to wait upon his bed-ridden master, whose despotic habits were greatly increased by exasperation at his own helplessness. He kept a cowhide beside him, and, for the most trivial occurrence, he would order his attendant to bare his back, and kneel beside the couch, while he whipped him till his strength was exhausted. Some days he was not allowed to wear any thing but his shirt, in order to be in readiness to be flogged. A day seldom passed with out his receiving more or less blows. If the slightest resistance was offered, the town constable was sent for to execute the punishment, and Luke learned from experience how much more the constable's strong arm was to be dreaded than the comparatively feeble one of his master. The arm of his tyrant grew weaker, and was finally palsied; and then the constable's services were in constant requisition. The fact that he was entirely dependent on Luke's care, and was obliged to be tended like an infant, instead of inspiring any gratitude or compassion towards his poor slave, seemed only to increase his irritability and cruelty. As he lay there on his bed, a mere degraded wreck of manhood, he took into his head the strangest freaks of despotism; and if Luke hesitated to submit to his orders, the constable was immediately sent for. Some of these freaks were of a nature too filthy to be repeated. When I fled from the house of bondage, I left poor Luke still chained to the bedside of this cruel and disgusting wretch.

One day, when I had been requested to do an errand for Mrs. Bruce, I was hurrying through back streets, as usual, when I saw a young man approaching, whose face was familiar to me. As he came nearer, I recognized Luke. I always rejoiced to see or hear of any one who had escaped from the black pit; but, remembering this poor fellow's extreme hardships, I was peculiarly glad to see him on Northern soil, though I no longer called it *free* soil. I well remembered what a desolate feeling it was to be alone among strangers, and I went up to him and greeted him cordially. At first, he did not know me; but when I mentioned my name, he remembered all about me. I told him of the Fugitive Slave Law, and asked him if he did not know that New York was a city of kidnappers.

He replied, "De risk ain't so bad for me, as 'tis fur you. 'Cause I runned away from de speculator, and you runned away from de massa. Dem speculators vont spen dar money to come here fur a runaway, if dey ain't sartin sure to put dar hans right on him. An I tell you I's tuk good car 'bout dat. I had too hard times down dar, to let 'em ketch dis nigger."

He then told me of the advice he had received, and the plans he had laid. I asked if he had money enough to take him to Canada. "'Pend upon it, I hab," he replied. "I tuk car fur dat. I'd bin workin all my days fur dem cussed whites, an got no pay but kicks and cuffs. So I tought dis nigger had a right to money nuff to bring him to de Free States. Massa Henry he lib till ebery body vish him dead; an ven he did die, I knowed de debbil would had him, an vouldn't vant him to bring his money 'long too. So I tuk some of his bills, and put 'em in de pocket of his ole trousers. An ven he was buried, dis nigger ask fur dem ole trousers, an dey gub 'em to me." With a low, chuckling laugh, he added, "You see I didn't *steal* it; dey *gub* it to me. I tell you, I had mighty hard time to keep de speculator from findin it; but he didn't git it."

This is a fair specimen of how the moral sense is educated by slavery. When a man has his wages stolen from him, year after year, and the laws sanction and enforce the theft, how can he be expected to have more regard to honesty than has the man who robs him? I have become somewhat enlightened, but I confess that I agree with poor, ignorant, much-abused Luke, in thinking he had a *right* to that money, as a portion of his unpaid wages. He went to Canada forthwith, and I have not since heard from him.

All that winter I lived in a state of anxiety. When I took the children out to breathe the air, I closely observed the countenances of all I met. I dreaded the approach of summer, when snakes and slaveholders make their appearance. I was, in fact, a slave in New York, as subject to slave laws as I had been in a Slave State. Strange incongruity in a State called free!

Spring returned, and I received warning from the south that Dr. Flint knew of my return to my old place, and was making preparations to have me caught. I learned afterwards that my dress, and that of Mrs. Bruce's children, had been described to him by some of the Northern tools, which slaveholders employ for their base purposes, and then indulge in sneers at their cupidity and mean servility.

I immediately informed Mrs. Bruce of my danger, and she took prompt measures for my safety. My place as nurse could not be supplied immediately, and this generous, sympathizing lady proposed that I should carry her baby[97] away. It was a comfort to me to have the child with me; for the heart is reluctant to be torn away from every object it loves. But how few mothers would have consented to have one of their own babes become a fugitive, for the sake of a poor, hunted nurse, on whom the legislators of the country had let loose the bloodhounds! When I spoke of the sacrifice she was making, in depriving herself of her dear baby, she replied, "It is better for you to have baby with you, Linda; for if they get on your track, they will be obliged to bring the child to me; and then, if there is a possibility of saving you, you shall be saved."

This lady had a very wealthy relative, a benevolent gentleman in many respects, but aristocratic and pro-slavery. He remonstrated with her for harboring a fugitive slave; told her she was violating the laws of her country; and asked her if she was aware of the penalty. She replied, "I am very well aware of it. It is imprisonment and one thousand dollars fine. Shame on my country that it *is* so! I am ready to incur the penalty. I will go to the state's prison, rather than have any poor victim torn from my house, to be carried back to slavery."

The noble heart! The brave heart! The tears are in my eyes while I write of her. May the God of the helpless reward her for her sympathy with my persecuted people!

I was sent into New England, where I was sheltered by the wife of a senator, whom I shall always hold in grateful remembrance. This honorable gentleman would not have voted for the Fugitive Slave Law, as did the senator in "Uncle Tom's Cabin;"[98] on the contrary, he was strongly opposed to it; but he was enough under its influence to be afraid of having me remain in his house many hours. So I was sent into the country, where I remained a month with the baby. When it was supposed that Dr. Flint's emissaries had lost track of me, and given up the pursuit for the present, I returned to New York.

XLI.

FREE AT LAST.

MRS. BRUCE, and every member of her family, were exceedingly kind to me. I was thankful for the blessings of my lot, yet I could not always wear a cheerful countenance. I was doing harm to no one; on the contrary, I was doing all the good I could in my small way; yet I could never go out to breathe God's free air without trepidation at my heart. This seemed hard; and I could not think it was a right state of things in any civilized country.

From time to time I received news from my good old grandmother. She could not write; but she employed others to write for her. The following is an extract from one of her last letters:—

"Dear Daughter: I cannot hope to see you again on earth; but I pray to God to unite us above, where pain will no more rack this feeble body of mine; where sorrow and parting from my children will be no more. God has promised these things if we are faithful unto the end. My age and feeble health deprive me of going to church now; but God is with me here at home. Thank your brother for his kindness. Give much love to him, and tell him to remember the Creator in the days of his youth, and strive to meet me in the Father's kingdom. Love to Ellen and Benjamin. Don't neglect him. Tell him for me, to be a good boy. Strive, my child, to train them for God's children. May he protect and provide for you, is the prayer of your loving old mother."

These letters both cheered and saddened me. I was always glad to have tidings from the kind, faithful old friend of my unhappy youth; but her messages of love made my heart yearn to see her before she died, and I mourned over the fact that it was impossible. Some months after I returned from my flight to New England, I received a letter from her, in which she wrote, "Dr. Flint is dead. He has left a distressed family. Poor old man! I hope he made his peace with God."

I remembered how he had defrauded my grandmother of the hard earnings she had loaned; how he had tried to cheat her out of the freedom her mistress had promised her, and how he had persecuted her children; and I thought to myself that she was a better Christian than I was, if she could entirely forgive him. I cannot say, with truth, that the news of my old master's death softened my feelings towards him. There are wrongs which even the grave does not bury. The man was odious to me while he lived, and his memory is odious now.

His departure from this world did not diminish my danger. He had threatened my grandmother that his heirs should hold me in slavery after he was gone; that I never should be free so long as a child of his survived. As for Mrs. Flint, I had seen her in deeper afflictions than I supposed the loss of her husband would be, for she had buried several children; yet I never saw any signs of softening in her heart. The doctor had died in embarrassed circumstances, and had little to will to his heirs, except such property as he was unable to grasp. I was well aware what I had to expect from the family of Flints; and my fears were confirmed by a letter from the south, warning me to be on my guard, because

Mrs. Flint openly declared that her daughter could not afford to lose so valuable a slave as I was.

I kept close watch of the newspapers for arrivals; but one Saturday night, being much occupied, I forgot to examine the Evening Express as usual. I went down into the parlor for it, early in the morning, and found the boy about to kindle a fire with it. I took it from him and examined the list of arrivals. Reader, if you have never been a slave, you cannot imagine the acute sensation of suffering at my heart, when I read the names of Mr. and Mrs. Dodge, at a hotel in Courtland Street. It was a third-rate hotel, and that circumstance convinced me of the truth of what I had heard, that they were short of funds and had need of my value, as *they* valued me; and that was by dollars and cents. I hastened with the paper to Mrs. Bruce. Her heart and hand were always open to every one in distress, and she always warmly sympathized with mine. It was impossible to tell how near the enemy was. He might have passed and repassed the house while we were sleeping. He might at that moment be waiting to pounce upon me if I ventured out of doors. I had never seen the husband of my young mistress, and therefore I could not distinguish him from any other stranger. A carriage was hastily ordered; and, closely veiled, I followed Mrs. Bruce, taking the baby again with me into exile. After various turnings and crossings, and returnings, the carriage stopped at the house of one of Mrs. Bruce's friends, where I was kindly received. Mrs. Bruce returned immediately, to instruct the domestics what to say if any one came to inquire for me.

It was lucky for me that the evening paper was not burned up before I had a chance to examine the list of arrivals. It was not long after Mrs. Bruce's return to her house, before several people came to inquire for me. One inquired for me, another asked for my daughter Ellen, and another said he had a letter from my grandmother, which he was requested to deliver in person.

They were told, "She *has* lived here, but she has left."

"How long ago?"

"I don't know, sir."

"Do you know where she went?"

"I do not, sir." And the door was closed.

This Mr. Dodge, who claimed me as his property, was originally a Yankee pedler in the south; then he became a merchant, and finally a slaveholder. He managed to get introduced into what was called the first society, and married Miss Emily Flint. A quarrel arose between him and her brother, and the brother cowhided him.[99] This led to a family feud, and he proposed to remove to Virginia. Dr. Flint left him no property, and his own means had become circumscribed, while a wife and children depended upon him for support. Under these circumstances, it was very natural that he should make an effort to put me into his pocket.

I had a colored friend, a man from my native place, in whom I had the most implicit confidence. I sent for him, and told him that Mr. and Mrs. Dodge had arrived in New York. I proposed that he should call upon them to make inquiries about his friends at the south, with whom Dr. Flint's family were well acquainted. He thought there was no impropriety in his doing so, and he consented.

He went to the hotel, and knocked at the door of Mr. Dodge's room, which was opened by the gentleman himself, who gruffly inquired, "What brought you here? How came you to know I was in the city?"

"Your arrival was published in the evening papers, sir; and I called to ask Mrs. Dodge about my friends at home. I didn't suppose it would give any offence."

"Where's that negro girl, that belongs to my wife?"

"What girl, sir?"

"You know well enough. I mean Linda, that ran away from Dr. Flint's plantation, some years ago. I dare say you've seen her, and know where she is."

"Yes, sir, I've seen her, and know where she is. She is out of your reach, sir."

"Tell me where she is, or bring her to me, and I will give her a chance to buy her freedom."

"I don't think it would be of any use, sir. I have heard her say she would go to the ends of the earth, rather than pay any man or woman for her freedom, because she thinks she has a right to it. Besides, she couldn't do it, if she would, for she has spent her earnings to educate her children."

This made Mr. Dodge very angry, and some high words passed between them. My friend was afraid to come where I was; but in the course of the day I received a note from him. I supposed they had not come from the south, in the winter, for a pleasure excursion; and now the nature of their business was very plain.

Mrs. Bruce came to me and entreated me to leave the city the next morning. She said her house was watched, and it was possible that some clew to me might be obtained. I refused to take her advice. She pleaded with an earnest tenderness, that ought to have moved me; but I was in a bitter, disheartened mood. I was weary of flying from pillar to post. I had been chased during half my life, and it seemed as if the chase was never to end. There I sat, in that great city, guiltless of crime, yet not daring to worship God in any of the churches. I heard the bells ringing for afternoon service, and, with contemptuous sarcasm, I said, "Will the preachers take for their text, 'Proclaim liberty to the captive, and the opening of prison doors to them that are bound'?[100] or will they preach from the text, 'Do unto others as ye would they should do unto you'?" Oppressed Poles and Hungarians could find a safe refuge in that city; John Mitchell[101] was free to proclaim in the City Hall his desire for "a plantation well stocked with slaves;" but there I sat, an oppressed American, not daring to show my face. God forgive the black and bitter thoughts I indulged on that Sabbath day! The Scripture says, "Oppression makes even a wise man mad;"[102] and I was not wise.

I had been told that Mr. Dodge said his wife had never signed away her right to my children,[103] and if he could not get me, he would take them. This it was, more than any thing else, that roused such a tempest in my soul. Benjamin was with his uncle William in California, but my innocent young daughter had come to spend a vacation with me. I thought of what I had suffered in slavery at her age, and my heart was like a tiger's when a hunter tries to seize her young.

Dear Mrs. Bruce! I seem to see the expression of her face, as she turned away discouraged by my obstinate mood. Finding her expostulations unavailing, she sent Ellen to entreat me. When ten o'clock in the evening arrived and Ellen had not returned, this watchful and unwearied friend became anxious. She came to us in a carriage, bringing a well-filled trunk for my journey—trusting that by this time I would listen to reason. I yielded to her, as I ought to have done before.

The next day, baby and I set out in a heavy snow storm, bound for New England again. I received letters from the City of Iniquity, addressed to me under an assumed name. In a few days one came from Mrs. Bruce, informing me that my new master was still searching for me, and that she intended to put an end to this persecution by buying my freedom. I felt grateful for the kindness that prompted this offer, but the idea was not so pleasant to me as might have been expected. The more my mind had become enlightened, the more difficult it was for me to consider myself an article of property; and to pay money to those who had so grievously oppressed me seemed like taking from my sufferings the glory of triumph. I wrote to Mrs. Bruce, thanking her, but saying that being sold from one owner to another seemed too much like slavery; that such a great obligation could not be easily cancelled; and that I preferred to go to my brother in California.

Without my knowledge, Mrs. Bruce employed a gentleman in New York to enter into negotiations with Mr. Dodge. He proposed to pay three hundred dollars down, if Mr. Dodge would sell me, and enter into obligations to relinquish all claim to me or my children forever after. He who called himself my master said he scorned so small an offer for such a valuable servant. The gentleman replied, "You can do as you choose, sir. If you reject this offer you will never get any thing; for the woman has friends who will convey her and her children out of the country."

Mr. Dodge concluded that "half a loaf was better than no bread," and he agreed to the proffered terms. By the next mail I received this brief letter from Mrs. Bruce: "I am rejoiced to tell you that the money for your freedom has been paid to Mr. Dodge. Come home to-morrow. I long to see you and my sweet babe."

My brain reeled as I read these lines. A gentleman near me said, "It's true; I have seen the bill of sale." "The bill of sale!" Those words struck me like a blow. So I was *sold* at last! A human being *sold* in the free city of New York! The bill of sale is on record, and future generations will learn from it that women were articles of traffic in New York, late in the nineteenth century of the Christian religion. It may hereafter prove a useful document to antiquaries, who are seeking to measure the progress of civilization in the United States. I well know the value of that bit of paper; but much as I love freedom, I do not like to look upon it. I am deeply grateful to the generous friend who procured it, but I despise the miscreant who demanded payment for what never rightfully belonged to him or his.

I had objected to having my freedom bought, yet I must confess that when it was done I felt as if a heavy load had been lifted from my weary shoulders. When I rode home in the cars I was no longer afraid to unveil my face and look at people as they passed. I should have been glad to have met Daniel Dodge himself; to have had him seen me and known me, that he might have mourned over the untoward circumstances which compelled him to sell me for three hundred dollars.

When I reached home, the arms of my benefactress were thrown round me, and our tears mingled. As soon as she could speak, she said, "O Linda, I'm *so* glad it's all over! You wrote to me as if you thought you were going to be transferred from one owner to another. But I did not buy you for your services. I should have done just the same, if you had been going to sail for California tomorrow. I should, at least, have the satisfaction of knowing that you left me a free woman."

My heart was exceedingly full. I remembered how my poor father had tried to buy me, when I was a small child, and how he had been disappointed. I hoped his spirit was rejoicing over me now. I remembered how my good old grandmother had laid up her earnings to purchase me in later years, and how often her plans had been frustrated How that faithful, loving old heart would leap for joy, if she could look on me and my children now that we were free! My relatives had been foiled in all their efforts, but God·had raised me up a friend among strangers, who had bestowed on me the precious, long-desired boon. Friend! It is a common word, often lightly used. Like other good and beautiful things, it may be tarnished by careless handling; but when I speak of Mrs. Bruce as my friend, the word is sacred.

My grandmother lived to rejoice in my freedom; but not long after, a letter came with a black seal. She had gone "where the wicked cease from troubling, and the weary are at rest."[104]

Time passed on, and a paper came to me from the south, containing an obituary notice of my uncle Phillip. It was the only case I ever knew of such an honor conferred upon a colored person. It was written by one of his friends, and contained these words: "Now that death has laid him low, they call him a good man and a useful citizen; but what are eulogies to the black man, when the world has faded from his vision? It does not require man's praise to obtain rest in God's kingdom." So they called a colored man a *citizen!* Strange words to be uttered in that region!

Reader, my story ends with freedom; not in the usual way, with marriage. I and my children are now free! We are as free from the power of slaveholders as are the white people of the north; and though that, according to my ideas, is not saying a great deal, it is a vast improvement in *my* condition. The dream of my life is not yet realized. I do not sit with my children in a home of my own. I still long for a hearthstone of my own, however humble. I wish it for my children's sake far more than for my own. But God so orders circumstances as to keep me with my friend Mrs. Bruce. Love, duty, gratitude, also bind me to her side. It is a privilege to serve her who pities my oppressed people, and who has bestowed the inestimable boon of freedom on me and my children.

It has been painful to me, in many ways, to recall the dreary years I passed in bondage. I would gladly forget them if I could. Yet the retrospection is not altogether without solace; for with those gloomy recollections come tender memories of my good old grandmother, like light, fleecy clouds floating over a dark and troubled sea.

APPENDIX.

THE following statement is from Amy Post, a member of the Society of Friends in the State of New York, well known and highly respected by friends of the poor and the oppressed. As has been already stated, in the preceding pages, the author of this volume spent some time under her hospitable roof.

L. M. C.

"The author of this book is my highly-esteemed friend. If its readers knew her as I know her, they could not fail to be deeply interested in her story. She was a beloved inmate of our family nearly the whole of the year 1849. She was introduced to us by her affectionate and conscientious brother, who had previously related to us some of the almost incredible events in his sister's life. I immediately became much interested in Linda; for her appearance was prepossessing, and her deportment indicated remarkable delicacy of feeling and purity of thought.

"As we became acquainted, she related to me, from time to time some of the incidents in her bitter experiences as a slave-woman. Though impelled by a natural craving for human sympathy, she passed through a baptism of suffering, even in recounting her trials to me, in private confidential conversations. The burden of these memories lay heavily upon her spirit—naturally virtuous and refined. I repeatedly urged her to consent to the publication of her narrative; for I felt that it would arouse people to a more earnest work for the disinthralment of millions still remaining in that soul-crushing condition, which was so unendurable to her. But her sensitive spirit shrank from publicity. She said, 'You know a woman can whisper her cruel wrongs in the ear of a dear friend much easier than she can record them for the world to read.' Even in talking with me, she wept so much, and seemed to suffer such mental agony, that I felt her story was too sacred to be drawn from her by inquisitive questions, and I left her free to tell as much, or as little, as she chose. Still, I urged upon her the duty of publishing her experience, for the sake of the good it might do; and, at last, she undertook the task.

"Having been a slave so large a portion of her life, she is unlearned; she is obliged to earn her living by her own labor, and she has worked untiringly to procure education for her children; several times she has been obliged to leave her employments, in order to fly from the man-hunters and woman-hunters of our land; but she pressed through all these obstacles and overcame them. After the labors of the day were over, she traced secretly and wearily, by the midnight lamp, a truthful record of her eventful life.

"This Empire State is a shabby place of refuge for the oppressed; but here, through anxiety, turmoil, and despair, the freedom of Linda and her children was finally secured, by the exertions of a generous friend. She was grateful for the boon; but the idea of having been *bought* was always galling to a spirit that could never acknowledge itself to be a chattel. She wrote to us thus, soon after the event: 'I thank you for your kind expressions in regard to my freedom; but the freedom I had before the money was paid was dearer to me. God gave me *that* freedom; but man put God's image in the scales with the paltry sum of three hundred dollars. I served for my liberty as faithfully as Jacob served for Rachel. At the end, he had large possessions; but I was robbed of my victory; I was obliged to resign my crown, to rid myself of a tyrant.'

"Her story, as written by herself, cannot fail to interest the reader. It is a sad illustration of the condition of this country, which boasts of its civilization, while it sanctions laws and customs which make the experiences of the present more strange than any fictions of the past.

AMY POST.

"ROCHESTER, N.Y., Oct. 30th, 1859."

The following testimonial is from a man who is now a highly respectable colored citizen of Boston.

L. M. C.

"This narrative contains some incidents so extraordinary, that, doubtless, many persons, under whose eyes it may chance to fall, will be ready to believe that it is colored highly, to serve a special purpose. But, however it may be regarded by the incredulous, I know that it is full of living truths. I have been well acquainted with the author from my boyhood. The circumstances recounted in her history are perfectly familiar to me. I knew of her treatment from her master; of the imprisonment of her children; of their sale and redemption; of her seven years' concealment; and of her subsequent escape to the North. I am now a resident of Boston, and am a living witness to the truth of this interesting narrative.

GEORGE W. LOWTHER."[105]

1. Andrews, *Free Story*, 241, 325.
2. Yellin, *Incidents*, xvi–xvii.
3. Ibid., xviii–xix.
4. Ibid., 237–238.
5. Ibid., xix–xx.
6. Ibid., 242.
7. Ibid., xxi–xxiv, 225, 244.
8. Titus, "'This Poisonous System,'" 199–207.
9. Carby, "Hear My Voice," 65.
10. Yellin, *Incidents*, xxxiii.
11. Andrews, *Free Story*, 258–259.
12. Yellin, *Incidents*, 276.
13. Andrews, *Free Story*, 277–278.
14. Goldsby, "'I Disguised My Hand,'" 12.
15. Yellin, *Incidents*, xxx. Also see Carby, "Hear My Voice," 74–75.
16. Andrews, *Free Story*, 252.
17. Yellin, *Incidents*, xxix.
18. Ibid., xxxiv.
19. Andrews, *Free Story*, 239–240, 260–263.

20. Yellin, *Incidents,* xxiv, xxv.

21. "Linda," 32–33.

22. Yellin, *Incidents,* xxv, 225; Yellin, "Jacobs, Harriet A.," 394.

23. Angelina E. Grimké (1805–79), *Appeal to the Christian Women of the South* (1836).

24. Lydia Maria Child (1802–80) wrote antislavery pamphlets, historical novels, a history of religions, and the popular *Frugal Housewife* (1829); she also edited the *National Anti-Slavery Standard* from 1841 through 1849.

25. Daniel Alexander Payne (1811–93) was the dominant figure in the African Methodist Episcopal Church throughout the second half of the nineteenth century. Elected a bishop in 1852, he was named president of Wilberforce University, the first black-controlled college in the United States, in 1863. Jacobs met him in 1842, before he had become a bishop.

26. Daniel Jacobs (?–c. 1826). Yellin, *Incidents,* 260. I am greatly indebted to this source for most of the following annotations.

27. John S. Jacobs (c. 1815–75). Ibid.

28. Molly Horniblow (c. 1771–1853). Ibid.

29. John Horniblow (?–1799); the hotel was in Edenton, North Carolina. Ibid.

30. Joe Horniblow (1808–?). Ibid., 261.

31. Delilah Horniblow. Ibid.

32. Margaret Horniblow (1797–1825). Ibid.

33. Mary Matilda Norcom (1822–?), who was actually only three years old. Ibid.

34. *Mark* 12:31.

35. *Matthew* 7:12.

36. Dr. James Norcom (1778–1850). Yellin, *Incidents,* 262.

37. John S. Jacobs ("William") explained his father's death as follows: "Being, as he was then considered, the best house-carpenter in or near the town, he was not put to field-work, although the privilege of working out, and paying his owner monthly, which he once enjoyed, was now denied him. This added another link to his galling chain—sent another arrow to his bleeding heart. My father, who had an intensely acute feeling of the wrongs of slavery, sank into a state of mental dejection, which, combined with bodily illness, occasioned his death." Cited in Yellin, "Through Her Brother's Eyes," 49.

38. January 1, 1828. Yellin, *Incidents,* 262.

39. Hannah Pritchard (?–1838). Ibid.

40. Betty Horniblow. Ibid., 263.

41. Mary Horniblow Norcom (1794–1868). Ibid., 262.

42. The number was actually closer to twenty. Ibid., 263.

43. James Norcom, Jr. (1811–?). Ibid.

44. Mark Jacobs (c. 1800–58). Ibid., 261, 264.

45. *Matthew* 23:27.

46. George Gordon, Lord Byron (1788–1824), "The Lament of Tasso."

47. Whipped and washed in brine. Yellin, *Incidents,* 266.

48. *Acts* 17:26.

49. Lydia Maria Child created this chapter by moving the incidents recounted here from elsewhere in Jacobs's original manuscript. Yellin, *Incidents,* 267.

50. Josiah Coffield (?–1837). Ibid.

51. "Thou shalt not steal." *Exodus* 20:15.

52. Thomas Campbell (1777–1844), "Pleasures of Hope" (1799).

53. William Mason (1724–97), *Elfrida* (1751).

54. Samuel Treadwell Sawyer (c. 1800–1865), an Edenton lawyer. Yellin, *Incidents,* 268.

55. Joseph Jacobs (c. 1829–c. 1863). Ibid., 269.

56. A portion of this chapter was written at Child's suggestion. In a letter to Jacobs dated August 13, 1860, she wrote: "My object in writing at this time is to ask you to write what you can recollect of the outrages committed on the colored people, in Nat Turner's time. You say the reader would not believe what you saw 'inflicted on men, women, and children, without the slightest ground of suspicion against them.' What *were* those inflictions? Were any tortured

to make them confess? And how? Where [sic] any killed? Please write down some of the most striking particulars, and let me have them to insert." Ibid., 244.

57. On August 21 and 22, 1831, the slave Nat Turner (1800–31) led an armed group of about sixty slaves in a revolt, killing between fifty-seven and sixty-five white men, women, and children. In the subsequent reprisals, at least two hundred blacks lost their lives. See Turner's narrative on pp. I:235–257. The revolt took place in Southampton County, Virginia, only about forty miles from Edenton.

58. A paddle with small holes in it. *Bucking* referred to tying or holding someone across a log for flogging.

59. This slave was known as Small's Jim; as a result of his false confession, nineteen slaves were jailed, and eight were indicted for conspiring to rebel. All charges were later dropped. Yellin, *Incidents*, 269.

60. On October 30, over two months after the revolt.

61. See *Matthew* 23:8.

62. John Avery (?–1837). Yellin, *Incidents*, 270.

63. *Ephesians* 6:5.

64. William D. Cairnes (c. 1803–50). Yellin, *Incidents*, 271.

65. Actually this was the action, under Cairnes's guidance, of a wealthy widow named Mary Bissell, who died two months after Cairnes's wife. Ibid., 271–272.

66. Rev. Nehemiah Adams (1806–78), a Boston pastor, published *A South-Side View of Slavery; or, Three Months in the South in 1854*.

67. Louisa Matilda Jacobs (1833–1917). Yellin, *Incidents*, 273.

68. See *Job* 3:17–19.

69. May 27, 1835. Yellin, *Incidents*, 274.

70. Three weeks later Norcom ran ads in the Norfolk, Virginia, *American Beacon*. They read as follows:

$100 REWARD

WILL be given for the apprehension and delivery of my Servant Girl HARRIET. She is a light mulatto, 21 years of age, about 5 feet 4 inches high, of a thick and corpulent habit, having on her head a thick covering of black hair that curls naturally, but which can be easily combed straight. She speaks easily and fluently, and has an agreeable carriage and address. Being a good seamstress, she has been accustomed to dress well, has a variety of very fine clothes, made in the prevailing fashion, and will probably appear, if abroad, tricked out in gay and fashionable finery. As this girl absconded from the plantation of my son without any known cause or provocation, it is probable she designs to transport herself to the North.

The above reward, with all reasonable charges, will be given for apprehending her, or securing her in any prison or jail within the U. States.

All persons are hereby forwarned against harboring or entertaining her, or being in any way instrumental in her escape, under the most rigorous penalties of the law.

JAMES NORCOM.

Edenton, N. C. June 30

Ibid., 215.

71. Patrick Henry (1736–99), speech to the Virginia Convention, 1775.

72. A song by J. Howard Payne (1792–1852).

73. A phrase from William Cowper (1731–1800), *The Task*.

74. A black festival tradition common to West Africa, the West Indies, the Carolinas, and New Orleans.

75. Albert Gallatin Brown (1813–80), one of the most prominent Southern politicans of his time, said these words during the 1854 debate in the Senate over the Kansas-Nebraska Bill. Yellin, *Incidents*, 278.

76. A follower of Samuel Thomson (1769–1843), a popular medical herbalist who believed that health could be restored through the "vital heat" induced by cayenne and steam baths.

77. While the Fugitive Slave Law of 1793, providing for the return between states of es-

caped slaves, was loosely enforced, the Fugitive Slave Act of 1850 commanded "all good citizens" to aid and assist federal marshals and deputies "in the prompt and efficient execution of this law," and imposed heavy penalties on anyone who assisted slaves to escape from bondage. When apprehended, any black man could be taken before a federal court or comissioner. Denied a jury trial, his testimony could not be admitted, while the statement of the man claiming ownership would be taken as the main evidence.

78. See *Job* 3:17.

79. James Iredell Tredwell (1799–1846), a Brooklyn merchant and Sawyer's cousin; his wife; and four daughters. Yellin, *Incidents,* 281.

80. The amount Judas was paid for betraying Jesus. *Matthew* 26:15.

81. Eleven cents.

82. Mary Stace Willis (c. 1816–45), wife of Nathaniel Parker Willis (1806–67); their daughter, born in 1842, was named Imogen. Yellin, *Incidents,* 285.

83. John S. Jacobs ("William") wrote of this meeting, "At first she did not look natural to me; but how should she look natural, after having been shut out from the light of heaven for six years and eleven months! I did not wish to know what her sufferings were while living in her place of concealment. The change that it had made in her was enough to make one's soul cry out against this curse of curses, that has so long trampled humanity in the dust." Cited in Goldsby, " 'I Disguised My Hand,' " 28–29.

84. Joseph Blount. Yellin, *Incidents,* 286.

85. Arent Van der Poel (1799–1870) was a Superior Court judge; John Hopper (1815–64) was a lawyer who would soon form the New York State Vigilance Committee, which attempted to protect fugitive slaves from kidnapping. Ibid.

86. Hon. Amelia Matilda Murray (1795–1884), *Letters from the United States, Cuba and Canada* (1856).

87. Mary Matilda Norcom had married Daniel Messmore in 1846. Yellin, *Incidents,* 287.

88. Mary Borham Howitt (1799–1888), "The Spider and the Fly."

89. The Young Ladies Domestic Seminary in Clinton, New York. Yellin, *Incidents,* 288.

90. John S. Jacobs's Rochester Antislavery Society and Reading Room was located one floor above the offices of Frederick Douglass's newspaper, *The North Star.*

91. Isaac (1798–1872) and Amy Post (1802–89) were antislavery pioneers and friends of Frederick Douglass and William Lloyd Garrison. Their house was a well-known station on the Underground Railroad. Formerly Quakers, they converted in 1848 to spiritualism, and in 1852 Isaac published *Voices from the Spirit World,* which included "communications" from the spirits of many famous men and women.

92. Willis's new wife was Cornelia Grinnell (1825–1904); their son, named Grinnell, was born in 1848. Yellin, *Incidents,* 289.

93. James Hamlet was the first New York victim of the 1850 Fugitive Slave Act.

94. Jenny Lind (1820–87) was a soprano who won worldwide fame as "the Swedish nightingale." At the time, she was touring the States under the management of P. T. Barnum.

95. At a meeting on October 1, 1850, more than fifteen hundred people, most of them black, met to protest Hamlet's arrest and to raise money to purchase his freedom. John S. Jacobs ("William") was one of the speakers. Yellin, *Incidents,* 289–290.

96. See *Daniel* 12:4.

97. Lilian, born in 1850. Yellin, *Incidents,* 290.

98. In Chapter IX of *Uncle Tom's Cabin* (1852), Harriet Beecher Stowe (1811–96) tells of a fictional Senator John Bird of Ohio who votes for the Fugitive Slave Act only to find Eliza, a runaway slave, and her son on his own doorstep. He takes pity on them and conveys them to a secure hiding place.

99. Actually Messmore cowhided Casper Norcom, not the other way around; Norcom then shot and wounded Messmore, and two months later Messmore was mobbed by thirteen men, including Dr. Norcom's son James. Yellin, *Incidents,* 291.

100. *Isaiah* 61:1.

101. John Mitchel (1815–75) was an Irish revolutionary who escaped to New York in 1853, where he edited the proslavery journal *Citizen.*

102. *Ecclesiastes* 7:17.

103. This was a lie. Dr. Norcom, as his child's legal guardian, had legalized the sale of Jacobs's children in 1837. Yellin, *Incidents*, 291.

104. See *Job* 3:17.

105. Lowther (1822–98) was a free black of Edenton who moved to Boston in 1838, where he worked as a hairdresser. Yellin, *Incidents*, 292.

JACOB D. GREEN

JACOB D. GREEN (1813–?) was the only slave narrator to make full use of a tradition of African American humor that stretches from African folktales to contemporary rap music. In this tradition, the protagonist is a *trickster*, a cunning character who continually tricks his adversaries, often with dire consequences—either for others or for himself. He lives in an amoral universe ruled by reversals of fortune; he lacks allegiances and is seemingly immune to social sanction. In his *Narrative*, Green, whom William Andrews has called "a human version of Brer Rabbit,"[1] displays little compunction in exposing both blacks and whites to his often cruel, though usually hilarious, trickery. The heroic stance of most narrators is here replaced by a kind of wicked glee.

Andrews cogently describes the main body of Green's *Narrative*:

> If there is one leitmotif that pervades Green's story, it is the principal of reversal, of things and people transformed into their opposites, of events cycling from humor to horror and back again. What goes around usually comes around with terrible, fateful logic in the world of J. D. Green, and triumph seems almost an inevitable prelude to tragedy. Everyone, white as well as black, must dance to an often-violent rhythm of metamorphosis.[2]

This leitmotif is continued in the appended material. Each of the three documentary appendices revolves around an ironic reversal: in the first, the ideal of democracy is divorced from that of liberty; in the second, the future vice president of the Confederacy argues against secession; and the third ridicules the claim of Confederate clergymen to be Christians. And Green plays his final trick in the last stanza of his concluding "song of deliverance," in which he transfers the appellation of Satan from himself to his old master—thus echoing his master's earlier comment, "you black vagabond, stay on this plantation three months longer, and you will be master and I the slave."

Nothing is known about J. D. Green except what can be gleaned from his narrative, which ends with Green's arrival in Toronto in the late 1840s. When or why he left Canada, how long he lived in West Yorkshire, and what happened to him subsequent to his narrative's publication there in 1864—all these will remain mysteries until further research turns up some answers. His book, which was never published in the United States, went almost completely unnoticed until 1986, when Andrews discussed it at length in *To Tell a Free Story*. There he calls Green "the supreme interstitial subversive of Afro-American autobiography in its first century," and claims that, along with Frederick Douglass's *My Bondage and My Freedom* and Harriet Jacobs's *Incidents in the Life of a Slave Girl*, his *Narrative* represents "the culmination of black autobiography in the first major period of Afro-American literary history."[3] It is here reprinted for the first time.[4]

NARRATIVE

OF

THE LIFE

OF

J. D. GREEN,

A RUNAWAY SLAVE,

FROM KENTUCKY,

CONTAINING AN

ACCOUNT OF HIS THREE ESCAPES,

In 1839, 1846, and 1848.

———

EIGHTH THOUSAND.[5]

———

HUDDERSFIELD:[6]
PRINTED BY HENRY FIELDING, PACK HORSE YARD.

———

1864.

TESTIMONIALS.

Jacob Green, a coloured man and an escaped slave, has lectured in my hearing, on American Slavery, in Springfield School-room, and I was much pleased with the propriety with which he was able to express himself, and with the capabilities which he seemed to possess to interest an audience.

GILBERT McCALLUM.
Minister of Springfield
Independent Chapel, Dewsbury.

Sept 2, 1863.

Hopton House, Sept. 10, 1863.

I have much pleasure in bearing my testimony in favour of Mr. Jacob Green, as a lecturer on the subject of American Slavery, having been present when he gave an able and efficient lecture here about a month ago. Having himself witnessed and experienced the fearful effects of that accursed "institution," he is well fitted to describe its horrors, and I have no doubt that amongst certain classes, his labours in the anti-slavery cause may be more telling and efficient than those of more highly educated lecturers who do not profess his peculiar advantages. I shall be well pleased to hear of him being employed by any anti-slavery society.

JAMES CAMERON,
Minister of Hopton Chapel.

Eccleshill, Sept. 11, 1863.

Mr. Jacob Green gave a lecture on Slavery, in our School-room here, about two months ago, which I considered a very able one; and it was so considered by my people.

JOHN ASTON.

I certify that Mr. Jacob Green has delivered two lectures in the Foresters' Hall, Denholm, to a very numerous audience; and on each occasion has given great satisfaction. The subjects were, first—Slavery,—second, the American War. He lectures remarkably well, and has a powerful voice; and I have not the least doubt would give satisfaction in lecturing elsewhere. The chair on each occasion was taken—first, by myself as incumbent—second, by the Rev. T. Roberts, Independent Minister.

J. F. N. EYRE.
Incumbent of Denholm.

Oct. 18th, 1863.

686

I can thoroughly endorse the sentiments of the Rev. J. F. N. Eyre, herein recorded.

T. ROBERTS.

———————

Mr. J. D. Green has lectured four times in our School-rooms, and each time he has given very great satisfaction to a large assembly. From what I have seen of him, I believe him to be worthy of public sympathy and support.

WILLIAM INMAN, Minister.

Ovenden, Nov. 14, 1863.

———————

NARRATIVE, &c.

_____

MY father and mother were owned by Judge Charles Earle, of Queen Anne's County,[7] Maryland, and I was born on the 24th of August, 1813.

From eight to eleven years of age I was employed as an errand boy, carrying water principally for domestic purposes, for 113 slaves and the family. As I grew older, in the mornings I was employed looking after the cows, and waiting in the house, and at twelve years I remember being in great danger of losing my life in a singular way. I had seen the relish with which master and friends took drink from a bottle, and seeing a similar bottle in the closet, I thought what was good for them would be good for me, and I laid hold of the bottle and took a good draught of (Oh, horror of horrors) oxalic acid, and the doctor said my safety was occasioned by a habit I had of putting my head in the milk pail and drinking milk, as by doing so the milk caused me to vomit and saved my life. About this time my mother was sold to a trader named Woodfork, and where she was conveyed I have not heard up to the present time. This circumstance caused serious reflections in my mind, as to the situation of slaves, and caused me to contrast the condition of a white boy with mine, which the following occurrence will more vividly pourtray. One morning after my mother was sold, a white boy was stealing corn out of my master's barn, and I said for this act we black boys will be whipped until one of us confesses to have done what we are all innocent of, as such is the case in every instance; and I thought, Oh, that master was here, or the overseer, I would then let them see what becomes of the corn. But, I saw he was off with the corn to the extent of half a bushel, and I will say nothing about it until they miss it, and if I tell them they wont believe me if he denies it, because he is white and I am black. Oh! how dreadful it is to be black! Why was I born black? It would have been better had I not been born at all. Only yesterday, my mother was sold to go to, not one of us knows where, and I am left alone, and I have no hope of seeing her again. At this moment a raven alighted on a tree over my head, and I cried, "Oh, Raven! if I had wings like you, I would soon find my mother and be happy again." Before parting she advised me to be a good boy, and she would pray for me, and I must pray for her, and hoped we might meet again in heaven, and I at once commenced to pray, to the best of my knowledge, "Our Father art in Heaven, be Thy name, kingdom come.—Amen." But, at this time, words of my master obtruded into my mind that God did not care for black folks, as he did not make them, but the d——l did. Then I thought of the old saying amongst us, as stated by our master, that, when God was making man, He made white man out of the best clay, as potters make china, and the d——l was watching, and he immediately took up some black mud and made a black man, and called him a nigger. My master was continually impressing upon me the necessity of being a good boy, and used to say, that if I was good, and behaved as well to him as my mother had done, I should go to Heaven without a question being asked. My mother having often said the same, I determined from that day to be a good boy, and constantly frequented the Meeting-house attended by the blacks where I learned from the minister, Mr. Cobb, how much the Lord had done for the blacks and for their salvation; and he was in the habit of reminding us what advantages he had given us for our benefit, for when we were in our native country, Africa, we were destitute of Bible light, worshipping idols of sticks and stones, and barbarously murdering one another, God put it into the hearts of these good slaveholders to venture across the bosom of the hazardous Atlantic to Africa, and snatch us poor negroes as brands from the eternal burning, and bring us where we might sit under the droppings of his sanctuary, and learn the ways of industry and the way to God. "Oh, niggers! how happy are your eyes which see this heavenly light; many millions of niggers desired it long, but died without the sight. I frequently envy your situations, because God's special blessing seems to be ever over you, as though you were a select people, for how much happier is your position than that of a free man, who, if sick, must pay his doctor's bill; if hungry, must supply his wants by his own exertions; if thirsty, must refresh himself by his own aid. And yet you, oh, niggers! your master has all this care for you. He supplies your daily wants; your meat and your drink he provides; and when you are sick he finds the best skill to bring you to health as soon as possible, for your sickness is his loss, and your health his gain; and, above all when you die (if you are obedient to your masters, and good niggers), your black faces will shine like black jugs around the throne of God." Such was the religious instruction I was in the habit of receiving until I was about seventeen years old; and told that when at any time I happened to be offended, or struck by a white boy I was not to offend or strike in return, unless it was another black, then I might fight as hard as I chose in my own defence. It happened about this time there was a white boy who was continually stealing my tops and marbles, and one morning when doing so I caught him, and we had a battle, and I had him down on the ground when Mr. Burmey came up. He kicked me away from the white boy, saying if I belonged to him he would cut off my hands for *daring* to strike a white boy; this without asking the cause of the quarrel, or of ascertaining who was to blame. The kick was so severe that I was sometime before I forgot it, and created such a feeling of revenge in my bosom that I was determined when I became a man I would pay him back in his own coin. I went out one day, and measured myself by a tree in the wood, and cut a notch in the tree to ascertain how fast I grew. I went at different times for the space of two months and found I was no taller, and I began to fear he would die before I should have grown to man's estate, and I resolved if he did I would make his children suffer by punishing them instead of their father. At this time my master's wife had two lovers, this same Burmey and one Rogers, and they despised each other from feelings of jealousy. Master's wife seemed to favour Burmey most, who was a great smoker, and she provided him with a large pipe with a German silver bowl, which screwed on the top; this pipe she usually kept on the mantel piece, ready filled with tobacco. One morning I was dusting and sweeping out the dining-room, and saw the pipe on the mantel-piece. I took it down, and went to my young master William's powder closet and took out his powder horn, and after taking half of the tobacco out of the pipe filled it nearly full with powder, and covered it over with tobacco to make it appear as usual when filled with tobacco, replaced it, and left. Rogers, came in about eight o'clock in the morning, and remained until eleven, when Mr. Burmey came, and in about an hour I saw a great number running about from all parts of the plantation. I left the barn where I was thrashing buck-wheat, and followed the rest to the house, where I saw Mr. Burmey lying back in the arm chair in a state of insensibility, his mouth bleeding profusely and from particulars given it appeared he took the pipe as usual and lighted it, and had just got it to his mouth when the powder exploded, and the party suspected was Rogers, who had been there immediately preceding; and Burmey's son went to Rogers and they fought about the matter. Law ensued, which cost Rogers 800 dollars, Burmey 600 dollars and his face disfigured; and my master's wife came in for a deal of scandal, which caused further proceedings at law, costing the master 1400 hundred dollars, and I was never once suspected or charged with the deed.

At this time two or three negroes had escaped, and I heard so much about the free States of the north that I was determined to be free. So I began to study what we call the north star, or astronomy, to guide me to the free States. I was in the habit of driving the master; and on one occasion I had to drive him to Baltimore where two of his sons were studying law; and while there, I stole some sweet potatoes to roast when I got home; and how master got to know I had them I never knew; but when I got home he gave me a note to Mr. Cobb, the overseer, and told me to tell Dick, (another slave on the plantation) to come to Baltimore to him on the following evening, and as soon as I took the note in my hand I was certain there was a flogging in it for me, though he said nothing to me. I held the note that night and following day, afraid to give it to Mr. Cobb, so confident was I of what would be the result. Towards evening I began to reason thus—If I give Cobb the note I shall be whipped; if I withhold the note from him I shall be whipped, so a whipping appears plain in either case. Now Dick having arranged to meet his sweetheart this night assumed sickness, so that he could have an excuse for not meeting master at Baltimore, and he wanted me to go instead of him. I agreed to go, providing he would take the note I had to Mr. Cobb, as I had forgot to give it him, to which he consented, and off I went; and I heard that when he delivered the note to Mr. Cobb, he ordered him to go to the whipping-post, and when he asked what he had done he was knocked down, and afterwards put to the post and thirty-nine lashes were administered, and failed seeing his sweetheart as well. When I arrived at Baltimore my master and young master took their seats and I drove away without any question until we had gone three miles, when he asked what I was doing there that night. I very politely said Dick was not well, and I had come in his place. He then asked me if Mr. Cobb got his note, I answered, yes, sir. He then asked me how I felt, and I said first rate, sir. "The d——l you do," said he. I said, yes sir. He said "nigger, did Mr. Cobb flog you?" No sir. I have done nothing wrong. "You never do," he answered; and said no more until he got home. Being a man who could not bear to have any order of his disobeyed or unfulfilled, he immediately called for Mr. Cobb, and was told he was in bed; and when he appeared, the master asked if he got the note sent by the nigger. Mr. Cobb said "Yes." "Then why," said master, "did you not perform my orders in the note?" "I did, sir," replied Cobb; when the master said, "I told you to give that nigger thirty-nine lashes," Mr. Cobb says, "So I did, sir;" when master replied, "He says you never licked him at all." Upon which Cobb said, "He is a liar:" when my master called for me (who had been hearing the whole dialogue at the door), I turned on my toes and went a short distance, and I shouted with a loud voice that I was coming, (to prevent them knowing that I had been listening) and appeared before them and said "here I am master, do you want me." He said "Yes. Did you not tell me that Mr. Cobb had not flogged you," and I said "yes I did; he has not flogged me to-day, sir." Mr. Cobb answered, "I did not flog him. You did not tell me to flog him. You told me to flog that other nigger." "What other nigger," enquired Master. Cobb said, "Dick." Master then said, "I did not, I told you to flog this nigger here," Cobb then produced the letter, and read it as follows:

"Mr. Cobb will give the bearer 39 lashes on delivery."

R. T. EARLE.

I then left the room and explanations took place. When I was again called in. "How came Dick to have had the letter," and I then said I had forgot to deliver it until Dick wanted me to go to Baltimore in his place, and I agreed providing he would take the letter. Master then said "you lie, you infernal villain," and laid hold of a pair of tongs and said he would dash my brains out if I did not tell him the truth. I then said I thought there was something in the note that boded no good to me, and I did not intend to give it to him. He said, "you black vagabond, stay on this plantation three months longer, and you will be master and I the slave; no wonder you said you felt first rate when I asked you, but I will sell you to go to Georgia the first chance I get." Then laying the tongs down he opened the door and ordered me out. I knew he had on heavy cow-hide boots, and I knew he would try to assist me in my outward progress, and though expecting it, and went as quick as I could, I was materially assisted by a heavy kick from my master's foot. This did not end the matter, for when Dick found out I had caused his being flogged, we had continual fightings for several months.

When I was fourteen years old my master gave me a flogging, the marks of which will go with me to my grave, and this was for a crime of which I was completely innocent. My master's son had taken one of his pistols out, and by some accident it burst. When enquiry was made about the damaged pistol William told his father that he had seen me have it; this, of course, I denied, when master tied me up by my thumbs and gave me 60 lashes, and also made me confess the crime before he would release me. From this flogging my back was raw and sore for three months; the shirt that I wore was made of rough tow linen, and when at work in the fields it would so chafe the sores that they would break and run, and the hot sun over me would bake the shirt fast to my back, and for four weeks I wore that shirt, unable to pull it off, and when I did pull it off it brought with it much of my flesh, leaving my back perfectly raw. Some time after this my master found out the truth about the pistol, and when I saw that he did not offer me any apology for the beating he had given me, and the lie he had made me confess, I went to him and said—now, master, you see that you beat me unjustly about that pistol, and made me confess to a lie—but all the consolation I got was—clear out, you black rascal; I never struck a blow amiss in my life, except when I struck at you and happened to miss you; there are plenty of other crimes you have committed and did not let me catch you at them, so that flogging will do for the lot.

Master had an old negro in the family called Uncle Reuben. This good old man and his wife were very good friends of my mother's, and before she was sold they often met and sung and prayed, and talked about religion together. Uncle Reuben fell sick in the middle of the harvest, and his sickness was very severe; but master having a grudge against uncle Reuben, and his old wife aunt Dinah, respecting a complaint that aunt Dinah had made to mistress about his having outraged and violated her youngest daughter, his spite was carried out by Mr. Cobb, the overseer, who forced Uncle Reuben into the field amongst the rest of us, and I was ordered to cradle[8] behind him to make him keep up with the rest of the gang. The poor old man worked until he fell, just ahead of me, upon the cradle. Mr. Cobb came over and told him to get up, and that he was only playing the old soldier, and when the old man did not move to get up Mr. Cobb gave him a few kicks with his heavy boots and told Reuben, sick as he was, that he would cure him. He ordered us to take off his shirt, and the poor old man was stripped, when Mr. Cobb, with his hickory cane, laid on him till his back bled freely; but still the old man seemed to take no notice of what Mr. Cobb was doing. Mr. Cobb then told us to put on his shirt and carry him in, for he appeared convinced that Reuben could not walk. The next morning I went to see him but he did not seem to know anybody. Master came in along with the Doctor, and master swore at Reuben, telling him that as soon as he was well enough he should have a good flogging for having, by his own folly, caught his sickness. The doctor here checked his master's rage by telling him, as he felt at Reuben by the wrist, he could not live many minutes longer; at this master was silent, and a few minutes Reuben was dead. Poor Aunt Dinah came in out of the kitchen and wept fit to break her poor heart. She had four sons and three daughters, and they all joined in mournful lamentation.

When I was sixteen I was very fond of dancing, and was invited privately to a negro shindy or dance, about twelve miles from home, and for this purpose I got Aunt Dinah to starch the collars for my two linen shirts, which were the first standing collars I had ever worn in my life; I had a good pair of trousers, and a jacket, but no necktie, nor no pocket handkerchief, so I stole aunt Dinah's checked apron, and tore it in two—one part for a necktie, the other for a pocket handkerchief. I had twenty-four cents, or pennies which I divided equally with fifty large brass buttons in my right and left pockets. Now, thought I to myself, when I get on the floor and begin to dance—oh! how the niggers will stare to hear the money jingle. I was combing my hair to get the knots out of it: I then went and looked in an old piece of broken looking-glass, and I thought, without joking, that I was the best looking negro that I had ever seen in my life. About ten o'clock I stole out to the stable when all was still; and while I was getting on one of my master's horses I said to myself—Master was in here at six o'clock and saw all these horses clean, so I must look out and be back time enough to have you clean when he gets up in the morning. I thought what a dash I should cut among the pretty yellow and Sambo[9] gals, and I felt quite confident, of course, that I should have my pick among the best looking ones, for my good clothes, and my abundance of money, and my own good looks—in fact, I thought no mean things of my self.

When I arrived at the place where the dance was, it was at an old house in the woods, which had many years before been a negro meeting-house; there was a large crowd there, and about one hundred horses tied round the fence—for some of them were far from home, and, like myself, they were all runaways, and their horses, like mine, had to be home and cleaned before their masters were up in the morning. In getting my horse close up to the fence a nail caught my trousers at the thigh, and split them clean up to the seat; of course my shirt tail fell out behind, like a woman's apron before. This dreadful misfortune almost un-manned me, and curtailed both my pride and pleasure for the night. I cried un-til I could cry no more. However, I was determined I would not be done out of my sport after being at the expense of coming, so I went round and borrowed some pins, and pinned up my shirt tail as well as I could. I then went into the dance, and told the fiddler to play me a jig. Che, che, che, went the fiddle, when the banjo responded with a thrum, thrum, thrum, with the loud cracking of the bone player. I seized a little Sambo gal, and round and round the room we went, my money and my buttons going jingle, jingle, jingle, seemed to take a lively part with the music, and to my great satisfaction every eye seemed to be upon me, and I could not help thinking about what an impression I should leave behind upon those pretty yellow and Sambo gals, who were gazing at me, thinking I was the richest and handsomest nigger they had ever seen: but unfortunately the pins in my breeches gave way, and to my great confusion my shirt tail fell out; and what made my situation still more disgraceful was the mischievous conduct of my partner, the gal that I was dancing with, who instead of trying to conceal my shame caught my shirt tail behind and held it up. The roar of laughter that came from both men and gals almost deafened me, and I would at this moment have sunk through the floor, so I endeavoured to creep out as slily as I could; but even this I was not permitted to do until I had undergone a hauling around the room by my unfortunate shirt tail: and this part of the programme was performed by the gals, set on by the boys—every nigger who could not stand up and laugh, be-cause laughing made them weak, fell down on the floor and rolled round and round. When the gals saw their own turn they let me go, and I hurried outside and stood behind the house, beneath a beautiful bright moon, which saw me that night the most wretched of all negroes in the land of Dixie: and what made me feel, in my own opinion, that my humiliation was just as complete as the triumph of the negroes inside was glorious, was that the gals had turned my pockets out, and found that the hundreds of dollars they had thought my pockets contained, consisted of 24 cents or pennies, and 50 brass buttons. Everything was alive and happy inside the room, but no one knew or cared how miserable I was—the joy and life of the dance that night seemed entirely at my expense, all through my unfortunate shirt tail. The first thing I thought of now was revenge. Take your comfort, niggers now, said I to myself, for sorrow shall be yours in the morning, so I took out my knife and went round the fence and cut every horse loose, and they all ran away. I then got on my horse and set off home. As I rode on I thought to myself—I only wish I could be somewhere close enough to see how those negroes will act when they come out and find all their horses gone. And then I laughed right out when I thought of the sport they had had out of my misfortune, and that some were ten to twelve, and some fifteen miles away from home. Well, thought I, your masters will have to reckon with you to-morrow; you have had glad hearts to-night at my expense, but you will have sore backs to-morrow at your own. Now, when I got home, the stable was in a very bad situation, and I was afraid to bring my horse in until I could strike a light. When this was done, I took the saddle and bridle off outside. No sooner had I done this than my horse reared over the bars and ran away into the meadow. I chased him till daylight, and for my life I could not catch him. My feelings now may be better imagined than described. When the reader remembers that this horse, with all the rest, master had seen clean at six o'clock the night before, and all safe in the stable, and now to see him in the meadow, with all the marks of having been driven somewhere and by somebody, what excuse could I make, or what story could I invent in order to save my poor back from that awful flogging which I knew must be the result of the revelation of the truth. I studied and tried, but could think of no lie that would stand muster. At last I went into the stable and turned all the rest out, and left the stable door open, and creeping into the house, took off my fine clothes and put on those which I had been wearing all the week, and laid myself down on my straw. I had not lain long before I heard master shouting for me, for all those horses, eight in number, were under my care; and although he shouted for me at the top of his voice, I lay still and pretended not to hear him: but soon after I heard a light step coming up stairs, and a rap at my door—then I commenced to snore as loud as possible, still the knocking continued. At last I pretended to awake, and called out, who's there—that you, Lizzy? oh my! what's up, what time is it, and so on. Lizzy said master wanted me immediately; yes, Lizzy, said I, tell master I'm coming. I bothered about the room long enough to give colour to the impression that I had just finished dressing myself; I then came and said, here I am, master, when he demanded of me, what were my horses doing in the meadow? Here I put on an expression of such wonder and surprise— looking first into the meadow and then at the stable door, and to master's satisfaction, I seemed so completely confounded that my deception took upon him the desired effect. Then I affected to roar right out, crying, now master, you saw my horses all clean last night before I went to bed, and now some of those negroes have turned them out so that I should have them to clean over again: well, I declare! it's too bad, and I roared and cried as I went towards the meadow to drive them up; but master believing what I said, called me back and told me to call Mr. Cobb, and when Mr. Cobb came master told him to blow the horn; when the horn was blown, the negroes were to be seen coming from all parts of the plantation, and forming around in front of the balcony. Master then came out and said, now I saw this boy's horses clean last night and in the stable, so now tell me which of you turned them out? Of course they all denied it, then master ordered them all to go down into the meadow and drive up the horses and clean them, me excepted; so they went and drove them up and set to work and cleaned them. On Monday morning we all turned out to work until breakfast, when the horn was blown, and we all repaired to the house. Here master again demanded to know who turned the horses loose, and when they all denied it, he tied them all up and gave them each 39 lashes. Not yet satisfied, but determined to have a confession, as was always his custom on such occasions, he came to me and asked me which one I had reason to suspect. My poor guilty heart already bleeding for the suffering I had caused my fellow slaves, was now almost driven to confession. What must I do, select another victim for further punishment, or confess the truth and bear the consequence? My conscience now rebuked me, like an armed man; but I happened to be one of those boys who, among all even of my mother's children loved myself best, and therefore had no disposition to satisfy my conscience at the expense of a very sore back, so I very soon thought of Dick, a negro who, like Ishmael, had his hand out against every man, and all our hands were out against him; this negro was a lickspittle or telltale, as little boys call them—we could not steal a bit of tea or sugar, or any other kind of nourishment for our sick, or do anything else we did not want to be known, but if he got to know it he would run and tell master or mistress, or the overseer, so we all wanted him dead; and now I thought of him—he was just the proper sacrifice for me to lay upon the altar of confession, so I told master I believed that it was Dick: moreover, I told him that I had seen him in and out of the stable on Saturday night, so master tied Dick up and gave him 39 lashes more, and washed his back down with salt and water, and told him that at night if he did not confess, he would give him as much more; so at night, when master went out to Dick again, he asked if he had made up his mind to tell him the truth, Dick said, yes, master;—well, said master, let me hear it. Well master, said Dick, I did turn the horses out; but will never do so again. So master, satisfied with this confession, struck Dick no more, and ordered him to be untied; but Dick had a sore back for many weeks. And now to return to the negroes I had left at the dance, when they discovered that their horses were gone there was the greatest consternation amongst them, the forebodings of the awful consequences if they dared to go home induced many that night to seek salvation in the direction and guidance of the north star. Several who started off on that memorable night I have since shook hands with in Canada. They told me there were sixteen of them went off together, four of them were shot or killed by the bloodhounds, and one was captured while asleep in a barn; the rest of those who were at the dance either went home and took their floggings, or strayed into the woods until starved out, and then surrendered. One of those I saw in Toronto, is Dan Patterson; he has a house of his own, with a fine horse and cart, and he has a beautiful Sambo woman for his wife, and four fine healthy-looking children. But, like myself, he had left a wife and six children in slavery. When I was about seventeen, I was deeply smitten in love with a yellow girl belonging to Doctor Tillotson. This girl's name was Mary, of whose lovliness I dreamt every night. I certainly thought she was the prettiest girl I had ever seen in my life. Her colour was very fair, approaching almost to white; her countenance was frank and open, and very inviting; her voice was as sweet as the dulcimer, her smiles to me were like the May morning sunbeams in the spring, one glance of her large dark eyes broke my heart in pieces, with a stroke like that of an earthquake. O, I thought, this girl would make me a paradise, and to enjoy her love I thought would be heaven. In spite of either patroles or dogs, who stood in my way, every night nearly I was in Mary's company. I learned from her that she had already had a child to her master in Mobile, and that her mistress had sold her down here for revenge; and she told me also of the sufferings that she had undergone from her mistress on account of jealousy—her baby she said her mistress sold out of her arms, only eleven months old, to a lady in Marysville, Kentucky. Having never before felt a passion like this, or of the gentle power, so peculiar to women, that, hard as I worked all day, I could not sleep at night for thinking of this almost angel in human shape. We kept company about six weeks, during which time I was at sometimes as wretched as I was happy at others. Much to my annoyance Mary was adored by every negro in the neighbourhood, and this excited my jealousy and made me miserable. I was almost crazy when I saw another negro talking to her. Again and again I tried my best to get her to give up speaking to them, but she refused to comply. There was one negro who was in the habit of calling on Mary whom I dreaded more than all the rest of them put together, this negro was Dan, he belonged to Rogers; and notwithstanding I believed myself to be the best looking negro to be found anywhere in the neighbourhood, still I was aware that I was not the best of talkers. Dan was a sweet and easy talker, and a good bone and banjo player. I was led to fear that he would displace me in Mary's affections, and in this I was not mistaken. One night I went over to see Mary, and in looking through the window, saw Mary—my sweet and beloved Mary—sitting upon Dan's knee; and here it is impossible to describe the feeling that came over me at this unwelcome sight. My teeth clenched and bit my tongue—my head grew dizzy, and began to swim round and round, and at last I found myself getting up from the ground, having stumbled from the effects of what I had seen. I wandered towards home, and arriving there threw myself on the straw and cried all night. My first determination was to kill Dan; but then I thought they would hang me and the devil would have us both, and some other negro will get Mary, then the thought of killing Dan passed away. Next morning, when the horn blew for breakfast, I continued my work, my appetite having left me; at dinner time it was the same. At sun-down I went to the barn and got a rope and put it under my jacket, and started off to see Mary, whom I found sitting in the kitchen, smoking her pipe, for smoking was as common among the girls as among the men. Mary, said I, I was over here last night and saw you through the window sitting on Dan's knee. Now, Mary, I want you to tell me at once whose you mean to be—mine or Dan's? Dan's, she replied, with an important toss of her head, which went through my very soul, like the shock from a galvanic battery. I rested for a minute or so on an old oak table that stood by. Mary's answer had unstrung every nerve in me, and left me so weak that I could scarcely keep from falling. Now I was not at that time, and don't think I ever shall be one of those fools who would cut off his nose to spite his face, much less kill myself because a girl refused to love me. Life to me was always preferable, under any circumstances; but in this case I played the most dexterous card I had. Mary, said I sternly, if you don't give Dan up and sware to be mine, I will hang myself this night. To this she replied, hang on if you are fool enough, and continued smoking her pipe as though not the least alarmed. I took out the rope from under my jacket, and got upon a three-legged stool, and putting the rope first over the beam in the ceiling, then made a slip-knot, and brought it down round my neck, taking good care to have it short enough that it would not choke me, and in this way I stood upon the stool for some considerable time, groaning and struggling, and making every kind of noise that might make her believe that I was choking or strangling; but still Mary sat deliberately smoking her pipe with the utmost coolness, and seemed to take no notice of me or what I was doing. I thought my situation worse now than if I had not commenced this job at all. My object in pretending to hang myself was to frighten Mary into compliance with my demand, and her conduct turned out to be everything but what I had expected. I had thought that the moment I ascended the stool she would have clung to me and tried to dissuade me from committing suicide, and in this case my plan was to persist in carrying it out, unless she would consent to give Dan up; but instead of this she sat smoking her pipe apparently at ease and unmoved. Now I found I had been mistaken—what was I to do, to hang or kill myself was the last thing I meant to do—in fact I had not the courage to do it for five hundred Marys. But now, after mounting the stool and adjusting the rope round my neck, I was positively ashamed to come down without hanging myself, and then I stood like a fool. At this moment in came the dog carlow,[10] racing after the cat, right across the kitchen floor, and the dog coming in contact with the stool, knocked it right away from under my feet, and brought my neck suddenly to the full length of the rope, which barely allowed my toes to touch the floor. Here I seized the rope with both hands to keep the weight of my whole body off my neck, and in this situation I soon found I must hang, and that dead enough, unless I had some assistance, for the stool had rolled entirely out of the reach of my feet, and the knot I had tied behind the beam I could not reach for my life. My arms began to tremble with holding on to the rope, and still my mortification and pride for some time refused to let me call on Mary for assistance. Such a moment of terror and suspense! heaven forbid that I should ever see or experience again. Thoughts rushed into my mind of every bad deed that I had done in my life; and I thought that old cloven foot, as we called the devil, was waiting to nab me. The stretch upon my arms exhausted me, with holding on by the rope, nothing was left me but despair, my pride and courage gave up the ghost, and I roared out, Mary! for God's sake cut the rope! No, answered Mary, you went up there to hang yourself so now hang on. Oh! Mary, Mary! I did not mean to hang! I was only doing so to see what you would say. Well, then, said Mary; you hear what I have to say—hang on. Oh, Mary! for heaven's sake cut this rope, or I shall strangle to death!—oh, dear, good Mary, save me this time: and I roared out like a jackass, and must too have fainted, for when I came round Doctor Tillotson and his wife and Mary stood over me as I lay on the floor. How I got upon the floor, or who cut the rope I never knew. Doctor Tillotson had hold of my wrist, feeling my pulse; while mistress held a camphor bottle in one hand and a bottle of hartshorn in the other. The doctor helped me up from the floor and set me in a chair, when I discovered that I was bleeding very freely from the nose and mouth. He called for a basin and bled me in my left arm, and then sent me over home by two of his men. Next day my neck was dreadfully swollen, and my throat was so sore that it was with difficulty that I could swallow meat for more than a week. At the end of a fortnight, master having learnt all the particulars respecting my sickness, called me to account, and gave me seventy-eight lashes, and this was the end of my crazy love and courtship with Mary.

Shortly after this, Mary was one Sunday down in her master's barn, where she had been sent by her mistress to look for new nests where a number of the hens were supposed to have been laying, as the eggs had not been found elsewhere. While in the barn, Mary was surprised by William Tillotson, her master's son, who ordered her to take her bed among the hay and submit to his lustful passion. This she strenuously refused to do, telling him of the punishment she had already suffered from her former mistress for a similar act of conduct, and reminding him at the same time of his wife, whose vengeance she would have to dread; but William was not to be put off, nor his base passion to go unsatisfied, by any excuse that Mary could make, so he at once resorted to force. Mary screamed at the top of her voice. Now the negro Dan was just in the act of passing the barn at the time, when he heard Mary's voice he rushed into the barn, and demanded in a loud voice what was the matter? when, to his horror, he beheld William upon the barn floor, and Mary struggling but in vain to rise. William, instead of desisting from his brutal purpose, with a dreadful oath ordered Dan to clear out; but the sight of the outrage on her whom, I now firmly believe he loved better than his own soul, made poor Dan completely forget himself—and made him forget too, in that fatal moment what he afterwards wished he had remembered. Dan seized a pitchfork and plunged it into young Tillotson's back; the prongs went in between his shoulders, and one of them had penetrated the left lung. Young Tillotson expired almost immediately, and Dan seeing what he had done, ran off at once to the woods and swamps, and was seen no more for about two months. Mrs. Tillotson, who had heard Mary scream, was on the balcony, and called out to Dan to know the cause, Dan made no reply but took to his heels. Mrs. Tillotson alarmed at this, and suspecting at once that something was wrong, hastened to the barn, followed by William's wife who happened to be there, and when they saw poor William's corpse, and Mary standing by, they both fainted. Poor Mary, frightened to death, turned into the house and informed her young mistress, Susannah, of what had happened. Miss Susannah spread the alarm, and called some of the slaves to her assistance. She went to the barn and found her mother and sister-in-law lying in a state of insensibility, and her brother William dead. With the assistance of old Aunt Hannah and several of the female servants, the two ladies were somewhat restored to consciousness; and William was carried into the house by the servants. The Doctor himself was away from home attending one of his patients, who was very sick. When Mrs. Tillotson had somewhat recovered, she sent for Mary and enquired as to how William came by his death in the barn. Mary told the whole story as previously related in the presence of about sixty or seventy of the neighbours, who had collected together on hearing of the murder. Of course Mary's story met with no credit from her mistress, and poor Mary stood in the eyes of all as an accomplice in the conspiracy to murder young Tillotson. When the doctor arrived it was dark, and after seeing the corpse and hearing from his wife the story that she had made up for him, he called for Mary, but she was nowhere to be found. The house and plantation were searched in all directions, but no Mary was discovered. At last, when they had all given over looking for her, towards midnight, a cart drove up to the door. Doctor, said the driver, I have a dead negro here, and I'm told she belongs to you. The Doctor came out with a lantern, and as I stood by my master's carriage, waiting for him to come out and go home, the Doctor ordered me to mount the cart and look at the corpse; I did so, and looked full in that face by the light of the lantern, and saw and knew, notwithstanding the horrible change that had been effected by the work of death, upon those once beautiful features, it was Mary. Poor Mary, driven to distraction by what had happened, she had sought salvation in the depths of the Chesapeake Bay that night. Next day the neighbourhood was searched throughout, and the country was placarded for Dan; and Doctor Tillotson and Mr. Burmey, young William's father-in-law, offered one thousand dollars for him alive, and five hundred for him dead; and although every blackleg in the neighbourhood was on the alert, it was full two months before he was captured. At length poor Dan was caught and brought by the captors to Mr. Burmey's where he was tried principally by Burmey's two sons, Peter and John, and that night was kept in irons in Burmey's cellar. The next day Dan was led into the field in the presence of about three thousand of us. A staple was driven into the stump of a tree, with a chain attached to it, and one of his handcuffs was taken off and brought through the chain, and then fastened on his hand again. A pile of pine wood was built around him. At eight o'clock the wood was set on fire, and when the flames blazed round upon the wretched man, he began to scream and struggle in a most awful manner. Many of our women fainted, but not one of us was allowed to leave until the body of poor Dan was consumed. The unearthly sounds that came from the blazing pile, as poor Dan writhed in the agonies of death, it is beyond the power of my pen to describe. After a while all was silent, except the cracking of the pine wood as the fire gradually devoured it with the prize that it contained. Poor Dan had ceased to struggle—he was at rest.

Mr. Burmey's two sons, Peter and John, were the ringleaders in this execution, and the pair of them hardly ever saw a sober day from one month to another; and at the execution of Dan, Peter was so drunk that he came nigh sharing the same fate. It was not a year after the roasting of Dan that the two brothers were thrashing wheat in the barn, which stood about a quarter of a mile from the house, and being in March, and an uncommon windy day, they had taken their demijohn full of brandy in order to keep the cold out of their bones, as it was their belief that a dram or two had that effect; so they were drinking and thrashing and drinking again until they reeled over dead drunk upon the floor. That same night the barn took fire over them. The first thing that excited the alarm of my master's negroes on Tillotson's plantation was a black smoke issuing from the barn. Suddenly there was a rush from all parts of the plantation, but it was all to no purpose, for scarcely had we got half way before we saw the flames bursting out on every side of the barn, still we continued to run as fast as we could. When we arrived we found the barn door shut and fastened inside. This Mr. Peter and Mr. John had done to keep out the wind which was very high. When old Mr. Burmey arrived with his daughter-in-law, Peter's wife, the first thing demanded was, where is your masters?—oh, my children! my children! while Mrs. Peter screamed, my husband! my husband! oh, pa! oh, pa! The strength of the flames inside at length burst open the barn door, when we beheld through the red flames the figures of the two wretched brothers lying side by side dead drunk and helpless upon the floor. The fire rapidly seized upon everything around. At this moment Mrs. Peter Burmey rushed into the flames to save her husband, but just as she attempted to enter, the beam over the door fell in upon her head, and struck her back senseless and suffocated to the ground; but, notwithstanding the most intense hatred to Burmey and his family, we negroes rushed forward to rescue them—but all in vain. After getting miserably scorched we were compelled to retreat and give them over, and with bleeding hearts to behold the fire consume their bodies. The barn was rapidly consigned to ashes, which being speedily swept away by the violence of the wind, left the victims side by side crisped skeletons on the ground. This was the dreadful end of the two chief actors in the roasting of poor Dan.

When I arrived at the age of 20, my master told me I must marry Jane, one of the slaves. We had been about five months married when she gave birth to a child, I then asked who was the father of the child, and she said the master, and I had every reason to believe her, as the child was nearly white, had blue eyes and veins, yet notwithstanding this we lived happily together, and I felt happy and comfortable, and I should never have thought of running away if she had not been sold. We lived together six years and had two children. Shortly after my marriage my master's wife died, and when he fixed upon Tillotson's daughter as his future wife, she made a condition that all female slaves whom he had at any time been intimate with must be sold, and my wife being one was sold with the children as well as any other female slaves. My wife was sold while I was away on an errand at Centreville, and any one situated as I was may imagine my feelings when I say that I left them in the morning all well and happy, in entire ignorance of any evil, and returned to find them all sold and gone away, and from then until now I have never seen any of them. I went to my master and complained to him, when he told me he knew nothing about it, as it was all done by his wife. I then went to her and she said she knew nothing about, as it was all done by my master, and I could obtain no other satisfaction; I then went to my master to beg him to sell me to the same master as he had sold my wife, but he said he could not do that, as she was sold to a trader.

From 18 to 27 I was considered one of the most devout christians among the whole Black population, and under this impression I firmly believed to run away from my master would be to sin against the Holy Ghost—for such we are taught to believe—but from the time of my wife's being sent away, I firmly made up my mind to take the first opportunity to run away. I had learned that if a Black man wished to escape he will have no chance to do so unless he be well supplied with money; to attain this I arranged with a Dutchman to steal small pigs, chickens, and any poultry that was possible to lay my hands on, and thus I proceeded for nine or ten months, when I found my accumulation to be 124 dollars. Among the plantations I visited was Mr. Roger's, and he had three large bloodhounds let loose about nine at night, but I had made them acquainted with me by feeding them at intervals quietly, unknown to him or his people, and this enabled me to carry on my depredations on his plantation quietly and unmolested. Rogers having suspected these depredations, and not being able to find the thief, set a patrol to watch, who, armed with a double-barreled gun, fixed himself under a fence about seven feet high, surrounded with bushes; but this happened to be my usual way of going to his plantation, and as I made my usual spring to go over, I fell right on the top of his head, and he shouted lustily, and I shouted also, neither of us knowing what really had occurred, and our fears imagining the worst and causing him to run one way and me another. After travelling about a quarter of a mile I thought of my bag, which had been dropped during my fright, and knowing that my master's initials were on the bag, and the consequences of the bag being found would be fearful, I determined to return for the bag and recover it, or die in the attempt. I searched for and found a club, then I returned to the spot and found the bag there, and by the side of it lay the gun of the patrol, and I picked the bag up and went home, and this narrow escape caused me to determine to give up my thieving expeditions for the obtaining of money from that time. About one week after the occurrence with the patrol, I took one of my master's horses to go to a negro dance, and on my return the patrols were so numerous on the road that I was unable to return home without observation, and it being past the usual hour for being at home, I was so afraid that when two of them observed me I left the horse and took to my feet, and made my way to the woods, where I remained all day, afraid to go home for fear of the consequences. But at night I returned to the barn, where my money was hid in the hay, and having recovered it, I started for Dr. Tillotson's (my master's father-in-law), and told him my master had sent me for a horse which he had lent him a few weeks before. After enquiring of the overseer if the horse had not gone home, and finding it had not, he ordered it to be given up to me. I mounted the horse and rode off for Baltimore, a distance of 37 miles, where I arrived early in the morning, when I abandoned the horse and took to the woods, and remained there all day. At night I ventured to a farm-house, and having a club with me, I knocked over two barn fowl, and took them to my place in the woods; I struck a light with the tinder, made a fire of brushwood, roasted them before the fire, and enjoyed a hearty meal without seasoning or bread.

The following night I went to the city, and meeting with some blacks I entered into conversation with them, and I asked if they had heard of any runaways at Baltimore, they said they had heard of one Jake having run from Eastern shore, and showed me the bill at the corner which had been put up that evening. I knew it was no other than me, so I bid them good evening, and left them saying I was going to church. I took a back road for Milford, in Delaware, and travelled all night; towards morning I met four men, who demanded to know to whom I belonged, my answer was taking to my heels, and the chase was hot on my part for about half an-hour, when I got into a swamp surrounded by young saplings, where I remained about two hours, and as soon as it was sufficiently dark to venture out, I made my way to a barn where I secreted myself all day, and in the morning I watched the house to prevent a surprise. At night I again commenced travelling, and at one o'clock in the morning arrived at Milford, where finding no means of crossing the bridge into the town, without being seen by the patrol, I was forced to swim across the river. I passed through Milford, and was ten miles on my road to Wilmington before daybreak, where I again made for the woods, and got into a marshy part and was swamped. I was struggling the whole night to liberate myself, but in vain, until the light appeared, when I saw some willows, and by laying hold of them I succeeded in extricating myself about seven o'clock in the morning. I then made my way to a pond of water, and pulled my clothes off, and washed the mud from them and hung them up to dry; and as soon as they were dry and night arrived, I put them on, and continued my journey that night in the woods, as the moon was so bright; though I did not progress much on my way, it was more safe. Towards morning I saw a farm-house, and being hungry I resolved to venture to ask for something to eat. Waiting my opportunity, I saw three men leave the house, and judging there then only remained women, I went up and asked if they would please to give me something to eat. They invited me in, and gave me some bread and milk, pitying my condition greatly, one of them telling me that her husband was an Abolitionist, and if I would wait until his return he would place me out of the reach of my pursuers. I did not then understand what was an Abolitionist, and said I would rather not stay. She then saw my feet, which were awful from what I had undergone, and asked me if I should not like to have a pair of shoes, and I said I should. They went in search of a pair up the stairs, and I heard one say to the other, "He answers the description of a slave for which 200 dollars are offered." When they returned I was sitting still in the position I was in before they went up stairs. She said to the other, "I will go and see after the cows;" and the other answered, "Don't be long." But my suspicion was confirmed that going after the cows was only a pretence; and when I thought the other had got far enough away, I laid hold of the remaining one and tied her to the bedstead; went into the closet and took a leg of mutton, and other articles, such as bread and butter, and made my way out as quick as possible; and when I got out outside I rubbed my feet in some cow dung to prevent the scent of the bloodhounds, and took to the woods, where I found a sand hole, in which I remained all day. The night was dark, with a drizzling rain; being very fit for travelling, I started again on my journey, but being very cautious, I only managed about 24 miles that night. Towards morning I met with a black, who told me that to Chester, in Pennsylvania, was only twenty-six miles. During the day I again remained in the woods, where I met a black man of the name of Geordie, whom I knew, belonging to Rogers, and who had left two months before me, and he said he had been in those woods five weeks. His appearance was shocking, and from his long suffering and hardships he was difficult to know; and, as he was hungry, I divided with him my leg of mutton and bread and butter, and I was telling him how unwise it was to remain so long in one place, when we were suddenly aroused by the well-known sounds of the hounds. In my fear and surprise I was attempting for a tree, but was unable to mount before they were upon me. In this emergency I called out the name of one of the dogs, who was more familiar with me than the others, called Fly, and hit my knee to attract her attention and it had the desired effect. She came fondling towards me, accompanied by another called Jovial. I pulled out my knife and cut the throat of Fly, upon which Jovial made an attempt to lay hold of me and I caught him by the throat, which caused me to lose my knife, but I held him fast by the windpipe, forcing my thumbs with as much force as possible, and anxiously wishing for my knife to be in hands. I made a powerful effort to fling him as far away as possible, and regained my knife; but when I had thrown him there he lay, throttled to death. Not so, Fly, who weltered in blood, and rolled about howling terribly, but not killed. The other two hounds caught Geordie, and killed him. After this terrible escape I went to a barn, and was looking through a hole and saw two men come to where Geordie's body lay, when a knot of people gathered round, and about ten or eleven o'clock he was buried. I shortly went to sleep among the hay, and slept so soundly that it was the morning after before I was awoke by a boy coming to get hay for the horses, and the prong of the fork caught me by the thigh, which caused me to jump up and stare at the boy, and he at me, when he dropped the fork and ran away. As soon as I recovered, I slipped down the hay-rack, and met six men and the boy, who demanded who I was and what I was doing there. Not knowing what to say, I stood speechless for a long time, and thought my hopes of freedom were now at an end. They again repeated their question, but I made no reply. I was then taken before a magistrate, when I was accused of being in the barn for some unlawful purpose; and as I made no answer to any questions put to me, they concluded I was dumb. When I remembered I had not given evidence of speech, I determined to act as if I was dumb; and when the magistrate called to me, I also thought deafness was often united with dumbness, and I made my mind up to act both deaf and dumb, and when he called "Boy, come here," I took no notice, and did not appear to hear, until one of the officers led me from the box nearer to the magistrate, who demanded my name, where from, and to whom I belonged, and what I was doing in the barn, which I still appeared not to hear, and merely looked at him, and at last acted as if I was deaf and dumb, and so effectually that he discharged me, convinced I was a valueless deaf and dumb nigger; and when told by the officer to go, I dared not move for fear of being found out in my acting, and would not move until I was forced out of the door, and for some time (for fear of detection) I acted deaf and dumb in the streets, to the fear of women and children, until it was dark, when I made for the woods, where I remained until eleven o'clock at night, when I again resumed my journey to Chester (Pennsylvania), which I had been told was only twenty-six miles. Shortly after resuming my journey, I saw four horses in the field, and I determined, if possible to possess one of them, and I chased them two hours, but did [not] succeed in catching one; so I was obliged to go on walking again, but shortly met with a gentleman's horse on the road which I mounted, and rode into Chester, and let the horse go where he liked. In Chester I met with a quaker, named Sharples, who took me to his house, gave me the best accommodation, and called his friends to see me, never seemed weary of asking questions of negro life in the different plantations. I let them see the money I had, which was in notes, and much damaged by my swimming across the river, but they kindly passed it for me, and I got other money for it; and I was presented with two suits of clothes. He sent in a waggon to Philadelphia and recommended me to a gentleman (who being alive, I wish not to reveal), where I remained in his employ about five weeks. This kind friend persuaded me to make for Canada; and it was with much reluctance I at last complied. My reluctance was in consequence of understanding that Canada was a very cold place, and I did not relish the idea of going on that account; and as a gentleman said he could find employment for me at Derby, near Philadelphia, I went and worked there three years, during which time I was a regular attendant at the Methodist Free Church, consisting entirely of colored people; at which place I heard the scriptures expounded in a different way by colored ministers—as I found that God had made colored as well as white people: as He had made of one blood all the families of the earth, and that all men were free and equal in his sight; and that he was no respecter of persons whatever the color: but whoever worked righteousness was accepted of Him. Being satisfied that I had not sinned against the Holy Ghost by obtaining my freedom, I enlisted in the church, and became one of the members thereof.

About this time, Mr. Roberts, for whom I worked, failed in business, and his property was seized for debt and sold, thereby throwing me out of employment. I was arrested and taken back to Maryland, where I was placed in prison, with a collar round my neck for eleven days.

On the twelfth day my master came to see me, and of course I begged of him to take me home and let me go to work. No, nigger, said master—I have no employment for a vagabond of your stamp; but I'm going to order that collar off your neck, not because I think that you are sufficiently punished, but because there are some gentlemen coming through the jail tomorrow, and they want to purchase some negroes, so you had better do your best to get a master amongst them—and mind you don't tell them that ever you ran away, for if you do none of them will buy you. Now I will give you a good character, notwithstanding you have done your best to injure me, a good master, and you have even tried to rob me by running away—still I'll do my best to get you a good master, for my bible teaches me to do good for evil. The next day I was called out with forty other slaves, belonging to different owners in the County, and we were marched into the doctor's vestry for examination; here the doctor made us all strip—men and women together naked in the presence of each other while the examination went on. When it was concluded, thirty-eight of us were pronounced sound, and three unsound; certificates were made out and given to the auctioneer to that effect. After dressing ourselves we were all driven into the slave sty directly under the auction block, when the jail warder came and gave to every slave a number, my number was twenty. Here, let me explain, for the better information of the reader, that in the inventory of the slaves to be sold all go by number—one, two, three, and so on; and if a man and his family are to be sold in one lot, then one number covers them all; but if separate, then they have all different numbers. An old friend of mine, belonging to William Steel, was also with his wife and six children in the same sty, all to be sold. The youngest was a babe in arms, the other five were large enough to walk; his number was twenty-one, but his wife's number was thirty-three, and notwithstanding the mournful idea of parting with relations and friends on the plantation, up to this moment they had indulged a hope of being sold as a family together; but the numbers revealed the awful disappointment. Even in this hoped for consolation, the painful distress into which this poor woman was thrown, it is beyond my ability to describe. The anguish of her soul, evinced by the mournful gaze first at her children and then at her husband, made me forget for the time being, my own sufferings and sorrows. Her looks seemed to say to her husband—these are your children, I am their mother—there is no other being in this world that I have to look to for love and protection; cant you help me? I am very much mistaken if these were not the thoughts running through that poor broken-hearted mother's mind. Reuben, for that was his name, called his wife and children into one corner of the sty, and repeated a verse of a hymn which may be found in Watts' hymn book:—[11]

> "Ah, whither shall I go,
>   Burthened, or sick, or faint;
> To whom shall I my troubles show,
>   And pour out my complaint."

Not daring to sing it for fear of disturbing the sale, they both knelt down with the children, and Reuben offered up a long and fervent prayer. In the interval of his prayer nineteen of the slaves were sold, and he had not concluded when my number being twenty was called, and my master handed me out under the hammer; when, after a few preliminary remarks on the part of the auctioneer, my master mounted the auction block and recommended me as a good field hand, a good cook, waiter, hostler, a coachman, gentle and willing, and above all, free from the disease of running away. So after a short and spirited bidding I went at 1,025 dollars. Here the sale policeman, whose business it was to take charge of the negroes sold until bills were settled and papers made out, led me from the block outside the crowd, and placing me by a cart, put on a pair of iron handcuffs; but being well acquainted with me as a troublesome tricky negro, he put the handcuff on my right wrist—took the other cuff through the cart wheel and round the spoke, and then locked it on my left hand, so that if I did start to run, I should carry the cart and all with me. Number twenty-one was now called, and out came poor Reuben, and was placed under the hammer; his weight was said to be two hundred pounds, his age thirty-two. Poor Sally, his wife, unable any longer to control her feelings, made her way out of the slave pen, with her babe in her arms, followed by her five small children, and she threw one of her arms around Reuben's neck; and now commenced a scene that beggars all description. Her countenance, though mild and beautiful, was by the keenest pain and sorrow distorted and disfigured; her voice soft and gentle, accompanied with heart rending gestures, appealed to the slave buyer in tones so very mournful, that I thought it might have even melted cruelty itself to some pity—coming as it did from a woman:—Oh! master, master! buy me and my children with my husband—do, pray; and this was the only crime the poor woman committed for which she suffered death on the spot. Her master stepped up from behind her, and, with the butt end of his carriage whip loaded with lead, struck her a blow on the side of the head or temples, and she fell her full length to the ground. Poor Reuben stooped to raise her up, but was prevented by the jail policeman, who seized him by the neck and led him over close to where I stood; and whilst he was in the act of selecting a pair of handcuffs for Reuben, voice after voice was heard in the crowd—she is dead! she is dead! But what was the effect of these words upon Reuben—one of the most easy, good-tempered, innocent, inoffensive, and, in his way, religious slaves that I ever knew—satisfied apparently that Sally's death was a fact—he tore himself loose from the policeman and made his way through the crowd to where poor Sally lay, and exclaimed, Oh! Sally! O Lord! By this time the policeman, who had followed him, undertook to drag him back out of the crowd, but Reuben, with one blow of his fist, stretched the policeman on the ground. Reuben's pain and sorrow, mingled with his religious hope, seemed now to terminate in despair, and transformed the inoffensive man into a raging demon. He rushed to a cart which supported a great number of spectators, just opposite the auction block, and tore out a heavy cart stave, made of red oak, and before the panic-stricken crowd could arrest his arm, he struck his master to the ground, and beat his brains literally out. The crowd then tried to close upon him, but Reuben, mounted with both feet upon the dead body of his master, and with his back against the cart wheel—with the cart stave kept the whole crowd at bay for the space of two or three minutes, when a gentleman behind the cart climbed upon the outside wheel and fired the pistol at him, and shot poor Reuben through the head. He fell dead about six yards from where the dead body of his beloved Sally lay, and where his children were screaming terribly. An indescribable thrill of horror crept through my whole soul, as I gazed from the cart wheel to which I was ironed, upon the dead bodies first of Reuben and then his wife, who but a few moments before I had seen kneeling in solemn prayer, before what they considered the Throne of Grace—and their master, whom I heard that very morning calling on God not only to damn his negroes, but to damn himself, now, in less than thirty minutes, all three standing before the awful Judgment Seat. After witnessing this dreadful scene I was led into Hagerstown jail, where I remained until my new master was ready, when I went with him to Memphis, Tennessee; but the remembrance of this awful tragedy haunted my mind, and even my dreams, for many months.

Reuben was the son of old Uncle Reuben and Aunt Dinah, and had been swopped away when about twelve years old to William Steele, for a pair of horses and a splendid carriage. Like his father and mother he was very religious, and I had often been to his prayer meetings, where poor Reuben would exhort and preach. Mr. Cobb had made him a class-leader long before he died; and, in fact, we all reverenced Reuben after the death of his father as the most moderate and gifted man amongst us. I had always loved Reuben, but never knew how much until that fatal day. After I went to Memphis I composed some verses on the life and death of Reuben, which run as follows:—

Poor Reuben he fell at his post,
    He's gone;
Like Stephen, full of the Holy Ghost,[12]
    Poor Reuben's gone away.
He's gone where pleasure never dies,
    He's gone,
In the golden chariot to the skies,
    Poor Reuben's gone away.

For many years he faced the storm,
    He's gone;
And the cruel lash he suffered long;
    Poor Reuben's gone away.
But now he's left the land of death,
    He's gone;
And entered heaven's happiness;
    Poor Reuben's gone away.

His friends he bid a long adieu,
    He's gone;
When heaven opened to his view,
    Poor Reuben's gone away;
His pain and sorrow of heart are passed,
    He's gone;
He arrived in heaven just safe at last;
    Poor Reuben's gone away.

Poor Sally, his wife, lays by his side,
    He's gone;
For whom poor Reuben so nobly died;
    Poor Reuben's gone away;
A mournful look on her her he cast,
    He's gone,
Five minutes before he breathed his last,
    Poor Reuben's gone away.

In Jordan the angel heard him cry,
    He's gone;
Elijah's chariot was passing by,
    Poor Reuben's gone away;
His body lays in the earth quite cold,
    He's gone,
But now he walks in the streets of gold,
    Poor Reuben's gone away.

After working in Tennessee three years and seven months, my master hired me to Mr. Steele. This gentleman was going to New Orleans, and I was to act as his servant, but I contrived to get away from him, and went to the house of a free black, named Gibson and after working four days on the levy (or wharf) I succeeded in secreting myself in a ship, well supplied by Mr. Gibson and friends with provisions, and in the middle hold under the cotton I remained until the ship arrived at New York; my being there was only known to two persons on board, the steward and the cook, both colored persons. When the vessel was docked in the pier thirty-eight, North river, I managed to make my way through the booby hatch on to the deck, and was not seen by the watchman on board who supposed I was a stranger, or what they call a "River Thief." I made a jump to escape over the bow and fell into the river; but before he could raise an alarm, I had reached the next dock, got out and made my way off as fast as possible. I wandered about the streets until morning, not knowing where to go, during which time my clothes had dried on my body. About ten o'clock in the forenoon I met with a colored man named Grundy, who took me to his house, and gave me something to eat, and enquired where I came from and where I belonged; I hesitated about telling my true situation, but after considerable conversation with him, I ventured to confide in him, and when I had given him, all the particulars, he took me to the underground Railway office and introduced me to the officials, who having heard my story determined to send me to Canada, forty dollars being raised to find me clothes, and pay my fare to Toronto, but I was only taken to Utica, in the State of New York, where I agreed to stop with Mr. Cleveland and coachman.

In November I was sent to Post-street on an errand, where I saw my master, who laid hold of me, and called to his aid a dozen more, when I was taken before a magistrate, and that night I was placed in prison, and next day brought before a court, and ordered to be given up to my master. I was taken back to prison that afternoon, and irons placed on my ancles, and hand-cuffed; but, previous to leaving, Mr. Cleveland and family came to take a kind leave of me, and gave me religious advice and encouragement, telling me to put my trust in the Lord, and I was much affected at his little girl, who, when I was placed in the waggon, screamed and cried as if she would fall into fits, telling her father to have me brought back, for these men intended to murder me. The waggon drove to the railway depot, and I was placed in the cars, and at three o'clock we started for buffalo, where I was placed on the steam boat "Milwaukie," for Chicago, Illinois, on Lake Erie. The next night I arrived in Cleveland, and was taken from the boat, and placed in prison, until my master was ready to proceed. While in prison a complaint was made that a fugitive slave was placed in irons, contrary to the law of the state of Ohio, and after investigation, my irons were ordered to be taken off. On the Monday following I was taken on board the steam boat "Sultana" bound for Sandusky, Ohio, and on my way there, the Black people, in large numbers, made an attempt to rescue me, and so desperate was the attack, that several officers were wounded, and the attempt failed. I was placed in the cabin, and at dinner time the steam boat started, and had about half a mile to go before she got into the lake and, on the way, the captain came down to me, and cautiously asked me if I could swim—I answered I could, when he told me to stand close by a window, which he pointed out, and when the paddle wheels ceased I must jump out. I stood ready, and as soon as the wheels ceased I made a spring and jumped into the water, and after going a short distance, I looked up and saw the captain standing on the promenade deck, who, when he saw I was clear of the wheels, waved a signal for the engineer to start the vessel. I had much difficulty in preventing myself from being drawn back by the suction of the wheels, and before I had gone far I saw my master and heard him shout, "Here, here, stop captain; yonder goes my nigger," which was echoed by shouts from the passengers; but the boat continued her course, while I made my way as fast as possible to Cleveland lighthouse, where I arrived in safety, and received by an inumerable company of both blacks and whites. I was then sent to a place called Oberlin, where I remained a week, and from there I went to Zanesville, Ohio, where I stopped for four months, when I was taken up on suspicion of breaking the windows of a store, and while in prison I was seen by a Mr. Donelson, who declared to the keeper that I belonged to him. I knew him well as the father-in-law of Mr. Steel, with whom I travelled to New Orleans. He was also a methodist minister. He had me discharged by paying the damage, and making affidavit that I was his slave, I was placed in prison, and kept in two weeks, when I was brought before the court for trial; and Mr. Donelson procured papers showing that he had purchased me as a runaway. I therefore saw it was of no use prolonging the matter, and I acknowledged myself. I was then taken and put into the stage and taken to Cincinnati, Ohio, where I was placed upon the steam boat, *Pike*, No. 3, to be taken to Louisville, Kentucky, and there placed in prison a week, and on Thursday brought out to auction and sold to Mr. Silas Wheelbanks for 1,050 dollars, with whom I remained about twelve months, and acted as coachman and waiting in the house. Upon a Saturday evening, my master came and told me to make my carriage and horses so that he could see his face in them, and be ready to take my young mistress, Mary, down to Centreville, to see her grandmother. So I prepared my horses and carriage, and on Monday was ready. The lady got in, and when about seven miles I drove into a blind road, distant about two miles from any house, where I made the horses stand still, and I ordered Miss Mary to get out: and when she asked me why, I thundered out at the top of my voice, "Get out, and ask no questions." She commenced crying, and asked if I was going to kill her. I said "No, if she made no noise," I helped her out, and having no rope, I took her shawl and fastened her to a tree by the roadside; and for fear she should untie the knot and spread the alarm, I took off her veil, and with it tied her hands behind her. I then mounted the box, and drove off in the direction of Lexington, and at a place called Elton I stripped the horses of their harness and let them go. I made my way to Louisville and arrived about 7 o'clock in the evening. I walked about the dock until *Pike* No. 3, the same vessel before spoken of, was nearly ready for starting and I got a gentleman's trunk on my shoulder and went on board, and when I had been paid six cents for carrying the trunk I watched a chance, and jumped down the cotton hold and stowed myself away among the cotton bags and the next day was in Cincinnati, Ohio, where I arrived about daylight in the morning. I waited until the passengers had left the boat and saw neither officer nor engineer about when I ventured to go on shore. On starting up the hill I met my master's nephew, who at once seized hold of me, and a sharp struggle ensued. He called for help but I threw him and caught a stone and struck him on the head, which caused him to let go, when I ran away as fast my legs could carry me, pursued by a numerous crowed, crying "stop thief." I mounted a fence in the street, and ran through an alley into an Irishman's yard, and through his house, knocking over the Irishman's wife and child, and the chair on which she sat, the husband at the time sat eating at the table, jumped into a cellar on the opposite side of the street without being seen by any one, I made my way into the back cellar and went up the chimney, where I sat till dark, and at night came down and slept in the cellar. In the morning the servant girl came down into the cellar, and when I saw she was black I thought it would be best to make myself known to her, which I did, and she told me I had better remain where I was and keep quiet, and she would go and tell Mr. Nickins, one of the agents of the underground Railway. She brought me down a bowl of coffee and some bread and meat, which I relished very much, and that night she opened the cellar door gently, and called to me to come out, and introduced me to Mr. Nickins and two others, who took me to a house in Sixth street, where I remained until the next night, when they dressed me in female's clothes, and I was taken to the railway depot in a carriage—was put in the car, and sent to Cleveland, Ohio where I was placed on board a steam boat called the *Indiana*, and carried down Lake Erie to the city of Buffalo, New York, and the next day placed on the car for the Niagara Falls, and received by a gentleman named Jones, who took me in his carriage to a place called Lewiston, where I was placed on board a steamboat called *Chief Justice Robinson*. I was furnished with a ticket and twelve dollars. Three hours after starting I was in Toronto, Upper Canada, where I lived for three years and sang my song of deliverance,—[13]

WHAT THE "TIMES"[14] SAID OF THE SECESSION IN 1861

(From the *Liverpool Daily Post*, Feb. 3, 1863.)

The following article appeared as a "Leader" in the *Times* on the 7th January, 1861:—

"The State of South Carolina has seceded from the Union by a unanimous vote of her legislature, and it now remains to be seen whether any of the other Southern States will follow her example, and what course the Federal authorities will pursue under the circumstances. While we wait for further information on these points, it may be well to consider once again the cause of quarrel which has thus begun to rend asunder the mightiest confederation which the world has yet beheld. One of the prevalent delusions of the age in which we live is to regard democracy as equivalent to liberty, and the attribution of power to the poorest and worst educated citizens of the State as a certain way to promote the purest liberality of thought and the most beneficial course of action. Let those who hold this opinion examine the quarrel at present raging in the United States, and they will be aware that democracy, like other forms of government, may co-exist with any course of action or any set of principles. Between North and South there is at this moment raging a controversy which goes as deep as any controversy can into the elementary principles of human nature and the sympathies and antipathies which in so many men supply the place of reason and reflection.

The North is for freedom, the South is for slavery. The North is for freedom of discussion, the South represses freedom of discussion with the tar-brush and the pine fagot. Yet the North and South are both democracies—nay, possess almost exactly similar institutions, with this enormous divergence in theory and practice. It is not democracy that has made the North the advocate of freedom, or the South the advocate of slavery. Democracy is a quality which appears on both sides, and may therefore be rejected, as having no influence over the result. From the sketch of the history of slavery which was furnished us by our correspondent in New York last week, we learn that at the time of the American Revolution slavery existed in every State in the Union except Massachusetts; but we also learn that the great men who directed that revolution—Washington, Jefferson, Madison, Patrick Henry, and Hamilton—were unanimous in execrating the practice of slavery, and looked forward to the time when it would cease to contaminate the soil of free America. The abolition of the slave trade, which subsequently followed, was regarded by its warmest advocates as not only beneficial in itself, but as a long step towards the extinction of slavery altogether, it was not foreseen that certain free and democratic communities would arise which would apply themselves to the honourable office of breeding slaves, to be consumed on the free and democratic plantations of the South, and of thus replacing the African slave trade by an internal traffic in human flesh, carried on under circumstances of almost equal atrocity through the heart of a free and democratic nation. Democracy has verily a strong digestion, and one not to be interfered with by trifles.

"But the most melancholy part of the matter is, that during the seventy years for which the American confederacy has existed, the whole tone of sentiment with regard to slavery has, in the Southern States at least, undergone a remarkable change. Slavery used to be treated as a thoroughly exceptional institution—as an evil legacy of evil times—as a disgrace to a constitution founded on the natural freedom and independence of humankind. There was hardly a political leader of any note who had not some plan for its abolition. Jefferson himself, the greatest chief of the democracy, had in the early part of this century speculated deeply on the subject; but the United States became possessed of Louisiana and Florida, they have conquered Texas, they have made Arkansas and Missouri into States; and these successive acquisitions have altered entirely the view with which slavery is regarded. Perhaps as much as anything, from the long license enjoyed by the editors of the South of writing what they pleased in favour of slavery, with the absolute certainty that no one would be found bold enough to write anything on the other side, and thus make himself a mark for popular vengeance, the subject has come to be written on in a tone of ferocious and cynical extravagance, which is to an European eye absolutely appalling. The South has become enamoured of her shame. Free labour is denounced as degrading and disgraceful; the honest triumphs of the poor man who works his way to independence are treated with scorn and contempt. It is asserted that what we are in the habit of regarding as the honourable pursuits of industry incapacitate a nation for civilisation and refinement, and that no institutions can be really free and democratic which do not rest, like those of Athens and of Rome, on a broad substratum of slavery. So far from treating slavery as an exceptional institution, it is regarded by these Democratic philosophers as the natural state of a great portion of the human race; and so far from admitting that America ought to look forward to its extinction, it is contended that the property in human creatures ought to be as universal as the property in land or in tame animals.

"Nor have these principles been merely inert or speculative. For the last ten or twelve years slavery has altered her tactics, and from a defensive she has become an aggressive power. Every compromise which the moderation of former times had erected to stem the course of this monster evil has been swept away, and that not by the encroachments of the North, but by the aggressive ambition of the South. With a majority in Congress and in the Supreme Court of the United States, the advocates of slavery have entered on a career the object of which would seem to be to make their favourite institution conterminous with the limits of the Republic. They have swept away the Missouri compromise, which limited slavery to the tract south of 36 degrees of north latitude. They have forced upon the North, in the Fugitive Slave Bill, a measure which compels them to lend their assistance to the South in the recovery of their bondmen. In the case of Kansas they have sought by force of arms to assert the right of bringing slaves into a free territory, and in the Dred Scott case they obtained an extrajudicial opinion from the Supreme Court, which would have placed all the territories at their disposal. All this while the North has been resisting, feebly and ineffectually, this succession of Southern aggressions. All that was desired was peace, and that peace could not be obtained.

While these things were done the South continued violently to upbraid the Abolitionists of the North as the cause of all their troubles, and the ladies of South Carolina showered presents and caresses on the brutal assailant of Mr. Sumner.[15] In 1856 the North endeavoured to elect a President[16] who thoughtfully recognising the right of the South to its slave property, was opposed to its extension in the territories. The North were defeated, and submitted almost without a murmur to the result. On the present occasion the South has submitted to the same ordeal, but not with the same success. They have taken their chance of electing a President of their own views, but they have failed. Mr. Lincoln, like Colonel Freemont, fully recognises the right of the South to the institution of slavery, but, like him, he is opposed to its extension. This cannot be endured. With a majority in both houses of Congress and in the Supreme Court of the United States, the South cannot submit to a President who is not their devoted servant. Unless every power in the constitution is to be strained in order to promote the progress of slavery, they will not remain in the Union; they will not wait to see whether they are injured, but resent the first check to their onward progress as an intolerable injury. This, then, is the result of the history of slavery. It began as a tolerated, it has ended as an aggressive institution, and if it now threatens to dissolve the Union, it is not because it has anything to fear for that which it possesses already, but because it has received a check of its hopes of future acquisition."

SECESSION CONDEMNED IN A SOUTHERN CONVENTION.

SPEECH

Of the Hon. A. H. STEPHENS,[17] made at the Georgia State Convention, held January, 1861, for the purpose of determining whether the State of Georgia was to secede. Notwithstanding this remarkable speech of an extraordinary man, the Convention decided on secession. Mr. Stephens was afterwards elected Vice President of the so-called Confederacy. This distinction shows the estimate of his powers, and adds force to the deliverance, the prophetic declarations of which are now being fulfilled to the letter.

This step of secession, once taken, can never be recalled; and all the baleful and withering consequences that must follow, will rest on the convention for all coming time. When we and our posterity shall see our lovely South desolated by the demon of war, which this act of yours will inevitably invite and call forth; when our green fields of waving harvests shall be trodden down by the murderous soldiery and fiery car of war sweeping over our land; our temples of justice laid in ashes; all the horrors and desolations of war upon us; who, but this Convention will be held responsible for it? and but him who shall have given his vote for this unwise and ill-timed measure, as I honestly think and believe, shall be held to strict account for this suicidal act by the present generation, and probably cursed and execrated by posterity for all coming time, for the wide and desolating ruin that will inevitably follow this act you now propose to perpetrate? Pause, I entreat you, and consider for a moment what reason you can give that will even satisfy yourselves in calmer moments—what reasons you can give to your fellow-sufferers in this calamity that it will bring upon us. What reasons can you give to the nations of the earth to justify it? They will be the calm and deliberate judges in the case? and what cause or one overt act can you name or point, on which to rest the plea of justification? What right has the North assailed? What interest of the South has been invaded? What justice has been denied? and what claim founded in justice and right has been withheld? Can either of you to-day name one governmental act of wrong deliberately and purposely done by the government of Washington, of which the South has a right to complain? I challenge the answer. While, on the other hand, let me show the facts (and believe me, gentlemen, I am not here the advocate of the North; but I am here the friend, the firm friend and lover of the South and her institutions; and for this reason I speak thus plainly and faithfully—for yours, mine, and every other man's interest—the words of truth and soberness), of which I wish you to judge; and I will only state facts which are clear and undeniable, and which now stand as records authentic in the history of our country. When we of the South demanded the slave trade or importation of Africans for the cultivation of our lands, did they not yield the right for twenty years? When we asked a three-fifths representation in congress for our slaves was it not granted? When we asked and demanded the return of any fugitive from justice, or the recovery of those persons owing labor and allegiance, was it not incorporated in the constitution, and again ratified and strengthened in the Fugitive Slave Law of 1850? But do you reply that in many instances they have violated this compact and have not been faithful to their engagements? As individual and local communities they may have done so; but not by the sanction of government for that has always been true to Southern interest. Again, gentlemen, look at another fact, when we have asked that more territory should be added, that we might spread the institution of slavery, have they not yielded to our demands in giving us Louisiana, Florida, and Texas out of which four States have been carved and ample territory for four more to be added in due time, if you by this unwise and impolitic act do not destroy this hope and perhaps, by it lose all, and have your last slave wrenched from you by stern military rule, as South America and Mexico were; or by the vindictive decree of a universal emancipation, which may reasonably be expected to follow. But, again, gentlemen, what have we to gain by this proposed change of our relation to the general government?

We have always had the control of it, and can yet, if we remain in it and are as united as we have been. We have had a majority of the presidents chosen from the South, as well as the control and management of most of those chosen from the North. We have had sixty years of Southern presidents to their twenty-four, thus controlling the executive department. So of the judges of the Supreme Court, we have had eighteen from the south, and but eleven from the North; although nearly four-fifths of the judicial business has arisen in the Free States, yet a majority of the court has always been from the South. This we have required so as to guard against any interpretation of the constitution unfavourable to us. In like manner we have been equally watchful to guard our interests in the legislative branch of government. In choosing the presiding president (*pro. tem.*) of the Senate, we have had twenty-four to their eleven. Speakers of the house we have had twenty-three, and they twelve. While the majority of the representatives, from their greater population, have always been from the North, yet we have so generally secured the speaker, because he, to a greater extent, shapes and controls the legislation of the country. Nor have we had less control in every other department of the general government. Attorney-Generals we have had fourteen, while the North have had but five. Foreign ministers we have had eighty-six and they but fifty-four. While three-fourths of the business which demands diplomatic agents aboard is clearly from the Free States, from their greater commercial interests, yet we have had the principal embassies, so as to secure the world's markets for our cotton, tobacco, and sugar on the best possible terms. We have had a vast majority of the higher offices of both army and navy, while a larger proportion of the soldiers and sailors were drawn from the North. Equally so of clerks, auditors, and comptrollers filling the executive department, the records show for the last fifty years that of the three thousand thus employed we have had more than two-thirds of the same, while we have but one-third of the white population of the republic. Again, look at another item, and one, be assured, in which we have a great and vital interest; it is that of revenue, or means of supporting government. From official documents we learn that a fraction over three-fourths of the revenue collected for the support of government has uniformly been raised from the North. Pause now while you can, gentlemen, and contemplate carefully and candidly these important items. Leaving out of view, for the present, the countless millions of dollars you must expend in a war with the North; with tens of thousands of your sons and brothers slain in battle, and offered up as sacrifices upon the altar of your ambition—and for what? we ask again. Is it for the overthrow of the American government, established by our common ancestry, cemented and built up by their sweat and blood, and founded on the broad principles of right, justice, and humanity? And, as such, I must declare here, as I have often done before, and which has been repeated by the greatest and wisest of statesmen and patriots in this and other lands, that it is the best and freest government—the most equal in its rights, the most just in its decisions, the most lenient in its measures, and the most inspiring in its principles to elevate the race of men, that the sun of heaven ever shone upon. Now, for you to attempt to overthrow such a government as this, under which we have lived for more than three-quarters of a century—in which we have gained our wealth, our standing as a nation, our domestic safety while the elements of peril are around us, with peace and tranquility accompanied with unbounded prosperity and rights unassailed—is the height of the *madness, folly,* and *wickedness,* to which I can neither lend my sanction nor my vote.

THE CONFEDERATE AND THE SCOTTISH CLERGY ON SLAVERY.

Some three months ago, we published an "Address to Christians throughout the world," by "the clergy of the Confederate States of America;" and yesterday we published a reply to that address, signed by nearly a thousand ministers of the various Churches in Scotland. The Confederate address begins with a solemn declaration that its scope is not political but purely religious—that it is sent forth "in the name of our Holy Christianity," and in the interests of "the cause of our most Blessed Master." Immediately after making this declaration, however, the Confederate divines commence a long series of arguments designed to prove that the war cannot restore the Union; that the Southern States had a right to secede; that having seceded, their separation from the North is final; that the proclamation of PRESIDENT LINCOLN, seeking to free the slaves is a most horrible and wicked measure, calling for "solemn protest on the part of the people of GOD throughout the world;" that the war against the Confederacy has made no progress; and there seems no likelihood of the United States accomplishing any good by its continuance. This may be esteemed good gospel teaching in the Confederate States, but in this country it would be thought to have very little connection with "the cause of our most Blessed Master." But the Southern clergyman reserve for the close of their address the defence of the grand dogma of their religion—the doctrine that negro slavery as carried out in the Southern States of America "is not incompatible with our holy Christianity." Stupendous as this proposition may appear to the British mind, it offers no difficulty to these learned and pious men. Nay, they are not only convinced that slavery is "not incompatible" with Christianity, but they boldly affirm that it is a divinely established institution, designed to promote the temporal happiness and eternal salvation of the negro race, and that all efforts to bring about the abolition of slavery are sacrilegious attempts to interfere with the plans of Divine Providence." "We testify in the sight of GOD," say the clergy of the Confederate States, "that the relation of master and slave among us, however we may deplore abuses in this, as in any other relations of mankind, is not incompatible with our holy Christianity, and that the presence of the Africans in our land is an occasion of gratitude on their behalf before GOD; seeing that thereby Divine Providence has brought them where missionaries of the cross may freely proclaim to them the word of salvation, and the work is not interrupted by agitating fanaticism. * * * We regard Abolitionism as an interference with the plans of Divine Providence. It has not the signs of the Lord's blessing. It is a fanaticism which puts forth no good fruit; instead of blessing, it has brought forth cursing; instead of love, hatred; instead of life, death—bitterness and sorrow, and pain; and infidelity and moral degeneracy follow its labours." There is no shirking of the question here. Slavery is proclaimed to be the God-appointed means for the regeneration of the African race, and those who seek to bring about the emancipation of the slaves are branded as apostles of infidelity. Upon these grounds, the confederate clergy appeal to Christians throughout the world to aid them in creating a sentiment against this war— "against persecution for conscience sake, against the ravaging of the church of God by fanatical invasion."

In their reply to this appeal, the Scottish ministers do what the Confederate ministers professed their intention of doing—they avoid every thing in the shape of

political discussion. Among those gentlemen there is no doubt considerable difference of opinion respecting the two parties in the civil war; but they say nothing of
that, and address themselves exclusively to the question of slavery. Happily, there
is no difference of opinion upon that point among men who take upon themselves
the high office of preaching God's word in this country. The Scottish Ministers, in
powerful and manly language, express the "deep grief, alarm, and indignation"
with which they have seen men who profess to be servants of the Lord Jesus Christ
defend slavery as a Christian institution, worthy of being perpetuated and extended, not only without regret, but with entire satisfaction and approval. "Against
all this," say they, "in the name of that holy faith and that thrice holy name which
they venture to invoke on the side of a system which treats immortal and redeemed
men as goods and chattels, denies them the rights of marriage and of home, con-
signs them to ignorance of the first rudiments of education, and exposes them to
the outrages of lust and passion—we must earnestly and emphatically protest." We
believe that this is the answer of the whole British community to the appeal of the
Confederate clergy. However much the public sentiment may have been misled respecting the rights and the wrongs of the two parties in the war, it cannot but be
sound at the core on the subject of slavery. There are many thousands of people
who have not the slightest sympathy with slavery, and who yet sympathise with the
slave-owners because they have a vague impression that the Southerners are brave
gentlemen and the Northerners base mechanics. They have managed by some
strange process to separate the cause of slavery from the cause of slave-owner, and
while they rejoice at every success which tends towards the establishment of a confederacy which is to have slavery as the "head stone of the corner," they continue
to pray as fervently as ever that the fetters of the slaves may be broken. All such
people—and they constitute the mass of the Southern sympathisers in this country—must be ready to repudiate with the sternest indignation this attempt to connect the holy religion of Christ with the most horrible oppression which the cruelty and cupidity of man ever created.

But it is not enough that the Confederate defence of slavery should be rejected. It was proper that the Scottish ministers of religion should deal only with
the religious aspect of the question, but it is the duty of every man who feels that
he has any influence in the world—and there is no man who has not some—to study
the political lessons which the address affords. There can be no doubt that the appeal expresses the genuine sentiment of the Southern States, softened down by
whatever softening influence there may be in their peculiar kind of Christianity,
and shaped to offend as little as possible the prejudices of British readers. And what
does it show us? Does it show us that emancipation is more likely to follow from
the success of the Southern society which assumes to be at the helm of all schemes
of religion and philanthropy, not only has no desire to put an end to slavery, but
regards it in such a light that it will be its duty *to extend it as much as possible.* The
Southern clergy say that the relation of master and slave is "not incompatible with
our holy Christianity:" why, therefore, should they seek to get rid of it? From a
thousand pulpits this language will be sent forth week after week, and it is clear
that the religion of the Confederate States will be employed only to convince the
slaveowner that he is doing perfectly right in perpetuating a system which enables
him to buy men and women as chattels, and to obtain command of human bodies
and minds at the prices current of the market. Then, the Southern clergy think it a

cause for gratitude to GOD on behalf of the negroes "that He has brought them where missionaries of the Cross might freely proclaim to them the word of salvation." Will it not, therefore, be the duty of the Southern clergy to extend those blessings to new millions of Africans, and thus carry out the "plans of Divine Providence?" Is the whole tendency of this argument not to elevate the horrible trade of the slave-catcher to the same high level with the noble office of the missionary? Proclaiming as they do that the capture of Africans and their removal into slavery in the Southern States is GOD's own missionary plan, the Confederate clergy and people will consider it as much their duty to equip slave-ships with cargoes of manacles and send them forth accompanied by the prayers of the churches, as it is now our duty to send forth missionary-ships laden with Bibles and preachers of the gospel. Then the heathen world will know what missionary Christianity really is. Thousand of Africans, caught on the west coast, will be torn from their families and taken chained on board ship; should they survive the horrors of the passage, they will be set to hard work under laws which permit of almost any degree of corporeal punishment and which deprive them of all the rights of men; and they will be told to thank GOD who has brought them into the blessed light of the Gospel! Let not the man who cannot reconcile his sympathies in the American struggle with his convictions on the question of slavery pooh-pooh this as an extravagant fancy picture of something that never can occur. It is exactly the missionary scheme which the Confederate clergy call "the plan of Divine Providence;" and supposing a powerful Southern Confederacy to be established, what is to prevent its being accomplished? Not the religious and philanthropic feelings of the Confederates; for the religious and philanthropic feelings of the confederates are all for a revival of the slave trade. Not treaties concluded with foreign nations; for a people holding such sentiments could never make a treaty shutting themselves out from the most promising field of missionary labour; or if forced by circumstances to conclude it, their religious convictions would urge them to break it at any moment. In fact, were a powerful nationality once established, with interests and religious convictions all pointing in the way of reviving the slave trade, it would be utterly impossible to prevent a resumption of that abominable traffic.

We have dealt with the professed convictions of the Southern ministers as sincere convictions. We should be sorry to accuse any body of men professing to be teachers of the Christian religion of intentional insincerity, and although we can hardly conceive the possibility of men who base their religion upon the same Bible upon which we rest ours, attempting sincerely to justify slavery upon religious grounds, we would rather attribute the extraordinary moral obliquity which the attempt exhibits to the demoralising influence of the slave system than to actual hypocrisy. The spectacle of a crowd of learned and no doubt pious men standing forth as the avowed apologists of a system which deprives their fellow-men of all the rights of humanity is, perhaps, the most distressing evidence of its blighting and blinding influence which has yet been exhibited to the world. It ought to have its effect. As we have said, it is the duty of every man to study the lessons which this address of the Confederate clergy has for him. If his sympathy and influence be given to the Confederates, let him understand the nature of the cause he is aiding. Let him learn from the statement of the Confederates themselves that their cause is the cause of slavery, and that they look forward to the perpetuation and extension of slavery as the prize of success.

SLAVERY AND LIBERTY.[18]

I'm on my way to Canada,
   That dark and dreary land;
Oh! the dread effects of slavery
   I can no longer stand.
My soul is vexed within me so
   To think I am a slave,
Resolved I am to strike the blow,
   For freedom or the grave.

     CHORUS—
   Oh, Righteous Father!
     Wilt thou not pity me,
   And help me on to Canada,
     Where coloured men are free.

I've served my master all my days,
   Without one dimes' reward,
And now I'm forced to run away,
   To flee the lash and rod.
The hounds are baying on my track,
   And master just behind,
Resolved that he will bring me back
   Before I cross the line.

Old master went to preach one day,
   Next day he looked for me;
I greased my heels and ran away,
   For the land of liberty.
I dreamt I saw the British Queen
   Majestic on the shore;
If e'er I reach old Canada,
   I will come back no more.

I heard that Queen Victoria said,
   If we would all forsake
Our native land of Slavery,
   And come across the lake:
That she was standing on the shore
   With arms extended wide,
To give us all a peaceful home
   Beyond the swelling tide.

I heard old master pray one night,
   That night he prayed for me,
That God would come with all his might,
   From Satan set me free.
So I from Satan would escape
   And flee the wrath to come,
If there's a fiend in human shape,
   Old master must be one.

1. Andrews, *Free Story*, 207.

2. Ibid., 211.

3. Ibid., 214, 265.

4. The faultiness of its typography makes Green's perhaps the least legible of the slave narratives: it is replete with typographical errors (which have been here corrected) and missing and broken type. This may be one reason it was not reprinted in the 1960s and 1970s like dozens of other slave narratives.

5. This signifies that eight thousand copies of the *Narrative* were printed.

6. Huddersfield and the towns mentioned in the testimonials are located in West Yorkshire, England.

7. On the Delaware Peninsula, across the Chesapeake Bay from Annapolis.

8. A *cradle* was a scythe with rods attached to it like fingers, used for harvesting grain.

9. In this context, *Sambo* simply means *black*.

10. Probably the dog's name (Carlo).

11. Isaac Watts (1674–1748), a prominent English dissenting divine, wrote several hundred hymns; the hymnbook Green refers to is an edition of his *Hymns and Spiritual Songs* (1707). The hymn he quotes, however, is by Charles Wesley (1707–88), not Watts.

12. See *Acts* 7:55. Stephen was stoned to death.

13. See song on p. 718.

14. The London *Times*.

15. The prominent abolitionist Charles Sumner (1811–74), U.S. senator from Massachusetts, was beaten with a cane by Congressman Preston S. Brooks of South Carolina, following Sumner's speech denouncing the Kansas–Nebraska Act. Brooks resigned, but was unanimously reelected by his constituents; Southerners presented him with gold-headed canes and a gold-handled cowhide.

16. John C. Fremont (1813–90), a popular Western explorer, mapmaker, military governor of California, and multimillionaire, was the first Republican presidential candidate.

17. Alexander H. Stephens (1812–83) served Georgia in the U.S. House of Representatives from 1843 to 1859 and was elected vice president of the Confederacy in 1861.

18. This song was most likely written by J. D. Green himself.

JAMES MARS

JAMES MARS(1790–c. 1877) was probably the only slave narrator to spend his entire life north of the Mason-Dixon line. His narrative has almost nothing in common with previous narratives, not only because of the difference between slave life in the North and South, but because Mars's purpose was avowedly to tell his story to his family rather than to arouse indignation, inspire lofty sentiments, or document current conditions. Although he recollects his early life with tranquility, it was full of strong actions: Mars escaped from one master, defied another, and insisted on his equality with whites. His is a coming-of-age story in which maturity arrives with the act of resistance.

Mars's narrative went through thirteen editions between 1864 and 1876; the second included an appendix that was expanded in subsequent editions. From it we learn that, subsequent to the events related in his first narrative, Mars aided a slave named Nancy to free herself from a Southern master who had taken her to Connecticut. A deacon and the father of eight children, Mars lived in Hartford about sixteen years, then moved to Pittsfield, possibly because Massachusetts laws imposed fewer restrictions on blacks.[1] In his old age he seems to have supported himself by the sale of his narrative. In the 1870 edition he stated:

> I am now in my eightieth year of age, I cannot labor but little, and finding the public have a desire to know something of what slavery was in the State of Connecticut, in its time, and how long since it was at an end, in what year it was done away, and believing that I have stated the facts, many are willing to purchase the book to satisfy themselves as to slavery in Connecticut. Some told me that they did not know that slavery was ever allowed in Connecticut, and some affirm that it never did exist in the State. What I have written of my own history, seems to satisfy the minds of those that read it, that the so called, favored state, the land of good morals and steady habits, was ever a slave state, and that slaves were driven through the streets tied or fastened together for market. This seems to surprise some that I meet, but it was true. I have it from reliable authority. Yes, this was done in Connecticut.[2]

Ever mindful of persistent inequality—blacks were denied the right to vote in the state until 1876, and racial discrimination persisted in virtually every area of public life[3]—Mars concluded, "Connecticut I love thy name, but not thy restrictions. I think the time is not far distant when the colored man will have his rights in Connecticut."[4]

LIFE

OF

JAMES MARS,

A SLAVE

BORN AND SOLD IN

CONNECTICUT.

WRITTEN BY HIMSELF.

HARTFORD:

PRESS OF CASE, LOCKWOOD & COMPANY.

1864.

TO WHOM IT MAY CONCERN:

These will certify that the bearer, DEA. JAMES MARS, has been known to me and to the citizens of this town for a long period of years, as an honest, upright, truthful man,—a good citizen, an officer in his church, and a man whose life and character have gained the approbation, the esteem, and the good wishes of all who know him. Born a slave, the good providence of God has long since made him free, and, I trust, also taught him that "where the Spirit of the Lord is, there is liberty."

JNO. TODD.

PITTSFIELD, Mass., June 23, 1864.

INTRODUCTION.

WHEN I made up my mind to write this story, it was not to publish it, but it was at the request of my sister that lived in Africa, and has lived there more than thirty years. She had heard our parents tell about our being slaves, but she was not born until a number of years after they were free. When the war in which we have been engaged began, the thought came to her mind that her parents and brothers and sisters were once slaves, and she wrote to me from Africa for the story. I came to Norfolk on a visit at the time the war broke out, and some in Norfolk remember that I was once a slave. They asked me about it; I told them something about it; they seemed to take an interest in it, and as I was in Norfolk now, and having an opportunity to write it, I thought I would write it all through. In telling it to those, there were a great many things that I did not mention that I have written. After I had written it out, I saw that my brother and my other sister would think that I might give them the same; and my children had often asked me to write it. When I had got it written, as it made more writing than I was willing to undertake to give each of them one, I thought I would have it printed, and perhaps I might sell enough to pay the expenses, as many of the people now on the stage of life do not know that slavery ever lived in Connecticut.

A SLAVE BORN AND SOLD IN CONNECTICUT.

THE treatment of slaves was different at the North from the South; at the North they were admitted to be a species of the human family. I was told when a slave boy, that some of the people said that slaves had no souls, and that they would never go to heaven, let them do ever so well.

My father was born in the State of New York, I think in Columbia county. He had, I think, three different masters in that State, one by the name of Vanepps, and he was Gen. Van Rensaeller's[5] slave in the time of the Revolution, and was a soldier in that war; he was then owned by a man whose name was Rutser, and then was owned in Connecticut, in Salisbury, and then by the minister in North Canaan.

My mother was born in old Virginia, in Loudin county; I do not remember the name of the town. The minister of North Canaan, whose name was Thompson, went to Virginia for a wife, or she came to him; in some way they got together, so that they became man and wife. He removed her to Canaan, and she brought her slaves with her, and my mother was one of them. I think there were two of my mother's brothers also. The Rev. Mr. Thompson, as he was then called, bought my father, and he was married to my mother by him. Mr. Thompson ministered to the people of Canaan in holy things; his slaves worked his farm. For a short time things went on very well; but soon the North and the South, as now, fell out; the South must rule, and after a time the North would not be ruled. The minister's wife told my father if she only had him South, where she could have at her call a half dozen men, she would have him stripped and flogged until he was cut in strings, and see if he would do as she bid him. She told him, You mind, boy, I will have you there yet, and you will get your pay for all that you have done. My father was a man of considerable muscular strength, and was not easily frightened into obedience. I have heard my mother say she has often seen her mother tied up and whipped until the blood ran across the floor in the room where she was tied and whipped.

Well, as I said, the South and the North could not agree; the South seceded and left the North;[6] the minister's wife would not live North, and she and her husband picked up and went South, and left my father and mother in Canaan to work the farm, and they lived on the farm until I was eight years old. My mother had one child when she came from the South; I was the first she had after she was married. They had five children born in Canaan,—three died in infancy. I was born March 3d, 1790.

Mr. Thompson used to come up from Virginia and talk about our going South. He would pat me on the head and tell me what a fine boy I was. Once when he was in Canaan, he asked me if I would not like to go with him and drive the carriage for my mistress. He said if I would go he would give me twenty-five cents, or as it was then called, twenty-five coppers. I told him I wanted the money first. He gave me a quarter, and then I would not agree to go, and he put me in the oven; that I did not like, and when I got out I would not give him the money, but his business I did not yet know. He had come to sell his farm and to take us all South. My father said he would not go alive; the minister told him he must go; my father said he never would. Well, the man that had formerly ministered to the people in holy things, sold the farm, and stock, and tools, and effects, with a few exceptions. He kept a pair of horses and harness, a wagon, a bed, and a few such articles. The harness and wagon he kept to take us to the South with. After he sold his place, he took us all to a wealthy friend of his, until he had settled up all his affairs, so as to show to the world that he was an honest and upright man. He would have them think that he feared God and let alone evil; for he was born or raised in the State of New York, and had taught the people of North Canaan the way to do, as you will see, for in former days he spoke to the people from the pulpit morally, and they thought much of the man. He had taught them slavery was right, and that the Great Almighty God had sanctioned the institution, and he would practice it. He now made his arrangements to set out on his journey; the day was fixed to leave his much-loved people and home for his southern home, where he had obtained a new home and friends and acquaintances.

My father, although a slave without education, was intensely watching the movements of the teacher of the people, but kept all that he saw to himself, yet he was steadily planning his escape. The set day had now within about thirty-six hours come; all went on well with the man from the South. He had had no thought but all was well; those fine chattels were his, and would fetch him in a southern market, at a moderate estimate, two thousand dollars; they would furnish him pocket change for some time, and also his loving wife could have a chance to wreak her vengeance on my father for what she called disobedience.

It was a matter of doubt with my father what course to take,—how he could get away with his family the best and safest; whether to go to Massachusetts, which joined Canaan on the north, or to Norfolk, which joined Canaan on the east. Very fortunately for us, there was at that time an unpleasant feeling existing between the two towns or the inhabitants of Canaan and Norfolk. He said that the people of Canaan would side with their former pastor, and he found that the people of Norfolk would take sides against Canaan and their pastor; then he thought the best that he could do would be to take his family to Norfolk, where they would be the safest. He concluded to take them to Norfolk, but how was he to get them there with what he wanted to take with them? He came to the conclusion that the horses he had for a long time driven might as well help him now in this hour of distress as not. He got a colored man to help him that was stout and healthy. They hitched up the parson's team, put on board what few things he had and his family, in the still of a dark night, for it was very dark, and started for Norfolk, and on the way we run afoul of a man's wood-pile, for it was so dark he could not see the road; but we got off from the wood-pile without harm, and arrived in Norfolk about one o'clock. I think we stopped at a tavern kept by Mr. G. Pettibone, and in him we found a friend. We unloaded what we had, and father and the man that was with him took the team back to Canaan, so that the parson might set out on his journey and not have to wait for his team, and father returned to where he had left his family. He felt that he had done all for the parson that he well could, for he had taken away his family off from his hands, so that the parson would be relieved from the care that must necessarily occur in such a long journey with a family on his hands to see to, and my father thought that the parson's old Jewel would be re-lieved from some of her pardoned habits and from a promise she had so often made to him when she got him South. Well, how the parson felt when he had got him-self out of bed, and found that he was left to pursue his journey alone, the reader can tell as well as I, for he was a big and bristle man; but I will leave him for a while, and see what is to be done with us.

It was soon known in the morning that we were in Norfolk; the first in-quiry was, where will they be safe. The place was soon found. There was a man by the name of Phelps that had a house that was not occupied; it was out of the way and out of sight. After breakfast, we went to the house; it was well located; it needed some cleaning, and that my mother could do as well as the next woman. We all went to work and got it cleaned, and the next day went into it and stopped some time. Father did what work he could get out of the way, where he would not be seen, and it was necessary for him to keep out of sight, for Norfolk was the thoroughfare to Hartford. Days and weeks passed on, and we began to feel quite happy, hoping that the parson had gone South, as we heard nothing from him. At length we heard that he said he would have the two boys at all hazards. It was thought best that the boys should be away. So one dark night we heard that the parson was coming out with his men to find the boys, for have them he would. A man that lived near to us said he would take the boys where they would be safe. His name was Cady. It was agreed on, and he went with us over a moun-tain, over rocks and logs. It was very rough and steep, and the night was so dark that we could only see when it lightened. At last we got through the woods on the top of what is called Burr Mountain. We could look down in low grounds and see logs that were laid for the road across the meadow; at every flash they could be seen, but when it did not lighten we could not see anything; we kept on,—our pilot knew the way. At last we arrived at the place. The name of the family was Tibbals. The family consisted of an old man, a middle-aged man and his wife and four children, and a very pleasant family it was. We had not been there long before it was thought best that my brother should be still more out of the way, as he was about six years older than I, which made him an object of greater search, and they were at a loss where to send him, as he was then about fourteen years of age. There was a young man by the name of Butler, from Mass-achusetts; he was in Norfolk at the time, studying law; he said he would take him home with him, and he did so, as I supposed, and I saw him no more for more than two years.

I stopped with the family a few days, and then went home, or what I called home. It was where my parents and sister were. I found them very lonely. I had not been home many days before our quiet was disturbed, for the parson had his hunters out to find our whereabouts. He somehow found where we were. My sister and myself were at play out at the door; we saw two men in the woods, a little from the house, coming very fast, and they came into the house. My father was not far from the house; mother was in the house. The men were Captain Phelps, the man who owned the house, and Mr. Butler, the law-student. They told us that we must now say whether we would go with the parson or not, and we must decide quick, for the parson was coming, and he would soon be on the spot, and there was no time to lose. Mother had said she was not unwilling to go herself, if it was not for father and the children, and the parson had made her such promises that she was somewhat inclined to go. The parson talked so fair to her, he beguiled her, I suppose, somewhat as our first mother was beguiled in the garden. The beguilers were both, I do not say preachers, but they were both deceivers, and he talked so smooth to mother that he beguiled her. He told her if she would go to Canaan and see to his things and pack them up for him, then if she did not want to go, she need not. Mother talked with father; he did not incline to go, but finally he consented. The parson ordered a wagon, and it was soon on the spot; but where was Joseph?—he is not here. "I want him to go with us, that we may be all together," said the parson. Father saw what the parson's plan was: he told him the boy was on the way,—he could get him when we got to Canaan. I should have said that those two men that came to tell us that the parson was coming, hid in the barn before the parson arrived, and were not seen by him. They had a few words with my father while the parson went for his team. We set off for Canaan, and in the land of Canaan we arrived that day. Where is Joseph? Father said he would go for him the next day in the morning, or in the day. Father went, as the parson supposed, for Joseph. The parson was loading; mother was packing; all was now going on well. Night came, and when all was still, for father had told some one it would be late before he got back, he came and took the parson's horses, and took mother and the two children on horseback, and instead of going South, went to Norfolk, and got there about two o'clock in the morning. We stopped at a tavern kept by Captain Lawrence. The horses were sent back for the parson, for he said he should start the next day; but it seemed that he did not start for old Virginia, for we often heard of him after that day.

We stopped with Capt. Lawrence a few days. It was thought best by our friends that we should not all be together, for it was found that the parson was still in the land, and on the lookout for us. I was sent to a woman in the neighborhood, by the name of Darby—a poor woman. I stopped with her a few days, with instructions to keep still. The old lady had but one room in her house. You may wonder why I was sent to such a place; most likely it was thought she had so little room that she would not be suspected of harboring a fugitive.

A man by the name of Walter lived near by; he was in the habit of coming in to see how his boy did, as he called me. He told me when any one came there I must get under the bed. I used to sit in the corner of the room, so that I should not be seen from the window. I stayed there a number of days,—I do not now remember how many. One day I ventured to take a peep through the key-hole; the door was locked. Some one came to the door; I made a bound, and then a roll, and I was out of sight. The door was opened, and it was my friend Mr. Walter. He was quite amused to hear the performance; he said he would take me with him the next day, he was going to work in a back lot where it would be out of sight. So the next day I went with him; it was quite a treat. At noon we ate our dinner in the field; that was new to me. After dinner Mr. Walter lay down on the ground; he told me he should go to sleep, and I must keep a look-out to see if any one came in sight. If I saw any one, I must wake him. I kept watch, but there was none came to disturb him in his repose. The day passed away, and we returned home at night—all well, as I supposed; but it seemed that the parson had his pickets out, and had got an idea that I was somewhere in the street. That night I had to leave my place at Mrs. Darby's, and went about a mile to a man's house by the name of Upson; he lived on a back street. I thought him to be a friend; I do not know but he was,—but as I find that men now act in relation to slavery, I am inclined to think otherwise. The next morning the man went to his work; he was painting for the minister in Norfolk. Mrs. Upson sent me to the brook, a little way from the house, to fetch a pail of water. I did not like going into the street very much, but being taught by my parents to obey, I went without any words. As I got to the brook, a man rode into the brook with a cocked hat on. I did not much like his looks. I did not know who he was. Said he,—"My boy, where is your father and mother?" I said, "I don't know, sir." "Where is your brother?" "I don't know, sir." "Where do you live?" "I don't know, sir." "Whom do you stay with?" "I don't know, sir." I did not then know the name of the man. He rode off, or rather I left him asking questions. He looked after me till I got to the house, and rode up. I asked Mrs. Upson who it was that came to the brook when I was there. She said it was Mr. Robbins, the minister. I thought nothing of it, for I thought all the people in Norfolk were our friends. In a few hours, the woman sent me to the neighbor's to get some water from the well. It was a widow woman where I went to get the water, and there I found my father. He said that Capt. Lawrence had been there and told him that Mr. Robbins had sent his son to Canaan to tell parson Thompson that he had seen one of his boys, and we must go in the woods, for he thought the parson would come out to look for me. Father took the water and went with it to the house that I brought the pail from. The family where I went for the water, I shall always remember with the kindest feelings. We have ever, from that day to the present, been on the best terms, and I believe three of them are living now. Two of them live in that same house that they then lived in, and the transactions of this narrative took place sixty five years ago. Their name is Curtiss.

When father came back, we set off for the woods pointed out by our friends; we went across the lots and came to a road, and crossed that into another open field. The woods were in the backside of the field. As we went on, we ascended a ridge of land, and we could see the road that led from Canaan to Norfolk. The road then went past the burying-ground, and we could see it from where we were. We saw fourteen men on horseback; they were men we knew; the parson was one of them. We hid behind a log that was near us until they got out of sight; we then went into the woods, and there we found my mother and sister; they had been sent there by the man that had told us of the parson's information of where I was. We all remained there. This I should think was about two or three o'clock in the afternoon. Very soon the thought of night came to mind; how we were to spend the night, and what we should do for something to eat; but between sundown and dark a man passed along by the edge of the woods, whistling as he went. After he had passed on, father went up where the man went along, and came back with a pail or basket, and in it was our supper. We sat down and ate. The man we saw no more that night, but how were we to spend the night I could not tell; it was starlight, yet it was out in the woods, but father and mother were there, and that was a comfort to us children, but we soon fell asleep and forgot all our troubles, and in the morning we awoke and were still in the woods. In due time the man that passed along the night before, came again with more food for us, and then went his way; his name was Walter. We spent several days in the woods,—how many I do not remember. I think it was the fore part of the week when we went into the woods; we were there over the Sabbath, for I well remember a man by the name of Bishop had a shop where he fulled and dressed cloth not very far from where we were, and he came to the back door of his shop and stood and looked out a while, and went in and shut the door. I felt afraid he would see us. We kept very still, but I think he did not know that we were there; if he did, it did us no hurt. We were fed by kind friends all the time we were in the woods.

One afternoon, or towards night, it was thought it would be safe to go to a barn and sleep. After it was dark we went to a barn belonging to a Mr. Munger and slept, but left it while the stars were shining, and so for a few nights, and then it was thought we might sleep in the house. The next night after dark, we went in the house of Mr. Munger for the night. My sister and myself were put up in a back chamber, behind barrels and boxes, closely put together, out of sight for safe-keeping. We had not been there long before mother came and told us we must get up, for Captain Lawrence, our friend, had sent word that the parson said he would have the boys at any rate, whether he got the parents or not. His pickets were going to search every house within a mile of the meeting-house that night, or search until he found them. But we went into the woods again; we were there awhile again; when it rained, we went sometimes into a barn when we dared. After a time it was rather still, and we were at one house and sometimes at another. We had pickets out as well as the parson. It was thought best that I should not be with the rest of the family, for the hunt seemed to be for the boys. My brother, I have said, was out of the State. I was sent to one family, and then to another, not in one place long at a time. The parson began to think the task harder than he had an idea; it rather grew worse and more perplexing; he did not know what to do. He was outwitted in all his attempts; every effort or trial he had made, had failed. He now thought of giving my father and mother and sister their freedom if they would let him have the boys to take with him; this they would not do.

After some time was spent, the parson or his pickets had an idea that we were all at Capt. Lawrence's house, shut up there; how to find out if we were there or not, was the puzzle. They contrived various plans, but did not succeed. Finally there was one thing yet. They knew that Mr. Lawrence loved money; they thought they would tempt him with that; so they came to his house and made trial. They met together one day and wanted to search his house; he would not consent for a time; they urged and he refused. He finally told them on certain conditions they might go into every room but one. They went into all the rooms but one. They then wanted to go into the room that they had not been into; they offered him money to let them go into the room,—how much he did not tell, as I know of. He finally consented. The much-desired room was a chamber over the kitchen. Mr. Lawrence opened the door at the foot of the stairs, and called and said, "Jupiter! (for that was my father's first name,) you must look out for yourself now, for I can not hide you any longer." He then told the parson's pickets they must take care, for Jupiter says he will kill the first man that lays hands on him. They hesitated some; they then went up stairs still, and stopped a short time, and then with a rush against the door, it gave way, and they all went in. They found the landlady sitting there as composed as summer, with her knitting-work, unconscious of an arrest to go south as a slave! but they found us not, although the room they last went into was the one we had occupied all the time we were in that house, sometimes one night, sometimes a week, and then in the woods or elsewhere, as was thought best to keep out of the way.

The pickets returned to the land of Canaan to see what was to be the next move. The parson then proposed to give my father and mother and sister their freedom, if they would let him have the boys. That they would not do; but the boys he said he must have. As my brother was away, it was thought best that I should be away. I was sent to Mr. Pease, well-nigh Canaan, and kept rather dark. I was there for a time, and I went to stay with a man by the name of Camp, and was with him a time, and then I went to stay with a man by the name of Akins, and stayed with him a few days, and went to a man by the name of Foot, and was with him a few days. I went to another man by the name of Akins, and was there some time. The parson was not gone south yet, for he could not well give up his prey. He then proposed to sell the boys until they were twenty-five, to somebody here that my parents would select, for that was as long as the law of Connecticut could hold slaves,[7] and he would give the other members of the family their freedom. It was finally thought best to do that if the purchasers that were acceptable could be found. Some friends were on the look-out. Finally a man by the name of Bingham was found; it was a man that my father was once a slave to; he would take my brother,—then a man by the name of Munger would buy me if they could agree. Mr. Bingham lived in Salisbury, Mr. Munger lived in Norfolk; the two men lived about fifteen miles apart, both in Connecticut.

The trade was made, and we two boys were sold for one hundred pounds a head, lawful money,—yes, sold by a man, a minister of the gospel in Connecticut, the land of steady habits. It would seem that the parson was a worshiper with the Athenians, as Paul said unto them when he stood on Mars Hill, he saw an inscription on one of their altars; and it would seem that the parson forgot or passed over the instruction of the apostle that God made of one blood all nations of men for to dwell on all the face of the earth.[8]

The parson was a tall man, standing six feet in his boots, and had no legitimate children to be heirs to his ill-gotten gains. The bargain was made on the

12th of September, 1798. Then I was informed that I was sold to Mr. Munger, and must go and live with him. The man I did not know, but the thought of being sold, not knowing whether I was ever to see my parents, or brother, or sister again, was more than I could endure; the thought that I was sold, as I did not then know for how long, it was hard to think of; and where were my parents I knew not: It was a sad thought, but go I must. The next morning (I was to go the morning of the 13th) was a sad morning to me. The morning was clear, without a cloud. I was told where the man lived, and I must go, for he had bought me. I thought of my parents; should I, oh! should I never see them again? As I was taught to obey my superiors, I set out; it was a little over a mile. The way was long. I went alone. Tears ran down my cheeks. I then felt for the first time that I was alone in the world, no home, no friends, and none to care for me. Tears ran, but it did no good; I must go, and on I went. And now sixty-five years have passed away since that time; those feelings are fresh in my memory. But on my way to my new home I saw my father; I will not attempt to describe my feelings when he told me he had taken rooms in the same neighborhood, and should be near me. That made the rough way smooth. I went on then cheerful and happy. I arrived at the place. I found a man with a small family; it consisted of himself and wife and three daughters. The oldest was near my age. The family appeared pleasant. I ate a bowl of bread and milk, and was told to mount a horse that was at the door with a bag of rye on his back, and ride to the field; that was about a mile off. The man went with me, and on the way we passed the house of Mrs. Curtiss, where I mentioned in the former part of this narrative of going for well-water for Mrs. Upson. We went to the field and worked that day; went home at night. The family appeared very pleasant, and I felt pleased to think that the parson had gone, for I was told that he went the same day that I went to my new home. In a short time my father and mother and sister came into the neighborhood to live. I was allowed to go and see them one evening in two weeks. They lived about sixty rods from where I lived. Things went on well. I was very contented, and felt glad that the fear of being carried south was at an end. The parson was out of town and out of mind. I soon became acquainted with Mrs. Curtiss' boys, for I passed the house where they lived every day, as Mr. Munger's farm was beyond where they lived. I soon was feeling contented and happy. There was one thing that was unfortunate for me; Mr. Munger was not a stout, strong man, and not very healthy, and had no other help but me, and of course I had many things to do beyond my strength. I do not complain of many things, yet there are two things more I will mention. One of them I feel to this day, and that I feel the most is that I did not have an opportunity to go to school as much as I should, for all the books I ever had in school were a spelling-book, a primer, a Testament, a reading-book called Third Part,[9] and after that a Columbian Orator.[10] My schooling was broken and unsteady after the first and second winters, as Mr. Munger had no help, and had to go something like two miles for his wood. He would take me with him to the woods, and he would take a load and go home, and leave me to chop while he was gone. The wood was taken off from a fallow where he had sowed rye. It was in piles. Some had to be cut once, and some twice, and some three times. I went to school the most of the first winter;

after that my schooling was slim. The other thing was, he was fond of using the lash. I thought so then, and made up my mind if I ever was the strongest I would pay back some of it. However, things went on, and I thought a good deal of Mr. Munger; yet I wonder sometimes why I was not more contented than I was, and then I wonder why I was as contented as I was. The summers that I was thirteen and fourteen, I was sick; they began to think I had the consumption. They sometimes would say to me, "If you should die we should lose a hundred pounds." I do not know as Mr. Munger ever said that, but it was said to me. But I will pass on with my story.

I soon found out that I was to live or stay with the man until I was twenty-five. I found that white boys who were bound out, were bound until they were twenty-one. I thought that rather strange, for those boys told me they were to have one hundred dollars when their time was out. They would say to me sometimes, "You have to work four years longer than we do, and get nothing when you have done, and we get one hundred dollars, a Bible, and two suits of clothes." This I thought of.

Some of the family or friends of the family would tell me what a good boy I should be, because Mr. Munger saved me from slavery. They said I must call him Master; but Mr. Munger never told me to, so I never did. If he had told me to, I should have done so, for I stood greatly in fear of him, and dreaded his displeasure, for I did not like the lash. I had made up my mind that I would not stay with him after I was twenty-one, unless my brother did with the man he lived with. My brother had been home to see us, and we went once to see him. I asked my brother how long he was going to stay with Mr. Bingham. He said Mr. Bingham said he should have his time when he was twenty-one. Well then, I would have my time, I said to myself. Things went on, and I found Mr. Munger to be a very good sort of a man. I had now got to be fifteen years of age. I had got my health, and had grown to be a big boy, and was called pretty stout, as the word is, yet I was afraid of Mr. Munger. I actually stood in fear of him.

I had now got to be in my sixteenth year, when a little affair happened, which, though trivial in itself, yet was of consequence to me. It was in the season of haying, and we were going to the hayfield after a load of hay. Mr. Munger and I were in the cart, he sitting on one side and I on the other. He took the fork in both of his hands, and said to me very pleasantly, "Don't you wish you were stout enough to pull this away from me?" I looked at him, and said, "I guess I can;" but I did not think so. He held it toward me with both his hands hold of the stale. I looked at him and then at the fork, hardly daring to take hold of it, and wondering what he meant, for this was altogether new. He said, "Just now see if you can do it." I took hold of it rather reluctantly, but I shut my hand tight. I did as Samson did in the temple; I bowed with all my might, and he came to me very suddenly. The first thought that was in my mind was, my back is safe now. All went on well for two months or more; all was pleasant, when one day he— or Mr. Munger, I should have said—was going from home, and he told me, as was usual, what to do. I went to my work, and did it just as he told me. At night, when he came home, he asked me what I had been doing. I told him, but he did not seem satisfied. I told him I had done just what he told me. He said I had not done what I ought to have done. I told him I had done what he told me. That was more than I had ever said before. He was angry and got his horsewhip, and said he would learn me. He raised his hand and stood ready to strike. I said, "You had better not!" I then went out at the door. I felt grieved to see him in such a rage when I had done just as he told me, and I could not account for it. If he had been a drinking man, I should not have wondered; but he was not, he was a sober man. I could not get over my feeling for some time, but all was pleasant the next day. I said to his daughters that I would not stay there a day after I was twenty-one, for I did not know what their father meant. I did just as he told me, and thought I was doing what he would be satisfied with. They told me not to mind it. Things went on from that time as well as I could wish. From that time until I was twenty-one, I do not remember that he ever gave me an unpleasant word or look. While I lived with him, after that time, I felt that I had now got as good a place as any of the boys that were living out. I often went with his team to Hartford and to Hudson, which the other boys did not that lived in the neighborhood. I now felt that I could do anything for the family; I was contented and happy.

The year that I was eighteen, Mr. Munger was concerned in an iron establishment, manufacturing iron. He had a sister living in Oneida county, and he learned that iron was high or brought a good price there. He told me he thought he would send a load out there and get a load of wheat, and asked me if I would go out with a load. I told him I would if he wished me to; he said he did. He got every thing ready, and I set out the 17th day of October, and thought it would take me about two weeks or thereabouts. On I went, and when I got there I could exchange my iron for wheat readily, but none had their wheat out, and their barn-floors were so full that they could not thrash. I had to wait a week. As soon as I got my load, I set out for home. I was gone a day or two over three weeks. After I got to Norfolk, I passed the house where my parents lived. They told me that it was very current with the people that I had sold the horses and wagon, and was seen by some one that knew me, and was on my way to Canada. They said that Mr. Munger said he did not believe it,—he said he should not trouble himself. Yet I went on home. He was glad to see me; asked if I had any bad luck. I told how it was, and he was satisfied, and said when he saw the team that they were in better condition than they were when I left home. "Now they may talk as much as they please; you and the team, wagon and load are here." And when I told him what I had done, he said he was perfectly satisfied, I had done well; he had no fault to find. Every thing went on first-rate. I did my best to please him, and it seemed to me that the family did the same. I now took the hardest end of the work. I was willing to do what I could. I was willing to work, and thought much of the family, and they thought something of me. Mr. Munger was receiving his share of offices of the town, and was from home a portion of his time. I felt ambitious to have our work even with others. He said his work went on as well as if he was there.

When I was in my twentieth year, a nephew of Mr. Munger came to board with him; he was studying law. Mr. Munger and I were accustomed to talk about my term of service with him. I told him I did not mean to stay with him until I was twenty-five. He said he thought I would if I meant to do what was fair and just. I told him that my brother had his time when he was twenty-one, and I wanted my time. He finally had some talk with his nephew, who said that he could hold me. But finally Mr. Munger made me an offer of what he would give me if I would stay. I thought the offer was tolerably fair. I had now become attached to the family. I told him that I would stay, as he had often said he thought I ought to stay after I was twenty-one. I thought I would divide the time with him in part, as the offer he made would not cover the whole time. All was fixed, and I worked on. Nothing more was said for a long time about it; then the thing was spoken about, and the same mind was in us both, and I felt satisfied. The fall previous to my being twenty-one came; all was right, as I thought. The winter came and nothing was said. The last of February came. I heard it hinted that Mr. Munger had said that he should not make any bargain with me, but if I left him he would follow me. The thing was understood by us, and I paid no attention to it. March came, and nothing was said. The third of March was my birthday. All was quiet, and I kept on as before until the first of April. It was told me that Mr. Munger said that his nephew had examined the law and found that he could hold me, and what he gave me would be his unless he was bound by a written agreement. As there were no writings given, I began to think it was time to know how it was. There was another thing now came to mind.

When I was thirteen years old, Mr. Munger bought a calf of my father, and gave it to me, and said he would keep it until it was two years old, and then I might sell it and have what it brought. He kept it. He had a mate for it, and when the steers were two years old he sold them for twenty-four dollars. He then told me that he would give me a heifer of the age the steer was, and when she had a calf he would take her to double in four years. When I was seventeen he gave me a heifer, and she had a calf that spring, and the first of April he said he would take her, and at the end of four years from that time he would give me two cows and two calves. That was agreed on. The next year, in March or April, one of his oxen hooked my cow; it hurt her so that the cow died. Well, now, what was to be done? He said at the time agreed on I should have my cows. I was content with that and worked on, feeling that all would be made right. I thought I should have two cows with those calves when I was twenty-one, and that would be a beginning. Afterward I agreed to stay with him until I was twenty-five; I could let them until that time. I will now go on with my story. I asked him for my cows and calves. He said he should not let me have any. He said if I stayed and did well perhaps he would give me a cow. I asked him if that was all that I was to have if I stayed until I was twenty-five. He said he would see. I asked when he would see. He said when the time came. I then told him I had been told that Warren (that was the name of his nephew) had told him not to give me what he had agreed to, and I wanted to know if he would do as he had agreed to or not. He said I belonged to him, and I could not help myself. I told him I would stay with him as I had said if he would give me a writing obligating himself to give me the sum we had agreed upon. After hesitating a short time, he said he would not give a writing; he would not be bound. I told him I had got that impression, "and if you say you will not give me what you said you would, I will not work another day." He then said if I left him he would put me in jail and keep me there a year at any rate. This was on Saturday. The next day I picked up what few duds I had, and at evening, as it was the Sabbath, I told him I had done all the work for him that I should do. I then bade him good night and left his house, and went to my father's. The next day in the afternoon, Mr. Munger and nephew came to my father's with a sheriff. I was not in the house. He told my father that he would pay my board in jail for one year, and I could not help myself. They took what few clothes I had, and went away before I got home. It was well it was so. I told my father that I would stay in jail as long as Mr. Munger would find money. I sent the word to Mr. Munger. He sent me word that I should have an opportunity to. My people wanted to have me go away for a time. I thought at first I would. Then I saw that I had nothing to go with, and had no clothes for a change. I would not leave. I told them I would go to jail. I thought perhaps I could get the liberty of the yard, and then I could earn something to get some clothes, and then I would leave for Canada or some other parts.

A few days after, I heard that Mr. Munger said he would leave it to men how it should be settled, and he sent me such word. I sent word to him, no, I was going to jail, if he would keep his word. He finally said as I had always been faithful, he would not or had rather not put me in jail. My parents said so much, they did not want to have me go to jail, that I finally said I would leave it to three men if they were men that I liked: if they were not, I would not. He said I might name the men; their judgment was to be final. The men were selected, the time and place specified. The day came, the parties met, and the men were on hand. Mr. Munger had his nephew for counsel; I plead my case myself. A number of the neighbors were present. Mr. Munger's counsel began by saying that his uncle had bought me, and had paid for me until I was twenty-five, and that he had a right to me. I then told his nephew that I would have a right to him some day, for he was the cause of all the difficulty. He said no more. The arbitrators asked Mr. Munger if he had anything against me. He said he had not. They asked him, in case they gave him anything, if he wished me to work it out with him; he said he did. They went out a few moments, and returned and said that I must pay Mr. Munger $90. He then asked me to go home with him, and he would hire me. I told him I would go and get my clothes, for that was in the decision. He said I could have them. His nephew did not want me to live with his uncle, if he boarded with him. I told Mr. Munger that I would not work for him. I hired to another man, and went to work in the same neighborhood. This nephew kept an eye on me for a long time, and always gave me the road whenever he saw me coming. Mr. Munger and family always treated me with attention whenever I met them; they made me welcome to their house and to their table. If that nephew had not interfered, there would have been no trouble.

Things all went on pleasantly. In about four years I went there again to work, and in a short time Mr. Munger and his two daughters joined the church of which his wife was a member. I joined the same church, and was often at his house. Mr. Munger was unfortunate and lost his property, not as people lose their property now. He was poor and not very healthy, and his wife and the daughter that was not married, not being healthy, and he being a man advanced in life, it wore upon him and his family, and his daughter went into a decline. I went west, and was gone about three months, and on my return went to see the family, and found the daughter very much out of health and wasting away. I called again the next day but one. As I had been accustomed to take care of the sick, she asked me to stop with her that night. I did so, and went to my work in the morning. The second day after, I called again to see her, and she made the same request. I staid and watched with her that night. She asked what I thought of her; I told her I feared she would never be any better. She then asked me to stay with her if she did not get any better, while she lived. I told her I would. A cousin of hers, a young lady, was there, and we took the care of her for four weeks. I mention this because it was a time to be remembered and cherished by me while I live. We were in the daily habit of speaking of her prospects and how she felt. She would speak of death with as much apparent composure as of any other subject. She said very little to her friends about her feelings. The day that she died was the evening of the Sabbath. About six o'clock in the afternoon, or rather all that day, she did not appear to be as well; but at the time just mentioned she sunk away and seemed to be gone for a short time, when she revived as one out of sleep, suddenly, and seemed surprised, and said, "There is nothing that I want to stay here for; let me go." She then bade her friends farewell, and told them not to weep for her, for she was going. Her countenance seemed as if lit up with heavenly love, and for a short time she seemed to be away from the world, and then was still and said but little. About eleven o'clock she wanted to be moved. She was moved. She then wanted to drink. I gave her, or put the glass to her lips. She did not swallow any. I saw there was a change, and before her friends could get into the room her spirit had fled.

That was a scene that I love to think of. It makes me almost forget that I ever was a slave to her father; but so it was. I staid until she was buried, and then I went West again. Her parents were broken-hearted indeed. I returned from the West, and spent a part of the summer with Mr. Munger. I afterwards worked where I chose for a few years. I was frequently at Mr. Munger's house. He seemed depressed, his health rather declined, and he finally sank down and was sick. He sent for me; I went to him, and he said he wished to have me stay with him. I told him I would, and I staid with him until he died, and closed the eyes of his daughter when she died, and his also. And now to look back on the whole transaction, it all seems like a dream. It is all past, never to be re-acted. That family have all gone, with one exception.

I am now seventy-four years of age, in good health, and the hay season that is just passed I took my scythe and went into the hay field and took my turn with the hands, day after day, with the same pay. Such health I feel thankful for; it is a favor granted me from my Heavenly Father.

1. Mars, *Life of* [1870 ed.], 55–58.
2. Ibid., 57
3. Miller, "Connecticut," 643.
4. Mars, *Life of* [1870 ed.], 58.

5. Henry Kiliaen van Rensselaer (1744–1816) was twice wounded during the Revolutionary War at the head of his regiment; he repelled the British at Fort Ann in July 1777.

6. Of course, no such secession took place at this time.

7. To quote a later edition of Mars's narrative, "the Legislature in 1788 [actually 1784], passed an act that freed all that were born after 1792, those born before that time that were able to take care of themselves, must serve until they were twenty-five." Mars, *Life of* [1870 ed.], 57–58; Miller, "Connecticut," 643. Accordingly, when Mars was freed in 1815, he was one of the last Connecticut slaves, since the law provided for freeing all slaves by 1817.

8. See *Acts* 17:22–26.

9. Probably *The Reader* (1802) by Abner Alden (1758–1820), which called itself "the third part of a Columbian exercise . . . an easy and systematical method of teaching and of learning the English language." The first two parts comprised Alden's *An Introduction to Spelling and Reading* (1797).

10. Caleb Bingham (1757–1817), *The Columbian Orator,* a collection of writings and rules "calculated to improve youth and others in the ornamental and useful art of eloquence."

WILLIAM PARKER

WILLIAM PARKER (1822–?) led an armed group of ex-slaves in battling would-be kidnappers; in 1851 they struck what many then considered the first blow of the Civil War.

The three thousand or so black residents of Lancaster County, Pennsylvania, relied on Parker and his men for protection against Maryland slaveholders and their hires, who would frequently raid the area in search of fugitive slaves to kidnap and return to bondage. Parker was, as Thomas Slaughter has written,

> a man of courage, intelligence, bravado, and justifiable pride, who was admired by Lancaster's black residents, and some of its whites, and rightly feared by those who wished ill to him and his cause. By all accounts, Parker was a tall, thin, well-muscled mulatto man, whom his African-American neighbors knew as "the preacher" during his twelve years in Lancaster County. . . . According to a local historian, Parker had "a reputation among both the colored people and the kidnapping fraternity for undaunted boldness and remarkable power." He was the one above all others whom the slave catchers "wished to get rid of." A white abolitionist from the region remembered that Parker was as "bold as a lion, the kindest of men, and the most steadfast of friends." He was the sort of man who made an impression, even on those who met him only once. Parker "could have commanded an army had he been educated, and he challenged the universal respect of all of them who did not have occasion to fear him," another white man recalled. Local blacks "regarded him as their leader, their protector, their Moses, and their lawgiver all at once."[1]

On September 11, 1851, the long-simmering, low-level war between Lancaster County blacks and Maryland slavehunters erupted into a full-scale battle thereafter known as the Christiana Riot, which Parker's narrative describes in great detail. The fighting sent tremors throughout the nation. A Lancaster paper proclaimed: "Civil War—The First Blow Struck." A Southern paper warned, "unless the Christiana rioters are hung . . . THE BONDS WILL BE DISSOLVED." President Millard Fillmore sent in a company of forty-five Marines and about forty Philadelphia policemen, who were joined by about fifty local ruffians; they arrested dozens of blacks and harassed scores more. Meanwhile, Parker and his associates were on their way to Canada.

In Rochester, New York, they stayed with Parker's old friend Frederick Douglass. He later wrote of their visit in his *Life and Times of Frederick Douglass*:

> I could not look upon them as murderers. To me, they were heroic defenders of the just rights of man against mansteaalers and murderers. So I fed them, and sheltered them in my house. Had they been pursued then and there, my home would have been stained with blood, for these men who had already tasted blood were well armed and prepared to sell their lives at any expense to the lives and limbs of their probable assailants. What they had already done at Christiana and the cool deter-

mination which showed very plainly especially in Parker, (for that was the name of the leader,) left no doubt on my mind that their courage was genuine and that their deeds would equal their words. . . . The hours they spent at my house were therefore hours of anxiety as well as activity. I dispatched my friend Miss Julia Griffiths to the landing three miles away on the Genesee River to ascertain if a steamer would leave that night for any port in Canada, and remained at home myself to guard my tired, dust-covered, and sleeping guests, for they had been harassed in traveling for two [actually eight] days and nights, and needed rest. Happily for us the suspense was not long, for it turned out that that very night a steamer was to leave for Toronto, Canada. . . .

I remained on board till the order to haul in the gang-plank was given; I shook hands with my friends, received from Parker the revolver that fell from the hand of Gorsuch [the slaveholder who had come from Maryland to recapture his fugitive slaves] when he died, presented now as a token of gratitude and a memento of the battle for Liberty at Christiana, and I returned to my home with a sense of relief which I cannot stop here to describe. This affair, at Christiana, . . . inflicted fatal wounds on the fugitive slave bill. It became thereafter almost a dead letter, for slaveholders found that not only did it fail to put them in possession of their slaves, but that the attempt to enforce it brought odium upon themselves and weakened the slave system.[2]

Back in Pennsylvania, federal prosecutors charged the rioters not only with resisting the Fugitive Slave Act of 1850, but also with treason. Thirty-six blacks and two whites were indicted and imprisoned in Philadelphia. Throughout the country, blacks raised money to defend the rioters, to make their imprisonment more comfortable, and to provide funds for their families. Because merely prosecuting blacks would not have mollified the South, Castner Hanway, a white man who had been present at the riot, was accused of having directed the blacks in their attack; his trial was to be a test case on which the fate of the other defendants would rest. Instead it became a farce. Hanway was handily acquitted, and the rest of the prisoners were released. As a whole, the riot and trial encouraged Northerners to resist enforcement of the Fugitive Slave Act, outraged Southerners, and moved the nation closer to civil war.[3]

As for Parker, he became a hero. The fugitive slave Henry Bibb welcomed him to Canada with the following words:

This man in our estimation deserves the admiration of a Hannibal, a Toussaint L'Ouverture, or a George Washington. A nobler defense was never made in behalf of liberty on the plains of Lexington, Concord or Bunker Hill than was put forth by William Parker at Christiana. We bid him, with his family, and all others, from that hypocritical Republic welcome to this our gracious land of adoption, where no slave-hunter dare to step his feet in search of a slave.[4]

Parker and his family eventually moved to Elgin, Canada, a settlement for fugitive slaves, where he learned to read and write. By March 1858 he had completed the first draft of his narrative. Although it was then "worked on" by three black men, as noted by the publisher of *The Provincial Freeman* in Chatham, Canada, it was never published in book form, and it was not until 1866 that it finally saw print. As "The Freedman's Story," it appeared in two parts in the February and March issues of *The Atlantic Monthly,* with introductions and minor revisions by James Gilmore, a frequent contributor to the magazine.[5] It has never been reprinted in full until now.

Among slave narratives, Parker's is perhaps the strongest example of black self-determination and quasi-revolutionary activity. Whether engaging in verbal braggadocio or physical battle, Parker never backed down, and his bravado made him an irresistible force. As Jonathan Katz writes:

> William Parker, born a slave, had reinvented himself as a free man, he had turned himself inside out. . . . He learned that the world can be turned upside down, that things as they are are not settled forever. He took his life into his own hands, he was no longer in the grip of fate. Who was he? One who had produced himself by his acts, an individual, impatient, critical, dissatisfied, who looked to the future, judging what was by what could be. Who was he? A disturber of the peace, an agitator, one who would be useful in the liberation battle, one who would be free.[6]

In 1872 William Parker returned to Pennsylvania, saw some old friends, and visited the site of the "battle for liberty." He stayed several months, attending a meeting of black voters who were supporting Ulysses S. Grant in his race against Horace Greeley for the presidency. He then returned to Canada, the land of his freedom.[7]

THE FREEDMAN'S STORY.

IN TWO PARTS.

PART I.

THE manuscript of the following pages has been handed to me with the request that I would revise it for publication, or weave its facts into a story which should show the fitness of the Southern black for the exercise of the right of suffrage.

It is written in a fair, legible hand; its words are correctly spelled; its facts are clearly stated, and—in most instances—its sentences are properly constructed. Therefore it needs no revision. On reading it over carefully, I also discover that it is in itself a stronger argument for the manhood of the negro than any which could be adduced by one not himself a freedman; for it is the argument of facts, and facts are the most powerful logic. Therefore, if I were to imbed these facts in the mud of fiction, I should simply oblige the reader to dredge for the oyster, which in this narrative he has without the trouble of dredging, fresh and juicy as it came from the hand of Nature,—or rather, from the hand of one of Nature's noblemen,—and who, until he was thirty years of age, had never put two letters together.

The narrative is a plain and unpretending account of the life of a man whose own right arm—to use his own expression—won his rights as a freeman. It is written with the utmost simplicity, and has about it the verisimilitude which belongs to truth, and to truth only when told by one who has been a doer of the deeds and an actor in the scenes which he describes. It has the further rare merit of being written by one of the "despised race"; for none but a negro can fully and correctly depict negro life and character.

General Thomas[8]—a Southern man, and a friend of the Southern negro—was once in conversation with a gentleman who has attained some reputation as a delineator of the black man, when a long, lean, "poor white man," then a scout in the Union army, approached the latter, and, giving his shoulder a familiar slap, accosted him with,—

"How are you, ole feller?"

The gentleman turned about, and forgetting, in his joy at meeting an old friend, the presence of this most dignified of our military men, responded to the salutation of the scout in an equally familiar and boisterous manner. General Thomas "smiled wickedly," and quietly remarked,—

"You seem to know each other."

"Know *him!*" exclaimed the scout. "Why, Gin'ral, I ha'n't seed him fur fourteen year; but I sh'u'd know him, ef his face war as black as it war one night when we went ter a nigger shindy tergether!"

The gentleman colored up to the roots of his hair, and stammered out,—

"That was in my boy days, General, when I was sowing my wild oats."

"Don't apologize, Sir," answered the General, "don't apologize; for I see that to your youthful habit of going to negro shindies we owe your truthful pictures of negro life."

And the General was right. Every man and woman who has essayed to depict the slave character has miserably failed, unless inoculated with the genuine spirit of the negro; and even those who have succeeded best have done only moderately well, because they have not had the negro nature. It is reserved to some black Shakspeare or Dickens to lay open the wonderful humor, pathos, poetry, and power which slumber in the negro's soul, and which now and then flash out like the fire from a thunder-cloud.

I do not mean to say that this black prophet has come in this narrative. He has not. This man is a doer, not a writer; though he gives us—particularly in the second part—touches of Nature, and little bits of description, which are perfectly inimitable. The prophet is still to come; and he *will* come. God never gives great events without great historians; and for all the patience and valor and heroic fortitude and self-sacrifice and long-suffering of the black man in this war, there will come a singer—and a black singer—who shall set his deeds to a music that will thrill the nations.

But I am holding the reader at the threshold.

The author of this narrative—of every line in it—is William Parker. He was an escaped slave, and the principal actor in the Christiana riot,—an occurrence which cost the Government of the United States fifty thousand dollars, embittered the relations of two "Sovereign States," aroused the North to the danger of the Fugitive-Slave Law, and, more than any other event, except the raid of John Brown, helped to precipitate the two sections into the mighty conflict which has just been decided on the battle-field.

Surely the man who aided towards such results must be a man, even if his complexion be that of the ace of spades; and what he says in relation to the events in which he was an actor, even if it have no romantic interest,—which, however, it has to an eminent degree,—must be an important contribution to the history of the time.

With these few remarks, I submit the evidence which he gives of the manhood of his race to that impartial grand-jury, the American people.

E. K.[9]

EARLY PLANTATION LIFE.

I WAS born opposite to Queen Anne, in Anne Arundel County, in the State of Maryland, on a plantation called Rowdown. My master was Major William Brogdon, one of the wealthy men of that region. He had two sons,—William, a doctor, and David, who held some office at Annapolis, and for some years was a member of the Legislature.

My old master died when I was very young; so I know little about him, except from statements received from my fellow-slaves, or casual remarks made in my hearing from time to time by white persons. From those I conclude that he was in no way peculiar, but should be classed with those slaveholders who are not remarkable either for the severity or the indulgence they extend to their people.

My mother, who was named Louisa Simms, died when I was very young; and to my grandmother I am indebted for the very little kindness I received in my early childhood; and this kindness could only be shown me at long intervals, and in a hurried way, as I shall presently show.

Like every Southern plantation of respectable extent and pretensions, our place had what is called the "Quarter," or place where the slaves of both sexes are lodged and fed. With us the Quarter was composed of a number of low buildings, with an additional building for single people and such of the children as were either orphans or had parents sold away or otherwise disposed of. This building was a hundred feet long by thirty wide, and had a large fireplace at either end, and small rooms arranged along the sides. In these rooms the children were huddled from day to day, the smaller and weaker subject to the whims and caprices of the larger and stronger. The largest children would always seize upon the warmest and best places, and say to us who were smaller, "Stand back, little chap, out of my way"; and we had to stand back or get a thrashing.

When my grandmother, who was cook at the "great house," came to look after me, she always brought me a morsel privately; and at such times I was entirely free from annoyance by the older ones. But as she could visit me only once in twenty-four hours, my juvenile days enjoyed but little rest from my domineering superiors in years and strength.

When my grandmother would inquire of the others how her "little boy" was getting on, they would tell her that I was doing well, and kindly invite me to the fire to warm myself. I was afraid to complain to her of their treatment, as, for so doing, they would have beaten me, after she had gone to the "great house" again. I was thus compelled to submit to their misrepresentation, as well as to their abuse and indifference, until I grew older, when, by fighting first with one and then with another, I became "too many" for them, and could have a seat at the fire as well as the best. This experience of my boyhood has since been repeated in my manhood. My rights at the fireplace were won by my child-fists; my rights as a freeman were, under God, secured by my own right arm.

Old master had seventy slaves, mostly field-hands. My mother was a field-hand. He finally died; but after that everything went on as usual for about six years, at the end of which time the brothers, David and William, divided the land and slaves. Then, with many others, including my brother and uncle, it fell to my lot to go with Master David, who built a house on the southeast part of the farm, and called it Nearo.

Over the hands at Nearo an overseer named Robert Brown was placed; but as he was liked by neither master nor slaves, he was soon discharged. The following circumstance led to his dismissal sooner, perhaps, than it would otherwise have happened.

While master was at Annapolis, my mistress, who was hard to please, fell out with one of the house-servants, and sent for Mr. Brown to come and whip her. When he came, the girl refused to be whipped, which angered Brown, and he beat her so badly that she was nearly killed before she gave up. When Master David came home, and saw the girl's condition, he became very angry, and turned Brown away at once.

Master David owned a colored man named Bob Wallace. He was a trusty man; and as he understood farming thoroughly, he was installed foreman in place of Brown. Everything went on very well for a while under Wallace, and the slaves were as contented as it is possible for slaves to be.

Neither of our young masters would allow his hands to be beaten or abused, as many slaveholders would; but every year they sold one or more of them,—sometimes as many as six or seven at a time. One morning word was brought to the Quarter that we should not work that day, but go up to the "great house." As we were about obeying the summons, a number of strange white men rode up to the mansion. They were negro-traders. Taking alarm, I ran away to the woods with a boy of about my own age, named Levi Storax; and there we remained until the selections for the sale were made, and the traders drove away. It was a serious time while they remained. Men, women, and children, all were crying, and general confusion prevailed. For years they had associated together in their rude way,—the old counselling the young, recounting their experience, and sympathizing in their trials; and now, without a word of warning, and for no fault of their own, parents and children, husbands and wives, brothers and sisters, were separated to meet no more on earth. A slave sale of this sort is always as solemn as a funeral, and partakes of its nature in one important particular,—the meeting no more in the flesh.

Levi and I climbed a pine-tree, when we got to the woods, and had this conversation together.

"Le," I said to him, "our turn will come next; let us run away, and not be sold like the rest."

"If we can only get clear this time," replied Le, "may-be they won't sell us. I will go to Master William, and ask him not to do it."

"What will you get by going to Master William?" I asked him. "If we see him, and ask him not to sell us, he will do as he pleases. For my part, I think the best thing is to run away to the Free States."

"But," replied Levi, "see how many start for the Free States, and are brought back, and sold away down South. We could not be safe this side of Canada, and we should freeze to death before we got there."

So ended our conversation. I must have been about ten or eleven years old then; yet, young as I was, I had heard of Canada as the land far away in the North, where the runaway was safe from pursuit; but, to my imagination, it was a vast and cheerless waste of ice and snow. So the reader can readily conceive of the effect of Levi's remarks. They were a damper upon our flight for the time being.

When night came, Levi wanted to go home and see if they had sold his mother; but I did not care about going back, as I had no mother to sell. How desolate I was! No home, no protector, no mother, no attachments. As we turned our faces toward the Quarter,—where we might at any moment be sold to satisfy a debt or replenish a failing purse,—I felt myself to be what I really was, a poor, friendless slave-boy. Levi was equally sad. His mother was not sold, but she could afford him no protection.

To the question, "Where had we been?" we answered, "Walking around."

Then followed inquiries and replies as to who were sold, who remained, and what transpired at the sale.

Said Levi,—

"Mother, were you sold?"

"No, child; but a good many were sold; among them, your Uncles Anthony and Dennis."

I said,—

"Aunt Ruthy, did they sell Uncle Sammy?"

"No, child."

"Where, then, is Uncle Sammy?"

I thought, if I could be with Uncle Sammy, may-be I would be safe. My Aunt Rachel, and her two children, Jacob and Priscilla, were among the sold, who altogether comprised a large number of the servants.

The apologist for slavery at the North, and the owner of his fellow-man at the South, have steadily denied that the separation of families, except for punishment, was perpetrated by Southern masters; but my experience of slavery was, that separation by sale was a part of the system. Not only was it resorted to by severe masters, but, as in my own case, by those generally regarded as mild. No punishment was so much dreaded by the refractory slave as selling. The atrocities known to be committed on plantations in the Far South, tidings of which reached the slave's ears in various ways, his utter helplessness upon the best farms and under the most humane masters and overseers, in Maryland and other Northern Slave States, together with the impression that the journey was of great extent, and comfortless even to a slave, all combined to make a voyage down the river or down South an era in the life of the poor slave to which he looked forward with the most intense and bitter apprehension and anxiety.

This slave sale was the first I had ever seen. The next did not occur until I was thirteen years old; but every year, during the interval, one or more poor souls were disposed of privately.

Levi, my comrade, was one of those sold in this interval. Well may the good John Wesley[10] speak of slavery as the sum of all villanies; for no resort is too despicable, no subterfuge too vile, for its supporters. Is a slave intractable, the most wicked punishment is not too severe; is he timid, obedient, attached to his birthplace and kindred, no lie is so base that it may not be used to entrap him into a change of place or of owners. Levi was made the victim of a stratagem so peculiarly Southern, and so thoroughly the outgrowth of an institution which holds the bodies and souls of men as of no more account, for all moral purposes, than the unreasoning brutes, that I cannot refrain from relating it. He was a likely lad, and, to all appearance, fully in the confidence of his master. Prompt and obedient, he seemed to some of us to enjoy high favor at the "great house." One morning he was told to take a letter to Mr. Henry Hall, an acquaintance of the family; and it being a part of his usual employment to bring and carry such missives, off he started, in blind confidence, to learn at the end of his journey that he had parted with parents, friends, and all, to find in Mr. Hall a new master. Thus, in a moment, his dearest ties were severed.

I met him about two months afterwards at the Cross-Road Meeting-House, on West River; and, after mutual recognition, I said to him,—

"Levi, why don't you come home?"

"I am at home," said he; "I was sold by Master William to Mr. Henry Hall."

He then told me about the deception practised upon him. I thought that a suitable opportunity to remind him of our conversation when up the pine-tree, years before, and said,—

"You told me, that, if you could escape the big sale, Master William would not sell you. Now you see how it was: the big sale was over, and yet you were sold to a worse master than you had before. I told you this would be so. The next time I hear from you, you will be sold again. Master Mack will be selling me one of these days, no doubt; but if he does, he will have to do it running."

Here ended our conversation and our association, as it was not in our power to meet afterward.

The neighbors generally called Master David, Mack, which was one of his Christian names; and the slaves called him Master Mack; so the reader will understand, that, whenever that name occurs, Master David is meant.

After the sale of Levi, I became greatly attached to Alexander Brown, another slave. Though not permitted to learn to read and write, and kept in profound ignorance of everything, save what belonged strictly to our plantation duties, we were not without crude perceptions of the dignity and independence belonging to freedom; and often, when out of hearing of the white people, or certain ones among our fellow-servants, Alexander and I would talk the subject over in our simple way.

Master Mack had a very likely young house-servant named Ann. She was between sixteen and eighteen years old; every one praised her intelligence and industry; but these commendable characteristics did not save her. She was sold next after Levi. Master told the foreman, Bob Wallace, to go to Annapolis, and take Ann with him. When Wallace told me he was going, I had a presentiment that the purpose was to sell the girl, and I told him so; but, man as he was, he had no fear about it. Wallace and Ann started for the city on horseback, and journeyed along pleasantly until they reached the town and were near the market-place, when a man came up to them, took Ann off the horse without ceremony, and put her into jail. Wallace, not suspecting the manoeuvre, attacked the man, and came well-nigh getting into difficulty. When Wallace returned, he said to Master Mack, "Why did you not tell me that Ann was sold, and not have me fighting for her? They might have put me in jail." But his master did not appear to hear him.

Poor Uncle Henry followed Ann. His wife lived in Annapolis, and belonged to a Mr. George McNear, residing there. Uncle Henry went one Saturday night to see her, when Master William put him into jail for sale; and that was the last we saw or heard of him.

Alex Brown's mother followed next. After the poor woman was gone, I said to Alex,—

"Now that your mother has been sold, it is time that you and I studied out a plan to run away and be free."

But so thoroughly had his humanity been crushed by the foul spirit of Slavery, so apathetic had he—though in the vigor of youth—become from long oppression, that he would not agree to my suggestion.

"No," he said, "'t is no use for you and I to run away. It is too far to the Free States. We could not get there. They would take us up and sell us; so we had better not go. Master Mack can't sell any more of his hands; there are no more than can carry on his farm."

"Very well," said I, "trust to that, and you will see what will come of it."

After that I said no more to him, but determined to be free. My brother Charles was of like mind; but we kept our thoughts to ourselves. How old I was then I do not know; but from what the neighbors told me, I must have been about seventeen. Slaveholders are particular to keep the pedigree and age of favorite horses and dogs, but are quite indifferent about the age of their servants, until they want to purchase. Then they are careful to select young persons, though not one in twenty can tell year, month, or day. Speaking of births,—it is the time of "corn-planting," "cornhusking," "Christmas," "New Year," "Easter," "the Fourth of July," or some similar indefinite date. My own time of birth was no more exact; so that to this day I am uncertain how old I am.

About the time of the conversation last narrated, Jefferson Dorsey, a planter near by, had a butchering. One of Dorsey's men met me, and said that they wanted more help, and that Master Mack said I might go and lend a hand. Thinking that he spoke truth, I did not ask permission, but went and stayed until noon. I soon learned, however, that the man had deceived me.

Master Mack, when told by some of the people where I was, sent my brother John after me, with the threat of a whipping. On reaching home, the women also told me that master would almost kill me. This excited me greatly, and I replied,—

"Master Mack is 'most done whipping me."

When I went in to see him, I saw plainly enough that his face foretold a storm.

"Boy," said he, "yoke up the oxen, and haul a load of wood."

I went at once, and did the task; but, to my dismay, there he stood at the stable. I had to drive near to him; and as he evidently intended to catch me, I was all vigilance.

"When you unload that wood, come to me, Sir," he said.

I made no reply, but unloaded the wood, left the oxen standing, and stole away to Dorsey's, where I staid until the next day. Then I prevailed upon Samuel Dorsey to go home with me. Master Mack told me to go to my work, and he would forgive me; but the next time he would pay me for "the new and the old." To work I went; but I determined not to be paid for "the new and the old."

This all occurred in the month of May. Everything went on well until June, when the long-sought-for opportunity presented itself. I had been making preparations to leave ever since Master Mack had threatened me; yet I did not like to go without first having a difficulty with him. Much as I disliked my condition, I was ignorant enough to think that something besides the fact that I was a slave was necessary to exonerate me from blame in running away. A cross word, a blow, a good fright, anything, would do, it mattered not whence nor how it came. I told my brother Charles, who shared my confidence, to be ready; for the time was at hand when we should leave Old Maryland forever. I was only waiting for the first crooked word from my master.

A few days afterwards all hands were ordered to the fields to work; but I stayed behind, lurking about the house. I was tired of working without pay. Master Mack saw me, and wanted to know why I did not go out. I answered, that it was raining, that I was tired, and did not want to work. He then picked up a stick used for an ox-gad, and said, if I did not go to work, he would whip me as sure as there was a God in heaven. Then he struck at me; but I caught the stick, and we grappled, and handled each other roughly for a time, when he called for assistance. He was badly hurt. I let go my hold, bade him good-bye, and ran for the woods. As I went by the field, I beckoned to my brother, who left work, and joined me at a rapid pace.

I was now at the beginning of a new and important era in my life. Although upon the threshold of manhood, I had, until the relation with my master was sundered, only dim perceptions of the responsibilities of a more independent position. I longed to cast off the chains of servitude, because they chafed my free spirit, and because I had a notion that my position was founded in injustice; but it has only been since a struggle of many years, and, indeed, since I settled upon British soil, that I have realized fully the grandeur of my position as a free man.

One fact, when I was a slave, often filled me with indignation. There were many poor white lads of about my own age, belonging to families scattered around, who were as poor in personal effects as we were; and yet, though our companions, (when we chose to tolerate them,) they did not have to be controlled by a master, to go and come at his command, to be sold for his debts, or whenever he wanted extra pocket-money. The preachers of a slave-trading gospel frequently told us, in their sermons, that we should be "good boys," and not break into master's hen-roost, nor steal his bacon; but they never told this to these poor white people, although they knew very well that they encouraged the slaves to steal, trafficked in stolen goods, and stole themselves.

Why this difference? I felt I was the equal of these poor whites, and naturally I concluded that we were greatly wronged, and that all this talk about obedience, duty, humility, and honesty was, in the phrase of my companions, "all gammon."

But I was now on the high-road to liberty. I had broken the bonds that held me so firmly; and now, instead of fears of recapture, that before had haunted my imagination whenever I thought of running away, I felt as light as a feather, and seemed to be helped onward by an irresistible force.

Some time before this, I had been able, through the instrumentality of a friend, to procure a pass, for which I paid five dollars,—all the money I had saved in a long time; but as my brother determined to go with me, and as we could not both use it safely, I destroyed it.

On the day I ceased working for master, after gaining the woods, we lurked about and discussed our plans until after dark. Then we stole back to the Quarter, made up our bundles, bade some of our friends farewell, and at about nine o'clock of the night set out for Baltimore. How shall I describe my first experience of free life? Nothing can be greater than the contrast it affords to a plantation experience, under the suspicious and vigilant eye of a mercenary overseer or a watchful master. Day and night are not more unlike. The mandates of Slavery are like leaden sounds, sinking with dead weight into the very soul, only to deaden and destroy. The impulse of freedom lends wings to the feet, buoys up the spirit within, and the fugitive catches glorious glimpses of light through rifts and seams in the accumulated ignorance of his years of oppression. How briskly we travelled on that eventful night and the next day!

We reached Baltimore on the following evening, between seven and eight o'clock. When we neared the city, the patrols were out, and the difficulty was to pass them unseen or unsuspected. I learned of a brick-yard at the entrance to the city; and thither we went at once, took brick-dust and threw it upon our clothes, hats, and boots, and then walked on. Whenever we met a passer-by, we would brush off some of the dust, and say aloud, "Boss gave us such big tasks, we would leave him. We ought to have been in a long time before." By this ruse we reached quiet quarters without arrest or suspicion.

We remained in Baltimore a week, and then set out for Pennsylvania.

We started with the brightest visions of future independence; but soon they were suddenly dimmed by one of those unpleasant incidents which annoy the fugitive at every step of his onward journey.

The first place at which we stopped to rest was a village on the old York road, called New Market. There nothing occurred to cause us alarm; so, after taking some refreshments, we proceeded towards York; but when near Logansville, we were interrupted by three white men, one of whom, a very large man, cried,—

"Hallo!"

I answered,—

"Hallo to you!"

"Which way are you travelling?" he asked.

We replied,—

"To Little York."

"Why are you travelling so late?"

"We are not later than you are," I answered.

"Your business must be of consequence," he said.

"It is. We want to go to York to attend to it; and if you have any business, please attend to it, and don't be meddling with ours on the public highway. We have no business with you, and I am sure you have none with us."

"See here!" said he; "you are the fellows that this advertisement calls for," at the same time taking the paper out of his pocket, and reading it to us.

Sure enough, there we were, described exactly. He came closely to us, and said,—

"You must go back."

I replied,—

"If I must, I must, and you must take me."

"Oh, you need not make any big talk about it," he answered; "for I have taken back many a runaway, and I can take you. What's that you have in your hand?"

"A stick."

He put his hand into his pocket, as if to draw a pistol, and said,—

"Come! give up your weapons."

I said again,—

"'T is only a stick."

He then reached for it, when I stepped back and struck him a heavy blow on the arm. It fell as if broken; I think it was. Then he turned and ran, and I after him. As he ran, he would look back over his shoulder, see me coming, and then run faster, and halloo with all his might. I could not catch him, and it seemed, that, the longer he ran, the faster he went. The other two took to their heels at the first alarm,—thus illustrating the valor of the chivalry!

At last I gave up the chase. The whole neighborhood by that time was aroused, and we thought best to retrace our steps to the place whence we started. Then we took a roundabout course until we reached the railroad, along which we travelled. For a long distance there was unusual stir and commotion. Every house was lighted up; and we heard people talking and horses galloping this way and that way, with other evidences of unusual excitement. This was between one and two o'clock in the morning. We walked on a long distance before we lost the sounds; but about four o'clock the same morning, entered York, where we remained during the day.

Once in York, we thought we should be safe, but were mistaken. A similar mistake is often made by fugitives. Not accustomed to travelling, and unacquainted with the facilities for communication, they think that a few hours' walk is a long journey, and foolishly suppose, that, if they have few opportunities of knowledge, their masters can have none at all at such great distances. But our ideas of security were materially lessened when we met with a friend during the day, who advised us to proceed farther, as we were not out of imminent danger.

According to this advice we started that night for Columbia. Going along in the dark, we heard persons following. We went very near to the fence, that they might pass without observing us. There were two, apparently in earnest conversation. The one who spoke so as to be distinctly heard we discovered to be Master Mack's brother-in-law. He remarked to his companion that they must hurry and get to the bridge before we crossed. He knew that we had not gone over yet. We were then near enough to have killed them, concealed as we were by the darkness; but we permitted them to pass unmolested, and went on to Wrightsville that night.[11]

The next morning we arrived at Columbia before it was light, and fortunately without crossing the bridge, for we were taken over in a boat. At Wrightsville we met a woman with whom we were before acquainted, and our meeting was very gratifying. We there inclined to halt for a time.

I was not used to living in town, and preferred a home in the country; so to the country we decided to go. After resting for four days, we started towards Lancaster to try to procure work. I got a place about five miles from Lancaster, and then set to work in earnest.

While a slave, I was, as it were, groping in the dark, no ray of light penetrating the intense gloom surrounding me. My scanty garments felt too tight for me, my very respiration seemed to be restrained by some supernatural power. Now, free as I supposed, I felt like a bird on a pleasant May morning. Instead of the darkness of slavery, my eyes were almost blinded by the light of freedom.

Those were memorable days, and yet much of this was boyish fancy. After a few years of life in a Free State, the enthusiasm of the lad materially sobered down, and I found, by bitter experience, that to preserve my stolen liberty I must pay, unremittingly, an almost sleepless vigilance; yet to this day I have never looked back regretfully to Old Maryland, nor yearned for her flesh-pots.

I have said I engaged to work; I hired my services for three months for the round sum of three dollars per month. I thought this an immense sum. Fast work was no trouble to me; for when the work was done, the money was mine. That was a great consideration. I could go out on Saturdays and Sundays, and home when I pleased, without being whipped. I thought of my fellow-servants left behind, bound in the chains of slavery,—and I was free! I thought, that, if I had the power, they should soon be as free as I was; and I formed a resolution that I would assist in liberating every one within my reach at the risk of my life, and that I would devise some plan for their entire liberation.

My brother went about fifteen miles farther on, and also got employment. I "put in" three months with my employer, "lifted" my wages, and then went to visit my brother. He lived in Bart Township, near Smyrna; and after my visit was over, I engaged to work for a Dr. Dengy,[12] living near by. I remained with him thirteen months. I never have been better treated than by the Doctor; I liked him and the family, and they seemed to think well of me.

While living with Dr. Dengy, I had, for the first time, the great privilege of seeing that true friend of the slave, William Lloyd Garrison,[13] who came into the neighborhood, accompanied by Frederick Douglass. They were holding anti-slavery meetings.[14] I shall never forget the impression that Garrison's glowing words made upon me. I had formerly known Mr. Douglass as a slave in Maryland; I was therefore not prepared for the progress he then showed,—neither for his free-spoken and manly language against slavery. I listened with the intense satisfaction that only a refugee could feel, when hearing, embodied in earnest, well-chosen, and strong speech, his own crude ideas of freedom, and his own hearty censure of the man-stealer. I believed, I knew, every word he said was true. It was the whole truth,—nothing kept back,—no trifling with human rights, no trading in the blood of the slave extenuated, nothing against the slaveholder said in malice. I have never listened to words from the lips of mortal man which were more acceptable to me; and although privileged since then to hear many able and good men speak on slavery, no doctrine has seemed to me so pure, so unworldly, as his. I may here say, and without offence, I trust, that, since that time, I have had a long experience of Garrisonian Abolitionists, and have always found them men and women with hearts in their bodies. They are, indeed and in truth, the poor slave's friend. To shelter him, to feed and clothe him, to help him on to freedom, I have ever found them ready; and I should be wanting in gratitude, if I neglected this opportunity—the only one I may ever have—to say thus much of them, and to declare for myself and for the many colored men in this free country whom I know they have aided in their journey to freedom, our humble confidence in them. Yes, the good spirit with which he is imbued constrained William Lloyd Garrison to plead for the dumb; and for his earnest pleadings all these years, I say, God bless him! By agitation, by example, by suffering, men and women of like spirit have been led to adopt his views, as the great necessity, and to carry them out into actions. They, too, have my heartfelt gratitude. They, like Gideon's band, though few, will yet rout the enemy Slavery, make him flee his own camp, and eventually fall upon his own sword.*

One day, while living at Dr. Dengy's, I was working in the barn-yard, when a man came to the fence, and, looking at me intently, went away. The Doctor's son, observing him, said,—

"Parker, that man, from his movements, must be a slaveholder or kidnapper. This is the second time he has been looking at you. If not a kidnapper, why does he look so steadily at you and not tell his errand?"

I said,—

"The man must be a fool! If he should come back and not say anything to me, I shall say something to him."

We then looked down the road and saw him coming again. He rode up to the same place and halted. I then went to the fence, and, looking him steadily in the eye, said,—

"Am I your slave?"

He made no reply, but turned his horse and rode off, at full speed, towards the valley. We did not see him again; but that same evening word was brought that kidnappers were in the valley, and if we were not careful, they would "hook" some of us. This caused a great excitement among the colored people of the neighborhood.

A short while prior to this, a number of us had formed an organization for mutual protection against slaveholders and kidnappers, and had resolved to prevent any of our brethren being taken back into slavery, at the risk of our own lives. We collected together that evening, and went down to the valley; but the kidnappers had gone. We watched for them several nights in succession, without result; for so much alarmed were the tavern-keepers by our demonstration, that they refused to let them stop over night with them. Kidnapping was so common, while I lived with the Doctor, that we were kept in constant fear. We would hear of slaveholders or kidnappers every two or three weeks; sometimes a party of white men would break into a house and take a man away, no one knew where; and, again, a whole family would be carried off. There was no power to protect them, nor prevent it. So completely roused were my feelings, that I vowed to let no slaveholder take back a fugitive, if I could but get my eye on him.

One day word was sent to me that slaveholders had taken William Dorsey, and had put him into Lancaster jail to await a trial. Dorsey had a wife and three

---

* This sentence was written before the beginning of our civil war. Viewed in the light of subsequent events, it is somewhat remarkable. —E.K.

or four children; but what was it to the slaveholder, if the wife and children should starve? We consulted together, as to what course to take to deliver him; but no plan that was proposed could be worked. At last we separated, determining to get him away some way or other on the day of trial. His case caused great excitement. We attended the trial, and eagerly watched all the movements from an outside position, and had a man to tell us how proceedings were going on within. He finally came out and said that the case would go against Dorsey. We then formed in a column at the court-house door, and when the slaveholders and Dorsey came out, we walked close to them,—behind and around them,—trying to separate them from him. Before we had gone far towards the jail, a slaveholder drew a pistol on Williams Hopkins, one of our party. Hopkins defied him to shoot; but he did not. Then the slaveholder drew the pistol on me, saying, he would blow my black brains out, if I did not go away. I doubled my fists to knock him down, but some person behind caught my hand; this started a fracas, and we got Dorsey loose; but he was so confused that he stood stock still, until they tied him again. A general fight followed. Bricks, stones, and sticks fell in showers. We fought across the road and back again, and I thought our brains would be knocked out; when the whites, who were too numerous for us, commenced making arrests. They got me fast several times, but I succeeded in getting away. One of our men was arrested, and afterwards stood trial; but they did not convict him. Dorsey was put into jail; but was afterwards bought and liberated by friends.

My friends now said that I had got myself into a bad difficulty, and that my arrest would follow. In this they were mistaken. I never was disturbed because of it, nor was the house at which I lodged ever searched, although the neighbors were repeatedly annoyed in that way. I distinctly remember that this was the second time that resistance had been made to their wicked deeds. Whether the kidnappers were clothed with legal authority or not, I did not care to inquire, as I never had faith in nor respect for the Fugitive-Slave Law.[15]

The whites of that region were generally such negro-haters, that it was a matter of no moment to them where fugitives were carried,—whether to Lancaster, Harrisburg, or elsewhere.

The insolent and overbearing conduct of the Southerners, when on such errands to Pennsylvania, forced me to my course of action. They did not hesitate to break open doors, and to enter, without ceremony, the houses of colored men; and when refused admission, or when a manly and determined spirit was shown, they would present pistols, and strike and knock down men and women indiscriminately.

I was sitting one evening in a friend's house, conversing about these marauding parties, when I remarked to him that a stop should be put to such "didos," and declared, that, the next time a slaveholder came to a house where I was, I would refuse to admit him. His wife replied, "It will make a fuss." I told her, "It is time a fuss was made." She insisted that it would cause trouble, and it was best to let them alone and have peace. Then I told her we must have trouble before we could have peace. "The first slaveholder that draws a pistol on me I shall knock down."

We were interrupted, just at this stage of the conversation, by some one rapping at the door.

"Who's there?" I asked.

"It's me! Who do you think? Open the door!" was the response, in a gruff tone.

"What do you want?" I asked.

Without replying, the man opened the door and came in, followed by two others.

The first one said,—

"Have you any niggers here?"

"What have we to do with your niggers?" said I.

After bandying a few words, he drew his pistol upon me. Before he could bring the weapon to bear, I seized a pair of heavy tongs, and struck him a violent blow across the face and neck, which knocked him down. He lay for a few minutes senseless, but afterwards rose, and walked out of the house without a word, followed by his comrades, who also said nothing to us, but merely asked their leader, as they went out, if he was hurt.

The part of Lancaster County in which I lived was near Chester County. Not far away, in the latter county, lived Moses Whitson, a well-known Abolitionist, and a member of the Society of Friends. Mr. Whitson had a colored girl living in his family, who was pounced upon by the slaveholders, awhile after the Dorsey arrest. About daylight three men went to Mr. Whitson's house and told him that the girl he had living with him was their property, and that they intended to have her. Friend Whitson asked the girl if she knew any of the men, and if any of them was her master. She said, "No!" One of the slaveholders said he could prove that she was his property; and then they forcibly tied her, put her into a carriage, and started for Maryland.

While the kidnappers were contending with Moses Whitson for the girl, Benjamin Whipper, a colored man, who now lives in this country, sounded the alarm, that "the kidnappers were at Whitson's, and were taking away his girl." The news soon reached me, and with six or seven others, I followed them. We proceeded with all speed to a place called the Gap-Hill, where we overtook them, and took the girl away. Then we beat the kidnappers, and let them go. We learned afterwards that they were all wounded badly, and that two of them died in Lancaster, and the other did not get home for some time. Only one of our men was hurt, and he had only a slight injury in the hand.

Dr. Duffield and Squire Henderson, two respectable citizens of the town, were looking on during this entire engagement; and after we had stopped firing, they went up to the slaveholders, and the following conversation took place:—

Squire Henderson. What's the matter?

Slaveholder. You may ask, what's the matter! Is this the way you allow your niggers to do?

Squire. Why did you not shoot them?

Slaveholder. We did shoot at them, but it did not take effect.

Squire. There's no use shooting at our niggers, for their heads are like iron pots; the balls will glance off. What were you doing?

Slaveholder. Taking our property, when the niggers jumped on us and nearly killed some of the men.

Squire. Men coming after such property ought to be killed.

Slaveholder. Do you know where we can find a doctor?

Squire. Yes; there are plenty of doctors South.

Being much disabled, and becoming enraged, they abruptly left, and journeyed on until they reached McKenzie's tavern, where their wounds were dressed and their wants attended to. So strongly was McKenzie in sympathy with these demons, that he declared he would never employ another nigger, and actually discharged a faithful colored woman who had lived a long time in his employ. Dr. Lemmon, a physician on the road to Lancaster, refused to attend the slaveholders; so that by the time they got to the city, from being so long without surgical aid, their limbs were past setting, and two of them died, as before stated, while the other survived but a short time after reaching Maryland.

A large reward was offered by the Maryland authorities for the perpetrators of the flogging, but without effect.

McKenzie, the tavern-keeper referred to, boasted after this that he would entertain all slaveholders who came along, and help them recapture their slaves. We were equally determined he should not, if we could prevent it.

The following affliction was eventually the means, under Providence, by which he was led to adopt other views, and become a practical Abolitionist.

A band of five men stood off, one dark night, and saw with evident satisfaction the curling flames ascend above his barn, from girder to roof, and lap and lash their angry tongues in wild license, until every vestige of the building was consumed.

After that mysterious occurrence, the poor fugitive had no better friend than the publican McKenzie.

Shortly after the incidents just related, I was married to Eliza Ann Elizabeth Howard, a fugitive, whose experience of slavery had been much more bitter than my own. We commenced housekeeping, renting a room from Enoch Johnson for one month. We did not like our landlord, and when the time was up left, and rented a house of Isaac Walker for one year. After the year was out, we left Walker's and went to Smyrna, and there I rented a house from Samuel D. Moore for another year. After the year was out we left Smyrna also, and went to Joseph Moore's to live. We lived on his place about five years. While we were living there, several kidnappers came into the neighborhood. On one occasion, they took a colored man and started for Maryland. Seven of us set out in pursuit, and, soon getting on their track, followed them to a tavern on the Westchester road, in Chester County. Learning that they were to remain for the night, I went to the door and asked for admittance. The landlord demanded to know if we were white or colored. I told him colored. He then told us to be gone, or he would blow out our brains. We walked aside a little distance, and consulted about what we should do. Our men seemed to dread the undertaking; but I told them we could overcome them, and that I would go in. One of them said he would follow at the risk of his life. The other five said we should all get killed,—that we were men with families,—that our wives and children needed our assistance,—and that they did not think we would be doing our families justice by risking our lives for one man. We two then went back to the tavern, and, after rapping, were told again by the landlord to clear out, after he found that we were colored. I pretended that we wanted something to drink. He put his head out of the window, and threatened again to shoot us; when my comrade raised his gun and would have shot him down, had I not caught his arm and persuaded him not to fire. I told the landlord that we wanted to come in and intended to come in. Then I went to the yard, got a piece of scantling, took it to the door, and, by battering with it a short time, opened it. As soon as the door flew open, a kidnapper shot at us, and the ball lodged in my ankle, bringing me to the ground. But I soon rose, and my comrade then firing on them, they took to their heels. As they ran away, I heard one say, "We have killed one of them."

My companion and I then rushed into the house. We unbound the man, took him out, and started for home; but had hardly crossed the door-sill before people from the neighboring houses began to fire on us. At this juncture, our other five came up, and we all returned the compliment. Firing on both sides was kept up for ten or fifteen minutes, when the whites called for quarter, and offered to withdraw, if we would stop firing. On this assurance we started off with the man, and reached home safely.

The next day my ankle was very painful. With a knife I extracted the ball, but kept the wound secret; as long before we had learned that for our own security it was best not to let such things be generally known.

About ten o'clock of a Sabbath night, awhile after the event last narrated, we were aroused by the cry of "Kidnappers! kidnappers!" and immediately some one halloed under my window,—

"William! William!"

I put my head out and demanded his errand. He said,—

"Come here!"

I answered,—

"You must be a fool to think I am going to you at this time of the night, without knowing who you are and what you want."

He would not satisfy me, so I took my gun, and went out to him. I was then informed that kidnappers had been at Allen Williams's; that they had taken Henry Williams, and gone towards Maryland. I called one of our party, who dressed and proceeded to arouse our men. Two of us then started for the Nine Points, in Lancaster County, and left instructions for the other men to meet us in the valley. They did so, and we hurried on to our destination. We had not gone far before we heard some one calling, "Kidnappers! kidnappers!" Going back some distance, we found the cry came from a man who had fallen into a lime quarry. He was in a bad situation, and unable to get out without assistance, and, hearing us pass, concluded we were kidnappers and raised the cry. We were delayed for a time in helping him out, and it provoked me very much, as it was important we should be in haste.

We started again for the Nine Points, but, arriving there, learned to our dismay, that the kidnappers had passed an hour before. The chase was given up, but with saddened feelings. A fellow-being had been dragged into hopeless bondage, and we, his comrades, held our liberty as insecurely as he had done but a few short hours before! We asked ourselves the question, "Whose turn will come next?" I was delegated to find out, if possible, who had betrayed him, which I accordingly did.

Lynch law is a code familiar to the colored people of the Slave States. It is of so diabolical a character as to be without justification, except when enforced by men of pure motives, and then only in extreme cases, as when the unpunished party has it in his power to barter away the lives and liberties of those whose confidence he possesses, and who would, by bringing him before a legal tribunal, expose themselves to the same risks that they are liable to from him. The frequent attacks from slaveholders and their tools, the peculiarity of our position, many being escaped slaves, and the secrecy attending these kidnapping exploits, all combined to make an appeal to the Lynch Code in our case excusable, if not altogether justifiable. Ourselves, our wives, our little ones, were insecure, and all we had was liable to seizure. We felt that something must he done, for some one must be in our midst with whom the slaveholders had communication. I inquired around, quietly, and soon learned that Allen Williams, the very man in whose house the fugitive was, had betrayed him. This information I communicated to our men. They met at my house and talked the matter over, and, after most solemnly weighing all the facts and evidence, we resolved that he should die, and we set about executing our purpose that evening. The difficulty was, how to punish him. Some were for shooting him, but this was not feasible. I proposed another plan, which was agreed to.

Accordingly, we went to his house and asked if a man named Carter, who lived with him, was at home, as rumor said that he had betrayed Henry Williams. He denied it, and said that Carter had fought for Henry with him, but the slaveholders being too strong for them, they had to give him up. He kept beyond reach, and the men apologized for intruding upon him, while I stepped up to the door and asked for a glass of water. He gave it to me, and to the others. When he was giving water to one of the party, I caught him by the throat, to prevent his giving the alarm, and drew him over my head and shoulders. Then the rest beat him until we thought we heard some one coming, which caused us to flee. If we had not been interrupted, death would have been his fate. At that time I was attending a threshing-machine for George Whitson and Joseph Scarlot.

It must have been a month after the Williams affray, that I was sitting at home one evening, talking with Pinckney and Samuel Thompson about how I was getting on with my work, when I thought I heard some one call my name. I went out, but all was quiet. When I went in, Pinckney and Thompson laughed at me, and said that I had become so "scary" that I could not stay in the house. But I was not satisfied. I was sure some one had called me. I said so, and that I would go to Marsh Chamberlain's to see if anything was wrong. They concluded to go also, and we started.

Arriving near the house, I told Pinckney and Thompson to stop outside, and I would go in, and if anything was wrong, would call them. When I reached the house, I saw a chair broken to pieces, and knew that something had happened. I said,—

"Hallo, Marsh!"

"Who is that?" said he.

And his wife said,—

"Parker, is that you?"

"Yes," I said.

"Oh, Parker, come here!" she called.

I called Pinckney and Thompson, and we went in. Marsh met us, and said that kidnappers had been there, had taken John Williams, and gone with him towards Buck Hill. They had then been gone about fifteen minutes. Off we started on a rapid run to save him. We ran to a stable, got out two horses, and Pinckney and I rode on. Thompson soon got the rest of our party together and followed. We were going at a pretty good gait, when Pinckney's horse stumbled and fell, fastening his rider's leg; but I did not halt. Pinckney got his horse up and caught up with me.

"You would not care," said he, "if a man were to get killed! You would not help him!"

"Not in such a case as this," I replied.

We rode on to the Maryland line, but could not overtake them. We were obliged to return, as it was near daybreak. The next day a friend of ours went to Maryland to see what had been done with Williams. He went to Dr. Savington's, and the Doctor told him that the fugitive could not live,—the kidnappers had broken his skull, and otherwise beaten him very badly; his ankle, too, was out of place. In consequence of his maimed condition, his mistress refused to pay the men anything for bringing him home. That was the last we ever heard of poor John Williams; but we learned afterwards why we failed to release him on the night he was taken. The kidnappers heard us coming, and went into the woods out of the way, until we had passed them.

Awhile before this occurrence, there lived in a town not far away from Christiana a colored man who was in the habit of decoying fugitives fresh from bondage to his house on various pretexts, and, by assuming to be their friend, got from them the name of their master, his residence, and other needed particulars. He would then communicate with the master about his slave, tell him at what time the man would be at his house, and when he came at the appointed hour, the poor refugee would fall into the merciless clutches of his owner. Many persons, mostly young people, had disappeared mysteriously from the country, from whom nothing could be heard. At last the betrayer's connection with these transactions was clearly traced; and it was decided to force him to quit the nefarious business.

He was too wary to allow himself to be easily taken, and a resort was had to stratagem. I, with others, thought he deserved to be shot openly in his daughter's house, and was willing to take the consequences.

At last this man's outrages became so notorious that six of our most reliable men resolved to shoot him, if they had to burn him out to do it. After I had sworn the men in the usual form, we went to his barn, took two bundles of wheat-straw, and, fastening them under the eaves with wisps, applied a lighted match to each. We then took our stations a few rods off, with rifles ready and in good condition,—mine was a smooth-bore, with a heavy charge.

The house burned beautifully; and half an hour after it ignited the walls fell in, but no betrayer showed himself. Instead of leaving the house by the rear door, as we had expected, just before the roof fell in, he broke out the front way, rushed to his next neighbor's, and left his place without an effort to save it. We had built the fire in the rear, and looked for him there; but he ran in the opposite direction, not only as if his life was in danger, but as if the spirit of his evil deeds was after him.

THE FREEDMAN'S STORY.

IN TWO PARTS.

PART II.

As the Freedman relates only events which came under his own observation, it is necessary to preface the remaining portion of his narrative with a brief account of the Christiana riot. This I extract mainly from a statement made at the time by a member of the Philadelphia bar, making only a few alterations to give the account greater clearness and brevity.

On the 9th of September, 1851, Mr. Edward Gorsuch,[16] a citizen of Maryland, residing near Baltimore, appeared before Edward D. Ingraham, Esquire, United States Commissioner at Philadelphia, and asked for warrants under the act of Congress of September 18, 1850,[17] for the arrest of four of his slaves, whom he had heard were secreted somewhere in Lancaster County. Warrants were issued forthwith, directed to H. H. Kline, a deputy United States Marshal, authorizing him to arrest George Hammond, Joshua Hammond, Nelson Ford, and Noah Buley, persons held to service or labor in the State of Maryland, and to bring them before the said Commissoner.

Mr. Gorsuch then made arrangements with John Agin and Thompson Tully, residents of Philadelphia, and police officers, to assist Kline in making the arrests. They were to meet Mr. Gorsuch and some companions at Penningtonville, a small place on the State Railroad, about fifty miles from Philadelphia. Kline, with the warrants, left Philadelphia on the same day, about 2 P. M., for West Chester. There he hired a conveyance and rode to Gallagherville, where he hired another conveyance to take him to Penningtonville. Before he had driven very far, the carriage breaking down, he returned to Gallagherville, procured another, and started again. Owing to this detention, he was prevented from meeting Mr. Gorsuch and his friends at the appointed time, and when he reached Penningtonville, about 2 A. M. on the 10th of September, they had gone.

On entering the tavern, the place of rendezvous, he saw a colored man whom he recognized as Samuel Williams, a resident of Philadelphia. To put Williams off his guard, Kline asked the landlord some questions about horse thieves. Williams remarked that he had seen the "horse thieves," and told Kline he had come too late.

Kline then drove on to a place called the Gap. Seeing a person he believed to be Williams following him, he stopped at several taverns along the road and made inquiries about horse thieves. He reached the Gap about 3 A. M., put up his horses, and went to bed. At half past four he rose, ate breakfast, and rode to Parkesburg, about forty-five miles from Philadelphia, and on the same railroad. Here he found Agin and Tully asleep in the bar-room. He awoke Agin, called him aside, and inquired for Mr. Gorsuch and his party. He was told they had gone to Sadsbury, a small place on the turnpike, four or five miles from Parkesburg.

On going there, he found them, about 9 A. M. on the 10th of September. Kline told them he had seen Agin and Tully, who had determined to return to Philadelphia, and proposed that the whole party should return to Gallagherville. Mr. Gorsuch, however, determined to go to Parkesburg instead, to see Agin and Tully, and attempt to persuade them not to return. The rest of the party were to go to Gallagherville, while Kline returned to Downingtown, to see Agin and Tully, should Mr. Gorsuch fail to meet them at Parkesburg. He left Gallagherville about 11 a. m., and met Agin and Tully at Downingtown. Agin said he had seen Mr. Gorsuch, but refused to go back. He promised, however, to return from Philadelphia in the evening cars. Kline returned to Downingtown, and then met all the party except Mr. Edward Gorsuch, who had remained behind to make the necessary arrangements for procuring a guide to the houses where he had been informed his negroes were to be found.

About 3 P. M., Mr. Edward Gorsuch joined them at Gallagherville, and at 11 P. M. on the night of the 10th of September they all went in the cars to Downingtown, where they waited for the evening train from Philadelphia.

When it arrived, neither Agin nor Tully was to be seen. The rest of the party went on to the Gap, which they reached about half past one on the morning of the 11th of September. They then continued their journey on foot towards Christiana, where Parker was residing, and where the slaves of Mr. Gorsuch were supposed to be living. The party then consisted of Kline, Edward Gorsuch, Dickinson Gorsuch, his son, Joshua M. Gorsuch, his nephew, Dr. Thomas Pierce,[18] Nicholas T. Hutchings, and Nathan Nelson.

After they had proceeded about a mile they met a man who was represented to be a guide. He is said to have been disguised in such a way that none of the party could recognize him, and his name is not mentioned in any of the proceedings. It is probable that he was employed by Mr. Edward Gorsuch, and one condition of his services may have been that he should be allowed to use every possible means of concealing his face and name from the rest of the party. Under his conduct, the party went on, and soon reached a house in which they were told one of the slaves was to be found. Mr. Gorsuch wished to send part of the company after him, but Kline was unwilling to divide their strength, and they walked on, intending to return that way after making the other arrests.

The guide led them by a circuitous route, until they reached the Valley Road, near the house of William Parker, the writer of the annexed narrative, which was their point of destination. They halted in a lane near by, ate some crackers and cheese, examined the condition of their fire-arms, and consulted upon the plan of attack. A short walk brought them to the orchard in front of Parker's house, which the guide pointed out and then left them. He had no desire to remain and witness the result of his false information. His disguise and desertion of his employer are strong circumstances in proof of the fact that he knew he was misleading the party. On the trial of Hanway, it was proved by the defence that Nelson Ford, one of the fugitives, was not on the ground until after the sun was up. Joshua Hammond had lived in the vicinity up to the time that a man by the name of Williams had been kidnapped, when he and several others departed, and had not since been heard from. Of the other two, one at least, if the evidence for the prosecution is to be relied upon, was in the house at which the party first halted, so that there could not have been more than one of Mr. Gorsuch's slaves in Parker's house, and of this there is no positive testimony.

It was not yet daybreak when the party approached the house. They made demand for the slaves, and threatened to burn the house and shoot the occupants, if they would not surrender. At this time, the number of besiegers seems to have been increased, and as many as fifteen are said to have been near the house. About daybreak, when they were advancing a second or third time, they saw a negro coming out, whom Mr. Gorsuch thought he recognized as one of his slaves. Kline pursued him with a revolver in his hand, and stumbled over the bars near the house. Some of the company came up before Kline, and found the door open. They entered, and Kline, following, called for the owner, ordered all to come down, and said he had two warrants for the arrest of Nelson Ford and Joshua Hammond. He was answered that there were no such men in the house. Kline, followed by Mr. Gorsuch, attempted to go up stairs. They were prevented from ascending by what appears to have been an ordinary *fish gig*. Some of the witnesses described it as "like a pitchfork with blunt prongs," and others were at a loss what to call this, the first weapon used in the contest. An axe was next thrown down, but hit no one.

Mr. Gorsuch and others then went outside to talk with the negroes at the window. Just at this time Kline fired his pistol up stairs. The warrants were then read outside the house, and demand made upon the landlord. No answer was heard. After a short interval, Kline proposed to withdraw his men, but Mr. Gorsuch refused, and said he would not leave the ground until he had made the arrests. Kline then in a loud voice ordered some one to go to the sheriff and bring a hundred men, thinking, as he afterwards said, this would intimidate them. The threat appears to have had some effect, for the negroes asked time to consider. The party outside agreed to give fifteen minutes.

While these scenes were passing at the house, occurrences transpired elsewhere that are worthy of attention, but which cannot be understood without a short statement of previous events.

In the month of September, 1850, a colored man, known in the neighborhood around Christiana to be free, was seized and carried away by men known to be professional kidnappers, and had not been seen by his family since. In March, 1851, in the same neighborhood, under the roof of his employer, during the night, another colored man was tied, gagged, and carried away, marking the road along which he was dragged with his blood. No authority for this outrage was ever shown, and the man was never heard from. These and many other acts of a similar kind had so alarmed the neighborhood, that the very name of kidnapper was sufficient to create a panic. The blacks feared for their own safety; and the whites, knowing their feelings, were apprehensive that any attempt to repeat these outrages would be the cause of bloodshed. Many good citizens were determined to do all in their power to prevent these lawless depredations, though they were ready to submit to any measures sanctioned by legal process. They regretted the existence among them of a body of people liable to such violence; but without combination had, each for himself, resolved that they would do everything dictated by humanity to resist barbarous oppression.

On the morning in question, a colored man living in the neighborhood, who was passing Parker's house at an early hour, saw the yard full of men. He halted, and was met by a man who presented a pistol at him, and ordered him to leave the place. He went away and hastened to a store kept by Elijah Lewis, which, like all places of that kind, was probably the head-quarters of news in the neighborhood. Mr. Lewis was in the act of opening his store when this man told him that "Parker's house was surrounded by *kidnappers,* who had broken into the house, and *were trying to get him away.*" Lewis, not questioning the truth of the statement, repaired immediately to the place. On the way he passed the house of Castner Hanway, and, telling him what he had heard, asked him to go over to Parker's. Hanway was in feeble health and unable to undergo the fatigue of walking that distance; but he saddled his horse, and reached Parker's during the armistice.

Having no reason to believe he was acting under legal authority, when Kline approached and demanded assistance in making the arrests, Hanway made no answer. Kline then handed him the warrants, which Hanway examined, saw they appeared genuine, and returned.

At this time, several colored men, who no doubt had heard the report that kidnappers were about, came up, armed with such weapons as they could suddenly lay hands upon. How many were on the ground during the affray it is *now* impossible to determine. The witnesses on both sides vary materially in their estimate. Some said they saw a dozen or fifteen; some, thirty or forty; and others maintained, as many as two or three hundred. It is known there were not two hundred colored men within eight miles of Parker's house, nor half that number within four miles; and it would have been almost impossible to get together even thirty at an hour's notice. It is probable there were about twenty-five, all told, at or near the house from the beginning of the affray until all was quiet again. These the fears of those who afterwards testified to larger numbers might easily have magnified to fifty or a hundred.

While Kline and Hanway were in conversation, Elijah Lewis came up. Hanway said to him, "Here is the Marshal." Lewis asked to see his authority, and Kline handed him one of the warrants. When he saw the signature of the United States Commissioner, "he took it for granted that Kline had authority." Kline then ordered Hanway and Lewis to assist in arresting the alleged fugitives. Hanway refused to have anything to do with it. The negroes around these three men seeming disposed to make an attack, Hanway "motioned to them and urged them back." He then "advised Kline that it would be dangerous to attempt making arrests, and that they had better leave." Kline, after saying he would hold them accountable for the fugitives, promised to leave, and beckoned two or three times to his men to retire.

The negroes then rushed up, some armed with guns, some with corn-cutters, staves, or clubs, others with stones or whatever weapon chance offered. Hanway and Lewis in vain endeavored to restrain them.

Kline leaped the fence, passed through the standing grain in the field, and for a few moments was out of sight. Mr. Gorsuch refused to leave the spot, saying his "property was there, and he would have it or perish in the attempt." The rest of his party endeavored to retreat when they heard the Marshal calling to them, but they were too late; the negroes rushed up, and the firing began. How many times each party fired, it is impossible to tell. For a few moments everything was confusion, and each attempted to save himself. Nathan Nelson went down the short lane, thence into the woods and towards Penningtonville. Nicholas Hutchings, by direction of Kline, followed Lewis to see where he went. Thomas Pierce and Joshua Gorsuch went down the long lane, pursued by some of the negroes, caught up with Hanway, and, shielding themselves behind his horse, followed him to a stream of water near by. Dickinson Gorsuch was with his father near the house. They were both wounded; the father mortally. Dickinson escaped down the lane, where he was met by Kline, who had returned from the woods at the end of the field. Kline rendered him assistance, and went towards Penningtonville for a physician. On his way he met Joshua M. Gorsuch, who was also wounded and delirious. Kline led him over to Penningtonville and placed him on the upward train from Philadelphia. Before this time several persons living in the neighborhood had arrived at Parker's house. Lewis Cooper found Dickinson Gorsuch in the place where Kline had left him, attended by Joseph Scarlett. He placed him in his dearborn,[19] and carried him to the house of Levi Pownall, where he remained till he had sufficiently recovered to return home. Mr. Cooper then returned to Parker's, placed the body of Mr. Edward Gorsuch in the same dearborn, and carried it to Christiana. Neither Nelson nor Hutchings rejoined their party, but during the day went by the railroad to Lancaster.

Thus ended an occurrence which was the theme of conversation throughout the land. Not more than two hours elapsed from the time demand was first made at Parker's house until the dead body of Edward Gorsuch was carried to Christiana. In that brief time the blood of strangers had been spilled in a sudden affray, an unfortunate man had been killed, and two others badly wounded.

When rumor spread abroad the result of the affray, the neighborhood was appalled. The inhabitants of the farmhouses and the villages around, unused to such scenes, could not at first believe that it had occurred in their midst. Before midday, exaggerated accounts had reached Philadelphia, and were transmitted by telegraph throughout the country.

Many persons were arrested for participation in the riot; and, after a long imprisonment, were arraigned for trial, on the charge of treason, before Judges Grier and Kane, of the United States Court, sitting at Philadelphia.

Every one knows the result. The prisoners were all acquitted; and the country was aroused to the danger of a law which allowed bad men to incarcerate peaceful citizens for months in prison, and put them in peril of their lives, for refusing to aid in entrapping, and sending back to hopeless slavery, men struggling for the very same freedom we value as the best part of our birthright.

The Freedman's narrative is now resumed.

A short time after the events narrated in the preceding number, it was whispered about that the slaveholders intended to make an attack on my house; but, as I had often been threatened, I gave the report little attention. About the same time, however, two letters were found thrown carelessly about, as if to attract notice. These letters stated that kidnappers would be at my house on a certain night, and warned me to be on my guard. Still I did not let the matter trouble me. But it was no idle rumor. The bloodhounds were upon my track.

I was not at this time aware that in the city of Philadelphia there was a band of devoted, determined men,—few in number, but strong in purpose,—who were fully resolved to leave no means untried to thwart the barbarous and inhuman monsters who crawled in the gloom of midnight, like the ferocious tiger, and, stealthily springing on their unsuspecting victims, seized, bound and hurled them into the ever open jaws of Slavery. Under the pretext of enforcing the Fugitive Slave Law, the slaveholders did not hesitate to violate all other laws made for the good government and protection of society, and converted the old State of Pennsylvania, so long the hope of the fleeing bondman, wearied and heart-broken, into a common hunting-ground for their human prey. But this little band of true patriots in Philadelphia united for the purpose of standing between the pursuer and the pursued, the kidnapper and his victim, and, regardless of all personal considerations, were ever on the alert, ready to sound the alarm to save their fellows from a fate far more to be dreaded than death. In this they had frequently succeeded, and many times had turned the hunter home bootless of his prey. They began their operations at the passage of the Fugitive Slave Law, and had thoroughly examined all matters connected with it, and were perfectly cognizant of the plans adopted to carry out its provisions in Pennsylvania, and, through a correspondence with reliable persons in various sections of the South, were enabled to know these hunters of men, their agents, spies, tools, and betrayers. They knew who performed this work in Richmond, Alexandria, Washington, Baltimore, Wilmington, Philadelphia, Lancaster, and Harrisburg, those principal depots of villany, where organized bands prowled about at all times, ready to entrap the unwary fugitive.

They also discovered that this nefarious business was conducted mainly through one channel; for, spite of man's inclination to vice and crime, there are but few men, thank God, so low in the scale of humanity as to be willing to degrade themselves by doing the dirty work of four-legged bloodhounds. Yet such men, actuated by the love of gold and their own base and brutal natures, were found ready for the work. These fellows consorted with constables, police-officers, aldermen, and even with learned members of the legal profession who disgraced their respectable calling by low, contemptible arts, and were willing to clasp hands with the lowest ruffian in order to pocket the reward that was the price of blood. Every facility was offered these bad men; and whether it was night or day, it was only necessary to whisper in a certain circle that a negro was to be caught, and horses and wagons, men and officers, spies and betrayers, were ready, at the shortest notice, armed and equipped, and eager for the chase.

Thus matters stood in Philadelphia on the 9th of September, 1851, when Mr. Gorsuch and his gang of Maryland kidnappers arrived there. Their presence was soon known to the little band of true men who were called "The Special Secret Committee." They had agents faithful and true as steel; and through these agents the whereabouts and business of Gorsuch and his minions were soon discovered. They were noticed in close converse with a certain member of the Philadelphia bar, who had lost the little reputation he ever had by continual dabbling in negro-catching, as well as by association with and support of the notorious Henry H. Kline, a professional kidnapper of the basest stamp. Having determined as to the character and object of these Marylanders, there remained to ascertain the spot selected for their deadly spring; and this required no small degree of shrewdness, resolution, and tact.

Some one's liberty was imperilled; the hunters were abroad; the time was short, and the risk imminent. The little band bent themselves to the task they were pledged to perform with zeal and devotion; and success attended their efforts. They knew that one false step would jeopardize their own liberty, and very likely their lives, and utterly destroy every prospect of carrying out their objects. They knew, too, that they were matched against the most desperate, daring, and brutal men in the kidnappers' ranks,—men who, to obtain the proffered reward, would rush willingly into any enterprise, regardless alike of its character or its consequences. That this was the deepest, the most thoroughly organized and best-planned project for man-catching that had been concocted since the infamous Fugitive Slave Law had gone into operation, they also knew; and consequently this nest of hornets was approached with great care. But by walking directly into their camp, watching their plans as they were developed, and secretly testing every inch of ground on which they trod, they discovered enough to counterplot these plotters, and to spring upon them a mine which shook the whole country, and put an end to man-stealing in Pennsylvania forever.

The trusty agent of this Special Committee, Mr. Samuel Williams, of Philadelphia,—a man true and faithful to his race, and courageous in the highest degree,—came to Christiana, travelling most of the way in company with the very men whom Gorsuch had employed to drag into slavery four as good men as ever trod the earth. These Philadelphia roughs, with their Maryland associates, little dreamed that the man who sat by their side carried with him their inglorious defeat, and the death-warrant of at least one of their party. Williams listened to their conversation, and marked well their faces, and, being fully satisfied by their awkward movements that they were heavily armed, managed to slip out of the cars at the village of Downington unobserved, and proceeded to Penningtonville, where he encountered Kline, who had started several hours in advance of the others. Kline was terribly frightened, as he knew Williams, and felt that his presence was an omen of ill to his base designs. He spoke of horse thieves, but Williams replied,—"I know the kind of horse thieves you are after. They are all gone; and you had better not go after them."

Kline immediately jumped into his wagon, and rode away, whilst Williams crossed the country, and arrived at Christiana in advance of him.

The manner in which information of Gorsuch's designs was obtained will probably ever remain a secret; and I doubt if any one outside of the little band who so masterly managed the affair knows anything of it. This was wise; and I would to God other friends had acted thus. Mr. Williams's trip to Christiana, and the many incidents connected therewith, will be found in the account of his trial; for he was subsequently arrested and thrown into the cold cells of a loathsome jail for this good act of simple Christian duty; but, resolute to the last, he publicly stated that he had been to Christiana, and, to use his own words, "I done it, and will do it again." Brave man, receive my thanks!

Of the Special Committee I can only say that they proved themselves men; and through the darkest hours of the trials that followed, they were found faithful to their trust, never for one moment deserting those who were compelled to suffer. Many, many innocent men residing in the vicinity of Christiana, the ground where the first battle was fought for liberty in Pennsylvania, were seized, torn from their families, and, like Williams, thrown into prison for long, weary months, to be tried for their lives. By them this Committee stood, giving them every consolation and comfort, furnishing them with clothes, and attending to their wants, giving money to themselves and families, and procuring for them the best legal counsel. This I know, and much more of which it is not wise, even now, to speak: 't is enough to say they were friends when and where it cost something to be friends, and true brothers where brothers were needed.

After this lengthy digression, I will return, and speak of the riot and the events immediately preceding it.

The information brought by Mr. Williams spread through the vicinity like a fire in the prairies; and when I went home from my work in the evening, I found Pinckney (whom I should have said before was my brother-in-law), Abraham Johnson, Samuel Thompson, and Joshua Kite at my house, all of them excited about the rumor. I laughed at them, and said it was all talk. This was the 10th of September, 1851. They stopped for the night with us, and we went to bed as usual. Before daylight, Joshua Kite rose, and started for his home. Directly, he ran back to the house, burst open the door, crying, "O William! kidnappers! kidnappers!"

He said that, when he was just beyond the yard, two men crossed before him, as if to stop him, and others came up on either side. As he said this, they had reached the door. Joshua ran up stairs, (we slept up stairs,) and they followed him; but I met them at the landing, and asked, "Who are you?"

The leader, Kline, replied, "I am the United States Marshal."

I then told him to take another step, and I would break his neck.

He again said, "I am the United States Marshal."

I told him I did not care for him nor the United States. At that he turned and went down stairs.

Pinckney said, as he turned to go down,—"Where is the use in fighting? They will take us."

Kline heard him, and said, "Yes, give up, for we can and will take you anyhow."

I told them all not to be afraid, nor to give up to any slaveholder, but to fight until death.

"Yes," said Kline, "I have heard many a negro talk as big as you, and then have taken him; and I 'll take you."

"You have not taken me yet," I replied; "and if you undertake it you will have your name recorded in history for this day's work."

Mr. Gorsuch then spoke, and said,—"Come, Mr. Kline, let 's go up stairs and take them. We *can* take them. Come, follow me. I 'll go up and get my property. What's in the way? The law is in my favor, and the people are in my favor."

At that he began to ascend the stair; but I said to him,—"See here, old man, you can come up, but you can 't go down again. Once up here, you are mine."

Kline then said,—"Stop, Mr. Gorsuch. I will read the warrant, and then, I think, they will give up."

He then read the warrant, and said,—"Now, you see, we are commanded to take you, dead or alive; so you may as well give up at once."

"Go up, Mr. Kline," then said Gorsuch, "you are the Marshal."

Kline started, and when a little way up said, "I am coming."

I said, "Well, come on."

But he was too cowardly to show his face. He went down again and said,—

"You had better give up without any more fuss, for we are bound to take you anyhow. I told you before that I was the United States Marshal, yet you will not give up. I 'll not trouble the slaves. I will take you and make you pay for all."

"Well," I answered, "take me and make me pay for all. I 'll pay for all."

Mr. Gorsuch then said. "You have my property."

To which I replied,—"Go in the room down there, and see if there is anything there belonging to you. There are beds and a bureau, chairs, and other things. Then go out to the barn; there you will find a cow and some hogs. See if any of them are yours."

He said,—"They are not mine; I want my men. They are here, and I am bound to have them."

Thus we parleyed for a time, all because of the pusillanimity of the Marshal, when he, at last, said,—"I am tired waiting on you; I see you are not going to give up. Go to the barn and fetch some straw," said he to one of his men. "I will set the house on fire, and burn them up."

"Burn us up and welcome," said I. "None but a coward would say the like. You can burn us, but you can't take us; before I give up, you will see my ashes scattered on the earth."

By this time day had begun to dawn; and then my wife came to me and asked if she should blow the horn, to bring friends to our assistance. I assented, and she went to the garret for the purpose. When the horn sounded from the garret window, one of the ruffians asked the others what it meant; and Kline said to me, "What do you mean by blowing that horn?"

I did not answer. It was a custom with us, when a horn was blown at an unusual hour, to proceed to the spot promptly to see what was the matter. Kline ordered his men to shoot any one they saw blowing the horn. There was a peach-tree at that end of the house. Up it two of the men climbed; and when my wife went a second time to the window, they fired as soon as they heard the blast, but missed their aim. My wife then went down on her knees, and, drawing her head and body below the range of the window, the horn resting on the sill, blew blast after blast, while the shots poured thick and fast around her. They must have fired ten or twelve times. The house was of stone, and the windows were deep, which alone preserved her life.

They were evidently disconcerted by the blowing of the horn. Gorsuch said again, "I want my property, and I will have it."

"Old man," said I, "you look as if you belonged to some persuasion."

"Never mind," he answered, "what persuasion I belong to; I want my property."

While I was leaning out of the window, Kline fired a pistol at me, but the shot went too high; the ball broke the glass just above my head. I was talking to Gorsuch at the time. I seized a gun and aimed it at Gorsuch's breast, for he evidently had instigated Kline to fire; but Pinckney caught my arm and said, "Don't shoot." The gun went off, just grazing Gorsuch's shoulder. Another conversation then ensued between Gorsuch, Kline, and myself, when another one of the party fired at me, but missed. Dickinson Gorsuch, I then saw, was preparing to shoot; and I told him if he missed, I would show him where shooting first came from.

I asked them to consider what they would have done, had they been in our position. "I know you want to kill us," I said, "for you have shot at us time and again. We have only fired twice, although we have guns and ammunition, and could kill you all if we would, but we do not want to shed blood."

"If you do not shoot any more," then said Kline, "I will stop my men from firing."

They then ceased for a time. This was about sunrise.

Mr. Gorsuch now said,—"Give up, and let me have my property. Hear what the Marshal says, the Marshal is your friend. He advises you to give up without more fuss, for my property I will have."

I denied that I had his property, when he replied, "You have my men."

"Am I your man?" I asked.

"No."

I then called Pinckney forward.

"Is that your man?"

"No."

Abraham Johnson I called next, but Gorsuch said he was not his man.

The only plan left was to call both Pinckney and Johnson again; for had I called the others, he would have recognized them, for they were his slaves.

Abraham Johnson said, "Does such a shrivelled up old slaveholder as you own such a nice, genteel young man as I am?"

At this Gorsuch took offence, and charged me with dictating his language. I then told him there were but five of us, which he denied, and still insisted that I had his property. One of the party then attacked the Abolitionists, affirming that, although they declared there could not be property in man, the Bible was conclusive authority in favor of property in human flesh.

"Yes," said Gorsuch, "does not the Bible say, 'Servants, obey your masters'?"[20]

I said that it did, but the same Bible said, "Give unto your servants that which is just and equal."[21]

At this stage of the proceedings, we went into a mutual Scripture inquiry, and bandied views in the manner of garrulous old wives.

When I spoke of duty to servants, Gorsuch said, "Do you know that?"

"Where," I asked, "do you see it in Scripture, that a man should traffic in his brother's blood?"

"Do you call a nigger my brother?" said Gorsuch.

"Yes," said I.

"William," said Samuel Thompson, "he has been a class-leader."

When Gorsuch heard that, he hung his head, but said nothing. We then all joined in singing,—

"Leader, what do you say
About the judgment day?
I will die on the field of battle,
Die on the field of battle,
With glory in my soul."[22]

Then we all began to shout, singing meantime, and shouted for a long while. Gorsuch, who was standing head bowed, said, "What are you doing now?"

Samuel Thompson replied, "Preaching a sinner's funeral sermon."

"You had better give up, and come down."

I then said to Gorsuch,—" 'If a brother see a sword coming, and he warn not his brother, then the brother's blood is required at his hands; but if the brother see the sword coming, and warn his brother, and his brother flee not, then his brother's blood is required at his own hand.'[23] I see the sword coming, and, old man, I warn you to flee; if you flee not, your blood be upon your own hand."

It was now about seven o'clock.

"You had better give up," said old Mr. Gorsuch, after another while, "and come down, for I have come a long way this morning, and want my breakfast; for my property I will have, or I'll breakfast in hell. I will go up and get it."

He then started up stairs, and came far enough to see us all plainly. We were just about to fire upon him, when Dickinson Gorsuch, who was standing on the old oven, before the door, and could see into the up-stairs room through the window, jumped down and caught his father, saying,—"O father, do come down! do come down! They have guns, swords, and all kinds of weapons! They 'll kill you! Do come down!"

The old man turned and left. When down with him, young Gorsuch could scarce draw breath, and the father looked more like a dead than a living man, so frightened were they at their supposed danger. The old man stood some time without saying anything; at last he said, as if soliloquizing, "I want my property, and I will have it."

Kline broke forth, "If you don't give up by fair means, you will have to by foul."

I told him we would not surrender on any conditions.

Young Gorsuch then said,—"Don't ask them to give up,—*make* them do it. We have money, and can call men to take them. What is it that money won't buy?"

Then said Kline,—"I am getting tired waiting on you; I see you are not going to give up."

He then wrote a note and handed it to Joshua Gorsuch, saying at the same time,—"Take it, and bring a hundred men from Lancaster."

As he started, I said,—"See here! When you go to Lancaster, don't bring a hundred men,—bring five hundred. It will take all the men in Lancaster to change our purpose or take us alive."

He stopped to confer with Kline, when Pinckney said, "We had better give up."

"You are getting afraid," said I.

"Yes," said Kline, "give up like men. The rest would give up if it were not for you."

"I am not afraid," said Pinckney; "but where is the sense in fighting against so many men, and only five of us?"

The whites, at this time, were coming from all quarters, and Kline was enrolling them as fast as they came. Their numbers alarmed Pinckney, and I told him to go and sit down; but he said, "No, I will go down stairs."

I told him, if he attempted it, I should be compelled to blow out his brains. "Don't believe that any living man can take you," I said. "Don't give up to any slaveholder."

To Abraham Johnson, who was near me, I then turned. He declared he was not afraid. "I will fight till I die," he said.

At this time, Hannah, Pinckney's wife, had become impatient of our persistent course; and my wife, who brought me her message urging us to surrender, seized a corn-cutter, and declared she would cut off the head of the first one who should attempt to give up.

Another one of Gorsuch's slaves was coming along the highroad at this time, and I beckoned to him to go around. Pinckney saw him, and soon became more inspirited. Elijah Lewis, a Quaker, also came along about this time; I beckoned to him, likewise; but he came straight on, and was met by Kline, who ordered him to assist him. Lewis asked for his authority, and Kline handed him the warrant. While Lewis was reading, Castner Hanway came up, and Lewis handed the warrant to him. Lewis asked Kline what Parker said.

Kline replied, "He won't give up."

Then Lewis and Hanway both said to the Marshal,—"If Parker says they will not give up, you had better let them alone, for he will kill some of you. We are not going to risk our lives";—and they turned to go away.

While they were talking, I came down and stood in the doorway, my men following behind.

Old Mr. Gorsuch said, when I appeared, "They'll come out, and get away!" and he came back to the gate.

I then said to him,—"You said you could and would take us. Now you have the chance."

They were a cowardly-looking set of men.

Mr. Gorsuch said, "You can't come out here."

"Why?" said I. "This is my place. I pay rent for it. I'll let you see if I can't come out."

"I don't care if you do pay rent for it," said he. "If you come out, I will give you the contents of these";—presenting, at the same time, two revolvers, one in each hand.

I said, "Old man, if you don't go away, I will break your neck."

I then walked up to where he stood, his arms resting on the gate, trembling as if afflicted with palsy, and laid my hand on his shoulder, saying, "I have seen pistols before to-day."

Kline now came running up, and entreated Gorsuch to come away.

"No," said the latter, "I will have my property, or go to hell."

"What do you intend to do?" said Kline to me.

"I intend to fight," said I. "I intend to try your strength."

"If you will withdraw your men," he replied, "I will withdraw mine."

I told him it was too late. "You would not withdraw when you had the chance,—you shall not now."

Kline then went back to Hanway and Lewis. Gorsuch made a signal to his men, and they all fell into line. I followed his example as well as I could; but as we were not more than ten paces apart, it was difficult to do so. At this time we numbered but ten, while there were between thirty and forty of the white men.[24]

While I was talking to Gorsuch, his son said, "Father, will you take all this from a nigger?"

I answered him by saying that I respected old age; but that, if he would repeat that, I should knock his teeth down his throat. At this he fired upon me, and I ran up to him and knocked the pistol out of his hand, when he let the other one fall and ran in the field.

My brother-in-law, who was standing near, then said, "I can stop him";— and with his double-barrel gun he fired.

Young Gorsuch fell, but rose and ran on again. Pinckney fired a second time, and again Gorsuch fell, but was soon up again, and, running into the cornfield, lay down in the fence corner.

I returned to my men, and found Samuel Thompson talking to old Mr. Gorsuch, his master. They were both angry.

"Old man, you had better go home to Maryland," said Samuel.

"You had better give up, and come home with me," said the old man.

Thompson took Pinckney's gun from him, struck Gorsuch, and brought him to his knees. Gorsuch rose and signalled to his men. Thompson then knocked him down again, and he again rose. At this time all the white men opened fire, and we rushed upon them; when they turned, threw down their guns, and ran away. We, being closely engaged, clubbed our rifles. We were too closely pressed to fire, but we found a good deal could be done with empty guns.

Old Mr. Gorsuch was the bravest of his party; he held on to his pistols until the last, while all the others threw away their weapons. I saw as many as three at a time fighting with him. Sometimes he was on his knees, then on his back, and again his feet would be where his head should be. He was a fine soldier and a brave man. Whenever he saw the least opportunity, he would take aim. While in close quarters with the whites, we could load and fire but two or three times. Our guns got bent and out of order. So damaged did they become, that we could shoot with but two or three of them. Samuel Thompson bent his gun on old Mr. Gorsuch so badly, that it was of no use to us.

When the white men ran, they scattered. I ran after Nathan Nelson, but could not catch him. I never saw a man run faster. Returning, I saw Joshua Gorsuch coming, and Pinckney behind him. I reminded him that he would like "to take hold of a nigger," told him that now was his "chance," and struck him a blow on the side of the head, which stopped him. Pinckney came up behind, and gave him a blow which brought him to the ground; as the others passed, they gave him a kick or jumped upon him, until the blood oozed out at his ears.

Nicholas Hutchings, and Nathan Nelson of Baltimore County, Maryland, could outrun any men I ever saw. They and Kline were not brave, like the Gorsuches. Could our men have got them, they would have been satisfied.

One of our men ran after Dr. Pierce, as he richly deserved attention; but Pierce caught up with Castner Hanway, who rode between the fugitive and the

Doctor, to shield him and some others. Hanway was told to get out of the way, or he would forfeit his life; he went aside quickly, and the man fired at the Marylander, but missed him,—he was too far off. I do not know whether he was wounded or not;[25] but I do know, that, if it had not been for Hanway, he would have been killed.

Having driven the slavocrats off in every direction, our party now turned towards their several homes. Some of us, however, went back to my house, where we found several of the neighbors.

The scene at the house beggars description. Old Mr. Gorsuch was lying in the yard in a pool of blood, and confusion reigned both inside and outside of the house.

Levi Pownell said to me, "The weather is so hot and the flies are so bad, will you give me a sheet to put over the corpse?"

In reply, I gave him permission to get anything he needed from the house.

"Dickinson Gorsuch is lying in the fence-corner, and I believe he is dying. Give me something for him to drink," said Pownell, who seemed to be acting the part of the Good Samaritan.

When he returned from ministering to Dickinson, he told me he could not live.

The riot, so called, was now entirely ended. The elder Gorsuch was dead; his son and nephew were both wounded, and I have reason to believe others were,—how many, it would be difficult to say. Of our party, only two were wounded. One received a ball in his hand, near the wrist; but it only entered the skin, and he pushed it out with his thumb. Another received a ball in the fleshy part of his thigh, which had to be extracted; but neither of them were sick or crippled by the wounds. When young Gorsuch fired at me in the early part of the battle, both balls passed through my hat, cutting off my hair close to the skin, but they drew no blood. The marks were not more than an inch apart.

A story was afterwards circulated that Mr. Gorsuch shot his own slave, and in retaliation his slave shot him; but it was without foundation. His slave struck him the first and second blows; then three or four sprang upon him, and, when he became helpless, left him to pursue others. *The women put an end to him.* His slaves, so far from meeting death at his hands, are all still living.

After the fight, my wife was obliged to secrete herself, leaving the children in care of her mother, and to the charities of our neighbors. I was questioned by my friends as to what I should do, as they were looking for officers to arrest me. I determined not to be taken alive, and told them so; but, thinking advice as to our future course necessary, went to see some old friends and consult about it. Their advice was to leave, as, were we captured and imprisoned, they could not foresee the result. Acting upon this hint, we set out for home, when we met some female friends, who told us that forty or fifty armed men were at my house, looking for me, and that we had better stay away from the place, if we did not want to be taken. Abraham Johnson and Pinckney hereupon halted, to agree upon the best course, while I turned around and went another way.

Before setting out on my long journey northward, I determined to have an interview with my family, if possible, and to that end changed my course. As we went along the road to where I found them, we met men in companies of three and four, who had been drawn together by the excitement. On one occasion, we met ten or twelve together. They all left the road, and climbed over the fences into fields to let us pass; and then, after we had passed, turned, and looked after us as far as they could see. Had we been carrying destruction to all human kind, they could not have acted more absurdly. We went to a friend's house and stayed for the rest of the day, and until nine o'clock that night, when we set out for Canada.

The great trial now was to leave my wife and family. Uncertain as to the result of the journey, I felt I would rather die than be separated from them. It had to be done, however; and we went forth with heavy hearts, outcasts for the sake of liberty. When we had walked as far as Christiana, we saw a large crowd, late as it was, to some of whom, at least, I must have been known, as we heard distinctly, "A'n't that Parker?"

"Yes," was answered, "that 's Parker."

Kline was called for, and he, with some nine or ten more, followed after. We stopped, and then they stopped. One said to his comrades, "Go on,—that 's him." And another replied, "You go." So they contended for a time who should come to us. At last they went back. I was sorry to see them go back, for I wanted to meet Kline and end the day's transactions.

We went on unmolested to Penningtonville; and, in consequence of the excitement, thought best to continue on to Parkersburg. Nothing worth mention occurred for a time. We proceeded to Downingtown, and thence six miles beyond, to the house of a friend. We stopped with him on Saturday night, and on the evening of the 14th went fifteen miles farther. Here I learned from a preacher, directly from the city, that the excitement in Philadelphia was too great for us to risk our safety by going there. Another man present advised us to go to Norristown.

At Norristown we rested a day. The friends gave us ten dollars, and sent us in a vehicle to Quakertown. Our driver being partly intoxicated, set us down at the wrong place, which obliged us to stay out all night. At eleven o'clock the next day we got to Quakertown. We had gone about six miles out of the way, and had to go directly across the country. We rested the 16th, and set out in the evening for Friendsville.

A friend piloted us some distance, and we travelled until we became very tired, when we went to bed under a haystack. On the 17th, we took breakfast at an inn. We passed a small village, and asked a man whom we met with a dearborn, what would be his charge to Windgap. "One dollar and fifty cents," was the ready answer. So in we got, and rode to that place.

As we wanted to make some inquiries when we struck the north and south road, I went into the post-office, and asked for a letter for John Thomas, which of course I did not get. The postmaster scrutinized us closely,—more so, indeed, than any one had done on the Blue Mountains,—but informed us that Friendsville was between forty and fifty miles away. After going about nine miles, we stopped in the evening of the 18th at an inn, got supper, were politely served, and had an excellent night's rest. On the next day we set out for Tannersville, hiring a conveyance for twenty-two miles of the way. We had no further difficulty on the entire road to Rochester,—more than five hundred miles by the route we travelled.

Some amusing incidents occurred, however, which it may be well to relate in this connection. The next morning, after stopping at the tavern, we took the cars and rode to Homerville, where, after waiting an hour, as our landlord of the night previous had directed us, we took stage. Being the first applicants for tickets, we secured inside seats, and, from the number of us, we took up all of the places inside; but, another traveller coming, I tendered him mine, and rode with the driver. The passenger thanked me; but the driver, a churl, and the most prejudiced person I ever came in contact with, would never wait after a stop until I could get on, but would drive away, and leave me to swing, climb, or cling on to the stage as best I could. Our traveller, at last noticing his behavior, told him promptly not to be so fast, but let all passengers get on, which had the effect to restrain him a little.

At Big Eddy we took the cars. Directly opposite me sat a gentleman, who, on learning that I was for Rochester, said he was going there too, and afterwards proved an agreeable travelling companion.

A newsboy came in with papers, some of which the passengers bought. Upon opening them, they read of the fight at Christiana.

"O, see here!" said my neighbor; "great excitement at Christiana, a—a statesman[26] killed, and his son and nephew badly wounded."

After reading, the passengers began to exchange opinions on the case. Some said they would like to catch Parker, and get the thousand dollars reward offered by the State; but the man opposite to me said, "Parker must be a powerful man."

I thought to myself, "If you could tell what I can, you could judge about that."

Pinckney and Johnson became alarmed, and wanted to leave the cars at the next stopping-place; but I told them there was no danger. I then asked particularly about Christiana, where it was, on what railroad, and other questions, to all of which I received correct replies. One of the men became so much attached to me, that, when we would go to an eating-saloon, he would pay for both. At Jefferson we thought of leaving the cars, and taking the boat; but they told us to keep on the cars, and we would get to Rochester by nine o'clock the next night.

We left Jefferson about four o'clock in the morning, and arrived at Rochester at nine the same morning. Just before reaching Rochester, when in conversation with my travelling friend, I ventured to ask what would be done with Parker, should he be taken.

"I do not know," he replied; "but the laws of Pennsylvania would not hang him,—they might imprison him. But it would be different, very different, should they get him into Maryland. The people in all the Slave States are so prejudiced against colored people, that they never give them justice. But I don't believe they will get Parker. I think he is in Canada by this time; at least, I hope so,—for I believe he did right, and, had I been in his place, I would have done as he did. Any good citizen will say the same. I believe Parker to be a brave man; and all you colored people should look at it as we white people look at our brave men, and do as we do. You see Parker was not fighting for a country, nor for praise. He was fighting for freedom: he only wanted liberty, as other men do. You colored people should protect him, and remember him as long as you live. We are coming near our parting-place, and I do not know if we shall ever meet again. I shall be in Rochester some two or three days before I return home; and I would like to have your company back."

I told him it would be some time before we returned.

The cars then stopped, when he bade me good by. As strange as it may appear, he did not ask me my name; and I was afraid to inquire his, from fear he would.

On leaving the cars, after walking two or three squares, we overtook a colored man, who conducted us to the house of—a friend of mine.[27] He welcomed me at once, as we were acquainted before, took me up stairs to wash and comb, and prepare, as he said, for company.

As I was combing, a lady[28] came up and said, "Which of you is Mr. Parker?"

"I am," said I,—"what there is left of me."

She gave me her hand, and said, "And this is William Parker!"

She appeared to be so excited that she could not say what she wished to. We were told we would not get much rest, and we did not; for visitors were constantly coming. One gentleman was surprised that we got away from the cars, as spies were all about and there were two thousand dollars reward for the party.

We left at eight o'clock that evening, in a carriage, for the boat, bound for Kingston in Canada. As we went on board, the bell was ringing. After walking about a little, a friend pointed out to me the officers on the "hunt" for us; and just as the boat pushed off from the wharf, some of our friends on shore called me by name. Our pursuers looked very much like fools, as they were. I told one of the gentlemen on shore to write to Kline that I was in Canada. Ten dollars were generously contributed by the Rochester friends for our expenses; and altogether their kindness was heartfelt, and was most gratefully appreciated by us.

Once on the boat, and fairly out at sea towards the land of liberty, my mind became calm, and my spirits very much depressed at thought of my wife and children. Before, I had little time to think much about them, my mind being on my journey. Now I became silent and abstracted. Although fond of company, no one was company for me now.

We landed at Kingston on the 21st of September, at six o'clock in the morning, and walked around for a long time, without meeting any one we had ever known. At last, however, I saw a colored man I knew in Maryland. He at first pretended to have no knowledge of me, but finally recognized me. I made known our distressed condition, when he said he was not going home then, but, if we would have breakfast, he would pay for it. How different the treatment received from this man—himself an exile for the sake of liberty, and in its full enjoyment on free soil—and the self-sacrificing spirit of our Rochester colored brother, who made haste to welcome us to his ample home,—the well-earned reward of his faithful labors!

On Monday evening, the 23d, we started for Toronto, where we arrived safely the next day. Directly after landing, we heard that Governor Johnston, of

Pennsylvania, had made a demand on the Governor of Canada for me, under the Extradition Treaty.[29] Pinckney and Johnson advised me to go to the country, and remain where I should not be known; but I refused. I intended to see what they would do with me. Going at once to the Government House, I entered the first office I came to. The official requested me to be seated. The following is the substance of the conversation between us, as near as I can remember. I told him I had heard that Governor Johnston, of Pennsylvania, had requested his government to send me back. At this he came forward, held forth his hand, and said, "Is this William Parker?"

I took his hand, and assured him I was the man. When he started to come, I thought he was intending to seize me, and I prepared myself to knock him down. His genial, sympathetic manner it was that convinced me he meant well.

He made me sit down, and said,—"Yes, they want you back again. Will you go?"

"I will not be taken back alive," said I. "I ran away from my master to be free,—I have run from the United States to be free. I am now going to stop running."

"Are you a fugitive from labor?" he asked.

I told him I was.

"Why," he answered, "they say you are a fugitive from justice." He then asked me where my master lived.

I told him, "In Anne Arundel County, Maryland."

"Is there such a county in Maryland?" he asked.

"There is," I answered.

He took down a map, examined it, and said, "You are right."

I then told him the name of the farm, and my master's name. Further questions bearing upon the country towns near, the nearest river, etc., followed, all of which I answered to his satisfaction.

"How does it happen," he then asked, "that you lived in Pennsylvania so long, and no person knew you were a fugitive from labor?"

"I do not get other people to keep my secrets, sir," I replied. "My brother and family only knew that I had been a slave."

He then assured me that I would not, in his opinion, have to go back.[30] Many coming in at this time on business, I was told to call again at three o'clock, which I did. The person in the office, a clerk, told me to take no further trouble about it, until that day four weeks. "But you are as free a man as I am," said he. When I told the news to Pinckney and Johnson, they were greatly relieved in mind.

I ate breakfast with the greatest relish, got a letter written to a friend in Chester County for my wife, and set about arrangements to settle at or near Toronto.

We tried hard to get work, but the task was difficult. I think three weeks elapsed before we got work that could be called work. Sometimes we would secure a small job, worth two or three shillings, and sometimes a smaller one, worth not more than one shilling; and these not oftener than once or twice in a week. We became greatly discouraged; and, to add to my misery, I was constantly hearing some alarming report about my wife and children. Sometimes they had carried her back into slavery,—sometimes the children, and sometimes the entire party. Then there would come a contradiction. I was soon so completely worn down by my fears for them, that I thought my heart would break. To add to my disquietude, no answer came to my letters, although I went to the office regularly every day. At last I got a letter with the glad news that my wife and children were safe, and would be sent to Canada. I told the person reading for me to stop, and tell them to send her "right now,"—I could not wait to hear the rest of the letter.

Two months from the day I landed in Toronto, my wife arrived, but without the children. She had had a very bad time. Twice they had her in custody; and, a third time, her young master came after her, which obliged her to flee before day, so that the children had to remain behind for the time. I was so glad to see her that I forgot about the children.

The day my wife came, I had nothing but the clothes on my back, and was in debt for my board, without any work to depend upon. My situation was truly distressing. I took the resolution, and went to a store where I made known my circumstances to the proprietor, offering to work for him to pay for some necessaries. He readily consented, and I supplied myself with bedding, meal, and flour. As I had selected a place before, we went that evening about two miles into the country, and settled ourselves for the winter.

When in Kingston, I had heard of the Buxton settlement, and of the Revds. Dr. Willis and Mr. King, the agents.[31] My informant, after stating all the particulars, induced me to think it was a desirable place; and having quite a little sum of money due to me in the States, I wrote for it, and waited until May. It not being sent, I called upon Dr. Willis, who treated me kindly. I proposed to settle in Elgin, if he would loan means for the first instalment. He said he would see about it, and I should call again. On my second visit, he agreed to assist me, and proposed that I should get another man to go on a lot with me.

Abraham Johnson and I arranged to settle together, and, with Dr. Willis's letter to Mr. King on our behalf, I embarked with my family on a schooner for the West. After five days' sailing, we reached Windsor. Not having the means to take us to Chatham, I called upon Henry Bibb,[32] and laid my case before him. He took us in, treated us with great politeness, and afterwards took me with him to Detroit, where, after an introduction to some friends, a purse of five dollars was made up. I divided the money among my companions, and started them for Chatham, but was obliged to stay at Windsor and Detroit two days longer.

While stopping at Windsor, I went again to Detroit, with two or three friends, when, at one of the steamboats just landed, some officers arrested three fugitives, on pretence of being horse thieves. I was satisfied they were slaves, and said so, when Henry Bibb went to the telegraph office and learned through a message that they were. In the crowd and excitement, the sheriff threatened to imprison me for my interference. I felt indignant, and told him to do so, whereupon he opened the door. About this time there was more excitement, and then a man slipped into the jail, unseen by the officers, opened the gate, and the three prisoners went out, and made their escape to Windsor. I stopped through that night in Detroit, and started the next day for Chatham, where I found my family snugly provided for at a boarding-house kept by Mr. Younge.

Chatham was a thriving town at that time, and the genuine liberty enjoyed by its numerous colored residents pleased me greatly; but our destination was Buxton, and thither we went on the following day. We arrived there in the evening, and I called immediately upon Mr. King, and presented Dr. Willis's letter. He received me very politely, and said that, after I should feel rested, I could go out and select a lot. He also kindly offered to give me meal and pork for my family, until I could get work.

In due time, Johnson and I each chose a fifty-acre lot; for although when in Toronto we agreed with Dr. Willis to take one lot between us, when we saw the land we thought we could pay for two lots. I got the money in a little time, and paid the Doctor back. I built a house, and we moved into it that same fall, and in it I live yet.

When I first settled in Buxton, the white settlers in the vicinity were much opposed to colored people. Their prejudices were very strong; but the spread of intelligence and religion in the community has wrought a great change in them. Prejudice is fast being uprooted; indeed, they do not appear like the same people that they were. In a short time I hope the foul spirit will depart entirely.

I have now to bring my narrative to a close; and in so doing I would return thanks to Almighty God for the many mercies and favors he has bestowed upon me, and especially for delivering me out of the hands of slaveholders, and placing me in a land of liberty, where I can worship God under my own vine and fig-tree, with none to molest or make me afraid.[33] I am also particularly thankful to my old friends and neighbors in Lancaster County, Pennsylvania,—to the friends in Norristown, Quakertown, Rochester, and Detroit, and to Dr. Willis of Toronto, for their disinterested benevolence and kindness to me and my family. When hunted, they sheltered me; when hungry and naked, they clothed and fed me; and when a stranger in a strange land, they aided and encouraged me. May the Lord in his great mercy remember and bless them, as they remembered and blessed me.

The events following the riot at Christiana and my escape have become matters of history, and can only be spoken of as such. The failure of Gorsuch in his attempt; his death, and the terrible wounds of his son; the discomfiture and final rout of his crestfallen associates in crime; and their subsequent attempt at revenge by a merciless raid through Lancaster County, arresting every one unfortunate enough to have a dark skin,—is all to be found in the printed account of the trial of Castner Hanway and others for treason.[34] It is true that some of the things which did occur are spoken of but slightly, there being good and valid reasons why they were passed over thus at that time in these cases, many of which might be interesting to place here, and which I certainly should do, did not the same reasons still exist in full force for keeping silent. I shall be compelled to let them pass just as they are recorded.

But one event, in which there seems no reason to observe silence, I will introduce in this place. I allude to the escape of George Williams, one of our men, and the very one who had the letters brought up from Philadelphia by Mr.

Samuel Williams. George lay in prison with the others who had been arrested by Kline, but was rendered more uneasy by the number of rascals who daily visited that place for the purpose of identifying, if possible, some of its many inmates as slaves. One day the lawyer previously alluded to, whose chief business seemed to be negro-catching, came with another man, who had employed him for that purpose, and, stopping in front of the cell wherein George and old Ezekiel Thompson were confined, cried out, "*That's* him!" At which the man exclaimed, "*It is, by God! that is him!*"

These ejaculations, as a matter of course, brought George and Ezekiel, who were lying down, to their feet,—the first frightened and uneasy, the latter stern and resolute. Some mysterious conversation then took place between the two, which resulted in George lying down and covering himself with Ezekiel's blanket. In the mean time off sped the man and lawyer to obtain the key, open the cell, and institute a more complete inspection. They returned in high glee, but to their surprise saw only the old man standing at the door, his grim visage anything but inviting. They inserted the key, click went the lock, back shot the bolt, open flew the door, but old Ezekiel stood there firm, his eyes flashing fire, his brawny hands flourishing a stout oak stool furnished him to rest on by friends of whom I have so often spoken, and crying out in the most unmistakable manner, every word leaving a deep impression on his visitors, "The first man that puts his head inside of this cell I will split to pieces."

The men leaped back, but soon recovered their self-possession; and the lawyer said,—"Do you know who I am? I am the lawyer who has charge of this whole matter, you impudent nigger. I will come in whenever I choose."

The old man, if possible looking more stern and savage than before, replied,—"I don't care who you are; but if you or any other nigger-catcher steps inside of my cell-door I will beat out his brains."

It is needless to say more. The old man's fixed look, clenched teeth, and bony frame had their effect. The man and the lawyer left, growling as they went, that, if there was rope to be had, that old Indian nigger should certainly hang.

This was but the beginning of poor George's troubles. His friends were at work; but all went wrong, and his fate seemed sealed. He stood charged with treason, murder, and riot, and there appeared no way to relieve him. When discharged by the United States Court for the first crime, he was taken to Lancaster to meet the second and third. There, too, the man and the lawyer followed, taking with them that infamous wretch, Kline. The Devil seemed to favor all they undertook; and when Ezekiel was at last discharged, with some thirty more, from all that had been so unjustly brought against him, and for which he had lain in the damp prison for more than three months, these rascals lodged a warrant in the Lancaster jail, and at midnight Kline and the man who claimed to be George's owner arrested him as a fugitive from labor, whilst the lawyer returned to Philadelphia to prepare the case for trial, and to await the arrival of his shameless partners in guilt. This seemed the climax of George's misfortunes. He was hurried into a wagon, ready at the door, and, fearing a rescue, was driven at a killing pace to the town of Parkesburg, where they were compelled to stop for the night, their horses being completely used up. This was in the month of January, and the coldest night that had been known for many years. On their route, these wretches, who had George handcuffed and tied in the wagon, indulged deeply in bad whiskey, with which they were plentifully supplied, and by the time they reached the public-house their fury was at its height. 'T is said there is honor among thieves, but villains of the sort I am now speaking of seem to possess none. Each fears the other. When in the bar-room, Kline said to the other,—"Sir, you can go to sleep. I will watch this nigger."

"No," replied the other, "I will do that business myself. You don't fool me, sir."

To which Kline replied, "Take something, sir?"—and down went more whiskey.

Things went on in this way awhile, until Kline drew a chair to the stove, and, overcome by the heat and liquor, was soon sleeping soundly, and, I suppose, dreaming of the profits which were sure to arise from the job. The other walked about till the barkeeper went to bed, leaving the hostler to attend in his place, and he also, somehow or other, soon fell asleep. Then he walked up to George, who was lying on a bench, apparently as soundly asleep as any of them, and, saying to himself, "The damn nigger is asleep,—I'll just take a little rest myself,"—he suited the action to the word. Spreading himself out on two chairs, in a few moments he was snoring at a fearful rate. Rum, the devil, and fatigue, combined, had completely prostrated George's foes. It was now his time for action; and, true to the hope of being free, the last to leave the poor, hunted, toil-worn bondman's heart, he opened first one eye, then the other, and carefully examined things around. Then he rose slowly, and, keeping step to the deep-drawn snores of the miserable, debased wretch who claimed him, he stealthily crawled towards the door, when, to his consternation, he found the eye of the hostler on him. He paused, knowing his fate hung by a single hair. It was only necessary for the man to speak, and he would be shot instantly dead; for both Kline and his brother ruffian slept pistol in hand. As I said, George stopped, and, in the softest manner in which it was possible for him to speak, whispered, "A drink of water, if you please, sir." The man replied not, but, pointing his finger to the door again, closed his eyes, and was apparently lost in slumber.

I have already said it was cold; and, in addition, snow and ice covered the ground. There could not possibly be a worse night. George shivered as he stepped forth into the keen night air. He took one look at the clouds above, and then at the ice-clad ground below. He trembled; but freedom beckoned, and on he sped. He knew where he was,—the place was familiar. On, on, he pressed, nor paused till fifteen miles lay between him add his drunken claimant; then he stopped at the house of a tried friend to have his handcuffs removed; but, with their united efforts, one side only could be got off, and the poor fellow, not daring to rest, continued his journey, forty odd miles, to Philadelphia, with the other on. Frozen, stiff, and sore, he arrived there on the following day, and every care was extended to him by his old friends. He was nursed and attended by the late Dr. James, Joshua Gould Bias, one of the faithful few, whose labors for the oppressed will never be forgotten, and whose heart, purse, and hand were always open to the poor, flying slave. God has blessed him, and his reward is obtained.

I shall here take leave of George, only saying, that he recovered and went to the land of freedom, to be safe under the protection of British law. Of the wretches he left in the *tavern,* much might be said; but it is enough to know that they awoke to find him gone, and to pour their curses and blasphemy on each other. They swore most frightfully; and the disappointed Southerner threatened to blow out the brains of Kline, who turned his wrath on the hostler, declaring he should be taken and held responsible for the loss. This so raised the ire of that worthy, that, seizing an iron bar that was used to fasten the door, he drove the whole party from the house, swearing they were damned kidnappers, and ought to be all sent after old Gorsuch, and that he would raise the whole township on them if they said one word more. This had the desired effect. They left, not to pursue poor George, but to avoid pursuit; for these worthless man-stealers knew the released men brought up from Philadelphia and discharged at Lancaster were all in the neighborhood, and that nothing would please these brave fellows—who had patiently and heroically suffered for long and weary months in a felon's cell for the cause of human freedom— more than to get a sight at them; and Kline, he knew this well,—particularly old Ezekiel Thompson, who had sworn by his heart's blood, that, if he could only get hold of that Marshal Kline, he should kill him and go to the gallows in peace. In fact, he said the only thing he had to feel sorry about was, that he did not do it when he threatened to, whilst the scoundrel stood talking to Hanway; and but for Castner Hanway he would have done it, anyhow. Much more I could say; but short stories are read, while long ones are like the sermons we go to sleep under.

1. Slaughter, *Bloody Dawn,* 47.

2. Douglass, *Autobiographies,* 724–726.

3. Finkenbine, "Christiana Revolt," 541; Quarles, *Black Abolitionists,* 212.

4. Cited in Katz, *Resistance at Christiana,* 270.

5. Ibid., 284–290. Katz convincingly argues against previous scholars, who denied that Parker wrote his narrative himself. The notations in the ledger of the publisher of *The Provincial Freeman* read: "Augusta took first manuscript of Parker's life to work upon. [Abraham] Johnson [a close friend of Parker's from his Pennsylvania days] came in from Buxton [Elgin] to see about it." "Joseph and Anderson working in office on Parker's life." While Katz assumes that these notations imply that these three men (whom Katz fully identifies) were revising the narrative, it seems entirely possible that they were typesetting it or otherwise readying it for publication in book or pamphlet form. At the least it can be adduced that Parker had completed a first draft of his narrative by March 1, 1858, the date of the first notation.

6. Ibid., 304.

7. Ibid., 290–291.

8. George Henry Thomas (1816–70) was a Virginian who fought with the Union army during the Civil War, and was nicknamed "The Rock of Chickamauga" for his bravery on that battlefield.

9. Edmund Kirke, the pen name of James R. Gilmore (1822–1903), a prolific writer of both fiction and nonfiction. During the Civil War, Lincoln had sent him to the South to sound out rebel leaders on the prospects of peace.

10. John Wesley (1703–91) was the founder and leader of Methodism. His commitment to missionary work gained him worldwide fame; his practical and religious writings fill thirty-two volumes. He was the first high-ranking religious leader to oppose slavery.

11. Because York and Wrightsville, Pennsylvania, are southeast of the Susquehanna River, they were not safe places for fugitive slaves; Columbia is on the other side of the river.

12. Actually Dr. Obadiah Dingee, an abolitionist sympathizer. Hensel, *Christiana Riot,* 28.

13. William Lloyd Garrison (1805–79) published *The Liberator,* the most popular abolitionist newspaper, from 1831 to 1865. He helped organize the American Anti-Slavery Society, of which he was president from 1843 to 1865. He advocated Northern secession, publicly burned the Constitution, and was widely regarded as the foremost leader of the antislavery movement.

14. This was probably in the fall of 1843. Nash, "William Parker," 25.

15. While the Fugitive Slave Law of 1793, providing for the return between states of escaped slaves, was loosely enforced, the Fugitive Slave Act of 1850 commanded "all good citizens" to aid and assist federal marshals and deputies "in the prompt and efficient execution of this law," and imposed heavy penalties on anyone who assisted slaves to escape from bondage. When apprehended, any black man could be taken before a federal court or comissioner. Denied a jury trial, his testimony could not be admitted, while the statement of the man claiming ownership would be taken as the main evidence.

16. Edward Gorsuch (1795–1851) was a prominent and prosperous citizen of Baltimore County and the owner of twelve slaves. By a provision in his father's will, he set his slaves free when they reached the age of twenty-eight. The four slaves who escaped—his only adult male slaves—still had several years to serve him. See Hensel, *Christiana Riot,* 20–21; Slaughter, *Bloody Dawn,* 3–6.

17. The Fugitive Slave Act (see note 15, above).

18. Actually Thomas Pearce.

19. A light, four-wheeled wagon.

20. See *Colossians* 3:22.

21. *Colossians* 4:1.

22. This popular spiritual also appears in Harriet Beecher Stowe's *Uncle Tom's Cabin* (1851).

23. See *Ezekiel* 33:2–6, from which this is freely adapted.

24. Although the facts are unclear, these numbers are unlikely. It is probable that between fifteen and fifty blacks, most of them armed, were on the scene by this time, and that the white men received no additional aid. See Katz, *Resistance at Christiana,* 94–95; Slaughter, *Bloody Dawn,* 215–216.

25. Pearce was wounded by bullets in his wrist, spine, and shoulder blade.

26. Gorsuch was a farmer, not a statesman.

27. Frederick Douglass.

28. Probably Julia Griffiths, a British abolitionist and Douglass's close friend, benefactor, and business manager.

29. The Webster-Ashburton Treaty of 1842 provided for the extradition of fugitives from justice.

30. Because Canada's unwritten policy was to to shelter fugitive slaves, and because no precedent for criminal extradition of such fugitives had been set, the British government apparently refused to honor Governor Johnson's request.

31. Parker refers to the Elgin settlement for fugitive slaves, also known as Buxton; its founder William King (1812–95), an Irish missionary; and Michael Willis (1799–1879), principal of Knox College in Toronto and president of the Anti-Slavery Society of Canada. Established in 1850, Elgin emphasized classical rather than manual education; it was doubtless there that Parker learned to read and write, since the colony required this of all heads of families.

32. Henry Walton Bibb (1815–54) was a fugitive slave and antislavery activist. He published his *Narrative of the Life and Adventures of Henry Bibb, an American Slave* in 1850, and moved to Ontario that year. There he became a leader of the Afro-Canadian community, establishing the first black newspaper, the *Voice of the Fugitive,* and advocating black emigration. See his narrative on pp. II:1–101.

33. See *Micah* 4:4.

34. James J. Robbins, *Report of the Trial of Castner Hanway for Treason, in the Resistance of the Execution of the Fugitive Slave Law of 1850* (1852).

Part I: Ten highly recommended slave narratives not included in this collection (listed in chronological order)

Smith, Venture. *A Narrative of the Life and Adventures of Venture, a Native of Africa: But Resident Above Sixty Years in the United States of America.* New London: C. Holt, 1798. Reprinted in Porter, *Early Negro Writing*, 538–558, and Carretta, *Unchained Voices*, 369–387. Smith grew up in Africa, where he witnessed a tribal war in which his father, a king, was tortured and killed. A rebellious and combative slave, he purchased his own freedom for an exorbitant price. He then bought his wife and children, some land, and a slave of his own. Despite a condescending amanuensis, Smith's bitter pride and rebellious spirit come through intact.

Bayley, Solomon. *Incidents in the Life of Solomon Bayley.* Philadelphia: Tract Association of Friends, 1820. *A Narrative of Some Remarkable Incidents in the Life of Solomon Bayley, Formerly a Slave, in the State of Delaware, North America.* 2d ed., London: Harvey and Darton, 1825. Reprinted in Porter, *Early Negro Writing*, 587–613. The most remarkable passage of this intensely religious self-penned tract is Bayley's mystical account of how a circle of birds in the woods protected him from fugitive slave hunters.

Prince, Mary. *The History of Mary Prince, a West Indian Slave.* London: F. Westley and A. H. Davis, 1831. Reprinted in Gates, *Classic Slave Narratives*, 183–242. Prince was sold at a young age to an extraordinarily cruel master; her description of the salt works comes as close to hell on earth as any passage in the slave-narrative tradition. Although dictated to a British amanuensis, her *History* is the first West Indian autobiography, and the first narrative of a female slave.

Williams, James. *Narrative of James Williams, An American Slave.* New York: American Anti-slavery Society, 1838. On-line, <http://sunsite.unc.edu/docsouth/narratives.html>. After a mild childhood, Williams was separated from his wife and children, taken to Alabama, and made a slave driver. His overseer, Huckstep, was a brutal murderer, and Williams escaped by befriending his master's bloodhounds. His popular narrative, dictated to the abolitionist poet John Greenleaf Whittier, was widely discredited not long after its publication, because certain details, such as names of places and people, had been falsified.

789

Lane, Lunsford. *The Narrative of Lunsford Lane, Formerly of Raleigh, N. C.* Boston: J. G. Torry, 1842. Reprinted in Katz, *Flight from the Devil.* After making money as a tobacconist and buying his freedom, Lane was banished from North Carolina under a law that disallowed the residence of free blacks in the state. When he returned to Raleigh to purchase his wife and child, he was brought before a local court, accused of giving abolitionist lectures in Boston, and tarred and feathered.

Gilbert, Olive. *Narrative of Sojourner Truth, a Northern Slave.* Boston: the Author, 1850. Numerous reprints. Although entitled a slave narrative, this book is actually a biography largely drawn from the recollections of Truth, and was instrumental in bringing her to the world's attention. Its most unforgettable scene comes near the end, when Truth disperses a group of rioters at a revival meeting.

Douglass, Frederick. *My Bondage and My Freedom.* New York and Auburn: Miller, Orton and Mulligan, 1855. Numerous reprints. Three times as long as Douglass's earlier *Narrative,* his second autobiography not only updates and expands his first, but is less heroic and more sophisticated, complex, playful, nuanced, humorous, detached, and inclusive—all without sacrificing Douglass's militancy.

Steward, Austin. *Twenty-Two Years a Slave, and Forty Years a Freeman.* Rochester [N.Y.]: William Alling, 1857. On-line, <http://sunsite.unc.edu/docsouth/narratives.html>. Steward was an important abolitionist who spent most of his life in Canada. His lengthy and militant autobiography not only deals with the evils of slavery, but the "black codes" common in the free states and the difficulties of life in the black settlements of Canada.

Keckley, Elizabeth. *Behind the Scenes, or, Thirty Years a Slave, and Four Years in the White House.* New York: G. W. Carleton & Co., 1868. Reprint: New York, Oxford University Press, 1988. Keckley was dressmaker both to Virginia Davis, wife of Jefferson Davis, and to Mary Lincoln, wife of Abraham Lincoln. She had intimate knowledge of the entire Lincoln family, and her anecdotal account is priceless for its insider's view.

Hughes, Louis. *Thirty Years a Slave: From Bondage to Freedom.* Milwaukee: South Side Printing Company, 1897. Reprint, Detroit: Negro History Press, 1969. On-line, <http://sunsite.unc.edu/docsouth/narratives.html>. This narrative includes perhaps the longest, most interesting, and most exciting firsthand account of slave life during' the Civil War.

Part II: Other works cited

Andrews, William L. "*Narrative of the Life of Frederick Douglass.*" In Andrews et al., *Oxford Companion,* 526–527.

———. "The Representation of Slavery and the Rise of Afro-American Literary Realism, 1865–1920." In Andrews, *African American Autobiography.*

———. "Slave Narrative." In Andrews et al., *Oxford Companion,* 667–670.

———. *To Tell a Free Story: The First Century of Afro-American Autobiography, 1760–1865.* Urbana: University of Illinois Press, 1986.

———, ed. *African American Autobiography: A Collection of Critical Essays.* Englewood Cliffs, NJ: Prentice Hall, 1993.

————, ed. *From Fugitive Slave to Free Man: The Autobiographies of William Wells Brown*. New York: Mentor, 1993.

Andrews, William L., Frances Smith Foster, and Trudier Harris, eds. *The Oxford Companion to African American Literature*. New York: Oxford University Press, 1997.

Andrews, William L., and William S. McFeely, eds. *Narrative of the Life of Frederick Douglass, an American Slave, Written by Himself: A Norton Critical Edition*. New York: W. W. Norton, 1997.

Aptheker, Herbert. "Turner, Nat." In Logan and Winston, *Dictionary*, 611–613.

Bibb, Henry. *Narrative of the Life and Adventures of Henry Bibb, An American Slave*. 3d ed, New York: the author, 1850.

Black, Alexander. *The Story of Ohio*. Boston: D. Lothrop, 1888.

Blackett, R. J. M. *Beating Against the Barriers: Biographical Essays in Nineteenth-Century Afro-American History*. Baton Rouge: Louisiana State University Press, 1986.

Blassingame, John W. "Bibb, Henry Walton." In Logan and Winston, *Dictionary*, 44.

————. *The Slave Community: Plantation Life in the Antebellum South*. Rev. & enlarged ed. New York: Oxford University Press, 1979.

————, ed. *Slave Testimony: Two Centuries of Letters, Speeches, Interviews, and Autobiographies*. Baton Rouge: Louisiana State University Press, 1977.

Blight, David W. Introduction and notes to *Narrative of the Life of Frederick Douglass, An American Slave*. Boston: Bedford Books, 1993.

Bontemps, Arna, ed. *Great Slave Narratives*. Boston: Beacon Press, 1969.

Brown, Henry Box. *Narrative of the Life of Henry Box Brown*. Manchester [England]: Lee and Glynn, 1851.

Brown, William Wells. *The Anti-Slavery Harp; A Collection of Songs*. 4th ed., Boston: Bela Marsh, 1854.

Byrd, William. *The Correspondence of the Three William Byrds of Westover, Virginia, 1684–1776*. Ed. Marion Tinling. Charlottesville: University Press of Virginia, 1977.

Carby, Hazel V. " 'Hear My Voice, Ye Careless Daughters': Narratives of Slave and Free Women before Emancipation." In Andrews, *African American Autobiography*, 59–76.

Carretta, Vincent. Introduction and notes to *The Interesting Narrative and Other Writings* by Olaudah Equiano. New York: Penguin, 1995.

————, ed. *Unchained Voices: An Anthology of Black Authors in the English-Speaking World of the Eighteenth Century*. Lexington: University Press of Kentucky, 1996.

Chernow, Barbara A. and George A. Vallassi. *The Columbia Encyclopedia*. 5th ed., New York: Columbia University Press, 1993.

Child, Lydia Marie. "Leaves from a Slave's Journal of Life." *National Anti-Slavery Standard*, Oct. 20, 27, 1842. In Blassingame, *Slave Testimony*, 151–164.

Costanzo, Angelo. *Surprizing Narrative: Olaudah Equiano and the Beginnings of Black Autobiography*. Westport, CT: Greenwood Press, 1987.

Davis, Arthur P. "Hammon, Briton." In Logan and Winston, *Dictionary*, 281.

Davis, Charles T., and Henry Louis Gates, Jr., eds. *The Slave's Narrative*. New York: Oxford University Press, 1985.

Davis, David Brion. "A Big Business." *New York Review of Books* 45, no. 10 (June 11, 1998), 50–53.

Douglass, Frederick. *Autobiographies.* New York: The Library of America, 1994.

———. *My Bondage and My Freedom.* New York and Auburn: Miller, Orton & Mulligan, 1855.

Doyle, Mary Ellen. "The Slave Narratives as Rhetorical Art." In Sekora and Turner, *Art of Slave Narrative,* 83–95.

Drewry, William Sidney. *The Southampton Insurrection.* Washington: The Neale Company, 1900.

Dziwas, Doris. "Hammon, Briton." In Salzman et al., *Encyclopedia,* 1178–1179.

Eakin, Sue, and Joseph Logsdon. Introduction and notes to *Twelve Years a Slave,* by Solomon Northup. Reprint, Baton Rouge: Louisiana State University Press, 1968.

Eaklor, Vicki L. *American Antislavery Songs: A Collection and Analysis.* Westport, CT: Greenwood Press, 1988.

Edwards, Paul. Introduction to *The Life of Olaudah Equiano.* Reprint, London: Dawsons of Pall Mall, 1969.

———. "Three West African Writers of the 1780s." In Davis and Gates, *Slave's Narrative,* 175–198.

Fabricant, Daniel S. "Thomas R. Gray and William Styron: Finally, a Critical Look at the 1831 *Confessions of Nat Turner.*" *The American Journal of Legal History* 37, no. 3 (July 1993), 332–361.

Farrison, William Edward. *William Wells Brown: Author & Reformer.* Chicago: University of Chicago Press, 1969.

Finkenbine, Roy E. "Christiana Revolt of 1851." In Salzman et al., *Encyclopedia,* 541.

Fisher[, Isaac]. *Slavery in the United States: A Narrative of the Life and Adventures of Charles Ball, a Black Man.* [2d ed.] New York: John S. Taylor, 1837. Reprint: New York: New American Library, 1969.

Five Black Lives. Middletown, CT: Wesleyan University Press, 1971.

Foner, Philip S. *The Life and Writings of Frederick Douglass.* New York: International Publishers, 1950–75.

Foster, Frances Smith. *Witnessing Slavery: The Development of Ante-Bellum Slave Narratives.* 2d ed. Madison: University of Wisconsin Press, 1994.

Franklin, John Hope, and Alfred A. Moss, Jr. *From Slavery to Freedom: A History of African Americans.* 7th ed. New York: Alfred A. Knopf, 1994.

Freedman, Florence B. Introduction to *Running a Thousand Miles for Freedom,* by William and Ellen Craft. Reprint, New York: Arno Press and The New York Times, 1969. ·

Galbreath, Charles B. *History of Ohio.* Chicago: American Historical Society, 1925.

Gara, Larry. "Craft, Ellen." In Logan and Winston, *Dictionary,* 139–140.

Garfield, Deborah M., and Rafia Zafar, eds. *Harriet Jacobs and* Incidents in the Life of a Slave Girl. Cambridge: Cambridge University Press, 1996.

Garland of Freedom, The: A Collection of Poems, Chiefly Anti-Slavery. London: W. and F. G. Cash & William Tweedie, 1853.

Gates, Henry Louis, Jr. "From Wheatley to Douglass: The Politics of Displacement." In Sundquist, *Frederick Douglass,* 47–65.

———. "James Gronniosaw and the Trope of the Talking Book." In Andrews, *African American Autobiography,* 8–25.

———, ed. *The Classic Slave Narratives.* New York: Mentor, 1987.

Goldsby, Jacqueline. "'I Disguised My Hand': Writing Versions of the Truth in Harriet Jacobs's *Incidents in the Life of a Slave Girl* and John Jacobs's 'A True Tale of Slavery.'" In Garfield and Zafar, *Harriet Jacobs*, 11–43.

Grandy, Moses. *Narrative of the Life of Moses Grandy, Late a Slave in the United States of America.* Boston: Oliver Johnson, 1844. 2d ed. reprinted in Katz, *Five Slave Narratives.*

Greenberg, Kenneth S., ed. *The Confessions of Nat Turner and Related Documents.* Boston: Bedford Books, 1996.

Grimes, William. *Life of William Grimes, the Runaway Slave, Brought Down to the Present Time.* [2d ed.] New Haven: the Author, 1855. Reprinted in *Five Black Lives*, 59–128.

Gross, Seymour L., and Eileen Bender. "History, Politics and Literature: The Myth of Nat Turner." *American Quarterly* 23, no. 4 (October 1971), 487–518.

Hammon, Briton. *A Narrative of the Uncommon Sufferings, and Surprising Deliverance of Briton Hammon, A Negro Man,—Servant to General Winslow, of Marshfield, in New England.* Boston: Green & Russell, 1760. Reprinted in Porter, *Early Negro Writing*, 522–528.

Hensel, W. U. *The Christiana Riot and the Treason Trials of 1851: An Historical Sketch.* Lancaster, PA: New Era, 1911.

Henson, Josiah. *An Autobiography of the Reverend Josiah Henson.* Reprint, Reading, MA: Addison-Wesley, 1969.

Higginson, Thomas Wentworth. *Black Rebellion.* Reprint, New York: Da Capo Press, 1998.

Hurd, John Codman. *The Law of Freedom and Bondage in the United States.* Boston: Little, Brown, 1862.

Jackson, Blyden. *A History of Afro-American Literature, Volume I: The Long Beginning, 1746–1895.* Baton Rouge: Louisiana State University Press, 1989.

Jefferson, Paul, ed. *The Travels of William Wells Brown.* New York: Markus Wiener, 1991.

Johnson, Charles, Patricia Smith, and the WGBH Series Research Team. *Africans in America: America's Journey Through Slavery.* New York: Harcourt Brace, 1998.

Jones, Thomas H. *The Experiences of Thomas H. Jones, Who Was a Slave for Forty-Three Years.* Boston: Daniel Lang, Jr., 1849.

Katz, Jonathan. *Resistance at Christiana: The Fugitive Slave Rebellion, Christiana, Pennsylvania, September 11, 1851; A Documentary Account.* New York: Thomas Y. Crowell, 1974.

Katz, William Loren, ed. *Flight from the Devil: Six Slave Narratives.* Lawrenceville, NJ: Red Sea Press, 1996.

Kolchin, Peter. *American Slavery 1619–1877.* New York: Hill and Wang, 1993.

"Life and Adventures of a Fugitive Slave, The." *Quarterly Anti-Slavery Magazine* 1, no. 4 (1836), 375–393. Excerpted in Davis and Gates, *Slave's Narrative*, 6–8.

"Life and Bondage of Frederick Douglass, The." *Putnam's Monthly Magazine* 6 (Nov. 1855), 547. Reprinted in Davis and Gates, *Slave's Narrative*, 30–31.

"Linda: Incidents in the Life of a Slave Girl: Written by Herself." *The Anti-Slavery Advocate* 53, vol. 2 (May 1, 1861), 1. Reprinted in Davis and Gates, *Slave's Narrative*, 32–34.

Logan, Rayford W. "Henson, Josiah." In Logan and Winston, *Dictionary*, 307–308.

Logan, Rayford W., and Michael R. Winston. *Dictionary of American Negro Biography*. New York: Norton, 1982.

Loggins, Vernon. *The Negro Author: His Development in America*. New York: Columbia University Press, 1931.

Logsdon, Joseph. "Northup, Solomon." In Logan and Winston, *Dictionary*, 473–474.

Low, W. Augustus, and Virgil A. Clift. *Encyclopedia of Black America*. New York: McGraw-Hill, 1981. Reprint, New York: Da Capo Press, 1984.

MacKethan, Lucinda H. "Metaphors of Mastery in the Slave Narratives." In Sekora and Turner, *Art of Slave Narrative*, 55–69.

Mars, James. *Life of James Mars, a Slave Born and Sold in Connecticut*. [1870 ed.] Reprinted in *Five Black Lives*, 35–58.

Mason, Theodore O., Jr. "Signifying." In Andrews et al., *Oxford Companion*, 665–666.

Merrill, Walter M., and Louis Ruchames, eds. *The Letters of William Lloyd Garrison*. Cambridge, MA: Harvard University Press, 1971–81.

Miller, James A. "Connecticut." In Salzman et al., *Encyclopedia*, 642–644.

Nash, Roderick W. "William Parker and the Christiana Riot." *Journal of Negro History* 96, no. 1 (1961): 24–31.

Nelson, John Herbert. *The Negro Character in American Literature*. Lawrence, KS: Department of Journalism Press, 1926.

Nichols, Charles H., Jr. "The Case of William Grimes, the Runaway Slave." *William and Mary Quarterly* 8, no. 4 (Oct. 1951), 552–560.

———. *Many Thousand Gone: The Ex-Slaves' Account of Their Bondage and Freedom*. Leiden: E. J. Brill, 1963.

Niemtzow, Annette. "The Problematic of Self in Autobiography: The Example of the Slave Narrative." In Sekora and Turner, *Art of Slave Narrative*, 96–109.

Oates, Stephen B. *The Fires of Jubilee: Nat Turner's Fierce Rebellion*. New York: Harper & Row, 1975. Reprint, New York: HarperPerennial, 1990.

Olmsted, Frederick Law. *A Journey in the Seaboard Slave States in the Years 1853–1854, with Remarks on Their Economy*. Reprint, New York: Putnam's, 1904.

Olney, James. "'I Was Born': Slave Narratives, Their Status as Autobiography and as Literature." In Davis and Gates, *Slave's Narrative*, 148–175.

Parker, William. "The Freedman's Story." *The Atlantic Monthly* 17, no. 100 (Feb. 1866): 152–166; no. 101 (March 1866): 276–295.

Parramore, Thomas C. *Southampton County, Virginia*. Charlottesville: University Press of Virginia, 1978.

Peabody, Ephraim. "Narratives of Fugitive Slaves." *Christian Examiner* 47, no. 1 (July–September, 1849), 61–93. Reprint: in Davis and Gates, *Slave's Narrative*, 19–28.

Porter, Dorothy, ed. *Early Negro Writing, 1750–1837*. Reprint, Baltimore: Black Classic Press, 1995.

Potkay, Adam, and Sandra Burr, eds. *Black Atlantic Writers of the Eighteenth Century: Living the New Exodus in England and the Americas*. New York: St. Martin's Press, 1995.

Quarles, Benjamin. *Black Abolitionists*. Reprint, New York: Da Capo Press, 1991.

———. Introduction to *Narrative of the Life of Frederick Douglass, an American Slave*. Cambridge: Belknap Press, 1960.

Redding, J. Saunders. *To Make a Poet Black*. Chapel Hill: University of North Carolina Press, 1939. Reprint, Ithaca: Cornell University Press, 1988.

Ripley, C. Peter, et al. *The Black Abolitionist Papers*. Chapel Hill: The University of North Carolina Press, 1985.

Ripley, Peter. "The Autobiographical Writings of Frederick Douglass." Excerpted in Andrews and McFeely, *Narrative*, 135–146.

Roper, Moses. "Moses Roper to the Committee of the British and Foreign Anti-Slavery Society." In Ripley, *Black Abolitionist Papers*, I:134–137.

———. "Moses Roper to Thomas Price." In Blassingame, *Slave Testimony*, 23–26.

———. *A Narrative of the Adventures and Escape of Moses Roper, from American Slavery*. 2d British ed. London: Darton, Harvey and Darton, 1838. Reprint, New York: Negro Universities Press, 1970.

Salzman, Jack, David Lionel Smith, and Cornel West. *Encyclopedia of African-American Culture and History*. New York: Macmillan, 1996.

Sartwell, Crispin. *Act Like You Know: African-American Autobiography and White Identity*. Chicago: University of Chicago Press, 1998.

Seager, Robert, II. *and Tyler too: A Biography of John & Julia Gardiner Tyler*. New York: McGraw-Hill, 1963.

Sekora, John, and Darwin T. Turner. *The Art of Slave Narrative: Original Essays in Criticism and Theory*. Macomb: Western Illinois University, 1982.

Slaughter, Thomas P. *Bloody Dawn: The Christiana Riot and Racial Violence in the Antebellum North*. New York: Oxford University Press, 1991.

Smith, Sidonie. *Where I'm Bound: Patterns of Slavery and Freedom in Black American Autobiography*. Westport, CT: Greenwood, 1974.

Starling, Marion Wilson. *The Slave Narrative: Its Place in American History*. Boston: G. K. Hall and Co., 1981.

Stearns, Charles. *Narrative of Henry Box Brown, Who Escaped from Slavery Enclosed in a Box 3 Feet Long and 2 Wide*. Boston: Brown and Stearns, 1849.

Stepto, Robert Burns. "I Rose and Found My Voice: Narration, Authentication, and Authorial Control in Four Slave Narratives." In Davis and Gates, *Slave's Narrative*, 225–241.

Stowe, Harriet Beecher. *A Key to Uncle Tom's Cabin, Presenting the Original Facts and Documents upon Which the Story Is Founded, Together with Corroborative Statements Verifying the Truth of the Work*. Boston: John P. Jewett & Co., 1853.

Stroud, George M. *A Sketch of the Laws Relating to Slavery in the Several States of the United States of America*. 2d ed. Philadelphia: the author, 1856.

Sundquist, Eric J. *To Wake the Nations: Race in the Making of American Literature*. Cambridge, MA: Harvard University Press, 1993.

———, ed. *Frederick Douglass: New Literary and Historical Essays*. Cambridge: Cambridge University Press, 1990.

Titus, Mary. "'This Poisonous System': Social Ills, Bodily Ills, and *Incidents in the Life of a Slave Girl*." In Garfield and Zafar, *Harriet Jacobs*, 199–215.

Tragle, Henry Irving. *The Southampton Slave Revolt of 1831: A Compilation of Source Material*. Reprint, New York: Vintage Books, 1973.

Volk, Betty. "Clarke, Lewis G." In Logan and Winston, *Dictionary*, 116–117.

Weiss, John McNish. *Free Black American Settlers in Trinidad 1815–16*. London: McNish & Weiss, 1995.

Williams, Kenny J. *They Also Spoke: An Essay on Negro Literature in America, 1787–1930*. Nashville: Townsend Press, 1970.

Winks, Robin W. "The Making of a Fugitive Slave Narrative: Josiah Henson and Uncle Tom—A Case Study." In Davis and Gates, *Slave's Narrative,* 112–146.

Wood, Peter H. "Nat Turner's Rebellion." In Salzman et al., *Encyclopedia,* 1970–1971.

Yellin, Jean Fagan. Introduction and notes in *Incidents in the Life of a Slave Girl* by Harriet A. Jacobs. Cambridge, MA: Harvard University Press, 1987.

———. "Jacobs, Harriet A." In Andrews et al., *Oxford Companion,* 394.

———. "Through Her Brother's Eyes: *Incidents* and 'A True Tale.'" In Garfield and Zafar, *Harriet Jacobs,* 44–56.